The Works of William James

Editors
Frederick H. Burkhardt, General Editor
Fredson Bowers, Textual Editor
Ignas K. Skrupskelis, Associate Editor

Advisory Board

Max H. Fisch	Eugene T. Long
John J. McDermott	Edward H. Madden
Maurice Mandelbaum	H. S. Thayer

*This edition of the Works of William James
is sponsored by the American Council of
Learned Societies*

*Introduction to this volume by
Ignas K. Skrupskelis*

William James in 1907

photograph by Alice Boughton; courtesy Houghton Library, Harvard University

Manuscript Lectures

William James

HARVARD UNIVERSITY PRESS
Cambridge, Massachusetts
and London, England
1988

CENTER FOR
SCHOLARLY EDITIONS
AN APPROVED EDITION
MODERN LANGUAGE
ASSOCIATION OF AMERICA

Library of Congress Cataloging-in-Publication Data

James, William, 1842–1910.
    Manuscript lectures.

    (The works of William James)
    Includes index.
    1. Psychology. I. Title. II. Series: James, William,
1842–1910. Works. 1975.
BF149.J343 1988   150   87–8804
ISBN 0–674–54826–4

1G
.J23m

Foreword

Manuscript Lectures, the final volume of THE WORKS OF WILLIAM JAMES, provides a nearly complete record of James's teaching career at Harvard University from 1872 to 1907. That career, as Professor Skrupskelis makes clear in his introduction, coincided with the transformation of Harvard into a modern university with a new curriculum based on elective courses for undergraduates and a strengthened emphasis on graduate studies. James, appointed by President Charles W. Eliot as one of a new, younger cadre of teachers who were incorporating in their courses the most recent advances in science and scholarship, was one of the first teachers in America to develop the implications of evolutionary biology in his courses in physiology, psychology, and philosophy.

The texts, which are drawn from the manuscripts in the William James papers in the Houghton Library at Harvard University, include extensive working notes for lectures in more than twenty courses, syllabi, reading lists, and examination questions. Some of the notes include summary statements of James's views on various subjects that have never been published before, such as his treatment in lectures of 1888-89 of the question of proof in ethics, in the only course in that subject that James ever taught. Other notes are illuminating in the way they show James contending with problems in early stages of the development of views that were published years later in their final form. Still others convey a sense of the contemporary controversies in philosophy, as in the Philosophy 9 course he shared with Josiah Royce in 1904-5 and 1905-6. It was that course that developed into the famous debate on Idealism and the nature of the Absolute.

In addition to the lecture notes, the manuscripts are a mine of information on other aspects of James as a classroom teacher: the books he used as texts, the reading lists for the students, and his examination questions. They show, among other things, that although James's enthusiasm and colorful personality may have made his courses popular, they were by no means easy or superficial in their treatment of subject matter. This material, almost all of which appears for the first time in this volume, adds a new dimension to our understanding of James's philosophy because his teaching was so closely involved with the development of his thought.

James as a lecturer outside of the classroom is more familiar to us. It was his lectures to a wide public that gained him world renown, and many of them were incorporated in his published writings substantially in the form in which they were delivered. Thus, the manuscript materials in the archives contain relatively few notes for public lectures that have not been published in other volumes of this edition in their final form. There are, however, several sets of notes and drafts of important lectures that James never wrote out for publication; these drafts are important enough in themselves as well as in James's intellectual development to warrant a place in his works.

The earliest of these are the notes for the 1878 lectures at Johns Hopkins University and at the Lowell Institute on the physiology of the brain and its relation to "mind." In them ideas are adumbrated that became important in James's later psychology and philosophy: his view of mental states as unitary and his antimaterialistic conception of consciousness as an organ of selective control.

The notes for the lectures on the physiological effects of alcohol and on abnormal psychology provide discussions of topics that, despite their sometimes fragmentary form, are more extensive than in any of James's published works. On the whole, however, James confined himself in those lectures to expositions of the contemporary state of knowledge on the subjects rather than developing new positions of his own. The notes for the lectures of 1902 on "Intellect and Feeling in Religion," on the other hand, present much new material. James wrote them as supplements to his *Varieties of Religious Experience*, and at least partly in response to those who reacted to the treatment of religion in *Varieties* as "morbid." They were intended to be his "last word" on the psychology of religion, after which he planned to devote himself to the difficult metaphysical and epistemological problems of his philosophy of radical empiricism.

Manuscript Lectures is the seventeenth title and nineteenth volume in THE WORKS OF WILLIAM JAMES. Since it is also the final volume of the edition, it is appropriate to give a brief valedictory summation of the history of the project and to thank those who have been important to its progress. Before doing so, however, the editors would like to express their appreciation of the assistance given them in the preparation of the present volume:

Harley P. Holden, the Curator of the Harvard University Archives, made available the *Syllabus in Philosophy D*, which was used to confirm that the extant portions were identical to the syllabus in the James Collection in the Houghton Library printed in this volume.

Deborah Wythe, Archivist of the Brooklyn Museum, provided information concerning James's lectures of 1896 on abnormal psychology given at the Brooklyn Institute.

Jennie Rathbun of the always helpful staff of the Houghton Reading Room checked and cleared up many dubious readings in our xeroxes of the manuscripts.

Page Nelson-Saginor attended to some necessary research at the Houghton Library.

Audrone and Daina Skrupskelis helped the Associate Editor in checking references and indexing.

David Miller, a graduate student at the University of South Carolina, provided information about Maeterlinck.

Professor Lance Schachterle of Worcester Polytechnic Institute inspected the volume for the seal of the Center for Scholarly Editions of the MLA.

Finally, Judith Nelson and Bernice Grohskopf, of the Editorial Coordinator's staff, helped to prepare the manuscript for the press.

The following chronology outlines the major steps in the progress of THE WORKS OF WILLIAM JAMES.

1973 In March 1973 an application was submitted by the American Council of Learned Societies to the National Endowment for the Humanities for a grant in support of research preparatory to the planning and execution of a definitive edition of the works of William James. NEH awarded the requested grant in May 1973, and in June, Fredson Bowers, then Linden Kent Professor of English at the University of Virginia, was asked to prepare the study. In August 1973 Professor Bowers submitted his report. Based on his investigation of the availability of textual resources needed to produce authentic texts, some trial collations, and a tentative editing of two chapters of *Pragmatism*, the general feasibility of the project was established and a workable editorial methodology for the edition was produced. On the basis of his report the ACLS, as sponsor of the edition, made a formal application to NEH for funds in support of editing the initial volumes of the edition.

1974   A grant for two years' support was made to the ACLS. The Council then invited Fredson Bowers to be Textual Editor of the Works. Ignas K. Skrupskelis, Professor of Philosophy at the University of South Carolina, was appointed Associate Editor, and Frederick Burkhardt, then President Emeritus of the ACLS, was appointed General Editor and Project Director.

An Advisory Board of leading scholars was also appointed by the ACLS to help establish general policy and to serve as consultants to the editors on substantive problems. The six members appointed were Max H. Fisch, Eugene T. Long, John J. McDermott, Edward H. Madden, Maurice Mandelbaum, and H. S. Thayer. Except for the sad loss of Maurice Mandelbaum in January 1987, the membership of the Board remained unchanged throughout the duration of the project. As will be seen below, three members of the Board also wrote introductions to some of the volumes of the Works.

Arrangements were made with the Harvard University Press for publication of the edition and, critically important to the initial stages of the project, a grant in aid of publication of the first four volumes was made to the ACLS by the Andrew W. Mellon Foundation.

A small staff of research and editorial assistants was formed and established in office space provided by the Alderman Library of the University of Virginia.

At the outset it was decided that the volumes of the edition would be edited according to the standards of the Center of Editions of American Authors, now the Center for Scholarly Editions, of the Modern Language Association of America.

In the spring of 1974, work was begun on *Pragmatism* and *The Meaning of Truth*.

1975   *Pragmatism* and *The Meaning of Truth* were published, with Introductions to both volumes provided by Professor H. S. Thayer of City College, City University of New York.

1976   *Essays in Radical Empiricism* was published, with an Introduction by Professor John J. McDermott, then at Queens College, City University of New York, now at Texas A & M University.

The National Endowment for the Humanities made a second two-year grant to the ACLS for support of the editorial work of the edition.

1977   *A Pluralistic Universe* was published, with an Introduction by Professor Richard J. Bernstein of Haverford College.

1978   *Essays in Philosophy* was published, with an Introduction by John J. McDermott.

1979   *The Will to Believe*, with an Introduction by Professor Edward H. Madden, State University of New York at Buffalo, and *Some Prob-

lems of Philosophy, with an Introduction by Professor Peter H. Hare of the State University of New York at Buffalo, were published.

1980   The National Endowment for the Humanities continued its support with a third two-year grant.

1981   *The Principles of Psychology* was published in three volumes. It was provided with two Introductions, one by Professor Gerald E. Myers of the Graduate Center of the City University of New York, the other by Professor Rand B. Evans of Texas A & M University.

1982   *Essays in Religion and Morality* was published, with an Introduction by John J. McDermott.

The National Endowment for the Humanities awarded another grant.

1983   *Talks to Teachers on Psychology*, with an Introduction by Gerald E. Myers, and *Essays in Psychology*, with an Introduction by Professor William R. Woodward of the University of New Hampshire, were published.

A three-year grant was awarded by the National Endowment for the Humanities.

1984   *Psychology: Briefer Course* was published, with an Introduction by Professor Michael M. Sokal of Worcester Polytechnic Institute.

1985   *The Varieties of Religious Experience* was published, with an Introduction by Professor John E. Smith of Yale University.

1986   *Essays in Psychical Research* was published, with an Introduction by Professor Robert A. McDermott of Baruch College, City University of New York.

A final grant was awarded to the ACLS by the National Endowment for the Humanities for the completion of the edition.

1987   *Essays, Comments, and Reviews* was published, with an Introduction by Professor Ignas K. Skrupskelis of the University of South Carolina and Associate Editor of the WORKS. This volume completed the editing of all the previously published works of William James.

1988   *Manuscript Essays and Notes* and *Manuscript Lectures*, two volumes of hitherto unpublished material from the William James Papers at Houghton Library, were published, with Introductions by Ignas K. Skrupskelis.

No review of the history of the edition can fail to mention the institutions and individuals that helped make the edition possible. The editors acknowledge their indebtedness, and express their appreciation, to the following:

The American Council of Learned Societies sponsored the project and provided administrative support. Robert M. Lumiansky, John

William Ward, and Stanley N. Katz, the three Presidents of the Council during the editing of the WORKS, took an active and supportive interest in its progress. Charlotte Bowman, Vice-President, and Executive Associates Thomas A. Noble and Richard W. Downer, all now retired, had charge of the administrative details of the grants during their tenure with the Council. Douglas Greenberg, Vice-President, and Hugh O'Neill, Director of Finance and Administration, have attended to the project's needs during the preparation of the last four volumes.

The National Endowment for the Humanities provided the continuing financial support without which this edition would not have been possible. Particular thanks are due to Ronald Berman, Chairman of the Endowment at the start of the project, and to William Emerson, Simone Reagor, Geraldine Otremba, David Wallace, George F. Farr, Jr., and Kathy Fuller, who were a steady source of support and guidance throughout.

Alexander R. James, William James's grandson and literary executor, gave the editors permission to publish material on which he holds copyright.

The University of South Carolina and its philosophy department have been closely associated with the project from its inception. The Associate Editor has been provided with working facilities and administrative assistance as well as support from his colleagues in the department. One of its members, James Willard Oliver, now retired, was one of the first to envisage an edition of the works of William James, and readily joined in support of the present project when it was launched. Davis Baird, also of the USC philosophy department, has helped the Associate Editor with advice and assistance with details of the history of science.

William H. Bond, Librarian of the Houghton Library, and Rodney Dennis, Curator of Manuscripts, facilitated access to the James Papers. Throughout the years, the staff members of the Houghton Library Reading Room helped the editors with innumerable problems of access and research.

The Alderman Library of the University of Virginia provided working space, and its staff helped the Textual Editor, the Editorial Coordinator, and her staff of research assistants on an almost daily basis throughout the project.

The Barra Foundation made two generous and timely matching grants in support of the editorial work.

Heritage Printers, Inc., of Charlotte, North Carolina, has set type for all but one of the nineteen volumes of the edition. The editors have had many occasions to be thankful for the high professional standards of the press's work.

The editors also thank the Director of Harvard University Press, Arthur J. Rosenthal, for his ready approval of the plan to publish the works of one of Harvard's most illustrious teachers. Throughout the fifteen years of work on the volumes, Maud Wilcox, the Editor-in-Chief, has superintended publication of the volumes and worked in close cooperation with the General Editor. Catherine Bayliss, Ann Louise McLaughlin, Vivian B. Wheeler, Maria Ascher, and Mary Ellen Geer have in turn been editors responsible for individual volumes at Harvard University Press.

A number of other individuals have been associated with the edition for a substantial period of its history. Charlotte Bowman has been administrative assistant to the General Editor since the project began. Audrone Skrupskelis has assisted the Associate Editor for the same period. Anne McCoy served from 1974 to 1984 as head of the staff of research assistants responsible for checking and preparing copy for the press. Her successor, Elizabeth Berkeley, first joined the staff in 1975 and has served as Editorial Coordinator since 1984.

Many other individuals and institutions have helped the editors by supplying documents, by examining the volumes for the seal of the Center for Scholarly Editions, and by responding to a multitude of requests for information. They have been thanked in the specific volumes to which their help has contributed.

A word of special thanks should be expressed to John J. McDermott, with whom the project for a complete critical edition of the works of William James was originally conceived and discussed at lunches during 1971. Since then he has been active as a member of the Advisory Board of the WORKS and has written the introductions to three of the volumes. He will now become the General Editor and Project Director of *The Correspondence of William James*, a position for which, as a leading scholar in American philosophy and an authority on James's life and thought, he is eminently qualified.

Frederick H. Burkhardt

Contents

Foreword   v
Introduction by Ignas K. Skrupskelis   xvii

Manuscript Lectures

I. PUBLIC LECTURES

1. Johns Hopkins Lectures on "The Senses and the Brain and Their Relation to Thought" (1878)   3
2. Lowell Lectures on "The Brain and the Mind" (1878)   16
3. Notes for a Lecture on "The Physiological Effects of Alcohol" (1886)   43
4. Draft and Outline of a Lecture on "The Effects of Alcohol" (1895)   46
5. Lectures on Abnormal Psychology (1895, 1896)   55
6. Summer School of Theology Lectures on "Intellect and Feeling in Religion" (1902)   83
7. Drafts and Notes for Addresses to Graduate Clubs (1902–1906)   100

II. COURSES

8. Fragments of Early Courses (1875–1885)   117
9. Notes for Natural History 2: Physiological Psychology (1876–1877)   126
10. Notes for Philosophy 4: Psychology (1878–1879)   129
11. Notes for Philosophy 3: The Philosophy of Evolution (1879–1885)   146
12. Notes for Philosophy 5: Psychology (1880–1881)   177
13. Notes for Philosophy 4: Contemporary Philosophy (1881–1882)   178
14. Notes for Philosophy 4: Ethics—Recent English Contributions to Theistic Ethics (1888–1889)   182

Contents

15. Notes for Philosophy 1: General Introduction to
    Philosophy (1890–1891)   186
16. Notes for Philosophy 10: Descartes, Spinoza, and
    Leibnitz (1890–1891)   198
17. Notes for Philosophy 20a: Psychological Seminary
    (1891–1892)   206
18. Notes for Philosophy 20b: Psychological Seminary—The
    Feelings (1895–1896)   212
19. Notes on Stout's *Analytic Psychology* for Psychology
    Course (1896–1898)   230
20. Notes for Philosophy 20b: Psychological Seminary—The
    Philosophical Problems of Psychology (1897–1898)   234
21. Notes on "Conclusions of Lotze Course" (1897–1898)   259
22. Notes for Philosophy 9: Metaphysics—The Fundamental
    Problems of Theoretical Philosophy (1898–1899)   265
23. Syllabus of Philosophy 3: The Philosophy of Nature
    (1902–1903)   267
24. Notes for Philosophy 20c: Metaphysical Seminary—A
    Pluralistic Description of the World (1903–1904)   273
25. Notes for Philosophy 20c: Metaphysical Seminary
    (1903–1904)   319
26. Notes for Philosophy 9: Metaphysics (1904–1905)   327
27. Notes for Philosophy 9: Metaphysics (1905–1906)   347
28. Lectures at Stanford (1906)   374
29. Talk with Cohen about Kant (1906)   377
30. Syllabus in Philosophy D: General Problems of
    Philosophy (1906–1907)   378
31. Report of a Discussion in Philosophy 20e: Seminary
    in the Theory of Knowledge (1908)   429

Notes   447

Appendixes
    I. Report of the Lecture on "The Physiological
       Effects of Alcohol"   513
   II. Report of the Lecture on "The Effects of Alcohol"   514
  III. Reports of James's "Lectures on Abnormal
       Psychology"   516
   IV. Notes of the 1906 Summer School of Theology
       Lectures on "Religious Philosophy and
       Individualism"   526

Contents

V. James's Annotations of His Private Copies of
    Syllabus in Philosophy and *Syllabus in
    Philosophy D*   529

A Note on the Editorial Method   536

Textual Apparatus   540

Index   660

Introduction
by
Ignas K. Skrupskelis

It is difficult to divorce James's teaching career at Harvard from the presidency of Charles William Eliot, who upon his election in 1869 embarked on a course that made Harvard the center of American intellectual life. James was one of the wave of Eliot appointees whose mission was to transform Harvard from a small college into a modern university. In 1894, on the twenty-fifth anniversary of his presidency, Eliot wrote James: "Your coming to the University and your career as a teacher and writer have been among my most solid grounds of satisfaction. So your words of cheer are of especial value to me."[1]

The election of Eliot—a controversial choice—decided numerous questions that had been agitating Cambridge for years. In his *Fair Harvard*, published in 1869 but depicting Harvard life in the 1850s, William Tucker Washburn has one of the students say: "Harvard College is looked upon by its students as a gladiatorial school, and by its officers as an amateur police station." To this another student replies:

If we had the wit of our fathers, who founded this college almost before they had pitched their tents in the wilderness, we should build it up to be a great University, and endow it with money enough to educate all the men and women of talents in the country: we should make it not a place for boys to be drilled in, and tutors to air their brief authority, but the centre of American thought, at which scholars and students, young and old, would gather to give and receive inspiration. It is only by such a union that a great literature can be produced.[2]

For Eliot, reform hinged on the elective system. By 1869 Harvard offered some electives, but most of the undergraduate program was prescribed, and a class studied and caroused through its four years as a single body. Opponents such as Noah Porter, president of Yale, argued that the elective system would make education more expensive and prevent a class from developing its own individuality. Eliot

[1] Henry James, *Charles W. Eliot: President of Harvard University 1869–1909*, 2 vols. (Boston: Houghton Mifflin, 1930), II, 87.

[2] William Tucker Washburn, *Fair Harvard: A Story of American College Life* (New York: G. P. Putnam & Son, 1869), pp. 235–236.

agreed that there would be a substantial additional expense because colleges would be required to hire additional faculty. But in his view this offered an opportunity for a school to become a research institution:

A college must either limit closely its teaching, or provide some mode of selecting studies for the individual student. The limitation of teaching is an intolerable alternative for any institution which aspires to become a university; for a university must try to teach every subject, above the grade of its admission requirements, for which there is any demand; and to teach it thoroughly enough to carry the advanced student to the confines of present knowledge, and make him capable of original research.[3]

In his early years Eliot hired new faculty at a great rate, and James was one of his many beneficiaries.

In the view of William James's son Henry, the elective system "afforded the instructors new and unequaled opportunities to teach what they were interested in instead of almost nothing except what it was thought wise to prescribe to the average undergraduate."[4] When one considers that up to this time American philosophical literature consisted almost exclusively of dreary textbooks, it is a sobering thought that James could easily have taught in an institution very different from Eliot's Harvard.

It was also important that Eliot was not a clergyman. The overwhelming majority of American colleges had clergymen for presidents, primarily charged with the supervision of the morals of their students and responsible for the teaching of philosophy. Granville Stanley Hall, recipient of a Harvard doctorate in psychology in 1878, noted in describing the condition of American philosophy: "Indeed there are less than half a dozen colleges or universities in the United States where metaphysical thought is entirely freed from reference to theological formulae."[5] In responding to a somewhat earlier but similar complaint by Hall, James agreed that the teaching of philosophy by clergymen was a major barrier to the advance of philosophical studies:

The philosophical teaching, as a rule, in our higher seminaries is in the hands of the president, who is usually a minister of the Gospel, and, as

---

[3] Charles William Eliot, "Liberty in Education" (1885), in *Charles William Eliot, Educational Reform: Essays and Addresses* (New York: The Century Co., 1898), p. 127.

[4] Henry James, *Charles W. Eliot*, I, 257.

[5] Granville Stanley Hall, "Philosophy in the United States," *Mind*, 4 (January 1879), 90.

he more often owes his position to general excellence of character and administrative faculty than to any speculative gifts or propensities, it usually follows that "safeness" becomes the main characteristic of his tuition; that his classes are edified rather than awakened, and leave college with the generous youthful impulse, to reflect on the world and our position in it, rather dampened and discouraged than stimulated by the lifeless discussions and flabby formulas they have had to commit to memory.[6]

The threat to academic freedom posed by a clergyman president was serious, especially in connection with James's favorite topics, evolution and Herbert Spencer, as is illustrated by the clash at Yale between the sociologist William Graham Sumner and Noah Porter, a clergyman and a major name in American philosophy of the time. In a letter to Sumner dated December 6, 1879, Porter objected to the use of Spencer's *Principles of Sociology* as a text:

The freedom and unfairness with which it attacks every Theistic Philosophy of society and of history, and the cool and yet sarcastic effrontery with which he assumes that material elements and laws are the only forces and laws which any scientific man can recognize, seem to me to condemn the book as a textbook for a miscellaneous class in an undergraduate course. . . . I feel assured that the use of the book will bring intellectual and moral harm to the students, however you may strive to neutralize and counteract its influence.[7]

Porter himself used Spencer's book, but only in graduate courses and apparently only in such a way as to "neutralize or counteract" him. The controversy became public and dragged on for a number of years. In a letter of June 1881 to the Yale Corporation, defending his right to choose the best book available, Sumner noted that he had failed to take into account "the horror of Spencer's name, which, as I have since learned, is entertained by some people."[8] There is evidence that James himself faced questions about his own orthodoxy in connection with his proposed Lowell Institute course in the late 1870s.[9]

In his inaugural address Eliot touched upon the teaching of phi-

---

6 William James, "The Teaching of Philosophy in Our Colleges," *Essays in Philosophy*, WORKS, p. 3.

7 *American Higher Education: A Documentary History*, ed. Richard Hofstadter and Wilson Smith, 2 vols. (Chicago: University of Chicago Press, 1961), II, 850.

8 Ibid., p. 852.

9 See note to 16.26 in the present volume.

losophy and emphasized academic freedom: "Philosophical subjects should never be taught with authority. . . . The notion that education consists in the authoritative inculcation of what the teacher deems true may be logical and appropriate in a convent, or a seminary for priests, but it is intolerable in universities and public schools." [10] Eliot's presence ensured that James could teach what he wanted to, at least as far as the university administration was concerned. He did, however, encounter objections from his colleagues. According to George Herbert Palmer, Eliot's first appointee in philosophy, in James's early years Palmer clashed with Francis Bowen over James's proposal to teach a course on Spencer. [11] Bowen, the main Harvard philosopher of the pre-Eliot years, was widely known as an opponent of evolutionary theory. In his review of *The Origin of Species* Bowen claimed that for the "defence of the great truths of philosophy and natural theology, it is hardly necessary to spend much time in the refutation of such fanciful theories of cosmogony as this by Mr. Darwin." [12]

A third issue decided by Eliot's election was the role of the sciences in the curriculum. Up to that time, college education at Harvard as everywhere else was based on the study of classical literature. And the classicists were the main opponents of Eliot's candidacy. Eliot's presence ensured that the curriculum would be expanded to accommodate more science and that there would be room on the faculty for a person with James's background.

The changes that took place during the Eliot years are indicated by some statistics: in 1869-70 there were 32 faculty members and some 600 students in Harvard College and the Lawrence Scientific School; in 1908-9, Eliot's last year, there were 165 faculty and 2,270 students. The graduate department in 1872-73, its first year, had 28 students; in 1908-9, there were 403. [13]

The philosophy department grew in a similar way. In 1872-73 the program consisted of five courses. There was a required course for juniors that used *Elementary Lessons in Logic* by William Stanley Jevons and works by William Hamilton as texts. It was taught

[10] Eliot, *Educational Reform*, pp. 7–8.

[11] Letter to James [December 25, 1900], in Ralph Barton Perry, *The Thought and Character of William James*, 2 vols. (Boston: Little, Brown, 1935), I, 435.

[12] Francis Bowen, review of *On the Origin of Species*, in *North American Review*, 90 (April 1860), 504.

[13] The figures for Harvard College are from Samuel Eliot Morison, *Three Centuries of Harvard: 1636–1936* (Cambridge, Mass.: Harvard University Press, 1936), p. 490.

by Palmer to 162 students in five sections. There were four electives available to juniors and seniors: Philosophy 1, which used Locke's *Essay* and works by Victor Cousin and John Stuart Mill as texts, taught by Bowen to 14 students, mostly juniors; Philosophy 2, ancient philosophy, taught by Bowen to 2 students; Philosophy 3, the "Schools of Descartes and Kant," taught by Bowen to some 30 students, mostly seniors; and Philosophy 5, ethics, which was offered by Andrew Preston Peabody, a Unitarian clergyman and professor of Christian morals, to 12 seniors. Peabody used Dugald Stewart's *Philosophy of the Active and Moral Powers of Man* and Cicero's *De Officiis* as texts, while Bowen included Kant's *Critique of Pure Reason* among the texts for Philosophy 3.

In 1906-7, the last year of James's teaching, the philosophy department offered five half-year introductory courses; nine half-year and seven full-year courses available to undergraduates and graduates; and six courses of special study for graduates. The philosophy staff consisted of Palmer, James, Royce, Santayana, Ralph Barton Perry, and James Haughton Woods. The psychology portion of the program was taught by Hugo Münsterberg, Edwin Bissell Holt, and Robert Mearns Yerkes. Included in the philosophy program were two theology courses, taught by William Wallace Fenn and Edward Caldwell Moore. The total enrollment was almost 1,000. Not included in these figures are the courses, students, and faculty of the divisions of social ethics and education, which in that year were still listed with the department of philosophy.[14]

One of Eliot's first appointees was John Fiske, a known evolutionist who was also suspected of religious infidelity. As a Harvard undergraduate, Fiske had been punished for reading Comte during chapel. Eliot appointed him university lecturer for 1869-70 to give a course on positivism, a course that turned into a defense of evolution. Fiske attended Eliot's inaugural and came away much impressed: "We are going to have new times here at Harvard. No more old fogyism, I hope."[15] Herbert Spencer, upon learning of Fiske's appointment, exulted in a letter to Fiske: "I congratulate

[14] Course titles, descriptions, and enrollment figures are based on Harvard presidents' reports and catalogues. Slight discrepancies between the two sources are treated silently. Additional information about James's teaching is provided by entries in his books and lecture notes.

[15] James Spencer Clark, *The Life and Letters of John Fiske*, 2 vols. (Boston: Houghton Mifflin, 1917), I, 353.

you, Harvard, and myself, on the event of which your letter tells me. It is equally gratifying and surprising. That eight years should have wrought such a change as to place the persecuted undergraduate in the chair of lecturer is something to wonder at, and may fill us with hope, as it must fill many with consternation."[16]

The precise circumstances of James's first appointment at Harvard remain obscure. His letter to his sister, Alice, dated July 27, 1872, suggests that he offered himself as a replacement for Henry Pickering Bowditch, who for some reason was resigning his appointment.[17] In any case, James was much like other Eliot appointees: young, with no prior university connections, interested in research, abreast with the latest in the sciences. Eliot was not interested in raiding other schools to staff the expansion of Harvard. According to Henry James, appointments "were more completely Eliot's personal affair than were other changes." He adds: "If, for instance, it was deplorable that old Professor Bowen should be the one and only fountain of instruction in both Philosophy and Economics, it was clear that the selection of other men to serve as correctives and antidotes and ultimately to replace him could not be guided by Bowen himself."[18]

In whatever way it came about, on August 3, 1872, the President and Fellows of Harvard College voted to appoint James instructor in physiology for the ensuing academic year and to pay him $300 for three exercises a week during half of the year.[19] The course was Natural History 3: Comparative Anatomy and Physiology, with an enrollment of 28 juniors and 25 seniors. Thomas Dwight, another of Eliot's young men, was responsible for the anatomy portion, and James for the physiology. Although the second term began on Monday, February 10, 1873, James began his lecturing in early January. Thus, in a letter to his brother Henry dated October 10, 1872, he wrote: "I keep up a small daily pegging at my physiology, whose duties don't begin till January, and which I shall find easy, I think."[20] James's father wrote in a letter to Henry dated January 14, 1873: "Willy is going on with his teaching. The eleven o'clock

16 Ibid., I, 356.

17 Original in the Houghton Library, Harvard University (bMS Am 1092.9 #1115). Hereafter, for materials in Houghton, only the call number will be given.

18 Henry James, *Charles W. Eliot*, I, 253.

19 The dates of the several appointments and salary figures are based on Corporation Records, Harvard University Archives.

20 Perry, *Thought and Character*, I, 330.

bell has just tolled, and he is on his platform expounding the mysteries of physiology." [21] And like most teachers, James enjoyed his vacations, as can be seen from a letter written to his brother Henry when he was only several weeks into his teaching career: "I am enjoying a two week's respite from tuition, the boys being condemned to pass examinations, in which I luckily take no part at present." [22]

The enrollment figures were good, a fact duly noted by Eliot: "As the course was experimental and a part of the new expansion of the Elective System, the President and the Faculty were interested in the fact that the new course under these two young instructors attracted 28 Juniors and 25 Seniors." [23] And the work was good for James's mental health, as he informed his brother Henry in a letter of November 24, 1872: "It is a noble thing for one's spirits to have some responsible work to do. I enjoy my revived physiological reading greatly, and have in a corporeal sense been better for the past four or five weeks than I have been at all since you left." [24] The improvement was noted by James's father, in a letter to Henry dated March 18, 1873: "Willy . . . came in here the other afternoon . . . and after walking the floor in an animated way for a moment, exclaimed 'Dear me! What a difference there is between me now and me last spring this time: then so hypochondriacal' . . . 'and now feeling my mind so cleared up and restored to sanity. It is the difference between death and life.' " [25] James himself thought that his teaching was going well. In a letter to Henry dated February 14, 1873, he wrote:

I find the work very interesting and stimulating. It presents two problems, the intellectual one—how best to state your matter to them; and the practical one—how to govern them, stir them up, not bore them, yet make them work, etc. I should think it not unpleasant as a permanent thing. The authority is at first rather flattering to one. So far, I seem to have succeeded in interesting them, for they are admirably attentive, and I hear expressions of satisfaction on their part. Whether it will go on next year can't at this hour, for many reasons be decided.[26]

21 Ibid., I, 334.
22 *The Letters of William James*, ed. Henry James, 2 vols. (Boston: Little, Brown, 1920), I, 167–168. The quoted portion of this letter is dated February 14, 1873.
23 Ibid., I, 166.
24 Ibid., I, 167.
25 Perry, *Thought and Character*, I, 339.
26 *Letters of William James*, I, 168.

On June 2, 1873, the Harvard Corporation appointed James instructor in anatomy and physiology for 1873-74, the appointment to begin on September 1, with no increase in salary.[27] But James decided to spend the year in Europe instead. His letters suggest that he was unwilling to spend so much time on anatomy. At the same time, uncertain of his mental condition, he was unwilling to commit himself to philosophy: "Philosophical activity *as a business* is not normal for most men, and not for me. . . . To make the *form* of all possible thought the prevailing *matter* of one's thought breeds hypochondria."[28]

When James returned to teaching in 1874-75, he was responsible for the whole of Natural History 3 and received a salary of $600. The course, now titled "Comparative Anatomy and Physiology of Vertebrates," had an enrollment of 6 seniors, 27 juniors, and 1 sophomore. In 1875-76, James offered Natural History 3 to 13 students. His texts were Emile Küss, *A Course of Lectures on Physiology*, and St. George Jackson Mivart, *Lessons in Elementary Anatomy*. The following year James had 65 students and used Mivart and Thomas Henry Huxley, *Lessons in Elementary Physiology*, as texts. In 1877-78, using Mivart and Küss as texts, James had 85 students. The next year was the last in which he taught the course under the title of natural history. That year the course was renumbered as Natural History 2 and had 94 students.

In summary, James taught Natural History 3 (once as Natural History 2) six times, with a total enrollment of 344. James continued to teach some of the material of the course for several more years under the title of "Physiology and Hygiene," a course meeting once a week and available to all students. In the catalogue it is listed under the heading of "Voluntary Instruction" and under the offerings of the Lawrence Scientific School. According to the Harvard *Crimson*, November 21, 1879, the course covered the less technical parts of James's natural history course. "Physiology and Hygiene" was given in 1879-80, 1880-81, and 1881-82. A report of one of the lectures on the effects of alcohol can be found in *Essays, Comments, and Reviews* (WORKS, pp. 19–21).

Harvard Corporation Records show that small amounts were appropriated for James to buy apparatus for anatomy and physiology. His appropriation was usually the smallest on the list of laboratories

---

27 It is not clear whether James was to teach for the full year or just for one term.
28 From James's diary, quoted in *Letters of William James*, I, 170.

voted special appropriations. On October 26, 1874, James was voted $150; on June 14, 1875, $250, for apparatus that Henry Pickering Bowditch was to buy for him; November 15, 1875, $50; December 11, 1876, $100; December 10, 1877, $100; November 25, 1878, $50. He received the sum of $35 for 1879-80, after he had given up Natural History 3. By then James was teaching other courses, and it is impossible to say which of these the money was meant to support. However, the appropriations usually specified anatomy and physiology, and this would connect the appropriations with Natural History 3 rather than the courses in psychology that James was teaching at the same time.

No manuscripts in the James Collection at Harvard's Houghton Library have been identified as notes for Natural History 3. In his *Thought and Character of William James*, Ralph Barton Perry reports several comments by students in the course suggesting that James often strayed into philosophy and into broad defenses of evolutionary theory: "A Harvard graduate who took this course in 1876–1877 tells me that James's weakness for philosophy was so well known that his students could always (sometimes in self-defense!) switch him from the scientific matter in hand and set him to talking on fundamental issues." Another student reported:

I took Natural History 3 in the college year 1877–1878. . . . The text books were Mivart's *Anatomy* and Huxley's *Physiology*; these books, by the way, received but little attention in the classroom, for the lecturer could but feel hampered by the tediousness of such class work, and launched out, at almost any occasion, into a lecture which took shape gradually in a course on evolution; these lectures were clear and illuminating and, as the lecturer was enthusiastic on the subject, did not fail to kindle a reflection of that enthusiasm in his hearers.[29]

After citing this testimony Perry notes that "James's tendency was to use comparative anatomy in the first half-year as affording proofs and illustrations of evolution, and physiology in the second half-year as an approach to psychology."

It is difficult to guess at the precise connection between examination questions and the contents of a course, especially because some questions can be interpreted as belonging either to physiology or to psychology. Most of the time James's examinations avoided broad theoretical issues and tested the students' knowledge of specific de-

---

[29] Perry, *Thought and Character*, I, 469.

tails.[30] For example, in an examination from 1874-75, perhaps the broadest question is the last one: "What is reflex action? Give examples." Not atypical are the questions of the final examination in 1878-79:

16. How is it that a man can remain with impunity in a heated oven?
17. How do you know that a large proportion of the waste of muscle consists of CO_2?
18. Where would you press your abdomen to ascertain tenderness in the coecal region?
19. What is the difference between whispering and speaking?
20. Diagram of intestinal villus. Functions thereof.
21. Give any one example of the way in which we mix up judgments with sensations.
22. What is the general distinction between actions performed by lower centres and actions performed by hemispheres?

Question 19 can be classed either with physiology or with psychology, depending on whether in class James talked about the different muscles used or the different sensations experienced. The last two questions are much broader and suggest that James tried out in class the ideas of the Johns Hopkins and Lowell Institute lectures of 1878.

During these early years James was an active member of the Harvard Natural History Society, perhaps one of his obligations as an instructor. The Harvard University Archives preserves the secretary's records (HUD 3599.505) for the period 1865–1890, and these provide some information about James's scientific interests. He was elected a member of the society on December 2, 1874. According to the records, he took part in a discussion on November 16, 1875; on December 7, 1875, he gave a paper on the dissection of a three-month-old fetus; on December 21, 1875, he described an unidentified machine invented by an Austrian physician; on February 1, 1876, he gave a talk on the causes of vertigo; on May 2, 1876, he asked the members to try experiments on vision; on February 20, 1877, he spoke on the hypnotism of frogs. James served as corresponding secretary in 1876-77 and 1877-78.

In 1877 the Natural History Society sponsored a course of popular scientific lectures at Sanders Theater. James lectured on March 1 on

---

[30] Numerous examinations are preserved in Houghton (bMS Am 1092.9 #4521, #4522).

"Recent Investigations on the Brain" to an audience of about 1,000. The report in the *Boston Daily Advertiser*, March 2, 1877, noted that James concluded "by deprecating any anxiety about materialistic consequences. If the spiritualistic faith of today finds central physiology a stumbling-block, that of tomorrow will be all the stouter for successful contact with it. The human mind always has been and always will be able to interpret facts in accordance with its moral interests."

On February 14, 1876, James was appointed assistant professor of physiology; his salary as an assistant professor was to start from December 1, 1875. His pay was $1650 for 1875-76 and $2000 thereafter. In 1875-76 he offered his first graduate course in psychology. He offered such a course almost every year through 1897-98, for a total of seventeen years.

The growth of graduate instruction at Harvard reflected Eliot's hopes for an institution where faculty and students would engage in advanced study and research. The Graduate Department was formally organized in January 1872, although for years it remained a loose organization and the lines between graduate and undergraduate instruction were never sharply drawn. The Graduate Department began to offer courses primarily for graduates in 1875-76. Two years later it became possible for graduate students to receive special instruction by arrangement with a professor. The courses numbered Philosophy 20 (followed by some letter) often reflected such special arrangements.

It is fortunate that James Eliot Cabot, who was in frequent contact with James through several philosophical clubs, was chairman of the Board of Overseers' Visiting Committee, for his reports prepared the way for the graduate course in psychology. Cabot himself had little background in physiology, and one suspects that James may have influenced Cabot's thinking. Some have even thought that James had a hand in the writing of the relevant portions of the reports.[31]

In 1873 Cabot's report concluded with a criticism of the teaching of psychology at Harvard: "We have no wish to reflect, or to seem to reflect, upon the Plummer or Alford professors, by whom philosophical studies have long been ably and faithfully taught. They

---

[31] Sheldon N. Stern, "William James and the New Psychology," in *Social Sciences at Harvard, 1860–1920: From Inculcation to the Open Mind*, ed. Paul Buck (Cambridge, Mass.: Harvard University Press, 1965), p. 301 n. 13.

> the philosophical problems of psychology (2 hours per week;
> 10 graduate, 2 divinity, 2 Radcliffe)

James offered an advanced course in psychology almost every year up to the coming of Hugo Münsterberg in 1892. With Münsterberg available to take over theoretical psychology, James was able for several years to offer advanced courses in abnormal psychology. The last two seminars in theoretical psychology were heavily philosophical. Their contents are known from the surviving lecture notes, published in the present volume as Nos. 18 and 20. There are also lecture notes from the year 1891-92.

The first student to complete the graduate program in philosophy was Granville Stanley Hall, who received his doctorate in 1878. Hall's dissertation dealt with "The Perception of Space," a Jamesian subject. An important glimpse of the advanced course is provided by a copy of an examination for 1879-80, preserved by Francis Almy, a student in that year. A number of the questions reflect James's theoretical preoccupations:

> 4. Can actions accompanied by intelligence be conceived under the form of reflex action?
> 5. What is the present state of the question of localization of functions in the cortex?
> 6. What were the most characteristic points in your instructor's sketch of space-perception?

One question suggests an excursion into philosophy: "Would the untruth of the 'conscious automaton' theory involve the truth of the free will theory?"[36] It is likely that James would not have posed such theoretical questions much before 1878. That year he was forced to work out his own position in connection with the Johns Hopkins and Lowell Institute lectures. The year also marks the beginning of his work on *The Principles of Psychology*. Thus it would have been interesting to know what the course was like in its earliest years, but no information concerning these years has been found.

Some of the work by students in advanced psychology found its way into print. A fragment by Ralph Waldo Black from the mid-1880s appears in *Principles*.[37] It is also plausible that the essay on

36 Ibid., II, 737. The Houghton Library has Almy's "Experiments on Optical Vertigo. April 26–27, 1880," apparently prepared for this class (bMS Am 1092.9 #4411).

37 William James, *The Principles of Psychology*, Works, p. 965n (hereafter *PP*).

the law of contrast by Edmund Burke Delabarre[38] was a product of the advanced course during 1888–1890 when Delabarre was a graduate student. James himself described the course for 1889-90 as follows:

The method is the so called seminary-method, no two men doing just the same work. Brain-anatomy, however, forms an obligatory part of the course, and human brains are dissected instead of the sheep's brains used by the undergraduates. The class meets two hours weekly at the Professor's house for lecture and discussion, and the students do their laboratory work at special individual hours.[39]

The level of the work done in the Harvard laboratory in its last years under James can be estimated from two "Contributions from the Harvard Psychological Laboratory" communicated by James to the *Psychological Review*, 4 (May 1897), 246–271: "Discrimination in Cutaneous Sensations" by Leon M. Solomons and "Studies in Sensation and Judgment" by Edgar Arthur Singer. There are numerous similar contributions in the *Psychological Review*, but only these two were communicated by James, suggesting that he had supervised the work to some extent.

Having introduced the advanced psychology course, in the following year, 1876-77, James offered undergraduate psychology, listed as Natural History 2: Physiological Psychology, using Spencer's *Principles of Psychology* as his text. Until then Harvard undergraduates had been exposed to psychology by Bowen, who used Locke's *Essay*, Mill's *Examination of Sir William Hamilton's Philosophy*, and Bowen's own *Principles of Metaphysics and Ethical Science Applied to the Evidences of Religion* as texts. The great distance separating Bowen and James is illustrated by the fact that of the hundreds of references in *The Principles of Psychology*, only two are to Bowen. Granville Stanley Hall suggested that James's proposal to teach psychology using Spencer encountered opposition, and, according to Palmer, the opposition came from Bowen. Commenting on the teaching of philosophy, Hall mentioned James's course as the fourth elective available at Harvard and noted:

The fourth course has been organized only two years, and is conducted by the assistant-professor of physiology. It was admitted not without some opposition into the department of philosophy, and is up to the

---

[38] Ibid., pp. 662–674.
[39] William James, *Essays, Comments, and Reviews*, WORKS, p. 31 (hereafter *ECR*).

den genesis. Whatever it is I am glad you like it. I often take an afternoon nap beside Herbert Spencer at the Athenaeum, and feel as if I were robbing *you* of the privilege."[44] Several years later, on April 21, 1879, in connection with this course, James asked Spencer to comment on his interpretation of his thought: "In teaching your *Principles of Psychology* here I am a good deal puzzled to make clear to my own mind the exact manner in which you conceive of the function of cognition."[45] Spencer's reply endorsing James's interpretation is at the Houghton Library (autograph file).

The fortunes of James's undergraduate psychology course are summarized in the following table:

1876-77 Natural History 2: Physiological Psychology. Text: Spencer's *Principles of Psychology* (19 students, mostly seniors)

1877-78 Philosophy 4: Psychology. Text: Taine's *On Intelligence* (23 students)

1878-79 Philosophy 4: Psychology. Text: Spencer's *Principles of Psychology*[46] (18 students)

1880-81 Philosophy 5: Psychology. Text: Bain's *Mental and Moral Science* (25 students)

1881-82 Philosophy 2: Psychology: the Human Intellect. Text: Taine's *On Intelligence* (27 students)

1883-84 Philosophy 2: Psychology. Text: same (first half-year; 81 students)

1884-85 Philosophy 2: Psychology. Text: Sully's *Outlines of Psychology* (first half-year; 55 students)

1890-91 Philosophy 2: Psychology. Recitations, theses, lectures, and illustrative experiments. Text: James's *Principles of Psychology* (28 students, including 4 graduate)

1891-92 Philosophy 2: Psychology (description and text same; 65 students, including 9 graduate)

1893-94 Philosophy 2 (with Hugo Münsterberg). First half-year: lectures, theses, and experiments; second half-year: demonstrations and exercises in the laboratory (42 students, including 6 graduate)

1895-96 Philosophy 2a: Psychology (advanced). Texts: Wundt's *Lectures on Human and Animal Psychology*, Höffding's *Outlines*

---

44 *Henry James Letters*, ed. Leon Edel, II (Cambridge, Mass.: Harvard University Press, 1975), 102.

45 Perry, *Thought and Character*, I, 480. For a possible draft of the statement sent to Spencer see ibid., I, 479–480.

46 According to the catalogue the texts that year were Bain's *Senses and the Intellect* and *Emotions and the Will*.

of Psychology (first half-year; 40 students, 9 graduate)
Philosophy 2b (assisted by Edgar Arthur Singer): Physiological
Psychology. Lectures, laboratory exercises, and special topics
treated in conferences and theses (second half-year; 22 students,
including 5 graduate)

The class met three times per week, except in 1881-82 when it met
twice a week. In 1883-84 and 1884-85 Philosophy 2 was listed among
introductory courses that could not be offered for honors. From
1885-86 through 1889-90, Philosophy 2, with James as the instructor, combined both logic and psychology. In 1890-91 and 1891-92
introductory psychology was offered as part of a general introduction to philosophy, while Philosophy 2 was listed among the systematic courses available to both undergraduates and graduates. In
1893-94, according to the catalogue, James taught the theoretical
part of the course and Münsterberg the laboratory part. In 1895-96
Philosophy 2 was available to both undergraduates and graduates.
Students completing it could proceed to 2b, 20b, or both, with the
permission of the instructor.

George Albert Burdett, a student in 1877–1881, took Philosophy
5 in 1880-81. His notebook is in the Harvard University Archives
(HUC 8880.370.5). The notebook shows that the course was heavily
physiological, although as it developed, James spent more and more
time discussing such subjects as will, spontaneity, feelings, perception, memory, and dreams. At one point Burdett records a suggestive
sequence of questions: "1. What test do we commonly use to decide
whether intelligence is present in phenomena or not? 2. Do actions
from the lower centers conform to this test? 3. If so, can they be
excluded from study of mind?"

The fragments of James's notes—published as Nos. 9 and 10 in the
present volume—are philosophical. Of special interest is No. 9,
which probably dates from the fall of 1876, because it is one of the
earliest of James's philosophical writings. The fragment shows that
even at this early date, James was distancing himself from some
aspects of British empiricism by drawing philosophical conclusions
from the more precise analysis of sensation which the new psychology was making available. James's point is that raw sensations are
not important in elaborating the body of our knowledge:

[Helmholtz] shows the sensations of the retina to be to the last degree
fluctuating and inconsistent; and yet the eye, *as its data enter into the*

ities of scholastic philosophy to realist pragmatism,"[52] from speculative philosophy to sociology and social activism.

James befriended Glendower Evans, who died in 1886 after graduating from Harvard in 1879. In *Pragmatism*, while quoting from an old letter, James referred to Evans as "a gifted friend who died too young."[53] He also befriended John Edward Maude, a student in the early 1880s. Maude also died young, bequeathing to James a manuscript that he edited and published as *The Foundation of Ethics*.[54]

The year 1878 was a pivotal year in James's life. In January he published his first signed essays, in February he lectured at Johns Hopkins, in June he signed the contract for *The Principles of Psychology*, in July he married, and in October he began the first of his Lowell Institute courses. James emerged in that year as a thinker with his own point of view; it was a decisive time in his shift from natural history to philosophy.

According to James's son, if "somebody like the Reverend Andrew Peabody had presided over Harvard during the seventies in place of young C. W. Eliot, and if D. C. Gilman had been made president of Yale instead of Noah Porter in 1871, the first American university would have grown up in New Haven instead of in Cambridge."[55] In 1871 Daniel Coit Gilman had been the favorite candidate of "Young Yale," a group seeking changes in the Yale charter to pave the way for educational reforms. The battle had been fought in public, including in the *Nation*, and probably James had been aware of it. Having failed at Yale, in 1875 Gilman became president of the about-to-be-established Johns Hopkins University. In September 1876 he invited Huxley to lecture. The fact that there were no prayers before or after Huxley's lecture gave rise to a public scandal. There is evidence that at the time of his negotiations with James, Gilman was under some pressure to hire a "safe" philosopher. In spring 1881 he explained to James that the trustees were not interested in a psychologist for the philosophy position and were looking at a European scholar, Robert Flint, a young Scottish theologian. It is suggestive that Granville Stanley Hall, negotiating

[52] *The Autobiography of W. E. B. DuBois* (International Publishers, 1969), pp. 148, 133.

[53] William James, *Pragmatism*, WORKS, p. 115.

[54] Reprinted in *ECR*.

[55] Henry James, *Charles W. Eliot*, I, 224.

with Gilman at about the same time, found it useful to emphasize his churchgoing habits.[56]

James was one of numerous applicants laying siege to Johns Hopkins, attracted by higher salaries and Gilman's educational reforms. The correspondence between James and Gilman is summarized in the notes and need not be repeated here. It is on the whole silent concerning motives and leaves unanswered the question who was courting whom. In any case, James's February 1878 lectures on "The Senses and the Brain and Their Relation to Thought," besides earning him some extra money, served to keep his name alive in the minds of the Hopkins authorities.

In the lectures he defined his standpoint in psychology along the lines of the 1875 letter to Eliot. James claimed to have a place in two camps, that of the physiologists and that of the introspective philosophers:

Where two lots adjoin with disputed boundary we find each owner disposed to push back the fence. If one man owns both lots, he does not care where the fence stands. I think we ought all to assume this attitude, and cast aside as ignoble this jealousy of the man on the other side of the fence. The truth is all our own whether it be truth of body or truth of mind. What truth the physiologist may have discovered belongs by equal right to any introspective philosopher who will take the trouble to understand it. What mental facts the latter notes, are for the benefit of the physiologist as well (*ML*, p. 3).

Given the academic politics of the day, it is likely that both scientists and religionists would have found such views reassuring. Somewhat later James called the "attention of persons who are fearful of the reduction by physiology of higher to lower powers of the mind" to the fact that Helmholtz and Wundt, leaders of the new science, recognize "innate potentialities in the mind which sensations merely awaken into exercise" (*ML*, p. 9).

At Johns Hopkins James developed an argument important for understanding his view that every mental state is a whole and is not composed of parts. In this early formulation his notes presented it as an antidote to skepticism: "When a man tells you he is cold, cold he is, however little cause you might see for it. In a word no distinct between real and phenomenal side. Consciousness is sole judge of

[56] The political background of James's negotiations with Gilman is discussed in Hugh Hawkins, *Pioneer: A History of the Johns Hopkins University* (Ithaca, N.Y.: Cornell University Press, 1960), pp. 188–189, 194.

its own constitution. To say now that pain is not really what it seems but is really composed of other smaller feelings that we know nothing of, seems to reduce all things to chaos again. No fulcrum of certainty" (*ML*, p. 5). At Hopkins James also argued that consciousness is causally efficacious, that men are not automata. No manuscripts related to this argument have survived, perhaps because they were used for "Are We Automata?" (1879).[57] Probably the argument was the one used in the Lowell lectures.

James presented his view of consciousness with reference to evolution, although the details are few. The only surviving reference to evolution is this: "Evolution accounts for mind as a product. First nervous system appeared, then consciousness" (*ML*, p. 4). Shortly thereafter the word "utility" appears, but at that point the notes are rather sketchy. These remarks can be interpreted in the light of a view James expressed in 1875: "Taking a purely naturalistic view of the matter, it seems reasonable to suppose that, unless consciousness served some useful purpose, it would not have been superadded to life."[58]

Since little information about the Johns Hopkins lectures has been found, it is impossible to compare them with the Lowell Institute course on "The Brain and the Mind" of the same year. James probably intended to use the same material in both cases, but when the Institute offered only six lectures, he decided to concentrate on theories of brain function and hope that the material on the senses could be used in a later course.[59]

When addressing the Lowell Institute James again tried to mark out a middle ground for himself:

As proprietors of a body we ought to feel the insufficiency of every theory of the mind which leaves the body out. As owners of a mind we ought to feel the worthlessness of all explanations of our feelings which leave out that which is most essential to be explained. I confess that in the past few years, owing to the divided duties I have alluded to, I have felt most acutely the difficulties of understanding either the brain without the mind, or the mind without the brain. I have almost concluded in my moments of depression that we hardly know anything (*ML*, p. 32).

James's main concern was to show that consciousness as an organ of selection is causally efficacious, and thus useful from an evolution-

[57] Reprinted in William James, *Essays in Psychology*, WORKS.
[58] *ECR*, p. 302.
[59] See note to 16.26 in the present volume.

ary point of view. There is evidence that in the early 1870s James viewed consciousness as an epiphenomenon,[60] but in the late 1870s he reached his mature view. The view that consciousness is useful is worked out in the context of an attack on "modern materialism." In terms of academic politics, James again appeared as a man completely at home in the latest sciences and yet mindful of spiritual values.

According to James, modern proponents of materialism such as Tyndall and Huxley—its "best exponents"—hold that the connection between mind and brain is inexplicable. Since they do not pretend to explain mind but simply insist upon the fact that for every mental event there is an event in the nervous system, they cannot be accused of "degrading the high by deducing it from the low." On the other hand, since they claim that mind is not causally efficacious, they do not escape the charge in the "practical sphere":

When I hear a man call our feelings impotent, deny them any independence, when he says they are passive creatures of physical conditions & not masters of such conditions, I call him a materialist for his utterances contain surely all that is repugnant or objectionable in materialism. It is absurd for such authors to indignantly deny that they are materialists, merely because they admit that the servile relation of mind to matter that they so strenuously affirm to be the truth, is an incomprehensible truth (*ML*, p. 23).

In support of his own view James offered an argument familiar from "Are We Automata?" and *The Principles of Psychology*. The higher nervous centers such as the cerebral hemispheres enable men to make fine discriminations and to act with reference to past experiences, to facts not directly present, to future possibilities. However, an organ "so multiform in its performances" is bound to suffer from "extreme instability," a "hair-trigger organization." As such, it would often act from "very slight disturbances, from accidental causes," and "caprice" would be its law. To a creature with such an unstable neural system, consciousness is useful because it can "load the dice, can exert a constant pressure in the right direction." This is so because consciousness can both keep the goal constantly in view and, as an organ of selection, focus attention upon those stimuli to which response is needed while ignoring the rest (*ML*, p. 26). The

[60] See the draft of an early essay published in *Manuscript Essays and Notes*, WORKS, pp. 247–256 (hereafter *MEN*).

argument thus developed became the cornerstone of James's philosophy of mind. Henceforth, he had his own point of view in philosophy.

In 1879-80, still an assistant professor of physiology but with his courses entirely in the philosophy department, James introduced two new courses, his first philosophical ones. He offered Philosophy 5: Contemporary Philosophy, using Renouvier's *Essais de critique générale* as a text, only once; there were 9 students, including 2 graduate and 2 law students. The other new course, Philosophy 3: The Philosophy of Evolution, was repeated several times.

James announced the Renouvier course in a lost letter to Renouvier. The latter replied on August 21, 1879: "I have allowed the many thanks which I owe you to accumulate. Receive them all at once, I beg you, with the expression of my intense gratitude for the great honour which you have done me in including my writings among those which you deem worthy of being assigned as university readings,—not merely *en passant*, but as something like subjects of instruction." [61] Apparently Renouvier did not prove a suitable text, for on February 3, 1880, James noted in a letter to Josiah Royce: "I've tried Renouvier as a text-book—for the last time! His exposition offers too many difficulties." [62] A few days before the final examination, James commented on the results of the course in a letter to Renouvier dated June 1, 1880:

My last lesson in the course on your *Essais* took place today. The final examination occurs this week. The students have been profoundly interested, though their reactions on your teaching seem as diverse as their personalities; one (the maturest of all) being yours body and soul, another turning out a strongly materialistic fatalist! and the rest occupying positions of mixed doubt and assent; all, however (but one), being convinced by your treatment of freedom and certitude. [63]

Nothing that can be definitively identified as notes for the course has survived, although it is possible that the dialogue between Renouvier and an evolutionist published in the present volume (*ML*, pp. 133–134) is connected with the course. The examination questions, however, suggest a strong preoccupation with infinity and freedom and contain nothing about mental activity, the subject of the dialogue.

[61] Perry, *Thought and Character*, I, 668.
[62] *Letters of William James*, II, 205.
[63] Perry, *Thought and Character*, I, 671.

James taught Philosophy 3: The Philosophy of Evolution four times:

1879-80   Text: Spencer's *First Principles* (2 hours per week; 17 students)
1880-81   Texts: Spencer's *First Principles* and *Data of Ethics* (2 hours per week; 21 students, including 2 divinity)
1883-84   Texts: same (second half-year; 3 hours per week; 89 students)
1884-85   Texts: same (second half-year; 3 hours per week; 55 students)

In its first three years Philosophy 3 was listed among the introductory courses recommended as preparation for those intending to take advanced work in philosophy. It thus initiated the long series of introduction to philosophy courses that James taught over the years. In 1884-85 the course was removed from the list of introductory courses.

A letter unusual for its exuberance and uninhibited banter even for James recorded his state of mind at the conclusion of one of the Spencer courses. It is dated simply May 26; the year remains uncertain. It is addressed to James Jackson Putnam:

Your insolent card of May 13 reached my eyes (by a strange coincidence) just as I return from the last crowning lecture of the course in wh. poor Spencer has been shaken in my jaws as a mouse is shaken by a tiger (as soon as the latter can conquer his native timidity and once fairly take hold of the mouse). The course (I need not say) closed amid the tumultuous, nay, delirious applause of the students. Poor Spencer, reduced to the simple childlike faith of merely timid, receptive, uncritical, undiscriminating, worshipful, servile, gullible, stupid, idiotic natures like you and Fiske! . . . Of all the incoherent, rotten, quackish humbugs & pseudo-philosophers which the womb of all-inventive time has excreted he is the most infamous and "abgeschmackt"—but even *he* is better than his followers. . . . Go! child of perdition . . . subscribe to the Popular Science monthly, hang at the breasts of "Cosmism" (—breasts yclept "falsehood" and "insanity",) go to bed with the Persistence of Force the unknowable, the Realism, the Empiricism . . . and all the other brats of the chromo-philosophy.[64]

The surviving notes, published as No. 11 in the present volume, suggest that the course had a strongly polemical flavor. James made

---

[64] Original in the Countway Library of Medicine, Boston. It is published in Nathan G. Hale, *James Jackson Putnam and Psychoanalysis* (Cambridge, Mass.: Harvard, 1971), pp. 68–69. Hale places the letter in 1877, but I think it is later. There are clear references to Spencer's *First Principles*, and James did not use the book in a course until 1879-80.

a common residence of hundreds of young men and women of immature character and marriageable age are very grave. The necessary police regulations are exceedingly burdensome."[68] But with Eliot's support, the Women's Annex—later to become Radcliffe College—began to offer courses in fall 1879 with an enrollment of 27 students. Men and women were not to attend the same classes, but Harvard professors were to offer regular courses to the women for additional pay. According to the records of Arthur Gilman, one of the organizers of the Annex, Gilman conferred with James on January 14, 1879, and received a favorable response.[69] Published accounts of James's involvement leave the impression that his motives were somewhat mercenary, as this example illustrates:

William James believed in wholesale rates. He would teach Psychology and Modern Philosophy, but not for more than four hours a week. He would charge "not less than four dollars an hour" and his price "would probably exclude any solitary pupil." For three pupils, he would charge six dollars, "for four, five and for five or six only $1.50 apiece." For any class larger than six, the charge would be ten dollars an hour.[70]

Although mercenary in inspiration, James's teaching at Radcliffe led to many warm, almost sentimental, attachments. The following letter to Mary E. Raymond, dated June 16, 1895, is a fair representative of many that could be quoted:

I thank you heartily for all the kind things you say about my instruction, and—Heaven save the mark!—moral influence. We are instruments in the hands of the Infinite, who can do extraordinary things with us! And I may truly say that your moral or spiritual influence upon me has been of the best—as indeed I am grateful to Radcliffe through and through for many subtle forms of good. The worst of it is the separating so soon.[71]

James did not teach at Radcliffe[72] very often, although the situation is sometimes confused by the fact that in some years his courses were announced but apparently not given. The following table represents his involvement in the education of women:

68 Eliot, *Educational Reform*, pp. 22–23.

69 Records of Arthur Gilman, Radcliffe Archives.

70 Louise Hall Tharp, *Adventurous Alliance: The Story of the Agassiz Family of Boston* (Boston: Little, Brown, 1959), p. 249.

71 Original in Colby College Library.

72 The account of James's teaching at Radcliffe is based on several reports and announcements in the Radcliffe Archives.

a common residence of hundreds of young men and women of immature character and marriageable age are very grave. The necessary police regulations are exceedingly burdensome." [68] But with Eliot's support, the Women's Annex—later to become Radcliffe College—began to offer courses in fall 1879 with an enrollment of 27 students. Men and women were not to attend the same classes, but Harvard professors were to offer regular courses to the women for additional pay. According to the records of Arthur Gilman, one of the organizers of the Annex, Gilman conferred with James on January 14, 1879, and received a favorable response.[69] Published accounts of James's involvement leave the impression that his motives were somewhat mercenary, as this example illustrates:

William James believed in wholesale rates. He would teach Psychology and Modern Philosophy, but not for more than four hours a week. He would charge "not less than four dollars an hour" and his price "would probably exclude any solitary pupil." For three pupils, he would charge six dollars, "for four, five and for five or six only $1.50 apiece." For any class larger than six, the charge would be ten dollars an hour.[70]

Although mercenary in inspiration, James's teaching at Radcliffe led to many warm, almost sentimental, attachments. The following letter to Mary E. Raymond, dated June 16, 1895, is a fair representative of many that could be quoted:

I thank you heartily for all the kind things you say about my instruction, and—Heaven save the mark!—moral influence. We are instruments in the hands of the Infinite, who can do extraordinary things with us! And I may truly say that your moral or spiritual influence upon me has been of the best—as indeed I am grateful to Radcliffe through and through for many subtle forms of good. The worst of it is the separating so soon.[71]

James did not teach at Radcliffe[72] very often, although the situation is sometimes confused by the fact that in some years his courses were announced but apparently not given. The following table represents his involvement in the education of women:

---

[68] Eliot, *Educational Reform*, pp. 22–23.

[69] Records of Arthur Gilman, Radcliffe Archives.

[70] Louise Hall Tharp, *Adventurous Alliance: The Story of the Agassiz Family of Boston* (Boston: Little, Brown, 1959), p. 249.

[71] Original in Colby College Library.

[72] The account of James's teaching at Radcliffe is based on several reports and announcements in the Radcliffe Archives.

sations and a realism for which substances are unperceivable some-things behind the phenomena:

My idea of substance is simply that it means that the present phenom-enon is not all—that its existence involves other existences—that in addition to its actuality it has a potentiality when it *is* not, and that such potentiality means that whatever *is* now calls for that phenomenon in its time & place. In other words, it is not an accident, but continuous with all the rest of things—*it is meant.* To be able to say of each phe-nomenon this is meant by all that is would be to achieve the philosophic task and bind all that is into unity (*ML*, pp. 147–148).

These fragments of his own somewhat tentative point of view were developed in the context of a general attack on Spencer.

Not only is Spencer vague, according to James, but his attempt to build a philosophy out of evolutionary ideas leads to vicious results:

We have all got to attack the problem of the *meaning* of the facts of evolution. The evolutionary *philosophy* is a monism. Nothing comes new—no new essence, and so far as it *dwells* on the common substance it shares the blame of all monisms. So far as it reduces the higher to the lower, "survival" etc.—the inverse process to Spencers development of cognition—it is vicious. Historically it has tended to this. Philosophies of selfishness etc (*ML*, p. 158).

It is noteworthy that in these early reflections James tried not to erect the evolutionary struggle for existence into a moral norm. Many years later his own pragmatism was sometimes attacked in the way in which he here attacked Spencer.

In the meantime, preoccupied with greater things, he was acting like a typical absent-minded professor. While in Europe during the summer of 1880 he asked his wife to send him the examination grades for Philosophy 3, only to realize several days later that he had had the grades with him all along.[67]

The early years of James's teaching career saw another change at Harvard: the beginning of collegiate instruction for women. Eliot raised the issue in his inaugural address, urging great caution. In his view, very little was known about the capacities of women and, in any case, it was not Harvard's task to decide such questions. Cau-tion was needed for practical reasons: "The difficulties involved in

[67] Letters of June 15, 1880, and June 18, 1880 (bMS Am 1092.9 #1213, #1214).

clear his intent at the very beginning, in a list of phrases under the heading "Reasons for Course." According to James, Spencer was a "mouthpiece" of the spirit of the age, with its ideas of progress and evolution. Spencer's views needed "polemic" treatment (*ML*, p. 150).

James insisted upon Spencer's essential vagueness, something which he does in most of his published comments about Spencer. To the class he explained that Spencer's Unknowable has ten different meanings: it is at one and the same time the self-existent, the first cause, the unity of things, the cosmos as completed, the *summum genus*, the ideal truth, bare abstract being, the correlative, power, and noumenon (*ML*, pp. 163–164). In his last philosophical reflections James insisted that philosophy cannot offer an explanation of the mystery of existence: "Philosophy stares, but brings no reasoned solution, for from nothing to being there is no logical bridge."[65] The same theme is sounded in his early criticism of Spencer and his arguments for the Unknowable: "But we have seen that they need not bring self contradiction into our data—only the *inexplicability* of their being data. Some time back I said that this might be dealt with either by exorcising the question as illegitimate, by ignoring it, or by answering it" (*ML*, p. 166). In this context James made several remarks important for understanding his early efforts to work out his own phenomenalism.[66] In one case James argued that Spencer began with facts accepted by everyone:

No doubt it is the living sense in everyone's breast that this fact has something more in it than is borne in upon his consciousness at any given moment, that he stands simply expectant of what it will bring forth, and passively at its mercy, unable by his thought to foresee its course in other than a tentative sort of way,—no doubt all this is why Spencer's asseverations awaken in the mind of every reader who takes things in an easy hospitable way, an immediate echo of adhesion. But I insist that the readers postulate is merely that of *more to be known*—not of still more unknowable (*ML*, p. 165).

Of great interest in connection with his early phenomenalism is James's definition of substance, whereby he tried to avoid both a pure nominalism for which substances are only collections of sen-

---

65 William James, *Some Problems of Philosophy*, Works, p. 27.
66 James's early manuscripts on phenomenalism appear in *MEN*.

James taught Philosophy 3: The Philosophy of Evolution four times:

1879-80   Text: Spencer's *First Principles* (2 hours per week; 17 students)
1880-81   Texts: Spencer's *First Principles* and *Data of Ethics* (2 hours per week; 21 students, including 2 divinity)
1883-84   Texts: same (second half-year; 3 hours per week; 89 students)
1884-85   Texts: same (second half-year; 3 hours per week; 55 students)

In its first three years Philosophy 3 was listed among the introductory courses recommended as preparation for those intending to take advanced work in philosophy. It thus initiated the long series of introduction to philosophy courses that James taught over the years. In 1884-85 the course was removed from the list of introductory courses.

A letter unusual for its exuberance and uninhibited banter even for James recorded his state of mind at the conclusion of one of the Spencer courses. It is dated simply May 26; the year remains uncertain. It is addressed to James Jackson Putnam:

Your insolent card of May 13 reached my eyes (by a strange coincidence) just as I return from the last crowning lecture of the course in wh. poor Spencer has been shaken in my jaws as a mouse is shaken by a tiger (as soon as the latter can conquer his native timidity and once fairly take hold of the mouse). The course (I need not say) closed amid the tumultuous, nay, delirious applause of the students. Poor Spencer, reduced to the simple childlike faith of merely timid, receptive, uncritical, undiscriminating, worshipful, servile, gullible, stupid, idiotic natures like you and Fiske! . . . Of all the incoherent, rotten, quackish humbugs & pseudophilosophers which the womb of all-inventive time has excreted he is the most infamous and "abgeschmackt"—but even *he* is better than his followers. . . . Go! child of perdition . . . subscribe to the Popular Science monthly, hang at the breasts of "Cosmism" (—breasts yclept "falsehood" and "insanity",) go to bed with the Persistence of Force the unknowable, the Realism, the Empiricism . . . and all the other brats of the chromophilosophy.[64]

The surviving notes, published as No. 11 in the present volume, suggest that the course had a strongly polemical flavor. James made

[64] Original in the Countway Library of Medicine, Boston. It is published in Nathan G. Hale, *James Jackson Putnam and Psychoanalysis* (Cambridge, Mass.: Harvard, 1971), pp. 68–69. Hale places the letter in 1877, but I think it is later. There are clear references to Spencer's *First Principles*, and James did not use the book in a course until 1879-80.

1879-80   Philosophy 3: The Philosophy of Evolution
1894-95   Philosophy 3: Cosmology
1895-96   Philosophy 2a: Psychology (first half-year; 19 students)
          Philosophy 3: Philosophy of Nature (first half-year; 16 students)
1896-97   Philosophy 3: Philosophy of Nature (first half-year; 15 students)
1897-98   Philosophy 3: Philosophy of Nature (14 students)

In 1895-96 James did not teach Philosophy 3 at Harvard. Concerning this course, he commented in a letter of August 13, 1895, to Théodore Flournoy: "I also repeated my course in Cosmology in the new woman's College which has lately been established in connection with our University. The consequence is that I laid by more than a thousand dollars, an absolutely new and proportionately pleasant experience for me. To make up for it, I have n't had an idea or written anything to speak of."[73] The list shows that James did not prepare any new courses for Radcliffe students but only repeated courses prepared for Harvard.

One other fact can be noted in connection with the education of women: according to Harvard Corporation Records, on October 1, 1890, Mary Whiton Calkins was granted permission to attend classes taught by James and Royce. Later there were women in many of James's Harvard classes.

As of December 1, 1880, James became an assistant professor of philosophy with a salary of $2000, to serve in that rank for five years. This amounted to no more than formal recognition of his actual status. James became a leading organizer of the philosophy department, constantly on the lookout for candidates who would fit Harvard's needs. The histories of his bringing Josiah Royce and Hugo Münsterberg to Harvard are well known and need no repetition here. In any case, this introduction is concerned with James as a teacher rather than as an academic politician. He certainly was active in the latter capacity, for example, in trying to find jobs for Harvard graduate students.

James next introduced a new course in 1881-82, Philosophy 4: Contemporary Philosophy, using Mill's *System of Logic* as a text. The course attracted 22 students. Apparently much the same course was given in 1886-87; it was called Philosophy 5: English Empirical Philosophy and drew 17 students. In a letter to Thomas Davidson

[73] *Letters of William James*, II, 24.

dated April 16, 1881, he noted: "I have been enjoying my class in Mill's *Logic* immensely."[74]

The fragment of James's notes for Philosophy 4, No. 13 in the present volume, suggests that James was critical of Mill as a methodologist of science. In James's view Mill was mistaken in treating the four methods of induction as methods of discovery. In fact, the four are methods for "*testing* not *making* guesses." Furthermore, Mill was mistaken in thinking that all uniformities in nature are causal. "Most 'laws of nature' relate to coexistence of properties, specifications of processes &c. that are ill-described in causal language" (*ML*, p. 179). One of the examination questions is tantalizing: "What does your instructor mean by 'postulates of intelligibility'? Name one of them." Unfortunately, the notes are silent on this point.

For some years the Harvard program had included a course on British empiricism. Originally taught by Palmer, it was taken over by Josiah Royce—James's replacement while James was on leave—in 1882-83 and by James in 1883-84. The course was Philosophy 5: English Philosophy. James offered it four times: 1883-84 (9 students); 1884-85 (13); 1885-86 (19); and 1887-88 (16). The texts were Locke's *Essay Concerning Human Understanding*, Berkeley's *Treatise Concerning the Principles of Human Knowledge* and *Essay towards a New Theory of Vision*, and Hume's *Enquiry Concerning Human Understanding*, except for the last year when Reid's *Essays on the Intellectual Powers of Man* was substituted for Locke. For this period James's main philosophical sources were Spencer and John Stuart Mill. From the mid-1880s he came to view himself as heir to the whole tradition of British philosophy, including in his extensive reading even minor figures. Notes for the course taken by Ralph Waldo Black in 1884-85 are preserved in the Houghton Library (bMS Am 1092.9 #4583a). They indicate a considerable interest in the differences between the empiricists and Kant.

On February 16, 1885, the Harvard Corporation approved James's promotion to the rank of professor of philosophy. In 1885-86 he began teaching an introductory course that covered several areas. The course was Philosophy 2: Logic and Psychology, which James taught a total of five times: 1885-86 (99 students, including 46 juniors); 1886-87 (85, including 33 juniors); 1887-88 (123, including

[74] Perry, *Thought and Character*, I, 742.

43 juniors); 1888-89 (87, including 39 juniors); and 1889-90 (128, including 36 seniors and 35 juniors). James's course was one of three lecture courses intended as introductions to philosophy and having large enrollments. Palmer offered an introduction to the history of philosophy, while Royce offered a third introduction which in some years covered the same material as James's course. The enrollment patterns were similar for all three courses: very few freshmen, more sophomores, many juniors and seniors, several graduate students, and a sprinkling of others.

For the logic portion of the course James used William Stanley Jevons, *Elementary Lessons in Logic*, the standard logic text at Harvard for many years. The book has the honor of being the only logic text that James employed in his classes. The text for the psychology portion varied. The first year it was Bain's *Senses and the Intellect*; the next two years, Bain's *Emotions and the Will*; the last two years, George Trumbull Ladd, *Elements of Physiological Psychology*. A notebook for Philosophy 2, 1887-88, compiled by Clarence A. Bunker (HUC 8887.370.2), is preserved in the Harvard University Archives. It is curious that what should have been the notes on logic are nothing but empty pages. In the class of January 4, 1888, James urged the benefits of early marriage.

For four out of the five times when it was taught, Philosophy 2 met at noon. This fact lends additional significance to the following passage, probably autobiographical, from *The Principles of Psychology*: "I know a person, for example, who will poke the fire, set chairs straight, pick dust-specks from the floor, arrange his table, snatch up the newspaper, take down any book which catches his eye, trim his nails, waste the morning *anyhow*, in short, and all without premeditation,—simply because the only thing he *ought* to attend to is the preparation of a noonday lesson in formal logic which he detests."[75] Perhaps this explains the gap in Bunker's notebook.

In the middle years of his Harvard career James played an active part in the discussion of questions concerning curriculum and student discipline. His published statements appear in *Essays, Comments, and Reviews* (WORKS, pp. 32–41, 62–67, 122–126, 128–130) and need only be mentioned briefly here. In 1885 and 1886 he published three letters in the Harvard *Crimson* concerning student celebrations, the Harvard custom of marking every athletic victory

---

[75] *PP*, p. 398.

with explosions and bonfires in the Yard. In James's view the students themselves should be responsible for making sure that such celebrations did not get out of hand. Several years later he commented on the proctoring of examinations, urging an honor system. In 1891 he published an essay on "The Proposed Shortening of the College Course." Harvard records show that James actively supported Eliot's plan to make it possible for Harvard undergraduates to obtain a degree in three years. In 1899, as a member of a committee, James signed a report on the proper use of academic regalia.

In 1888-89 James offered his first and only course in ethics, Philosophy 4: Recent English Contributions to Theistic Ethics. The course attracted 37 students, most of them seniors. The texts were James Martineau's *Types of Ethical Theory* and volume II of Martineau's *Study of Religion*. According to the president's report, "Each student was expected to employ half of the time devoted to this course in the preparation of a thesis involving the reading of several volumes; the theses averaged 50 pages in length." In a letter of October 7, 1888, to G. Croom Robertson, James wrote: "I am teaching ethics and the philosophy of religion for the first time, with that dear old duffer Martineau's works as a text. It gives me lots to do, as I only began my systematic reading in that line three weeks ago."[76] Number 14 in the present volume and, probably, No. 62 in *Manuscript Essays and Notes* (WORKS, pp. 301–311) are notes used in the course. The notes show that James rejected utilitarianism on psychological grounds: "I firmly believe that we have preferences inexplicable by utility, or by the direct influence of the environment, preferences for certain kinds of behavior, as consistency, veracity, justice, nobility, dignity, purity etc etc. Those who contend for an innate moral faculty are therefore right from a *psychological* point of view" (*ML*, p. 183). It is interesting that James treated Kant's imperatives as psychological facts, as feelings, and that he applied what appears to be the pragmatic maxim to elucidate the notion of obligation: "The *effective*ness of a feeling of obligation depends on the circumstances. *If not effective*, what we mean by calling it an obligation is that we haven't heard the last of it" (*ML*, p. 185).

James's letters to his wife provide several glimpses of James as a

---

[76] *Letters of William James*, I, 283.

teacher in the late 1880s. On February 20, 1888, he wrote that the philosophy club had just left "bearing away six planchettes, which I will charge to my college appropriation." On October 20, 1889: "spent a couple of hours over brains with Phil 20a." On November 3, 1889, he expressed his pleasure at becoming professor of psychology: "how badly I teach my logic, and to be responsible for the limited field of psychology, instead of the whole howling waste of philosophy is a good load off my mind. I shall *do* philosophy all the same." [77] The change in James's title was approved on November 11, 1889. He remained a professor of psychology until October 4, 1897, when he resumed the title of professor of philosophy. His pay as professor was $5000.

For the 1890-91 academic year the teaching of introductory philosophy was completely reorganized. The new course was Philosophy 1: General Introduction to Philosophy, covering logic, psychology, and metaphysics, with a different instructor responsible for each segment:

1890-91   Palmer, James (metaphysics), Santayana (201 students)
1891-92   Palmer, James (psychology), Royce (176 students)
1893-94   Palmer, James (psychology), Santayana (200 students)
1894-95   Palmer, James (psychology), Santayana (285 students)
1895-96   Royce, James (psychology), Santayana (310 students)
1896-97   Palmer, James (psychology), Royce, assisted by Benjamin Rand (338 students)
1905-6   James (general introduction to philosophy), Royce, Münster-berg (226 students)

In all cases most of the students were sophomores or juniors. In 1893-94 the course was numbered 1a to distinguish it from Philosophy 1b, a general introduction taught by Royce. In 1895-96 and 1896-97 the students would have Royce for logic and introductory lectures on philosophical study during the first half-year, and for the second half-year they would choose between psychology and history of philosophy. Enrollments for James's segment are not given separately. When he taught metaphysics, James used Lotze's *Outlines of Metaphysics*; when he taught psychology, his text was his own *Psychology: Briefer Course*. Since *Briefer Course* was published in 1892, in 1891-92 he used partial prepublication printings,

[77] bMS Am 1092.9 #1534, #1700, #1707.

which are identified in the Harvard catalogue as "James's Outlines of Psychology."[78] James's notes for 1905-6 are preserved (bMS Am 1092.9 #4516) but are not published here to avoid duplication. That year he was responsible only for the first several weeks of the course, which was numbered 1a to distinguish it from 1b, an introduction to the history of philosophy.

James's notes for the metaphysics segment of the course in 1890-91 are published as No. 15 in the present volume. They show that James approached the task of introducing students to philosophy in historical terms, emphasizing the connection between philosophical and scientific developments. The Harvard University Archives preserve student notes for 1891-92 and 1893-94. The latter set of notes, compiled by Edward Waldo Forbes (HUC 8893.369.1), show that James taught the course that year, a fact noted in neither the president's report nor the catalogue. According to Forbes, on February 12, 1894, James lectured on immortality, claiming that the question could be settled either by revelation, intuition, or scientific evidence. James suggested that the first two ways could be ignored and in connection with scientific evidence mentioned the case of Mrs. Piper. According to the notes, James's segment of the course began on December 20 and ended on March 16.

When George Santayana began teaching at Harvard in the fall of 1889, he took over James's course on the British empiricists. In its place, in 1890-91, James offered a course on the continental rationalists, Philosophy 10: Descartes, Spinoza, and Leibniz, with 6 students. The following year the course was taken over by Santayana, and James did not teach it again. Number 16 in this volume represents the surviving notes.

James's teaching load during these years consisted either of three full courses per year or of two full courses and either a half-course or one segment of introduction. Almost every year he offered graduate psychology, undergraduate psychology, and one of the several courses in philosophy listed above. It is not clear whether James changed his philosophy courses because of departmental needs or because of a desire to broaden his own reading. According to Palmer, the departmental organization at this time was rather loose, with a rotating chairman whose job was to call meetings and communicate

[78] For the prepublication printing see William James, *Psychology: Briefer Course,* WORKS, p. 480.

with the president.[79] Palmer suggests that the teaching schedule reflected the wishes of the professors themselves.

James's philosophy courses to this point were largely historical, focusing either on the work of one writer or on a period. As a result, he made up the deficiencies in his own education and became unusually learned in the history of modern philosophy. According to Palmer, historical courses were the rule in American colleges, a habit started "in modesty and the conscious need of knowledge," but incompatible with creative work and in the end "enfeebling." Palmer claims that he himself offered the first systematic course—a course entitled systematic ethics—in 1889.[80] In the 1890s James's teaching pattern changed gradually. In the area of psychology, he moved from physiological psychology to abnormal and philosophical psychology. In effect, having completed work on *The Principles of Psychology*, he was carrying out part of the plan he had indicated in a letter to Henry dated September 18, 1887: "When this book is out I shall say adieu to Psychology for a while and study some other things, Physics a little, and History of Philosophy, in which I'm awfully in arrears."[81] He did drop the physiological psychology, but in philosophy he began gradually to shift his attention from historical to systematic courses. Dickinson Sergeant Miller was a Harvard student in the early 1890s. His detailed reminiscences of James as a teacher during this period are published in *The Letters of William James*, II, 11–17.

Number 17 in this volume represents the notes for the graduate psychology course in 1891-92. This was the last year in which James's graduate course dealt with physiological psychology. The notes indicate a strong interest in physiological aesthetics.

When in 1893-94 James returned to teaching after a year's leave, he took over from Royce the course Philosophy 3: Cosmology, "a study of the fundamental conceptions of Natural Science, with special reference to theories of Evolution and Materialism." Whereas the older Philosophy 3: The Philosophy of Evolution had been primarily a course on Spencer, the new one was a systematic course

---

[79] George Herbert Palmer, *The Autobiography of a Philosopher* (Boston: Houghton Mifflin, 1930), p. 50.

[80] Ibid., p. 44.

[81] bMS Am 1092.9 #2634. The letter was begun on September 1 but was completed on the 18th.

dealing with a variety of problems. In fact, in 1897-98 the course description was changed from the one just quoted to "The Philosophy of Nature, with especial reference to Man's place in Nature." The texts for the course were changed frequently: 1893-94 (42 students), Spencer's *First Principles* and Lotze's *Outlines of the Philosophy of Nature*; 1894-95 (33 students), Spencer; 1896-97 (34 students), Spencer, and Paulsen's *Introduction to Philosophy*; 1897-98 (34 students), Lotze's *Microcosmus*; 1902-3 (57 students), Pearson's *Grammar of Science* and Ward's *Naturalism and Agnosticism*. In the last year James was assisted by Dickinson Sergeant Miller. The course, which met three times per week, usually attracted a few graduate students and many seniors. Information concerning this course at Radcliffe has been given earlier.

There is much information concerning this course. Two student notebooks are preserved from 1896-97: one by Roger Bigelow Merriman in the Harvard University Archives (HUC 8896.369.3.54), the other by Ralph Barton Perry in the Houghton Library (bMS AM 1092.9 #4590). There are three sets of notes from 1902-3 in the Archives: by Eugene Lyman Porter (HUC 8902.370.3); by Jared Sparks Moore (HUC 8902.370); and by Edwin DeTurck Bechtel (HUC 8899.321). James's own notes are available as well for that year (No. 23 in the present volume). It is also possible that No. 21 is connected with this course.

Merriman's notebook shows that in 1896-97 for most of the year students were asked to read portions of Paulsen's book, and that in class James commented on Paulsen's views. James emphasized the need to reconcile science and religion, and apparently presented "The Will to Believe" as effecting such a reconciliation. According to Merriman, James explained that although Kant was primarily a rationalist, he had another side: he was also a "great dirationalist" because his great aim was to destroy reason in order to establish faith. At the end of the course James argued that the philosophy of nature leads to pluralism.

Merriman's notes and other evidence show that from the mid-1890s James's teaching became more philosophical and constructive. The ideas tested in class became the core of his philosophical writings. At this point James began to preserve his class notes more systematically: there are notes for most of the courses of the later period, and these notes are much more complete. To preserve chronology, James's 1902-3 notes for Philosophy 3 will be discussed later.

There is still one nonphilosophical course to be noticed, the course in abnormal psychology. The following table summarizes James's teaching in this area:

1893-94 Philosophy 20b: Psychological Seminary, questions in mental pathology (2 hours per week; 11 students, including 8 graduate)

1894-95 Philosophy 20b: Psychological Seminary, questions in mental pathology, embracing a review of the principal forms of abnormal or exceptional mental life (2 hours per week; 7 students, including 4 graduate)

1896-97 Philosophy 15: Abnormal Psychology, a study of the various types of insanity, and of recent investigations into exceptional mental phenomena (first half-year; 3 hours per week; 11 students, including 3 graduate; text, Henry Maudsley, *The Pathology of Mind* [1880])

1898-99 Philosophy 20b: Psychological Seminary. Abnormal Psychology, a study of the various types of insanity and of exceptional mental phenomena (3 hours per week; 12 students, including 6 graduate)

In the last year each student was required to make three visits to asylums and write two reports.

No notes connected with the abnormal psychology course have been identified. Probably James used the same material in three courses of public lectures on abnormal psychology, published in the present volume as No. 5. Abnormal psychology was just then coming into existence as a distinct field, and James, realizing that the field was in its infancy, was primarily interested in assembling and classifying the facts. The public lectures—and probably the Harvard courses—were in the main descriptive, although he hoped that eventually there would be theories and therapeutic applications. He suggested that the notion of a subliminal consciousness could provide the basis for a general theory of these strange and diverse phenomena. There are signs (*ML*, p. 70) that James was trying to decide between two different interpretations of the subliminal: Janet's, that the subliminal results from degeneration of normal consciousness, and Myers's, that by means of the subliminal we come into contact with superior consciousness. In the first case abnormal phenomena could only be signs of disease; in the second they could serve as vehicles for deepening our understanding of reality. In a letter to George Holmes Howison dated April 5, 1897, concerning the Lowell lectures, James wrote: "In these lectures I did not go into psychical research so-called, and although the subjects were decidedly morbid, I tried to shape them towards optimistic and hygienic conclusions, and the audience regarded them as decidedly anti-morbid in their tone."[82]

As we have seen, James's teaching was gradually shifting from psychology and exposition to philosophy and construction. In 1895-96 his graduate psychology course was no longer a course in physiological psychology, but belongs with his efforts to work out a philosophy of radical empiricism. Its affinities are with "The Many and the One," the Miller-Bode notebooks—both published in *Manuscript Essays and Notes* (WORKS, pp. 3–129)—and the *Essays in Radical Empiricism*. James's notes for the course appear as No. 18 in the present volume. Clearly by then James was committed to working out a phenomenalism for which experience was the only stuff and the subject-object distinction represented only two different ways of grouping experience:

The datum in itself & intrinsically considered is no more inner than outer. It *becomes* inner by *belonging* to an inner, it becomes outer by *belonging* to an outer, world. It can be strung (in its intrinsic entirety) either on a vertical thread so to speak which unites it to associates that together with it make the inner world, and also on a horizontal thread with associates that together with it make an outer world. But these latter associates, when severally *realized as data*, also belong to the inner world, and it is only as *supposed* termini of relations with the datum that they constitute an outer world with it (*ML*, p. 217).

The advantage that radical empiricism has over common sense and absolute idealism is its "concreteness": "That is, when asked what we *mean* by knowing, ego, physical 'thing,' memory, etc. we can point to a definite portion of content with a nature definitely realized, and nothing is postulated whose nature is not fully given in experience-terms" (*ML*, pp. 228–229). In the course James used the expression "pure experience" (*ML*, p. 213), one of the earliest occurrences of this term in James. From the point of the history of this term, it is suggestive that in these notes he mentioned Richard

---

[82] *Letters of William James*, II, 54n.

Avenarius, who in 1888 began the publication of his *Kritik der reinen Erfahrung.*

The notes are extensive and coherent, mostly complete sentences and paragraphs rather than phrases serving as cues for lecturing. The same can be said for the notes for the graduate psychology course in 1897-98, No. 20 in the present volume. James's central problem was the problem of the Johns Hopkins and Lowell lectures of 1878, whether consciousness is a mere epiphenomenon or is causally efficacious: "But can we now frame any suggestion as to how the world of bewusstheit, thus centralized congruently with the teleological interests of the brain in the physical world, actually is useful in steering the latter?" (*ML*, p. 235). The difficulty arises in part because the mind and the brain stand in different relations to time: "In the brain-world past and future as such are ineffective, and whatever happens has a present cause, whereas in conscious world memories and futures appear as incentives to activity" (*ML*, p. 236). Common dualism cannot solve the problem because, for it, self and thing are contentless. A solution can be worked out only within "the system of 'pure experience'" (*ML*, p. 238).

The two sets of notes serve to emphasize the side of James obscured in his published writings: James as a technical philosopher struggling with difficult conceptual puzzles. They also provide links between the James of *The Principles of Psychology* and James the radical empiricist. Some of the continuities were set out by James himself: "The whole *use* of the 'change of base' to pure-experience is to see whether one may thereby solve certain problems which are *stickers* on the usual dualistic categories." James listed six problems:

1) The paradox that though sensations & sensible attributes are one, the former are deemed inextensive, the latter extensive;
2) psycho-physical causality;
3) the idealistic paradox—brain being a condition of consciousness, whose creature brain nevertheless is.
4) the discrepant cycles of "activity"—cerebral and psychological.
5) the perceptual & conceptual worlds
6) the "composition" of mental states (*ML*, p. 242).

Work on radical empiricism was set aside, at least as far as the surviving records show, until the 1900s when James began work on "The Many and the One." In the meantime, he introduced a new course on the philosophy of Kant. The earliest mention of this occurs in a letter to Eliot, dated February 22 [1896]: "What is proposed by me so far for next year is the psychology-part of Phil. I, a 1/2 course in English Philosophy, the 'Philosophy of Nature' course, and a seminary in Kant's Philosophy."[83] He did not give the course in English philosophy. In a letter of October 9, 1896, to Henry William Rankin, he wrote: "I am beginning a course in Kant's Philosophy now, strange to say, for the first time in my life, and have to read much in connection with it."[84] He offered a course on Kant three times:

1896-97 Philosophy 20c: Metaphysical Seminary, on the philosophy of Kant, a study of the three Critiques (2 hours per week; 9 students, including 5 graduate)

1897-98 Philosophy 8: The Philosophy of Kant (first half-year; 3 hours per week; 6 students)

1898-99 Philosophy 8: The Philosophy of Kant (first half-year; 3 hours per week; 16 students)

Scattered notes for the course survive. Since James associated these notes with a planned article on Kant, they were published in *Manuscript Essays and Notes* (WORKS, pp. 199–203). His attitude toward Kant during this period is most clearly expressed in "Philosophical Conceptions and Practical Results" (1898).[85]

In 1898-99, his last year of full-time teaching, James took over from Royce the course Philosophy 9: Metaphysics. The course attracted 38 students and was described as follows: "The fundamental problems of Theoretical Philosophy. The unity or plurality of the World-Ground, and its knowability or unknowability; Realism and Idealism; Freedom, Teleology, and Theism." It met three hours per week, and students were required to prepare two reports each. Together with Royce, James taught Philosophy 9 in 1904-5 (35 students) and 1905-6 (34). This course was the legendary battleground of the Absolute.

Much information about the course has survived. James's own notes are preserved for all three years, in Nos. 22, 26, and 27 of the present volume. The American Jewish Archives on the Cincinnati Campus of the Hebrew Union College has notes by Horace M.

83 *William James: Selected Unpublished Correspondence, 1885–1910*, ed. Frederick J. Down Scott (Columbus: Ohio State University Press, 1986), p. 142.

84 *67M–96 #21.

85 Reprinted in William James, *Pragmatism*, WORKS; see especially p. 269.

Kallen for 1905-6. James's notes for the first year suggest that the course was a polemic against monism. He argued that the unity of the universe is no more than the unity of a collection, and that nothing is gained by claiming that things have their source in one "primal being" (*ML*, p. 266). Absolute idealism fails because the notion of the Absolute explains nothing. The concrete connections and lines of influence are just as they are found to be, and the existence or non-existence of the Absolute simply makes no difference.

Because of a heart condition and work on the Gifford lectures, James did not teach in 1899-1900 and 1900-1. When he returned, he did so with thoughts of retirement on his mind and taught only part-time, at half pay. The only course he taught in 1901-2 was Philosophy 6: The Psychological Elements of Religious Life, with 22 students. No notes for this course have been identified. Its content most likely was much the same as that of the Summer School of Theology lectures of 1902, published as No. 6 in the present volume.

In 1902-3 he taught only Philosophy 3: The Philosophy of Nature, assisted by Miller. The syllabus for the course, published as No. 23, was clearly regarded by James as a general summary of his philosophical position. Thus, he sent a copy to Bergson and, on February 25, 1903, noted: "The *Syllabus* which I sent you the other day is (I fear), from its great abbreviation, somewhat unintelligible, but it will show you the sort of lines upon which I have been working."[86]

In 1903-4 he taught Philosophy 20c: Metaphysical Seminary, with 20 students; the subject of the course was a pluralistic description of the world. His notes appear as Nos. 24 and 25. The two provide a very extensive record of James's reading and interests at a time when he was trying to work out his own system of philosophy. Much of the notes consists of phrases, but there are some coherent pages. His intent in the course was "to come *out* with collective *pluralism*, purposive impulse, and *nextness* as principle of unity" (*ML*, p. 275). To accomplish this, James insisted on the reality of external relations, as opposed to the idealists, who recognized only internal ones. In his published work he rarely formulated his conflict with idealism as a conflict over external relations, and thus these notes add to our understanding of James's favorite polemic. He noted:

[86] Perry, *Thought and Character*, II, 610.

My philosophy and common sense both assume that things whose being is independent, can nevertheless come into relations, which are adventitious & external, not neccessarily involved in the being of each thing, but possible only, or conditional on other things arising, between which and the first thing the relations obtain.

Absolutists say that no such external relations are possible (*ML*, p. 290).

Against the absolutists, he insisted on the categories of possibility and chance:

In books on probability chance is regarded as *revealer* of a regular order, if such exist. Perturbations neutralize each other; frequencies come to light. My theory goes farther. Chance *production* occasions effective increase in certain regularities, because other chances are eliminated and these remain & accumulate. If *n* men toss pennies, there will be accumulation of wealth in a few hands, by the elimination of those whose stock gives out (*ML*, p. 304).

He then goes on to point out the similarities between his position and evolutionary theory.

The text contains an interesting summary of panpsychism (*ML*, pp. 278–279) and suggests additional reasons for preferring radical empiricism to the ordinary dualism (*ML*, p. 322). There are also interesting remarks on academic philosophy in the form of reflections on the program for the Congress of Arts and Sciences at the Universal Exposition, St. Louis, 1904, prepared by Münsterberg:

Münsterberg's Congress-program seems to me, e.g. to be sheer humbug in the sense of self-infatuation with an idol of the den, a kind of religious service in honour of the professional-philosophy-shop, with its faculty, its departments and sections, its mutual etiquette, its appointments, its great mill of authorities and exclusions & suppressions which the waters of Truth are expected to feed to the great class-glory of all who are concerned. To me "Truth," if there be any truth, would seem to exist for the express confusion of all this kind of thing, and to reveal itself in whispers to the "meek lovers of the Good" in their solitude, the Darwins, the Lockes, etc., and to be expressly incompatible with officialism (*ML*, p. 326).

James claimed that the difference between himself and Münsterberg was a "splendid expression of pragmatism. I want a world of anarchy, M. one of bureaucracy, and each appeals to 'Nature' to back him up."

Numbers 26 and 27 are the notes for the course Philosophy 9: Metaphysics in 1904-5 and 1905-6. According to James, every metaphysical system "breeds its own problems"; the goal is to find "the one that breeds fewest" (*ML*, p. 327). In the course he launched numerous attacks on monism and emphasized the importance of the categories of chance and possibility. The pragmatic method made numerous appearances, with James insisting that it provides the key to the solution of philosophical problems. Of some interest is the pragmatic definition of sameness (*ML*, p. 336).

In both years Royce took over the course for the second semester. James rushed a number of articles on radical empiricism into print so that he could distribute offprints to the students before Royce's advent.[87] In 1904-5 James concluded his part in late January 1905; the next year he ended somewhat earlier because he had agreed to teach at Stanford University in spring 1906. In the last year of James's Philosophy 9 he used Höffding's *Problems of Philosophy* as a text, the translation of which James had supervised closely.

On November 10, 1905, James wrote to Dickinson Sergeant Miller:

"Phil. 9" is going well. I think I *lecture* better than I ever did; in fact I know I do. But this professional evolution goes with an involution of all miscellaneous faculty. I am well, and efficient enough, but purposely going slow so as to keep efficient into the Palo Alto summer, which means that I have written nothing. I am pestered by doubts as to whether to put my resignation through this year, in spite of opposition, or to drag along another year or two.[88]

In January he went to Palo Alto to teach at Stanford. Shortly thereafter, on February 1, 1906, he wrote to his brother Henry:

I got here . . . on the 8th, and have now given nine lectures, to 300 enrolled students and about 150 visitors, partly colleagues. I take great pains, prepare a printed syllabus, very fully; and really feel for the first time in my life, as if I were lecturing *well*. High time, after 30 years of practice! It earns me $5000, if I can keep it up till May 27th.[89]

To avoid duplication, James's notes for the course (bMS Am 1092.9 #4516) are not published. However, two fragments on religion related to his Stanford stay appear as No. 28. Number 30 in the present

---

[87] William James, *Essays in Radical Empiricism*, WORKS, pp. 201–202.
[88] *Letters of William James*, II, 235.
[89] Ibid., II, 240.

volume is a revised version of the syllabus mentioned in the letter to Henry. The great earthquake put an end to James's California work: "The earthquake has knocked Stanford University 'into a cocked hat,' and stopped lecturing for this year," James wrote to Giovanni Papini on April 24, 1906, adding that he was sending to Papini sheets of the syllabus prepared at Stanford.[90]

In the first half of the academic year 1906-7 James taught his last course, Philosophy D: General Problems of Philosophy, with an enrollment of 133. On January 20, 1907, he wrote to his daughter Margaret Mary: "I have spent all day preparing next Tuesday's lecture, which is my last before a class in Harvard University, so help me God amen!"[91] On March 26, writing to Théodore Flournoy, James expressed his feelings of relief:

I thank you for your congratulations on my retirement. It makes me very happy. A professor has two functions: (1) to be learned and distribute bibliographical information; (2) to communicate truth. The *1st* function is the essential one, officially considered. The *2nd* is the only one I care for. Hitherto I have always felt like a humbug as a professor, for I am weak in the first requirement. Now I can live for the second with a free conscience.[92]

For his last year as a "humbug" he chose Paulsen's *Introduction to Philosophy* as his text. The syllabus for the course is printed as No. 30. It has many affinities with *Some Problems of Philosophy*, but since the book was never completed, the syllabus represents the fullest statement of James's general philosophical position, albeit in outline form.

With the publication of this second volume of unpublished manuscripts, most of the material in the James Collection at Harvard is now available in published form.[93] It is much too early to speculate on what effect the wider dissemination of the manuscript material will have on James studies. At first glance there appears nothing radically new, but there is much that helps to fill out the details. Readers of the last two volumes of the Works should have a much better grasp of James's sources: his philosophical publica-

90 Courtesy of Signora Paolo Casini.

91 *Letters of William James*, II, 262.

92 Ibid., II, 268.

93 Diaries and autobiographical writings, notes compiled while James was a student, and marginalia are not included in the edition; for a more complete statement, see the introduction to *MEN*.

tions often lack documentation; his class lectures, if anything, provide too much. To mention just one example, Nos. 18 and 20 contain several references to Avenarius and constitute the best point of departure for studying the role of Avenarius' concept of pure experience in the development of James's own radical empiricism. The manuscripts should lead to more balanced interpretations of James: he should emerge as a complete philosopher, rather than as merely a defender of religion and founder of pragmatism. Interesting from this point of view, for example, is James's attempt to dissociate himself from social Darwinism, mentioned earlier in this introduction. Finally, the publication of James's manuscript essays and notes should establish beyond doubt that it is the cluster of problems associated with radical empiricism that forms the core of James's work in philosophy and provides the thread needed to bind together his seemingly disconnected published works.

I. Public Lectures

1. Johns Hopkins Lectures on "The Senses and the Brain and Their Relation to Thought" (1878)

Every misf. has good side. The good side of spreading out ones instruction rather thin over a broad surface seems to be this, that one is obliged to form *responsible* opinions concerning a variety of matters about which irresponsible opinions are very frequently & loudly expressed. The difficulties of decision in a question are not often felt by a man who is not responsible for the decision. Most of all are they felt by the umpire of both sides. A physiologist may form opinions in psychology with the utmost carelessness & good conscience & say etc. because he is not in duty bound &c. A philosopher who follows subj. method may equally scorn physiol. &c. Each owns a common share in human nature. Where two lots adjoin with disputed boundary we find each owner disposed to push back the fence. If one man owns both lots, he does not care where the fence stands. I think we ought all to assume this attitude, and cast aside as ignoble this jealousy of the man on the other side of the fence. The truth is all our own whether it be truth of body or truth of mind. What truth the physiologist may have discovered belongs by equal right to any introspective philosopher who will take the trouble to understand it. What mental facts the latter notes, are for the benefit of the physiologist as well.

I propose then to choose latter course & take subject of broad general interest even at risk of treating it rather meagrely. I shall try to atone for this by being as impartial as possible in a field where partizanship has too often held sway. Easy to day,　Names. If at end of short course, we find that the mysterious problems which so long have baffled & fascinated the human mind are no nearer definitive solution, at least we shall have gained some facts by the way. And the contemplation of the difficulties will at least be edifying if not scientifically instructive, will make us patient and charitable. After all wise men have always felt the difficulties of belief and the difficulties of unbelief. To have forcibly bro't home to us that even after the most refined scientific investigation these diffi-

3

culties & facilities are essentially what they always were, will be a valuable result for it will corroborate, confirm the wisdom of the past and make us feel again that there is no such breach.

Science gained her laurels in narrow fields by verification and modesty of aim. Now physics and chemistry are running together, whilst geology, zoology, astronomy, & human history all seem to be coalescing into a vast system called the theory of evolution, whose aims whatever they may be are not modest, and to whose results no laboratory verification but only the large vague v. of circumstantial evidence can be applied. Evolution accounts for mind as a product. First nervous systems appeared, then consciousness. Superinduced. Org. of harmony. Tree, man, anemone. Utility. At first nascent, Romanes. ◁ ⫶⌐ Consciousness = retardation. Section of motor proce

Study afferent side. 5 senses. Data of some subjective, smell, taste, colour sound. Resistance & space remain, to form outer world. Given by touch. This the mother tongue, because important, and because its data untranslatable. The world a system of motions of atoms. Senses organs of *selection*. Important mental principle. First motion that of contact of part of surface. Most authors make space prior.

$\frac{1}{20}$ $\frac{1}{70}$
Mistake. Skin, Exner. 0.044, ″ 0.015. Watch, fly, tickle, retina, stars. Vierordt's illusions. Sub & ob. undifferentiated. Pressure & position. Pass to air. Bat. Air sense anticipatory touch. [Lateral line.] Same sense in tymp. membr. Cochlea.

I have no time to speak of the function of hearing. All who wish to understand it in its full physiologic and psychologic extent have now in the eng. tr. of H. the opportunity to do so. I cannot however resist pausing for a moment to discuss the use which Spencer and Taine have made of the facts of sound-perception to support a vast and fundamental theory—the theory that all the feelings of which we are directly conscious are built up of unconscious units. The theory in fact that mind as well as matter has a molecular composition. They rely mainly on pitch & harmony. A single stroke or snap affects the ear once—repeated, often, until 40 a″ it passes into a new quality of pitch. Subsequent increase only alters the pitch till 40 or 50000. Two pitches in the same way are felt as timbre. Now this proves according to these authors that ⌣⌣⌣⌣ ⊤ ⊤ ⊤ ⊤ ⊤ ⋅ They entirely forget the alternative that the psychic event does not follow immediately upon the outward irritant but that the latter produces its immediate effect upon the nerve. Now in the physical world repeating the cause does not always repeat the effect. quantitative change of cause qualitative of effect. Deflection. Camel's back. melt ice. heat gunpowder. Summation in muscle N. and so in this case the rapidly increasing waves may summate themselves in the N. and the resulting Cons. not come from the coalescence of psychic but be the direct concomitant of a complex nervous state. The alternative not only possible but probable. This may at first sight seem a trifling point—but not so. It is a fundamental point. Because if it be admitted that the real constitution of our feelings is diff⁺ frm. what it is felt to be there seems no limit to uncertainty. Hitherto it has been g'ally supposed that however phenomenal outer things might be, in our feelings, at any rate we know the thing in itself—when we were joyful the joy *was* just what we felt it to be. When a man tells you he is cold, cold he is, however little cause you might see for it. In a word no distinct between real and phenomenal side. Consciousness is sole judge of its own constitution. To say now that pain is not really what it seems but is really composed of other smaller feelings that we know nothing of, seems to reduce all things to chaos again. No fulcrum of certainty. Descartes cogito. Many ramifications obscure—must pass on. But I repeat the question is a fundamental one. and that it should not be solved shows the deplorably backward state of psychology. How about chemistry.

½ can. anatomy. Long tho't to preside over sounds. It is almost certain now that they are organs of an hitherto unrecognized sense, The sense of our movement in space. This proved by the [*fol.* 11 *missing*]

We now pass to the subject of vision—the most anticipatory of all the ministers of touch. Anatomy. Subject so vast that I must select one special point and that is the part played by our direct sensation. Certain philosophers analyzing our finished thought about *things* come to the conclusion that it is wholly made up of sensations. They are the bricks whilst space and time are the mortar that join them together into unity. This bowl a certain possibility of sensations coexisting in space—No substance. You can name no property you can tell nothing about the bowl which does not end when brought back to the *fact* it imports, a sensation which under certain circumstances you receive. Its shape. Sensations are always spoken of by this school as perfectly definite ultimate bricks absolute and distinct packages. This comes of starting fm. the study of the objects. Now physiologists begin at more humble end & study sensations themselves. And they come to the exactly reverse conclusion. The great lesson of H. is that a sensation in itself is the most fluctuating and indefinite of mental occurrences. So far is it from being the stable and solid foundation of knowledge, that it is wholly plastic in the hands of our thoughts of things. The same sensation may be ambiguous enter into many objects, and according to the thought of the object will alter its felt quality. To use H.'s own words, they are *signs* of outward things, whose meaning it is the duty of our understanding to learn. According to this view of Helmholtz the perceptions cognitions thoughts of the mind are far from being merely constituted by the sensation. The sensation merely wakens the mind from its slumber, and when the mind puts forth its power it may do so in the way of overriding, altering or ignoring altogether the sensation. Examples will make all this clearer. I will begin by trying to show you that numbers of sensations exist which we do not attend to because they are of no practical value to us as signs. What is a visual sensation. The *immediate* result of a certain optical change. A certain movem't. shd. always give a fixed sensation, a certain color a certain retinal shape and size. Our ignorance. Blind spot. Schattenfigur. Entoptic appearances. Inability to estimate angular distances. We don't know *what eye* we look with, nor *which part* of each, for that is of no consequence so long as we do somehow see the object. Squinter's. Microscopists. Choice. Nachbilder. Obvious in case of sun. Unnoticed elsewhere. $+ \equiv \circ$. Change of colour according to previous excitement. According to illumination. Peripheral retina. Change of illumination. Moon & sun. We care nothing about sensation we only need to define what the object is. Even tho' the sensation of black velvet in the sun be the same as that of white paper in moon, as long as I know that the one sensation belongs to one object, the other sensation to another, I feel them as different. The thought engulphs the sensation, swallows it up absorbs it. And so of color blue & red. H H. simultaneous contrast. H's explanation. We think not of the sensation but of the *thing*. Woods, thunder storm, sunset, afternoon. Disks. Col'd shadows.

Hole through hand. Indirect vision of color, sky & grass. All these monocular. Pass to binocular. Animals Man monocular to some extent: Retinal rivalry. Colours won't mix, disproving

Spencer & Taine. Aiming, candle shadow. Image of l. eye cast to r. & *ignored*. This leads to double images. Generally overlooked. Why do we see single? Not to be dismissed by reference to two ears &c. The fact is that we have sometimes two sometimes one image. The two retinal sensations fuse into one whenever we distinctly refer them to one object in one position. When we don't they keep their separateness, but under these circumstances, not being useful signs are wholly over looked. The sensations on the two yellow spots have during all our ancestral history converged upon a single object and that the one we were interested in: we can't fix them on vacancy. Thus we always think of *one thing* when we get as in stereoscope two similar sensations on the yellow spots. If dissimilar, rivalry, but not two things. Some Physiol. have tried to prove single vision to be due to the fact that there were identical points in the two retinae. Yellow spots the only connate ones. Others again impossible to fuse (extreme nasal). Other points ambiguous. That is are seen double if we think the object in one position, single if we think it in an other. Our thought of the object thus again determines our feeling of the sensation. Before going further it will be well to explain our judgment of position. It depends largely on convergence. Jeffries threads. Shut one eye. Intersection of optic axes gives a sensation but the *distance* seems to be a tho't: (Try with eyes shut.) Helmholtz. Wundt. Sensation nonspatial. Intersection point the one whose distance we for the moment are distinctly conscious of.

The best way to begin the discussion of binocular vision is to speak of dogs birds, of retinal rivalry, the candle exp^t, Graefe's malingerer and Rogers' exp^{ts} Then of the estimate of distance as dependent on feeling of convergence of optical axes the object being judged to lie at their intersection. [Jeffries threads. Closing one eye. Thaumatrope.] This the distance of the object that most interests us, the distance we are for the moment distinctly conscious of. We become distinctly conscious of other distances by rapidly converging or diverging upon them. An object at another distance as soon as it attracts our attention will instantaneously produce a movem^t of this sort, and its distance be judged. Alteration of convergence in stereoscope: we converge for the upper end and so judge it nearer. But still / \ further. The changed convergence may not actually occur, it need only be started, or suggested and the proper judgment of distance will result from it as if it did occur.

That is if rays of light fall on the two retinae so as to *suggest* a certain rotation of each eyeball to bring the rays upon the yel. sp^s then the distance of the point which emits the rays will be rightly felt by the mind even though the rotation be not effected; and according as the rotation is outward or inward the point will be judged farther or nearer than the point of fixation and in each case judged single. [Dove. Donders' electric spark.] But sometimes this suggestion imperfectly occurs. F⟨ ⟩gers, changed size of double image. Then each retinal spot projects image in direction where cause usually lies. R. of retina usually affected by objects to l. of axis, l. by obj. to r. When then both nasal or both frontal sides simultaneously affected object seen in 2 directions or double. But to see them single we need only vividly imagine the position in wh. one object wd. cast the two pictures. I.e. *imagine the object and we get a new sensation.* Wundt's law. The same thing occurs with pictures: Sensation ambiguous, but alters its quality instantaneously according to suggested notion. ⌐⌐ ⟋⟋ mask mosquito. steam whistle. toads—dogs. Bunch.

Wundt and Donders have tried to show how all the peculiarities of our double images etc may be explained by ancestral experiences of objects having become so organized that sensations immediately excite the tho't in some cases in others not. The sensation itself being thus a sign of some existence beyond itself and not constituting that existence.

What is that existence? that thing? that shape? that position which the sensation *is* not but suggests. Sensationalists would say it is nothing but a mass of absent sensations, voluminous eno' at times to swallow up the present one & alter it it is true, but still themselves sensations locomotor tactile and other. The tho't is identified with some sensation, tho' not the present one. Helmholtz in one place after finding the evasive instable character of visual sensations says the sensible properties of the *thing* must be distinctly and definitely given by the sense of touch. But touch is equally evasive. My observations. Crossed fingers. In short the eye man may wash his hands of the matter by referring to the skin man, but the skin man must then roll the ball back to the eye man. Wundt who goes into both concludes that the spatial determinations of the object contain a *plus* which is not sufficiently accounted for by any of the sensations. The thought he says is a synthesis. & H. in another place seems to admit this. It is an idea put forth by the mind to account for the causation of the sensation. The latter is a psychic stimulus merely or occasion of the minds independent activity. Sensation not even spatial. These are very difficult matters. To me not even W. & H. seem adequate but impossible to go more deeply into the matter here. I merely wish to call the attention of persons who are fearful of the reduction by physiology of higher to lower powers of the mind that H. & W. both absolutely incapable of sentimental bias, put forth a doctrine as the result of their elaborate result of sensation per se, which has been hailed by followers of Kant as the most striking experimental verification ever made of a doctrine originally deduced a priori, the doctrine of innate potentialities in the mind which sensations merely awaken into exercise.

Retinae of birds rodents &c. independent
Double and single vision is a matter less of sensation than of perception. That is, it depends not so much on what the retinal image in itself is as on what we think the position of the object is in space. If we think the object at one distance we see it double, if at another single. There are it is true limits to this power of thought to make a double image single. Beyond them it must either continue to appear double or cease to appear at all—generally the latter is what occurs—and these limits seem traced by the habitual experience of the race. If the points on the two retinae which the rays affect are hardly ever affected normally by rays coming from one spot double vision occurs. If they are sometimes so sometimes not, single or double vision according to the mind's interpretation; if generally, vision is always single. The yellow spots are in the latter case. In our habitual looking at things the point we "fixate" falls on both yellow spots; in other words the eyeballs are always turned so that some object lies at the point of intersection of the optic axes. In the case of secondary axes this does not occur. There may be no object

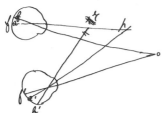 at p, but there always is at o. On the other hand there may be an object at r, the point of intersection of the secondary axes from a and b'. So that a and a' may not, while a and b' may constantly receive rays from the same object whilst f. always does. This tenor of experience explains our perception. The two retinal images fuse into one when we refer the object of each to the same position as

that to which we refer the object of the other, or refer objects of both to one and the same spot. They remain separate when we refer each to a different spot. Now the reference to a spot is merely a thought of a direction and a distance, and the reason why we refer affections on the left of the retina to a direction on our right is habit. Therefore when the l. of l. retina is affected by a spot simultaneously with the right of r. retina, our first tendency is to project the two images into opposite directions, unless we expressly think of the image as being so near to our nose that both directions may be correct. In like manner the nasal side of both retinae if affected projects images outward and these can only be united in a point more distant than that at wh. we are looking. If we lose consciousness of this increased distance we project the r. hand image to the r, the l. to the l. Wundt's law.

The best way to begin the discussion of binocular vision is to speak of dogs birds, of retinal rivalry, the candle exp^t, Graefe's malingerer and Roger's exp^{ts} Then of the estimate of distance as dependent on feeling of convergence of optical axes the object being judged to lie at their intersection. [Jeffries threads. Closing one eye. Thaumatrope.] This the distance of the object that most interests us, the distance we are for the moment distinctly conscious of. We become distinctly conscious of other distances by rapidly converging or diverging upon them. An object at another distance as soon as it attracts our attention will instantaneously produce a movem^t of this sort, and its distance be judged. Alteration of convergence in stereoscope: we converge for the upper end and so judge it nearer. But   still further. The changed convergence may not actually occur, it need only be started, or suggested and the proper judgment of distance will result from it as if it did occur. That is if rays of light fall on the two retinae so as to *suggest* a certain rotation of each eyeball to bring the rays upon the yel. sp^s then the distance of the point which emits the rays will be rightly felt by the mind even though the rotation be not effected; and according as the rotation is outward or inward the point will be judged farther or nearer than the point of fixation and in each case judged single. [Dove. Donders' electric spark.] But sometimes this suggestion imperfectly occurs. In that case each retinal spot projects the image in the direction where most usually the object that affects it lies. Thus on the whole the right side of each retina is affected by objects to the left of its axis, the left side by objects to the right of its axis. When therefore both nasal sides or both frontal sides are affected by the same rays the object emitting the rays is judged to be in different directions by each retina. In other words two objects. Ex^{pt} with pins. So soon however as the convergence is made actual they fuse. And they also fuse whenever we strongly realize their distance, or in other words associate with our sensation of them the idea of a distinct convergence. You will note how your double vision is always accomp^d by an inaccurate feeling of the distance. Double images are therefore most distinct when we think of things as being in one plane. Disparate points only fuse when we have the feeling of perspective.[1] Wundt's law.—Now it is obvious here that the sensation is ambiguous, and is overridden by the mind's notion of its outward cause. If it be objected that the feeling of the third dimension is nothing but the associated feeling of convergence, I deny it, because with closed eyelids we have the latter per se with no feeling of third dimension. Third dimension in general is a retinal quale, like the sky—a particular determination of position therein can only be called a *thought* of the objective reality, wh. here as everywhere has the power of altering the sensation.

In a single picture eyes converge always equally on every point. In stereoscope eyes converge unequally in order to look at the different points. Hence it was supposed that the relief was due to the motions. Dove's disproof. We may say that for every degree of convergence of the eyeballs there is a distance within and beyond the point of fixation where images are seen single *provided* we give mentally the proper perspective. If we fail to do this we see double. And conversely within these limits we may unite any two retinal pictures into one by imagining vividly the spatial position in which one object would cast the two pictures. Beyond these limits fusion will not occur, unless movements are made.

If when first attacked with external rectus paralysis, I move my eyeball so $\longrightarrow$ and feel as if I had moved it so $\longrightarrow$ a strange confusion occurs—it seems as if the distances across objects in front of me had increased, and the usual correspondence between movements of my limbs and of my eye is broken up. An object looks far to the right but if I rapidly place my hand upon it I find I have struck too far. All this confusion causes vertigo which disappears

---

[1] WJ wrote 'perspective' above undeleted 'relief'.

when I have shut my eyes. Soon a squint is developed & then I actually see a double image of the object lying off to the r.

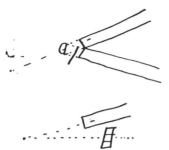

Certain philosophers define the mind as wholly constituted of sensations present and remembered. The thought of a thing is the sum of all possible sensations which the thing might give us briefly glimpsed. It has no other substantiality than that. The study of sensations accordingly is the base of psychology. Skepticism (Spencer) tries to show by the way in which our sensations vary that we have no true knowledge. Such however is not the verdict of those physiologists who study sensation per se. Helmholtz and Wundt elaborately study the sensations of the eye and conclude that those present at any time are the most insignificant part of the object tho't of. They are ingulphed caught up, used, neglected, or altered, by the idea we gain of the *thing*. I will show this in some

Space

Intensity in a sensation is relative. To feel a given intensity as such we must have compared it with a greater or a less one, and it therefore might be contended that the intensity as an affection of consciousness does not arise at all until comparison has been made. If this be granted, then the question will arise, when the comparison is made what shall force us to assign the greater intensity to the sensation A, the lesser to the sensation B, & not vice versa? Evidently some sensible quality in each sensation which, though not itself felt as intensity, may be called a sign or mark of the order of intensity of the sensations, a sign to be translated by the mind. It is obvious enough that this conception is complicated in the extreme, postulating in order to attain one system of feelings—the scale of intensities,—another preliminary scale which runs parallel to it and reduplicates it point for point. It demands a text and a translation, whereas we are aware only of a simple text that we seem to read right off. Each sensation has a quale of intensity—when a sensation of another intensity succeeds to it, we arrange the two in a certain order, and the *order* no doubt is a separate feeling or cognition on the minds part, but it is an order of which the items as such have been already felt separately—and as I think, felt as intensities or at least as *muchnesses* or littlenesses. This sensation of muchness is the *sensible* quale of intensity as distinguished from the intellectual cognition of position in a scale of intensities. It is the sign for the position, but the ordering in position confers no new sensible quality.

Let us now take the question of extension. Those who say it is not a sensible quality given in any single retinal sensation, do so for the reason that to their minds it is a "relation" between at least two points, and that the two points must be discriminated before the relation is perceived. But *two* points cannot be given in any single sensation. Multitudinousness in like manner is not an attribute of any one sensation. It seems to require distinct acts of attention to each unit of the multitude, and these can only occur in successive moments of time.

But now if I say that both extension and multitude *are* given as such, in their specific *qualia*, in single sensations, what do I mean? I mean that when we open our eyes for the first time we see a totality either of room, or of colored objects, which is yet neither topographically mapped out nor numerically counted, but which contains already the sensible quale of muchness, and contains it too in the peculiar specific form of extensive and of numerical as distinguished from intensive muchness. The sensation is an aggregate of coexistent discernibles. Discrimination arises from the fact that in the eye selective attention can wander from point to point of the field and emphasize now one and now another, without at the same time in any degree losing the coexistent whole. Thus discriminations arise, and relations are established, of distance, of direction, of form, & of number. These I am willing to admit, result from an additional intellectual set of acts, and so far forth they are exactly comparable to that ordering of intensities into a system with which we began our study. But the difference between the earlier case & this is that the several intensities arranged in a scale need not be simultaneously felt, whilst the several extensions and positions even whilst we are arranging them into their system of relations are all already given together in the total retinal sensation of spatial vastness—and this sensation clinging to them, always envelopes and colours so to speak their order and makes it the particular order we call spatial. *Qua order* the spatial may be represented by the same scheme as any other—and it is only qua *order* that it can be called a product of relating thought.

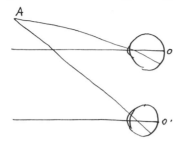

When the eyes are looking thus in the open air, most objects cast their images on corresponding sides of the retina (like A.) Only very near objects in the centre of the field affect the two outsides, whilst the two insides cannot possibly be affected by any single object.[2] This case can only occur when with convergent axes an object B, beyond the point of convergence, is pictured. Now the far look is at least as frequent as any. It is the

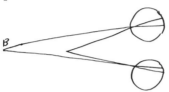

position of repose. When thinking our eyes always assume it. Images then like those which a single body casts in that position of the eyes will be habitually referred to one point, i.e. projected in the line of the secondary axis. Near objects are therefore seen double unless by an especial correction on the part of thought their true distance is very vividly imagined. Anything which helps that imagination, like a contour line, helps the localization and the fusion. In the same way with convergent axis a double inside image will be projected upon two points unless it be vividly conceived as distant. The trouble is that as a rule we most distinctly feel the distance of the point of fixation other images are as a rule referred to that point. Double images seem too small if they belong to a far object, too large if to a near one. Nachbilder vary their size according to the point of fixation.

In reviewing the facts we have been through one point must have struck you—the number of sensations we are receiving that we know nothing about. Not only do we remain ignorant of muscae volitantes, vascular shadows, blind spots, chromatic aberration, peripheral failure to discriminate and change of colour, double images and the feelings of position in the eyeballs, not only are we ignorant of angular magnitude, not only does the actual perception of the colour of an object depend very little on the actual sensation but

---

[2] In the left margin WJ wrote vertically, 'It ou[gh]t to be easier to blend near than far double images.'

immensely on the notion we have of what it should be, but even such a gross point as which eye we see with is ignored by us so that a man may be blind of one eye for years and only learn it by accident. Helmholtz's work a long commentary on this law. He explains it by saying that our sensations are means for making us acquainted with facts, outward facts of practical importance. So far as a sensation is always associated with a particular fact it becomes a mere sign of that fact. The mind passes right on to the fact and forgets the sensation in se. Invariable sensations like Purkinje's shadows are of no practical consequence and are wholly ignored. Signs like convergence, accommodation, position of double images, have the greatest interest as signs but none in se, so that when they occur apart from their outward cause we have got so used to thinking merely of that that we can't abstract from it and notice the sign at all, the object seems nearer, larger &c. Thus a sensation redintegrates always a thought of a *thing*. And where the sensation is ambiguous the thing comes and goes in the oddest manner. What is the tho't of the thing. Philosophers

I Deny *quale*: Associational empiricists. (Mill Bain?)

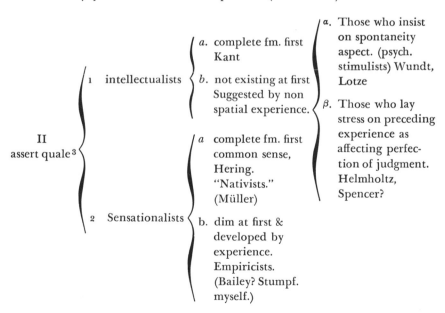

II assert quale[3]
  1 intellectualists
    a. complete fm. first Kant
    b. not existing at first Suggested by non spatial experience.
      a. Those who insist on spontaneity aspect. (psych. stimulists) Wundt, Lotze
      β. Those who lay stress on preceding experience as affecting perfection of judgment. Helmholtz, Spencer?
  2 Sensationalists
    a complete fm. first common sense, Hering. "Nativists." (Müller)
    b. dim at first & developed by experience. Empiricists. (Bailey? Stumpf. myself.)

[3] In the space below WJ wrote vertically in brown crayon 'Space'.

The division between apriorists & empiricists may be made a cross division. Thus in II 1 we have an empirical & an intuitional wing; in its b division the same; in II. 2. the same. This suggests that we begin by thinking of a priori & empirical rather as representing two tendencies than 2 sharply defined things.

means that there is a choice between several appropriate directions of advance. Consciousness is the *section* of the nervous string, *constater*ing the link laid down, and feeling among the lot of possible ends presented to its choice for the one which best fits. Its effectiveness lies in this, that being due to the nascent excitation of nerve tracts, by its attractive or repulsive quality it decides whether that excitation shall abort or shall become complete.

Such a case as that of space consciousness may easily be brought under this same conception of a pause between two nervous events, affording the means of a better coadaptation of them. For instance, if a prick on the outstretched leg means a certain point of space, *all* centrifugal events which mean or reach that same point become appropriate to succeed the prick. They rise as possibilities into consciousness and the most attractive becomes plenary. Here, to be sure, I postulate nervous tracts as theatres of the incipient consciousness, equivalent in number to the sum total of the several possible next steps, and so get no economy of anatomical arrangement, but I get

2. Lowell Lectures on "The Brain and the Mind" (1878)

[*Outlines of the Six Lectures*]

Lecture 1

Introd.—metaphysics. For past 10 years— . . devoted to this question—and celebrating new light . . . or defending orthodox truth. This most natural . . . . all partizans—Some . . enthus. for new knowledge, others see brutal materialism lurking like idol behind the brilliant veil. Some feel that there is an element of stagnant dogmatism in Orth., others . . insol. & barb. in sc. The worst is . . . eager partizans on slender basis. . . Pop. Sc. speak of superstit. of introsp. Psych. Others—open. phys. declaim agst. degrad. soph. of med. mat.

To be regretted. 6 hours. Take subj. of brain & see exactly how much recent &c. All ought to gladly join in sober review, for as human beings are we not alike proprietors. . . As propr. of body . . . insuff. of account of mind leaves body out. . As owners . . . . worthlessness of all explan. of feeling etc. The phys. & psych. professionally considered . . . . It is surprising that each shd wish to encroach on the domain of the other. Each owns a lot & 2 lots lie side by side. Each tries to push . . fence & reduce . . . for benefit. But we who are neither . . . ought to aspire to attitude. . . . He cares not . . . . & being master of all . . . tries to cultivate.

In thinking of my duties . . . deplore wide surface . . . thin. In standing here . . . misf. . . good side. A teacher must form . . . a reader need not. Difficulties not felt. . Judge . . . Mere physiol. careless . . . & keep good conscience. In a philosoph. very light treatment of phys. diff. is excusable. I confess that owing to my divided & multiform resp., I have felt acutely diff. of b. s̄. m. or of m. s̄ b. At moment . . . hardly anything. But those momentary. In time that I think we can see *beginning* of knowledge if no more.

Anat. Remind   Cells & fibres

Sp. cord. eff^t & aff^t roots not conductor.

Develop^t Slides.

Human diag^s & model. Course of fibres. Inner capsule & crura.

Rank: absol. size. Flint.

size to body. Diag.

Convol.

Hem: rest. Meynert's diag.

Really resultant—like muscle.

quality = chem. or microscop. properties

Microscopic structure.

Luys slide—imaginary.

Gerlach's—Schmidt.

Henle's.

Only *one* certain—do *not* connect by broad— —Supposed that excitement *must* pass—network not known—broad p. must be bridge.

— —apriori notion of phys. necc. give rise to fictitious anat. In like manner psych. necc. . . fict. physiol. Whole theory of diff^t local hab^ns for diff^t ideas with connecting fibres—schema of way in wh. feelings awaken each other—Reduplication in brain terms . . of

introspection
Grounds pro & con.
Meanwhile theory before grounds—even now
Psych. first. physiol. takes cue.
Ps " established " gropes for light
Ludicrously false assertions . . . .
Only facts directly known . . . .
Between them physiol—processes among cells & fibres. Of these we *guess* Outward effects = motions. In lower animals we know roughly localities. In higher we shall see—we know paths. Negative variation. Acid Excretions, waste products: cholesterin, urea, phosphates.
Where motions absent, or delayed, physiologists wd. have no reason to suspect action . . . . . . reagent
Leave aside processes—take localizations. Natural unit of nervous function—3 segments, factors. Middle delayed—read book. Minimum delay—reflex action—wink, repair balance.
Great law; functions differ in diff^t animals. Lower centres independent in low forms, in high can do nothing without hemis. Frog & bird.

Lecture 2

Common features
1st. Response to *near* stimulus—not spontan.
2nd invariable & determinate. J.—j.
string—vis a tergo—water boil. organist.
3rd. useful—safer.
Fish, turtle
Headless bird, rattlesnake. Robin
Bird s. hemis. rodents
In general no response to the remote
Sum up centres below hemis. series of platforms for executing in fatal response.
Is it not remarkable that machine . . . . is rational? What explanation?
Some deny machine, Lewes & Co. Frog, eel—both sensibility & intelligence, end in view. But what intelligence? No space idea, no cause & effect, no memory.
Possible sensibility ? Facts exaggerated. Eel, snake.
The best explanation that drawn from human habit. These appro-

priate acts result from previous acts of intelligence so often repeated that lower centres have learnt the trick.

Cases in human beings. Music, stand, walk, ride, skate, read aloud &c. Conscious first,—then lower C. suff^t. Grow to modes. Sleeping horseman, Onimus.

Authors suppose when N.S. of parent exercised, N.S. of offspring tends to act. Thus instincts—suck, calves, lambs, chickens run to hen.—*learnt* by ancestors.

Few instincts in man, not even walk; Individual learn afresh.

Possibly wrong. Spalding's s   Time of birth accidental. Dogs—children deaf, don't wink.

Be this as it may, whether parent's acts leave trace or not, man's *own* acts do. Every act modifies and makes easier. Importance in moral education. We think when tempted start afresh tomorrow as well as to-day. Self-deception—not same man. R.V.W N.S. resultant. Clay   Habits the great thing—they liberate hemis. for higher flights. Keep unbroken. One lapse . . . . weeks cannot reorganize. Carpenter.

No habit wholly performed by lower centres,—even in dogs, dependent. Hence, ignorance. Hemispheric superintendance.

How do hemis. differ?

1st, distant—eye & ear.

2nd, incalculable, physiologist impotent—not a pipe.

3rd Sentiments.

4th Spontaneity,

Machine-character lost.

Intelligent agent—choice.

Variety . . . . open. Mans foot.

Meaning?

Lecture 3

Last lecture—Organ—Add hemis. incalculable, choice, spontaneity.

Motives—considerations. = Emotions, ideas of circumstances not present. Represented goods and evils constitute sentiments memories expectations & considerations alike. Assume hemis. to be reservoir—make distinct later. Simple scheme of action: direct & loop line—seat, Rip v. W. All reflex. All leave trace—scoop out path.

Understand now why *choice*: remote suggestions infinitely more numerous—unstable equilib. Jelly. Resultant indeterminate. In lower centres paths few—direct line simple. Present sensations few. Slave—free, spontaneous.

Utility obvious. Slave of present sensation cannot deliberate, pause, postpone, weigh—prudence impossible. Now every animal dealing with complex . . . . needs prudence. Polyp can do without it. High animal must think of remote consequences—the higher . . . the fewer. . . . . . The more hemispheres control him—the more widely extended in time and space is the sphere the more remote are the suggestions . . . which enter with present into . . Feeding Frog & hen. Leave cerebrum organ of absent vs. present

Rank in scale. In human life we deem . . . . . tramp. . . saint

Before closing these preliminary generalities

These thoughts along loop line, what?—psychological digression. Few elements—images all schools agree are bricks. Mortar.

Images motor & sensory. Lowell Institute. Way hither. Few, but enough. No more wonder . . . . . than that 26 letters.

Now make details of sketch distinct

But now if mental life composed of images how *can* hemis. subserve . . . . by keeping images?

Physiologists claim . . . . examine. Remark something analogous.

Habit in lower centres. Bruise, scar. Even in inorganic: violin, razor, phosphorescent, dry plate, glass mirror. Clock at night. String round finger. Muscles at night. After-image. All cases of revival, reproduction. Quickly perish *here*, last for years in hemis.

Mind I say *revival*, not memory— —practically same thing—if at sight of liquor—this is drunkard. Once is enough in hemis—imperishable. In other cases, transient—great diff., diff. of permanence— what causes it?

Answer: each element separate pigeon-hole—no need to lodge, to wipe out. On retina all parts used, impressions interfere.—Wipe slate.[1] In lower centres few habits possible at once. Drill, box, shoot, no loss of time. Where numerous, hesitant, loss of time, hemis. come in. Same cells &c used.

In hemis. there must be separate pigeon-holes, into which ideas, or several elements which compose them, are switched off. If each acquisition is laid up in its own cells and fibres, no need to wipe slate. Impressions not superposed—lie side by side.

This the postulate. See whether experiments corroborate it.

[1] Above the dash WJ wrote in pencil 'raspberry'.

Lecture 4

Last lecture *a priori*. Memory a common property. Hemis. reproductions both numerous and permanent—elsewhere numerous *or* permanent, not both—explained by same tracts serving for all acquisitions elsewhere whilst in hemis. each acquisition has separate tracts.

Experiments. Flourens. Unexcitable time. Hitzig & Ferrier: Motor & unexcitable regions.

Effects of destruction: anesthesia. Paralysis of volitional movements, because loop-line required. Pigeons wink, dodge   Even defensive movements of head because in dog intelligence involved.

Auditory & optic centres. Munk vs Ferrier. Mental blindness—sees but don't understand. "Hear" fight, runaway horse. "See" guilty, home to dinner.

Sensation sign—rest supplied by mind.—no discrimination, direct line. Dish, whip, masked figure, sign & word of command, loop-line. Education

Goltz's method. Like bird, fear, love, lost. Idiocy. Can't find meat.

Conclude that each motor and sensory element has its home. When that destroyed representation wiped out; remaining representations not enough to constitute thought—house wd. tumble if bricks &c knocked out.

Human. Aphasia—gestures. copy, conscious. Anatomy.

Analyze. Say "Lowell Institute." . . . . . Among properties, written word. When I *see* this, I may be so accustomed that the sight prompts utterance,—but not as a rule. Sight of letter . . . . . When I *hear* L.I. . . . .

4 Elementary factors. Explanation.

Psychology the torch, ... Nemo . . . . No faculty—process, resultant—Entire brain—outlet of funnel.

Phrenology. Complex tendencies   Pigeon-hole theory corroborated.

Lecture 5

Were there no conflicting evidence Physiologists might fairly claim to have explained the succession of our thoughts by the changing stream of nervous action, as it shoots through the cortex, awakening now one set of localities, now another. They may explain why thought is mutilated or weakened when a given locality is destroyed, just as a building is weakened and crumbles when some of its component bricks are knocked out. The succession of our thoughts, on this theory, wd occur in very much the same way that the succession of figures occurs in a kaleidoscope. Every change in the instrument, as in the brain, causes the few elements present to shoot out from each other in arrangements whose total number is inexhaustible.

Phrenology . . . discrepancy in locality is a noteworthy conflict. Still greater discrepancy however in the principle of the two doctrines. For the Phrenologist, brain-spots represent *faculties*—for the Physiol. Psyc., elementary processes, sensory & motor. Such faculties as conscientiousness, self-esteem, causality, hope, philo-progenitiveness, designate the entire man in a particular attitude of his being and are built up of many elementary processes.

The Phrenologist, in short, imagines a little homunculus sitting in each bump and guiding the destinies of the individual. You will observe that there is not even an attempt here to explain the faculties or the action of the brain out of anything simpler. To explain that a man loves children because his brain has large philop. is a purely verbal explanation, quite antediluvian in its simplicity. The Psychologist, whether he succeeds or not, at any rate tries to explain such a general tendency in the man as the love of children, by showing the sort of images which compose it and building it up from them, as elements.

All this is not meant to disparage Phrenology as an art of reading character. It may be that without being a science of character. I am inclined to think that prominent eyes are a sign of fluent speech, just as a prominent nose is a sign of decision, and delicate hands of sensibility. But the brain behind the eye need no more be the organ of the first peculiarity than are the nose and the hand of the other two.

Thus we seem to have achieved most brilliant results. Psychology & Physiology like two sisters, may hence forward wander hand in hand. I regret however to dampen the enthusiasm which in some of you the evidence brought forward may have aroused, by saying now that that evidence was picked. The fact that Munk & Ferrier assign . . . . . . should show us how insecure as yet, is the experimental basis. I already told you that in human pathology innumerable cases are recorded which contradict the notion of immutably fixed localities for motor & sensory processes.

B. Séquard has brought them before you.

H.J. long ago showed that whatever part of the cortex . . . . . . same symptoms were observed viz. disturbance of powers most recently acquired, least automatic, least heritage of race—Aphasia.

Goltz also . . . . . Restitution.

Are we then to say that we know nothing of the brain and that everything is a chaos? By no means! this hopeless conclusion wd. be very wrong. It is not a chaos. The matter is only more complicated than at first appeared. There is a tendency for functions to localize in particular tracts, but it is like that of water to flow . . . . .

I do not say that all writers on the connection of body & mind are guilty of such confusion. I imagine that with more reflection Maudsley & Spencer wd. both admit that to account for my knowledge of the past by saying that my brain has the property of recollection, is quite as unscientific as to account for my love of children by saying that my head has a bump of philoprogenitiveness.

Tyndall & Huxley who popularly pass for rank materialists wd most vehemently repudiate the pretension to *explain* the connection between a certain brain-action & the mental state which corresponds to it. The connection is perfectly inexplicable, they say—Tyndall page 121.

It is thus a mistake to suppose that modern materialism pretends to be a philosophy in the sense of being a *rational* explanation of everything. All it does, in the person of its best exponents, is to say that however irrational, however inscrutable the fact may seem, it is a fact that no conscious event can occur without some parallel event occurring in the nervous system on which the conscious event depends. In this couple the bodily event is the condition, the mental event the consequence. What we esteem as highest is at the mercy of what we esteem as lowest and must ask its permission to exist.

Thus the charge of degrading the high by deducing it from the low which these authors escape in the theoretical sphere, is a charge which they cannot escape in the practical sphere.

When I hear a man call our feelings impotent, deny them any independence, when he says they are passive creatures of physical conditions & not masters of such conditions, I call him a materialist for his utterances contain surely all that is repugnant or objectionable in materialism. It is absurd for such authors to indignantly deny that they are materialists, merely because they admit that the servile relation of mind to matter that they so strenuously affirm to be the truth, is an incomprehensible truth.

This servile relation, this impotence of consciousness has been lately so loudly heralded by Prof. Huxley & so welcomed as the last word of scientific wisdom, that it demands a somewhat careful consideration at our hands.

Lecture 6.

Restate theory. Thoughts follow[2] each other in certain order because brain tracts awaken each other in that order. All actions down to . . . . . . human history written . . . . . if we knew nerve processes completely.

Feeling inert, uninfluential, a passenger.

Our common sense deludes itself when we think that we put on our coats, draw to fire because *feel* cold; or that we eat ice cream because it tastes good. The reason . . . . . .

Also victims of delusion when we think that our thoughts produce each other, Good news joy—premises, conclusion—disappointed hopes, sadness—by inward congruity. No such thing. Diag. . . . .

All cause & effect in physical chain. Mental items juxtaposed.

Now observe that this is a perfectly possible conception.

Once reflex action grasped, it follows as a conception. The men who advocate it are illustrious and not triflers. What are their arguments?

Nothing but this; that since frog's legs twitch and automatic habitual acts may be performed by men without consciousness and yet outwardly appear rational, then when rational acts appear with consciousness, this consciousness is unconcerned with their production.

Observe the inverse of Lewes's reasoning. He starts from brain & says, "no rational action without feeling" . . . . .

No proof either way. Pure hypothesis. Conception of possibility.

Only direct proof given by Clifford: because my thoughts can't directly affect yours, then they can't directly affect each other, can't directly affect their own brain, have no causality. Literally only direct evidence, & yet . . . . . savages.

To such wild & whirling utterances have men of science come. Science will lose all the credit which has distinguished her from metaphysics . . . . converting "may be s" into "must be s."

---

[2] Above 'Thoughts follow' WJ wrote in pencil 'Collateral product'. On the evidence of deleted pencil 'Collateral product' after 'feeling" . . . . .' (24.28) this would appear to be a memorandum.

The true motive like most philosophic motives, aesthetic. Read 9.
But we may also have aesthetic demands. Read 11.

The aesthetic demands confront each other like G & G, & the only thing for us . . . . . . seek objective evidence.

What kind? . . . . . Direct testimony of Consciousness is that nerve action, awakening unpleasant feeling, is checked because of feeling, that feeling of effort increases action etc. But this ruled out of court as lying, *mendacious*

Seek circumstantial evidence, & to do so look a little at peculiarities of C. It appears gradually—[3] develops.

Resembles organ added for use. If we cd. find use of C. and find at same time that it wd. lose this use if deprived of causal efficacity, there wd be strong presumption that it existed, because of efficacity, because not inert.

This then my argument—try to show whether a N.S. with C. added wd. be more useful . . . . . wd. perform as well as more complicated—In a word does C. economize Nervous Machinery?

First see defects in N.S., then attributes of C.

We saw that simple N.S. or N.S. made simple by deprivation of hemis. formed machine remarkable for regularity and accuracy, responding to few stimuli but to them strongly, & well. We saw that when hemis. were added the animal capable of reacting on slight variations in environment, faint sounds, motions of points in field of vision; & we saw that these were responded to, not directly but indirectly, through processes whose subjective side we call "considerations," & which are composed of complex & shifting vibrations in the hemis.

Recollect how I compared extreme mobility of hemis. to that of jelly. . . . The indeterminateness, incalculableness of result when animal acts from hemis., we deemed to be due to equal permeability of this organ by currents in every direction. The line of considerations a process may strike through, determined by influences so slight . . . . . accident.

Hemis. in short most instable of bodies. But observe that their very essential function necessitates instability. They are there to adapt animal to minute variations in complex environment. Where animal responds to few circumstances, hemis. small. Where he re-

---

[3] Above the dash WJ interlined in blue pencil 'evolved'.

acts to many, to distant & future as well as present, like man, large & all-controlling.

Extreme instability, liability to be discharged by minutest differences—hair-trigger organization—a necessity in an organ so multiform in its performances.

But is it not evident that the price of such instability, such multiple powers, is extreme delicacy & liability to act ill from very slight disturbances, from accidental causes, such as variations in nutrition. Happy go lucky   Hit or miss. Caprice its law. Like sonorous plate with Chladnis

Read 17 & 18.

If[4] consciousness can load the dice, can exert a constant pressure in the right direction, can feel what nerve processes are leading to the goal, can reinforce & strengthen these & at the same time inhibit those which threaten to lead astray, why, consciousness will be of invaluable service. To resume plate simile = finge⟨r⟩ of physicist.

But nature of C. as we know it is just this & nothing else. In first place, it feels the goal, it knows the interests, it is the sole standard of use. Apart from some C. staking, positing, creating some particular end, as good we could not talk about the brain being useful or efficient, its actions being appropriate, at all.

In physical world idea of good don't exist. Matter has no ideals. Entirely indifferent to C.N.O.H. whether they combine in a live or a dead organism. They do with equal cheerfulness whatever they are fatally necessitated to do, without any thought of an alternative possibility. Whether the result of their action be the perfume of a rose or the odour of carrion, the words of a Shakespeare or the crackling of thorns under a pot, it is brought forth with as little reluctance in the one case as in the other. The notion that to generate life is better than to decompose it, can only come from the judgment of some consciousness looking on at the process.

Mr Darwin's C. looks on & says survival is the *summum bonum* & then he measures the utility of every creature's organs by this end. Such a reaction of the N.S. is efficient⟨.⟩ Such an instinct appropriate, such a habit fit etc. In short, he decides which of the animal acts is worthy of approbation & encouragement, as measured by this interest of survival.

---

4 The text from 26.12 to 27.4 is marked by blue-crayon lines in the margin and the notation 'read' at 26.12,19,32.

But if D.'s C. can do this . . . . . surely animal's can for itself. It can say "survival or pleasure or what not is my end, and no action shall be called useful, no nervous tendency encouraged which fails to minister to this end." Thus first requisite filled. C. knows end.

And now can C. go farther and *not* only as an inert looker-on approve & disapprove of actions & nerve processes but also further & check? . . . .

I think if we survey the field of C. from lowest to highest, we shall find that it always seems to be comparing & selecting. Regret lack of time for function of selection not enough noticed . . . . . . Comparison admitted but authors fail to see that always for sake of choice. Impartial C., nonentity. C. in short, at each of its stages is busy picking out from data offered it by lower stage, some one item, noticing, emphasizing, attending to, pursuing it & ignoring all the rest.

Brief survey. Sensation the lowest. 29. 28 bottom

Perception the next stage. Groups sensations into objects, & out of all present sensations picks out only such as are signs of objects, ignoring the rest. Among eye-sensations are many which are constant, present in all objects; useless as signs. These we overlook. Read 29, 30.

The mental industry goes on to deal with objects in same way. Of the innumerable objects that come before us we attend to very few. Read 35, 36.

Reasoning is the next higher faculty & is obviously of most extreme utility. If an animal reasons he can guide himself though unexperienced. If not he is lost in unfamiliar circumstances. Less obvious but perhaps most striking case of mental choice. Regret no time, but may say that reasoning simply & solely ability to break up & pick out———. . . . . Point connected with interest.

Genius is he . . . . . .

And now passing to higher faculties still, does not every one know that aesthetic activity consists in selecting items, rejecting colours, tones, shapes which do not harmonize with each other & with artist's main purpose?

In ethics choice reigns supreme. The choice in the moral life is between the interests. Which is my true interest, to be rich or to be just? To be powerful or to be pure? To escape pain or at any cost of pain to do some service to humanity. In fact we choose one, out of several equally possible future selves.

A striking panorama; the highest products of C. are filtred from the data offered by the faculty next beneath; this faculty sifted them from still simpler materials &c. Impartial C., monstrosity.

Now pause & ask what are data present at any one time? They are nerve processes. C. thus seems, at any rate, for the sake of the interests & ends which she has staked to be uninterruptedly encouraging some nerve processes & discouraging others, pressing constantly in the right direction, recognizing what is congruous with purpose & reinforcing that. The instable brain throws its dice & may hit or miss, but consciousness loads the dice. It is a constant force in the midst of fluctuating ones & determines the acts of a naturally indeterminate brain to drift in one way. These are the appearances but if Huxley & Clifford say they lie, how can we defend them? By no direct evidence, but by several grounds forming strong chain of circumstantial evidence. Distribution

1st Long ago noticed that useful actions, pleasurable; noxious, painful. Spencer tries to account by Nat. Selection. Supposing C. efficacious . . . . .

If animal liked suffocation——4 minutes.

Grant Allen . . . . . distribution.

2nd Historical appearance of C. corroborates. Least in lowest animals, whose least instable brain least needs a rudder. Appears step by step as brain defect grows more prominent.

Inference that it is introduced to remedy defect of brain.

3rd Now C. if added for this purpose wd. only be needed when the nerve currents were not sure to flow in beneficial channels. The fact that it is so weak in us when we execute habitual, well organized actions which our N.S. performs with security & rapidity, wd. lead us to think that being useless here Nature has not produced it.

On the other hand, it becomes intense the moment nerve processes hesitant or difficult. In cases of great indecision, agonizing. Here brain not sure to do right. C. steps in to reinforce right tendencies . . . . . . Compared to cross-section. Read pencil.

4th Phenomena of vicarious functions very strong argument for efficacity. A machine in order functions fatally in one way. We call it the right way. Out of order, it functions in another way. We call it the wrong way.

But the machine itself works fatally when wrong as well as right. It has no ends to pursue. Don't care—Steam engine runs through drawbridge . . . . . . If brain machine why not just so? Scoop out portion, diff^t machine, diff^t function.

Nevertheless we saw brain educate itself. How explain falling into old grooves again without guiding pressure? C. recognizes what goes right way, forms habit.

In fact this notion of C. as educator of N.S. which when educated can dispense with it, harmonizes many facts.

Remember theory of instinct & reflex action of frog being inherited habit; flight of swallow.

If N.S. can be moulded by C. like clay under thumb of sculptor, labour of Nat. Selection shortened. Darwin supposes appropriate instincts to arise by fortuitous variations in N.S. Nature a gaming-table . . . . . Only lucky throws survive.

But on my theory when once C. reached, reign of chance over—reign of intelligence begins.

Thus however we look at the matter, the Common Sense theory & not the C. Automaton theory gains ground. We have combatted it solely on the plane of facts without appealing to any *a priori* or metaphysical ideas.

If men of science are those who are guided by concrete facts, & metaphysicians be those who dogmatically proclaim as true whatever unverified conceptions may occur to their minds as possible & may flatter their taste then we here are men of science and Huxley, Clifford & Co. are metaphysical dreamers.

Many persons now-a-days seem to think that any conclusion must be very scientific if the arguments in favor of it are all derived from twitching of frog's legs—especially if the frogs are decapitated—& that on the other hand any doctrine chiefly vouched for by the feelings of human beings—with heads on their shoulders, must be benighted & superstitious.

They seem to think too, that any vagary or whim, however unverified, of a scientific man must needs form an integral part of science itself; that when Huxley for example has ruled feeling out of the game of life, and called it a mere bystander, supernumerary, the matter is settled.

I know nothing more deplorable than this undiscriminating gulping down of every thing materialistic as peculiarly scientific.

Nothing is scientific but what is clearly formulated, reasoned & verified.

An opinion signed by the Pope if it have these merits will be a thoroughly scientific opinion. On the other hand an opinion signed by Prof. Huxley if it violate these requirements, will be unscientific.

To talk of Science as many persons do whose mental type is best represented by P.S.M. is ridiculous. With these persons it is forever science against Philosophy, Metaphysics, Religion, Poetry, Sentiment, against all that makes life worth living, in short.

The truth is that science & all these other functions of the human mind are alike results of man's thinking about the phenomena life offers him. No mode of thinking is *against* any other, except false thinking & illogical thinking. If we think clearly & consistently in Theology or Philosophy we are good men of Science too. If we think logically in Science we are good theologians & philosophers. If, on the contrary, our thought is muddled in one field, it is worthless in all the rest. It must be that truth is one & thought woven in one piece.

I, for one, as a scientific man & a practical man alike, deny utterly that Science compels me to believe that my conscience is an *ignis fatuus* or outcast, & I trust that you too after the evidence of this evening will go away strengthened in the natural faith that your delights & sorrows, your loves & hates, your aspirations & efforts are real combatants in life's arena, & not impotent, paralytic spectators of the game.

[Drafts of Lecture 1]

In these recent days we hear a great deal of the marvellous achievements of science, how Darwinism has made us understand so much about animal and vegetable forms and how in particular the physiologists by the deep insight they have been acquiring into the nervous system and the brain, have to a great extent banished the mystery which used to hang about the action of the mind and constituted a new psychology which explodes and renders obsolete the old views of mental action all based on a priori speculation and metaphysics. Whilst this is triumphantly repeated by the sectaries of physical science it is as indignantly denied by another class of persons. The latter fancy that they see the most brutal materialism lurking behind what the former call enlightenment and scientific progress, like some hideous heathen idol whose form is dimly seen through the glare of fireworks and golden dust and dazzling vapours of incense with which its followers continually fill the air before it. Both sides alike are confident and often bitter. Each one of us probably is to some extent a partizan in the matter for few educated men are devoid of some small bias either against what seems the stagnant dogmatism of orthodoxy or the no less insolent barbarism of science. The worst of it is that in this matter of the brain and the mind people are ready to become very eager partizans on a very slender basis of study. Those whose highest flights are articles in the *Popular Science Monthly* will talk of the exploded superstitions of introspective psychology and those who have hardly opened a treatise on physiology will declaim against the degrading sophistries of medical materialists.

It has seemed to me that the 6 hours which the trustees of the Lowell fund have done me the honor to place at my disposal, could not be better spent than in taking a single subject, the brain, and in seeing exactly how much recent investigations have explained its action and in particular how much they may be said to have cleared up or made less mysterious the action of consciousness in each one of us. A sober review of this kind ought to do good to the over hasty partizans of both sides. It may perhaps make the scientific ones feel themselves prematurely sanguine, and the others feel over jealous and timid. I have for some years past in thinking of my duties as teacher in Cambridge, been inclined to deplore the rather wide surface over which my instruction had to be spread. I have been obliged to teach a little Anat., a little Phys., a little Psychology; and I have felt that where one's wisdom tried to cover so much ground it must needs be thin at any given spot. But in standing before you now I feel that my misfortune has had its good side. A teacher must form responsible opinions; a reader need not. But the difficulties of deciding a question are not often felt by one who is not responsible for his decision. The judge feels them more than the two lawyers. A physiologist may form the most careless opinions in psychology and keep a good conscience. The only thoroughness obligatory on *him* is physiological. The philosopher on the other hand who follows the subjective method may in like manner scorn the crudities of the physiologists. He does not feel the dignity and the difficulty of their problems any more than they do of his. Each owns a lot in the field of human knowledge and each, provided he cultivates his own lot conscientiously feels tolerably indifferent about what happens in his neighbor's. Each, it is true wishes to shove back the fence and reduce the size of his neighbor's lot for the benefit of his own and the disputed boundary leads to the jealousies we have seen. I think we ought tonight to aspire to the attitude of one who should own both lots. He does not care where the fence stands and being master of all the land tries to cultivate every sq. ft. of it impartially. We are each alike proprietors of a body and a mind. We are as much interested in having a sound science of the one as of the other. As proprietors of a body we ought to feel the insufficiency of every theory of the mind which leaves the body out. As owners of a mind we ought to feel the worthlessness of all explanations of our feelings which leave out that which is most essential to be explained. I confess that in the past few years, owing to the divided duties I have alluded to, I have felt most acutely the difficulties of understanding either the brain without the mind, or the mind without the brain. I have almost concluded in my moments of depression that we know hardly anything.

Anat. Remind.—Nerve roots on Bkbd.—Aff. and Eff.

Centres Sp. Cord on Bkbd. Enlargements. Not mere conductor. Dev^t of Brain on Bkbd. Slides of lamprey, cod, turtle, bird, beaver, horse, porpoise, elephant, monkey,

Human Diag. and Model. Course of fibres. Inner Capsule and crura.

Rank in scale of intelligence. Absolute size. Size relative to body. Convolutions. Intelligence, resultant of many factors; among them probably chemical or microsc.—like muscle. Hem.; Rest. Meynerts.

Physiol.[5] outward effects manifested by motion. What happens when motion occurs? Physiologist only knows that current passes. Partly he knows its paths e.g. ant. lat. columns for motion—en. caps. Neg. variation now doubtful. Acid. Phosphates, Cholest., Urea. Processes without outer effect only known to exist from subj. accomp.; their form guessed by analogy. In short we directly observe anat. and Psyc. facts—physol. hypoth.

We will examine now the processes, so far as we know them to occur, in the diff^t centres from below upwards. Sp. cord   Reflex action. Tickling feet, frog's arms.

Sp. cord. Defensive movements—rattle-snake—Robin.

Medulla. Breathing, swallowing.

5 Before '*Physiol.*' WJ wrote in brown pencil 'Insert (1)'.

Cerebel. Locomotion, turning over.
Optic lobes. Locomotion perfect, swims, stops.

Dift. kinds of cell. Spinal cord diag—Gerlach. Convolution—
Meynert. Cerebellum. What becomes of cell-processes in brain we
do not know by direct observation. In the Sp. cord reason to think
that fibres from roots pass in to process—never, if at all, directly
observed. No direct observation of connection of cells with each
other—Gerlach. Schmidt has affirmed minute net-work in convolutions; all conjectural. Only one thing certain, that cells do not connect by broad processes except in unusual cases and it has been
suggested that these cases are embryonic. Nevertheless we see figured by many authors such broad connections—Luys slide. Such
representations are *a priori*, or imaginary anatomy invented because
of certain supposed physiological necessities. It was supposed that
nervous action must pass from cell to cell and that it could not pass
without a definitely formed anatomical channel. Not knowing the
fine net-work, these authors supposed that the coarse processes were
the only possible bridges from cell to cell and figured them accordingly. The fact really is, that there may be no necessity for a definite
anatomical bridge to carry the excitement from one cell to another.
We know nothing of how it passes. It may not pass along the fibres
of the minute net-work at all. It may go right across them.

I dwell on this because it is a little instructive with regard to the
order in which we form our ideas about the nervous system. In this
case we have seen an *a priori* notion of physiological necessity give
rise to a fictitious anatomy. But in just the same way our notions of
psychological necessity may give rise to an imaginary physiology.
The whole theory of different local habitations in the brain for
different classes of ideas with fibres connecting the localities together, so that when one locality is excited the excitement may
travel along the fibres and waken up the other locality, this whole
theory I say was originally derived from our introspective knowledge of the way in which our feelings awaken each other. A certain
school in Psychology explains every mental fact by ideas and their
associations. Consider that each idea corresponds to a definite cortical cell group, each association to a bundle of fibres, and you have
an exact reduplication in brain terms, of what you directly know by
introspection. If the sensation of hearing the door-bell ring awakens
the notion of someone standing on the steps, this was considered to

be because the cells which give us the feeling of ringing when excited discharge themselves through special fibres into other special cells which give us the notion of a human figure standing in a certain place. One cell group, one idea. Another cell group, another idea, and no association possible without fibres. We shall see hereafter that there exist strong experimental grounds for holding this view, but that there also exist strong grounds for doubting it. Meanwhile the theory existed and was dogmatically stated in books, long before the grounds either way were fully known. In a word Psychology with its associations went first and from it Physiology took its cue, and Psychology today as far as all this matter goes, is definitely established whilst Physiology still gropes for light. There is nothing then more ludicrously false than the assertions so loudly made by some authors that the only sound psychological science is that founded on Physiology. Page after page of Maudsley's book, for instance, are filled with denunciation of the subjective method in Psychology—the truth really being that the subjective method has not only given us almost all of our permanently secure psychological knowledge but has also suggested all our interpretations of the facts of brain-physiology. Instead of our knowledge of the mind being based on our knowledge of the instrument, the latter leans on that of the mind and will probably do so for many years to come. The only facts we directly know are the subjective facts and the anatomical facts and we have seen how limited is our knowledge of the latter. Between them lie the facts of Physiology, the processes and currents in the cells and fibres. What these are we can only guess at and indeed should not have guessed their existence, where they give no outward sign except for introspective observation.

[Appendix]

[*List of Slides*]

1   Lamprey
1–9   Series of brains
10   Human base
11   Flechsig
12   Lebon
13   Dog and Ox
14   Porpoise

15 Meynert
16 Luys
17–18 Gerlach
19 Henle.
20 Cerebellum
22–28 Frogs & Pigeon

[*Table of Brain Sizes*]

Bricklayer	67.00 oz
Cuvier	64.33
Abercrombie	63.00
Congenital epileptic idiot,	60.00
Ruloff	59.00
James Fisk Jr	58.00
Boy, aged 13, healthy & intel.	58.00
Spurzheim	55.06
Adult man. idiot since 2.	54.95
Laborer	53.79
Daniel Webster	53.50
Celebrated mathematician	53.41
Celebrated mineralogist	43.24

[*Drafts of Lecture 2*]

croaks, compensates tilting. Indistinguishable by the vulgar from ordinary frog. Notice three common features in all these reactions. 1st. They are not spontaneous but in response to a stimulus, and this always a *near* stimulus.

2nd Invariable and determinate, machine-like. They resemble the movements of a jump.-jack, whose legs *must* fly. Present stimulus = string—it pushes the action into being by a sort of *vis a tergo*, from which there is no more escape or choice than there is choice for water to boil when a fire is put under it. Physiologist like organist.

3rd Useful. Animal safer for wiping, turning over, compensating etc.

Other instances, rattle snake, decapitated bird, locomotion. Robin. Bird without hemis. No response to distant objects.

We may state these results by saying that centres below hemis.

constitute a series of platforms superposed each of which contains an arrangement of cells for executing in a machine-like manner the particular combination of movements constituting a more or less useful action; and executing these in fatal response to immediately present changes of sensibility.[6]

Add Cerebrum—1st Great difference. In the first place response to distant sensorial impression, eye and ear. 2nd Response incalculable; no fixed order. Physiologist impotent. Frog not a pipe for fortune's finger. Moreover actuation by sentiments, hunger, fear; in bird, love. Spontaneity. The machine-like character lost. The creature has every appearance of an intelligent agent. Intelligent agents seem to have freedom of choice from the manner of their response to present solicitations of sense—a variety of reactions to any given excitement seems always open. Suppose I try to irritate a man's foot; he may withdraw it, he may scream out, he may kick me, attack me with his fists or move off as soon as he sees me coming. And the intact frog shows a like indeterminateness. What is the reason of all this? It is that the sensorial stimulus in an intelligent creature does not discharge directly into the muscles as it seems to in the machine-like animal, but acts by first suggesting *considerations*. These are what incite the motions. Now what are considerations?

Remarkable that machine should act in so rational a way;—what explanation? No time for thorough discussion but will allude to one explanation drawn from formation of habits in human being. Piano-playing, standing, walking, reading aloud, writing, skating and so forth. Conscious mind at first involved, after which lower centres seem sufficient. They grow to modes in which they have been exercised. Sleeping horseman. Onimus. Ducks and pigeons. Many authors suppose that when nervous system of parent has been exercised in one way, N.S. of offspring tends spontaneously to act in that way and that instincts are thus developed. The manner in which young mammals suck, calves and lambs walk as soon as born. Chickens peck at grain and run to hen when she calls. Cases of this deposition in N.S. of habits consciously learnt from former generations. Man has very few such instincts. It would seem as if walking, throughout all ancestral generations had not organized itself in his centres. He

---

6 After 'sensibility.' WJ wrote in pencil 'insert (a)', perhaps a reference to 'Remarkable . . . considering?' (36.23–37.24). See the Textual Apparatus, p. 549.

must learn afresh each time. This interpretation possibly untrue. Spalding's swallows. Spontaneous ripening. Moment of birth accidental. Dogs blind; children deaf, don't wink. Parent's habits, may then descend even in man. At any rate every act leaves trace in individual. Importance in moral education. We think when tempted that we may not count this time and make a fresh start tomorrow as well as today. Grievous self-deception. Not the same man after this lapse—cannot start as well. N.S. at this moment literally moulded result of our past acts. If they be acts of virtue, well. If sins, woe unto us. The great thing is to form habits which then leave hemis. free for higher flights and in forming habits, to keep them unbroken. One lapse dissolves, undoes what weeks can't firmly organize again. Carpenter's Mental physiology.

I have spoken of habits performed by lower centres in man. No habit, however, in man is wholly so performed. Even in monkeys and dogs lower centres seem not wholly independent. This accounts for the fact that with all our experimentation we are still ignorant of their functions in higher animals. We only know that they have something to do with coordinating movements and that optic lobes particularly control eye-movements. We must suppose that in even the most automatic habit in man, at least a minimum of hemispheric superintendence occurs.

Now how do acts of cerebrum differ from those we have been considering?

Rip Van Winkle may delude himself and excuse himself for yielding to temptation by saying "I won't count this time." His poor muddled mind may not count it, but does he think for that, that it escapes counting altogether? An indulgent heaven may not count it, but the eternal laws of nature to which one fact is as another, which overlook and which know nothing of excuses, they count it as much as they count the fortitude of   or the constancy of   . The cells and fibres in his hemis. & thalami & optic lobes are appropriating it, adopting it, registering it and storing it up to use it against him when the next moment of temptation comes.

His N.S. can never again be exactly what it was before this lapse.
Never can the marks of that which once hath been
Be wholly wiped away.
Our organizations are the literal resultants of our past sins and good deeds.

[Drafts of Lectures 3, 4, and 5]

In the last lecture we saw that hemis. enabled an animal to act from ideas instead of stimuli, and that ideas presupposed the storing up of past experiences; cerebrum is then a reservoir of reminiscences. The animal who has it will be an educable animal not subjected to unvarying instinct but able to resist the present solicitations of sense, if from previous experience he has learnt their results to be disastrous. The past and the future enter into his determinations along with the present.[7]

We must then seek to understand how in the hemis. ideas *can* be imperishably preserved. If there is one mental thing which physiologists claim to have explained by the properties of matter, it is this function of memory, and we must in an impartial manner examine the claim.

Begin by remarking that something analogous to memory exists not only in lower centres but in other tissues; not only there but in inorganic matter. The photographic surface often appealed to as an example; a dry plate may be exposed to a scene and carried about for months in the dark and then at the touch of the developing fluid, the scene will reproduce itself with its minutest details. The plate is reminded of the scene by the fluid. Again there are substances, (BaS) which are phosphorescent i.e. they retain the light and emit it for minutes after exposure. Every one knows how the touch of a finger will mark a bright steel surface. Breathe on the surface and the mark of the finger will reappear; wipe it, and still the mark is there. Glass once sullied in this way can never be cleaned; the spot in spite of every washing will show like a ghost and not fade out until an entirely new surface. What again is the tenderness which a bruise or blow leaves behind? A scar which never fades is the memory of a cut. Violin.

These examples show that memory is not an unparalleled phenomenon, if we take it merely to mean revival of past modes of activity. It is indeed no peculiar property of hemis. It is only the growing to habitual modes of activity which, when we studied the lower centres we called the law of habit. It exists, not only in lower centres but in nervous tissue everywhere;—in sensory organs. How often listening to distant clock at night do we hear the strokes con-

[7] Following deleted text after 'present.' (see Alterations entry 38.9) WJ wrote in brown pencil 'Insert (3)'.

tinue? This is in the ear just what after-images are in the eye. Every-one knows after-image of sun. Not everyone knows that every object gives an after-image. Practice enables us to attend to them. String round finger. Muscles after skating, riding and so forth. These all cases of reproduction, like that of cerebrum only less permanent. The permanence seems the only difference.

Why this difference of permanence in the storing-up power of different parts of the N.S.? And what consequences are bound up with it? What would happen if retina stored up forever all its after-images? Obviously they would interfere with present impressions falling on the same spot. Raspberry story. Figures on slate. We must wipe old ones off before writing down new ones. These peripheral organs then, used in their entirety for each impression, permanent reproductive power would be detrimental. In lower centres how is it? We have the reproductive power stored up in the form of habit. And it is most noteworthy that many of these habits originally learnt under the superintendence of hemis. end by being performed when hemis. asleep or removed. Robin. Sleeping horseman. Walking. *Onimus*, ducks and pigeons. The centres grow to the modes in which exercised. Habits organized and automatic. No reflexion, or deliberation. No loss of time. All-important in feats of skill. In drilling, boxing, shooting and so forth. But note now that number of such automatic acquisitions is restricted; two similar ones cannot coexist without losing promptitude i.e. without requiring reflexion, deliberation. Whenever action is hesitant, hemis. come in—full con-sciousness awakens. Muskets, skates. These examples show that in lower centres the condition a good deal resembles that of retina. An old acquisition has to be wiped out before a new one can be in-grained. The interference shows that same cells and fibres are used. If now we could find an organ where each acquisition could be switched off to a separate group of cells and fibres, there would be no need of ever wiping the slate clean. Successive impressions would not be superposed as on retina but would lie peacefully side by side, and might be preserved forever. Before passing on to show how this conception of the cerebrum, forming a collection of pigeon-holes, as it were, in which our mental acquisitions are singly stored away, and ticketed, I must pause to make sure that we understand what the acquisitions are. Psychologists have analyzed our thoughts and have found them composed of few elements, viz. images of past sen-sations whose permutations and combinations form the mind. All schools agree in this, that the bricks of mental architecture are vestiges of sensation left in the memory—sensory images and motor images,—Lowell Institute, benches, way hither. Schools only differ in account of mortar, relations, such as likeness, unlikeness, causality and so forth, but even those who hold these to be mental functions additional to faculty of reproducing images, also admit that without images no mental life would be. Be not surprised that elementary sensations are so few—the variety comes from the endless combination. No more wonderful that a few colours, a few sounds, feelings of contact and of motion should build up all our thoughts, than that 26 letters should build up all the literatures of all Europe. Reverting now to hemis. we need only assume that certain cells are reserved for certain elementary impressions. The cells for instance which are strongly excited when we see a flame and less strongly when we think of it, are never excited when we see black or hear a sound. They become active whenever we think of an object containing flame. The other cells simultaneously active and containing like elements of sensation determine the rest of the object. Street. Lowell Institute. If flame-cells were equally excited by sounds and so forth, and their former memories permanent, we should have all these memories and present sensation arising together when the cell became active—confusion. If, on the contrary, flame-cells have nothing but flame, no confusion, because their activity at any moment awakens nothing discordant with its present object.

Hemis. might then be conceived as organ of thought by supposing each of their component cell-groups to correspond to an elementary sensation. The particular groups excited at any time would determine entire thought in mind at that time.

This all *a priori* reasoning. Confirmed by experiment. Flourens. Unexcitable period. Hitzig and Ferrier. Slides. Motor and Sensory regions. Unexcitable regions. Munk's localizations.

Phenomena of mental blindness; usually interpreted not as failure to see but as failure to understand. When we say we see a thing, we really see or hear very little of it. We say "hear" a fight in next room, horse run away in street, "see" that the man is guilty or "see" that he was in a hurry to get home to his dinner.

Sensation a sign—rest supplied by mind. Dog has the sensation but mind being gone it has no meaning—like pigeon. Whip, dish, sign of command, word of command. Direct line and loop line. Masked figure. Shuns obstacles.

Paralyses. Walking suffers little. Leg moved in concert with others by help of lower centres. Special volitional movements impaired. Won't give paw because that performance result of individual education, requiring loop line. Goltz' results. Even defensive movements impaired because in dogs these involve intelligence.

As a result of these experiments one might conclude that special centres were found for different elementary images which constitute bricks of the mental edifice. In the human subject, data less precise. Aphasia. Paralysis of right half. Various symptoms. Can't speak at all, or babbles, or uses a few unmeaning words, or miscalls words. Perceives this and grows angry, swears. Can understand. Sometimes can't understand and babbles without knowing it. Can understand gestures. Sometimes understands reading and can write, sometimes not, but can never spell. Can repeat words immediately after they have been uttered. Pathol. Anat. How are we to explain this curious medley by the functions of the brain? How account for the fact that one patient can understand but not speak whilst another can't even understand? That one can't read words whilst another can read words but not the letters of which they are composed? Utterly inexplicable without psychological analysis of language. What is psychological process when I say this is Lowell Institute? Optic sensation awakens optic images.—Recognition. They awaken auditory image. Auditory image discharges into articulatory centre, that, into tongue. When I hear the words *Lowell Institute* and understand them, what happens? Sensation awakens auditory image, that, representation. Among images in representation, possibly written words. When I read L.I. what happens? Optic image awakens properties of thing, and I understand, but cannot read aloud unless also optic image awakens sound. For vocal centre prompted by idea of sound. It may be that owing to my great practice in reading and so forth the mere sight of word and thought of meaning will discharge itself vocally without preliminary thought of sound.

Analysis shows three elementary factors, vocal, motor, auditory, optic and other notion images. In monkey Ferrier finds, and so forth. Now the supposition that one of these centres is destroyed &c. Observe here how Psychology is the torch that casts a light over the paths which physiology must tread. Nemo &c. Certainly without analysis the anatomical observation *Broca* would never have lead to anything beyond his crude assumption of a "localized faculty of language." The truth is, there is no "faculty." There is process, or function, the resultant of many elementary faculties. The entire brain is at work when we speak. *Broca's* spot only its outlet. Mouth of funnel.

Digress here to show difference between phrenological and scientific analysis. Diff⸞ locality, but great difference consists in this, that organs of phrenologist are not elements of mind, but entire mind working in special way; language, hope, benevolence, causality, combativeness conscientiousness &c. Each faculty involves all elementary processes, is a little homunculus sitting in a certain part of the brain. Psychological analysis does not deny supreme importance of particular localities for expression of faculty but it shows how each faculty is built of images, motor and sensory, combining in peculiar proportions, and it assumes that the elementary functions of the brain are the production of these images. To localize the images would be an achievement compared with which the clumsy performances of phrenology would seem really of antediluvian simplicity.

Phrenology in a word makes no analysis either of the mind's powers or of the brain's functions, it merely takes certain broad general tendencies in the individual's temperament, gives them a general name such as hope, firmness conscientiousness self-esteem, caution and says that a particular fullness in the skull designates their presence. Observe that there is nothing scientific here, no explanation. The psychologist on the contrary really tries to explain such complex tendencies as caution, self-esteem &c, by showing the sort of images of which they are composed. No man can have much caution without a large development of fear; this fear wd. play a part in all his expectations of the future, the latter, doubtless, wd. involve the entire brain. If physiologist could show what localities or processes produced fear, we wd. have to suppose in cautious person exaggerated activity of those localities. This wd. *explain* his caution. Science attempts this. Phrenology does not even attempt. Phrenology a useful art.

Thus we see how the hemis. if they constitute pigeon-holes for elements of our thought, and reproduce these elements in the order of previous experience, constitute a machinery for rational action.

Evidence laid before you most beautifully points to this conclusion. But that evidence picked. If *all* facts taken, many seem irreconcilable with result. In human brain it is true, Ferrier can find many corroborative instances, but many exceptions. H. Jackson has found that no matter what part of cortex is affected, tendency to disturbance of those movements which are most artificial, most educated, most recent acquisitions in history of race—most voluntary. Thus fingers first, then hand, then arm, toes &c.

Same thing

3. Notes for a Lecture on "The Physiological Effects of Alcohol" (1886)

Alcohol

Physiological vs. empirical evidence.
Primary vs. secondary effects.
Acute effects often reverse chronic.
    opium, pain wakefulness alcohol trembling.
    tobacco nervousness, goneness.
Is alcohol food—Lallemand & Co.
More than 1½ oz appears in Urine.
Bichromate test.
Cases of nourishment by it.
In beer, malt extract plays a part.
In wine, salts & ethers.
Hammond's Exp^{ts} MR. ii, 721
Edinb. Rev. July 1875
Aliment d'Epargne
Dim's CO_2
Increases Heartbeats—followed by fall.
Dilates blood vessels of surface, chronically
Dim's heat slightly—diagnosis in dead drunk.
Muscular weakness—want of precision.
Sensorial anaesthesiae.
Cerebral effects—higher parts, *judgment* first—imagination feelings.
Anaesthetic[1] qualities are the secret of its fascination.

---

[1] On the facing page WJ wrote: 'All anaesthetics alike—differ only in spread over time.'

Ether & Chloral topers
Man at Dinner party
No judgment.

Its uses—stim^n of trigeminal & stomach Nn.
Chewing—candy—raisins.
Insufficiency of dinner.
May help digestion
Cardiac effects good
But soup or even saline water will do this.
Parkes' exp^{ts} c̄. beef extract coffee & alcohol.
Arctic and army results
Bad to work on
Better to rest on—anaesthetic.
Never on empty stomach.
Parkes's q^{ty} 1½ fluid oz. per diem. = 7½ oz sherry   15 oz claret, 30
   oz beer.

Empirical data.
Chronic alcoholism—short life—degeneration of tissues.
Drink craving—a disease wh. may be superinduced by habit.
Hospital statistics in favor of teetotalism.
Insurance ditto

	Teetotalers lives		General lives	
	expected	actual	expected	actual
9 years	1110	801	2002	1977

On the other hand ethnic experience.
Sum up—risk—especially for us Americans.
Don't enter race of life handicapped. O.W.H.

Alcohol

1 Apology
2 Physiological vs empirical evidence
3 Primary vs. secondary effects
      (Often reversed—opium—tobacco)
4 Food dispute—bichromate test.
   Jaillet: it combines with hemoglobin & is burned, Ā, CO_2 &
      H_2O.—

This dim^s respiratory capacity of blood and accumulates
  CO_2—
Slow asphyxia—
Aliment d'Epargne—Hammond MR ii. 721
Smith on CO_2 elimination.
S'ts real food
Ales, wines, etc not alcohol
5 Increases pulse.
  Parkes: 106,000 + 25,488
    122 foot tons + 24
6 Dilates superficial vessels—chronic
7 Dim's heat—dead drunk diagnosis.
Arctic.
8 Muscular weakness—no precision
    Exner.—Parkes
9 Sensorial Anaesthesia—Ether
    Secret of charm.—Dinner party
10 Cerebral effects.
    No judgment—bad for work.

11 *Uses*
in disease.
digestion
Cardiac effects good
3geminal N.
  (Candy etc)
sp^t arom. ammon. 20 or 30 M
+ 5 to 10 tinct capsicum
+ 2 oz inf. gentian or cascarilla
Even soup
    milk
    star water
Bad to work on
Better to rest on.
    (read Parkes p. 298)

Empirical data.—despair
"Fortifying" Parkes 305 note
Chronic alcoholism.
Drink craving—disease of habit

Surgical & army statistics
Insurance Parkes 292.
On other hand ethnic experience.
Sum up—risk—

J. J. Ridge. (Med. Temp. Journ. April 1882) Exp^{ts} on sensibility.
    Estimation of 2 points. Distance had to be incr^d from 115 to
        189 (on average) after taking 3 ii of abs. alcohol.
        ————— weight. Average error rose from 6.060 to 9.095 when
    two weights had to be made equal. (Mostly 2 drachms)
        ————— sight. With one eye letters had to be brought nearer
    (from 9.375 to 8.538) to be read. (mostly 2 drachms)
Gustafsen, Foundation of death p. 118.
Edinb. Rev. July 1875 & Littell
E. A. Parkes: Practical Hygiene, Book I, Chap VII, § I.
————— Experiments on Alcohol, Transactions of Royal Soc.
  1874 ————— on Ration
T. L. Brunton, Text Book of Pharmakology etc page 647–57.
D. Merriman: A Sober view of Abstinence, in Bibliotheca Sacra
    Oct. 1881
Edwd Smith: Foods, Chap XXXVI
Contemp. Review 1878

4. Draft and Outline of a Lecture on "The Effects of Alcohol" (1895)

The Effects of Alcohol

I have accepted the invitation with pleasure.
Total abst. League small but important.
Matthew A. conduct ¾ etc. better 99/100
But if so, fashion & imitation are 99/100 of conduct.
The drinking habits of a community are purely matters of fashion
Why don't women smoke?
Why don't women as a rule drink with us?
Why don't Hindoos drink?

Whether a given youth now shall grow into a drinker or an abstainer depends more than on anything on the fashion he finds set.

There are countries in which drinking is so universal that it is almost impossible to be a water drinker

Europe—hard to get water—just beginning to recognize a set of persons.

Restaurants advertize 50 cent dinners "ohne Weinzwang"—

In old times it was thought that wine gave strength—Prescribed now for children whenever weakly etc. in Europe.

In the old army and navy of great Britain, Capt. Marryat's and Nelson's & Wellington's time, the function of getting drunk was idealized as the one duty of martial & manly human beings, just as it now is in savage races whose indulgences can only be occasional. Read Parkes, 334 note.

In the German universities the same ideal prevails to a great extent—

The northern romantic ideal of manhood always involved enormous powers of drinking as one of its elements.[1] Die Knochen voll von Rittermark der Becher angefullt . . is the description of a german hero in one of G's most exquisite lyrics. Curious association of the idea of *strength* . . .

The academic habits of youth continue into the mature life of academic heroes.

In 1890 The City of Berlin gave a great banquet . . . 4000 guests.

bottles	
5308	Champagne
4721	Claret
3853	Rhine
1500	Mosel
15382	bottle
22000	litres of beer
300	goes of brandy.

Anecdotes . . . . .

In our country thank heaven the individual does n't find this incubus of conformity to the duty of drinking imposed on him.

So many people are water drinkers that one need make no individual apologies and explanations.

Great wave in England in same direction.

[1] In the left margin WJ wrote, 'form of *prowess*'.

In Germany it is beginning

In the latin countries, it is hardly understood yet.

Now one condition of this change is the creation of a large number of invariable abstinents who set an example. Every man of prominence who habitually drinks water is the starting point of a wave of imitation. challenges, rebukes or encourages.

I think we must thank and respect this League, even if we do not join them. Their existence is either a challenge or a rebuke.

I do not join them . . . . but they help me none the less.

Individuals differ:

Whole men—half men

firm men—waffling men.

Some men to whom the bare fact of an irrevocable decision is enough to cause a frenzy of desire to back out. Berenson

Don't like to turn key, lock themselves in

Others who get relief and peace by settling a question once for all and never opening it again.

These differences we must respect.

When league was founded I lectured etc etc.

I will give a somewhat diff^t lecture now and add some moral words

But first let us review the facts.

2 kinds of evidence

1 Physiological : 2 empirical

experimental (statistical)

Primary vs. Secondary effects.

(Often reversed)—opium

tobacco

pain wakefulness

tremor, goneness

Experiment can only study primary effects of gross and measurable kind.

C_2H_5HO—First question is it food?

Chromic & SO_3 test.

Anstie, Binz & others show agst. Lallemand Perrin & Duroy that it disappears in system. Hence can be called food.

Just what becomes of it we don't know.

Added to fresh blood 10% disappears (Schulinus)

Brain[2] absorbs most of it (id).

---

[2] In the left margin WJ wrote vertically, 'Anstie's cases' and drew a rule underneath.

Increases saliva

apparently *gastric juice*

But *retards* artificial *digestion* and apparently also natural (fistule dog, Ogáte)

Later improves digestion by being absorbed and increasing gastric juice (Glusinsky)

Hammond: Aliment d'Epargne

Temp. (from ½ to 1° F.) 2 or 3 degrees Fever.

Sweat

Heart.[3] Injected into heart temporary enfeeblement

Cut out heart does less work when fed by alcoholized blood (Martin)

Absorbed by stomach quickens pulse somewhat, but soon paralyzes vasomotor centres relaxes vessels and lowers pressure

(Castillo)—4.8 fl ℥ abs. alcohol per diem made heart perform 15.8 foot tons of work (Parkes, p 325).

N—output dim^d? (Richardson's conclusions)

Respiratory gas-exchanges give contradictory results.—No obvious difference.

Reaction time, first quickened—then slowed—no great effect—increases range of error

Muscular strength—at first may be slightly incr'd

Later dim'd.

Chronic changes in all organs—the very genius of degeneration

Subjective experience

    Immediate exhilaration

        reflex effect

    Happiness

        Stimulation or anaesthesia?

    Certainly emotional stim^n.

        From paralysis—(after apoplexy).

    Possible intellectual stim^n from small doses

Narcotic effect is main effect

    Belongs to class of chloroform, ether—

    Same phases—diff. of speed.

    Dead drunk total anaesthesia . . .

    Compass points—weight—error—precision—narrowing of consciousness—associations

Fascination of drunkenness a mystery.

---

[3] In the left margin WJ wrote vertically '(apud Warren)'.

incapable of anything, yet happy.

paralytic dementia

From periphery to centre. Rapture of N_2O

Top goes first—judgment

speech first or later "British Constitution"

cerebrum—cerebellum—cord

Mania

Restraints removed . . . .

The sort of "courage" which this brings, especially when emotion is irascible, and the "happiness" are probably at the root of the delusion that a man full of wine is more of a man.

Anaesthesia the seduction.

"Drives away care"—"don't care a rap" Worry disappears

Feeling of numbness on lips and fingers.

Pain—cold—fatigue disappear.

But all come back sevenfold.

The great *excuse* is conviviality . . .

You arrive cold, morose, tired and presently are laughing, and gabbling and gobbling as full of enthusiasm as you can be. When one considers that some of the business of the world is transacted over the table etc.

Even here you *pay* . .

But here if anywhere is what you pay for worth the price

Elsewhere it is n't.

To *work* on alcohol is a most treacherous business, even where it does stimulate, if it does.

In most cases it merely masks the fatigue and makes the work worse.

Whipping and spurring the brain to go on when the best guide is the fatigue feeling.

Neurasthenic insensibility to fatigue.

What I say here is true of tobacco, tea coffee and all other stimulants used as whippers up of fatigue.

What I say also is hardly the sort of thing to be understood by youth, because the kind of fag that needs an anaesthetic to overcome is not felt.

The whole bill against alcohol is its *treachery*. Its happiness is an illusion and seven other devils return—*So far as* it has an appreciable effect.

Parkes sets down 1½ fl ℥ as the daily dose.

Don't give oration under its influence . . .

Hitherto only temperate use . .

Now intemperance.

Of course no one defends that as a habit.

2 sorts. Congenital & acquired.

Dipsomania . . .

Neurasthenic craving—innate

acquired by starvation, bad air, insipid food, etc.

Mere drink *habit*.

Here comes in the importance of changing social habits.

From every point of view we see one conclusion. It is *safer* to drink cold water, or hot water, or any kind of water.

In this overburdened, especially here in America, every ounce of handicap that is added should be avoided, and the daily use of even the smallest amount of alcohol is probably a real handicap, increasing the fatigue and wear and tear of life, diminishing reserve force and elasticity, and tending to shorten existence.

Say what you will about quality of existence, the quality, the gas lit spurious hilarity with sickness afterwards is not the real quality. And indeed it seems a pity and a mean way of deciding a question like this by fear.

Spinoza long ago said . . . .

The best way to wean people from intemperance is to fill them with a love of temperance for its own sake. In other words replace the drink idol, & ideal by another ideal. What is the other ideal. It is the ideal of having a constitution in perfect health that is as elastic as cork and never creaks or runs rusty or finds any situation that it can't meet by its own buoyancy. I remember a passage that I read in 1862 in Leland's sunshine . . .[4]

That intoxication is not

Customs etc.

Drunkenness

---

4 The quotation from Charles Godfrey Leland, written on a loose leaf in ink mostly in Alice James's hand, is found with the notes for the lecture on the "Physiological Effects of Alcohol." In the upper left hand of the leaf is a note written by WJ 'Bunge, 26', followed by the quotation in Alice's hand: '*Leland: | Intoxication [WJ *hand*] is not the pleasantest and most desirable state of mind. *. . . [*intrl.*] I know, for I never felt even from Veuve Cli[c]quot—no, nor after the opening of those stupendous yellow seals which reveal apocalypses of Johannisberg, such exhileration as one feels from simple, sober, perfect *health* on a fine Indian-summer morning. I have tried both—the one in Schloss Johannisberg itself, and the other everywhere—and of the two, the best excitement was that of my own bounding life-blood.'

Physiology.
Subjective.
Safety.
Spinosa

Alcohol

Invitation
League small but important
Conduct ¾ of life
Fashion ¾ of conduct
Women . . . Hindoos . .
Whether a youth shall drink depends . . .
In Europe almost impossible not . . .
Just beginning to recognize . .
"Ohne Weinzwang"
In old times ideal of manhood
"Gives strength."
Sick children
Army & Navy. Parkes. 334
Ideal human function . . . as in savages.
      Goethe
Academic ideal . . . prowess.
Berlin banquet

5308	Champagne
4721	Claret
3853	Rhine
1500	Mosel

15382
22 litres beer
300 goes Cognac
Read Bunge, p. 29—then p. 24
Our country, thank heaven . .
In England too one need no longer apologize
Even in Germany . . .
One condition existence of body of teetotalers
Each one starts a wave,
We must respect League

I do not join but they help me—
Individuals differ.
>   Whole men & half men—
>   (Berenson) "key"
Others like to close . . . .
Respect these differences!

My last lecture . . .
>   different now.
First, drunkenness.
>   2 sorts.

1 $\begin{cases} \text{Dipsomania} \\ \text{Neurasthenia} \end{cases}$

Acquired habit . .
Here the importance of teetotal fashions.

Now temperate use—& *Facts*!
2 kinds of effects.
>   effects often reversed.
>   Alcohol relieves its own symptoms.
Primary effects. C_2H_5HO
Food? It disappears in body
Fresh blood destroys it.
Small fraction only, found in urine tissues brain $\Big\}$ Schulinus
Anstie's cases of old topers—etc
Saliva & gastric juice both incr'd (altho' artificial digestion stopped)
Hammond.
Temperature $\frac{1}{2}$ to $1°/2$ or 3.
Fever.
Circulation.
>   Skin sweat.
>   Heart (*directly* applied dim[s] work done Martin)
>   P. incr[d] in soldiers (Parkes)
>   4.8. oz. = 15.8 foot tons. about $\frac{1}{5}$ more.
N—output? . . (*Probably* diminished)
Gas exchanges . . probably no great effect
Reaction time, quicker at first, then slower
Muscular strength . . . . .
>   Parkes . . .
Chronic changes post mortem
>   "Genius of degeneration"

Subjective experience
      Immediate exhilaration (reflex)
      (Ginger, sweets, tobacco soup—star water)
Intellectual stimulation—rare.
Emotional always
Narcotic cause in part.
We say stimulant. we mean anaesthetic.
Ether Chloroform.
Dead drunk. Surgery.
Compass points—weights
Error. no precision.
Incoordinate. "Brit. Con"
Judgment goes . . then cerebellum—sp. cord . . .
Mania. Restraints removed.
Courage, irascibility and happiness account for delusion that *full*
  man is more man . . .
Happiness a mystery.
  paralytic dementia
Lower degrees are anaesthesia
"Cave" Don't care . .
Numb lips . . .
Pain—cold, fatigue vanish
tedium . . . Germans over beer.
Dinner party . . .
     Ami Fritz
Obvious that you can't *work* on alcohol
Fatigue feeling best guide
Treacherous remedy. (tobacco coffee, etc.)
Reaction time delusion.
     N_2O
     Crisis
If ever, then, *provided* it stimulates.
But often treacherous.
    (Chicago dinner)
Convivial excuse
temper brittle next day
Whole bill against it is its *treachery*!
Shortens life.
Sceptre Company   1884–9

	expected	actual	%
General § ——	569	434	76
Teetotal	249	143	57
General Temp & Prov. Inst 1866–81			
	4080	4044	99
	2418	1704	70

Benefit Society.

abstinents.	non abstinents
7.48 weeks	26 weeks.

One conclusion

Safer to drink cold(?) water.

Handicap.

Advantage of not beginning.

This talk about temptation to relieve fatigue does n't appeal to
   young.

Very real danger when old.

But after all, mean form of appeal.

Fear!

Spinosa

Best way implant *contrary ideal*

Bunge,—Leland to be read

Gas light . . . fever . . . vs sound as bell—Clear as crystall.

Elastic as cork that never creaks or runs rusty or finds situations that
   can conquer its own buoyancy.

Ideal of perfect *health*

This the coming ideal.

Athletics are helping it.

If it once get root, it will dispel the ideal of turbid excitement as
   the mists of night are dispelled by the risen sun.

5. Lectures on Abnormal Psychology (1895, 1896)

[*Notes for a Lecture on Degeneration*]

Neurasthenia—*phobias*: of spaces, of enclosure, crowds; solitude;
   disease; contamination; of s'thing dreadful.

Germ in most people when unnerved.

Single out *mysophobia*: Kaan, p. 117

We see here *obsessive idea*, but no real delusion.

    Normal germ: seal letter; lock door; wind watch   put out gas; look under bed.

In morbid cases idea returns & insists.

    Patient must open mouth—Kaan 30

In these cases the obsessive idea is a *doubt*

The act gives relief. Folie du doute

A good example is the *recherche angoissante du mot*?

Its normal germ.

Case in Magnan Rech. 283 Georgette—notebook photographs

Arithmomania. Normal germ, Candlesticks

Case in Magnan, 281. Counts spoonfuls, mouthfuls   appleseeds cherry stones

Metaphysics.—orange to apple

          fig to pear   but what to greengage?

          lemon to quince

New element. Anxiety and dread if idea not obeyed. Harm will follow. Things *not right*. Must be made so.

Dressing; arranging of things etc. *repeat!*

Here also normal germ.

Cochran case.

Clothes—Cowles.

Case: Am J. I. 240 Harm to a person by thoughts conjured by other thoughts or other persons—complicated system

Note exorcism and cancelling.

All sorts of devices.

Legrand du Saulle: pretty women

Van Eedens Case. R. de l'Hyp. VI, 12.

Shades into general anxious melancholy.

Different are the pure motor impulses where the act is primarily the thing suggested.

We have the so called manias.

Dipsomania, (periodical)

Kleptomania,

Pyromania, (mostly in imbeciles.)

Suicidal & homicidal mania

All sorts of impulses belonging to the sexual sphere.

These show graver trouble.

Though they exist in germ in the healthy.

E.g. Kleptomania: we pay at desk but our will is overpowered, all the same.

Money-spending mania (oniomania).

Suicide—of two kinds

Sudden impulse: musician the other day.

Rev. de l'hyp. VII, 292

Homicide: Descourtis, p. 24.

I will say nothing of those blood thirsty types—Safe to say. Jack the Ripper.

Cruelty in general—moral insanity—anti-social impulses. Usually but not always weakness of intellect. Cunning.

Weakness of intellect still greater in pure motor impulses, 'tics.' Prichard 42–3. Murder: hat

No end to the possible kinds of obsession

Anti-vivisectionist mania.

anti-slavery mania—unity of Italy mania.

Munsterberg's bathing case.

Love a case—Danville.

Superior—challenge, Bergh, Parkhurst Somerset

Transition to genius.

These persons are not *insane*. Not maniacs—not melancholics—not deluded.

Yet not sane. 'Monomaniacs': 'mattoids.'

They have divided selves. Can't *control*.

They show under a microscope the play of the elements of human nature.

Ideas and their association

All ideas being impulsive . . or inhibitive

Déséquilibrés Horses and driver.

The question is why certain ideas are so strong

Why such associations are formed

Such emotions of doubt—of wonder—of fear.

When bad enough we pity—elsewhere blame.

Irresolute type

Descourtis, 16. Délire des négations.

In some cases we begin to know where the ideas come from.

Transition to hysteria.

[*Notes for a Lecture on Genius and Insanity*]

Genius & Insanity

Myers explains genius by 'uprush'—not certain that it contains organized thinking. It does influence our moods and conclusions.

Turn now to another view of genius.

Academic view: divine, miraculous, conflagration on mountain top, don't trace conditions but be grateful & adore.

Not only the intellectual gifts but the character of the genius must be heroic & god given—no selfishness or jealousy, no meanness or cruelty—one effulgence of light.

Contrast with this hero-worship the realistic tendency.—[*fols.* 17–19 *missing*]

All this sounds amusing—and is so.

Lombroso flies in face of logical rules.

Simple enumeration. . . . *Friday*—Blue eyes   count—don't count.

Ought to compare ratio of $\dfrac{\text{psychop.}}{\text{geniuses}}$ with $\dfrac{\text{psychop.}}{\text{to population}}$

For this must know $\dfrac{\text{geniuses}}{\text{to pop}^{\text{n}}}$ sedentary life business men

[Compare with verid. halls.?]

Let us see if we can't ourselves . . . .

In first place not a psychol. Conception . . .

Social conception . . . does s'thing excellent.

What psych type depends on what is done.

No common measure betw. Paderewski & Bonaparte; Shelley & Jay Gould; S. Bernhardt & Washington; St Paul & Thos. C. Platt.—yet all geniuses.

Public opinion restricts to *artistic* genius, and even there to *capricious*—romantic rather than classic—Mark Twain—Holmes; Dickens—Thackeray.

Of course if you *mean* that by genius, you get neurotic temperament . . . . . . Susceptibility . . . . excess.

But then affair of words.

Even within artistic temperament immense differences of type. Men of moods & steady men[1]

---

[1] In the left margin WJ wrote in pencil, 'Boston list [*short rule*] Lowell, O.W.H. Longfel. Emerson'.

Goethe .. Schiller
Mozart .. Beethoven (confession)
De M.—G. Sand

If you take in all types of genius, it means nothing short of Marion's def.

> superior reason
> powerful imagination
> ardent sensibility
> strong will

This the ideally complete man who may be Goethe, Moltke, or Helmholtz according to his interests.

If you say, W. not original—*originality!*

Then Bain's definition— —truly psychological.

But this carries no consequences.

Maniac's o. due to lack of inhibitions.

Degenerates obsessions not original in this sense. Englishman

Liability to obsession, sensibility & impulsivity are however conditions of *effective* genius.

If you have an idea the impulse to work it out. Gen. Booth, John Brown   Howard   F. Willard

This a quality quite distinct from the intellectual quality

With $\left\{ \begin{array}{c} \text{strong} \\ \text{weak} \end{array} \right\}$ intellect, it makes $\left\{ \begin{array}{c} \text{genius} \\ \text{crank} \end{array} \right.$

My own opinion

No one element makes a mind sound or unsound, but the mixture.

We are all resultants of ideas impulsions & inhibitions

Affair of *balance*

> Strong horses need strong drivers
> Goethe—Washington

One leg too short . . .

Every *combination possible* of will, intellect, & feeling.

> Geo. III—Philip II—Bonaparte
> Leibnitz or Coleridge
> Shelley, Poe, de Musset.
> Gladstone, Holmes, Longfellow

Great men; g^t intellects or emotions; cranks; weaklings.

Practical conclusion important

> Tendency to pessimism—cynicism—drag higher down.

— — —it all tends to contract field of health

We should rather expand it.
Health a relative conception—term of praise.
Evolution . . . Venn's results, Monist, IV, 5
    Genius are the sallying points.
Nordau—biceps profi

[Fragment of a Lecture on Exceptional Mental Phenomena]

difference, consequent on the proportionate activity of the different factors involved. What is shown to be true in a strong degree in one class of persons, is certainly true in some degree in all, and may be true in special individuals to a degree quite indeterminable *a priori*.

In many grave and inveterate cases of hysteria one of the most characteristic symptoms consists in local losses of sensibility or anaesthesias. The skin may be affected, the mucous membranes and deeper tissues, or the sight of one or both eyes. Now this anaesthesia is very curious, and it was not till 1886 or thereabouts that its nature began to be cleared up, thanks to the observations of a number of french physicians. It is an anaesthesia that comes and goes, an anaesthesia that gives the patient little trouble, an anaesthesia that is there only when the patient thinks about it, an anaesthesia that, in short is not a genuine insensibility, but an insensibility in certain relations and for certain purposes. Just the sort of defect that in old times brought upon the whole class of hysteric subjects the accusation of being wilful shammers and malingerers.

Here for example is a patient the skin of whose whole left side is supposed to be insensible. Lying with bandaged eyes he is told to say "yes" whenever he feels a pinch, whilst the surgeon goes over his skin now here, now there, to test the power of sensation. To every pinch on the right side the patient replies yes but whenever the left side is touched, instead of no reply at all being made, the patient says 'I feel nothing there.' But he must feel something in order to reply so opportunely.

Here again is another patient who when her right eye is closed sees nothing, her left eye is totally blind. By certain artifices it may be proved that this eye sees perfectly well when used along with the other. For instance, arm the patient with a pair of spectacles of which the right glass, being red, stops all rays coming from green objects, making them invisible to the right eye which it covers. Then exhibit to the patient, looking with both eyes, a prepared card on which are both green and red letters. The patient reads them all; she must therefore have used her left eye for the right eye cannot possibly see the green letters. Similarly hold a prism before her right eye, both of her eyes being open. She will forthwith say that she sees double, an effect optically impossible unless both eyes be simultaneously used.

The spectacles and the prism are contrivances originally made to catch malingerers in the army; and a few years ago, after such an exposure, the poor hysterics would have been incontinently discharged as impostors. But the study of certain analogous phenomena in hypnotic subjects has revealed the real complexity of the case, and enabled us to treat them more sympathetically.

A good hypnotic subject may, as is well known, have all sorts of hallucinations suggested to him. He will see things and animals where they are not; marks, drawings, etc, will appear to him on a blank sheet of paper if you only tell him they are there. Not only this, but you may suggest to him *negative* hallucinations. He shall *not* see a certain mark, a certain word in a printed sentence, a certain object in the room, he shall not hear a certain person's words. Now in these latter cases the conditions are often such, many similar marks, things, words, being present, that he must first *discriminate* the object, before he can know that it is the identical one to whose presence he is supposed to be insensible. If the pencil-stroke has no distinguishing mark on it to distinguish it from others, he will very likely see it like the rest. If on the contrary there be some peculiarity in it he will be blind to it every time. Dᴿ Bernheim tells of a subject to whom he suggested deafness to everything that he the doctor, should say. The subject became incontinently deaf, to all appearance. But when the doctor said "now you are able to hear me again," she forthwith ceased to play the deaf subject. She had doubtless heard him with her ears all the time; but the hearing had entered into no connection with her thoughts or behavior, until the permissive suggestion was made.

The state of mind is here very peculiar. There is no real sensorial insensibility produced, and no mere failure to notice through ordinary inattention, but a mental deafness and blindness which is more complex, something like an active dissociation or shutting out of certain feelings and objects from the field of consciousness that counts as thought and governs conduct. It is as when one cuts an acquaintance, ignores a claim, or refuses to be influenced by a consideration of which nevertheless one remains 'marginally' and ineffectively aware. I say marginally, but the difficult question to answer, even in these cases, is whether the idea excluded from influence is really inside the margin of the conscious field or outside of it altogether, forming a separate coexistent bit of consciousness flocking all alone by itself. It would seem to quiver directly *on* the limit in these simple hysteric and hypnotic instances, sometimes being in and sometimes out, and at all times ready to make connection.

But in other cases it is surely extra marginal altogether, and the subjects mind loses its quality of unity, and lapses into a polypsychism of fields that genuinely coexist and yet are outside of each others ken and dissociated functionally. From all quarters of the pathological and experimental horizon this state of facts is borne in upon us. I can only give a few examples to familiarize you, if you are not already familiar, with so strange and unsuspected a phenomenon.

It was first brought to light in a distinct way by Edmund Gurney's investigations into post hypnotic-suggestion. In a considerable number of hypnotic subjects, an order given, during the induced sleep, to do something at a designated moment after waking, will be punctually obeyed, even altho on being waked the subject's mind will preserve no recollection of the order, nor indeed of any other of the trance-occurrences. The order may be to perform an act when a certain appointed signal is made or it may be to perform it simply after the lapse of a designated interval of time, whether days, hours, or minutes.

> Dessoir's case.
> Bernheim, & Janet

Make remember touches, nose, roll of paper in ear etc.

> Give Gurney's Expts.
> Proceedings Vol IV 282 +

Crystal vision cases.

> Miss X's
> Prince's
> Binets hand to eye.

Janet's Lucie, birth of Adrienne etc. R. Phil. XXII p. 584

Hysteric cases   Marie   etc

Automatisms as above

Mediumships.

There is a deep and laudable desire of the intellect to think of the world as existing in a clean and regular shape. The mass of literature, growing more abundant daily, from which I have gathered my examples, consisting as it does almost exclusively of oddities and excentricities, of grotesqueries and masqueradings, incoherent, fitful, personal, is certainly ill calculated to bring satisfaction either to the ordinary medical mind, or to the ordinary psychological mind. The former has its cut and dried classifications and routine therapeutic appliances of a material order; the latter has its neat notion of the cognitive and active powers, its laws of association and the rest. Everything here is so lawless and individualized that it is chaos come again; and the dramatic and humoring and humbugging relation of operator to patient in the whole business is profoundly distasteful to the orderly characters who fortunately in every profession most abound. Such persons don't wish a *wild* world; a world where tomfoolery seems as if it were among the elemental and primal forces. They are perfectly willing to let such exceptions go unnoticed and unrecorded. They are in too bad form for scientific recognition. So the Universe of fact starts with the simplest of all divisions the respectable and academic system, and the mere delusions. Thus is the orderlyness which is the great desideratum, gained for contemplation.

[*Notes for the Lowell Institute Lectures on
Exceptional Mental States*]

Lowell Lectures
I
Dreams—Hypnotism
Unwholesome—etc. No S. P. R.
The less we can think of the morbid . . . .
Think of it. *morbidly*
Common distinction: "healthy" & "morbid"
Can't make it sharp.
No one thing is morbid. Saint Paul. Lombroso. Kant.
Melancholy! gives truer values.
A life healthy on the whole, must have some morbid elements.

Sleep. "dreadful disease"—but for its familiarity.

Really dreadful for hysterics. Krafft-Eb.'s case.

If dreams don't interfere with waking life, they only enlarge our
    knowledge.

Various intoxicants.

NO.—What we call normal consciousness is but a fragment.

Now of some states, *dreaming* is the type; so it behoves us to ask.

Diff. betw. d. & waking mind.

Associations complete. Whole of knowledge brought to bear.

"House on fire."

3 types: level head, rattled, & half awake.

Ideas detached from usual consorts.

My dream of Seth.

2 conditions of dream:

    (1. negative)—narrow ⎱
                           ⎰ field.
    (2. positive) —vivid ⎰

These found in many of the disorders . . .

So get clear idea of fundamental fact!

The sound mind is a system of ideas *in gear*. Integrated.

Field . . focus . . . margin.

Margin *controls*. .

In healthy life no *single* ideas!

If we could have a single idea, it would be believed & acted on.

This happens in dreams.

Electric wire & chandelier metaphor.

In waking life approaches to condition:

        day-dreaming—milk maid.

         Castles in air: Absorption. Newton.

         Drunkenness: Ami Fr. Modern Inst 304

         Sleep—drunkenness: Wundt VIII. 31.

Now some minds get easily out of gear, & go to pieces, others keep
    together.

Why? is one great question in theoretic psychology. Janet.

Natural somnambulism.

        Pilot stories: Crothers, 18

                     Beard. 87

In these states memory gone.

Now hypnotism— —

You know its history.

Hypnotic *state*. Fluid?—Will?

Behavior of profession.
Only partial sleep.
> leave patient—either wakes or snores.
> Explain hypnotizers function.

Main symptom *suggestibility.*
This means vividness and motor efficacy.
Some persons suggestible when awake.
"You can't do it!" Not only is doing paralyzed, but opposite mus-
cles contracted. Peggy on bicycle. Hammond's case breaks table.
Hypnotized subjects, item.
Suggestibility due to narrowness of field.
(Cf. dreaming. Senses dead: but *if* . . .
> Maury: feather pitch mask.
> head on anvil: water
> Tissié: lantern of nurse: tickle forehead—Bees.)

Hence hallucinations—dramatic scenes.
Why doesn't he wake?—He will if suggestion produces disturbance—
as in dream—synthesis will occur.
So long as he *does n't* wake. analogy between his state & dreamer's
complete.
> *a.* Both wake when you *say* wake.
> *b.* ___ anaesthetic to most impressions.
> *c.* In both, possible *rapport.*
> *d.* Suggestions obeyed. *Delboeuf. Hudson!*

Mrs. Morris's cases[2]

---

[2] Found with the notes for these lectures are two typescripts, each one signed in ink
'Alice Vanderbilt Morris.' The first, foliated by WJ 'p. 9ᵃ' and 'p. 9ᵇ', has the heading
'Skating.' on the first page and 'Skating. 2' on the second: '[¶] Shortly after Christmas
1894 when I was just twenty years old, I spent a week with some friends in Lenox,
Mass. The house was filled with young people all bent on having a jolly holiday. I
was one of two or three who knew nothing about skating. When I put on my skates
on my high laced shoes I could neither stand up alone nor make a single stroke on the
ice. It seemed to me that I was peculiarly *awkward, [*comma ink added*] even much
more than one or two other girls who were making first efforts with me. It was all two
men could do to hold me up without themselves being pulled down. After a half hour
of failure, greatly discouraged I took off my skates and walked back to the house. [¶]
I was much ashamed of my inability to learn. I kept thinking of it constantly for two
*days, [*comma ink added*] during which time I did not go on the ice. The night of
the second day I dreamed that I put on my skates and begged my friends to make one
more attempt at teaching me. I fell down while they laughed hopelessly. Determined,
however, to turn failure into success I kept on struggling until at last could maintain
my own balance. With much pride I skated once around the pond;—then I woke *up.
[*period ink added*] [¶] The next morning, New Year's Day, 1895, I put on my high

e. Memory often gone in both. Sometimes preserved from one dream, as from one hypnosis, to another. From hypnosis to dream, Bernheim 220.

f. *"Post"*—effects (as above) and Albert's "fugues" in Tissié

In all this we notice *dissociation.*

Polyzoism—polypsychism!

This conception, held to, throws flood of light on matter of later lectures.

Two phenomena especially bring it out.

1) Negative halls: system. anaesthesias

Skin—eye.

Proved not sensorial by many facts.

negative after image.

Line not seen if not marked

(must first recognize)

Bernheim makes subject deaf—then says "hear"—he hears. (p. 71)

makes other girl *remember* touches (nose, roll of paper in ear)

One eye blind, yet prism doubles.

Looks like shamming.

Curious state: "cutting."

Rapport. "Head here."

---

laced boots, and strapped my skates over my arm and went down to the ice. On my way I told four or five of my friends about my dream and made a wager that in it I had mastered the art of skating. The men who had helped me three days ago looked provokingly skeptical. But I surprised them. After screwing on my *skates, [*comma ink added*] without a single helping *hand, [*comma ink added*] I went around the pond, quite alone, and feeling that for years I had known how to skate.'

The second, foliated by WJ 'p. 9ᶜ', is titled 'Singing.': '[¶] I had been reading several books on the Power of the Mind over the Body. I had come in contact with a mental healer who inspired me with enthusiasm. My interest finally turned to faith and I determined to try my own power. [¶] I was taking singing lessons and was greatly discouraged. My throat seemed to be constantly contracted and I had no control over my voice. I gave up practicing for three days. The evening before the day of my lesson, after I had gone to bed I firmly concentrated my mind upon my own voice. I finally imagined myself singing as easily as Melba and with the force of Lehmann. Concomitant with my beautiful imagining I was willing myself to obtain all this power of song while I slept. The next morning in calm but breathless excitement I went to my singing master. I had sung hardly two lines before he stopped me and said with a surprised ring of delighted enthusiasm in his *voice: [*colon ink alt. fr. period*] *"What has happened to you since your last lesson? If you could sing like this every day I can promise you that your voice would be great." [*db. qts. ink added*]'.

Split-off system. Two minds not on speaking terms.—Command to *forget.*

But *where* is the part ruled out?

Post-hypnotic suggestion throws some light.

Define it: paralysis, sleep, dreams, cures, anaesthesias, acts, hallucinations.

16th Tuesday from last Tuesday (Moll)

one year of interval Liegeois 340

Gurney's experiments:

P__ll[3] told to mail letter on 123rd day.—No memory. But in trance gives record of days. Gives minutes. Sovereign offered.

P__ll you will poke the fire in 6 minutes

Pierce and Landmann's view, disproved by case where command has to be intellectually worked out. Additions and multiplications. Write backwards. Count letters in sentence. Give anecdote of childhood. Meanwhile either reading loud, talking or engaged in conversation.

Same result in Janet's Lucie who counts signals (to sleep) up to 43.

Multiplies 739 by 42. (Rev. Phil XXII p. 584+)

Results: either split consciousness

or rapid alternation

or unconscious cerebration.

After all, only a development of walk & talk, read loud and think.[4]

Myers' "Subliminal Self." (Vol VII.+)

Possible automatism in Barkworth's adding (Vol VI); or alternation in Dessoir counting steps p. 4

But there are cases which look otherwise.

Dessoir's observation

Like the systematized anaesthesia case of Bernheim, above

Miss X's crystal vision. Split-off?

Andrew Lang. Morton Prince's case

This leads us to *automatisms*:

Sensory & motor. "messages."

Mrs Shaler's case. Glines case   Kettle case

Planchette writing makes Myers' notion more plausible.

Drawer full—all varieties. mirror-script.

Read Albee

[3] In the left margin WJ wrote, 'Vol IV 286, 323'.
[4] In the left margin opposite this sentence WJ wrote, ' "field of inattention." '

Spirit type. Underwood.

Hieroglyphs. Dean.

Gift of tongues. St Paul. Waters.[5]

All which looks not like the immediate triumph of any simple theory.

These phenomena alternate, but *two* spheres

Lecture III.

RECAP. The notion of subliminal—simultaneous

I showed its presence in post-hypnotic suggestion; in negative hall^n
In automatic writing.

(Nichols   Newbold.)

Lately applied to hysteria.

This a disease . . . .

My excuse is that it sheds new light on our mind's structure, leads to simple cure, and converts a dark chapter of human opinion into one relatively bright. Optimistic! . . .

No definite symptoms. Pains, insensibilities, palsys & contractions. Lethargies, fainting fits, & convulsions. Loss of voice, hiccup. vomiting. mimicries of inflammation, peritonitis, joints, ph[*illeg.*]is, dyspepsia.

Quickly cured . . . . . Come & go. magnets etc.

Grave hysteria with attacks . . . unconsciousness therein . . . . "passional attitudes."

Poor hysterics! First treated as victims of sexual trouble . . . Then of moral perversity & mendacity . . . . Then of *imagination*.

Among the various "rehabilitations" wh. our age has seen, none more deserved or humane . . .

Real disease, but *mental* disease. "Psychosis" of very peculiar kind. Charcot's school

We get an entrance by the anaesthesias
    Skin; eye; ear. Pseudo, not genuine.

Such things as this may happen:
    Janets pt. with yes and no
    Blindness of one eye. Prism. Stereoscope.
    Plays ball.

---

[5] A slip now pasted-on at the foot of blank fol. 14^v but attached to the foot of fol. 14 and intended to apply to 68.3: 'Gift of tongues. XIV of Corinthians. | (I thank my God I speak with tongues more than ye all, yet in the church I had rather speak 5 words with my understanding than 10 000 in an unknown tongue).'

Elective anaesthesia: hair pin, ear rings hair; scissors; match; mouse:

Shamming? No! Just like hypnotic suggested anaesthesias of last time, where Bernheim *says* "you can hear," where the p^t later is made *to remember* what she didn't feel, where he must *single out* a particular line on a black board in order *not* to see it.

Not sensorial but intellectual blindness.

Elective:

Mouse!

Match!

Self-suggested!

Janet finds memory of pictures shown to blind eye come back when sensibility is restored. Serpent on tree, etc.—just as in the hypnotic cases mentioned last time.

Something sees and feels in person—but person does n't. That something may be hyperaesthetic. Binet, 125. Limb insensible to passive movements performs active ones well.

Alterations, 108, 120, 184–7, 190

Binet's and Kriegers cases.

Janet's Lucie with papers in lap, made posthypnotically blind to certain ones which by automatic writing she says she sees.—Her hand and arm sensibility tested in same way.

Consciousness splits—the two halves share the field.

Binets "Marguerite."—Adamson

Not shammers then.

But how does such splitting come to pass.

Janet says synthetic weakness.

Breuer says weakness due to splitting.

Question open!

Anyhow a shock often starts . . . & here comes interesting chapter. "Janet, Breuer, Freud."

Memory of shock becomes subconscious & parasitic.

Often a regular *collection* of sick ideas

Tapped in hypnosis, dreams, automatic writing attack. Breuer's method, of mere talk-cure.

Cases: Isabelle. ("accidents m.")

Justine: cholera—cokorico.

Marie:

Marcelle

Gib. red flowers. Cause unknown when awake
Vel's tic
Breuer's Lucy.
Sub-conscious fixed ideas can have their effect—Not sole types
From these depths etc . . .
New hopes for insane delusions

Lecture IV

We are by this time familiar with the notion that a man's consciousness need not be a fully integrated thing. From the ordinary focus
and margin, from the ordinary abstraction, we shade off into phe-
momena that look like consciousness *beyond the margin.* Hypno-
tism & automatic writing the means of approach. In the relief of
certain hysterias by handling the buried idea, whether as in
Freud, . . or in Janet . . we see a portent of the possible usefulness
of these new discoveries. The awful becomes relatively trivial.
Pass now to cases where the division of the personality is obvious.
From time immemorial *"alienati a se."*.
Of late years many cases of *alternating* personality. "Fugues"
Epileptic cases
Psychopathic cases—dreamy states.
Tissié's case. Raymond's case of P. (read) Mine of Miss O.
Hysteric(?) cases.
 Mary Reynolds.
 Ansel Bourne. Jan 17. 87 Norristown Earle Dr Read. Mch 14.
 Hypnotised May 1890
Mollie Fancher. Mason Osgood's case of No 1, Twoey, & the Boy.
Felida X
Madame B. (Leonie.)
Janet's theory. plain sailing
Birth of "Adrienne." Rev. Phil XXII 589
Mediumship.
Produced by suggestion & imitation. Cadwell & other "developing
 circles."
This expl^n fits many cases.
 N. & N's of automat. writing.
But . . . Mrs. Underwood's?
What shall we say to the case of Lurancy V.?
The truth is that we see here the complexity of Nature. Janet's
 formula not descriptive.—Myers' better.

At the portal of P.R., into which I said I would not enter.

But I suppose that it would be over-cautious in me, and disappoint some of my hearers if I did not say here frankly what I think of the relation of the cases I have dwelt on to these supernormal cases. I put forth my impression merely as such, and with great diffidence. The only thing I am absolutely sure of, being the extreme complication of the facts.

Some minds would see a marvel in the simplest hypnosis—others would refuse to admit that there was anything new even if one rose from the dead. They would either deny the apparition, or say you could find a full explanation of it in Foster's physiology.

Of these minds one pursues idols of the tribe. another of the cave. Both may be right in respect to a portion of the facts. I myself have no question that the formula of dissociated personality will account for the phenomena I have brought before you. Hypnotism is sleep. Hysteria is obsession not by demons, but by a fixed idea of the person that has drop^t down. J.'s phrase suffices here. But to say that is one thing and to *deny any other range* of phenomena is another. Whether supernormal powers of cognition in certain persons may occur, is a matter to be decided by evidence. If they can occur, it may be that there must be a chink. The hypnotic condition is not *in itself* clairvoyant, but is *more favorable* to the cause of clairvoyance or tho't transference than the waking state. So alternate personality, the tendency for the Self to break up, may if there be spirit influences, yield them their opportunity. Thus we might have hysteric mediums; and if there were real demons they might possess only hysterics. Thus each side may see a portion of the truth. I believe that Hodgson Myers & Sidgwick in obstinately refusing to start with any theories, in patiently accumulating facts, are following the footsteps of the great scientific tradition. Mosely.

I myself am convinced of supernormal cognition. Supernormal healing. But not a vestige of a theory. So now return to our lectures!

Demon possession.

Lecture V.
Demoniacal Possession.

Recap.   Alternate personality—3 types.
Insane—hysteric—somnambulistic—Cadwell

Fourth type = mediumship.

History shows that mediumship is identical with demon-possession.

No one regards it as insanity. *Diff. from insane delusion* of altered personality.[6]

Obsolescence of this disease and of the belief in it is strange. Xian belief

Every land & every age has shown the facts that make for the belief. India. China Egypt Africa, Polynesia, Greece, Rome, & all mediaeval Europe believed that certain nervous disorders were of supernatural origin.

Inspired by gods and sacred; or by demons. When the pagan gods became demons all possession was deemed diabolic,[7] and we have the mediaeval condition.

4th type mediumship

Replaced by our optimistic mediumship.

Complex of symptoms. Convulsion. Altered character. New name. 3rd person. Supernormal powers Amnesia. Well between intervals.

Oracles. Samoa. Ontaké Percival Lowell: p. 153, Nevius, p. 104 *Foxes!*

Caldwell. Contemp. Rev. vol 27. (Madura, Capt. Pole *Dancing*).

Nevius: Case of Kwo. p. 23.

Boguet: p 1. 142–9 One sees that the type is modified by the traditions of the country. Globus. Hysteria.

Imitative. Chorea. W. Mitchell. 69

Constans.   1861. Morzine ⎫
Chiap.   1878. Verzegnis ⎭

Read. Constans 23.+

      Chiap   97. Michael Zilk in Bataille I 930. 1891 Wemding Bavaria

"Hystero-demonopathy." suggestive disease.

If there are devils—if there are supernormal powers it is through the cracked Self that they enter!

We see the accusations. Transition to witchcraft.

Lecture VI
Witchcraft.

Recap. Accusations of Rollande, of Jean Berger, of Herz (by Zilk).

Witchcraft not extinct then. Cape Cod.

---

[6] In the left margin opposite this sentence WJ wrote in pencil, 'postpone'.
[7] In the left margin WJ wrote in pencil, 'Montaigne'.

At all times sorcerers—evil spirits.

But the witch period proper is that of belief in Compact with Satan: 1250–1650

the proper devil's period: 1475 1600

This the time of highest bloom.

revival of learning

birth of modern thought

Protestant reformation

Discovery of new world

Renaissance in Italy—Arts

Copernicus, Shakespeare, Bacon, Vesalius, Kepler Galileo Descartes.

Evil ploughed under. Good survives.

Don't judge an age . . . Apply to our time.

The inquisition (estabᵈ in 12th Century) helped to organize the belief. Heresy, Albigenses. Waldenses. Templars.

1484. Innocent VIII's bull *summis desiderantes affectibus* inaugurated the epidemic witch trials that raged for a century.

Sprenger's Malleus 1487 confirmed by successive popes as manual of canon-law.

Dominican inquisitors worked up . . . . Protestants need n't, however . . Scotland

Hold up book. Spiritual atmosphere drips with blood. *Quote Snell* Babylonian . . . Antediluvian etc.

Ghastly combination of authority with feebleness of intellect. Powers of life & death with a mental makeup that is almost idiotic for its meanness, timorousness and unmanliness. A mind no bigger than a pins head, guiding a will that stuck at nothing in the way of cruelty and a conscience raised to fever heat by the idea that the battle was directly waged with God's enemy Satan, there in the very room. The most curious gruesome rathole feeling—

Complete *philosophy* of W. in 3 parts 1) the Devil, the witch, and the divine permission. 2) the Varieties of W. their cures & proofs 3) the procedure.

Questions: Specimens: (regret time so short).

Why poor?

Why women? (monkish *fé.-minus*)

Why so much more sinful than devils themselves (baptized—sin agst Xᵗ)

What works.

Hail, storm, ruin harvests
kill horses, dry cows
Kill & eat unbaptized children make their flying salve with
the fat.
Substitute changelings—Marks: lean, heavy, dry 3 nurses; cry except
when something wrong done in house then laugh. Die before
seven.
Aid demons to possess. (This the later subject of debate.)
Sign contract.
Sabbath. Mock mass orgies.
Love spells. Change themselves & men to beasts.
Turn people into beasts.

Signs.

Can't weep
Feel no pain in torture
Teats—shave their skin.
Stigmata diaboli. (our hysterics!)
Must n't touch ground—mustn't see judge first.

Rules of trial. Crimen exceptum

May be arraigned s̄. complaint, on suspicion
Witnesses anonymous; No advocate; Children & wives & husbands
may testify against each other, etc.
Confession must be extorted.
Malleus[8] says judge may falsely promise life to get confession. he
won't condemn her. "She shall not be put to death"
Conjures them to shed tears if innocent.
    (Diabolically malicious!)
The confessions rarely failed to come. Accused was shown the in-
struments—then confined fasting & visited by hangmen and others
who advised confession
Torture "continued"—not repeated.
Sabbath fully described
All were executed on Sufficient Evidence.
Cases:
    Anna Eve   Soldan   Baissac 670
    Junius   Baissac 592   Soldan II, 125–128
    Salem: 1692: 22 hanged, 51 confessions, 150 rele⟨ased⟩
All were executed on sufficient evidence!

[8] In the left margin WJ wrote '*Read!*'

Lecky..

How comes so much evidence for what *we* can't believe?

4 Theories[9]

    1. Calmeil's.

    2) Michelet's

    3) Weier's & Mejer's (henbane—datura aconite, belladonna)

    4) Torture.

Snell's refutation of Stramonium

No reports of sabbath's seen.

Not witches but accusers[10] were insane, possessed persons; or hysterics

Remember Jean Berger, the Herz woman in the recent bavarian case.

Read newspaper extract.

halls. looked at. "pinched"

Salem case. Almost everywhere.

In the eyes of so-called enlightened criticism we have in these accusers malicious invention.

No tertium quid between possession and fraud

Reply of Montpelier faculty. Baissac 541 (Calmeil II. 49)

Honest disease not thought of.

So Upham of the Salem girls. "Carried out with consummate policy & skill in acting."

Hysteria & all sorts of convulsions, were deemed due to witchcraft & demons.

Malleus[11] says diseases that where the organs of the p^t seem healthy, and which don't come from poison; also such as are made worse and not better by the doctor's remedies; prefacing that this is the opinion of the doctors themselves.

It was the Doctor who invoked the devil in the Salem epidemic.

Fortunately the doctors have got now a better understanding. The study of hysteria, hypnotism, imitation and all the automatisms... explain in the most innocent way . . . and also give us modes of treatment more efficacious as well as more humane.—though exorcisms also will work.

---

[9] In the left margin WJ wrote circled '2nd hour'.

[10] WJ wrote 'accusers' above undeleted 'victims'.

[11] In the left margin WJ wrote in pencil, 'There couldn't be a better description of functional nervous disease.'

This does not mean that there were no insane delusions in the witches. (Tituba)

Occasional cases of melancholiacs.

Nor does it wholly exclude Michelet's theory. Black Art. Paris. Mediumship.

But beyond all question *torture* accounts for the *evidence*.

Spee's Cautio 1631. Philip von Schönborn.

We thus get a rational understanding of this whole nightmare episode of our race's history. In the origin a form of disease, which if rightly handled is innocent enough. But fanned & encouraged by fanatical delusion, made horrible beyond conception. Yet its prime agents the friars of the Inquisition & other judges were the most conscientious of men, the puritans of their day. The whole story is an example of the good intentions with which hell is paved. To diminish the power of the Prince of hell, a hell wantonly & of whole cloth was manufactured upon earth. There is no worse enemy of God & Man than zeal armed with power and guided by a feeble intellect. We had it in Robespierre and the terrorists, we have it in the commune & the anarchists. The great lesson of history is to keep power of life and death away from that kind of mind, the mind that sees things in the light of evil and dread and mistrust rather than in that of hope.

I have entertained you with a gloomy subject. But I believe it does one good in one's carelessness, to stop now and then and realize what human life really has been, and may be again if the best men do not keep up a constant fight not against an imaginary satan but the real devil of intolerance and ignorance inflamed with the lust of power, and the conceit that they alone can save the world, and getting all the legitimate professional & legal authority into their hands. Strange as it may sound there can be little doubt that a good natured scepticism, and willingness to let the devil have his head a bit, is for public purposes a better state of mind than too exalted a notion of one's duty towards the world.

Lecture VII

I now pass to *Degeneration*:

A morbid subject: but again my excuse is that looking directly at facts makes the Devil's sphere seem less broad and deep.

Squeezing the thistle.

Humaner view.

In the eye of the Law one must be sane or insane. *No tertium quid.*
    Room light or dark.

Human nature can't be dealt with by these simple disjunctions.

Guiteau: "crank" Screw loose. excentric Insane temperament
    "Off his base." desequilibré. "Borderland."

Hereditary character. Morel.

Two classes of mental disease $\begin{cases} \text{valid \&} \\ \text{invalid brain} \end{cases}$

"Degeneration." "Psychopathic temperament"

Stigmata

Neurotic constitution

Oversensitive—excessive response fear anger, pity tears fainting

Unbalanced.—Mind discordant—doesn't keep together.

Impulses and obsessive ideas.
    (reminding us of the conception of integrated & non-integrated
        mind from which we started.)

Confine ourselves to these.

Normal germ. Seal letter; gas; lock door, wind watch; look under
    bed.

In morbid cases idea returns. *Doubt* Wine in cellar: open mouth.

Act gives relief.
    Recherche du mot (Magnan, 283)
    Mysophobia—just mention.
    Arithmomania. (Magnan, 281)

"Infinite." Grübelsucht. Metaphysical mania.
    Orange — apple
    lemon   quince
    fig   — pear
    ?   greengage.

Caricature of scientific theory

Kant's "how is nature possible?"

Things not right. Cochran case. Cowles's clothing.

Exorcism. Suggestion. Pretty women case.

Van Eeden's case. Mysticism

Impulses.
    Münsterberg's.
    Money spending.
    Kleptomania. (*we* pay—but.)
    Pyromania

Suicide
Cruelty
Homicide.
Anti vivisectionist mania.
In all these cases *anxiety*—relief.
A certain process *vibrates independently.*
Whence the source?
Post hypnotic sugg[n] reminds us. As in hysteria. Demon possession.
But as yet these ideas not applied.
Anti Viv.
Moreau.
Love. Danville.
Anti-vivisectionist mania.

> Bergh.
> Parkhurst
> Miss Dix.
> J. Brown   }   one-idea
> General Booth.
> Lady H. Somerset.
> Frances Willard.

Lecture VIII.
Genius

RECAP. No end to kinds!

Leads[12] to question of genius.

Divine: miraculous; god-given; no meanness; no selfishness; effulgence of light. Adore!

Contrast the realistic tendency. Not only blots on sun, but sun itself a blot. p. 57

Lélut 1836. Read p. 57 [ed., 78.30–37]

Lélut, 1836   *Moreau,* 1859. *Lombroso* 188- -

Lélut on Socrates "visionary = halluciné = fou."

"Forgetting that it is S. who is in question; turning from the greatness of the name and seeing only the reality of the fact; following imperturbably the chain of my deductions; passant from one term in them to another by this purely algebraic process: a = b; b = c; c = d; therefore a = d, I arrive at this definitive equation "Socrates = madman." "

---

[12] With a pencil guideline WJ transposed 'Lecture VIII. . . . kinds!' from before 'Love. . . . Willard.' (78.12–20). Before 'Leads' he wrote in pencil 'Begin', with a line drawn below.

But the ball was set rolling by *Moreau* 1859, who showed psychopathic heredity and discussed many cases. . . . . . Madness ferments
in the dough of which great men are made. M. & G. are congeners,
in radice conveniunt. 6 branches to tree: On left bodily diseases,
anaesthesias, neuralgias, epilepsy, spasmodic disorders, hysteria,
paralyses, tumors of the brain etc. On the right mental branches,
idiocy at the bottom, then insanity proper, then excentrics, & im-
pulsives, utopists, criminals, cranks, finally geniuses at the top.
Moreau 1859.[13]

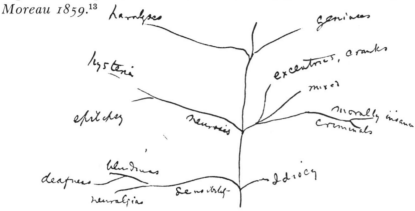

Lombroso (188–) squarely calls g's "degenerates" at first. Explain
Later epileptics. (g. a neur. of ep. variety).
Methods of proof very simple:
    1 Family $\Big\}$ history
    2 Self
    3 Mortality from neuropathic disease.
Astonishing how many persons you can show to have had some ner-
vous trouble.
Read Lombroso's first book—its list of eccentricities that accompany
    both g. & deg[n]
Describe Lombroso first.
    Short stature
    Rickets
    Leanness
    Odd physiognomy, unlike parents & nation
    Anomalies in skull & brain.

[13] In the manuscript '*Moreau 1859.*' and the diagram appear on p. 56, following
'*Lélut 1836.* Read p. 57' (78.29). WJ drew pencil lines around '*Moreau 1859.*' and the
diagram and in pencil wrote, 'Psychol. Morbide | illustration To p. 58' (79.1–11).

Stammering
Left handedness
Sterility
Precocity
Vagabondage
Absent mindedness, unconsciousness, impulsiveness
Somnambulism
Inspiration—double personality.
Stupidity in other matters
Over-sensibility
Forgetfulness
Originality
Word-conning
Epilepsy
Melancholy
Delusions of conceit of greatness
Doubting mania
Drunkenness
Hallucinations.
No moral sense
Longevity.
His second book.
Dante, Guido, M.A.
Dante confesses epilepsy in 11 places
Exhaustion-theory: out of 313 symptoms only 6 in geniuses:
Somnambulism
pallor
unpracticality—helplessness.
irritability
depressed spirits.
Portraits:
Burns—Coleridge ⎫
Bryant—Darwin ⎬ Common degenerate type
G. Eliot—Bulwer ⎭
Swift's dog latin.
"More fun than a goat!"——
Nisbet's book. 1891.
His method XVI. 250 cases
His list. *Total* number   neuropathic

Nordau 1890. Wagner, Ruskin, Ibsen   Tolstoi, Zola, Morris, pre
   rafaelites
When all is said,
A formidable indictment of the classic flawless superhuman view.
By ferreting, prying, d____l's advocacy.— —Concrete view of h.n.
   superior.
To begin with, nothing proved by method.
Brown eyes, born on Sunday . . .
You living in odd numbers.
No numerical comparison with rest of population!
Nisbet alone tries this in case of death:
Prop^n of nerve disease to all disease $3\frac{1}{2}$ times in geniuses than in
   g'al pop^n
Sedentary men were the right term of comparison
Negative instances all left out.
        What shall we say to Walter Scott, Goethe, Browning, G. Sand?
Poets too! Take Emerson, Longf. Low., O.W.H.   Whittier.
No *neccessary* connexion with morbidness, then.
Why so *frequent* a connexion?
To answer that, look ourselves!
Genius not a homogeneous conception.
For purposes of Lombroso it means any such eminence as will get a
   person's name into a biog. dictionary.
But what affinity between Bonaparte and Paganini;
        Jay Gould and Shelley;
        Sarah Bernhardt & Rockefeller, or Mark Twain & Washington.
        Rudyard Kipling & St Paul?
It is a *social* conception . .
To make it psychological, we have to bring it down to the *intellect.*
First class originality of Intellect!
Bain has analyzed that . . . —
But in the permutations of human nature this may combine with
   any state of health or nerve, or temperament.
Steady men or men of moods.
Eager ambitious men or lazy men.
Feeling or no feeling.
Conscience or none.
Pertinacity or fickleness.
Love of rule or humility.

This being the case, which man is likely to get into dictionary.
Those who in addition to intellect, have zeal, ambition & dogged-
ness.
These alone with good enough intellect will get a man in.
We know examples in every profession.
One-idea'd men, by that fact alone get in. Garibaldi, John Brown.
Liability to Obsession! Work off.
Psychopathic temperament does n't then *constitute* . . . for
Most psychopaths have weak intellects.
But where a powerful intellect is psychopathic *as well* . . . .
In the artistic life the excessive sensibility of the psychopath.
Everywhere the haunting . .

    Doubts.
    Arrangements (Myself with hymn-books)
    Number-combinations.
    Search for what is lost
    Metaphysics.
    Moral intensity
    Belief in mission.

The neurosis theory of genius is in one sense true, then but not in
that in which the authors mean it.
Hirsch's book. .

One more lurid, picturesque and smoky idea gone!
Let us look back. .
We have taken up many lurid things & made them tamer.

    Hypnotism = sleep.
    Hysteria, with all its . . = hypnotism.
    Double personality simply conceived
    Demon possession = mediumship.
    Witchcraft explained simply.
    Insane genius more romantic but also flattens out.
    The result is to make disease less remote from health.

No *one* thing can make a man unsound. Affair of balance "one leg"
Susceptibilities, obsessions on the contrary. Goethe. Gladstone.
Line of health *not* narrow!
Nordau & Co. Jury of
The "normal man" a nullity.
S. love, poetry, art, religion or any sentiment but pride in his non
neurotic constitution.

temperance hotel.

Biceps!

pounds chest.

Welcome sensibilities.

broaden health idea

Fear not life.

All these geniuses & their mental peculiarities are organs by which mankind works out that experience which is its destiny.

Who shall absolutely say that the morbid has no revelations about the meaning of life? that the healthy-minded view so called is *all*?

A certain tolerance, a certain sympathy a certain respect . . .

Above all a certain lack of fear . . . seem to be the best attitude we can carry in our dealings with these regions of human nature,

And in thanking you for the attention with which . . . . tedious lectures

Let me express a hope that you go away from them with that attitude increased & confirmed

6. Summer School of Theology Lectures on "Intellect and Feeling in Religion" (1902)

Lecture I

When I accepted . . . book unpublished.

Title provisional.

Change of program needed, yet must connect with book.

My point of view is *anthropological*, outside . . .

Can we *define the normal significance* of religion, *what it stands for in human life?*

First struck by enormous ambiguity of term & *extent of variations,* which it covers.

Some of them *subjective*, temperamental.

Obvious hopelessness of conformity here.

Some take it intensely, acutely, zealously;

Others wish it moderate, reasonable.

{For some it means nothing if not *dogma and ecclesiastic* institution
{Others, *private experience*—"man in bush."
{Some make it *combine with morality,* continue it
{Others make it *supersede morality.*
{*Pessimists* demand *a new birth*
{Optimists find in *natural good* a religious object.
{In some it takes an *other worldly* character
{In others it but *softens this world's outlines.*

Finally, some men lead *lives consecrated* to ideals, and are *yet incapable of any* beliefs or *sentiments* which others would call *religious.* Their hearts are hardened "Godward."

And these different persons *abhor each other.*

Mystical attitude }
Amorous commerce } viewed with loathing

{The moderate wince at crude zeal of the enthusiastic
{The enthusiastic in turn wonder at the platitude & philistinism of the moderate.

{To the individualist the formalist & votary of sacerdotalism appears a strange spiritual idiot or baby,
{On the ecclesiast he in turn makes the impression of a sort of tramp or mangy vagrant, almost like a spiritual street cur.

{The intense egotism of the religious consciousness of some persons seems diseased to minds framed on the academic pattern.
{Academic or philosophical religion, on the other hand, consisting in a noble way of thinking about the general laws of things, rather than in a concern for ones personal salvation, appears to the devotee of personal experience to be a hollow abstraction which omits the gist of the whole matter.

In general, antagonism between *depth and breadth* in inner life, between the *hot and passionate* and the *cool and temperate* character

Characters of *emphasis* and of *harmony*

Hebraism and Hellenism—remember M. Arnold.

{Poise and balance, equal mixture, *avoidance of onesided excess,*
{Intensity of devotion to the *one thing needful,*
{Readiness to be sacrificial

The hellene *hates shrillness,* and often lets evils drift rather than make a rupture with the conditions, and lose any of the collateral goods that these entail.

The hebraist's vital element is shrillness, and to strew his path with
  ruins gives him a righteous joy.

From generation to generation both are needed, first one then the
  other, and the two sway society in alternation

Reactions on my book—For most men the subjective reaction conclusive, they *won't* train with that brutal gang, that snivelling
  psalm-singing band.

Useless to conciliate such antipathies. They are fundamental.

Radical divergencies of character.

Different needs and faculties.

and if the world is wide enough to produce the individualities of
character in all their variety, it ought surely to afford a large enough
map of spiritual truth to allow each of them to carve out of it what
suits his own neccessities.

As regards such subjective contrasts, to one who is not in them
himself, "live & let live" is the only possible motto. If one be in them
oneself, as champion of a certain type, one must of course become a
propagandist, and make as many converts as possible by one's example. But if one be an outside spectator, a general critic and seeker
for what is true objectively, one has to admit that magnificent specimens of human nature abound in all the types, and that to seek to
reduce them to one type would be to oversimplify humanity. Even
the distinction between the religious as a whole and the highest
class of men who are non-religious, has little or nothing to do with
that between the sheep and goats. The non-religious doubtless lack
a faculty, an insight; but each specialized religious type lacks
also something which another has; and a man is often made non-
religious, or calls himself so and is called so, because of the presence
in him of some human strength or some capricious kind of mental
magnanimity, in which ordinary religious men may be deficient.

We need all types in order to garner in the plenary revelations.
The broad and the deep, the hot and the cool, the emphatic and
the equable all play their part in working out the problem. We
need not narrow the sphere of application of such a word as "religion." Vast collection.

[Above all, not use *eulogistically*.

Terrible to use words "   "   " .

No clear solution of any controversy . . . .

Those who throw away the meaning still cling to the word, and no clear understanding is possible.]

If we are to use any word eulogistically it ought to be the word *wisdom*.

The wise man is the man who is supposed to employ all human faculties in the right mixture and measure. Religion would then be only one element in perfect human wisdom. The religion of the wise man would thus never be a one-sided or intolerant rival of his other interests, it would simply be their enlightener and animator. But historically the besetting drawback to all this breadth and harmony is lukewarmness in moral crises such as in a world like this men are perpetually called to play a part in. The indifference to political & social right and wrong which has been so often charged against a wise man like Goethe is a case in point. There are two ways of measuring men—the one static, by their immanent perfection, the other dynamic, by their power to effect results outwardly. The temper of depth and preferential emphasis, the exclusive interest in the "one thing needful," is often better for this latter purpose than the temper of wisdom. The individual may be the victim of his office, pay with his person for his utility, and present on the whole a sorry spectacle to those who judge by purely aesthetic standards, but he "gets there," and in the worlds workshop his function is indispensable. [Luther   Wesley]

So far then this conclusion: *Science of religions must not take sides in these subjective issues.* Hardly even can she tip the beam in favor of wisdom as against one-sidedness. In our father's house are many mansions, the individual must gravitate in the direction in which his genius leads him.

I call these differences *subjective*.

They are largely matters of *personal attitude* in which there is a more or less.

Even *the twice born and the once born* are extremes in a continuous series, and other-worldliness admits of degrees

If our would-be "Science of religions" is to have real questions to arbitrate they must be more *distinct and objective issues* than these.

They must relate to the *content* of religion, not to men's ways of taking it.

They must be questions of *fact*.

There may be many such questions for science of religions to study and discuss.

86

I desire in these two lectures to press one of them upon your attention,—an issue of fact which seems to me extremely momentous, which dumbly or explicitly has been the centre of discussion ever since modern thought, scientific and philosophical, began her slow aggressive inroads upon primitive belief and ancient ways of philosophizing. It is an issue not yet definitively settled. I think it is nowadays too much the fashion to *evade* it & not to focus one's attention on or try to solve it by choice of one alternative to the exclusion of the other.

It is possible that the style of thought which may be called *hegelian* is partly responsible for this haziness. *Contradictories are both true* in the hegelian philosophy—you only have to ascend to the higher synthesis which reconciles them. So the tendency ever is to minimize our differences.

I think that in this instance the evasion has gone too far.

To name bluntly & grossly the issue of fact which I have in mind, it is the question of there being a *supernatural world*. The issue is between the old dualistic way of thinking which set divine things over against the natural world, and modern thinking which makes the two worlds one.

Primitively, no sharp distinction between natural and supernatural.

Personal agencies, *polytheistic*. No *"law"* sympathetic magic.

Later, a more *dualistic* scheme. Nature *versus* supernat! Boundary & *system*. *Contraction* of supern^{tl} Peripateticism. [Summa theologiae.]

This dualistic view overcome by *science*.

Naturalism wipes away "other world."

No miracles

No prayer—only "law."

No ends—only elements

No persons—only mechanism.

A completely deanthropomorphized world.

And now a very *trostlos*, hopeless one!

In this, religion seems *undone*!

"Scientists" think we must abandon altogether.

For many anthropologists religion a survival of primeval demon-worship, magic, and every kind of obscene savage vagary—simply made more refined and expurgated.

Yet simultaneously another movement.

Religion rescued by *natural supernaturalism*.

No dualism,

No clinging to particular facts, or proofs of divine,

No "arguments from design" even,

No dependence on fact at all, but a *transfer of the whole interest* from *facts* to *values*.

Let me explain:

There *are* but two sorts of question.

$\begin{cases} \text{Existential—}fact \\ \text{Spiritual—significance, }value \end{cases}$

$\begin{cases} \text{What }is\text{ it?} \\ \text{What is to be done about it?} \end{cases}$

How has this come about?

Christian controversy has largely been over facts.

Within the Church what truths of fact does bible reveal?—and, now, what is Bible's origin?

Between Church and the irreligious, fact of existence or not, of supernatural beings and of positive world beyond nature.

Historically, fact after fact abandoned, yet something not abandoned: claim to feeling.

Habit of abandoning, waiving literalness, in liberal wing of Church.

Provided *a myth* be an apt vehicle for symbolizing truths of sentiment, we keep its place among religious instruments, . . in vocabulary

To many of *you*, unneccessary to pin your faith on any one decisive view of order of Nature, or any one determinate way of conceiving being of Deity.

The essence of the situation, *whatever the order of nature be*, whatever be the power behind Nature, is that both should be worthy to elicit religious sentiment.

The gratitude the thing, not the existential constitution.

Very diff^t ideas of fact in men with similar religious reactions.

Ethnic creeds and similar sainthood.

To day miracle and no-miracle; free will and law; immortality and annihilation; world of nature alone, and other world; God as distinct person, and as suffused influence or energy

All held by persons in the same communion.

Only they must not pronounce themselves *too emphatically*.

[This the secret of broad church success.]

Such pronouncement deemed a relapse into scholasticism with its belief in the adequacy of (absoluteness) formulas,

The more religious a man, the more contented with his ignorance

And with his faith that whatever the facts be, they must be worthy of devout reaction.

We must all share this disrespect for formulas—respect it.

Conceptual thought never does more than pick out from life fractional bits and elements, and fix them for our attention to deal with

These very fragments it picks out only for their *value*.

If a mythical conception can be so used as to have the same value for life as a real one, why not continue to use it? It would seem to make little difference which kind of term we thought in.

Transcendentalism methodically cultivates this indifference to literalness in fact.

Truth is when we see things in the total; but

The total is divine anyhow;

So, sure in advance that the truth must be good, why need we be anxious that its details should even now be certified as of one sort rather than another?

So important seems this general abstract insight into the ideality of the *ensemble* of things that for the transcendentalist all questions concerning concrete particulars dwindle into insignificance. In its place in the whole, any kind of existent is sure to be justified, and a limitless hospitality and complacency with all stages of being supposable or proposable is characteristic of the transcendentalist philosopher. His optimism chokes at nothing, the meannesses and atrocities of human history, the cruelties and brutalities of nature are all so many stepping stones of Spirit, so many momenta in the all inclusive body of perfection. "Miracles," he does not need them. The common order of nature is miraculous enough for him. Special providences? They are uncalled for in a world whose general laws are wholly providential. He does n't pit spirit against matter, mechanism against teleology, all is of one substance, and such antitheses as these are merged when we ascend to the Absolute Unity. He is willing to be passive when Science talks, to accept without cavil any of her explanations of higher things by lower, to be a darwinian, a mechanical determinist, a cerebral psycho-physicist, to listen without a murmur to all our speculations about the running down of the solar system. He has his inner remedy, his notion of the saving total, and the only thing we find him radically objecting to is the tendency of old fashioned religious thought to continue dualistic, and to treat the spiritual as a particular element in things that has to be perpetually distinguishing itself from the material with which it finds itself entangled or from the diabolical with which it finds itself in opposition. It is all *one Divine* taken at different stages of completeness.

This new tendency in modern thought is too familiar to need particular illustration. It characterizes liberalism in Christianity. It may be called natural supernaturalism, to use Carlyle's term or immanent supernaturalism as compared with the older dualistic supernaturalism, with its two concrete worlds, its angels and demons and prophets and revelations, joining hands with ghosts and hobgoblins and oracles and magic and propitiation and all sorts of mumbo jumboisms of the primeval savage world. Other world! there is no other world, it says with Emerson. Either nowhere or here at this point of this pencil converges the whole divine.

$$\left.\begin{array}{l}\text{Natural Supernaturalism} \\ \text{Universal } \text{"} \text{ "} \text{ "} \text{ "} \text{ "}\end{array}\right\} \text{ makes } \left\{\begin{array}{l}\text{piecemeal} \\ \text{particular}\end{array}\right. \text{S'}^{\underline{m}}$$

       needless for religious purposes.

Short circuits problem of divine.

Appeals to all of us, especially certain minds.

Clean, intellectual, abstract, general, elevated.

Worthier view of God than placing him in dusty particulars, & setting him *against* facts.

No wonder it succeeds!

Still less wonder, since it capitulates to "Science."

All right too, as *provisional faith*.

But mark the situation!

The partnership makes *breach* between ancient and modern thought.

For common sense, Divine has always been a *part*.

My purpose!—to ask:

Is this expulsion of dualism *definitive*? or incidental to growth of a new view, is it true as far as it goes but inexhaustive?

[Always new views make clean-sweep, till reaction arrives]

Is supernaturalism's account closed prematurely?

Is a *reaction* possible?

Clear issue of fact! Question of World's *constitution*?

Is there a larger world of individual facts than "science" allows?—
to wh. personal experiences bear witness?—as in older tho't.
Or is the natural world of one mechanical consistency—"scientific"
facts the sole ones?
Is the only "other world" one not of fact, but only of abstract elements & relations, truths and values?
[Santayana, Lasswitz, Münsterberg.]

Religious doctrines would do well to withdraw their pretension
to be dealing with matters of fact. That pretension is not only the
source of the conflicts of religion with Science, and of the vain and
bitter controversies of sects; it is also the cause of the impurity &
incoherence of religion in the Soul, when it seeks its sanctions in
the sphere of reality, and forgets that its proper concern is to express the ideal.

Santayana, p. V.

"The reconciliation [of Science and Religion] is to be reached
only by assuring perfect independence and freedom to each, and
by gradually training the popular mind to understand that those
two different orders of reality, the content of natural knowledge
and the content of religious faith *can* never come into conflict because they belong to altogether different fields of existence." ... "We
know that alongside of the reality which natural events enjoy, there
is another sort incomparably more important to us, the *value* namely which they have for our feelings. In this valuation on our part
things gain a new reality independent of scientific laws, and through
it religion becomes independent of all particular matter of knowledge." "To quote the blind rages of Nature as a ground against the
existence of a God, is as wrong as to prove his existence by the
apparent purposiveness of organisms . . . It drags God out of his
unapproachable height above Nature down into the sphere of our
knowledge, and degrades him to being an instrumentality inside of
Nature." "God is an object of *trust*; trust is a relation between free
personalities. . . . . It can obtain, no matter what the actual course
of the world is ascertained to be. . . . So that religion as a relation of
feeling is independent of all actual results of Science, and of all her
future discoveries." (Lasswitz, Wirklichkeiten, pp. 250, 251, 253,
256, 257.)

So Munsterberg says: "Religion is the adding of a complement
to existence. . . . . . But if what is thus religiously supplied is thought
of as so much existence and not simply as so much value, then

God becomes merely a gigantic psycho-physical apparatus, heavenly goods turn into physical stimuli, immortality into an endless succession of conscious processes. All this is merely matter of knowledge, not of faith, it is psychophysical material (whether true or false makes no difference) but it is *not religion.*"

Grundzüge, p. 168

Spoke of diversity

Each thinks to be like *him* is to be truly religious

We eliminated subjective

Objective matters of belief

Found issue

Science & Phil. of Absolute rule out particular facts . . .

The one because there is no divine world

The other because it coalesces with Nature as Science gives it.

I say *facts* are *not* irrelevant

I side with spontaneous thought, with metaphysicians & scientists both against me.

I wish to plead the "reaction," to ask you to consider piecemeal supernaturalism as again a possibility, to beg that dualism's account, and the notion that God is one element of things rather than the whole of things, be left open to discussion a little longer.

Desperate!—for metaphysicians and scientists are both against me.

The Universe is One! *Once law*, always law! Her constitution not private, but universal. This point of view once attained, shall the dog return . . . , the sow . . . . ?

Within the churches just as bad. Genuine saintliness repulsive. Methodistic type of experience odious. Shall we relapse into childish miracle, forget the dear-bought gains, join hands again with savage anthropomorphisms, and worship mumbo jumbo?

Great vice of thinking men: sweeping formulas—all embracing.— "either—or."

Talk as if *all* law or *no* law!

Forget possibility of different spheres of reality.

States enveloped by federal gov![

Ship enveloped by meteorological order[1]

2-dimensional being by third dimension

Exterior agencies seem to impinge—unaccounted for by inner law: *Miracle?*

---

[1] WJ drew a vertical line beside the two lines 'States . . . order' and in the right margin wrote: 'Bees—: Maeterlinck'.

So if supernaturalism were right, it might be here.

No question of denying law *in principle*!

No need to revert to *older notion of miracle*.

Question of *fact!*—solely & simply.

But if the *facts* are there, Science of religions ought to acknowledge them.

Lecture II.

What facts are assigned.

Facts of individual personal experience:

> Leadings, responses to prayer, mystical persuasions, senses of higher presence, phenomena consequent on self surrender, new energy, happiness, health, *regeneration*.

See my book.

The tepid, even within the churches, officially pooh-pooh these things

But wherever you have *intensity* you have them.

Matter of *level* in experience.

Science denies all "objective" significance.

Admits as phenomena, but grudgingly. [L. Stephen.]

Vagaries, delusions, hysterics

Dogmas from physics extended universally.

What is the great scientific objection to these facts.

I believe it is that they are *too individual*.

Too individual!

Both science and philosophy aim at the *general*—they *hate exceptions*.

What they recognize must enter into *formulas*.

And here the official religion of the churches joins them.

It always tries to keep religion "reasonable," condemns extravagance, preaches moderation, etc.

Reasonable views can always be exprest in general formulas.

But the individual as such, struggling with his problems feelingly, knows that they escape all general formulas.

Conflict more general than that of science and religion!

Conflict of intellect & feeling. My title.

Individuality based in feelings

Never exhausted by general adjectives

The way an individual's life comes home to *him*, his intimate needs, ideals, desolations, consolations, failures, successes, always exceed the formulas by which common sense of others subsumes them.

93

At least they are different from these formulas—"unreasonable" if he have any acuteness of sensibility.

Reasonable judgment sets up Procrustes' bed—abolishes idiosyncracy, despises the exceptional person, and holds by norms and averages.

Against this sovereignly shallow and unjust treatment individuality protests.

It leaves the essence out.

Somewhere in this world I must be recognized for what I am.

The individual takes *refuge* in his religion, escapes from the falsehood of the common intellectualized classifications of him by his fellows.

God is his only adequate understander and companion.

Don't you agree?—can there be doubt? isn't this religion?

The question of fact then is whether beyond the more general abstract laws and forces [which ignore individuality] there is a region of being in the world which is there purely for individual experience.

Are there realities beyond the individual which are pertinent only to him *as such*? which well up *within*, and not without, him? Whose existence discredits *abstract* philosophizing

There *might* be.

[Illustration of fourth dimension.]

Mere question of fact.

I, for one, reading all these autobiographies, do not feel free to deny authority of mystical experience of which they are so redolent. I cannot ignore all this unanimous tradition.

"Imitation!" "suggestion!"—but there must be *originals*!

It looks like a genuine *region*.

That religious persons are repugnant to *us* is no proof that they may not have perceptions closed to ourselves.

No one type grasps truth's fulness.

Sickness and privation have their revelations.

Religious man possibly not best man, yet he might gain peculiar insights wh. science might accept.

We recognize this elsewhere—

Genius generally a victim of its function. We use its results, but would n't swap places. Too extreme, queer, measly.

Hearers of concerts may be finer animals than composer.

Pro tanto, man with eyes has truth, yet blind man may excel in character.

Love is a revelation, yet to outsiders lovers are ridiculous, even loathsome.

All this subjective talk is *irrelevant.*

Once more, *is it a fact* that Rel. stands for?

Is this world declared a fragment not only by its wrongness, incompleteness?

But have we also contents of perception that go beyond it?

Positive experimental contacts with a wider world?

Assurance of more than barely conjectural sphere of deliverance?

Historically religion has stood for this *perceptively verifiable* enveloping order

Science scouts it as merely ideal conception tinged with emotion, and unverified by outer sense. (Munsterberg)

My familiarity with observations on subconscious life makes me hospitable . . .

Science resists—then pooh-poohs and minimizes.

Instead of studying says "nothing but"—"rot."

Jastrow on fence.

Nevertheless investigation, observation, continue.

[Facts individual, sporadic, capricious. Myers, Janet, Flournoy, Prince Hodgson Hyslop.]

Memory, cognition.

Obviously wider order of *some* kind exists.

Myers's *problem*—topography.

Dissolutive phenomena?

                    [Myers's book]

Supra-normal phenomena?

If the latter, they enter *via* subliminal.

My hypothesis. ["Soul of a Xian": Granger]

Mere program and suggestion.

I only ask you to leave it open

I can't prove it. Long investigation!

Details only can settle.

Let me show its *philosophic bearings* if it *be* true at all.

1 Gives dignity & backbone to witness facts.

  Mere sentiment inferior.

  Hindlegs—contradicted.

2 *Heals historic breach.*

Shocking to suppose pure *insane perversity.*

Early religions full of subliminal phenomena, oracles, possessions, mediumships

[Yet Frazer . . . .]

My view would reestablish *continuity.*

3 It rehabilitates the *individual* as such. As he has problems, so solutions, accessible only to himself. Science can't well deny former, yet denies latter.

[*Methodistic theology* may fall, yet methodism as experience be real.]

It confirms *Tolerance*—respect for personal *secrets.*

It makes those personal *antipathies* irrelevant, instead of making them conclusive, as now.

4 Yet it leaves room for general science, to *study* facts—they *must* be studied, Science only a *method*

Not simply suppressed as "rot."

Physiology of senses ought to warn "scientists."

Too soon to pass sentence of death on view that Divine is interpolated, interjected.

Still under discussion—must be worked out.

I confess to philosophic reasons . . . . . .

First, my interest in individual fact.

Moments of experience the reservoirs of truth.

Conception abstracts, relates, collects.

Then grows exclusive and substitutes her abstractions.

Aesthetic cleanness.

Concrete seems like mud—rooted in dirt.

Scholastic vice: put world into *book,* and admit things through *words.*

I am shocked at the abstract and remote ways of considering individual facts.

It would be comic were it not tragic.

Philippine situation.

Doctrinaireism in general—the philosophic sin.

Second, when transcendentalists say the Divine is independent of particular matter of fact revelations of his presence, something very deep in me resists.

Every difference in principles must make a difference in facts.

Particular facts!

Pragmatism.

Whole meaning of general conception lies in particular results to
 be deduced.

God, to be real must carry consequences.

Suppose facts *were* indifferent

Suppose world run down.

Theistic controversy would have no meaning

Read—p. 9 15. Berkeley address.

You see at last what my contention is.

You see the issue

The particular facts supposed may be elusive

My own idea is vague.

Yet these are there, for study.

Both methods required   But

My closing word is to encourage you to think that by following up
 the clues set by all this private regenerative methodistical experience we may gain insight into the meaning of the Universe.

However it may be with methodist theology—methodist connexion
 with experience may be a normal path.

One may be a methodist in this sense without even being a christian.

[Appendix: Notes on Religion]

Ecclesiasticism.—To minds brought up on the contemplation of
Nature as science now reveals her, it is quite impossible to believe
that a God who founded Nature should stand in any specially
loving relation to ecclesiastical institutions or be pleased by thinking of the difference between laymen & clergymen. The spirit of
the two systems is so utterly diverse that to an imagination nurtured
on the one it is hardly conceivable that the other should yield sustenance. It would be foolish to describe the difference—it is patent
to all of you that the two systems are incongruous worlds, and
demand opposite faculties for their appreciation and enjoyment. I
must personally confess that my own training in natural science has
completely disqualified me for sympathetic treatment of the ecclesiastic universe. To treat seriously, as having positive importance in
God's eyes, the distinction between deacons and archdeacons, bishops, archbishops and Cardinals, to imagine him——

Impossible to believe that the same God who established "Nature" should also feel a special pride at being more immediately represented by clergymen, than by laymen, or find a sweet sound in church-phraseology and intonation, or a sweet savor in the distinction between deacons, archdeacons, and bishops. He is not of that prim temper.

He who gives up the world possesses it supereminently & excellently,

Sainte Beuve

"Reasonable" versus passionate religion. The former lays the emphasis and gravity on this world and uses the unseen world to soften its outlines and suffuse it gently. The latter places the accent on the other world. It is an alternative to this world, it brings tragedies into this world, upsets this world's values, and commands sacrifices in its own honour. It is in the acuteness of its note, in the exceedingness over sense of what it believes in, that the characteristic of impassioned religion lies, and to the passionately religious mind, "reasonable" religion, levelling everything down to the level of this world's decencies, seems mere pooh-pooh and dull propriety. In the organization of religion the reasonable type of man always acquires authority, so within the churches impassioned religion is always at a discount, as something for which apology must be made, and towards which indulgence is needed.

The question is: to which kind of religion should an outside judge award the truer function?

which twice-born religions everywhere profess and stand for.

Your ordinary "well mixed" man has his religion, his sense of mystery, and of the infinite, of total responsibility and paramount obligation to his feeling of the deepest, his dissatisfaction with his actual & aspiration to the ideal, and the like. But in him these things remain moderate, and harmoniously combine with his equally moderate and reasonable worldly impulses, of whatsoever kind. They help rather than hinder his worldly life, and between the ordinary churchgoer and the passionate saint there is the inveterate feud of those who instinctively tend to keep religion "reasonable," and those who would obey it in ways that are uncompromising and inconvenient.

At bottom it is the feud between a naturalism with a softened outline, and a positive supernaturalism with its centre of emphasis outside the margin of this world altogether.

My own solution seems to favor this latter view. But I think that to apprehend it rightly one should keep in mind the intense individualism of my thought. A man's religious desolations and consolations

Against this sovereignly unjust and shallow treatment, individuality always protests. The general leaves the essence of reality out, individuality says, and I insist

If Consecration to any large ideal is enough to make a man religious, the term seems widened so as to mean active ideality überhaupt. But is not the species of active ideality which I have called religious distinct enough to merit a specific name? I am willing to accept any name whatever provided it doesn't lead us astray from the discussion of the *thing*. The *function of the thing* in human life seems to me an issue of sovereign importance. The thing asserted by the religious (in my sense) is the existence of unseen powers, our relations with whom are the most real of all the relations which we possess. They assert that the centre of gravity of our emotions or sentiments, and even of our practice lies in a supernatural world, a world of over-belief. Of those who object to them, many, while not *denying* these assertions, nevertheless rather wince at hearing them emphatically or dogmatically made. Religion for them must be a penumbral thing, a softener of this world's otherwise hard outlines, not a giver of another world with outlines of its own, an introducer of air, of alternatives, of perspective, in short of "more" than the finite, a permitter of tender hopes, but not a destroyer of any already existent finite values. Religion (in my sense) has always tended to make havoc of this world's values.

It is a terrible thing when words get used eulogistically. The habit then is to save the word, long after you have abandoned what it ori-

fashions, with our own ideals. As a rule we are shy of imparting what they are. We believe in them on condition that they should remain in the shade, and strangely enough, if any one insists on making them articulate and definite in formula, we incline to deny that formulation, and what it trust in just those places like the vinegar or the bitter without which the characteristic savor of a pickle or a cocktail would be lost.

The trouble with this way of taking things is its extreme abstractness, from any attainable human point of view. For the Absolute's

Add them to the more abstract truths which transcendentalism professes.

Not logically a case of alternation but a possibility of combination.

My study makes me believe in dualistic supernaturalism.

I wish to rehabilitate it.

I cannot ignore all this tradition.

L. Stephen's question.

When I combine it with the study of subconsciousness, it seems more than ever to point to a real experimental region.

Subconsciousness. Myers, etc.

Mere program and suggestion.

Tremendously important, however, if true.

It reinstates the individual.

Confirms respectful tolerance.

7. Drafts and Notes for Addresses to Graduate Clubs (1902–1906)

[a]

I have long been struck by indestructibility of ascetic impulse. We don't fast flagellate or mutilate. Too refined. But we bore. Out of 10 dinner Clubs, 9 listen to a paper or a talk, or an address before they can abandon themselves to conviviality. They have to pay that tax to culture & conscience. So you can't hold this meeting without asking a prof to add one to the 500 lectures. Your willingness to listen to professorial voice is a standing marvel. Equally wonderful the willingness of the professorial voice. I accepted immediately, though I had n't the least idea what I had to say. Experience had taught me, that with the audience, something would come, even though it might be only a repetition of some old lecture in Phil 2 or 3. And let me tell you, since you are to be professors, that your day too will come. I will guarantee you that if carried from your death bed . . . the lecturing function will continue. As long as you breathe you can lecture. Prop you up at a desk, etc. though you may drop dead, you will have died in harness, and your professorial function will be the last one to expire.

Now whatever I do, I must not repeat Phil 3. When a man of 60 meets youngsters in the same profession, the thing most natural for them to wish to hear would be his feelings about the profession itself. What does it mean to him. What on the whole, now that he knows all sides of it does it seem to him worth.

If you will let me ramble on somewhat incoherently I will talk to you of this.

You belong to the highly educated élite of our country. What is the higher education worth? What is any intellectual education worth?

For three generations schools & popular education have been the pet panacea of political liberalism throughout the western world. The school master & schoolmistress have in this country always been looked to to raise the moral level of the nation, to teach people what is right, to make them straight reasoners, and to check poverty discontent and crime, of which evils ignorance was supposed the natural source. President Eliot lately, reviewing certain social defects of our time, expressed an ordinary American sentiment when he charged that the schools of our country were at fault, that if more money were expended on education, there would be more virtue in our national life.

But recently many critics—I need only mention Spencer, have expressed an almost total disbelief in intellectual education as such to raise the moral level of Society. And I think, in spite of the high level of popular instruction and the great amount of reading that goes on in our country and in european countries today, that a survey of social conditions is very disappointing and calculated to make one doubt whether education be a moralizing agency at all. Brutal crimes may have diminished, but mean crimes have increased. Swindling has developed on the most intellectualized scale. We find college graduates on every side of every public question in about equal numbers, both among the leaders, and in the rank and file. They sell their services to the great corporations, not to defend them, but ingeniously to aid them in getting round the law. There is not an interest so selfish, or an abuse so vile, that educated partisans, either hired or naturally sympathetic, do not spring up by the hundred to prove by specious sophistry that the eternal order requires it to exist. The newspapers, supposed to teach the people truth in their editorial page, are elaborately organized for the sole purpose of telling them what it is supposed they want to hear and will buy. With hardly an exception[1] they are absolutely venal & insincere, and your modern journalist of the knowing sort may almost claim to be the lineal descendant of those old parasites bravoes & panders whom great nobles supported to do their dirty & criminal work. They prostitute their wits; they glory in their shame.

It makes one think of Goldsmith's epigram: For what was Reason given to man, unless to invent reasons for what he wants to do? In fact, one may well ask ones self whether the intellectual part of man have any substantive vitality at all. Whether it be not there merely to discover means, and set forth arguments for ends which instincts, desires & passions have already fixed.

Look at the Dreyfuss case in France, with father parted from son, brother from brother partner from partner, all with the same education, & half the country in two camps almost ready for civil war. Look again at our Philippine war. Nothing has given such a blow to my belief in any definite and positive results from education, in the way of telling men what is right. To me it has seemed, and still seems, an almost insanely blundering enterprise. All that I can see in it is the crushing out of the beginnings of a national soul, and the nipping in the bud of one of the most interesting experiments in history, the spontaneous effort of a yellow race to organize itself after western ideals. We seem to me to be doing this with all our inherited traditions pointing the other way, & no imperial prestige to keep up, such as England had to be mindful of in the boer war, doing it by fire and sword and treachery, making ourselves implacably hated enemies where we already were beloved friends, and spitting upon our own national soul and taking on every quality we have been accustomed to execrate since our own revolution. All this makes it seem to me, as I said, an almost insane adventure. Yet friends of my own youth, educated just as I was, in liberalism, philanthropism, old time abolitionism, clergymen, men from whom I

1 In the left margin WJ wrote '(Sp. Rep.)'.

least expected it, are enthusiastic over the new departure, say that every step was dictated by unmistakeable duty, and that it will all result in an inestimable second youth for our nation.

If intellect and education can lead to no unambiguous conclusion as to what is right in issues as simple as these, can we say that intellect is anywhere more than an advocate pleading the foregone cause of passion? My passion in the philippine case is for ancient american sentiments. My friends' passions are for power & new responsibility and enlargement. Their intellects are certainly better than mine. Many of them are Harvard PhDs in history. I myself am a PhD, tho' not of Harvard. But if PhD.s can be so divided, need a nation full of them neccessarily be anything but a more bewildered and sophisticated crowd than ever.

Nobody can live to 60 and not have *some* of his young faiths disappointed. Yet, although such pessimistic doubts about education as I have exprest are beginning to spread widely, & some of you perhaps are already touched by the tip of their bat's wing, I myself still firmly believe that we ought not to give way to them. There is an extravagant trust in the intellect which indeed we can no longer indulge in. But I still think that when the sphere of the intellect's power is properly limited, intellectual culture is at least one of our two sheet anchors, and that our Ph.D's and you, our candidates for PhD. are in a true sense the élite and the hope of the Nation.

The *great* sheet anchor of a nation is its customs, political and moral, and these are habits obeyed not so much intelligently as blindly. They are taught not at school, but at home, in business offices, at clubs and dinners, at caucuses and conventions, polling booths, on trains and in the streets. The kind of men whom a country admires, the calls & catchwords it responds to, the sort of taxes it will pay, and orders it will take from leaders, the amount of public unfaithfulness it will make jokes about, and the amount which it will smite sternly, the kind of license it will tolerate from individuals, and the kind it will stop business for and take up arms against, the sort of national crazes which can inflame it, and the sort that can't inflame it, the fashions it will follow, and the amusements it will pay for, these are the vital soul of a nation, because these are its unhesitating impulses to action, and the intellect can do little more than review such impulses, weigh one against the other, and proclaim the balance. Its function in a word is *critical*. This is a cold and disillusioned word, and hard to conjure by, yet, and this is what I wish to insist on, it defines a force which in the long run, may work irresistibly.

You remember in Darwin's Descent of Man, how he explains the origin of conscience. It is in after reflection, too late for the fair, upon the fruits of passion. The bird overtaken by autumn leaves her nest and follows the migrating flock, but the thought of her young haunts her. So far, the mischief is done, and the regret is unavailing.

It must be confessed that the function of intellect's critical judgments is too often of this unavailing kind. When the passion-gust is on an individual, or a great popular craze is on a nation, intellectual criticism is usually absolutely powerless. The intellect's appeal is then from Philip drunk to Philip sober. But by that time the evil is perpetrated, its victims have suffered, and the later academic verdict of history that they suffered unjustly comes as a derisive consolation. Dreyfuss has been to prison, and the Filipino patriots are under the sod.

We can't rely on intellectual judgments as a force against present passions; present passions of an opposite sort are the only things that we can trust to. But all present passions are inconstant, and subject to reactions and revulsions, while Cortical judgment, on the other hand, is a constant function. Now a small force, if it never remits, will often accumulate effects more considerable than those of much greater forces, if these but alternate and neutralize one another. The popular craze may sweep the PhDs, and even the DD's before it, and our personal interest or corporate passion may make our intellect play the sophist, but the quiet hour comes round for us, just as for Darwins bird, and then we face the eternal incorruptible judgment, the judgment of condemnation. In these sober intervals, when no passion is uppermost, our intellect may even devise measures to prevent the craze's recurrence. It may erect organized obstacles. Wars are popular crazes, often sweeping unwilling rulers before them. Hague tribunals are instituted to lead away the electricity; and in general it may be said that most of the institutions that characterize modern society are inventions of the intellect for delaying passionate action, and thus evening out social disturbance.

So far, then, as the mission of the educated intellect in society is not to find or invent reasons for the demands of passion, it reduces itself to this small, but incessant criticizing, or equalizing function.

It re-establishes, because it never forgets the normal perspective, of interests, and keeps things in their proper places in the scale of values. For this it has to blow cold upon the hot excitement, and hot upon the cold motive; and this judicial, and neutral attitude sometimes wears, it must be confessed, a priggish expression and is generally unpopular and distasteful. The intellectual critic as such knows of so many interests, that to the ardent partisan he seems to have none, to be a sort of bloodless bore and mugwump.

Those who anticipate the verdict of history, the abolitionists, *les intellectuels*, as the university professors were called who stood out for Dreyfuss, the present anti-imperialists, etc., excite an almost corporeal antipathy. Living mugwumps have indeed a harder row to hoe than members of the regular organizations. Often their only audience is posterity. Their names are first honored when the breath has left their bodies, and, like the holders of insurance policies, they must die to win their wager.

But this is far from being inevitably the case. Oscar Wilde once, extolling the intellectual onlooker above the man of action, said, "Any one can make history, the test of genius is to write it." The intellectual critic of course can always write history; but he sometimes makes it also even tho' he makes it slowly. The stars in their courses, the eternal laws of truth are with him, small as his strength may seem, at the moment, for the steady insensible tug of justice warps things round in the end to his conclusions.

If you graduates of colleges, of both sexes, are not to use your education solely in the service of some temporary passion, but for ends worthy to be called ideal & eternal, you must then resign yourself to possibly occupying somewhat humble places in this temporal order. You must stand outside of popular crazes. You must even stand somewhat out of your own time, and country, and be cosmopolitans. "Les intellectuels"—this epithet, invented ironically at the time of the Dreyfuss trial, names after all, as fine a Club as any of which one might aspire to be a member. Surely there is a higher mother-country of general human truth and reason to which an American may belong along with frenchmen, Russians, germans, english men, even more intimately, because more subtly, than he belongs to his own country, and for the sake of which he may cease that envious snarling at other countries, which so far has always been the cheapest form of patriotism. Who unless it be these intellectuals see all things in their right proportions?

If you ask me in what direction it seems to me to day that the weak but steady pressure of the highly educated is to be exerted congruently with the everlasting pull of truth and justice, I should say of course that in general it is in the direction of deeper realities, as opposed to shows and shams and transient unreal values, and in particular that it turns away from some of the ideals of success that in the world about us reign almost undisputed. People never realize how much the idols they worship are idols of the tribe, imitated ideals, caught from suggestion, & followed because we are ashamed to appear isolated. The idol of the American nation to day is what is called "big success." To be big, a success must be immediate and flagrant; and as the *immediate* test of success is always market-value, it has come about that the only success that strikes our national imagination as big is the making of a fortune. We may indeed use our fortune for other ideals when we have it, but we must first "get there." If we share not this kind of ambition, we are, in the contemptuous slang of the street, simply not "in it." We are "back numbers." Most of us blindly obey the tide that irresistibly sets in this direction. We should be ashamed of our lack of spirit if we were from the outset content to be financial failures. So we load up with houses, goods, servants, furniture, bric a brac, responsibilities, a burden all assumed for the sole purpose of making ourselves like other people, correct in their eyes, we become mean, dishonest, cruel, everything that the market-war demands, and die vitiated and satiated, and bored, without knowing why we were created. If the other people had been simpler, we should have been so too; If none of us had been so rich, we all would have been happier; but of the spirit of the age, the idol of the tribe, we all are both accomplices and victims. We have blindly followed the vulgar herd and drawn others to follow us instead of setting an example of distinction. Emerson we read, Ruskin we read, Carpenter & Tolstoi we read, but they are far off literary unrealities. Even the religions of the day are filled with this curious financial success-worship. I speak not of orthodox congregations only, but of followers of new lights, mind curers, theosophists and transcendental mystics generally. For some reason unknown to me, I am flooded with their literature, and smeared all over the gospel of relaxation, and union with the One soul of things I find this curious cult of the dollar. Business success is mentioned on every page as being one of the ripe fruits of spiritual regeneration.

Quote.

It seems to me that the fraternity of the intellectual have got to resist *this* craze. People have been happy in other ages & are happy in other countries now without this "big success" of getting richer. They make themselves happy in their native circumstances. Intellectual men must stand for the dignity of smaller worldly successes, or of worldly failures. Later generations will recognize the wisdom, history will vindicate it, when the present success-craze, born of our material expansion, shall have spent its vitality.

[b]

We don't flagellate—we bore.
Wonderful   listen—add 1 to 500
                    —professorial voice.
Your day will come.
                    die in harness.
                    prof. function last to expire
I must not repeat Phil 3.
What does it mean? what worth?
Pet panacea.
Eliot . . . . more money more virtue
Recently many critics . . . total disbelief
Survey . . . doubt whether Ed. be moralizing agency
Crimes . . Swindling
Graduates on every side.
Corporation lawyers.
No interest . . . . eternal order requires it to exist.
Newspapers.
Panders . . . glory in shame.

Goldsmith . . . invent reasons . . substantive vitality at all? find
    means & set forth arguments for ends . . . already fixed

Dreyfuss case

Philippine case

If intellect & education lead to no unambiguous conclusions as to
    what is right . . . can we say anywhere . . not advocate for passion.
My passion . . . *their* . . .

PhD's all round . . . . bewildered crowd.

No body can live till 60 & not . . . disappointed. I confess to some.
  I expect less than I did, but still not pessimistic. Progress slow,
  but real.

Give up extravagant trust.

Intellect *one* sheet anchor.

PhD's the real élite.

Great sheet anchor custom, blindly followed. learnt at home.

catch words, taxes, orders, jokes   crazes which inflame. These the
  soul.

Intellect plays the critic . . .

Cold word, disillusion, conjur⟨e⟩

Yet in long run irresistible.

Darwin.

So of critical judgments of the intellectual
Read p. 9, 10 [*ed.*, 104.10–37]

Our intellects may invent pretexts but have this higher function.

normal perspective

scale of values.

Blow hot, blow cold.

Elite
panacea
Eliot
Spencer
Swindling
Sell services
Newspapers
panders
Goldsmith
my formula
Dreyfuss
Philippine
One result of education

Live till 60
pessimism?
one of our sheet anchors, *you* the élite
Great sheet anchor

Intellect only critical.
(Darwin)
Powerless during passion fits.
constant function
incorruptible, quiet hour condemnation

Hague
delay!

normal perspective
scale of values
cold . . hot
bloodless bore

Wilde
Make history—but slowly
stars in courses
eternal laws
tug of justice
Liberal atmosphere
We can't all be prophets. We can't all follow prophets blindly.
But we can applaud, support.
Know difference.
Carried to abstract extreme—you have Emerson, Thoreau, Carpen-
    ter, Tolstoy.
Individuals.
Democracy gives shelter—bitterness not required.

Intellectual education
Serves individual.

How is *community* better . . ?
Both sides, sell services,
            newspapers,
            panders.
Free trade, Philippines, Dreyfuss.
One result! Goldsmith . . . already fixed

Pessimism. Not clear.
Not intellectual ed.—*Customs!*
habits obeyed blindly.
men

taxes
orders
unfaithfulness
crazes
fashions   amusements
Customs change.
In my memory (Bryce)
Inventions, leaders, types.

Education does n't make these.
It lets us *weigh* them better.
critical!
Powerless during fit.
Darwin's bird. quiet hour
condemnation
Constant force
Normal perspective
Scale of values.
eternal laws
tug of justice.
So many interests . . . . hot cold
mugwump
Les intellectuels.
Cosmopolitans, snarling

Humble place in temporal order.
Applaud—Support
Know the better . . . .
Know what's what.

Individualism.
        Emerson, Thoreau, Carpenter, Burroughs
Democracy gives shelter.

Intellectual
Serves individual
How is community better?
not clear.
Customs are *the* sheet anchor.
But customs change.
Bryce's lectures.
Leaders.

Bryan, Roosevelt, Debs, Eliot, Volk, B Washington, Jerome, Adler,
   Tolstoy   Kipling.
Enthusiasts, prophets.
Educated critics.
Evident that *some* more rational distribution must occur—
Line of deeper realities as opposed to shams and transient values
Idols of the tribe.
Equalizer   normal perspective.
hot—cold.
humble place in temporal order.

Graduate Club—begin as at Brooks House   Great unifying Guild.
   Universities our aristocracy. Humanities mean civics. Imitation.
   Success worship. Chesterton.

The trouble about asking a Professor is that he begins by "having
nothing to say" . . . etc. But I will curb professional loquacity and
not lecture either about Philosophy or Psychology . . . Gossip social-
ly about your profession. Am struck in coming here by the cosmopolitanism of our Guild. . One would call us the great go-betweens
& equalizers until one thinks of commerce, politics & the press. And
then one asks what differences are going to remain any where. But
if we ourselves contribute to the equalizing—also to individualiz-
ing. This, *é* . . *g* . . , is a very individualistic institution. But every
where in U__s, originality is encouraged. Excentricity results. 'Characters' . . Lotze. "Academic freedom." Strongly marked individual
characters in Germany, in part due to university inspiration. We are
the aristocracy—and *noblesse oblige*. It is for us as far as possible to
keep alive ideal of full manhood. Contrast of U-spirit to teacher
spirit, to technical spirit. Said to be due to humanities, but what are
they? Not languages, not literatures not art as such—but *all* human
products, all human history, Civic righteousness, today. Why study
such. To imitate! Tarde. We are here to know the variations, and to
judge. To hold up standards of other possibilities[2]

Trouble about a professor speaking.
But I won't lecture. This I understand to be a convivial occasion.
Gossip about our guild.
Struck by cosmopolitanism.

[2] In the left margin WJ wrote: 'All this conformity to public success leads to a kind
of Humanity-and-water. Establish ourselves in our individualities regardless of success*—[*dash ov. period*] and the country will end by being *full* of vigorous humanity.'

111

One would call *us* equalizers until . . .
What differences will be left—such monotony.
Shall *we* increase it?
Well, we can't diversify it much by our *mode of life*
We ought to by our intellectual & moral individuality of character.
Academic freedom. German characters. Lotze
We are the aristocracy   umpires   knowers of good things.
Noblesse oblige. Keep alive ideals of full manhood.
Compare U-spirit with teacher's, with technical—
Claimed for "humanities" but what are they?
All human products, history, civics.
Study of *men.*
Forces here are *individuals to imitate.*
Tarde.
We must be such individuals, in our small way, sticking up for
    tweedledum
Our national disease is success-worship. .
Big success. Little success not worthwhile.
I don't speak of money aspect, but a little paper, little cause, etc
Little things can be more real.
Can allow for individuality.
Big systems always unjust.
When I look round, I see that the need is reinstatement of the small
    in esteem. Lust am kleinen

fortunate enough to make their own tone contagious. These individuals are variations, geniuses. If not geniuses in any other way,
they are geniuses at least in being magnetic. Boulanger, Blaine,
Butler as examples. Bryan. They stand for nothing but they are
magnetic. They make parties. Partisanship is the great human passion. Nothing great can be done without it. Often a party is temporarily built of mere antipathy. It is anything to beat the opposite
party—whose tone we dislike. Down with the mugwumps, anti im-
perialists, reformers! Down with Harvard and its conceit & priggish-
ness! Down with the peace party, the goo goo "holier-than-thou"
crowd. The leader who, appealing to these antipathies, can make
them victorious, is certainly a great man for that occasion. Speaking
broadly, there are never more than two fundamental parties in a
nation: The party of red-blood, as it calls itself, and that of pale
reflection; the party of animal instinct, jingoism, fun, excitement,

bigness; and that of reason, forecast, order gained by growth, and spiritual methods. Briefly put, the party of force and that of education.

Now as Burke says, you can't indict a whole people, nor can you indict either of these human tendencies wholesale, for both play a part in history that is indispensable. Each has its faults—now it is too much wildness from the reign of the jingo, now too much tameness from the friends of moderation, and countries advance by oscillating too far first in one and then in the other direction.

The tories in any country and the mob will always pull together in the red-blood party, when the catch words are properly manipulated; as a while ago they were by Disraeli; and liberalism will be between the upper and the nether millstone if *it* has no magnetic leader and they have one. The chronic fault of liberalism is its lack of speed & passion. Over and over again generations get into such a deadlock that a hole in the dam must be made somewhere—then the flowing water will enlarge it. A rifle bullet makes a hole by its mere speed, where the dead pressure of a weightier mass does nothing. But occasionally a leader with liberal ambitions has the vis viva of the rifle bullet. He may be a fanatic, a Cromwell, a Garibaldi or he may be a Bismarck, or he may be an adventurer like Napoleon. Happy the country that proves able to use such men for what they are worth, & to cast them off before they victimize it. That country indeed is educated! But I must not let you think that I am talking only of politics. Heaven forbid—I am talking of the *tone of human assemblages*, of which assemblages countries and their politics are only one example.

Great political crises are rare; and the ability of the *tone* of us to stand the strain decides whether we shall meet them successfully or unsuccessfully. See the

Education suggested!
What is man . . . .
Know *good man* when you see him.
_____ human being.
Chicago anecdote!
What I did say . . . .
modest aim . . . "critical judgment."
Small force, but steady.
It works in fields in wh. we have experience.

Passes but little to other fields.
But there is a *general* field . . . .
Human life. National and civic affairs. *Tone of the community.*
Decides fate in great crises.
Built up—
Born into it.
Not taught at school or college.
Habits, catchwords, leaders, jokes, amusements, newspapers, amount
   of abuses, vice, sin. smite, condone
Then God's Assizes! Fools to top of bent, then hangs up!
Franco-Prussian. Russia   Japan.
Life-Insurance here. Depew.
Permanent contrast of parties red-blood—reflection.
Then fanatics— —exploiters like football
But what can you & I do?
Few genius . . . . . orders fm bosses
Disease of societies . . .
Boulanger
Antipathies . . down with . .
Great man for *that occasion.*
Spirit vs. tameness
Intensely difficult problem . . .
Where education comes in.
Every generation forgets history
Bernard Shaw's def[n]
Reading does give standards
Cheap jack type . . . .
Our jingoism
Thucydides.
Like Dreyfuss case . .
Narrow squeak.
Tie to the best. the finished.

II. Courses

8. Fragments of Early Courses (1875–1885)

[a]

Reasoning, etc.

We have seen train of ideas in association.

   "   "   " feeling of relation as tho't.

   "   " studied assimilation of sensation by idea in the form of concept or classificatory judgment. & we have studied the actual time it takes to decide whether a sensation is of this or that class so as to react in this or in that way upon it.

Now we must take creature with this power of assimilation, place him in world, and see what he assimilates, and how he ends by reasoning. In other words study Transformation of perceptual into conceptual order.

Perceptual order an unemphasized continuum

"Manifold of intuition!" bah!

Conception makes manifold by its partiality & emphasis.

"Notice"

Wundt's inner field of view & point of sight.

Involuntary notice

Voluntary attention determined by interest.

Impossible not to notice without conceiving.

Pre-existence of assimilating image often determines notice. We only bring back what we take. We only receive what we have a matrix prepared for.

Difficulty of finding good observers. Layman in library or museum. "Foreign stuff." "Dirt." "Impure results" Physiological experiments. "Experiment failed" "Rubbish." "guts." grass vs grasses.

We all assimilate[1] different sets of things. 4 tourists in Europe. Colored female homoeopathist in florence.

Hobbies—fanatics—Spencer's & Darwin's learning.

Lover—sportsman—ghost seer.

---

1 WJ wrote 'assimilate' above undeleted 'observe'.

Concept[n] depends then on assimilation of character in accordance with interest.

Disinterested conception impossible.

Temporary insensibility to other features (Bain overlooking points of difference)

Selection, selection! discrimination! Most abundant in creatures with most interests. Dog's lack.

Study then discrimination. Have seen that in educated person it depends on preexisting and interesting image.

Overtones.

Can't see a thing till we have seen it, then wonder why we did n't.

Hearing speech—foreign language

Reading print—proof reading.

But this don't account for *original* discrim.

Interesting *things* first.

Qualities later.

Law of dissociation by varying concomitants.

Martineau.

Read B. & H. I. p 250+

Enough said about dissociation.

Pass to reasoning.

How does a reasoned knowledge differ from an empirical one?

Find things together—see that they belong together.

> Brain & consciousness—cortex and lower centres. Refraction. Fire blacken paper.

Confirm & justify connexions.

By reasoning then we not only can show how 2 given facts are linked by a bond which passes from the heart of one to that of the other; but we can pass from what is given to what is not given, and so forestall experience.

Association only presents things—we obey its laws but do not understand them. In reasoning we seize the inward pulse of the machine.

Pass from an end to the means—practical Reasoning.

Pass from a given juxtaposition to its connexion.

From a given condition of things to their consequences, or their causes.

We see the inconsistency of certain alleged connexions etc.

In a word, we bridge over gaps which had no bridges and clinch the
   bridges that were there already.

This is part of that reconstruction of the perceptive order, of wh. I
   spoke.

Now how does reasoning do this. With the answer will come an
   understanding of the way all the facts we have been over hang
   together. Treat psychologically

R. is the substitution of parts & their couplings for wholes and their
   couplings.

The parts I speak of

[b]

Find examples of explanation

Examples of a given "reality" being conceived of in diff^t manners
according to the purpose in hand. (Exposure to air of ink and Pasteur's solution dust-evaporation)

Lewes's assertion that every truth is neccessary means that so far
as the terms are *rightly conceived* in any case of truth they will be
intuited as identical; and can never again be conceived in *that* way
as not identical. But the terms he admits may be conceived another
time ("under other conditions") not in that but in new ways, and
then the identity will have disappeared. There seems really no fer-
tility in Lewes's principle. It only amounts to saying: a = a even
when latent. The changed conditions he speaks of are not change of
accompaniments, they are changes of *a* itself. That changed accompaniments may compel changes of *a* is a thing that Lewes gives no
account of—he does not show when the conditions *b* & *c* of the subject term become b′ & c′, why a can't stay what it is and the proposition keep its truth. And yet *these* are the conditions which being
known to change make us wonder if the term we deal with may still
be regarded as a case of *a*. What is the coupling between b and a
that changes both at once? that is not identity. Mill says it is juxtaposition—chance. Taine says it is an ultimate primordial synthetic
nature.

Either we must analyse everything down to simple elements 1)
identical everywhere 2) or to simple elements empirically juxtaposed; or thirdly to bilateral or synthetic elements.

If A & B are each analysed down to the same simple ultimate element, say x, then they are a case of identity—of buried identity it is true, but still of true identity, *so far* as each is essentially constituted by that element. Whence then their differences? From the other characters they possess, either one of which may serve to represent their essence on some different occasion from the present. What will make the difference of the occasion? The particular A which B is confronted with. Thus, a knife will remove ink blots from paper; india rubber will remove pencil marks; citric acid will remove ink from cloth; KC, spots from indelible ink &c. In each and every case of spot from one point of view that of the purchaser, say the essence is the same, it is disfigurement, involving the rejection of the spotted article. From the point of view of the owner they are all identical cases, involving the need of erasure. But from the point of view of the remedy they are different. The first is a case of adhesion so strong as to require the fibres of the paper to be removed; the second so weak that a counter adhesion to bread or india rubber will suffice to overpower it; the third a case of tannate of iron, the 4th of nitrate of silver, the fifth, grease, of solubility in ether etc etc. The entire fact is the totality of all its relations, requiring before we are through with it that each and all of its attributes should in turn have figured as its essence.

If this jar be hermetically sealed its contents will taste good next year. Why? because sealing keeps out mould spores—(i.e. keeping these out is the essence of the sealing *pro hac vice.*) and freedom from mould is the essence of good flavor in food. Now if the food be meat, or sweetmeats, or biscuit etc we shall be quite right in saying that the essence of good taste depends on freedom from mould and the like. Our reasoning may be symbolized thus: Even though the 2nd datum, "good tasting contents" largely overlap the intermediate term, yet if its essence be involved therein, the latter is the "raison explicative."

the dotted circle represents the other properties of the food.

But suppose that the contents be Stilton or Roquefort cheese. Then the essence of its tasting good would lie in a wholly different place. Absence of mould would not explain the preservative effect of sealing. Retention of moisture might however.

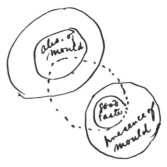

A similar case wd. be: Keeping vessels open spoils the fluids they contain, in the case of ink by evaporation making it gummy, syrup spores making mouldy; wine making sour, Ferrous solutions precipitating ferric hydrate, permanganate of potash bleaching, sulphuric anhydride attracting moisture, potassic hydrate attracting CO_2, argentic nitrate decomposes by light. A, or "keeping open" involves each and all of these causes of B, or "spoiling." What the particular cause we shall assign may be in any present case depends on our genius.

Liebreich for example knowing chloroform to cause sleep and chloral mixed with alkali to make chloroform, thought that chloral introduced into the alkaline blood would produce insensibility

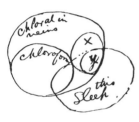

through chloroform. It does. And Liebreich concluded that this concrete case of sleep was a case of chloroformization. But there is no chloroform formed, so that the essence of the injection must be represented by another circle x, and that of the sleep by y, both unknown.

The ether undulations wh. are supposed to be intermediaries uniting all consequent luminous phenomena to their antecedents may turn out not to be really such, inasmuch as the terms may not at all contain such waves as their essence, but something entirely diff^t The single fluid & the double fluid accounts of electricity are also good examples of phenomena being possibly cases of either this or that essence indifferently as far as our knowledge goes, but they must be one or the other as far as real existence goes.

Courses

[c]

Syllogism

Mill's

Facts in Evidence	Two coordinate inferences
A, B, C, D, ... are P	**Major**
	Anything like A, B, C, &c is P
	Conclusion
	S, which is like A, B, C, &c is P.

Complete form.

Facts	Inferences
A, B, C, D, ... quâ M, = P.	*All M's* are P
	S (wh. is M) is P

The difference consists in Mill's leaving the *ground* of the P ness unanalyzed out of his facts. The moment we see to what element in A, B, C, etc, their being P is due, we get a test for true and false analogues of them in this respect. If M & P are ideas between which an a priori relation obtains, then the conclusion is neccessary. But then also we can do without the "Facts."

On the Syllogism apropos of Mill

Mill says, if S is like A, B, C, &c., then it is P.

This is an inference by analogy. & it is obvious that it is valid only in case the likeness of S to A, B, C, &c., is in those respects which carry P with them.

These respects are the *ground* why the inference about S is valid. To be sure of our inference, we must then exhibit it *with* its ground.

& this is what casting it into the syllogistic form does.

The major premise, by naming no longer $A, B, \& C$ as so many individuals, but as a class, (that is as "all things" that possess a certain common essence, the character M, namely connoted by the class name,) assigns in *form* (of course materially there may be a mistake) the *ground why A, B, & C* are P. It is *as cases of this essence M,* & not by dint of any other properties they may possess.

S, in its turn, cannot be proved to be P, unless it too be classed as a case of the same essence, M. & this is what the minor premiss does for it.

It is obvious that classing A, B, & C, on the one hand, & S on the other, as so many cases of M, as a preliminary to seeing that they are P, is a very different thing from simply noting the "coexistence" of P with them as so many "resembling" totals.

The right classification of the sensible phenomena is thus what the Syllogistic form of statement ensures, & as all classification is with regard to a purpose, it follows that to deduce another conclusion than P, we must use another class essence than M. But the ascent to "*all* M" is important not by reason of the all, but by reason of the M; Not by reason of its being an *universal* but by reason of its being an *essential* judgment.

The syllogistic form expresses just the transition between Psychology & Logic. To make an inference in that roundabout way *postulates* that there may be a *justification* for our inferences. And altho' our major premisses were never neccessary yet, their existence would express a *claim* of there being somewhere such things.

[d]

Unintelligible "law" of connexion (Tyndall   Huxley, Fechner?) nervous event a premiss from which consciousness concludes (Wundt?)—what? The 1 nervous event itself?—2 its outward cause?— 3 its relations to other nervous events?—4 certain of its abstracted attributes?—Each of these alternatives is in turn alleged. 3 & 4 cover the comparison of intensities (Weber's law) and qualities (contrast)

But why this choice different at different times? the unintelligible law seems really just as satisfactory.

Aesthetics

Influence of habit in making ideas agreeable.

All ease is agreeable, habit produces ease.

Rest has an element of the agreeable. And in intellectual matters, the intelligible, rational, are synonyms for that in which we tranquilly rest or feel mentally at home; whereas the nonsensical, the doubtful, or the uncomprehended signify representations in which the mind is agitated to pass on to something different, only without a definite direction being afforded. Now according to a certain school the rational is nothing but the habitual. And it may therefore be that the rational owes its pleasant quality to its rest, & that therefore this may be considered a mere result of habit.

Pleasure inversely as habit in most purely sensual delights. Novelty gives a zest to most of them.

We get accustomed (blunted) by repetition to both pains & pleasures of the body. Yet altho' the pleasure an experience gives is blunted by habit, another aesthetic effect comes out instead viz: that the omission[2] of an experience that has grown habitual causes uneasiness, distress or pain.

Psychologic physiology has to determine what classes of emotion accompany certain classes of cerebral activity. It is presumable that a constancy of correspondence will be found.

Start fm. the very general law that unimpeded energy is pleasurable—but a strong tendency to energy painful if checked. Habit means an empirically marked out tendency to energy. Habits are not however neccessarily positively pleasant, altho' their checking causes discomfort as above.

On the other hand there are tendencies to energy which are far from habitual, & which are very pleasant, what relates to the sexual relation.

The pursuits of food & drink warmth, rest, sexual gratification, air, soft skin contact, &c may be all empirically organized reflexes. The pleasures and pains that are connected with them may pertain to the general nervous law that an unimpeded tendency to a particular nervous discharge is agreeable whereas its check, either within or without, is unpleasant. It is true that the discharge in many actions is neutral and only the arrest painful. But in others as in eating, relieving bladder or bowels or vesic. seminales it rises to a positive pleasure.

The question whether there is in the mind a progressive combination of elements of representation forming a set of powers so to speak in our interests, representations on one plane combining to produce another of a higher denomination, by virtue of their subjective quality, and this combining with another of its own rank again to produce still another and so on, this question I say can only be solved by an appeal to facts. Here follow a few.

1 The pleasure of consistency.

2 In morals do the "will" criterion and the beneficence criterion conjointly used issue in a distinct quality of pleasure? Do any or all of the elements (see "Morals" 1) so combine?

2 WJ wrote 'omission' above undeleted *'intermittence'*.

That high consistency of ideas with each other and with conduct recommended by Maudsley, and wh. is a great source of the serenity of the sage must be one of the greatest moral pleasures. Yet it is not utilitarian in its origin. On the contrary, our knowledge is so fragmentary, that inconsistent thought is no doubt truer than consistent. Both in mere consistency of doctrine then, and in the above moral consistency, which are strong passions in some minds, we have an instance of a pleasure arising from purely subjective conditions, from the formal relation to each other of representational elements derived themselves from outward experience.

Spamer's theory of pleasure, that it results from an addition of motion to nerve matter "adequate" to the intrinsic motion, is in harmony with the laws of composite pleasure, in which different representations harmonize when they support & reinforce each other.

It also explains why habit makes a thing pleasant which at first was not so. The intrinsic movements may tend by habit to alter themselves in conformity with the outward influence, which thus gets adequate.

Impressions too intense or prolonged are unpleasant, because the intrinsic movement is so feeble.

The pleasure of an intrinsic tendency being *assisted,* (itching &c).

Craving for stimulants as a case of the law of stimulation—normal state being one of uneasiness we drown it by a strong buccal or gastric sensation, glass of liquor; when effects pass away uneasiness redoubles, we don't feel right, smoke; then eat sweets; chew tobacco, take snuff; another drink; each successive indulgence being the production of a strong and interesting sensation which veils & smothers the discomfort of the organism when left to itself.

In "nervous" states the uneasiness is tremendous. In such cases excitement of any sort, however intense acts as an anaesthetic to the organic disease.

Authoritativeness of pure aesthetic element over mixed.—Contempt of artists for sentimentalists. British couple in Venice academy. Application to intellectual rationality. Chauncey Wright &c.

Ennui

We tire—need change—

It is a consequence of the "law of stimulation" that, apart from motor effects and per se, feeling is reckoned as a good. Which lives most, the orderly man whose life runs on oiled rails of propriety, who never does ill or makes a mistake or has a regret, or a pang, because on every occasion the right *action* presents itself to his mind and he simply does it, or the passionate tumultuous blunderer, whose whole life is an alternation of rapturous excitement, and horrible repentance and longing for the ruined good? *He* feels; the other does. If his type should be extinguished, surely would not one of the divinest of human gifts, the gift of intense feeling, be lost from life?

9. Notes for Natural History 2: Physiological Psychology (1876–1877)

Spencer on Relativity of Feelings & Relations

This arg^t for Agnosticism is entirely diff^t fm. the one Sp. has used in his chapter on the substance of mind. One may be true without the other being true. I think this argum^t is at least imperfect. It professes to be a reductio ad absurdum. He assumes at the start that sensation confers knowledge and then finds that diff^t sensations give a diff^t knowledge of the same object. In this conflict, which is right? he asks, and answers, "neither." But another may answer, "*one*, the rest, wrong." In truth this is the answer physics gives, when she ends by defining the universe in purely mathematical terms. She don't doubt these but calls them reality, and explains our non-mathematical feelings as partial events of extremely restricted scope, existing merely as such, as feelings. From this conception, Spencer's only agnostic escape is by way of the first argument. That we won't consider here.

What I want to consider here is his assumption that at any rate sensation alone constitutes the knowledge we possess. For an examination of this assumption is connected with many of the fundamental questions in Philosophy; and Sp's. way of thinking, simply *assumed* as it is, ignores a mass of familiar facts which other men lay their main stress upon and so reach on the whole a very different conclusion from Spencer's. To avoid misunderstanding let me say what I am *not* going to do: I am not going at first to consider the question at all of whether there is an *outward* reality or not corresponding to the ideas we end by receiving as true. There may or there may not be a truth *extra mentem*; at any rate we all admit that *intra mentem* there are certain conclusions we regard as more tenable than others, in other words there is a division of our notions into erroneous and correct. And leaning on this familiar fact I proceed to ask, what *constitutes* the correct conclusions. Spencer like the British school generally, says they are constituted of sensations. The sensations segregated, integrated &c, are *themselves* the conclusions. (J. Mill a succession, change &c of feelings is a feeling of succession, change, &c.) Certain of these organized sensations live and enter into the formulas we accept as veracious, others are extruded from such formulas and under the name of error or fancy sooner or later perish. But the true and the erroneous formulas alike have no other substantiality or content than they receive fm. the sensations out of which they are built. If these sensations, in the case of the true formulas are flickering, uncertain, mutually contradictory, then the formulas are equally so; and the "truth" they contain lacks the first requisite of truth as ideally conceived, namely, immutability.

Now as matter of natural history Spencer's account of the variability of feelings is admirable. He might even have made his case still stronger by quoting the German investigations in optics, color contrast, &c.

But equally as matter of natural history we are entitled to examine the actual way in which practically the variable sensations in question are used in forming the entire system of consciousness which each one of us here terms his mind or his tho't. The first thing that strikes us in attending to this question, is the small stress we lay upon the present sensation as such in most of our moments, and the immense importance relatively to it of the ideal mass which apperceives it. It is engulphed and corrected, reduced by the system of thought into which it is immediately caught up, to its standard or average significant value. The different feeling of 10 lbs on the back or on the little finger need never deceive our judgm^t of the objective weight. The diff^t retinal projection of a table top in diff^t positions don't mislead us as to what its shape really is. Nor do the diff^t "angles subtended in memory" by the past 24 hrs, & 24 hrs. spent a year ago make us in the least believe them to be truly diff^t spaces of time. The particular feelings become guides to constant conclusions, no matter how much they may, regarded merely as feelings, vary *inter se*, and our main attention is given to the conclusions, because our main interests lie with them. All this is matter of perfect familiarity which no one will dispute. It is, regarded as mere phenomenal description, so patent, & so influential practically that it has received almost exclusive attention from one type of philosophic minds which we may call the logical idealists and of whom Hegel, Green & C. S. Peirce may be taken as types. Such minds point to the fact that as a rule our sensations are merely contributory to our *opinions* about *things*. The *things* are the matter of knowledge, the sensations are overlooked. So true is this that every one who learns to draw has painfully to discover what his sensations actually are. He never has been accustomed to noticing or caring what they are, so much more has he been concerned with the thing they reveal. Helmholtz's Optics is one long commentary on this law. He shows the sensations of the retina to be to the last degree fluctuating and inconsistent; and yet the eye, *as its data enter into the system of thought*, and are there used, is an instrument of admirable precision giving most exact and constant results. One may go farther & affirm that it makes no difference at all *what* the sensation is in itself, its function in tho't, its connections with the other ingredients of the mental organism so *determine* it, that if time enough is given it will in all cases contribute to one identical conclusion. Thus blind persons seem to have built up the notion of space as perfectly as those who see it. Laura Bridgmans ideas about things indistinguishable fm. Dr Howe's. Peirce's example of blind & deaf man witnessing murder. There is an inevitable drift in tho't, a logical destiny precipitated out of all experience, which takes up every sensation and makes it contributory to its ends, if it can correct it, reduce it, or interpret it; & if not, extrudes it as error, (and even then uses it, for counted *as error*, errors are facts & part of the body of ascertained truth.) This conclusion to which all sensations, all men, all opinions converge is inevitable, if time & experience enough are given, & is "the Truth." According to the school of writers I have mentioned, it is the fundamental reality, the alpha & omega, the Absolute. Exactly how they understand this, I won't here explain.

But I call attention to the fact that Spencer ignores this whole consideration, and that it really so far as relates to our thought regarded as an actual phenomenal matter of fact, refutes his opinion that the fluctuation of feelings, prevents the truths to which those feelings lead, from being fixed and consistent.

So far, good. But reaching this point, we are compelled to make further inquiries which again seem to return the ball to Spencer's hands. What are these truths we get to at last? Judgments about things. What are things? Substantialists in philosophy say they are outward entities existing in se and producing effects on us. I expressly postpone entering into the question of their outwardness just now, as it is wholly irrelevant for our immediate purpose which view is held on that point. Substantialists whether realistic or not, admit that as we *know* the thing, it is a tho't in us, if realistic, like the outward, if idealistic, not like the outward but intended fixed & determined by nothing extraneous to the outward. Nihilists of course say that there is nothing but the thought. So in either case we may assume the true thought to be equivalent to the thing, and say Things are true thoughts. Now in general our truer thought of a thing defines it by its relations to other things rather than by its relations to our subjectivity. In the examples above given the real 10 lbs was s'thing which wd. objectively tip a certain balance, the *real* table top was square to a T rule, the real 24 hours had properties connected with the motion of clocks and the sun. But these objective properties, are again themselves nothing but wider & wider referring groups of sensations, and our thoughts in the last analysis thus seem again to resolve themselves into the particular subjective elements, wh. severally appeared in our former account to be of such insignificant moment.

10. Notes for Philosophy 4: Psychology (1878–1879)

The[1] relativity of knowledge school finding that we only know things as related to each other, nothing absolute & self contained, proceed further to assert that this universal attribute of our knowledge constitutes an imperfection, and justifies skepticism of its

---

1 At the top of the page WJ wrote, '*Spencer's Psych. [*underl.*]. i. 146'.

results. Of course their judgment implies at least that they have the notion of an other kind of knowledge, a knowledge of things as unrelated, and since this hypothetical knowledge is assumed to be superior or more *real* to the usual sort, it implies that they have the further notion that the *real existence of things* is of this interior self contained unrelated sort. Now, if all that we know of things presents them in relation, how did the notion ever awaken in us of their having a being out of relation, and how again did that being ever come to seem to us their truest most ideal form of being?

In Spencer's polemic against our "knowing" substance he falls back on this peculiar conception of knowledge. The substance it is "impossible to know" is "unmodified" substance, i.e substance unrelated to attributes. But if our only notion of substance is that of the unifier or *locus* of attributes, what guarantees to Spencer that it *has* any "real" existence in itself as unrelated to its attributes? It is a gratuitous assumption from which no sure conclusion can be drawn as to the imperfection of our knowledge. If substance has no "unmodified" being at all, of course we must be ignorant of such being; but we may know all the while most adequately the substance *as such*, i.e. as support of such and such attributes, rigidly determinate too and distinguished from other substances, which support other groups of attributes but not this particular group. All that Spencer says on p. 146 is: you cant know substance in a form different from that of substance, or as other than itself.

On p. 147. Sp. takes up the other fork of the relativity reasoning—the relativity of the known to the knower. He says there *must* be a difference or duplicity between the two. Then if the "unmodified" substance is the *known*, the *knower* or the knowing act (which is neccessarily different from it) must be a mode of it, and thus *it* not known (!) [This argument assumes that the knower must *be* the known.] If on the contrary the unmodified substance is *the knower*, then *the known* wh. labors under the neccessity of being diff^t from it, *can* only be a mode at most & not the desiderated substance in question.

Read[2] to the class Tyndall's Fragments p. 121. Then say that both Tyndall's and Spencer's doctrine amounts to this, that the consciousness wh. accompanies nerve tremors is not a consciousness of the tremors themselves. If this were so, the coalescence and integra-

---

[2] At the top of the page WJ wrote, 'Spencer's Psych. p. 158' and drew a line beneath.

tion of psychic events (which according to Sp. constitutes developed intelligence) wd. result in a complete representation of the system of tremors, or in other words in a complete knowledge of the *anatomy & physiology of the brain,* or nervous system which we must admit to be something wofully different from the truth. The brain is not *self* conscious, whatever it may be. What its movements reveal to us is not their own peculiarities but their outward *causes.* These provoke the movements and then the concomitant consciousness *reconstructs* them as causes; and developed intelligence is regarded as knowledge of the world, in which as a small fragment the brain is included.

But there is a class of cases of nervous change or *mode of* nervous action to which the concomitant mental action runs *parallel.* The same schema covers both. The psychic and the physical fall under common categories. The thoughts *a* corresponding to A, & b corresponding to the nerve event B, may be as wholly unlike our cognitions of A & B as hate is like a left hand spiral movem^t &c but the *relations* between a & b may be identical with the relations between A & B. Thus succession in time may be common to the two orders, objective & subjective, &c.—i.e anteriority of one representation to another may be due to the anteriority of the nerve discharge supporting the former to that of the other. In like manner the first tho't may be more intense than the last because its nerve discharge is more violent, or the thought may be accompanied with slowness & effort because the nerve discharge is impeded and tardy; or the thought may be complex and voluminous because its nerve tract is the same; easy and brief because the discharge is immediate & so on. In other words *some* peculiarities of the thought are identical with peculiarities of the cerebral event. The representation is *partially* a revelation of the brain's condition. But in the vastly great part of our nervous life there is not even the remotest analogy. The particular tremors of the optic lobes which respectively correspond to the sensations white & black, are not themselves white & black tremors; the disturbance caused in our brain by cologne water has itself no different odor from that caused by carrion; nor does the hatred awakened in the mind by the tho't of a certain man, reveal to us any such state of feeling as existing between the nerve tracts involved in the two representations in question. Nevertheless certain vague writers (Luys, Maudsley) aware of the partial analogy above pointed out extend its limits far beyond legitimacy, and write as if the *essence* of the connexion between tho't and brain action were this fact of the brain cell becoming conscious of its *own* action or condition, a thing which could only result, if consistently completed, in an intuitive consciousness of the nervous system.

It is in the realm of aesthetics that this vague treatment is particularly confusing. A plausible hypothesis makes pleasure to be the concomitant of changes in nerve tissue beneficial to its nutrition. Benefit is thus the physical *condition* of the pleasure; but in many cases of pleasure, if asked for its logical *reason* we also reply "benefit." Thus is suggested the notion that in the pleasure of a simple sensation the mind is cognizant of the objective prosperity of the sensation's substratum. The change *is* beneficial, so we feel it beneficial, and the feeling is thus not subjective but cognitive.[3]

Thus an iconoclastic aesthetician seems to speak with great authority. His materialistic explanation of an aesthetic judgment is not a nervous event *arbitrarily* connected with it as a substratum, but a nervous event of such a kind as legitimately to serve (if cognized) as a *reason* for the judgment; and which may therefore claim to replace the transcendental reasons we may at first allege, with some show of propriety. Not so the nervous events underlying pure objective cognitions, for that seems to have no logical connexion whatever with the latter. In the esthetic case however the connexion is *logical* between substratum & feeling, and what seems a lower cognition may drive out a higher, by offering itself as a simpler premise for a conclusion once for all given (viz. the pleasurable feeling.)

We here reach through physiological considerations a very similar kind of result to that attained in other cases by psychological analysis, or by the study of mental development. A complex feeling is proved to consist of conscious factors and they are then called its sole import, as movements of space. Or it is learned to have arisen incidentally to certain objective uses and *they* are called its sole import (as social approbation and survival of morality.) In every case a transmutation of something intrinsically felt as more interesting into something less, of a high into a low.

But now note a frequent confusion in this aesthetic matter. Pleasure is sought by us for its own sake. It is regarded not as a sign of benefit, but as being itself benefit. If the nervous prosperity were

---

[3] At the top of the page WJ wrote, '*Spencer's ['Sp' *ov.* 'Co'] Psych p. 158. (2)'.

unaltered by it, a world of pleasures wd. still be considered a beneficent world. Writers like Allen therefore slip into the habit of thinking that a pleasurable response of the organism is per se beneficial provided only it dont injure, and the physiological assumption with which they started (that pleasures *accompany* benefits) is reinforced unconsciously by this belief that pleasures *are* benefits.

Renouvier says to the Evolutionist: you explain the mental forms by facts which assume them.

The E. replies: I assume them *qua* existents, I explain them *qua* cognitions.

R. replies: then you neccessarily allow for a capacity in the mind cognizing just for these forms of existence. The knowledge *is* not the existence, but has in its quality of true knowledge the aptitude for exactly mirroring existence. Not a fact in Nature but is reduplicated by mind. A wonderful harmony. The ultimate Being then consists of things with tho'ts of them, and the things and the capacities for tho't are coequal, not to say coeval.

The E. retorts: It is not fair to speak of definite capacities in the mind. It is pure receptivity and indefiniteness of itself. Existence just pours itself in.

R: Like the old species sensibiles! That won't wash. We know by our fallacious secondary qualities that the mind is not purely receptive. And we can only understand cognition as an awakening in the mind of a mental fact already slumbering there. But this if true cognition be, presupposes aboriginal correspondence & harmony.

E. Well then, I admit it. I was wrong in calling the cognitions true. I am an agnostic, and my mental and physical geology are symbolic of a truth inconceivable.

R. But your cognition is true at least in so far as it affirms *existence* in something extra-mentem, from whose action the mental forms come. Those two propositions are true though time space etc are false.

E. Yes! Those are absolutely true.

R. Mental states then transcend themselves *so* far,—become the subjects of a "miraculous revelation,"—but no farther.

E. There is no "revelation" about it. The Real simply gives us true cognition so far, & farther gives us illusive cognition.

R. But how do you know this?

E. I simply can't doubt it.

R. But I can. Falsus in uno, falsus in omnibus. It seems to me that if cognition be possible at all, it is arbitrary for it to be limited to existence and psychogenetic activity. If the further determinations of my thought be illusory, its belief in the extra mental and its powers are probably no less so.

E. Well, I admit it seems queer.

R. Then your position really is that you find your self fatally impelled to excogitate geologies &c, the objects of which may have no existence at all. Your position is really the extreme of subjective idealism. The object *is* only as it is thought. So that in either case, cognition being assumed true or untrue, my thesis remains the right one. The thought and the thing are coequals. In the first case as members of a dualistic harmony, in the second place as aspects of an inseparable Phenomenon.

We must start by recognizing the truth that *some* of our mental forms are illusory. Secondary qualities, e.g. are so admitted by everyone. Primary qualities are so asserted by Agnostics, & Kantians. The only true judgments that Spencer allows are the judgement that a Reality extra-mentem *exists*, and the judgment that it *operates* to produce *our mental forms*—producing them as cognitions consequently so far as they express these 2 judgments, producing them as delusions so far as they express anything else.

Now they express a theory of physical evolution in time and space. This of course is part of the delusion. They express a mental ditto—also part of the delusion; for the "outer relations," which make the inner ones, don't exist. This whole industry of the mind then *makes* its objects as it thinks them, they having no existence out of the thought. It creates geology & cosmogony regressively by thinking up the stream of time. It is pure subjective Idealism— tho't fatally obeying a destiny—with no real object.

As for the 2 veracious judgments, the question immediately arises, how do we know them true when all the rest is false? Spencer's attempt to explain the genesis of cognition is simply silly—the only answer he can really make, is that *he* can't doubt these two. But if we can and do doubt them, Idealism triumphs along the whole line. Thought and thing are correlates & coequals mutually involved. Renouvier's position triumphs.

If on the other hand we allow them true, the question arises, why are not some of the other judgments true also?—Cosmogony given in molecular terms e.g. But this admitted, Renouvier's position also triumphs. For it is equivalent to the admission of a pre-established harmony between objective forms and subjective forms. The veracious judgments *are* not the things simply pouring themselves into the mind like the "species sensibiles" and "intelligibiles" of the scholastics. The things awaken them from the mind—in themselves they are mental facts, but by a wonderful harmony they repeat the outer Reality. The world is aboriginally dual—each aspect is a match for the other, but neither is derived. This differs from R. only in asserting separability. The only third course is that of sticking tight to the Spencerian position, but that is so absolutely arbitrary that I can't conceive it to be adopted on a large scale.

Picture languages institutions etc in these terms—ms. of Hamlet. Automatism.

A history of the world expressed in these terms wd. truly be a doctrine of mechanical evolution. The office of physical science to day, her ideal, is to fill in the interstices of the sketch. Be as radical as we can!

Notice that in our sketch *not one* point due to Spencer. Merely the tendencies of the g'al tho't of the time!

Note too that the only *facts* are the molecules & their positions and motions. The wholes are names, the "kinds" are appearances to us. Water is not H_2O + something else.

But here is the fact of consciousness. Is it a shadow? Or is it as Spencer seems to think, a link? Two theories.

Take Spencer's account of genesis of C.   Psych. vol i, pp. 403, 435, 560

To sum up, We start by *assuming* atoms and elementary laws (wh. we don't know in detail) of attraction and repulsion between them, such that any arrangements we now find real might at one time or another have been mechanically produced. These elementary laws lead to a result which may be expressed by a statistical "law of evolution," thus: As Evolution proceeds the world will contain more and more of those aggregations of matter whose *parts* have become *organs* acting in such a way as to promote the survival of the whole aggregate. This applies to separate animals, and to their habits & actions, which must be *organized*. It applies to communities and their institutions and accumulations, material & ideal.

Spencer's "Law of Intelligence"

Sp.'s law makes the outer relations do all the work. The inner ones are plastic and without spontaneity.

Empirical vs. a priori schools always represented. One lays most stress on *thing*, t'other on *thinker* in the product *thought*.

Sp.'s law and statement of evolution form the most thorough going statement of empiricism yet formulated.

Along with the antithesis between inner & outer there runs another which has at all times been more or less confounded with it, but which a little reflection shows us to have no necessary connection with it at all. I mean the distinction between the natural and the supernatural. The outer experience contains nothing but *natural* facts: the inner by its faculty of getting at necessary truth by its conscience and by its free-will seems to grasp into a region not tributary to nature, consequently above nature, or spiritual. But it is obvious that there might be in the mind principles quite as natural as those of the outer world which nevertheless altered the shape taken by the outer facts in thought. In other words the antithesis between inner and outer may subsist on a purely natural plane and a Philosophy accentuating the inner element be true without in any sense being a supernatural Philosophy.

In our discussion on free-will we shall have to inquire how far the mind may be said to contain a supernatural element. I now express my belief that we can give no clear scientific description of the facts of Psychology considered as phenomena belonging to a purely natural plane without restoring to the inner at every step that active originality and spontaneous productivity which Spencer's law so entirely ignores. The trouble in all discussions of this kind lies in the fact that so few people analyze the elements of the problem. Most disciples of Spencer assume if you criticize his law that you must be doing it in the interest of miracles or scholasticism or theology. *Aut* Spencer, *aut* catechism.

Now criticize Spencer. But I assume complete determinism.

His law leaves out an immense mass of mental fact.

My objection to it best expressed by saying that in Psychology he repeats the defects of Darwin's predecessors in biology.

Explain—Fortunate to have so good an illustration.

Animal forms determined by 3 factors

    Heredity conservative

Adaptation

Spontaneous variation

Pre-Darwinians thought only of adaptation. They made organism plastic to environment—lungs, giraffe's neck, speed, change of medium, change of food, sunned skin, strength, skin of hand the type. The outer relation corresponded to produces the correspondence.

Darwin almost wholly discards this. *Darwin's Principles.*

Distinction between stimuli and transitive forces;

Operative and regulative forces.

Operative factors of organic form intrinsic and molecular—acorn and palm seed in same pot.

Discharged by unknown stimuli they produce spontaneous variations.

Environment regulates these.

Spencer admits this in his *Biology*, ascribing however to environment considerable operative or adaptive power (direct equilibration).

Darwin never means that spont. var.s. are causeless; nor that they are not fatally implied in the environment since they and it are both parts of the same natural whole.

He means to emphasize the truth that the regulator or preserver of the variation, the environment, is a different part from its producer, is moreover sensible to us and matter of scientific discussion. To clump it with the stimulus and say "variations are caused by outward relations" is to revert from scientific distinctness to speculative vagueness. The main point is that the variation or inner relation does *not* "correspond" with its *cause* but with some environing relation utterly removed from its cause.

This outward relation has a perfectly definite function: to take the variation once made and preserve or destroy it.

It is thus fair to say that organism differentiates *itself*.

Manifold ways of adjusting to environment.

Examples.

Consequence: Resultant form determined more by material of organism than by environment.

Read Wallace.

Objection: Common ancestral fauna came from adaptation.

But why are descendants not adapted?

Conclusion: In Zoology environment plays no such part as that which Spencer ascribes to it in Psychology.

2$\underline{\text{nd}}$ Example: Social evolution. Environment theory. Buckle, Taine, Allen,

When I say that Spencer's account of the way in which the ideal law of intelligence becomes realized, (namely by adaptation to the frequency of relations in the environment) repeats the error of Darwin's predecessors in not allowing for the unaccountable factor of spontaneous variation (incidental interests &c, men of genius) let me not be understood to undervalue the enormous part which direct adaptation, i.e. the teachings of experience, play in mental evolution. The environment, meaning the *sensible* facts of our experience is a vastly more potent agent in mental evolution than in physical. All the individual's acquisitions properly so-called, come from it, and so very likely do many of his inheritances. The whole enormous field of habitual expectation and contiguous association is its domain. So far am I from ignoring this, that it is precisely *because* our adjustments to the sensible facts of the environment are produced by direct experience of those facts themselves, and thus may be said to be evolved by adaptation, that it is precisely because the action of the environment moulds the mind in so peculiar and distinct a way, that I object to allowing Spencer to say that it moulds it in every way. To say this we must perform a retrograde step in science. We must exchange for a true and perfectly definite conception, a conception which can only be kept true by being made indistinct. If we alter the meaning of the word "environment" so as to make it include the unknown physiological conditions of variation, we make it synonymous with universal nature and we then lack a term by which to specify those particular sensible parts of nature, the experience of which does produce direct adaptations. In short we have pulled the blanket "environment" or experience which was only long enough to cover our feet, up over our shoulders, but we are no more covered than we were before and need a new blanket to cover our feet. I hold it to be vastly more scientific to restrict experience to the sensible environment whose function we definitely know to be great and of a specific sort, and then to say that mental advances of other specific sorts tho' they flow from nature, do not result from *experience* of that part of it known as the environment.

[Pop. Sc. Monthly Sup. Dec. '71 & Gentleman's Mag.]

Great-Man theory repudiated by Allen and Sp.

Both Spencer and Allen in falling back on the environment as implicating the causes of the great man are clumping into one term things which it is very useful to have distinguished. The operative cause, the ferment or stimulus which results in a certain ovum producing a great man is no doubt part and parcel of that entire system of nature of which the environment is also a part. In this vast sense it and the environment imply each other. But how useless for any particular scientific inquiry into the causes of a change is it to fall back on an empty universal abstraction and say: "Change is produced by Nature." We want to know in what part of nature to look for the cause—the *proximate* cause.

If I have a trunk &c.

So here, it makes a great difference scientifically to know whether the cause of social changes lies inside the social organism itself or outside, lies in adaptation or spontaneous variation.

In the case of social evolution we can actually see the proximate cause. We can note with our eyes the way in which the great man works and to abandon this solid foundation for the emptyness of an unknown ultimate cause is in the highest degree unscientific.

[Diagram on back of page [*ed.*, 139.28–37]]

To the social evolutionist advent of great man is a datum which he accepts from Physiology as Darwin accepts spontaneous variations.

Difference is interposition of social organism.

Great man a ferment.

Like individuals, societies have many slumbering potentialities. Which shall become actual depends on great man—lactic vs. alcoholic fermentation.

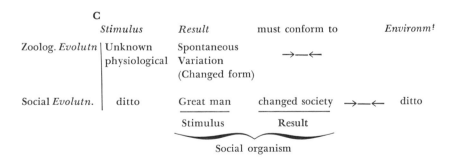

Great man + changed society is the variation of form from inward causes which the environment, national & physical, *regulates*.

Read Bagehot.

I accept this. Examples trivial but so are Darwin's & Lyell's.

True method advances from observed to unobserved.

To make more plausible take examples of Luther & Mahomet.

Bismarck. Effect on national characters of Franco-Prussian War. "Ces bons ces naifs allemands," political herbivores. Yet either of 3 or 4 individuals might have averted it. King Wm. might have changed its end.

Disraeli may commit England to Asiatic policy.

Influence on English tone of J. S. Mill, Cobden &c.

Social organism of course regulates. Read Spencer. (Contemp. Rev. vol 19. 1872 p. 707–9)

But to say its potentialities are not determined by great men is to say that the fate of a wood-pile is not determined by the presence or absence of spark.

Physical Geog. theorists always reason after the fact. They prove only that national characteristics are *compatible* with environment. But such compatibility indeterminate. Sardinia & Corsica. Iceland. Rome.

Practical consequences of Spencer's system have been extolled. In regard to the Great-Man question they constitute a return to oriental fatalism, removing all theoretic incitement to individual energy. Scientific determinism like *Mill's* says: Society follows a fated destiny but the laws of that destiny work themselves out through individuals and their initiatives. Spencer says they work themselves out in spite of all that individuals may do.

Return to the book. Instinct.

Spencer makes it = habit. His example shows how the circumstance to which the action is adjusted is the operative, not merely the regulative cause of the action. On 439, bottom he says this is sole explanation.

But it fails to explain cases where action is adjusted to an outer relation which the agent never experiences. Cuckoo. Read Darwin 6th Ed. p. 206, 211.

Changed society itself in a larger environment which preserves or destroys.

Mental evolution.

Invention and discovery produced by Spont. Var. = Hypothesis.

Aristotle

Baconian Method; Jevons.
So in music, art, religion, morals.
Many modes of corresponding.
Spencer's law.—Persistance
Pre-Darwinian.
Darwin adds Spont. Var. Production vs. Selection
Ambiguity of correspondence. Wallace.
Social evolution
Environment theory; Allen.
Great-man theory; Spencer.
Both true.
Great man a spont. var.
Produced physiologically
Selected by social environment
Changes it.
Many potentialities. Corsica &c
Sugar
Wood-pile

Spencer's Chapter on the Assumptions of Metaphysicians

The important theoretic point introductory to all this is that, (as expounded in Spencer's chapters on the Relativity etc) we get at diff* times & places sensations which are held *to conflict,* i.e. to be contradictory versions of the *same* facts. Were this not so, each primary "direct perception" cd. stand by itself for ever with no need for "reconciliation" or interpretation.

The conflict however compels interpretations. These take place through the interventions of *hypotheses,* hardly ever, if ever themselves direct perceptions, which explain the latter as so many *appearances to the Subject.* The hypotheses of "Science," stop short at the primary qualities. But even here metaphysicians find conflicts, which compel them to assert these to be subjective appearances too—so that little by little the idealistic hypothesis drives direct perception out of the entire field.

Spencer in his chapter on the Assumption of Metaphysicians maintains that it is absurd to suppose that reasoning can, by its manipulations of data evolve out of them any conclusions which were not already involved in them. If it seem to result in anything new the seeming is illusory. In a word nothing can come out of our reasonings which was not put into our premises.

The first thing wh. strikes one here is the strange inconsistency of Spencer's doctrine with his practice in trying to deduce a true *cognition* of an objective existence *extra mentem* from the mere ʳepetition of feelings, themselves non-cognitive, and differing only in vividness and other subjective qualities.

But leaving aside this personal cavil, let us turn to the question of how far reasoning does or does not transform the data it gets from sense into something entirely new. At the first glance it seems as if it did, and my own dilemma is just this: if I admit that it does, I ought also to admit that shuffling of sensations may transform them into cognitions which I have already denied; whilst if I contend that it does not, I must yield to the remainder of Spencer's argument in favor of realism, and also retract my objections to the sceptical conclusions of his chapters on "The Relativity &c" in the first volume.

Possibly a little exercise of discrimination will show us wherein reasoning does add to experience, and wherein not.

The first dawn of consciousness is, as I contend, cognitive, is a feeling of something spread out in space and time, and endued with a certain quality. As we go on acquiring farther experiences it comes to pass that the same *something* gets different qualities attached to it, and so a conflict arises as to which is the one under which we should rightly conceive it.

Spencer in his chapters on the Relativity gets discouraged by the conflict and says that neither of the attributions brought forth by experience is true, and that the only truly cognitive element in the whole conscious train is that in which all its parts agree, namely the existence of a something to be determined. He calls this the unknowable reality, and in insisting that it cannot be doubted he squarely places himself with those who feel as I do that the form of consciousness is essentially, inexplicably, and intuitively *cognitive*.

Let us now ask whether the cognitive power of this consciousness be, as Spencer says, limited to the assertion of a bare Something, or whether, out of the contradictory determinations woven upon it by experience and thought, some may not prove more reliable than others and displace them.

Primitive experience says the heavenly bodies are small round things revolving about the earth at a comparatively small distance. It says that sound flows from the bell and warmth from the fire.

Combining however in our thought various past remembered positions of planets with our present impression of seeing them move round the earth, suddenly there dawns in the mind of genius the conception that they may be really revolving round the sun, and that the Earth too may be whirling in the same direction and also producing night and day by turning on its axis. These contradictory determinations of the same appearance are not held to neutralize each other, but the latter is retained as true for its truth is not only compatible with, but explanatory of, the original perception *regarded as an appearance* to an observing consciousness placed in just such determinate conditions as those which the developed conception affirms actually to exist. The primitive judgment of perception is, in short, reinterpreted by being made an incidental consequence of the facts as they are finally conceived—a consequence involved in the particular relation in which the percipient consciousness stood to the real facts. This relation again was due to peculiarly determined conditions of the act of perception which were at first ignored by the percipient, but being now noticed give the key to the whole situation. The *something* has become a certain objective reality *plus* a certain manner of perceiving it.

The cases of the warmth and the sound are similar. To the original impression of sound flowing from the bell are associated further impressions of its ceasing to flow in a vacuum; puffs of air rapidly repeated by a sirene producing a similar sound; of congestion of the head similarly causing it until from the various associations and disassociations due to these experiences the *something* flowing from the bell is held to be, not sound, but undulations of air; whilst the sound is seen to have a close connection with the brain; and finally the appearance of the sound in the bell is seen to result from the mysterious and inscrutable connection of perception with the brain, and the mechanical connection of this latter with the object by means of the tympanic membrane and the ear.

Taking these instances as typical we may say that the act of reasoning about a first impression always clings fast to the belief that the impression corresponds to something; but it multiplies the conditions under which the *something* appears until out of their mutual discrepancies a conception suddenly starts, of which the discrepant appearances—the original perception included among them—are seen to be only so many disguised *cases*. We believe all along that something is: our cognitive effort from moment to moment is always directed to answering the question *what* it is. The *what*, as I have frequently said, in these scientific cases shoots into the mind by a sort of "sport" among the ideas of the brain. It is never generically new but always derived from some already experienced order of impression, only not *obviously* present in the case in hand. In short, it is *transferred* from a remote experience to the one immediately in hand; and the sole way in which the new-born, definitive, and conceived *what* is made not to contradict the primitive provisional & perceived *what*, is by determining the former as a reality and the latter as its appearance to a subject standing in certain conditions. The sensation in ceasing to be held as the *what* of the reality in no wise ceases to exist. It exists with absolute reality as a sensation, and as such becomes a *sign that* something exists whose *what* is given us in some other conceived form.

You end by determining your *something* definitively and conceiving it rightly (after you have gone on to reason about it) through the ability which you have gained of conceiving it as one part of a world much wider than itself, with whose other parts, including the percipient subjects, it stands in relations now for the first time made clear and comprehensible. But if, at any moment of this procedure perplexities seem to multiply rather than diminish, our hope lies, not with Spencer in returning to the minimum of cognition, to the original psychoplasm, not in making it vomit out like an amoeba the nutrient contributions of experience which it has just begun to assimilate, not in saying that we can believe no further than that *something* is, and that we can never know it; not in this, but in going on to think still more and more, confident that if things be not radically self-contradictory, more experience and reason will fill the gaps which separate the experiences already in our hands.

In a word, the two elements involved in the most rudimentary action of consciousness, the element which says there is something there, and the element which seeks to define what that something is, are alike preserved in all the later evolutions of thought. But the determination of what the something is, becomes more and more perfect in proportion as the phenomenon we began with gets more and more embedded in that total mass of phenomena which we call the existing universe. The other items, which range themselves alongside of it and *with* which we know it when we come to *conceive* it through reason, are needed for its full understanding. One of these items tho't with the primitive must always be the percipient subject with his experiences. We start with a *something* determined as simple p. We end with a something determined as S——p——O. The O, granting the S, must be always capable of producing this particular experience p in the S, if it be acceptable as a true O.

But now you will rightly ask how it comes that if conceptions or wide inductions when true determine things more adequately than simple impressions, they nevertheless are more *fallible* than these impressions. The astronomer and chemist whom Spencer instances both yield to the perceptions and let the conceptions go. What constitutes the peculiarity of these instances?

To understand this we must reflect that the perception as such, can never be doubted. Considered as a perception pure and simple it *is* as it appears. Should a concept turn up affirming the *what* of the reality to be such that this perception cannot possibly flow from it, the concept must give way; because the reality present to us at any time must, as said above be able to produce this experience in us which we undergo at that moment of time. In fact, one may say that the essential meaning of reality is, That which produces these experiences considered as experiences. If the Conception we form of the reality be such that these experiences cannot be produced, then it must needs be a false conception.

In Spencer's instance of Venus we cannot believe that her presence on the sun's face would not produce the appearance of a black spot. In the case of the Chemist we cannot believe that a real 1 grain of matter would counterpoise the 2 grain weight in the opposite scale. We cannot believe that our senses in these cases are playing us tricks. The conception which contradicts the experience must then be denied, for the experience itself *can't* be denied.

In many cases of this sort the contradiction has proved temporary; further information about the conditions of the apparent phenomenon have shown that it was at heart a case of that which the conception postulated. Such spurious exceptions have always been held to be brilliant confirmations of the theories which at first they seemed to overthrow.

But leaving such mistakes and reverting to Spencer's point we have the following general rule that perception has absolute authority to declare whether something, viewed as *appearance,* is there or not. Where conception denies the appearance, and perception affirms it, perception must prevail. In short there is no contradiction possible save where reason and sense both make a deliverance about the appearance taken as such. Conclusions about the cause of sensations cannot contradict sensations.

See also *Lewes* Problem II, Ch. IV & Problem VI, Chaps. II & III
"On Residual phenomena" in Fraser's Magazine April '79, &
Pop. Sc. Monthly May '79

11. Notes for Philosophy 3: The Philosophy of Evolution (1879–1885)

[*On* First Principles]

Definition of philos.
Unknowable = "other world"
      farther experience.
Truth = totality
Panpsychistic view.
What is the *rest* of experience?
Ours is shot through with purposes.
So is animals.
But is it so with the larger world?—Is there *one* purpose?
We saw the difficulty with teleology
Not that things are produced mechanically, because that may be
    part of the purpose. (Football game.)
But What the purpose can be?
It exceeds us.
We can't forecast it.
Yet it *may* be there all the time,
And teleology is a standing problem.

Philosophy 3

1. *a)* What does Spencer mean by the Unknowable Reality?
   b) By what reasons does he prove its existence?
   c) Are the reasons good?
2. What is the relation of Part I to Part II, in the System.

3. Give the law of Evolution *verbatim*.
4. Compare the usefulness, etc. of a law of this kind with that of an elementary law like that of refraction.
5 How does he use "the persistance of force" to prove various subordinate clauses in his law? Compare Spencer's Persistance of Force with the Conservation of Energy.
6 Sincerely state at as great length as the time allows, both the sins and the merits in your own eyes of Spencer's attempt.
7 Name any one truth that has struck you most in the Course.

"Evolution" is an essentially teleological conception.
Elementary order, vs. resultant order.
"Weather."
Subjective illusion in teleology. fog. Harvard.
Is there an End of ends? A sovereign end?
Hypothesis merely!
Heterogony alternative.
Plural world more *naturalistic.*
Leave out epistemological proofs
Take induction.

Canst thou bind the Unicorn—hast thou given the horse strength?
Then Job answered the Lord & said Behold I am vile. What shall I answer thee. I will lay my hand upon my mouth.
Then the Lord answered Job out of the whirlwind, and said who is this that darkeneth counsel by words s̄ knowledge?
Gird up thy loins now like a man and answer me. Where wast thou when I laid the foundations of the earth . . .
Have the gates of death been opened unto thee?
Canst thou bind the sweet Influences of the Pleiades, or loose the bonds of Orion.

Sp.'s two cardinal faults.
Philos. of vagueness vs
    "   " clearness.
The first substantialist, fatalist but attractive by its semblance of unity. monstrous abridgement.
The second systematic, complex, but does not attain an illusory simplicity by wiping out differences.

My idea of substance is simply that it means that the present phenomenon is not all—that its existence involves other existences—

that in addition to its actuality it has a potentiality when it *is* not, and that such potentiality means that whatever *is* now calls for that phenomenon in its time & place. In other words, it is not an accident, but continuous with all the rest of things—*it is meant.* To be able to say of each phenomenon, this is meant by all that is would be to achieve the philosophic task and bind all that is into unity. It wd. moreover achieve the moral and religious task. For each phenomenon that confronts us is an occasion for our reaction. We know it by meeting it actively—in the *kennen* sense— If moreover in the *wissen* sense we know that it is meant here & now to meet us we know it all round. The christian who says our experiences are sent us by Providence to try us only says this in other words.

One important point then is this practical meaning of knowledge.

Another point which I wd reiterate is that relative to mind as a selective agency. If we consider our mental life as a series of representations we are always sustaining some and letting the others slip. The essence of character both in action & belief is the power[1] to sustain representations that are disagreeable. They tend to vanish from the mind—arguments against a temptation can't be considered. But he who will consider them will be guided by them. The will obeys the arrested motive.

Course next year.

*Mean*ing of facts of evolution.

One interpretation is materialistically monistic

It gratifies desire for unification. Each stage essentially identical c̄ the preceding.

Its disadvantages are fatalism, explanation of higher by lower (mind as correspondence to outward relations)—all right reduced to fact, and independent validity and prophetic character denied to higher emotional interests.

It is true that the material processes turn the mill wheel for the Ideal, but they only cast it off *inter alia*, and are themselves entirely indiff᪲ to it. They will end as Sp. himself allows by dissolving it out of existence again. They seem moreover incompatible with ideal. Status belli, utilitarianism

They are blind, they mean nothing, yet they are eternal, and the

---

1 WJ drew a vertical line beside 'power . . . year.' (148.18–23) and wrote vertically in the margin 'Force, reality, being, substance'.

things in which our emotional interests most centre are at their mercy. Either might = right, or right is powerless as such.

Now unity is but one factor of philosophies. Other emotional factors. Don't despise them for love of truth itself is one of them. They are postulates all.

Expectancy

Huxley's formulas.

Rule for the will.

Easy to see that latter demand leads to postulation of some real object commensurate with our highest powers. We wish a supreme determinant. Instead of which reverence for the All becomes nonsense, truth ceases to be a duty etc. If we act self sacrificingly it must be for the sake of something as good at least as self sacrifice itself, and more enduring. What shapes my will must also have power to protect me, if faithful, against the lower world. In short—right must also be might. Or to put it in another way, the *perfection* for which we act *must be eternal.* This the formula of moral creeds.

But why then any imperfection? why the need of evolution? Why not perfection from the start?

This the everlasting crux of religions. It only enlarges, makes universal the paradox of body & soul. Sin, Manichaeism.

Negative element. A "lack" etc invoked. Practically accepted as basis for struggle, with confidence of issue. Great theoretic postulate.

Idealism, does it help.

R $\longrightarrow$ experience.

But here as species we have the same division. What do we mean by calling some experiences *true,* real. Criteria of reality—Coerciveness—Read! (Simplicity, persistency, relations, effectiveness, independence, transparency).—a *plus ultra* the immediate phenomenon. This sorts the actual. And not only a plus ultra, but an *other* of truth. The immediate phenom. may be an error—the truth may end by correcting it—it lay lurking under it—independent of what at any given time the phenomenon was. Bricks. Bricks—will be judged *to have been.*

Now what is this truth, this plus ultra, this reality? in what state? As actual the true phenomenon is continuous with a system. As potential the truth is not phenomenal at all as yet, and still seems to be the condition of phenomena appearing.

In both ways we seem led to the notion of   continuity between the
    actual or potential and *s'thing* outside
       as regards the actual—system
           "   "   potential   "
also for all drift to *this* permanent phenomenon. Bricks again. The
    transitory and erroneous drops off.
But what is system? the assertion that the rest demands this—there
    is a place for this, it is meant that we *shd. so* perceive.
C. S. Peirce's criterion.
Thus the thing and a duplication of it in the shape of an it is meant.
    Why for us to react upon.
Christian providence sending us experience.

Reasons for Course.
Spirit of age—understand.
Need of Polemic treatm^t
Spencer's personality.
Only one mouthpiece.
Task of this century.
No progress idea before.
Hindoos   Hebrews
Chinese

fragmentary $\left\{\begin{matrix} \text{Greeks} \\ \text{Romans.} \end{matrix}\right.$ Anaximander
                             Cicero, Lucretius, Seneca

The Platonic & Scholastic philosophy prevented Christianity—"each
    after its kind."
Even the opponents—Voltaire
Rousseau.
Leibnitz
However—Geology
Kant—La Place.
Lamarck—Geoffroy
Diderot.
Then Science of Language beginning with Sanscrit. Grimm, Bopp,
    Benfey.
Religions & Mythologies.
Niebuhr. Assyriology.
General search for origins
At last Darwin.
Contemporaries

Haeckel
Tylor
Lubbock.
Fiske
Encyclop. Brit.
Ward.
Continuity.

Persistance of Force

Begin[2] by saying to what extent I mean to criticize Sp. I don't object to his saying we have an intuitive belief in the principle. If it is any thing at all it is intuitive. But the principle itself is so vague that I object to saying we can use it to deduce anything from it. Sp. does try to deduce his whole system from it. Just as if Darwin had tried to deduce his system from Natura non facit saltum.

The principles belong to the same class. Others are causa aequat effectum, Nature does everything by simplest means, &c. Aesthetic demands.

The preceding ones are false. There is another: Every change has a cause, or nothing happens without sufficient reason. These may both be expressed by saying: Nature must be completely *intelligible*, for as Helmholtz says they are postulates of our *understanding* of Nature.

That this ideal should be real is the hope of all of us. We assume it even where unproved, hoping it will be proved.

It is really the principle Spencer works with, esp^y in his chapter on persistance of relations among forces, although it smells so of the enemies' camp that he disguises it under another name.

To show how diff^t the Qu^{ty} of Existence or Persistance of Force principle is from it, we need only ask *why* Force or Existence can't change their quantity; and the only possible reply is "there is no visible reason why they should." Say it does change. Is the change + or − ? Like the so called proof of the principle of inertia. If anyone could provide us with such a reason, we should not have the slightest objection to admit the change. The change plus the reason would be intelligible.

2 At the top of the page, above the heading, WJ wrote in pencil 'Ch VI'.

Now the reason might be of many orders,—especially moral. Karma. "leave not a grease spot[3] behind." Aesthetic reasons, final cause, eternal fitness, all make happenings seem intelligible. The world is morally unintelligible, i.e. no sufficient reason for our judgment of better or worse, if fact is determinate. To reconcile the different postulates of intelligibility is the great task.

3 Defects:

1. He reverts to an obsolete standpoint in speaking of "Force" in general.

2 He calls it non phenomenal and yet says we can make judgment about its quantity.

3 He makes this judgment independent of conscious experience.

Begin by speak[g] of conceptions—and their aesthetic worth.
4 examples: Causa aequat effectum.

Natura non facit saltum.

Nature uses the simplest means.

Quantity of existence never changes.

You may say that the first three differ fm. the last in that *that* is a true divination, and verified.

Well, let's see!

Certainly the quantity of *any given phenomenon* changes. If candle blown out here, no other candle need be lighted in Madagascar. Stop walk, wake up, storm cease etc etc. No conservation of any *one* phenomenal quantity whatever.

It must be then that the sum of *all* phenomenal quantities is constant. When one sort disappears, another arises in equal amount to take its place.

But how can we know the equivalents of heterogeneous phenomena? Certainly not intuitively. They are sensibly incommensurable. Even when the same substantive phenomenon is affected by heterogeneous adjectives it is impossible to make equation. Is cold duration greater or less than hot? Is sleep with or without dream the larger? You can't make a sum of heterogeneous magnitudes: Beethoven's 7th Symphony + smell of 12 lbs of roast beef + rainbow, is it greater or less than a walk to Boston + a scientific discovery + $3.25 divided by an anthracite coal fire.

The only way is to find if possible some common *aspect* of all these phenomena and measure that. Let us suppose it possible to

---

[3] WJ wrote 'grease spot' above undeleted 'rack'.

conceive motion at the bottom of all the diff^t kinds of phenomenon. Motion is a distinct phenomenon which is measurable, and so is mass. Masses + motions regarded as effects of Force wd. then give a measure of this hyperphysical entity, and Spencer's dictum wd. then be that we have an intuitive knowledge, the opposite of which is unthinkable that the sums of all the masses, and of all the motions in the world is constant.

Were this true we ought to find that in the most familiar cases of motion we have an intuitive measure of equivalent quantities. Where we cause motions by exerting force of our own (since this is said to be the nearest symbol we have of the outward Force) we ought spontaneously to be able to judge how much more motion we should get as an effect if we doubled the cause, etc. At any rate when one motion expires in giving rise to another we ought intuitively to feel the equality of the two. Well, try.

I pull out an india rubber string one foot. Will pulling twice as hard lengthen it 2 feet?

I draw a boat by a rope with force of 10 lbs, 1 inch a second. Will 20 lbs move it 2 inches?

I throw a stone with a certain velocity. It rises 20 ft. Will doubling velocity send it 40 ft.

I blow into a tube and get a sound of a certain loudness. Will doubling blow give double loudness? etc etc.

I apply a certain force to a lever. It gives a certain motion.

I apply the same force to throw a stone. Can I tell from my lever experience how far the stone will go? etc

These cases show that we have absolutely no a priori or native sensibility whatever to the quantities of phenomenal motion which correspond to different exertions of our personal force, or of the ratios of different motions to each other, considered as effects of force.

We must utterly abandon the notion of an intuition of the same quantity of motion being in the world all the while, for the simple reason that we never are sure what the same quantity is under slightly diff^t conditions. It might swell or shrink indefinitely and we be none the wiser. It is then false that we can measure how much force there is by the existing amounts of motion.

Physicists, abandoning point by point the early notion of *sensible* amounts of force or motion have ended by discriminating a number of relations in which motions may be considered and consecrating a special name to each: velocity, momentum, vis-viva, force, work, etc. etc. All these are highly artificial, though absolutely precise, conceptions. Not one of them is a sensible notion, or can be said to enter into an intuitive judgment except in the vaguest most general way.

Now it is found that measured in each of these ways the quantity of motion in the world varies indefinitely.

Mass is another conception, which is found to persist in the world, it is Spencers intrinsic force. Here he is right. Qu^{ty} of existence $=$ number of atoms.

But, you may ask, what is the "Conservation of energy?"

Nothing like spencers dictum. It assumes certain very special conditions, and says that *if* they are fulfilled in nature then a certain sum of two quantities, neither of them intuitively expressible, will be preserved. The nearest approach to an intuitive consequence which the theorem contains is the conservation of *vis viva*. The[4] assumptions are that bodies move with rapidities dependent only on their distances. If time, quality or velocity affect motion, then theorem not true. If there be in world any fact which is not motion in disguise, then theorem not true. If forces produce rotations instead of translations, theorem not true.

Interesting to trace way in which Helmholtz reached theorem. Read.

Observe he does not say, "It *must* be true" but, "it must be true *if* we are to understand nature." It is a postulate we make for the practical benefit of our theoretic life, just as we might postulate indeterminism for the benefit of our moral life.

Identical with principle of sufficient reason which is only such a theoretic postulate.

This is what Spencer really has in view in his chapter on Persistance of Relations. That chapter a perfect muddle. Strange that an author whose corner-stone is the unintelligibility of things, should base his entire construction on the principle of sufficient reason.

Ask now, whether Uniformity of Nature follows either from conservation or principle of sufficient reason.

Not from the former if other than central motor forces are involved. Will force at least is *sui generis*.

---

4 Opposite this sentence in the left margin WJ wrote vertically, 'vol X p. 303.'

Not from the latter—free will, energy, karma.

Spencer keeps slipping all the while into the admission that our only suggestion of the existence of force comes from conscious effort. It is inconsistent that he should immediately deny all the properties which the prototype suggests. Idealistic theism is the only consistent philosophy of non-phenomenal force.

Conservation of energy treats the matter phenomenally and rests on the simplest empirical basis. The experience that perpetual motion is impossible, and that a reversible engine is the most perfect one which nature allows, is what lies under the whole deduction. But the notion of another kind of engine is conceivable and is constantly tried after. The hypothesis that it is not attainable is verified for all combinations of matter hitherto experimented on.

Give conception of world wh. grows more and more intense by cumulative moral effort.

Rythm of Motion

A body set in motion by force A may come within the sphere of
  force B.
    [medium, other bodies, position etc]
B may then destroy the body's motion.
  1. If after destroying it, B ceases to act, the case will be one of *no*
  rythm.
    [inelastic impact, stone to earth, ball stopped by hand]
  2. If B does n't stop acting it will send the body back again. And if A
  meanwhile has stopped acting this will end the matter: there will
  be *one cycle* of rythm
    [stone thrown up.]
  3 But if A acts again, and then B again, &c. we shall have *recurrent
  rythm*.
    [Every case of motion against elastic medium—including fluid.]
Nature's forces sometimes stop acting, sometimes go on, so that all
  three cases may be realized. Class 3 is very numerous owing to the
  fact that the attractions and repulsions which matter exerts never
  stop but keep reversing all motions against the direction of their
  influence. And every motion that begins must in this crowded
  world run counter to one or more of these *constant forces.*

Rythm of Motion.

means return either to same spot or to same level.

In case of single body in empty space no rythm.

In case where only forces are impacts,

    no rythm where bodies inelastic,

    but   "   "   "   " are elastic.

In case where position is a force (which is the real case) rythm comes, from the fact that the original motion exhausts itself in attaining the position, when the position itself becomes operative in reversing the motion.

An important point in this case is that the position force is *constant*. No matter how long the body moved may be *caught* in the position, if it endures and is *ever* uncaught the motion is reversed.

Elasticity is a case of energy of position.

All motions of bodies through resisting media are the same. The motion exhausts itself in crowding the medium into a violent position. This then undoes the force.

But if the force regenerates itself then the same rythm recurs.

Variations of no. of animals, supply & demand etc., come from the interaction of two forces both self reproducing. The plants produce the animals and exhaust themselves in so doing. Then the constant force of oxidation makes the animals die and the plants have time to regenerate.—The high prices produce the supply and lower themselves in so doing. Then the constant force of social need makes the supply rot away till the high prices regenerate.

Nerve centres exhaust themselves in discharging. They must then regenerate.

Take out the regenerating power, and you get but a single beat of the rythm.

In nature we have cases of single beat, of continued beat, of no beat. The dissipation of energy is a case of no beat.

Sp.'s peculiarity is that he describes the average statistical resultant of a complex lot of conditions and refuses to analyse the conditions.

The latter is what the scientific man does and by it is alone able to predict what may happen in a given case.

Napoleon, republics. Does a man or a nation exhaust himself in reaching a certain height and is there then a constant force to press them down.

The Direction of Motion[5]

Spencer's account of "social movements" is that men always do the mechanically easiest thing. As they notoriously often do the mechanically hardest thing, the law has next to be explained as including future things: Men do the thing which will "cost least," or involve "least exertion" in the future, even though the first step have to overcome the maximum present resistance, as when tunnels are built or emigration resolved on. But future facts can't determine present movements *mechanically*. A mechanical force must be *present*. We must frankly say then that there is *no* law connecting men's social movements with the present mechanical resistances and that what determines "social movements" is not their actual mechanical ease or difficulty, but *ideas*, among which ideas, of course, those of ease and difficulty, either present or future, figure. But here again there is no law; for the idea of gaining future ease sometimes does, and sometimes notoriously does not nerve men to attack a present difficulty. To get a law, we must say, not that a social movement follows the idea *of* the greatest ease, but that it follows the *easiest idea*, even though that (on occasion) may be the idea of making the most tremendous effort. And since ideas correspond to brain-processes, we can translate now into mechanical terms by saying that a social movement is always determined by the *brain-molecules* tumbling in the easiest path, even though the consciousness attached be one of greatest exertion, and the social movement take the line where resistances are thickest. When asked for empirical evidence that the brain paths followed are the easiest, we have none. We can only say "they *must* be easiest because they *are* followed." In other words Spencer's whole show of establishing the law inductively is not only needless but harmful, for it leads to the intolerable confusions of the chapter, in which future obstacles are spoken of as if they acted mechanically as present checks; in which the openness of paths in one country is made to determine movements over closed paths in another; in which such ideal things as "cost" figure as mechanical forces, and ideas are spoken of as if they immediately pushed and pulled not brain molecules but outer things; in which

[5] At the top of the page, above this heading, WJ wrote in pencil 'Ch IX'.

finally elementary processes are never clearly abstracted or distinguished from gross results. It would have been much better policy simply to postulate in a single page the law of least resistance as an elementary law needed for the establishment of a thorough-going mechanical philosophy. To such postulation no one could interpose the slightest objection, as a working hypothesis to be judged later by its consistency with all the facts.

Concluding Lecture on Spencer

Sp. psych. 492 & 493, 453

1st Princ. p. 156

passages illustrative of the way in wh. he assumes that what is not cognitive can by rearrangement end by becoming cognitive. If he wd. simply assume this there cd. be no objection—a matter of faith. But he pretends to explain it. His passages against Kant, Hamilton etc, have no meaning unless they signify that he positing an outward really does show how its cognition arises, whilst they are lost in bottomless unreality. His mediation between Kant & the empiricists seems to show this. Read, & criticize

Now there are several ways of stating the cognitive difficulty. Read Phenomenalism, 1.2. Chloroform article Mind Oct 1878

Will return on Saturday to the question of what the otherness is.

At present g'al estimate

His learning—Fiske

Lack of style, side lights, like student.

Best in details. Essays. expression   Most important point relations. Biology. affirms unity of consciousness. Inherited habit. Forensic power—aggressive and popular form.

We have all got to attack the problem of the *meaning* of the facts of evolution. The evolutionary *philosophy* is a monism. Nothing comes new—no new essence, and so far as it *dwells* on the common substance it shares the blame of all monisms. So far as it reduces the higher to the lower, "survival" etc—the inverse process to Spencers development of cognition—it is vicious. Historically it has tended to this. Philosophies of selfishness etc.

The higher has no *meaning* but the lower. Brute fact is right. No thing prophetic in cognition—no teleology. This the great point involved in materialism.

Now common men care not much for explanation or unity. That is but one factor of philosophy. They want to *expect*

They want a rule for action which shall be congruous with their power—a rule for their will

And a sanction for that rule—an authority to enforce it.

> A harmony of might & right
>
> perfection is eternal.

Now mechanism evolving its products does not this.

Spencer's First Principles

Part I.

Chap. I.

What is the purpose of his illustration from the various forms of gov.?

What do all the beliefs about gov.^t imply? ("subordⁿ of individ. to social requiremts." p. 9)

How can we generalize our procedure here, so as to find truth? p. 11 & solve conflict between Religion & science?

Why does he feel sure that the source of religions is deep seated & not superficial? 14.

Whence comes sentiment of R.? Two suppositions? But what follows from either? 16

What is Science? How does he describe it?

What kind of a truth must that one be which is common to the two? (Abstract)

Bibl. Kant-Müller p. 351+

Hamilton Discussions—I. & Lectures   Chaps. 39, 40, & Appendix III.

Mansel, Lectures II & III.

Monck's Hamilton Chap V.

Mill's Examⁿ Chaps VI, VII.

Chap. II

He describes symbolic conceptions & the way in wh. they shade into adequate ones.

—*How* does he then proceed to distinguish betw. the symbolic ones that are legitimate & those that are vicious? 29

Origin of Universe—3 hypotheses—

What are they?

Why is self existence unthinkable? (31) (it is existence s̄ beginning—
infinite past time)

Why is self creation ditto? 32—3 (Change s̄ cause & infinite past.)

Why creation by ext. agent ditto? (Whence the elements or the
emptiness? Whence the creator? *His* self existence leads to same
difficulty as that of world.)

What common difficulty then in all the 3? (self-existence, involving
unlimited duration?) 36!

Nature of Universe—neccessary supposition of 1st Cause, finite or
infinite.

What objection to thinking it finite? (37)

It must be *what* next. (Independent)

What obj. to that? (38)

It must consequently be Infinite & Absolute. 39

What contradictions between 1st Cause & *Absolute*
            between causality & infinite?

Why must first cause operate by freewill & consciousness?

What contradiction here? (*Absolute* consciousness)

The Absolute? what does he say of it?

Wherein do religions agree? (a need of explaining)

Discuss the Infinity Question

Grote's Plato vol i, p 96+. Mill on H. last pages of Chap. XXIV
Renouvier: Crit. Rel. 5me Année pp. 248, 353
———— Logique Tome 1$^{er.}$ pp. 40–99
Wundt. 4teljsch. I. p. 80
Lasswitz. ib. 329
Lester H. Ward. J of Spec Phil. Oct 1881, p 381
Geo. S. Fullerton, ibid January 1884. p. 38

Chapter III.

Why can't S. & T. be entities [1. no attributes]
       [2 neither limited nor unlimited]

Why not Kantian forms of the mind?
       [contradicts consciousness.—Form & matter]

What results? [incomprehensible]

Matter? [Inf. div^n not *realizable* (terminable) in *tho't*:—Limit to
division ditto. (Possibly there in *fact*)]

Solidity? [abrupt change of speed after impact]

Boscovich's theory? [unthinkable]

Assume atoms—what wd. disciple of Boscovich reply? [atom's cohesion due to force.]

What results? [Matter absol. incomp. choice betw. opposite absurdities.]

Motion? Why can't we think absolute M.

Transfer of M.? What is transferred? [Neither a *thing*, nor an *attribute*.]

Motion & Rest? [Zeno's]

Force used in lifting chair. [absurd to suppose like our sensation, yet unimaginable in any other way.]

Action of force, why unintelligible? [because it must be *at a distance*, even if ether be assumed, its lack of mass neccessitating g^t distance betw. its particles.]

Gravitation indiff^t to fulness or emptiness of space.

Consciousness' chain? Cannot be infinite, but why not finite? [we know neither end. Last end wd. not know itself.]

Self? Why not impressions & ideas? ["something impressed."]

Remains that it is an *entity*—Why unjustifiable by Reason? [C. is a dualism & in self consciousness, which is which?]

Jas *Martineau*: Essays, vol i. Sc. Nesc. & Faith. p. 171. Review of Mansel p. 213.

J. B. *Stallo*: Concepts of Mod. Physic. Tho't.

John. *Caird*: Philos. of Religion Ch. I.

Malcolm *Guthrie*: Mr Spencer's Formula of Evolution, Part V.

G. H. Lewes: Problems, vol ii, Problem VI, Chaps II & III

Spencer. Replies Essays vol iii

Jas. F. Ferrier, Institutes, §I, Props XIII to XXI.

Chap. IV

Analyze product of tho't. *What* is explanation? [assimilation to general class]

Is this a limited process? [yes! by summum genus.]

What is Mansel's arg^t from the process of knowing to prove we can't know Absolute & Infinite. [Consci. involves *distinction* betw. one object & another—involves *relation*. 76–78]

What arg^t does Sp. add? [*recognition*]

   [Then inf. and abs. being insusceptible either of relation, distinction, or classification, *cannot* be known.]

Now he takes up an important def^n of Life & Mind. *What* is it.

How now does it prove our knowledge to be only of the relative?

    P. of B. Pt. I, Ch. IV, V, VI

    P. of Psych. Pt. III

What do Hamilton & Mansel call the Absolute & Infinite? What grave error? (negation of thinking)

What does Sp. try to prove throughout rest of Chapter. [That Absolute is a positive obj. of Tho't.]

What arguments does he use? [1. term can't be denied if *meaningless*.—2 Residuary consciousness of *what* is conditioned.—3. Correlative.—4 Momentum of tho't.   5. Abstract Existence common to all concepts.]

What is the only measure of validity among beliefs? [persistance]

Why then has "Absolute" the highest validity?

Do you understand him to mean merely that *we* practically are unable to attain to knowledge of Absolute? Or rather that A. & knowledge have an eternal & essential repugnance. So that A. can't know itself

Chapter V.

One may either deny ultra phenomenal or say we can attain to its knowledge. But Sp. says we must think the ultra phenomenal[6] exists, & yet cannot (not accidentally we—but it *cannot be tho't*) think it *as it is.* (p. 99) *Do you understand* him to impute this to our knowledge as a *defect* or not? cf. 108, 110 bottom

(Ferrier's Institutes. p 404–7)

Is he right in calling phenomena "manifestations" of the

    Unknowable. $\left[\begin{array}{c} \text{p. 100} \\ 108 \end{array}\right]$

Suppose I say the seasons, the tides, life & death, sleep & waking are due to a *principle of periodicity*; or that chemical actions are due to struggles of *affinity.* *What* will be the religious part of my assertion? Suppose I invoke *Force.* *How* must religious element be made complete? [p 103–105]

Would a purely scientific account in terms of phenomenal relation be adequate accord[g] to Spencer? [No]

But what is really, apart from Spencer, our feeling that such laws are inadequate? [demand for more *comprehensibility*.]

---

[6] WJ wrote 'ultra phomemal' above undeleted 'Absolute' and drew lines around the words. WJ's 'phomemal' has been corrected to 'phenomenal' by the editor.

Does it warrant his unknowable? [No. On the contrary, it repels it. Cf. p. 106]

[Give physicist's account of Force]

Suppose we grant Unknowable. *Is he right* in calling it "higher" or "greater" than anything we know?

Can it be called *impiety* to say we won't worship it unless it have qualities with which we have some kinship? (Mill's to hell.)

How about watch simile? p. 111 (Martineau 208)

[Sp. really an Atheist. Folly of pretending to satisfy Religion with such negations. Gov^t composed of submission & authority—you take S. I will take A. Pope—Slaves.]

S. H. Hodgson. Philos. of Refl. Book I. Chap III

Chauncey *Wright*: Philos. Disc. p. 43

F. *Paulhan*: Revue Philosophique, VI. 270

H. *Vaihinger*: Vierteljsch. f. wiss. Phil, II 188.

Fiske's Cosmic Phil. Pt. III Chs. I, II, III. esp. Ch. III on "Cosmic Theism"

Criticism

Establish fact that unknowable is a *derationalizer.*

Most metaphysic principles invoked to rationalize.

Spencer gives us Phenomenal World *plus* unknowable.—two mysteries instead of one. (infra p. 17 [*ed.,* 165.1–15])

Obvious advantages in getting rid of Unknowable if possible. (Confessed uselessness 86)

Examine Spencer's Proofs of its existence. He seems to consider it equivalent to each & all of the following notions.

1. The *self-existent.* 36 Neither neccessarily unrelated nor unknown.

1 Self existent

2. *First Cause,* 30, 43. ditto.

3. The *Unity* of things, 41   Bosh.

4. The *Cosmos as completed* under the forms of Space, Time, Matter, Motion 48,–58. This the notion of something *phenomenal.* The difficulty lies in the contradiction between completion & infinity. (Postpone.) But whether completed or infinite, the existence of the phenomenal world proves nothing as to Absolute or Unknowable.

5. The *Summum Genus.* 73, also 50. This is the s. g. of the phenom-

enal, with whose Nature we may be absolutely acquainted—
nothing more to be known.

6. *Ideal Truth*, 88. Postulate of more to be known. Exact opposite
of his Unknowable absolute.

7. *Bare abstract Being*, named also consciousness of an indefinite
(88) raw material (90) residuary (91) objective reality (93)
unformed & unlimited (94) general existence, or something
(95) which persists indestructibly in all our thought. This is
the *grammatical subject*, about which we assume that the
more we think, the more we get to know. So far from being
unrelated to tho't, it is nothing but the minimum of tho't.
We must suppose it present to all consciousness, as its starting
point, the bare form of *objectivity* of presence. Cf. Mind III.
556. S'ts it means *Matter*. Guthrie "Formula" 169

8. *Correlative*. 91.

9. *Power*, Substance. 98–9. Analogy of Soul. Is it Unknowable?
By its essence it is related? Does it exist?

10 The *Noumenon*. Ding *an sich*. Not even this is irrelative. We
know it is. Observe Sp's. strange theory of cognition. Every
step forward from admission of its existence *falsifies*. Common assumption.

Noumenon a gratuitous assumption. Kant. Why may not things
exist in relation? Post Kantians. Renouvier, Hodgson, Mill &
Bain. Emerson. "Other world! There is no other world." At this
pen's point lies the whole of reality. "Natur hat weder Kern noch
Schale."

Its genesis moreover is from the Truth Ideal. It is a perversion of
this. A dog in the manger. That Ideal postulates a Reason beyond, an *explanation*. This is the one thing that Sp's Unknowable
cannot be. Take watch. Suppose watchmaker says your watch is
relative. Here is an absolute one wh. will not go at all. Sp. says:
attainable explanations are relative. They postulate absolute one.
I present it in form of Unknowable, debarred by its definition
fm. being any expl^n at all.

Is there then no Mystery? Assuredly: plenty—*3*

First the mystery of *more* truth to be known.[7]

---

[7] Following 'known.' WJ wrote '(Skip to p. 18 [*ed.*, 165.23–31])', and on the next
page, numbered 17, below the heading 'Spencer's 1st Principles', which he partially
deleted with blue crayon, he wrote '(*Omit this in order*)'. It is likely that these notes
were used several times and the instruction to skip to p. 18 was introduced after the

The peculiarity of Spencer's attitude is that he supposes 1st)

that the real truest being of things is in se, or out of relation, ignoring the other possibility that being in relation may be the only form of being.

2nd) That if our knowledge is to be considered true at all, it *ought* to be knowledge of this being, which nevertheless is precluded by its essence from ever being known even to an infinite intelligence. This leads to the grotesque conclusion that knowledge *ought* to do something which in its nature it can't do. One may well reply that ignorance of the Unknowable is no defect, there can be no ignorance of that which is not potentially subject to be known. Ferrier

3rd) That we are driven to suppose this unknowable Entity in se as a relief to the mind from the unexplained acceptance of the Cosmos. If the Unknowable assuaged our demand for explanation of the given this would be an ample cause for believing it. But its presence only baffles still more our reason. We have not only our given cosmos then, but our Unknowable being also, to account for. Every rule of sobriety should lead us then to cut short the labyrinth of inexplicability, and content our selves with that of the simple given-ness of the Kosmos as an empirical fact. Confessed uselessness p. 86

No doubt it is the living sense in everyone's breast that this fact has something more in it than is borne in upon his consciousness at any given moment, that he stands simply expectant of what it will bring forth, and passively at its mercy, unable by his thought to foresee its course in other than a tentative sort of way,—no doubt all this is why Spencer's asseverations awaken in the mind of every reader who takes things in an easy hospitable way, an immediate echo of adhesion. But I insist that the readers postulate is merely that of *more to be known*—not of still more unknowable. Those philosophers and religious Mystics like Pascal Hamilton & Mansel who thought that to our understandings there were *contradictions* in the Known, and so insisted that there must be a world where our minds would be changed and we should see the eternal verities face to face with an entire set of new faculties, were in a far healthier and more strictly reason-

---

first delivery. Thus, the decision to retain the deleted portion (165.1–22) is based on the fact that WJ gave this lecture sometimes with the deleted portion and sometimes without.

able state of mind. For they did not enthrone self contradiction in the heart of Being, in the essence of knowledge, as Spencer does in saying the only thing that ought to be known is the only thing that can't be known—they admitted it, but as a stage to be outlived.

But we have seen that they need not bring self contradiction into our data—only the *inexplicability* of their being data. Some time back I said that this might be dealt with either by exorcising the question as illegitimate, by ignoring it, or by answering it . . . . . .

1 to 9 all in relation to mind

  7 to its properties.

Noumenon hypothesis

  motives

    make World less of an accident

    explanation fails.

? Things are in relation

  Brute fact mystery.

Givenness of Cosmos the only probl.

Mysticism, Wordsworth's peace of God

Active nature.

limit to powers scales drop.

lack

dog.

Dog in Laboratory.

Not a technical point at all. Is the world only unfathomed, or unfathomable? Aristotles *Wonder*. Read Jackman 1884

You can decide as well as Sp.

Region beyond science. *Aberglaube*. Gives accent & character to life according as we treat it.

Spencer uses it to forestall criticism on the shortcomings of his matter & motion universe. "Whatever I don't tell you is unknowable." It consecrates the dryness in him.

But which way is the way of treating it that is of most worth to our lives?

Read Carlyle S.R. 284, 286–9.

Conclude in favor of leaving it *open*.

    ——————— End of mystery no 1.

—But suppose we find out *what* it is, and suppose it to be completely transparent,—*a God*.

There still remains the mystery (No. 2) *that* it is, instead of nothing.

Existence *überhaupt*—not "*self-existence*" as Spencer puts it p. 36 is mystery number 2. The givenness of the Cosmos. The mystery of *Fact.*

Maybe a vicious question. (Romanes)

Sp. apparently supposes answer to it, then defines answer so as to be no answer.

I venture to suggest: The *that* of things is knowable *a posteriori* but not *a priori. Fact* is only known *after* the fact, i.e. your will by me, I know *that* it is, I know *what* it is. But I can't get in front of it & say what it *shall* be. So of the Universe—it conditions our intellect but is not conditioned by it.[8]

Empiricism—we find. But this is not the Unknowable.

("Am Anfang war das *Wort.* am anfang was die *That*")

Perhaps the whole opacity of *being* means only its numerical *otherness* from the tho't that knows it.

(S^t of Rat^y VIII, Mind vol. iv, pp. 340,–6)

3rd mystery, or rather self contradiction. The given Universe appears to us in infinite form.

Infinite not a constant or a quantity. Name for an endless *process.*

However much is actual, more is possible.

Composed therefore of actual + possible parts.

Solution: to so conceive time past, space, composition of matter, &c as to admit of actuals + possibles.

This impossible if they are *reals* extra mentem.

Possible if they are *thoughts.*

God's actual tho't of Universe, only finite.

So far as he thinks the past, he *starts* somewhere with it.

Infinity of Cosmos: *Wundt, Lasswitz* in Vierteljsch. f. w. Ph. vol i *Lester H. Ward* in Journ. of Spec. Phil. Oct 1881, p. 381.

Part II. Chap. I.

Paulsen, in 4tljsch. I. 15—Greek and mediaeval ideal that of omnitudo scientiarum. Descartes, Leibnitz, Wundt.—Locke & Hume began—Kant completed the change of base which made questions of knowledge the main ones. For Kant Knowledge *ex principiis* meant something different from K. *ex datis.* Later idealists pur-

---

[8] In the left margin WJ wrote vertically, 'Don't know how being *made itself. Did* it?'

sued the way ex principiis. Science retaliated by cutting off, so
that only unfinished sciences and insoluble questions were left to
philosophers. Now a revival—but the philosoph von Fach . .

Chap. II.

Can philosophy start by assuming *nothing?* (No)
What is the remedy? (assume *provisionally*—justify or refute later)
How justify? (Show *consistency*)
        [Hypothesis—circle. 539–552. True method.]
What are the data we must assume? (Objective likeness & unlike-
ness corresponding to subjective.)
What is the principal *subjective* 154 difference? (That between
vivid & *faint* manifestations)
What *objective* 156 difference does he conclude that this reveals?
    (Two powers, object & subject)—ego & non-ego. p 154.
Are these two powers *ultimately* two? (No! manifestations of *One*
    p. 157)
What other differences separate faint from vivid manifestations?
                                        Exceptions

1.	vivid—faint	——	p. 144
2	originals—copies	——	p. 145 (& emotions)
3	Two unbroken series	——	not quite
	Each *self* coherent	——	but also with other
4	Cohesions more dissol-		
	uble in faint order	——	matter of degree
5	Vivid unmodifiable by		
	faint.	——	p. 149
6	Vivid order has vivid		
	antecedents, faint or-		
	der faint ones.	——	p. 151
7	Faint order has trace-		
	able antecedents, viv-		
	id not	——	about equal in this respect

(Element of *coerciveness* left out)[9]

Spencer on the Data of Philosophy

Spencers object to *justify* belief in world extra mentem by showing
    how we come to believe it

[9] In the space between this line and the last two lines ('Same . . . –XIX' 169.24–25)
on fol. 27, WJ wrote and circled the note: 'pp. 28 *& 29 [*intrl.*] [*ed.,* 168.34–169.23] on
separate sheet'.

Bain, Mill, seek to *explain it away* by same showing. (B's E. & W. last Chapter)

All point out certain *marks* in our representations by which they segregate themselves into groups.

The question is do these marks point to differing realities beyond themselves?

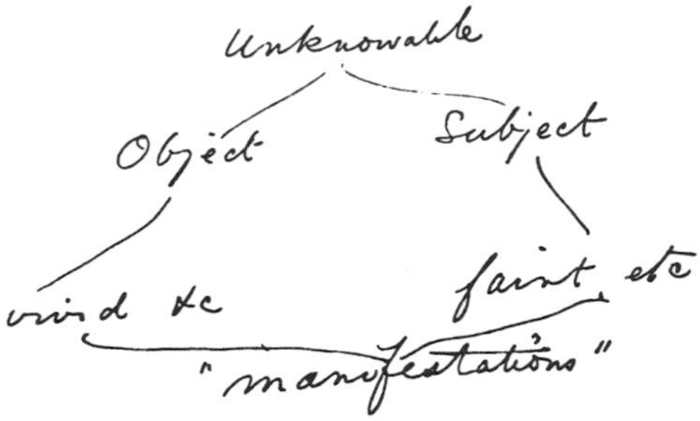

Called on p 157 "one Power"

Called on p 154, "2 Powers"

Or do they themselves *constitute* the differences?

If the latter, we are idealists, since they are but differences in the behavior of representations.

[handwritten diagram: Unknowable at top, branching to Object and Subject; below, "mind &c" and "faint, etc"; "manifestations"]

If the former, sheep parable.—Humming birds! Masters! Inference only of what is generically known.

We must have "revelation."

Impossible to evolve cognition out of the non-cognitive. This is Sp's attempt.

It must be begged.

Every sensation cognitive in form.

Itself numerically other than its content.

Minimum S : O

Same argument more expanded in P. of Psych. Part VII, Chs. XI–XIX

Chapter III

(Comment on "insanities of idealism" p. 159, & on his "going back" on his Unknowable 159)

What means the word *real*? (persistent *"in consciousness,"*—forsooth why *in c* only?)

How does he square phenomenal reality with doctrine of Unknowable? [*"Equivalent for us"* 162]

What is the purport of the rest of the Chapter? (Space, Time, Matter and Motion are notions traceable to experiences of Force. Force is underivable and is a direct manifestation of Unknowable.)

Explain the extraordinary farrago of this chapter by a desire to put himself on record in case of his death before Psychology came out.

Vulgar Scholasticism. Entity behind entity.

Chap. IV.

He begins by certain remarks on the mental condition requisite for
the perception of neccessary truths. *What* are these? (mental
structure & deliberate & definite representation p. 174–5.)

What confusion has made possible diff͡t opinions about destructi-
bility of matter? (176)

What is the real datum of consciousness? (177)

What "phenomenon" of matter do we perceive to be indestructible?
("Force" = weight)

(Weight varies with distance etc. It is a phenomenon, whose indestructibility is simply a well verified hypothesis. Lavoisier.)

Recommend B. Stewart: The C. of E.–D.D. Heath: the D. of E.–
J. Clerk Maxwell: Matter & Motion.–P. G. Tait: Recent Advances in Physical Science.–E. Mach: Mechanics.

Chap. V.

What does he mean by the C. of M. (apparently (187) the *continuance* of a metaphysical "principle of activity" now shown by
translation, now by strain.)

Is translation continuous? (No (183))

What is translation? (*Sign* of an existence 183)

Of What is this "existence" correlative? (of our muscular activity)
("*Invisible*" activity, "*latent*" do, strain, tension.)

What does he finally call this? (Force 188.)

(Metaphysic method! What is gained?)

Read Comte's first lesson, p 87–8

Controversy in Nature vols IX, X. Bowne, Studies Ch. V.

Birks, Chaps with same names. Wright pp 77–87

Chap. VI

Two kinds of force—*which*? (space occupying, intrinsic, passive;—
active, extrinsic worker of change)

Can P. of F. be *proved*? (No)

Why?

What is the F. that persists? (Unknowable correlate of muscular
effort.)

(mass—motion—position. Is anything gained by the metaphysic
treatment.)

Insist on fact that *phenomena are* lost. The scientific postulate is that something shall be invariable, but *what?* See *Delboeuf.* Rev. Phil. IX, p. 137 + (1880), & XIII, p. 610 + (1882)

Chap. VII.

What does he mean by the "p. of r." (Uniformity of sequence & coexistence among phenomena.)
(Note on p. 196)

Comment on Chap. VIII
Correlation
No intuition of equivalence.
Heterogeneous q^{ts} incommensurable.

Conjecture that these may be *motions* in disguise
Force = musc. motion
Comment on 192 note, & *d.*
No intuition of q$^{\underline{ties}}$ of motion.
Read III.
Motion varies.
What does n't?
What law, relation, value is permanent?
Mariotte, index, *g.*
Conservation of energy.
A conjecture.
Its postulates
Its expression
Its proofs—no reversible engine.
Read Helmholtz.
Postulate of intelligibility.
Not "it *must* be true," but *if.* IV. etc.
Principle of sufficient reason.
Variation of weights.
World shall be intelligible the only demand.
Relations among forces.
Principle of symmetry.
Sp's strange inconsistency.

Chap. IX.[10]

What is its thesis?
    "   two corollaries? (Movement continues in same direction 226.

---

10 In the left margin WJ wrote in pencil 'Leuba | VII, 309'.

Direction hardly ever straight. 227. Sp. fails to distinguish. Some movements bank up obstructions, some sweep them away. Drive hole in clay. Crowd at theatre exit. Filtration under pressure. Homoeopathy.)

Give some of his examples.

What is his a priori proof? (246–8)

This, so far as parallelogram goes is no deduction from P. of F. And so far as final move^t in direction of larger of 2 forces goes, it is merely a definition of "larger" as applied to "Force."

Does it ever help us to say which *is* larger force? in an untried case? It wd. do so if we could use past experience immediately, If e.g. force *a* was previously larger than *b*, we cd. then say it wd. now be larger than *b* and produce motion in its own direction.

Where forces are merely of impact this is the case.

Distinguish forces of detent from these.

In an immense number of phenomena, *discharges* lie between "cause" & effect.

These discharges are locked up by resistances which may be very small for the right *kind* of key, but insuperably large for every other force.

In such cases the internal resistance to the discharge must be carefully distinguished from the external resistance it overcomes. (The pyramids of Egypt are a great ext^l res^e to human muscles. A king's breath however is adequate to discharge the muscles to their construction. Vastly greater natural forces would not so discharge them.) The most *explosive* might also be the most *sensitive* dynamite.

Where then we say "the motion is in the line of the strongest force or the least resistance," we must, where forces of detent are involved, recognize that the greatest *outward* resistance may be the one overcome, and the smallest *outward* force be the one to do it.

Chapter X

What is the thesis of Chapter?

What means "rhythm"?

Will stone thrown on mountain ledge & weathering be rhythm?

    You returning to this room?

    Regulus to Carthage?

    The transformation of impact into heat?

    Of *any* motion into another?

Are fluctuations of price, taste, religious beliefs properly *motions*? (only by analogy. If we map the change as a line then each of its extremities will be an extreme of the change, & the latter can be symbolically represented as motion in the line.)

Can we deduce in any particular case from Sp's law, *how, when,* or *whither* the return of a motion shall occur?

Can persistence of force tell us that the original motion must be reversed?

All Sp's law amounts to is that on the whole few bodies come to an absolute rest in this world, that when one motion stops, another begins, and that sometimes the two make a rhythm which may under certain conditions be repeated. Usually when a body has got into a snug position, something comes along and knocks it out.

What are the conditions of Rhythm?

Difference between statistical law and causal law.

Sp's law like Hegel's, or Emerson's of Compensation. 5 Nature's No. All things go in 3's

Note to p 253. Lester H. Ward i. 160. Holt.

Mortality of living things. . Sexes at birth. Decay of Empires.

Can't we in motion get at conditions? Assuredly. See Beilage.

There is nothing in the nature of motion taken by itself which should make it rhythmical. On the contrary, law of inertia . . .

It can only be made rhythmical by some force outside the moving body, which, when the latter has gone long enough in one direction, stops it, & makes it return.

Chapter XI.

He recapitulates these laws—do they severally or together make a philosophy? Why not? [Philosophy = "synthesis."]

["*Combined consequences.*"]

What general formula would be a philosophy? [Law of redistrib. of matter & motion! p. 270]

Note here the frankly materialistic position =

Law of change of position.

Chapter XII.

What must the entire history of anything include? p. 278.

What is first foreshadowing of law? [all changes of position imply either concentration or dispersion of matter 279]

How about the motion? p 281

What mean *dissipation* & *absorption* of Motion? [Assume either]

Define "integration." 282,–4. (both accretion & condensation.)

Note the *neccessary* character of the two aspects—If we take a certain distribution of matter, its changes of position can only consist of approaches and withdrawals. And approach towards one is withdrawal from another.

Approach is called what?

Withdrawal   what?

Chapter XIII.

What are the *secondary* re-arrangements he speaks of which make Evolution *compound*?

Note that the problem with him always supposes "incident" forces.

What internal state favors secondary rearrangement by incident forces?

[Contained motion.]

Examples? [Shaking—heating helps. precipitation etc.]

How is it with the changes where internal motion is very great, as in liquids & gases? [Instable]

_____Solids? [Small]

What is *optimal* matter to show these changes? [*Plastic*—p. 292]

How do chemical compounds illustrate this law?

How do organic tissues show themselves to be the best possible seat for evolutionary changes.

What does he mean by "the imperceptible"? 278

                by "concrete form"? 280

                "diffused state"? 280

Opposed[11] to this philosophy there always exists a philosophy of ultimate kinds. So many natural forces, so many chemical elements, so many laws of nature, so many kinds of sensation, so many forms of mental action as volition, cognition, feeling and sensation, so many principles of motivation as self-love and brotherly-love, conscience and sensuality

Bunch of asparagus

[11] Inserted into the bundle of notes in #4492 are two separate leaves. The first (174.26–32) comes after 161.16 ('. . . infinite,') and is numbered '6a'. It is in Alice James's hand except for the last line. The second (175.1–25), written on recto and verso in WJ's hand, comes after 162.3 and is numbered '7' and '8'. These two leaves are clearly out of place and their proper locations were not established. Hence, they are placed at the end of this section.

The position of tension may be kept indefinitely. But a supervening stimulus may unclamp the materials, and the fall ensue at any moment.

Traps thus prevent rythm or postpone it indefinitely and make it irregular.

Rythm no general law!

Now postponement of rythmical return is the very essence of all highly evolved arrangements. Energy is *stored*, and ready for the proper occasion.

Take organic matter. First it has no "retained motion" such as Spencer talks about. That wd make it hot. It is simply a trap.

Single cell. The matter has got accidentally knocked into such a trap that when certain parts fall they occasion rise of other parts which take their place as in candle flame.

Ciliary or amoeboid movem⁺ comes from fall but is condition of rise in food. Effect of exercise.

Gemmation etc is a disintegration but is a condition of more aggregation.

Higher animals = republics, of which the rise of some depends on the fall of others. Just as growth of child depends on destruction of mothers milk cells, so destruction of stomach & pancreas cells is condition of alimentation of body. Muscle cells get food. Nerve cells waste in starting muscles.

Feeding, dodging, breeding.

In all this not a grain of integration after

[*On* Data of Ethics]

Kant's form of action, perfection, happiness, survival, knowing "the Truth" etc, Schopenhauer's *neminem laede*, etc, love, justice,

To be a basis for ethical reasoning the good must be acquiesced in by both parties.

If one denies it, there must be more reasoning to prove it, by showing that its goodness follows from some higher good of which it really is a case.

Somewhere there must be an uncriticized good, which is simply obeyed.

To treat an alleged good as not objective but as relative to a certain given sensibility, is really to envelope the ethical judgment in a scientific judgment.

And to make it collapse or lose its authority & coerciveness.

The good of survival, from the moment the instinct of self preservation is reflected on, (as it is by evolutionists) lapses thus from an objective uncriticised good into a fact relative to subjectivity.

The deepest truth ceases to be, "we must survive" but becomes: "we feel that we must survive."

If we *don't* feel so, nothing can coerce us to except a further ethical proposition: "to feel so is itself good."

This is the proposition Evolutionary ethicists ought to prove.

But dont prove.

The natural way of proving it would be to show that what survives has an intrinsic worth, an ideal perfection which makes its survival good. But for Evolutionism all worth means mere furtherance of survival. The survival can borrow no excellence from the mere means of its realization since it lends to the means whatever goodness the latter show.

For evolution *whatever* survives has all its qualities *ipso facto* made good.

If we call the qualities objectively good we may then consent to the survival.

Spencer's confusion: he avails himself of popular belief in the qualities, says survival's law maintains these qualities, ergo survival must be good.

The Germans clearer headed

Read Hellwald: enlightenment consists in "seeing round" and no longer being duped by Ideal, which we once for all now know as a mere fact of subjectivity.

Curious junction of evolutionary materialism with pessimism in Germany.

But no matter: let us accept survival as Ideal.

Still ambiguous as to practical conclusions. Objective evidence all for war. Read Hellwald again.

Even if we abandon complete status belli, ambiguity eno' remains.

When shall we begin to be peaceful? Wipe Zuloos & Modocs out?

All things have small beginnings, the best have the biggest endings.

Suppose we recognized a tribe etc.

And after all, can final state be a practical guide? Sidgwick—punishment?

Is not the absence of friction an ideal like that of Kants dove.
Is not pain an essential factor.
Richness? tragic? pathos?
Read Stephen.
Can we ever approach equilibrium?
Mediaeval & brute joy.
Pessimism a disease of satisfied epochs & classes.
The more we approached Spencer's equilibrium, the more thorough
   our scientific back look & outlook, the more chance for vanitas
   vanitatum! & cui bono?
Survival principle *in*ferior to elder ones, because not eternal.
Admits of arbitrary application being an indeterminate standard:
   Very little diff. betw. one man & another &c.
Granted equilib! *whose* shall it be?
Most of all tho', Sp. sins in reducing ethical to scientific proposition.
We need either the absolute or the infinite ought,—good.
Read Mallock: p. 111–3
The earnestness, the infinite appeal to energy etc will be gone.
Religion means: All is not vanity.

12. Notes for Philosophy 5: Psychology (1880–1881)

Sentimentality

Cases where sensations in becoming ideal form sentiments stronger
   than the parent sensation in determining the will.
1. We do a disagreeable thing now rather than look forward to it.
2. Valuing the potential more than the actual. Our liberty rather
   than its use, as in marrying &c.
3. The miser.
4. Rousseau glows with ideal parental love.
   French radicals
Enthusiasm for the abstract quality may coexist with perfect insensibility to its particular manifestations, as where the goodness
   of God is used for denying all goodness in his creatures.

The way Carlyle, Ruskin, Kingsley, Froude and all that fry idealize the past and dont see in the present the very qualities they prate about.

As where we do a thing now because we shall be glad to have done it.

Or where we enjoy a present experience the more for representing the pleasure with which in future we shall look back upon it.

A sailor goes to sea for the pleasure of landing.

A woman has all her own sound teeth extracted so that she may be relieved of the dread of it for some future day.

Escape from fear, acquisition of the feeling of safety, is gained by many a present sacrifice.

See Bain's Chapter on "Ideal Emotion."

Rather *deserve* a thing and not have it, than have it as a matter of course.

Rather keep the *power* of having or doing a thing and go without the thing than have the thing "over" and lose the power. (See also no. 2)

13. Notes for Philosophy 4: Contemporary Philosophy (1881–1882)

Mill on Induction

The psychological process of Inference in all cases is the same.— from presence of A to affirm B.

Ignore for the present cases where A & B are a priori syntheses, felt intuitively to belong together.

Attend exclusively to *empirical* couplings

Couplings of particular concretes inconstant and unimportant.

The important couplings are those of general terms. *Taine* II, 292

They form laws of Nature.

That Nature has such uniformities is an empirical peculiarity, very useful for our intellectual ends. *Lotze* Metaphysik §58.

Planes of cleavage. *Venn*

As we stand opposite Nature the great question is which characters

are the uniformly coupled ones? Which laws the general laws?
Very hard to answer. "Discovery."

No rules or method, but look about and guess.

Mill's "four methods" are methods for *testing* not *making* guesses.
This is Mill's first great blunder.

His second is talking as if all uniform couplings were "causal"
couplings. *Sigwart* II. 419

Most "laws of nature" relate to coexistence of properties, specifications of processes &c. that are ill-described in causal language.
Definite proportions, specific heat, Kepler's ellipses, etc mammals
have 4 chambered heart.

All these laws so far as we consider them may fail; they are generalizations of incomplete induction, throwing on the future only
the light of analogy.

Mill's third mistake is to treat "Induction by the four methods" as
something superior to analogy, simple enumeration, hypothesis
&c.

Each "law" of coupling is only true provided Nature be "uniform"
in this law.

Now Nature's couplings notoriously variable in point of uniformity.

Uniformity when absolute can only result from *necessity* of coupling, *zusammengehörigkeit* of terms.

The mind's postulate of Uniformity covers a postulate of rational
belonging together.

If *A* & *B belong* together, a single case of their coupling lets us perceive it to be a uniform law.

The result is that instead of seeking couplings that are *uniform* our
problem is to find such couplings as are rational, essential, necessary. Then uniformity will be "added unto us."

Mill himself talks of "strong" & "weak" Inductions, "derivative" vs.
"ultimate" laws.

Let us ask then what the strength of a coupling consists in, and how
we may get the strongest ones possible.

Mill gives the answer, vol i. p. 368–72: *Strong* are those inductions
based on experience of a *kind* that, through wide diversities, has
been found invariable. The law gains the strength of its *kind*, of
what it is.

"Weak" inductions can be made stronger by *deducing* them from
strong ones, p. 370.

Deduction thus enters into the heart of the Inductive method.

Supposing it possible to "derive" all subordinate inductions de-
ductively from some few supreme couplings our system wd. be as
strong throughout as in those couplings.

(According to Mill those wd. be non-rational juxtapositions.

According to us, belongings together or a priori syntheses.

Reserving this difference,) speak of the deduction itself.

By deducing, Mill means "composing" from "causes." Chaps. vi, x,
xi, xii, or "subsumption." p. 546 vol i

Example of composing
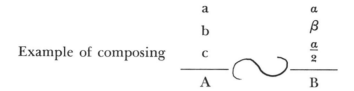

We must conceive *what* A is, and what B is. (e.g. planets are bodies
started tangentially to Sun but drawn towards it. Summation of
these movements gives ellipse).

Example of subsuming. Falling body is a case of two material masses
attracting. Pump a case of fluid pressed more by wgt. of outer
than by elasticity of inner air. Small pox recurring every dozen
years a case of consumption of fresh fuel. (Contrast with "natural
motion, abhorrence of vacuum, law of periodicity")

Here again we must conceive *what* the law is, or *what* one of its
terms, or both, are.

The deduction consists in substituting a coupling of this new *what*
for the coupling of the original term, terms or law.

It is a substitution of more general concepts & their couplings for
less general ones & their couplings.

Of a genus for a species, so that the genus of the genus, (or what is
true of the genus, its predicate) becomes the genus of the species,
(true of it, its predicate).

Of parts & their couplings for wholes & theirs

Diagram

a carries b

this is a

this carries b

(Respiration-burning, muscular contraction-discharge, earth-glob-
ular, a magnet, light-undulation)

The couplings substituted are more general (Chap. XII) "Elementary laws."

The top-most of all are the so called axioms, a priori syntheses
according to us, generalizations according to Mill.

But whatever they be mark that even by Mills confession *the form
of deduction from them* is the ideal form of expression of the
inductive philosophy. We substitute the deductive expression of
a coupling for its direct inductive expression wherever we can.
We refrain from the form "a *always* carries *b*" and adopt the form,
"*a, as an m* must carry *b*."

So paramount is the need of the deductive form that to gain it we
make the strangest mathematical hypotheses. (Open works on
optics, heat, gases, electricity & magnetism.)

Now observe that the living moment in the whole process is the
moment of classing, subsuming, saying *what*, picking out character.

Mental decomposition, breaking up totality. (vol i 437; ii, 199, 201,
208, 209 Whewell, Nov. Org. 44, W. J. Atlantic Oct 1880 Bowen's
Logic 410)

Observe also that Character picked out is an *extract*. The whole
scientific process is an *elimination* of what is immaterial to your
purpose. The purpose is special. The substitutes are partial, they
mutilate the living truth. Molecular world *vs.* religious man's
world. (Sentiment of Rationality p. 19) But however partial, they
are true as far as they go. (Bain's Logic, Induction, 141)

Now take highest couplings! Are they "belongings"? We said yes to
some. (Taine)

How numerous? Arbitrary answer.

Take physical world. Axioms of geometry, mechanics, laws of attraction & repulsion, privative numbers motions and collocations of
atoms, make a plurality.

Add mind; laws of sensation, laws of classification; laws of logic,
another pluralism. (Mill, Chap XIV, §2, xxii p. 117. Sentiment
of Rationality p. 21. Bain's Induction Chap. XII.)

System of categories.

Where is the unity.

Time, space, Ego. *Continuity.*

How much does this exclude real chance?

Monism and rationality.

Induction = *Re*duction to a concept from which *de*duction will be possible.

14. Notes for Philosophy 4: Ethics—Recent English Contributions to Theistic Ethics (1888–1889)

Resumé of My Lectures in Ethics 1888–9

Preface

Martineau's point of view is narrow. The relative worth of springs of action is a subjective question altogether, a question of *merit*. Martineau himself confesses that we must also consult the objective consequences to know the full wisdom or rightness of an act. The best spring of action is the will to do the best you know. This gives merit, however imperfect the knowledge. The belief that there *is* a best, which must be ascertained and acknowledged, seems postulated in the very fact of beginning a systematic ethical enquiry. There is a moral kingdom, we say, but what is its constitution? The broader ethical question is, then, "what *things* (of any sort) are good?" not merely "what springs of action are good?"

1) Things are either immediately admitted to be good, without discussion, or there is discussion. To *prove* a thing good, we must conceive it as belonging to a genus already admitted good. Every ethical proof therefore involves as its major premise an ethical proposition; every argument must end in some such proposition, admitted without proof.

2) How come such ethical propositions to be admitted?

This question is psychological. There are innumerable ways in which men have been led to their judgments that things are good and bad. The satisfaction of any desire or impulse is good, its frustration bad. From the conflicts and harmonies between our instinctive constitution and the circumstances of our life there must necessarily arise innumerable goods and bads, social & physical. And remote things (either real or imaginary) by association with immediate things, come to be esteemed good and bad themselves.

3) Analogy leads us, moreover, to admit that apart from the instinctive preferences and repugnances which are neccessary to life, there must be others arising spontaneously or by "accidental variation" in minds which contain these. I firmly believe that we have preferences inexplicable by utility, or by the direct influence of the environment, preferences for certain kinds of behavior, as consistency, veracity, justice, nobility, dignity, purity etc etc. Those who contend for an innate moral faculty are therefore right from a *psychological* point of view.

When, however, they go beyond psychology and utter the *ethical* propositions that the absolutely best is what that faculty approves this (like other ethical propositions) remains subject to the conditions of all ethical discussion. It must be either itself admitted as ultimate, or if doubted, proved by an argument which contains another ethical prop^n that *is* regarded as ultimate. (See 1)

4) The ulterior prop^n usually bro't forward is that whatever seems to us *obligatory* is better than what seems not so. The intuitive school thereupon says that our ethical system can be founded very simply: Things are good in proportion as they are *obligatory*; and the sense of obligation attaches to certain goods inexplicably. Our estimate of the intuitive ethical systems must thus depend on what we think of the *feeling of obligation*.

5. I discussed this feeling psychologically. Kant calls notions of obligatory goods "imperatives." But impulses and imperatives run together, and the same act may seem imperative to one man, but not so to another. Neither will the criterion of giving us no peace till we do it, or that of returning to plague us if we do the opposite, serve to differentiate moral from non-moral or even immoral impulses; for *any* act may be imperative in *these* ways. Moreover there are two sorts of obligation, 1) internal and 2) external. 1) The inner dignity of an act has an urgency of its own. Our outer responsibility for it has another urgency. The two obligations may conflict. Martineau admits that the "total wisdom" of an act is a compound of its dignity with its utility—so that more utility with less dignity may sometimes be best. We sometimes must 'pocket' our dignity for moral ends. Our responsibilities also may conflict, among themselves. The feeling of obligation taken alone is thus too wavering and fallible a thing upon which to found a definitive system of ethics. Its

data must themselves be compared, discussed & judged. But how?

6   What does one mean by seeking a *system* of ethics? It means that one admits the distinction between apparent goods and true goods, and demands that one's own ethical judgments shall be true. Now nothing can be good at all except as *felt* so *by some consciousness*. So far as I feel anything good, I make it so. It *is* so, for me. Good & bad therefore can exist in a universe in which there is even one mind pronouncing ethical judgments. These judgments themselves can't be *true* or false, however, unless there are at least two such minds, of which one is *authority* for the other.

When therefore I seek the *true* good, that implies that my judgments are already subject to a preexisting authority. Mine must conform to his.

Two minds, of whom one is authority for the other, are enough to constitute a systematic moral universe. But what constitutes authority itself? I can find nothing but the *claim* on the one part and the *submission* on the other. Where both elements coexist the authority may be called *perfect*, otherwise imperfect.

7   Where rival claims or refused submissions arise, the only possible way of restoring harmony is the way of submission to some pontifical authority whom both parties acknowledge.

The moral character of the universe is thus *created* by certain relations amongst persons. These relations moreover are created by the *wills* of the persons. Abolish either the wills or the persons and what remains in the universe is non-moral.

8   Our philosophic quest for the real system of goods, is a quest for that system which has the real authority behind it. In a subjective sense we enter the moral kingdom, the moment we become serious ethical students. We make the assumption that there *is* a moral kingdom, with an authority in it which we must seek; and so we leave ethical skepticism behind us. The objective problem, however, (what things are goods for that authority?) remains untouched.

9)   Prima facie, goods form a multifarious jungle. Must we so leave them, or can they be unified? If there were any quality by participating in which all concrete goods are made good, that would be a unifying and subordinating principle. Of all the proposed *summa genera*, pleasure and perfection have the best claim to be considered.

So far as enjoyment is a part of perfection, & so far as the consciousness of perfection brings pleasure, these two standards do not conflict, but involve each other.

10 Inquiry presently shows us that, whether we take a unifying principle or whether we treat goods as irreducibly plural, in either case we practically bring up against problems insoluble by a priori rules. The abstract best would be that *all* goods should be realized. That is physically impossible, for many of them exclude each other. The whole difficulty of the moral life consists in deciding, when this is the case, which good to sacrifice & which to save. The difficulty is the *good excluded*; and exists where pleasures and perfections are the goods as much as when these have no common denominator. "Whose pleasure? which perfection?" etc etc. shall be sacrificed. If we say the pleasure of the *best* person, or the *best* kind of perfection etc. we are right back on our problem again, by what test shall the best be known.

11 The solution is by Royce's "moral insight"—consider *every* good as a real good, and *keep as many as we can.* That act is the best act, which *makes for the best whole*, the best whole being that which prevails at least cost, in which the vanquished goods are least completely annulled.

Criticize "Science"

It may show some good (e.g. eternal happiness, escape from pain on earth etc) to be *unrealizable* or make some other very *explicit* (e.g. adjustment, survival etc).

No psychologic fact as to how an ethical judgment arose can prove (or disprove) its validity, unless combined with the ethical major premise it is good (or bad) to obey a judgment so arising. Sidgwick, Mind I, 52; V. 216 XIXth Cent Feb. 1880.

The ultimate question always remains: *Shall* I obey it? *Shall* it bind me? *Shall* I hold it good?

This leads to next point—*Obligation.* Goods as mere objects of preference *versus* imperative goods.

Kant's hypothetical and categorical imperatives.

The *effectiv*eness of a feeling of obligation depends on the circumstances. *If not effective,* what we mean by calling it an obligation is that we haven't heard the last of it.

An imperative motive is one which we yield to, even if only to escape the uneasiness of its urgency. It may be moral or non-moral, even immoral. It gives us "no peace" till obeyed.

A *morally* imperative motive is one

15. Notes for Philosophy 1: General Introduction to Philosophy (1890–1891)

Hard task! Use of Philosophy
Touchstone to Corin.
Metaphysics—the word.
Knowledge exhaustive & final
"Completely unified" vs. "partially unified"
Knowledge of the most *general*.
Schopenhauer as example of (1. W. a W. II. 189
Comte   "   "   (2 Principes, 87
2 tendencies { ontological, transcendental (1
             { positivistic, naturalistic (2
Noumena—phenomena; Absolute—relative.
Things in themselves; things for us.
God; substance; Will; Unconscious; Unknowable; Anima Mundi.
Agnostic vs. Gnostic transcendentalism

Lecture II.
Agnostic: Spencer "the Reconciliation"——
Gnostic: Scholasticism, Descartes   Leibnitz   Hegel.
Positivism: Littré, Principes, p. 66–7
          Fiske I, 25
Shortsighted talk!
Go back 300 years   Copernicus denied, circulation of blood unknown, optical glasses just invented, laws of motion undiscovered, world supposed to be 5 or 6000 years old, common pump could n't be explained, no thermometers, no physics, no chem-

istry, no gravitation, spirits moved the planets, substantial forms explained corruption & generation, alchemy & magic reigned.

5 *men* would carry oral tradition back to this time, just as 120 to black unknown of race.—Descartes, Newton, Voltaire, Dalton Huxley

Kepler Astronomia	1609			
Bacon's Nov. Org	1620	Modern	Copernicus 1543	
Harvey	1628	Science		
Galileo Dialogs	1632	begins		
Descartes Principles	1644			
Newton's Prin	1687			

We don't realize how young science is, or how ridiculous the thought that its race is run. I hope to show you that Philosophy *does* make progress.

The emancipation of the sciences from Scholasticism was wrought by Philosophers

Kepler, Galileo, Descartes, Bacon

Atomism—conservation—

mechanical view of life—evolution, determinism

Read Ward: Mind XV, 219 April 1890

Moreover as soon as questions are settled they cease to be "philosophy" & are "science." "Philosophy" thus always is left—

Evolution

Logic

Psychology

As sciences we must leave them

They assume—Philosophy criticizes

These most general ideas & relations which they assume *we* must study, as Reality, Space, time, Cause, Motion, Change, Knowledge

Lotze's book

Lectures on History of Phil.

Kant: All the interests of my reason unite in 3 questions: was kann, soll, darf etc.

Cousin's 4 types:—

We may say: Materialistic & Idealistic for matter, and *rationalistic, mystic, and skeptical* for manner.

(So far as one takes *revelation* one is skeptical, or at least non-philosophical)

The One & the Many

In earliest antiquity contrast between materialistic & idealistic way
was crudely & energetically defined.

		hot cold wet dry		
Pre Socratic	(water)	slim ἄπειρον	(air)	
	Thales,	*Anaximander,*	*Anaximenes*	
	(number)	(Being)	Monism	
	Pythagoras,	Xenophanes,	Parmenides Zeno	
	κοσμος			
2 centuries.	Heracleitus	(change)		
Thales *b.* 640	*Empedocles*	(4 elements	mingling & separation φιλία	
		(roots)	νεῖκος	
Empedocles *d.* 432	*Leucippos,*	*Democritus*	(atoms)	
	Anaxagoras	χρήματα, ὁμοιομερῆ & νους.		

Decay & generation
Evolution
Heracleitus—change fire strife universal order— Patrick
Empedocles elements roots, Evolutionism
Democritus. atoms void soul Gods. perception—many worlds—don't
   vex.
Anaxagoras,
Socrates   *b.* 469   *d.* 399
Plato   428   347
Aristotle   384   322
Books: πάντα ῥεῖ
Socrates disdains physics—moralist.
Always talking of "cobblers"
His method. Dialectic. Midwife. example: Theaetetus. Jowett III.
   381
Concepts.   knowledge = virtue
His piety
His character   Jowett I. 535.
His martyrdom   *ibid*. I. 466
His Demon
No writings
Xenophon
Antisthenes   b. 444
Aristippus   b 435
Plato—Morning! His genius. Journeys: in Sicily. Dionysius sells him
   in Ægina

All the better because of unsystematic form.
His writings. Dialogues.
S's antagonists not men of straw—the worldly side: III. 77; II. 182
His philosophy:

    Ideas = universals. μέθεξις
    Senses despised, I, 409–427
    Anamnesis.
    Timaeus.

The type of Idealists: logical Realism, apriorism, absolutism, spir-
  itualism, teleology, transcendental ontology, mysticism.
Plato vs. anti platonists! Sophists.
Beauty I. 526
Aristotle   Stagira 384   342 to Alexander   Lyceum
           After Alexander's death fled to Chalcis
His works.   Agst Materialism   Agst. Ideas
          ὕλη Individual real. εἶδος
          4 causes. Entelechy. God.
Nature   Eternal universe & genera, cycles
         No atoms no void
         qualitative change
         teleology.
         Imperishable stars in circular motion
         Changing things embodying opposition
         Fifty six heavenly spheres
Man   3 kinds of soul.
         Perception through body memory imagination
         Common Sense αἰσθητήριον κοινόν
         Its seat the heart
         νοῦς no organ
Ethics

    Good perfection of activity
    For man virtue = activity of reason
    theoretic vs practical
    the mean—bravery, temperance vs Socrates
    4 cardinals

Read his ideal of philosophy
He objects in limine to Plato's ideas as *redundant* and as *stagnant*.
Plato's *geometrical* ideal.
For Aristotle things *happen*

He objects to materialism that they happen for purposes.
The fulfilment of each things end is the cause of change
World filled with things tending towards their ends.
Supreme unmoved perfection the cause of all motion.
In each thing 4 causes:
Concrete alone real
Yet universals only known.
—*ante rem*; —*in re*; —*post rem*
Nature
No void or atoms
qualitative change.
teleology
universe & kinds eternal—cycle—
Spheres.
God.
     Man
Three kinds of soul.
    Ethics.
Chief end? welfare
Proper work
Mans is energy of soul accordingly
Habit of virtue.
Virtue a mean
Chief virtues
Read passage
Anti Socrates.—full life richer etc.
Deficient in gentleness

Aristotle   384 322
During Aristotle's life (d. 322)
1) Skepticism   Pyrrho   360–274
2) Stoicism   Zeno   350–258
3) Epicureanism.   Epicurus 341–270
1   Arcesilaus, Carneades   Sextus Empiricus (Alexandria)
2)
    Both aim at practical life.
3)
Stoicism a Religion. God the soul of the world
Vivere convenienter Naturae.
Heraclitean Physics.

M. Aurelius. Cicero de Finibus. Seneca   Arrian   Epictetus

Like modern transcendentalism—virtue for its own sake. People say
the jews bro't religious ideas—all they bro't was intensity.

Read Epictetus pp. 50, 114, 53, 82   56, 104, 106, 146. Emerson

Epicureanism = Materialism—Atoms—void—soul made of atoms—
no Gods—no immortality—

Refined pleasures—serenity—

Avoid pain! anaesthesia

Easy going & strenuous mood

Utilitarianism

Lucretius, Pliny jr, Caesar, Horace

Philo BC-AD

Plotinus Porphyry	3rd century
Augustine (Proclus)	400
Scotus Erigena	9th century
Anselm	11th "
Abelard	1100
Thomas Aquinas	1225–74
Duns Scotus	1274–1308
(Dante 1265–1321)	
Ockam	1300 1347

Augustine founds Xian theology

Anselm's Ontologic proof—
    credo ut intelligam

Study of Aristotle begins in 13th century

Rapidly becomes official.

Scholasticism

Read C. S. Peirce N.A.R. CXIII, 451+

S⁺ Thomas

Read Leo XIII's Encyclical
   "   Extracts from contents

Catholic Education to day.

Read more contents—Bible & Aristotle

Innumerable principles all self evident.

Substance only one of them.

Distinctions

"Real" distinctions

Duns Scotus says in a man the *thisness* is really distinct from the
matter & from the form

Thos. says the matter gives the thisness

Everything depends on what you mean by "really"

Not *separable*.

Practical consequences—angels having no material *thisness*, D.S. says are each a species

Trans substantiation.

Thos says real accidents.
    aptitudinal inherence

Occam & nominalism.

In sum, no doubts as to 1st principles.

Composite system.

Idealistic as opposed to materialistic. Ontological not phenomenal

Includes a sort of materialism, therefore not idealistic in modern sense. Substantialist.

Kills atomism—strenuous.

Finally breaks down by ponderosity.

On the whole much richer than any ancient philosophy.

Weak spot: matter & form!

H.O.H example.

Lotze's aim is to show that we are led to consider that all real beings are parts of One supreme reality which is the whole fact. He thus stands amongst those who in seeking what is the deepest ground, the ultimate reality of truth or face towards the concrete total, and say *that* comes first; other things are explained through being implied in it. He neither builds up the total out of its parts, supposed to be absolute existents, like the atomists; nor does he face backwards (like the Eleatics, Spinoza   Spencer etc) towards the most abstract element of the total, and say the source of reality is a Being or Substance or Unknowable, or Unconscious, or God (Spinosa's) from which things emanate.

⟨L⟩otze Chap II.

We don't immediately perceive the Thing, as owner of the qualities

We perceive it no better in a simple element than in a compound thing.

Sensible qualities are affections and actions

The Thing itself can't be conceived after the pattern of a quality

For each quality is homogeneous and each "thing" unfolds a great variety. Unity *in* variety.

Nor will abstract quality determined do

Microcosmus Bk IX. Chap I. (vol II, 578)

Don't mind scaffolding—get result!
Essence—existence—position.
Thing = Subject + properties:
  Water, man, gravitation.
Properties = acts & affections (Helmholtz)
Unity of subject = *law.*
Law a mental conception.
We want a *ground* (p 40) for law
Belonging together.

Montaigne dies 1589
1543 Copernicus de Revol. condemned 1616
Bruno burnt 1600
Kepler's Astronomia nova 1609
Vanini burnt 1618
Bacon's novum organum 1620
Galileo's dialogs. 1632 trial 33
Hobbes Leviathan 1651
Descartes *b.* 1596 Discours 1637. dies at Stockholm 1650
Renaissance   Reformation
Philosophy of all nature
Dubito ut intelligam
His life. Read from method
His character—Galileo
"Method" Geometrical, non syllogistic analytical geometry
Cogito
God
Things
Soul distinct from body—adversaries—eucharist
Bête machine
2ndy qual.
Vortices. | laws of motion *gravity*
Optics refraction. Perception
Physiology | Reflex action | Brain pineal gla
Meteorology, magnets.
Rainbow
Passions.
Great popularity of the system.

"What we conceive clearly and distinctly to belong to the nature, essence, or immutable and true form of a thing, may be said or affirmed with verity of that thing." Existence belongs thus to God's essence; therefore he exists.

Body a machine. Reflex action.

Soul distinct   Eucharist reply.

"Parallelism or automatism"   Spinoza   Leibnitz

Materialism.

Circulation

Brain—pineal gland

Psychology of perception.

Refraction

Rainbow.

Embryology

First phil. of Evolution in modern times.

A priori method—slights experiment.

His results differentiate into "Science"

Leaving the unsolved behind

Gassendi

Descartes broke thought & extension

Geulincx & Malebranche

"Interaction of substances"

Separate things! Where is the unity?

in God?

Wordsworth—Bhagàvat Gita

Spinoza | Pantheism | Lotze

Walt Whitman

Goethe.

Sp's. Life. 1632–1677

Saint—Demon!

Atheist Acosmist. Gottestrunken

Not a physicist.

His works   His style

p. 104   108 Geometrical ideal   men = triangles

His God. =   ∽ ✗ ∾   = Nature

Space & thought—parallel—harmony

No evil 185, 239–40 No freedom

No final causes 182

Self preservation by adequate ideas

Summum bonum = knowledge of God. = knowledge of things by
    their causes
joy & sadness
pity repentance hope fear all bad
so is esteem & humility   shame—227–8 230–1
knowledge of evil is inadequate (240)
reason can do all that passion does
Equanimity 247   255
Death 242
God's impossibility 272, 273
Intellectual love of God. From 284 onwards

Retrospect—materialistic & idealistic systems
    Platonism
    Atomism
In Descartes & Spinoza the material and the ideal worlds break
    apart.
Spinoza unites them by a *machtspruch*
The peripatetic unity is gone!
No final causes in the physical world!
Leibnitz a philosopher of reconciliation.
1646–1716 State of Germany
Autodidact—Livy—300 hexameters at 13   at 15 decides for Car-
    tesian
Studies law Court of Mainz
Hanover—Berlin—Austria—
            Peter the Great
Politician—Egypt scheme—Paris   London.
Conciliation of Churches
Librarian   Historiographer
3 vols records of middle ages
Hist of Brunswick
Code of internat¹ law
Academics.
Mines—mint—geology
Mechanics—submarine boat
Calc^g machine.
Universal alfabet
Diff¹ Calculus.

Theodicy—monadology. N^{x} Essais
Non-polemic character.
Mode of work & person Fischer 279; 31
Easy to give catch words:
1) Monads = live atoms simple substances—alive—indestructible
    their perceptions
    their hierarchy
2) Unconscious mental life
3) Identity of indiscernibles
4) Continuity
5) Preestablished harmony: mechanism with teleology
6) Evolution
7) Neccessary & Contingent truth
8) Optimism.
One permanent thing had been accomplished.
Mechanical view of Nature.
Things explained—their changes,—generations and corruptions—by
    separations and aggregations of *more elementary things*—at bot-
    tom *atoms*
These *are*; other things come & go.
But what are these primal *things*.
Resistance? a relation! a *something* which determines other things.
No *quality* for Lotze's reason! simple homogeneous.
Blind, dead, "matter"—how does it make other blind dead matter
    change?
Leibnitz makes these things alive.
Chess game! Contrapuntal Concert! Read Monadology §7–15
    Change inward à la Lotze
Teleological view.
Matter an *object*. Read Nx Es. 14–16
L. does n't explain *how this is all done.*
Dwell on Lotze's distinction.
But the *nature* of what *is* done is freed from contradictions
A kind of thing which *we* know

Idealism in modern sense begins.
Substances are minds.
"Things" are mind's *objects.*
        Locke. 1632–1704
Make connection with former *skepticism.*

His life—Oxford. F.B. 47, 45, 61 Essay 512–3

Greek lectureship

Rhetoric do.

Censorship of Moral Phil. takes him to aet. 30

Flees "Whig."

Studies medicine—enters service of Ashley (Shaftesbury) family

Politics in and out. Shaftesb. Chancellor

    Sec. of Presentations

       "   " Council of trade & foreign plantations

Flees to Holland

Essay 1689 Letter on Tolerance

Lady Masham

Newton, Boyle etc.

Liberty of Printing.

Reasonableness of Xty.

Epistles

Comagi

Commission of Bd. of Trade.

Linen Trade of Ireland.

Character F.B.

Read

Innate Ideas

Simple ideas. "way of ideas"

Personal identity example of practical spirit

Substances nominal essence—compare with scholastic view. Read
   328   439

Locke still believes in *real essence* or substance.

Progress towards idealism, 395 (secondary qualities)

Berkeley 1685 b Kilkenny—1753 Oxford

Dean of Derry 1724

1729–32 America

Bishop of Cloyne 1734

Theory of vision 1709

Principles 1710

Read Mill.

Immaterialism

The table is *there*, the room *here*, *this* table, this room, both real
   with the plenitude of reality, because there is no *more* real.

They are there, but they are there for *us*—that is Berkeley's doctrine.

Panpsychism—Nothing is but thinkers & their objects or ideas. When we know what all the other thinkers are thinking we know the *whole* of truth.

Hume 1711–76 (Huxley)

Skepticism—Descartes—Locke—Berkeley

Hume like an antique sk.   precocity—letter to D.—Treatise 544

Miracles—Immortality—Suicide—Belief

Cause p. 60–2

Ego. 533+

Easy-going—death—Wesley—Johnson

All this clearing away brings relations between thoughts into view.

16. Notes for Philosophy 10: Descartes, Spinoza, and Leibnitz (1890–1891)

Look up Bouillier, Caird, Mahaffy, Cousin, Rosmini Whewell, Lange, Mach, Dühring, Bacon, Stöckl's history, Kleutgen, Renouvier, Windelband. Substantial forms.

D's argument for God from our imperfection is analogous to Spencer's for the Absolute.—It will prove the existence of anything conceived as violating our experience

Ask somebody to collate passages about clear & distinct.

Opposition of the Church   Fischer, 404–5

Descartes philosophy agrees with Paulsen's idea
By making body = extension, Physics becomes Mathematics

1635 French Acad. founded by Richelieu.
1636 "Cid" published
1637 Discours de la Methode, & Essais pub^d
1666 Acad of Sciences founded by Colbert

D. ignores law of action & reaction, Fischer 394.

Say early that I must talk as if the monarchical conception of God was absurd.

God bro't in usually to carry off any absurdity—Could n't God have so arranged it?—useful as inlaying imagination.

How utterly lax the distinction is between obscure &c & clear etc—It seems s'times as if it were invented only to enable him to affirm what he likes. Cf. Hobbes 221. His "Clear" ideas are so highly abstract (produced expressly by rejecting all that we learn from the senses) that most men can't tell whether a proposition concerning them is either true *or* false, & are at the mercy of anyone who makes a sturdy affirmation. e.g. p. 188, 185 VI, VII VIII & IX, p. 43 158 266 280

Read pretty early the *demands* on p. 184

The lumière intérieure is like la grace divine. All who have it are sure, but not all who are sure have it.

Circle of reasoning 250 288—resulting in God's veracity being a warrant for *memory* and not for our certainty of clear and distinct perceptions. No harm in a circle.—on the contrary it is inevitable if this be a universe. One element is on condition that the other is—you must have the whole or nothing; and the question is do you assume *that* whole.

His meditations pursue the analytic method

modal entity? look up! (291,–3)

In discussing the ontologic proof, don't forget my own so often felt but never formulated aperçu like Pascal's *sait qu'il meurt* etc

Descartes

1596 born
1612 Leaves la Flèche   spends a year at home in gentlemanly exercises   no books
—13 goes to Paris with Valet. One year in Society—gambling etc.
   14 Mersenne.
   15 Hides himself in Paris for study
   16
   17 aet 21. Goes with Prince Maurice of Nassau to Netherlands. Breda 2 years of armistice.
   19 Bavarian service   winter at Neuburg (Pfalz)
   20 Hungarian campaign. Vow. leaves army.

23 ⎫
25 ⎬ Italy
  ⎭

|

28 St. Germain & Paris
28 Seige of la Rochelle   royal staff.
28 goes to Holland—stays 20 years.

|

48 Visits England, Denmark, Paris 2 or 3 ts.
1637 Discours
  41 Meditations
  44 Principles (dedicated to Elizabeth)
  49 Sweden to Queen Christina   Chanut
  50 Dies, Stockholm

Leibnitz[1]

Spinoza = causal philosophy
Leibnitz = causal + teleological
Leibnitz's political schemes
His universal genius 16
Gedanken alfabet 21, 54
Uncritical nature 23
Antisectarianism 25
His occupations 30

born 1646, Leipzig, juristic-academic family learns Livy by himself.—300 hexameters in 1 day at 13—Scholasticism.
University at 15—studies law—Modern philosophy—mechanics prevail 15 years old. Quote p. 62
p. 66–8 Autodidakt like Descartes
1666 Graduates at Altdorf near Nurnberg
  Declines academic place at A.—like Spinoza
  Goes to Nurnberg—Rosicrucian
  Boineburg advises him & he
1667 goes to Mainz; where the Elector Joh. Philipp v. Schonborn
  employs him on the code
1670 On Nizolius' style, with defence of German
1669 on the polish election, more geometrics, Boineburg an envoy
  to warsaw

---

[1] To the right of this heading WJ inserted 'Descartes + 1650 | Spinoza *1677 ['6' *ov.*
'8'] | Locke 1704 | Newton 1717 | Leibnitz 1716'.

1670 Bedenken etc on the safety of the German Empire—a peaceable league for defence—let france attack the Turks

1672 goes to Paris with a plan of french invasion of Egypt, already submitted to Louis XIV

62 to 76 Stays in Paris & London—becomes a *french* writer

Mechanical inventions—submarine boat—calculating machine

1676 Differential Calculus—

Quarrel with Newton through Oldenburg about priority, then about plagiarism finally a trial by the Royal Academy in 1712 which gave the verdict to Newton.

On his way back to Germany visits Spinoza at the Hague—knew van den Enoc in Paris.

Takes service with Duke of Brunswick in Hanover, had corresponded with him for some years. (remains there 40 years)

Throws himself into the Guelph family's politics, later becomes historiographer etc.

Librarian in both Wolfenbuttel & Hanover

In Berlin a part of the time—great confidant of Sophia Charlotte, Frederic II's grandmother—founds Academy

In Italy 3 years 87–90—

In Vienna 2 years—interested & writes about politics the whole time. Great enemy of France. At last however returns to Hanover 1714 to his own study. Apart from honors etc—his outward ambitions may be considered to have failed.

Geology—mines—mint

Codex of international law—3 vols

Historical records of middle ages—175 annotated documents

History of Brunswick

Plan[2] of uniting Cath. & Prot. Churches

Spinola—Molanus—L.'s own friends Boineburg, Elector of Mainz, Duke of Brunswick

He never would be a Catholic accused by both sides of indifference.

Bossuet's Exposition de la Foi, & L's systema theologica as a basis

Plan of uniting evangelical & reformed parts of Protestantism.

1700 Founds Societät der Wissenschaften in Berlin.

[Schemes to give it book trade!]

L. its 1st president

---

2 In the left margin WJ drew a vertical line against 'Plan . . . Brunswick' (201.29–31) and wrote '1683'.

1705 Sophie Charlotte dies
1711 With Peter the Great. Karlsbad & Dresden
1716 Dies at Hanover (*read* pp. 277–282).
Theodicy 1710 Monadology 1714

Bacon's Opus majus	1266	
Thos Aquinas Summa	1264	
Dante's Comedy	1319	
1st printed Vulgate	1450	Constantinople taken 1453
Pomponatius	1462–1524	
Luther's theses	1517	
Copernicus de Revolutionibus	1543, condemned 1616	
Agrippa's de Incertitudine Scientiarum	1531	
Suarez Disputationes Metaphysicorum	1597	
Telesius de Rerum natura	1565–87	
Montaigne's Essais	1580	
Bruno burnt	1600	
Kepler's Astronomia nova	1609	
Vanini burnt	1618	
Bacon's novum organum	1620	
Shakespeare	1623	
Galileo's dialogues	1632	trial '33
Descartes Discours de la M.	1637	
Meditations	1641	(1643 Louis XIII–XIV)
Principles	1644	
Gassendi Syntagma	1649	
Malebranche Recherche	1673	
Spinoza's theol. polit. tract	1670	Ethics 1677
Newtons Principia	1687	
Locke's Essay	1689	
Leibnitz Theodicy	1716	

Pomponatius
Telesius b. 1508   nature—Parmenides
Picus Mirandola & Patrizzio   Platonizers
Lipsius   Stoic
Campanella de sensu rerum
Certainty in senses, love, emanation   triads, astrology

Roger Bacon

1200 -50 1300 50 1400 25 -50 75 1500 25 50 75 1600 25

Luther.

Suarez 48 Hobbes 85 Leibnitz 17
Bacon 26
1651

Ramus St. Bartholomew † 1572
Galileo 64
Campanella 68
Nov. org. 1620 Historia mind. 1687 Ramus 72
Ramus
33 Montaigne et al. 1580
Pomp. b 1462 – 1524 Gassendi
Descartes
Vanini 1585 1618
Marsilio Ficin. translat. Plato † 1543 Bruno
Thos. Aquinas 1225 Plotin. 1616 Malebranche 38
Dante 1265 before 1500 Copernicus † de Revolutionibus Optica
Spinoza 1632. 1633 Copernicus de Revolutionibus condemned †
Galileo † 1632 Newton 42
Galileo † Dialogue. Leibnitz 46

Agrippa de Incertitudine 1531
Erasmus b. 1466 d 1536

Occam.

Böhme, Helmont   Agrippa
Montaigne   Charron   Sanchez

The evil *nature* is hatable, in whatever *fact* it is embodied. But one
 must distinguish between the nature and the fact in ones reaction. The *producer* of the fact is "responsible" for that, whoever
 he may be. The fact itself is not *responsible*, but removable or
 suppressible. The nature is simply hatable. Hate the nature, pity
 its bearer, blame the latter's creator.
The reconciliation with evil $=$ *it is good to have been.*
Chaos of sensible experiences
All unity the work of the mind
Need of unity! *Need* of finite reality.
The rhythm of life

peace╲aspiration╱
Spinoza's finale 1)╲ 2)╱
Leibnitz╲
Reject Spinoza—*unless* mysticism!
The voice of the silence.
We will be non mystical.
The question is as to the last word of *clear* and *reasoned* thinking
Leibnitz's conception is *clear*: Pluralism in the original *natures*—
 Unity in the deed by which they are actualized. The Natures are
 "spontaneous," "free" & "independent" *of each other* §§291–302.
 They become a block-universe so far as they *exist*, however.
This is the same thing as Kant's transcendental character etc. Each
 may have once *voted*—but the votes were *lumped* in the one
 primal creative decree, and after that all is fate.
The natures form a pluralism
The *Being* forms a unity.
But what *need* to lump? Why not disseminate?—leave something
 over to be finished—beings actualizations in the plural?

L's world has unity only as ideal—
Reality only as separateness.

What do we *mean* by unity?
1) Generic unity.
2) Unity of "Continent" (e.g. space)

3) Unity of Object to thought.
4) Unity defined in Lotze's Naturphilosophie p. 26
5) Unity of relatedness überhaupt.
Only 3 in this list is thoroughgoing, but it excludes the finite.
No 4 does n't seem neccessarily to have the One realized for itself—
  seems to merge into 5, except that 5 for Lotze itself demands 4.

Does the other question, as to what is meant by the particular, come
  in here? All particulars resolve themselves into congeries of universals—the singular being contentless by itself—a mere *that
  which*. No! because the universals quâ *natures* are multiple es-
  sences, and the problem of the One and the many is not the same
  as that of the one essence in the many individuals.

In Royce's conception the primal fact is that the thought supposed
  (if finite) starts towards its object & touches it, without enveloping
  it. To envelope it demands a larger thought.
In

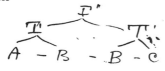 it suffices that T′ start similarly toward
B without enveloping more than its
place, to identify it, to make the world
of objects continuous.

The great thing, with Leibnitzs principle, is to keep *at least his*
  elements of reality, and to do without his superfluities.
The former seem the monads. The latter seems the unity.

We may assume unity.
Then the lapse is insoluble!
Whereas if we assume plurality the progress towards unity is nat-
  ural.

Difficulty not as to what can be, for complex can be as easily as
  separate
But which content of what is is the more rational.

17. Notes for Philosophy 20a: Psychological Seminary (1891–1892)

Aesthetics

To arrest even sadness, when under way, is a pain: Malebranche,
    Entretiens, 77–8   Cesca 4teljsch. x. 137
Major triad: ut^3 mi^3 sol^3 big 3rd below little on top
Full chord   ditto $+ ut^4$

Minor   little 3rd below, big on top
                la^3 ut^4 mi^4
$ut^3 = c' = 256$

1	2	
ut	ut	Monochord

Chro- matic scale	tem- pered scale	Leave out flats & sharps from 1 and you get the modern diatonic scale.

Essential pleasures and pain?
sweet   bitter
              shortness of breath
              hunger & thirst
              colic
              nausea
              fear of falling
              "nervousness"
              apprehension
              flickering, intermission
              (fear is on this account less tolerable than grief and
                  hope more exciting than the certainty of good.
                  Volkmann II 306)

Pleasure of crescendo.	*Pain* of check or restriction of activity
itch	Elastic thread snaps
sneeze	bad success
yawn	labor in vain
orgasm	
music	

finding something lost

any deferred expectation gratified

Insight by many mutually corroborating grounds

Pleasure of rest.

Pleasure of getting more than we looked for.

Pleasures	Pains
The morbid fascination of the horrible, of gooseflesh etc.	volitional effort.

Alcohol & ether intox^{n}

Is desire a pain (Marshall)? or a pleasure (Delboeuf)?

Hope & dread seem the best cases on which to ground the Herbartian view. And yet *as a triumph of Vorstellungen* the triumph of the hopeful and that of the dreadful image are on a par.

Food gives pain when we are full, pleasure when we are hungry. (Disgust's connexion with movement, rê Miller)

Conflict of ideas produces doubt, etc rather than pain (Dumont 62, 100)

Unification of total sentiment of pleasantness or unpleasantness (see Dumont p. 99 etc)

Mantegazza

G'al musc. contractions give incr^{d} heartbeat

Rise of P. in pain explained by musc. action simultaneously provoked. Excessive pn seems to slow P. (21—2)

Pain causes refrigeration which begins immediately and lasts 20 minutes or more—1.30° C. average

Effects on pulse demand integrity of sensory nerve and pneumogastrics.

Respiration not affected with any constancy 47

On p. 58 he says it is almost always made more frequent. In rare cases without cries or struggles less frequent

CO_2 exhalation is pretty constantly dimin^{d} (as much so as 67% in one case)

In cases with strong struggling it may rise greatly.

The Pons is traumatically sensitive, not so the corp. striata, & thalami   Cerebellar peduncles are sensitive   Longet

Associative relations: Since the expressions of grief (e.g.) are associated with many occasions why doesn't one occasion remind us of
other occasions?—it does n't, I think. Cf Lehmann on tears.

Facts which every theory must keep account of,

1 *Accommodation*: the blunting of both pleasure and pain by
long continuance of the experience.—Pleasure departs soonest.

2 *Contrast*: this is perhaps only the converse aspect of the fore-
going.
a) The stoppage of a pain is a pleasure:
b) the stoppage of a pleasure a pain. (Marshall says that in *a*
the pleasure is in other organs than the one wh. was the
seat of the pain.)

3 Crescendo,

4 More moderate in higher senses, especially eye—"don't threaten
our self"

5 Wider seat than any one sensation—*e.g.* tactile sensibility almost
absent in inner parts.

6 Excited by touching nerve-trunks

7 Analgesia

8 Anaesthesia dolorose—hyperalgia

9 Retardation of feeling of pain. (Burkhardt p. 81.)

10 Pain goes with strong impression

10 Cravings result when habitual stimulations cease

11 The beginning of an activity which may become very pleasant
often requires a painful effort at the outset (Sheffield)

12 Relative non-localization (*irradiation*) of both pleasure and
pain.

13 Long duration, longer than in sensations

14 Aroused by long continued weak, as well as by intense stimuli
Pleasure of novelty—pain of novelty
"   " familiarity—tiresomeness of ditto.

The alternative most dwelt on this year was that, due to Dr Nichols,
between specific-*nerve* theories and specific-*process* theories.

I confess that when one takes the sp. n. theory *generally* there are many facts which seem to me to make it extremely improbable. So many p's & p's arise on the occasion of a certain manner of experiencing a "content," that one is almost irresistibly led to assume that the pp. is *directly due* to the manner. If we adopt the sp. n theory we have to suppose that the various "manners" stimulate additional nn. and this seems strained. E.g. the pain of craving or inhibition, & the pleasures of release, the pleasure of a gradual crescendo, say of sound; the pain of sudden stimulation, that of irregular intermittences etc., and the pleasure of regular rhythms; the pains generally of disappointment and baffled expectation, and the pleasures of general excitement and copious stimulation—all these facts demand on the sp. n. theory an *overflow*, from the nerves immediately involved, into p. & p. nerves; and without dogmatically saying that a scheme of such overflow is impossible, I feel as if it were a very difficult thing to make plausible.

The retardation, the bad localization of sensations of p. & p. do point to *diffused* processes of some sort (Cf. Kröner Meynert etc) to irradiation—but why into the pain nn. in some cases and into the pleasure nn. in others?

The rapid blunting to pleasure, and the habituation to a certain extent to pain (to many "disagreeables" and disgusts etc) are odd if the nn. are separate here. Why should *these* nn. be so much very easily thrown out of gear? The "getting into the mood" of an activity, begun with effort, looks more like chemical change etc etc. Then again take eczema—one has to suppose pleasure nerves of the most intense sort slumbering there for the scratching, which does nothing but harm. But if the scratching pleasure can come from the form of the process in the ordinary nn. so may the venereal pleasure and that of sneezing and gaping.

The only case, it seems to me, where Nichols can make his stand strongly, is that of bodily pain proper. Not *that*, but only disagreeableness or uneasiness is produced by changes in the form of experiencing the content. *That* we do not grow blunted to etc., that *per se* can be understood as due to overflow etc.

Separate that as the properly *painful*, from all the *disagreeables* and *unpleasants* (which have nothing in common with it in intrinsic quality, but only resemble it in all being "intolerables," and you may be able to treat one set of phenomena in one way, and the other the more properly aesthetic ones in another way.

Are feelings per se associable? Hoffding, 240

The Wundt   Schliemann-Horwicz   Angell controversy

The Hamilton-Mill ditto }
Spencer   } Roberts

Thompson   Hodder

Dumont   Nichols

Bouillier   Santayana

Lotze   Miller

Herbart   }
Nahlowsky   } Sheffield
Volkmann   }

Höffding   Thomas

Richet—Mantegazza

Fechner

Gurney. Allen   Bakewell

Bain   McLeod

                  (Physical Basis of—Mind XVI 327
                  { Classification of
H. R. Marshall   (Pleasure & Pain: Mind XIV, 511

Bain: on Feeling as Indifference   ibid. 97

H. M. Stanley:_____   ibid. 537

Bradley:_____   Mind XIII, p. 1

Johnson on Feeling as Indifference   " 253

Sully: Harmony of Colours: Mind IV, 172

Jas. Ward: Article Psychology

Meynert: Psychiatrie p. 171+

Mosso in Virchow's Archiv Bd 106, p. 119

Sorel in Rev. Phil XIX, XXX.

Lipps, 195–210ff. 59–64

Meynert, 183ff.

H. M. Stanley, Feeling & Emotion, Mind XI, 66

"   "   "   Relation of Feeling to Pn & Pleasure Mind XIII, 537

C. L. Herrick. Modern Algedonic Theories

Journ. of Comp. Neurology, March 1895

33 pp., mainly summarizing other authors

Ch. *Richet*: l'Homme & l'Intel. Essays I, II, & appendix (on **Pain**)

Mantegazza: la Douleur.

Nahlowsky: Das Gefühlsleben.

Dumont

Bouillier   G. Sergi: Psychol. physiol Book IV.

Schopenhauer: W. als W. §58

Ulrici:

Lotze: Microcosmus   Bk II. Chap. V; Bk III Chap. III, §3.; Bk V.
    Chap. II.

   " " Med. Psychol. pp. 233–286.

M. Maher Bk I, Pt I. Chap XII, p 223. 355–60

H. Ulrici Leib u. Seele II Thl. 3. Abschnitt Chap I. vol II. pp.
    164–207

E. Rabier: Psychol. Chap XXXV

C. J. Levesque de Pouilly, The Theory of Agreeable Sensations,
    (H. L. 24–25)

E. Beneke: Lehrbuch d. Psych. Chap VII (p. 170)

Th. Waitz: "   "   "   " 3. Abschnitt (p. 272–422)

Wundt pp. 129, 342 & Horwicz p. 308 4tljsch. III

Jaeger Prinzip d. kleinsten Kraftmasses in der Aesthetik. 4tljsch.
    415, vol V

Lipps. Bemerk^{gn} z. Theorie der Gefuhle ibid. vol XIII, p. 160

Kröner Gemeingef. u. sinnliches Gef. ibid vol XI, p. 153

Külpe. Zur Theorie d. sinnl. Gefühle. ibid. XI, 424; XII, 50

Hoffding: Outlines, p. 221 to 308

Volkmann: Psychol. (8th part). II, 289–386

Horwicz: Vol II, 2te Hälfte. Vol I. p. 168

Hamilton: Metaphys., Lects. XLI,–XLVI.

Mill: Exam^{n} of H. Chap XXV

Spencer: P. of Psych. Vol I, p 476 (The feelings)

Grant Allen: Physiol. Aesthetics.

D. G. Thompson: System of P. Pt. VIII., Vol ii pp 293–495

F. T. Palgrave: "the Decline of Art [Fortnightly (?) Jan. 1889]

J. A. Symonds: Article on Evolution of Arts (also on Style) in his
    vol. of Essays ("? & Suggestions") pub^{d} in 1890

I. H. Fichte: on Herbart's doctrine, Psychol. I. 233 ff.

18. Notes for Philosophy 20b: Psychological Seminary—The Feelings (1895–1896)

The man living in a certain train of experience finds it e.g. painful— The painfulness seems to flow by inner logic from the nature of the experience. This nature seems to the man to be the *ground* of the pain which he feels, and would be deemed a rational ground even if others (through disease or what not) failed to feel the pain as a matter of fact. In all this we are considering what determines the pain's *nature*. It is the nature of the objects in the man's experience. If he feels, what he feels should be pain.

But now another question arises. By what means is the man enabled to have the pain at all as a matter of fact? This is different from the question why, supposing the man to have a feeling, the latter ought to have the pain-character. We ask now why as a matter of fact the man feels at all—a question not of essence but of cause.

Possible meaning of the Self.

1) Soul
2) Subject or transcendental Ego
3) Sum of states
4) the passing state
5) The will or active element in each state
6) The Bewusstheit.

The content with the vessel (container)
  "   "   "   "   " stuff of which is made bewusstheit

Brentano 166 ff The tone the primary the hearing the secondary object of consciousness

M—g. 154 ff. universal self 128, –30, –31.

Bowne. Psych 71. 11+ 244+
         Metaph. 362+

Baumann: Philos. als Orientierung p. 114+

Rehmke: 133, 145, 153.

Natorp 16+ 30,+ 37+

Lotze: Microcosmus. Metaph.

Hodgson: T. & S. 164+

Fouillée's books, Green, Spencer

Hamilton Jas. Mill Reid. Kant. Scholastic theory Cornelius

Ferrier Phil. of C. Baldwin Avenarius.

M. de Biran Stumpf. Meinong

Questions.

The I as personal or impersonal. What is the Thinker?

The Phenomenist view.

What then is knowledge?

How can the same appear twice? (Singer)

Composition & combination Apperception

Mind stuff (Strong)

Monistic Ego (Royce)

Free will.

All our terms are suggestive of 2 aspects. Datum, phenomenon, experience, vorfindung or vorgefundenes (Avenarius), object, content.

On the phenomenist view the *objects* are separate, the system is in the tho't. The thought is the systematic way of taking them, the thing the separate way. But it is *more* or *less* systematic. Apperception & mind stuff come in there. The ground of synthesis, what is it?

First the phenomenon the datum "pure" experience which we find that common sense has already dirempted

But what do you *mean by* the object*ivity*? We mean connexion with certain concepts. We don't mean difference in nature.[1] There is no other *whatness* in the objective than in the subj. world, but we change the whatness. We break the datum into conceived units which enter into remote systems located in conceived places and times, & finally with altered qualities

The datum meanwhile becomes regarded subjectively as immediate, not remote, but as objectively caused by the object, and this subjective keeps its whatness. It enters into the system of such whats as have preceded & will follow. (also new whatnesses as by J.L. & M—g.[2])

---

1 Opposite 'nature . . . qualities' (213.26–30) WJ drew a vertical line in blue pencil. In the left margin he wrote in ink: 'these places & times are however *postulated*—as given they are subjective'.

2 In the manuscript WJ wrote 'also . . . M—g.' above undeleted 'also here conceived new units like Soul'.

All this because datum comes as an insufficient and has to be defined or conceived. The order[3] of conception proves to be diff! fm. that of perception and the latter remains as part.

But do we not silently here describe a process of thinking and are not both orders and the immediate datum itself assumed as objects to a thinker?

If so, why? and who is the permanent thinker in all this? The object-subject world of the epistemologist presupposes *him*. Why?— Marginal object? Imminently next tho't? No! for supposed to be now. Why, since we dont feel it, can't we doubt it? Why can't world be absolute? It is only for reflection & discussion that Thinker is supplied. Directly thinker is there but not known to be there. The next instant he is known to have been there. All our *past* objects are thus objects *of ours*, and thus comes habit of anticipating regarding the present. The moment question or discussion arises about any content, that moment refers it to future judges, and considers it as *opinion* even now.

The other alternative presupposes immediate self consciousness of I. Everything easy on that basis except to define the I. (Schuppe, Rehmke manage that sweetly.)

My hypothesis that there is no immediately given I is much harder to durchführen. The I is to the whole content as the *me*-part is to the *it*-part of the content. Why not presume some such ideal term by mere habit?

Suppose we do, then what happens? *Nothing*; for we have only supposed a *locus* but no content.

Object-stuff & tho't-stuff are the same in whatness. But the *me*-s are shed off into their own string or stream. 'Shed off' by whom? By the next datum. And are not the conceptual determinations also immediate content? Yes. But *significant* content—significant of other content for in the end all is content.

That the same *can* be meant again seems to be the foundation of it all.

The me in the act of being distinguished from the not-me, does n't distinguish *itself*. Therefore the distinguisher is either felt or supposed.

The datum is part of a stream, is immediately continued, becomes determined & qualified by what follows—that also becomes

---

[3] In the left margin WJ wrote 'Hodgson | Newman'.

connected with it retrospectively, and (as things turn out) experience shells apart into two great series or lines of connexion the data as such or "thises" and the predicates or whatnesses attached to them. These latter form a system of permanents spread out & "describable." The former not describable

Why[4] are not the data themselves describable by the predicates which they involve as "things," even as their primary appearance?[5] Why do we say a feeling *of a* red square? and not a red square feeling? Why do we attribute an intrinsic plurality to the datum as thing, and a unity to it as feeling?—That is the great question. Uphues says it proves the "transcendence" of the thing.

One reason is that it is of the object-*units* that these determinations are predicated, and that they work causally by means of them on each other. The red mixes, the squareness fits, the heat burns, the one loudness overpowers another, the hardness indents etc. etc. Whereas none of these things *operate* when considered as intra mental. They only operate logically then but not temporally. They assign to each other places in schemes of classification but dont determine time and space fillings. The space of one datum does n't have any particular connexion with that of another. Movement as represented doesn't annul other movement. Pluses and minus coexist without making a sum. Things are distinct without being separate

A content can be used substantively (as concept or mental state) or adjectively (as determination of reality). Substantively it *is* not in itself that (blue e.g.) which adjectively it makes something else to be, because to it as subject *other* adjectives then come.

> Munsterberg p. [12]
Read Natorp p. 15–21, 32, 42
> Schuppe 16–24
> Rehmke: 52, 133,153, 454–5, 460–1

Assume as hypothesis. Easy if directly cognized.
Harder if shown to result from Experience.
Try latter course, however.
Suppose datum in itself neutral.

---

[4] WJ marked 'Why . . . thing.' (215.6–11) with a vertical line in blue pencil and wrote in ink 'Cf. *infra*, p. 17–18'.

[5] In the manuscript WJ interlined 'il' above the 'ry' in 'primary' and wrote 'experienced' above undeleted 'appearance'. Because some ambiguity exists about his intentions, the original reading has been retained.

The diremption comes from fact of Datum's continuity

Each moment refers to next for completion.

Predicate & subject.

C. S. Peirce (neccessity examined?) argues for extensity of mental states.

Our assumption of integral datum.

Maybe it can't be made to work; but *try!*

Datum always complex. Former data figure as its parts.

Don't start with present datum and say what it becomes prospectively; but treat retrospectively the old datum given in the present one.

Retrospectively then we find every past datum shelling into two parts, things cognized and the cognizing thereof.

E.g. *Your* datum now is of me, and your having seen and heard the same me 5 minutes ago. The me as such shells itself out of your experience as such. The past mes fall into one series, the knowing of them by you into another.

The datum $= it +$ me—two coordinate parts.

The *it* part connects itself with past and remote its.

The me part with past mes.

The question is: "How does the whole datum come to be treated now as it, now as me."

The it as then is to the it as now as reality to ghost.

Real vs intentional existence.

That experience is now given in 2 ways.

    1.) as *it* really *is* (now judged)

    2.   As it then appeared.

          The real being of it involves a world of attributes etc

          The appearances a world of my thoughts.

        The *me* has the thoughts. But they are not its attributes, but each other's.

The whole past datum is an experience (connects itself with or refers to) something that is no longer my datum, yet something that belongs with my datum. It is an experience *of that* thing *to this* me. That owns it, this owns it.

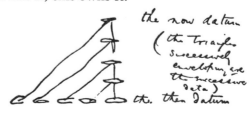

216

Things perceived and things tho't of—both experiences

Not tantamount to real & fictitious things for real things may be tho't of.

But wherever *the connexion* exists the things (whether tho't of or not) are real.

But then (when the reals are present) they are *both* real *and* tho't of.

The point is to decide why they should be deemed to be *both*.

They are not by common men, and not by Kantians & philosophers. For the transcendental Ego is only the space etc. or substance, not *content*.

Yet as tho't of, reals are of diff^t stuff from what they are as present.

The datum in itself & intrinsically considered is no more inner than outer. It *becomes* inner by *belonging* to an inner, it becomes outer by *belonging*[6] to an outer, world. It can be strung (in its intrinsic entirety) either on a vertical thread so to speak which unites it to associates that together with it make the inner world, and also on a horizontal thread with associates that together with it make an outer world. But these latter associates, when severally *realized as data*, also belong to the inner world, and it is only as *supposed* termini of relations with the datum that they constitute an outer world with it.

It leads to the question

1. Why don't the immediate experiences break into units.

2 How comes the same object known in two tho'ts

Bradley: App. & R., Chaps IX, X.

Lasswitz in Monist, April 1896

Miller: Truth & Error 1893   } *Stein*
     Content & Function Nov. 1895 }

Stumpf: Mehrheit's theorie T. E. II. 1–86   Holt

Cornelius: 4tljsch. verschmelzung u. Analyse XVI, XVII

Meinong: Begriff d. Empfindung XII

Uphues

Twardowski

Piat—*Spindler*   Knauer

Baldwin Nov 95 Origin of Thing & Nature

Rickert   *Rice*

Brochard d l'Erreur.

Fonsegrive. April. 1896

---

[6] In the manuscript 'by *belonging*' is represented by ditto marks placed under the first 'by *belonging*' in the sentence.

Reid: Inquiry
Hamilton: Discussions, p. 39. Metaph. XXIII–XXVI
Avenarius.
Seth: vols I, II, III *Huntington*
Royce.
Hodgson   *Thorndike.*   Bergmann: Das Bewusstsein
Spencer   *Holt.*
Green
Bain Consciousness E. & W 538 *Solomons*
Cabell[7]

Singer

What we *mean* by Unity & by Consciousness
A large class of unities are classes of similars put together as such.
   This emphasizes the common feature, & the heterogenous ele-
   ments sink into background.
All unities are of this kind. (NB)
Take the unity of an object.
Sounds paradoxical
Take a piece of space & time. A cubic foot = the common extension
   of all the inches + their differences.
Dozen, bushel connote differences as well as common features.
In the cb′ the parts must be·*contiguous.*
Contiguity is a kind of similarity. The contiguous portions of space
   are probably filled with the same objects. The cb′ is an empha-
   sized identity like a genus.
Desk-case. Not mere aggregate—not s'thing additional to aggregate.
   Unity is a category added to the colour, hardness etc. All parts
   associated in the same function have a common meaning. Here
   again a manifold with common elements emphasized, just as in a
   diversity the differing elements are emphasized.
Can we call an infinite or absolute universal a *whole*? A finite makes
   a whole.
To be distinguished from other wholes is essential.
Any manifold can be made into a unit.
Which u__ __s are so?
Those which it is useful so to consider.
A given unit is opposed to a manifold ab extra, to parts ab intus.

---

[7] In the left margin WJ wrote vertically in pencil: 'For a future Seminary: Cyples;
Clay's *Alternative [*intrl.*] Laas (4tljs, IV)'.

The series of points of view occupied is consciousness

That series which is independent of points of view is the objective series

A unit is determined by a point of view.

As the proof of any consciousness is to act so proof of a unit consciousness is to act as a unit.

A certain subjective stream goes on. It contains a lot of presentations changing more & more; but also a lot of tho'ts coexisting with them and entirely irrelevant to them quâ objects

The collocations & sequences follow entirely diff^t laws in the inner & outer worlds. A & B, two "objects," come together in my thot but as outer realities they are separated by the diameter of the globe.

The *presented portion* of the datum has pretty similar neighbors in the two worlds. The tho't portion is freer.

The order of the world which we end by conceiving to be real is never presented. What is presented is a multitude of its appearances from particular standpoints. We supplement any one of those by supposing the rest. Nevertheless the supposition *as such* is not the outer real. It is *of* the latter, which thus is a postulate.

Is it then fair to say that the "datum" is used twice over, as belonging &c.?—as belonging to what, in the case of its being used objectively? Well, as belonging after all with other data, or with things imagined like other data, although they may be insufficient to fully give the outer real. It belongs with them, *etc, etc.*[8]

The thot's reference to the real is to something developable, to possibility.

There *is* no stuff anywhere but data. The entire world (obj. & subjective) at any actual time is a datum.[9] Only within that datum there are two parts, the ob. & the subjective parts, seen retrospectively; and as, within the datum, the one part is to the other, so will the datum itself in its entirety appear as the subjective part in the next datum which will contrast it with the objective part of its own content. We have, in discussing all this to assume the cognitive or self transcending function on the datum's part, subject possibly to the duty of explaining it later on

[8] In the left margin WJ wrote vertically: 'Start with incompletely dirempted experience as emotion, [*opening paren del.*] aesthetic life (Santayana-Calkins), movement feeling. Vierordt etc.'

[9] In the right margin WJ wrote vertically: 'The *whole* tho't world is identical with the *whole real world*—Thorndike's thesis | Cf. Hegel.'

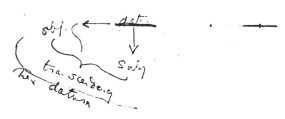

[*retouched for clarity*]

The thing can be expressed solipsistically without altering any of the relations. Let the "datum" be a *nunc stans*.[10] Its content goes on increasing without its bulk changing, as the landscape seen from the back window of a RR. train might, if new marginal (or physical) matter kept pouring in whilst the older matter concentrically withdrew towards the centre filling a constant space that stood there to represent the subjective part. The original datum might be altogether objective in content. The next datum would have it shrunk into the subjective area, and would say that area represents or represented these (physical) facts. There are, however, parts that are ab initio subjective—i.e. feelings. Do they violate our original hypothesis? They would if they were of a diff^t substance. But the difference is transient anyhow for in the next moment the originally physical part falls into the subjective; and the originally subjective may (as in the James-Lange theory) figure as objective.

The only questions then are why when the margin has become central does it lose its spatiality, etc. as attributes, and also lose its parts.

The passage to centrality means anyhow a loss of vividness; and whatever loses vividness loses at the same time a lot of other peculiarities. It can coexist with what it could n't when vivid. It is transformable at will. It can violate all sorts of "laws" which as objective it keeps. I.e. real water puts out real fire. Imagined water may or may not put out imagined fire,—it will not put out real fire. Imagined fire will not burn real wood. Imagined space bears no particular relation to real space. Imagined motion has no Newton's "laws," etc.[11]

[10] In the left margin WJ wrote: 'use the word "field" here for "datum"—it is conveniently ambiguous.'

[11] This paragraph is scored and in the left margin WJ wrote vertically: 'An adjective attribute always expresses a relation of something to s'thing else (Helmholtz pop sc. lect)'.

The Feelings

The rules which relate these attributes in one "subjective" fact to those in another being absent, the attributes become non-essential and uncharacteristic. The facts don't act according to them. They are not adjectives of the fact as such, altho the fact "*has*" them in the sense that they are not absent from it. To have a property as an adjective means to wear it outwardly, to be subject to its limitations in regard to other things, to be dealt with in accordance with it. These laws of attributes that make them adjectives are laws of coexistence and sequence, whereas the only laws that attributes as subjective follow are laws of comparison. Where attributes obey other laws, as where we say that feelings of love and anger can't coexist, we call them adjectives and say the feelings *are* angry & *loving* respectively.*

This explains the difference of adjective determination. Can we similarly explain the difference of *composition* ascribed to the same content when regarded now as physical now as ideal? When physical we say it *consists* of parts entitatively separate, when ideal we say it is *of* parts inseparable yet distinguished.

It all hinges on what we *mean* by being made, or consisting, of parts. Physically we know very well. And when, like the associationists, we frame the hypothesis that subjective data are made, analogously, of "ideas," we abolish all difference. When, however, we bethink us of "combination" we see no parallel in the subj. world to its medium in the physical.[12]

In the physical, parts obey definite laws of collocation and sequence, mutual besideness etc. Each one comes and goes and leaves the others intact. The whole is altered thereby but not the other parts, they stay.

So far as this occurs in the mental, so far we should say the mental whole consists of mental parts. All *additive* fields of consciousness are of this sort. The fields of space and of time are such additive fields. But where the field is not additive, where either the whole changes, or nothing changes, where the discernable elements have no mutually adjective properties but only logical differences, the

---

* We also say they *are* intense, they are prolonged, or brief, they are homo- or hetero-geneous, they are natural & easy or the reverse, they are interesting, focal or marginal, insipid, wise, idiotic, appropriate or not, accidental or rational, etc., vague or precise, general or particular subject or predicate etc. Cf. Monist II, 548–51.

12 In the left margin WJ wrote vertically: 'Say both worlds are "spatial"—the outer one alone has "extension"—its parts limit each other definitely'.

parts are not analogous to physical parts, & the whole is not "composed" of them in that way, even if composed at all.[13]

And in *any* way, what does composed or united into a whole mean here? In the physical it means affecting together a medium. The medium must be supplied. What is it in the subjective? [It means not separated—it is *given* together.]

Where *one part* of a field can be replaced by a new idea, we may call the *field* the vehicle. Where the *entire* field changes we ought to say that there is no *composition*, even if the parts discerned should be significant of physical separates. In this case the many "parts" mean plural *outward relations* of the whole. Substantive whatness and significance of a not yet fully given other whatness twinkle into each other so evasively that one easily merges the two.

"Our little datum at any given time is but a small fragment yet this fragment is surrounded by a fringe of symbols, like the visible area around a man walking in a fog which in the same way is ever changing, and so our fragment by intermediary data, might lead to any possible experiences."

Cabell's examination-book

"The wall of dark seen by small fishes eyes that pierce a span in the wide ocean." Spanish Gypsy, p. 196.

Here comes in the fact of *significance*—what do we *mean* by that?

As the field alters and the older content shrivels, it forms connexion in its new subjective value with the new objective content that marginally comes in. *That* was an appearance of *this* from the earlier point of view. This is a predicate, then unknown, of that, this belongs with that, etc. Solipsistically speaking still, in the changed content the central parts although immanently having their own quality and whatness, no longer figure as the whole world but as parts thereof that did so figure once, but are now superseded and corrected. As so corrected, they are inner, but *significant* of that larger outer. The "water" field or datum has developed into the H_2 & O field *continuously*. That is now the physical fact, but the ladder has been pulled up and preserved in this other shape, and what we mean by signifying is *leading* in this continuous way.[14] Of course the paths of the continuity must be ulteriorly defined and described.

[13] In the left margin WJ wrote: ' "Parts" that are merely directions of outer relation are not parts in the former sense'.

[14] In the left margin WJ wrote: 'The ellipse changes its look to a circle etc'.

Continuity & discontinuity are themselves a part of the content. Continuity may mean the mere absence of discontinuity—it probably does mean this. In the field *the same* abides either unaltered (in which case we may not expressly make it shrink to centre) or accreting new predicates or changing old ones. Singer's community of function may come in here.

But *when* the development is in *divergent* directions [lemon, sugar, H_2, O, etc] we have no right to say the many new things already *constituted* the one old one, but only that the old one *stood for* the many new. In spite of its possibilities the old datum was actually an integer, with plural functional relations. Resemblance is such a relation; and is also part of the total content of the field (Cf. Meinong).

We thus reach the abstract notion of an inner part of the field Meaning and knowing an other (probably outer) part. We can explain what signifying and knowing mean; & generalizing the notion, we can say by anticipation that all fields, even the present and the future one, are vehicles of knowledge, appearances to a self of a content that transcends the appearance, and is not yet given. This judgment *is* the "field" given to the epistemologist as his datum the conditions of whose possibility he has to ascertain.

Around every field a wider field that supersedes it, that yields more truth, the truth of every moment lying thus beyond itself. Not that the present datum need feel insufficient or carry a trans subjective reference at all times. But only when *you raise the question* of its sufficiency then the judgment is always *no,* (as *when you ask* whether this is *all space,* & the judgment must be *no*). An "eject," a not yet realized, is continuously connected with the realized, such being the analogy of all experience and consequently an unavoidable induction.

But this kind of eject is not Clifford's—the unrealizable! It seems unnatural, however that that should obey a diff^t law of production. Cf Avenarius. When once the notion of a not actually given is formed, of a merely possible experience it seems quite in order that it should be indeterminate as to who should have it. As well postulate it as mine as postulate it as yours. It is so far only an abstract notion, which may later be determined as excluding mine, or as excluding yours, or as including both. The important point is that the abstract notion itself should be an inevitable generalization from the content of every field.

The solipsistic character of the present field seems then by *implication* removed—and removed *actually* so far as the question is raised. Who *asks* "is there *nothing* beyond the present moment" can on grounds of analogy only be answered no, there is *something*. The only way to disbelieve the eject is to abstract from its imminence by not asking whether it be there or no, in other words *not to think of it,* as ordinarily indeed we do not, the present datum being our absolute for the time.

Now the eject, the more, the reality, quâ physical, tends to assume a certain form whenever we represent it—The invincible form of a stable permanent world of matter in space. *It there* is the fountain of all our data, fields; our experiences, as its aspects from shifting points of view.

But what is this but a more than *any* experience, a solid supposed as the source of all these points. They never exhaust it, it always exceeds, therefore it falls under the general category of a more or eject. No special mystery here.

What is the difference between a field in which a memory (of my past tho't) figures, and a field that contains "your thought" among its objects? Only a species of the great generic difference that must first be explained, between the *presented* überhaupt and the merely *meant.* Your thought is never presented, always meant, but I know the kind of thing it is. My past tho't is now meant, but was once presented. "Matter" is never presented, always meant.

My whole explanation being by continuity, Royce's substantialist argument for Monism drops out. Royce says tho't and object must be objects for a higher tho't. This is what they are on my system only not *already,* as he says. Unless they are so already according to him they can never be so for they never are the same terms again. But sameness means "with no difference"; & he must point out the difference, if he says that the tho't or the object are not the same when they have continued into a new datum. The continuously enduring *comes as* the same.

On my pluralistic scheme, the oneness of the universe comes from the parts overlapping. But can the *Same* figure in 2 contexts? Can a thing exist twice over?—Why *not*? Singer's analysis might come in here. Being *known* twice over would fall under the general head[15] of figuring twice over. But now how do "data" figure twice over?

---

15 WJ wrote 'general head' above undeleted 'genus'.

Once in actu, once in *immediate* memory. In this case that which came as Object changes into *Object from that point of view* or that idea of object (a phase of the subject-life) whilst the *"real"* Object that that *meant* is now the margin.

But in changing thus the field breaks into two parts that are ejective to each other. The "object from that point of view" is n't part of the physical world at all—the margin is. The "thing" gets duplicated. Avenarius tries to eliminate the duplication.

To say that the datum serves in two contexts etc. is as much as to say that each datum can stand as meant and as meaning. When as meant it is altered by the margin. When as meaning, it retains its substantive nature.

The great simple problem is this: Common sense believes not only in this physical world but in a lot of 'representative' editions of it in so many diff^t heads, all ejective to each other. This *is* the datum for common sense. My problem should be to explain the growth or origin of this datum $\bar{s}$. destroying its validity. It is a form of the "communication of substance's" problem.

How can what is a datum for you stand for my datum? How can one datum mean another überhaupt?

The point is to show how within the solipsistic datum the division arises between a part meant and a part meaning that, even though only one, or even neither, may be completely given.

All that is needed is the giving of a "start"—that involves the possibility of its complement. The start is itself part of the datum's content.

My assumption that the problem is the analysis of a given solipsism does n't preclude our finding that the content of that solipsism should be a world of mutually objective parts, or eventually that the solipsism itself should proleptically appear with a function in such a world.—One must, however, apparently not assume a *static* solipsism—it must be something that rolls over itself and developes.[16]

The *value* of the whole attempt would however, be insignificant if one were obliged after all already to assume in the *mechanism of the unrolling* as many principles as common sense, its pretended product, finds in its own world.

The whatness of the datum can in any case be expressed in con-

16 In the left margin WJ wrote vertically: 'Rice in his thesis says that unless "mental" states have some sort of spatial character they cannot be *continuous* with physical objects.'

ceptual form—such and such natures, whose ever they be. (Adjectives?) *Its* THAT*ness, however, is that the being-conscious of it, its relation to a self or knower?* Cf. what Green *et al.* say about a sensation not being a "fact," unless it is more than a sensation. The machinery[17] of unrolling, in implying that what is originally an entire "datum" forthwith becomes part of another, does it *eo ipso* imply that everything is for a knower, and so *lug in the immediate duality that we have been trying to expel?* We admit a duality, indeed, in admitting the transition of the one datum to another. The datum itself, as immediate, seems to be an abstraction, something incomplete. But the duality is not immediate, as in the common theory, it is a relation outwards. Only in the system of related data do known & knower appear as such.

But now back to the big question: What is the *medium of continuity* on our scheme between the many various *ejective fields* or points of view. As parts of my solipsistic datum, one sees how they come to be postulated. But *as so postulated they differ from other unrealizable postulates (such as matter by itself) in that (although their* WHATNESS *can be perfectly expressed) their* THATNESS *cannot be realized even possibly in this continuum, but is defined expressly as an* OTHER *continuum.* They are not grenzbegriffe, one of the other, they are discontinuous with each other.

Royce solves this by saying they *are* continuous. Can such continuity grow out of our assumptions?

Perhaps the best approach is *via* history and the relations of the various fields to the NS. (Cf. Avenarius). The solipsistic datum acquires outer realities & tho't as divisions of its content and the NS. which is one of the outer realities comes to be believed in as condition of the *thatness* of there being tho'ts, and even of there being things *from that point of view.* Proleptically then, from any point of view! Part of the content of our absolute tho't is that the two worlds are mutually conditioned, and, without both neither is. I.e., an NS. of some sort must be given before a thought of any kind can be given. Proleptically for the absolute datum or immediate solipsism to be a that, it must be a *certain* peculiar what.—In other words no datum can *be*, whose content is not *developable* into one with an

---

[17] WJ marked 'The machinery . . . *expel?*' (226.5–8) with a vertical line and 'NB' in brown ink.

NS. as its part, the part figuring there as the conditio existendi of the content itself,—or of the thatness of that what.[18]

—All this does not lead us very far towards clearness! Revert then to the big simple question: How do the many ejective data form a continuous world. But first *in what respects is* the world which they form continuous?—and *in what respects* discontinuous?

Is this "epistemological" problem after all one with the psychological problem of "noetic synthesis"? In the latter we find data which we suppose to be ejective to one another at one time, nevertheless made continuous at another? The ejective data (your thots, e.g. and mine) are continuous in that they vary as functions of each other (your tho'ts functionally vary with the expressions of your body in *my* field, e.g.). They are continuous also in that they *resemble* each other (both of us e.g. suppose an N.S. as causa existendi for each). If the functional variation had a "causal nexus" of any sort, *that* would make my field and yours more continuous still. My own N.S. has some sort of causal nexus with my field of thought, *because* they vary functionally. By parity of reasoning, it ought to have causal nexus with your thoughts, and mutatis mutandis, your N.S. with my tho'ts. Whatever *discontinuity* I predicate *in this respect* between my thots and yours, obtains just as much between any "field" of my own and my own NS., or my own bodily expression, so far as these vary together.

What must be sought is the diff. between the *relation of* an NS. as *condition* of a field, in which it may not figure at all as an object, and the field, and the relation of the same NS to the rest of the field of objects when it does figure as partial object therein. All the terms are in any case *datum-stuff* so to speak, *field stuff*, and the relations are also field stuff, though this stuff is used subjectively or objectively as the case may be, by the judging Immediate. "How do the *relations differ?*" that seems to be the question. Now the relation of NS. to ejective field (the psychophysical relation) is a great problem, the other relations (apart from "causality") are simple enough. Physical causation and psycho-physical causation are both unknown relations, postulating something as yet in no field given; and *in so far forth* both the physical and the psychophysical systems offer discontinuity. And the discontinuity is not more in the psychophysical than

18 In the left margin WJ wrote vertically, 'Mach   Facts & Mental Symbols, Monist, II, 198'.

physical system, for the physical system can never be realized completely from the point of view of him who represents it. Some of its determinations escape that point of view as much as the contents of other minds do—the physical system is in fact tho't of as so much possibility of appearance to other minds.

If therefore one wants to describe the process of experience in its simplest terms with the fewest assumptions one must suppose:

1) "fields" that "develope" under the categories of continuity with each other:—sameness and otherness in things, sameness and otherness in tho't-streams, fulfilment of one field's meaning in another field's content, "postulation" of one field by another, cognition of one field by another etc.

2) But nothing postulated whose whatness is not of some *nature* given in fields, that is not of field stuff, datum-stuff, experience stuff, "content."—[19]No pure ego, for example, and no material substance. This *is* the hypothesis that we are trying to work out.

3) All the fields commonly supposed are incomplete, & point to a complement beyond their own content.—The final content for common sense is that of a plurality of fields, more or less ejective to each other, but still continuous in various ways.

4) Transcendental monism insists that this conception logically implies a single all-embracing field in which the others are not only continuous but given as one content.

The questions that stare us in the face then are:

a) Is transcendental monism right?

b) What have we gained by substituting mutual "fulfilment" and "postulation" of fields or the Same "figuring" in 2 fields, for 'knowing & known.' What by substituting various contents continuing in certain respects (which "respects" are also contents) into each other, for stable things and changing "tho'ts," the latter of which know the former? What by substituting "fields" or "points of view" for egos?

We certainly have gained no *stability*. The result is an almost maddening restlessness. The transcendental ego at any rate gives some stability to the view.

But we have gained concreteness. That is, when asked what we *mean* by knowing, ego, physical "thing," memory, etc. we can point to a definite portion of content with a nature definitely re-

[19] Opposite this sentence on the facing page WJ wrote: 'Oliver: Free will (mathematical view of) in Phil. Rev. I., 292.'

alized, and nothing is postulated whose nature is not fully given in experience-terms. Whereas the common sense terms, with all their stability are "mysteries," so-confessed. E.g. common sense expressly posits its object, & subject, as *discontinuous*, its knowing as conquering the discontinuity. Whereas our view defines object subject and knowing as terms continuous in certain verifiable ways, and discontinuous in others, with no need of mysterious conquering. (Of course eventually the causal and psychophysical nexuses ought also to be thus verifiably defined; and with the psycho-physical nexus we should probably define the problem of "knowing-together," so far as the *thatness* or history of its conditions *fiendi* go.)

(Pure ego doesnt exist on this view

Desires & feelings are parts of content that don't get physical adjectives attached to them.)

How can 2 tho'ts know the same?

How can the same be twice over?

This is only a mystery if we *begin by defining* "same" in such a way that it *can't* be twice over etc. (See p 38 [*ed.*, 228.37–229.10])

Lecture.

Ask for statement, and amend it.

Take solipsistic view. Immediate content is absolute.

Its deliverance is complex world of things and memories.

But it itself developes, by marginal inroad & shrinking. Window perspective.

We must *assume* this process.

Centre is no longer the whole world, but stands corrected by margin which it *meant*. ("Ellipse," "Water")

The same abides—continuity between fields.

"Sameness" is itself a part of the content.

Abstract notion of knowing. Explain this.

Proleptically even round *this* field an imminent *more* supposed.

Logically it makes no diff. whether this more be object or eject.

Even when object it is eject.

Only the *start* is given, the postulation & fulfilment.

Difficulty where eject is *your* tho't.

But even here a kind of continuity, though the *medium* of continuity the psycho-physical relation is still mysterious. (But in physical continuity the medium *causality* is yet to seek).

Whole system a pluralism of "points of view."

Every "field" incomplete.

Now what do we gain? (p. 37 [*ed.*, 228.24–37]) Transcendental monism.

19. Notes on Stout's *Analytic Psychology* for Psychology Course (1896–1898)

Competing systems, 235

Comment on prolixity of Stout's impeachment of pleasure pain as determinants. Explained by anti-*Bain*ism. The deeper conception being *excitability*.

Attention the system making state 245, 185–6 247, 55

The distincter vs. the completer idea.

Is attention only a name for the fact that the *content gets widened*— only a name for *judging*?

History = reactions.

Vital series.

activity sentience.

Habits formed with *end* not by mere repetition

Conation tends to disappear. 267, 190. Does this prove its inefficacy? This is the question

I discuss under the head of will, P. of P. II. 584+ especially 591 [*The Principles of Psychology*, WORKS, pp. 1186+, 1192]

Topic vs. idea 273

Noetic syntheses vs. association. 3

Perception vs association 6.

Both Ward[1] & Stout think that perception is not recall of *ideas*, but Ward denies it to be recall of anything, whilst Stout would make it recall of impressions with psychic synthesis.

I Repetition without finality would not give rise to habits. 265–9. Discuss this . . Refer to my Will chapter. Compare with doctrine

[1] In the left margin WJ wrote, 'Ward | Read p. 353+'.

of association in vol II. Say "I began with associative explanation translated into brain terms."

Brain terms have the great advantage that they explain non conative, non-rational non-"active" trains and the others together.

Stout seems to make perception association and habit sequence depend on felt significance. But obviously this can be no absolute principle, otherwise there would have to be an infinite forward-reference. There must be provisional objects of attention which are significant of nothing beyond themselves. The question is how far down in the mental life do these extend. Can they become mere *impressions*? If so, we *can* have simple perception s̄. noetic synthesis.

Discuss the Aphasia cases on p. 7 in the light of Ward's articles.
[Mental Chemistry] J. S. Mill p. viii
Lotze Mic 204.—Ward Complication   Encyc. p. 57. My notes on Hoffding etc.

Relative suggestion.
Explain pure association from next to next.
Must assume constellation. What mode *that* constellation? its systematic unity. The next items will be *in completion* of the unity (conative) or they will be suggested in part by relations within the unity.

Inchoate conception 197
appercipient systems = concepts

The noetic & the psychologic point of view = function vs. content = object vs psychosis etc

Drunkenness as mystical—note in religious philosophy—escapes through hole & pulls hole in after.
Shows *some* defect in normal mind.

Completely concrete vs. elementary abstract. Stout is neither.

to obey vs. to infer.

The moment of *life* is that in which novel or hitherto raw content becomes apperceived and thus changes form of habit-system. All appercipient systems as such are habits.

The world grows by intussusception—the ultimate subject is always the universe of discourse. 214

Subject-predicate relation not a part of the objectively referred content 219

The extraordinary fewness of *acts* as compared with the extraordinary multitude of thoughts. Thus in passing into act most of the qualifying shades of the thought must simply be ignored, and a blunt single behavior express equally a host of different species of motivation. *Language* is the only possible act, culminating in poetry and music, through which thought can escape without injury to its specificity. (But language is the "act" not of heroes or of moralists, but of phrasemongers)

The translation of an individual time history no two parts of which are the same, into a timeless system of permanent elements and constant laws from which each phase of the history can be potentially deduced. The many expressions of the single "being" with its "nature" or "character."

Apperception: We make "systems" which formally considered are subjective, being so many modes chosen for our convenience in carving out the flux of experience. Things, with their "inner form" of space arrangement or organic subordination, and their position in a classification by genus and species, which latter involve attributes are such systems; and so are histories and events, with the time arrangement & causal dependance of the data. We hate wild experiences (except when we give way to the concrete moment as *action*) and we try to systematize all data that come in.[2] *Intussusception!*

To explain apperception is to explain formal apprehension, which is always by abstracts & universals, and to show how it differs from the immediately lived matter, a continuous broth

Universe of discourse, 212.

Transition from inchoate[3] to explicit system, from system obeyed to system abstracted & recognized, from "influent" to "reason,"—

[2] In the left margin WJ wrote: 'But even the angry man & the drunkard to some extent systematize.'

[3] WJ wrote 'inchoate' above undeleted 'implicit'.

from automatic to noetic determination—in what does it consist?—and wherein lies its advantage? See my chapter on reasoning.

On the associationist scheme the separate ideas are vehicles of permanent forces—those of "association" namely. On the concrete reason-scheme, the scheme of logical or noetic sequence the "force" lies not in the elements singly taken but in their form of relation. The psychological explanation is by *habits*. The elements are habits

In the physical world one can exhaustively deduce the resultant if one knows the elements. There is no real novelty—all is repetition, for the configuration does n't count as a separate fact. In the mental world it does so count; so there is always something really new, (Wundts psychic synthesis) and not given in the mere sum of the elements. This new as such becomes one of the determinant conditions of further action, as is especially evident wherever it takes the form of *feeling*. For the reception of new experience is not simple addition, feeling and conation are simultaneously aroused, and the farther additions proceed along lines of attention and desire, thereby set in motion. Thus Stout is right with his apperception etc. What happens can only be described as action & reaction—i.e. the objects conflict, or agree, choice and rejection are among them etc.

But this is all from the noetic point of view, of the inner subject realizing the significance of what happens. It is conceivable that what does happen should be *brought about in detail* by an extraneous machinery. The significance of a concert for the ear is one thing, the causes of the sounds another. Ditto of a tapestry. My explanation of ass^n by similarity is an instance in point. The "causal" factors are a prepotent nucleus and its contiguities—the noetic result is a new thought of which we are "reminded by its similarity" to the old one.

Reid
Postulates activity.

no passive elements in a *process*

20. Notes for Philosophy 20b: Psychological Seminary—The Philosophical Problems of Psychology (1897–1898)

The Self

1) The *what* of it, 2) the *whence* 3) the *whither*.

1) we got from Stout etc.

2) from cerebral physiology (provisionally)

3) must remain undecided, at present.

3) can be expanded into a) philosophy of knowing, into b) immortality, into c) practical efficacy.

Grant with M—g et al. the bewusstheit & its content; and in the content the division of self and non-self, and in the self, of activities and passivities.

The question comes up: Why should the content arrange itself, segregate itself organize itself in this way?

Suppose first utilities: Brain is organ of practical connection with physical world. Mind ditto.

Brain a centre of action

Self a centre of knowledge & interest

Brain adjusts action to the remote in space by adjusting itself for the future act. Space and time, as Bergson says, are equivalent to each other in this way.

The Present is for the brain the action-centre, for mind the knowledge-centre.

Assume that with brain bewusstheit uberhaupt shall be connected. Can we from the obvious neccessities of the case deduce any special determinations of the B—ᵗ?

If it were a consciousness of things with which the brain were not practically concerned, I do not see that one could. Could *you*?

But if it were of the other things, a few points immediately appear
  as probable.

As the things are more or less *important* for the brain they shd.
be more or less so for the C—ness. More or less remote, infrequent,
etc. So much we can broadly say, if the brain and consciousness are
to show any sort of teleological harmony whatever. And we *do* see,
accordingly, that the content of consciousness has a centre, the self,
corresponding to the body, which is the centre of the physical world.
Where the body is is the "here" of the self, when the body acts is the
"now" of the self. Other remoter things and actions are "theres" and
"thens"; so the field of consciousness is at all times systematized with
reference to a focus of feeling whose position is in the body, and
with which the other contents connect themselves in an ordered and
shaded manner, as they become less and less important or near. As
there are things constantly near and important for the body's actions these with the body form the apperceptive system of the me,
contrasted as a whole with the various not-me systems.

All this, you see, is on the dualistic supposition of a world of
Bewusstheit additional to the physical world. Granting the B—t. to
be a sort of neutral impersonal manner of existence[1], we see that
personality would arise in it as a kind of differentiation of its content, contrariwise to those who would make personality a pre-
supposition of there being B—t. at all. There *might* be B—t. s̄
personal form.

This keeps what I call the psychological point of view, which is
dualistic. All real masses of bewusstheit exist in this centralized
form. Whatever is known in them is known positionally, as from a
here, a now, a this, a self. Of masses of b—t. not thus centred we have
no information—probably they do not exist.[2]

Of the activities which appear, some also are attributed to the
self, others to extraneous objects, which thus appear as obstructions,
the activity of the entire business being called *my* activity.

But can we now frame any suggestion as to how the world of
bewusstheit, thus centralized congruently with the teleological interests of the brain in the physical world, actually is useful in steering the latter?

[1] WJ wrote 'ce' above the undeleted 't' of 'existent'.
[2] Opposite this paragraph WJ wrote in the right margin, 'Experience is a "collection
of points of view." A self and a point of view seem synonymous'.

235

We have assumed the brain-changes to be its "whence." The activities *appearing* in the conscious world are effects of other activities in the brain world. Activity involves *direction*. The conscious activities might be conceived in some way to reinforce the brain-activities if they tended in an identical direction.

The chief difference that one sees between the brain world and the conscious world is that in the brain-world past and future as such are ineffective, and whatever happens has a present cause, whereas in conscious world memories and futures appear as incentives to activity.

As incentives in this sense, that, were the future not to appear in the content, the resultant action might be quite different. And yet one can't say that the future *as such acts* now, for it only acts now through its representative idea, which is present. It is only "intentionally inexistent" as a motive, just as it is only so as an object of knowledge. The dynamical situation at each instant in the field of consciousness is the change of equilibrium of its present content, just as it is in the brain-field.

The *apparent* change is due to the idea of the future soliciting the activity of the self, determining the direction of that activity. The activity *terminates* in the real future just as the cognition (on my theory) terminates therein, but also (for the matter of that) just as the brain tendencies terminate therein.

The sole point would be to show that the brain tendencies terminate differently on account of the *representative* character of the present ideas.

Can this be shown? Possibly the mere notion of representation involves it. A representation is a present idea that physically terminates in a remote reality. Such representations, such termini. As the representations fall out, so the termini are determined. To represent is to terminate in. The issue of a conflict of representations is the ratio fiendi of a certain terminus. So the question of what decides the termini is the question of what decides the present conflicts.

That question is answered in a general way in the psychology of volition. The struggle goes on between the ego-system and other apperceptive systems. Pleasure, pain, effort, all are co-factors in the result. No general laws can be laid down. Only this is true that in the unity of the conscious field the various termini which as remote are separate from each other are represented together, with their relations, condensed as it were, and in that shape equilibrated in such way, that what happens results in action taking the direction of one of them, and no other. We *call* it decision or selection, and the selection of the idea determines the selection of its terminus.

Ditto, however, of the ideational psycho physical processes. The static, or dynamic pressures may be symbolized as *tendencies,* each coupled with a terminus as the ideas are, so the struggle towards an equilibrium, at each successive moment decided by the resultant of the tendencies may be called a process by which one of several possible termini is selected to become actual. The bond of union here would be the motor outlet on which the various tendencies converge.

In other words a mechanical diagram seems applicable throughout.

And yet the question is not decided whether the conscious form as such which is added may not alter the issue. In other words the arguments of my Chapter on the Automaton theory remain unaffected one way or the other.

The dualistic view thus seems an *impasse* so far as the question of the teleology of the self-form of all consciousness goes.

Let us try then a new departure and see if any better results come from the analysis of pure experience—call it for short:

THE PHENOMENISTIC VIEW.

According to this view there are not 2 worlds, one of bewusstheit the other of physical things, but only two species of experience, percepts and concepts. And the problem is to get the simplest expression for describing their relations. The self is a system of percepts (feelings & sensations) and concepts (memories, ideals etc). Physical things ditto.

The nucleus of reality is the *experience continuum,* with its transitive and substantive content. The "vital series" idea comes in here. The transitive portions are changes towards positions of equilibrium, which are usually perceptual in character—sensations of effected movement for the most part, or other sensations thereby achieved. The transitive parts *terminate* here; have their *significance* here; and where they are distinctly conceptual are often called representations of termini. The brain is hardly ever given as a terminus. Its activities never so. Some things are never given as termini—molecules, etc. But whether given as percepts or concepts things may be given as causes of each other. An experience continuum may as part of its conceptual content contain another experience continuum.

Define the assumptions of the common dualistic view. They are:
1) a self with thoughts and fields (affections of Self) *cognitive* of
2) a world of physical and psychical existents; and *produced* by
3) a brain (which is connected with 2)
2) and 3) are stable ejects to 1); 1.) continuously changes save for its central Self.
On this view the selves and the physical "things" are stable, but contentless, in their abstract substantiality. The only motive one can see for wishing to eliminate them is this contentlessness.
Taken as content 2 & 3 have no other content than 1, which latter is all that is *immediately verifiable*. But the immediately verifiable field of consciousness is almost always *an insufficient*. It developes like the field of a man walking in a fog, and *terminates* elsewhere. The parts within develope in different directions, too, some predominating in associational power so that the field has many potential termini, of which it becomes *significant*. Prospectively, the actual content *knows* these termini.

The objects known are often large systems—(can these be treated as "termini"? doubtfully!) The knowledge of them takes place in so many several "fields," which are among the fields that develope. Thus the system of platonic ideas is one way of looking at the whole of experience, one system in which its contents can appear arranged. So "the world of values" is another, the system of moral and aesthetic discords and accords. The system of the physics-books, strung say on the conservation of energy, or on the molecular hypotheses, etc., is a third. Finally the system of "pure experience" which I am aiming at, will be a fourth.

What is required in *this* system is, assuming only one sort of content to show how part of it segregates into inner experience or knowledge and part into things. But this is just one more case of the system-shedding which I have just noted in other instances.

One matter of experience with a curious sort of segregation or classification of it as it developes, or rather its development *being* such classification. The shortest description of it is to say that beginning with mere "immediacy" it ends by consisting of "ideas" (in the old broad sense of the term) *reporting* "things" to a "self."

Otherwise of a "self" becoming aware of, or cognizing, perceiving, or thinking various objects. The *what* of it all is however the one sort of what, experience stuff, to which nothing heterogenous is ever added.

The *how* of it is as follows.[3] Owing to the continuity of field with field through the melting and growing margins or fringes, contents change and yet retain through time a noetic identity, the later content supersedes the earlier as its fulfilment, or as that which the other meant. The "disturbances" terminate in provisional equilibria, forming so many "vital series," and various portions of content in the terminal fields "refer" to each other and make report of each other as of so many "objects." From the analytic or purely descriptive point of view there is *nothing transsubjective or mystical in such cognitive function. It is itself a definite portion of content, namely the feeling of certain definite sorts of continuity or absences of rupture in the developing process itself.* Where that feeling is, the fact of "terminating" is given; and this is what the phenomenist "means" by knowing, or what knowing is "known as." It is a definite sort of connexion, *within* the unrolling scroll of experience, between termini—both of which are immediate phenomenal content.[4]

But observe now how the relations between different fields multiply, the moment these feelings of connexion and continuity between them multiply and diversify their kinds. A part of field A connects itself in one way with a part of field M, in another way with a part of field N, etc.[5]

If one entire field melted into another entire field, we should have "total redintegration." But that is the exception in man. Certain parts are prepotent in the associative process, and the fields fulfil each other and terminate each other in all sorts of specially felt ways, pursuing as we say diverse threads of relation, logical, teleological, descriptive, etc., and succeeding and superseding each other so that the most varied forms of result accrue, and the most varied functional connexions between a given term and other terms.

---

3 Opposite this sentence WJ wrote in the left margin, 'explain that the how is due in the last resort to associative processes. Stream of thought.'

4 In the left margin WJ wrote vertically, 'Distinguish the conceptual from the perceptual mode of appearing.'

5 Opposite this paragraph WJ wrote vertically in the right margin, 'Interpolate here an acct of the diff. betw. perceptual and conceptual order, and how the secondary figuring of objects as in this or that system, is more often than not in a conceptual field.'

Thus a given term S may be simply held-to, in its identity, through a long series of fields, and reported at the end as "that same S." But then in the final field it may be conjoined with an adjective P, or classed as an M and then presently so conjoined; or it may be connected causally with a C; or it may be contrasted with a non-S; or it may be assigned to a certain place or a certain function in a system, of whatsoever nature, aesthetic, classificatory, chronological, or what not, all according to the various concomitant terms in relation to which it figures in the new fields. These terms themselves in turn may have figured in past fields, even as the S of which we speak has so figured. To sum up: various original contents, preserving their "logical" identity, can figure in various combinations with each other, forming parts of diverse systems, each system as such being the main content of some subsequent field.

Examples of such systems are the 1) field of Plato's classificatory conception of "ideas," where the originals meant are the various abstract "qualities" or types-of-nature that may appear in any field. The relations here are those of *comparison*.

2) The system of ideal values, aesthetically or ethically arranged. The relations are those of worth, and the field is one of appreciation.

3) The system of physical nature, where the terms are sensations or hypothetic objects sensationally defined, and the relations those of sequence and coexistence or quantitative equivalence. The field is one of scientific conception, and its great peculiarity is that it is verifiable, or that all its parts *terminate* in some sensation definitely datable or placeable.

4) The psychologic system of individual streams of consciousness, if such a collection can be called a system. Ordinarily we think more of the single streams than of their systematic union, but we also often think of that. This system furnishes the sensational termini for system 3; and it contains in their immediacy those abstract types of quality that figure conceptually in systems 1 and 2.

For the important point to notice is that the contents that figure in systems 1, 2 & 3 are conceptual contents that terminate in, and arise from, and mean, originals that are given somewhere in system 4.

The system that unites by some definite relation all the minor systems would be the absolute system, the philosophic system. System 4, *e.g.*, connects itself with system 3 by the "psychophysical" relation. And systems 3, 2, & 1 connect themselves with system 4 by the epistemological relation. The absolute system would have to exhibit the harmony of 2 such at present discrepant relations as these 2 between 3 & 4 and 4 and 3, respectively.

Now what places the same content now in one system, now in another system, is the fact that there are so many relations in which it can stand, and each of these relations makes the inner form of one or other of the various systems. Thus as compared by mere difference of quality things connect themselves into system 1. By mutual *fitness* or desirability into system 2. When referred as effects to a set of entities conceived with quantitatively measureable properties as having a permanent existence in space, with definite position there, and movement, they enter into system 3. But when conceived in their immediacy, as limiting each other merely in time without reference to space and without reference to epistemologic function, they enter into system 4, abstractly considered by itself.

The relation that is characteristic in system 4 is the relation of the various contents to the Self. This self appears to be a definite part of the content, more continuously there than the rest which figures in a central position as the agent (where there is activity) or at any rate as *that to which* the other contents make report, & appear as "objects," whether of perception, conception, or conation. This sort of "appearance as object" we may call noetic function to distinguish it from the transsubjective cognitive function termed epistemological just previously. Probably it will be better *in limine* to distinguish the noetic relation *within* system 4 (as where we speak of "objects" of thought, or of imagination, or objects of mistaken belief) from the noetic relation to realities outside the system. One might call them respectively immanently and transcendently noetic—or subjectively and objectively or transsubjectively noetic, or one might call one noetic, & the other epistemologic. The point is that the relation in the first case is between the Self and the other parts of an immediately given psychologic field; in the second case between that field in its immediacy and a remote field (representative it may be of a system 1, 2, or 3,) in which it terminates.

Now since within each system, the relations that govern the content in other systems are abstracted from, we have so many mutually exclusive points of view of the content, and what is true of it from one point of view is either false from another or is so irrelevant that it cannot be treated as positively true. Thus in System 1 the various contents have no time or place relations, no relations of number, to each other. Nothing happens to them, they do not causally affect each other, etc.

(Sunday, April 3. 98.)   The whole *use* of the "change of base" to pure-experience is to see whether one may thereby solve certain problems which are *stickers* on the usual dualistic categories. *E.g.*:

1) The paradox that though sensations & sensible attributes are one, the former are deemed inextensive, the latter extensive;

2) psycho-physical causality;

3) the idealistic paradox—brain being a condition of consciousness, whose creature brain nevertheless is.

4) the discrepant cycles of "activity"—cerebral and psychological.

5) the perceptual & conceptual worlds

6) the "composition" of mental states.

Could the facts that enter into these problems be smoothly formulated without paradox or contradiction on the basis of the pure-experience or pure-phenomenon hypothesis then the latter wd. certainly score a great triumph.

Avenarius's attempt, so far from being a reconciling one, appears to aim at the absolute expulsion of system 4, considered as such, and the installation of system 3 as the only system compatible with the pure experience hypothesis.

Take psycho-physical causality, on pure experience terms: What does it reduce to? first, on the parallelistic view:

To this, that a certain field as such, belonging with other fields in a system 4, enters into no such homogeneous relations with those parts (brains etc.) of other fields which form portions of a system 3 as these latter enter into with each other. You must turn your back on the relations that characterize the brain-system, when you treat of the stream of consciousness system, and conversely.

Second, on the common sense view of psycho-physical causality, the pure experience statement would be that between a field in its entirety belonging to system 4, cross-relations are possible to such portions (brains) of other fields as enter into system 3, and that these cross relations are of the same kind as those that obtain betw. the terms of system 3.

The *stuff* of both the systems is homogeneous, being experience-stuff. The whole point of the pure-experience hypothesis is that what figures or reports itself as the *same* stuff can figure over and over again, and then in diverse relations. In relation to the next total field (the subjective stream of the individual) the stuff bears the relation of purely psychological development, with the self-part of it active, etc. In relation to that *portion* of (either that same or) another field which under the name of "brain" figures repeatedly in various system 3's, commonsense says *it is*, the parallelists say it *is not*, capable of entering into a relation of causality. Since it is *that stuff anyhow*, the argument of the parallelists based on the *difference of stuff* wont hold. The only valid argument for them is that the relations of the brain in system 3 are so *continuous* that there is *no room* for a cross relation with any term taken from a system 4.

We strike thus upon the notion of a *continuum*. Is that perhaps the key? Does "pure experience" fall into discrepant continua each characterized by a certain dimension, so to call it, of relationship? Just as the same point in space may belong to various lines which pass through it in as many directions?

Certainly each system 4 forms a continuum. And certainly each system 1 and each system 2 forms severally a homogeneously progressing series which would be violently jerked out of its own line of direction, in case it were simultaneously to figure causally in a system 3. And yet just those *same terms* do figure causally in systems 3 as well as in systems 4; only then we consider them along with other associates, and it seems hard to combine the two points of view into one solid picture.

The great point, however, is that when they figure thus discrepantly they are not usually the same *entitative* terms, but figure in one series entitatively and in another series representively. For example my *percept* of this pen *can* figure entitatively in two systems, a 3, and a 4; but then only as a "terminus" in 3, since for the *most* part in the same system 3 (*as experienced*) it exists only as a portion of a conceptual field, or representively, as something *tending towards* that terminus.

Possibly this is then the point at which one must *anknüpfen*. It is the *termini*, and they alone, which develope in different *conceptual* directions in systems 1, 2, & 3, whereas in system 4 the termini are continuous, so far as that system consists of a sensational succession.

Yet it consists of more than that, for the sensational succession is only one element of it, a large part being representative or conceptual. In spite of this objection, however, the fact remains that the development of objects into systems is always traceable back to sensible originals as its starting point, and so far as it in any way connects with practice terminates in other such originals (words or acts, concretely taken, for example).

The primal *facts* which the pure-experience hypothesis must recognize are, first, the *continuity* of experience in concreto (giving systems 4); second, its *decomposability* into objects; third, the *identifiability* of these objects in diff.ˡ fields, or in other words the noetic function of fields relatively to each other (developability of them from and towards termini); and fourth the *discontinuity* of the various sorts of objective (or "noetic"?) relation on which the different systems are based. In space we have a similar discontinuity. By no prolongation of a straight line can we strike into another angular direction; by no amount of movement in a plane can we enter the third dimension. Just so, no prolongation of subsumptive judgments will lead to a judgment of cause, and no number of judgments of cause will end with one of worth anymore than a number of j's of worth will give one of time-succession.

Is it owing to the existence of all these discontinuous kinds of relation that pure experience does fall into so many independent systems? Should the philosophic establishment of the systems be preceded by a sort of logical discrimination of the relations?—And finally might a synthetic account be found by following out the analogy of a line getting into an angular direction by curving gradually, or does no such gradual mediation exist between (say) the sort of continuity that runs through a system 4, and the relation which might connect it causally with the "brain"-part of a system 3? If *not*, then one could express the fact that experience develops into so many diverse systems by saying that experience offers diverse ultimate *points of view*, mutually exclusive, or insusceptible of combination into one point of view. In other words it forms an irreducibly plural collection of systems of fact.

Start with simple cases: make a violent contraction of the hand. You feel it, at the same time you see it, both times it is an object of sensation. Or you may feel it without seeing it; only thinking visually of it; or you may simply think of both the feeling and the seeing conceptually. Work out from this simple case, of one item of experience taking part in 3 diff.ˡ systems.

(Sunday, April 10th.)   It seems to be a case of "many-dimensional continuum."

I ought perhaps to have divided system 4 (on page 17½ [*i.e., page* 18; *ed.,* 240.28–33]) into two parts, 1) the individuals sensation continuum (Hodgson's perceptual order) and 2) the same individuals inner life taken in its totality as including his sensation continuum, together with all his thoughts and feelings.

In its immediacy the sensation continuum has no noetic relations. But, as concretely functioning, parts of it (gestures, words etc) are as noetic, symbolic, or representative as any of the individuals conceptual states (thoughts etc) are. That is they are not only continuous with the other sensations immediately annexed to them in time but terminate or are terminable through later parts of the same sensations continuum with remote sensations. The individual's total stream yields both the noetic and the sensational continuity, inasmuch as he can't get from a present representative state to its terminus (what it represents), without being led thither through his chain of sensational life. But the *focal part* of the said chain may be all that his *attention* follows, and most of his sensational continuum may remain marginal and inadvertently experienced, the logical path or path of continuous meanings following an exclusively conceptual line, until the very last steps certain movements of his own, namely, previous to the sensational terminus, are reached. Here the two different continua run side by side within the individual's experience, and they ought to be easily distinguished from one another. The basis of continuity in the total series is *mere time* sequence, whilst in the narrower noetic series it is this, but also (for the *most* part! since one must allow for lapses of attention) *interest* in the "topic" to which the terminus belongs.

Such series as 1, 2, & 3 (Bk II, p. 17½ [*ed.,* 240.15–27]) fall under this distinction, being all noetic series whose thread of continuity is interest in a certain point of view, as well as the relation which the point of view envisages. One might perhaps say interest in following certain kinds of relation. *Selection* (within an individual stream of consciousness) of certain interesting lines of relation would thus appear to be the actual subjective condition which permits experience to fall into so many different systems; whilst the objective condition would be from the fact that a plurality of relations are logically there in the content, and may logically and possibly be found and followed out.

And the *occurrence*, in the stream, of objects which, *when they occur, occur with specific noetic fringes developable into termini* is the initial peculiarity of experience to which all I write about may be traced. We call this a *recurrence of the same object*, often; often a mere continuation of the same topic of discourse; and it is quite indifferent to the existence of such a system whether time-continuity be there or not. In such ways are systems 1, 2, and 3 formed within our several concrete minds.

Entitatively considered, the system as such is always a conceptual field, a field of which the representative or noetic function consists in its having such or such termini, mostly remote.

Provisionally then, this may be considered a sufficient *psychological analysis* of the matters which concern us. But such an analysis does not yet throw a ray of light on the questions asked in Book II, p. 28, 29 [*ed.*, 242.4–36]. Let us revert to them.

The trouble with them seems rather to be of a *logical* order.

Take question 3,[6] the idealistic paradox. No brain is entitatively or immediately *realized* except as a portion of some subjective field in an individual stream of experience. And yet, it has gradually come to be realized there, by us psychophysicists, with a peculiar conceptual fringe around it which unites it in a system A of causal relations according to which the entire field in question, together with all the other fields of the same individual subjective stream, figure *as its effects.* It obviously contradicts logic to say that a portion of a field is the cause (in the ordinary sense of that word) of the entire field itself; or rather such words seem quite devoid of any intelligible meaning. By what discriminations, then, might the matter be cleared up?

Will the distinction between object in its sensational immediacy and object *quâ* remote terminus help? Go back to the *hand*-illustrations (Book II, page 34 [*ed.*, 244.33–38]). My hand-feeling (which is a portion of my field) *is* the supposed "real" physically moving hand which gives itself and at the same time causes its concomitant visual appearance, figuring thus as remote cause of the entire field of which it forms a part. Are the cases analogous? Can we treat the "field" as corresponding to the *hand as seen*, and the "brain" as corresponding to the *hand as felt*? [This would be somewhat like the Fechner, Clifford, Taine "double-aspect" theory.]

Or can we simply say that it is not the brain in *the field* which is

---

[6] In the right margin WJ wrote vertically, 'Avenarius insists that "system C" is not sole cause but only one (immediate) condition, of which "R" is the co-condition, of the E-value which is ausgesagt.'

cause of that field? The cause of any field as such is a brain in some *other* field—either some other person's field, or a field merely potentially terminative, in the same person, of *that* field? This would hardly seem to suffice. We might make the same quibble about the eye or any other instrumental cause. The eye which I think of is not entitatively the eye which I see with, etc.

Generalize the notion of instrumental cause. The brain thought-*of* is not entitatively the brain thought-*with*. But if diverse "entitatively," in what sense *are* they the same? The one tho't-of potentially *terminates* in the one tho't-with. It is as *terminus* that it *causes* the field[7] of which entitatively it forms a portion. Here we come up against the same diremption of real outer thing from tho't which dualistic common sense affirms. How can we wrest it to our purposes?

The "field" is a concrete individual datum. And as you can't hang a real chain on a painted hook, so the "cause" of it must be a concrete individual brain. Only, then, as direct sensational terminus concretely intuited, can the brain be the brain tho't-with.[8] But it is only as such that it can be cause of *anything*, that it can be cause of heat, creation, nerve-currents etc. It has then a bifurcating causation, 1st. of these latter parts of system 3, 2nd of an individual system 4; and yet the *matter* of both systems is the same matter, which in one system is thrown into one kind of form, and into another kind of form in the other system. The systems however as such seem discontinuous; for the term "brain," which figures in each, and through which they communicate is at the apex, so to speak, of an angle, such that in passing to it up one set of effects you have to start from it in a diff.[t] direction to strike into the other. It figures in other words in two contexts, incongruent inter se.

But is this strictly so? Cant you schematize the thing on one plane? probably not! Let the entitative brain-history flow along one of the ruled lines on this paper, its physical causes, food, stimuli etc, would flow into it from above, its physical effects out of it below, and its mental effects would have to be schematized as floating in the space between the paper and the reader's eye.

(Friday April 15th.) Does n't it seem like the wrigglings of a worm on the hook, this attempt to escape the dualism of common

---

[7] WJ wrote 'field' above undeleted 'thought'.

[8] WJ wrote 'the brain tho't-with.' above undeleted 'cause of thought.', and drew lines around both phrases.

sense? And is not the contrast I have been forcibly led to between the brain terminatively or entitatively considered and the brain "in the field" (= the brain *representatively* considered) indistinguishable from the common sense contrast between the objective brain and the brain thought-of? It looks so. Let me then try some one of the other problems for better luck!

Try question 4 (Bk II, p. 28 [*ed.*, 242.12]) of the discrepant cycles of "activity," cerebral and psychical. [For the distinction see this book, *supra* p 10+ [*ed.*, 236.19–237.20]]

This question and the previous one are hard to dissever, for the sphere of psychic activity is a succession of fields of consciousness continuous in time, and the field of cerebral activity is a coinciding[9] succession, the *what* of which (were it given) would be given in just such another succession of fields. Meanwhile it is n't actually given but only conceived, and has thus only a potential existence quâ phenomenon.

All things are phenomena, but there are immediate phenomena and remote phenomena. The termini of our psychic "activity" are remote phenomena ("acts") in the line of development of the psychic field-series. The termini of the cerebral phenomena are the *same termini*—the difference being that the psychic activity series doesn't go beyond that, whilst the cerebral series, being less limited, has still more remote termini, termini which do not figure even potentially among the goals of psychic activity.

Consider one of those more proximate termini which are common to the two series, and let it be a *phenomenon of movement.* In it the series are entitatively one, for on the psychic side it is a sensation, on the physical side the "objective" motion of a limb. Developing it retrospectively, we find it leading backward in 2 directions; associating itself with two entirely diverse series of content, which have hardly anything in common save their parallelism in time. Both masses of content, as given retrospectively, are given in conceptual fields. Where we try to unite them in one field that field takes the form of a puzzle—the problem of their union.

Common sense partly solves the problem by its dualism. The cerebral content exists ejectively to the psychical content. To the "subject" of the latter it is only a potential object; but it is all the

9 WJ wrote 'coinciding' above undeleted 'synchrous', (i.e., synchronous) and drew lines around both words.

while an actual object in itself, or to itself, or at most to some other subject, as, *e.g.* to Berkeley's god.

If Phenomenism is to make things work, it can't be solipsistic. Existents may be only phenomena, but the total collection of them contains groups ejective to each other. The remarkable thing about it is that these groups *coalesce* at certain points—as in the "movement" spoken of, which is common to 2 groups. Common sense would double up on this phenomenon too; and the *great difference betw. phenomenism and common sense would seem to be that the former is monistic as regards such points,* or at any rate tries to make things work on that supposition.

Does it revert to the dialectic question of how one and the same thing *can* have diverse relations?

The question thereupon takes this form: What is gained by a monistic over a dualistic treatment of the points where experience of objects is *immediate* (sensations, etc.)?

I can see an immediate advantage for my own pluralistic yet continuous universe—but let that pass for the time being. Take the concrete case again. The moved limb is known both as kinaesthetic, tactile, and optical content. Both in the object- and the subject-worlds it consists of such content—at least it does so in the object-world of common sense, as contrasted with that of molecular physics.

Do the associations which make the content a *perception* in the subject-world cast any light on the general problem of the way in which a content develops in one direction or another?

It is in the kinaesthetic feelings that the movement seems to be most immediately given as an "original." These "suggest" an optical limb in the psychic field which fuses with them. In the physical world these also connect themselves with optical space-content, and with other purely optical matter, namely muscles, nerves etc., which matter, is however (or may be) quite discrete (ejective) from the optical matter in the subject's perception of the limb. The connexion is "association" in the subjective field. It is not association in the physical field, as so meant, it is *location*, or some other objective attribution. In the mind the

(Friday, April 29, '98.)   The great diff. between the phenomenist and the common sense view is that the latter gives *stable* elements, whilst the former is afflicted by a restlessness which is painful to the mind. In it one never gets out of the conception of flux, or process; although it might well seem that all the *actual* found its place in the flux. For common sense the actually experienced is only a very small extract of the whole.

In phenomenism fields develop & terminate in other fields, and that is *knowing* them. Tufts (Psych. Rev. VI.) says that to know is to "interpret." In the form of judgment the predicate interprets the subject, etc. So I might say that the later fields interpret the earlier; and if asked what that means, reply that *the whole process or flux of fields can be described as a substitution of later for earlier values.* Of course succession is in any case *time*-substitution, but this means more. The earlier is completed or fulfilled, and thus a functional connection between the terms remains over and above the mere succession. It is a continuous experience of the same world, the value of which, as knowing, developes. And this of course is a fair description of *my* experience, or *yours.* But what does it develope into? Into a view of the dualistic world of common sense, first. Can it develope farther into a phenomenism? That is what I am trying to ascertain.

My[10] great trouble seems to lie in the diremption of real thing from sensation in the phenomenon of perception. Common sense dualism takes the same fact 2'ce over—makes it figure first in the outer world say as that chair, then secondly as my mental copy of that chair. For phenomenism this is inadmissible: the one fact is in my inner world and yet is entitatively the objective chair.

(Sunday, May 1st)   Conceptual fields on the whole are "transitive states"; we feel ourselves active in them, they are "insufficients." Whereas sensational fields are "substantive states" and "sufficients." Any field, to him who is absorbed in it, is an *absolute* for the time being, and the universe is then just "that." At such time the questions are not asked: "is there aught more?—is this all? *What* is this?— how shall I interpret it?" But the moment the question *is* asked, there can only be one answer: "This is *not* all—it is *in*sufficient." And the "more" thus postulated is the "transsubjective," no matter under what quality it may be looked for. "Molecules" are transsubjective, other "minds" are, future experiences of my own are, "truth"

---

[10] In the left margin opposite this paragraph, WJ wrote, vertically, 'This is Avenarius's "E-werth" without introjection.'

is, all are transubjective in so far as they postulate somewhat beyond the present field.

My point must be to show that *the beyond is part of the same continuum*, whereas for common sense dualism, it is discontinuous, and separated by the epistemological chasm.

Well, one point ascertained seems to be that established in "Book I, (loose sheets," pp. 32ff. [*ed.*, *pp.* 227ff.]) namely that the other minds, varying synchronously with the variations of objects in my field, are no more "ejective" than the molecules supposed also to vary synchronously with those variations of objects. From the logical point of view they are both possibilities of farther experience, and it might be in both cases of *my* experience, since your mind and mine might conceivably become continuous hereafter (in directions made conceivable by such ideas as Janet's and such facts as those of mediumship).

The "more" as a mere logical object need not be determined temporally any more than it is qualitatively. It may be conceived as contemporaneous as well as future. It may be defined as my future experience, or yours or anyones; it may be conceived as your present experience, or it may be conceived as a lot of "things" (molecules etc.) by whomsoever experienced existing *now alongside* of the immediate field. If asked, we reply that such contemporaneous things do exist in the part of the room from which our faces are turned. It is only a question of defining the *what* of them—the *that* of them stands fast—and panpsychistic monadism is only a theory of the what.

What does it mean now to say that he answers "truly" who answers "yes" to the question of their *that*—the question "*do* they now exist?"

It means on dualistic principles that the epistemological chasm is leaped, and that even now he in some way grasps the more.

On phenomenist principles it seems also to mean that—only it gives a more verifiable turn to the conception. In what way more "verifiable"? Verifiable namely by *him*.

Is n't the difficulty this?—*to get out of a solipsism without jumping a chasm*? So far, with my question about the more, and my necessary "yes" in reply, I am solipsistic. For the "more" is continuous (being only a marginal object) with the focal "that" first posited absolutely; and the yes is a relation between the more and the that on the one hand and the self and the whole field on the other. The whole thing is immanent in my experience, when simply so described. Yet my "yes" is supposed to *mean* something ejective to that whole immediate experience of which itself is an element. In what sense is my yes *verified* by me, (or in fact *verified überhaupt* from the point of view of any speaker) as distinguished from the sense in which according to dualists it is even now "true," whether verified or not?

Well, from the point of view of actual experience, *is* it ever true until verified? That is, is it ever surely true?—ever more than hopefully true? Certainly it is not:—unless the Over-soul be there. If that were there truth might be interpreted by verification through the Over-soul. But epistemologically or logical it seems doubtful whether this would remedy matters. For, even assuming the Over-Soul as one's hypothesis the passage from my present field to the rest of the Over soul is as much a chasm, as the passage to the "more," substantively taken. The Oversoul seems indeed merely to be another name for *that continuity* between *the objective "truth" and my "verification" thereof* which common sense dualism breaks by its chasm, and which I am saying that phenomenism is obliged to work out in some way or other. The Oversoul theory says that nothing is verifi*able* by any finite which is not actually verifi*ed* already by the Absolute. It denies *conterminousness* in plurality as an interpretation of knowledge, whilst such *conterminousness is the denkmittel which I am forced to make work, if I can.*

My central task should then be to make clear the conditions and implications of conterminousness.

Suppose there *were* conterminousness, suppose the notion clearly established: What would result? how should my description run?

Why thus, that my field with the question "more?" and the answer "yes!" terminates where yours begins—say in this table or that human body, and yours terminates where someone else's begins, and so *de proche en proche* until the whole world gets covered. It *is* covered, *now*, just as common sense thinks it is, and independently of my verification; but it is not *one field* now, as monistic absolutism declares it to be. Arrived at the table in my field I say "more"—namely that it is your table too, or that molecules are in it (ditto of your body in my field), and so far as *my* verification goes I end there, getting no farther. But the "truth" of my "more" consists in the fact that my "table plus more" which is my terminus is *conterminous* with you and with the molecules—there is no "chasm."

So THE *notion of conterminousness has to be defended.*

Not only percepts seem conterminous; concepts seem so too—minds meet in truths as well as in facts.

Whoso says my table etc. is not one with yours has to prove that they *are different.* Primâ facie they are the same; so the burden of proof lies on him.

Well, his task at first seems easy.

(Friday May 13th. '98.)

(Sunday May 15—)

Concepts merge into sensible originals, and in such, *many concepts may be conterminous—e.g.* quality, intensity, and extent of a sensation, all start forth into different directions from the individual concrete sensation into the conceptual world, even if the sensation be a simple one, and still more of such concepts start forth if the sensible experience be complex. In what we call a "perceptual" experience there is perfect fusion of conceptual and sensible material, like the fusion of painted background and real foreground in one of those circular panoramas of battles etc. where to inspection the line of division cannot be made out. Moreover, yon bed e.g. as I turn my head becomes first a marginal present object, then in immediate memory a conceptual object, then grows as I turn back (or still farther round) into a sensibly present object again, all the while with no "chasm" of otherness to break the continuity of its objective self-identity as meant or known by me through all these changes. It stays always the "same" bed, numerically. And for common sense dualism this numerical sameness becomes the element of "objective reality" in the experience, the stable constant existent, whilst the varying qualifications of the content pass over to the subjective aspect of the experience. But there is no break *in* experience of the two aspects. It is always *that* bed which is in question for me, and if I bring you in as a second participant, it is *that* bed which I understand *your* deliverances (E-werthe of Avenarius) to concern themselves with.

The "that" remains for Avenarius on the common sense stage of experience (the stage without introjection?) as the permanent remote "complementär bedingung," whilst the Schwankungen of system C in both of us are the immediate bedingung of our several "experiences."—"*duality* without *dualism.*"

But for me the problem still is this: To describe all that occurs without ontological dualism between the *that* as object, & the that as "subjective" "content." One can simplify the problem by supposing the real physical world to be one of stagnant spatial coexistents without change, which the experiencer merely describes and classifies. His experiences are in a constant flux, but what they are "of" is this stagnant system of termini. Thus they are "there" "for" him in several ways, of which he distinguishes the subjective from the objective way (notwithstanding leaving them continuous); and ascribes a (conceived) constancy to the latter which the former lacks. The "things" and my "experience of" them thus come to be in a manner opposed. And indeed the primary "thing" (the sensational terminus) stands midway between the finally credited thing (as scientifically defined) and the subjective appearances. The scientific thing is an object of conception,* and so to a great extent is the apparent thing. Reality vs. appearance is not therefore the same contrast as immediate sensation and concept or memory. Sensation mediates between both object and subject worlds, figuring in both, and yet not figuring dualistically there, as in the common sense-philosophy.

For science the *what* is reduced to subjectivity, but the *that-there* remains common to both worlds. For Kant, the *that* remains (Dinge an Sich) but the *"there"* is reduced to subjectivity. For absolute idealism the whole *that-there* is reduced, and what remains is zero—all has become inner, i.e. variable—the constant element is totally eliminated, or at most remains in the "timeless" "truth" that the idealist utters when he says that the flux of experiences, perceptual and conceptual, *is* All.

The diremption of experience into 2 worlds (inner and outer) would thus seem to be stateable as the capacity for the sensible termini to figure in two contexts: 1st. as parts of the (inner) flux, second, as parts of the (outer) system conceived as permanent, or relatively so. But the *that* in the one system is numerically one with the *that* in the other. [Cause in the one, it is effect in the other!—look to this!]

Both *conceptual* systems are insufficients in their immediacy, and are felt to be so. Both point to a terminus, and the terminus is a sensible experience.

---

* Causally conceived, however whilst the apparent thing is an effect only.

(For class, Monday, May 22nd 1898, & 29th.)

The process of experience must be a homogeneous growth. So begin with the elements of the common sense world.

Show how, as fields of experience continuously succeed each other (meaning sense of sameness and difference, & time, by continuity), there arise, through the alternation and displacement of one content by another, the categories or time- and place-tags of

> this — that — other
> here — there — elsewhere
> now — then — soon — hereafter
> always, *more*

together with the various kinds of percept, their samenesses and differences, and the difference between faintness and vividness in them,—all as data of the later fields. These data or elements may figure interrogatively, negatively or affirmatively there.

Take the alternation of three $\left(\begin{smallmatrix} ao \\ I \\ co \end{smallmatrix} b\right)$ as I turn from them successively and back. I presently make, whilst a and b are vivid, the affirmations "c now faint, soon vivid again," and "c not here now" "there elsewhere," not faint there, vivid there.

Begin[11] with account of "experiences" as a time-succession, with *memory* and a sense of *sameness*, and *continuity* of one experience with another, as meaning nothing mystical, but only the experienced phenomenon of "no break" or "conterminousness."

Show next, as on p. 41 [*ed.,* 255.4–15]. how the later fields acquire a margin as well as a centre. There is "more" than that centre; & in the more, *directions*, as "then," "soon," "beyond," "behind" etc. Fields develop or succeed each other along such lines of direction ("activity," "search," "fulfilment," "going right," "going wrong," come in here.)

At last a field comes with some of its content segregated into a physical world with a fixed dynamic order and the time & space tags "always-there," and mental states with time-tag "sometimes" & no "space-tag," strictly so called. This is the common sense dualistic stage.

It next develops the dualistic epistemology. The mind-states know the world facts by duplicating them in copy, even when the

---

[11] Opposite this line WJ drew an arrow pointing to 'So begin . . . world.' (255.2–3) on fol. 41.

world is vividly "present" & the mind state is direct "perception."

This may change into the transcendentalist epistemology, in which each content is for bewusstheit or impersonal consciousness. All the "content" both inner and outer is homogeneously treated as so much matter of "experience," but coextensive with it all is the consciousness which it is "for." The dualistic point of view is only partially abolished; and the fact of knowing is left more of a mystery than ever.

In me it has changed into the pure experience epistemology which I proceed to explain.

Take me solipsistically if you will. My talk is merely a description of my present field of experience. That field is an experience of physical things immediately present, of "more" physical things "always there" "beyond" the margin, of my personal self "there," and of thoughts and feelings belonging to that self, together with "other" thoughts and feelings connected with what I call "your" personal selves. Of these various items some, as fully realized are "sufficients"; others, the physical things "beyond" and "your" thoughts come as insufficients—they connect themselves with the marginal "more."

But in the first instance that marginal more is part of the experience under description. No one can use it mystically and say that self-transcendency or epistemological dualism is already involved in the description, that the "more" is a reference beyond the *experience*. The "more" is more than the vividly presented or felt; the "beyond" is beyond the centre of the field. The field so far lays hold of nothing beyond *itself*, and *if the world began and ended with that field of experience, it would be an Absolute*, and nothing would *be* except as therein experienced. In it the All would find its prison and its grave. So my actual field as I speak is full of *thises & thats, thens, theres, thuses, sames, & soons*, all as portions of its content, in the first instance, & in so far forth without the transcendent reference which dualism ascribes to cognition. *They* BECOME *cognitive only through the field changing into later fields* (or through having developed out of earlier fields) between which and the parts of itself definite relations of succession & feeling obtain, those viz: accounted for in Mind. Vol. X. p. 27. Such development is an ultimate fact which no philosophy can get along without admitting.

The "continuity" of one field with another is known as the "more" margin of the earlier growing into the centre of the later. It would seem as if the whole dualist and transcendent-question might lodge itself in this event. The same more, we say, is in a measure common to two successive fields. Their contents overlap there. But quâ successive *existents in time* they can't overlap; there must be a *cut* which marks the present instant in the event of change, and from what one might call the physical point of view, all content behind that line belongs to the *gone* field, all after it to the *coming* field. These two fields, *conterminous* in that line, or cut, have no *being* "in common," for the cut is a mere boundary and not a being with content of its own. What is "common" can only be present entitatively, or as an *object* in one field, and "intentionally" or as a *knowledge* of that object in the other field. So the cut is bridged and the chasm filled, by the immediate miracle of self-transcendency in that spot, whichever it be, where the "knowing" state is found.

The force of this reasoning ceases if one sticks consistently to the empiricist account of 'knowing,' as I give it. On one side is the knowing bit of experience, on the other the known bit; and whether we take them far apart in time or immediately next to each other, that makes no difference in the noetic relation, for the latter *is* nothing but the fact that as earlier content is replaced by later (entitatively), subjectively a portion of the content is a feeling of some sort of "sameness," or a feeling of "no-otherness," or whatever you please to call it, in what comes, whereby *discontinuity never appears*. And where that does n't appear, continuity obtains. We can partly express this by distinguishing between objective time or the time in which the experience changes, and subjective time, or the time which the experience is "of." The latter is always more extensive than the former. So that as the subjective time-fields replace each other, they never have a *wholly* different content, the going field drops its stern, gains a new bow, but remains "the same" amidships, and thereby "becomes" the coming field, without any sense of breach. Such as a matter of fact, *is* the form of our experience, and the noetic relation between its pulses is only the name for that fact, realized and given in the very tissue of the experiences themselves and not provided for outside of them, by any transcendental machinery whatever.

Each field has a *that* & *thus* in it which is the directly presented thing, a *now* which is the directly presented time, a *here* which is the directly presented place, and an "*I*" which is the directly presented seat of activity. The three latter elements coalesce into one position, and the essence of our theory is that in all four of these focal experiences object and thought-of-object are identical. It is by varying contexts in later fields that they get first distinguished and then "introjectively" doubled up.

The "now," for example, changes into a "then," as another now comes in. But when you think of it along with the *I* and the *here* that went with it you think it as an element of your past stream of consciousness, as the *feeling* you then had of "the present." When, however, you think of it along with the *thats* and *thuses* you think of it as part of *real time*. Meanwhile it is *that same* object which both was a now for your mind, and a bit of the objective time in which history was unrolling itself.

The "thing," when we proceed to think of it in relation to certain other "things" is physical, but mental when we think of it in relation to the I and its feelings, and to that part of the content of adjacent field which is "physically" incoherent with it.

Now take apparent contradiction, that if our theory be true, mental states must smell good, be hot, big, hard etc. since they are identical with the objects to which these qualities are ascribed.

Distinguish betw. intentional and attributive possession of a quality. As physically realized all attributes are relations to other things, determinations in something by which something else is *affected*, or changed. A thing possesses its physical attributes adversely, so to speak, or wears them on its outside. An experience therefore figures *as physical* when taken in relation to such other experiences as it dynamically alters. In that context its determinations are *adjectives* or *attributes*. In relation to things towards which its determinations are inert, it figures as a state of mind; and the determinations are its "objects" or contents. In the former case we say the Exp. *"is"* P; in the latter, "it is *of*" P. (Compare Book I, p. 17–19 [*ed.*, 220.13–222.6].) In the former case it is the thing, in the latter the consciousness of the thing. "Composition" of mental states similarly explained.

Substitution. My account of knowledge makes the object identical with the consciousness, or else it treats the one as a *substitute* for the other. The presented thing supersedes the image which terminates therein; and the concept supersedes the sensational "that" which it proceeds to define. But you can only substitute a term whilst keeping its function. And we must define the function or purpose for which concepts and percepts are thus mutually substitutable.

Entitatively every later bit of experience is substituted for all earlier ones. It supersedes them, bodily crowds them out—assuming their relation to the constant Self [easily make this free from cavil!] Sometimes with sense of satisfaction, sometimes otherwise, since we proceed towards querying states, as well as towards answering states. In either case the relation takes a noetic form, and can be analyzed into substitution of the entitative kind.

But where the series is still under way & incomplete, how shall we clearly define substitution? A passing conceptual field is a substitute for a lot of original objects (which we say it knows or is "of" because it could terminate in them) when it terminates actually in things in which they would terminate. Thus the perceptual and conceptual orders are conterminous, and touch and coalesce at a lot of points common to both, whilst between these points they form two distinct things. The substitution is in respect of the identical function of *leading to and from* these points which both orders possess.

Most all the "termination" of which I write remains only potential. It is realized only in the conceptual form of a direction in which "more" lies. It is ejective to any given experience. My "presentation" of your body e.g. is the centre of a field whose "more" points on the one hand in the direction of anatomy and physiology, on the other in that of your mind. Even thus summarily referring to these things, I now "know" them, however. In what sense? In the sense that my thoughts of them terminate in what they terminate in (CO_2 out of your lungs e.g. on the body side) adaptations to your future acts on the mental side. They are functionally substitutable as leading to these experiences.

21. Notes on "Conclusions of Lotze Course" (1897–1898)

Unity

because it violates the principle of practicalism, and because plurality meets all logical requirements.—There is therefore no Absolute, as object of serious belief.

The monistic arguments all rest on the plea that if there be any connexion at all among things, there must be complete union. The lesser connexions, logically or in point of fact, *involve* the greater, and so on, up to the greatest, so that we have the sharp disjunction: either an absolutely disconnected manifold, or a manifold of members of one organic unity of fact.

Applying the principle of practicalism to the conceptions of unity, connexion etc. we find that unity and connexion are "known-as" many different kinds of thing, and that some kinds make one practical difference, other kinds another.

E.g. complete identity, or absence of any differences is one meaning of unity, but that meaning cannot apply to our universe.

The unity meant must be a means of practical connexion between things. The more obvious means of this sort are

The noetic unity[1] of the things, by one knower.

Their affinity[2], permitting of passage by logic from one to the other. Things are of "kinds."

Their existence in *one time & one space.*

Their *unity of origin.*

Their *dynamic unity* or capacity for mechanical interaction.

The practical results of these kinds of union are realized between certain parts of the universe, on every hand. But as far as our own experience goes, the *time-unity* is the only one that is all-inclusive, and mediates between anything and everything else.

Some of the connexions due to these forms of unity involve others, some do not.

Knowableness-together, and being-in-time seem to involve *no* farther connexions.

Dynamic connexion seems not to involve generic unity, for differents seem to interact.

Some generic connexions involve others, as where "like causes—like effects," of which the extreme case is where "things of a kind have one origin" (living species, manufactured articles).

Some dynamic connexions involve others (telegraphic connection requires land or water connexion to lay wire. Connexion by sound involves air; by sight ether; by love knowledge, etc). Others seem

---

1 WJ wrote 'noetic unity' above undeleted *'knowableness-together'* and drew lines around the words.

2 WJ wrote 'affinity' above undeleted 'commensurability' above undeleted *'generic unity'* and drew lines around the words.

independent. There can be water-connexion without telegraph. Knowledge without love, mechanical without chemical influence, etc.

Purely physical connexions seem to involve no noetic connection. Where living beings come in, their interactions do often involve noetic connection.

One noetic connexion may or may not involve another. You may know of me, but I not of you. Even things known to one knower, are not known by him all at once.

In general there seem to be deeper and more general, and shallower and more special levels of connexion between things. The deeper do not involve the shallower, though the shallower do involve the deeper, as their prerequisite.

Prima facie the parts of the universe hang together in *all* these ways, some in one way, some in another. Any one way would save these parts from being *absolutely dis*connected. It would be a *universe of that grade*, or type. Mere temporality, mere knowability, would suffice, even without further commensurability, interaction, or common origin. The mind could roam from one such item to another, or hold them all together. "With"-ness or "after"-ness "for" this mind would be the principle of unity. The world would be a barely *"noetic collective"*—and its parts would be *"additives"* or *"subtractives."* There would be no logical aesthetic, physical, or any other connexion. One might imagine other connexions added between certain of these parts, and the universe would thus acquire a higher grade of unity *in those parts.*

Finally it is conceivable that *absolute organic unity* should be attained; though how to define this in detail is hard at present. It would involve one origin; knowledge at-once; complete logical system, so that one could deduce the whole from any part; complete dynamic connection, so that a change anywhere would involve change everywhere else, etc., etc. But more than that one can't well say.

Now such an *absolute unity* is supposed by Monism to be susceptible of logical proof. A unity less "organic" is too lean and low for their demands, which only an *Absolute Unit* can quench.

The only arguments which we need this year consider are that of Royce from *Truth and Error*, and those of Lotze, from *Commensurability*, and from *Interaction.*

1. The *argument from Truth and Error* maintains that if there is

noetic connexion between any two things, there must be also a wider *noetic* connexion, etc. till finally all things stand in "absolute" noetic connection, i.e. are known in a single fact of knowledge from which no item escapes. Partial knowledge anywhere involves Omniscience elsewhere. This violates appearances. The Cuban war for example hangs together by noetic connexions between its parts, knowers and known, but no total knowledge of it exists on earth. The argument is an abstract a priori argument.

Give Royce's form.

Test it now by principle of practicalism. What is noetic connexion known-as? What is the cash equivalent of your "knowing" the memorial hall clock-tower?

It is the tendency to move so as to terminate at the clock tower. If you move otherwise you don't know it. You know it, as a gun in Boston Harbor might aim at it. The knowing and the aiming are *constituted by the fact of the outer intermediaries*. Without them, a knowing state of mind is practically indistinguishable from a merely imagining, or from a deluded state. (Give my view Mind, X. [*The Meaning of Truth*, WORKS, pp. 13–32], Psych. Rev. II. [*Essays in Philosophy*, WORKS, pp. 71–89]).

My mouse just caught. That I should know that secret does not imply that another should know it. Another *may*, an absolute mind *may* (Mrs. Piper and the cat.) but they may not, and it is a question merely of fact, if they do.

The state of mind as such does *not* transcend itself, does not *refer*, does *not* mean, is *not* mysteriously "present" to, its absent object—it *leads* to it.

So I conclude: Noetic connection does not neccessarily imply any wider noetic connection—least of all an absolute mind. As a matter of fact the universe may be in *noetic continuity*, as the Cuban War will be, though no one ever shall know it all at once.

Noetic connexions, so far as realized through nervous systems, imply all sorts of physical connections between their terms. "Clairvoyance" would involve such a connexion, and "thought-transference" wd. involve a psychic connexion (whether simultaneous or successive), if the "resemblance" of the state of mind to its original were not to be classed as "coincidence."

To sum up, the universe, even if *knowable in toto*, need not be *known* in toto either successively or all at once.

2. *The Argument from Commensurability.*

The actually found affinities of things prove, it is said, their *common origin*. Of empirical things (living things and things manufactured by man) this is undeniable. But where we are dealing with *first* things (like atoms), with no machinery of production, the analogy hardly holds. Suppose the primal things to arise independently. What is there to *prevent* them from being mutually similar? Ought we not if they were *in*comparable to postulate by the same logic an efficient principle of diversification of some sort, just as positively as we assume a principle of unification, finding them congeneric?

Can we go behind the *fact*? Need we to explain the amount of unity *in* the fact (*generic* unity) invoke a still earlier *substantial* unity in addition? For the "one origin" sought, is the primal source as *cause*, and must be regarded as a unit-Being. Is n't the argument either a false analogy with secondarily produced things, or else a case of that explanation of all determinations of *actuality* by the antecedent *possibility* of just those determinations. "The fact of unity demands a principle of unity, the fact of diversity a principle of diversity," etc.—We fail to ask how these respective principles get their *own* possibility.

However, even if a principle of possibility does precede the facts, that would determine nothing as to the dates of their emergence, whether simultaneous or successive. Whatever the kinds, whatever the differences, whatever the dates, it would be a principle of origin for those kinds, those differences & those dates. In itself, nothing could be deduced from it by us. Even were it a knower as well as a source, it would be a knower of those facts, *whatever* they might be. The conception of it would add nothing to the actual determination of the facts for us. *Pragmatism should rule it out.*

It is only by making the principle a *God*, in other words invoking *an hypothetical fact*, that pragmatism finds its account.

The "one origin" idea thus evaporates into indeterminate abstract possibility, or hardens itself into a God. A God might truly both know and produce everything in just the order that is, and the idea of him would practically determine our expectations concerning the yet unknown. The kinds would be numbered, the laws fixed, the things assigned each to its place and date, yet the whole known in one act of Omniscience, if there were *such* a god as the primal fact. Meanwhile the primal fact might be otherwise constituted—no God, many gods, etc: In either case there would be a universe and no pure disconnection.

3. *The argument from Interaction.*

(See Schiller Phil. Rev,) Once more, say the monists, if things have that amount of affinity which is expressed by their mutual influence they must have a still deeper unity as its ground. But grant the deeper unity: why should *its parts* be such as to respond mutually in those ways?—why but that as a matter of fact it is that kind of a unity and not another? If you need *it,* to explain the unity of the things, you need another principle to explain its own constitution. In the end you must leave off with a "constitution," whether of the substantial principle or of the empirical universe.

And don't retort that those who work without the unifying principle sin through beginning with terms ("separate" things) on which interconnexion is impossible. Of course abstract separateness contradicts abstract connexion. But separateness in space, in nature, etc. does not contradict connexion in other ways. As a matter of fact changes in things *are* temporally connected, and it is as odd (as a mere matter of chance happening) that there should be extant something that can make them so as that they should "be" so *schlechthin.*

We ask for Lotze's mind-unity to embrace them, not for its ontological clearness, but simply because it hypothetically represents the facts in analogy with a type of connexion that both satisfies us and is familiar. The facts would not be more intelligible *a parte ante*, but practically, *a parte post.*

Immanent change, in the Absolute mind, is as far as its mechanism goes, just as unintelligible as transeunt change. It is moreover incredible, if said mind be already perfect, as the absolutists say it is. Lotze's description of the absolute "compensating" its own inner "disturbances," shows how far away we are from living intelligibility. Once more the substantial unity postulated is assumed for pragmatic purposes, and it only fulfils those purposes when represented as an ordinary pluralistic "God."

Concluding, then, I say that 1. proves nothing, leaving the universe as known or unknown as it finds it. Royce's Absolute in his latest book, evaporates into just the abstract knowability of all things.

2. Proves no more unity than it finds, either.

3. is a pretty hypothesis.

The word "unity" when applied to the universe needs all sorts of specifications before you can deny or affirm it. One sort of unity may be there, another not. Absolute unity in the sense given on p. 19 [*ed.*, 261.27–33] is not only not proven, but, if hypothetically admitted, appears both sterile practically and even, the moment the attribute of perfection is added to it, inwardly absurd.

With what then are we left? With a universe certainly containing all the unity we find, and possibly more, both noetic and dynamic.

How much more? is a question of fact not for logic but for science & faith to decide.

Panpsychism would answer

22. Notes for Philosophy 9: Metaphysics—The Fundamental Problems of Theoretical Philosophy (1898–1899)

Uniformity of nature such as to call for Bowne's argument for Intelligent creator. But we mustn't forget Darlington's objection, that if beans be thrown down we can pick them out so as to make a pattern—the laws of nature are laboriously *picked*. Bradley on many times spaces, and causal system.

Still all sorts of things have got into *interaction*, and this is said to be impossible on our pluralistic scheme.

To discuss interaction we must recollect:

1. That *Hume has triumphed*. No *power*. The phenomenon is law, functional variation.

2. This is said to contradict the supposed separateness of the things. For their changes are inward activities, and how can an outward fact get *in* to instigate such an activity. The only two solutions are monistic.

a) Leibnitzs preestablished harmony originating in Creator

b) Lotze's "One Being"—*M*.

But it does n't explain *how a* influences *b* to say that they are both parts of one being, ideas in one mind, etc. It only amounts to saying in another form of words that *a does* influence *b*, that they are less separate than we thought, that they run parallel and can be described under a common law. That the *full* fact is not *a*, *b*; but a = f (b).

But it is just as much a mystery how this full fact *comes to be* if you describe it monistically as if you describe it pluralistically. The One original being has that sort of constitution. We beg the details singly if we say it grew up, & we beg them in a lump otherwise. But it is the same identical ontological "beg"; and *what* is begged is the plain fact that distinct things do run parallel. (*Esse = fieri.*)

The only inward way of interpreting the parallelism is psychically, by fitness, love, sympathy etc. Suppose then that the variations the summation of which makes progress are increments of this sort of sympathetic synchronous, or functional variation. The result would be *system-building*. Uneasiness and satisfaction.

Difficult to carry out in detail, but my point is simple enough, that granting the amount of system we find in Universe, and the actual relations of influence we do find we add nothing to our understanding of them by saying they have their source in one primal being. They are the peculiar things they are, anyhow, and the "Being" is just a name for the whole system of them considered at once.

Nay, say Royce, Bradley, Lotze, etc. The being *realizes* itself at once, and is an *additional* fact to the several relations. Yet Royce gives this up, with his separate will acts.

I reply that this is a distinct hypothesis. And a bad one!

Something wrong about this being! Lapse from his full unity! The wrong is that the parts *are* realized singly, anyhow.

I believe that the One being is only the abstract idea of the collection, made into an entity and put behind the collection as its cause. (pentadactyles.) The world thus exists 2ce over. The monistic god does n't help at all. It only derealizes.

What is the God, on our principles. Neither Bradley's, nor Royce's; nor Bowne's. But the not-me which makes for my ends & of which I feel the presence.

Paulsen's panpsychism. Are we the highest? the wisest? Conterminousness comes in.

Now as to God? Lutoslavski's horse race.

Religious *experiences*!

But to be admitted only so far as actual. The ordinary absolute God is only a description of the fact taken after the fact, and then placed behind the fact as its ground.

The only absolute thing so far as the intellect goes is history,—process.

A restless moralistic world: Yet philosophy's only world.

Peremptorily rejected by many.

Frank mysticism.

> Whitman
> Trevor
> Bucke. Blood.
> Plotinus
> Ribet.
> Light on Path etc
> Vivekananda,
> Bhagvat Gita

Yet even in this world of the mystic One there is something wrong. The rest, the peace, is broken by the Maya.

In short—*the Universe is not concluded*. As Blood says—what is concluded? etc. This means that Time is real. Pragmatically Time means that beyond what you can't act on or expect from, there are action and expectation possible. The timeless Absolute denies this, pluralism asserts it as the untranscendable truth.

23. Syllabus of Philosophy 3: The Philosophy of Nature (1902–1903)

What Philosophy is: an investigation into object-world as well as into subject-world.

"Pragmatism" as our method.

Berkeley's Idealism as an example thereof.

Kant's argument for Idealism.

Post-Kantian Idealism makes experience absolute.

Pluralistic Panpsychism: material objects are "for themselves" also.

Idealism is not necessarily Ideality, for us—even the Absolute may will human frustration.

"Facts," "laws," and ultimate "elements." Elements and laws (the conceived order) have usually been considered to have a deeper reality than facts (the perceived order).

Recent criticism treats them as a subjective short-hand for descriptive purposes: our laws do not pre-exist, Nature verifies them only approximately; and our elements (atoms, ether) involve logical absurdities.

The Energy-theory tries to reduce this artificiality and to describe perceptual experiences simply.

Yet "conservation of energy" is also an ideal conception which the facts fit, so Nature does meet our rational demands.

How explain this harmony?

Theistic view: God's design.

Transcendentalist views: Eternal Reason evolving.

Pearson's suggestion: co-evolution of intellect and sense.

Peirce's suggestion: Order results from chance-coming, and survival of the more coherent.

Question of Unity of World.

Description of world as a multitude of moments of experiences, connected by relations (also experienced) which constitute so many grades of "unity," such as sharing one Space and Time, being of a kind, being known together, interacting, having one origin, etc. Any sort of unity makes a universe of that grade. Our universe is of many grades. It shows, *e. g.*:

Noetic Unity: Complex objects are perceived or conceived;—but there is always some ignorance. The various knowers are not immediately conscious of one another. I only *postulate* your mind, as correlative to what I see your body do.

"Pure Experience" thus agrees with common sense: Our various minds "terminate" at percepts (physical things), which they experience in common.

Objections to this conterminousness of minds:

I. Pluralistic:

a. "Two can't have the same object, because each has its object inside of itself." Pragmatic answer: How can I tell *where* your object is except by your acts? To show where, you point to *my* object with your hand which *I* see. It is only as altering *my* objects that I guess you to have a mind. If your object is not where mine is, the objector must show where else it is; he probably introjects it into your head.

b. "Two minds can't have one object because they are two." Answer: A purely verbal objection! The objector should show a *hindrance* to their being one in that point.

c. "Pre-established harmony is a better theory." Answer: No, for it violates parsimony, precludes eventual increase of conscious union, and involves universal predestination.

II. Monistic objections: They assert that there is no half-way position between absolute unity and absolute disconnection.

a. Royce's argument for Noetic Unity: it assumes self-transcendency of knowing state. Answer by pragmatic description (1.) of perceptual knowledge as identity of state and object, and (2.) of conceptual knowledge as transition through harmoniously developing intermediary experiences to a terminus (or *towards* such terminus, assumed to be possible if no hindrance appears). On this view knowledge becomes an external relation, and no All-Knower is required.

b. External conjunctions in general are absurd: The conjunctions would have to be conjoined in turn. "Independence" contradicts "connexion." A, related, is another A from A not related, etc.—No adventitious union of things is possible, through and through unity is required.

Answer: Such arguments are purely verbal, and even verbally, "partial independence" is an admissible term. Pragmatically, adventitious relations *are* intelligible. Need a space-interval be "linked"? Does A "resemble" before its like exists? etc.

Pragmatic discussion of Likeness, Change, Possibility, comes in here.

c. "An absolute Many is absurd on idealistic principles; for then every fact exists only by being known, and if the manyness be a fact, it is established as such by being present to an All-Knower." Answer: If unnoticed, the manyness is (on idealistic principles) no fact. If noted or questioned, it is *we* and not the All-Mind, who make it a fact.

d. "You can't say 'many' without uniting them into a universe of discourse." Answer: But need they for that be a universe of more than discourse?

The constitution of a multiple and additive universe is thus perfectly intelligible after the fact. Questions of *genesis* are more difficult.

Monism affirms one *origin.* Even to get into adventitious relations, things must have been pre-adapted to the relatedness. In the order of Being, the idea of the whole system had to come first. Block-universe!

Sterility in human hands of the abstract idea of system. It would apply to any universe whatever, after the fact. A chaos has its parts systematically interadapted to that chaotic effect.

No economy of data in one origin: our universe of discourse remains as numerous as if things came singly.

Monists, whenever they study details, have to adopt the pluralistic and empirical method.

All the appearances make for unity being of gradual growth. In concrete experience each step brings new ends into view. "Heterogony of purposes" and substitutability of "fulfilments." The larger systems are only retrospective results.

"Tychism" as an ultimate hypothesis. Some spontaneity is required by every philosophy. As ultimate terms, freedom, chance, necessity, truth, fact, mean one and the same thing—namely *datum* or *gift*; what (since we find it) we must accept as having *come*; what, for theory, is *taboo*. Is what has actually come *incompatible* with plural origin?

The details which we find could come in some way or they would not be here; Monism ought to show something to *prevent* their having come piecemeal.

In a world without previous hindering necessity, everything *may* come as a chance; the more stable chance products will accumulate, and if connected, will make a universe which will grow in unity also.

Interaction might also come (hindrance of it would be a case of it). Things instead of interpenetrating and making no difference, might, first, interfere with and *bound* each other, and then grow gregarious,—associations, habits, and compound units thus accumulating by degrees. What should prevent such variations?

Lotze's proof of Monism by interaction. Purely verbal: *call* them "One," they can, call them "many" they can't, interact. The real question is, What is interaction known as? Whatever it be, it *came*, whether it came in the one, or with the many.

The originals of all that we know as interaction are subjective aspects of experience. Continuity, activity, causality, change, development, help, hindrance, fulfilment, etc., are forms of consciousness of transition.

"Interaction" therefore was realized whenever consciousness of transition came, when boundaries as such became objects, and conterminous experiences were known together. Vast empirical differences in the *spread* of consciousness.

There may, even now, be much more spread than we are aware of. Royce's "time-span" hypothesis. Divine consciousness a question of fact, not of logic.

The wider the span the more is unity realized. "Organic" unity the form of unity most likely to accumulate, if once produced.

Limitless cumulative power of minute variations in conservative direction. Conformably to Science, the increments have been incredibly minute and our universe, now inconceivably old, is already enormously evolved towards order.

Reasons in Tychism's favor.

I. Scientific reasons:

1. No concrete experience ever repeats itself. The usual explanation of concrete variety by permutation of unvarying elements, is, if taken absolutely, only an assumption. Scientific laws express only aggregate results, compatible with individual variation in the elements—recent science abounds in the admission of such variation.

2. We fail to absolutely exclude originality, by assuming that elements only *repeat*. Repeat what?—original models!

3. Our own decisions suggest what "coming into existence" might be like: "Chance" from without, self-sufficing life from within. *What* comes is determined only *when* it comes. *Ab extra* it appears only as a possible gift or "graft."

II. Moral Reasons.

1. Absolutely to deny novelty, as monism does, and to assume that the universe has exhausted its spontaneity in one act, shocks our sense of life.

2. Tychism, essentially pluralistic, goes with empiricism, personalism, democracy, and freedom. It believes that unity is in process of being genuinely won. In morals it bases obligation on actual demand. Tychism and "external relation" stand or fall together. They mean genuine individuality, something to *respect* in each thing, something sacred from without, *taboo*.

III. Metaphysical reasons.

1. Tychism eliminates the "problem of evil" from theology.

2. It has affinities with common-sense in representing the Divine as finite.

3. It avoids Monism's doubling-up of the world into two editions, the Finite repeating the Absolute in inferior form.

Infinity.—For Tychism, things come in instalments, causing *change*. Continuous change would give us the *completed infinite*.

Zeno's argument conclusive. Continuity is only an ideal construction. In actual experience, there are "thresholds," and change is always by finite increments.

Where the world's elements are represented as standing (space), or as having come already (past time), there seems no incompatibility between their infinity and their actuality.

Kant's antinomies. Fallacy of K.'s argument against infinity. Each condition must indeed be there; but need the "each"-es make an "all" in the sense of a bounded collection? To say so, begs the question. All that logic requires is that no one (distributively taken), must be lacking.

Renouvier's *principe du nombre*: Same fallacy. Real things may be countable *ad infinitum* if each number finds its thing already there.

For the more in these cases is defined as something previous, and not, as in the case of continuous change, as something yet to be produced.

Empirical discussion of infinity of world.

Conclusion.—In any case the "quantity of being" is finite, since, by Tychism, beings have come in successive instalments, each of finite amount, just as our experiences now come. Time and space may be infinite without contradicting logic.

Pragmatically, infinity means that more may come, infinitesimal means that something is lost, has sunk below the pragmatic threshold. "Experience," swinging between the two infinites, is thus most naturally describable in pluralistic or tychistic terms.

The *inanity* of infinite time and space disinclines the mind to their acceptance, and panpsychic idealism, for which infinity no longer forms a problem, seems the most satisfactory theory to adopt.

24. Notes for Philosophy 20c: Metaphysical Seminary— A Pluralistic Description of the World (1903–1904)

Rationalist vs empiricist *temper* again!

Objections to monism.

1. Does n't account well for finite consciousness.

(Represents us as characters in a novel, but they don't walk off. . . . .

Absolute knows us *cum alio*, we know ourselves *sine alio*.[1]

With our ignorance goes pain)[2]

2. Introduces problem of evil.

If Perfection came first why any imperfection?

(Lotze on Leibnitz etc.)

3. Its eternal world contradicts character & expression of reality.

Novelty, achievement, gain!

4. Fatalistic. Violates free will. Makes notion of 'possible' illusory.

Against this, only religious peace, & authority of mysticism. "Central peace abiding at the heart of endless agitation."

Contrast between religion & morality.

Pluralism the *moralistic* view

Perfection necessary, vs.

      "   "   conditionally possible.

Would you accept the latter world?

Of course!

"Reality grows, for we are at once its dark husk and its radiant core,

---

[1] In the left margin WJ wrote, 'my griefs at least are mine'.

[2] In the right margin WJ wrote, '*privation* the essence of us.'

the battlefield of its hard won conquests, and also ourselves the conquerors. And these battles, once gained, are gained for eternity, seeing that the path of the spirit moves not in a blind circle but with upward and widening sweep.[3] In so far as we discern & identify ourselves with its trend, we share that upward & onward movement. In so far as we are blind or wayward, we necessarily lag behind. To be passively borne along would be barren of results to the universe; only the permeation of nature (which is impulse) by spirit (which is free will) can actualize for us the Ideal. Thus nature becomes spiritualized & spirit naturalized without flaw in the immemorial sequence of cause & effect." Chas. J. Whitby (The ethical review, May 12. 1906, p. 14).

Set up frankly the pluralistic view.

"God rested the 7th day with parts of his world unfinished—those are the parts that we are finishing now."

Hoffding: Our knowledge is unfinished   his anecdote of Child: In what business now is God?

Say a word about the God of religious experience, as *working*

Hegelian whirlpool dialectic.[4]

Parallelism—mind & body

Causation. Activity etc

Monism. Absolute etc.

Evolution. Tychism.

Conservation of Energy

Determinism

Infinite.

Cognition. Royce's argument

Pragmatism.

Man thinking

Hypotheses   Pragmatism

Abstract & Concrete

Connection   Unity

Continuity   Infinite.

Possibility   Actuality

Nextness   Conterminousness   adjacency

Evolution

Objectivity   Subjectivity

---

3 In the left margin WJ wrote, 'Cf. Hume's metaphor of stage actor & audience'.

4 In the left margin WJ wrote vertically, 'Sameness & Identity See Fullerton'.

Being as absolute datum—the amount of it irrelevant. Renouvier.

reality = objectivity

Perceptual vs. conceptual order.

I want to come *out* with collective *pluralism,* purposive impulse, and *nextness* as principle of unity.

Best to *foreshadow this* rather early, as my intention.

Begin construction by question of *Realism vs. Idealism.*

Meaning of *real,* of *being.*

Criticism of *matter.*

Idealism. Berkeley's pragmatism.

Two forms of Idealism.

Berkeleyan—Transcendentalist

Whether "Nature" be material or mental the question is as to the *history* of it, the plan and pattern, pragmatic outcome rather than the substance.

Leave question of idealism undecided therefore!

In any case Nature is congruent with our intellectual interests, is *intelligible.*

    (Logarithms, analytic geometry, etc).

    Statistics   life insurance.

    parallelogram of forces.

    Centre of gravity

    lines & "pencils" of light

    Uniformity

    Law

    Molecular mechanics

    Conservation of energy.

    Obedience to simple formulas.

Result: Natural*ism*!

Other mental interests baffled.

Still there is *some* order.

How explain this?

Theism: "design."

Monism: Lotze's argument.

Question of connexion: Bradley. Possibility.

Nextness.

Evolution à la Peirce.

Zielstrebigkeit

Pluralistic appearance.

What[5] *is matter?*

Aristotle Metaph. Bk VII. ὑλη, ὑποκείμενον,

T. Harper. Metaph. of the School vol II. p. 183+ esp. pp. 189

J. Rickaby: Gen. Metaph. 86+

Explain as *nature* and *being*

Matter gives reality.

Descartes: 2 Substances.

What is matter?

Basis of real existence

Nature & being

Ideals & reals have same *nature*.

In reals a substance supports it.

Material substance.

1) First step to undermining it is criticism of the Senses,—their variations. *Which* true?—if not one, neither.

Modern physiology[6]—"specific energies."

Trace history.

Democritus: real atoms slumbered and opinion

Protagoras: all opinion.

Aristotle Metaph. Bk VII.

         Psych. Bk III beginning

Renaissance: Mechanical philosophy

    Hobbes. Human Nature, Ch. II

    Descartes

    Locke: Bk II. Ch. VIII, p. 75.

2) *Berkeley*: Selections, 33, 36, 39, 47, 57–8–9

Edwards: 668,–74[7]

The beyond on theistic idealistic principles *confirms* the given; on realistic principles it undoes its truth.

Don't think that B. means: we can't *prove* by our having an idea of matter that *said matter really exists*. He says we have no other idea of it than as a percept.

B's question is "What does matter *mean*?"—not "does it exist?"

Obj. Is n't the desk *there*?

Reply: If it is at all it is "there."

---

5 On the facing blank page WJ wrote, 'J. J. Thomson: on electrons | vol 59. Pop. Sci. Aug 1901'.

   6 In the left margin WJ wrote in pencil, 'atoms + subjective effects.'

   7 In the left margin WJ wrote vertically, 'Ideal rain can wet an ideal skin, etc. | Descartes | Geulincx and occasionalism. Malebranche | Leibnitz'.

Read Edwards: 669

Berkeley's ideas of Space. Primary qualities mental.

Theistic *pluralistic* idealism

Absolute experien*ces* (plural). Howison—Emerson.

    Harvard Square. Curtain *is* picture.

3) Kant[8] made further argument

Certain things given and actual, yet infinite in form.

K's def of "infinite."

Incompatible with actuality. Potentiality

Yet for every actual thing the totality of its conditions must have
    been realized.

How can these take infinite form?

    Past time?

    Composition?

    Rest of space

    Continuous change.

Kant solves by distinction betw. extra-mental and phenomenal
    givenness.

Phenomenally, *aufgegeben*—potential.

Regress *indefinite*.

Universe follows laws of mind. K's Physics

"Transcendental idealism." Müller p. 426 428

K. still kept *D.a*S.—but not in space—as correlative to our "receptivity."

4) Fichte & Hegel expel the D.a.S.

No transcendent, unapproachable reality.

Experien*ce* (sing) is absolute.

Phenom. vs. real = private, transient, vs. general & stable.

---

[8] On a folded sheet pasted-in between fols. 6 ('B's question . . . been realized.'
276.33-277.11) and 7 ('How can these . . . the D.a.S.' 277.12-25) WJ wrote: 'Actual ex-
istence and infinite form are incompatible. At least so Kant admits. | No repugnance
between infinite and what is merely *potential [ab. del. 'possible']. Things can be *possible* in infinitum without paradox. If *continuous change [ab. del. 'the Space'], past
time, the parts of matter exist *per se* apart from representation, we have the contra-
diction. *Antinomies*. | But if these things be only as represented, the contradiction
vanishes. ['What' *del.*] Times, Spaces, subdivisions, as actually represen*ted*, are always
finite, but ['are' *del.*] more of them always remains representable in infinitum. | Calling
them *phenomena* reliefs us from the contradiction. Only a part of them is then *gegeben*,
the rest are auf[ge]geben, form an *Aufgabe* for the mind to follow and find. | *Nature
[ab. del. 'It'] obeys this law of indefinite regress in the conditions, which ['law' *del.*]
which the structure of the mind prescribes to it. | Transcendental Idealism. | Muller,
p. 426. | Kant's rationalistic physics.'

The phenomenal is that in which reason can't *rest*. Dialectic method
   Truth is thought's *destiny*.
Kant's transcendental Ego interpreted as a World Soul led to mo-
   nistic Phil of Absolute. To think as the Absolute thinks.
Question as to *constitution of Nature* recurs just as for materialism.
What if world-soul be imperfect?
Within Idealism a materialistic wing.
5) *Panpsychism*—"World of Spirits"
Lotze: being in itself = being *for* self.
Paulsen. monadism
Possible pluralistic interpretation.
Dictate (?) sheet about panpsychism.

               Panpsychism says:

1 The only Realities are Minds with their Thoughts—psychical
   facts.
2 All knowledge to be definitively true must be knowledge of these
   facts.
3 All I can truly know is *what* some other thinker is thinking.
4 All he can truly know is what I am thinking.
4a not because of any limitation in our knowing faculty—but because mental facts are the only existences there are.
S + Physical Object in se
S.+ Secondary qualities + Physic. Object
S + Sec. + prim. qualities + ?
S + Thought + S
I lay stress on the point that the actual presence of the other S there
   is what constitutes the *veracity* of our consciousness that the matter of our own tho't is objective. The form of our consciousness
   must always be objective. But only when the other S is there is it
   veraciously so.
5 Each then knows s'thing which exists without his thinking it.
6 The consciousness of each is thus cognitive in form & veracious.
7 The thought of a physical object existing in *se*, though cognitive
   in form is not veracious.
8 The physical object to be truly known must be conceived as a
   psychical one.
9 theism conceives it thus by saying *God means* I should think just
   that physical object. In knowing what God means for me, I
   know the whole truth as a psychic fact and yet I preserve the
   physical appearance.

10 It is hylozoistically done by supposing that the physical fact is really or *in se* a feeling which however appears to me as something else. Atoms. Hard to think out.

11 The theistic solution explains the physical world as a phenomenon intended for us all to think just as we do think it. When all the thinkers know each other's thoughts of it and God's purposes in sending them all will have the same Object Which will be the full truth. So long as any one's Object bears a pur⟨ely⟩ physical form, or so long as any one thinker ignores the thoughts of another thinker, error will remain in the world.

6. Criticism of Scientific conceptions.

Until quite recently men believed that the hypotheses of science were *truths*. Just as for scholastics matter & forms, so for Kant all the Newtonian apparatus.

Phenomenal for Kant, but inalterable. His rationalism.

So of us: Matter and its properties, in the form of atoms & molecules, and the "laws" thereof are objective entities.

Self contradictions:—atoms & elasticity etc.

Unintelligibilities:—hardness.

Paradoxes:—ether.

Mysteries: attraction.

Sigwart, Lotze, Riehl,

Stallo, Pearson, Jas. Ward

Mach, Ostwald.

James, Psychology II, 633, 641 [*The Principles of Psychology*, WORKS, pp. 1229, 1237]

Le Roy: Rev. de M. 1899   Bergson.

Stallo's book.

New conception.

 Nature a chaos, torrent,
 like foreign tongue.

We carve out "things"

We class them & abstract properties.

We discover laws.

 All for *descriptive* purposes
 "economy."

You[9] see, 2 idealisms.

---

9 On the facing page WJ wrote: '[*penc.*] Pearson 86 | [*ink*] le. Donné, cette pâte plastique et malléable où l'activité vivante trace des figures ['où' *del.*] et dispose des

monistic (derived fm. "transcendental Ego")
    pluralistic
In either case reality not transcendent
Experience is absolute.
In first case, how account for separate consciousnesses?
In second, How for unity, or union?
In either case, account for appearance of external world.
Here, in deeper criticism of our scientific conceptions of nature, a
    new set of arguments for idealism come in.
Secondary qualities subjective anyhow
But *laws* supposed universal & objective.
Berkeley's view
Kant's view: inalterable, Nature rational.
Truths! objective existents.
Popular realism: Caloric, electric fluid, attractive & repulsive
    forces—and now ether, chemical molecules, energy, etc.
Remarkable harmony between mathematics and natures laws.
Nature seems to have a mathematical and rational structure.
Theistic explanation: Bowne, 66, 74.
Transcendentalist: Schelling, Hegel.
Meanwhile the succession of scientific theories has bro't out their
    artificiality.
Authors to day who assert their subjectivity.
It is only *as if* they were "laws" of nature.
    Analytic coordinates—curves
    Centre of gravity
    lines & pencils of light
    "Geometrical addition"
    "lines" & "pencils" of light
    Averages
    Pearson, 86. +   Poincaré, Cornelius.
    Mach Monist II, 198
    Triumph of *formulas* over hypotheses.
Matter becomes "mass" (reines Gedankending)
Force is that which in the effect is correlative to acceleration, Ward
    I, 59–63.
Molecules become points of position (Boscovich)
Bare description of functional variations of phenomena

---

systèmes de relations. | Le Roy, Rev. de M. VII, 389 | Cf. Schiller in *P. [*ov.* 'I'] Id.,
p. 60 | [*penc.*] Sail & ballast | We drain out uniformity'.

As if atoms, as if continuous medium, *as if* attractive forces, either
as if a spiral spring.

"Metaphors" (Maxwell II, 227) which we choose according to our
taste.

Any hypothesis good which gives elegant formulas

Science a *language*

$$mgh = \tfrac{1}{2}\, mv^2 \mid \sum S + \tfrac{1}{2} \sum mv^2 = const$$

how unanschaulich!

Don't try!

All our laws approximations

Ostwald on hypotheses, 206

"Energetic." Explain

No conservation of any one phenomenon
(candle, sleep, storm, walk)

Sum?

How make it? (Symphony, rainbow, $1.50, 12 lbs beef, walk to
Boston)

Common aspects—measure those!

Difficulty—no intuitive measure.

Pull elastic one foot

Draw[10] boat 1 in with 10 lbs. 2 with 20?

Throw stone with v. rises 20 ft. will 2 v give 40?

will they do the same work?

No intuition. Leibnitz Newton controversy.

Conserved thing discovered. 3 facts.

1 Levels.

2. Work done in falling, must be done to rise

3. Amount of work depends only on level.
Reversible process the ideal   Galileo   Carnot
No perpetual motion.

Pendulum, planet

Configuration, inner stress.

Heat specific, & temperature

Chemical separation—affinity

Quantity (Coulomb)—potential (volt)

---

[10] On the facing page WJ wrote: 'Entire elimination of "force," as ['an' *del.*] a
*factor [*ab. del.* 'cause'] constant throughout time, by the energy-conception. This
substitutes two factors, both variable in time,—*viz. [*intrl.*] level and work, and
"forces" need n't be mentioned at all.'

Galileo's assumption
Carnot's
Law that things pass to lower level
In doing so drive other things to higher
Pendulum
Steam engine.
Luminous current
Zn Cu.
But you can't get higher level than you started from, on reversing.
Measurement in terms of equivalence.
Equiv. of heat 430 kgmt. for 1°C. 1 kg
Formula of form $mgh + \frac{1}{2} mv^2 = $ Const
What is the energy *itself*?
A *name*—for what?—for *sensibles*. "pure experience"
Description of actual experiences.
One thing is transmuted into another.
Ostwald's pamphlet, 12.
World running down. 2nd law.
No perpetual motion
Artificial formulas
Mosaic of experience
Back to Berkeleyism.
Or to Transcendentalism
Why do formulas fit?
Whence come the experiences?
Why do they resist other formulas?
(Le Roy vol IX, pp 413+)

Philosophy of "pure" experience, reverting to something like berke-
   leyan idealism. except that "God" acts less directly.
Idea that Nature's "unity" & "law" are subjective.
We drain off unity into our formulas.
We might drain disorderliness, if we would
Nevertheless Nature contains classes.
She has a grain, has cleavages.
Various attempts to conceive this. *Flexibility*
Ward's[11] last two chapters.
Pearson's: p. 100–104

[11] To the right of 'Ward's . . . –638' (282.36–283.2) WJ wrote: ' "Nature" *is* what we
make it, but she cooperates in the making, and resists certain attempts. She contains
classes and can only be *generalized* in certain ways.'

Schiller: p 59+
Wilbois, vol 9. p 634–638
Scepticism? Intellectualism?
Uncanniness of both
Familiarity of more religious idealism
And yet even that is ambiguous
If God is defined only as the God of that experience.
Experience only *becoming* ideal.
"Matter" is perhaps displaced, but is the victory barren?
Subtler materialism—"nothing but"
Here comes in a reflection
Our judgment of dissatisfaction
Pascal's roseau.
In a sense the thinker overlaps
"Imperfection" implies standard of perfection a principle of infinity[12] that makes us know our finitude. In the consciousness of it we rise above it   Caird.
Were you *merely* imperfect you could not know the fact
Possibility of perfection, then, anyhow might be condition of reaching it.
  This the empiricist evolutionary view.
Transcendentalist view not so modest.
Royce says not merely possible, but neccessarily now actual.
For[13] assume any defect in the universe—that defect is a *fact*. As fact, it has a *knower*—that knower knows that there is no remedy. But knowing is willing; so he wills thus—and so his world is perfect.
At this rate any world whatever, provided it were the Absolutes, would be perfect, for what he thinks he wills to think, and it must fulfill his will, whatever its content may be. (For "possibilities" excluded by the Absolute, See W. & I. I, 574) (Subjective contentment of the Knower with an unrelieved desire vs possession of desideratum)
Absolute therefore guarantees no perfect world *from human point of view*. Philos. of A. might be pessimistic, have a materialistic or naturalistic "wing." "Perfection" might be one of the excluded possibilities.
  Problem of "Knowledge."

12 WJ wrote 'infinity' above undeleted 'perfection'.
13 To the left of this paragraph WJ wrote, 'Conception of God, p. 38+ W. and I. II, 365–8 371, 409 Religious Aspect p. *443–5 ['3' *ov.* '4']'.

Locke's & Berkeley's representationism

Atomistic theories of perception, Lucretius.

Scholastic doctrine. (Maher.)

"Intentional" species. Intentional possession

Popular dualism, self transcendency, quasi miraculous presence in absence.

Royce's argument involves this element.

Demands Absolute to relieve the paradox.

My formula[14]—implies no transcendency.

(Mind, X, 27, (1885); Psych. Rev. II, 105 1895   Miller: Phil Rev. II, 408, 1893)

Cases:[15] 1) immediate perceptive knowledge, object & subject are identical. "Acquaintance."

   2) k. of distant or future, intermediate experiences develope into perceptional terminus.

   3) k. of past, regressive associates harmonious

   4) Conceptual k. of general truths can be potentially resolved into one of the other kinds. Always knowledge "about" some percept.

3 points implied:

   1) No transcendency[16]

   2) Feeling of prosperous development or of contradictory development

---

[14] On the facing blank page WJ wrote: ' "Knowledge," on my theory, can be predicated of a *printed [*intrl.*] word or name as well as of a state of mind. *Either [*ov.* 'Each'] is connected by intermediaries with its term. But the state of mind *lives in the transitions* and the name does n't (a propos of W. Walsh's demand for the names of my family).'

[15] On the facing page WJ wrote: 'Distinguish complete knowledge from incomplete (where terminus is not reached). Most knowledge is incomplete, sometimes forever so, as in case of ejects. The peculiarity of my theory is that the ideal terminus, even here, ['can only' *del.*] must always be represented as a bit of "experience." "Panpsychism," always, whereas dualism may make it "matter" or "spirit" or something else. An experience might always be potentially reached or shareable, for it is the same *sort* of thing which we already have. *Absence of contradictory consequences is practically the equivalent of a terminus that fulfils [*added diagonally*]'.

[16] On the facing page WJ wrote: 'The peculiarity of this "pure experience" description is that it eliminates transcendency, and makes of "subjects" and "objects" one kind of *Being ['B' *ov.* 'b'], simply viewed in different practical relations. One experience['s' *del.*] "knows" another when it connects with it in certain definable ways. The outward functions of replacing, continuing, fulfilling, practically superseding, etc. take the place of the supposed miracle of cognizing, which latter thus falls within the objective description of the world among all the other objective relations to be found there.'

3) The knowledge may be created as well as verified by the terminus being reached.[17]

Have we not here the full pragmatic equivalent of what any one means by knowledge? *Write* me objections!

Whatever may be the truth of *mill's statement* that objects are permanent possibilities, it is true that to be an *object of knowledge* is to be a possible sensory experience.

We can paraphrase Kant, and say that "to call an object a *known* thing before it is perceived means that in the possible progress of our experience we shall *perceive* it." Cf. Muller, p. 428. If we claim knowledge "about" anything—that task is *aufgegeben*.

General type of Philosophy of pure experience.

Mosaic without backing. All that is is experiences, possible or actual.

Immediate experience carries *sense of more*.

Each experient distinguishes the actual from the potential—actual being a narrow thread.

The "more" developes,
    harmoniously, or
    inharmoniously
Terminates in
    fulfilment, or
    check
Treat hospitably.

The problem is to describe universe in these terms.

Certain difficulties:

1) "Develope" implies either
    "change" of one being

17 On the facing page and on two lines of the next verso WJ wrote: 'One case is that of knowledge about things ['with' *del.*] which, a moment before, we were considering *without [written orig. as two words, but then joined]* noticing the relation (e.g. of similarity, causality or what not,) between them. Here again it is an experience-continuum, and no transcendency is required, anywhere. [The importance of the case lies in the retrospective attribution of the relation. If now similar, they were so then, before the similarity was noted. All the *objective* factors of the similarity pre-existed to the subjective judgment. *If ['f' *ov.* 't'] the question of similarity *in ['n' *ov.* 's'] ['raised about' *del.*] the things as they existed uncompared is raised, the only answer can be that they *were* similar, even then. You *certainly ['c' *ov.* 's'] can't say that they were not similar, and *you* can't not say that they were similar, being asked. [¶] If things concerning which a judgment is made pre-existed to the judgment, and the judgment does n't *alter* ['an' *del.*] them, then what the judgment says of them was already true previously. [*fol.* 24ᵛ] [Bradley ought to contend that it must necessarily *alter them!*]'

or "continuity" in succession of many

2) We imply many experients, yet one world. The experients are ejective to each other—How can they know one another or the same objects?

3) "Possible"—so much remains only possible for each experient, that the question comes: *what is* being that is only *possible*?

4) How can the diverse come into relation at all? Bradley, Royce, Lotze's monism.

5) What do we mean by "One"?

6) "   "   "   " by "Same"?

You see how many puzzles.

My program is to solve them by the principle of *nextness*, conterminousness.

Pluralism with continuity.

Nowhere all realized together.

Modest program, defending common sense.

"*The moment of experience*." Hodgson I. Ch II.

The minimum involves time

Explain the sense of *more* and its fulfilment, $\bar{s}$. self transcendency. ("them" "there" soon other elsewhere)

Fields succeed and supersede, fulfilling.

The confidence in each that we are to verify or fulfil, the feeling of onrushing life is what we mean at any moment by our knowledge of the existing world beyond. More experience possible. *Termini* to the various conceptual members of our field.

Many experients: how can they know same objects?

How be conterminous?

For dualism or representationism this is an impossibility or a paradox.

Not so for "pure experience," using the principle of nextness.

Define nextness as outer relation with "nothing between." (Give *physical* examples)

Why do you infer my mind at all?

As cause of movement in your object, my body!

Like *sight* & *feeling* of *your own hand*.

They terminate[18] at each other.

18 On the facing page WJ wrote: '*How *can* you and, each with his idea inside his own mind, know the same object?—so says "epistemology," but *this* philosophy of ours asks: [*written ab. and bel. del.* 'No sense of continuity over the terminus'] Why *can't* you & I ['hav' *del.*] know same object? | If I terminate *at* yours and you *at* mine, and nothing between, the two objects are at any rate *continuous*, and the question of same-

(Berkeley's denial of anything in common)

My consciousness of my body terminates at your object.

The rest of my consciousness is continuous with that body c.

As my body, so this lamp.

We all terminate *at* it, if not in it.

There may be *in* it something that lies *between* us all, but it may be numerically one thing.

No paradox! so long as the between is represented as a *more* which might continue the experiences.

Remember that I am only describing the *what* or nature of experience as it presents itself. Questions of *genesis* are postponed. If objections are to be made they must be logical objections, based on contradiction between the parts of what is described, not on the physical difficulty or impossibility of bringing what is described, to pass.

I am rehabilitating common sense—a process which always *sounds* queer.

Common sense supposes one world open to us all, we share its objects, though we each have private experiences.

Now is my sensible world the "same" as yours?

You sit here—I enter. My body for you is part of the same world with the lamp, with your body. We can pull against same lamp.[19]

That body seems to express mind, so you infer *my* mind as animat-

---

ness becomes philological. | If aught lies between, (molecules etc) it may be a "more" for each of us, exploring which, we may terminate again at an identity.'

[19] On the verso of this leaf WJ drew the following diagram, joined by guideline to the text:

'Our two trains terminate inside this circle, and they may get nearer each other than their first termini— much interpolation is possible, and their real point of coalescence may be ideal. Yet since they are dynamically one in the sense explained over the page, since each drags the other along in its alterations, they unite the two trains of consciousness to that extent. ['Operations in one have effects in the other' *del.*] They are subject to one operation'.

ing it. But it is your object; so *my* mind is taken as altering *your* object—our two minds have relations to that same object. It is only as animating that object of yours that you assume my mind at all.

Our two minds therefore share that object, both terminate (one noetically the other dynamically) in this body. And this body carries with it the case of all other material things, for they are homogeneous with human bodies and terminate at them.

Rope & two bodies.

If you mistrust the argument, it is probably because of certain prejudices.

1st. How *can* an object in your mind be the same as an object in my mind. "*In.*"

"Introjection": If in head, my object must be located differently from your object.

But where *are* our objects (supposed two) located if not in the same place?

In study of vision we answer question "where?" by *acts*.

So here:[20] You ask me where *my* lamp is and I point to the lamp which *you* see, with the hand *you* perceive as the hand of my body. The only mind you assume to exist as mine, when appealed to, locates its objects where you locate yours.

If you say this *can't* be, for since 2 minds are out of each other, their "contents" must be numerically two, their spaces two spaces, etc.,

I ask what is to *prevent* partial coalescence of two trains of tho't? The burden of proof lies with you. You must show, if you say my object is not where[21] your object is, that it is s'where[22] *else*.

Say then they are the *same!*[23]—same world. What do we mean by "same"?

---

[20] On the facing page WJ wrote: 'My theory shd. be classed with Royce's *"realistic" [*intrl.*] theories. It says that *of [*intrl.*] two beings "independent" of each other in *other* respects, one may become a "knower" the other a "known," through certain definitely stateable intermediaries being realized. Royce's argt is silly: He starts by saying the independence is "total," and of course finds that this contradicts *all* relations! Who ever said that the known did n't depend on the knower for its quality of being an "object."? Who said that the *knower* as such does n't depend on there being an object for it to know?'

[21] Above 'where' WJ wrote 'same'.

[22] Above 'where' WJ wrote 'other'.

[23] Opposite this sentence WJ wrote on the facing page, 'Or don't say "same": say "conterminous." Conterminousness *brings [*ab. del.* 'is'] a certain ['kind of' *del.*] type of union into the world.'

Pragmatically at least this, that you, operating on your object, also
operate on mine, or at any rate, mine changes.

This might be the case were they numerically two, yet with a *pre-
established harmony.*

Why not adopt that view?

The 2 weltbilder, Leibnitz's & mine are comparable.

Leibnitz says beforehand that continuity of consciousness, personal
union, *can* never obtain.

Furthermore everything predetermined with reference to everything else.

My theory allows for possibility of completer unity (not only conterminousness, but *conscious union* between parts beyond the
bridge). The world may actually be *achieving* unity. (Illustration
of *hand.*)

It allows of freedom—mutual independence

It is "economical." [Hardly as much so as either Berkeley or
Leibnitz!]

Its essential peculiarity is to discriminate between different grades
of unity, sameness, oneness.

It gives a world hanging together by intermediaries, whose parts
need not all be *immediately* together; as in the theory of the
absolute.

Discuss now the doctrine which says there can be no unity unless an
absolute one.

The general principle[24] involved here is that if you start with any
kind of uniting relation between things you are forced on towards
a still deeper relation till you end by seeing that what you took
to be distinct or independent things are only elements in one
being.

First example: Lotze's argument[25] about interaction.

Is *contact* action

Influence must pass, force, action, state

---

24 On the facing page WJ wrote, 'Correlative principle that if you assume any disconnection whatever it forces you on to absolute disconnection. Marvin works this in
his Chaps. on Pluralism and on Causation.'

25 On the facing page WJ wrote: 'Micr. Bk IV. Ch. III; Bk IX, Ch. I | Metaph. Bk I.
Chaps V & VI. | Outlines of Met. Ch. V. | Schiller Philos. Rev. V, 225 (1896) | "M"
['simply' *del.*] does n't *acct. for* interaction, say how it takes place, how *done*, it simply
['co' *del.*] says the things are not "independent" *so far*. It renames the fact. *In* the
absolute it is just as enigmatical as *out* of it, *how* the things move together'.

But these can't *pass*, detaching themselves.

Even then how does the inner state of B alter?

Transeunt has to become *immanent* action.

 Relations are "between," but

Any *between* becomes a third entity, & the problem recurs. Microc. II p. 596[26]

My philosophy and common sense both assume that things whose being is independent, can nevertheless come into relations, which are adventitious & external, not neccessarily involved in the being of each thing, but possible only, or conditional on other things arising, between which and the first thing the relations obtain.

Absolutists say that no such external relations are possible. The relations must be founded on something *in* the several things, or not exist at all. If there be any relation whatever "between" things it must be based on a communion of their being, and from one relation to another you are finally driven to admit that there is only one being really with all the things and relations inside of it as its elements or parts. The arguments are subtle. I will enumerate some of them. A few abstract statements

General contrast of Absolutism with my position is on opposite [*ed.*, 290.7–19].

Ideal of a most super-intimately grounded truth—every shallow state of facts must be rooted in a deeper state of facts. *mystical* terminus.

E.g. If it be apparently a fact that A is "after" B or "beside" B, or "like" B, there must be a ground for this fact, and a reason why it is true of *this* A; and if the intimate name of it do not involve the reason, why *this* A? If the reason were outside, any other A would do. A must "contribute" (Bradley 575), so must B. They must not only *come* together de facto ideally belong to each other beforehand. Even when still unrelated they must *be for* each other essentially, form an intended system before the fact.[27]

---

[26] Opposite this sentence WJ wrote on the facing page, 'See also Royce, II, 128'.

[27] On the verso of this leaf WJ wrote, 'Pringle-Pattison in Bradley in Man & the Cosmos, espy pp. 110+ | Hodder, Psych. Rev. I. 307'. Below a line drawn across the page he wrote, 'Bring in, without naming him, Royce's contention long ago, in opposi-

$$\overset{\text{I}\quad\text{I}}{\overbrace{}}$$

tion to my notion of plural noetic relations holding a universe together A B C, etc that the B-known-by-A could n't possibly be the same as the B-known *or knowing

Through[28] & through union, or pure irrelevance!

Positive model of such union in a thought or sentence. The whole is the minimum that can *be*. Like soap bubble.

"An external qualification is a mere conjunction, ... an attempt of diversities simply to identify themselves, and such an attempt is what we mean by self contradiction . . . . Since diversities exist, they must therefore somehow be true and real, and since, to be understood and to be true & real, they must be united; hence they must be true and real in such a way that from A or B the intellect can pass to its further qualification without an external determination of either. But this means that A & B are united, each from its own nature, in *a whole which is the nature of both alike*. And hence it follows that in the end there is *nothing real but a whole of this kind*." p. 570–1.

Read p. 574 ff. of Bradley.

Abstract habits of speech help to the same conclusion.[29]

How can "the separate" become "conjoined"? If so, it is no longer the separate. You simply have two worlds instead of the synthetic phenomenon of union.

How can A when in relation, be the *same* A wh. was out of relation? You contradict yourself, are talking of two worlds. If your A is identically to enter into relation, it must always have contained the relation as a virtuality—it must somehow have been inwardly represented. It cannot be purely adventitious.

Each term must be antecedently adapted, must implicitly refer to

---

[*intrl.*] by C, so that there would be an impassable chasm making 2 universes, thus:

A - B chasm B - C. Cf. notes in "Royce" envelope; and infra, p. 39½ [*ed., fn.* 30]'.

28 In the left margin WJ wrote vertically, ' "Parts" are *abstracts*.'

29 On the facing page WJ wrote: 'Likeness is grounded in *the [*intrl.*] inner nature of the two like things—it is the "same" in both. Absolutists tend to regard outer relations as similarly grounded. But [' "likeness" itself' *del.*] the capacity for likeness itself in noway presupposes the existence of *the [*ab. del.* 'the'] like elsewhere. ['['It is' *del.*] The ['T' *ov.* 't'] nature' *del.*] Anything with a nature of its own is *ipso facto* potentially like all other things which may arise and have that nature. Till they come, and the likeness is observed, it is not actualized or realized. Not that they are *not* alike, *if the question be raised*. If raised, "*they [*ov.* 'yes'] are alike" is the only answer. We must admit *2 [*ov.* '3'] ['states of a relation.' *del.*] sorts of relation, grounded inwardly & grounded outwardly. In either, the relation may be grounded without being realized. Yet it is "there," in the sense that you can't *call* it *not* there. *On likeness compare Royce's almost incredible rubbish, W. & I. I, 130. [*added vertically in mrgn.*]'

the other terms, if *those* terms are to come together in synthetic union. The union must be *through* the parts, must preexist.

Subject & predicate: "A is B." You lie, A is just *A*. To be true A can be no stark self identical. It is the A which is already potentially B which is B. But the union is then the first thing, the minimum of reality, and the form of your proposition, representing A & B as if disjoined and then united afterwards, or *per accidens*, falsifies truth.

"Sugar is white & sweet."[30] Another lie. The sugar which is white is *as such* not that which is sweet. It takes three things in one already to make your account of sugar true.

Qualities are relative to other things, "sweet," "white," "brittle." It takes many things to make one thing what it is. Unity again precedes.

Relations. How can two things ever become related at all if they are originally independent and irrelative? Must n't the relation be grounded *in* the things as a susceptibility? E.g. *Likeness.* But it can't be in them singly—Platos "taller." And it can't be a third fact "between" them, for its own linkage to both recurs etc. (Bradley p. 33). It must be that in the order of being the entire related system pre-exists throughout, and determines all the terms which we talk of as separates. They are conformed *for* each other.

Things really irrelative never *can* get linked?

Refer back to Lotze on Interaction

      "   "   " Royce on Cognition.

Read Royce on "Realism": W. & I. I, 127–131. If "independent" they *cant* get linked.

---

30 On the facing page WJ wrote: 'How can one thing stand in many relations? They tear the thing to pieces. *That* which is white is not *that* which is sweet, etc. No abstract name ['of a name' *del.*] explicitly names anything else than just what it denotes. It may be said to exclude, or even deny anything else, quâ name. Bradley etc. treats the names as if they were the things. | We assert something of something else *([*ov.* '4'] 57) | How anything can possibly be anything else . . . | It (change) asserts two of one. (45) | (Bradley)'. Below a line drawn across the page, he wrote: 'A & B have 100 dollars apiece. A gives one of his to B, so now one has 99, the other 101. Royce, Bradley & Co. insist that the (dollar-given-by A) can't be identical with the (dollar-received-by B) because forsooth these two "terms" are not identical. | Same example when I buy a strip of land from Turner. can't identically figure in both transactions. | ['See' *del.*] *See above, p. 37ᵉ [*ed., fn.* 27] [*added vertically in mrgn.*]'.

Royce's[31] *general reductio ad absurdum* of a *plural world*. W. & I.
   I, 398–9.
"Let there be many facts. Each, by the idealist principle *is* by being
   known to a knower. There are then, so far, many knowers. This
   last proposition however expresses a fact. But this fact as fact,
   exists only as present to a knower. The manyness of the knowers,
   in short, can exist as fact only on condition of there being one
   ultimate knower to whom the manyness is present as an object.
   Pluralism, if a fact, is based on monism."
A monism tends to become a "block Universe." Where no relations
   are adventitious, it is clear that all those which are actually found
   to obtain must obtain neccessarily. They cannot be mere possibilities which either may or may not occur. Where on the contrary, relations are adventitious, the terms may or may not get
   into them, according to the conditions which rule. Their inner
   natures are consistent with either result, and the relations are
   possible in the strict sense.
Absolutism denies possibility as a category. It seems easy to prove
   this by Royce's argument. If a fact be merely possible, that means
   that we cannot know now how it will turn out. But our ignorance
   is itself a fact, present to the all-knower, who to know it as ignorance must also know what it is ignorant of, namely how the so
   called possibility *will* turn out. What for us is an unknown future
   is thus known to the Absolute, and what we call possibilities do
   not genuinely exist.

Criticism of Monism

1st. Don't talk[32] abstracts, which *ignore*, but don't *deny* the existence of relatedness of the things they name. "Liquid" does n't
   mean "sweet," yet this does n't prove a sweet liquid to be self-
   contradictory.
2nd. Remember that we are not discussing *how* many things in
   connection *can* fisically have originated, but, they being there,

---

31 On the facing page WJ wrote: 'Miss Sears's *reductio ad absurdum* of pluralism:
Assume a fact *disconnected* with others. Its disconnection is a fact, and by the idealist
principle must be known to be one. There must therefore be noetic connection for any
['other' *del.*] disconnection to be. At this rate every negative must be known. There can
be no ignorance; for the ignorance, to be, must be known, as such, along with what it
ignores. *Not to be* turns into *to be not*, etc.'
32 On the facing page WJ wrote: 'Bradley p. 570'.

whether certain sorts of connection are absurd. Question of *logic* not of *genesis*!

3rd Use concrete illustrations.

Immediately[33] we find various grades of relation, some more inner, some more outer.

A	Resembles	B	
"	is better than	"	seem to depend on inner nature of
"	knows	"	the terms
"	changes into	"	
"	causes	"	
A	coexists with	B	
"	succeeds	"	
"	is near	"	seem to be extraneous to the inner
"	far	"	nature.
"	above	"	
"	below	"	
"	next to	"	

In the former case alter the nature of either term, and the relation vanishes or alters, & vice versa.

In the latter case either term may alter and leave the relation, or the relation may vanish and leave one term.

Take case[34] of lamp being on desk. Desk placed; exterior changes, & makes something "true" of desk.

Need either term inwardly alter.

Does the relation need a "link" to the terms?

The lamp "there" *is* the relation—no intermediary is conceivable.

Is n't the very form of the intellect satisfied? Is n't the perception complete, transparent?

1st Case:[35] hat and desk: hat alongside of/"near" desk. Is there any

[33] On the facing page WJ wrote: 'In a thought, or word the whole precedes the parts (although when these are once abstracted, we can make new wholes out of them[)]. | Ditto in such systems as partnership, marriage, debt, etc.'

[34] On the facing blank page WJ wrote: 'Bradley p. 568'.

[35] On the facing blank page WJ wrote: 'Bradley says: "Every bare conjunction is *. . . . [intrl.] contradictory when taken up by thought, because thought in its nature is incapable of conjunction and has no way of mere "together" ["] *([ov. period] p. 571). If by thought we mean consciousness uberhaupt, is n't the space interval absolutely 'conjunctive' by its nature? B. says: "What in the end would satisfy the intellect, *supposing [ab. del. 'provided'] it could be got?*" [aft. del. db. qt.] and continues by describing an imaginary "process" "which would be itself the intellect's own *proprius motus*["] etc. p. 568, but says (569) that he is himself unable to verify a solution of this kind. Is n't the *perception [ab. del. 'sensible phenomenon'] of the hat near the table a process of just this very kind?'

hidden mystery in understanding this relation? If the terms have an "outside" don't they "contribute" to it by that outside? The relation here *is* a third thing—viz the space interval. Does n't this interval *touch* each term by one of its ends, come literally next to it? *Are* additional things required to "link" it? Can they be conceived? Would n't they frustrate, if there? Is n't the whole intimacy of the continuity here due to the fact that there is nothing more involved than what the experience gives, no farther go-betweens required. (Once more, I don't ask how the space came to *be,* and the objects got *made,* and *introduced themselves* into the space, but what their relation *consists* in, or is known-as when once bro't about.) Is n't it absolutely transparent and complete? Does nt it follow the very motion of our understanding? If there can be space, if a thing can get into it, then without inwardly altering, it will be able to assume innumerable external relations to other things which may equally succeed in getting into the same space. The naked facts per se here are the related facts.

To make a paradox[36] here would be *perverse.* Logically therefore, *this* type of external connexion[37] between things has to pass.

Same argument as to *time-relations.*

2nd case: *Resemblance* of this desk with other desks. (Once again, not how a thing can *get itself made* in the likeness of another thing, but what the likeness as a constituted fact logically involves.)

It involves a *ground* in the quality of the things. If one desk is to resemble another, it must be of a determinate quality, but the resemblance follows the quality, not the quality the resemblance. The resemblance is annihilated if one quality alters, but the other quality in that case may remain just as it was.

"Resemblance" is thus an adventitious relation to any *one* thing, since it depends *wholly* on a fact external to that thing, viz. the existence of another thing of determinate quality.

You[38] *understand* the likeness completely the moment you perceive

---

36 On the facing blank page WJ wrote: 'The point is that you don't have to alter your notion of what a thing which you have already thought of *is,* *when you pass on [*intrl.*] to consider it either as *with,* or as *like,* or *as [*intrl.*] *unlike* something else. | The term enters into the relation with its ['barely being determi' *del.*] bare ['determinate' *del.*] being to which the other factors are bare additions. | *Burn* one of two similar pictures—etc.'

37 Above 'external' WJ wrote 'adventitious', with an opening parenthesis bracing the two words, and above 'connex-' | he wrote 'relat-' | .

38 On the facing blank page WJ wrote: 'Mr. Frantz asks whether things so ['te' *del.*]

its ground. So far from anything more being required to "satisfy the intellect," it is the *absence* of anything more, the absence of any difference, which makes the relation so transparently what it is. It is "known-as" absence of difference.

Although grounded in the *nature* of each thing, the resemblances into which the thing may enter, are among the thing's *possibilities* only. The nature as such does not logically imply any particular number of specimens. There might be only one of the kind. [Of course, in the order of genesis, the minimum producible might be more than one—e.g. two half apples, two ends to a cut string etc. "manifolding" of writings etc.]

Implicit vs explicit possibilities

Former not noticed: yet the moment question raised only one answer can be given. You can never *say* they "don't" obtain.

Manyness of universe as an example.

Royce's argument (p. 41 above [*ed.*, 293.1–9]):

Grant idealistic premiss: even then arg^t wont hold, for we can't say *fact* to the many if no one observes. Each as a singular is all that *idealistically* exists then. But pass that by.

Take "likeness" again as example

No need of higher knower in either case.

If each partial fact exists, then whole ground of complex fact exists, & the latter may become explicit

Pragmatically things are many if they can be *counted*: They are then "numerically distinct." Whether distinct in other respects is a farther problem.

Joachim on simple greenness, 40–42 49 (You can allow no inner complexity if you disallow the absolute)

---

heterogenous as not to belong to the same universe at all, "absolutely disconnected" things, do not, so far as subsumed under that idea, form a unity. This is the trump-card of transcendentalist monism, & confers a peculiar beatitude.* | [*fn. added vertically in mrgn. w. guideline to asterisk in text*] *The pluralist's "speech," they say, "bewrayeth him." | Of course you can't say "no-universe," or "multiverse,["] without thereby constituting a "universe of discourse." But is it *more* than a universe of discourse?—that is the pragmatic point; and *it [*intrl.*] naturally must be decided in the negative. A universe of discourse need show no *other [*intrl.*] specific connexion whatever among its parts. *The [*intrl.*] Noetic unity involved *in making the conception [*intrl.*] may be the alpha and omega of the unity realized by what the ['hypothesis asserts' *del.*] conception denotes. We are talking about these residual manners of being unified. Who says "disconnected universes" says that none of them obtains within his universe of discourse.'

2. Allow any connexion and you involve absolute union.

> Lotze's monism
>
> Royce on error.
>
> Royce W. & I. **56–7, Loyalty, "To deny that there is truth or that there is a real world, is simply to say that the whole truth is that there is no whole truth, and that the real fact is that there is no fact at all." Derives its speciousness from play on words.

Abstract comfort only! As if a doctor admired the general beneficence of medicine, but couldn't prescribe a single remedy.

The logical intellect must therefore allow that *the being of a thing with a determinate nature is "independent" of the resemblances in which it may figure as a term.*[39]

Case 4.[40] *Changes.* [Not how they can physically occur, but what they are "known-as" when they have occurred]

Known as something existing which did not exist, or s'thing not-existing which did (Cf. Baldwins Dict)

2 Sorts:

> Discontinuous: Kinetoscope.
>
> Continuous, by interpolation, or by partial alteration.

Consciousness of continuity.

Ground of possibility here means:

> 1. Presence of initial member;
>
> 2. Absence of frustrating condition.

---

39 On the facing page WJ wrote: 'But derealizes, and produces indifferentism. The comfort is only "this *also* is *worthwhile [*ab. undel.* 'rational'],—therefore pluralistically applies.["] | Dickinson, p 78 | St Michael & the fiend, *we* the fiend s̄. the saint | my griefs are mine'.

40 On the facing page WJ wrote: 'In discussing the "many," one's interlocutor is pretty sure to pose *one [*ab. del.* 'you'] with the dialectic question "Can there be a many without a *One ['O' *ov.* 'o']?" meaning sometimes that each member of the many is a unit, sometimes that "many" itself is one *conception.* Of course unity of *both* these kinds is implied in the realization of manyness; and I not only concede but especially emphasize it. It's of no use however for the Absolute's interests, for the *first of these [*ab. del.* 'one'] unities ['ies' *ov.* 'y'] is distributive, the other is *merely [*intrl.*] ['the' *del.*] noetic unity, relative ['merely' *del.*] to the finite discusser, ['and' *del.*] No ['N' *ov.* 'n'] *ulterior* or *deeper* unity is logically implied than *these two which are [*ab. del.* 'what is'] explicitly accorded.' Below a line drawn across the page he wrote: 'Kants: "Nur das Beständige *kann ['k' *ov.* 'c'] sich verandern." etc. with the dialectic comments therefrom accruing. Emphatically not required. The finite observer of the Change is enough, and it is a toss-up in many cases whether he shall describe the experience as an expulsion of one being by another, or a succession of "states" in the same being.'

Possible chicken = actual egg—not broken or addled.

Ordinarily a possibility is tho't of as something intermediate between nothing and complete reality—A way of being even now of the future or doubtful thing. On pragmatic principles everything must be treated of as far as possible in terms of reality, and possibles in all their grades of possibility are known as determinate actuals.

A *bare* possible is anything of which you can frame an idea which is neither self-contradictory, nor contradicted by something known as real.

A *grounded* possible is anything of which part of the conditions exist. When *all* the conditions exist, the thing is actual. Absence of known hindrance is also here supposed.

By the grounded possibility of an entire fact you mean then only the actuality of its component parts. Until the last of these is supplied, we call the fact possible only. If the fact be a future terminus of change, its possibility means that the initial step is there.

In general then, a possibility means, pragmatically, something actual, either a component or an antecedent of something future, with the absence of a frustration.

If[41] Royce insists that such absence is also a fact demanding an infinite knower, I say that if unnoticed, it is not a fact; if noticed, the finite knower is enough. (Comment on superfoetation of negative knowledge in Royces Absolute)

Take now case of *knowledge*. Does my definition as development towards terminus without check require the Absolute?

No, for the terminus is only a possibility in the sense assigned. It consists entirely of things actual viz terminus a quô, with no frustration. Change with sense of continuity.

Real[42] puzzle here is that of completed infinitive—treat later under questions of genesis.

Case 5. *Interaction*.[43] Lotze.

---

[41] In the left margin WJ wrote, 'Hindoo goddess 3 heads 6 arms 8 breasts. "All the hairs on our head are numbered"—to wh. J. L. Motley replied—"as if that were any object!" '

[42] On the facing page WJ wrote, 'Lutoslawski in Monist, (1899?) | *Cf. ['C' *ov.* 'S'] Schiller, Phil. Rev. vol V. p. (225 May 1896)'.

[43] On the facing page WJ wrote: 'What pluralist says is that things *whose existence is mutually "independent" in other respects may nevertheless [*ab. del.* '['whose existence' *del.*] which do not depend on each other for existence'] may interact. | Lotze

Treatment too abstract. L. calls them nothing but *"separates,"* or many which word of course connotes non-contact, awayness, outness non-intercourse. He gets over it by the word "One."

Grant the One—does it really explain?

Why should its parts be such as to interact just thus?

Why but that it is in point of fact just that kind of a unity. If you need it to explain the interaction, you need another thing to explain its constitution.

In the end you leave off with a "constitution," whether of the many or the One, so that all that your abstract One has done for you is to correct the denial of impossible intercourse which your abstract word Many was falsely supposed to involve.

The concrete Many evidently do interact, and the question is as to the *what*ness or process.

Immanent change in an absolute mind is also hard to understand, especially if that mind be perfect [Lotzes "compensation" of "disturbances."]

Question of process of interaction must also be postponed to genesis.

Unity of that grade must at any rate be allowed to the Universe.

Case 6.[44] *Commensurability—Affinity*

In point of fact we find various degrees of union realized:

    1. Co-existence, withness, togetherness in space & time.

    2. noetic unity. (Kant.)

    3. Likeness, and difference.

    4. Change } law, classification, synchronous variation.
    5. Interaction

The monist says that these require admission of

    6. Unity of substance (subject in change)

    7. Unity of origin (Maxwell)

    8. Absolute noetic union, with final theory that universe is constructed on the pattern of a single thought—together with the universal interdependence and inter-determination of all things (block-universe) which this involves.

---

says *that this contradicts meaning of ['word' *del.*] [*intrl.; orig. intrl. aft.* 'word' *del.*] word independent, *wh [*intrl.*] means without relation, having no business with. If you call the things "one," he says, they *can* interact. | Meanwhile question of what *process of [*intrl.*] interaction *consists-in* remains unanswered. | Only when ['it is' *del.*] process is concretely known can we tell whether it be compatible or not with the things possessing mutually independent existence.'

44 On the facing page WJ wrote, 'Mahaffy's Fischer on Kant, pp. vi–vii. | Lotze: Metaphysic, §§13–14'.

6, 7, 8, are hypotheses which *may* be true, but I contend that they
need not be true. My own hypothesis is that a succession of conterminous subjects is enough;
> that the origins can be many;
> that no knowledge of whole is extant anywhere.

Make a picture!

Even if we make the ultra-monistic hypothesis, it remains an abstract
Machtspruch.

When the monist has said "One" in the abstract he is still forced in
the concrete to describe the multiplicities and incomplete stages
of unity which we find. He has to let us interpret his unity for
him empirically. He can deduce no definite consequences from
it. The absolute mind realized its universe in that pluralistic
way—it hangs together piecemeal thus. *That* was what the absolute origin brought to birth.

Paulsen & Lotze[45] as examples of the neccessity of falling back on
pluralism concretely.

Everything that happens produces unforeseen results, which produce neccessity of readaptation

Paulsen 190, 206

Lotze: Micr. I 175, 181, 190, 419, 438–441

Royce, C. of G. 292–4, 312–14.

Thus individualism, piece meal world.

Unity *in posse*.

"But possibility supposes capacity"

Refute.

At bottom whole monistic arg^t resolves itself into dictum of *genesis*:
> Unless things had one *origin* they could n't ever get into relation
> at all

Not only like things as "manufactured articles" (Maxwell) but
things in relation überhaupt, must be made "for" each other.[46]

World on these terms an "organic unity." There are things which
can only be produced together, like words in sentence. Quarters
of an apple. You can get a feather, a hand only by getting a whole

---

[45] On the facing page WJ wrote: ' "Empiric knowledge of the purpose in the world,
*. . . [intrl.] taken alone would much more easily produce the polytheistic view of a
plurality of divine beings, ['each of whom' *del.*] . . . which agree so far as to produce a
certain general compatibility, but not not a harmony without exceptions." Lotze. Mic.
II, 667. | See his Bk VII, Ch. III. The forces that work on history.'

[46] On the facing page WJ wrote, 'According to Darwin *unfitnesses get cancelled out*'.

bird, a whole man etc. So of the parts of a universe, the whole comes first. Rain-drops.

Legitimate hypothesis.

Old teleological view: 1) whole aimed at, parts designed in view of it. 2) physical forces inadequate. 3) Carpenter-God required.

What do you mean by "fit"?[47] All things fit in some way. Eyes with cataract, stch. s̄. gastric juice. Hunchback. Lisbon earthquake. Forests fit fire. Dead body fits bacterium.

In every collective unity the parts must fit so as to produce *some* result—*that* result.

Teleological argument would apply to *any* world, if one could only *believe such a world aimed at.*

Production by mechanism may be part of aim.

Question thus liquefies.

Once more, Absolute unity[48] indifferently absorbs all possible empirical findings, but determines none. Anything is *compatible* with One Source, one whole.

Even new production of things in time wd. be compatible.

Sterility of this theory!

The question is, is what we find, incompatible with plural origin.

We find things related.

Must things with different origins remain unrelated?

Take question from far back: How does a *what* ever become a *that,* a bare *possibility* become a *fact*?

(Distinguish from question of *grounded* possibility)

From whatness of universe to thatness, no logical bridge.

Creative fiat[49]—Leibnitz.

Even the whatness which has become a thatness is non logical, in spite of Hegel, Oken, etc. Indifferentism of Absolute.

Empiricism is the only method.

We find certain whatnesses realized, others not.

Their[50] *numbers, places, collocations,* all mere found facts, that must be begged, and are given. *Gifts.* "Laws" don't determine.

---

47 On the facing page WJ wrote: 'Any state of things whatsoever may have had all its parts created to fit each other for that design. The difficulty is to suppose that certain states of things could ever have been *wanted* by any being whatsoever.'

48 WJ wrote 'unity' above undeleted 'thought'.

49 On the facing page WJ wrote, '['No r' *del.*] "Being" a wonder! Fechner, Tagesansicht, p. 52. Fine passage to quote. | Lotze Micr. I, 548, 554'.

50 In the left margin WJ wrote circled: 'Irreducible plurality!'

In the order of existence, behind the facts, for us there is *nothing*.

Even if we admit one source, there might be different dates for the appearance of different members of the variety.

Since[51] what comes is anyhow unaccountable it makes no difference in principle whether we shove it all back into one initial act, and say that that exhausted the universe's spontaneity, or take the pluralism as of piecemeal origin, and distribute the spontaneity through time—

No ontological difference, only phenomenal difference.

If piecemeal coming seems to be the fact, we must, for aught logic can say to the contrary, admit it.

Upshot of this hour has been to make us see that

1. Whatever has come in point of fact has been able to come; and

2. that since unity of origin is *compatible* with any order and manner of coming in detail, it can't help us a priori to decide about how or in what shapes things actually *did* come.

Drop then the notion of unity, as fruitless, until we have considered the hypothesis of aboriginal plurality of origins.

"Tychism"—theory of chance origin

"Chance" means such a relation between two things that you can't deduce the one from the other. They are *additives* in the respect in which the chance obtains, not mutual consequences. Chance is thus a term of *logical ignorance*.

The chance may obtain in various respects. From the being of a "parent" you can deduce the *being* of a child, but not his grade of intelligence. From the being of a branch, that of a root, but not its shape. From the being of Stratford you can't deduce the being of Shakespeare, though you may, granted his being, deduce *some* of his qualities. From the being of this desk, you can't deduce the being of an electric car, nor in general from the being of one thing can you deduce *how many* things either like it (or different) you will have. [In some cases (packs of cards, etc.) you can.][52]

---

51 On the facing page WJ wrote: 'No *cheaper* to beg one origin. Every individual item had to get produced then, just as much as if they had come piecemeal. Either way the *entire number* had to come.'

52 On the facing page WJ wrote: 'There is no discernable "law" in the distribution of matter in cosmic space. If you say it is the result of laws of attraction, they suppose *primal [intrl.] collocations in which no law can now be discerned; but even if there were "law" then in the distribution, that was a bare datum.'

Suppose things to have come "independently," first A, then B, etc. An *abstract* supposition. Pure "chance."

Can they be "like"? Can they share a common "space," if space there be? etc

If you say "no," I ask what's to *prevent*.

If union as such requires a positive "principle," then disunion as such must require one also.* Show the principle that keeps *A & B asunder* in these respects.

Anything is "barely possible" of which we can frame a conception, and to which we know of no hindrance. Our present hypothesis assumes nothing but the bare fact that A & B do come. In the absence of a principle either way, may they not, when here, resemble, etc., as well as not?

Certainly this is absolutely possible, for aught that our logic tells us to the contrary, and if to day there were a spontaneous addition to being (increase of being) there is no reason why it might not add itself, & contract extraneous relations to the mass of being that already is, even though it could not logically be deduced beforehand from what is.

Absolute origination, "free-will."

In abstracto, then, unity of origin is *not* required to enable many things to form a universe after they have arisen.

In such a universe the things would be *"matters of chance"* in respect to one another.

Define chance. It means such a relation between two things that you can't deduce one from the other, nor both from a single origin or end. They are mutually *contingent*, *meet* and *touch* each other, but we can't go behind the *fact*. They are *additives*. No connection *logically neccessary*.

Word of logical ignorance. It *means plurality*, irreducible by logical means.

Collateral series, inosculating. Aristotle's example of debt paid in agora. Other examples

Multiple worlds. As Cournot says: the way in which we pass our days in our houses is not influenced by what happens in a chinese household.

Only ideally, if we ascend to origin of universe, should we find that

---

* But absence of law needs no explanation, according to Peirce, Monist III, 559

they are one. But that is an *hypothesis*. Logically this *might* be a chance-universe after all, also hypothesis.

The essence of my contention is that in a world where connexions are not logically neccessary, they may nevertheless adventitiously *"come."* Series of independent origin and purpose may inosculate by "chance-encounter," and thereafter mingle their causalities, and combine their effects.

The idea reverts to the distinction between the *neccessary* and the merely *possible*, I contending that there are such things as "possible" relations, even between things of the same origin, provided the origin started them on merely collateral serial lines.[53] Possibility being defined as partial actuality, each factor in a chance-encounter would be a condition of the possibility of the compound result. This latter *from the point of view of either single factor* would be a matter of chance. Call it here "relative" chance if you will, since the origin may have predetermined all the series together. It would be absolute chance only if origins were irreducibly distinct.

In books on probability chance is regarded as *revealer* of a regular order, if such exist. Perturbations neutralize each other; frequencies come to light. My theory goes farther. Chance *production* occasions effective increase in certain regularities, because other chances are eliminated and these remain & accumulate. If *n* men toss pennies, there will be accumulation of wealth in a few hands, by the elimination of those whose stock gives out.

"Tychism." Peirce: Monist II. 321.

Radical evolutionary theory. If your only description of the way things come is that anything is as possible as anything else, then you can get order as a chance result, by survival of the permanent and *withness* of the *gregarious*, if gregariousness be among the chance variations.[54]

Speculative hypothesis this; but its existence proves that a chance-universe is *possible* at least.

53 Below 'them . . . lines.' WJ wrote, 'Rev. de Mét. et de M. Nov. 1902 | "Dilemma of determinism." | "Great men" article.' and then added 'Rev. de Phil. Nov. 1904', drawing lines around the notes to separate them from the text. He then continued with 'Possibility' on the same line immediately after 'lines.'

54 On the facing page WJ wrote: 'Remember that *pastness* is a kind of annihilation of ['things that' *del.*] everything that ever *is*, an annihilation that seems absolute in most cases; that they are *superseded* by new things that come into being, and that, so far as these also die, there is annihilation.'

Is it probable? Consider the matter now more concretely.

If we adopt physical theories absolutely, the doctrine of the conservation of mass would lead us to suppose that all the atoms came at once, from one origin, like rain drops from a cloud.

Yet the minuteness of the entities supposed here, & the fact that our laws are only statistical, might allow for variations of mass inside the errors of observation. [Thomson's "corpuscles," "electrons," Reynolds's "granules."]

Coarseness of the human time & number span. [Red light vibrates about 400,000,000,000,000 times a second. Bergson 229]

Tendency of recent science[55] to statistical explanations (see foot of p. 61½ [ed., 304.19–25])

In the elements, only a general similarity need be supposed, and the appearance of uniformity is due to the "large numbers," in which the minute variations every which way neutralize each other.

[Free-will, and Quetelet's statistics as example.]

The finer our observations the more they vary, & *approximate uniformity* is all that Science can claim.

Distinguish here between elementary and phenomenal uniformity. As *experienced*, nothing repeats itself. All our names are like the names "winter" or "summer," rough appellatives that cover endless variation. Where is the plesiosaurus? Where Helen of Troy? Alexander?

The "uniformity of nature" means then nothing but imitation, and self same repetition in the *elements*. Even science must admit that, within the limits of variation which elements so minute comport, her observations require us to suppose no such thing.

If we drop the notion of elements and take the energetic view it is with the concrete experiences that we have to deal. Their uniformity is only a "limiting" ideal.[56] The general law of conservation of energy determines nothing in detail. The special laws are only approximately verified (mechan. equiv. of heat an average figure. Difficulty of getting chemical substances "pure." Argon, helium etc.—are we sure that *they* have n't impurities ad infinitum?)

What we know from physical science is that the realm of spontaneity

---

55 On the facing page WJ wrote, 'Wandering of ions, Crookes phenomenon,'.

56 On the facing page WJ wrote, 'Solomons: Phil. Rev., VIII, 146'.

and aboriginal chance must be *incredibly minute* in the physical
world if it exist. That's all. It *may* exist.

Being so minute, it simplifies our philosophy to ignore it altogether
and talk as if it did n't exist.[57]

Admit, then, that physical uniformity although it may have *arisen*
by Tychism, is now complete. Many things are alike, and their
relations are alike. Variety as good a postulate as uniformity.

Next for the *interrelations* of the many. Changes and causations
are according to law. The properties of things *are* their interrelations and interactions.

For the atomistic philosophy the only changes are of collocation,
configuration. $H_1 H_1$ & O are called water in the position H–O–H.

But they *influence, affect.*

Only condition requisite is continuity, nextness. [Actio indistans.
vs. plenum. Faraday   Maxwell   Hertz.]

Can't this be a variation?

Whats to *prevent*?

In a world without interaction the existence of one object would
make no difference to others. If they were roomy their rooms
would interpenetrate and no sign given. They would be mutual
ejects, as in point of fact the conceptual and emotional worlds of
human individuals now are.

Only when interaction comes in, can they be "objects," "present,"
one to another. The minimum of interaction would seem to
consist in bounding each other's room. This would be their
"Anerkennung" and the germ of everything else in their relation. It would give the "withness." A similar bounding of their
durations would give their successiveness. "Repulsiv-kraft."

Thus *boundary-making* would be the critical step in the formation
of a coherent universe. If things stopt there, there would be no
relational habits—the only law would be Spinoza's Unaquaeque
res in suo Esse perseverare conatur. "Mere aggregate." Logically
nothing else follows from such mathematical nextness. The adjacent beings each contain their boundary—well and good; but
in point of fact that is not equivalent to *"affecting"* each other

---

[57] On the facing page WJ wrote: 'Parallel [*alt. fr.* 'Parrallel'] with sheep flock, or
perfected social order with stationary population. France. To an outer observer there
would be constancy | Yet to the beings involved, the variations realized might be
important to the last degree. Games of whist, chess etc. Difference between musical
performances, pictures etc. Football games.'

otherwise, and such affecting is what we actually find. This is the world of mere mathematical coexistence & succession, functional variations of position etc. which· "Science" knows.

Since it is actually here, it could *come*, and if the monist can beg it as a specification of his one, then we also can beg it as a specification of our many, in the absence of any known hindering cause. It seems in fact to lie among the "bare possibilities," for a hindering cause could hinder only by affecting, and could therefore not be supposed without admitting the possibility of affectibility itself.

Assume, then, that in addition to bounding, affecting *comes*. What kind of affecting would increase the coherence of the many?

Associability, plainly; for this means gregariousness, following, and habit-forming, and the creation of compounds, which are units of a higher order.

Attraction, then, in the physical world, and association in the mental, being what we find to exist, must have "come." Also consciousness in the sense of experiencing differents together, synthetic experience.

If this latter could come as One, it could come. Why not then piecemeal?

All we require is a *tendency* towards consciousness at the boundaries.

There would thus be *compound units*.

What kind of a universe would tend most to accumulate, what character would "prevail"?

Or rather what kind of variation would tend to make the universe more stable & coherent, more "One."

Permanence in units, and in compounds too, and organic unity is the condition of this.

Spencer.

I must consider possibility of physico-chemical order being due to wearing down of friction. This supposes random *affectibility* to be primal, involving all sorts of interferences, habit taking second and the evolution is exactly like that of social organism. Non-interfering habits get preserved.

Peirce: law of mind. Monist, II. 531

Universe grows more coherent as gregariousness increases, and things draw each other near. *Compound units* arise.

Then we say that one "thing" *changes*, then we say that things "interact" by "integrating" as well as by keeping each other at a distance.

Cohesion & chemical affinity the great physical examples. But in physical world process is opaque.

In "moment of experience," as the only concrete real which we know, it is transparent.

Here we have the originals of memory & expectation, causal activity, desire and fulfillment, development, elsewhere the outer shell.

This is why panpsychism leaves a minimum of opacity in things.

The chance-variation required for making the universe most coherent is therefore either that *consciousness should arise at the boundaries,* and the first beings thus grow consciously continuous, or that *conscious continuity* in the sense of change being felt as such, differents being known together, should come as a spontaneous variation.[58]

The absolute idealists believe in its coming when the One came. It *can* come, then, according to them. It may therefore be admitted to come piecemeal, in the absence of known hindrance.

Mere nextness[59] thus gives way to mutual *suffusion* at the boundary. *Overlapping, sharing* of boundary. (Peirce & Clifford.)

Continuity[60] is thus the form of the universe's unity. And it is needed only at the boundaries.[61] There alone the universe need

[58] On the facing page WJ wrote: 'With consciousness (overlapping at the boundaries) the ['bringing together of the things by' *del.*] simple continuity [*comma del.*] becomes concatenation, *nextness* changes into *chain*-structure ⟨⟨⟨⟩⟩⟩ '. Below a line drawn across the page he wrote: 'So far as consciousness adds itself to nextness, it brings this *chain-structure [*intrl.*] directly about— the nextness *is [*ab. del.* 'becomes'] a condition of the *possibility* of interpenetration; for the consciousness which outstrips one member has no place to drop into between it and the next member, and so flows over upon the latter; and the interpenetration thus is *realized*, the "unity" is realized *as such*.' In the left margin at the end of this note WJ wrote 'unity' and then deleted it.

[59] On the facing page WJ wrote: ' "Linkage"—Royce *& absolutism generally [*intrl.*] have ['ve' *ov.* 's'] to account for *non*-linkage, which *R. [*ov.* 'the'] does by lapses of the finite attention.'

[60] In the left margin WJ wrote in pencil, 'Line of fire in burning grass.'

[61] On the facing page WJ wrote: 'The boundary, become sensibly alive, is the firing line, the line of action. Behind it lie *the [*ov.* 'a'] ashes of the past, in front the non-existent future, *in neither of [*insrtd.*] which [*alt. fr.* 'where'] *does any [*insrtd. for del.* 'no'] thing wear['s' *del.*] its adjectives "adversely," [See Seminary of 1897–8 [*No.* 21 *in this ed.*]] ['thou' *del.*] or dynamically, though all the adjectives are there. ——Two pro[b]lems here, on this fire-line: 1st. The fact of *there being überhaupt

live, as a *universe.* Elsewhere its elements live only each in itself, as an element. Where they *meet* the common life is realized, bridging takes place.

In our present sensible perceptions our lives meet dynamically, there is a bridge, but no conscious suffusion thereof or there-over.

Within our inner life we know how the suffusion varies. Items dissociate and associate again. "Span of consciousness" idea.[62] (My psychology; Royce, II, 227)

Mere question of fact how far conscious suffusion extends. It may extend very far. Telepathy. Myers's ideas. Anima mundi. Fechner. Preyer. Paulsen et al.—"God," or "Gods."

Highly speculative territory here.

Meanwhile one abstract condition stands out clear: The many includes more and more of a universe, in proportion as compound units grow more abundant in it; as the span of consciousness among them increases; and as they grow more permanent through assuming more and more the form of *organic unity.*

Spencers formula: "definite, coherent, heterogeneous, integrated"— it means wholes of which the parts help each other to *stay.*

That universe *accumulates.* It is *stable.*

It has already formed itself on an enormous scale, existing where we don't expect it, so that we know not its extent. *Physical* universe properly so-called seems to be one organic unity, of which "conservation" is a characteristic. [Enigmatical character of tendency to descend in level. Ability to draw on other things for reascent is consonant with organic unity tendency].

Limitless[63] power of small increments to accumulate in statistical direction, when conservative tendency exists among the chances. Our universe has already enormously evolved.

Have we any evidence of the favorable variations being due to chance?

How about our own moments of choice?

Two futures seem alike possible when their beginnings are actual.

[*intrl.*] a "present," ['*überhaupt*,' *del.*] a place of action; and 2nd the particular linkages and bridges that traverse it.'

62 On the facing page WJ wrote, 'Telescoping of one state into another. Drunkenness. Bergson. Mysticism.'

63 On the facing page WJ wrote in pencil, 'All pre-astronomic time for physics & chemistry to have consolidated'.

Up to the bifurcation, either future will fit. *In* the moment the variation seems to occur. *After* the moment one can trace the line of causal uniformity. But this means repetition. And concrete mental states never repeat themselves exactly. The alternative chosen came as an *additive,* of which the reason only lived at the moment of choice. See Bergson's "Essai."

Free-will means what is intelligible only after the fact. When mere antecedents introduce by uniform law, their consequents, the habit of *that* consequent must be already formed. How did the habit begin? If ideals start habits we have the answer. And in conflict, which ideal shall *prevail?* It feels like real decision, as if we were in the workshop of being.

If 2 alternative futures are to be possible, and if their possibility is to be *grounded,* that means that one at least of their components or antecedents has become actual. Among the antecedents of our acts of choice are our *ideals.* [An ideal not only antecedes, it prefigures; so an ideal seems a peculiarly privileged ground of possibility. It is then somebody's possibility, something says hurrah for it.] The ideals gather strength, the ideas and motives accumulate, and *whichever* the decision be, it would retrospectively fit the antecedents and be representable as a continuous process. It would be an *additive* of which the last actualizing condition came only at the last moment. Determinists, following the analytic method, & seeing only "ideas," "motives," and uniform "laws of association," will tell us that no other result *could* come. They would tell us so retrospectively, because this result did come; but they would equally have told us so if the other result had come. Their "laws" demand *repetition.* But concrete states of mind do not repeat, and abstract elements, "ideas" etc, are fictions *here,* whether or not physical elements be such. *What* comes is really decided *when* it comes. If it ever came by chance (wh. simply means non-deducibility from the outside) this would be an actual experience on our part of the way world developes. In many cases it feels like that! The whole conception stands or falls with the admission of extraneous relations.

In these experienced cases, since what comes continues something else & is preceded by an ideal, it may be likened to a *graft.* A graft is an *additive* to a tree. No body can contend that it is essential. Yet it combines harmoniously, replaces another branch that would have come, or another scion that might equally well have been grafted, and redefines the "whole tree." It is strictly among the tree's possibilities.

Assume this as the prototype of what happens universally, and you get the living attitude of the pluralistic or personalistic philosophy. Individualism.

Unity is in process of achievement. What is already "one" and "whole" is already static. What is dynamic lives only in the parts—the line of fire. *The moment of experience.*

Moreover the achieved unities appear such only in retrospection. Zielstrebigkeit and heterogonie der Zwecke.

Stevenson: A bargain just that bargain—whereas it is a link in the policy of mankind.

Small systems the truer systems.

Graft-theory

It means *Anarchy* in the good sense. [Hegel.]

It means *individualism, personalism*:

 that the prototype of reality is the *here & now*;

 that there is genuine novelty;

 that order is being *won*—incidentally reaped.

 that the more universal is the more abstract

 that the smaller & more intimate is the truer. the man more than the home, the home more than the state, or the church. Anti-slavery.

It means tolerance, and respect. Skepticism

It means democracy as against systems which crush the individual. Good systems always can be described in individualistic terms.

It means hero-worship & leadership.

It means the vital and the growing as against the fossilized & fixed, in science, art, religion, custom, government.

It means faith and help. In morals, obligation respondent to demand.

Question of Infinite

Things, I said, come in small instalments.

Novelty is by *change* in actual.

But change I described as gradual or abrupt. In either case creation. If we suppose the change to be continuous, we are met by the paradox of the Infinite. Not matter of *size* of world—too big to be. Not matter of finite grasping infinite. That relates to our sensibility merely.

Infinitely *growing* things offer no difficulty. Standing inadequacy on our part to complete them. They figure as variables. Infinites *in potentia*. Number series.

Standing infinite, or I *in actu*, maximum which growth can never reach, "so great that nothing can be or be thought greater." *Theological* conception, = "Perfect," "Absolute." *God*.

Mongrel infinite, as if it were both growing and standing growing quâ represented, but the remainder standing as if it had a private value, like the balance of a partly paid debt.* Past time. Space subdivisions

Cantor's ω. Two growing infinites, of different laws of formation.

Symbol ∞ reached by continuity in mathematics has a definite value. Couturat.

Standing infinite? Tangent of $90° = \dfrac{\sin: 1}{\cos: 0} = \infty$

Infinite convergent series $1 + \frac{1}{2} + \frac{1}{4} \ldots$

Limit gets itself into being independently of series, is a standing infinite.

Can never be actualized by successive addition of those terms.

Achilles & Tortoise. Principe du no⟨m⟩bre   Best paraphrased by saying that if anything exists the whole of it must be there. Nothing can lack. You can say "that's all." But this seems to make it finite.

Fullerton, Rev. Phil. 1901

Evellin: Infini et Quantité

The usual refutations of Zeno say that the expression "never can overtake" is ambiguous. The words suggest infinite time, when they only mean infinite subdivisions of finite time. That time may be as short as a second; and since the second elapses, the overtaking occurs. But the difficulty in overtaking is not relative to the *amount* of time required at all. It is positive, and applies to the time's elapsing, as well as to the distance to be traversed.

A bounded quantity is not involved in the notion of a lot of parts of which each must be real. It is the *parts* that stand & pre-exist, not their quantity. They must have always been as copious as our counting ever becomes. The denial of bounds to them contradicts nothing. The denial of their preexistence would contradict their reality.

* The remainder really is that ever recurring variable, the next greater number

Quantity of standing things vs. standing quantity

Evellin, Bergson Essai 76–87 & ff, Fullerton.

Keyser on Royce etc., in Journ. of Phil. I, 29

Each part must exist, nothing still due. But then *all* the parts must.
  They must be numerable. But there is no infinite number.
    Cauchy—Dedekind.[64]

Ergo they are finite.

But the conditions of certain things take infinite form:

Kants "Unconditioned" = totality.

His antinomies.

Renouvier.

Read R.'s évolution personelle, Esquisse II. 376+

Conclude that it is a question of fact, not of logic, in the static
  antinomies

Change seems different, so does time.

Idealism lets us out here. Also Elsewhere
    Best hypothesis.

Taken in the pure experience sense it gives us a real world of
  minima, and helps us to harmonize an individualistic philosophy.

Any, each, are terms of possibility. "All" a term of actuality, but
  only marking abstractly a class by exclusion & inclusion. The
  class is one of possibles, unless we have an intuition excluding
  any "more," in wh. case there is a last term, and the whole is
  finite.

The Russell-Cantor aim is to ascend to conceptions so highly abstract that they embrace relations common to number & to other
  logical entities as well, Classes, defined so as to ex- and in-clude
  any proposed term. Such is the class of cardinal numbers, which
  has only so far a logical existence. To prove that "a_0" or "ω" have
  a 'real' existence, would require additional ontological reasoning. Royce supplies this addition by his arguments for an Absolute, which is supposed to have a special form of intuition for the
  totality of infinite classes. The classes "real" for humans to which
  the logical entities correspond are formed by adding sensible
  determinations to the logical definitions. These determinations
  (successive existence, priority of elements over whole, or what
  not) might defeat certain consequences with which the bare abstract definition of the classes was not at variance, givenness all at

[64] In the right margin WJ wrote circled, 'Cf. Phil 3 notebook pp. 21–23'.

once, e.g., or infinity of number. [Might not also the abstract definition import certain associates or suggestions of its own, such as "ideal" existence, which the real material could dispense with?] The more abstract def^n of number, according to which order, and relation to a predecessor are irrelevant, contradict (by omission leastways) the ordinal numbers, which are in a growing order, and formed by $+ 1$ to the previous idea of another.

"Free-will"

Ambiguity of word

> Good to be able to *do* what one wills. If told we can only do one thing we rebel. Similar insult if we can only will one thing.

Determinism says this:

Uniform law

Character, circumstances, motives.

One future, & that certain;

No possibilities. No real novelty.

Kant

Schopenh. 42, 50 (Mill.)

If, abandoning abstract analysis, we place ourselves on pure experience, things look different.

1. Uniformities cover only a part of life.

> Routine character is relatively dead and capitalized.
> On the firing line it is character itself which seems ambiguous & fluid.—What character shall I *be*?

2. Moreover, circumstances never the same.

Concretely the issue is both

> novel,[65] & }
> unique.   } a graft.

Pluralistic description is alone applicable.

At most we can ascribe *likeness*

But lives differ immensely in this respect, so no *exact* conclusion is possible.

Fullerton.

One decides by one's general philosophy.

Monism & fate. } only one future
Uniformity.   }

---

[65] On the facing blank page WJ wrote: 'Novelty—Delboeuf on Helen of T. | Reptiles etc. | Where are all the ancient summers and falls ['s' *del.*] of the leaf—['the' *del.*] of the world?— — —the snows of yesteryear?'

But uniformity involves fiction of elements, that repeat.

If no concrete moment repeats, then you have "uniform" sequence
  = *unique* sequence (Royce), and the graft-world

What[66] comes decides itself *when* it comes.

"Character" incomplete till then.

"More" career. Something "comes."

Baldwin (Rev. Psych II) protests against adequacy of retrospective
  category.

Always the conflict between habit & novelty

So that in the end we conclude that the appearance is the truth.
  The moment of experience itself decides which future is to be.

Otherwise why have moments of experience at all?—if they exert no
  function?

Evolution, Teleology etc

Our account of the world is "evolutionary."

2 ways of taking Ev__n:

  1. Metaphysical, monistic, pantheistic
  2. Historical.

1. "Nothing evolved which was not *in*volved." Universe comes to
  consciousness of what it is. Equation of universe permanent:
  Potential + actual = constant.[67]

Connexion of this view with *Teleology.*

What is evolved was potential, was designed.

Older teleology assumed

  1. Reality of "things," as ends.
  2. Inability of general physical laws to produce them.
  3. Need of planner, contriver.

---

[66] On the facing blank page WJ wrote: 'Wundt's law (System, 314) of wachsthum der geistigen Energie gives the additive relation. On pp. 343–5 he gives a good passage to quote.'

[67] On a leaf pasted-in on the facing page, numbered '4 ['5–6' *del.*]', WJ wrote: '*Energy of [*intrl.*] Chemical ['explosives—heat absorbed' *del.*] separation—undone produces heat. Produced absorbs work as in formation of explosives, chlorophyllian function etc. | Fall of some parts rise of others but most of what falls ['is' *del.*] remains. [*short rule*] Relapse of raised part is rhythm. Permanent rhythm—waves elastic bodies etc. [*short rule*] Bodies important for us are those embodying quasi permanent strains | Balance of tensions ['—Traps.' *del.*] [*in the bottom right-hand corner of the page* WJ *wrote* 'over' *and circled the word*] [*verso of the leaf, numbered* '5–6'] 1) simple | logjam. [*start of letter del.*] boulder. Iceberg ['Ratchet' *del.*] Derrick—Ratchet | Bow—Hydraulic ram—Gun-powder—['muscle' *del.*] | 2) ['moving–' *del.*] self renewing—fountain—vortex—candle—living body. | Traps—in vicissitudes of matter things constantly moved into positions from which they can't escape.'

4. Supernatural physical agent to carry plan out.

Carpenter-theory!

Evolutionary teleology 1) can't specify what are "ends" & what not.

    2. Conceive physical forces as adequate.

    3. Conceive mechanical production as possibly itself an end. Pantheism *must*.

The question thus liquefies:

What is *fit* to be a purpose?[68] Anything *might* be.

Question of *character* of universe.

It is in any case a machine, and one that works *agreeably* to the guidance, *compatibly* with the ends which *we* feel worthy.

If it did n't produce those it might have produced others which someone else would have found worthy.

Are all ends therefore subjective & partial?

Transition to scientific evolutionism.

Non-teleological.

Molecular naturalism keeps up equation, & denies ends.

But what, if world is always identical, are the pure experiences in which there is real novelty? (Wundt, System, 314)

Transition to historic conception of evolution.

Additive universe. Ends *many*.

Only to be assumed where we have reason to suppose an actual *will*.

Not neccessarily mutually harmonious.

"Heterogony[69] of Ends," Wundt, 336.

Harmony in process of being won, by weeding out of irreconcileables.

How diff.^t from monistic view.

With panpsychism we have to suppose Will everywhere.

Atoms—gravitation—gregariousness.

Aggregate results need not have been aimed at, yet may be constant and desirable by spectators. "Bye products." "Chance," in so far forth. Yet teleology can work it in

How different from monistic view.

---

68 On the facing page WJ wrote: 'To 'prove' design, you have to prove a purpose. Impossible to prove this by mere inductive reasoning for everything *may* have been purposed. Only some purposes seem to us more incredible than others.' Pasted-in on this page, partially covering the inscription, is p. 3 of No. 23, "Syllabus of Philosophy 3: The Philosophy of Nature" (269.16–270.6).

69 On the facing blank page WJ wrote, 'Like the incidental properties of a mathematical figure. Ambiguity of "fulfilments." '

Last lecture

The wider order which we espouse when we see it, was it not pre-figured?

In what shape did it exist when it was merely a possible, not an actual?

If the grounded possible is the fractional actual, then there are as many g—d possibles as there are conceivable grafts upon the actual.

Are ideals, as such, grounds?

Abstract & vague ideals welcome various fulfilments as grafts.

Tychism pure & simple leaves direction of chances wholly indeterminate.

Ideals define direction.

The trouble with *us* is that we are unwilling that our higher ideals should be simply subjective. We feel ourselves their servants, and for our willingness to serve we ask countenance and requital. The wider order (opposite page [*ed.*, 317.2]) etc, must have been prefigured.

Where? It has always been objectified by men as a Divine existent s'where.

Beauty, harmony, struggling through, and more eternal than any finite embodiment.

"Perfection is eternal."

"Stars in their courses" fighting for righteousness.

If ideals are mere biological variations, the trouble they give, and the "problem" of them, can be solved for the onlooker, in two ways, by their fulfilment, or by their abolition. This is the retrospective, static, point of view. From the point of view of the ideal itself there is one only way, viz. fulfillment, answer; for the ideal in suo esse perseverare conatur. It is a fact of the creative order. The fulness of experience can be described only in voluntaristic terms. To know about it is never an adequate equivalent to living it, or cooperating with it, by as M—g says *Anerkennung*.

We, who are describing, get as near to our object as possible when we define all its voluntaristic peculiarities. Then we make another step when we say "*that* object commands my sympathy and loyalty."

Well, experience holds to ideals and holds to this further ideal about them that they shall be shared, imposed. It is when considered as imposed that we are most reluctant to give them up.

How can this postulate be fulfilled?—To some extent by a gregarious life: "Kingdom of Man."

But man is too helpless against the cosmic forces, unless there be a wider Ally. Religion, the belief in this Ally has thus the simplest of *Motives*. Its *arguments* for me lie in the conviction that our normal experience is only a fraction, and in the mystical phenomena. But by this extension of experience only *possibilities* are opened, and what most men want are certainties.

They are not *bare* possibilities however. To make a live possibility, more than an existent stock for a graft is required. The stock must, by idealizing the graft, exert tractive force upon it. Habit-taking seems also to require this continuity between the actual & the potential worlds. How to formulate it? I don't know; only Bergson's idea of brain and memory may help.

The great metaphysical question is as to the *extension* of consciousness, in the downward as well as in the upward direction.

More important conclusion.

Evolution is by addition, not only of experienced content, but of ends & wills.

If we cling to pure experience, it is in part experience of *activity*. The world evolves by its activity.

Consider activity. Bradley.

Activity *is* the feeling of it. It is a kind of experienced transition, a part of the content. (Causality, efficacity, dynamic energy etc, are not elsewhere to be found.)

Involves sense of *direction*.

Our wills welcome grafts in the right direction. Others are obstructions.

Pure tychism leaves direction of chances indeterminate. Gains may be lost.

Absolute eventual disappointment thus possible.

Natural demand for assurance.

Religion's demand for Ally against cosmic accidents.

Metaphysical demand for "whence."

Harmony, beauty, ideally pre existent, & struggling through.

Perfection eternal. Stars in courses.

Motive for monism.

Not omega solely—alpha & omega.

Against this tychism's open doors & windows.

☞Does pure experience philosophy offer any guarantee beyond *possibility*

We want more than a *bare* possibility.

Metaphysics of relation of ideal & potential to actual, of past & future to present.

If present experiences can not only welcome, but introduce . . . . then there are *live* possibilities.

Leave as problem!

Meanwhile I ask whether a world of hypothetical perfection conditional on each part doing its duty be not as much as can fairly be demanded.

Something must be lost.

But is n't this the inexpugnably serious side of life?

(Most religious men want certainty not possibility. They want to lie back to become 'quietistic':—"The eternal God is my refuge, and underneath the everlasting arms.")

Every additional ground, champion of ideal already there is a *pledge*.

25. Notes for Philosophy 20c: Metaphysical Seminary (1903–1904)

Seminary of 1903–4   Cognition etc.

(Nov. 6. 1903.)— Working towards the non-dualistic conclusion. Pragmatically, what diff. does it make whether we say thoughts & things à la Descartes, the former knowing the latter, or make our division of a common experience-stuff into objects presented and objects[1] represented, of which in certain series & systems the latter terminate in the former, after the fashion of the foreground and the background of a panorama?

   1.) You escape the noetic "chasm," with its discontinuity. [One

---

[1] Opposite this line ('rience-stuff . . . objects' 319.25–26) WJ placed a question mark in the right margin.

object does n't "know" another—it leads to another, such leading being called "knowing" when the whole process is an object for someone else.]

2.) You escape *duplication* in the case of presented objects, which duplication violates common sense. (Common sense assumes "thought" only in the case of *absent* objects.)

3.) You escape the quasi-gaseous material, "consciousness" with its unverifiability.

4) You let the physiological description of the Ego come to its rights. (No ego of 'apperception' is required, so long as the synthetic and continuous quality of the smallest parts of experience is admitted at the outset.)

5.) You frankly make connexion with the principle of *experienced continuity* as the general unifier of the world.

The "whole process" "leads to" another bit of experience which we say remembers or conceives it. These are terms of knowing also. It seems as if Dewey's notion of successive replacements and substitutions of one term by a functionally better one within the limits of one sheet of experience would do the work here sufficiently well. Only in so far as the latter term re-interprets the earlier one should we have to use it in describing the earlier. In the present case our own terms now are the latest.

It sounds paradoxical to say that one *object* "knows" another; and indeed that would be a mixture of terminologies. If we talk "objects" we must say "leads to." If we say "knows" we must talk "states of mind."

Munsterberg says the reine Erfahrung point of view is that of living. When we proceed to talk-about, we have to break the world into thoughts & things, psychic & physical objects, introject, duplicate etc. In so far as talking is a kind of living, the talker himself is in the reine Erfahrung position.

In my view, self-transcendency is everywhere denied. Instead of it, and performing the same function, we have the continuity of adjacents. It is clear that too much attention cannot be brought to bear upon this notion.

Bewusstheit (See Natorp, 112   G.E. Moore, Mind, 449–50) does not exist at all on my view. The beziehung auf eine Subject by which N. explains it, is a perfectly assignable phenomenal relation realized in finite experience between two parts of the total object-field.

Avenarius:—does he mean by Erfahrung in the singular to say Erfahrungen in the plural, so that what *is* is not the tree and I and the mitmensch and our several thoughts of the tree, but just tree, I, & mitmensch, objectively meant, *posited three times over*. This would have some sense. Yet this is Berkeleyism without the transcendent "reductive," and the problem of intercommunication between the numerical many comes up and is ignored by Avenarius.

Natorp 88–9, 94–5 says that Psychology has to *reconstruct* the pure experience before it has been conceptualized. M—g. echoes him (p.   ). I say that Philosophy must do this and describe all Reality in the terms thus gained.

If the world stopt for a million years, & recommenced, the various experiences before and after would be continuous, so far as their contents had certain definable peculiarities, discontinuous otherwise. In either case the 1000 000 years, being supposed not to be "experienced," would not affect either the con- or the dis-continuity. The next thing one of the previous experiences could change into (in the line of experience) would be one of the subsequent ones.

"Bewusstheit" might be devoid of personal form

For[2] the question why, if there be only one "experience" or given, handled now as physical now as mental, the mental can't have the same "adjectives." Cf. Book I, pp. 5, 17, 18 [*ed.*, 215.6–11, 220.17–221.18]. Cf. Aristotelian Proc.

While sitting here, or in Chapel, or anywhere in the midst of a sensible situation, I suddenly have a train of tho't about a distant situation. It is so unreal relatively that introjection is quasi-spontaneous & self-transcendency predicated almost inevitably. Yet *per se* this is a bit of pure experience and just as objective as the sensibly present situation. It is the sensible successors and concomitants which so immediately "reduce" it. In their absence, it

---

2 In the left margin beside this paragraph, WJ wrote vertically, 'The *time*-category *is* common'.

would be a dream, with full reality, and the place- & time-tags which are part of its content might even change to "here" & "now."

"Experiences," "data," "phenomena"—yes, the objector says, but *whose, for whom?* Do not the very words imply an inner dualism, a self to whom the content reports itself, is known, appears, etc., and which in turn is aware of, cognizant of, conscious of that content? You talk of the experiences as of simple objects existing. If they were only that, then when one ceased to exist there would be an absolute end of it. Yet there is a remembrance of it; and how is it possible to account for this without the common-sense supposition of an element in the experience which survives it into the next one, to which the objective element or content *reported* itself, and which now makes possible—knowing as it does the two contents together— a perception of whatever relations may obtain between them. This element is the self, it is what we mean when we call the experiences *conscious* experiences, not dead objects.

I have to reply to such objectors pragmatically, taking the experiences as "dead" data, and yet so describing their content as to eliminate the need of dual constitution, or of Bewusstheit as their menstruum, and to preserve without loss everything that the objector rightly claims in the way of *outcome* or *result*.

Work the menstruum-simile, in which oil, size, or water stands for consciousness, while the object is made of the pigments held in suspension or solution.

In expounding the pure-experience view, state the problem thus, as a genetic one:—Here we are, with a certain resultant experience— "Self" and a certain field of objects, present and remote. Which description of the process that led to this experience is the better, that of dualism or that of "pure experience"?

(Dec 1. 1903.)[3]   Santayana's paper on Schiller. Royce objects to Sch.'s acc^t of truth, that unless the man who says "truth is what I find easiest" also thinks that he *ought* to say so, he has no power to meet others with his truth—the content of his statement contradicts the fact that he takes the trouble to state it.

---

3 On the facing page opposite this paragraph WJ wrote: 'The question is:—Is the world best described ['as' *del.*] in terms of fact, or in terms of meaning of fact? So far as meaning is *realized* it is part of a fact, the fact that some one realizes it.'

Scepticism.[4] Schiller's and Dewey's views of truth are supposed to lead to *damned-please philosophy.* Those who assert an external archetype or absolute standard say it is the only way of escape from the capriciously sceptical condition. In what sense does it make that condition less easy? Certainly not in the practical sense, for if there BE sceptics, it simply leaves them, saying it must be that the Absolute requires such organs. It can only say they *ought* to change. If they disobey, then the absolute requires the disobedience. The real force that works against scepticism is the train of experience, which makes belief more convenient. Where would be the harm in scepticism, if the dream part of life were its only part? It makes no difference to us now what dreams anybody has, because they share no practical points of application to clash in. If we acted on our dreams it would be otherwise. We do act on "reality," and share it and there it is important that we should conform to a standard.

Royce tries in general to show that belief in an 'independent' reality is the only non-contradictory position. Every statement about knowledge has to include itself by anticipation. The 'deliverance' therefore, and the fact that one makes it, must not contradict each other. The absolutist's deliverance is that there is objective truth and that he is objectively true in declaring so. The series here is homogeneous throughout. Not so, says Royce, with the sceptic or pragmatist, for his deliverance, being that "truth is matter of feeling," is contradicted by his dogmatic attitude in saying that it IS matter of feeling—the 'is' evidently affirming here something independent of the statement.

Not so, say I. There is no contradiction whatever. The pragmatist's deliverance "Truth is what one feels like saying" includes his own saying of it proleptically, if you don't slip into non-pragmatic thought. "It is what one feels like saying, and I feel like saying that," etc ad infinitum—where is the contradiction? Is there in fact any *serial* contradiction in any sort of account of truth. Whatever definition you give of it must apply to the definition itself, but you always can apply it, it is merely the prolongation of encapsulating terms. Whatever truth be said to be, that is the sort of truth which the saying carries. Take "systematic" scepticism. It declines to affirm

4 In the left margin WJ wrote vertically: ' "How can pragmatism distinguish betw. bluff & sincerity?" R. Cabot'.

or deny, and declines even to affirm or deny its own declining, i.e. take a consistent attitude about it. Anything may or may not be true, even my own saying so. There may be no truth, not even in the statement that there may be none.

All these homogeneous series are logically faultless. Inconsistency would only come in with heterogenous mixture.

Nextness.— It assumes 2 objects, a change from one to the other, and no consciousness of interval. What is meant by the 'change'? If one object simply lapses and the other comes into being, there is no nextness involved. The nextness must be verified, experienced as such. Mere time succession does n't make nextness. All sorts of things are now succeeding each other in time without being in any positive sense adjacent. There must be co-consciousness of the two objects for their nextness to be matter of experience. Something must move out of object 1 and find that the only thing to move into is object 2. *We* are now that something, as we talk about the two objects hypothetically. But the question is what takes our place in a world where the objects themselves are all there is? How is the nextness, which we might find and talk about, verified or experienced when we are not there?

The condition of the verification is the memory-form. The continuity itself must be part of object 2. When 2 has this constitution, that its object is (1—just past) and naught between, then the nextness is a verified thing.

Continuity, as a basis of Union, or a means of making a universe. Things may be continuous with each other in many ways, forming universes of as many grades of union.

The simplest is where a collection of objects (of knowledge or discourse) are so experienced by an external describer, that he discerns *nothing between them*. Such absence of aught between makes them next, contiguous, adjacent. Adjacency is thus the lowest grade of union. (This seems to be Aristotle's continuity.)

A collection of terms thus co-adjacent from next to next would have to be described as one world. Its parts would hang together. They would not be separated by anything in the line of that observer's[5] experience. When he left one, the next would be the only thing that offered itself. "Space" & "Time" are such worlds for our

---

[5] WJ wrote 'observers's', emended to 'observer's' in the present edition, above undeleted 'describer's'.

description. It seems immaterial whether we say one Space, or many contiguous parts of Space. If the observer ceased between two objects, to be conscious for a certain interval, the world of objects would be discontinuous for another observer who might perceive the empty time-interval, but for the first observer it would still be a continuous world.

Co-aptation, or co-adjacency is thus the simplest way in which a many can form a universe.

If the observer, instead of being external, is one with the experiences, then the same thing holds. They form a continuum so long as he experiences no gap. If he experienced empty time-gaps between his "objects," the latter would not form one object-world. It would be a lot of scattered objects. It would however be one time-world for him.

If two objects were both contiguous to a 3rd object, in this kind of a world, that intermediary would be the medium of their continuity.

Distinguish between the contiguity wh. suffices for my pragmatic purposes and the continuity of the mathematicians. Avoid the latter word. The mathematicians[6] are dealing with number series originally discrete, & made continuous by infinite interpolation, the result being a scale of continuously shaded values with no *step*. Between contiguous things there may be any amount of step, and there must be no intermediary value of any kind.

Activity = "doing":—A common sense *denkmittel* of which the factors must be analyzed out.

Change is one. *Direction* towards a *terminus* seems to be another. *Agent* seems to be a third. *Tendency*.

Common sense uses this category both ob. and subjectively; and for it any motion involves it as well as any thought. The *origin* of the activity is a great point for common sense. Who's to blame?— and the *transmission* of activity has to be admitted and investigated. Imputation of responsibility.

TRUTH. How can I, as a Deweyite, justify the strong antithesis I constantly feel, namely that certain philosophic constructions, (Kant's whole system, e.g., Münsterberg's classification scheme, the

---

[6] In the manuscript 'mathematicians' is represented by ditto marks written below 'mathematicians' in line 19.

scholastic statically arranged concepts & principles, etc) to be subjective caprices, redolent of individual taste, while other constructions, those which work with concrete elements, with change, with
indeterminism, are more objective and cling closer to the temperament of Nature itself. Surely Nature itself and subjective construction are radically opposed, one's higher indignations are nourished
by the opposition. What, on pragmatist terms, does "Nature itself"
signify? To my mind it signifies the non-artificial, the artificial
having certain definite aesthetic characteristics which I dislike, and
can only apperceive in others as matters of personal taste—to me
bad taste. All neat schematisms with permanent & absolute distinctions, classifications with absolute pretensions, systems with pigeon
holes etc., have this character. All "classic" clean, cut & dried, "noble," fixed, "eternal" Weltanschauungen seem to me to violate the
character with which life concretely comes & the expression which
it bears, of being, or at least of involving, a muddle and a struggle,
with an "ever not quite" to all our formulas, and novelty and possibility forever leaking in.

Münsterberg's Congress-program seems to me, e.g. to be sheer
humbug in the sense of self-infatuation with an idol of the den, a
kind of religious service in honour of the professional-philosophy-
shop, with its faculty, its departments and sections, its mutual etiquette, its appointments, its great mill of authorities and exclusions
& suppressions which the waters of Truth are expected to feed to
the great class-glory of all who are concerned. To me "Truth," if
there be any truth, would seem to exist for the express confusion of
all this kind of thing, and to reveal itself in whispers to the "meek
lovers of the Good" in their solitude, the Darwins, the Lockes, etc.,
and to be expressly incompatible with officialism. "Officials" are
products of no deep stratum of experience. M—g's congress seems to
be the perfectly inevitable expression of the system of his Grundzüge, an artificial construction for the sake of making the authority
of professors inalienable, no matter what asininities they may utter,
as if the bureaucratic mind were the full flower of Nature's self-
revelation.

It is obvious that such a difference as this, betw. me & M—g, is a
splendid expression of pragmatism. I want a world of anarchy, M.
one of bureaucracy, and each appeals to "Nature" to back him up.
Nature partly helps & partly resists each of us. How should her
"resistance" be interpreted here? [ὕλη—but with a cleavage?] The

326

sensible and the intellectual, what comes fr outside & what comes from the mind, fuse into unity in *"perception."* The real foreground & the canvass background in the panorama.

26. Notes for Philosophy 9: Metaphysics (1904–1905)

(Oct 6th. 1904)

"Metaphysics."[1] Ordinarily referred to things beyond experience—"entities."

Special sciences deal with uncriticized postulates. *Physics*: space matter, force. *Psychol.*: bodies, life; states of mind, knowledge. *Sociology*: good & bad as measures of progress.

Metaphysics discusses these assumptions, and eke in relation to one another.

Does not necessarily "transcend" experience, find origin of world. Rationalizes "experience" "Obstinate attempt to think clearly."

Being,[2] change, matter, mind, activity, connection, cause, force, time, space, number, possibility

All present obscurities, paradoxes especially if we take them in relation to each other.

Most exquisite work of human mind!—yet how pathetic
    Teichmüller[3] vs. my article

Great thing to find right entrance   basis.

    Each one breeds its own problems.

Find the one that breeds fewest.

---

1 On the facing page WJ wrote: 'A. Definition. | Refer to Baldwin's Dictionary'.

2 The text is braced to the left, originally from 'Being' to include 'All' but then extended to include the text through 'mind!', the line breaking before the dash; a guideline leads from the brace to the third entry on the facing page: 'Expatiate on puzzles'. Above this entry, beginning at the head of the page WJ wrote: '['B. Materials *treated ['ed' *ov. poss.* 'ment']' *del.*] | Well, we find common sense in possession | Read!'

3 On the facing page WJ wrote: '*Great antitheses*: ['Universal vs particular.' *del.*] | Universal vs. particular | Material vs. spiritual. | *Changing [*ab. del.* 'Instable'] vs eternal | ['Empiricism | Eternal particular   atomism | Monadi | Atomism | Monadism | Pantheism' *del.*]'.

Matter
God
Ego: Berkeleyan & Absolute
Pure experience.
Common sense[4] system.
Change!
Being
Plato: Knowledge of reality[5] vs. opinion. *True idea* of thing! definition!
World of change & becoming—being & non-being.
Real world of ideas fixed.
Partaking μέθεξις
Aristotle:
Actuality & potentiality
4 Causes
Unmoved first mover
Pure activity
God's pure contemplation
Atomism
Monism (idealistic)
Monadism.
Nobility without reality
Abstractness.
Clearness with lowness. etc
Empiricism
Rationalism.

(Oct 8)
The dilemma today.[6]
Pathetic.
Find right entrance.
Each breeds its own problems
God
Matter
Ego

---

4 On the facing page WJ wrote: 'C. Some attempts at systems.'

5 On the facing page WJ wrote: 'Two kinds of reality, "Phenomena" *(Democritus) [*intrl.*], & essences | Windelband §9.'

6 On the facing page WJ wrote: 'For this see "Envelope I["] | Give empiricist authors | *Give rationalist authors ['Give' *and* 'authors' *are indicated by ditto marks in the* MS] (Royce)'.

Interpret[7] whole by part
(Envelope II)
1. Thought or sentence (rationalist)
2. Struck by disconnectedness—order
Secondary.
     a. Divine artificer
     b. evolution   attrition
3. Grab-bag
4. We *carve* order.
(Oct 11)
My own system:
5. Drawn from social sphere.
     (Read II, 12–16)
Growth by addition & subtraction
Purpose, accident & passive drift
Designs change to meet events.
Results mixed with collaterals
"Plans fulfilled" are abstract & retrospective
Many jostling aims, both in individual & in social life.
Heterogonie der Zwecke.
Compromise   modus vivendi
Lyell's method
Panpsychism.
"Pure experience." (Define "exp." later)
Conjunctive relations.
radical empiricism
reconciles with spiritualism
Unnaturalness[8] of any ultimate datum.
Fluency within a system.
Relations to Nothing   Schopenhauer.
Being—it must be begged
Wholesale or piecemeal? 21–37
Gradual nascency   Spencer imperceptible
God, Mind. Organic unity

---

[7] On the facing page WJ wrote: 'paint pictures'.

[8] On the facing page WJ wrote: '*Dictate*: *The ['T' *ov*. 'I'] idea of a Nothing that might be instead is the parent of ontological wonder. No philosophy successfully accounts for *there ['re' *ov*. 'ir'] being anything rather than nothing. All are alike in having to beg being, and confess the *gift*. (Refer to will to believe volume.) The problem is to describe *Being ['B' *ov*. 'b'] adequately and in terms that leave the fewest dissatisfactions.'

Hegel's attempt. (McTaggart)

Pure[9] experience. Phenomena
Provisional convenience of double barrelled word.
Pragmatic[10] method. Substance. Matter: Self.
God and matter as illustrations.

Experience as an ultimate term. Baldwin
Its connotations
    1 Object & Subject.
    2. concrete, "sensible."
    3 Discrete from others.
In[11] the older metaphysics the soul *had* experiences.
In Kant's the Ego is a *constituent* of them
Experiences *per se,* we are told, are disconnected.
Association psychology.
Radical empiricism
Conjunctive relations
Dualistically, exp. implied soul & body.
Berkeley introduced alteration.
Neutrality of pure experience
Noetic unity: The world is "one," to talk about.
(Oct 20) Recap. Ostwald
Application to problem of Unity of World.
Various connexions
All save world from *disconnectedness* (multiverse)

---

9 On the facing page WJ wrote: '['Note ['N' *ov.* 'p'] p' *del.*] Admit nothing that is not *matter of **either actual['ly' *del.*] or possible [*intrl.*] [*intrl.*] experience['d' *del.*] ['somewhere, somewhen,' *del.*] and find some place for whatever is *actually [*intrl.*] experienced.'

10 On the facing page WJ wrote: 'Question of Unity of world. | ['1 can collect.' *del.*] | 1½ can't divide. Can collect | 2. Continuous—pass s̄ let go. minds discrete | 3 One substance *3 [*ab. del.* 'continuity'] ? [*ov. comma*] 4? | 4. Generic unity | 5 Origin | ['6 can collect (noetic)' *del.*] | 7 Mechanical connexion more than physical continuity.'

11 On the facing page WJ wrote: '[*fol.* 8ᵛ] Hoffding's lecture. Main points: "Critical Monism." Continuity vs. Discontinuity: Rational = Irrational. One—Many. Ideal is the One. bel. every many is dragged out.—Concedes possible novelties.—Our tho't part of world: So long as our tho't incomplete, world incomplete.—Ethical relativity. [*fol.* 9ᵛ] "Withness" seems all. | *Some* unities involve others, others not. differents interact. Generic U. not required for dynamic. | Love involves knowledge not vice versa | Chemical [*ditto marks*] mechanical [*ditto marks*] | Sound [*ditto marks*] air [*ditto marks*] | Sight [*ditto marks*] ether. | Physica[l] & noetic reciprocally independent | *You [*ov.* 'Que'] may know me, I not you. | Things known to one Knower not all at once. | Shallower *involve [*ab. del.* '&'] deeper leve[l]s. Read p. 17.' The ditto marks represent 'involves' and 'not vice versa'.

Universes of different grades:
Temporality, knowability, without interaction, commensurability
  or common origin. "Withness."
Noetic "collective." "additives" "subtractives"
There would be no logical, aesthetic, physical or other connexion.
You can imagine other connexions added.

    Generic.
    physical
    mechanical
    chemical
       Non-reciprocal:
    Sound added to air
    light to ether.
    love to knowledge
    generic added to dynamic unity
    You may know me: I not you
    One knower *may* know all, but may know it successively.
Finally absolute organic unity is *conceivable*.
Style of argument.
    Criticize later.
Meanwhile for *us* synechism or concatenation is enough.
Shallow accusations!
Let us avoid vagueness and temper.
Start then with our *partly connected* & *partly disconnected* universe
Connexions & disconnections equally real *prima facie*.

I proposed "Experience" as our primal term.
Its advantages:
  1. Neutrality: double barrelled.
    It admits object & subject but
    Does n't prejudge "soul" "matter" etc.
  2. Its concreteness. clearness.
  3. Its convenience pragmatically.
  4 Its inclusiveness: matter alone or mind alone exclude. Duality
    precludes Idealism, etc.
But, we are told, experiences *per se* are incoherent.
Ego as unifying principle. Caird   Green etc.
Vulnerability of associationism.
Radical empiricism
(Oct 25)

Chaos Whence the disconnections? are they experienced?

If[12] so—they are *coordinate* with the conjunctions.

1 Describe chaos

Presentative and representative exp[s]

Thoughts *about* . . . tracing relations or non relations.

(Mind's passivity or activity)

Dreams—delusions—Jean

Sympathetic magic (hair, nails, name, portrait, footprint)

    wear iron to impart hardness

    chew wood to make interlocutor soft

Dyak's head.

But experiences are intrinsically *double.*

    whose? for *whom*?

Does n't the word imply reporting, awareness.

Not flat, dead data.

The immediate—unverified—yet *responsible* to a future.

The sense of 'more' is followed by the real 'more,' that verifies it.

Into this short state of fact the whole mystery of "transcendence" shrivels.

Cohen stands out for self transcendency in cases where the terminus is not presented. Admit it: but what is it *known-as*? What does it *do for us*? It is only *known* as knowledge when the terminus is reached   until then it is not known as *knowledge* but as tendency.

Astonishing how much rubbish the pragmatic acc[t] of knowing scuffs away. E.g.—Bert. Russell's diseased stuff in Mind Oct '04

In a sense a "hand sapolio" advertisement is self-transcendent. It refers to an object, exactly as much and as little as my tho't of the object does. Why don't we say it *knows* the object? Because the conjunctive transitions thereto are missing, so long as the advertisement is regarded as a physical object.

Knowing is only one way of getting into practical relations, relations, in the end, of presence, contact.

We are really *advertisements* of Memorial Hall, just like Hand Sapolio advertisements in the cars.

The account of the knowing function must be built up gradually:

12 On the facing page WJ wrote: 'Conjunctions need no more explanation of their power to join than disjunctions need of their power to disjoin.'

1. Suppose a physical world & one knower. His ideas lead to a presentation

2 *Identity* there of tho't & thing—so long as no other knower, or better (further) knowledge of thing exists.

3. Other knowers come

4. Better knowledge comes.

> The simple identity at first assumed naively has to be replaced by a more elaborate diagram, but the schematic form need not be altered.

> Through that place experiences of various kinds are *confluent*.

The *nature* of the physical & of the mental is the same.

The Dyak's head metaphor can be used for the part as well as for the whole. Any "that" which belongs to a mental series also has physical streamers attached to it. Compare a point of strain in a solid or sheet of india-rubber. A particle of air is the place of transit of many sonorous messages, a point of ether of many luminous waves.

Solipsism

1 "That" passes for true. At the same time that is only his opinion.

2. Add other minds. "That" is common to them.

3. They may predicate different *whats* of it. Still the *that* remains as the *place* of the whats, and the centre of interactions of all the elements involved.

There the minds are *conterminous* without being *confluent*.

3 degrees:

> Conterminous
>
> Continuous (or contiguous superficially)
>
> Confluent.

Royce's arg^t from error.

If you say there is nothing but opinion, neither truth nor error, *that* opinion at least claims truth, the opinion that there *is* truth is at least an error. So truth & error come back upon us, and we contradict ourselves.

Is this so? *distinguons!*

1st., there is no contradiction if instead of claiming truth for our dictum we merely suggest the dictum, but don't maintain it as more than *our* opinion.

2nd., also none if declaring our dictum we say no *other* dictum is true.

Royce seems to imply that

My hand felt kinaesthetically and at the same time seen. The places are confluent. So are the sensations.

(Nov 10th. '04.)
The immediate or living experience runs smoothly.
Reflection introduces paradox
Philosophy seeks to recover the best sense of life.
Common sense introduces as its denkmittel:
>One time, one space.
>
>Minds & bodies, with the minds knowing objects in common.

Idealism finds paradox: minds can only know their own ideas. Solipsism etc. results.
Hume,[13] Bradley etc. deny conjunctive relations überhaupt as experienced
Kant reinstates them by a complicated machinery.
So do Royce, Hegel, Taylor, Bradley, with their absolute.
I leave them as parts of experience, and restore the living sense of continuity, abolishing "consciousness" "matter" etc. by bringing back everything to what it is immediately "known as."
The world then appears as the sum of your actual experiences, & mine, with indefinitely numerous possible experiences, all mediated with each other by experienced relations—the whole forming an enormous web or net with streamers at its knots.
The only great difficulty is the relation of conceptual to perceptual experiences überhaupt. The physical world is partly conceptual—the mental partly perceptual.
The combustibility etc. of the table are really there with the percept, as well as really here with me.
They are insufficients. So is the percept.

>So is everything.
>Everything is a substitute that has to be superseded. The present experience, whatever it be "of" is ever the cross section of an onrushing stream.

[13] On the facing page WJ wrote: 'Quote Hume from Inquiry §7.'

In so far forth my phil. joins hands with the sense of life. *This* absolutists deny.

(Nov 12.) *Dialectical Objections.*
1. Royce on the same in diverse relations.
          " Unity of Things
2. Lotze's argument for Monism.
3. Royce's refutation of realism
Dictate.

The dialectical objection is that "B-as-related-to-A" is not numerically one with "B-as-related-to-C." Verbally not, assuredly, for B with its two contexts is *named* twice over. But what the words mean, not what they *are* is the real question. They mean a train of experience. In that train of experience a term B is given; and given in its two relations to A & to C in such wise as to be the medium of union or of transition or of communication between these latter terms. No element in the immediate experience suggests any self diremption of the B into 2 Bs, one related to A the other to C. On the contrary B is expressly and positively experienced as the one and only B, a self same *that*, which, just because it is self-same, mediates conjunctively between the A & C. There is no trace whatever of doubling up in the B as originally given, the experience being one of conjunctive transition from A to C with no point of disjunction, or discontinuity about it, beyond the logical distinction of the terms themselves. Whoever undertakes to prove the experience to be discontinuous must abandon the "pure" estate of it, and show by a reflective process that it is the appearance of some deeper and discontinuous object which is more real.

The arguments to this effect, even when they profess to be logical seem purely verbal. They substitute, not deeper realities, but words, for the original experience. The integral phrase "B as related to A" is a different phrase from "B-as-related-to-C." But whoever tells us that because we have to use 2 Bs in this way of analyzing the phenomenon by 2 successive phrases, therefore the phenomenon itself *can't* have been of one B, fails to distinguish between words and facts. Every word is separate from every other word, but it does n't follow that every aspect of fact which the words denote is similarly separate. The abstract concept of B to A is other than the abstract concept of B to C. The mind distinguishes and fixes & eternalizes its distinctions by naming them apart; but so far is it from being true that "the mind never perceives any real connexion among distinct existences" (in this case its own mental objects) that in using them and the words that name them it sees immediately what they mean, and restores the fluency of the original experience.

The only *real* proof that B is not the same would be to show that it is *different*. The pragmatic test of sameness is inability to show difference. So far as things are the same, you can show no difference. So far as you can show difference they cease to be the same. B to A, & B to C differ in the contextual part alone, not in the B. It is *that* B in both cases, there, now, intrinsically self identical, in all points indistinguishable—in short one B.

Bradley A & R., 20, 23, relations must be linked 33, 108–*109*–12, 118 123 146, *159*

Such an arrangement may work, but the theoretical problem is not solved.

how? 113, 104 118

may work 23

Stout: Arist. Proc. 1901–2 p. 7

Where does Bradley get the separateness with which he finds all things infected? That also must be appearance—and I suppose he thinks it so, as seen by the Absolute. Yet it is appearance of a higher denomination than the continuity which also appears and appears as its coordinate, for it is used by B. to expel the continuity.

The point for me to stick to is the denial of conjunctive relations, of the union of a many.

Obviously pure experience gives conjunctions. Every sensation passing away leaves what we call a memory of itself, in which it figures as the "same." The sameness means no break, no discontinuity. These are not given. Time-continuity is. The self, which is part of every experience is similarly given as unbroken. Every field of experience gives multitude. Vaguely apprehended its parts are "with" each other, conjoined by *ands*. More clearly they are *placed*, classed, etc.

Defy Bradley to show that these conjunctions are *not* found.

His reply is that "they are not, when there, as they are when you by an abstraction have taken them out." (564)

But even if they were there thus "and your intuition of them were a fact, it is not an *understanding* . . . it is a mere experience and furnishes no consistent view . . . ." (109.)

"The question is how thought can think what is offered, so that we are led to inquire what (in B's words) would satisfy the intellect provided it could be got?" (568)

"There must [in the experience-manifold] be an identity, and in that identity a ground of distinction & connection" (568). But an external ground won't do, because that calls for synthesis itself. Yet "in the intellect no intrinsic connections are found." "If the process were the intellect's own proprius motus, the case would be altered. Each aspect would of itself be a transition to the other aspect, a transition intrinsic & natural at once to itself and to the intellect. . . . There is no how or why beside the self-evident process." (568) "But for myself, unable to verify a solution of this kind." "I cannot say that to me any principles of diversity in unity are self-evident." "Thought in its own nature has no 'together' "

The experiences offered as facts or truths, "I find that my intellect rejects . . . because they contradict themselves. They offer a complex of diversities conjoined in a way which it feels is not its way and which it cannot repeat as its own. . . . For to be satisfied my intellect must understand, and it cannot understand by taking a congeries in the lump. . . . To understand, it must go from one point to another, and in the end also go by a movement which it feels satisfies its nature. Thus, to understand a complex AB I must begin with A or B. And beginning say with A if I then merely *find* B, I have either lost A or I have got beside A something else, and in neither case have I understood. For my intellect cannot simply unite a diversity, nor has it in itself any form or way of togetherness, and you gain nothing if beside A & B you offer me their conjunction in fact. For to my intellect that is no more than another external element."

Royce's Religious Asp. Phil 3 & 17
Its argument.
Lotze's argument
Royce on Realism 112–138
Taylor p 86–91

(Nov. 21)
Revert to central point, which is *concatenated* vs. *consolidated* Universe. [Nextness, conterminousness, etc]
Supposes a privacy in the being of the parts, and that relations can be adventitious.

Recall Royce on independence.

Read & criticize Taylor, p. 86. [Mention W. to B]

Then explain Bradley's proof that there can be no 'external' relations. As I understand it it is s'thing like this.

"The lamp is *on* the table." The elements here are 3: Lamp, table, on. Do they themselves give the concrete fact. They might severally be given and yet the fact be other. The fact is *that* lamp in *that* relation to *that* table. Some thing *in* the lamp & in the table that determines that relation. What draws a bare "on" to these 2 terms. Read *supra*[14]

He seems to desiderate a ground of the connexion previous to the fact thereof to make it that fact, and this ground must be synthetic of all the elements.[15]

Read what he says of the intellect's proper motion, p. 568.

"How" "Understand"—seems as if he got into genetic questions.
> Lamp *near* book
> Chair *like* chair

To seek paradox is perverse.

If each partial fact exists then whole exists.

Distinguish question of intelligibility & constitution when object *made* from genesis.

Miss Sears's edition of it.

Assume disconnection as a fact: there must be noetic connexion at least. Every negative must be known. Ignorance must be known, along with what it ignores. "The Absolute is ignorant." "There is no knower" "There is no world"—all prove the absolute.

Frantz's remark: "affirm a Chaos & your speech bewrayeth you." etc. Universe of discourse only.

Can there be a many without a one

(Nov 26) General question of Monism. Royce's reduction of a pluralism to a monism by the idealistic argument that every fact has its knower.

Answer: the finite knower is enough. Where there is no knowing there is no fact.

---

[14] In the left margin WJ wrote: 'Read Ap. & R. p. 33' and on the facing page: ' "If it is external to the terms ['what' *del.*] how can it possibly be true of them?" 575 Read this passage, first!!'

[15] On the facing page WJ wrote: ' "A & B are united *each in its own nature* in a whole which is the nature of both alike." 570, 1.'

Royce says but the no knowing is itself a fact

Yes! but for whom? for its noticer, who may well be finite.

The only consequence which the idealistic postulate carries is that if a thing can't be shown to be a fact for any finite consciousness. It is no fact at all.

A zero universe would equally prove the Absolute.

Then discuss monism as an hypothesis.

1. One time ⎞
2. One space ⎠ contiguity etc ⎞
3 Generic unity (*kinds!*)   ⎬ Concatenation type
4 Change   ⎠
5 Interaction
6 Noetic union ⎞ but to what extent
7 Unity of origin ⎠

(Nov 28)

Resume. All that follows from Idealistic principle is that if a thing is n't a fact for a finite consciousness it is n't a fact at all.

If you plead absolute to know the finite's finiteness, it opens the door to negations impossible to follow.

Ignorance[16] treated as a fact means absence of knowledge treated as a presence.

   Take absurd cases:
   Absolute is ignorant
   There is no knower
   There is no world
      All prove the Absolute.

Conclude that even Idealism does n't prove the Absolute.

We are not even Idealists!

Nevertheless[17] it is a perfectly intelligible hypothesis that the world may possess complete noetic unity.

My reasons for aversion to that hypothesis.

Its religious value to many men.

It contains all fulfilments (Royce II. 302.)

1. Yet its fulfilment is not *our* fulfilment.
   Aesthetic delight in a tragedy—devil!

16 On the facing page WJ wrote: 'G. LeBon | La Dematerialization de la matiere | Rev. Scient. 12 *et [*intrl.*] 19 Nov. 1904 | Id La Materialization de l'Energie. | 15 Oct. 1904 | La Solution des Rayons N., 705'.

17 On the facing page WJ wrote: 'On time-span Cf. Royce II, 221ff. 418 | Marshall. J. of Phil. July 7. I. 365'.

In any result the parts fit.

3. Superfoetation. Abs. must contain all the odds & ends of our ideas[18]
4. Lion's den character.
5. Block universe.

(Dec 1)
Superfoetation on mind view.
Block universe
    1. as mechanical
    2. rational (symphony)

(Dec 3)   Sum up. Finite experiences less weird. Piece meal world Raindrops etc
Unity of *origin* & generic unity. Maxwell
Teleological argument.
Voltaire.[19]
"fit" "for"
Any world planned if one cd. believe such a world *aimed at* at all.
Production by mechanism may be part of aim. Like football.
Every thing *compatible* with absolute unity of origin.
Question is, is what we *find*, *in*compatible with *plural* origin?
Transition to question of genesis.
(Dec 6)   Genesis.
Hitherto *constitution* discussed. the question is *what*?
      that to what
From *what* to *that* a non-logical step.

$$0 = +1 - 1$$

$$\frac{0}{0} = \frac{1-1}{1-1} = 1$$

Hegel's doubly negated truth

Empiricism the only method.
Numbers, places, collocations pure *data*
    Other book, p. 58 [*ed.*, 301.26–302.8]
(Dec 15)

18 At the head of the facing page, opposite deleted text (see Alterations entry 339.34), WJ wrote in pencil: ' "Why need the Absolute be made into hash? I don't want a world hashed over." Gray's *book ['b' *ov.* 'w'].

19 On the facing page WJ wrote: 'eyes c̄ cataract | stch s̄. gastric juice | Hunchback | forest fire | bacterium. | *Some* result, always!'

Chance[20] means occurrence without known reason. Reason is
 grounded in *fact*

Chance production means *spontaneity,* grounded in no other fact

Chance coincidence means two factors   the action of neither of
 which is the ground of the others action.

A world in which chance is found means one in which things occur
 without ground in other things.

Ultimate	chance	= no grounds	
	freedom	= no constraint	
are	necessity	= no possibilities	outside
synonyms	law	= no disturbances	
	truth	= no hypotheses	
	fact	= no reason	

A world of Chance is a world where *novelty is possible*. Not a block
 Universe.

Hark back to the *being*-question

Does n't prevent *graft* when here.

Peirces *tychism*   Monist II, 321

Out of chance can come order

Out of order no chance

Compatible with nature's uniformity

Conservation[21] of energy,

Things like 'summer' 'winter'

This table

Constancy to an outside observer

(Dec 17)

To the beings involved, differences important to the last degree.

Difference in games, chess, Shah of Persia. Musical performances,
 pictures. Football.

Sheep flock—stationary country.

Could physical order have arisen?

Suggest possible evolution of laws of nature

1st. Space bounding. Universe of withness
     Spinoza: unaquaeque res—conatur.

2nd Affecting? If it *could* come. [But if it could n't, the preventer
 would have to affect]

What kind of affecting?

[20] On the facing page WJ wrote: 'Taylor—Bk. III Chap III p. 216'.
[21] On the facing page WJ wrote: 'Solomons: Phil. Rev. VIII, 146.'

'Gregariousness'—which makes compounds.
'Attraction' & 'association.'
Refer to Bowne
(Dec 22)   "Free will"

Causation over sufficient.
Possibility vs. necessity
Reality of phenomena
Real loss—real gain
Workshop of being
fact in the making.
World *grows*, by *whats* as well as by *thats*
How it grows—2 ways
Individualism.
Motive for supposing:
  abolition of evil as "problem."
  Possibly ideal world.
Royce
[Transition to possibility, necessity, and cause.]

(1905)
(Jan 3)
Begin by saying freedom has no value *per se*, only from its opening
  possibilities of content, Huxley wound up like a clock.
Since *b*'s possibility is *a* (and not a 3rd estate of *b*) the question of
  possibility merges into that of procession, change, causality etc.
(Jan 10)
Change what *known-as.*
  s'thing exists which did not
  s'thing ceases wh. did exist.
     Baldwins Dict.
Discontinuous kinetoscope
Take discontinuous first.
  kinetoscope.
Witness required, for conjunctive relation—like eye.
Continuous change due to mixture of discontinuous novelty &
  identity.
Zeno on motion.

Refer to Infinite.

But what introduces the new when it is not a matter of chance.

This opens question of causality.

Only 3 views:

    Identity. Scholastic.

    Succession of differents.

    Activity

          Causality.

(Jan 12. 05)

Lewes. Problems II.

    Prob. V.

F. Bowen's gleanings.

John Venn. Emp. Log. Chap II. p. 45

C. Sigwart. Logic, §73. (II. 92)

A. E. Taylor. El. of Met. Bk II. Ch V. p. 158

Also Mill, Riehl etc. Hobhouse.

A. Stöckl Lehrb. d. Phil. II. 90

J. Rickaby: G'al Met. Bk II. Ch III. p. 298

Aristotelian 4

The savage's demand looking forward is for *means* of *production,* of

    fire, of drunk, of death—or looking backward, "who's to blame,"

Efficiency! }

Real activity } Regularity subordinate.

Read scholastic principles (Stöckl)

Activity involved!

Attempts to *eliminate efficiency* & introduce *regularity.*

Hume first.

"Law"—popular misunderstanding of it as coercing—to be *obeyed*

Kant's vague use of "rule."

    What does it bind? the next phenomenon? The observer? The

    whole future series.

Sum-total theory.

Popularly taken "cause" and "effect" are both abstracts.

2 forms of sum-total theory

1) Scientific: *equation* phases of process in movement. Riehl.[22]

2) Teleologic: Taylor. Royce

Resumé. 4 views.

[22] On the facing page WJ wrote: 'receptacle vs. link, *co.,* between.'

1) Cause obtains *between* individuals.
   Efficient—active.
2 Means procession of *identicals.*
3. *Law* of succession of differents.
4. Purpose, expression etc.
(Jan 14)
Surely notion of efficacy must be added to functional variation
   ("law") of differents to give the full popular meaning to the word
   cause.
Pass on to "Activity"
Differents must be admitted.
(Jan 17)   Relation of long to short span activities is the urgent
   problem.
Either pluralism or monism.
If the former, either panpsychism or a devitalized word.
But monism fails.
(Taylor's *one* purpose!?)
Panpsychism then.
Healthy type of speculation inasmuch as it makes hypotheses
Science vs. analysis. Paulsen
Shallow ordinary view of experience.
      (Absolute directly beneath)
Go back to theory of cognition.

Your lamp & mine, your body & mine *conterminous* } because of
                        not contiguous. } activity
                                          } passing

How represent the activities?
We have only one paradigm.
Our inner life.
Idea & percept are confluent.
Percepts engender ideas
Ideas engender percepts.
Activity, *if efficacious*, means *creation*[23]
Desire—ideal.
The only *rational* ground why anything should be is that it is de-
   manded.
(Jan 19)

[23] On the facing page WJ wrote: 'Read paper | Huntington | This stuff not exam-
inable'.

Were this the only ground extant our world would be like a fairy
   tale—every desire would instantaneously be satisfied.[24]
But our world is pluralistic.
Intermediaries have to be worked upon & resistances overcome.
Short-span activities, relatively blind, have to be propitiated and
   harnessed
(wireless telegraphy, and the instant lighting of a whole city by
   some one pressing a button in the power house show the concentration & approach to immediacy)
You have to pay for what you get (Conservation of energy.)
Whatever other intermediaries, there is always the neural chain.
Our activity has to pass through that to reach the outer world—to
   reach other minds.

$$I : \frac{(\text{motor}) \; line}{\times \; \times \; \times \; \times \; + \; +} \quad I^2$$

Problem of mind & brain.
If we discard old fashioned epiphenomenalism we get
Two chief types of theory:
Strong's,
& Bergson's
Their essential difference is that for Strong the "I" is homogeneous
   with the rest of the chain
For Bergson . . .
On Strongs theory
What I think now is the reality—there is no cortex.
For B. there is a cortex.
If you re-think my tho't you *know* it—terminate *at* it—influence it—
But don't penetrate it.
Telepathy would penetrate.
Talk informally about this. brain is seat of *action*
Bergson a new force
Fechner. Carpenter   Royce
The only surely false theory would be a perfectly clear & final one
If there were telepathy there would be another line of conjunction.
The synthesis within the person is telepathic.
Meanwhile insulation, ignorance
(Jan 21)   Religion.

[24] On the facing page WJ wrote: 'The world of wishing caps and Aladdin's lamps.'

345

Last lecture.
Read case. Janet
Question of synthesis
Post hypnotic suggestion
Psych. Rev. Vol 2.
Wider world.
My varieties. private: concrete work done
Leuba
My reply
Starbuck & Leuba in Hall, No 2.
God infinite or finite?
Is mysticism authority for Monism?
If One why breaking?
If Many why connexion?
Lotze on Leibnitz.
Monism an *absolute guarantee.*
Partridge & Cooper book, p 95 [*ed.,* 318.33–319.3]
If time, ibid 74 [*ed.,* 311.4–14]
Do we need one
(Jan 24)   *Quiz & Résumé.*
  1. Pragmatic method
  2. Principles of pure Experience
  3 Conjunctive relations,
  4. Concatenated world
  5. Theory of knowledge—Realistic
  6. Mind & matter functional terms.
  7. "Absolute" rejected because (a) useless; (b) enigmatical.
  8. Additive universe—Graft
  9. Tychism and indeterminism
  10. "Truth" newly interpreted.
  11. Causality is real activity
  12 Theology.

A vital point is that perception is fixed as the practical stage. Theory inter- and extra-polates beyond it. But that *through* it we do act and are acted on shows it to be dynamically continuous with what profounder realities there may be. It is their substitute, for practical purposes, but they also must be real.
"Truth" is timeless—i.e. if a statement was ever true it is always true—of *that* subject, *then*; But subjects change so that what was

true of then is never true of any other time. The real is that of which our statements can be true. The real changes, adds to itself. The train of experiences had by J. Caesar in Gaul were real. It is eternally true that they *were*. But that J.C. is a torture to American boys of 13 is an addition

Begin synechistic discussion by a few concrete schemes, e.g of a burden needing 2 men to support it, yet being continuously supported though the men shd. change. (In that case man 1 & man 4 would have no contemporaneous relation). Or of an electric connecter ⌒ ⌒ ⌒ ⌒ ⌒ ——

27. Notes for Philosophy 9: Metaphysics (1905–1906)*

[a]

Dewey's & Spencer's Ethics
    Price
Something about
        Plato   *Reed*: P's Idealism
        Aristotle: *Cohen*
        Plotinus
        Sᵗ Augustin
        John Scot Erigena
        Saint Anselm
        Saint Thomas
        Duns Scotus
        Ockham
        Howison

* The first thirteen leaves plus two tipped-in leaves (pp. 347.13–352.30) of #4511 contain a class list, two examinations, and a few notes that pertain to the 1904–1905 course (No. 26 in the present edition). Why this 1904–1905 material prefaces the 1905–1906 notes is not known, but there are notes within these pages that probably were intended for use in both courses. Therefore, it is the editors' decision to preserve the arrangement of the material as found in #4511.

DATE Sept 5 D. S. S. Robins

PHIL. 9.

Robinson, Strong's book

05 Atherton, H. F. — *Truett* gr. Knapp, J. H.
06 Blagden, A. C. — 06. Lewis, C. I. Perfection
Gr Breed, F. S. — Consciousness, 06. J. Gray Association
05 Byard, L. B. — Infinity
06 Clements, E. T. — Immortality
Gr Cohen, M. R. — Aristotle, Bradley, etc.
05 Dorrance, S. M. — Berkeley
Gr Emerson, L. E.
Gr Fisher, G. M. — Lao-Tse
05 Greene, J. A.
05 Hackett, L. W. — Sh. Schlesinger. A A
05 Hale, S. (Knowledge as Value)
05 Heathcote, G. M.
~~Gr Hertzog, W. S.~~
06 Hooper, W. E. — Strong's book
05 Lathrop, J. H. — Ritschl
Gr Lindley, E. H.
06 Lord, R. H. — Augustin on predestination
~~05 McLeod, K.~~
05 Mayer, L. — Brain physiology
Gr Merrington, E. N.
05 Miner, C. E.
06 Monasmith, H. B. — Matter, Dualism, anti Kant
Gr Reed, C. C. — Plato
05 Smith, A. G. — Teleology
Gr Stowe, A. R. M.
Gr Surrey, F. M.
Gr Toll, C. H. — Maher
05 Swain, P. L. — Chance
05 Washburn, C. C. — Idealism
Sp Watts, R. H. — J. S. Mill
Gr Waugh, K. T. — Reality - Idealism

'06. Foerster R W.
Sh Burnett A R. Gr. Gulick A C

Davidson, Laws of History
06. C. J. Lewis
D. Parker, N. H. Strong's book.
G. Coleman, J. Truth
G. Tilley, Determinism
D. Vail, A. R. Religion as feeling
Toll? Dorrance, Foerster.

[*Opposite* 'Perfection', WJ *wrote* 'W.J., Mill. Aristotle.' *on the facing recto.*]

Read:

        Locke

        Berkeley: *Dorrance*: Fraser's Sel

                   Mill

                   Huxley

       Hume

       Kant

       Mill   Foerster

          Extracts from 3 books

      Jevons

      Mach

      Pearson

                   Concepts

Unity	— multiplicity
Sameness	difference
Individual	universal
abstract	concrete
Relation	
Continuity	
Percept	— concept
Being	non-being
Reality	
Possibility	
Cause	
Chance.	*Tilley* (my Essay, Sidgwick, Green's Proleg)
Experience	
Necessity	
Free will	
Teleology	*A.G. Smith* (Martineau Bowne)

Where the terminus is not reached, but an ideal, Cohen says the *salto mortale* exists. There is transcendence.

Pragmatically what does the transcendence mean unless either 1) that we *shall* reach it, or 2) that it defines a direction for our progress. In both cases, that is what the denier of transcendence asserts. Does n't it seem then that the dispute is verbal? This must be developed.

Metaphysical.

Knowledge

    Plato

    Aristotle

    Saint Thomas

Metaphysical
 Matter.
 Soul
 Soul & Body
  Descartes
  Spinoza
  Clifford Huxley
 Panpsychism.
Infinity *Byard.*
Immortality *Clements*
Kant's antinomies
Atoms
Progress
Evolution
  Davidson (Tarde)
Laws of History
Energy
Fourth Dimension
Origin of Life
Heredity
Materialism
Pragmatism.
Body and Mind: Tait: Strong's book
Truth[1]   *HARVARD UNIVERSITY*

PHILOSOPHY 9

1. Define " empiricism " and " rationalism " ; — " radical " empiricism.

2. " Philosophers interpret the World after the analogy of certain parts thereof." Give examples.

3. "The Universe is One"; "It is Many." Criticise such statements.

4. Define the pragmatic method.

5. The term " experience." Why is it advantageously non-committal?

6. Define representative knowledge.

Hour Examination. November 1, 1904.

[1] On the facing blank page WJ wrote, 'Religious Truth. Perry: Internat! J. of E. Oct 1904'.

(Dec 10.)

1. Why is Lotze's argument for monism from interaction 'verbal'?
2. Common empiricism & Idealism deny conjunctive relations: explain this, and argue for their recognition.
3. In what sense is it that many knowers can know one thing?

—explain the term.

How does W. J.'s account of "knowing" remove some of its difficulties?

Difference between concatenation and conflux, as types of world-structure.

How does he define religion?

Build up tychistic theory of the universe, making use of the concepts of being, additive relation, possibility, chance, indeterminism, pluralism, & explaining these concepts so far as time allows.

Compare Höffding's discontinuities & irrationalities.

Being question.

"One thing can't be in two relations"—say anything about this.

How, in the article "Does consciousness exist," does W.J. explain the difference between physical objects and 'ideas.'

On this theory, must ideas possess physical properties?

The pragmatic method—mention any instances of its use that may have struck you.

"Radical empiricism"

"Truth" is what has a claim to be acknowledged (Taylor). Give an empiricist account of what the claims may consist in.

"Sensations are the tent-pins of truth"—Can the sensations themselves be called true?

Flux broken

Phil. to restore   Present day dilemma

Paint pictures—name types

Common sense

Universal & particular | percept & concept

Pure experience

Pragmatic method

Radical empiricism
Genesis vs. analysis "Being."

Theory of Knowledge   Natl. Realism

Criticize Absolute.

heterogony   Lotze   Royce etc.

HARVARD UNIVERSITY

1904–5

PHILOSOPHY 9

1. Discuss the self-transcendency implied in "knowing." Compare that involved in your thought of Memorial Hall with that involved in a "Hand Sapolio" advertisement, etc.

2. "In sense-perception, object and subject are one fact." Developing the divergent relations of this fact, account for the dualism of mind and matter in terms of a "pure experience" philosophy. Be as complete as you can.

3. Why did W. J. attach so much importance to conjunctive relations?

4. "'Being' has to be *begged* in all philosophies." Explain this.

5. Define "chance." "Things are produced by chance," "by freedom," "by necessity," "by law;" "they are blank data;" "they are facts":— Compare these phrases as to their meaning and worth.

6. Define "possibility" (*a*) as bare; (*b*) as grounded.

7. Compare the popular, the scientific, and the absolutist conceptions of "cause." Which did W. J. favor?

8. Compare a solidified universe with a concatenated one of tychistic type, as to their general satisfactoriness, treating "activity" as the medium of continuity between possibles and reals in the latter.

9. How far can any state of facts experienced be taken either as proving "design," or as being incompatible therewith? Compare the monistic with the pluralistic notion of design in the universe.

10. Express your personal reaction on pluralism candidly.

Mid-Year. 1905.

Pluralistic world.
Grades of universe   Dyak's head
One origin. teleology
Question of origin. genetic probs.
Tychism. Chance.
Possibility   Continuity
Necessity   activity etc.
Confluence etc.

Evolution scheme. Graft.

Moral consequences.

    Religious

Infinite.

Body & Mind.

    Strong   Bergson

Humanism

Truth

Faith etc.

                  Theses

Atherton: the Self.

Berry: Heymans (Soul & body)

Bloomfield: Reid & Common Sense

Bruce:

Caldwell: Pragmatism.

Cate: Taylor's Metaphysics.

D. Arnold: Freewill

Cogswell:

Coleman: Emerson

Dueberg:

Sc) R. W. Pumpelly: Will to Believe, etc.

Hale: Freedom of will

Hatch Freedom of will

Jenckes: Schopenhauer

Lambe J. Ward's N. & A²

Mc.Cormick

Mitchell

Musgrove: the Self (Hume, James, Mill)

Parker: Theism or religious principle

Perry: Religious experience   Mysticism

Peterson: Common Sense

Price: Dewey's Ethics

Reed: Mind & Body (Tuke etc)

Savage: Materialism

Seipt: Teleology: Paulsen, Bowne

2 'J. Ward's N. & A' was added in pencil, the 's N. & A' written on a calling card that was pasted on the page of the notebook. The calling card bears the name of 'Mr. George William Tupper', a student of James's. On the card WJ had written 'Gr.' in ink to the left and just above the 'Mr.', and below the name he had written, also in ink, '1654 Mass. Avenue'. On the notebook page above the calling card, WJ wrote in pencil, 'Phil 9 | 1905–6'.

Shurtleff:

Strother:

DATE

PHIL. 9.

Tu., Th., Sat., at 11

Sever 11

Professor James

Dv	Archibald, W. S.
Dv	Arnold, H. G.
06	Atherton, H. F.
Gr	Berry, C. S.
06	Bloomfield, L.
07	Bruce, E. E.
Gr	Caldwell, M. A.
06	Cate, S. R.
Dv	Cobb, S.
07	Cogswell, W. C., Jr.
Gr	Coleman, N. F.
Dv	Freeman, L. E. W.
Dv	Gunderson, A. L. G.
Gr	Hale, R. L.
08	Hatch, R. C.
Dv	Hutcheon, R. J.
Gr	Jenckes, E. N.
~~Sp~~	~~Lambe, R.~~
Dv	Leavens, R. F.
08	McCormick, W. J.
Gr	Musgrove, W. J.
Dv	Ogawa, C.
08	O'Reilly, W. F.
06	Parker, DeW. H.
06	Perry, E. R.
Gr	Peterson, H.
07	Price, J. L.
Sc	Pumpelly, R. W.
07	Reed, W. W.
Gr	Savage, T. F.
06	Seipt H. A.
06	Shurtleff, H. R.
Sp	Strother, S. F.
Gr	Tait, W. D.
07	Thompson, R. W.
Gr	Tupper, G. W.
06	Turley, L. A.
Dv	Wauchope, W. C.
06	Wheeler, F. C.
06	Wiley, F. T.
Gr	Wolfman, N.

Theses

Tait:

Turley:

Kallen:

Dvn Ogawa, Mill

Wiley: Spencer's & Fiske's religion

Dᵛ Wauchope Janets final cause

Wolfman: Spencers Sociology

Dv. Gundersen

Brundage: Fichte

Dv. Leavens,

Wheeler: (Plato Lutoslaw)

'07. O'Reilly: Lotze

Ogawa: Mill

Dᵛ Cobb: Marcus Aurelius & Santayana

'07. Thompson R. N.

D. Freeman L.E M. Pessimism

Dv. Pyle?

Archibald (Freewill)

D. Hutcheon—Santayana's book

D Gundersen Evolution & Immortality

354

(Sept 30. 1905)
1st. meeting.

> Ask how many know Berkeley & Kant.
> Explain dual nature of course.
> State my program.
>> to unite empiricism with spiritualism.
>
> *Radical* empiricism
> Pluralism.   Contrast empir¹ & rationalism
> Teleology   Start from facts
> Connexion   work up to principles or vice versa

(Oct 3. 1905)

Metaphysic seeks the last deepest truth about things

Science of the possible as such (Wolff.)

Science of the *Ens reale* (as distinct from *ens morale* or *ideale*) in its
   essence, relations & laws (Read Stöckl, II, p. 1.)

Science of the first principles of human knowledge (Baumgarten)

"Inventory of what pure reason gives us, systematically arranged"
   (Kant)—a priori truth

"Systematic interpretation of experience" (Pringle Pattison in Baldwins Dict).

Science of the most universal principles of reality, whether experienced or beyond experience, in their connexion with each other,
   and with our powers of thought.

In any case, s'thing quintessential in the way of knowledge—irre-
   versible, absolute and coherent.

"Completely unified knowledge."

"Knowledge of the *One*."

1) Positivistic disdain:
   Reply: only unsolved prob⁵ remain. Ward: Mind XV, 1890

2) "Unpractical"
   Reply: gives religion to live by
            Harris's motto.

3) Anti scientific spirit:
   Sound objection.

Metaphysicians as a priori dogmatists closed systems

Science stands for indefinite increase.

Philosophers say "take or leave my whole system" (Kant)

A merit to preserve open door,
      positivistic spirit

4) opposed to life.[3]

    last year's student.

    Morrison Swift. p 7

Shallow optimism.

    Leibnitz 114, 147

Howison "exquisite but pathetic"

"Smugness"

True philosophy must redeem itself from this reproach.

(Oct. 5th 1905)

Science of problems & hypotheses[4]

How comes there to be a world?

What is the most real reality? higher or lower?

Is oneness or diversity most fundamental

What connects things? ground of oneness?

Is everything predestined

Infinite or finite?

God?

Mind & body?

Interaction? Change

Knowledge?

Cause of all things?

Outcome " " " ?

Meaning " " " ?

Substance " " " ?

How should we act?

What is our fate?

Are we free?

How do we know?

Kant { What can I know? What may I hope?
       { What should I do?

Universals & particulars?

Truth vs. opinion.

Contrasted types of answer to all these questions

    One vs many   continuity vs. discontinuity

---

[3] On the facing blank page WJ wrote: 'Used by most people *abstractly, [*intrl.*] merely as a corrective, ['an['d' *del.*]' *del.*] a aesthetic adjunct to the ignoble mess of experience. Cf. *infra.* Nov 16th'.

[4] On the facing blank page WJ wrote: 'Recommend | Taylor's Elements | Fullertons System | Marvin's Introduction | Paulsen's *Introduction [*indicated by ditto marks in the* MS]'.

Spiritual vs material
Universal vs. particular
Reason vs. Experience
Freedom vs Necessity
Renouvier's list
    Things facts vs ideas
    Infinite vs. finite
    Evolution   creation
    Necessity   liberty
    Evidence   faith
One may sum up
    Nobility s̄. reality
    Continuity s̄. clearness
    Abstractness
        vs.
    Concreteness & lowness
       clearness.
Terms of discussion so wide and abstract as to be full of ambiguity
   and misunderstanding.
Principle[5] of method: pragmatism.
Locke, Berkeley, Hume
Mill on Substance
Squirrel anecdote.

(Oct 9)
Case of completed world.

Schiller's use of word Humanism.
What do you mean by "truth."
Wider Philosophy of Prag.
Involves (according to Papini)
     1) nominalism (appeal to particulars)
     2) utilitarianism
     3) positivism (avoidance of useless inquiries.)
     4) Kantism (practical reason)
     5) voluntarism (cooperation of will c̄. intellect.)
     6) fideism (pietism)
Later we will consider humanism
My first application of pragmatic method is to knowledge

[5] On the facing blank page WJ wrote: 'Personal Idealism (Sturt) | Humanism:
(Schiller) | Sturt: The Logic of Prag. Arist. Soc. Proc. 1902–1903'.

But postpone!

Roughly class philosophies into

     1) Common Sense (scholasticism)

     2) Empiricisms

     3) Transcendentalisms

     3. goes from whole to part—is apt to be monistic but pantheist.[6]

     2. from part to whole, materialist pluralist.

     1. pluralist & theist.[7]

Two ways of working *phenomenalism*

     1. Rationalistically (Absolute)[8]

     2. Empirically.

(Oct. 12)

Define these two words:—

     1. Whole[9] to parts

     2. Parts to whole.

For Rationalism, things co-determine each other like notes in a concert, bits of glass in a mosaic.

That is the type-phenomenon, that or words in sentence.

     (Explain priority of whole here)

     Lotze's M.

Explain need of type-phenomenon.

     Theism: artificer

     Evolutionism:[10] growth of plant.

        (Pearson)

     Peirce, grab-bag (sampling)

     Philosophers paint pictures

Empiricism uses "collection."

(Oct. 14)

Where are we?

we have abolisht transphenomenal principles.

We[11] have substituted intra-experiential connexions for magical powers.

---

6 WJ wrote 'pantheist' above undeleted 'spiritualist'.

7 WJ wrote 'theist.' above undeleted 'spiritualist.'

8 On the facing blank page WJ wrote: 'Knox on "uniformities of Exp.["] (Mind)'.

9 In the right margin WJ wrote ' "Substance" turns into "subject" '.

10 On the facing blank page WJ wrote: 'Aristotle: biology | W.J. Sociology'.

11 On the facing page WJ wrote: 'Mosaic—hanging together, not planted. | philosophy of *co*, not *in*, or *by*,'.

These connexions are *feelable*.

The problem is to define what kinds of feeling *belonging* can mean.

Logical,[12] aesthetic, dynamic . . . . roughly!

In any case, interest and importance revert to the real world

"Aus diese Erde quellen meine freuden etc."

The *more* becomes its *prolongation*.

Piety towards life in the concrete.

May well be pitted against the school philosophy

Homeliness vs. majesty.

Santayana's book, I. 96–7   dont read it

Remember, we got here by pragmatic method.

Now two ways of conceiving:—

    1) Monistic[13]—through & through.

    2) Pluralistic—. next to next. concatenation.

Transcendental idealism's hypothesis.

The absolute Mind.

(Oct 17)

All-knower—noetic unity.

Argument based on "epistemological chasm."

Berkeley's phenomenalism made knowledge impossible.

A plurality of solipsisms.

Common[14] objects strictly impossible.

Common sense ignores this: proceeds to act *as if* secondary qualities
    were extra mental, and as if objects were common and is not dis-
    appointed.

The epistemological chasm does not exist!

Knowing is a perfectly definite relation.

Give[15] my theory.

(Oct 19)   There is no leaping *over* the intermediaries of experience

But orderly progress *through* them.

They unite, they do not separate.

---

12 On the facing page, with an arrow pointing to this sentence, WJ wrote: 'Cognitive
['C' *ov.* 'K'] not included'.

13 On the facing blank page WJ wrote: 'plenary *co-implication [*ab. del.* 'commix-
ture ['of' *del.*]'] in *absolutely [*intrl.*] all respects of everything with everything else.'

14 On the facing blank page WJ wrote: 'D. S Miller. Truth & Error, Phil. Rev. II,
408 | *D. S Miller [*indicated by ditto marks in the* MS] Function & Content, Psych.
Rev. II, 535'.

15 On the facing blank page WJ wrote: 'What do you mean by *pointing*? | What do
you mean by self-transcendency. | One part of experience knows another part.'

No immediate presence of the termini to each other.

No "pointing" other than what the chain of context creates.

Thoroughly phenomenal relation.

Nothing peculiar in it; only a sum of the usual nextnesses.

Which ultimately enable you to make practical connexions with the object.

Knowledge is only a way of getting into practical connexion with your object.

Importance of context, of neighborhood.

Where *no* context (telepathy) what would knowing signify? There would simply be two facts, like 2 eggs.

We[16] tend to call that knowledge, because we always invoke possibility of context. We extrapolate.

Concepts mean perceptual termini.

On the common sense level, sensations are *absolute* termini.

(Oct 21)   Remaining on that level, let us discuss presentative knowledge.

Berkeley's answer.

His[17] reply to the question: what becomes of the idea-things in our absence? pluralistic

Common sense's answer:

It interpolates them *tels quels*.

So we "know" things that never *can* terminate our experiences

Most of the time our knowledge only takes a *start* towards the terminus, then stops.

When perceiving, we act *on* object immediately

When conceiving, we act *about* it.

And if right, things fall out as if the percept had been there.

All that chapter is plain enough.

---

16 On the facing blank page WJ wrote: 'If telepathy superabounded, or if *the sense- [ab. del. 'our'] termini of individuals were proved to be different, either by equals of equals *not* equal, or by requiring diff! practical adjustments, what would "knowledge" consist in? In the same sort of thing; only the individual would be the measure of his own truth, and there would be no common *stock* of knowledge. | As the world is formed common sense can treat its termini as *absolute*, for the difference between them as diff! individuals have them leads to no diff! conduct (*I* can easily get *your* view of the table, and *you* operate through *your* view on *my* table) and their kinds keep stably harmonious—sensations equal to a third are equal *inter se*'.

17 On the facing blank page WJ wrote: 'Were there no criticism of the senses the common sense belief that esse = percipi and that we all know the same objects would pass for absolutely true. | Common sense attains its harmony by simply *neglecting* certain facts, *of [intrl.] which pure scientific curiosity takes note.'

But what of common sense's notion that different minds know *the same*? (See Common Sense in the other red book)[18]

[Note for next year]

Best, after describing conceptual knowledge of percepts, to begin perceptual knowledge with the common sense treatment of percepts as absolute objects.

Then show that even common sense must distinguish betw. the individual percept and the absolute object.

It takes it vaguely.

But science comes and defines it more closely.

Call it the "thing in itself," as Strong & Heymans do

Then the scheme re-enters that of Conceptual knowledge, our original percepts not being things in themselves, but our views of them—i.e. representatives.

But the scheme is one scheme. We extrapolate from the original termini. The things in themselves are only remoter termini.

No room for much dispute about transcendency, admit it if one likes, only give the pragmatic equivalent.

Only the thing in itself can be the thing common to two minds—and it is common only as their ideal terminus.

Yet through that terminus, only as yet a *possible* perception, *action* runs. By every pragmatic test it really mediates between the minds. Both, if asked *where* the object is, point to one & the same place. Either, when acting on its own representation, makes the other mind's representation change. This requires either a pre establisht parallelism of representations or else a medium of transmission of influence from one to the other. This medium we all suppose to be the thing in itself.

(Oct 26)   Review:—We applied pragmatic method to conceptual knowing, and got the notion of *leading to a terminus*, and of one kind of experience knowing another representatively.

Turning to that other, we found that common sense took it as both in the mind and out of it. "Thing" in space & percept are *identical*.

This notion breaks into something less simple when we analyse the

---

18 The reference is to #4514, a red-bound notebook. In the panel pasted on the reversed back cover, WJ wrote 'Emerson | [short rule] | Common Sense | [short rule] | Miller-Bode'. "Common Sense" does not appear in the notebook; "Emerson" and "The Miller-Bode Objections" have been published in *Manuscript Essays and Notes*, WORKS.

facts more curiously. Our first percepts are not ultimate termini. The real terminus lies beyond them. *Something* lies beyond which is a centre whereby influence passes from my mind to yours.

We can't, with Mill, suppose *nothing*, nor is either Berkeley or Leibnitz satisfactory.

How about Strong & Heymans? Explain, & confess difficulty of explanation.

Conclude by explaining *pure experience* notion.

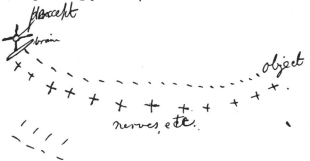

One[19] thing in itself produces an entirely diff^t remote one

That remote one is (on my theory) a phenomenal object, with energetic relations that cover psychic relations

(Oct 28)   With *possible confluence* in the end allowed. That's why Leibnitz is unsatisfactory.

The pure experience view is *pluralistic* and its universe works by *nextness*. Dwell on the continuity implied in nextness[20]

(Nov 5)

It[21] would seem as if this required change *throughout*, when *any* change

Mere abstract rhyming.

Instead of argument, reiteration that there *must* be absolute union, if any.

We find things connected in a vast number of diff^t ways.

Some of these ways may run all through.

Yet what does it *mean* to say that they are all expressions of *one way*?

---

[19] In the manuscript the diagram and the text, 'One . . . relations' are found on the facing page, but belong with the text dated by WJ 'Oct 26'.

[20] On the facing page after an earlier false start in ink, 'Concate', which he deleted in pencil, WJ wrote in pencil: 'NB. I think I must bring in very early a full enumeration & description of the different transitive relations and means of continuity in experience, including "activities" and other psychic causations.'

[21] On the facing blank page WJ wrote: 'Stern: Veränderungsauffassung.'

That is the point: Connexion within each partial system, and each
  p.s. connected in the unity of the total system.

What *are* the partial systems?

a) Dramatic—esthetic—expressive.
    Stories: imagine one story to whole universe! Cross section!

b) Purposes: one result.
    Trying to realize their unity you have to make it purely formal
      as richness, harmony etc., leaving the items independent, and
      the result secondary.

c) Logical:[22] all the *kinds* derivable from each other.

Read the concessions:

to a) Paulsen; 205–6, 190
    "We live forward, u'd backward."

to b) Paulsen 172
    Lotze, Mic. I, such passages as 440–1

(Nov 7)

to c) Lotze " I, 175
    Cognition, feeling, will, 181
    Polytheism, ibid II, 667

The systems we actually find realized are partial. One may easily
  break the chain by stepping sideways. Some involve one another
  some not. Implication s'ts reciprocal, s'ts not.

Noetic union seems to involve *nothing*.

Time, ditto.

Causal union seems not to involve generic unity.

telegrafic connexion involves land water or air

Sound involves air

Sight, ether

love, knowledge

But these cases are not reciprocal.

There can be knowledge s̄. love, copper without telegraf.

Mechanical influence s̄ chemical

Physical connexion s̄ noetic.

Noetic not reciprocal.

Deeper and shallower levels

---

22 On the facing page WJ wrote: '*Why must the purpose be realized thro[u]gh
such a *number* (neither more nor less) of beings that in so many cases seem simply *to
repeat* it [*penc. added*] | Mill on number of elements, laws, etc. | Stellar matter dis-
tributed according to no "law." '

Shallower involve deeper.

(External connexions denied   postpone!)

Any connexion makes a universe *of that grade*

Time, space, *and, with. co*

Network!

Question for Science, not a dogma

Gothic, not Classic.

Classic idea goes with notion of our intellectual relations being exact copies of archetypes.

Read Humanism & Truth.

Outline (Sauberer Umriss) drawing vs. full one[23]

(Nov 9) Absolute noetic unity.

Criticize it.

You see the pragmatic method and attitude. If the oneness is worth anything, it ought to show these concrete results:—What *does* it show?

If in addition to these it can awaken a sense of sublimity, all the better; but we can't live on sublimity alone.

These results ARE *the Oneness.* It doesn't exist before them as a previous principle, any more than "health" as a principle exists before all the functions whose good performance is what we mean *by* health.[24]

1.   Idealistic[25] argument requires absolute knowledge of every negation; of every ignorance in every man; of every whim & insanity. Superfoetation.

All the hairs in our head are numbered.

Omniscience of this silly sort so far from being sublime is idiotic, or dropsical.

You can't get over obj. 1 by saying that to think all these negations (A is not b, not c, not d etc) it suffices that the absolute should think A simply and not think that it is b, that it is c, etc., for on Royce's principle the fact of "A-not-b" can't be established by

---

[23] In the left margin WJ wrote 'Kant' and circled the name.

[24] In the left margin WJ wrote vertically: 'Cf. remarks on Emerson's *on Art [*ab. undel.* 'Monism' w. *lines drawn around the words*], fm [*ov.* 'in'] my earlier note book on him, in the other red note book [*published as* No. 66, "Emerson," *Manuscript Essays and Notes*, WORKS]. If a doctor undertook to admiring the general beneficence of medecine [*stet*] instead of working it for all it was worth on *his [*ov.* 'a'] single patient, etc.'

[25] In the left margin WJ wrote: 'Bloated & puffy with superfluous consciousness, & information'.

the absence of thought, but by thought positive & explicit. A negation or an absence cannot, as *facts*, function per se or exist per se. Their esse being cogitari, they must be reported in full. The whole point is that no fact can help being formulated for all that it is.

According to Absolutism, the absolute mind makes both the that and the what of us by thinking us. Its way of thinking us is all there is of us. There seems no room for any other way than its way of our being thought. Yet it thinks each of us *with* all the rest, we think ourselves *without* the rest, and the privation (as Lovejoy & others have said) becomes the essential feature in the thought.

2. It is barren[26]

Compatible with any details

Lion's den.

Materialistic? Chaotic

Pluralistic in age etc.

Metaphysical difficulty of understanding how I know *without* when Absolute knows with[27]

Royce's concessions amount to making it a collection—parts first.

Royce on free will C. of G. 292-4, 312-4

3. It is fatalistic anyhow.

Problem[28] of evil ⎫
—————— of freedom ⎬ come up.

(Nov 11)

4. Pessimism vs. optimism

Absolute has the victory as well as the defeat; but even for him it is both. For the defeated party it is nothing *but* defeat.

To redeem the Absolutist position from the sheerest abstractness, there is no half-way house short of complete surrender to empiricism, to making It only a name for the details in themselves. It in them, not they in It!

We see that shame etc of an overscrupulous psychasthenic are absurd. So may the Absolute see all our stings of conscience. He will then know of our shames & compunctions: but will he feel them

26 In the left margin WJ wrote vertically: 'It is as if, by the fact of being written in a novel, the characters should each have a life of his own, additional to their life for the author or the reader.'

27 In the left margin WJ wrote: ' "One" knows not all, my griefs at least are mine, by me their measure & to me their lesson" | Blood.'

28 WJ drew an arrow from 'Problem' to his comment on the facing page: '= Prob. of fall—disruption in the absolute. | Lotze's criticism of Leibnitz's God.'

as we do?—for we *don't* feel them as absurd, and that is just the difference.

Absolute usually held optimistically

Royce's argument: Read blank book 1903–4, p. 20–1 [*ed.*, 283.23–36]
        Read religious Asp. 443–5

Leaves particular content of satisfaction indeterminate

Victory of absolute's will

But whose *defeat?*

Conclude that Noetic Unity raises more difficulties than it solves.

It is only an *hypothesis,* for us, and useless both morally & intellectually.

Express firmly the counter-hypothesis.

Many[29] knowers

Private experiences.

Union progressing.

As ignorance disappears *sympathy* spreads.

No one purpose.

(Nov. 13)

Reign of possibility.

Absolutism excludes this category. Note bk. 1903–4. p 42 [*ed.*, 293.18–25].

Postpone farther inquiry into poss—ʸ—

What remains? Religious faith.

Indulge it, optimistically!

(Take Chicago note-book—V [*Pragmatism*, WORKS, pp. 294–295])

(Nov 16)   Where are we?

Neither as a necessity of tho't nor as a desirable hypothesis should the Absolute tempt us.

Our pragmatic theory of knowledge cut us loose from Royce's epistemological argument.

Our pragmatic discussion of unity inclined us to treat the oneness not as a principle, but as a collective name for various experienced connexions.

These could only be talked of in plural terms. Even Monists so talk of them.

Discussing noetic unity we found it full of difficulties.

---

[29] On the facing page WJ wrote: 'Royce reviewed by | R. B. Perry, Monist, XII, 446 | Montague, Phil. Rev. XI, 43 | Lovejoy: American J. of Theol. VI, 399 | Schiller on Absolute: Mind Oct. 1905'.

1. Useless information.
2. Sterility—compatible with any facts.
3 Fatalistic. Problem of evil.
4. Its ambiguity morally.

If interpreted religiously (not dialectically) and believed in as warrant for security, it commits us to one type of religion which may not be the best.

Remember[30] that the slightest break destroys it. A general proposition is contradicted by a single instance.

It must be held abstractly (with no attempt to use it intellectually) or else must make complete surrender to the empiricist position. Most men do hold it abstractly, as an aesthetic adjunct to their world, a reason for vague admiration. The pluralist who feels loyal to the old mother that bore us any way does n't need this help.

No doubt that empiricism is the moralistic doctrine.

Let us work now positively as our hypothesis, and trace its most congenial consequences.

It redeems us from abstraction, from carrying on our book keeping in two accounts, like Sunday Christianity.

It[31] restores to philosophy the temper of science and of practical life, brings the ideal *into things.*

It allows order to be increasing—therefore is a philosophy of *progress.*

It makes *us* factors of the order.

(Nov. 18) It[32] frankly interprets the universe after a *social* analogy.

It[33] admits different systems of causation relatively independent,—
Chance, therefore, in so far forth.

Take evolution au grand serieux.

Recent speculations about elements.

Physics now highly speculative.

We may be sure of farther developments in this line.

---

[30] On the facing blank page WJ wrote: 'Hindoo's letter with his *330,000,000 [2'3' *ov.* 'o'] gods—one need not go so far! | *Read [*penc. added*] Hoffding's critical monism: J. of P. II, 85 | *Universe is *wild* [*penc. added*]'.

[31] On the facing page WJ wrote: 'Raises *definite* problems.'

[32] On the facing page, below a line drawn across the page, WJ wrote: 'Set it up on its hind legs, let it scratch for itself!'

[33] On the facing page WJ wrote: 'Biological, social. Meteorological, matrimonial | Agricultural—meteorological'.

An abstract hurrahing for chance seems to the naturalist silly.

He knows how formidably oppressive is law, & that no efforts of ours can exhaust it.

But equally silly is abstract dogmatism about uniformity.

Some of each—the "ever not quite" baffles us as much as the absoluteness.

So far I have been *atheistic*.

But[34] if evolution—Gods may be one of the results.

[*upper half of notebook page cut off*]

(Dec 12)[35]

Two types of a⟨rg⟩

1 Rationalist

  a) "ontological"

  b) "less can't *explain* greater," therefore there must be a greatest.

2 Empiricist

  a) *objective*. "Design."*

  b) Subjective: "Personal experience"

Criticize 2a. Any state of things may be designed. Question of "what is character of world?"

How far is its character *congenial*?

Broadly[36] any feeling that world is friendly is a religion. But men differ as to the sort of friendliness they are satisfied with. friendly to heroism?—or to weakness?

Character[37] of world defined by diff^t emphases.

Santayana's book as example.

Antipathies play a part just as in political life "goo goo" "slumming"

Personal religious experience discovers friendliness in the depths.

---

* Any kind of world *after the fact* may have been designed—by that kind of designer namely. It is just like the lion's den Absolute. The really important thing is the pragmatic thing, what *is* the kind of world before us? If its *character* turns out empirically "divine," it makes no difference whether it have a designer or not. We can lead an adequate life in its presence. Cf. Perry's A to P. Chap. IIII

34 On the facing blank page WJ wrote: 'Grote's Aristotle, I, 295 | 1903–4 note book p. 50 [*ed.,* 298.19–30]'.

35 On the facing page, within lines drawn across the page, WJ wrote: 'Do we live in presence of a world that is divine in Character? If we do, the question of its having a 'designer' is a merely formal one. The essential practical thing is the Character. That lets us be religious. Obviously its empirical character is the stumbling block, *to remove [*insrtd. for del.* ⌄or'] which all the ['sp' *del.*] theologies are bro't in.'

36 In the left margin WJ wrote: 'Question of *life* first, *belief* second.'

37 On the facing blank page WJ wrote: 'Plenty of love, plenty of justice (God's assizes) Also plenty of their opposites.'

Read Sartor Resartus p. 175.

(Dec. 14)

There are forces that annul our inhibitions & put us on our feet.

We have a reserve of vital resource.

Ab- or praeter-normal states of mind.

Mysticism. Character *most* congenial.

To[38] confide in that is a religion.

Are our various reserves confluent?—that is the God-question.

Naturalism allows no mind above the human

Yet there may be such. Dogs.

On[39] the other hand "the Divine" may be impersonal. That also a religion.

Emerson's Oversoul, 252

    "The Soul" "the Intellect"

(Dec. 16) I left matters too open. Experimental religion may claim more than Emerson does.

Superhuman consciousness.

Super*canine* consciousness—analogy!

Fechner's views.

All may have evolved

The *important* point is "are they here *now*?"

Pluralism possible, with a choice for each man of which part of the divine is *his* God.

Those who live in this communion will continue to.

Do you then say "no truth!"

Nay!—but that every experience has its "say," only those that are organizable with others surviving to the end.

This[40] is only the pluralistic philosophy in another guise.

For[41] myself, not getting beyond the Emersonian stage, I should be happy to be at the Fechnerian.

38 On the facing page WJ wrote: 'Hoffding's argt for the perpetuity of religion.'

39 Below a line separating it from the comment in fn. 38 and with a line drawn to connect it to 'On' in the text, WJ wrote the comment: 'Just as E. says ["]we eat, drink, & wear perjury & fraud," so we eat drink an[d] wear truth, beauty, justice. It is life in us finding an answering life. "Thus is the Universe alive!" [*short line*] Fechner's view. General question of relations'.

40 On the facing page WJ wrote: 'The world has many characters. | Don't *select one*; but *reconcile all!*'

41 In the top half of the facing page WJ wrote vertically: 'Something preposterous in the naturalistic *methoden lehre*, wh. forbids us to *determine the nature of the Universe by any sort of experience [*insrtd. for del.* 'use any data'] save sense-observation *& [*ov.* 'm' *or* 'or'] mathematical reasoning, they being so small a part of *experience,

I would accept the assurances of others, were parts of them not inconsistent with what I believe, e.g.

1 Fact:—Specifications of visions, at variance with facts elsewhere known
2 Logic:—Compounding of selves.
3 metaphysics.—"Souls" vs. pure experience.

In any case religion is indestructible because private life is indestructible

"Monument to egotism"

Personal life the only concrete

Whole is greater than part. Intellectual life a part.

Pure naturalism an abstraction.

An *ascetic* abstraction, when held up as a deity to sacrifice to.

Once more it is a *character* in the world—its impersonality—taken to be an essence.

Remaining points.

Dialectic difficulties.

Royce on absolute sameness

Bradley on additive relations

Refer to my reprint: Thing & its relations.

(Dec 19)   *Question of Truth.*

Pragmatic method asserts that what a concept *means* is its consequences

Humanism says that when these are satisfactory, the concept is *true*.

Discuss this:

The popular view: *copying*, derived from relation of concepts to sensations. Abstract relations copy absolute mind.

Only possible in infancy of Science.

Admit it of things like memorial hall, does the percept itself copy?

Is it true? No, it simply *is*. Substantive term.

[*ab. del.* 'the life of the mind,'] which is ['a life' *del.*] of good as well as of *physical [*intrl.*] truth, and which refuses to believe that *to [*intrl.*] the objective constitution of things the *categories ['ies' *ov.* 'y'] of good, of importance, meaning, higher & lower, cause, activity, achievement, ['etc [*intrl.*] are' *del.*] the concrete living categories in short, are so much pure irrelevance. *In [*insrtd. for del.* 'The' *insrtd. for del.* 'In' *ab. del.* 'Wh'] feeling that certain things are fit to be true, ought to be true, must be true, shall be true, we obey a logic as natural as that of identity'. Earlier, he had written horizontally on the bottom half: 'Naturalism abolishes causation | Activity experience gives real causation. | Tychism is called *irrational*. What would be a rational ground for being. | Experience of decision—fact in the making. Not without cause. too much cause'.

Similarly of relations. Unlikeness *is*, distance *is*.

Truth consists in saying something about these terms & relations, what about *that*? *what* is like that?

Humanism says we must say what is *satisfactory*. What *works*?

Anti humanists[42] say we must say *truth*; because most of our beliefs have no relation to work (Cain; higher mathematics, π ad libitum) and when they do work, it is because they are *true*. $(2 + 2 = \quad)$

Taylor[43] then defines truth as what has a *claim* to be acknowledged.

But what does the claim *consist* in? Are there no reasons for it? and have the psychological reasons why we *accept* it for true nothing to do with the reasons why it *is* true?

Hoernle, Mind Oct 05, vol 15 NS, p. 448 calls the satisfactoriness and the truth two complementary aspects of the same thing. Neither is "cause." When we say a theory "works" we mean it explains systematizes, harmonizes. When we say "true" we mean the same thing.

Do[44] we throw away standard? Believe what we "damned please"? Taylor says so

Absolutist standard. Eternal, fixed. No growth.

I think Lotze's remark luminous. Hoffding.

Erhohung des vorgef. Daseins.

There are facts independent. They coerce us.

But *what* are they? Sensations & relations, of time & space, and of comparison. These the tent-stakes.

The immediate won't stay
    we must expect . . . . . .

This leads to universals.

These depend on interests

42 In the left margin WJ wrote: 'Satisfactoriness accidental & irrelevant'.

43 In the left margin WJ wrote horizontally 'Phil rev. | July, 05' and then vertically '['If' *del.*] Taylor's defⁿ is set up to kill humanism, so he must mean that Truth can give no reasons for her claim and we must n't ask them. It is a Machtspruch. Humanism starts by admitting the claim and gives pragmatic reasons for it; just as in the case of Oneness.'

44 In the left margin WJ wrote vertically: 'Two spheres of truth: 1. the narrower, of perceptions, constant, coercive. [this is the sphere that Taylor alone considers in his arguments with humanism (Cf. Mind, XV, 81)] and 2. the wider, our buildings out of 1., into constructions, principles and generalizations of various sorts. Here the true is the *satisfactory on the whole & in the long run, including in satisfactoriness, of course, *consistency* with the perceptions. Taylor would seem to interpret consistency as meaning unequivocal logical implication. [*written in the right margin and connected to text in the left margin with a guideline*]'.

Hence linear progressions.

But the tent-stakes must be acknowledged.

Parts of experience must respect one another. Past & future tenses
involved.

> Pluralistic, socialistic view.

Copying not required.

> Truth is an immediate aspect. a good in itself.
> One kind of *good*.

A way of getting into useful relations with reality.

Suppose you are to know me. Should I think of *copying*?

I am M's enemy. Need you copy how I feel? No. Only don't invite
us to dinner together etc.

Absurd is the notion that a reality is there complete, "*claiming*" to
be copied or known in countless inferior editions.

[b]

Unforeseeable novelty from the point of view of any one system.

Novelty from *every* extant point of view.

Tychism, then. *Possibility*

Free will.

Our next topics therefore are

> possibility.
> Chance
> free-will.

Possibility: *What may either be or not be.* Opposed therefore to the
impossible & to the necessary.[45]

> Vulgarly supposed to be a twilight mode of existence *of the
> possible* thing

Whatever is not impossible

> that is the first half.

Whatever is not neccessary.

> what makes a thing necessary? the existence of conditions ade-
> quate to make its production certain [express relation of
> "necessary" to "certain"]
> that is the second half.

> Possibility in the fullest sense means then *real contingency*

If *all* the grounds of a thing are either actually given or certain

---

[45] In the left margin WJ wrote, circled, 'Common sense view'.

to come from what is actually given then the thing is now necessary. If there be a *single* ground neither given, certain, nor impossible then the thing is possible sensu stricto.

What makes a thing *impossible*?

Self-contradiction, or contradiction by some actual fact.

Leibnitzian def^{n}. *logical* as opposed to *real* impossibility.

This leads to *real possibility*.

Grounded in fact. possible chicken; possible statue, recovery of sick man, decay of commonwealth.

Aristotle's matter. form by itself was only a possible nature. 405.

When the last condition comes, the thing is neccessary.

Gap between impossibility & necessity filled in by conditions, making more or less *probability*.

Possibility[46] again applies to the conditions, so we have the question of its being an ultimate category.

This leads to question of *Chance*

Postpone a while.

(Nov 21)   Meanwhile *absolutism must deny* possibility except as a name for our ignorance. (Note book 1903–4 p. 42 [*ed.*, 293.18–25])

As conditions are realized, world *changes*

Possibility bound up with *Change*.

What is it known-as?

     S'thing existing which did not

       "   not existing which did.

Alternatives:

     Total: partial

     Discontinuous: continuous.

Phenomenally we can mistake discontinuous for continuous.[47]

Empiricist pluralism must prefer *discontinuous* change avoiding antinomy of infinite.

---

46 In the left margin WJ wrote vertically, '[*beginning of note torn off*] grounds — — *all* the grounds. The more grounds, the more *probable* is the thing.' On the facing page he wrote, 'On possibility compare blue copy book in big envelope marked "Possibility" [*Manuscript Essays and Notes*, Works].' Below a line he wrote, 'Of ['O' *ov.* 'o'] the thing treated as possible *are ['a' *ov.* 'A'] either the "hindrances" or the "grounds(")' [*tr. by guideline fr. bef.* 'Of'] that have not yet come, *necessarily co-implicated* with what has come and is here? If so, no possibility. If not, genuine possibility.'

47 In the left margin WJ wrote vertically, 'Give concrete examples of the discontinuity: Positive differences next each other, and nothing between. This (m)eans, in case of time, specious presents coming by drops; and in case of motion positions given discretely in specious presents just as they empirically are.'

World thus gets additive structure

"Graft"—idea. Novelty.

The *possible*[48] as irrepressible category.

coincides here with that of the *uncertain*. If the grounds are *no where*, chance means absolute novelty, possibility, or *fact*, (without reason). = Gift.

    Well! diff^t cycles in nature.

    (Examples) Rev. de Metaph. Nov 190⟨2⟩ vol 10

S'ts the events irruptive from the other cycle *fit* the first one. "Coincidences"

Aristotle's debtor.

Absolutely, not chance. Go back far enough you find one universe with grounds for all future things in it. Fate

Pauper meets man who has sworn to give 100 to the first poor man he meets.

Darwinism.

Both mechanical & teleological ways of explaining this.

Both *exclude* absolute chance.

28. Lectures at Stanford (1906)

Faith

Its natural logic is the sorites: fit to be, ought to be, may be, must be, shall be, is, etc. . . . Intellectualism says we must *resist* stren-

---

[48] On the facing page WJ wrote: 'Omit or adjourn question of Ego matter or permanent element in change. It suffices that *anything* should remain when something old has gone & new has come [*short line*] Mr. Brundige [*i.e.*, Brundage] asks ['if' *del.*] "what *makes* the new thing *come* in discrete change if ['no old' *del.*] nothing fills the intervals? Where does it come *from*?["] "Continuous" means ['po' *del.*] interpolation possible ad libitum. This is *its [*intrl.*] methodological & pragmatic *rôle [*intrl.*]. But it evidently plays *for most minds [*insrtd.*] a['s' *del.*] metaphysical rôle also. If namely the change be ['posited' *del.*] posited as resulting in alterations that are of no sensible amount, that you can't really call different from their predecessors, the miracle of addition is softened. And yet *since [*intrl.*] in the end *your full amount comes*; ['so' *del.*] not only have you *that ['at' *ov.* 'is'] miracle, but you have the dialectical one superadded, *of supposing that it comes from an infinite summation of zēroes. [*cont. at foot of facing recto*]'.

uously that logic. This is the best order in wh. to bring in its veto. It also throws "will" on the opposite side of belief; and turns the tables on poor Miller's polemic.

When intellectualism would be "scientific" it forgets one thing. It forgets that you can't possibly formulate "facts" without using your faculty of *emphasising*. The sensations indeed must be given you, and they are indeed given independently of your will in the matter. But you can *say* nothing *about* them, they mean, signify, stand for nothing till your mind has put a perspective into them by making some essential & emphatic and ignoring or subordinating others. This is not part of the given-ness; it is your own contribution. The sensations say or express entirely different truths according as your mind uses them. How impossible then is the command to take our interests out when we establish truth. It is n't as if the sensations had an independent perspective & meaning of their own which we interfere with by our meddling desires. There is no meaning whatsoever in them, humanistic or anti humanistic prior to their elaboration by our desires. So that the question is not as to desire or non-desire, but as to which is the more prophetic, fruitful, sort of desire, the one which cooperating with sensations leads to the most satisfactory results.

Lecture to Miss Martin's Class

Co-incidence with Phil 1.

Here, psychology alone.

Is there any specifically religious psychology.

It depends on what you mean by religion.

Müller: Sentiment of the Infinite.

    Criticize

Spencer: A religious creed is definable as an *a priori* theory of the Universe.

    Criticize.

Religion is not intellectual only. It is a function of the whole man.*

Vital function, almost; biological; men *live* by their religion.

---

* But there can be a religion constructed of knowledge feeling & will without anything peculiar in its elements. Evolutionists; single-taxer; civil service reformers. Is there aught more specific?

Leuba on the faith-state (Varieties, 505 [*The Varieties of Religious Experience*, WORKS, pp. 397–398])

"Religious sentiment."

 Criticize—no specific emotion.

It would be more true to say specific *perceptions,* which arouse emotion.

What do I mean by perceptions?

Mystical & ½ mystical states.

Series: déjà vu, deeper insights, open air, sense of presence; Cases like Bucke; (399 [WORKS, pp. 316–317]). Jefferies; Obermann (476 [WORKS, pp. 375–376]).

 Conversions:

Intoxicants: normal consciousness only one case.

Resultant notion: Myers's conception of Subliminal life. Partition moveable

 Criticize it.

Specifically religious region of it.

Some can't pray or feel a God.

Yet they have the germ—Amen!

Mind curists vs. Ashburners.

We use only a part of our resources.

Mystical *training*

Conversion by imitation.

No reproach. Everything in us is elicited by imitation.

In Evangelical experience (Luther) one does seem to have something specific.

Contrast solemnity of pagan moralists.

No hypocrisy: no irony about values.

Twice born—after nature's death!

One could n't have *deduced* this psychologically.

Here then we seem to have a specific content.

A new range of life opens—resources that we had no reason to suspect.

Experimental contact with the wider world.

People who live either originally or by example in this world are working out our religions.

As psychologists we have to say that the classic psychology covers only a small part of the ground.

29. Talk with Cohen about Kant (1906)

(May 27. 1906.)— Talk with *Cohen* about Kant. He reduces Kant's apriorism to a matter of "method"—the whole content of experience, including apparently Kant's own structural categories, is inessential & may be adventitious. But there is a residual structure in the method which we must eternally and perforce apply, and this (if I understood C. rightly) consists in the logical minimum, the 3 laws of tho't, identity, contradiction & excluded middle. Who talks at all, even to deny these, or affirm their empirical origin, must use them. (He does n't transcend them, they transcend *him*)—He therefore contradicts himself if he denies their finality.

The pragmatic value, according to C., of this is that it cuts off Protagoreanism and standardless empiricism.[1] It gives a πον στω. This is an important pragmatistic consequence, if the ruling out of Protagoreanism be itself pragmatically important.

But wherein would consist its importance, if the *inconcussum* were reduced to the 3 logical principles, and all "content," even relational content, were handed over to "experience" in the empiricist's sense? The empiricist would have to admit that we can talk of the same and of not the same, and that we must n't confuse them when we do talk. A rather barren confession to extort from him, and I doubt whether any Protagorean ever cared to contradict it. Does n't the whole value of having fixed and final principles of truth depend on the value of the content of truth guaranteed by them? Is finality *per se* of any consequence? Surely not! It is the finality of *good things* that we are after. Bad things may be as unguaranteed and ephemeral as possible, and all the better. If the principles have no preference for one content over another and apply equally to all possible universes that can be talked about, their eternal, apodictic, regulative, a priori, necessary character, or whatever you please to call it, is trivial in the extreme—not worth

[1] On the facing blank page WJ wrote, 'Cf. Heim: Psychologismus etc., p. 17'.

contending for. It always has been the marriage of eternal principles with certain sorts of fact-content that the rationalistic philosophies affirmed. Give up the marriage, and what remains is an insignificant formalism.

[I may not have apprehended Cohen exactly—but this is the impression that remains.]

30. Syllabus in Philosophy D: General Problems of Philosophy (1906–1907)

I. General Characterization, and Defense

Objection 1. Unlike Science, Philosophy makes no progress.

Reply. A false opposition. The 'Sciences' are branches of the original tree of 'Philosophy.' As they grow minute and accurate, they drop off, and only the unsettled questions remain to be treated under the ancient name. In our own day we have seen general biology and psychology drop off from the parent trunk of philosophy, and grow into independent 'sciences.'

(On all this, see James Ward, Mind, Vol. XV. 1890.)

The evolution of philosophy shows this.

The earlier philosophers were encyclopædic sages, as in Greece those from Thales to Aristotle (say from 550 to 300 B.C.); in the middle ages Saint Thomas Aquinas, *b.* 1225; in modern times Descartes, *b.* 1596.

All gave accounts of *everything*, physical as well as moral.

After Locke's 'Essay' (1689) philosophy turned to questions about *knowledge*, and became "critical."

The older tradition is the better one.—Read Paulsen, pp. 19–44.

Philosophy and Science have no different methods. Both are only man thinking—observing, comparing, classifying, tracing analogies, making hypotheses.

Both have evolved from 'primitive thought' of the 'animistic' type or of the 'sympathetic magic' type, for which consult J. JASTROW, Fact and Fable, etc., chapter on Analogy; E. B. TYLOR, Primitive

Culture; F. B. JEVONS, Introd. to History of Religion, chap. IV; J. G. FRAZER, The Golden Bough, chap. I, § 2.

The more dramatic aspects and relations of things were the only ones noticed at first.

Only after 1600 did the more insipid mathematical aspects attract attention, and lead away from occult agencies to 'laws' describing Nature's phenomenal order.

These have proved so fruitful that a 'mechanical philosophy' has arisen, denying anything else to be 'scientific' and disparaging inquiry into anything spiritual.

Science is only 300 years old. Five lives could span its marvelously successful history. The less mechanical aspects of things await their day of equally successful treatment.

In one sense Science has made less progress than Philosophy; its most general conceptions would astonish neither a Greek nor Descartes. The composition of things from elements, universal determinism, the conservation of energy, etc., would sound familiar to them. But the whole idealistic, subjective, critical attitude in present day philosophy would sound strange, and require much explanation.

Objection 2. Philosophy is dogmatic, appeals to 'Reason' *a priori*; Science appeals to concrete experience.

Reply. The objection is historically valid. Too many philosophers have aimed at closed systems, established *a priori*, which had to be *taken or left*, as totals. The sciences, on the contrary, admit of indefinite correction and increase. At the present day it is getting difficult for dogmatic system-making minds, claiming finality, to have sway in philosophy. Philosophy *should* become as empirical as any science.

Objection 3. Philosophy is out of touch with real life, and treats of abstractions. Its inveterate optimism is artificial. The world is various, tangled, painful. Philosophers paint it as noble, dignified and simple, shutting their eyes to evil facts. [Leibnitz, Schopenhauer, M. Swift quoted.]

Reply. Objection historically valid, but true only because of the undeveloped state of Philosophy. No permanent reason why a philosopher should not keep in as close touch with life as any realistic novelist.

Conclusion. In the original sense, Philosophy *includes* all sciences,—logic, mathematics, physics, psychology, ethics, politics and metaphysics,—and aims at making of them what Spencer calls a system of "completely unified knowledge." In the modern sense, of something *contrasted* with the sciences, Philosophy means 'metaphysics.' The older sense is the more worthy sense; and as the metaphysical questions get more settled, and the sciences more coordinated, the term will revert to its original meaning.

II. Some Typical Problems and Metaphysics

In this course we shall take Philosophy in the sense of 'metaphysics.'

No exact definition possible. The term denotes various obscure, abstract, and universal questions which the sciences suggest but do not solve: questions *left over*; all very broad and deep, and relating to the whole of things, or to the last elements thereof. Instead of definition, take examples at random:

What is the meaning, character, significance of Nature, or of the whole of things?

Is there a common stuff of which all things are made?

How comes there to be a world at all? Might it as well not have been?

Which is the most real reality?

What binds things into one continuous world?

Is the unity, or the diversity of things more fundamental?

Have all things one origin?

Is everything predestined? or are some things (*e.g.*, our wills) free?

Is the world infinite or finite?

Are its parts continuous, or are there vacua?

What is God? or the Gods?

How are mind and body joined? Do they act on each other?

How does anything act on anything else?

How can one thing change into another?

Are time and space Entities? or what?

In knowledge, how does the object get into the mind? or the mind *at* the object?

We know by means of *universal notions*—are these also real? or are only particular *things* real?

What is meant by a 'thing'?

'Principles of reason'—are they inborn or derived?

Are truth and good matters of opinion? or have they objective validity? And if so, what does the phrase mean?

Such are types of metaphysical question—all very general and abstract. Kant sums them up in three heads: What can I know? What should I do? What may I hope?

One may say that metaphysics inquires into the cause, the substance, the meaning, and the outcome, of all things.

A rough definition is now possible: Metaphysics is the science of the most universal principles of reality (whether experienced or beyond experience), in their connection with one another and with our powers of thought.

['Principles' here may mean either *'things'* (such as 'atoms,' 'souls'), or *laws of connexion* (such as 'a thing can only act where it is'; or 'to operate, a thing must first *be*.')]

Metaphysical questions are real. They may be insoluble, but they exist. Things, *e.g.*, either *are* or *are not* of one stuff; either *have* or *have not* one origin, etc.

Someone must take charge of such problems, and of the solutions that are proposed. The latter must be classified and discussed. (For instance, how many hypotheses are possible as to the origin of the world? Spencer says only three: it must be either eternal, self-made, or by an outside power.)

Some hypotheses may be absurd on their face; others insusceptible of proof; others probable. A science of the hypotheses, as well as of the problems, is thus inevitable: in short, there must be metaphysicians.

Let us in this course be metaphysicians!

III. Two Types of Mind Fill the History of Opinion with Their Warfare

(*a*) The rationalistic, dogmatic, system-building type reasons from whole to parts, and aims at sweeping statements and finality.

(Examples: Older Greeks, ARISTOTLE, SCHOLASTICS, DESCARTES, SPINOZA, LEIBNITZ, KANT, HEGEL, SCHOPENHAUER.)

(*b*) The empiricist, critical, sceptical type reasons from parts to whole, aims at accuracy of detail, and is contented to be fragmentary. Men of 'hard facts.'

(Examples: Socrates, Protagoras, Locke, Berkeley, Hume, the Mills, and most contemporaries.)

Type *a* have usually set up optimistic theories, supplementing the experienced world by clean and pure ideal constructions.

Type *b* have kept more in touch with actual life. More objective, but less inspiring.

Our study will largely follow the clash of these types, for which see W. James, 'The Sentiment of Rationality,' in The Will to Believe, p. 63 [Works, p. 57].

Take some special problems as examples of metaphysical inquiry.

IV. The Problem of Being, or Ontological Problem

How comes there to be a world at all? Need there have been anything? (See Schopenhauer on the metaphysical craving of man: World as Will, Appendix XVII. English tr., vol. II, p. 359.)

The *what* as well as the *that* of Being is mysterious.

If it began in time, why at just that date?

If it be eternal, you have the paradox of a past infinity already having elapsed.

Dilemma of choosing either an absolute first, which baffles comprehension, or a completed infinite, which seems self-contradictory. A frequently recurring 'antinomy,' of which Kant, Hamilton, Spencer say much.

Kant's 'dialectic' solution: in Time are only phenomena; realities are out of Time.

Most philosophers have preferred to suppose something necessary & eternal, whether God or matter.

God's Being treated as eternally *necessary* by Saint Anselm: From His definition as *Ens perfectissimum*, it follows that we cannot think of Him as non-existent, for that would be a defect, and contradict the definition. Therefore, says Anselm, we must believe Him to exist. Compare similar proofs in Descartes: Meditation V; and Spinosa: Ethics, Book I, Prop. XI, and Scholium.

Kant is considered to have demolished this 'ontological' proof of God's existence, which even St. Thomas could not fully accept.

To prove Being to be necessary, we should have to show that 'Nothing' and 'Being' are not alternatives, but mutually involve each other. This is Hegel's pretension. The nature of Reality, he says, is always to include and negate its own negation. Heroic, but vain attempt! I pass over pseudo-mathematical attempts to deduce Being, such as Oken's who, finding 'polarity' to be a character of reality, writes the equation

$$+\, 1 - 1 = 0. \quad \left(\text{Compare} \frac{0}{0} = \frac{1-1}{1-1} = 1.\right.$$

Compare also KANT, R. & S. edition, pp. 148–152.)

We cannot rationally deduce Being or prove it 'necessary.' We cannot banish ontological mystery. Whether what IS be divine or undivine, theoretically we can only *find* it or *beg* it, while practically we must accept it as a *gift*. Thus is a bound set to *Rationalism*. Reality gets itself made, we know not how; our Reason cannot go behind the *fact*. This also is the lasting truth of *Empiricism*. Philosophy more and more tends to admit that her task is to ascertain the *character* of what is, no matter how it may have come to be. Our quest lies with the *what* of it, rather than with the *that*.

But a question of fact remains: Is the *quantity* of Being always the same? Most philosophers say 'yes,' neither God nor primordial matter, nor 'energy' being supposed to admit of increase or decrease. The foundations are eternally fixed in amount, and the waxing and waning of certain phenomenal parts of experience are superficial appearances, which leave the deeps untouched.

Nevertheless, *within experience*, phenomena come and go. There are novelties; there are losses. The world seems, on the concrete and proximate level at least, really to *grow*. So the question recurs about experience: how do our finite experiences come into being from moment to moment? By inertia? By perpetual creation? Do the new ones come at the *call* of the old ones? Why don't they all go out like a candle?

Who knows? The question of Being is the darkest in all Philosophy. All of us are beggars here. No one school, whether rationalist or empiricist, can speak disdainfully of another, or give itself airs.

V. The Problem of Universal Notions

We know things through 'concepts,' or general notions (verbs, nouns, adjectives, etc.). Are these as 'real' as percepts are? Or are they less so? [Read as a lesson, PAULSEN, pp. 378–389.]

[A 'percept' is an individual thing, present to the senses now and here.]

An immediate percept as yet unnamed, is a mere *that*. Our field of sense at any time comes as a continuum. Our attention carves 'things' out of it. In the sky we see 'constellations.' On the earth we distinguish 'beach' from 'sea,' and 'cliff' from beach, 'bushes' from cliff, and 'grass' from bushes. We break the flow of time into 'days' and 'nights,' 'summers' and 'winters.' We say *what* each part of the immediately given continuum is.

A '*what*' is a general head under which we class a '*that*.' We class less general under more general *whats* (*e.g.*, that is a man, a biped, an animal, a living-thing, a body, a substance, a being, an object of our thought).

All these *whats* are *concepts*. Traditionally, a concept is said to consist of the *essential character or characters* of a thing, by which our intellect knows it. A 'man' is a compound of weight, shape, color, temperature, strength, intelligence, etc., etc., these being concepts.

Thus we live mentally by *translating the perceptual or sensible order of our experience into a more intelligible order*. We conceive instead of experiencing, substituting generals for singulars, and names for things.

But note that the substitute is always *emptier* than the original. Every concrete thing or situation, every present piece of experience's flow, has a potential infinity of characters. In selecting any aspect of it as essential, we neglect the others. Our concept may be *more general* than the fact of perception, but it is *less full* (in the language of logic, its *extent* is wider, but its *intent* narrower). It is an '*abstraction*.'

Why then do we pursue such abstractions?

First, the world seems in point of fact *made* of general characters. Its particulars do have attributes in common. If you analyze, you will find the same character, quality or property cropping up in different things.

Secondly, our mind is partial. It cannot disperse itself over many things at once. It gets one percept, then another; and, in a given percept, attends first to one aspect and then to another of it. It takes the world piecemeal, in successive percepts; and it takes each percept piecemeal, in successive concepts. It analyzes. [See W. JAMES, Principles of Psychology, vol. II, pp. 332–7 [WORKS, pp. 959–963].]

Now, like animals, we *can* react on some situations by mere perception without conceptual analysis (instinctive reactions). But these are few and must be very familiar. To deal with a *new* situation, its immediacy must be analyzed, its fullness broken up. We must discern in it some general character that we know already, and react on *that*. It thus gets 'mediated' to us by our concept. We can then *reason* about it.

[Legend of Cuvier.] Habitually, as we meet things, we name and class them, and so dispose of them conceptually. If we cannot, if they are 'nondescripts,' we are at a loss. *This is why we seek to convert the perceptual into a conceptual order.*

We try to conceive each particular perceptual situation by the character essential to *our purpose* then and there. For its sake we neglect the other characters, which *then* would only confuse us. This abstract treatment proves so useful that we work with abstract concepts almost exclusively, content at all times to be blind and deaf to most of the characters of the reality that lies before us, well knowing that on another occasion we can make amends for our partiality.

Conceptualism and Nominalism

This state of facts has given rise to two opinions. Plato and his successors, struck by the singleness, steadfastness and fruitfulness of each concept, worship them as a diviner order of realities, with which our Reason can hold commerce, while our senses lie immersed in matter. They and their mutual relations exist eternally, and *ante rem*. To know them is true knowledge. Knowledge of individual things by the senses is inconstant, and is mere opinion. (*e.g.*, Cudworth.)

Nominalists, on the other hand, as Berkeley and James Mill, explain concepts by our need of economy in naming. Unable to provide a name for each individual thing, we sort things by resemblance into classes, they say, and just name the class. A concept thus has only a mental existence, *post rem*. It is a *flatus vocis*, a name that denotes any individual of a class indiscriminatingly. A tool, an instrument.

[Notice here clash of rationalist with empiricist temper.]

We need not enter into the subtleties of the dispute. Concepts and percepts are both 'real,' in the sense that we have practically to *take account of them*. But the relative hollowness of the concepts makes conceptual knowledge forever incomplete. No perceptual experience is exactly like another (read W. T. Marvin, Introduction to Philosophy, pp. 22–25). When we class an experience under some general head, we are always blind and unjust to some of its immediate concreteness.

The best example is the contrast of our inner life as known to ourselves in immediate feeling, and the same life as known to outsiders through conception. The abstractness and injustice are flagrant.

If 'things' were conscious, they would make the same complaint.

So we have the paradox that while only singulars really *are*, what are *known* are only universals (Aristotle).

The only part of reality *present* and *actually here*, the only part that immediately *acts* on us and that we *act* on, comes in the shape of sensible perception. Through this it is that we encounter the rest of reality. But we habitually meet this perception and handle it, both theoretically and practically, by the intermediation of concepts that necessarily ignore much of its particular content, but which are useful now because they remind us of what proved useful on former occasions of similar perception. What infinite power does this conceptual handling yield us! What hidden relations among our singulars does it disclose!

This cleanness, economy, and power of conceptual thought is what has led to its deification by intellectualist philosophers, from Plato and Aristotle downwards. Particulars and singulars are low, being contaminated with sensation, which is of the flesh. Generals and universals alone have dignity. Our Reason deals with these, showing its own nature to be divine.

But the hollowness of general concepts, on the other hand; the fact that the individual thing or situation always exceeds and overflows them; together with the fact that we handle the same situation (name it, class it) variously and by different concepts, according as our temporary purpose with it varies; these facts, I say, have led empiricist minds since Berkeley to make light of universal notions, to consider them as secondary human conveniences, and to treat sensible perception, which presents the concrete facts, as the fountainhead, not only of reality, but of truth. The abstractness of universals thus is made their crime.

Now *the truth is that each side favors its own pet abstraction.* If conception abstracts from Reality's fullness by cutting out one character, and ignoring the others that coexist with it in a particular present fact of sense, no less does pure perception abstract from Reality's fullness by cutting out that particular fact of sense from the rest of the world, and by ignoring the past, future and distant facts of sense with which it really is continuous.

An Absolute Knower who could know all things together in one indivisible act, would probably know the whole as we perceive a particular. He would have no such need of general concepts to connect present particulars with absent particulars as we have, for he would see all particulars at once. The limited character of our human perception, aware only of what one point in space and one moment in time reveals, is what drives us to use concepts to remedy its imperfection.

God's knowledge has been supposed to be of the perceptual type, only complete, his perfect intuition of singulars requiring no help from general notions (ST. THOMAS; recent idealists). But these are so ingrained in our own mental structure that we cannot easily imagine a consciousness to go on wholly without them.

Conclusion.—The practical outcome, for this course, is this: that, since metaphysical systems are but so many sweeping ways of conceiving the essential character of the world, they must all lie open to the reproach of abstraction. They gratify us intellectually, inspire us morally or help us practically. They are in short most useful, but they always err by defect, they *acquaint* us with very little of the actual world; and if they dogmatically claim finality and do not expressly provide for their own completion and correction, they are false, or at most true partially. (Science, by its method of hypothesis and verification, provides for its own perpetual correction.)

Examples of metaphysical abstraction.—Materialism calls 'Matter' and its laws, Spiritualism calls 'Mind,' the *essential* reality. But *what* matter? Concretely, and in point of fact, the kind of matter that produces mind. *What* mind? Concretely, the kind that is produced by matter. The *full* truth is Matter-producing-mind, or Mind-produced-by-matter, and it is a mere affair of emphasis which term you treat as the more essential. Either alone tells us very little.

Similarly, Theology calls God the *essence.* But the abstract term 'God' means little. We need to know what kind of a God. And to answer that, we have to bring in the world again. He is the kind of God that makes this kind of a world. This world defines the actual God and becomes His measure. The name 'God' thus needs farther qualification in order to be really instructive.

Monists call the unity of the world its essence; Pluralists, the diversity. But either term needs the other to redeem it from abstractness. The unity means the union of just *that* diversity; the diversity, the inner composition of just that kind of a unity, etc. [On the abstractness of all philosophic formulas, etc., see W. JAMES: 'The Sentiment of Rationality,' in the Will to Believe and other essays, pp. 63–70 [WORKS, pp. 57–62].]

Comments on Paulsen

Important points in the lesson pp. 378–389 are these:

Pp. 379–80.—Rationalism's claim that our mind owns infallible and sufficient principles of knowledge was required in order to found closed systems. So natural an aspiration! 'Scepticism' of this claim arose early (PROTAGORAS, SOPHISTS generally, SEXTUS EMPIRICUS) but systematic Empiricism may be said to have begun with LOCKE—synonymous with 'critical' philosophy.

P. 380.—The two problems: (1) genesis of principles in mind; (2) how can mind-born principles apply to extra-mental realities?

380.—Plato's doctrine of 'ideas' or eternal natures, each one of them single and unchangeable, of which phenomenal things partake, has had great importance in philosophic history. The question is whether to place them *ante rem, post rem,* or *in rebus*.

381, near bottom.—Truth, for rationalism, always means *copying* an archetypal reality.

382.—DESCARTES' innate ideas, chief of which is that of the infinite God. This idea can neither be 'adventitious' nor 'factitious.' D.'s argument.

383.—God's veracity the guarantee for DESCARTES that clear and distinct ideas are true.

384.—SPINOSA says, "I will treat of human actions and affections as if it were a matter of lines, surfaces, or solids." (Ethics, Pt. III, preface.)

384.—*Empiricism.* PAULSEN himself is an empiricist.

385.—LOCKE first called mathematics a system of 'mental' truth.

Only by first *finding* triangles and circles to exist in point of fact in Nature can we apply our mathematical intuitions about such bodies to the world of realities. Previous philosophers had omitted the link of *fact to be observed* ere the mental conclusions could apply. They had dogmatized about Nature, supposing thoughts to carry things with them. LOCKE admits necessary truths *a priori*, but in the first instance they only express the relations which the mind finds among its *own ideas*. They are not true of things, unless things corresponding to those ideas happen to exist, and only our own senses can teach us whether they do or not.

385.—Empiricism not only insists that only sense-experience can teach what facts exist, but it insists also that facts exist only in individual form. *Generals* are mental abstractions.

387.—Before HUME, 'Cause' was defined as '*an activity proceeding from one being* whereby another being is altered.' HUME taught that we can nowhere detect the activity or 'power' *as such* in its passage, but only the alteration. Since his time the notion of 'laws of causation' (*i.e.*, habitual sequences of special fact, empirically ascertained) have tended to drive out from 'Science' the older notion of a 'principle of causality.'

389.—The trouble with HUME's *argument against miracles* is that if a miracle actually *did* happen, it would preclude him from admitting it.

Important Points in Paulsen on Materialism

Read pp. 44 to top of p. 48; and pp. 53 to top of 57.

P. 56.—Aristotle's philosophy and the 'peripatetic' scholasticism based upon it are only common sense expressed in very technical terms and made articulate.

Read §2, pp. 60 to 67.

P. 61, near top: "the real thesis of materialism."

Argument 1:—the supposed invariable connexion.

Common sense and scholasticism explain conscious life by a Soul, Power, or Being *behind* what we immediately experience.

61–2.—Science explains it by relating it to its *conditions*. These are *other experiences,* previous or simultaneous. It brings the explanation *inside* the tissue of our experiences. For materialism, the other experiences in question are brain-conditions. Consciousness is 'nerve-glow,' nerve-'phosphorescence,' etc.; or the 'inner aspect' of what through our outer senses appears to us as a brain-change.

Three subdivisions of the Argument:

(*a*) Parallel development of soul-life and nervous system in animal kingdom, p. 63.

(*b*) Cerebral pathology and injuries, p. 64.

(*c*) Parallelism in geological evolution, p. 65.

P. 66.—Materialism concludes against immortality.

To-day the names *Monism* and *Naturalism* are more popular than that of Materialism, which was a dogmatic rather than a critical system, and whose last great flowering period was in Germany from about 1860 to 1870.

Read §3, pp. 67–74.

P. 68.—Distinction between *judgments of facts* and *judgments of value*. All the perspective of the world and the varying degrees of interest of its content are due to the latter. Apart from an onlooking mind with its judgments of value, one thing in nature would have no more importance than another. [See W. H. MALLOCK: Is Life Worth Living, pp. 109–113.] To us the mental facts are the higher and more precious ones.

69–74.—Materialism, deriving these, as it does, wholly from physical facts, puts the higher at the mercy of the lower, and may engender apathy, cynicism, or pessimism.

But to argue against a doctrine merely from its bad moral effects, is a bad sort of procedure. Therefore, Is materialism *true*?—whatever be the consequences. [For the consequences, see W. JAMES: Journal of Philosophy, etc., N. Y. Dec. 8, 1904, vol. I, p. 677ff. [*Essays in Philosophy*, WORKS, "The Pragmatic Method"]]

Read §4, pp. 74–78.

P. 75.—For materialism, the physical world exists *absolutely*. For idealism it exists only *for consciousness*, or as a *phenomenon*. As an *object* in our own experience matter thus depends on our own perceiving minds; of what it is, apart from our minds, we know nothing. This line of argument, which he calls 'epistemological,' PAULSEN postpones for the present.

76.—*Agnostic objections* to materialism (DU BOIS REYMOND and TYNDALL): Even if matter does produce thought, we can never *ex-*

plain the process of production. Materialism is no *explanatory philosophy.*

79.—PAULSEN replies that Science never explains the *how* or *why* of any effect in Nature, only *that* it comes when certain conditions are fulfilled. *That* consciousness is dependent on brain states, is all that materialism asks us to admit.

80.—He begins his own criticism by showing how materialists waver between two different views:

(1) Thought is *correlated* with brain-action, and

(2) Thought is a *form, kind,* or property of brain-action.

This latter view is absurd, he says. Only the first view merits discussion.

83.—It subdivides into two theories: (*a*) Thought is an *effect,* and (*b*) Thought, although not an effect, is an invariable *concomitant,* of brain-action.

84.—In theory *b* ('*parallelism*') the brain-processes form a continuous and uninterrupted chain of physical causes and effects.

85.—Theory *a* ('*interaction*') allows of breaks in the physical chain, and imagines states of consciousness interpolated between the physical events, engendered by them and reacting on them.

We cannot experimentally decide between these theories.

86.—But physicists, P. says, will never be willing to admit mental links of causation thrusting themselves between the links of a chain of physical events. It is too incongruous. With them, therefore, PAULSEN postulates parallelism and rejects interaction.

Read §5, pp. 87–111.

87–90.—He expounds the view of radical '*automatism,*' as necessitated by the rejection of interaction. Our brain is a self-sufficing automatic machine for the performance of the most intelligent acts. Materialism ought to be satisfied with this.

90.—But of what then *are* our feelings and thoughts *effects*? As we have them, they are interrupted by sleep, by sensations that break in and interfere with our cogitations, by ideas that pop up, etc.,—in short, our trains of consciousness show *discontinuity.* Where do such discontinuous bits come from?

91.—P. answers by the hypothesis of *universal parallelism.* The discontinuous feelings and ideas whose origin seems not to be in *our* consciousness are effects of *other* consciousness, *not* 'ours,' connected with parts of our nervous system other than that cerebral cortex whose activities *our* consciousness accompanies. There are thus two series, each causally continuous in itself. To each term of the physical, there corresponds a term in the mental series; only *our* mental series is a broken and imperfect extract from the great continuous mental series that totally exists.

92.—Of the two series, the mental might well be the *more real* ('Idealism.'—Compare below, pp. 111).

From here onwards P. tries to make it seem likely that every physical fact without exception has its mental correlate (hypothesis of *panpsychism* or *hylozoism*—of all matter being animated). In the first place, if brains alone are animated, mind would seem to be a paltry and relatively unreal incident in an infinitely vaster world of purely brute events, and materialism, in the bad sense of subordinating the higher to the lower, would seem to triumph.

93.—But all philosophic thinkers have admitted, and we also must feel, that mind is something central and essential. After all, it is only through our consciousness that we know that there *is* any matter. Matter is only *known* in terms of mind—this is the idealistic position.

94–99.—P. argues for souls in *plants* on the principle of continuity:—where so much is similar, why not all? Great objection: Mind in animals is knit-up with *nervous system*; but plants have no nervous system. Reply: Lowest animals have none; in those which have one, it is an organ of adaptation to their *life of action* in response to environing objects distant as well as near. Plants lead a far *less active* life, responding only to immediate contacts; they need no nervous system, and their consciousness is probably more sensitive and diffused.

99–102.—May *inorganic matter* be conscious? Continuity again: whence comes the mind in any growing embryo, unless from the nutriment it absorbs? Whence its first appearance on our Earth, if it were not in some shape in *the elements*? We have *defined* life *out* of "matter" in our class-rooms, but all matter is full of life in the form of characteristic spontaneous activities.

102–105.—P. quotes authorities in his favor. The forces found in living things are all derived from inorganic nature. Why not mind also?

105.—What *is* a piece of matter, anyhow, apart from *our feeling* of it? What is it in *itself*? The question must be changed, to be intelligible, into "What is it *for* itself?" and would be answered if we know just how it felt—it would be that feeling.

106–111.—P. now defends the notion of a collective *world-soul*, leaning much on FECHNER's reasoning, which is purely by analogy. Materialism, thinks P., is vanquished, not by denying that everything has a physical side and a physical explanation, but by seeing that the physical side that things have is secondary and external. The mental side is the innermost and realest side, not only of ourselves but of all things. The bodily side which they present is their *phenomenon*, or *appearance to us*. This is the fundamental conception of *Idealism*.

Comments on Paulsen's Account of Materialism

As a general mental attitude, Materialism means the tendency to explain higher things by lower things, or to reduce them to lower things, to take the lowest and leanest view of everything, to say that things are "nothing but" . . . etc. In this sense, some philosophers, as well as other men, are born materialists.

From this vague practical tendency Materialism as a *doctrine* must be distinguished. It takes two forms (PAULSEN, p. 80):—

1. Thought *is* material. Spirit *is* breath, vapor, gas, "ghost." LUCRETIUS, *e.g.*, says that mind is composed of smooth, fine, round atoms. Easily refuted.

2. Thought is an *activity* of matter, a "movement," a "phosphorescence," an "energy," etc.

Both these doctrines make mind dependent on body, and consecrate physiological explanations of mental facts.

The same is true of *Spinosistic parallelism*, or *epiphenomenalism* (which on the whole PAULSEN seems to favor). Here the primordial Substance is neither mind nor matter, but something of which mind and matter are two inseparable *aspects*, like the concave and the convex aspects of a circle. But the inner aspect, according to PAULSEN, has no efficacy (*i.e.*, we *feel* what happens to us; but our bodies *bring it about*; and we, as minds, *can't alter it*) and to get at the productive *causes* of anything, philosophy must study its physical antecedents and concomitants exclusively; and these work "blindly," as if pushed *à tergo*, not drawn by a purpose. This makes the higher aspects dependent on the lower aspects of things, and is, in so far forth and in spite of Paulsen, materialistic in the vague practical sense first described.

Parallelists like PAULSEN, when reproached with this, reply that minds are indispensable, for, by their *judgments of value*, they decide what *is* higher and what *is* lower, and communicate *perspective* to the physical facts (compare p. 68).

This is the position of F. A. LANGE, in his important book, 'The History of Materialism,' which allows the realm of *ideals* to be mentally determined, but contends that the realm of *facts* obeys laws of matter exclusively, and can only be studied by using the materialistic method. The world is a material machine, with a mental *significance* only.

But, so long as minds are causally inert and can only judge, while all the world's *work* goes on by physical causation exclusively, minds not being able even to check, encourage, or steer the brains to which they run parallel, parallelism as a doctrine still lies open to the reproach of being materialistic in the practical sense of the term. It leaves the higher at the mercy of the lower. It says that *ideals* (which are mental facts) have *no power over matter*. Matter may *work out* our ideals, but it does not *obey* them. It works them out *blindly*.

If, as a matter of fact, material forces *always* made for higher ends (ideals), they would themselves be "higher." But they also bring about the horrors that the world is full of, and seem to be indifferent what they make for. Minds are champions of ideals; and to give minds *influence* as well as the power of judging puts into the world ideal *forces*, which the physical forces are not; and seems to make the world more rational than parallelism makes it;—even though parallelism thinks it irrational to imagine that mind-energy can influence brain-energy, because that would make a break in the closed physical chain (pp. 85–6).

The *theory of interaction* assumes that mind-energy can influence. It is the common-sense theory. But if mental states be supposed to influence brain-processes by interpolating themselves between them, interactionism becomes a theory not so much of the parallelism as of the *alternation* of the mental and the physical. Thus does PAULSEN take it, and the final reason he gives for rejecting it is that physicists will never allow of an interpolation of mental links between the parts of a physical chain of events. (See pp. 85–6.) In case of a voluntary action, interaction would mean that, when our brain-cortex had been excited by an experience, *it* couldn't directly excite our lips—to name the experience, for example; for, to do that it must first excite our thought, which in its turn must excite our speech-muscles; and the stream of causal energy, when it thus hopped up into the mental world, would momentarily be lost to the physical world and so would violate the principle of conservation of physical energy, which must be held sacred.

This is highly speculative reasoning. Needless to say that even if interaction required such momentary leakages of energy from out of the physical into the mental world, so that the existing amount of physical energy would fluctuate, we have no means of measuring whether the fluctuations actually occur or not. If mental action were a form of 'energy,' its 'mechanical equivalent' might well be exceedingly small. Our brain acts purely as a *detent* or *instrument of discharge*, causing this or that set of muscles to explode. The minutest force might suffice to this. Our mind at any moment, deciding "no" rather than "yes," might similarly act as a trigger to the various possible brain-actions themselves, and be a minuter force still, impossible for physicists to measure. [The total physical *results* meanwhile might be enormous, as when Caesar said "yes" to the idea of "Crossing the Rubicon," or Luther to that of disowning papal authority.] Physicists have no right to dogmatize here.

What our sense of concrete life demands is that the world should not be run by its 'blind' aspect, 'Matter,' exclusively, while 'Mind' stands by and *judges*, but is impotent to *execute* its judgments. In part, life seems to be run blindly; in part to be steered by mental foresight, preference and will. The biological evolution of consciousness suggests that, like everything else, it too, has a useful function, and that that function is to reinforce those brain-processes whose results it foresees and judges to be good. (See W. JAMES: Principles of Psychology: 'The Automaton-theory,' vol. I, p. 140 [WORKS, p. 143].) This would make 'interaction' plausible, and would be less materialistic (in the more general sense) than PAULSEN's view.

A still less materialistic view would be the kind of panpsychism recently urged with great skill by C. A. STRONG (Why the Mind has a Body, N. Y. 1903) and G. HEYMANS (Einleitung in die Metaphysik, 1904). These authors assume that the real energy *everywhere* is mental, that what we call causation of one physical event by another, is only the phenomenal appearance to us of a chain of events whose inner reality "for themselves" is something conscious. The whole physical world would thus unroll itself by mental forces exclusively, and not be run 'blindly.' In a recent review of the work of HEYMANS, PAULSEN favors this theory. Not only (as on pp. 110–111 of our text-book) is the mental aspect called the more *real* aspect of things, but it is the more *active* aspect also. In our own mental experience of activity we apprehend the kind of activity that *works* everywhere, he grants even underneath the physical appearances.

Thus there are two main types of theory:

1. Parallelism or panpsychism, which calls *all* matter animated.

2. Interactionism, which allows us to say that only nerve-centres may be animated.

No. 1 splits into two sub-types:

1 *a*. Epiphenomenalism, which says that the mental side of things, though omnipresent, is inert, impotent, a 'shadow'; and

1 *b*. Which says that it alone is really active, and thus that the world is not run 'blindly' (idealistic panpsychism).

All three theories are *compatible* with known facts. Ordinary common-sense interactionism violates, however, the long list of reasons given by PAULSEN (from p. 92 to p. 105) for extending consciousness downward from brains into all living cells and thence into all matter.

Epiphenomenalism in turn violates, not only our sense of Life, but evolutionary probabilities.

Idealistic panpsychism has neither defect; and in some shape or other will probably be the theory of the future.

The Character and Outcome of the World Are the Real Issue

But, after all, *why* do we claim that the feeling side and not the blind side of things shall "run" them? Is it not because they seem then more sure of being run *right*, that the more ideal issues, those which we care for most, seem then in safer hands? If we knew beforehand just *how the world was certainly predestined to turn out*, it would make no difference to us whether its blinder or its more seeing side were the 'active' one. If the world's *character* were so obviously good already that we could fully trust its safe upshot, we could admire and love material forces, however blind, if it were they that insured us such an outcome. If, on the contrary, the world's character were already obviously *bad*, we should have no remedy, even though the active energies of it were mental.

From this fatalistic point of view, then, the alternative between epiphenomenalism and idealistic panpsychism has no practical significance. The *good issue* of the world is really what concerns us; and only because we suppose the mental forces to aim at this, is the idea of their activity so precious, and is epiphenomenalism displeasing.

But in point of fact, *the character of the world is not as yet obvious*. Death and life dog each other through every part of it, and we don't know which will have the final ascendant. All our ideals are menaced by their enemies. Issues seem open and uncertain, futures ambiguous and indeterminate. Now it *may be* that this appearance corresponds to the reality, and that to some degree and in some respects the world is still in the making, still really growing, still to be lost or saved, according as the forces active in it work well or badly. In such a case, the choice between the two types of panpsychism would have a deep practical meaning. Believers in free-will or indeterminism ought therefore to insist on its importance; while conversely those who believe that efficient causality runs through the mental series, ought also to incline favorably towards indeterminism. 'Minds' in point of fact do seem always *choosing*; if they be *forces*, why not admit that *their choices may be decisive*, no matter whether the minds belong to the human, the infra-human, or the super-human level?

We have here the hypothesis of a world not wholly determined beforehand, but determined by what its parts may do from moment to moment with their own possibilities, a world therefore of which the total outcome is not predestinate. This is the world of free-will, the kind of world that common sense believes in, so far as human life is concerned. Such a view is wholly immaterialistic, for it treats the higher or mental aspect of things, not only as everywhere accompanying the physical aspect and judging its results, but as carrying the power of directing as well as the power of judging in its hands.

One aim of this course will be to make such a free-will view of the world seem more and more probable. Here the lecturer's tendency will differ from Paulsen's, though in other respects they agree.

The Pragmatic Method

One sees that the whole materialistic controversy, which thinks itself to be about the *principles that move things,* is really about the *results of the movement.* What do we care for mind or matter in themselves, or for their activity or passivity, except as significant of practical results to be looked for? To quarrel over them without reference to the results is 'metaphysics' in the bad sense of the term, is *bad* metaphysics. If matter will give us immortality and the final triumph of ideals, then matter is precious and holy. If mind will not do this, then mind is despicable. As we know minds, they are champions of ideals, and as we know the laws of matter, they seem blind; so, the world seems to need minds to direct it, and we rightly prefer either Interactionism or the idealistic form of panpsychism, they being equally consistent with the present facts, to Epiphenomenalism.

Because they mean to us these consequences! This is a good example of what nowadays is meant by "Pragmatism." Pragmatism says that *the meaning of any concept must be sought in its consequences.* Two concepts that have identical consequences have the same meaning. For any concept to be *true* or *not-true* is a circumstance that *must make some assignable practical difference* in our experience. The truth of materialism in any form (even in that of epiphenomenalism) must entail final defeat of ideals; the truth of mind-supremacy in either form (interaction or idealistic panpsychism) must warrant the final triumph of those ideals. Apart from this, it makes no difference whatever which theory be true—they mean the same thing, if the defeat or the triumph be predestined anyhow.

Later we shall meet other examples of the pragmatic method of discussing theories by tracing their practical consequences and so giving their true meaning. (Compare W. JAMES: Philosophical Conceptions and practical results, reprint from University Chronicle, Berkeley, 1898 [*Pragmatism,* WORKS, pp. 257–270].)

Comments on Paulsen

Pp. 145–9.—Our world a cosmos, not a chaos. What do these words denote? They denote organization *versus* disorganization. But what kind of organization makes a cosmos? Evidently an organization into *things* that we can name, and of which we can describe the *histories*, things that are interrelated and coordinated with one another, while together they enter into larger aggregates, that are also things with histories, and these in turn are subordinate to the one great total cosmos, with one all-inclusive history, that we can write down in some more or less simple formula, like SPENCER's "law of evolution."

Example: Muscles, bones, glands, etc., correlated are things; not able to exist except in a whole body, the higher thing to which they are subordinate. *That* can't exist except in a social and terrestrial 'environment.' Both the human and the climatic part of this are still more inclusive things that have had and will have *their* history, subordinated in turn to the history of the earth and of mankind. These are in turn subordinate to the solar system, etc. The parts here seem to presuppose the wholes, these latter being the *minimum that can exist.* If you want a feather, or a drop of rain, or a man you must have a whole hen, or a whole shower, or a human race, as the indispensable condition of the part's existence.

Things wholly diverse in *origin* seem in this world *fitted* in advance, one being unable to live without the other. [The woodpecker's feet, bill, tongue, *e.g.*, are fitted to a world of trees, with grubs in their bark to feed on.]

Such unity is unity of *design*: things seem organized *in view of one another*. Does this point to one Designer? If so he must *execute* as well as design. Who and what is he? Or can *blind atomic forces* have worked out such results?

PAULSEN, on pp. 149–50, gives the three possible answers, and his account of Greek thought on the matter is clear and interesting.

Pp. 150–151.—P. is right in saying that theology or religious philosophy has always tended to make God immanent in the world, or to become pantheistic, 'Creation' from without being too hard to understand. Common sense, on the other hand, with no ideas about Creation, tends to take a purely practical view of God. He is an *existing power* that makes for righteousness, and will help men to that end. Apart from that, common sense pretends to know nothing of him.

P. 155, bottom.—"The irrational factor, matter." The design gives the *nature* of the Universe, conceives of *what* things it shall be composed, but merely to think out a universe is not to execute it.

What determines *that* it is? What makes a *percept* of the concept of the world?

Here we have the *problem of Being* again. How does thought get realized? By 'informing' matter, replied ARISTOTLE and the SCHOLASTICS. But this is a blank dualism. *How* does thought 'inform' matter?

P. 156.—In our own lives, we know how mind informs matter. Thought appears to influence our cerebral hemispheres immediately and they influence our muscles, and our muscles then shape the material world according to our aims. Thus the hemispheres are the *one known place* where immediate action of mind on body occurs. The execution of our designs elsewhere is contingent on this action first occurring.

On the theistic theory of a God outside the physical world, yet shaping it to his designs, the analogy fails us. There is *no one place* which seems particularly open to his mental action as our brains are to our mental action. We can't represent that action by any analogy in our experience. To call it 'creation' tells us nothing definite. This is what PAULSEN means by the second paragraph on p. 156, and is what ultimately drives him over from the dualistic theism, which places God's mind over against matter and outside of it, to the pantheistic panpsychic form of monism.

Critique of the Teleological Argument

(Teleology is from τέλος, meaning *end, purpose.* It considers the world with respect to its final purposes.) PAULSEN'S discussion subdivides into three parts, *viz:*—

A. Pp. 159–165.—He criticizes the propriety of interpolating purposes into the chain of outward events, treating them as if they were physical causes, God, for the usual design-argument, being such an external purposive cause.

B. 165–172.—He shows the difficulty of finding any one intelligibly consistent purpose or system of purposes actually realized in animal life. Later, from 217 onwards, he seems on the contrary to think that all the lesser purposes are parts of the World-Soul's one purpose.

C. 172–180.—Ditto in human history.

Remarks on A.—PAULSEN seems in these pages to revert pretty clearly to the epiphenomenalist view that mind is a concomitant shadow rather than a directing force. It judges, it sees that things reach ends or fail to reach them, but it can't put its finger in to help. It appreciates values, and that is all. (See Syllabus, p. 14 [*ed.*, 394.4–31].)

The conception of a world entirely run by physical forces, but with a *value* or *significance* for mind, keeps dominating PAULSEN. His state of mind is a natural reaction against the trivial way in which teleological philosophers have made purposes and physical causes alternate, as if some things came by physical causes and other things for a divine purpose. [Thus liquids freeze for physical reasons; but when water freezes it acts differently from other liquids, it *expands* into ice that floats, *in order that* the sea may not grow solid and interfere with navigation, etc.]

Of course there is no logical conflict between the mechanical production of a thing and its being purposed. It need not be one *or* the other. That the cloth of my coat is woven by a machine doesn't prevent it being designed. The machine itself is designed to weave that cloth.

God's world may be like such a machine or like a game of football. The production of spiritual life or of civic righteousness may indeed be God's aims. But evidently not spiritual life *straight*, not civic righteousness *immediate*, are aimed at; but these purposes *only as realized by all the tortuous mechanical processes* of cosmic and animal evolution, and by all the crimes of history,—realized as a *victory*, amid just such restrictions, and over just such obstructions. *That* must be God's *total* aim.

The notion expressed on p. 162 (bottom) that *everything* is mechanical, but *designed to be* mechanical, has been very popular of late, LOTZE being its ablest defender.

If taken to mean that no particular purposes act singly anywhere, only the vast general purpose of having this cosmic machine everywhere work out its results, it comes near to epiphenomenalism, and also seems to violate the pragmatic principle (above, p. 17 [*ed.*, 398.1–33]). For it lets minds exist, with their purposes, but refuses to let them make *any difference in any particular fact*.

Remarks on B.—The great difficulty here is to conceive *what* the final and absolute purpose, the veritable significance, of the cosmic machine is. There seems no one inclusive purpose in Nature except to realize the greatest diversity of contrary experiences possible.

Different creatures have *their* purposes; but these frustrate one another, and Nature deals out birth and death impartially. The old view that the world's peculiarities are all for human purposes, even culinary ones, is outgrown. What is *the* purpose? Every creature will judge the world from his own point of view, and differently from every other creature.

P. 171, bottom.—*We* can't sympathize with the *character* of a cosmic mind whose purposes are fully revealed by the strange mixture of good and bad that *we* find in the world. How can such warring ends be conceived as parts of one enveloping end? Nature tells no single story.

Observe that the point here is not to prove that, some end being assumed, the physical means that led to it were well adapted. Of course they were, or they would not have led to it. The point is, rather, to decide *what* or which end is the *really purposed* end. What has nature really aimed at with all her machinery? We can only guess at that by ascertaining what she has produced. Then, *no matter what* she may have produced, the means were fitted to *that production*; and the argument from design would apply, whether the product were good or bad. The recent Mont Pelée eruption required all previous history to produce that exact combination of ruined houses, human and animal corpses, sunken ships, ashes, etc., in just that configuration of positions. *If* God aimed at just *that* result, the means by which it was led up to through the centuries were exquisitely designed. And so of any state of things whatever, either in Nature or in History, which we find actually realized: the parts of it must form *some* kind of a resultant, and must appear 'fitted' to each other to that effect. The cosmic machine *may* have been designed for just that result.

Our inquiry thus takes the same turn here which it took on pp. 16–17 [ed., 396.27–397.39] of the syllabus. What we are *practically* interested in is not *whether* design exists in the world, but *what* the design is. What is the world's *character*? its *outcome*?

The reason why the argument from design has been so popular is that certain parts of the world are so good in our human sight, and the means of their production so apt, that we infer a humane and intelligent contriver for *them*. Then, generalizing our conclusion, we are reassured as to the total process, even if we can't well understand it. In some vague way, this must be God's world, we say. His proved presence in any part of it is a guarantee of its whole character. The abstract or empty notion that he is a benevolent Power is enough for us, even though we fail to fathom his purposes in detail.

Remarks on C.—We know what ideals history has succeeded in preserving. We do not know what ideals may have suffered shipwreck.

Pp. 179–80.—PAULSEN here seems to end by despairing of any proof that things have worked out under any general intelligent guidance. At this point he seems rather to treat the world (in spite of his panpsychism) as the result of its blind material energies.

Conclusion.—For us, three rather important points now come into sight:—First, the 'pragmatic' form which the cosmological problem takes: What is the world's *character*, so that we may know what to expect from it.

Second, the empiricist method of ascertaining that character,—so that even if we believed in God as the designer, we could only read the design by consulting the facts of Nature.

Third, the question whether panpsychism should be interpreted monistically or pluralistically. That is, is there *one all-inclusive purpose* harbored by a general world-soul, embracing all sub-purposes in its system? Or are there *many various purposes*, keeping house together as they can, with no overarching purpose to include them? In other words are the different parts of matter 'informed' by diverse souls that obey no one unifying principle, but work out their mutual harmony as best they can?

Rationalism going from whole to parts, would favor the monistic view; empiricism, going from parts to whole, the pluralistic.

General Estimate and Criticism of Paulsen's Handling of the Cosmological-Theological Problem

[In studying P.'s book, pp. 198 to 202, 249 to 251, 266 to 288, 290 to 300, 303 to 307, finally 322, will not be required for examination and may be omitted.]

First of all, P. and the lecturer seem to agree in thinking that the proof of an external designer fails.

A will-less intellect, viewing our world, could only say that its details *may* have been designed to produce the results observed.

But it could say that of any world whatever, so its conclusion is un-important. A God *may possibly* exist, adequate to the production of this world,—that is the intellect's last word in the matter. It is like an indeterminate solution in mathematics: anything on one side of the equation may be equal to anything on the other:—$0 = 0$.

The question *"Does* God *really* exist?"* could only be answered by the intellect after causes more 'natural' than God were proved im-possible. But how prove them impossible? The sections on Evolu-tion (pp. 180 to 206) show natural causes to be probable; and after all, the God himself may have designed to produce his world by natural causes.

P. therefore is right in saying that the step from seeing God to be possible to believing him to be real, is a step beyond the intellect (coerced, as that is, solely by logic) into the life of the 'Will' (in the broad sense of the term) which freely says that what *may* be real, and is *fit* to be real, *shall* now be treated as real. Our *life*, meet-ing something akin to itself in the expression of the world, greets it, espouses it, and acts upon it. This is 'faith'; and P.'s Section on 'Knowledge and Faith' (pp. 313–335) is surely sound, and connects itself happily with his 'voluntaristic psychology' on pp. 112–120. Compare also pp. 245–248.

Whether faith has a *right* to act thus is a question for later treat-ment.

Monism or Pluralism.—Revert now to the alternative at the bot-tom of page 21 [*ed.*, 403.18–27] of this Syllabus. P. seems never to have grasped the alternative sharply, and the two points of view vacillate in a perplexing way in his successive sections.

Assuming panpsychism to be true, rationalism would interpret it monistically. The least that exists is the One World-Soul. The finite portions of consciousness are parts of it, as letters are of words, and words of sentences.

Empiricism on the contrary would interpret it pluralistically giving primacy to the parts, and calling the world-soul a resultant. (If radically taken this might lead to atoms of mind-stuff as the ultimate realities out of which the larger consciousnesses were built up—CLIFFORD, TAINE, SPENCER, etc.)

PAULSEN is neither a radical monist nor a radical pluralist. In §1 (pp. 145–149) he seems monistic—all motions are a single motion, the cosmos is organized throughout, a universe of 'law,' etc.

Monistic also in the whole of §6 (pp. 207–217), where the parts of reality are treated, following HUME, as being without connection; unless, following LOTZE, we regard them as members of one all-inclusive Being which, living all over if it lives at all, involves and includes the mutually adapted changes of its constituent parts in its own total changes. This is most naturally interpretable as SPINOSA'S "Unity in which every particular thing is absolutely determined by the whole" (see p. 292), or as the 'Absolute Mind' of the 'transcendental idealists' such as HEGEL, the CAIRDS, ROYCE, etc.

P. is monistic also in §8 (Pantheism and World-Soul). Compare 'the All-One' on pp. 255, 258.

On the other hand, §4 is pluralistic (pp. 180–206). Evolution is said to take place as an unintended result, the will to live being lodged in a collection of distinct beings, half-blindly moving from step to step, 'purposive impulse' taking the place of clear design, but aggregate results accruing which we can retrospectively interpret as forming a history with a tendency. No real designed invention in either language, morals, or law (197–202); sciences arise without anticipatory reason. Men and nations go through their careers without designs—the facts are truly and well described. But the parts here have the primacy over the whole, and it does not even appear that the latter may be conscious, except in the dimmest way, of what the parts are doing.

In §7 (Causality and Finality), P. blows hot and cold. Everywhere, we are told, there is purpose; but it appears in the first instance as disseminated through the various creatures, in the form of *Zielstrebigkeit* (218) and we don't learn clearly whether the whole World-purpose is clearly conscious of itself at all, or is only a subconscious Will.

Our own discussion must be more radical than this, for the choice between monism and pluralism is fraught with momentous philosophic consequences.

Two different doctrines receive the name of monism, viz.

1. All Things are compounded of *one Stuff*, material atoms, or units of mind-stuff, as the case may be, and this Stuff is the sole ultimate reality.

2. The ultimate reality is the integral whole of things, which

forms an Individual Being of which all lesser things are the constituent parts. 'God' or 'Nature' are names for this Being in the Spinosistic form of monism. In contemporary philosophy it usually receives the name of 'the Absolute' (HEGEL, BRADLEY, ROYCE).

Both forms of monism imagine the things and events immediately known in our experience to be subordinate to something profounder. In form 1, the profounder thing is lower and simpler; in form 2 it is higher and richer than what we know.

We shall confine our discussion to form 2.

Neither form allows 'freedom' to be, or freedom not to be, to any single experienced fact. In the Absolute Unit of Being, all the parts must necessarily be just what they are. They co-implicate each other, and each is required to make the Absolute the individual Being which it is. If any part altered, the change would run through the whole, and the Absolute Being would be another Individual. This consolidation of all things into one Block-universe, with everything in it necessarily determining everything else, is the great achievement of the rationalist state of mind. When rationalists say: "reality is a unity," "the Cosmos is one system," "the World is one great fact," etc., they usually have this sort of consolidated Being in mind. The 'Oneness' of the Universe is often treated by pantheists as a diviner and more illustrious attribute than its diversity, and as something which it would be almost blasphemous to deny.

Pragmatic Method of Discussing Monism

What does it mean to call the world *One*? What is its oneness known-as?

1. Some say it means that it is a 'Universe,' not a 'Multiverse'; a Cosmos, not a chaos; a system, not a collection. (PAULSEN, 232, 235.)

To say this without specifying farther what the systematic character consists in, is to remain in hollow abstraction. By thinking it all together in one act of conception, you make of it indeed a 'universe of discourse,' but if you thought of it as a chaos, that would be equally your universe of discourse. What exactly is *meant* by the Oneness?

2. *Mystical Unity.*—Certain persons have states of insight in which

they seem actually to see and feel the identity of all things, of the self with God, etc. (PLOTINUS, VEDANTISM, WALT WHITMAN, etc.) This, if it could be articulately demonstrated, would be the paragon of a through and through consolidated Monism. Such insights cannot, however, be reasoned out or analyzed. So philosophy (dealing only with *reasoned* results), has to leave them on one side.

3. *Unity of Substance.*—Some say that all the parts of the Universe are supported by one Substance, be it 'God' or 'Matter.' The particulars 'inhere' in the substance. Recent idealism has in general got beyond this conception of Substance. The notion of a mere 'substratum' has no positive content. It is at bottom only a clumsy way of claiming that things *are* not disconnected, but connected rather. The real pragmatic question of "*how* connected?" gets here no intelligible answer.

4. *Unity of Time and Space.*—These receptacles hold all things and form one pragmatic specification of the world's unity. You can travel through space from one thing to another, they are joined by intervals of time. But also *dis*joined, etc.; so the unity of the world in this respect is no more vital than its diversity.

5. *Generic Unity.*—This is the basis of the *logical* connexion of things. So far as they belong to *kinds*, you can *infer* concerning them. But the kinds are notoriously many, and ultimately irreducible. So here again the world's oneness is no more essential than its many-ness.

6. *Unity of Origin.*—It is a common belief that all particular beings have one origin and source, either in God, or in atoms all equally old. There is no real novelty, it is believed, in the Universe, the new things that appear having either been eternally prefigured in the Absolute, or being atoms or 'monads,' results of the same *primordia rerum* getting into new mixtures. But we saw (Syllabus, p. 5 [*ed.*, 383.8–32]) that the question of Being is so obscure anyhow, that whether realities have burst into existence all at once, by a single 'bang,' as it were; or whether they come piecemeal, and have different ages (so that real novelties may be leaking into our universe all the time), may well be left an open question. It seems a question to be solved empirically rather than rationalistically; though it is undoubtedly intellectually *economical* to suppose that all things are equally old, and that no novelties leak in.

7. *Noetic Unity.*—(*a*) The universe in all its parts exists as one

undivided Thought of the Absolute Mind. *We* know the whole universe abstractly, whenever we throw the word universe at it, and make it one object of discourse. But the Absolute knows every minutest detail of it concretely, along with every other detail, in one undivided act of omniscience which you may call either eternal or instantaneous, as you prefer, for it is 'out of time,' time being only a feature of the Universe as *known*. Kant first made this *monistic* view possible; his successors, the philosophers of the Absolute or 'Transcendental Idealists' (ROYCE, among ourselves), have made it relatively popular.

(*b*) But the noetic union of things may also be interpreted *pluralistically*. The whole world may be known, but not by the same Knower, or in one single act, just as all mankind is knit in one network of acquaintance, A knowing B, B knowing C . . . Y knowing Z, Z knowing A again, without the necessity of anyone knowing everybody at once. This 'concatenated' knowing, going from next to next, should be distinguished from the 'consolidated' knowing of the Absolute Mind. It makes a coherent type of Universe, yet a universe in which the widest knower that exists may yet remain ignorant of *something*.

8. *Systematic Union.*—Different things are related in different ways, 'masses' gravitate to one another, people love or hate one another, animals prey on others, electrical conductors equalize their tensions, heat distributes itself, chemical action spreads through bodies from next to next, etc. Each group of things related in any one of these ways forms a distinct 'system,' thermal, gravitational, affectional, or whatever it may be. Most of these systems are limited. Light, electricity, heat, stop when they meet a non-conducting body. Love stops when acquaintance stops. But taken all together, they form a number of networks that cover the universe, the knots of the nets standing for 'things,' the threads for relations between them. The nets are larger or smaller, and the same knot or 'thing' may belong to several nets, as when a man belongs to the gravitational system, to a thermal, and to an affectional system.

From this point of view the world is unified in different degrees. Its parts cohere. Following a given sort of connection, and choosing your steps, you can travel from one object to another very far without finding the objects disconnected. In any one of these ways the world is a *Universe* of *that* kind, grade and extent. It is more instructive to specify concretely the kinds than abstractly to proclaim that "the world is One."

Many of these systems coexist without interacting. All bodies gravitate, and all exchange heat; but not all exchange love, not all *know* each other. We men are adding constantly to the connexions of things, establishing postal, consular, mercantile, railroad, telegraph and other systems that bind us and things together in ever wider unions. Some of these systems involve others, some do not. You can't have a telephone system without air or copper, but you can have air and copper without telephones. You can't have love without knowledge, but you can have knowledge without love, etc.

From the point of view of these partial systems, the world hangs together from next to next in a variety of ways, conforming to the concatenated type of union. Gravitation is the only sort of connexion among things that reminds us of the consolidated or through-and-through form of union. If a mass should change anywhere the mutual gravitation of all things would instantaneously alter.

9. *Unity of Purpose, Meaning, Story.*—Teleological and aesthetic unions are one form of systematic union. The world is full of partial purposes, of partial stories. But that they all should form chapters of one supreme purpose and history is a pure conjecture. They seem to run along side of each other, either irrelevantly, or where they interfere, leading either to frustrations or to mutual compromises. On pp. 20–21 [*ed.*, 401.36–403.3] of this syllabus we saw how hard it is to find one single harmonious story in the world.

Conclusion.—These results are what the Oneness of the Universe is *known as.* They *are* the oneness, pragmatically considered. A world coherent in any one of these ways would be, not a chaos, but a universe of such or such a grade. (Its parts, *e.g.*, might have space-relations, but nothing more; or they might also gravitate, or exchange heat, etc.)

Such is the *cash-value* of the world's unity, empirically realized. Its total unity is the sum of all the partial unities. It follows upon them. Such an idea, however, outrages the rationalistic mind, which despises all this practical small-change. It insists on a deeper, more through-and-through union of all things in the Absolute, "each in all and all in each," as the *prior condition* of these empirically ascertained connexions. But this seems only a case of the rationalistic worship of abstractions. It is like calling 'bad weather' the cause of to-day's rain, etc., or accounting for a man's vigor, good digestion and sleep, etc., by his 'healthiness,' when really the rain *is* the bad weather, is what you *mean by* 'bad weather,' just as the vigor, good sleep, etc., are what you mean by healthiness.

To sum up, the world is 'one' in some respects, and 'many' in others. But the respects must be distinctly specified for either statement to be more than the emptiest abstraction.

Objections to Absolute Monism

Monism, radically taken, holds the oneness of things to be more real than their manyness. We understand a thing the more truly the more we take it along with other things. To take it separately is to take it falsely. This leads to the belief that the entire Cosmos is a Consolidated Unit of Being, within which no part has any independence of the rest. Each part is determined by the Whole to be just *that*; and the slightest tremor of disunion is ruled out. The Universe is *tight*, not *loose*.

Pluralism shows no such absolutist temper. It is free to allow any amount of union among things, provided there be *some* disunion, however small, as well. It allows that *some* parts of the world may simply be added externally to the rest, and might vanish without the rest having to change. For Monism, such merely additive relations between things are inadmissible.

The kinds and amounts of union or disunion that actually obtain among things can only be ascertained through experience, pluralism thinks.

The most important form of Monism to-day is Absolute Idealism, which asserts the world to exist as one Object for an all-knowing Mind ('noetic' unity). KANT said that every part of experience must be an appearance to *some* self. His successors changed this notion into that of One Absolute Self, giving reasons which this course cannot discuss (see T. H. GREEN, the CAIRDS, ROYCE, etc.). In the lecturer's opinion they are not cogent; so that noetic monism has to be treated as a bare hypothesis, alongside of pluralism, and their results compared.

One must immediately admit the sublimity of the monistic hypothesis and its power to confer religious stability and peace. "The everlasting arms are beneath." It can also invoke mystical insights in its favor.

On the other hand it introduces into philosophy puzzles peculiar to itself, as follows:

1. *It doesn't account for our finite Consciousnesses.* If nothing exists except as the Absolute Mind knows it, how can anything exist *otherwise than* as that Mind knows it? That Mind knows each thing in one act of knowledge, along with every other thing. Finite minds know things *without* other things, and this ignorance is the source of most of their pain. We are thus not simply objects to an all-knowing Subject: we are subjects on our own account, additional to It, and knowing *differently* from It.

2. *Monism creates a 'problem of Evil.'* Evil, for pluralism, presents only a *practical* problem. For monism the puzzle is *theoretical*:—how, if Perfection be the Source, should there be Imperfection? If the world as known to the Absolute be perfect, why should it be known otherwise, in myriads of inferior finite editions *also*? The perfect edition surely was enough. How do the breakage and dispersion and ignorance get in?

3. *It contradicts the character of reality as experienced by us.* Of our world, Change seems an essential ingredient. It has a history. There are novelties, struggles, losses, gains. But the world of the Absolute is represented as unchanging, eternal, or 'out of time,' and is foreign to our powers either of apprehension or of appreciation. Monism usually treats our world as a *mirage* or illusion.

4. *It is fatalistic.* Possibility, as distinguished from necessity on the one hand and from impossibility on the other, is an essential category of our human thinking. For monism, it is a pure illusion; for whatever *is* is necessary and aught else is impossible, if the world be such a Unit of fact as monism pretends.

Our sense of 'freedom' supposes that some things at least are decided here and now, that the passing moment may contain some novelty, be an original starting-point of events, and not merely transmit a push from elsewhere. We imagine that in some respects at least the future may not be co-implicated with the past, but may be really *added* to it, and indeed added in one shape *or* another, so that the next turn in events can at any given moment genuinely be *ambiguous, i.e.,* possibly *this,* but also possibly *that.*

Monism rules out this whole conception of possibles, so native to our common sense. The future and the past are given in one, she is obliged to say; there is no genuine novelty anywhere, and an additive constitution is repugnant to the world.

Conclusions

Monism in all this is rationalistic. She would gladly say with Spinosa that all things follow from the essence of God as necessarily as from that of a triangle it follows that the angles should equal two right angles; the whole explains the part, not the part the whole. Pluralism, relying on experience, protests against making such statements too absolutely. Some parts indeed can't exist out of their wholes; but others can. To some extent the world seems genuinely additive; it may really be so. We can't *explain how* a genuine novelty can come; but we could *experience that* it came if it did come. Experience overlaps reason. The *that* transcends the *why*. So the common-sense view of life, as something really dramatic, with work done, and things decided here and now, is acceptable to pluralism. 'Free will' means nothing but real novelty; so pluralism goes with free will.

But pluralism, accepting a universe unfinished, with doors and windows open to possibilities uncontrollable in advance, gives us less religious certainty than monism, with its absolutely closed-in world. It is true that monism's religious certainty is not *rationally* based, but is only a faith that "sees the All-Good in the All-Real" (Paulsen, p. 252). In point of fact, however, monism usually exerts this optimistic faith: its world is certain to be saved, yes, is saved already, unconditionally and from eternity, in spite of all the phenomenal appearances of risk.

Pluralism is neither optimistic nor pessimistic, but *melioristic* rather. The world, it thinks, *may* be saved, *on condition that its parts shall do their best*. But shipwreck in detail, or even on the whole, is among the open possibilities.

There is thus a practical *tension* about pluralism, which contrasts with monism's *peace of mind*. The one is a more *moral*, the other a more *religious* view; and different men will usually let this determine their preference.

Experience cannot as yet finally conclude for either view. Monism scouts pluralism as absurd, a Unit-universe being for it the only rational world. A real world, actually working out an uncertain destiny, as the phenomenal world appears to be doing, is an intolerable idea to the rationalistic mind.

Melioristic Pluralism

Nevertheless, if the question had been put to us before the Creation, whether we would ourselves enter a world, not perfect, but only perfectable, and that on condition that its parts should severally do their best; or whether we should prefer to have no world rather than go in for such irrationally uncertain conditions; we probably would most of us have accepted the pluralistically constituted world. We are champions of certain ideals, we know there are other champions, and the 'fighting chance' of success would have been enough. The element of venture is a part of human life; why may it not be an element in the universe as a whole?

The lecturer favors this pluralistic view. Even religious men think that some extremes of religious feeling are too sickly sweet and devoid of moral backbone. The fact that monism imposes no limits on religious feeling cannot therefore be regarded as conclusive in its favor as against the pluralistic idea.

Faith and the Right to Believe

Paulsen's chapter on Knowledge and Faith shows a certain courage, for in Germany Intellectualism is to-day in the ascendent.

'Intellectualism' is the belief that our mind comes upon a world complete in itself, and has the duty of ascertaining its contents; but has no power of re-determining its character, for that is already given.

Among Intellectualists two parties may be distinguished. Rationalizing intellectualists lay stress on deductive and 'dialectic' arguments, making large use of abstract concepts and pure logic (Hegel, Bradley, Taylor, Royce). Empiricist intellectualists are more 'scientific,' and think that the character of the world must be sought in our sensible experiences, and found in hypotheses based exclusively thereon (Clifford, Mach, Pearson).

Both sides insist that in our conclusions personal preferences should play no part, and that no argument from what *ought to be* to what *is* is valid. 'Faith,' being the greeting of our whole nature to a kind of world conceived as well adapted to that nature, is forbidden, until purely intellectual *evidence* that such *is* the actual world has come in. Even if evidence should eventually prove a faith true, the truth, says CLIFFORD, would have been 'stolen,' if assumed and acted on too soon.

Refusal to believe anything concerning which 'evidence' has not yet come in, would thus be the rule of intellectualism. Obviously it postulates certain conditions, which for aught we can see need not necessarily apply to all the dealings of our minds with the Universe to which they belong.

1. It postulates that *to escape error* is our paramount duty. Faith *may* grasp truth; but also it *may* not. By resisting it always, we are sure of escaping error; and if by the same act we renounce our chance at truth, that loss is the lesser evil, and should gladly be incurred.

2. It postulates that in every respect the universe is finished in advance of our dealings with it;

That the knowledge of *what* it thus is, is best gained by a passively receptive mind, with no native sense of probability, or good-will towards any special result;

That 'evidence' not only needs no good-will for its reception; but is able, if patiently waited for, to neutralize ill-will;

Finally, that our beliefs and our acts based thereupon, although they are parts of the world, and although the world without them is unfinished, are yet such mere externalities as not to alter in any way the significance of the rest of the world when they are added to it.

In our dealings with many details of fact these postulates work well. Such details exist in advance of our opinion; truth concerning them is often of no pressing importance; and by believing nothing, we escape error while we wait. But even here we often *cannot* wait but must act, somehow; so we act on the most *probable* hypothesis, trusting that the event may prove us wise. Moreover, not to act on one belief, is often equivalent to acting as if the opposite belief were true, so inaction would not always be as "passive" as the intellectualists assume. It is one attitude of will.

Again, Philosophy and Religion have to interpret the total character of the world, and it is by no means clear that here the intellectualist postulates obtain. It may be true all the while (even though the evidence be still imperfect) that, as PAULSEN says, "the natural order is at bottom a moral order." It may be true that work is still doing in the world-process, and that in that work we are called to bear our share. The character of the world's results may in part depend upon our acts. Our acts may depend on our religion,—on our not-resisting our faith-tendencies, or on our sustaining them in spite of "evidence" being incomplete. These faith-tendencies in turn are but expressions of our good-will towards certain forms of result.

Such faith-tendencies are extremely active psychological forces, constantly outstripping evidence. The following steps may be called the "faith-ladder":

1. There is nothing absurd in a certain view of the world being true, nothing self-contradictory.

2. It *might* have been true under certain conditions;

3. It *may* be true, even now;

4. It is *fit* to be true;

5. It *ought* to be true;

6. It *must* be true;

7. It *shall* be true, at any rate true for *me*.

Obviously this is no intellectual chain of inferences, like the *Sorites* of the logic-books. Yet it is a slope of good-will on which in the larger questions of life men habitually live.

Intellectualism's proclamation that our good-will, our 'will to believe,' is a pure disturber of truth, is itself an act of faith of the most arbitrary kind. It implies the will to insist on a universe of intellectualist constitution, and the willingness to stand in the way of a pluralistic universe's success, such success requiring the good-will and active faith, theoretical as well as practical, of all concerned, to make it "come true."

Intellectualism thus contradicts itself. It is a sufficient objection to it, that if a "pluralistically" organized or "co-operative" universe (the "melioristic" universe of p. 30 [*ed.*, 413.3–13], above) were really here, the veto of Intellectualism on letting our good-will ever have any vote would debar us from ever admitting that universe to be true.

Faith thus remains as one of the inalienable birthrights of our mind. Of course it must remain a practical, and not a dogmatic attitude. It must go with toleration of other faiths, with the search for the most probable, and with the full consciousness of responsibilities and risks.

It may be regarded as a formative factor in the universe, if we be integral parts thereof, and co-determinants, by our behavior, of what its total character may be.

How We Act on Probabilities

In most emergencies we have to act on probability, and incur the risk of error.

"Probability" and "possibility" are terms applied to things of the conditions of whose coming we are (to some degree at least) ignorant.

If we are entirely ignorant of the conditions that make a thing come, we call it a "bare" possibility. If we know that some of the conditions already exist, it is for us in so far forth a "grounded" possibility. It is in that case *probable* just in proportion as the said conditions are numerous, and few hindering conditions are in sight.

When the conditions are so numerous and confused that we can hardly follow them, we treat a thing as probable in proportion to the *frequency* with which things of that *kind* occur. Such frequency being a fraction, the probability is expressed by a fraction. Thus, if one death in 10,000 is by suicide, the antecedent probability of my death being a suicide is 1-10,000th. If one house in 5000 burns down annually, the probability that my house will burn is 1-5000th, etc.

Statistics show that in most kinds of thing the frequency is pretty regular. Insurance companies bank on this regularity, undertaking to pay (say) 5000 dollars to each man whose house burns, provided he and the other houseowners each pay enough to give the company that sum, plus something more for profits and expenses.

The company, hedging on the large number of cases it deals with, and working by the long run, need run no risk of loss by the single fires.

The individual householder deals with his own single case exclusively. The probability of his house burning is only 1-5000, but if that lot befal he will lose everything. He has no "long run" to go by, if his house takes fire, and he can't hedge as the company does, by taxing his more fortunate neighbors. But in this particular kind of risk, the company helps him out. It translates his one chance in 5000 of a big loss, into a certain loss 5000 times smaller, and the bargain is a fair one on both sides. It is clearly better for the man to lose *certainly*, but *fractionally*, than to trust to his 4999 chances of no loss, and then have the improbable chance befal.

But for most of our emergencies there is no insurance-company at hand, and fractional solutions are impossible. Seldom can we *act* fractionally. If the probability that a friend is waiting for you in Boston is 1-2, how should you act on that probability? By going as far as the bridge? Better stay at home! Or if the probability is 1-2 that your partner is a villain, how should you act on that probability? By treating him as a villain one day, and confiding your money and your secrets to him the next? That would be the worst of all solutions. In all such cases we must act wholly for one *or* the other horn of the dilemma. We must go in for the more probable alternative as if the other one did not exist, and suffer the full penalty if the event belie our faith.

Now the metaphysical and religious alternatives are largely of this kind. We have but this one life in which to take up our attitude towards them, no insurance company is there to cover us, and if we are wrong, our error, even though it be not as great as the old hell-fire theology pretended, may yet be momentous. In such questions as that of the *character* of the world, of life being moral in its essential meaning, of our playing a vital part therein, etc., it would seem as if a certain *wholeness* in our faith were necessary. To calculate the probabilities and act fractionally, and treat life one day as a farce, and another day as a very serious business, would be to make the worst possible mess of it. Inaction also often counts as action. In many issues the inertia of one member will impede the success of the whole as much as his opposition will. To refuse, *e.g.*, to testify against villainy, is practically to help it to prevail.

Read here W. JAMES's Essays entitled "The Will to Believe," and "The Sentiment of Rationality," pp. 90–110 [*The Will to Believe*, WORKS, pp. 13–33, 75–89] (not for examination).

The Pluralistic or Melioristic Universe

Finally, if the "melioristic" universe of p. 30 [*ed.*, 413.3–13] of this syllabus were *really* here, it would require the active good-will of all of us, in the way of belief as well as of our other activities, to bring it to a prosperous issue.

The melioristic universe is conceived after a *social* analogy, as a pluralism of independent powers. It will succeed just in proportion as more of these work for its success. If none work, it will fail. If each does his best, it will not fail. Its destiny thus hangs on an *if*, or on a lot of *ifs*—which amounts to saying (in the technical language of logic) that, the world being as yet unfinished, its total character can be expressed only by *hypothetical* and not by *categorical* propositions.

[Empiricism, believing in possibilities, is willing to formulate its universe in hypothetical propositions. Rationalism, believing only in impossibilities and necessities, insists on the contrary on their being categorical.]

As individual members of a pluralistic universe, we must recognize that even though we do *our* best, the other factors also will have a voice in the result. If they refuse to conspire, our good-will and labor may be thrown away. No insurance-company can here cover us or save us from the risks we run in being part of such a world.

We *must* take one of four attitudes in regard to the other powers: either

1. Follow intellectualist advice: wait for evidence; and while waiting, do nothing; or

2. *Mistrust* the other powers and, not sure that the universe won't fail, *let* it fail; or

3. *Trust* them; and at any rate do *our* best, in spite of the *if*; or, finally,

4. *Flounder*, spending one day in one attitude, another day in another.

This 4th way is no systematic solution. The 2nd way spells faith in failure. The 1st way may in practice be indistinguishable from the 2nd way. The 3rd way seems the only wise way.

"*If* we do *our* best, *and* the other powers do *their* best, the world will be perfected"—this proposition expresses no actual fact, but only the complexion of a fact thought of as eventually possible. As it stands, *no* conclusion can be positively deduced from it. A conclusion would require another premise of fact, which only we can supply. The original proposition *per se* has no pragmatic value whatsoever, apart from its *power to challenge our will to produce the premise of fact required.* Then indeed the perfected world emerges as a logical conclusion.

We can *create* the conclusion, then. We can and we may, as it were, jump with both feet off the ground into or towards a world of which we trust the other parts to meet our jump—and *only so* can the *making* of a perfected world of the pluralistic pattern ever take place. Only through our precursive trust in it can it come into being.

There is no inconsistency anywhere in this, and no "vicious circle" unless a circle of poles holding themselves upright by leaning on one another, or a circle of dancers revolving by holding each other's hands, be "vicious."

The faith circle is so congruous with human nature that the only explanation of the veto that intellectualists pass upon it must be sought in the offensive character *to them* of the faiths of certain concrete persons.

Such possibilities of offense have, however, to be put up with on empiricist principles. The long run of experience may weed out the more foolish faiths. Those who held them will then have failed; but without the wiser faiths of the others the world could never be perfected.

(Compare G. Lowes Dickinson: Religion, a criticism and a forecast, N. Y. 1905. Introduction; and chaps. III, IV.)

Paulsen, Book II

Skip pp. 339 and 340. No harm in reading 341 to 343, but not for examination.

Poor account of scepticism on p. 342. Scepticism has been accused of self-contradiction, inasmuch as its thesis "there is no certain judgment anywhere," seems to cut the ground from under itself, for itself professes to be certain truth. It is easy to escape this accusation by changing the form of statement into: "There is but one certain judgment, which is that all other judgments are uncertain." Also said to be self-contradictory in using the very notion of truth to deny the fact of it. But the notion is one thing, the fact another, and you use the notion of any false thing (as a centaur) when you deny or doubt the fact of it.

Such objections to scepticism are too childish. As a will-attitude of habitual doubt, not as a dogmatic system, scepticism is irrefutable. The sceptic, whatever is proposed to his belief, simply *declines to conclude*. It may be, but also it may not be, he says. He takes this attitude successively in single cases, without professing to generalize it, otherwise than as a prudent habit. In so far as such a habit keeps him from espousing reforms or voting, he adds his weight to the forces of inertia. He pooh-poohs faith; he may thereby escape error but he runs the same risk as the faith-man does, of losing truth.

Idealism

In what follows, the word "idea" must be taken to mean any mental act, affection, or experience, as percept, concept, emotion, desire, or volition.

Study Paulsen from p. 344 to p. 377.

§1 (pp. 344 to 351) traces the successive steps of the argument from the fallibility of our senses to the radical phenomenalist or idealist conclusion that "ideas" are the only things we know.

Next (pp. 352–367), Paulsen, starting from the universal conviction that every idea is the idea of *some reality*, seeks to show that the reality is in no case a transcendent "thing-in-itself," lying outside of all our ideas, but rather the *rest* of that very system of ideas to which the first idea may belong.

In §2 (pp. 352–367) he applies his reasoning to the inner world, and criticises the popular notion of a soul-substance as the "support" of our ideas, continuing here his earlier criticism on pp. 128–144. "Souls" and their "powers" are only names for the fact that the world contains innumerable collections of ideas so conjoined together as to constitute what we call personal lives. A personal life obtains whenever in a stream of ideas the later ones remember the earlier ones and continue their purposes. The word "I" is the natural name for such a stream of ideas. But where we have a name we almost inevitably think we have a separate thing; so the soul-substance has come to be believed in as a transcendent reality, of which the ideas are the transient appearances or "states." But a soul *means* only a concrete personal life, and we know our own reality absolutely when we livingly experience the flow of our ideas as such. There is no deeper reality connected with us. "Self" or "soul" are only *names* for this verifiable flow.

On p. 368 Paulsen, pursuing his pantheistic or monistic tendency, tries to make it appear that our various inner lives may be unified still farther in the total or "timeless" consciousness of the divine world-self.

In §3 (pp. 369–377) he applies his reasoning to the outer world.

By physical "things" we mean in the first instance our actual percepts. Secondarily we mean remoter percepts which the first percepts may cover (as the desk's surface covers woody-fibre), or to which they may lead (as when a smell of smoke leads us to a distant or hidden fire). The remoter percepts then often get treated as the realities of which the more immediate ones are the signs.

The substitution of remote or possible percepts for immediate and actual ones, with the remote regarded as the more real, may be pushed very far. Physics and chemistry push it as far as ether, atoms, electrons, etc. These hypothetic realities are represented as much as possible in perceptual form (as filling space and having mechanical properties at any rate) so that they belong to no transcendent realm of "things in themselves."

We may stop here if we like. Mill, Mach, and others do so. They think that the world is just a system of percepts, actual and possible, whose habitual groupings and sequences are expressed as "laws"; and behind the bare fact of this constitution of things, there is nothing to write down.

But Paulsen suggests that we should go farther, and take the panpsychic view, which says that behind the fact of the possibility of a perception (say of woody fibre in the table's substance) there is a *ground* of that perception's possibility in the actual existence of the table's substance *for* itself, or as an "inner" life or feeling, of which the woody fibre is the outer appearance to us.

With this, Paulsen rejoins the conclusions of Book I. The upshot, then, is that the universe is essentially a system of inner experiences or "ideas," some of which run together directly into "personal consciousnesses," while others only influence these so far as to give them outer perceptions. These latter, then, stand as symbolic physical representations of what, in and for themselves, are facts of a spiritual order.

Comments

The vulgar view of Berkeley's idealism is that "Berkeley denied the existence of the external world."

A mistake! What he denied was "matter," as an inaccessible and non-perceptible "thing in itself" *supporting* the external world. He admitted the latter; and only undertook to show what it *consisted of*. It consists, he said, of material things; and these, when analyzed, prove to consist of "ideas of sensation," such as hardness, round-ness, sonority, whiteness, weight, etc., grouped in determinate ways. Tell off all such qualities, and you have a whole billiard ball, with no *caput mortuum* of matter left over. God sends us such groups of percepts, which exist for Him when we don't get them, and which consequently are *out* of our minds as well as in them. They are out of our *heads* also. They are *there*—in outer space, for the space itself is just another idea of sensation, and a billiard ball is "there" if anywhere, and is as real as the space is. Berkeley consequently didn't *derealize* our experience; on the contrary he made it absolutely real; for by expelling the notion of there being a more real metaphysical substance beneath the appearances, and by saying that the only thing beyond them is God, sending them to us, and *meaning us to have them just as they are*, he *continued* and *corroborated*, instead of undermining them.

He introduced the whole "phenomenalist" way of thinking, which analyzes the world into concretely verifiable things, individual experiences of somebody, somewhere, somewhen, connected together by relations which are themselves experienced. According to this view reality is not something behind all experience, which experience veils and masks, it is the *more* of experience, the *fuller* experience, compared with which the experience of the moment is always inadequate and unreal.

(You can interpret this phenomenalist way of thinking monistically or pluralistically, as you prefer.)

Phenomenalism or idealism is usually accused (in spite of all this) of denying the "objective" import of experience. It is important in discussion to disentangle certain ambiguities in the word "objective" as used here. That an idea represents an "object" may mean that it represents something either:—

1. Trans-*personal*—as when my object is also *your* object; or

2. Trans-*corporeal*—as when my object is outside of my body; or

3. Trans-*cerebral*—as possibly in my body, but out of my brain; or

4. Trans-*visible* or trans-*palpable*—as when it is defined either as a "scientific" entity (like the atom or ether-wave) or as a panpsychic entity; or finally,

5. Trans-*mental* altogether, as when it is said to be altogether "unknowable."

If, with Paulsen, we deny the last kind of object, we still have other kinds to fall back on. Exercise yourselves in defining how much of an "object" Science, Panpsychic Phenomenalism, Berkeleyan Idealism, Common Sense, and "Solipsism," or radical Scepticism, respectively admit into their worlds.

The ordinary pathway towards idealism from the *"naïf"* realism that accepts every immediate percept as absolutely real, is by way of successive steps of critical reflection, as follows:

1. Our senses vary in their accounts of the same object. Which account is true? Perhaps neither!

2. Hallucinations, illusions, dreams, feel just like reality, until you wake from them. Why may not the whole world be a dream from which we haven't awakened?

3. Brain-physiology shows that our percepts are due to brain-excitements, *however aroused.* People feel amputated limbs as if they were still there, because the brain-centres for feeling them are there, and subject to excitements from within.

4. Physical science explains the order of nature better by assuming that only the "primary" (i.e., the mathematical and mechanical) properties of bodies are real. Heat, color, sound, smell, taste, etc., are thus only effects on our sensibility. But so are shape, hardness, softness, etc.; in the end only geometrical properties, and number, remain as non-subjective attributes.

5. Kant thought that space and time themselves were subjective for reasons some of which Paulsen gives on pp. 349–350. The "antinomies," K. thought, are overcome by idealism. What is infinite can't be completed by successive synthesis, can't therefore be *wholly* given. Yet past time comes as now wholly given, in spite of the infinite regress to which we are led in trying to imagine it. Kant gets over this "antinomy," or contradiction between the infinite form of time and its givenness when past, by assuming, idealistically, that past time exists not in itself, but *only for our imagination*, which is

bound, by a law of its own being, to imagine ever more of it previous to the most previous bound. Its infinite recession means thus a finite amount of it imagined or conceived, with an indefinite more, always conceiv*able* or imagin*able*, behind it. An infinite series of this sort, partly real, partly possible only (uncompleted therefore *a parte ante*), involves no contradiction.

6. Our only intelligible notion of an object *in itself* is that it should be an object *for* itself, and this lands us in panpsychism and a belief that our physical perceptions are effects on us of "psychical" realities.

7. Even if we don't become panpsychists, we can still describe the entire course of our experience as a system of possible sensations connected by definite laws with actual sensations (Mill), and keep a place in our description for every verifiable fact, without invoking any entity of which sensation does not constitute the nature.

That something exists when we, as individuals, are not thinking it, is an inexpugnable conviction of common sense. The various stages of idealistic reflection are only as many successive attempts to define *what* the something is that thus exists. The upshot tends pretty strongly towards something like panpsychism. But there are various shades of opinion here, with which later philosophy courses will acquaint you in more detail.

A useful distinction is that between epistemological and ontological idealism. Epistemological idealism says: "I know nothing but my own ideas." This opinion, consistently held, would amount to "Solipsism":—nobody seriously defends it. Epistemological realism says: "I know, *through* my ideas, other realities." *Ontological* idealism may then define these other realities as spiritual entities (panpsychically, for example). Ontological realism on the other hand, defines them as something material, unknowable, or at any rate non-psychical.

The Question of "Free Will"

Better state it as the question of ambiguous or indeterminate futures. It is primarily a general cosmic question: Are there in the universe futures not fully determined by all that has gone before? Monism, affirming that everything is co-implicated with everything else, answers: "No!" An all-seeing mind would see the future to be fully determined as the past. Pluralism, on the contrary, believing in a world some of whose parts may be merely added to the others, sees no objection to admitting that what is added *may* be this or *may* be that. What *is now*, is compatible with various supplements; and whichever future came and grafted itself on to the present, the results would hang together, and form a connected universe in either event.

The *proximates* of experience are full of individuality and novelty. No "person" absolutely repeats another; no two "things" or "events" are just alike. Each adds itself as what it is, to the pre-existing mass of being; and the mass tolerates the addition. Scientific monism gets over this appearance of novelty by resolving the "proximates" into "ultimate elements," more real than they, that produce them by their mixtures. These elements are eternal, and there is no novelty in *their* behavior. The atoms repeat and imitate their ancient conduct in *secula seculorum*; but, forming always different mixtures, they produce on us the appearance of novel things and events.

For radical monism there is thus no real novelty, and nothing really *happens* to the universe. It is a vast eternal unit of fact. Our idea that it has more than one possible future is a delusion. Its one future is necessary—any fancied alternative is impossible.

On the other hand the monist and the pluralist alike confess that *being* is a mystery. The world comes into being by processes into which we have no insight. Monists insist that it has come all at once, or "eternally," in a single act; pluralists, that it may just as well come piecemeal, or in single drops. (Equivalent amounts of Being must be assumed or begged by the philosopher in either case.)

So far as the physical universe goes, the plural view is restless, and monism agrees sufficiently with what we know of nature; so hardly any one doubts determinism in the physical world. The weather and the fate of the stars we believe to be absolutely fixed in advance.

In human life, however, and in history, we have strong feelings the other way. The future offers itself as an *either-or*. The world seems to us genuinely unfinished, and as if our beliefs and acts might be additions, originating *now*, and giving it a turn this way or that, according to their nature.

This ambiguous possibility in our decisions is what people mean by free-will. Doubtless the ambiguity is to a great extent deceptive:

we are more predestined than we think. But is it an absolute delusion? Does indeterminism *nowhere* exist? Are there nowhere genuine *possibles*?

Obviously facts cannot decide this question. Determinists appeal to the principle of causality. Two issues, equally possible, to one antecedent situation, would, they say, be absurd. They would mean one cause, with two possible effects, and no cause to determine *which* effect?

Still, if new beings can come into the world piecemeal, this may be just the place. We are often surprised by the way "the cat jumps" in us. It may be that at such moments we catch being in the making, and assist at pulses of creation. Such a view tallies with the intense feeling of ambiguity that goes with our consciousness of self. What we are is always lined with the notion of what we *might* be, or *might have been.* We continue our past, but we seem to ourselves not always to be passively transmitting its push, but from time to time to re-direct it ourselves. Why need our feeling that something really *happens* at such moments, that events take a turn, that new series begin, be false, as monism insists it is? Somewhere in the universe something must genuinely happen. Why not here, in the bosom of our several phenomenal lives?

Faith is what dictates the answer on both sides. The determinist pins his faith on the rational co-implication of all things, and gives up the notion of possibilities and genuine happenings and history, rather than admit a universe in which uncontrollable accidents and miracles (for such are new beginnings) can occur.

That sort of universe is too irrational for him. If we are indeterminists, on the other hand, we pin our faith on the instinctive sense of life, telling us that we have here a world genuinely incomplete and growing by addition of new parts, that its fate quivers, and that among the forces that decide its history are ourselves.

Monism and pluralism, as two opposite types of world-constitution, are the truest names for the rival views that appeal here to our faith. It is important to extricate this central fact from the confusion that covers the subject. Free-will means simply pluralism. It is less an ethical or psychological than a cosmological hypothesis.

Pluralism clings to certain appearances, as incompleteness, "more," uncertainty, insecurity, possibility, fact, novelty, compromise, remedy, success, etc., as being authentic realities; and to certain contrasts, as better and worse, loss and gain, retrospect and prospect as never to be superseded or effaced. Its world is dramatic in essence as well as in form. These categories are the pigments with which its world-picture has to be painted.

Monism, passing from the finite to the absolute or eternal point of view, has to treat all these dramatic determinations as illusions. They are true of the finite as such, but not of the absolute reality.

Remember the two disconnected universes of my student: that of the philosophic class-room and that of the street! Your lecturer chooses one world that, namely, of which the street yields the type.

Materialism Again

Paulsen's discussion of materialism and his transition to pan-psychism use technical terms, and enumerate many opinions. The following will perhaps help to clearness:—

There are three kinds of materialism:—

1. The "crass" kind, which says thought is a *modification,* or *secretion,* or *motion,* or *property,* of matter. Thought in short, is of material nature.

2. More refined, saying: "thought, though not of material nature, is an *effect* of matter, especially of brain-matter."

3. Most refined, saying thought is not an effect, but merely a *concomitant* or inner aspect, uniformly correlated with matter. This is *parallelism.* When parallelists insist not only that thoughts are not effects, but that they do not *react* on matter either, they make them causally *inert.* This doctrine of thoughts' inertness is called *automatism* when you view it from the side of matter, and *epi-phenomenalism* when you view it from the side of mind. Matter automatically performs all the work, mind merely appears alongside of it, commenting, or judging.

Parallelism may be taken to hold either partially or universally. Brain-matter might be the only kind that had an inner aspect. But Paulsen (and most of those who call themselves parallelists) believe that *all* matter is thus *"beseelt,"* or animated. This is *panpsychism.*

Paulsen must be classed as a panpsychist of the epiphenomenalist stripe. He believes that matter does all the work by its uniform laws, and that mind, though present everywhere, is only conscious of what is done. Conscious both in the sense of knowing, and in the sense of approving, condemning, wishing and regretting. But the wishes and regrets are powerless, since thought has no causality.

From this point of view, Paulsen, although he calls the inner aspect of his parallelism the more real aspect (since it alone gives *meaning* to what the other aspect *does*) is liable to the reproach of being a materialist, if "materialism" be taken in the wider sense of asserting the world to be run by its lower forces. The blinder aspect *does* things, the seeing aspect only *records* them, for Paulsen.

Against this materialistically flavored panpsychism (on the whole a monistic doctrine) we may set a frankly dualistic spiritualism. Mind and matter here would not be aspects of one real Being, but two sorts of beings that interact, both of them remaining causal agents. They might be co-extensive with each other or not. Paulsen uses the word "interactionism" to designate the opinion that they are not co-extensive, but that thoughts accompany brains only, and interrupt the continuity of brain-events by inserting themselves as another kind of link in the chain of causation. He thinks that "Science" has a right to refuse such links.

Can thought *move* the matter of our brain? The very idea, he thinks, materializes it (Cp. p. 84)!

But on the other hand mind and matter might be co-extensive, and "interactionism" might take a more panpsychic form. Matter might *everywhere* make mind conscious of what matter was doing, and mind might then everywhere either acquiesce in the performances, or encourage, hinder, or redirect them.

Some such interactionist view as this your lecturer favored, as harmonizing better with our feeling of life. It is very subtly interpreted by Strong and Heymans. No physiological facts refute it, and it goes well with the general pluralistic view of the world.

31. Report of a Discussion in Philosophy 20e: Seminary in the Theory of Knowledge (1908)

Philosophy 20 E
Report of meeting of March 5, 1908
Pragmatism

HOLT: I want to find out just what you mean by 'reality.' How do we know it? You appeal to this reality for verification of the question whether an opinion is true or not. In order to appeal to this reality, you must know, I should think, what the extent and limits of this reality are. It goes on further than what we get in the verification process?

JAMES: That has nothing to do with pragmatism. Pragmatism simply establishes the method by which opinions about reality may be reached. Therein, exactly, it differs from other philosophies, which seem to think that their method itself involves some notion of reality. The dialectical method supposes that reality is implicitly present in every thought we make, and that it is a complete, self-sufficing unit of truth. Pragmatism says, Let reality be what it will, the truth of an idea concerning it consists of certain things which the pragmatist tries to define. The truth of an idea is the manner in which it gets us. The connection of the idea with reality is the particulars of our experience, in the first instance.

HOLT: At the outset, in my reading of pragmatism, I saw statements that that was true which led one to the maximum number of satisfactions—

JAMES: Provided the reality were there, of course.

HOLT: Well, doctrines that had turned out highly satisfactory to many, had yet been held, by many others, to be untrue. Then this word 'reality' crept in. So the opinion became true if it led you straight up to some 'reality'—e.g. if it is true about *this* desk. Then, if the satisfactoriness of the doctrine, and so its truth, is going to

429

depend upon its reality, we must know what reality is, and how far it extends.

JAMES: That comes in in the particulars. The pragmatist account is a definition of an abstract thing which may never be realized anywhere. The question you are asking is, How is the actual reality to be realized, which exists for some actual thinker? It is true that a man is mortal because all men do die. Mortality means that men will die, some time or other. Meantime, we account a man mortal before he is dead. The pragmatist isn't called upon to show how the reality, the true connection with which, on the part of an idea, consists in the event or chain of events called verification—how that reality is to be reached by any particular individual, nor what it shall be when it is reached.

HOLT: If I am supposed to define my truth by its application to reality—. There are things I don't suppose to be real things. To test the truth of an idea, say Alice in Wonderland, when am I to use reality, and where, to test the truth of the idea?

JAMES: Test it anywhere. Look for Alice in Wonderland.

HOLT: You will find her, but she is not real.

JAMES: All right; why is that? She is ultimately unreal because she is unsatisfactory to some thinker. As the thinkers are many, and as their experiences are diverse, such realities are always, in themselves, not possessed by us, but independent; that is the assumption of the ordinary definition of truth with which pragmatism starts; he has no standard of truth except his satisfactions. These are the actual marks and signs of truth. All the while, since these satisfactions are so diverse, since they lead to so many of these ideas that claim to be true, we set up a reality that is independent of all these individuals, and an ultimate truth, that shall be the final verdict about reality. The reason each of these others proves to be false is that it proves to be unsatisfactory. If, at last, reality should be defined by all men in a way which was entirely satisfactory, which left nothing out, then the human race would consider—and there is no other person that can come and rectify the human race, except itself, in that respect—it would consider that it had an account of reality that is true.

HOLT: Then in speaking of reality you have not to distinguish against any realm of objects called unreal objects?

JAMES: Absolutely not! Pragmatism holds good, whatever reality may ultimately be defined to be. Whatever truth may ultimately prove to be, as to its *content*, this definition holds good as to what you mean by *true opinions concerning it.*

HOLT: Well, then, reality means very much for philosophy what being means for logic?

JAMES: Yes, undoubtedly.

HOLT: Reality, then, doesn't figure, after all. There is no test in appealing to reality. You can't appeal to anything *but* reality; it is all real. It comes down to the greatest number of satisfactions?

JAMES: Yes, but satisfactions can't get along with each other without correcting each other.

THOMAS: Who should be regarded as the judge of satisfactoriness and unsatisfactoriness?

JAMES: Anybody.

THOMAS: Suppose that two men are in an argument, and one is more or less uneducated, but holds to the evidence of his senses that the earth stands still and that the sun and other heavenly bodies revolve about it. That is a perfectly satisfactory hypothesis, for him. Is it true?

JAMES: Certainly—it is true for him. People fail to get together; truth isn't the same for us all. We can only compare and discuss and try to come to some workable understanding.

THOMAS: Doesn't this make truth a merely personal matter?

JAMES: Why, what else can truth possibly be, when you are debating? Of course truth is a merely personal matter for people who are debating. The only appeal from one thinker is to a better thinker, to a thinker who has better and wider, truer relations with the reality that you are concerned with. How can you get away from thinking that the only truth, the only approach to reality is through thinking? How can any philosopher say that his philosophy enables men to escape from the possibility of difference of opinion?

THOMAS: Not from the possibility of difference of opinion, but from the possibility of one man's saying that his opinion is better than another.

JAMES: One man's opinion is a *great deal better than another.* But who is the superior man? That is the question. Pragmatism doesn't say anything, there, that common sense doesn't know. It is only a presumption that the man who knows a lot about the subject, who has been in close relations with it, probably has the superior opinion.

THOMAS: Then the truth for any given society at any given

stage is made up of the consensus of opinion of those who are qualified to say?

JAMES: Certainly.

THOMAS: We have a right, then, in argument, to bring to bear upon the truth of any individual opinion the light of the truths that these better-qualified men hold?

JAMES: Of course we have. What kind of truth is there which enables the individual who holds it to step out of this general liability of life, to which his fellows are exposed, and to possess a truth which nobody can differ from, in opinion—to possess absolute truth, warranted by the fact that he speaks it? There is nothing of this sort in the field. Certain philosophers say there is. They say their system is true because anything else is self-contradictory. They make truth that which you can't deny without affirming it. But it seems to me the history of mankind shows what a curiously *thin* and vain pretension this is. If men did have a system such as that, it ought to have some persuasive power over others. Take the Hegelian Dialectic. It seems natural to suppose that if there were a method of that kind, which would do for the rationalization of the world—and that is just what science is—one would think that, on some occasion, somewhere, it would have occurred to someone to use it. But science has never, I believe, in any one instance, thought of using the Dialectical Method.

THOMAS: Pragmatism can say, absolutely, that truth is in a flux, can it not?

JAMES: Do you say that? Isn't that an absolutely incorrect opinion about what we concretely mean by any definite truth? Against that the pragmatist urges—and it is the breath of his life to urge— that there *is* an ultimate *reality*, concerning which the *truth* is to be *obtained*, and that all these particular truths that individuals believe in are steps toward. When the pragmatist begins by saying that truth is agreement with reality, *he assumes that there is reality there*. That *reality* stands there; and because your attempts to get into satisfactory relations with it today, on the basis of your small experience, although they are the best attempts for you—because your experience is so small, because your attempts are so finite, does that shut you out from believing that more experience, more satisfactory relations with that reality, may be reached? The reality is indispensable, of course. The pragmatist postulates a world of experience, a world of reality.

THOMAS: The attitude of pragmatism toward history is that, in studying history, we are simply studying the evolutionary development of truth?

JAMES: The history of thought? Yes; isn't the history of philosophy generally thought to be the evolution of truth by all philosophers agreed upon?

The pragmatist view of truth lends such a cordial hand to the evolutionary side of Hegelianism! It lends a very cordial hand to Royce's philosophy—except to the Absolute. And to empiricism. It has no theory of reality of its own; it is simply a set of postulates of what truth would be, as agreement with any reality, at all.

MUSGROVE: Someone asked, last week, at your lecture, whether, if we now believed in Caesar, and so far our verification was satisfactory; and if, at a later time, it were proven that Caesar had not existed—whether that opinion was false when it was held.

JAMES: In the ultimate sense, undoubtedly. A belief means that an opinion is true for the man who holds it. If any number of persons believed in Caesar, that belief was true, for them. It was a truth that counted as such, at the time. But it was not an ultimate truth. We now don't believe in Adam, but the belief in Adam was true enough.

It is unfortunate that truth should be used, now for the temporary belief of men and now for a purely abstract thing that nobody may, perhaps, ever be in possession of. The pragmatist definition of truth applies to both. Since the word, however, is the same, I wish someone here present might invent distinct words for ultimate truth and for temporary belief.—Schiller says 'truth as claimed' and 'truth as validated.' That gives the distinction, and if those adjectives could always be used, it would obviate the trouble. It has given a great deal of trouble to Mr. Schiller and myself, because our critics say that, because we call temporary belief true, therefore we have no right to believe in ultimate truth. It is really, I should say, an uncandid way of pinning on us one thing, the inferior thing; and because we say 'yes' to that, therefore, they say, you are cut off from ultimate truth.

MUSGROVE: One of the most puzzling things in pragmatism is just that you don't know to which kind of truth it is being applied.

JAMES: Yes. Well, they should have different names, to be sure. They *have* different names applied to them, sometimes. They are called truth and opinion, for instance. But what is the use of talking about ultimate truth? It is such a purely abstract ideal that it only serves as a vanishing point. The only truths that men ever have anything practical to do with are those truths that they severally believe in, at any given time. Therefore, so far as pragmatism pretends to be a useful doctrine it establishes its utility far more by applying itself to the truths that concern us than it would by applying itself to an abstract ideal. *There*, in the truths that concern us, there is nothing more to be said than this definition. Can you suggest any way in which we may use the standard and ultimate truth to help us to choose between the beliefs which are candidates for our acceptance now?

MUSGROVE: We use it simply as an ideal. It seems to me that, unless we do use it, we are at sea.

JAMES: Yes, we are at sea, but how does ideal truth help you? How can any truth that isn't real truth help you? The pragmatist is just where everybody else is.

MUSGROVE: So long as I believed that there was an ultimate truth, I should continue to discuss; when I lay that aside I come to the point where, as people say, we agree to disagree, and then discussion would cease.

JAMES: What under the sun is there, in your notion of ultimate truth, that will ever help you to agree or disagree with anyone? Does your belief that there is such a truth help you to choose between an opinion of Dr. Huntington's and an opinion of mine?

Perhaps there is some gentleman here who thinks that the notion of an ultimate truth can be so filled with content that certain opinions can be shown to be more in agreement with ultimate truth than others?

HOLT: I think so. You ask if the ideal of ultimate truth helps in establishing the truth or falsity of any statement. Surely nothing else ever helps. I say there are certain ear-marks whereby a statement is known to be true; otherwise you have to run around and ask all your friends what they think. What do we do? We always say, Is this thing consistent with the other things that I know to be true? Consistency is just the ear-mark of ultimate truth; it is ultimate truth within our inner realm. In scientific investigations we make images, as Hertz says, which represent outer objects. We give them certain properties and relations, and deduce what they will do. In order to find out whether this is true or not, we compare the image with the object. If the object has the same positions and motions as the image, the image is verified—that is, it is verified by its consistency. That is not a personal nor a social standard, at all. It may be interesting that Newton has done such and such a thing at such and such a time; his opinion is of great importance, but it has nothing to do with my verification.

JAMES: Is that verification in the consistency with *ultimate* truth?

HOLT: With the rest of truth.

JAMES: With the rest of *ultimate* truth, or the rest of your own opinions?

HOLT: With the rest of my opinions.

JAMES: There you are, right plump in the middle of pragmatism! In order to be true, an idea must be consistent with other truths that the believer believes in. Your ultimate truth doesn't help you a bit, there. That whole system, you think, must be consistent: this demand for consistency is one of the standard impulses of our nature, and by virtue of it we make a postulate: we say that reality itself shall be consistent with itself. Meanwhile that is a pure postulate. You are speaking entirely from the pragmatist state of mind, only you don't know it.

HOLT: It remains perfectly true that, as the human race goes on, the things people call true are the things most people think to be so. Truth is consistency, it seems to me, and ultimate truth would be, in the end, what the whole body of consistent knowledge is, whatever that may prove to be. You are looking for consistency, not for people's opinions.

JAMES: You couldn't mean anything by 'consistency with ultimate truth' but consistency with reality. You postulate it. Isn't consistency quite indeterminate? You can make A and B consistent by altering them.

HOLT: But it isn't A and B, then.

JAMES: No, and so we have to alter our opinions. We are in an infinite series; the position we are in is determined by other positions, *ad infinitum*, and we can't play fast and loose with the system. I think that if you read my lecture on Truth, you will see that you are speaking from out of the very heart of pragmatism, and that this simple counting of opinions is a gross caricature.

HOLT: It is always true that I may be wrong. Truth comes to me as a sort of flux of men's opinions. I am always limited to my consciousness. Everything, then, is consciousness. We get the same thing about truth; everything is real. I think the pragmatist and the idealist both mix up the distributive and the collective use of 'all.'

JAMES: I don't recognize anything, there, that touches me. The pragmatist, having postulated ultimate truth, then falls back on the practical ways of getting there, just as the man who is on his journey doesn't keep his eye on the thing that is around on the other side of the horizon, but on the steps he makes. So the beliefs that claim to be true become the serious concern of people who are trying to work out a doctrine of truth. The *thinness* of the notion of absolute truth, in philosophy, used without all this other practical interest, is, to me, very surprising. Idealists make the pretension that their notion of absolute reality, of absolute truth, puts them in a far better position, somehow, than the outsider. But the extraordinary *thinness of the results* is astonishing. 'The truth is that, to deny which is absurd, to deny which is self-contradictory. The truth is that which you have to affirm in order to deny.' Golly! If we only had a truth like that!

MUSGROVE: As a matter of usage, would you prefer to define truth as claimed truth?

JAMES: Yes. I think it is a great pity that we can't find a pair of terms. I have said, in a short article which I hope will appear soon, that, since these misunderstandings seem so inveterate, suppose we use the terms 'true' and 'truthful.' Let truth be an inherent virtue that a thing has, and then let the kind of truth that depends upon working be called the truthfulness of the idea. An idea is truthful so far as it puts us in possession of truth. It is true so far as it hits reality, though nobody knows whether it does, or not.

MISS BARNETT: Would a scientific hypothesis be truthful in the same way as the facts the scientist finds out by means of it, even though the scientist himself does not regard it as true in the same way?

JAMES: Yes; Mr. Hertz, whom Mr. Holt quoted, would only make that claim. If consistent, he would regard them as true in the same way.

POPE: Will you tell us a little more explicitly about these satisfactions?

JAMES: There comes in your real logic of science. There is a real study, which the pragmatists haven't developed, a bit. These satisfactions are exceedingly diverse in nature. The chief among them is the satisfaction of consistency.

POPE: Isn't that fundamental to them all?

JAMES: I rather doubt that. I think consistency comes in rather late. The primitive satisfactions are much more practical, material satisfactions.

POPE: Wouldn't it be possible to define those satisfactions as purposes for organization? Consistency is rather abstract, perhaps; I suppose it would come rather late.

JAMES: Yes, but I think certain thinkers have made a deal too much of this; because, if you go back to the original jungle of motives, they are so *little* organized.—That is the sort of thing that Prof. Palmer represents.

POPE: Of course this goal of organization is not conscious, but how else can you define the purposefulness of experience—save in terms of a search for organization? This ideal is present in all experience, of whatever kind?

JAMES: Yes, in that extremely general way, it is; the ideal of organization is pretty explicit and consistent.

POPE: Isn't this purpose for consistency, or organization, the most fundamental purpose, in terms of which, alone, truth can be defined?

JAMES: That would be a definite opinion about what the content of truth consists in. The pragmatist is perfectly willing that that shall be—or that anything else shall be—the ultimate truth; but he isn't willing to assume it, at the beginning. The great satisfactions that truth brings us, the first crude, early satisfactions, the first crude utilities, are when the reality that the truth puts us into connection with is the useful object. So it is very important for us to know the truth about a thing like that. The truth then becomes a substitute, in our mind, for the thing; it has the same consequences for us that the thing has.

But the object may be of no importance to us, practically, and yet it may be useful to us, or it may be satisfactory to know about it, for more refined reasons. There is an infinite number of satisfactions. And all these things must be studied in the psychological part of logic.

POPE: Would you say that truth might be any other satisfaction than organization?

JAMES: Oh yes; unity and organization can be made too much of an idol. Our mind has grown up and organized itself. It has an historic organization, which accounts, certainly, for a great many of its peculiarities, if not all of them. It is partly adapted and partly unadapted to its present experience. Are we certain in advance—of course, we can practically assume in advance, but are we theoretically certain in advance—that reality will be plastic to our categories? In other words are we theoretically certain in advance that reality will prove itself consistent? I think it is a postulate we must make, but, theoretically, no one can warrant its truth. For it is a statement about ultimate reality, which no one can make.

SHEFFER: Doesn't pragmatism undertake to tell us anything about being?

JAMES: I think not. A pragmatist may—I may, for example—but not pragmatism.

SHEFFER: Then how will you choose between your realism and your idealism and other 'isms'?

JAMES: Choose them as true because they are satisfactory.

SHEFFER: Then it does influence you to choose one or the other?

JAMES: Yes; but the method, *per se*, is impartial.

SHEFFER: You are a pragmatist; you will say that this theory of pragmatism must make you a realist, in the end, or an idealist, or some other 'ist'?

JAMES: You can't define truth in any such way as to imply what the truth is, except in some of those 'thin' ways.

POPE: Suppose the idealist can show that ultimate reality is perfect organization of experience; it has certainly given us a method to work by? It has given us an interpretation of experience as a whole, and has shown us what we are trying to accomplish in all aspects of our life?

JAMES: Certainly, and that is the method we adopt. We must work so that our experiences organize themselves into a set of beliefs. That is what we are all doing; we are trying to compare our beliefs with other beliefs. In that process we find that all sorts of things occur: the organization got in the simplest way will be got by ignoring certain things that won't organize; the other way is finding a higher conception which will reconcile these apparent contradictions. The pursuit of organization is the pursuit of satisfactions, really. What you call organization, when you carry it into the concrete field, is exactly what the pragmatist means by pursuing the most satisfactory set of satisfactions.

HUNTINGTON: If it is permissible for an outsider to propose

a question on this occasion, there is a matter that interests me very greatly; and I thought that, as Professor James has come to answer any questions and clear up any difficulties that might arise in the discussion of pragmatism, one might serve as well as another, to put a question.

I don't pretend to know what 'reality' means, in this august assembly. We mathematicians have a habit of seeking for very concrete, accurately specified details. We are baffled by abstractions, abstract speculations; and I am a little bit baffled by the use of the word 'satisfaction.' I would like to have a little more concrete illustration of that word. I will contrast two sorts of satisfaction: the greatest satisfaction I know of, as a mathematical teacher, is that of being perfectly sure I am right, and being able to make others know that I am right. I could never be so about Caesar, for instance; but there are certain things about which I am perfectly sure I can convince anybody else who is willing to listen—unless, of course, I make some bull blunder, but we can leave that out, in supposing. The nature of these things doesn't connect up in my mind, very well, with what you call satisfactions. Thus, I know that, if certain things are true, certain other things will follow. Logical deduction seems to me to be something which I *watch*; I follow the logical activity of these propositions, wherever it may lead. They are there, absolutely in themselves. What is the relation which the pragmatist word 'satisfaction' has toward the belief in reality of that logically-deductive kind?

JAMES: That is a separate realm of realities, isn't it? It is an independent realm?

HUNTINGTON: Yes, no doubt.

JAMES: It is a realm of realities, by itself. You have a certain opinion, there. We will allow that it is a true opinion. So far that is only an idea in your mind, which, as yet, isn't verified; it doesn't connect with reality, yet; it is only your opinion. If it is true, it will be able to lead you up to reality. It is verified by certain figures, certain auxiliary lines you draw—either on the blackboard or in imagination—and then by directly comparing the realities. These auxiliary lines, which are the workings of your idea, lead you to perceive that this opinion about, say, the interior angles of a triangle, is true. You see the two triangles there before your eyes. The satisfaction now consists in having been led up to the reality itself. Through these workings, it has led you to a true idea of the reality.

I consider that these eternal objects and relations are, in our intellectual life, what sensible objects are in our sensible life. It is true if it so works as to lead you to verification, which, in this case, consists in direct inspection, comparison. The principle of pragmatism works absolutely the same way in the intellectual world as it does in the physical world.

HUNTINGTON: You stated the case, there, very clearly, and I agree with what you said. The geometrical illustration, though, brings in an ideal object of some sort, which isn't the case, for instance, in applied mathematics. Applied mathematics doesn't deal with ideal objects any more than it deals with physical objects. It doesn't deal with eternal triangles, any more than it deals with Memorial Hall. The kind of mathematics I am speaking about now, would be better described as logic, in which we don't have any concrete objects, ideal or physical, before our eyes, or minds, at all, simply an empty proposition: If such and such a thing is true, then other things are true. Algebraic illustrations, therefore, are better, in this case, than geometrical ones. The *deduction* is the thing the validity of which I am certain I can convince you of. How does that assurance connect up with your other satisfactions?

JAMES: Isn't there a relation, there, of identity or difference?

HUNTINGTON: No, I should think there was no such relation.

JAMES: Isn't 'is' a relation? Give a simple example of the kind of proposition whose truth—. You say your propositions are established, verified, by demonstrations all similar to this, are they not? You have to have demonstrations, verbally exhibited?

HUNTINGTON: The demonstration always consists in starting from the set of fundamental propositions, and watching them develop. And you will come out with a much more complicated proposition. You don't get that proposition first, but watch it grow.

JAMES: What is the relation of what grows out of it and what is already in it?

HUNTINGTON: I don't know.

JAMES: Aren't you in the presence of a reality whose latent properties—look what occurs when you look at an object and after a while you see that there is something in it that you don't see at first. It is the reality which you directly inspect; for the inspection is really inspection of relations, there. There is no verification about it. It is inspection.

HUNTINGTON: Then what is the satisfaction? Pure curiosity?

JAMES: Curiosity partly; elegance; aesthetic appreciation. There are a good many satisfactions there, I should say.

MISS DAVIS: Why is it that it seems to us as if truth were the thing we can't do without? It seems like a step backward when you reduce truth to a mere satisfaction.

JAMES: You admit that the truths are thus connected with particular satisfactions?

MISS DAVIS: No; I don't seem to accept the expression, that I understand to be the expression of pragmatism, that one thinks it true because one is satisfied.

JAMES: We do a great many things because the doing satisfies us, without doing them for the sake of the satisfaction. There are all sorts of things which you pursue, the result of which pursuit is to give you satisfaction. Almost everything that we pursue takes the form, in our mind, of an absolute goal, and yet, if we examine the concrete thing, we find that we pursue so long as satisfaction is not reached, and we stop when satisfaction is reached, even though someone standing by may think we have not reached the goal.

It is just so with truth. The satisfaction has to figure in the definition of truth. It is not a psychological factor realized by the person. Truth at any time is that quality in a belief, which is satisfactory. Truth is the quality which satisfactory beliefs possess—truthfulness we will call it, if you like. Now, meanwhile you ask the person why he is pursuing that object, and he won't say, for the sake of satisfaction; yet that *is* why. No mother thinks she nurses her baby for the sake of the satisfaction; she nurses it because it is just the thing to do with it; because it ought to be nursed, of all things in the world. But she would stop nursing it the moment nursing it ceased to be satisfactory. If it wasn't a satisfaction, she would have nothing more to do with the baby; she would throw it into the fire. When you say that the true belief is the satisfactory belief, you are accused, immediately, of saying that the true belief is a belief in the satisfaction. It is a belief in the *object,* but it is only belief in *that* object, which is satisfactory; a belief in any other object is not satisfactory. Therefore I say that the true belief is the satisfactory belief. It isn't fair to say that therefore the satisfactory belief is a belief in satisfaction. It is the belief in the thing that is satisfactory, and if you don't believe in that thing, it is not satisfactory. The satisfaction runs alongside of the belief. The pragmatist is not making out that the satisfaction is the thing believed in.

MISS DAVIS: Does pragmatism say that, in the case of two objects, of belief, in case we knew, on theoretical ground, that there is no difference between them, that we should be able to believe in one to the exclusion of the other, provided they couldn't both be believed in, and provided that one would be more satisfactory for other reasons? That I don't understand. I can't get that point of view. It seems to me that wouldn't alter our belief in regard to the object, if it be a good thing to have one truth rather than the other.

JAMES: That is a belief about goodness, not about the existence of the object.

MISS DAVIS: I understood it was a belief in the existence of the object.

JAMES: Why, no; there are a lot of beliefs of this sort, of course, which really don't depend, for their usefulness, on the existence of the object. And they have their truth—or their truthfulness—for the people that believe them; they are good beliefs for them to have; and yet they have very little connection, some of them, probably, with ultimate reality. It doesn't follow that, because that kind of truth exists, the pragmatist admits no other kind. *Satisfaction is indispensable, for truth, but it isn't sufficient.* Between the indispensable and the sufficient, there is a wide chasm. It is indispensable, for a belief to be true, that it should be satisfactory, but it isn't sufficient.

CALDWELL: What would you say about propositions that refer to the future? Can a proposition be true before it is verified?

JAMES: Yes, in the same sense that you are mortal now. The truth is constituted by its verifiability, not by the act of verification. That would be like saying that a man ceases to be married as soon as the wedding ceremony is over.

CALDWELL: Then you can say that a thing is true without regard to its verification?

JAMES: Yes; we do that in the case of mortality and other things. We deal with things by their classes. We assume that the kind of thing that has been verified in other instances can be verified in this instance.

HUNTINGTON: The kind of mathematical truth I spoke of a moment ago doesn't seem to be either verified or verifiable. What is the pragmatic attitude toward that kind of opinion?

JAMES: You are in direct contact with the reality, there. In intuition you possess the reality; you can't lead up to it, therefore; well, leading up to reality is just what verification means.

Royce's argument for the existence of God is based on something like the pragmatist conception. He applies himself sincerely to a hypothesis. Royce is the only one who has shown any sense of there being any problem there, at all. Royce is the only absolute idealist I know of who sees any problem of truth. The other critics of pragmatism have nothing but the word 'truth' to offer. The idea is born true. With nothing to propose as an alternative, they proceed to annihilate this account.

I think, however, that things are changing; that the discussion has led to the elimination of misunderstandings. I think the fact is beginning to be understood, a little, that we have said nothing but to emphasize, a little, facts which everybody knew.

Notes

Appendixes

A Note on the Editorial Method

Textual Apparatus

Index

Notes

All of the manuscripts printed in the present volume are housed in the Houghton Library of Harvard University and belong to the James Collection. Their main call number is 'bMS AM 1092.9'; individual manuscripts are further identified by four-digit numbers. Throughout, it is only the latter that are indicated; the former is understood.

Many books from James's library are in Houghton; most of these are identified by call numbers that begin with either 'WJ' or 'AC'. Other books from his library are in Harvard's Widener Library and elsewhere, and in such cases their location is stated. Still others were sold and have not been located. However, Ralph Barton Perry made a list of the books from James's library, noting markings and annotations; this unpublished list may be consulted at Houghton. Notice should be taken of the fact that the Collection is constantly changing. Widener has discarded many books from James's library, others have been moved out of Widener into Houghton, still others have been found or lost. Some manuscripts have been reclassified and letters have been added. The Collection will no doubt continue to change.

In the text, James mentions the names of various students. No identification for these students is provided in the notes, but their full names are given in the index when they could be ascertained with reasonable confidence from Harvard directories.

Since all of James's published works have appeared in the present edition, all references to them are to this edition without further notice.

3.3 Every] James's early teaching at Harvard fell within the Department of Natural History, where he was primarily responsible for a course on the "Comparative Anatomy and Physiology of Vertebrates." But since physiology took time and energy away from mental science, James viewed his position as temporary—a pause until something more in line with his interests should turn up. Around April 1877 he informed Charles William Eliot, president of Harvard, that he would like to be considered a candidate for the first "philosophical vacancy that should occur here." But because nothing at Harvard was definite, in a letter dated April 23, 1877, James also informed Daniel Coit Gilman, president of Johns Hopkins University in Baltimore, of his availability. Apart from considerations of income, the lectures that James gave at Johns Hopkins in February 1878 were motivated by a desire to present himself as a candidate for a permanent appointment. It is difficult to know how sincere James was in his dealings with Gilman. Possibly he was using the Johns Hopkins threat to put pressure on the Harvard authorities, a conclusion that Gilman himself eventually reached.

James's very complicated negotiations with Gilman are recorded in his letters to the latter preserved among the Gilman Papers at Johns Hopkins. These letters have been published by Jackson I. Cope, "William James's Correspondence with Daniel Coit Gilman, 1877–1881," *Journal of the History of Ideas*, 12 (October 1951), 609–627. Cope gives much of the background of the negotiations. Copies of some ten letters from Gilman to James are preserved at Johns Hopkins, in Letter Books 3 and 4, Special Collections. Most of these are not published by Cope and seem not to have been known by him.

The earliest surviving reference to the lectures occurs in a letter to Gilman dated December 30, 1877. James writes:

> I have seen President Eliot, & can now say that it will be entirely convenient to me to spend a fortnight, in the latter half of February, in Baltimore & give any number of lectures within ten, if the University authorities should think it worth while to make arrangements for so short a course.
>
> The subject would be in a general way expository & critical of recent speculations concerning the connection of mind & body.

Gilman replied on January 4, 1878, with a definite offer. James's acceptance is dated January 7:

> I have the honor to acknowledge the receipt of your letter of January 4th, inviting me, on the part of the Executive Committee of your University, to give ten lectures in February. I will gladly do so, beginning, probably, on February eleventh.
>
> You have omitted to enclose one of the printed announcements which you speak of, so I do not know how detailed mine ought to be.
>
> Meanwhile, I suggest as a title for the course, "The Brain & the Senses; and their Relation to Intelligence."
>
> As regards the audiences I will try to make them popular without being trite, so that they may interest almost any educated person.
>
> You make no mention of compensation, but, I suppose, that was accidental.

Gilman remedied some of his oversights on January 11. The lectures would begin on February 11th and end on the 22nd. Payment would be $500. James replied on January 14:

> I thank you for your note of the 11th and for the specimen announcements that preceded it. I enclose herewith an announcement drawn up after their pattern; but I confess the brief enumeration of topics has such an outlandish and pretentious sound that unless you insist on specification, I should rather confine myself simply to saying that as the shortness of the course requires selection only such points shall be treated as are either novel or important.

No copy of an announcement was found either at Johns Hopkins or at Harvard; nor were any descriptions of the lectures found in either Johns Hopkins publications or Baltimore newspapers. Thus the titles and contents of the lectures as delivered remain unknown. In *The Thought and Character of William James*, 2 vols. (Boston: Little, Brown, 1935), II, 27, Ralph Barton Perry quotes the following description of the last of the Baltimore lectures provided by Francis J. Child in a letter to James Russell Lowell: "I had William James with me a fortnight in Baltimore. He gave ten lectures on the brain as the organ of the mind, and made a decided impression. I heard the last, in which he offered reasons for not accepting the theory that we are automatons unreservedly."

According to the *Fourth Annual Report of the Johns Hopkins University*, the announced title of the lectures was "The Senses and the Brain and Their Relation to Thought." The average attendance is given as 62.

In the James Collection, no attempt is made to distinguish between manuscripts related to the Johns Hopkins lectures and those related to the similar Lowell lectures. Of the latter, there survives an outline of the six lectures (#4397), with internal references that leave no doubt that these are the Lowell lectures. There are also fragmentary drafts that closely correspond with the outline. Furthermore, the bulk of these manuscripts is in the hand of James's wife, Alice. Since their wedding took place on July 10, 1878, the Baltimore lectures precede the marriage, while the Lowell lectures follow it. The manuscripts grouped here as the Johns Hopkins lectures are in James's own hand; the title "Baltimore lectures" appears on one verso. Furthermore, the problem of the perception of space so prominent in these manuscripts fits the general subject of the Baltimore lectures, dealing as they do with the senses. The topic is not prominent in the Lowell outlines. Thus, the distinction between the Baltimore and the Lowell manuscripts is reasonably firm.

In the summer of 1878 James wrote "The Spatial Quale," reprinted in *Essays in Psychology*. But there is little risk of confusion between this paper and the Baltimore material. For one thing, "The Spatial Quale" is a response to an essay that appeared in July 1878 and is very polemical. Furthermore, James says that he dictated that paper to his wife (*Essays in Psychology*, p. 398). Thus, both handwriting and contents make it clear that the discussions of the perception of space are correctly included among the Baltimore lectures and are not related to the essay.

4.13   Romanes] George John Romanes (1848–1894), Canadian-born naturalist.

4.22   Exner] Sigmund Exner (1846–1926), Austrian physiologist. For possible references see *The Principles of Psychology*, pp. 578, 811.

4.23   Vierordt's] Karl von Vierordt (1818–1884), German physician. For the reference see *Principles*, p. 811.

4.28   H.] Hermann Ludwig Ferdinand von Helmholtz (1821–1894), German physiologist and physicist, *On the Sensations of Tone as a Physiological Basis for the Theory of Music*, trans. Alexander J. Ellis (London: Longmans, Green, 1875).

4.29   Spencer] For the references to both Spencer and Taine see *Principles*, pp. 154–156, 162n.

5.24   ½ can.] Semicircular canals.

6.3   H.] For the reference to Helmholtz see *Principles*, pp. 274, 666.

6.21   Schattenfigur] See note to 15.9.

6.34   H's] For the reference see *Principles*, p. 665.

7.1 Spencer] James could be claiming that the failure of colors to mix disproves Spencer's general theory of the composition of mental states. For a possible reference see *Principles*, pp. 154–156.

7.1 Taine] For a possible reference to Taine see *Principles*, note to 162.31.

7.21 Jeffries] Benjamin Joy Jeffries (1833–1915), American ophthalmologist. James could be referring to the thaumatrope described by Jeffries in *Proceedings of the Boston Society of Natural History*, 12 (1869), 94–96.

7.23 Helmholtz] For references to Helmholtz see *Principles*, pp. 867, 897–898, and elsewhere.

7.23 Wundt] For references to Wundt see *Principles*, pp. 868, 906–907, 1110, and elsewhere.

7.27 Graefe's] James could have in mind the work of Alfred Karl Graefe (1830–1899) on the effects of paresis on the innervation of the eyes; see *Principles*, pp. 1117–18. But there are others with similar names with whose work James was familiar.

7.28 Rogers'] William Barton Rogers (1804–1882), American naturalist. For a possible reference see *Essays in Psychology*, note to 47.15.

8.7 Dove] Heinrich Wilhelm Dove (1803–1879), German physicist. Dove describes his work involving vision and electric sparks in "Über Stereoskopie," *Annalen der Physik und Chemie*, 110 (1860), 494–498.

8.7 Donders'] Franciscus Cornelis Donders (1818–1889), Dutch ophthalmologist; for the reference see *Principles*, p. 863.

8.15 Wundt's] For a possible reference see *Principles*, p. 675.

8.19 Wundt] For possible references see *Essays in Psychology*, note to 74.35.

8.34 Crossed] For this illusion see *Principles*, pp. 731–732.

8.36 Wundt] For fuller treatments of Wundt and Helmholtz see *Essays in Psychology*, p. 80, and *Principles*, pp. 906–910.

15.9 Purkinje's] Johannes Evangelista Purkinje (1787–1869), Czechoslovakian physiologist. Purkinje observed shadows cast by blood vessels on the retina. In *Principles*, p. 489, James quotes Helmholtz on Purkinje's discovery.

15.19 Deny] The views of most of the writers mentioned in the diagram are discussed in "The Spatial Quale," reprinted in *Essays in Psychology*, and throughout *Principles*.

15.19 Mill] John Stuart Mill.

15.31 Hering] Ewald Hering (1834–1918), German physiologist.

15.33 Müller] Johannes Müller (1801–1858), German physiologist. James does not usually cite him in connection with problems of the perception of space.

15.38 Bailey] Samuel Bailey (1791–1870), British economist and philosopher.

15.38 Stumpf] Carl Stumpf (1848–1936), German psychologist.

16.26   Lecture] After the February 1878 lectures James continued negotiations with Gilman for future courses at Johns Hopkins, while at the same time offering the material to the Lowell Institute and driving Gilman to despair. A memo by Gilman preserved in the Gilman Papers at Johns Hopkins tells the whole story:

1877 Ap. 23. Offers himself as Professor
This leads to talk in Newport
Dec. 30— agrees to lecture &
1878 April 22 agrees to lecture in Feb. 1879
May 4 proposes 1880
May 15 requests 1879
May 29 telegraphs *stop*
1879 asks 1880
Sept 19 tel. asking 79
    23 *de permanence*
Oct 8 gives up 79
[illegible] 1880

In a letter to Gilman dated May 4, 1878, James asks that his proposed 1879 lectures be postponed to 1880 and that Gilman send him endorsements of the 1878 lectures for use in support of his Lowell application. On May 15, James informs Gilman that it is too late to apply for a Lowell course in 1878. But on May 30, James notifies Gilman that he has secured a Lowell appointment as a replacement for one of the original appointees who has withdrawn.

During this period Augustus Lowell was serving as trustee of the Lowell Institute, and James's letters to him are preserved in the Lowell Institute Papers at Houghton. No call numbers have as yet been assigned to this collection. On May 19, 1878, James sent Lowell testimonials supporting his application and in his covering letter notes:

The course I propose is on the subject to which I have given most attention—the Senses and the Brain and their relation to the Mind. I feel confident of my ability to make the course both entertaining to the many by its abundance of new facts and illustrations, and instructive to the few by its theoretic conclusions. I think I can safely say that I am neither a materialistic partisan nor a spiritualistic bigot.

James wanted twelve lectures, but Lowell offered only six. This forced James to omit the material on sense perception used in Baltimore and to restrict his topic to "The Brain & the Mind." This is the sense of James's letter to Lowell of May 30, in which he still indicates his hopes for twelve lectures if another appointee should retire.

The remainder of the correspondence has nothing to do with the present manuscript but is important as a record of James's intellectual and financial dreams of the period. His letter to Lowell of February 27, 1879, indicates that he applied for a course in 1879 to be titled the "Senses and the Mind," intending to use the Baltimore material on sense perception not used in 1878. The difficulty, James informs Lowell, is that James's course is too much like the one proposed by Granville Stanley Hall. Thus, should Lowell prefer, James would lecture on "The Theory of Evolution as Applied to Mind," a criticism of Herbert Spencer. An interesting aside in this letter involves the question of religious orthodoxy. James writes: "And recollecting the question you asked me last spring, I may say their tendency will be decidedly 'conservative.' " On February

22, 1880, James reminds Lowell that he is still a candidate for a course on "The Senses and the Intellect," for the "sake of my butcher's and baker's bills." Apparently, nothing came of these applications, and James dropped negotiations with the Lowell Institute until 1896 when he proposed the exceptional mental states lectures.

According to the *Boston Evening Transcript* James began his lectures on "The Brain and the Mind" on Tuesday, October 15, 1878, at 7:30 P.M. He lectured on October 18, 22, 25, and 29. The course was concluded on November 1. On October 23, p. 1, the *Transcript* reports that James gave the third of his Lowell lectures,

> showing how animals in full possession of their nervous systems act from sentiment or considerations of good and evil, as distinguished from the lower animals or those in which a part of the brain is no longer operative— with a psychological digression on the nature and sources of these considerations. He spoke in a familiar way of the manner in which emotions, sentiment, thought and will, developing into action, are produced in the brain, and of the theory, which he would explain and defend in a subsequent lecture, that the cerebral hemisphere, as an organ of memory, consisted of an infinite number of cells or compartments, in which an infinite number of impressions or experiences might be stored away, infinitely permanent, and called into mental life and action by an access of mental energy.

Reports of the other five lectures were not found in the *Transcript*.

Internal evidence indicates that James first wrote drafts of the lectures and then prepared the outline used in the delivery. Only fragments of the former have survived, whereas the outline has remained pretty much intact. Given James's habits, the lost drafts probably were used in other projects. It is unlikely that the surviving drafts go back to the Baltimore lectures because the manuscripts are in Alice's hand. This fact suggests that the drafts were dictated shortly after their marriage in July 1878.

James showed slides during the Lowell lectures; his list of the slides appears in the present volume.

16.33　Pop.] The *Popular Science Monthly*, a major supporter of Herbert Spencer.

17.22　eff^t] Efferent and afferent.

17.25　Flint] Austin Flint (1836–1915), American physician and physiologist.

17.26　size] James appears to be referring to the table of brain-sizes on p. 35.

17.28　Meynert's] Theodor Meynert (1833–1892), psychiatrist, active in Austria. For works by Meynert from James's library see *Principles*, note to 27.8.

17.32　Luys] Jules Luys (1828–1897), French anatomist and physician. For works from James's library see *Principles*, note to 72.23; James's review of Luys is reprinted in *Essays, Comments, and Reviews*. The list of slides James used for the course appears on pp. 34–35.

17.33　Gerlach's] Joseph von Gerlach (1820–1896), German anatomist.

17.33　Schmidt] Perhaps Henry D. Schmidt (1823–1888), American physician.

17.34 Henle's] Jakob (Friedrich Gustav Jakob) Henle (1809–1885), German anatomist.

18.28 Robin] Charles Philippe Robin (1821–1885), French anatomist.

18.35 Lewes] George Henry Lewes (1817–1878), English philosopher and writer. For Lewes's view see *Principles*, p. 22.

19.4 Grow] The phrase is borrowed from William Benjamin Carpenter; see *Principles*, p. 117.

19.9 instincts] In *Principles*, pp. 1022–57, James takes a different view of human instincts.

19.10 Spalding's] Douglas Alexander Spalding (c.1840–1877), British naturalist. For a possible reference see *Principles*, p. 1014.

19.15 R.V.W] See p. 37.

19.18 Carpenter] William Benjamin Carpenter (1813–1885), British physiologist; for the text see *Principles*, pp. 114–117.

21.7 Flourens] Jean Pierre Marie Flourens (1794–1867), French physiologist, usually connected with a holistic view of brain function; see *Principles*, p. 42.

21.7 Hitzig] Eduard Hitzig (1838–1907), German psychiatrist. For James's view of his work see *Principles*, p. 42.

21.7 Ferrier] David Ferrier (1843–1928), British physician and neurologist. In *Principles* Ferrier is one of James's major sources for the localizationist theory of brain function.

21.12 Munk] Hermann Munk (1839–1912), German physiologist. In *Principles* Munk is presented as a localizationist whose findings differed from those of Ferrier. They agreed that a given region of the brain performs a distinct function, but disagreed as to what that function is.

21.18 Goltz's] Friedrich Leopold Goltz (1834–1902), German physiologist. In *Principles* Goltz is the major source of the holistic view of brain function.

21.24 Aphasia] Throughout *Principles* aphasia is presented as important evidence in favor of localizationism.

22.40 B. Séquard] Charles Édouard Brown-Séquard (1817–1894), Mauritian physiologist. Brown-Séquard suggested that the loss of function may be due to inhibition resulting from the wound rather than to the removal of a region.

23.1 H.J.] John Hughlings Jackson; see p. 43.

23.12 Maudsley] Henry Maudsley (1835–1918), British physiologist and psychologist. For James's criticism of Maudsley on memory see *Principles*, pp. 617–618.

23.16 Tyndall] John Tyndall (1820–1893), British physicist, *Fragments of Science for Unscientific People* (London: Longmans, Green, 1871).

23.16 Huxley] Thomas Henry Huxley (1825–1895), English biologist and essayist. James often cites Huxley's "On the Hypothesis that Animals Are Automata, and Its History" (1874).

24.30 Clifford] William Kingdon Clifford (1845–1879), British mathematician and philosopher. For Clifford's view see *Principles*, pp. 135–136. #4401 contains several pages of quotations from Clifford's *Lectures and Essays*, ed. Leslie Stephen and Frederick Pollock, 2 vols. (London: Macmillan, 1879), II, 57, 164, on the relations between brain and mind. These quotations are not printed in the present edition.

25.1 Read] This appears to be a reference to a draft no longer extant. It is likely that James used some of the Lowell drafts in "Are We Automata?" (1879) and that he has in mind the discussion reprinted in *Essays in Psychology*, pp. 39–40.

26.10 Chladnis] Ernst Florens Friedrich Chladni (1756–1827), German physicist. For James's meaning see *Essays in Psychology*, p. 52.

26.11 Read] This appears to be a reference to a draft no longer extant. It is likely that the material appears in "Are We Automata?", *Essays in Psychology*, pp. 52–54.

27.20 Read] The material probably appears in "Are We Automata?", *Essays in Psychology*, pp. 46–50.

27.30 Genius] For the sentence see *Essays in Psychology*, p. 50.

28.20 Allen] Charles Grant Blairfindie Allen (1848–1899), Canadian-born naturalist and writer. For James's meaning see *Essays in Psychology*, p. 56.

34.15 Maudsley's] For similar remarks on introspection see *Essays, Comments, and Reviews*, pp. 336–337; for a reference to Maudsley on introspection see *Essays in Psychology*, note to 142.2.

34.34 Flechsig] Paul Emil Flechsig (1847–1929), German physiologist and psychiatrist.

34.35 Lebon] Not identified.

35.9 Cuvier] Georges Cuvier (1769–1832), French naturalist.

35.10 Abercrombie] John Abercrombie (1780–1844), Scottish physician.

35.12 Ruloff] Edward Howard Ruloff (1819–1871), convicted murderer.

35.15 Spurzheim] Johann Kaspar Spurzheim (1776–1832), German phrenologist.

35.18 Webster] Daniel Webster (1782–1852), American statesman and orator.

37.2 Spalding's] For the text see *Principles*, p. 1025.

37.25 Winkle] In *Principles*, p. 131, James mentions a similar excuse offered by Rip Van Winkle as played by Joseph Jefferson (1829–1905), American actor. For a fuller version of the excuse see *Principles*, note to 131.3.

41.39 *Broca*] Pierre Paul Broca (1824–1880), French physician and anthropologist. For a fuller discussion of Broca and aphasia see *Principles*, pp. 49–50.

43.1 Jackson] John Hughlings Jackson (1835–1911), British neurologist. For the reference see *Essays in Psychology*, note to 84.21.

43.10 Physiological] James lectured before the Harvard Total Abstinence League on the evening of October 26, 1886, at Sever Hall. The Harvard *Daily Crimson* carried a brief report of the lecture on October 27. This report is reprinted as Appendix I in the present volume. James dealt with the subject of alcohol in his course on "Physiology and Hygiene" in the late 1870s; see *Essays, Comments, and Reviews*, pp. 19–21, and note to 19.18.

43.21 Hammond's] William Alexander Hammond (1828–1900), American physician, published several papers on the effects of alcohol, but nothing fitting James's reference was found.

43.22 Edinb.] An unsigned review article on "The Physiological Influence of Alcohol," *Edinburgh Review*, 142 (July 1875), 145–173; reprinted in *Littel's Living Age*.

44.10 Parkes'] Edmund Alexander Parkes (1819–1876), British physician, *A Manual of Practical Hygiene*, 5th ed., ed. F. S. B. François de Chaumont (London: J. & A. Churchill, 1878). For Parkes's text see *Essays, Comments, and Reviews*, note to 20.31.

44.15 Parkes's] P. 298.

44.21 Insurance] Parkes, p. 292n.

44.27 O.W.H.] Oliver Wendell Holmes (1809–1894), American physician and author.

44.34 *Jaillet*] Jules Jaillet (b.1852), French physician, *De l'alcool: sa combustion, son action physiologique, son antidote* (Paris: Octave Doin, 1884).

45.5 Smith] Edward Smith (1819–1874), British physician and medical writer, *Foods* (New York: D. Appleton, 1873).

45.9 Parkes] Edmund Alexander Parkes and Cyprian Wollowicz, physician, "Experiments on the Effect of Alcohol (Ethyl Alcohol) on the Human Body," *Proceedings of the Royal Society of London*, 18 (1870), 362–393. The number of heart-beats per day was 106,000 when the subject was given no alcohol; on a day when the subject was given 8 ounces, his heart beat 25,488 more times. On a normal day, the heart does work equal to "122 tons lifted one foot." Alcohol caused it to do additional work equivalent to 24 tons.

45.36 Parkes] On p. 305n Parkes presents evidence showing that alcohol does not strengthen soldiers as is alleged, but rather weakens discipline and leads to crime.

46.5 Ridge] Axel Carl Johan Gustafson (b.1849), Swedish-born reformer, *The Foundation of Death: A Study of the Drink-Question*, 3rd ed. (Boston: Ginn, Heath, & Company, 1885), pp. 116–118, quotes from a paper in the *Medical Temperance Journal* by John James Ridge (1847–1908), British temperance writer. In the first series of experiments, using touch alone subjects were required to place a dot exactly midway between two other dots. Failure was measured by degrees. The sum of the averages for five abstainers was 115 degrees; for the five subjects given two drachms of alcohol each, 189.8 degrees. The other experiments also tested sensitivity without and with alcohol. The doses varied somewhat.

46.13   Edinb.] See note to 43.22.

46.14   Parkes] Pp. 277–308, the section on alcoholic beverages.

46.15   Experiments] Edmund Alexander Parkes, "On the Influence of Brandy on the Bodily Temperature, the Pulse, and the Respirations of Healthy Men," *Proceedings of the Royal Society of London*, 22 (1874), 172–190.

46.17   Brunton] Thomas Lauder Brunton (1844–1916), British physician and pharmacologist, *A Text-Book of Pharmacology, Therapeutics and Materia Medica*, adapted to the United States Pharmacopœia by Francis H. Williams (Philadelphia: Lea Brothers, 1885). Alcohol is discussed on pp. 647–657.

46.18   Merriman] Daniel Merriman (1838–1912), American clergyman, "A Sober View of Abstinence from Intoxicating Stimulants," *Bibliotheca Sacra*, 38 (October 1881), 707–759.

46.21   Contemp.] James Paget (1814–1899), British surgeon, Thomas Lauder Brunton, Albert James Bernays (1823–1892), British chemist, "The Alcohol Question," *Contemporary Review*, 33 (November 1878), 683–706.

46.25   have] James lectured before the Harvard Total Abstinence League at 7:30 in the evening of January 22, 1895. The *Harvard Crimson* carried a brief report of the lecture on January 23. This report is reprinted as Appendix II in the present volume. For additional information on James's view of alcohol see Perry, II, 301–302.

46.27   Matthew] Matthew Arnold (1822–1888), English poet and critic, in *Literature and Dogma* writes that "conduct is three-fourths of our life and its largest concern" (*Literature and Dogma*, in *Dissent and Dogma*, ed. R. H. Super [Ann Arbor: The University of Michigan Press, c1968], p. 180).

47.10   Marryat's] Frederick Marryat (1792–1848), British naval officer and novelist.

47.18   Die] Johann Wolfgang von Goethe, from the poem "Hoch auf dem alten Turme," *Goethes Werke*, ed. Erich Trunz, 5th ed., I (Hamburg: Wegner, 1958), 81.

47.32   litres] In this account the quantity of beer seems excessive for the number of guests, while on p. 52, it seems too modest. The correct figure is unknown since James's source has not been located.

48.14   Berenson] Bernhard Berenson (1865–1959), Lithuanian-born art critic, a student at Harvard.

48.34   Anstie] Francis Edmund Anstie (1833–1874), British physician. For Anstie's view see *Essays, Comments, and Reviews*, p. 20.

48.34   Binz] In the manuscript the name is almost illegible. James could be referring to Karl Binz (1832–1913), German chemist, whose work is sometimes cited in the literature on alcohol used by James.

48.34   Lallemand] Ludger Lallemand (1820–1862), French physician, Maurice Constantin Perrin (1826–1889), French surgeon, and J.-L.-P. Duroy, French pharmacologist, *Du rôle de l'alcool et des anesthésiques dans l'organisme: recherches expérimentales* (Paris: F. Chamerot, 1860).

48.37 (Schulinus)] Hugo Schulinus, physician associated with the University of Tartu, "Untersuchungen über die Vertheilung des Weingeistes im thierischen Organismus," *Archiv der Heilkunde*, 7 (1866), 97–128.

49.6 (Glusinsky)] C. Anton Gluziński, Polish physician, "Über den Einfluss des Alkohols auf die Function des menschlichen Magens," *Deutsches Archiv für klinische Medicin*, 39 (1886), 405–430.

49.11 (Martin)] Henry Newell Martin (1848–1896), Irish-born biologist, active in the United States, and Lewis T. Stevens, "The Action of Ethyl Alcohol upon the Dog's Heart," *Memoirs from the Biological Laboratory of the Johns Hopkins University*, 3 (1895), 69–85 (first published in 1883).

49.16 Richardson's] Benjamin Ward Richardson (1828–1896), British physician and temperance lecturer, "The Action of Alcohol on the Mind," included in *Ten Lectures on Alcohol* (New York: National Temperance Society and Publication House, 1881).

49.39 Warren] Joseph Weatherhead Warren (1849–1916), American physician, "Alcohol Again: A Consideration of Recent Misstatements of Its Physiological Action," *Boston Medical and Surgical Journal*, 117 (July 7, 1887), 1–6; (July 14), 25–29.

50.39 Parkes] *A Manual*, p. 298.

51.28 Leland's] Charles Godfrey Leland (1824–1903), American author, *Sunshine in Thought* (New York: Charles T. Evans, 1862).

51.34 Bunge] Gustav von Bunge (1844–1920), Estonian-born physiological chemist, active in Switzerland, *Die Alkoholfrage*. James is known to have owned a copy of this pamphlet (Basel, 1894). The edition consulted for the present notes, 5th ed. (Zürich: Verlag des Vereins zur Bekämpfung des Alkoholgenusses, 1890), has slightly different paging from that owned by James. James is referring to a section titled "Alcohol an Enemy to True Pleasure."

53.33 oz.] Parkes, *A Manual*, p. 324.

53.40 Genius] James at this time was interested in theories that genius is a kind of degeneration. See the lectures on exceptional mental states in the present volume.

54.25 Ami] See p. 64.

55.32 Neurasthenia] In the 1890s James read extensively in abnormal psychology and published numerous reviews (reprinted in *Essays, Comments, and Reviews*). He used the material in at least three courses of public lectures, a lecture before the New York Neurological Society, and four Harvard courses. A report of the lecture in New York, together with James's letter explaining his view of demon possession, is included in *Essays, Comments, and Reviews*. No material connected with the Harvard courses survives. In 1893–1894 James gave Philosophy 20b: Psychological Seminary on "Questions in Mental Pathology." The same course was given in 1894–1895 on "Questions in Mental Pathology, embracing a review of the principal forms of abnormal or exceptional mental life." In 1896–1897 he offered Philosophy 15: Abnormal Psychology, "A study of the various types of insanity, and of recent investigations into exceptional mental phenomena," a half-year course using *The Pathology of Mind* (1880) by Henry Maudsley as a text. In 1898–1899 he taught Philosophy 20b: Psychological Seminary, over the full year, described in much the same way as Philosophy 15. For the seminary, three visits to asylums and two reports were required. In 1898–1899 Philosophy 20b was offered at Radcliffe, but was not given.

Notes related to three different courses of public lectures survive and are here published as No. 5.

The earliest of the public courses is known only from a printed announcement which James apparently enclosed in a letter to his brother Henry, February 11, 1895 (#2751), with the remark on the announcement that "this is what I'm sunk to. $50 a 'talk.' " He was to give "Three Talks on Recent Investigations into Abnormal Mental States and Types of Character. Feb. 12.—The Doctrine of Degeneration. Feb. 19.—The Subliminal Self and Hysteria. Feb. 26.—The Nature of Genius." Neither year nor place of delivery is indicated. There is evidence that on February 12, 1895, James was in Cambridge, suggesting that the lectures were given in the Boston area. There is some possibility that the 1895 dating of the lectures is in error, since it is based on the association between the announcement and the letter which could have resulted from an archivist's mistake.

In 1896 James gave a course of six lectures on "Recent Researches into Exceptional Mental Phenomena" before the Brooklyn Institute of Arts and Sciences. The dates and titles of the lectures are as follows:

Jan. 11 "The Hypnotic and Other Trance States"
Jan. 18 "Automatism. Secondary Personality and Subliminal Consciousness"
Jan. 25 "Hysteria"
Feb. 1   "Demoniacal Possession & Witchcraft"
Feb. 8   "Degeneration"
Feb. 15 "Genius"

The information is taken from *The Brooklyn Institute of Arts and Sciences. Prospectus for 1895–'96*, 3rd ed. (September 30, 1895), pp. 91–92. It is confirmed by the Minutes of the Department of Psychology, 1890–1896, preserved in the Brooklyn Museum Archives. The lectures were given on Saturday mornings at 10:30, the first four in the Art Building, the last two in the Large Lecture Hall of the Young Men's Christian Association. According to *The Eighth Yearbook of the Brooklyn Institute of Arts and Sciences, 1895–96* (Brooklyn, 1896), p. 179, on February 15 James conducted a conference on "Recent Research in Psychology," assisted by James McKeen Cattell and Miss A. E. Wyckoff of the Packer Collegiate Institute in Brooklyn. It is not clear whether or not this conference is the lecture on genius James gave on the same day. Reports of several of the lectures were found in the *Brooklyn Eagle* and are reprinted as an appendix to the present volume. According to a letter to his brother Henry, dated January 26, 1896 (#2765), James received $300 for the six lectures.

The first two fragments (#4404, #4405) appear to belong together: they are very similar in appearance and are foliated in the same way. Because the arrangement of subjects best fits the plan of the three lectures of 1895, it is likely that they were originally written out for these lectures. The first fragment deals with the general topic of degeneration and concludes with references to hysteria; the second fragment deals with genius and begins with a reference to a preceding discussion of the subliminal consciousness. This suggests that they are parts of the first and third lectures of the 1895 course and that the second lecture on the subliminal self and hysteria is missing. Both manuscripts show signs of revision for another delivery. For example, the reference to the subliminal consciousness with which the lecture on genius originally began is deleted. This deletion has the effect of fitting the lecture on genius into the program for the Brooklyn Institute. Given James's working habits, it is likely that the same material was presented to Brooklyn Institute audiences in 1896.

The third fragment (#4403) is more difficult to place. The sequence of topics fits neither the 1895 course nor the Lowell Institute course. Thus, by elimination, the fragment is assigned to the Brooklyn Institute. Dealing as it does with several mental states, it could be part of the first lecture on "Hypnotic and Other Trance States." But since this conjecture is quite uncertain, in the present text the fragment appears under the indefinite title of "Fragment of a Lecture on Exceptional Mental Phenomena."

James proposed the Lowell course in a letter to Augustus Lowell, dated April 18, 1896, preserved in the Lowell Institute papers at Houghton:

> I have on hand material already arranged which I think might make a course of ten timely and interesting lectures with some such title as "Recent investigations into exceptional mental states." There is a mass of floating matter that is hardly yet codified and organized, but that is becoming more and more so, and that has great practical and historical importance, to which for some years past I have been giving a good deal of attention, and which I think I could bring together in an instructive way. The subjects would be somewhat as follows:
>
> > Sleep and Dreams
> > Hypnotism
> > The Subconscious Self
> > Hysteria
> > Multiple Personality
> > Demoniacal possession
> > Mediumship
> > Witchcraft
> > Degeneration
> > Genius

So much of this is in the air that an impartial treatment on lines as scientific as possible would undoubtedly be useful.

In his letter to Lowell of May 15, 1896, James thanks Lowell for the appointment for a course of eight lectures on "Recent Researches into Exceptional Mental States":

The dates and titles of the lectures are as follows:

Oct. 21   Dreams and Hypnotism
Oct. 24   Automatism
Oct. 28   Hysteria
Oct. 31   Multiple Personality
Nov. 4   Demoniacal Possession
Nov. 7   Witchcraft
Nov. 11   Degeneration
Nov. 14   Genius

Many of the lectures were reported in Boston newspapers. These reports are reprinted in an appendix to the present volume.

James proposed to repeat the lectures in California in 1898, but since nothing came of the plan, it had no influence on the composition of these manuscripts. The lectures were reconstructed by Eugene Taylor, *William James on Exceptional Mental States: The 1896 Lowell Lectures* (New York: Charles Scribner's Sons, ᶜ1982). In his reconstruction, Taylor collapses several courses into one, interpolates material from newspaper accounts, and fills the text out with quotations from *Principles* and published reviews. Since he tends to present his own views as if they were James's and since there are numerous misreadings and omissions, Taylor's reconstruction can be used only with great caution. His rather detailed commentary is sometimes helpful, but at times is inaccurate and misleading. Brief excerpts from the lectures appear in Perry, II, 169.

56.1 Kaan] Hanns Kaan, German physician, *Der neurasthenische Angstaffect bei Zwangsvorstellungen und der primordiale Grübelzwang* (Leipzig and Vienna: Franz Deuticke, 1893). The remark "Classic example of wash-mania, 117" is found on the cover of James's copy in Widener (Phil 6960.9).

56.11 Magnan] Valentin Magnan (1835–1916), French toxicologist and psychiatrist, *Recherches sur les centres nerveux: Alcoolisme, folie des héréditaires dégénérés, paralysie générale, médecine légale*, 2nd series (Paris: G. Masson, 1893). Magnan describes the case of a man who became so obsessed with remembering names and faces that he began to carry with him a notebook and to collect photographs.

56.22 Cochran] No information was found.

56.23 Cowles] Edward Cowles (1837–1919), American psychiatrist, "Insistent and Fixed Ideas," *American Journal of Psychology*, 1 (February 1888), 222–270. Cowles describes a female patient who became obsessed with the idea that her thoughts would cause harm to a friend. In the earlier stages of her illness, this patient dressed and undressed repeatedly to ensure the correct performance of these actions.

56.26 cancelling] Cowles's patient sometimes performed actions with the intent of cancelling the supposed harmful effects of her thoughts.

56.28 Legrand du Saulle] Henri Legrand du Saulle (1830–1886), French physician. In *La Folie du doute (avec délire du toucher)* (Paris: Adrien Delahaye, 1875), pp. 35–36, Legrand du Saulle describes the obsessions of a man who wanted to learn everything about every pretty woman he met.

56.29 Van Eedens] Frederik Willem van Eeden (1860–1932), Dutch psychiatrist and author, "Les Obsessions," *Revue de l'Hypnotisme*, 6 (1892), 5–14.

57.6 Rev.] Paul Brémaud (1846–1905), French physician, "Observation d'un hystérique," *Revue de l'Hypnotisme*, 7 (1893), 289–297.

57.7 Descourtis] Gabriel Descourtis, French physician, *Du fractionnement des opérations cérébrales et en particulier de leur dédoublement dans les psychopathies* (Paris: A. Parent, 1882). On p. 24 Descourtis describes a laborer who became obsessed with the idea of killing his own children. The copy in Widener (Phil 6953.4) was used by James.

57.13 Prichard] James Cowles Prichard (1786–1848), British physician, *A Treatise on Insanity and Other Disorders Affecting the Mind* (Philadelphia: E. L. Carey & A. Hart, 1837). At regular intervals, the patient would cry 'murder' twelve times and throw his hat into the air a precise number of times. The book was first published in 1835; the citation is that of the copy in Widener (Phil 6965.4).

57.17 Munsterberg's] Hugo Münsterberg (1863–1916), German-born psychologist, James's colleague at Harvard. The case has not been identified.

57.18 Danville] Gaston Danville (b.1870), *La Psychologie de l'amour* (Paris: Alcan, 1894).

57.19 Bergh] Henry Bergh (1811–1888), American reformer, in 1866 founded the American Society for the Prevention of Cruelty to Animals.

57.19 Parkhurst] Charles Henry Parkhurst (1842–1933), American clergyman and reformer, noted for his efforts to expose governmental corruption in New York.

57.19 Somerset] Perhaps Isabella Caroline Somerset (1851–1921), British temperance leader.

57.23 'mattoids.'] For this term see *Essays, Comments, and Reviews*, note to 507.20.

58.3 Myers] Frederic William Henry Myers (1843–1901), British essayist and psychical researcher. The "uprush" is "an emergence into ordinary consciousness of ideas matured below the threshold" of consciousness. This description is found in *Human Personality and Its Survival of Bodily Death*, 2 vols. (New York: Longmans, Green, 1903) (*AC 85.J2376Zz903m), I, 20. But the thought would have been available to James in 1895. James's review of the book is reprinted in *Essays in Psychical Research*.

58.14 Lombroso] Cesare Lombroso (1835–1909), Italian sociologist and physician. For James's review of Lombroso and other "genius-books" see *Essays, Comments, and Reviews*, pp. 505–513. Most of the hints in this lecture can be interpreted in terms of those reviews.

58.27 Paderewski] Ignace Jan Paderewski (1860–1941), Polish pianist and statesman.

58.27 Shelley] Percy Bysshe Shelley (1792–1822).

58.28 Gould] Jay Gould (1836–1892), American financier.

58.28 Bernhardt] Sarah Bernhardt (1844–1923), French actress.

58.28 Platt] Thomas Collier Platt (1833–1910), American politician.

58.32 Thackeray] William Makepeace Thackeray (1811–1863), English author.

58.38 Lowell] James Russell Lowell (1819–1891), American author.

58.39 Longfel.] Henry Wadsworth Longfellow (1807–1882), American poet.

59.3 De M] Alfred de Musset (1810–1857), French poet and novelist.

59.3 Sand] George Sand (1804–1876), French writer.

59.4 Marion's] Perhaps Henri Marion (1846–1896), French philosopher of education.

59.10 Moltke] Helmuth von Moltke (1800–1891), Prussian field marshall.

59.13 Bain's] Alexander Bain (1818–1903), Scottish philosopher and psychologist, identified genius with an extraordinary capacity for association by similarity. See *Principles*, p. 984.

59.19 Booth] William Booth (1829–1912), British clergyman, founder of the Salvation Army.

59.20 Brown] John Brown (1800–1859), American abolitionist.

59.20 Howard] John Howard (1726–1790), English philanthropist, advocate of prison reform.

59.20 Willard] Frances Elizabeth Caroline Willard (1839–1898), American educator and reformer.

59.33 Geo.] George III (1738–1820), British king, who, according to James, combined a stubborn will with a mediocre intellect (see *Essays, Comments, and Reviews*, p. 512).

59.33 Philip] Philip II (1527–1598), Spanish king, who, according to James, combined a stubborn will with a mediocre intellect (see *Essays, Comments, and Reviews*, p. 512).

59.34 Coleridge] Samuel Taylor Coleridge (1772–1834), English poet.

59.35 Poe] Edgar Allan Poe (1809–1849), American poet.

59.36 Gladstone] William Ewart Gladstone (1809–1898), British statesman.

60.3 Venn's] John Venn (1834–1923), British logician, "Correlation of Mental and Physical Powers," *Monist*, 4 (October 1893), 5–19.

60.5 Nordau] Max Simon Nordau (1849–1923), German physician and writer, advocate of the view that genius is a form of degeneration. For James's review of Nordau see *Essays, Comments, and Reviews*, pp. 507–509.

60.18 physicians] Alfred Binet (1857–1911), French psychologist, and Pierre Janet (1859–1947), French psychologist. James often mentions a series of articles by Binet in the *Open Court* and the *Revue Philosophique* (see *Principles*, note to 201.6), and *L'Automatisme psychologique* (1889) by Janet. James's "The Hidden Self," based on Janet's book, is reprinted in *Essays in Psychology*.

61.15 hypnotic] For a description of an experiment in hypnosis by James see *Essays in Psychical Research*, pp. 382–383.

61.28 Bernheim] Hippolyte Bernheim (1840–1919), French hypnotist. For James's review of Bernheim see *Essays, Comments, and Reviews*, pp. 467–468. On a flyleaf of his copy of *Hypnotisme, suggestion, psychothérapie: Études nouvelles* (Paris: Doin, 1891), James notes pp. 131–136, a possible reference for the case described. The book was in Widener (Phil 6671.5), but was later sold (see Taylor, pp. 177–178). For another possible reference see p. 66.

62.19 Gurney's] Edmund Gurney (1847–1888), British aesthetician and psychical researcher, "Peculiarities of Certain Post-Hypnotic States," *Proceedings of the Society for Psychical Research* (English), 4 (May 1887), 268–323.

62.29 Dessoir's] Max Dessoir (1867–1947), German psychologist, *Das Doppel-Ich* (Leipzig: E. Günther, 1890). James's copy is in Houghton (*Phil 7042.2).

62.35 Miss X's] Ada Goodrich Freer (1857–1931), using the pseudonym Miss X. For a reference to her writings on crystal vision and for evidence that she was a fraud, see *Essays in Psychical Research*, note to 97.15.

62.36 Prince's] Morton Prince (1854–1929), American physician and psychiatrist. James could have in mind the case of Mrs. R. described by Prince in "Some of the Revelations of Hypnotism," *Boston Medical and Surgical Journal*, 122 (May 8, 1890), 463–467; (May 22, 1890), 493–495. According to the proceedings of the Massachusetts Medical Society, James was present when Prince read the paper and made the following comment: "It is very easy in the ordinary hypnotic subject to suggest during a trance the appearance of a secondary personage with a certain temperament, and that secondary personage will usually give itself a name. One has, therefore, to be on one's guard in this matter against confounding naturally double persons and persons who are simply temporarily endowed with the belief that they must play the part of being double" (*Boston Medical and Surgical Journal*, 122 [May 15, 1890], 475).

62.37 Binets] Perhaps the experiments discussed in *Principles*, p. 202.

62.38 Janet's] Pierre Janet, "Les Actes inconscients et le dédoublement de la personnalité pendant le somnambulisme provoqué," *Revue Philosophique*, 22 (December 1886), 577–592. Lucie and Adrienne are patients with multiple personality.

62.39 Marie] See note to 69.38.

63.29 Unwholesome] These notes appear to be cues prepared by James for use during delivery of the lectures. The notes do not indicate where the second lecture was to begin. From newspaper accounts it can be conjectured that it began with the discussion of negative hallucinations at 66.10.

63.29 S. P. R.] Society for Psychical Research.

64.2 Krafft-Eb.'s] Richard von Krafft-Ebing (1840–1902), German neurologist.

64.13 Seth] The reference to Seth is not established.

64.20 Field] In *Talks to Teachers on Psychology*, p. 20, James claims that consciousness is complex, with some ideas at the center and others near the margins.

64.22 *single*] James holds that an idea which alone occupies consciousness will have motor effects; see *Principles*, pp. 1132–34.

64.25 chandelier] Taylor, p. 18, suggests the following interpretation of the chandelier metaphor: normal consciousness is like a chandelier with all of its burners burning brightly; sleep, like one with all the burners barely burning; trance, like a chandelier with only one burner burning.

64.28 Newton] For the anecdote about Newton see *Principles*, p. 396.

64.29   Ami] Émile Erckmann (1822–1899) and Louis Gratien Charles Alexandre Chatrian (1826–1890), French writers, *L'Ami Fritz* (Paris: Hachette, 1867). A drinking bout is described on pp. 304–310.

64.30   Wundt] Wilhelm Wundt (1832–1920), German psychologist and philosopher, "Hypnotismus und Suggestion," *Philosophische Studien*, 8 (1892), 1–85.

64.35   Crothers] Thomas Davison Crothers (1842–1918), American physician, *The Trance State in Inebriety: Its Medico-Legal Relations* (Hartford, Conn.: The Case, Lockwood & Brainard Company, 1882).

64.36   Beard] George Miller Beard (1839–1883), American physician. Beard contributed an introduction to the work by Crothers. James's "87" could be an error for pp. 7–8 of Beard's introduction, where Beard claims that automatic states can be produced both naturally and artificially.

64.41   Fluid] In *Principles*, p. 1197, James rejects the view that in hypnotism a magnetic force passes from operator to subject.

65.9   Peggy] Apparently James's daughter, Margaret Mary (b.1887).

65.9   Hammond's] Not identified.

65.13   Maury] Louis Ferdinand Alfred Maury (1817–1892), French scholar, *Le Sommeil et les rêves*, 3rd ed. (Paris: Didier, 1865), p. 132. For James's description of the incident see *Principles*, p. 770. A bundle of notes on sleep and trance (#4417) contains several pages of notes on Maury, describing cases in which external stimuli initiated more or less appropriate dreams. Maury is cited by Tissié, p. 8.

65.15   Tissié] Philippe Auguste Tissié (b.1852), French physician and librarian, *Les Rêves: Physiologie et pathologie* (Paris: Alcan, 1890), p. 164. On p. 102 Tissié describes a patient who dreamed of flies when tickled on the forehead.

65.24   *Delbœuf*] Joseph Remi Léopold Delbœuf (1831–1896), Belgian philosopher and psychologist. For a possible case see *Principles*, p. 1211.

65.24   *Hudson*] Thomson Jay Hudson (1834–1903), American author, proposed suggestion as a basic mental law in *The Law of Psychic Phenomena* (c1893).

65.25   Morris's] Alice Vanderbilt Morris (Shepard) (b.1874).

66.3   Bernheim] This and the subsequent reference to Bernheim fit Hippolyte Bernheim, *De la suggestion et de ses applications à la thérapeutique*, 2nd ed. (Paris: Octave Doin, 1888).

66.4   Albert's] Albert is a patient in whom Tissié induced various dreams. The report in the *Boston Herald*, November 1, 1896, of the lecture on multiple personality contains the following remark: "The French call the phenomena of double personality, the speaker said, 'fugues' or flights, in which one personality alternates with another." For the full report see Appendix III.

67.7   (Moll)] Albert Moll (1862–1939), German psychiatrist, *Hypnotism* (London: Walter Scott, 1890), p. 143. Moll suggested to a subject that the subject come to his house on the sixteenth Tuesday after last Tuesday and the suggestion was carried out.

67.8   Liegeois] Jules Liégeois (1833–1908), French jurist. In *Principles*, p. 1211, James attributes the same view to Liégeois without citing a source. An experiment to this effect is found in *De la suggestion et du somnambulisme dans leurs rapports avec la jurisprudence et la médecine légale* (Paris: Doin, 1889), p. 340. Liégeois hypnotised a patient and made certain suggestions. These were carried out exactly a year later.

67.9   Gurney's] The experiments involving P___ll are described in "Peculiarities of Certain Post-Hypnotic States." The letter episode is found on pp. 290–291. On another occasion, P___ll was asked to poke a fire; instead of doing so, he automatically wrote out the words (p. 296). Another subject was asked questions while in a trance; he could not repeat the questions in his normal state even after Gurney offered to pay him a sovereign (p. 285).

67.13   Pierce] James's review of Arthur Henry Pierce (1867–1914), American psychologist, "Subliminal Self or Unconscious Cerebration?", *Proceedings of the Society for Psychical Research* (English), 11 (July 1895), 317–325, and Samson Landmann, German physician, *Die Mehrheit geistiger Persönlichkeiten in einem Individuum. Eine psychologische Studie* (Stuttgart: Enke, 1894) is reprinted in *Essays, Comments, and Reviews.* James objects to their view that the supposed evidence of multiple personality really shows the workings of unconscious cerebration.

67.18   Lucie] See note to 62.38.

67.24   Myers'] Frederic William Henry Myers, "The Subliminal Consciousness," *Proceedings of the Society for Psychical Research* (English), 7 (February 1892), 298–355; continued as "The Subliminal Self." For additional references see *Essays in Psychical Research*, note to 98.5.

67.25   Barkworth's] Thomas Barkworth, member of the Society for Psychical Research, "Duplex Personality," *Proceedings of the Society for Psychical Research* (English), 6 (December 1889), 84–97.

67.31   Lang] Andrew Lang (1844–1912), British writer. James could be thinking of several cases of presentiment reported by Lang in *Journal of the Society for Psychical Research* (English), 5 (June 1895), 101–102.

67.31   Prince's] See note to 62.36.

67.34   Shaler's] James's connection with psychical research was widely known and he received numerous reports of psychic occurrences. The three cases were not reported in any of the publications of the Society for Psychical Research and no records of them were found in the James Collection.

67.35   *Planchette*] For James's view of the importance of the planchette in psychical research see "Notes on Automatic Writing" (1889), reprinted in *Essays in Psychical Research.*

67.37   Albee] Perhaps Helen Rickey Albee (1864–1939), American writer and rug-maker. In her autobiographical *The Gleam* (New York: Henry Holt, 1911), pp. 74–75, Albee states that at one point she produced automatic writing which James afterward quoted "in his class-room as an authentic and typical instance of this form of phenomenon." The early 1890s is a possible date for this episode.

68.1   Underwood] Sara A. Francis Underwood (1838–1911), English-born American journalist and spiritualist, *Automatic or Spirit Writing, with Other Psychic Experiences* (Chicago: Thomas G. Newman, 1896). James's copy is in Widener (Phil 7068.96.15).

68.2   Dean] Sidney Dean (1818–1901), American clergyman and author. James discusses his automatic writing in *Principles*, pp. 373–374, and in "Notes on Automatic Writing," *Essays in Psychical Research*, pp. 45–47.

68.3   Waters] Henry Guy Waters (b.1856), spiritualist writer. Under the pseudonym of Albert Le Baron, he is the subject of "A Case of Psychic Automatism" (1896), reprinted in *Essays in Psychical Research*.

68.11   Nichols] Perhaps Herbert Nichols (1852–1936), American psychologist, an instructor at Harvard.

68.11   Newbold] William Romaine Newbold (1865–1926), American educator. At the time Newbold was publishing numerous articles in abnormal psychology and it is impossible to say which of these James has in mind. The following seem more likely: "Experimental Induction of Automatic Processes," *Psychological Review*, 2 (July 1895), 348–362; "Suggestibility, Automatism, and Kindred Phenomena," *Popular Science Monthly*, 48 (December 1895), 193–198; (January 1896), 375–380; (February 1896), 520–526.

68.22–23   passional] In "The Hidden Self" James writes: "One stage in the great convulsive attack of hystero-epilepsy is what the French writers call *la phase des attitudes passionnelles*, in which the patient, without speaking or giving any account of herself, will go through the outward movements of fear, anger, or some other emotional state of mind" (*Essays in Psychology*, p. 255).

68.29   Charcot's] Jean Martin Charcot (1825–1893), French neurologist. Charcot is usually credited with developing the view that hysteria is mental in origin, or in the terminology sometimes used by James, is a psychosis rather than a neurosis. (For the terms see *Principles*, pp. 185–186.) In Charcot's view, the symptoms of hysteria are produced by autosuggestion.

68.33   Janets] James gives numerous examples of hysterical anaesthesias taken from Janet in "The Hidden Self," reprinted in *Essays in Psychology*, and in *Principles*, pp. 200–210.

69.4   Bernheim] See note to 61.28.

69.16   Binet] Alfred Binet, *Les Altérations de la personnalité* (Paris: Alcan, 1892). James's annotated copy is in Houghton (*AC 85.J2376.Zz892b). In back of his copy James has written "continuity of consciousness, 124–5" and "hyperaesthesia of insensible skin, 125."

69.19   Kriegers] No such case was found in the literature. In *Principles*, p. 359, James discusses a case of multiple personality described by Conrad Rieger. It is possible that the name Krieger represents a lapse of memory on James's part.

69.24   Binets] Several hysterical Marguerites appear in the literature of the time, but no Marguerite studied by Binet was found.

69.24   Adamson] Neither an investigator nor a subject named Adamson was found in the literature on hysteria and multiple personality. This suggests that

James has in mind a case which does not appear in the published literature. The stock of patients was small and these are discussed over and over again by the same handful of investigators. Thus, it is reasonable to expect that any published case would be mentioned in most of the works of the time.

69.27   Janet] In *Principles*, p. 207, James writes: "How far this splitting up of the mind into separate consciousnesses may exist in each one of us is a problem. M. Janet holds that it is only possible where there is abnormal weakness, and consequently a defect of unifying or co-ordinating power." Janet expresses this view in *L'Automatisme psychologique: Essai de psychologie expérimentale sur les formes inférieures de l'activité humaine* (Paris: Alcan, 1889) (WJ 642.59), p. 314.

69.28   Breuer] Josef Breuer (1842–1925), Austrian psychoanalyst. James discusses the views of Breuer and Freud on hysteria in his notice of Breuer and Freud, "Über den psychischen Mechanismus hysterischer Phänomene" (1893), reprinted in *Essays, Comments, and Reviews*. The paper is reprinted in *Studien über Hysterie* (Leipzig: Deuticke, 1895). James's copy of the book is in Houghton (Phil 6720.6*A).

69.30   shock] In 1894 James reviewed Janet's *État mental des hystériques*, 2 vols. (Paris: Rueff, 1892–1894), reprinted in *Essays, Comments, and Reviews*. According to James, Janet believed that the intellectual weakness of hysterics results from shocks which shatter the mind.

69.34   Breuer's] For Breuer's method see *Essays, Comments, and Reviews*, p. 475.

69.36   Isabelle] Isabella is an anorexic patient described by Janet in *État mental des hystériques*, vol. II (*Les Accidents mentaux*), pp. 66–67. For James's summary of the case see *Essays, Comments, and Reviews*, p. 473.

69.37   Justine] Justine is a patient described by Janet in "Histoire d'une idée fixe" (1894). In his review of this article (*Essays, Comments, and Reviews*, p. 486), James notes that Justine acquired a great fear of cholera as a result of having to deal with cholera patients. Since her fear was associated with the automatic repetition of the word 'cholera', part of her cure involved the substitution of 'cocoriko' and similar sounding words for 'cholera'.

69.38   Marie] Marie is a patient discussed by Janet in *L'Automatisme*, summarized by James in "The Hidden Self," *Essays in Psychology*, pp. 266–267. Marie tried to stop menstrual bleeding by immersing herself in cold water and this brought about her illness. It is interesting that in his summary of the case James omits references to menstruation.

69.39   Marcelle] A patient described by Janet in *État mental des hystériques*. For James's account of the case see *Essays, Comments, and Reviews*, pp. 472–473.

70.1   Gib.] A patient discussed by Janet in *État mental des hystériques*. When awake, Gib. had no memory of what she had done during one of her attacks. Nothing about red flowers was found in connection with her.

70.2   Vel's] Vel., another of Janet's patients, suffered from a tic that was eventually cured by suggestion. For James's account of the case see *Essays, Comments, and Reviews*, p. 473.

70.3   Lucy] Probably a patient described in *Studien über Hysterie* whose symptoms included the loss of the sense of smell and olfactory hallucinations. The case is described by Freud and not Breuer.

70.18   "Fugues"] See note to 66.4.

70.21   Raymond's] Fulgence Raymond (1844–1910), French neurologist, *Leçons sur les maladies du système nerveux (année 1894–1895)*, I (Paris: Doin, 1896), 592–616. The case is described in a chapter titled "Les délires ambulatoires ou les fugues."

70.21   Mine] In several instances James attempted to investigate the cases personally. No information about the case of Miss O. was found.

70.23   Reynolds] Mary Reynolds, a case of multiple personality, is discussed by James in *Principles*, pp. 359–363.

70.24   Bourne] The case of Ansel Bourne was studied by James extensively in person; see *Essays in Psychology*, p. 269, note to 269.2, and p. 411. It is a case of multiple personality.

70.26   Fancher] Abram Hoagland Dailey, *Mollie Fancher: The Brooklyn Enigma. An Authentic Statement of Facts in the Life of Mary J. Fancher, the Psychological Marvel of the Nineteenth Century. Unimpeachable Testimony of Many Witnesses* (New York [1894]). For evidence that James investigated the case in person see Taylor, p. 187.

70.26   Osgood's] Rufus Osgood Mason (1830–1903), American physician, "Duplex Personality," *Journal of Nervous and Mental Disease*, 18 (September 1893), 593–598. For James's review see *Essays, Comments, and Reviews*.

70.27   Felida] The case of Félida X, one of the most frequently mentioned cases of multiple personality, was first described by Eugène Azam (1822–1899), French physician. James discusses the case in *Principles*, pp. 358–359.

70.28   Madame B.] Madame B. or Léonie is one of the hysterical patients described by Janet in *L'Automatisme*. For James's account see *Principles*, pp. 365–367.

70.29   Janet's] Apparently a reference to Janet's view that multiple personality results from weakness of the unifying power (see note to 69.27).

70.30   Rev.] See note to 62.38.

70.32   Cadwell] J. W. Cadwell, *The "Delusion" of Spiritualism Compared with a Belief in the Bible* (Meriden, Conn., 1884). Cadwell gives instructions for developing mediumship. The mediums of the day routinely advertised "developing circles" for the purpose of developing mediumistic powers.

70.35   N. & N's] See p. 68.

70.36   Underwood's] See note to 68.1. James seems to be suggesting that Janet's explanation of multiple personality as the result of abnormal weakness does not fit the case of Mrs. Underwood, and that like the case of Lurancy Vennum, it appears to be a case of possession.

70.37 Lurancy] In *Principles*, p. 375, James writes: "The case of Lurancy Vennum is perhaps as extreme a case of 'possession' of the modern sort as one can find." For extended periods of time, Lurancy seemed to assume the personality of Mary Roff, a neighbor's daughter who had died some years previously. The impression was so strong that Mary's parents took Lurancy in as if she were their daughter. For further details see *Principles*, pp. 375–377.

70.39 Myers'] On numerous occasions James discusses Myers' view of multiple personality. Much of this material is reprinted in *Essays in Psychical Research*. James writes: "The 'supernormal' becomes thus for Myers synonymous with the 'evolutive' as contrasted with the 'dissolutive' with which the ordinary neurologist would prefer to connect it. The supernormal faculties of the subliminal take us into the cosmic environment; and for Myers this cosmic environment takes on more and more, as the volumes proceed, the character of a 'spiritual world' " (p. 207). For Myers it is possible that multiple personality and similar phenomena represent invasions of the ordinary consciousness by a consciousness lying beyond it. And this is why Myers' view leads from abnormal psychology into psychical research.

71.11 Foster's] Michael Foster (1836–1907), British physiologist.

71.17 J.'s] For James's interpretation of Janet's view of the connection between hysteria and fixed ideas see *Essays, Comments, and Reviews*, pp. 471–472, 486.

71.28 Hodgson] Richard Hodgson (1855–1905), Australian-born psychical researcher. Hodgson served as secretary of the American Society for Psychical Research and was closely associated with James in this work.

71.29 Sidgwick] Henry Sidgwick (1838–1900), president of the Society for Psychical Research (English) in 1882–1884 and 1888–1892.

71.31 Mosely] Perhaps Henry Nottidge Moseley (1844–1891), English naturalist, noted for his emphasis on the collection of data.

71.37 Possession] Additional information concerning James's view of possession can be found in a report of a lecture James gave before the New York Neurological Society, February 2, 1897, and in a letter to the spiritualist periodical *Light*. Both are reprinted in *Essays, Comments, and Reviews*, pp. 51–56. Also important is his letter to Henry W. Rankin, February 1, 1897, quoted in part in *Essays, Comments, and Reviews*, note to 51.16.

71.39 Cadwell] The placement of this name in the manuscript cannot be established with certainty. If James has in mind J. W. Cadwell and wants to connect the name with somnambulism, he would be emphasizing the connection between hypnotism and the third type of alternating personality. Cadwell had published a book on hypnotism (see *Principles*, note to 1214.20).

72.19 Lowell] Percival Lowell (1855–1916), American astronomer, *Occult Japan or the Way of the Gods: An Esoteric Study of Japanese Personality and Possession* (Boston: Houghton, Mifflin, 1895). James's copy is in Houghton (Jap 1308.94.75.12*). Lowell describes the various rites performed in trance which he witnessed while climbing Mount Ontaké in Japan.

72.19 Nevius] John Livingston Nevius (1829–1893), American missionary in China, *Demon Possession and Allied Themes: Being an Inductive Study of*

Phenomena of Our Own Times (Chicago: Fleming H. Revell [1894]). James's copy of the second edition (1896) is at Houghton (24244.43.2B*). His two reviews of the book are reprinted in *Essays, Comments, and Reviews*. According to Nevius, the belief that persons could be possessed by foxes was widespread in Japan. The case involves a girl possessed by a fox who was eventually cured by a Buddhist priest.

72.21 Caldwell] Robert Charles Caldwell, "Demonolatry, Devil-dancing, and Demoniacal Possession," *Contemporary Review*, 27 (February 1876), 369–376. Caldwell witnessed various rites in southern India. He reports that near Madura there are temples dedicated to local demons and that for the burial of a Captain Pole, who died on the way to Madura, the natives engaged a devil-dancer to propitiate his spirit.

72.22 *Nevius*] James summarizes the case of Kwo in *Essays, Comments, and Reviews*, p. 517. Kwo was possessed by a demon who left him when Kwo became a Christian.

72.23 *Boguet*] James is referring to the case of Louyse Maillat, in Henri Boguet (c.1550–1619), French judge, *Discours exécrable des sorciers* (1602). Louyse was possessed by five demons who were eventually driven out by exorcism.

72.25 Mitchell] Silas Weir Mitchell (1829–1914), American neurologist and author, *Lectures on Diseases of the Nervous System, Especially in Women* (Philadelphia: Henry C. Lea's Son, 1881). James's marked copy is in Widener (Phil 6322.11). On p. 69 Mitchell begins his account of the "most amazing illustration of mimicked disease I have ever seen." The outbreak took place in an orphanage and began when a healthy girl started to have "convulsive twitches" for no obvious reason. There are markings in James's copy at this point.

72.26 Constans] Augustin Constans (b.1811), French civil servant, *Relation sur une épidémie d'hystéro-démonopathie en 1861*, 2nd ed. (Paris: Delahaye, 1863). The outbreak in the village of Morzine began with hysteria among some children. Eventually some 110 exhibited symptoms of demon possesssion. For more details about the case see *Essays, Comments, and Reviews*, pp. 52–53.

72.27 Chiap] Fernando Franzolini (1840–1905), Italian physician, *L'Epidemia di istero-demonopatie in Verzegnis studiata dai dottori Giuseppe Chiap e Fernando Franzolini* (Reggio Nell'Emilia: Stefano Calderini e Figlio, 1879). The outbreak began when the rumour spread that a hysterical subject was in reality possessed by the devil. When it became apparent that the attacks were triggered by exorcisms and other religious rites, the epidemic was stopped by banning public religious displays. On p. 97, certain villagers are described who claimed to be able to arrange contracts between the devils and their victims. For a price, the devil would leave his victim alone for an agreed-upon period of time.

72.29 Bataille] Doctor Bataille, *Le Diable au XIXᵉ siècle*, 2 vols. (Paris and Lyon: Delhomme et Briguet [1892–1894]). Doctor Bataille is the pseudonym of a group of writers, most prominent of them being Gabriel Antoine Jogand-Pagès (1854–1907), French journalist. The book, describing satanic rites allegedly practiced by Masons, was probably written with the intent of embarrassing the Roman Catholic Church. Using material supplied by Bataille, various ecclesiastical officials condemned the Masons for practicing satanism. On April 19,

1897, Jogand-Pagès admitted that the work was a hoax and that the main character of this book and several other related works, Diana Vaughan, a convert from satanism to Catholicism, was fictitious. On I, 930 of *Le Diable* begins the account of Michel Zilk, a ten-year old boy in Wemding, Bavaria, who was possessed. Zilk accused a neighbor named Hertz of bewitching him. Given the nature of the book, it is unclear whether the case is purely imaginary or is based on actual reports.

72.37   Rollande] No accused person with that name was found.

72.37   Berger] Jean Berger was one of several persons accused by the townspeople of witchcraft during the outbreak in Morzine described by Constans.

72.38   Cape Cod] No references to witches on Cape Cod were found. It was one of the few regions of New England not to hold witch trials during the seventeenth century.

73.11   Vesalius] Andreas Vesalius (1514–1564), Belgian anatomist.

73.17   Innocent VIII's] Innocent VIII (1432–1492), pope in 1484–1492. His bull *Summis desiderantes affectibus* (1484) was primarily intended to support the work of the two inquisitors, James Sprenger and Henry Kramer (Insistoris), authors of the *Malleus Maleficarum* (c.1487). The bull notes that while Sprenger and Kramer have been appointed inquisitors for certain areas of Germany, there are still those who hinder their work. Such persons are commanded to desist, while the Bishop of Strasbourg is commanded to give the two inquisitors assistance and protection. According to many historians, while the bull did not initiate the outbreak, it was a major addition to a movement which had been gathering strength for some time.

73.21   Dominican] Both Sprenger and Kramer were Dominicans, but many inquisitors were not. Numerous trials before episcopal and secular courts are known. In some areas, the persecution intensified after the Reformation, but there were Catholic regions in which comparatively few trials took place. New England and post-Reformation Switzerland and Scotland had relatively high witch trials to population ratios.

73.22   Scotland] James was familiar with Charles Kirkpatrick Sharpe (1781–1851), Scottish scholar, *A Historical Account of the Belief in Witchcraft in Scotland* (1884). See *Essays in Psychical Research*, p. 133.

73.23   *book*] Houghton preserves the *Malleus Maleficarum*, 2 vols. (Lyons: C. Landry, 1620) (24244.13*) with markings by James.

73.23   *Snell*] Otto Snell (b.1859), German physician, *Hexenprozesse und Geistesstörung: Psychiatrische Untersuchungen* (Munich: J. F. Lehmann, 1891). The copy in Widener (24244.34) is marked by James. On p. 22, Snell states that the *Malleus* is so injudicious and full of brutality that it is impossible to comprehend how it could have been accepted in Germany as recently as four hundred years ago.

73.32   W.] James is summarizing the titles of the three parts of the *Malleus*.

73.36   poor] In part I, question 18 of the *Malleus*, the question is raised why witches are generally not rich. The explanation is that "devils like to show their contempt for the Creator by buying witches for the lowest possible price. And also, lest they should be conspicuous by their riches" (*Malleus Maleficarum*, trans. Montague Summers [New York: Dover, 1971], p. 87). James's list of page numbers in the back of the copy in Houghton is difficult to interpret. But one of the entries could be interpreted as a reference to question 18.

73.37 women] The authors of *Malleus* had to explain why so many more women than men are seduced into witchcraft. Part of the explanation is that the faith of women is weak, as is indicated by the derivation of 'femina' from "*Fe* and *Minus*, since she is ever weaker to hold and preserve the faith" (p. 44 [part I, question 6]). In the copy in Houghton, James notes p. 63, apparently a reference to this section.

73.38 sin] The crimes of witches are greater than those of devils because while devils sin only against the creator, witches sin against both the creator and Christ (p. 83 [part I, question 17]).

73.40 works] The list of the works which witches can accomplish and of witches' marks seems based on *Malleus*, with James picking out bits of information from various parts of the book. But the Houghton edition used by James includes other works on witchcraft, and James could have drawn some of his material from them.

74.20 complaint] It was possible to accuse and convict persons without any complaint having been made simply on the basis of observed suspicious behavior (p. 237 [part III, question 19]). In order to keep witnesses from harm, their names were not to be revealed to the accused, except where the witnesses themselves agreed to a confrontation (p. 216 [part III, question 9]).

74.24 Malleus] Pp. 371–372 are noted in the Houghton copy, apparently a reference to part III, question 14 (pp. 225–226 in the Summers translation). This question deals with the issue of making misleading promises in order to obtain a confession. James obviously intended to read some portion of this discussion.

74.26 tears] The question of tears is treated in part III, question 15: "And it is found by experience that the more they are conjured the less are they able to weep" (p. 227).

74.35 Eve] The case of Anna Eve is discussed in Jules Baissac (1825–1898), French writer, *Les Grands jours de la sorcellerie* (Paris: C. Klincksieck, 1890), and Wilhelm Gottlieb Soldan (d.1869), German educator, *Geschichte der Hexenprozesse*, ed. Heinrich Heppe, 2nd ed., 2 vols. (Stuttgart: J. G. Cotta, 1880). The copy in Widener of Baissac (24244.59) is annotated by James. Anna Eve was executed in 1660 upon conviction of sorcery. The fact that she showed no signs of pain under torture was important evidence against her.

74.36 Junius] John Junius, burgomaster of Bamberg, was burned at the stake in 1628. A letter from him to his daughter, written while Junius was in prison, is frequently cited.

75.1 Lecky] William Edward Hartpole Lecky (1838–1903), Irish historian and essayist. In an 1887 review (*Essays in Psychical Research*, p. 26), James reports Lecky's view that often even the best-attested evidence for facts can be discredited. Thus, no one now accepts evidence for witchcraft which in the past was deemed so powerful.

75.4   Calmeil's] Louis Florentin Calmeil (1798–1895), French psychiatrist. In his view, many of the accused were suffering from various mental illnesses.

75.5   Michelet's] Jules Michelet (1798–1874), French historian. In *La Sorcière* (1862) Michelet argues that some of the accusations describe actual practices. In his view, witchcraft was a revival of pagan religions among peasants as a protest against oppression.

75.6   Weier's] Johann Wier (sometimes Weier) (1515–1588), and Ludwig Christian Mejer (b.1825), both held the view that witches suffered from hallucinations induced by various drugs. Their view is discussed by Snell, pp. 78–81.

75.7   Torture] James apparently wants to reject the first three explanations in favor of the view that under torture the accused persons said anything that their torturers wanted them to say. It follows on this view that the literature of witchcraft describes purely imaginary incidents. In the discussion that follows, James seems to claim that often the witnesses at witch trials were suffering from various mental disorders. Thus, the girls at Salem were hysterics and not actresses.

75.8   Stramonium] Snell, p. 80, describes experiments involving stramonium, a drug obtained from thorn apples with effects similar to those of belladonna.

75.20   Montpelier] Around 1640 an outbreak of demon possession occurred in southern France. Several clergymen after describing the symptoms of the possessed asked the faculty of medicine of the University of Montpellier whether such symptoms always indicated the presence of demons. The faculty replied that other explanations were possible. An extensive account of this, without exact dates, is found in Louis Florentin Calmeil, *De la folie*, 2 vols. (Paris: J. B. Baillière, 1845), II, 48–53. Baissac's account is based on Calmeil's. The copy in Widener of the first volume of Calmeil's book (Phil 6952.1) was used by James.

75.22   Upham] Charles Wentworth Upham (1802–1875), American clergyman and author, *Salem Witchcraft; with an Account of Salem Village, and a History of Opinions on Witchcraft and Kindred Subjects*, 2 vols. (1867; rpt. Williamstown, Mass.: Corner House Publishers, 1971). The Salem girls usually went into convulsions in the presence of those they were accusing of witchcraft, a fact that the judges thought significant. According to Upham, the girls were skilled actresses acting out assigned roles. In his opinion, the tragedy showed signs of planning.

75.26   Malleus] The *Malleus* reports the view of doctors that there is sufficient reason to attribute a condition to witchcraft when no physical defects can be observed, when there are no signs of poisoning, and when drugs instead of relieving the disease appear to aggravate it (p. 87 [part I, question 18]). The reference to pp. 141–142 in back of the copy used by James can be interpreted as a reference to this section.

76.2   (Tituba)] A slave woman from the West Indies, one of the first in Salem to be accused and an important witness against others. According to Upham (II, 32), Tituba was imprisoned and later sold "for her fees."

76.7   Spee's] Friedrich von Spee (1591–1635), Jesuit writer, *Cautio criminalis* (1631). Spee was one of the leading Catholic critics of the witch trials.

76.7   Schönborn] Johann Philipp von Schönborn (1605–1673), German prince, Roman Catholic bishop. He suppressed witch trials in his territories at the urging of Spee.

76.19   commune] The Paris Commune, 1871.

76.39   thistle] In *The Will to Believe*, p. 120, James states: "I fancy that squeezing the thistle boldly will rob it of its sting."

77.5   Guiteau] Charles Guiteau was executed in 1882 for the assassination of James Garfield. In *Talks to Teachers*, p. 99, James refers to Guiteau with the remark that "the word 'crank,' which became familiar at the time . . . fulfilled the need of a *tertium quid*." James lists additional terms that fall in the range between sanity and insanity.

77.7   Morel] Bénédict Auguste Morel (1809–1873), French psychiatrist. In his *Traité des dégénérescences physiques, intellectuelles et morales de l'espèce humaine* (Paris: J. B. Baillière, 1857), Morel introduced the term degeneration for a variety of mental disabilities that fall short of insanity.

77.8   valid] The remark about the "valid & invalid brain" is difficult to interpret. James could be indicating the two classes of mental disease: those which are not associated with brain disorders and those which are. In that case, he would be using 'valid' in the sense of 'strong', a sense recognized by the *Century Dictionary* in the 1890s as archaic.

77.22   mouth] See p. 56, line 6.

77.24   Magnan] See note to 56.11.

77.34   Cowles's] See note to 56.23.

77.35   women] See note to 56.28.

77.36   Eeden's] See note to 56.29.

78.11   Moreau] Jacques Joseph Moreau (de Tours) (1804–1884), French physician.

78.16   Dix] Dorothea Lynde Dix (1802–1887), American philanthropist, active in prison reform.

78.29   *Lélut*] Louis François Lélut (1804–1877), French psychiatrist. James is referring to the excerpt from the preface to the second edition of Lélut's *Du démon de Socrate, spécimen d'une application de la science psychologique à celle de l'histoire*, 2nd ed. (Paris: J. B. Baillière, 1856), p. 7.

78.30   *Moreau*] Jacques Joseph Moreau, *La Psychologie morbide dans ses rapports avec la philosophie de l'histoire ou de l'influence des névropathies sur le dynamisme intellectuel* (Paris: Masson, 1859). James's annotated copy is in Houghton (Phil 6322.12*).

78.30   *Lombroso*] Cesare Lombroso, *L'Homme de génie*, trans. Fr. Colonna d'Istria (Paris: Alcan, 1889). James's annotated copy is in Widener (Phil 5425.4.5). James usually used the French translation rather than the Italian original or the English translation (1891).

79.4   tree] A reference to the diagram from Moreau, opposite p. 576.

79.11   g.] The abbreviation seems to be a reference to "genius a neurosis of epileptic variety."

79.19   Lombroso's] *L'Homme de génie.* The list of characteristics from "Short stature" to "Longevity" reproduces with omissions the table of contents for part I, chapters 2–3.

80.22   second] Cesare Lombroso, *Entartung und Genie: Neue Studien*, trans. Hans Kurella (Leipzig: Georg H. Wigand, 1894). James's copy is in Houghton (Phil 5425.4.15*). James reviewed the German translation (reprinted in *Essays, Comments, and Reviews*, pp. 506–507).

80.23   Guido] Guido Reni (1575–1642), Italian painter.

80.23   M.A.] Michelangelo.

80.24   Dante] In his review of Lombroso, James remarks that in the *Divine Comedy* Dante mentions swooning eleven times (*Essays, Comments, and Reviews*, p. 506).

80.32   Burns] In *Entartung und Genie*, p. 95, Lombroso claims that many of the portraits resemble each other. Robert Burns (1759–1796), Scottish poet, resembles Samuel Taylor Coleridge; William Cullen Bryant (1794–1878), American author, resembles Darwin; George Eliot (1819–1880) resembles Edward George Earle Lytton Bulwer-Lytton (1803–1873), English novelist and dramatist.

80.35   Swift's] Jonathan Swift (1667–1745). For the allusion see *Essays, Comments, and Reviews*, p. 507.

80.37   *Nisbet's*] John Ferguson Nisbet (1851–1899), British miscellaneous writer, *The Insanity of Genius and the General Inequality of Human Faculty Physiologically Considered*, 3rd ed. (London: Ward and Downey, 1893). The 1891 date is that of the first edition; James in other places cites the third. For James's criticism of Nisbet's argument see *Essays, Comments, and Reviews*, pp. 510n–511n. On p. xvi Nisbet describes his method; that he studied 250 men of genius is noted on p. 315.

81.1   *Nordau*] Max Simon Nordau, *Degeneration*, trans. from the 2nd German edition (New York: D. Appleton, 1895). The German *Entartung* was first published in 1892–1893. James's review of the book is reprinted in *Essays, Comments, and Reviews*.

81.1   Wagner] In *Degeneration* Nordau discusses Richard Wagner (1813–1883); John Ruskin (1819–1900), English essayist and critic; Henrik Ibsen (1828–1906), Norwegian playwright; Tolstoi; Émile Zola (1840–1902), French novelist; William Morris (1834–1896), English poet and artist.

81.5   h.n.] Human nature.

81.16   Scott] Walter Scott (1771–1832), Scottish novelist and poet.

81.16   Browning] Robert Browning (1812–1889), English poet.

81.17   Emerson] In *Essays, Comments, and Reviews*, p. 512, James lists Emerson; Henry Wadsworth Longfellow; James Russell Lowell; Oliver Wendell Holmes;

and John Greenleaf Whittier (1807–1892), American poet, as "geniuses of the community in which I write," who are noted for their "balance of character and common sense."

81.24   Paganini] Nicolo Paganini (1782–1840), Italian violinist.

81.26   Rockefeller] John Davison Rockefeller (1839–1937), American business-man and philanthropist.

81.27   Kipling] Rudyard Kipling (1865–1936), English author.

81.31   Bain] See note to 59.13.

82.6   Garibaldi] Giuseppe Garibaldi (1807–1882), Italian statesman.

82.22   Hirsch's] William Hirsch, German physician, *Genie und Entartung: Eine psychologische Studie* (Berlin: Coblenz, 1894). James's marked copy is in Houghton (Phil 5425.5.6*). In his review, reprinted in *Essays, Comments, and Reviews*, pp. 509–513, James writes: "It really reanimates one, after so much farce-comedy writing on the subject of genius, to come upon a book based on psychological analysis, logic, and common-sense" (p. 509).

82.35   narrow] For a more complete statement of the same thought see *Essays, Comments, and Reviews*, pp. 512–513.

82.38   Š.] Sans. For his concluding comments, James relied heavily upon his review of Hirsch; see *Essays, Comments, and Reviews*, p. 513.

83.21   When] The fourth session of the Summer School of Theology, sponsored by the Divinity School of Harvard University, was held from July 1 to July 18, 1902, and dealt with the general theme of "Current Problems in Theology." The session consisted of forty-five lectures given by twelve lecturers, from Harvard and other universities. The audience consisted of seventy-eight students, some sixty of them being ordained ministers. The fee for the session was fifteen dollars. James lectured on July 14 and 15 on "Intellect and Feeling in Religion."

James's point of view in the lectures is expressed in a letter to Henry William Rankin, July 8, 1902:

> I am you see a methodist, whilst hardly being a Christian, but that my account of religious life is *objective* would seem to be proved by the opposite reactions which the book elicits from different people. To some it offers a displeasing, to others a sympathetic picture, just as religion itself does as the world exhibits it. Very frequent is the complaint that as I exhibit it, it is too "unwholesome," and that normal religion should be more academic, and intellectual, and less personal and experimental.
>
> I am now writing a couple of lectures for the Harvard summer school of theology to defend this point—they come off Monday & Tuesday of next week (Houghton, *67M-96, letter 37).

On July 11, to Hugo Münsterberg, James wrote: "I lecture in Cambr. on Monday and Tuesday. If I go on at this rate, they'll make me a bishop" (Perry, II, 332). James initially thought of the lectures as his last word in religious psychology. With that chore out of the way, he would at last be able to concentrate on philosophical topics. At least, this is the sense of his letter to Wincenty Lutoslawski, dated July 18:

I have had to come down here to give a couple of lectures to the Harvard Summer School of theology,—lectures *eigentlich* supplementary to my aforesaid book, and now that they are over I feel free and as if that religious psychology phase of my existence were wound up, and, the burden once removed, I might get well with a great deal more *essor* and stimulus, and address myself to more properly philosophical tasks (*William James: Selected Unpublished Correspondence, 1885–1910*, ed. Frederick J. Down Scott [Columbus: Ohio State University Press, ᶜ1986], p. 291).

The book is of course *The Varieties of Religious Experience*, published in June 1902.

The eighth session of the Summer School was held from July 5 to July 21, 1906, and was devoted to the topic "Christian Theology in Its Origin and Development." James contributed five lectures on "Religious Philosophy and Individualism," from Tuesday, July 17, to Saturday, July 21, at noon. The School had six lecturers and sixty-eight students, fifty-three being ordained ministers.

James did not bother to prepare a new set of lectures. Rather, he inserted sheets with subject headings into his 1902 notes and thereby stretched two lectures into five. Because James's 1906 additions, consisting primarily of subject headings, are barely intelligible and because there are few connecting links between the additions and the original text, it seemed best to print the 1902 lectures and relegate the 1906 additions to an appendix.

James himself was not happy with the lectures. On the cover of the manuscript he wrote: "Trash never to be printed."

84.34 Arnold] The distinction between Hebraism and Hellenism is developed in Arnold's *Culture and Anarchy* (1869). Hellenists emphasize knowledge and the spontaneous play of thought; Hebraists, conduct and obedience to law.

86.18 "one] Luke x:42.

86.23 Wesley] John Wesley (1703–1791), English evangelist, founder of Methodism.

90.10 Carlyle's] Thomas Carlyle (1795–1881), Scottish essayist and historian. "Natural Supernaturalism" is the title of a chapter in *Sartor Resartus*.

90.16 Emerson] For the reference and fuller text see *Essays in Religion and Morality*, note to 114.16.

91.7 Santayana] George Santayana (1863–1952), American philosopher, *Interpretations of Poetry and Religion* (New York: Charles Scribner's Sons, 1900), p. v.

91.36 Lasswitz] Kurd Lasswitz (1848–1910), German philosopher, *Wirklichkeiten; Beiträge zum Weltverständnis* (Berlin: Emil Felber, 1900) (WJ 748.83.4), pp. 251, 253, 256, 257.

92.6 Grundzüge] Hugo Münsterberg, *Grundzüge der Psychologie* (Leipzig: Johann Ambrosius Barth, 1900) (WJ 757.62.2).

92.40 Maeterlinck] Maurice Maeterlinck (1862–1949), Belgian poet and dramatist. In *La Vie des abeilles* (1901) Maeterlinck emphasizes the subordination of individuals to the common good.

93.19 Stephen] Leslie Stephen (1832–1904), English philosopher and critic.

95.20 Jastrow] Joseph Jastrow (1863–1944), American psychologist. James could have in mind Jastrow's *Fact and Fable in Psychology* (1900).

95.22 Flournoy] Théodore Flournoy (1854–1920), Swiss psychologist. For a possible reference see *Essays in Psychical Research*, note to 219.12–13.

95.23 Hyslop] James Hervey Hyslop (1854–1920), American philosopher and psychical researcher.

95.26 Myers's] For James's statement of Myers's problem see *Essays in Psychical Research*, p. 374.

95.27 Dissolutive] See note to 70.39.

95.28 Myers's] See note to 58.3.

95.31 Granger] Frank Stephen Granger (1864–1936), British educator, *The Soul of a Christian: A Study in the Religious Experience* (New York: Macmillan, 1900).

96.5 Frazer] James George Frazer (1854–1941), Scottish anthropologist. For a possible interpretation of James's meaning see *The Varieties of Religious Experience*, p. 33.

97.8 Read] "Philosophical Conceptions and Practical Results." James is citing the pamphlet version (Berkeley: The University Press, 1898). P. 9 of the pamphlet is *Pragmatism*, pp. 260–261; p. 15 is p. 264.

97.22 *Ecclesiasticism*] The notebook (#4513) from which these notes are drawn, in respect of content, is one of the most miscellaneous in the James Collection. It contains brief notes, various quotations, and fragments of what once was a longer manuscript. An archivist dated the notebook 1903–1906, and these dates fit the content. Some of the jottings were made when James was working on "The Many and the One" in 1903–1904 (published in *Manuscript Essays and Notes*). In listing the contents, the same archivist noted that there are notes on religion "apparently for course in Harvard S.S. of Theology." This identification seems reasonable, but no evidence supporting it was found. It is possible that the notes were made in connection with *The Varieties of Religious Experience*.

It is clear that James used this notebook for a variety of purposes on different occasions and that no useful purpose would be served by reproducing such a miscellany as a whole. The text given in the present volume is what survives of the longer and continuously foliated manuscript.

98.8 Sainte Beuve] Charles Augustin Sainte-Beuve (1804–1869), French author and critic.

100.22 have] No. 7 contains drafts and notes for several addresses, preserved in two folders in the James Collection (#4523, #4524), on the role of college graduates.

The Harvard Graduate Club was the club for students in the Harvard Graduate School, which was often thought of as the professional school of arts and sciences primarily devoted to the training of teachers. Several remarks in the text indicate that James was addressing an audience of prospective teachers, and the references to Harvard philosophy courses make it plausible that many in the audience were Harvard graduates. According to the Harvard Catalogue,

James joined several other professors at the Club in a discussion of "The Idea of a University" during the 1897–1898 academic year. The present notes do not seem to go back that far, as indicated by the references to having reached age 60, which, if taken literally, would give 1902 as the earliest possible year. But the material could be later. According to a later catalogue, James addressed the Graduate Club in a talk entitled "The Vocation of the Scholar" during the 1904–1905 academic year.

In a diary (#4553) entry of December 5, 1905, James notes that he gave an address before the Radcliffe Graduate Club. "Know a good man when you see him" served as his theme. A deleted passage on #4523, fol. 17, includes a reference to Radcliffe. Furthermore, the theme of knowing a good man is repeated several times in the notes. Thus, it is likely that some of this material was used at Radcliffe and revised for another delivery. Notes for what may have been the same address at Radcliffe are found in the Miller-Bode notebooks (see *Manuscript Essays and Notes*, p. 420).

It is also likely that the same notes were used at Stanford in 1906. This is suggested by the following note on an envelope in James's hand: "Possible Assembly address—Graduate Club address (possibly work up for commencement)." The term 'assembly' was not a Harvard term, but was used at Stanford where James taught in spring 1906. There was also a Graduate Club at Stanford which, according to his diary (#4554), James addressed on January 26, 1906: "Graduates Club at Jordan's in the evening, where I made a short address. Ach! No more 'addresses' if I can avoid them." David Starr Jordan was president of Stanford. A further link with Stanford is provided by the reference to Chesterton on p. 111. James read Chesterton's *Heretics* while traveling by train to California (see *Pragmatism*, note to 9.2).

On the same p. 111 there is an indication that James had spoken at Brooks House prior to his Graduate Club address. Phillips Brooks House at Harvard was opened on January 10, 1900, as the religious center for Harvard students. While the House itself sponsored some lectures, other lectures that were sponsored by separate religious associations were also given at Brooks House.

The situation is further confused by the fact that James sometimes wrote out a full text and then prepared an outline for use during delivery. Thus, it is impossible to tell how many different occasions are represented in the group and how one fragment is connected with the others. Part A of No. 7 represents the one continuous manuscript that survives. The text itself or the delivery notes based on it could well have been used at Radcliffe on December 5, 1905. Part B contains the delivery notes that correspond to the manuscript in part A, as well as notes and drafts used on other occasions.

101.24   Eliot] Charles William Eliot (1834–1926), American educator, president of Harvard.

101.29   Spencer] Included in Spencer's *Facts and Comments* (New York: D. Appleton, 1902) is the essay "State Education" in which Spencer argues that education without moral training is undesirable. He contends that education makes the masses more susceptible to arousal by the lies appearing in the popular press, and as evidence points to the popular passions aroused by the British newspaper reports of the Boer War.

102.13   Goldsmith's] Oliver Goldsmith (1728–1774), British author.

102.19   Dreyfuss] For James's view of the Dreyfuss case see *Letters*, II, 97–101.

102.39 (Sp. Rep.)] The *Springfield Republican*, a leading supporter of American anti-imperialists. Many of James's own statements on American foreign policy (reprinted in *Essays, Comments, and Reviews*) appeared in the *Republican*.

103.10 PhD] In 1892 James received an honorary doctorate of letters and philosophy from the University of Padua. It is perhaps this degree that James has in mind.

105.17 Wilde] Oscar Wilde (1854–1900), Irish author, in the essay "The Critic as Artist" (*Intentions*, vol. vii of the *Complete Writings of Oscar Wilde* [New York: The Nottingham Society, c1909], p. 132).

106.31 Carpenter] Edward Carpenter (1844–1929), English poet and essayist. James quotes Carpenter's view of property in *Varieties*, p. 256.

110.7 (Bryce)] James Bryce (1838–1922), British historian, jurist, and statesman. In fall 1904 Bryce gave the Godkin Lectures at Harvard on "The Study of Popular Governments" and lectured before the Lowell Institute on changes in ideas during the past fifty years.

110.29 Burroughs] Perhaps John Burroughs (1837–1921), American poet and writer on natural history.

111.1 Bryan] William Jennings Bryan (1860–1925), American statesman.

111.1 Roosevelt] Theodore Roosevelt (1858–1919).

111.1 Debs] Eugene Victor Debs (1855–1926), American socialist.

111.1 Volk] Perhaps Douglas Volk (1856–1935), American painter.

111.1 Washington] Booker Taliaferro Washington (1856–1915), American educator.

111.1 Jerome] Perhaps William Travers Jerome (1859–1934), American jurist and reformer.

111.1 Adler] Felix Adler (1851–1933), American educator, founder of Ethical Culture.

111.13 Chesterton] Gilbert Keith Chesterton (1874–1936), English author. James read Chesterton's *Heretics* (1905) in January 1906 (see *Pragmatism*, note to 9.2).

111.22 *é . . g . .*] Possibly an abbreviation for *égalité*.

111.31 Tarde] Jean Gabriel Tarde (1843–1904), French sociologist, known for the study of imitation; see *Talks to Teachers*, pp. 38–39.

112.27 Boulanger] Georges Ernest Jean Marie Boulanger (1837–1891), French general.

112.27 Blaine] James Gillespie Blaine (1830–1893), American statesman.

112.28 Butler] Perhaps Benjamin Franklin Butler (1818–1893), American general and statesman.

113.4 Burke] Edmund Burke (1729–1797), British statesman and orator, in "Speech on Conciliation with America, March 22, 1775" (*Burke's Speeches* [London: Macmillan, 1963], p. 93).

113.12 Disraeli] Benjamin Disraeli (1804–1881), British statesman and author.

114.12 Depew] Chauncey Mitchell Depew (1834–1928), American statesman.

114.25 Shaw's] George Bernard Shaw (1856–1950), Irish dramatist and critic.

117.3 Reasoning] The group of manuscripts in No. 8 represents two folders in the James Collection (#4415, #4393). From internal evidence it is clear that they are fragments of James's early courses and that notes of different date have been placed together. It is likely that some of the fragments were used several times. It proved impossible to link the fragments with definite courses. The dates given indicate the most likely period of their use.

117.18 Wundt's] In 1875 James reviewed Wundt's *Grundzüge der physiologischen Psychologie* (1874), drawing attention to Wundt's experiments on reaction time and the concepts *"field of vision"* and *"inward point of sight"* (*Essays, Comments, and Reviews*, p. 299).

117.28 tourists] This example is developed in detail in "Are We Automata?" (1879); see *Essays in Psychology*, pp. 49–50.

117.29 female] The episode probably occurred in 1873–1874.

118.18 Martineau] James Martineau (1805–1900), English clergyman. James quotes Martineau on association in "Brute and Human Intellect" (1878); see *Essays in Psychology*, p. 15. James's reference is to "Brute and Human Intellect," *Journal of Speculative Philosophy*, 12 (July 1878), 236–276. P. 250 corresponds to pp. 13–14 of *Essays in Psychology*.

119.14–15 Pasteur's] Louis Pasteur (1822–1895), French scientist.

119.16 Lewes's] George Henry Lewes, *Problems of Life and Mind*, 1st series, 2 vols. (London: Trübner, 1874–1875), I, 390–414 (problem I, chapter 8). For a similar remark see *Manuscript Essays and Notes*, pp. 163–164.

119.31 Mill] For a similar criticism of John Stuart Mill see *Manuscript Essays and Notes*, p. 161.

119.32 Taine] Hippolyte Adolphe Taine (1828–1893), French philosopher and psychologist. For a similar criticism of Taine see *Manuscript Essays and Notes*, pp. 162–163.

120.8 Thus] James never completely worked out the example that follows, and the two parts do not fit together.

120.10 KC] KC is probably potassium chloride.

121.15 Liebreich] Matthias Eugène Oscar Liebreich (1839–1908), German physician and pharmacologist.

122.25 Mill] The text from 122.26 to 123.11 is typed on a typewriter that James used in 1882–1884 (see *Manuscript Essays and Notes*, note to 261.3).

123.21 Tyndall] For possible references to Tyndall and Huxley see "The Sentiment of Rationality" (1879), *Essays in Philosophy*, p. 47.

123.21 Fechner] Gustav Theodor Fechner (1801–1887), German philosopher, physicist, psychologist. In "The Teaching of Philosophy in Our Colleges" (1876) James writes: "It is more than doubtful whether Fechner's 'psychophysic law' (that sensation is proportional to the logarithm of its stimulus) is of any great *psychological* importance" (*Essays in Philosophy*, p. 6).

123.26 Weber's] Ernst Heinrich Weber (1795–1878), German physiologist.

124.40 "Morals"] A reference to a set of notes that has not survived.

125.11 Spamer's] Karl Spamer (1842–1892), German physician.

125.34 Venice] For a detailed account of the incident, which probably occurred in 1874, see *Principles*, p. 1085.

125.35 Wright] Chauncey Wright (1830–1875), American philosopher. In James's opinion, Wright's life was dominated by the craving for "consistency or unity in thought" (*Essays, Comments, and Reviews*, p. 16).

126.12 This] The manuscript (#4490) bears in Perry's hand the notation "Lecture Notes for 'Natural History 2' 1876–1877." This assignment is consistent with the handwriting, while the content of the notes fits the questions of an examination for the course in December 1876. James asked the following: "2. What does Spencer mean by the relativity of feelings and relations?". The fact that the topic of relativity was covered by the end of 1876 suggests that the notes were made in fall 1876. It is likely that James used the same notes in later courses.

The text for the course was Spencer's *Principles of Psychology*. James used the drastically revised second edition, 2 vols. (New York: D. Appleton, 1871–1873) (WJ 582.24.6). "The Substance of Mind" is the title of chapter 1, part II, in volume I, while chapters 3 and 4 of part II deal with the question of relativity.

127.10 Mill] James Mill (1773–1836), British philosopher and historian. For a fuller development of Mill's view see *Essays in Psychology*, p. 43.

128.7 Green] Thomas Hill Green (1836–1882), English philosopher.

128.14 Helmholtz's] Hermann Helmholtz, *Handbuch der physiologischen Optik* (Leipzig: Voss, 1867). For a possible text see *Principles*, pp. 873–874.

128.24 Bridgmans] Laura Dewey Bridgman (1829–1889). Samuel Gridley Howe (1801–1876), American educator and philanthropist, was her teacher.

128.25 Peirce's] Charles Sanders Peirce (1839–1914), American philosopher, in his review (1871) of Fraser's *Works of George Berkeley*, in *Writings of Charles S. Peirce: A Chronological Edition*, II (Bloomington: Indiana University Press, ᶜ1984), 468.

129.13 Nihilists] For the term nihilist see *Manuscript Essays and Notes*, note to 133.5, and "Against Nihilism."

129.28 relativity] The manuscripts in No. 10 represent three folders (#4494, #4493, #4491), prepared for Philosophy 4: Psychology in 1878–1879. It is, of course, likely that James continued to use the material for some years. Having used Spencer's *Principles of Psychology* in Natural History 2, James changed to Taine's *On Intelligence* for 1877–1878, when the psychology course was renamed Philosophy 4. In the following year, however, he returned to Spencer. That No. 10 is not earlier than 1878 is indicated by the fact that parts of the manuscript are in the hand of James's wife. It is unlikely that she would have served as his amanuensis prior to their marriage on July 10, 1878. The examination questions for 1878–1879 also support this dating. Thus the final examination on June 13, 1879, included the following two questions: "Interpret and criticize Spencer's ideas about the origin and validity of Cognition" and "What is Spencer's criterion of certitude, and why is it practically unavailable?" The examination for 1876–1877 in Natural History 2 placed less emphasis on difficulties in Spencer's theory of knowledge. Furthermore, several examinations in Philosophy 4 in 1878–1879 contained questions dealing with Spencer's law of intelligence.

More difficult is the assignment of the dialogue between Renouvier and an evolutionist (133.8–135.12) because James first taught Renouvier in 1879–1880 in Philosophy 5. However, the examinations in Philosophy 5 suggest that the dialogue does not fit the course, which emphasized the paradoxes of infinity and Renouvier's treatment of categories. It is furthermore quite possible that James introduced Renouvier in earlier courses, and it thus seemed safest to leave this fragment in the company of the manuscripts with which it has been associated.

130.25   Sp.] References in the text are to Spencer's *Principles of Psychology*, vol. I.

133.2   Allen] For James's review of Allen's *Physiological Æsthetics* (1877) see *Essays, Comments, and Reviews.*

133.8   Renouvier] Charles Renouvier (1815–1903), French philosopher. For the relations between James and Renouvier see *Essays in Philosophy*, note to 23.1. The correspondence between them began in 1872.

135.33   law] Spencer's *Principles of Psychology*, I, 407–417.

136.14   free-will] The final examination for Philosophy 4 included the question "Give briefly your instructor's statement of the problem of free-will."

137.15   *Biology*] Herbert Spencer, *The Principles of Biology*, 2 vols. (London: Williams and Norgate, 1864–1867). Marked copies of both volumes were sold from James's library, with vol. I dated 1864.

137.36   Wallace] Alfred Russel Wallace (1823–1913), British naturalist.

138.1   Buckle] Henry Thomas Buckle (1821–1862), British historian. In James's view both Buckle and Taine consider climate the primary determinant of social evolution. See *The Will to Believe*, p. 174.

138.38   Pop.] The text to 139.28–37, while part of the present notes, can also be viewed as an early draft of "Great Men and Their Environment" (1880). It is printed in *The Will to Believe* as Appendix III. James's article is a criticism of Allen's views expressed in "Hellas and Civilisation" and "Nation-Making: A Theory of National Characters," both reprinted from the *Gentleman's Magazine* in supplements to the *Popular Science Monthly*, no. 17 (September 1878), pp. 398–406, and no. 20 (December 1878), pp. 121–127. James's "Great Men and Their Environment" is reprinted in *The Will to Believe*.

140.1 Bagehot] Walter Bagehot (1826–1877), British economist and essayist. For James's view of Bagehot see *The Will to Believe*, p. 174.

140.2 Lyell's] Charles Lyell (1797–1875), British geologist.

140.10 Cobden] Richard Cobden (1804–1865), British statesman. Cobden was a leading opponent of the Crimean War.

140.11 Spencer] Herbert Spencer, part II of "The Study of Sociology," *Contemporary Review*, 19 (May 1872), 701–718.

140.33 Darwin] Charles Darwin, *The Origin of Species by Means of Natural Selection*, 6th ed. (London: John Murray, 1873).

141.1 Jevons] William Stanley Jevons (1835–1882), English logician and economist. James's review of *The Principles of Science* (1874) is reprinted in *Essays, Comments, and Reviews*.

141.20 important] "The Assumption of Metaphysicians" is chapter 2 of part VII of Spencer's *Principles of Psychology*. One of the questions on the final examination for Philosophy 4, June 13, 1879, refers to part VII.

146.3 *Lewes*] Vol. II of *Problems of Life and Mind*, 1st series.

146.4 "On] Matthew Moncrieff Pattison Muir (1848–1931), Scottish chemist, "Residual Phenomena," *Popular Science Monthly*, 15 (May 1879), 101–109, reprinted from *Frazer's Magazine*.

146.9 Definition] James offered Philosophy 3: The Philosophy of Evolution four times: 1879–1880, 1880–1881, 1883–1884, 1884–1885. The first year he used Spencer's *First Principles*; in later years he added *The Data of Ethics*. The manuscripts in No. 11 (#4487, #4489, #4488, #4484, #4492, #4486) are connected with this course and were probably used several times. Parts of them are in the hand of James's wife, characteristic of manuscripts from the late 1870s and early 1880s.

146.30 Part] Herbert Spencer, *First Principles of a New System of Philosophy* (New York: D. Appleton, 1877) (WJ 582.24.4). Part I is titled "The Unknowable," part II, "The Knowable." The numbers and titles of chapters given in the notes are taken from this edition.

147.4 "the] Chapter 6 of part II.

147.12 "Weather"] Probably a reference to Chauncey Wright; for the text see *The Will to Believe*, note to 49.10.

147.20 Canst] Job xxxix:10, 19; xl:4, 6, 7; xxxviii:31.

149.7 Huxley's] For a possible text see *The Will to Believe*, p. 17.

150.9 Peirce's] For Peirce's criterion see *Manuscript Essays and Notes*, p. 151.

150.32 Geoffroy] Étienne Geoffroy Saint-Hilaire (1772–1844), French naturalist.

150.33 Diderot] Denis Diderot (1713–1784), French encyclopedist.

150.34 Grimm] Jakob Ludwig Karl Grimm (1785–1863), German philologist.

150.34 Bopp] Franz Bopp (1791–1867), German philologist.

150.35 Benfey] Theodor Benfey (1809–1881), German philologist, an authority on Sanskrit.

150.37 Niebuhr] Barthold Georg Niebuhr (1776–1831), German historian.

151.2 Tylor] Edward Burnett Tylor (1832–1917), British anthropologist.

151.3 Lubbock] John Lubbock (Baron Avebury) (1834–1913), British banker and naturalist.

151.4 Fiske] John Fiske (1842–1901), American historian and philosopher.

151.6 Ward] Lester Frank Ward (1841–1913), American sociologist.

151.9 Begin] "The Persistence of Force" is chapter 6, part II of *First Principles*.

151.21 Helmholtz] For the text see *Essays, Comments, and Reviews*, pp. 324–325.

151.25 chapter] Chapter 7, part II.

152.2 "leave] Apparently an allusion to Shakespeare's *Tempest*, act iv, scene 1, line 146. Quoted in *First Principles*, p. 173.

154.22 Helmholtz] Hermann Helmholtz, "Über die Erhaltung der Kraft" (1847). For a possible text see *Essays, Comments, and Reviews*, pp. 324–325.

154.30 chapter] Chapter 7, part II.

155.17 A] "The Rhythm of Motion" is the title of chapter 10, part II of *First Principles*.

157.4 Spencer's] "The Direction of Motion" is the title of chapter 9, part II.

158.20 Phenomenalism] Preserved in the James Collection (#4455); printed in *Manuscript Essays and Notes*, pp. 170–179.

158.20 Mind] Herbert Spencer, "Consciousness under Chloroform," *Mind*, 3 (October 1878), 555–558, described as an addition to the appendix "On the Actions of Anæsthetics and Narcotics" in vol. I of Spencer's *Principles of Psychology*.

158.21 Saturday] The reference to Saturday indicates that the "Concluding Lecture on Spencer" dates from 1879–1880 or 1880–1881. James did not teach the course in 1881–1882, while in 1883–1884 and 1884–1885 the course was taught on Mondays, Wednesdays, and Fridays.

158.23 Fiske] John Fiske was one of the major expounders of Spencer in the United States.

159.15 p. 9] The page numbers, unless otherwise indicated, refer to Spencer's *First Principles*.

159.25 *Kant-Müller*] *Immanuel Kant's Critique of Pure Reason, Second Part Containing Kant's Critique*, trans. F. Max Müller (London: Macmillan, 1881).

James's copy is in Houghton (*AC 85.J2376.Zz881k). James is referring to the transcendental dialectic, book II, chapter 2, on "The Antinomy of Pure Reason."

159.26 *Hamilton*] William Hamilton (1788–1856), Scottish philosopher, *Discussions on Philosophy and Literature, Education and University Reform*, 2nd ed. (London: Longman, Brown, Green and Longmans, 1853). The copy from James's library is in Widener (Phil 2035.30.1). In *Principles* James used the *Lectures on Metaphysics and Logic*, ed. H. L. Mansel and John Veitch, 4 vols. (Edinburgh: William Blackwood and Sons, 1859–1860). James is referring to volume II.

159.28 *Mansel*] Henry Longueville Mansel (1820–1871), English philosopher, *The Limits of Religious Thought Examined in Eight Lectures* (Boston: Gould and Lincoln, 1859) (WJ 553.62).

159.29 *Monck's*] William Henry Stanley Monck (1839–1915), Irish philosopher, *Sir William Hamilton* (London: Sampson Low, Marston, Searle, & Rivington, 1881).

159.30 Mill's] John Stuart Mill (1806–1873), *An Examination of Sir William Hamilton's Philosophy* (1865). For James's copies see *Principles*, note to 166.37.

160.23 Grote's] George Grote, *Plato and the Other Companions of Sokrates*, 3rd ed., 3 vols. (London: John Murray, 1875). On I, 96, Grote discusses Zeno as the "inventor of dialectic."

160.24 Renouvier] Charles Renouvier, "Esquisse d'une classification systématique des doctrines philosophiques," *Critique Religieuse*, 5 (1882–1883), 182–209, 248–305, 353–416; *Traité de logique générale*, 2nd ed., 3 vols. (Paris: Bureau de la *Critique Philosophique*, 1875) (WJ 675.61.2).

160.26 Wundt] Wilhelm Wundt, "Über das kosmologische Problem," *Vierteljahrsschrift für wissenschaftliche Philosophie*, 1 (1876–1877), 80–136.

160.27 Lasswitz] Kurd Lasswitz, "Ein Beitrag zum kosmologischen Problem und zur Feststellung des Unendlichkeitsbegriffes," *Vierteljahrsschrift für wissenschaftliche Philosophie*, 1 (1876–1877), 329–360.

160.28 Ward] Lester Frank Ward, "Kant's Antinomies in the Light of Modern Science," *Journal of Speculative Philosophy*, 15 (October 1881), 381–395.

160.29 Fullerton] George Stuart Fullerton (1859–1925), American philosopher, "The Mathematical Antinomies and Their Solution," *Journal of Speculative Philosophy*, 18 (January 1884), 38–47. The reference to Fullerton could have been inserted at a later date.

161.1 *Boscovich's*] Roger Joseph Boscovich (Rudjer Josip Bošković) (1711–1787), Jesuit scientist.

161.21 *Martineau*] James Martineau, *Essays, Philosophical and Theological* (Boston: William V. Spencer, 1866), "Science, Nescience, and Faith," pp. 171–212, and "Mansel's Limits of Religious Thought," pp. 213–243.

161.23 *Stallo*] John Bernard Stallo (1823–1900), German-born American philosopher of science, *The Concepts and Theories of Modern Physics* (New York: D. Appleton, 1882) (WJ 483.3).

161.24   *Caird*] John Caird (1820–1898), Scottish philosopher, *An Introduction to the Philosophy of Religion* (New York: Macmillan, 1880). James's annotated copy is in Widener (Phil 8582.1.2).

161.25   *Guthrie*] Malcolm Guthrie, English businessman and philosophical writer, *On Mr. Spencer's Formula of Evolution as an Exhaustive Statement of the Changes of the Universe* (London: Trübner, 1879). James's review is reprinted in *Essays, Comments, and Reviews*.

161.26   Lewes] First series.

161.27   Spencer] Herbert Spencer, *Essays: Scientific, Political, and Speculative*, 3 vols. (London: Longman, Brown, Green, Longmans, and Roberts, 1858–1874). Several essays in volume III would fit.

161.28   Ferrier] James Frederick Ferrier (1808–1864), Scottish philosopher, *Institutes of Metaphysic: The Theory of Knowing and Being* (Edinburgh: Wm. Blackwood, 1854) (WJ 527.78).

162.2   P.] Spencer's *Principles of Biology.*

163.7   Mill's] For Mill's text see *Essays in Philosophy*, note to 17.40.

163.12   Hodgson] Shadworth Hollway Hodgson (1832–1912), British philosopher, *The Philosophy of Reflection*, 2 vols. (London: Longmans, Green, 1878) (WJ 539.18.4).

163.13   *Wright*] Chauncey Wright, *Philosophical Discussions*, ed. Charles Eliot Norton (New York: Henry Holt, 1877).

163.14   *Paulhan*] Frédéric Paulhan (1856–1931), French psychologist, "La Théorie de l'inconnaissable," *Revue Philosophique*, 6 (September 1878), 270–285.

163.15   *Vaihinger*] Hans Vaihinger (1852–1933), German philosopher, "Der Begriff des Absoluten (mit Rücksicht auf H. Spencer)," *Vierteljahrsschrift für wissenschaftliche Philosophie*, 2 (1878), 188–221.

163.16   Fiske's] John Fiske, *Outlines of Cosmic Philosophy, Based on the Doctrine of Evolution, with Criticisms of the Positive Philosophy*, 2 vols. (London: Macmillan, 1874).

163.31   Bosh] An expression derived from William Kingdon Clifford; see *Essays, Comments, and Reviews*, p. 40.

164.13   Mind] See note to 158.20.

164.24   "Other] For the reference in Emerson see *Essays in Religion and Morality*, note to 114.16.

166.19   Wordsworth's] William Wordsworth (1770–1850), English poet.

166.24   Dog] For this example see *Essays, Comments, and Reviews*, pp. 11–12.

166.26   Jackman] Wilbur Samuel Jackman (1855–1907), American educator, a Harvard student in 1884.

166.35   Carlyle] Thomas Carlyle, *Sartor Resartus: The Life and Opinions of Herr Teufelsdröckh*, 3rd ed. (London: Chapman and Hall, 1849) (*AC 85.J2376.Zz849c).

167.5   (Romanes)] For a possible reference see "The Sentiment of Rationality," in *Essays in Philosophy*, p. 61.

167.14   "Am] Johann Wolfgang von Goethe, *Faust*, ed. Erich Trunz (Hamburg: Vegner, 1963), p. 44 (lines 1224, 1237).

167.17   Mind] William James, "The Sentiment of Rationality," *Mind*, 4 (July 1879), 317–346; reprinted in *Essays in Philosophy*.

167.29   *Wundt*] See notes to 160.26, 160.27, 160.28.

167.32   Paulsen] Friedrich Paulsen (1846–1908), German philosopher, "Über das Verhältniss der Philosophie zur Wissenschaft," *Vierteljahrsschrift für wissenschaftliche Philosophie*, 1 (1876), 15–50.

169.1   B's] Alexander Bain, *The Emotions and the Will*, 3rd ed. (London: Longmans, Green, 1875) (WJ 506.41).

170.12   Stewart] Balfour Stewart (1828–1887), Scottish physicist, *The Conservation of Energy* (1873).

170.12   Heath] Douglas Denon Heath (1811–1897), British jurist and writer, *An Elementary Exposition of the Doctrine of Energy* (1874).

170.13   Maxwell] James Clerk Maxwell (1831–1879), Scottish physicist, *Matter and Motion* (1876).

170.13   Tait] Peter Guthrie Tait (1831–1901), Scottish physicist, *Lectures on Some Recent Advances in Physical Science* (1876).

170.14   Mach] Ernst Mach (1838–1916), Austrian physicist and philosopher, *Die Mechanik* (1883).

170.16   C.] Spencer speaks of the continuity of matter.

170.25   Comte's] Auguste Comte (1798–1857), *Cours de philosophie positive*, 6 vols. (Paris: Bachelier, 1830–1842). James's edition has not been identified.

170.26   Nature] The controversy in *Nature*, vols. 9–10 (1874), concerned Spencer's assertion that there are a priori truths in physics and mathematics. The first to enter a protest was Peter Guthrie Tait (*Nature*, 9 [March 26, 1874], 402–403). He was followed by numerous others.

170.26   Bowne] Borden Parker Bowne (1847–1910), American philosopher, *Studies in Theism* (New York: Phillips & Hunt, 1879). Chapter 5 is on "The Conservation of Energy."

170.27   Birks] Thomas Rawson Birks (1810–1883), English theologian. James could be referring to *First Principles of Moral Science* (London: Macmillan, 1873) or *Modern Physical Fatalism and the Doctrine of Evolution, Including an Examination of Mr. H. Spencer's First Principles* (London: Macmillan, 1876).

170.27   Wright] *Philosophical Discussions*.

171.1 *Delboeuf*] Joseph Remi Léopold Delbœuf, "Le Sommeil et les rêves," *Revue Philosophique*, 8 (October 1879), 329–356; 8 (November 1879), 494–520; 9 (February 1880), 129–169; "Déterminisme et liberté," *Revue Philosophique*, 13 (May 1882), 453–480; 13 (June 1882), 608–638; 14 (August 1882), 156–189.

171.4 "p.] Persistence of relations.

171.19 Mariotte] Edme Mariotte (1620–1684), French physicist.

171.37 Leuba] James Henry Leuba (1868–1946), American psychologist, "A Study in the Psychology of Religious Phenomena," *American Journal of Psychology*, 7 (April 1896), 309–385. This reference was added later.

172.32 Chapter] Chapter 10 of part II is on "The Rhythm of Motion."

172.37 Regulus] Marcus Atilius Regulus (d. c. 250 B.C.), Roman general. Captured by the Carthaginians, he was sent on a mission to Rome. According to legend, he returned to Carthage knowing that he would be put to death.

173.18 Ward] Lester Frank Ward, *Dynamic Sociology, or Applied Social Science*, 2 vols. (New York: D. Appleton, 1883).

173.18 Holt] Perhaps a student.

175.27 form] James added as a text Spencer's *The Data of Ethics* (New York: D. Appleton, 1879) (WJ 582.24) in 1883–1884.

176.27 Hellwald] Friedrich Anton Heller von Hellwald (1842–1892), ethnologist, wrote in German. Hellwald expresses such views in *Culturgeschichte in ihrer natürlichen Entwicklung bis zur Gegenwart*, 2nd ed., 2 vols. (Augsburg: Lampart, 1876–1877), II, 738–739.

176.39 Sidgwick] Henry Sidgwick, *The Methods of Ethics* (London: Macmillan, 1874). Sidgwick argued that in order to make our ethical views coherent we need to suppose a power which rewards and punishes.

177.1 Kants] Apparently a reference to the opening remarks in the preface to the first edition of the *Critique of Pure Reason* that reason, having risen with the aid of experience, strives to rise even higher without experience.

177.4 Stephen] Probably James Fitzjames Stephen (1829–1894), English jurist. For a possible text see *Talks to Teachers*, pp. 166–167.

177.17 Mallock] William Hurrell Mallock (1849–1923), British author, *Is Life Worth Living?* (London: Chatto & Windus, 1879).

177.22 Cases] In 1880–1881 James taught Philosophy 5: Psychology, using Bain's mental science as a text. Preserved is *Mental and Moral Science* (London: Longmans, Green, 1868) (WJ 506.41.2). In later editions the work was divided into two parts, with the first part devoted to psychology and the history of philosophy (London: Longmans, Green, 1872). It is probably this part which served as James's text. The dating of the manuscript is conjectural, based on the association with Bain. Part of it is in the hand of James's wife, characteristic of manuscripts from this period.

178.1 Kingsley] Charles Kingsley (1819–1875), English clergyman and novelist.

178.1   Froude] James Anthony Froude (1818–1894), English historian.

178.12   Chapter] There is a chapter on ideal emotions in the first part of *Mental and Moral Science* and in *The Emotions and the Will*.

178.21   psychological] In 1881–1882 James taught Philosophy 4: Contemporary Philosophy, dealing primarily with Mill's logic. In 1886–1887 he taught Philosophy 5: English Empirical Philosophy, also on Mill's logic. Since a part of these notes is in the hand of James's wife, they probably go back to 1881–1882, although they easily could have been used later. Preserved is *A System of Logic: Ratiocinative and Inductive*, 8th ed., 2 vols. (London: Longmans, Green, Reader, and Dyer, 1872) (WJ 555.51).

178.27   *Taine*] The reference fits *De l'intelligence*, 2 vols. (Paris: Hachette, 1870) (WJ 684.41).

178.30   *Lotze*] Rudolph Hermann Lotze (1817–1881), German philosopher, *Metaphysik* (Leipzig: S. Hirzel, 1879) (WJ 751.88.8).

179.7   *Sigwart*] Christoph Sigwart (1830–1904), German philosopher, *Logik*, 2 vols. (Tübingen: Laupp, 1873–1878).

181.20   Whewell] William Whewell (1794–1866), British philosopher and historian of science, *Novum Organum Renovatum* (second part of *The Philosophy of the Inductive Sciences*, 3rd ed.) (London: John W. Parker, 1858).

181.20   Atlantic] William James, "Great Men, Great Thoughts, and the Environment," *Atlantic Monthly*, 46 (October 1880), 441–459; reprinted under a different title in *The Will to Believe*.

181.20   Bowen's] Francis Bowen (1811–1890), American philosopher, professor at Harvard, *A Treatise on Logic; or, the Laws of Pure Thought* (Cambridge: Sever and Francis, 1864).

181.27   Bain's] Alexander Bain, *Logic*, second part, Induction (London: Longmans, Green, Reader, & Dyer, 1870).

182.9   Martineau's] The dating is James's. Texts for the course were volume two of James Martineau, *Types of Ethical Theory*, 2 vols. (Oxford: Clarendon, 1885) (WJ 553.78.2), and *A Study of Religion: Its Sources and Contents*, 2 vols. (Oxford: Clarendon, 1888) (WJ 553.78).

185.16   Royce's] Josiah Royce (1855–1916), American philosopher, one of James's closer personal friends, *The Religious Aspect of Philosophy* (Boston: Houghton, Mifflin, 1885) (WJ 477.98.4).

185.27   Sidgwick] Henry Sidgwick, "The Theory of Evolution in Its Application to Practice," *Mind*, 1 (January 1876), 52–67; "On Historical Psychology," *Nineteenth Century*, 7 (February 1880), 353–360.

186.7   Hard] The dating is James's. Philosophy 1: General Introduction to Philosophy.—Logic, Psychology, and Metaphysics was taught by George Herbert Palmer, James, and Santayana in 1890–1891. James was responsible for the metaphysics portion. His text was Lotze's *Outlines of Metaphysic*, trans. by George T. Ladd (Boston: Ginn & Co., 1886) (WJ 751.88.16).

186.8   Touchstone] For the quotation see *Some Problems of Philosophy*, p. 11.

186.13 Schopenhauer] Arthur Schopenhauer (1788–1860), *Die Welt als Wille und Vorstellung*, 3rd ed., 2 vols. (Leipzig: F. A. Brockhaus, 1859) (*AC 85.J2376.Zz859s).

186.14 Comte] Auguste Comte, *Principes de philosophie positive* (Paris: J. B. Baillière, 1868).

186.23 Spencer] "The Reconciliation" is chapter 5 of part I of *First Principles*.

186.25 Littré] Émile Littré (1801–1881), French positivist philosopher and writer, in his "préface d'un disciple" to Comte's *Principes*.

186.26 Fiske] *Outlines of Cosmic Philosophy*.

187.4 Dalton] John Dalton (1766–1844), English chemist.

187.7 Bacon's] Francis Bacon (1561–1626), *Novum Organu...* (1620).

187.8 Harvey] William Harvey (1578–1657), English anatomist.

187.10 Descartes] James's annotated copy of *Les Principes de la philosophie*, 4th ed. (Paris: Theodore Girard, 1681) (*AC 85.J2376.Zz681d) is preserved.

187.20 Ward] James Ward (1843–1925), British philosopher and psychologist, "The Progress of Philosophy," *Mind*, 15 (April 1890), 213–233.

187.30 Lotze's] *Outlines of Metaphysic*.

187.32 Kant] *Critique of Pure Reason*, A805=B833.

187.34 Cousin's] Victor Cousin (1792–1867), French philosopher and historian of philosophy. James is referring to Cousin's well-known division of philosophical systems into sensualistic, idealistic, skeptical, and mystical.

188.17 Patrick] George Thomas White Patrick (b.1857), American philosopher, *The Fragments of the Work of Heraclitus of Ephesus on Nature* (Baltimore: N. Murray, 1889).

188.28 Jowett] *The Dialogues of Plato*, trans. Benjamin Jowett, 4 vols. (Oxford: Clarendon, 1871) (WJ 835.70).

189.13 Aristotle] For works by Aristotle from James's library see *Some Problems of Philosophy*, note to 11.6.

191.1 Arrian] Arrian (b. c.100), Greek philosopher and historian, editor of the lectures of Epictetus.

191.4 Epictetus] James's references best fit *The Works of Epictetus. Consisting of His Discourses, in Four Books, the Enchiridion, and Fragments*, trans. Elizabeth Carter and Thomas Wentworth Higginson (Boston: Little, Brown, 1865).

191.28 Peirce] Charles Sanders Peirce, review of *The Works of George Berkeley*, ed. Alexander Campbell Fraser, in *North American Review*, 113 (October 1871), 449–472; reprinted in volume II of *Writings of Charles S. Peirce*.

191.30 Encyclical] In 1879 Leo XIII published the encyclical *Aeterni Patris* which initiated a revival of Thomism.

193.1 Microcosmus] Hermann Lotze, *Microcosmus: An Essay Concerning Man and His Relation to the World,* trans. Elizabeth Hamilton and E. E. Constance Jones, 2 vols. Vol. I of James's set (WJ 751.88.14) is (New York: Scribner and Welford, 1885), while vol. II is (Edinburgh: T. & T. Clark, 1885).

193.15 Vanini] Lucilio Vanini (1585–1619), Italian philosopher, executed as an atheist and magician.

194.33 works] *Œuvres de Spinoza,* ed. Émile Saisset, 3 vols. (Paris: Charpentier, 1861) (WJ 871.82). Page references are to vol. III, *Ethics.*

196.3 Fischer] James's page references best fit Kuno Fischer, *Geschichte der neuern Philosophie,* 2nd ed., vol. II (*Leibniz und seine Schule*) (Heidelberg: Friedrich Bassermann, 1867).

196.27 Monadology] *Œuvres philosophiques de Leibniz,* ed. Paul Janet, 2 vols. (Paris: Ladrange, 1866) (WJ 749.41), II, 595–596.

196.30 Read] *Nouveaux essais sur l'entendement humain,* in *Œuvres,* vol. I.

197.1 F.B.] Henry Richard Fox Bourne (1837–1909), British reformer and author, *The Life of John Locke,* 2 vols. (London: Henry S. King, 1876). James's references are to vol. I.

197.1 Essay] John Locke, *An Essay Concerning Human Understanding* (London: William Tegg, 1853) (WJ 551.13).

197.31 America] The dates of Berkeley's stay in America are 1728–1731.

198.4 (Huxley)] Thomas Henry Huxley, *Hume* (New York: Harper & Brothers, 1879).

198.6 Treatise] David Hume, *A Treatise of Human Nature,* ed. T. H. Green and T. H. Grose, 2 vols. (London: Longmans, Green, 1874) (WJ 540.54.2). The reference is to vol. I.

198.8 Cause] David Hume, *An Enquiry Concerning Human Understanding,* vol. II of *Essays Moral, Political, and Literary,* ed. T. H. Green and T. H. Grose (London: Longmans, Green, 1875) (WJ 540.54). For the texts see *Some Problems of Philosophy,* pp. 99–101.

198.9 Ego] *Treatise,* vol. I.

198.10 Wesley] Following Hume's death, Wesley preached a sermon attacking Hume's character.

198.10 Johnson] According to Ernest Campbell Mossner, *The Life of David Hume* (Austin: University of Texas Press, 1954), pp. 605–606, Samuel Johnson claimed that Hume was lying when he expressed his indifference at the prospect of annihilation.

198.14 Look] The dating of No. 16 is Perry's. This is the only year in which James taught a course on Descartes, Spinoza, and Leibniz.

198.14 Bouillier] With the exception of Bacon, the persons listed are authors either of studies in the philosophy of Descartes, or of general histories of philosophy, or who in their writings have dealt with historical figures. Francisque

Cyrille Bouillier (1813–1899) is the author of *Histoire de la philosophie cartésienne* (1854).

198.14   Caird] Edward Caird (1835–1908), Scottish philosopher.

198.14   Mahaffy] John Pentland Mahaffy (1839–1919), Irish scholar.

198.14   Rosmini] Antonio Rosmini-Serbati (1797–1855), Italian philosopher and statesman.

198.15   Lange] Friedrich Albert Lange (1828–1875), German philosopher.

198.15   Dühring] Eugen Karl Dühring (1833–1921), German philosopher.

198.15   Stöckl's] Albert Stöckl (1823–1895), German scholastic philosopher.

198.15   Kleutgen] Joseph Kleutgen (1811–1883), German Jesuit theologian and philosopher.

198.16   Windelband] Wilhelm Windelband (1848–1915), German historian of philosophy.

198.21   Fischer] Kuno Fischer, *Descartes and His School*, trans. from the 3rd German ed. by J. P. Gordy, ed. Noah Porter (London: T. Fisher Unwin, 1887).

198.25   "Cid"] James is referring to the tragedy by Corneille.

199.5   Hobbes] James seems to have in mind Objection 13 of the third set of objections, by Thomas Hobbes. The page reference fits James's copy, *Les méditations métaphysiques*, 3rd ed. (Paris: Chez Michel Bobin & Nicolas Le Gras, 1673) (*AC 85.J2376.Zz673d). The editors of this edition introduced paragraph numbering, using roman numerals, not reproduced in other editions. The numbering starts anew for each meditation and each set of objections.

200.27   Quote] The page numbers for Leibniz refer to Kuno Fischer, *Geschichte der neuern Philosophie*, 2nd ed., II (Heidelberg: Bassermann, 1867). Perry reports that an annotated copy was sold from James's library.

201.30   Spinola] Cristobal Rojas de Spinola (1626–1695), Roman Catholic bishop, noted for efforts to reunite Protestants and Catholics.

201.33   Bossuet's] Jacques Bénigne Bossuet (1627–1704), French clergyman and theological writer, *Exposition de la doctrine de l'église catholique* (1671).

202.12   Agrippa's] Henricus Cornelius Agrippa von Nettesheim (1486–1535), Renaissance adventurer and writer.

202.14   Suarez] Francisco Suarez (1548–1617), Spanish scholastic philosopher.

202.16   Telesius] Bernardino Telesio (1509–1588), Italian philosopher.

202.27   Gassendi] Pierre Gassendi (1592–1655), French philosopher, *Syntagma Philosophiae Epicuri* (1649).

202.33   Pomponatius] Pietro Pomponazzi (1462–1525), Italian Aristotelian philosopher.

202.35   Picus] Giovanni Pico della Mirandola (1463–1494), Italian humanist.

202.35   Patrizzio] Francesco Patrizi (1529–1597), Italian Platonist.

202.36   Lipsius] Justus Lipsius (1547–1606), Flemish humanist.

202.37   Campanella] Tommaso Campanella (1568–1639), Italian philosopher, *De sensu rerum et magia.*

204.1   Helmont] Jean Baptiste van Helmont (1577–1644), Flemish physician.

204.2   Charron] Pierre Charron (1541–1603), French philosopher.

204.2   Sanchez] Francisco Sanchez (1552–1623), Spanish philosopher and physician.

204.18   voice] *The Voice of the Silence* is the title of a book by Elena Petrovna Blavatsky (1831–1891), Russian traveler, one of the founders of theosophy.

204.23   *other*] From Leibniz's *Theodicy* (*Œuvres*, II, 326–334).

204.36   "Continent"] The Latin source of the word 'continent' means continuous. James often connects discussions of space with unity in the sense of continuity.

205.2   Lotze's] Hermann Lotze, *Grundzüge der Naturphilosophie* (Leipzig: S. Hirzel, 1882) (WJ 751.88).

206.4   To] The notes are connected with Philosophy 20a: Psychological Seminary for 1891–1892. The catalogue does not describe the course beyond noting that "subjects and hours will be determined after consultation with those who apply." The identification is based on the following remark by Dickinson Sergeant Miller: "In my second year [1891–1892] I was with him in one of these for both terms, the first half-year studying the psychology of pleasure and pain, and the second, mental pathology. Here each of us undertook a special topic" (Dickinson Sergeant Miller, *Philosophical Analysis and Human History*, ed. Loyd D. Easton [Dordrecht: Reidel, 1975], pp. 49–50). Miller goes on to list some of the students in the course, and his list matches the list of students on p. 210.

206.4   Malebranche] Nicolas de Malebranche, *Entretiens sur la métaphysique*, in *Œuvres de Malebranche*, I (Paris: Charpentier, 1871) (WJ 653.49).

206.5   Cesca] Giovanni Cesca (1858–1908), Italian philosopher and educator, "Die Lehre von der Natur der Gefühle," *Vierteljahrsschrift für wissenschaftliche Philosophie*, 10 (1886), 137–165.

206.28   Volkmann] Wilhelm Fridolin Volkmann, Ritter von Volkmar (1822–1877), Czechoslovakian philosopher and psychologist, *Lehrbuch der Psychologie*, 2nd ed., 2 vols. (Cöthen: Schulze, 1875–1876).

207.17   (Marshall)] Henry Rutgers Marshall (1852–1927), American architect and writer, "The Classification of Pleasure and Pain," *Mind*, 14 (October 1889), 511–536; "The Physical Basis of Pleasure and Pain" (part I), *Mind*, 16 (July 1891), 327–354.

207.22   Miller] Apparently Dickinson Sergeant Miller (1868–1963), American philosopher, then a graduate student.

207.23   Dumont] Léon Dumont (1837–1877), French author, *Théorie scientifique de la sensibilité* (Paris: Germer Baillière, 1875).

207.27   Mantegazza] Paolo Mantegazza (1831–1910), Italian physician and anthropologist, *Physiologie de la douleur* (Paris: Librairie Illustrée, 1888).

208.3   Longet] While James's hand is not clear at this point, the reference could be to François Achille Longet (1811–1871), French physiologist.

208.6   Lehmann] Alfred Georg Ludwig Lehmann (1858–1921), Danish psychologist. James discusses Lehmann's view of association in *Principles*, pp. 634n–635n.

208.24   Burkhardt] Gottlieb Burckhardt (b.1836), Swiss physiologist, *Die physiologische Diagnostik der Nervenkrankheiten* (Leipzig: Wilhelm Engelmann, 1875).

208.35   Nichols] Herbert Nichols served as instructor of psychology at Harvard in 1890–1893.

209.17   Kröner] Eugen Kröner (b.1861), German physician, *Das körperliche Gefühl* (Breslau: Eduard Trewendt, 1887). The copy in Widener (Phil 5400.16) is annotated by James.

210.1   Hoffding] Harald Höffding (1843–1931), Danish philosopher, *Outlines of Psychology*, trans. Mary E. Lowndes (London: Macmillan, 1891) (WJ 816.39).

210.2   Wundt] Schliemann is a student, probably William Emil Schliemann, a divinity graduate student in 1891–1892. His paper was on Wundt. James Rowland Angell (1869–1949), American psychologist, then a graduate student, wrote on Adolf Horwicz (1831–1894), German philosopher. See also note to 211.16.

210.6   Thompson] Daniel Greenleaf Thompson (1850–1897), American author, *A System of Psychology*, 2 vols. (London: Longmans, Green, 1884).

210.6   Hodder] Alfred Hodder (1866–1907), American author.

210.10   Herbart] Johann Friedrich Herbart (1776–1841), German philosopher.

210.11   Nahlowsky] Joseph Wilhelm Nahlowsky (1812–1885), *Das Gefühlsleben*, 2nd ed. (Leipzig: Veit, 1884).

210.16   Gurney] Apparently a reference to Edmund Gurney's *The Power of Sound* (1880).

210.16   Bakewell] Charles Montague Bakewell (1867–1957), American philosopher.

210.21   Bain] Alexander Bain, " 'On Feeling as Indifference,' " *Mind*, 14 (January 1889), 97–106.

210.22   Stanley] Hiram Miner Stanley, "Relation of Feeling to Pleasure and Pain," *Mind*, 14 (October 1889), 537–544.

210.23   *Bradley*] Francis Herbert Bradley (1846–1924), English philosopher, "On Pleasure, Pain, Desire and Volition," *Mind*, 13 (January 1888), 1–36.

210.24   *Johnson*] W. E. Johnson, "On Feeling as Indifference," *Mind*, 13 (January 1888), 80–83; F. A. Mason, "On 'Feeling as Indifference,' " *Mind*, 13 (April 1888), 253–255.

210.25   Sully] James Sully (1842–1923), British philosopher and psychologist, "Harmony of Colours," *Mind*, 4 (April 1879), 172–191.

210.26 Ward] James Ward, "Psychology," *Encyclopædia Britannica*, 9th ed. (1886) (WJ 592.75.2).

210.27 Meynert] Theodor Meynert, *Psychiatrie*, pt. 1 (Vienna: W. Braumüller, 1884). James's annotated copy is in Widener (Phil 6962.5).

210.28 Mosso] Angelo Mosso (1846–1910), Italian physiologist, "Einfluss des Nervensystems auf die thierische Temperatur," *Archiv für pathologische Anatomie und Physiologie und für klinische Medicin*, 106 (October 1886), 80–126.

210.29 Sorel] Georges Sorel (1847–1922), French philosopher, "Contributions psycho-physiques à l'étude esthétique," *Revue Philosophique*, 29 (June 1890), 561–579; 30 (July 1890), 22–41.

210.30 Lipps] Theodor Lipps (1851–1914), German psychologist and philosopher, *Grundtatsachen des Seelenlebens* (Bonn: Max Cohen und Sohn, 1883) (WJ 750.71).

210.31 Meynert] In back of his copy of *Psychiatrie* James has written: "Childish explanation of outer perception, p. 183."

210.32 Stanley] Hiram Miner Stanley, "Feeling and Emotion," *Mind*, 11 (January 1886), 66–76.

210.35 Herrick] Clarence Luther Herrick (1858–1904), American naturalist and psychologist, "Modern Algedonic Theories," *Journal of Comparative Neurology*, 5 (March 1895), 1–32.

210.38 *Richet*] Charles Robert Richet (1850–1935), French physiologist, *L'Homme et l'intelligence* (Paris: Alcan, 1884). James's annotated copy is in Widener (Phil 5257.6).

211.2 Sergi] Giuseppe Sergi (1841–1936), Italian anthropologist, *La Psychologie physiologique*, trans. from the Italian by M. Mouton (Paris: Alcan, 1888).

211.3 Schopenhauer] I, 376–381.

211.4 Ulrici] Hermann Ulrici (1806–1884), German philosopher, *Leib und Seele*, 2nd ed., 2 vols. (Leipzig: Weigel, 1874).

211.7 Med.] Hermann Lotze, *Medicinische Psychologie* (Leipzig: Weidmann, 1852) (WJ 751.88.4).

211.8 Maher] Michael Maher (1860–1917), Jesuit philosopher and psychologist, *Psychology* (London: Longmans, Green, 1890).

211.11 Rabier] Élie Rabier (b.1846), French philosopher, *Leçons de philosophie*, I (vol. I is titled *Psychologie*) (Paris: Hachette, 1884).

211.12 Levesque] Louis Jean Lévesque de Pouilly (1691–1750), French writer, *The Theory of Agreeable Sensations* (Boston: Bradford and Read, 1812). In this edition chapter 3—"There is a pleasure connected with whatever exercises, without fatiguing the organs of the body"—begins on p. 24. The "H.L." could stand for Harvard Library in which the edition cited is preserved.

211.14 Beneke] Friedrich Eduard Beneke (1798–1854), German philosopher, *Lehrbuch der Psychologie*, 3rd ed. (Berlin: E. S. Mittler, 1861).

211.15 Waitz] Theodor Waitz (1821–1864), German philosopher, *Lehrbuch der Psychologie als Naturwissenschaft* (Braunschweig: Vieweg, 1849).

211.16 *Wundt*] Wilhelm Wundt, "Über das Verhältnis der Gefühle zu den Vorstellungen," *Vierteljahrsschrift für die wissenschaftliche Philosophie*, 3 (1879), 129–151; "Psychologische Tatsachen und Hypothesen. Reflexionen aus Anlass der Abhandlung von A. Horwicz über das Verhältnis der Gefühle zu den Vorstellungen," *Vierteljahrsschrift*, 3 (1879), 342–357; Adolf Horwicz, "Das Verhältnis der Gefühle zu den Vorstellungen und die Frage nach dem psychischen Grundprozesse," *Vierteljahrsschrift*, 3 (1879), 308–342.

211.17 *Jaeger*] H. Jäger, "Das Prinzip des kleinsten Kraftmasses in der Ästhetik," *Vierteljahrsschrift*, 5 (1881), 415–447.

211.19 *Lipps*] Theodor Lipps, "Bemerkungen zur Theorie der Gefühle," *Vierteljahrsschrift*, 13 (1889), 160–194.

211.20 *Kröner*] Eugen Kröner, "Gemeingefühl und sinnliches Gefühl," *Vierteljahrsschrift*, 11 (1887), 153–176.

211.21 *Külpe*] Oswald Külpe (1862–1915), Latvian-born psychologist, "Zur Theorie der sinnlichen Gefühle," *Vierteljahrsschrift*, 11 (1887), 424–482; 12 (1888), 50–81.

211.24 *Horwicz*] Adolf Horwicz, *Psychologische Analysen auf physiologischer Grundlage*, 2 vols. (WJ 739.78). Vol. I (Halle: C.E.M. Pfeffer, 1872); vol. II, pt. 2 (Magdeburg: A. & R. Faber, 1878).

211.28 *Allen*] Charles Grant Blairfindie Allen, *Physiological Æsthetics* (London: Henry S. King, 1877) (WJ 503.49). James's review is reprinted in *Essays, Comments, and Reviews*.

211.30 Palgrave] Francis Turner Palgrave (1824–1897), English poet, "The Decline of Art," *Nineteenth Century*, 23 (January 1888), 71–92.

211.31 Symonds] John Addington Symonds (1840–1893), English writer, "On the Application of Evolutionary Principles to Art and Literature," *Essays: Speculative and Suggestive*, 2 vols. (London: Chapman and Hall, 1890), I, 42–83. The "Notes on Style" are in I, 256–331.

211.33 Fichte] Immanuel Hermann Fichte (1796–1879), German philosopher, *Psychologie*, I (Leipzig: F. A. Brockhaus, 1864) (WJ 728.12).

212.3 man] The title and date are James's. On the label, following the identification of the course, there is the following note: "Beginnings of Philosophy of Pure Experience." In the catalogue the course is described as "Psychological Seminary.—First half-year: the Feelings.—Second half-year: Discussion of certain theoretic problems, as Consciousness, Knowledge, the Self, the relation of Mind and Body, etc." According to James he concluded this seminary with some quotations from Benjamin Paul Blood and the words "There is no *Absolute*" (Perry, II, 231–232).

212.25 Brentano] Franz Brentano (1838–1917), German philosopher, *Psychologie vom empirischen Standpunkte*, I (Leipzig: Duncker & Humblot, 1874) (WJ 709.24).

212.27 M—g.] Hugo Münsterberg, "Über Aufgaben und Methoden der Psychologie," *Schriften der Gesellschaft für psychologische Forschung*, 2 (1891), 93–272. James's copy is of the separately paged off-print (WJ 757.62.4), inscribed to James, July 1891. The reference fits the journal version.

212.28 Bowne] Borden Parker Bowne, *Introduction to Psychological Theory* (New York: Harper & Brothers, 1887); *Metaphysics: A Study in First Principles* (New York: Harper & Brothers, 1882). For the latter reference see *Principles*, p. 221.

212.30 Baumann] Julius Baumann (1837–1916), German philosopher, *Philosophie als Orientierung über die Welt* (Leipzig: S. Hirzel, 1872) (WJ 706.89).

212.31 Rehmke] Johannes Rehmke (1848–1930), German philosopher, *Lehrbuch der allgemeinen Psychologie* (Hamburg and Leipzig: Leopold Voss, 1894) (WJ 775.39). James's index contains "One Universal Subject 133, 153, 52, 454,–5; 460,–1."

212.32 Natorp] Paul Natorp (1854–1924), German philosopher, *Einleitung in die Psychologie nach kritischer Methode* (Freiburg i. B.: J. C. B. Mohr [Paul Siebeck], 1888) (WJ 758.87). For marginalia see *Essays in Radical Empiricism*, note to 3.12.

213.2 Hodgson] Shadworth Hollway Hodgson, *Time and Space: A Metaphysical Essay* (London: Longman, Green, Longman, Roberts, and Green, 1865) (WJ 539.18.6).

213.3 *Fouillee's*] Alfred Fouillée (1838–1912), French philosopher. For the books see *Essays, Comments, and Reviews*, note to 457.16. James's review of Fouillée is reprinted in that volume.

213.4 Cornelius] Hans Cornelius (1863–1947), Monacan-born philosopher.

213.5 Ferrier] James Frederick Ferrier, "An Introduction to the Philosophy of Consciousness," *Blackwood's Magazine*, 43 (February 1838), 187–201; (April 1838), 437–452; 44 (August 1838), 234–244; (October 1838), 539–552; 45 (March 1839), 419–430.

213.5 Baldwin] James Mark Baldwin (1861–1934), American psychologist and philosopher.

213.5 Avenarius] Richard Avenarius (1843–1896), German philosopher. Preserved are *Philosophie als Denken der Welt* (Leipzig: Fues, 1876) (WJ 706.24) and *Der menschliche Weltbegriff* (Leipzig: O. R. Reisland, 1891) (WJ 706.24). James's annotated copy of *Kritik der reinen Erfahrung*, 2 vols. (Leipzig: Fues, 1888–1890) was sold. For James's view of Avenarius see *Letters*, II, 301.

213.6 M. de Biran] François Pierre Maine de Biran (1766–1824), French philosopher and statesman.

213.6 Meinong] Alexius Meinong (1853–1920), Austrian philosopher. For James's view of Meinong see Perry, II, 485.

213.11 (Singer)] Edgar Arthur Singer (1873–1955), American philosopher, a student in the course.

213.13 (Strong)] Charles Augustus Strong (1862–1940), American philosopher and psychologist. Nothing on mind-stuff by Strong was found.

214.19 Schuppe] Ernst Julius Wilhelm Schuppe (1836–1913), German philosopher.

214.39 Hodgson] Shadworth Hodgson; for a possible reference see *Principles*, p. 455.

214.39 Newman] Apparently John Henry Newman (1801–1890), Roman Catholic cardinal.

215.11 Uphues] Goswin K. Uphues (1841–1916), German philosopher. For a possible reference see *Principles*, p. 689.

215.28 Munsterberg] P. 12 fits the off-print version (p. 102 in the journal). On p. 12 James has the note "well is that a part of the inhalt? or a relation of it? or what."

215.30 Schuppe] Perhaps Wilhelm Schuppe, *Das menschliche Denken* (Berlin: W. Weber, 1870), or *Grundriss der Erkenntnistheorie und Logik* (Berlin: R. Gaertners Verlagsbuchhandlung, 1894).

216.4 Peirce] Charles Sanders Peirce, "The Doctrine of Necessity Examined," *Monist*, 2 (April 1892), 321–337.

217.25 Bradley] Francis Herbert Bradley, *Appearance and Reality* (London: Swan Sonnenschein, 1893) (WJ 510.2).

217.26 Lasswitz] Kurd Lasswitz, "Nature and the Individual Mind," *Monist*, 6 (April 1896), 396–431.

217.27 Miller] Dickinson Sergeant Miller, "The Meaning of Truth and Error," *Philosophical Review*, 2 (July 1893), 408–425; "The Confusion of Content and Function in Mental Analysis," *Psychological Review*, 2 (November 1895), 535–550. Miller was discussed by Gertrude Stein (1874–1946), American author, then a student at Radcliffe.

217.29 Stumpf] Carl Stumpf (1848–1939), German psychologist. *Tonpsychologie*, 2 vols. (Leipzig: S. Hirzel, 1883–1890) (WJ 783.89). James apparently confused the title of Stumpf's book with *Die Lehre von den Tonempfindungen* by Helmholtz. Stumpf was discussed by Edwin Bissell Holt (1873–1946), American psychologist, then a graduate student.

217.30 Cornelius] Hans Cornelius, "Über Verschmelzung und Analyse," *Vierteljahrsschrift für wissenschaftliche Philosophie*, 16 (1892), 404–446; 17 (1893), 30–75.

217.31 Meinong] Alexius Meinong, "Über Begriff und Eigenschaften der Empfindung," *Vierteljahrsschrift*, 12 (1888), 324–354, 477–502.

217.33 Twardowski] Kazimierz Twardowski (1866–1938), Polish philosopher, *Zur Lehre vom Inhalt und Gegenstand der Vorstellungen* (Vienna: Hölder, 1894). James's copy was sold with the following note on a flyleaf: "40, my feeling is not hot, square etc., its object is; does this same datum come thus to contain and to exclude, according to its different contexts, these attributes?"

217.34   Piat] Clodius Piat (1854–1918), French Catholic philosopher. Spindler is Frank Nicholas Spindler, then a graduate student.

217.34   Knauer] Vincenz Knauer (1828–1894), Austrian philosopher.

217.35   Baldwin] James Mark Baldwin, "The Origin of a 'Thing' and Its Nature," *Psychological Review*, 2 (November 1895), 551–573.

217.36   Rickert] Heinrich Rickert (1863–1936), German philosopher.

217.37   Brochard] Victor Charles Louis Brochard (1848–1907), French philosopher, *De l'erreur*, 2nd ed. (Paris: Alcan, 1897).

217.38   Fonsegrive] George Fonsegrive (1852–1917), French philosopher, "Généralisation et induction," *Revue Philosophique*, 41 (April 1896), 353–379; (May 1896), 516–536.

218.1   Reid] Thomas Reid (1710–1796), Scottish philosopher, *An Inquiry into the Human Mind on the Principles of Common Sense* (Edinburgh: A. Kincaid & J. Bell; London: A. Millar, 1764) (Phil 2240.30 [B]*, James's copy in Houghton).

218.4   Seth] James appears to be referring to a series of papers on epistemology in the *Philosophical Review*, vols. 1–3 (1892–1894) by Andrew Seth Pringle-Pattison (1856–1931), Scottish philosopher. The report is by Edward Vermilye Huntington (1874–1952), American mathematician, then a graduate student.

218.6   *Thorndike*] Edward Lee Thorndike (1874–1949), American psychologist, then a graduate student.

218.6   Bergmann] Julius Bergmann (1840–1904), German philosopher, *Grundlinien einer Theorie des Bewusstseins* (Berlin: Otto Loewenstein, 1870). James's marked copy was sold.

218.9   *Solomons*] Leon M. Solomons, a student.

218.39   Clay's] Edmund R. Clay, *The Alternative: A Study in Psychology* (London: Macmillan, 1882); see *Principles*, pp. 573–574.

218.39   Laas] Ernst Laas (1837–1885), German philosopher, "Die Kausalität des Ich," *Vierteljahrsschrift für wissenschaftliche Philosophie*, 4 (1880), 1–54, 185–224, 311–367.

219.37   Calkins] Perhaps Mary Whiton Calkins (1863–1930), American philosopher, a former graduate student, at the time teaching at Wellesley College. But there were other students of that name. Santayana was then teaching at Harvard.

220.16   James-Lange] The James-Lange theory of emotion; see *Essays in Psychology*, note to 168.9.

220.32   Helmholtz] Hermann Helmholtz, *Popular Lectures on Scientific Subjects*, trans. E. Atkinson (London: Longmans, Green, 1873).

221.38   Monist] Charles Sanders Peirce, "The Law of Mind," *Monist*, 2 (July 1892), 533–559.

222.21   Spanish] *The Spanish Gypsy* is a poem by George Eliot, but the lines quoted were not found in several editions of it.

223.31   eject] For this term and its origin see *Principles*, p. 74.

226.3   Green] For the view of Green and other idealists on the relativity of knowledge see *Principles*, pp. 659–660.

227.38   Mach] Ernst Mach, "Facts and Mental Symbols," *Monist*, 2 (January 1892), 198–208.

228.39   Oliver] James Edward Oliver (1829–1895), American mathematician, "A Mathematical View of the Free-will Question," *Philosophical Review*, 1 (May 1892), 292–298.

230.6   Competing] The manuscript of No. 19 was removed by an archivist from James's copy of Stout's *Analytic Psychology*. Clearly the notes are for a course. The *Analytic Psychology* was first advertised in the United States in late May 1896. In a letter to Théodore Flournoy, August 30, 1896, James states that he was engaged to review the book for *Mind*, kept it for two months without reading it, and passed it on to Royce (*Letters*, II, 47). This would make the summer of 1896 the earliest possible date for No. 19. The notes could have been prepared for any one of several courses in 1896–1897 or 1897–1898.

230.7   Stout's] George Frederick Stout (1860–1944), English philosopher and psychologist, *Analytic Psychology*, 2 vols. (London: Swan Sonnenschein, 1896) (WJ 583.67).

230.10   state] In vol. I.

230.23   association] In vol. II.

230.30   Ward] James Ward, "Assimilation and Association," *Mind*, n.s. 2 (July 1893), 347–362; n.s. 3 (October 1894), 509–532.

231.13   p. 7] The remaining references to Stout are to vol. II.

231.14   Mill] John Stuart Mill in his preface to James Mill, *Analysis of the Phenomena of the Human Mind*, ed. John Stuart Mill, 2 vols. (London: Longmans, Green, Reader, and Dyer, 1869) (WJ 550.50), I, vii.

231.15   Mic] *Microcosmus*, vol. I.

234.5   The] The dating is James's. He did not offer the psychological seminary in 1896–1897, and 1897–1898 is the first year in which the seminary dealt with "The Philosophical Problems of Psychology." The seminary met on Mondays, from 9–11 in the morning. The dates on p. 255 should be May 23 and 30.

234.21   Bergson] Henri Bergson (1859–1941), French philosopher.

237.17   Chapter] In *Principles*.

242.4   Sunday] The seminary met on Mondays.

246.38   Avenarius] In the *Kritik der reinen Erfahrung*, system C stands for the nervous system of an individual, R represents the environment, and E-values, the experiences.

250.6   Tufts] James Hayden Tufts (1862–1942), American philosopher, "Can Epistemology Be Based on Mental States?", *Philosophical Review*, 6 (November 1897), 576–592.

256.36 Mind] James's "On the Function of Cognition," *Mind*, 10 (January 1885), 27–44, reprinted in *The Meaning of Truth*.

259.32 because] The title is James's. In 1897–1898 James offered Philosophy 3: The Philosophy of Nature, "with especial reference to Man's place in Nature." The text was Lotze's *Microcosmus*. The course was also offered at Radcliffe. In vol. I of James's copy of the *Microcosmus* there is a list of students in Philosophy 3 at Radcliffe, and although James taught Philosophy 3 at Radcliffe in other years, 1897–1898 was the only year in which the *Microcosmus* was used as a text. In vol. II there is a list of students with 38 names, somewhat more than what is reported for Philosophy 3 at Harvard. But 38 is the number of students in Philosophy 9 in 1898–1899, suggesting that the lecture could be connected with the later course.

262.23 Piper] Leonora Evelina Piper (1859–1950), American trance medium.

264.2 Schiller] Ferdinand Canning Scott Schiller (1864–1937), British philosopher, "Lotze's Monism," *Philosophical Review*, 5 (May 1896), 225–245.

265.14 Uniformity] The dating is James's. The course description is as follows: "The fundamental problems of Theoretical Philosophy. The unity or plurality of the World-Ground, and its knowability or unknowability; Realism and Idealism; Freedom, Teleology, and Theism." Philosophy 9: Metaphysics was offered by Royce in 1897–1898.

265.14 Bowne's] Borden Parker Bowne, *Philosophy of Theism* (New York: Harper & Brothers, 1887), pp. 68–69.

265.15 Darlington's] Apparently Lionel Chester Darlington, a graduate student.

266.38 Lutoslavski's] Wincenty Lutoslawski (1863–1954), Polish philosopher and writer.

267.10 Trevor] John Trevor (b. 1855), British reformer.

267.11 Bucke] Richard Maurice Bucke (1837–1902), Canadian physician. James quotes Bucke extensively in *Varieties*.

267.11 Blood] Benjamin Paul Blood (1832–1919), American writer and mystic; for James's view see "A Pluralistic Mystic," reprinted in *Essays in Philosophy*.

267.13 Ribet] Jérôme Ribet (1837–1909), French Catholic clergyman, author of works on mysticism; see *Varieties*, note to 244.39.

267.15 Vivekananda] Swami Vivekananda (1863–1902), Indian religious leader.

267.19 Blood] For the text see *Essays in Philosophy*, p. 190.

267.26 What] The course is described as the "Philosophy of Nature, with especial reference to Man's place in Nature.—The Fundamental Conceptions of Science; the relation of Mind and Body; Evolution." The texts were by Karl Pearson (1857–1936), English scientist, *The Grammar of Science* (London: Walter Scott, 1892); and James Ward, *Naturalism and Agnosticism*, 2 vols. (London: Adam and Charles Black, 1899) (WJ 592.75). Houghton preserves a copy of *The Grammar of Science*, 2nd ed. (London: Adam and Charles Black, 1900) (*AC 85.J2376.Zz900p) from James's library.

271.16   Royce's] Josiah Royce, *The World and the Individual*, 2 vols. (New York: Macmillan, 1899–1901) (WJ 477.98.6), I, 421–422.

272.26   Renouvier's] For the *principe du nombre* see *Some Problems of Philosophy*, note to 84.30.

273.8   Rationalist] The dating is James's.

273.21–22   "Central] William Wordsworth, "The Excursion," book IV, lines 1146–47 (*The Poetical Works of William Wordsworth*, V [Oxford: Clarendon, 1949]), 145.

274.12   Whitby] Charles Joseph Whitby (b.1864), English poet and writer, "The Ideal and the Actual," *Ethical Review*, 9 (May 12, 1906), 146–147.

274.16   Hoffding] For the anecdote see *Letters*, II, 216.

274.38   Hume's] For Hume's text see *Principles*, p. 333.

274.39   Fullerton] George Stuart Fullerton, *On Sameness and Identity* (Philadelphia: University of Pennsylvania Press, 1890).

276.3   Harper] Thomas Morton Harper (1821–1893), English Jesuit theologian and philosopher, *The Metaphysics of the School*, 3 vols. (London: Macmillan, 1879–1884).

276.4   Rickaby] John Rickaby (1847–1927), English Jesuit theologian and philosopher, *General Metaphysics* (New York: Benziger Brothers, 1890).

276.23   *Hobbes*] Thomas Hobbes, *Human Nature: Or the Fundamental Elements of Policy* (1650).

276.26   *Berkeley*] Alexander Campbell Fraser, *Selections from Berkeley* (Oxford: Clarendon, 1874).

276.27   *Edwards*] Sereno Edwards Dwight, *The Life of President Edwards* (New York: G. & C. & H. Carvill, 1830).

276.36   Thomson] Joseph John Thomson (1856–1940), "On Bodies Smaller than Atoms," *Popular Science Monthly*, 59 (August 1901), 323–335.

276.40   Geulincx] Arnold Geulincx (1624–1669), Flemish philosopher.

277.4   Howison] George Holmes Howison (1834–1916), American philosopher.

279.23   Riehl] Alois Riehl (1844–1924), Austrian philosopher.

279.25   Ostwald] Wilhelm Ostwald (1853–1932), German chemist.

279.28   Le Roy] Édouard Le Roy (1870–1954), French philosopher, "Science et philosophie," *Revue de Métaphysique et de Morale*, 7 (1899), 375–425, 503–562, 706–731; 8 (1900), 37–72.

280.31   Poincaré] Henri Poincaré (1854–1912), French scientist.

280.39   Schiller] Ferdinand Canning Scott Schiller, "Axioms as Postulates," in *Personal Idealism: Philosophical Essays by Eight Members of the University of Oxford*, ed. Henry Sturt (London: Macmillan, 1902) (WJ 583.89). For the text see *Pragmatism*, p. 117.

281.3   Maxwell] The reference appears to be to *The Scientific Papers of James Clerk Maxwell*, ed. W. D. Niven, 2 vols. (Cambridge: Cambridge University Press, 1890). For a similar remark see *Pragmatism*, p. 104.

281.29   Carnot] Nicolas Léonard Sadi Carnot (1796–1832), French physicist, known for his work on reversible engines.

281.35   (Coulomb)] Charles Augustin de Coulomb (1736–1806), French physicist.

282.8   Zn Cu.] Zinc and copper, used in making batteries.

282.17   Ostwald's] Wilhelm Ostwald, *Die Überwindung des wissenschaftlichen Materialismus* (Leipzig: Veit, 1895). For the text see *Some Problems of Philosophy*, p. 77n.

282.27   Le Roy] Édouard Le Roy, "Sur quelques objections adressées à la nouvelle philosophie," *Revue de Métaphysique et de Morale*, 9 (1901), 292–327, 407–432.

283.2   Wilbois] Joseph Wilbois (b.1874), French physicist and writer, "L'Esprit positif," *Revue de Métaphysique et de Morale*, 9 (1901), 154–209, 579–645; 10 (1902), 69–105, 334–370, 565–612.

283.13   Pascal's] See *Manuscript Essays and Notes*, note to 208.7.

283.39   Conception] Josiah Royce, *The Conception of God* (New York: Macmillan, 1897) (WJ 477.98); *The Religious Aspect of Philosophy* (Boston: Houghton, Mifflin, 1885) (WJ 477.98.4).

284.10   Mind] "The Function of Cognition," reprinted in *The Meaning of Truth*; "The Knowing of Things Together," reprinted in *Essays in Philosophy*.

284.10   Miller] See note to 217.27.

286.17   Hodgson] Shadworth Hollway Hodgson, *The Metaphysic of Experience*, 4 vols. (London: Longmans, Green, 1898) (WJ 539.18.2).

288.29   "realistic"] One of the four conceptions of being discussed in *The World and the Individual*.

289.34   Marvin] Walter T. Marvin (1872–1944), American philosopher, *An Introduction to Systematic Philosophy* (New York: Columbia University Press, 1903).

289.37   Schiller] See note to 264.2.

290.29   Bradley] Francis Herbert Bradley, *Appearance and Reality*, 2nd ed. (London: Swan Sonnenschein, 1897).

290.34   Pringle-Pattison] Andrew Seth Pringle-Pattison, *Man's Place in the Cosmos and Other Essays* (Edinburgh: William Blackwood and Sons, 1897).

290.35   Hodder] Alfred Hodder, review of *Appearance and Reality*, in *Psychological Review*, 1 (May 1894), 307–311.

291.27   "Royce"] No such envelope has been identified.

296.27 Joachim] Harold Henry Joachim (1868–1938), British philosopher, *The Nature of Truth* (Oxford: Clarendon, 1906) (WJ 542.63). The reference could have been added later.

297.17 Baldwins] The article "Change" by George Edward Moore (1873–1958), British philosopher, in *Dictionary of Philosophy and Psychology*, ed. James Mark Baldwin, 3 vols. (New York: Macmillan, 1901–1905).

298.35 Motley] John Lothrop Motley (1814–1877), American historian.

298.37 Lutoslawski] Perhaps Wincenty Lutoslawski, "In Search of True Beings," *Monist*, 6 (April 1896), 351–355; but the reference could be to one of several reviews of books by Lutoslawski.

298.38 Schiller] See note to 264.2.

299.40 Mahaffy's] John Pentland Mahaffy, *A Commentary on Kant's Critick of the Pure Reason: Translated from the History of Modern Philosophy by Professor Kuno Fischer, of Jena* (London: Longmans, Green, 1866).

300.20 Paulsen] Friedrich Paulsen, *Introduction to Philosophy*, trans. Frank Thilly (New York: Henry Holt, 1895) (WJ 350.68). James's introduction is reprinted in *Essays in Philosophy*.

301.29 Oken] Lorenz Oken (1779–1851), German naturalist and philosopher of nature. For a possible reference see *Some Problems of Philosophy*, note to 29.1.

301.38 Fechner] Gustav Theodor Fechner, *Die Tagesansicht gegenüber der Nachtansicht* (Leipzig: Breitkopf und Härtel, 1879) (WJ 727.13.2).

303.34 Cournot] Antoine Augustin Cournot (1801–1877), French mathematician and philosopher. The example is found in *An Essay on the Foundations of Our Knowledge*, trans. Merritt H. Moore (New York: Liberal Arts Press, 1956), p. 40.

303.38 Peirce] Charles Sanders Peirce, "Reply to the Necessitarians," *Monist*, 3 (July 1893), 526–570.

304.26 Peirce] See note to 216.4.

304.34 Rev.] Gaston Samuel Milhaud (1858–1918), French philosopher, "Le Hazard chez Aristote et chez Cournot," *Revue de Métaphysique et de Morale*, 10 (November 1902), 667–681.

304.34 "Dilemma] Both of the essays are reprinted in *The Will to Believe*.

304.35 Rev.] Perhaps James has in mind the review by Théodule Ribot of Théodore Ruyssen, *Essai sur l'évolution psychologique du jugement*, in *Revue Philosophique*, 58 (November 1904), 524–528; for Ruyssen see *Pragmatism*, note to 34.3.

305.7 Thomson's] Joseph John Thomson.

305.8 Reynolds's] Osborne Reynolds (1842–1912), British physicist.

305.10 Bergson] Henri Bergson, *Matière et mémoire* (Paris: Alcan, 1896) (WJ 607.75).

305.17   Quetelet's] Lambert Adolphe Jacques Quetelet (1796–1874), French statistician.

305.38   Crookes] William Crookes (1832–1919), British physicist.

305.39   Solomons] Leon M. Solomons, "The Alleged Proof of Parallelism from the Conservation of Energy," *Philosophical Review*, 8 (March 1899), 146–165.

306.15   Faraday] Michael Faraday (1791–1867), English chemist and physicist.

306.15   Hertz] Heinrich Rudolf Hertz (1857–1894), German physicist.

307.37   Monist] See note to 221.38.

309.8   Royce] *The World and the Individual.*

309.11   Preyer] Wilhelm Thierry Preyer (1841–1897), German physiologist and psychologist; see *A Pluralistic Universe*, p. 70.

310.6   Bergson's] Henri Bergson, *Essai sur les données immédiates de la conscience* (Paris: Alcan, 1889) (WJ 607.75).

311.12   Stevenson] Robert Louis Stevenson; for the text see *Essays in Radical Empiricism*, note to 88.9.

312.11   Cantor's] Georg Cantor (1845–1918), German mathematician; for James on Cantor see *Some Problems of Philosophy*, p. 90.

312.13   Couturat] Louis Couturat (1868–1914), French philosopher; see *Some Problems of Philosophy*, p. 93n.

312.21   Principe] For Renouvier's *principe du nombre* see *Some Problems of Philosophy*, note to 84.30.

312.25   Fullerton] George Stuart Fullerton, "The Doctrine of Space and Time," *Philosophical Review*, 10 (March 1901), 113–123; (May 1901), 229–240; (July 1901), 375–385; (September 1901), 488–504; (November 1901), 583–600.

312.26   Evellin] François Jean Marie Auguste Evellin (1836–1910), French philosopher, *Infini et quantité* (Paris: Germer Baillière, 1880) (WJ 625.23).

313.3   Keyser] Cassius Jackson Keyser (1862–1947), American mathematician, "Concerning the Concept and Existence-Proofs of the Infinite," *Journal of Philosophy*, 1 (January 21, 1904), 29–36.

313.6   Cauchy] Augustin Louis Cauchy (1789–1857), French mathematician.

313.6   Dedekind] Richard Dedekind (1831–1916), German mathematician.

313.12   Esquisse] Charles Renouvier, *Esquisse d'une classification systématique des doctrines philosophiques*, 2 vols. (Paris: Bureau de la *Critique Philosophique*, 1885–1886) (WJ 675.61).

313.25   Russell] Bertrand Russell (1872–1970).

313.31   Royce] In the supplementary essay to vol. I of *The World and the Individual.*

313.39   Cf.] Not identified.

314.40 Delboeuf] For Delbœuf on novelty, but without Helen of Troy, see *Some Problems of Philosophy*, pp. 76–77.

315.7 Baldwin] See note to 217.35.

315.28 Wundt's] Wilhelm Wundt, *System der Philosophie* (Leipzig: W. Engelmann, 1889) (WJ 796.59.6).

318.16 Bergson's] According to James, for Bergson the "brain is an organ of *filtration* for spiritual life" (Perry, II, 606).

319.16 "The] Deut. xxxiii:27.

319.23 Working] The dating is James's. The course is Philosophy 20c: Metaphysical Seminary, on "A pluralistic description of the World." The seminary met on Fridays, and thus would have met on November 6.

320.17 Dewey's] John Dewey (1859–1952). James seems to have in mind Dewey's *Studies in Logical Theory* (Chicago: University of Chicago Press, 1903) (WJ 417.93). James's review is reprinted in *Essays in Philosophy*.

320.36 Moore] George Edward Moore, "The Refutation of Idealism," *Mind*, n.s. 12 (October 1903), 433–453.

321.11 M—g.] Hugo Münsterberg discusses the notion of pure experience in *Grundzüge der Psychologie* (Leipzig: J. A. Barth, 1900) (WJ 757.62.2), pp. 44–55.

322.30 Dec] December 1 fell on a Tuesday in 1903.

322.30 Santayana's] The paper has not been identified.

323.38 Cabot] Perhaps Richard Clarke Cabot (1868–1939), American physician and writer on social ethics, at the time a lecturer in philosophy at Harvard. It was not unusual for faculty to attend seminaries.

326.19 Münsterberg's] Münsterberg was involved in drawing up the program for the Congress of Arts and Sciences, Universal Exposition, St. Louis, 1904.

327.5 Oct] The dating is James's. Philosophy 9: Metaphysics is described as follows: "The Fundamental Problems of Theoretical Philosophy. The Nature of Reality; Monism and Pluralism; Freedom, Teleology, and Theism." The Harvard academic year began in late September, and the course met on Tuesdays, Thursdays, and Saturdays. October 6 fell on a Thursday in 1904. James taught the first half, into late January 1905, while Royce took over the second half. James rushed some of the essays on radical empiricism into print in order to be able to distribute them to the students before Royce's advent; see the textual introductions to *Essays in Radical Empiricism*.

327.20 Teichmüller] Nothing on James by a Teichmüller was found. Gustav Teichmüller (1832–1888), German philosopher and historian of philosophy, was concerned to restore the dignity of philosophy, and James could have intended some contrast between Teichmüller's approach and his own. Two works by Teichmüller were sold from James's library.

328.37 Windelband] The reference fits Wilhelm Windelband, *A History of Philosophy with Especial Reference to the Formation and Development of Its Problems and Conceptions*, trans. James H. Tufts (New York: Macmillan, 1893).

328.38 Envelope] Not identified.

329.22 Lyell's] For Lyell's method see *The Will to Believe*, p. 171.

330.1 (McTaggart)] John McTaggart Ellis McTaggart (1866–1925), British philosopher.

330.33 Hoffding's] In late October 1904, Höffding visited James and gave a lecture in James's class; see *Letters*, II, 216.

332.20 Cohen] Morris Raphael Cohen (1880–1947), American philosopher, at the time a graduate student at Harvard.

332.26 Russell's] Bertrand Russell, "Meinong's Theory of Complexes and Assumptions," *Mind*, n.s. 13 (April 1904), 204–219; (July 1904), 336–354; (October 1904), 509–524.

334.18 Taylor] Alfred Edward Taylor (1869–1945), British philosopher.

336.18 Stout] George Frederick Stout, "Alleged Self-Contradictions in the Concept of Relation—A Criticism of Mr. Bradley's 'Appearance and Reality,' Pt. I, Ch. III," *Proceedings of the Aristotelian Society*, n.s. 2 (1902), 1–14.

336.36 (564)] 2nd ed.

337.32 Royce] *The World and the Individual*, vol. I.

337.33 Taylor] Alfred Edward Taylor, *Elements of Metaphysics* (London: Methuen, 1903) (WJ 584.98).

339.36 LeBon] Gustave Le Bon (1841–1931), French sociologist. The following appeared in the *Revue Scientifique*, 5th series, vol. II: "La Matérialisation de l'énergie" (October 15, 1904), pp. 481–495; "La Dématérialisation de la matière" (November 19, 1904), pp. 641–651; unsigned, "La Solution du problème de l'existence des rayons N." (December 3, 1904), pp. 705–709.

339.39 Marshall] Henry Rutgers Marshall, "Of Simpler and More Complex Consciousnesses," *Journal of Philosophy*, 1 (July 7, 1904), 365–372.

341.39 Solomons] See note to 305.39.

343.10 Lewes] *Problems of Life and Mind*, 1st series, vol. II.

343.12 Bowen's] Francis Bowen, *Gleanings from a Literary Life: 1838–1880* (New York: Charles Scribner's Sons, 1880).

343.13 Venn] John Venn, *The Principles of Empirical or Inductive Logic* (London: Macmillan, 1889).

343.14 Sigwart] Christoph Sigwart, *Logic*, trans. Helen Dendy, 2 vols. (London: Swan Sonnenschein, 1895).

343.16 Hobhouse] Leonard Trelawney Hobhouse (1864–1929), British sociologist and philosopher.

343.17 Stöckl] Albert Stöckl, *Lehrbuch der Philosophie*, 4th ed., 2 vols. (Mainz: Franz Kirchheim, 1876).

344.38 Huntington] Perhaps Edward Vermilye Huntington; for a possible reference see *Some Problems of Philosophy*, note to 93.36.

345.30 Carpenter] For a possible reference see *Some Problems of Philosophy*, p. 108.

346.8 Leuba] James Henry Leuba reviewed *The Varieties of Religious Experience* in *International Journal of Ethics*, 14 (April 1904), 322–339.

346.10 Starbuck] Edwin Diller Starbuck (1866–1947), American psychologist, "The Feelings and Their Place in Religion," *American Journal of Religious Psychology and Education*, 1 (November 1904), 168–186; James Henry Leuba, "The Field and the Problems of the Psychology of Religion," *American Journal*, 1 (November 1904), 155–167. The *American Journal* was edited by Granville Stanley Hall, and both essays appeared in the second number.

347.13 Dewey's] The dating is James's. For a description of the course see note to 327.5. The course was offered on Tuesdays, Thursdays, and Saturdays. The students mentioned in the text, with rare exceptions, are not identified in the notes. Their full names as indicated in Harvard directories are given in the index.

349.25 Green's] Thomas Hill Green, *Prolegomena to Ethics*, ed. A. C. Bradley (Oxford: Clarendon, 1883) (WJ 535.22).

350.15 Davidson] Perhaps Thomas Davidson (1840–1900), Scottish-born writer.

350.25 Perry] Ralph Barton Perry (1876–1957), American philosopher, "Truth and Imagination in Religion," *International Journal of Ethics*, 15 (October 1904), 64–82.

351.15 Höffding's] The subjects are treated in Harald Höffding, *The Problems of Philosophy*, trans. Galen M. Fisher (New York: Macmillan, 1905) (WJ 350.39); James's preface is reprinted in *Essays in Philosophy*.

353.33 Tuke] Daniel Hack Tuke (1827–1895), English physician; for a possible reference see *Principles*, note to 712.41.

354.10 Janets] Paul Janet (1823–1899), French philosopher; for a possible reference see *Essays, Comments, and Reviews*, note to 319.26.

354.15 Plato] Lutoslawski is the author of *The Origin and Growth of Plato's Logic* (1897).

354.24 Santayana's] Perhaps George Santayana, *The Life of Reason*, 5 vols. (New York: Charles Scribner's Sons, 1905–1906) (WJ 479.62).

355.1 Sept] September 30, 1905, fell on a Saturday.

355.13 (Wolff.)] Christian Wolff (1679–1754), German philosopher.

355.16 (Baumgarten)] Alexander Gottlieb Baumgarten (1714–1762), German philosopher, *Metaphysica*, par. 1.

355.19 "Systematic] "Metaphysics" (II, 73).

355.29 Ward] See note to 187.20.

355.32 Harris's] For a number of years the *Journal of Speculative Philosophy*, edited by William Torrey Harris (1835–1909), American philosopher and educator, used as its motto "Philosophy can bake no bread; but she can procure for us God, Freedom, and Immortality," attributed to Novalis.

356.3 Swift] Morrison Isaac Swift (b.1856), American anarchist writer, *Human Submission*, second part (Philadelphia: Liberty Press, 1905) (WJ 483.94); James quotes Swift at length in *Pragmatism*.

356.5 Leibnitz] From the Théodicée (secs. 19, 72), *Œuvres*, vol. II; for the texts see *Pragmatism*, pp. 19–20.

356.38 Fullertons] George Stuart Fullerton, *A System of Metaphysics* (New York: Macmillan, 1904).

357.29 Papini] Giovanni Papini (1881–1956), Italian writer; for the reference see *Essays in Philosophy*, note to 146.5.

357.38 Humanism] Ferdinand Canning Scott Schiller, *Humanism: Philosophical Essays* (London: Macmillan, 1903).

357.39 Sturt] Henry Sturt (b. 1863), British philosopher, "The Logic of Pragmatism," *Proceedings of the Aristotelian Society*, n.s. 3 (1903), 96–122.

358.25 Peirce] See note to 216.4.

358.35 Knox] Howard Vincenté Knox (1868–1960), British military officer and philosopher. The paper was not identified.

359.5 "Aus] Goethe, *Faust*, p. 56 (line 1663).

359.10 Santayana's] *The Life of Reason*.

359.36 Miller] See note to 217.27.

361.11 Heymans] Gerardus Heymans (1857–1930), Dutch philosopher.

362.31 Stern] William Stern (1871–1938), German philosopher, *Psychologie der Veränderungsauffassung* (Breslau: Preuss und Jünger).

363.13 "We] From Søren Kierkegaard; see *Pragmatism*, note to 107.15.

364.10 Humanism] William James, "Humanism and Truth" (1904), reprinted in *The Meaning of Truth*.

365.10 Lovejoy] Arthur Oncken Lovejoy (1873–1962), American philosopher.

365.40 Blood] For the reference see *Essays in Philosophy*, p. 186n.

366.37 Perry] Ralph Barton Perry, "Prof. Royce's Refutation of Realism and Pluralism," *Monist*, 12 (April 1902), 446–458.

366.38 Montague] William Pepperell Montague (1873–1953), American philosopher, "Professor Royce's Refutation of Realism," *Philosophical Review*, 11 (January 1902), 43–55.

366.38 Lovejoy] Arthur Oncken Lovejoy, "Religion and the Time-Process," *American Journal of Theology*, 6 (July 1902), 439–472.

366.38 Schiller] Ferdinand Canning Scott Schiller, "Empiricism and the Absolute," *Mind*, n.s. 14 (July 1905), 348–370. Nothing by Schiller appeared in October.

367.34 Hoffding's] Harald Höffding, "A Philosophic Confession," *Journal of Philosophy*, 2 (February 16, 1905), 85–92.

368.33 Perry's] Ralph Barton Perry, *The Approach to Philosophy* (New York: Charles Scribner's Sons, 1905).

368.34 Grote's] George Grote, *Aristotle*, ed. Alexander Bain and G. Croom Robertson, 2 vols. (London: J. Murray, 1872).

369.13 Emerson's] Ralph Waldo Emerson, *Essays*, first series (Boston: Fields, Osgood, 1869) (*AC 85.J2376.Zz869e).

369.31 Hoffding's] *The Problems of Philosophy*, pp. 180–181.

369.33 E.] "Thus is the Universe alive" is from Emerson's *Essays*, p. 91.

371.12 Hoernle] R. F. Alfred Hoernlé (1880–1943), German-born philosopher, active in the United States, "Pragmatism V. Absolutism," *Mind*, n.s. 14 (October 1905), 441–478.

371.30 Phil] Alfred Edward Taylor, "Truth and Practice," *Philosophical Review*, 14 (May 1905), 265–289.

371.37 Mind] Alfred Edward Taylor, "Truth and Consequences," *Mind*, n.s. 15 (January 1906), 81–93.

374.8 Rev.] See note to 304.34.

374.21 Its] To avoid duplication two sets of course notes are not printed in the present volume. In 1905–1906 James, Royce, and Münsterberg offered Philosophy 1a: General Introduction to Philosophy, Logic, Psychology. James was responsible for the first part, and his notes for the course are preserved (#4516). The same notebook contains his notes for the introductory philosophy course James taught at Stanford from January 10, 1906, until the earthquake of April 18. Although these notes contain a few references not found elsewhere, on the whole they represent additional arrangements of familiar material. Much the same reflections can be found in the courses and syllabi printed in the present volume and in James's published works, especially *Some Problems of Philosophy*. Two fragments, however, seemed worth printing. The first consists of notes on faith and introduces the faith-ladder developed in *Some Problems*. The second represents notes for a talk on religion that James gave to Miss Martin's class on April 17. Miss Martin is Lillien Jane Martin (1851–1943), American psychologist.

375.3 Miller's] For Dickinson S. Miller's criticism of *The Will to Believe* see *The Will to Believe*, note to 7.23.

375.27 Müller] Such views are expressed by Friedrich Max Müller (1823–1900), German-born philologist, *Introduction to the Science of Religion* (1873).

376.10 Jefferies] Richard Jefferies (1848–1887), English writer.

376.10 Obermann] A novel by Étienne Pivert de Sénancour (1770–1846), French ethical writer.

376.20   Ashburners] Family name of several of James's acquaintances.

377.2   Talk] Morris Raphael Cohen received his doctorate in 1906.

377.32   Heim] Karl Heim (1874–1958), German historian and philosopher, *Psychologismus oder Antipsychologismus?* (Berlin: C. A. Schwetschke und Sohn, 1902).

378.10   *Objection*] James had a syllabus printed for use at Stanford. This syllabus was revised for Philosophy D: General Problems of Philosophy in 1906–1907 at Harvard. Paulsen's *Introduction to Philosophy* served as the text.

378.17   Ward] See note to 187.20.

378.32   TYLOR] Edward Burnett Tylor, *Primitive Culture* (1871).

379.1   JEVONS] Frank Byron Jevons (1858–1936), British philosopher and historian of religion, *An Introduction to the History of Religion* (London: Methuen, 1896).

379.2   FRAZER] James George Frazer, *The Golden Bough*, 2nd ed., revised, 3 vols. (London: Macmillan, 1900). A marked copy of this edition was sold from James's library.

382.14   English] For the text see *Some Problems of Philosophy*, p. 26.

383.3   Oken's] For a possible reference see *Some Problems of Philosophy*, note to 29.1.

383.6   edition] Immanuel Kant, *Versuch den Begriff der negativen Grössen in die Weltweisheit einzuführen*, in vol. I of *Sämmtliche Werke*, ed. Karl Rosenkranz and F. W. Schubert, 14 vols. in 12 (Leipzig: Leopold Voss, 1838–1842) (*AC 85.J2376.Zz838k).

385.27–28   CUDWORTH] Ralph Cudworth (1617–1688), English philosopher. For the reference see *Some Problems of Philosophy*, note to 34.32.

390.37   REYMOND] Emil Du Bois-Reymond (1818–1896), German physiologist.

394.8   book] For James's copy see *Principles*, note to 40.37.

395.36   STRONG] Charles Augustus Strong, *Why the Mind Has a Body* (New York: Macmillan, 1903) (WJ 483.77).

395.37   HEYMANS] Gerardus Heymans, *Einführung in die Metaphysik auf Grundlage der Erfahrung* (Leipzig: J. A. Barth, 1905) (WJ 820.37).

410.36   "The] Deut. xxxiii:27.

414.5   CLIFFORD] For the reference see *The Will to Believe*, p. 18.

419.22   DICKINSON] Goldsworthy Lowes Dickinson (1862–1932), English writer, *Religion: A Criticism and a Forecast* (New York: McClure, Phillips, 1905) (WJ 518.13).

429.3   *Philosophy*] The course was Philosophy 20e: Seminary in the Theory of Knowledge, dealing with idealism, pragmatism, and realism. The instructor was Ralph Barton Perry. Identifiable are Edwin Bissell Holt; Henry Maurice Sheffer (1882–1964), American philosopher, then a graduate student; William James Musgrove, a graduate student and assistant; and Edward Vermilye Huntington.

Appendix I

Report of the Lecture on "The Physiological Effects of Alcohol"

James's lecture on "The Physiological Effects of Alcohol," given before the Harvard Total Abstinence League, was reported in the *Daily Crimson*, 27 October 1886.

Meeting of the H. T. A. L.

LECTURE BY PROFESSOR JAMES.

A fair-sized audience gathered in Sever 11 last evening to hear Prof. William James' lecture on the Effects of Alcohol. "Alcohol," said the lecturer, "has the effect of stimulating the pulsation and dilating the superficial blood-vessels in all parts of the body and of the face. The latter is peculiarly noticeable in confirmed drunkards. The effects of this dilation is perspiration followed, if exposed to cold, by rapid cooling, if to heat, by rapid heating. Alcohol thus makes a man *feel* warm, but in reality, *cools* him. There is no stimulating effect on the nerves by alcohol, as is supposed, but the influence is anaesthetic; indeed this is its charm and attraction. All the senses and organs are dulled, and pain vanishes. But the action of the brain also is impaired by it, so that no good work can be accomplished after taking alcohol. Its effect on sick people is often beneficial; and affords a stimulating tone to the nerves of the mouth and stomach. This, however, can as well be gained by such drinks as milk or effervescent waters. One and a half fluid ounces of alcohol, the equivalent of a half glass of sherry, in twenty-four hours is the limit of its useful effect. The craving for alcohol is a disease brought about by exposure to hurtful influences or by excessive drinking. All statistics go to show the superior strength of the abstainer from alcohol. In our rapid American life especially, we should put ourselves on the safe side and endeavor to gain strength and longevity by abstinence from alcoholic drink."

Appendix II

Report of the Lecture on
"The Effects of Alcohol"

James's lecture on "The Effects of Alcohol," given under the auspices of the Harvard Total Abstinence League, was reported in the *Harvard Crimson*, 23 January 1895.

Professor James's Lecture.

Sever 11 was well filled last evening by those who had gathered to hear Professor James lecture on "Alcohol," under the auspices of the Total Abstinence League. Mr. Trotter, the president of the league, introduced Professor James, after making a few remarks on the platform and objects of the league.

The fashion of the community in which a man lives is the greatest factor in deciding his habits. In Europe, and especially in Germany, every one drinks beer as a matter of course throughout the day, and even in England it is a difficult matter for a water drinker to travel without being practically forced to drink wines of various sorts. But these customs are now giving way to modern ideas, which, fortunately for us, have been characteristic of American life since its beginning.

Formerly he was considered a strong man who could hold the greatest amount of wine; wine was considered to be so healthy in its effects that it was very generally given to young children. Man then lived only to drink all he could all the time; the veteran soldiers and sailors of Wellington and Nelson are notorious for their drinking propensities and powers. In Berlin, at a meeting of famous naturalists and doctors, about four thousand in number, no less than fifteen thousand three hundred and eighty-two bottles of different kinds of wine were consumed, to say nothing of quantities of beer.

This state of things is very generally passing away and no one thing is of more importance in its extinction than a constantly growing body of people who are total abstinents. Some people with diseased nervous systems are utterly incapable of resisting the desire to drink, it comes to them like a mania, while others have simply contracted the habit of indulgence from time to time. Although at one time alcohol was thought to pass through the system without suffering a change, it has been discovered more recently that it is destroyed in the system and in this sense is a food.

Professor James then spoke of the discoveries from experimental investigations and the more common results, or accompanying effects of inveterate drinking. Although alcohol warms the skin by increasing the circulation, yet in

514

a person who is paralyzed by liquor the temperature of the body is found to be several degrees below normal. The really strong plea for drinking is that it acts as an aid to conviviality, also that it helps at a crisis, but though it may produce temporary happiness, the following effects will be deeper melancholy and though it may stimulate for the moment, it leaves its victim all the more demoralized afterwards. The real state of happiness which we should strive for is one of perfect health.

Appendix III

Reports of James's "Lectures on Abnormal Psychology"

Two reports of the lectures that James gave in early 1896 at the Brooklyn Institute of Arts and Sciences are found in the *Brooklyn Eagle*. In the fall of that same year his series of Lowell Lectures, delivered at Huntington Hall in Boston, were reported in the *Boston Evening Transcript*, the *Boston Globe*, and the *Boston Herald*. These accounts are reprinted below.

[*Brooklyn Eagle*, 20 January 1896]

OUR SUBLIMINAL CONSCIOUSNESS.

HOW IT MAY BE AT ONE TASK WHILE WE ARE OTHERWISE EMPLOYED.

Professor William James of Harvard college delivered another interesting lecture in his course on "Recent Researches Into Exceptional Mental Phenomena" before members of the institute at the Art building Saturday morning. The subject was "The Subliminal Consciousness and Hysteria." The late term subliminal, derived from the Latin below-threshold, stands for that moiety of the mind which is outside of the common consciousness. It is a definition of hypnotism and all states foreign to usual consciousness.

"The mind is supposed to be divided into all these two republics, more or less distinct from each other," said the speaker. "Examples of such dual existence of the intellect are constantly presented in every day life. So called automatic actions are but actions of the subliminal being. A man walks with a friend and holds a conversation with him. He adjusts his steps to inequalities of the pavement, avoids col[l]lision with other pedestrians, turns corners and waits for vehicles to pass at the crossing; yet he remembers none of these things when he arrives home, having been exclusively occupied with the conversation. His subliminal consciousness guides his feet while his thoughts are elsewhere. An anecdote is given of a person who sat reading a book in a room where several others were talking. He was very much absorbed, but at the mention of a certain name he lifted his head and inquired what was being said about that one. The inquirer, for the sake of an experiment, was immediately hypnotized. He was then asked if he had heard any of the conversation. He replied in the affirmative and forthwith repeated all that had been said. Though his waking mind was taken up with the book, it was evident his subliminal economy had carefully gather[e]d in everything uttered within hearing. One experiment of the French investigator, Pierre Janet, accords well with the theory of divided consciousness. Hy[p]notizing a young woman he placed in her lap a number of slips of paper marked from 1 to 10. He told her that when she awoke she would count only the odd numbers. She awoke and could only perceive numbers 1, 3, 5, 7 and 9. Being returned to the hypnotic state she was asked to count the slips again. This time she perceived but the even numbers; her other consciousness had counted and done away with the odd. Hysteria has been long considered, even by medical men, as a willful mendacity. As a matter of fact most hysteric persons are sincere in their delusions, which are no more anomalous than the phenomena of hypnotism. A girl, who declares that she has lost the sense of feeling in a certain part of her body is pinched there. "Yes," she says, "I don't have any sensation there." She is of course accused of deceit. The truth is she is aware of the pinch sensorially and sublimilarly [*stet*], but her common mind refuses to note it. Hypnotism allows the modern healer to discover the mental cause of the hysteric malady and then to cure it by proper suggestion."

[*Brooklyn Eagle*, 16 February 1896]

PROFESSOR JAMES ON GENIUS.

HE DISAGREES WITH THE THEORIES OF OF [*stet*] NORDAU AND LOMBROSO.

Professor William James of Harvard university concluded his series of Brooklyn institute lectures on psychological subjects with an address on "Genius," delivered at the Y. M. C. A. building yesterday morning.

"The first man," said Dr. James, "who began the study of human nature on the modern more or less scientific basis, was a Frenchman named Leult [*i.e.*, Lélut], of the first half of this century. He wrote a book in which he proved to at least his own satisfaction, by algebraic and other methods, that Socrates was a madman; that the master of Plato was subject to hallucinations; he saw visions and he believed himself inspired by a demon. Since then the science of psychology has greatly advanced and Lombroso and Nordau have endeavored to place under its ken all mental phenomena which mankind once regarded as sacred. Catchwords of indefinable dread import, such as 'degeneration,' have been invented and the modern achievement has been to overthrow the classic belief that wise men were wise and inane men fools. The marks of degeneration, according to the nineteenth century scientist, are as numerous as the diseases which the patent medicine vendor professes to cure by his nostrum. They include such items as pallor, bow-leggedness, enthusiasm, fixed idea, short stature, melancholy, insane aunt, egotism, sensitiveness, neuralgia, inspiration, pious sentiments, moral depravity, cruelty, excessive lofty admiration of the fair sex, and a great many more. Genius is a branch of the human nature tree which is but slightly elevated above pure insanity and in it are to be found many of the degenerate signs. Lombroso was challenged to show that Dante and Michael Angelo belonged to his psychopathic class. He met the challenge by alleging that Dante was afflicted by epilepsy, as told by himself in several passages of the 'Divine Comedy,' where he swoons, and that the great painter had hallucinations which he transferred upon his canvas. It is to be noted, says Lombroso, that Byron, Bismarck, Von Moltke and other men of genius have not the national characteristics in their features, they belong to a brotherhood of their own. A certain similarity between the faces of geniuses is also to be remarked. Lombroso has gathered a large number of facts about geniuses of all ages, and he maintains that they all come under his classification. Nordau has made a similar noise in the world by his like strain.

"While we are indebted to Lombroso for the valuable collection of concrete facts which he has given us, we easily perceive his error and that of the common alienist. The degenerate theory of genius is not founded upon any logical ground. The mistake has been made of considering geniuses in a class by themselves and all their defects, whether physical or other, have been regarded absolutely instead of relatively. Lombroso finds that his thousand geniuses have certain disposition, histories, certain common faults, abnormalities, and he passes judgment on the species. If he would pick out another thousand men, say from the ranks of lawyers or from those of any sedentary, highly intellectual occupation, and still found that his geniuses were birds of unique feathers, then his conclusions would be worth something. It is easy enough to find any number of coincidences in this world to support particular position. The question hinges on the nature of sanity, which the extreme psychologist imagines to be a narrow crack, on either side of which is the devil and the deep sea. Your Nordau strikes his breast and thanks heaven that he is a perfectly sane man, because he doesn't believe in poetry, religion or anything else. According to this standard the dullest ploughman is to be accounted the paragon of humanity. The materialist and cheap cynic delights in such a conclusion. It is incorrect to put rigorously in one class all geniuses. Except in the higher sense there is no comparison between Napoleon Bonaparte and Paderewski, or Shakspeare and Thomas C. Platt. The geniuses of art and letters, however, should not be considered entirely apart from their brothers of exploration, invention and of the military field. The first, naturally from their calling, have more of the unearthly about them. Their feelings are highly cultivated and the passions of their souls are more intense than those of the multitude. Often a powerful sensibility is linked to a weak will, or the will is strong, but the passion stronger. The colossal proportions of these disproportionate elements stand out in bold contrast and the genius' falling is greater because of the height from which he descends.

"The obsession of idea, which every person understands somewhat from personal experience, is that which makes the genius effective. Many men have sufficient understandings to be the world's leaders, but they lack the everlasting doggedness and faint by the wayside. The genius' idea pursues him continually and he ever wrestles with it until he can work it out. If it is an impossible idea, the man is other than a genius. However, most genius' ideas have been considered absurd at first.

"The disproportionate mental makeup which may be shown in Lord Byron, Shelley and others, does not exist at all in many eminent men of letters. Goethe had a very strong spirit, but it was admirably controlled by his will, which was as strong. Such men as Emerson and Longfellow were as nearly perfect in their constitutions as could be desired. Dr. Johnson believed in his Cock Lane ghosts and other geniuses have had other private eccentricities; all of which, if they occurred in common men, would be considered as insignificant mental specks. It is because of the elevation of the genius and the strong light that is cast on his every action that his aberrations are so remarked. Homer is an intimate of the gods and, therefore, it is a crime for Homer to nod. The ordinary man has small temptations and small vices. Medioc[r]ity goes neither very high nor very low."

[*Boston Evening Transcript*, 22 October 1896
Report of Lecture I]

On "Dreams and Hypnotism."

At Huntington Hall last evening Professor William James of Harvard gave the first of his course of Lowell Institute lectures upon "Exceptional Mental States." The subject of the lecture was "Dreams and Hypnotism," and the hall was filled, many probably expecting sensational treatment of the subject. They were quickly undeceived, for he dealt with the subject in a thoroughly scientific manner and explained clearly the differences between the sleeping and the waking mind. Dreams, he said, were a disease of sleep. Hypnotic phenomena were to be explained on the theory of suggestion. It is not the result of a stronger mind operating upon a weaker one, the influence depending upon the subject. The mind of the subject can be hypnotized only in its passage from the waking to the sleeping state. If the mind of the subject is caught at this point and is given a suggestion, it immediately acts upon that idea. Hypnotism, he said, is harmless in itself, its right or wrong use depending upon the suggestion given.

[*Boston Globe*, 22 October 1896
Report of Lecture I]

"DREAMS AND HYPNOTISM."

Difference Between the Waking and Dreaming Mind Explained.

•   •   •

Dreams, he said, were a disease of sleep. The lecturer showed the difference between the waking and the dreaming mind and dwelt upon the dream consciousness and its characteristics. All hypnotic phenomena were to be explained on the theory of suggestion. It was not the influence of a strong mind or will over a weaker one. In hypnotism everything depended upon the subject, and nothing upon the operator. The mind of the subject could be "hypnotized" only on its passage from the waking to the sleeping state. If the operator caught it at the right instant and suggested an idea, the subject would be hypnotized. There was a great difference in the degree of the suggestibility of which a subject was capable. Hypnotism was neither right nor wrong nor harmful in itself. It all depended upon the use made of it.

[*Boston Herald,* 25 October 1896
Report of Lecture II]

POWER OF HYPNOTIC INFLUENCE

Second Lecture in Lowell Institute Course by Prof. James on "Mental States."

Almost as great as on the first night was the crush at Huntington Hall, in the Rogers building, last evening, when Prof. William James gave the second of his course of Lowell Institute lectures on "Mental States."

Prof. James began by saying that the mind seems to embrace a confederation of psychic entities, said that there are two kinds of phenomena met with in the hypnotic trance. The first, he went on to say may be designated as negative [*two lines illegible on microfilm*] illustrate, he said that when under the hypnotic influence, the patient may be told that he does not see a thing, and immediately he becomes blind to that particular thing, though seeing other objects. The second of the phenomena mentioned the lecturer spoke of as throwing some light upon post hypnotic suggestion. A patient may be told during hypnotic sleep, he said, that upon awakening he will not see a given object. The mind, obedient to the suggestion impressed upon it, will not, when the patient wakes up, recognize the object named. Nor will there be any memory of the suggestion. Similarly, the patient may be told that on a future day he must perform a certain action and not knowing why he does it, he will carry out the suggestion when the day comes.

The lecturer then proceeded to say something about where the mind stores the order, and quoted Edmund Gurney of London, narrating some of his experiments as indicating that there is a sub-consciousness in the background, attending to its own affairs and not interfering with the consciousness ordinarily active. This theory of simultaneous double consciousness the speaker considered the most plausible of the explanations offered. The workings of those two spheres, two systems of consciousness, were dealt with and the demonstrations, which were described, were termed by the lecturer after Phillip Meyers [*i.e.,* Frederic Myers], motor automatisms.

[*Boston Evening Transcript,* 29 October 1896
Report of Lecture III]

Professor James on "Exceptional Mental States."

Professor William James of Harvard University addressed a large audience in Huntington Hall last evening, on "Hysteria," under the general subject of "Exceptional Mental States." "Hysteria," he said, "has some connection with most of the diseases to which flesh is heir, for all sorts of diseases are reproduced in hysteria patients. In the case of hysteria, however, the symptoms of a disease, though at first very pronounced, may fly away and leave behind no bad effects. In grave hysteria, the patient has attacks which are usually dramatic performances, but such cases are rare. Hysteria usually takes the form of trembling, or agitation and anxiety. It is a disease of unbalanced nerves, and even persons of the strongest will and most vigorous intellect may be subject to it. It is also a mental disease, anæsthesia being one of the most common symptoms. But the anæsthesia is not real, but pseudo-anæsthesia. Having discovered the psychological cause of hysteria, the physician can cure the patient by hypnotic suggestion, imposing upon the patient's mind a pleasant idea, where an unpleasant one had previously existed."

[*Boston Evening Transcript,* 31 October 1896]

PROFESSOR JAMES'S LECTURES.

The interest and suggestiveness of the Lowell lectures now being delivered by Dr. James on "Exceptional Mental States" can hardly be realized by those who know them only through the scanty reports that the politics-crowded columns of the press allows. Everybody knows the authority, the exceptional authority, with which they come, and can understand why the crowds which attend them are drawn by something more than a sensational interest. The subject is in the air, and haphazard faiths are so common that such scientific deliverances as these have special attractiveness. Not because they seem to be about "damnation in general," as the lecturer feared the public would suppose, but because they bear so vitally and broadly upon life are the audiences large, intelligent, and appreciative. Even to those who may be familiar with the later conclusions of psychologists about hypnotism, the fresh illustrations and verifications are valuable, and to all hearers the clear, easily understood principles, binding together experiences not generally associated and suggesting applications in every-day life, are worth storing in mind.

If it is an unwholesome subject, Dr. James is right in saying that a sound treatment is better than leaving it alone; and his treatment of the subject is preëminently sound. "No one symptom by itself," he said, "is a morbid one—it depends on the part that it plays." "We speak of melancholy and morbid tendencies, but he would be a bold man who should say that melancholy was not an essential part of every character. Life must admit elements which in isolation or in another mixture would be morbid elements. We do not regard dreaming as morbid, because it is customary, but if it were not customary, it would be the subject of much medical wonder."

"Our consciousness is but a fragment surrounded by other possible experiences. Who shall say that the ordinary experience is the only one possible?" "In the sound mind there is a field of consciousness in which every idea is in gear with every other, a field with a focus and a margin. In the dreamer there is no control of the margin and the focus is narrow. Some minds easily get out of gear. Others have a broad field. Why this is so, why minds differ is one of the most important theoretic questions in psychology, but as yet there is very little contribution to its solution."

As to hypnotism, Dr. James showed how it consisted of that same breaking up of the mind into two or more parts. Discovered by Mesmer and rediscovered since, it met first with denial of the facts by scientists, until suddenly orthodox opinion admitted them. "The theory of suggestion robbed hypnotism of its former marvel." Mesmer's theory of a fluid through all nature, later theories that it was a power possessed by few persons, that it was magnetism, and now the mind theory that it is the will of the strong over the weak,—all these explanations Professor James declared are now exploded. "You need n't have a strong will at all; you need only suggest an idea which the mind itself takes hold of." "All persons go through the hypnotic state twice a day." "A good subject is one who can be caught on the road to sleep and suspended—prevented from deep sleep." "This is unquestionably the true explanation." "Everything depends on the subject, and hardly anything on the operator. Suggestibility is the explanatory word. It is not peculiar to the hypnotic state. The inward suggestion of one's fear may be more powerful than the outward one of command."

Such are some of the salient points of the first lecture, which in subsequent evenings have been shown also in relation to double personality, automatism and hysteria. The main result is positive, encouraging, optimistic in the best sense. It leads to sanity of opinion on subjects about which many of the soundest minds have been a little crack-brained. And the suggestion of the last lecture, that just as hysteria has been cured by reaching the subconscious strata from which it arises, and through hypnotism correcting its direction, so delusional insanity may in time be reached on the same principle and the level from which it springs joined with the whole mind and integrated with it—this suggestion opens a new field of hope and effort. It really seems as though Franklin, in discovering the identity of lightning with electricity, opened a realm of power not more useful than this which modern psychology reveals in proving that the play of seemingly abnormal forces may be used in redeeming mankind from some of its worst evils.

[*Boston Herald*, 1 November 1896
Report of Lecture IV]

PECULIAR MENTAL STATES.

Distinct Orders of Double Personality Described.

Prof. William James of Harvard University Lectures to Lowell Institute
Patrons in Huntington Hall—The Case of Mary Reynolds an Example
of the Hysteric Order.

Prof. William James, the head of the department of psychology in Harvard University, addressed an audience of Lowell Institute patrons last evening, in Huntington Hall, on "Exceptional Mental States." The subject is one on which Prof. James is a world known authority. The number of those who listened to his entertaining lecture was almost the capacity of the hall.

He reviewed in the beginning some things he had said in a preceding address, pointing out that many mental problems and phenomena which, not long ago unexplainable and awful, have become known and comparatively trivial. We have come to know, he said, that consciousness is not consolidated.

The gist of his lecture was a series of observations and comments on three relatively distinct orders of double personality: Epileptic, psychopathic and hysteric.

The French call the phenomena of double personality, the speaker said, "fugues" or flights, in which one personality alternates with another. Persons change periodically into other persons—that is, mentally. They sometimes leave their homes unexpectedly, without giving notice to their families or friends, stay away for days or weeks, experiencing entirely unusual mental careers, and turn up in some remote or unaccustomed place, utterly unable to account for themselves.

Tissier [*i.e.*, Tissié], psychologist of France, instances a case of "fugue," in which a workman carried out this programme unintentionally, and afterward in a hypnotic state accounted for his travels and experiences. The workman left his home as another personality after he had had a dream. His case was psychopathic, neither epileptic nor hysteric.

An instance of the hysteric order is the notable case of Mary Reynolds, who died in 1854, 60 years of age. According to Dr. Mitchell of Philadelphia, who reported the case, she was a melancholy person normally. When she fell into a second, abnormal state, she became jocose. The two states alternated at intervals of a month or more. Finally the second state became permanent, and she lived in it for 25 years, until her death.

One explanation of this double personality is, Prof. James said, that the normal, complete personal consciousness is split; part of it becomes detached, and to a certain extent independent. One set of the subject's mental possessions go to one centre of his consciousness, the other set is outside the threshhold [*stet*], below.

Prof. James believes that this formula covers a large number of cases. It would seem, however, not to account for an instance of a child who went out of her normal self entirely, and lived in the spirit and memories of another child who had died.

The most common sort of alternate personality is the phenomenon of ordinary trance mediumship, which, Prof. James observed, might be cultivated by many of his audience, if they took time and were persistent in cultivating a second mental state.

[*Boston Evening Transcript*, 5 November 1896
Report of Lecture V]

Demoniacal Possession Merely Modern Spiritual Mediumship.

Another in the series of lectures which Professor William James of Harvard, is giving on mental states, was delivered in Huntington Hall, last evening, upon the subject of "Demoniacal Possession." Professor James pointed out that this kind of possession, which has existed in every country, is no other than the historical counterpart of modern spiritual mediumship. He cited examples of demoniacal possession in proof of his assertion that, wherever it occurred, its characters were practically the same. The spirit, or demon, was believed to enter the person and use the organs of speech. Trances or convulsions were a frequent feature of the possession. Foreign languages were spoken, strange countries seen, distant occurrences described and future events prophesied. The possession took various forms, according to the country and the time in which it occurred, but the general features were the same.

In his next lecture Professor James will deal with witchcraft.

Appendix III

[*Boston Herald*, 15 November 1896
Report of Lecture VIII]

GENIUS NOT A DISEASE.

Lecture by Prof. James in the Course on "Exceptional Mental States."

In Huntington Hall, last evening, Prof. James of Harvard delivered the last lecture in his series on "Exceptional Mental States." "Genius" was his specific subject.

He referred to the psychopathic constitution which had been supposed to be the foundation of genius. This was the temperament of persons, he said, controlled by one idea, such as Dr. Parkhurst, Frances Willard and Lady Henry Somerset. The classical conception of genius, he went on to say, was that it was a divine thing, a perfect effulgence, and that it was blasphemy to critically analyze it. The literary conception of genius is that it is a pathological condition of the individual.

The psychopathic temperament does not constitute genius; indeed, most psychopaths have weak intellects, yet a psychopathic temperament may assist in the development of genius. Genius is not insanity or any disease. It does not consist of any one part of a man, but of all together.

[*Boston Evening Transcript*, 17 November 1896]

PROF. JAMES'S LOWELL LECTURES.

Professor James's lectures on "Exceptional Mental States" have been the means of attracting to the Lowell Institute twice a week a large number of people interested in these subjects, which are today pressing upon us at all sides. Because the lectures, as Professor James wittily said, seemed to have to do with "damnation in general," the audiences were at first tremendous. Latterly, however, the attendance has come to be less large though more even. The people who were attracted by the somewhat sensational titles of the addresses have ceased to come, while those who found that the lecturer was giving them new ideas and more light upon what have formerly been regarded as very morbid subjects, have grown more intensely interested as the course has progressed.

For though the subjects were, perhaps, morbid enough—Hysteria, Hypnotism, Demoniacal Possession, Witchcraft, Degeneration—their treatment throughout has been eminently sane and above all hopeful. Hypnotism, for instance, which to the minds of many people seems a strange, dread thing, was shown to be only partial sleep, a neutral state in itself, without character either good or bad, dependent for its ultimate effect upon the suggestion made to the patient while in the trance state. This comparatively new idea of suggestion from without as a means of coping with delusional insanity of various kinds, was one of the hopeful thoughts to which Professor James kept recurring throughout these lectures. In hysteria, the physician, having discovered the psychological cause of the disease, can cure the patient by imposing on his mind a pleasant idea where an unpleasant one had previously existed. In France, where this wonderful fact of suggestion has been very much more deeply studied and widely experimented upon than here, the comparative cures wrought by its utilization are very remarkable. Of the vast amount of literature which the French have put forth on psychological subjects, we particularly remember "La Suggestion," which came out a couple of years ago and is decidedly interesting reading.

To negative suggestion, too, Professor James attributes many of the disastrous consequences formerly brought upon unoffending old women by so-called "witchcraft." The witches seldom cried and the inquisitors used to say to them: "If you're not a witch, cry. There! you can't cry, so you're a witch!"

But there were many other interesting thoughts thrown out upon the subject of "witchcraft." Michelet's theory, that in the oppression and dearth of every kind of ideal interest in rural populations some safety valve had to be found, and that there were real organized secret meetings, witches' Sabbaths, to supply this need of sensation, was suggested by the lecturer, but discarded because of the lack of evidence. Torture, in Professor James's opinion, is the only explanation of the so-called "confessions." A person was suddenly found to be suffering from what we today should call hysteria, perhaps, but what in those old days was called a "witch disease." A witch, then, had to be found, a scapegoat must of necessity be brought forward. Some poor old woman was picked out and subjected to atrocious torture. If she "confessed" the torture ceased. She "confessed" and was executed. To us of this end of the nineteenth century these witch stories are utterly incomprehensible. Michelet's theory is certainly very attractive, but we will follow Professor James's example and leave the question hanging.

Perhaps the most interesting lecture of the whole course was that on "Multiple Personality." That such cases as that of "Dr. Jekyll and Mr. Hyde" have been almost paralleled in this country came to many of those present with a startling sense of strangeness. The "almost," however, represents much difference. For Dr. Jekyll was conscious of his connection with Hyde, while in the case of Mary Reynolds—by far the most interesting case quoted—there was no knowledge of the other state. This case, which has been published at considerable length by Dr. Weir Mitchell, is that of the child of some Pennsylvania settlers, who, a melancholy person, normally, became jocose in her second and abnormal state. In the second state, too, she knew nothing of what had been taught her in her first and normal state. The two states alternated at intervals of a month or more, until finally the second state became permanent. In this abnormal state she lived for twenty-five years, dying in it at the age of sixty-one. In neither state was she conscious of the other. Janet's theory of "split personality"—that the normal and complete consciousness is divided into two parts, each half being inferior to the whole—covers the case of Mary Reynolds and many similar cases, notably the cases of so-called test-mediumship, but it is not broad enough to account for the complexity of nature. As Meyers [*i.e.*, Myers] has well said, "the outskirts of our personality reach we know not where." Many of us, however, have a much more comprehensive knowledge of the possibilities of the human mind as a result of Professor James's Lowell lectures. Those who felt that the people at large would be interested in the psychological questions of the day have been proved to be in the right. Boston may well be thankful for the privilege which she has enjoyed in listening to scholarly, carefully prepared addresses upon these intensely interesting subjects, by one whose authority is unquestioned.

Appendix IV

*Notes of the 1906 Summer School
of Theology Lectures on "Religious
Philosophy and Individualism"*

In July 1906 James delivered a series of five lectures on "Religious Philosophy and Individualism" before the Harvard Summer School of Theology. Preserved in the James Collection, bMS Am 1092.9 (4479), is the manuscript of the first series of Theology School lectures given in the summer of 1902 (No. 6 in the present edition). Interspersed among the leaves of this manuscript written in ink are foliated leaves written in pencil and intended as 1906 alterations. (For a complete description of the 1902 manuscript and its rearrangement for the 1906 series, see the Textual Apparatus, pp. 568–570.) Transcribed below are the 1906 leaves, with indication of their position in relation to the 1902 text. Following the transcription is a list of the 1906 pencil alterations that were made in the 1902 ink text.

[*fol.* [1]; *written on the back of a false start for fol.* [1], 'Non-devotional. |
    Eulogistic']
Devotion
Eulogistic word, religion, "wisdom."
Religion a part of the wise man.
What is it? Ambiguous
"Varieties."
A content or theology
A spirit or temper, a *devotion*
[*del.* 'What repels is partly the content partly the spirit.
Cruel Gods
Exclusive interest.']
Some take *their religion [*intrl.*] acutely, zealously, [*in the bottom right-hand
    corner* WJ *wrote, with a half-circle separating it from the text,* 'p. 2', *referring
    to p. 2 of the 1902 series*]
[*fols.* 2–4½: *ed.*, 83.32–85.22] Others . . . humanity.

[*fol.* 5] Each man's problems are peculiar, and his solutions must be so too. If our several religions are what we live by, we have to find out our own way.

I spoke of wisdom. If all *could* be wise, it might perhaps be better, but in a world like this, some characters are only accessible to one sided-solutions. It is that or nothing for them.

In ['judging ['of' *del.*]' *del.*] perceiving the grotesqueness of some religious [*fol.* 5½] lives, from the point of view of *what is abstractly conceivable* we must not forget ['the point' *del.*] what is *concretely possible.*

It may well be that the narrowest revivalism has made for the best ['possible'
del.] result possible in *those men.*

We outsiders can't judge well.

I spoke of *wisdom.*

Even that! *not [*ab.* 3 *dashes*] for all.

If religion were but one element

[*fols.* 6–7; *ed.,* 86.3–28] If . . . him. If he is faithful to his own light, it is enough.

[*fol.* 8; *written on the back of a del. trial for fol.* 5, 'As individual has problems,
so he has solutions, accessible only to himself.']

So much for the *devotion!*

Often inspired by the theology.

Persecution etc.

Change the theology and the temper will change, but always contrast of strenuous & easy-going.

Turn then to the theology.

Aught *in common?*

Yes supernatural world.

[*fol.* 9] This world swims in wider ideal order.

Our lives *terminate,* are *next.*

The alternative:—

Naturalism defined.

Ideal order conceived

    (1.) reasonably   } 2 types.
    (2.) experimentally }

Even (1) must affirm *more experience* to give significance to this.

[*fol.* 10] So both *beg facts.*

Experimentalist says he *feels* them

"Science" says they are *subjective.*

What does this mean?

[*fols.* 11–14; *ed.,* 93.24–95.20] Too individual . . . fence.

[*fol.* 15] Here I re-enter my radical empiricism.

We terminate at sensations

They are *gifts.* *Unformulable, [*comma ov. period*] *experiences in themselves.
    [*insrtd.*]

['But doorways to a more.

Sensation is individualistic.' *del.*]

We [*insrtd.*] *Encounter* a *that*

Which our theories define as a world of *general law*

    (Atoms—energy etc.)

*Work ['W' *ov.* 'F'] is done on us. we receive.

[*fol.* 16] We share this world.

In religious life we also have unformulable feelings of encounter with an *ideal
that.*

Mystics can't *describe.*

They define according to their general *theories.*

This are *termini of natural world*

Work done on our *individuality.*

[*fol.* 16½] World *may* follow in those directions towards *another order of experience*

Where forces are *for the individual as such.*

When an individual draws strength our denial is vain.

My own view, hospitable to many dimensions, to continuity, to nextness without overlap, cannot but be hospitable to [*fol.* 17] the religious contention.

Our naturalistic consciousness is certainly but a part.

The religious C. may point to the most significant direction for the balance.

Faith

Tolerance.

Pluralism.

Individualism.

1906 ALTERATIONS IN THE 1902 MANUSCRIPT

Recorded below are the 1906 pencil alterations made in the 1902 ink manuscript. The lemmata are drawn from No. 6, "Summer School of Theology Lectures on 'Intellect and Feeling in Religion.' "

85.5–6 Reactions . . . *won't*] *separated fr. preceding text by line drawn across the page; del. by five vert. lines*

85.19 an . . . seeker] 'an . . . critic *and [*undel. in error*]' *del.;* 'a' *intrl. bef.* 'seeker'

85.22–24 Even . . . are] *separated fr. preceding text by line drawn across the page; del. by three vert. lines;* 'Omit' *in left mrgn.*

85.24–34 non-religious . . . as] *del. by vert. line;* 'Omit' *in left mrgn.*

86.3–7 If . . . wisdom.] *del. by oblique line*

86.8 thus] *del.*

86.14–15 two . . . measuring] *underl.*

86.15 the one static,] *del., but comma undel. in error*

86.16 the other dynamic,] *del., but comma undel. in error*

86.16 power . . . results] 'use' *ab. del.* 'power . . . results'

93.28–31 And . . . formulas.] *opening and closing sq. bkts. added;* 'Parenthesis' *in left mrgn.*

93.34–35 Conflict . . . title.] *del.*

94.21 Whose . . . philosophizing] *del.; in left mrgn. an arrow points to text* 'There *might* be.' *written bel. an ink line drawn across the page*

94.36–95.6 We . . . for?] *del. by vert. line*

95.7 wrongness] 'general' *insrtd. bef.* 'wrongness'

95.12–20 Historically . . . fence.] *separated fr. preceding text by line drawn across the page; del. by vert. line;* 'x' *in left mrgn. bef.* 'Historically' *and bef.* 'My familiarity' [95.16]

Appendix V

James's Annotations of His Private Copies of
Syllabus in Philosophy *and* Syllabus in Philosophy D

This appendix contains transcripts of all the autograph markings that James made in his private copies of the [1906] (SP) *Syllabus in Philosophy* (bMS Am 1092.9 [4467]) and the [1906–1907] (SPD) *Syllabus in Philosophy D* (bMS Am 1092.9 [4466]) preserved in the James Collection in the Houghton Library, Harvard University. The first page-line reference is to the present edition; the page-line reference within parentheses following the sigil is to the original Syllabus, whether SP or SPD. Bound-in in *Syllabus in Philosophy D* are three each of pages 11, 12, 13, and 14; in each case the present editor has assigned the letters a, b, and c (within inferior brackets) to the duplicate pages (see Textual Apparatus, pp. 653–654). The lemma is that of the original Syllabus, whether SP or SPD; in entries that include annotations in both SP and SPD, the lemma is that of SPD. The exact text referred to is not always to be identified precisely, this being especially true of general notes placed at the head and at the foot of a page. Annotations made by James in the top or bottom margin of a page, therefore, are keyed to the first or last words on that page, unless joined by guidelines to specific passages.

Professor Skrupskelis has provided the commentary notes. References to James's published works are to this edition.

380.15 What] [*ink*] '1' *joined by guideline to* 'What' SPD (2.36)

380.28 What] [*penc.*] Complete save for pp 18–24 [*vert. in left mrgn.*] Obscure & uncertain speculations into the intimate nature & causes of things SPD (3.1)

381.24 absurd] [*ink*] 'like the infinite' *joined by guideline to underl.* 'absurd' SPD (3.35)

381.25 proof] [*ink*] 'like 1' *joined by guideline to* 'proof' SPD (3.36)

381.29 III.] [*penc.*] Glendower Evans's phrase SPD (4.1)
      Glendower Evans (1859–1886), graduated from Harvard in 1879.
For the phrase see *Pragmatism*, p. 115.

381.31–32 (a) The . . . finality.] [*ink*] dessicators [*penc.*]—often *weak* like Prat with his moral law—thin blooded SPD (4.3–5)
      Perhaps Louis Prat, French philosopher, a disciple of Charles Renouvier.

381.36 fragmentary] [*ink*] 'hard headed—irreligious' *joined by guideline to* 'frag-' | SPD (4.9)

381.37   hard] [*blue penc.*] *underl.*; cold, stubborn SP (4.3)

382.7   Our . . . types] [*ink*] Place in Gore Hall SPD (4.17)

382.11   ONOTOLOGICAL] [*ink*] 2'o' *del.* SP (4.18)

382.13–14   SCHOPENHAUER . . . 359.] [*ink*] recommend to read SPD (4.24–26)

382.36–37 | volve each other.] [*ink*] domestic animals | ['So shall' *del.*] SPD (5.1)

383.1   negate its own nega- |] [*ink*] "The perfect could not be so imperfect as not to exist" (Emil Reich?) | Leibnitz adds "if it *could* exist." SP (4.47)
     Perhaps Emil Reich (1854–1910), Hungarian-born historian.

383.6   +1] [*ink*] action & reaction SPD (5.7)

383.9   Whether what IS] [*penc.*] What must be, & can be, *is* (Bradley SPD (5.10)

383.26–27   how . . . moment?] [*ink*] Only one *reason* why a thing shd. be. SP (5.29–30)

384.10   A '*what*'] [*ink*] Examination ['am' *ov. illeg.*] replies: When you call it a "desk," it is a percept; "object weighing 200 lbs" is a concept "Percept leaves no room for any other article; concept covers the whole ground." [*vert. in left mrgn.*] Question: "Why are concepts so useful?" Answers: "Useful on account of their great handiness"; "Useful because they give us a passing enjoyment—they help *us physically and morally.* SP (6.1)

384.31–34   First . . . things.] [*ink*] ' "Philosophy ['com' *del.*] is subdivided into Logic, Ethics, Metaphysics and Anaesthetics." ' *written vert. in right mrgn. and joined by guideline to end of paragraph* SP (6.20–23)

385.3   new] [*ink*] *underl.* SP (6.34)

385.18   amends.] [*ink*] "The usual view is that the cause precedes the effect. Hume showed that the effect precedes the cause." | "I can *at present [*intrl.*] suggest no remedy for the belief that this is God's world" SP (6.48)

385.29   MILL] [*ink*] 'I. 260' *joined by guideline to* 'MILL' SPD (7.13)

385.34   indiscriminatingly.] [*ink*] immutability vs. generality. SP (7.14–15); [*ink*] universe of uniques. | every *species ['sp' *ov.* 'ab'] waggles about in its definition. Every tool loose in its handle SPD (7.17–18)

386.13–14   So . . . (ARISTOTLE).] [*ink*] Plato: "The many are seen but not known, the ideas known, but not seen." SP (7.31–32)

386.15   The only part] [*ink*] *Brain* here! SP (7.33)

386.30   divine.] [*ink*] Contemptibleness of the immediate, in Santayana L. of R., V, 160+ SP (7.47)
     George Santayana, *The Life of Reason*, 5 vols. (New York: Charles Scribner's Sons, 1905–1906) (WJ 479.62).

387.21–31   *Conclusion* . . . correction.)] [*ink*] we need make no extravagant claims SP (8.32–42)

387.39   Similarly] [*ink*] Foot-ball SP (9.3)

388.5–11   Monists . . . –70] [*ink*] Philosophy called quest for unity. *Totality* rather. SPD (9.20–26)

388.12   COMMENTS ON PAULSEN.] [*ink*] His 3 great topics. SP (9.15)

388.14–16   Rationalism's . . . systems.] [*ink*] Plato on knowledge & opinion SPD (9.29–31)

388.14   ownsinfallible] [*ink*] *vert. line separates words* SP (9.17)

388.15   knowledge] [*ink*] *caret aft.* 'knowledge'; underived [*on* 8ᵛ]—does n't exclude some empiric knowledge (Continental) SP (9.18)

388.19   philosophy.] [*ink*] *line drawn across the page separates this paragraph fr. the foll. one* SP (9.23)

388.20–21   The . . . realities?] [*ink*] Kant. [*on* 8ᵛ] no matter for P.s notes. SP (9.24–26)

388.22   Plato's] [*red-brown penc.*] Recommend Fullerton's book SPD (10.1)
     George Stuart Fullerton, *Introduction to Philosophy* (New York: Macmillan, 1906) (WJ 430.50).

388.22   each one] [*ink*] '*Knowledge* is of true immutable Being, the one beauty, the one justice etc. | *O*pinion of being & non being' *joined by guideline to* 'one' SPD (10.1)

388.24   history.] [*ink*] 'Phaedo' *del.* SP (9.29)

388.26–27   Truth . . . reality.] [*ink*] Case [*on* 8ᵛ] of Great bear. SP (9.32–33)
     For the Great Bear illustration see *Pragmatism*, pp. 121–123.

388.28–30   DESCARTES' . . . argument.] [*ink*] [*in left mrgn.*] 2nd type of rationalism [*in right mrgn.*] 'D's notion of cause, 157' *joined by guideline to* 'facti-' | SPD (10.7–9)

388.28–32   DESCARTES' . . . true.] [*ink*] [*in left mrgn. the two paragraphs are braced*] Couple of points [*in right mrgn.*] reasoning by cause SP (9.34–38)

388.33–34   SPINOSA . . . solids.''] [*ink*] Glen. Evans's dictum. SPD (10.12–13)

388.36   empiricist.] [*ink*] —Derives [*on* 8ᵛ] *all* knowledge fm. senses—excludes all rational (['English' *del.*]) Refutes innate ideas SP (9.42); [*ink*] = Sensualism SPD (10.15)

389.1–3   Only . . . realities.] [*ink*] Read 385–6 SPD (10.17–19)

389.12–13   ²facts . . . abstractions.] [*ink*] Occasionalism SP (10.9–10); [*ink*] 'My definition of empiricism.' *joined by guidelines to underl. text* SPD (10.28–29)

389.14–20   Before . . . causality.'] [*penc.*] Geulinx etc. SP (10.11–17); [*ink*] The general is only of use *to [*ov.* 'in'] return['ing' *del.*] to the particulars with. Rationalism stays with it aloft, hugs it. *"Cause." [*insrtd.*] Agassiz [*red-brown penc. underl.*] dictum. *B. Peirce's [*red-brown penc. underl.*] SPD (10.30–36)
     Arnold Geulincx (1624–1669), Flemish philosopher. For his view see *Some Problems of Philosophy*, p. 99.

389.21   The trouble] [*ink*] Read H. SP (10.18)
     Apparently James has in mind some excerpt from Chapter 10 of Hume's *An Enquiry Concerning Human Understanding*.

389.23   it.] [*ink*] *Intuitive vs. sensitive knowledge | **is [*joined by guideline to* 'Intuitive'] of connexion among ideas—reaches a very little way. Weight, malleableness fusibility etc of gold—don't see why they are together. Don't see why God hasn't attached thought to matter. Little *necessary* connexion or repugnancy to be found. [*braced*; 'Locke' *to the right of the brace*] | Hume. Which is less miraculous—falsehood of witness or event? Weigh the two miracles reject the greater. SPD (10.39); [*recto of leaf insrtd. between pp.* 10 *and* 11 *of* SPD] Pure reason deals with generals. | Empiricists accuse *this [*intrl.*] of unreality and abstraction. | "Abstract" a term of reproach. We must never forget to correct ['it.' *del.*] our abstractness. | Take an example. Materialism & Spiritualism | Concrete world shows both kind of fact. Which is *essence*? [*verso*] [¶] Agassiz: No one can understand a general formula any farther than his knowlege of Particulars goes. [*short rule*] [¶] B. Peirce:— — —But I say unto you: "theorize, and again ['& aga' *del. intrl.*] theorize. Theorize *ad limitum*. Let there be no bound to your theorizing. *only [*ab. del.* 'But'] have something to theorize *about*. ['Get *facts*, facts.' *del.*] The more you theorize, the more facts you require. Let there be no bound to the stock of facts which your *theories ['es' *ov.* 'ze'] relate to. [*vert. in right mrgn.*] Unity vs. totality. Bellanger | My sentiment of R.

    For a fuller exposition of Louis Agassiz's view see *Essays, Comments, and Reviews*, pp. 49–50.

    Benjamin Peirce (1809–1880), American mathematician, professor at Harvard.

    A. Bellanger, *Les Concepts de cause et l'activité intentionnelle de l'esprit* (Paris: Alcan, 1904). For Bellanger's view see *Pragmatism*, pp. 64–65 and note to 65.35.

    "The Sentiment of Rationality" in *The Will to Believe*. A somewhat different version is in *Essays in Philosophy*.

389.24   IMPORTANT . . . MATERIALISM.] [*ink*] [*in left mrgn.*] Vague dualism, 54 bottom [*in right mrgn.*] Two meanings of term. | Mechanism vs. teleology. | "Blind" forces vs. purposes. SP (10.21); [*penc.*] Examination [*vert. stroke*] Agassiz & Peirce anecdotes [*rule*] SPD (11[a].1)

389.25–28   *Read . . . articulate.*] [*ink*] Naturalness of materialism and dualism [*rule*] SP (10.22–25); [*penc.*] Comment on p. 55 | p 56 [*rule*] SPD (11[a].2–5)

389.29–31   *Read . . . connexion.*] [*ink*] Aristotle vs. Democritus! [*rule*] SP (10.26–28); [*penc.*] Explain omissions [*rule*] SPD (11[a].6–8)

389.32–33   Common . . . experience.] [*ink*] Scholastic— (breath etc) SP (10.29–30); [*ink*] Buchner 239+ SPD (11[a].9–10); [*penc.*] Soul, ghost SPD (11[c].9–10)

    Ludwig Büchner (1824–1899), German philosopher. James appears to have in mind some edition of *Kraft und Stoff*. For a possible text see *Essays in Religion and Morality*, p. 85n.

389.34–390.3   Science . . . brain-change.] [*ink*] Read Cabanis, Lowell. [Refer to *Ostwald* | —— to W.J.] | 'effervescence' *joined by guideline to* 'brain-change.' SPD (11[a].11–17)

    Pierre Jean Georges Cabanis (1757–1808), French philosopher. For a possible text see *Essays in Religion and Morality*, p. 95n.

    Percival Lowell (1855–1916), American astronomer. For a possible text see *Essays in Religion and Morality*, p. 85.

390.4–8 *Three . . . 65.*] [*ink*] Read SP (10.37–40)

390.7 (*b*) . . . 64.] [*ink*] —Alcohol, tea, opium, hashisch, fever. SPD (11[a].21)

390.9 Materialism . . . immortality.] [*ink*] 'Balfour.' *joined by guideline to text and then del.* SPD (11[a].23)

390.10–13 To-day . . . 1870.] [*ink*] 'Read Haeckel, 280 | Levelling down—higher to lower—"nothing but" ' *braced* SPD (11[a].24–27)
    Ernst Heinrich Haeckel (1834–1919), German biologist and philosopher. Perry reports that a copy of *Les Énigmes de l'univers*, with p. 280, among others, noted on a flyleaf, was sold. Thus, James could be referring to *Les Énigmes de l'univers* (Paris: Schleicher Frères, 1902).

390.15–19 Distinction . . . another.] [*ink*] Even if mind be a dependent product, *it alone sets values.* (Drop of milk, drop of wine, drop of water) SPD (11[b].29–33)

390.15–16 *of value*] [*ink*] *two converging lines point to words* SP (11.3)

390.19–20 [See . . . –113.]] [*ink*] Good & true pages—read them, lay them to heart SPD (11[a].33–34)

390.23 puts . . . lower,] [*ink*] *underl.*; Matter produces results, mind estimates them. We shall see later that this is Paulsen's own position. SPD (11[b].37)

390.27 the consequences,] [*ink*] 'are admitted to be trostlos. But compare Santayana. Like Paulsen, 71, 73' *joined by guideline to underl. text and then del.* SPD (11[b].41)

390.28 p. 677ff.]] [*ink*] Good account of contemporary state of opinion. | Read to p. 144, to understand. | He defines | a) criticizes crude mat^m & crude spiritualism *with its soul [*insrtd.*] | b) sets up *correlation* of two different things | c) rejects *interaction.* Adopts *parallelism* | denying *effects.* | making it *universal* | d) But he makes of matter the independent variable, and of mind an epiphenomen *Gives [*ov.* 'Pass'] causation to the *blind* thing. | So the materialistic view is not "overcome" *p. 110 [*insrtd.*] SPD (11[a].43); [*ink*] Good account of contemporary opinion But read to p. 144 to understand. After criticizing *crude* materialism *83 [*intrl.*], and popular *"soul" philosophy*, he stops with *correlation*, 83 Rejects *interaction.* Adopts *parallelism*, making of matter the independent and causal variable, while mind is epiphenomenal. Universal panpsychism the result. | Mind & matter like two hands [*period poss. del.*] Santayana, [*comma ov. period*] *like Paulsen on pp. 71, 73. [*insrtd.*] | Mind judges, with no force to execute. SPD (11[b].43)

390.37–38 *Agnostic . . .* TYNDALL] [*ink*] *Read Tyndall [*penc. underl.*], but don't comment on this page which is clear. SPD (12[a].8–9)
    John Tyndall (1820–1893), British physicist. For a possible text see *Essays in Philosophy*, note to 46.33.

391.24 too incongruous] [*ink*] *underl.*; Purely aesthetic reason. SPD (12[a].34)

391.26–30 *Read . . . this.*] [*ink*] [*in left mrgn.*] *Comment on p. 88 | Clifford, Huxley [*penc. underl.*] | Body [*ov. penc. illeg.*] & Mind vol ii | Science & Culture,

IX. | (Douglas A. Spalding, Hodgson) | W.J. vol i. chap V. [*penc.*] [*in right mrgn.*] '90' *opp.* 'Materialism . . . this.' *penc. underl.* SPD (12[a].37–41)

William Kingdon Clifford (1845–1879), British mathematician and philosopher. James is referring to Clifford's "Body and Mind" in volume II of *Lectures and Essays,* ed. Leslie Stephen and Frederick Pollock, 2 vols. (London: Macmillan, 1879).

Thomas Henry Huxley (1825–1895), English biologist and essayist. Essay IX of *Science and Culture* (New York: D. Appleton, 1882) is titled "On the Hypothesis That Animals Are Automata, and Its History."

Douglas Alexander Spalding (c. 1840–1877), British naturalist. He is sometimes associated with the view that animals are automata; see James's *Principles of Psychology,* p. 134.

Chapter V of *The Principles of Psychology* is titled "The Automaton-Theory."

392.6 the mental . . . more] [*red-brown penc.*] *underl.*; [*ink*] 'Taine: text & translation' *red-brown penc. underl. and joined by red-brown penc. guideline to text* SPD (13[a].13)

392.16 mind . . . essential.] [*red-brown penc.*] *underl.* SPD (13[a].24)

392.35 P. . . . favor.] [*ink*] 'Hackel, Strong, Heymanns.' *red-brown penc. underl.* SPD (13[a].44–45)
Gerardus Heymans (1857–1930), Dutch philosopher.

392.36 derived] [*red-brown penc. and ink*] *underl.*; [*ink*] '*Talk about this [*red-brown penc. underl.*]—question of Being. | "What is evolved must have been involved." Abbot | Question of "Being." ' *joined by ink guideline to* 'derived' SPD (13[a].45)
Perhaps Francis Ellingwood Abbot (1836–1903), American philosopher.

392.38 What] [*ink*] 'Nut: Lotze' *red-brown penc. underl.* SPD (14[a].1)

392.39 in *itself*] [*red-brown penc.*] *underl.* SPD (14[a].2)

393.1 "What . . . itself?"] [*red-brown penc.*] *underl.* SPD (14[a].3)

393.3 P. now defends] [*ink*] For *Haeckel*: "gaseous vertebrate." SPD (14[a].6)

393.5 Materialism . . . vanquished] [*red-brown penc.*] *underl.* SPD (14[a].8)

393.8 The mental side] [*red-brown penc.*] Read Fechner SPD (14[a].11)

393.13–394.3 As . . . described.] [*ink*] Voluntaristic [*ink arrow and guideline ab. this word lead to* 'Materialism' [393.5], *but then guideline red-brown penc. del.*] psychology | Reign of intellectualism | Schopenhauer, p 113+ | *Education [*red-brown penc. underl.*] 116–7 | Transition to "blind" impulse *120 [*insrtd.*] | Thence to subconscious life. | (Jastrow) | Dessoir experiments. | Marginal field | Atom-soul. p. 130 | *Seat of soul is entire body [*red-brown penc. underl.*]—this panpsychic view indubitably has a future. But there are *two types. [*red-brown penc. underl.*] | ['Syllabus defends interactionist type.' *del.*] Syllabus, p. 15 | ['Paulsen's plea against' *del.*] Syllabus defends 1*b*. | [*short rule*] | Read. Spencer Give his agnostic conclusion | Read Herschell.—Read my notes. | Then

what's the matter with Materialism? | Read Syllabus above & p. 14½. SPD
(14[a].16–44)

Schopenhauer, p. 113+ is a reference to the discussion of Schopenhauer in Paulsen.

Max Dessoir (1867–1947), German psychologist.

John Frederick William Herschel (1792–1871), British astronomer.

393.36–394.3   This . . . described.] [*red-brown penc.*] 'This . . . materialistic in
the' *underl.; joined by guideline to* 'vanquished' [393.5] SPD (14[a].43–46)

396.18–26   All . . . future.] [*red-brown penc.*] *vert. line in left mrgn.* SP (16.1–9)

401.14–29   Of . . . defender.] [*ink*] *vert. line in right mrgn.* SP (20.4–19)

402.20–23   recent . . . positions] [*ink*] Paulsen p. 172 SP (21.1–4)

402.30–403.3   Our . . . detail.] [*ink*] *vert. line in right mrgn.* SP (21.11–24)

410.7   abstraction.] [*ink*] Hypostatization of the possibility of the thing. SP
(27.22)

417.11   how] [*ink*] Surgeon may be in doubt but he must act fully or not act.
Not cut open an abdomen and leave it. SP (34.1)

426.22–23 | terminist pins his] [*penc.*] only these two copies of this SPD (43.1)

427.9   type.] [*penc.*] end of syllabus SPD (43.33)

A Note on the Editorial Method

All headings in this volume, which is drawn primarily from James's unpublished manuscripts, are editorial. Subheadings enclosed in square brackets are also editorial; otherwise, internal headings are James's own.

The manuscripts are reproduced according to the system known as 'diplomatic transcript'; that is, save for the few silent alterations listed below and the recorded emendations, the readings of the manuscripts are exactly reproduced although no attempt has been made, in the manner of a type facsimile, to follow the lineation of the originals. In all cases of James's alterations, the final reading has been transcribed as representing his latest intention, the altered earlier readings then being recorded in the apparatus list of Alterations according to the system detailed in the heading to the Textual Apparatus. Rarely James might interline a word or phrase without deleting the original. One cannot say with certainty whether this failure to delete was inadvertent or designed; that is, whether James left the choice of readings for a later time but did not return to make a final decision, or whether in the rush of composition he neglected to mark a rejected reading. Although ambiguity must always attach to these readings, the editorial decision has been made invariably to print the later form, the earlier reading then being specially noted for emphasis in a footnote.

Whether in facsimile or diplomatic form, exact transcription of manuscripts will always involve a certain amount of editorial decision. Outside of questions of indention, remarked below, the chief problem in dealing with James's hand is his frequent lack of distinction between the majuscule and minuscule of certain initial letters, chiefly 'c' and 's'. In cases like these, context and custom have generally guided the editorial interpretation of James's intention. Somewhat similar problems may occur in connection with his linkage of words. No question of intent can arise for some words—as when James sometimes spaced words like 'together' as 'to gether'—since he was not always careful to link syllables, especially initial ones. It would be pedantic in the extreme, and often difficult to adjudicate the exact physical structure, to attempt to reproduce such anomalies that could never have been intended. On the other hand, this occasional characteristic of James's hand may cause problems of intention when a legitimate question may arise whether a division or compounding was intended in words like 'any one' or 'any-one', and even 'every where' or 'everywhere'. Ordinarily James's usual practice is well established, and frequently his intention may be assumed from the incidence of a narrow or of the normally wide space such as he was accustomed to use between two distinct words. Difficulties come when there is ambiguity in the spacing for words where he had a preference but might at random violate his custom either of separation or of linkage, such as may occur, for instance, even with his usual 'anyone' and 'everyone'. Such ambiguities the editor has ordinarily resolved by the retention of James's usual practice when the spacing is narrow; but if a major space appears between two words so that ambiguity cannot be asserted, the unusual (for James) form is transcribed and no attempt is made to impose an artificially invariable practice where James did not trouble to be consistent.

Underlined words are transcribed in italic and double-underlined words in the full capitals that James intended, except for his variable underlining of headings outside of the text, where the typographical suggestions of the Harvard University Press have been adopted as to capitalization and punctuation. James's footnotes are indicated by his customary asterisk, dagger, and so forth. These footnotes are preserved as he wrote them without expansion or normalization of his references. However, for the convenience of the reader James's internal references are followed by editorial bracketed identification in the pages of the present edition. References to other volumes already published in the WORKS are added in brackets after James's original page numbers. Editorial footnotes are numbered.

Quotations are reproduced exactly as James or his wife, Alice, wrote them out; unlike the treatment of quotations in the edited volumes of printed texts, no attempt is here made to collate quotations with their sources and to note variation in James's version. Professor Skrupskelis' Notes may be consulted for the identification of quotations. Missing diacritical marks in otherwise correctly spelled foreign words are not supplied by editorial intervention. Ralph Barton Perry worked over various of these manuscripts for possible inclusion of excerpts in his *Thought and Character of William James* and in the process marked them by various indicators, including square brackets. Fortunately, his medium usually differed from James's inscription, so that these accretions may be ignored, but in cases of ambiguity only those brackets in the manuscripts that one can be reasonably certain are James's own are admitted. In some cases James used square instead of round brackets to enclose parenthetical remarks or references, and these have been included in the text. In a few manuscripts James bracketed text that he may have intended for transfer but with no indication as to where this text was to be placed. Because of the ambiguity of purpose surrounding these particular brackets, they have not been included in the text but instead are listed in the respective textual introductions.

A strict diplomatic transcript would annoy and sometimes confuse the reader to no purpose by reproducing the trifling errors inevitable in composition that James did not review for publication. This volume drawn from his unpublished manuscripts, two printed syllabuses, and a typescript, therefore, follows the modifying principles of a scholarly reading edition formulated in the preceding volumes of the WORKS. Two levels of editorial intervention are present. The first, consisting of silent alteration, has been kept to a minimum. In James's holographs the exact position of punctuation in relation to quotation marks may vary or is sometimes in doubt, but his usual characteristic was to follow the American system of placing commas and periods within the quotation marks, colons and semicolons outside, and question or exclamation marks inside or outside depending upon the sense. This practice has been made uniform without record, especially because sometimes the punctuation may come directly beneath the quotation mark so that no significant position could be reproduced. In various of these manuscripts James was in the habit of drawing a short horizontal line in the left margin to mark a new thought or to break the discourse into sections. Instead of these intrusive lines the present edition has adopted the use of a white space to mark such divisions. Occasionally James marked text with a vertical line in the left margin. Only those lines with an attached 'NB' or other comment are noted in the editor's footnotes. In several of his course notes James included dates of composition or possibly of class meetings. These dates, which in the manuscript may be variably circled and written either in the margins or in the line of text, have been set in the present edition within parentheses and immediately preceding the text to which they refer. James's customary practice of using dots to indicate ellipses has been made uniform throughout, even though on occasion, and probably as a result of haste, his dots resemble hyphens. While all editorial alteration of the holographs is recorded as emendation, obvious typographical errors in the two printed syllabuses and in the typescript have been corrected silently.

In some of his discourses, especially when he was writing a series of topic sentences, James began flush with the left margin and indented the run-overs. In others, he made conventional paragraph indentions. On occasion he used both systems somewhat at random in the same manuscript, and the problem may become compounded when his wife, Alice, was writing at his dictation, so that her system (or lack of one) has little or no significance. Editorial discretion seems to be called for in this situation, and in general the prevailing system has been silently made uniform unless some purposeful distinction could be seen.

All remaining editorial alteration of the holographs is recorded as emendation so that the exact form of the original may be reconstructed from the apparatus whenever required for scholarly purposes. These emendations may note the insertion of missing periods at the ends of sentences as well as missing opening or closing quotation marks. Question marks are inserted only in the obvious cases when James's periods do not supply the necessary sense. Rarely, and only when ambiguity is present about the meaning, a missing genitive apostrophe is supplied, or a vital comma necessary for the sense. Misspellings are corrected, but James's characteristic 'neccessity' and 'neccessary' have been preserved. Dittographic error has been repaired. Rarely, a missing word necessary for sense has been supplied. James's various idiosyncracies of presentation, as for example his use of 'reform' spellings, as well as his use of variant spellings, and his characteristic use of minuscules in names and adjectives such as 'hegelian', 'greek', 'france', have been preserved since these cannot be classified as mistakes. Also preserved are his abbreviations such as 'wh.' for *which* and 'fm.' for *from* and his contractions with the apostrophe missing, as for example 'cant' and 'dont'. Errors that can be linked to James's alterations are recorded not in the Emendations but in the list of Alterations in the Manuscript in order to avoid overlap. Emendations in Alice's inscription are distinguished from those in James's holographs.

In various of James's manuscripts, passages are occasionally marked with a vertical or diagonal line through the text. In contrast to the cross strokes that indicate firm intent to delete, James used these strokes ordinarily to indicate passages that he might use elsewhere, or felt he should cut for lack of time. Because of this distinction these passages have been transcribed as an ordinary part of the present text.

All line numbers keyed to the text include headings and subheadings but do not include spaces after these headings or subheadings or spaces within the text itself.

The format of the apparatus differs in these manuscript volumes from that in the preceding editions of James's printed works. The description, or textual introduction, to each manuscript is followed immediately by its Emendations list and then by its list of Alterations in the Manuscript, so that all material in the apparatus is conveniently arranged under one heading instead of being grouped by kind for the whole volume.

F.B.

Textual Apparatus

All manuscript numbers in the headings are in the bMS Am 1092.9 series as catalogued in the Houghton Library of Harvard University. The single exception is No. 30, "Syllabus in Philosophy D," which includes a copy of the syllabus found in the Harvard University Archives. Following the description of each manuscript are the list of Emendations and the list of Alterations for that particular manuscript. For No. 30 the Historical Collation follows the list of Emendations.

Every editorial change is recorded save for such typographical adjustments as are remarked in the Note on the Editorial Method. The reading to the left of the bracket, the lemma, represents the form chosen in the present edition. (A prefixed superior 1 or 2 indicates which of any two identical words in the same line is intended.) In the list of Emendations the rejected reading of the manuscript appears to the right of the bracket. When the phrase *et seq.* occurs, all subsequent readings within the manuscript are to be taken as agreeing with the particular feature of the reading being recorded (save for singulars and plurals and unessential typographical variation, as between roman and italic), unless specifically noted to the contrary by notation within the entry itself, or by the use of *stet* within the apparatus. Readings grouped together with multiple page-line references may also be concerned with only the particular feature being recorded and not with unessential types of variation.

For convenience, certain shorthand symbols familiar in textual notation are employed. A wavy dash ($\sim$) represents the same word that appears before the bracket and is used exclusively in recording punctuation or other accidental variants. An inferior caret ($_\wedge$) indicates the absence of a punctuation mark (or of a footnote superscript) when a difference in the punctuation constitutes the variant being recorded, or is part of the variant. A vertical stroke (|) represents a line ending, sometimes recorded as bearing on the cause of an error or fault.

All alterations made during the course of writing and of revision are recorded here except for strengthened letters to clarify a reading, a very few mendings over illegible letters, and false starts for the same word. The medium is the black ink of the original inscription unless otherwise specified. It is certain that many of the alterations were made *currente calamo* and others as part of one or more reviews. The two are ordinarily so indistinguishable in the intensity of ink or in the kind of pen, however, as not to yield to systematic recordings by categories on the physical evidence. In the description of the alterations, when no record of position is given the inference should be that the change was made in the line of the text and during the course of the original writing. *Deleted* or *deletion* is given the abbreviation *del.*; *double quotation* and *single quotation* marks are abbreviated *db. qt.* and *sg. qt.*; *initial* is abbreviated *init.*; *lower case* and *capital* are given the abbreviations *l.c.* and *cap.*; *below* (*bel.*) is used when a word is written below another; *over* (*ov.*) means inscribed over the letters of the original without interlining; *altered from* (*alt. fr.*) indicates the changing of letters in a word in order to form a new word, as in 'she' *alt. fr.* 'they'; *above* (*ab.*) always describes an independent interlineation. When an addition is a simple interlineation, either with or without a caret, the description *intrl.* is used; when an interlineation is a substitute for one or more deleted words, the formula reads, instead, *ab. del.* 'xyz'. The word *inserted* (*insrtd.*) ordinarily refers to marginal additions or to squeezed-in letters, syllables, and words that also cannot properly be called interlines but are of the same nature. When reference is made to one or the other of two identical words in the same line of the present edition, some preceding or following word or punctuation mark is added for identification, or else the designated word is identified with a superscript [1] or [2] according as it is the first or second occurrence in the line. A superscript is also used to indicate which of more than one identical letter in the same word is referred to.

In order to ease the difficulty of reading quoted revised material of some length and complexity, the following convention is adopted. The quoted text will ordinarily be the final version in the manuscript, whereas the processes of revision are described within square brackets. To specify what words in the text are being affected by the description within square brackets, an asterisk is placed before the first word to which the description in brackets applies; thus it is to be taken that all following words before the square brackets are a part of the described material. For example, at 68.2 in *Some Problems of Philosophy* (WORKS) James altered 'one' to 'One' when he deleted four succeeding sentences. In the first sentence, which he subsequently may have independently deleted, he wrote 'We may mean' and then interlined 'for instance', following it with 'that' and a false start 'it is our' which he deleted. For the false start he substituted 'we treat the whole of it', deleted that, and wrote above it 'the whole of it can be taken', ending the sentence with 'as one topic of discourse.' He began the second sentence with 'We do this by the' which he deleted. He started again with 'Whenever we use the word 'universe' we' in which he wrote 'W' over 'w' in 'Whenever', interlined 'take it thus,' above deleted 'do this,', interlined 'for', continued with 'we mean that no item of reality shall', wrote 'escape' above deleted 'be left out', wrote 'from what' and inserted 'our word covers;' in the margin for deleted 'we point to,' which he inscribed above deleted 'is signified,'. He carried on beyond the semicolon with 'but this unity of abstract reference, altho it has been made much of by', crossed out 'some rationalists,' above which he wrote 'idealistic writers,' and ended with 'is insignificant in the extreme.' In the third sentence James wrote 'It carries no', altered 'other' to 'further', continued with 'sort of connection with it, and would apply as well to', interlined 'any' above deleted 'an utter', and ended with 'chaos as to our actual world.' The final sentence reads 'Both would be *knowable-together* in the same barren way.' with 'the' written over 'this'. In formulaic terms the alteration entry is transcribed as 68.2 One] ('O' *ov.* 'o'); *bef. del.* '[*del.* 'We may mean *for instance [*intrl.*] that *the whole of it can be taken [*ab. del.* '['it is our' *del.*] we treat the whole of it'] as one topic of discourse. We do this by the'] Whenever ['W' *ov.* 'w'] we use the word 'universe' we *take it thus, [*ab. del.* 'do this,'] for [*intrl.*] we mean that no item of reality shall *escape [*ab. del.* 'be left out'] from what *our word covers; [*insrtd. for del.* '*we point to, [*ab.

del. 'is signified,']'] but this unity of abstract reference, altho it has been made much of by *idealistic writers, [*ab. del.* 'some rationalists,'] is insignificant in the extreme. It carries no *further [*alt. fr.* 'other'] sort of connection with it, and would apply as well to *any [*ab. del.* 'an utter'] chaos as to our actual world. Both would be *knowable-together* in *the [*alt. fr.* 'this'] same barren way.'

In formulaic transcriptions double asterisks can also be used to set off subsidiary alterations occurring between the single asterisk and the bracketed description that applies to this single asterisk, as, for example, 'In all these modes of union *some parts **of the world [*intrl.*] prove [*ab. del.* 'several aspects seem'] to be conjoined'. Inferior brackets clarify subsidiary bracketed descriptions within or before the main bracketed entry with or without the use of asterisks according to circumstances. The full details of this system may be found in Fredson Bowers, "Transcription of Manuscripts: The Record of Variants," *Studies in Bibliography*, 29 (1976), 212–264.

In the list of Alterations, the lemmata are ordinarily drawn from the present edition and agree with the manuscript. Occasionally, however, twin daggers (††) warn the user that the lemma is not the reading of the present edition but instead is that of the manuscript. This convention is employed only when the two readings are so similar that a reader following the edition-text in the Alterations list will be able to identify with certainty the reading that is intended without recourse to the Emendations or when the manuscript reading is an error that can be linked to the alteration described to the right of the bracket.

The use of three dots to the right of the bracket almost invariably indicates ellipsis rather than the existence of dots in the manuscript. This is the only violation of the bibliographical rule that material within single quotation marks is cited exactly as it appears in the original document.

Passages in Alice James's hand are always indicated as such, and within these passages alterations that appear in her hand are indicated by '(AJ)'.

Deleted and undeleted rectos and versos that do not apparently relate to revisions in the main body of the Alterations list or that are revisions of continuous deleted material already set out therein are transcribed in a separate section following the list of Alterations for each manuscript.

I. Public Lectures

1. JOHNS HOPKINS LECTURES ON "THE SENSES AND THE BRAIN AND THEIR RELATION TO THOUGHT" 1878 #4395, #4401

The manuscript bMS Am 1092.9 (4395) is written on a series of leaves of white wove unwatermarked paper measuring 8½ x 6¾". Its foliation is irregular. The initial sequence runs from 2 to 4, 6 to 10, and 12 to 17, each leaf numbered at top center. On fol. 3 verso appear five lines of undeleted text (see Undeleted Versos following the list of Alterations) without specific link to any preserved leaves, but the contents suggesting that fol. 3 ('If . . . then to' 3.15–23) had been written on the back of a discarded early leaf containing introductory remarks. The foliation number 6 is written over an original 5, and the upper text ('what . . . breach' 4.1–3) is a revision, linking with the bottom of fol. 4, interlined above original matter that may have been intended as a continuation of fol. 4. Folio 7 ('Study . . . Cochlea.' 4.15–25) is a part-page and therefore associated with the revision. Folio 11 is missing so that the text is interrupted between 5.26 'by the' ending fol. 10 and 5.28 'We now' beginning fol. 12. Folio 15 is a part-page ('belongs . . . shadows.' 6.31–36). Folios 16–17 ('Hole . . . conscious of.' 6.37–7.25), though properly numbered, have had inserted in the upper left corner the letters 'a' and 'b' respectively, each with a closing parenthesis.

Folio 18 is anomalous and starts a major rearrangement of the original text. The number 4 appears in the upper right corner and the page originally began, without foliation, with three lines of text 'consciousness . . . law.' (10.13–14) that complete text found on a later leaf unfoliated except for the number 3 in the upper right corner. The foliation number, centered 18, has been inserted below these out-of-place three lines, and the text 'The best way . . .' (7.26) begins below it after a short horizontal line drawn to the left margin. Halfway down the page, the letter 'c' with a closing parenthesis has been inserted in the left margin. This transferred leaf joins with fol. 19, lettered 'd' in its upper left corner and beginning 'be judged' (7.36). Folio 19 is also interpolated on the evidence of its lettering 'd' and the number 5 in its upper right corner, indicating that the centered foliation 19 is a later addition, as was 18. The normal bottom line ending to the right margin with 'spark.' (8.7) has added below it, to the right margin, the words 'But some['th *del.*]times this' which link with the start of fol. 20 ('suggestion . . . sensa-' 8.7–26). This leaf is lettered 'e' at the left but has no number in the right corner. The centered foliation 20 is crowded in. The lettered sequence concludes with 'f' and 'g' on centered fols. 21 and 22 ('tion *is* not . . . into exercise.' 8.26–9.12). Folio 22 is written on the back of a leaf inscribed in a different ink 'Baltimore Lectures', underlined.

A new series begins on the same paper with the next leaf. From this point on the centered foliation stops. This first new leaf is numbered 1 in the upper right corner and headed 'Retinae of birds rodents *&c [ov. 'an'] independent', the text being continued on pages numbered 2 and 3 ('or double . . . . If we lose' 9.24–10.12). Folio 3 is written on the back of a deleted unnumbered trial that had originally continued the text of fol. 2. To complete the text of fol. 3 one must return to the leaf numbered 4 which had been abstracted and transferred to the fol. 18 position, with fresh text written under the original conclusion of fol. 4 ('consciousness . . . law.' 10.13–14). The leaf numbered 5 at upper right and lettered 'd' was transferred to become fol. 19. It is evident that the text headed by fol. 18 below that which had originally started numbered 4, i.e., the text beneath the short horizontal line marking a section and beginning 'The best way' (7.26)—continued on fol. 19 numbered 5 and lettered 'd'—creates a gap in the later sequence numbered at the right. It is also evident that fol. 20, lettered 'e', is a revision of fol. 6, lettered 'e', in the later sequence of leaves numbered at the upper right. In order to preserve continuity of text in this later sequence the editor has repeated the text on the abstracted fols. 4–5 to fill the gap between fols. 3 and 6, this fol. 6 ('suggestion . . . points' 10.37–11.10) representing the original form of the matter now found revised on fol. 20. Although the text is continuous between numbered fols. 6–7 (the 7 written below a deleted 6), this fol. 7 ('only . . . due to' 11.10–22) drops the lettering of the leaves, which does not return thereafter. Folio 8 ('the motions . . . are made.' 11.22–30) is a part-page that may represent recopied revision, since its successor fol. 9 is also a shorter page than usual; but fol. 9 may not be evidential since the large figure (12.3) that begins fol. 10 could not have been included toward the foot of fol. 9. Folio 10 breaks off with an incomplete sentence ('. . . I will show this in some' 12.18).

Hereafter the leaves are unnumbered and their order is decided contextually. For convenience they may be identified by numbering within square brackets for inference as if they followed fol. 10. The first set comprises three leaves written on white laid unwatermarked paper 8¾ x 6¼", a section headed underlined 'Space' (12.19), the first two leaves inscribed on recto and verso, the third leaf on recto only, ending with 'relating thought.' (14.3). This paper is the same as the draft found in #4397 and #4398.

Four unnumbered leaves of the main wove paper, fols. [14]–[17], are written on the rectos only ('When . . . . Philosophers' 14.4–15.18), the last ('He . . . . Philosophers' 15.4–18) written on the back of a single part-line of undeleted matter, the continuation of a deletion at the foot of the preceding leaf (see Alterations entry 15.4).

Folio [18] is written on a lightweight wove unwatermarked paper of different quality measuring 8⅜ x 7". At the top of the page is the word 'Space' written in brown crayon at some earlier time. The outline and following comment ('I Deny . . . things.' 15.19–16.5) are written vertically in ink. On the verso is printed 'W. James'.

Included in #4395 are miscellaneous notes and fragments not connected with the Baltimore lectures and not printed here.

Found in bMS Am 1092.9 (4401) is a leaf of cheap thin ruled paper, measuring 8¼ x 6", torn from a notebook. This leaf is numbered 9 in the upper right corner; in the upper left corner is an arrow pointing to a 7, the whole enclosed by a parenthesis. The text 'means . . . get' (16.6–23), written on the recto and halfway down the verso numbered 10 in the upper left corner, belongs with the Baltimore lectures.

Emendations

4.18	untranslatable] untranslateable	7.33	by] by by
4.24	anticipatory] anticpatory	8.6;9.14;10.35	than] that
4.36	pitch.] ~∧	8.7;10.36	spark.]] ~.∧ │
4.36	²pitch∧] ~.	8.15	law.] ~∧
5.2	quantitative] quantitive	11.3	retina.] ~∧
5.3	change] chang	12.29	sensations,] ~∧
5.3	effect.] ~∧	14.2	called] call
5.3	back.] ~∧	14.32–33	volitantes,] ~∧
6.21	ignorance.] ~∧	14.35	eyeballs,] ~∧
7.1	Taine.] ~∧	15.11	accommodation] accomodation
7.12	spots.] ~∧	15.19	∧Bain] (~
7.16	nasal) .] ~) ∧	16.18	prick.] ~∧
7.19	sensation.] ~∧		

Alterations in the Manuscripts

3.3	of] 'o' *ov.* 't'	3.8–9	Most . . . sides.] *intrl.*
3.4	thin] 'h' *ov.* 'in'; *bef. del.* 'of'	3.11	conscience] 'ence' *ov. illeg.*

3.11–12 philosopher] ¹'h' *ov.* 's'

3.12 physiol.] 'h' *ov.* 's'

3.14 disposed] 'os' *ov. doubtful* 'el'

3.18 truth] *ab. del.* 'land'

3.18 our] *ab.* 'own' | *undel. in error*

3.18 be] *bef. del.* 'body or'

3.19 What] *aft. del.* 'The gaps in it are'

3.20 any introspective] *ab. del.* 'the religious'

3.22 well.] *bef. del.* 'Happily it seems as if the old animosity were dying away. Helmoltz & Wundt. *Hodgson ['H' *ov.* 'S'] and Lewes. Science against philosophy. Science with philosophy.'

3.23 to] *bef. del.* 'speak in as impartial a spirit as I can command of certain'

3.23 broad] *intrl.*

4.1–3 what . . . breach] *insrtd. ab. del.* 'very novel or striking, be perhaps welcome as a re-corroboration of what has been the feeling of the wisest heads ['ha' *del.*] at all times'

4.25 Same] 'S' *ov.* 'O'

4.26 who] *bef. del.* 'wh'

4.30,31 *(second)* the] *aft. del.* 'our'

4.33 has] *aft. del.* 'is com'

4.34 pitch] *aft. del.* 'acoust'

4.35 once] 'ce' *ov.* 'e'

4.36 40] '4' *ov.* '3'

††5.2–3 quantitive . . . effect] *intrl.*

5.3 Camel's back] *intrl.*

5.4 Summation] *aft. del.* 'Ca'

5.5 increasing] *init.* 'i' *ov.* 'r'; *bef. del.* 'light'

5.6 of psychic] *intrl.*

5.7 direct] *bef. del.* 'accom'

5.8 This] 'T' *ov.* 'I'

5.9 point.] *bef. del.* 'Most p'

5.11 ¹it] *aft. del.* 'it'

5.12 that] *bef. del.* 'wh'

5.13 ¹in] *ov.* 'ou'

5.14 When] 'W' *ov.* 'w'

5.14 a man] *ab. del.* 'we'

5.14–15 tells . . . ²is] *ab. del.* 'suffers ['s' *ov.* 'ed'] pain, however ['unjusti *del.*] little cause there might be for it, ['still' *del.*] if *he [*ov.* 'we'] said it was pain, pain it was'

5.16–17 Consciousness . . . constitution.] *intrl.*

5.18 not] *bef. del.* 'what'

5.20 No] *bef. del.* 'pou sto'

5.21 obscure] *intrl.*

5.22 and] *bef. del.* 'it'

5.24 anatomy.] *intrl.*

5.29 Anatomy.] *intrl.*

5.29 so] *bef. del.* 'fa'

5.31 Certain] *insrtd. bef.* 'Philosophers' *not reduced in error*

5.31 thought] 'ho' *ov.* 'ou'

5.32 of] *bef. del.* 'the'

5.33 mortar] *aft. del.* 'molta'

5.34 join] 'j' *ov.* 'c'

5.34 into unity] *intrl.*

5.35 No] *aft. del.* '*No substance [*intrl.*] Such events as the breaking of the bowl wd. be explained by consecution in'

5.38 you] *final* 'r' *del.*

5.40 packages] *intrl.*

6.5 stable] *aft. del.* 'certain'

6.6 hands] 'h' *ov.* 'n'

6.9 *signs*] *bef. del.* 'for our consciousness,'

6.10 According to] *ab. del.* 'In'

6.10–11 of Helmholtz] *intrl.*

6.14 its] 'ts' *ov.* 's'

6.21 Our ignorance] *intrl.*

6.21 Blind] *aft. del.* 'Limitation of field of view.'

6.21 Entoptic] *aft. del.* 'De'

6.22 Inability] *aft. del.* 'Nachbilder [*intrl.*] Chromatic fringes.'

6.29 Even] *aft. del.* 'If I know that the object is a black hat in the sun I think of'

6.30 black] *aft. del.* 'a'; *bef. del.* 'hat in'

6.39–7.1 Retinal . . . Taine] *intrl.*

7.3 do] 'o' *ov.* 'oe'

††7.4 image,] *comma not altered to period in error bef. del.* 'one when we think we have before us one object in one position, two when we think of objects in two positions. But what makes us'

7.6 When] 'h' *ov.* 'e'

7.10 and] 'n' *ov.* 't'

7.11–12 as in stereoscope] *intrl.*

7.12 two] *aft. del.* 'those'; *bef. del.* 'sensations'

7.16 Other . . . ambiguous.] *tr. by guideline fr. aft.* 'ones.' *to bef.* 'that' *not cap. in error*

7.18 Our] *ov.* 'The'

7.18 again] *intrl.*

7.21 Jeffries . . . eye. ['Invert head.' *del.*]] *intrl.*

7.23 Sensation nonspatial.] *intrl.*

7.23–24 Intersection] 'I' *ov.* 'T'

7.35;10.24 will] *aft. del.* 'may'

7.40;10.29 judgment] *alt. fr.* 'judgement'

8.1;10.30 if] *bef. del.* 'a point of'

8.3;10.32 which] *aft. del.* 'fm. wh' *aft. del.* 'will sugge'

8.4;10.33 though] *final* 't' *del.*

8.7;10.36 sometimes] 'times' *aft. del.* 'th'

8.8 F⟨⟩gers . . . image.] ('c' *of* 'changed' *ov.* 's'); *intrl.*

8.15 Wundt's law] *intrl.*

8.15–16 Sensation] 'S' *ov.* 's'

8.17 mask] *intrl.*

8.23 being] *ab. del.* 'being'

8.29 other.] *bef. del.* 'I must candidly confess that this seems to me'

8.31 place] *bef. del.* 'refers to'

9.2–3 Sensation . . . spatial.] *intrl.*

9.8 put] *bef. del.* 'of'

9.9 as] 's' *ov.* 'n'

9.10 verification] 'v' *ov.* 'e'

9.13 &c.] *ov.* 'an'

9.17 at one distance] *ab. del.* 'here'

9.17 at another] *ab. del.* 'there'

9.19 Beyond] 'B' *ov.* 'b'; *aft. comma not alt. to period in error*

9.19 them] *ab. del.* 'which'

9.22 If the] *ab. del.* 'Positions from which rays start to the retina'

9.22 on] *bef. del.* 'which'

9.22 retinae] *ov.* 'rays'

9.23 hardly] *bef. del.* 'ef'

9.23 affected] *bef. del.* 'by'

9.26 yellow] *final* 's' *del.*

9.37–38 tenor of] *intrl.*

9.38 The] *bef. del.* 'near finger appears single so long as we think of it as'

10.1 refer] *final* 'red' *del.*

10.4–5 affections] *aft. del.* 'l. hand retinal s' *aft. del.* 's[ov. 'a']p'

10.9–10 correct] *aft. del.* 'right.'

10.10 if] *aft. del.* 'can never'

10.12 lose] *alt. fr.* 'loose'

10.38 where] *intrl.*

10.40 of its axis] *intrl.*

11.10 Disparate] *ab. del.* 'Non identical'

11.11 here] 'h' *ov.* 'r'

11.13 of] *bef. del.* 'relief' *bef. del.* 'pers'

11.15 per] 'p' *ov.* 'w'

11.18 reality] *aft. del.* 'reall'

11.20 In] *aft. del.* 'O'

11.21–22 different] *aft. del.* 'sa ['a' *ov.* 'm']'

11.23 every] *aft. del.* 'ey'

11.23–24 degree of convergence] *ab. del.* 'position'

11.27 within . . . limits] *intrl.*

11.30 unless] *aft. del.* 'but'

11.37 which] *bef. del.* 'obliges me'

12.2 object] *bef. del.* 'near'

12.3 Certain] *aft. del.* 'Beg | What are our sensations' |

12.4–5 present] *aft. del.* 'and'

12.14 per] *aft. del.* 'by'

12.15 that] *bef. del.* 'they are the m'

12.22 might] *ab. del.* 'may'

12.24 question] 'q' *ov.* 'r'

12.27 sensible] *intrl.*

12.29 of] *aft. del. comma; bef. del.* 'So'

12.29 translated] *aft. del.* 'interp'

12.30 in] *aft. del.* 'enough'

12.35 ¹a] *ab. del.* 'its peculiar'

12.36 another] *ab. del.* 'higher'

13.2 This] 'is' *ov.* 'e'; *bef. del.* 'quale or'

13.8 any] *aft. del.* 'a s'

13.19 yet] *aft. del.* 'not'; *bef. del.* 'topogra'

13.21 already] *intrl.*

13.22 and of numerical] *intrl.*

13.26 emphasize] 's' *ov.* 'z'; *aft. del.* 'pick out'

13.26 another] 'o' *ov.* 'y'

13.27 Thus] *bef. del.* 'relations'

13.29 These] *ab. del.* 'But the difference between these, which'

13.29 to] *bef. del.* 'call'

13.29 from] *bef. del.* 'different'

13.31 with] *intrl.*

13.32 our] *aft. del.* 'with'

13.32 earlier] *aft. del.* 'fo'

13.35   their] *aft. del.* 'our [*ab. del.* 'the']
spatial [*aft. del.* 'system'] system are'

13.37   clinging] *aft. del.* 'col'

13.37   always] *intrl.*

14.1   ¹spatial] *alt. fr.* 'space.'

14.4   eyes] 's' *added*

14.4   are] *ov.* 'is'

14.5   air] *aft. del.* 'ey'

14.12   axes] *alt. fr.* 'axis'

14.12   B] *ov.* 'be'

14.13   at] *aft. del.* 'on the whole the
most frequent'

14.15   Images] *bef. del.* 'cast'

14.18   i.e.] *intrl.*

14.21   true] *intrl.*

14.28   ¹too] ²'o' *added*

14.28   small] *insrtd. for del.* 'large'

14.35   and . . . eyeballs] (¹'the' *ov.
illeg.*); *intrl.*

14.36   does] *ab. del.* 'is'

14.36   perception] *ab. del.* 'feeling'

14.36   ²of] *aft. del.* 'we get'; *bef. del.*
'the coo'

15.1   what] *aft. del.* 'its'

15.2   a] *insrtd.*

15.2   point] *final* 's' *del.*

15.4   law.] *added ov. period bef. del.*
'He expresses *it [*undel. in error*] in
the form of a law by saying that only
those parts of our sensations are
noticed by us which are of practical

consequence in themselves. All [*undel.
verso*] those points on the contrary
which are'

15.7   particular] *ab. del.* 'given'

15.16   always] *aft. del.* 'an object'

15.23   intellectualists] *ov.* 'psychic';
'(psychical stimulus)' *written underneath and then del.*

15.25   experience.] *bef. del.* 'psch. stim'

16.3   suggests] *bef. del.* 'whether there
be a very fundamental differen'

16.6   there is] *intrl.*

16.6–7   directions] *bef. del.* 'of consecution.'

16.8   down] *ab. del.* 'behind'

16.8   among] *aft. del.* 'for the'

16.8   lot] *aft. del.* 'pos'

16.9   fits] *bef. del.* 'it'

16.10   that] *bef. del.* 'the nascent'

16.11   by] *aft. del.* 'it'

16.14   this] 'is' *ov.* 'e'

16.15   affording] *aft. del.* 'with the
result'

16.15   them.] *period added bef. del.* 'to
each other.'

16.16   if] *intrl.*

16.16   outstretched] *aft. del.* 'leg'

16.16   all] *bef. del.* 'other'

16.19   becomes] *aft. del.* 'is'

16.21   sum] *intrl.*

16.23   , but I get] *ink added*

Deleted and Undeleted Versos

[*undel. fol.* 3ᵛ] 'ficulties unaltered. Same facilities & difficulties for both belief & skepticism. I will therefore bring before you some of the difficulties. But there will be some new facts by the way; and if our conclusions have no very ringing sound'

[*del. fol.* 3ᵛ: *orig. continuation of fol.* 2, 'images fuse', 9.38–39] 'together so long as we *interpret them to proceed from one [*ab. del.* 'locate their object in the point']'

2. Lowell Lectures on "The Brain and the Mind" 1878 #4397, #4396, #4398, #4401, #4399, #4400

Lecture 1 in the series (#4397) consists of a series of leaves of unwatermarked white laid paper measuring 8¾ x 6¼", the same paper represented by three leaves of isolated text on Space in No. 1 (#4395). The text is written for the most part on both sides of the leaves, which are paged 1–6 [7–8] 9–25 47–72 [73] 74–81.

Pages 1–3 are in James's hand, although on p. 2 'each . . . lot ['in' *del.*]' (17.8–9) is in the hand of his wife, Alice. On p. 4, the verso of the second leaf, at 18.10 after James had squeezed in 'roughly' to end a line after 'know', Alice inscribes the rest of the page and continues to the end of part-page 5 ending 'Frog & bird.' (18.19–20), its verso blank. James begins Lecture 2 on p. 6 but Alice enters again halfway down the page with 'Headless bird' (18.28) and continues through the second lecture on p. 9 (19.29). There are additions in pencil made at a later time by James, as well as his revisions in ink. Alice begins the next page, 10, with Lecture 3. Page 12 is a part-page, the first line 'Before . . . generalities' (20.12) squeezed in in James's hand. Its verso is blank save for deleted 'Lecture', the following number illegible under the heavy deletion. Page 13 ('Now . . . hemis.' 20.17–24), the recto of the eighth leaf, continues the lecture in Alice's hand after James has deleted and revised the start of the page with 'Now . . . images'.

The third lecture concludes, still in Alice's hand, on p. 15, a part-page which is the recto of the ninth leaf, its verso blank. Leaf 10 consists of the first two pages of James's "Are We Automata?" cut from a copy of *Mind* for January 1879. The text, ending with 'I have heard a most intelligent', may be found at 38.1–40.2 in *Essays in Psychology*, WORKS.

The eleventh leaf begins Lecture 4 with p. 16 in Alice's hand and continues through p. 19, the verso of the twelfth leaf. Leaves 13–16 consist of pp. 15–22 (the end of the article) of "Are We Automata?" *Essays in Psychology*, beginning 'so may the accentuating finger' (52.35–61.4). In these pages James's first footnote on p. 17 (*Essays*, p. 55, fn. 8) has been scored through in ink and a deletion mark inscribed in the right margin.

Lecture 5 begins p. 20 in Alice's hand, which continues to the foot of its verso, p. 21, ending with 'many elementary processes.' (22.13). Leaves 18–20 follow with pages 3–8 of "Are We Automata?" (*Essays*, 40.2–46.18 'biologist say . . . *attention*. There'). That this was the original position of these printed leaves in the lecture notes is indicated by a few ink offsets from handwritten p. 22, toward the foot of the verso of the twentieth leaf, p. 8 of the printed article. The twenty-first leaf begins with p. 22 ('The Phrenologist . . .' 22.14) in Alice's hand and continues to the foot of p. 25, the verso of leaf 22, ending with 'water to flow . . . . .' (23.9). In the latter leaves of this sequence beginning on p. 23 a few words are underlined for sight emphasis with a black crayon. These have not been reproduced as italic in the present text.

The twenty-third leaf jumps from p. 25 to begin p. 47 in Alice's hand with 'I do not say' (23.10). After p. 50 ('. . . This servile' 24.1), leaves 25 and 26 consist of pp. 7–10 of James's "On Some Omissions of Introspective Psychology," *Mind*, 9 (January 1884) (*Essays*, 147.37–151.40 'the first instance, . . . is not, when'). The late date demonstrates that these leaves are a subsequent interpolation. Alice's handwritten text continues from p. 50 in mid-sentence on p. 51 with 'relation, this impotence' (24.1) to end the chapter with a part-page, leaf 27 with blank verso. Lecture 6 in Alice's hand begins leaf 28, p. 52, with more crayon underlining, this time in blue, not reproduced in the present text. For emphasis, or attention-calling, this same blue crayon adds marginal vertical strokes against various passages. After p. 55 ('. . . we may also have' 25.2), the verso of leaf 29, a leaf is intercalated, the last two pages, 25 and 26 (*Essays*, 166.14–167.41 'note of its existence . . . best specific name.'), of "On Some Omissions of Introspective Psychology." Alice's handwritten text continues on the thirty-first leaf, p. 56, with 'aesthetic demands.' (25.2) up to p. 61 'being useful' (26.20), the verso of the thirty-third leaf, after which appear two pages 19 and 20 from "Are We Automata?" (*Essays*, 57.12–59.22 'is subserved . . . possible selves'). Alice's inscription of p. 62, which is leaf 35 recto, follows, continuing the text of p. 61 with 'or efficient,' (26.21). The manuscript ends on the verso of the forty-sixth leaf, p. 81. (Leaves 42 and 43, numbered 1 and 2, are not a part of this sequence and are discussed below.) Page 73 is unnumbered. On p. 76 the number has been crossed through in pencil, a centered 4 added, and to the right of the 4 what appears to be 'L4—cli'. On p. 77 the number is again crossed through in pencil and 'L5—cli', centered, added. Starting with p. 78 and continuing to the end on p. 81 the separate foliation gives way to centered 'L6—cli' and so on to 9 on p. 81. The significance of this notation is not clear and the hand is probably not James's. Found in #4397, but not printed in the present edition, are quotations from W. K. Clifford's *Lectures and Essays*, inscribed in Alice's hand on the rectos of three leaves foliated 1–3.

A draft for Lecture 1 is preserved as #4396, which consists of six leaves of wove paper 10 x 8", ruled vertically, inscribed by Alice on the rectos and foliated 1–6 ('In . . . anything.' 30.25–32.17). Folio 6 is written on the back of a discarded leaf containing a trial of the opening sentence on fol. 1.

Notes concerning the lecture are found in #4397 on the forty-second and forty-third leaves, numbered 1 and 2 respectively ('*Anat*. . . . stops.' 32.18–33.2), of the sequence described above. They are in Alice's hand written on laid paper, measuring 9¾ x 8", watermarked with a crown and the legend Royal Irish Linen | Marcus Ward | & Co. On the verso of the first leaf Alice had written the first two words of the first line 'Anat. Remind', but then turned the leaf over for the full inscription.

A trial for part of Lecture 1 is catalogued as #4398, three leaves of the same laid paper as the main lecture in #4397. This trial ('Dift. . . . observation' 33.3–34.28) is written in Alice's hand on recto and verso, the leaves unpaged, with the verso of the third leaf blank. Associated with the first lecture (reprinted here as an appendix) is a sheet of wove paper 10 x 8", folded to form two leaves, the watermark Partridge & Cooper Vellum Wove. On the recto of the first fold is a list of twenty-two slides in Alice's hand. The inner folds are blank, but on the verso of the second fold Alice wrote a table of brain sizes. These lists (34.31–35.20) are catalogued as #4401.

A draft for part of the second lecture comes in #4399, the first fold measuring 8¾ x 6¾" of unwatermarked white laid paper written in Alice's hand on rectos and versos. The pages are numbered 3–6 in upper center, the text beginning on p. 3 in mid-sentence ('croaks . . .' 35.22) and ending on p. 3 with 'considerations?' (36.21–22) before a long deletion that had ended the page in mid-sentence (see Alterations entry 36.21–22). Following 'of sensibility' (36.5) on p. 4 James wrote 'insert (a)', perhaps a reference to 'Remarkable . . . considering?' (36.23–37.24), text written by Alice on the rectos and versos of four unnumbered pages of a second fold. In the upper left corner of the first page a circled 'a', written in red pencil, is probably not in James's hand. The note 'insert (a)' may have been referring to this text or it may have been referring to some other text, now missing. Since these notes and drafts were used more than once, no significance can be attached to this notation. A single leaf of the same paper, unnumbered, again written by Alice on the recto and the upper half of the verso ('Rip Van Winkle . . . deeds.' 37.25–39) is catalogued as #4400 but belongs with the drafts of Lecture 2.

Textual Apparatus

Drafts of Lectures 3, 4, and 5 are preserved in #4400, which consists of folds of the same laid paper written in Alice's hand on the rectos and versos. The recto of the first page is numbered 13 at the upper center, the number written after a deleted 1, the pagination thus changed from 11 to 13. Circled in the upper left corner is a pencilled 4. The next pages 14–20 are altered from 12–18 respectively. The upper text of p. 14 is deleted, continuing the deletion at the foot of p. 13 (see Alterations entry 38.9). When undeleted text follows after a white space (38.10), James wrote in brown pencil 'Insert (3)'. It is not known to what page or text this '(3)' refers. Starting with p. 21 ('how this conception' 39.34–35) and continuing to the end of the preserved manuscript on p. 32 the pagination numbers are unaltered. On p. 21 opposite the seventh and eighth lines ('understand . . . analyzed' 39.37–38) James wrote the number 2 with a parenthesis in the left margin. James made a few corrections and revisions throughout the leaves.

Emendations

17.5   proprietors] proprieters
17.7   feeling etc.] feelng $\sim_\wedge$
[*begin* Alice James *hand*]
18.16   segments,] $\sim_\wedge$
19.10;37.2   Spalding] Spaulding
19.36;38.4   reservoir] resevoir
20.8   the more] *om.*
20.21   violin,] $\sim_\wedge$
20.27   of] of of
20.38   corroborate] coroborate
21.7   Hitzig] Hitsiz
21.32–33   corroborated] coroborated
22.11   conscientiousness] consciencious-
ness
23.16,19   Tyndall] Tyndal

28.3   monstrosity] monstrocity
31.2   incense] insense
31.35   physiological] phyiological
32.21   horse,] $\sim_\wedge$
34.21   the latter] *om.*
34.28   observation.] $\sim_\wedge$
36.8   impotent] impotant
37.13   Mental] Metal
39.11   Raspberry] Rasberry
40.4   mortar] morter
40.40   obstacles.] $\sim_\wedge$
42.25   tries] trys
43.5   &c.] $\sim_\wedge$
[*end* Alice James *hand*]

Alterations in the Manuscripts

16.29–30   new knowledge] *ab. del.*
'science'
17.4   review] 're' *ov.* 'vi'
17.7   all] *ov.* 'of'
[*begin* Alice James *hand*]
17.9   lot] *bef. del.* 'in' (AJ)
[*end* Alice James *hand*]
17.15   Judge] *aft. del.* 'A'
17.15   careless] *aft. del.* 'm'
17.16   philosoph.] *bef. del.* '. . . only
thorough oblig. is'
17.29   Really] 'R' *ov.* 'r'
17.29   muscle.] *bef. del.* 'chem'
17.38   theory] *ab. del.* 'idea'
17.39   way] *aft. del.* 'wh'
18.3   now] *bef. del.* 'called a physiol.
postulate.'

18.6   Ludicrously false] 'ly false' *intrl.*
18.8   processes] *final* 'es' *added*
18.9   guess] *ab. del.* 'know almost'
18.9   Outward] *aft. del.* 'Ou'
18.9   In] *aft. del.* 'Paths.'
[*begin* Alice James *hand*]
18.16   segments] *added*
18.18   Lower] *aft. del.* 'Frog & bird' (AJ)
[*end* Alice James *hand*]
18.26   safer.] *bef. del.* | '*This* has *led
[alt. fr.* 'lead'] Lewes etc.'
[*begin* Alice James *hand*]
18.27   Fish, turtle] *penc. added*
18.29   rodents] *penc. added*
19.3   ride] *aft. del.* 'wa' (AJ)
19.14   We . . . tempted] *ab. del.* 'Not
count,'

550

19.14–15   as . . . to-day.] *intrl.; period aft.* 'tomorrow' *undel. in error*

19.15   R.V.W.] *intrl.*

19.16   Clay] *penc. added*

19.22   1ˢᵗ] *ov.* 'First' (AJ)

19.33   considerations. = Emotions] *period ov. comma;* '=' *added;* 'E' *ov.* 'e'

19.34–35   constitute . . . alike.] ('memories expectations' *insrtd.*); *intrl.*

20.2   Slave] *bef. del.* 'of'

20.3   Utility] *aft. del.* 'Preliminary, rough.' |

20.6–7   . . . the fewer.] *intrl.*

20.7   The] 'T' *ov.* 't'

20.7   hemispheres] 'es' *ov.* 'ic'

20.7   him] *ov. dash*

20.8   widely . . . sphere] ('extended' *aft. del.* 'the sphere'); *intrl.*

20.9   the suggestions] *ab. undel. three dots*

20.9   into] *ov. two periods*

20.10   Frog] *aft. del. intrl.* 'Polyp' (AJ)

20.10   cerebrum . . . present] *intrl.*

20.12   Before . . . generalities] *insrtd.*

20.17–18   Now . . . images] *added for del.* 'One criterion applied from first to last—emancipation from imme-diate. | No one disagree. But'

20.18–19   subserve] *aft. del.* 'keep' (AJ)

20.21   Bruise, scar.] *intrl.* (AJ)

20.21   violin] *intrl.* (AJ)

††20.22   mirror,] *comma not alt. to period in error bef. del.* 'violin'

20.23   All] *aft. del.* 'Rasberry'

20.25–26   if . . . drunkard.] *ab. del.* 'if [*undel. in error*] Catarrh revives.'

21.10   Pigeons wink, dodge] *penc. added*

21.15   mind.] *bef. penc. del.* 'Pigeons winking. Frogs, rodents dodging'

21.17   Education] *intrl.*

21.18   love] *aft. penc. del.* 'anger'

21.27   utterance,] *bef. del.* 'but'

21.36   ¹the . . . thoughts] *intrl.* (AJ)

21.37   stream] *aft. del.* 'activities' (AJ)

21.38   of] *insrtd.* (AJ)

22.3   occurs] 's' *added*

22.17   out . . . simpler] *penc. added*

22.17   explain] *ab. del.* 'say'

22.18   loves children] *ab. del.* 'is cautious' (AJ)

22.18   philop.] *ab. del.* 'caution'

22.29   first] *ab. del.* 'our'

22.29   are] *intrl.*

23.5   Are . . . and] *ab. del.* 'It would seem thus'

23.6   is a] *ab. del.* 'became'

23.6   chaos?] '?' *insrtd. bef. del.* 'is again.'

23.6   By no means!] *ab. del.* 'But'

23.6–7   wd. be] *intrl.*

23.9   localize] 'ize' *added* (AJ)

23.12–13   knowledge . . . past] *ab. del.* 'memory'

23.13–14   has . . . recollection] ('the' *ov.* 'a'); *ab. del.* 'remembers' (AJ)

23.15   my head] *ab. del.* 'I' (AJ)

23.15   has] *alt. fr.* 'have' (AJ)

23.15   bump] *aft. del.* 'large' (AJ)

23.16   who] *aft. del.* '&c'

23.24   ¹however] *aft. del.* 'whether rational or not' (AJ)

23.30   degrading] 'ing' *ov.* 'ation' (AJ)

23.30   high] *final* 'est' *del.; bef. del.* 'things we know' (AJ)

23.31   the] *ov.* 'a' (AJ)

23.33   When . . . man] *ab. del.* 'They' *insrtd. for del.* 'To' (AJ)

23.33   deny] *aft. del.* 'to' (AJ)

23.34   when he says] *ab. del.* 'to make' (AJ)

23.34   they] 'y' *ov.* 'm' (AJ)

23.34   are] *insrtd.* (AJ)

23.34   creatures] *aft. del.* 'receiv' (AJ)

23.34   physical] *aft. del.* 'the' (AJ)

23.35   ¹conditions] *intrl.* (AJ)

23.35   masters] *aft. del.* 'dictators of s' (AJ)

23.35–36   I . . . utterances] *intrl.*

23.36   contain] *final* 's' *del.*

23.37   absurd] *ab. del.* 'therefore uncandid'

23.37   to] *bef. del.* 'screen themselves from the'

24.10   Feeling] *in left mrgn. is penc. del. penc.* 'Col'

††24.10   a passenger,] *tr. by guideline fr. aft.* 'Feeling'; *comma not alt. to period in error*

24.15   joy—] *dash ov. comma*

24.15 conclusion—] *dash ov. semicolon*

24.28 feeling" . . . . .] *bef. penc. del.*
blue penc. 'collateral product'

25.3 ²&] *intrl.*

25.5 is] *intrl.*

25.7 But this] *intrl.*

25.8 lying,] *aft. del.* 'min' (AJ)

25.8 *mendacious*] *added*

25.16 perform] *bef. del.* 'better' (AJ)

25.19 or] *ov. illeg.*

25.25 processes] *aft. del.* 'consider-ations' (AJ)

25.27 the] *final* 'se' *del.*

25.29 jelly. . . .] *bef. del.* 'which'

25.31 by currents] *intrl.* (AJ)

25.31 The] *aft. del. start of letter*

25.34 instable] 'in' *blue penc. insrtd.*
aft. 'in-' |

25.36 minute] 'mi' *blue penc. insrtd.*
aft. 'mi-' |

26.3 discharged] *aft. del.* 'upset'

26.6 instability] *aft. del.* 'multi'

26.9 Happy go lucky] *penc. insrtd.*

26.9–10 Caprice . . . Chladnis] *insrtd.*

26.14 at] *aft. del.* 'can'

26.16 To . . . physicist.] *insrtd.*

26.17 this] *aft. del.* 'exa'

26.20 we] *aft. del.* 'such words as utility'

26.21 its] *aft. del.* 'or'

26.21 all.] *period added for del.*
comma

26.22 exist] *bef. del.* '; [*undel. in error*]
it must be entirely indifferent'

26.22 ideals.] *period ov. semicolon*

26.23 Entirely] 'E' *ov.* 'e'

26.27 words] *ab. del.* 'voice'

26.27 a] *intrl.*

26.27 Shakespeare] *blue penc. ab. del.*
'Tennyson'

26.28 brought] *aft. del.* 'done f' (AJ)

26.29 that] *bef. del.* 'one result is better than' (AJ)

27.4 Thus . . . end.] *blue penc. insrtd.*

27.11 choice] *aft. del.* 'selection' (AJ)

27.15 survey.] *bef. del.* 'Senses empha-size . . . . . . Read 28, *29, 30 [*vert. stroke*] [*insrtd.*] makes world discon-tinuous. | Perception only picks out signs'

27.15 29] *aft. del.* 'Read 28,'

27.15 28 bottom] *penc. added*

27.19 present] *aft. del.* 'use' (AJ)

27.24–25 extreme] 'ex' *blue penc.*
insrtd. aft. 'ex-' |

27.28 time,] *comma ov. period bef. del.*
'Have tried to show'

27.37 just] *ab. del.* 'good' (AJ)

27.38 do] *aft. del.* 'leave our footprints on the sands of time' (AJ)

27.38 one] *aft. del.* 'be' (AJ)

28.1 A striking] *ab. del.* 'To sum up this' (AJ)

28.4 Now] *aft. del.* 'T' (AJ)

28.6 & ends] *intrl.* (AJ)

28.7–8 constantly] *aft. del.* 'with her fingers' (AJ)

28.9 throws] *aft. del.* 'in a' (AJ)

28.11 ²the] *aft. del.* 'a n' (AJ)

28.14 grounds] *aft. del.* 'cir' (AJ)

28.15 Distribution] *blue penc. added*

28.17 Supposing] *aft. del. start of letter*
(AJ)

28.21 corroborates] 2'r' *intrl.* (AJ)

28.25 Now] *ab. del.* 'As' (AJ)

28.26 channels. The] *period ov.*
comma; 'T' *ov.* 't' (AJ)

28.28 actions] *aft. del.* 'performances whi' (AJ)

28.28 wd.] *aft. del.* 'but that it becomes intense' (AJ)

28.29 not] 't' *insrtd.*

28.30 hand,] *bef. del.* 'Read 49' (AJ)

28.31 In . . . agonizing.] *added aft.* 'H'
del. (AJ)

29.4 recognizes] *aft. del.* 'knows' (AJ)

29.6 In] *aft. del.* 'T' (AJ)

29.6 which when] *aft. del.* 'agrees with so'; *bef. del.* 'tho' (AJ)

29.8 instinct] 'in' *blue penc. insrtd.*
aft. 'in-' |

29.10 If] *aft. del.* '[¶] If ancestral C.
N.S.' (AJ)

29.14 C] *blue penc. ov.* 'S'; *aft. blue*
penc. del. 'N'

29.20 If] *aft. del.* '[¶] If the word "scientific" be meant to cover.' (AJ)

29.21 who] *bef. del.* 'follow me' (AJ)

29.22–23 & . . . taste] *intrl.*

29.25 conclusion] *ab. del.* 'opinion'
(AJ)

29.26 all] *insrtd.* (AJ)

29.28 doctrine] *ab. del.* 'opinion' (AJ)

29.32 man] *bef. del.* 'like Huxley'

29.33   itself;] *semicolon ov. period*
29.33   ruled] *ab. del.* 'declared' (AJ)
29.36   this] *bef. del.* 'partizan' (AJ)
29.37   thing] *bef. del.* 'that seems' (AJ)
30.1   the Pope] *aft. del.* 'Prof. Huxley which' (AJ)
30.5   With] *aft. del.* 'These p' (AJ)
30.9   phenomena] *ab. del.* 'facts' (AJ)
30.10   is] 's' *ov.* 'n' (AJ)
30.11   If] *aft. del.* 'If religious thought' (AJ)
30.12   Theology] *aft. del.* 'Ph'
30.12   men . . . too.] *ab. del.* 'scientists.'
30.13   philosophers.] *penc.* 'phers.' *aft. penc. del.* 'phe' |
30.13   If,] *bef. del.* 'our thought' (AJ)
30.14   muddled] *bef. del.* 'for one' (AJ)
30.14   worthless] *aft. del.* 'muddled' (AJ)
30.15   It] *aft. del.* 'For truth is one' (AJ)
30.20   strengthened] *aft. del.* 'with' (AJ)
30.20   natural] *penc. insrtd.*
30.27   animal] *aft. del.* 'organic' (AJ)
30.29   nervous] *aft. del.* 'mysteries of the' (AJ)
30.35   persons.] *period added bef. del.* 'who think' (AJ)
30.35   most] *intrl.* (AJ)
30.35   materialism] *aft. del.* 'idol of'; *bef. del.* 'lying in ambush behind the dazzling g' (AJ)
31.1   fireworks] *aft. del.* 'light' (AJ)
31.2   with] *intrl.* (AJ)
31.2   its] *insrtd. for del.* 'his'
31.6   stagnant] *aft. del.* 'stupid'
31.11   introspective psychology] *tr. by guideline fr.* 'psychology introspective'
31.11   hardly] *aft. del.* 'never' (AJ)
31.12   degrading] *aft. del.* 'shallow' (AJ)
31.17   exactly] *intrl.*
31.20   2to] *bef. del.* 'both sides' (AJ)
31.21   It] *aft. del.* 'The scien' (AJ)
31.22   and] *intrl.* (AJ)
31.29   that] *insrtd. for del.* 'a great advantage in this multifarious scientific apprenticeship. He who teaches any branch of learning becomes much more responsible for his opinions than he who merely reads'

31.34   conscience.] *period added bef. del.* 'because' (AJ)
31.38   owns] *bef. del.* 'hi' (AJ)
32.3   jealousies] 'ies' *aft. del.* 'y' (AJ)
32.6   every] *aft. del.* 'one' (AJ)
32.6   impartially] *ab. del.* 'as well as all the rest'
32.7   each] *ab. del.* 'all'
32.8   As] *aft. del.* 'As physiologists we ought' (AJ)
32.9   feel] *bef. del.* 'now' (AJ)
32.14   understanding] *ab. del.* 'explaining' (AJ)
32.16   in . . . depression] *intrl.* (AJ)
32.18   Nerve] *aft. del.* 'Fibres on Bkbd. Cells, diag. and Slide—Anastomoses.' (AJ)
32.19   Sp.] *aft. del.* 'Cor' (AJ)
32.20   Devᵗ] *aft. del.* 'E' (AJ)
32.24   *Rank*] *aft. del.* 'Cells and Fibres on Bkbd. Kinds of Cell *Connection unknown [*intrl.*] A priori anatomy'; *bef. del.* 'an' (AJ)
32.35   below] *aft. del.* 'above downwards.' (AJ)
32.36   Tickling] *aft. del.* 'Robin.' (AJ)
32.37   Sp.] *aft. del.* '[¶] *Whatever be inward* prac. ['it' *del.*] they make of brain a machine to transform impinging forces into motor responses. Current runs in at ['skin' *del.*] eyes, out at claws; middle part of journey more or less complex. Man on seat—reflex, change posit., loopline change seat. ['Action *useful.* Robin.' *del.*] If appropriate behavior be criterion, spinal cord a rational machine. [¶] Examine now degree of rationality in diff᷑ centres. Frog's brain on Bkbd.'
32.38   Breathing] *aft. del.* 'Cerebel. Cent' (AJ)
33.4   Meynert] 'eynert' *ab. del.* 'inot ['t' *undel. in error*]'
33.17   were] *aft. del.* 'must form brid' (AJ)
33.25   notion] *aft. del.* 'physiolog' (AJ)
34.17   Psychology—] *dash ov. comma bef. del.* 'but we should have to sweep away the' (AJ)
34.18   us] *bef. del.* 'the better half of our' (AJ)

34.24 and we] 'and' *intrl. w. caret ov. period bef.* 'We [*not reduced in error*]'

35.11 Congenital . . . 60.00] *insrtd.* (AJ)

35.17 53.79] '7' *ov.* '9'

35.20 Celebrated] *aft. del.* 'Agassiz [*line*] 53.40 [*undel. in error*]' |

35.25 stimulus.] *bef. del.* '2nd they'

36.4 immediately] *aft. del.* 'pre' (AJ)

36.6 1st] *insrtd.*

36.7 impression,] *comma ov. period bef. del.* 'In the'

36.9 finger.] *period added bef. del.* 'to fr' (AJ)

36.9 actuation] *aft. del.* 'spontaneity' (AJ)

36.9 sentiments] 'en' *ov.* 'po' (AJ)

36.14 irritate] *aft. del.* 'apply sulphuric acid to a' (AJ)

36.16 off] *bef. del.* 'be' (AJ)

36.19 discharge] *ab. del.* 'act' (AJ)

36.21-22 considerations?] *qst. mk. ov. comma bef. del.* 'They ['T' *ov.* 't'] are ideas or notions of *distant* circumstance distant good or distant evil. They are emotions, like love and so forth. ['The spontaneity which we notice' *del.*] The intact frog whose foot you irritate makes no defensive movements but tries to escape and hide himself. His motive is the consideration of danger which your presence suggests. The intact bird goes in search of worms. Her motive is the consideration of the chicks just hatched in her distant nest. [¶] The hemis. then would seem to be the resevoir for considerations, and the spontaneity or causeless activity that we observe in intact'

36.23 Remarkable] *aft. del. illeg.* (AJ)

36.24 No] *insrtd. for del.* 'Can [*start of letter*]' (AJ)

36.29 Sleeping . . . pigeons.] *intrl.*

37.9 our] *aft. del.* 'all'

37.9 2acts] *aft. del.* 'm' (AJ)

37.12 firmly] *intrl.* (AJ)

††37.13 Metal physiology] *orig. written as one word, then separated by vert. line* (AJ)

37.16 This] *aft. del.* 'All we can say is, that they help hemis' (AJ)

37.22 superintendence] *ab. del.* 'influences' (AJ)

37.25 himself] *ab. del.* 'his poor, muddled mind,' (AJ)

37.25 excuse] *ab. del.* '['keep yiel' *del.*] justify' (AJ)

37.28 escapes] *aft. del.* 'is not counted?' (AJ)

37.29 which] 'ich' *ov.* 'om' (AJ)

37.29 fact] *ab. del.* 'thing'

37.30 which overlook] *intrl.*

37.30 2which] *alt. fr.* 'who' (AJ)

37.30 know] *final* 's' *del.*

37.36 ∧Never] *db. qt. del.*

37.38 Our organizations] *intrl. aft. del.* 'We' (AJ)

38.2 hemis.] *aft. del.* 'an' (AJ)

38.6 resist] *aft. del.* 'modify the actions' (AJ)

38.8 disastrous] *alt. fr.* 'disasterous'

38.9 present.] *bef. del.* 'The dog is such an educable animal. If he is enclosed in a dining-room with the table set present ['exc' *del.*] incitement is etc. but past experience of whipping after a similar incitement has been yielded to, arise in memory along with the incitement itself and he resists the temptation.'

38.11 mental] *intrl.* (AJ)

38.12 claim] *aft. del.* 'can'

38.15 exists] *bef. del.* 'in lower' (AJ)

38.20 with] *ov.* 'in'

38.21 is reminded of] *ab. del.* 'recalls' (AJ)

38.24 on] *bef. del.* 'a bright' (AJ)

38.26 there.] *bef. del.* 'It is found' (AJ)

38.32 if] 'i' *ov.* 'I'

38.33-36 2It . . . organs.] ('habitual' *intrl.*); *insrtd.* (AJ)

38.37-39.1 continue?] *qst. mk. added bef. del.* 'long after' (AJ)

39.1 1in] *aft. del.* 'a' (AJ)

39.5 cases] *aft. del.* 'the' (AJ)

39.9 all] *bef. del.* | 'all'

39.14 lower centres] *ab. del.* 'spinal cord' (AJ)

39.20 or] *ab. undel. comma* (AJ)

39.24 requiring] *aft. del.* 'losing' (AJ)

39.33 side,] *comma ov. period bef. del.* 'Since the hemis. enable this peaceful coexistence in memory and indefinitely multiplied reproduction, we must suppose them to contain a provision for *giving ['g' *ov.* 'd'] ['disti' *del.*] to each separate idea ['of' *del.*] which man's memory is capable of retaining a distinct local habitation'

39.34 Before] *aft. del.* 'Instead, for example of the' (AJ)

39.36 away,] *bef. del.* 'labeled' (AJ)

39.37–38 understand . . . are.] *in left mrgn. is circled* '2'

40.5 mental] *aft. del.* 'addition' (AJ)

40.16 They] *aft. del.* 'In this way' (AJ)

40.22 If] *aft. del.* 'As it' (AJ)

40.22 flame-] *insrtd.* (AJ)

40.30 Slides] *aft. del.* 'I[*start of letter*]' (AJ)

40.33 ¹see] *underl. del.*

40.34 or] *aft. del.* 'bu' (AJ)

40.40 Masked] *aft. del.* 'P' (AJ)

40.40 Shuns obstacles] *added*

41.16 by] 'b' *ov.* 'B' *aft. del. qst. mk.*

41.22 —Recognition.] *dash insrtd.; period insrtd. for del. dash*

42.7 organs] *ab. del.* 'faculties'

42.9 conscientiousness] *intrl.*

42.9–10 involves . . . processes,] *intrl.*

42.15 To] *aft. del.* 'Not till the' (AJ)

42.16 an] 'n' *added bef. del.* 'f' (AJ)

42.17 ²of] *intrl.* (AJ)

42.19 Phrenology] *aft. del.* 'But now' (AJ)

42.21 a] *final* 'n' *del.* (AJ)

42.22 conscientiousness] *aft. del.* 'or' (AJ)

42.22–23 self-esteem, caution] *intrl.* (AJ)

42.23 that] *aft. del.* 'at' (AJ)

42.23 designates] *aft. del.* 'g' (AJ)

††42.25 trys to] *intrl. bef.* 'explains ['s' *undel. in error*]' (AJ)

42.37 action.] *bef. del. start of letter* (AJ)

42.38–39 conclusion. But] *period ov. comma;* 'B' *ov.* 'b' (AJ)

43.1 corroborative] ²'r' *intrl.*

[*end* Alice James *hand*]

Deleted and Undeleted Versos

[*del. fol.* 12ᵛ (#4397) *in* Alice James *hand*] 'Lecture [*illeg.*]'

[*undel. fol.* 6ᵛ (#4396): *trial for start of fol.* 1, *corresponds to text* 30.25–26] 'In these recent days we hear a great deal of the marvellous achievements of science, how Darwinism ['has upset all previous notions of the way in which living forms came' *del.*] to exist'

[*undel. fol.* 1ᵛ (#4397) *in* Alice James *hand: trial for start of fol.* 1, *corresponds to text* 32.18] 'Anat. Remind'

3. Notes for a Lecture on "The Physiological Effects of Alcohol" 1886 #4527

An assortment of notes is contained in #4527. The first set consists of two folds (4 leaves) of thin wove paper, ruled vertically, the leaves measuring 7¾ x 4¾", the versos blank except for short notes on the versos of the first and fourth leaves. This series ends with 'Don't enter race of life handicapped. O.W.H.' on 44.27. The second set consists of two folds (4 leaves) of laid unwatermarked paper 8¾ x 6½", written on rectos and versos, except for the second leaf of the first fold which is blank on the recto but contains three lines on the reversed verso. The text in the second set runs from 44.29–46.4. A single leaf of the same paper follows, 46.5–12, its verso blank. Another single leaf of the same paper but written horizontally contains the notes found in 46.13–21. Included in #4527 is a postcard from Henry Pickering Bowditch, postmarked Boston, February 28, 1894, concerning three articles on alcohol. A report of the lecture given before the Harvard Total Abstinence League appeared in the *Daily Crimson*, 27 October 1886, and is reprinted in the present edition as Appendix I.

Emendations

43.16 1½ oz] 1 oz ½
45.34 298)] ~∧

46.8 9.095∧] ~. |

Alterations in the Manuscript

43.10 Physiological] *aft. del.* 'Need of stimulus.' |
43.13 pain wakefulness] *intrl.*
44.4 stomach] *aft. del.* 'fucia'
44.15 7½] *ov.* '5'
45.5 Smith] *aft. del.* 'Sometimes real food. | (Remember wines' |
45.9 +] *ov.* 'ru [*doubtful*]'
45.15 Parkes] *bef. del.* | '9 Sensorial anaesthesia *Ridge* | Like aether | ['10 C' *del.*] Secret of its fascination |

Parkes | 9 Cerebral Effect'
45.20 Uses] *bef. del.* 'in'
45.26 20] '2' *ov.* '1'
46.1 statistics] *bef. del.* | 'Parkes 305 note | In'
46.2 292.] *bef. del.* | '9 years'
46.8 6.060] 2'6' *ov.* 't'
46.10 letters] 'le' *ov.* 'al'
46.14 Chap] 'C' *ov.* '§'
46.14 VII, §I.] *intrl.*

Undeleted Verso

[*undel. verso of second leaf in second set*] 'Port & sherry 16 to 25% vol. | ['Claret & Burg. 7 13' *del.*] | Light wines 6 or 8 to 16'

4. Draft and Outline of a Lecture on "The Effects of Alcohol" 1895 #4525, #4526

This manuscript #4525 is written in a blue covered exercise book from the Harvard Coöperative Society, ruled, measuring 8¼ x 6⅞", rectos and versos usually inscribed, unnumbered. The verso of the sixth leaf is deleted, continuing a deletion at the foot of 6 recto after 'No obvious difference.' (49.17–18). Leaf 7 verso is blank, a new section beginning on 8 recto with *Subjective experience*' (49.24), the verso inscriptions then continuing to the end on the verso of leaf 13 with a series of notes (51.30–52.4). The panel on the front cover has 'Alcohol' in James's hand.

Rough notes on alcohol come in #4526, which appear to be related to #4525 and may indeed have been notes for actual delivery, on the evidence of the especially large handwriting. This manuscript consists of 19 leaves of wove paper watermarked Merchants Bond, measuring 10 x 8", foliated [1] 2–5 5½ 6–18. Leaf 5½ (53.9–16) follows leaf 5 (53.2–8), deleted by a single vertical stroke but transcribed here, this deletion continuing from the foot of fol. 4 (52.37–53.1), the single vertical stroke extending through two deleted lines preceding 'We must respect League' on fol. 4 (see Alterations entry 52.36) and extending through the deleted final lines on fol. 5 (see Alterations entry 53.8). The margins of the first leaf are browned from exposure, the unexposed section just fitting the blue-book #4525, which seems to have been placed on top of #4526 for a considerable length of time and exposed to the light. A separate leaf on the same wove paper containing a quotation from C. G. Leland written in Alice's hand belongs with these notes although preserved in #4527. A note in Perry's hand identifies the quotation as from *Sunshine in Thought*, 1862.

A report of the lecture appeared in the *Harvard Crimson*, 23 January 1895, and is reprinted as Appendix II in the present edition.

Emendations

46.27   Matthew] Mathew
47.10   Marryat's] Maryatt's
48.1   beginning] begining
48.24   statistical] statitical
48.37   Schulinus] Schulainus
49.6   Glusinsky)] ~∧
49.16   (Richardson's] ∧~

49.33   chloroform] chlororoform
50.13   "don't] ∧~
50.20   considers] consders
52.8   ∧Conduct] "~
52.16   strength."] ~·∧
54.28   etc.)] ~·∧
55.29   risen] rison

Alterations in the Manuscripts

46.29   a] *ab. del.* 'the'
46.29   fashion] *aft. del.* 'habit'
47.2   fashion] *final* 's' *del.*
47.4   be] *aft. del.* 'rema'
47.5-6 just . . . persons.] *tr. by guideline fr. aft.* 'Weinzwang'—[*closing db. qt. poss. sg. qt.*]'
47.10   In] 'I' *ov.* 'T'
47.11   & Wellington's] *intrl.*
47.12   martial &] *intrl.*
47.17   romantic] *intrl.*
47.19   description] *aft. del.* 'ge'
47.20   G's] *ab. del.* 'his'
47.20   lyrics] *aft. del.* 'b'
47.21   ¹of] *aft. del. start of new line* 'The'
47.28   Rhine] *ab. del.* 'Hock'
47.35   In] *insrtd. bef.* 'Our [*not reduced in error*]'
47.35   the] *aft. del.* 'is not'
47.35   does n't] *aft. del.* 'not'
47.36   to] *bef. del.* 'alco'
48.3   one] *aft. del.* 'the'
48.4-5 prominence] 'ce' *ov.* 't'
48.6   challenges . . . encourages.] ('challenges,' *aft. del.* 'encourages,'); *insrtd.*
48.8   Their . . . rebuke.] (¹'a' *ab. del.* 'an'); *insrtd.*
48.14   desire] *bef. del.* 'to [*del. in error*] g'
48.15   Don't . . . in] *added at top of page*
48.16   relief] 'f' *ov.* 've'

48.18   These] 'T' *ov.* 't'; *aft. del.* 'To'
48.19   league] 'l' *ov.* 's'
††48.24 experimental (statitical)] *added*
48.30   gross] *bef. del.* 'kind'
49.3   retards] 't' *ov.* 'd'
49.13   vasomotor] *ab. del.* 'nerve'
49.14-15 abs. . . . 325).] ('Parkes' *ov.* 'Ric'); *insrtd.*
49.16   Richardson's conclusions)] *insrtd.*
49.18   difference.] *bef. del.* | 'Aliment d'Epargne—Hammond. | Turn to common subjective experience. | Immediate exhilaration—probably due to reflex from coats of stch. on cerebral circulation. Soup—CO_2 waters—ginger-bitters s̄ alcohol. gentian, bark—smoking, chewing—candy—snuff   3 geminal nerve, & pneumogastric. | *Mental ['M' *ov.* 'S'] stimulation? | varies | In general, happiness, *emotional* stimulation | *Turn to subjective experience. [*added at top of page*]'
49.20   error] *bef. del.* | 'Sensibility to weight, compass points ditto.'
49.29   stimɳ.] *bef. del.* 'From paralysis of upper centres? | Read Ami Fritz—'
49.37   associations] *bef. del.* | 'Ami Fritz | Howells.'
49.38   mystery.] *bef. del.* | 'Describ'

50.3   From . . . N$_2$O] *added at bottom of page*

50.6   cord] *bef. del.* | 'breathing heat—Vasomotor centre early—so that "shock" may not occur. | *Anaesthesia.* Pain—worry—cold—fatigue "don't care "a rap" '

50.13   "Drives] *aft. del.* 'Takes a'

50.18   You] *aft. del.* 'But only when | Read Ami'

50.20   ²the] *ov.* 'a'

51.4   2] *ov.* '3'

51.4   Congenital] 'C' *ov.* 'a'

51.4   acquired.] *bef. del.* | 'Neurasthenic craving . . .'

51.6   Neurasthenic] *aft. del.* 'Acquired by habit.' |

51.10   to] *aft. del.* 'to'

51.11   cold] *intrl.*

51.12   ounce] *aft. del.* 'ouce'

51.15   diminishing] *aft. del.* 'ge'

51.16   tending] 't' *ov.* 's'

51.17   the quality] *aft. del.* 'it'

51.25   perfect] *bef. del. start of letter*

51.25   as] *ab. del.* 'all'

51.26   creaks] *aft. del.* 'ran appro'

51.27   ¹that] *aft. del. poss.* 'or'

51.27   I] *aft. del.* '['The' *del.*] I cant express better than in Mr Leland's words.'

52.17   Sick] *aft. del.* 'Sick children. | Old army and | Goethe.' |

52.31   ²p.] *ov.* '2'

52.36   wave,] *bef. del.* | 'Challenges encourages or rebukes'

53.8   now.] *bef. del.* | '*Facts!* | 2 kinds of evidence.'

53.21–22 It . . . Fresh] ('Fresh' *added bef.* 'Blood' *not reduced in error*); *added w. finer pen*

53.22   it.] *added w. finer pen*

53.23   Schulinus] 'S' *ov.* 'C'

53.24   Small . . . only,] ('only,' *bef. del.* 'found in'); *insrtd. w. finer pen bef.* 'Found' *not reduced in error*

53.24   urine] *intrl. w. finer pen*

53.25   of . . . etc] *added w. finer pen*

53.26   both . . . stopped)] *added w. finer pen*

53.32   (directly . . . Martin)] ('done' *bef. del.* 'by'); *parens and* 'applied . . . Martin' *added w. finer pen*

53.33   in . . . (Parkes)] *added w. finer pen*

53.35   (Probably diminished)] (*opening paren ov. ellipsis dot*); *added w. finer pen*

53.36   probably . . . effect] *added w. finer pen*

53.37   quicker . . . slower] ('quicker' *ab. del.* 'incrᵈ'); *added w. finer pen*

53.41   degeneration] 'd' *ov. start of* 'g'

54.3   water)] *bef. del.* | 'Then *happiness . . —* | Emo'

54.15   delusion] *aft. del.* 'ideal.'

54.18   dementia] *bef. del.* | 'N$_2$O'

54.19   are] *ab. del.* 'all'

54.23   tedium . . . beer.] *insrtd. aft. del.* 'But all come back 7 fold.' |

54.28   (tobacco . . . etc.] *added*

54.31   Crisis] *aft. del.* 'Orator.' |

54.36   temper] *aft. del.* 'Bad'

55.13   Advantage] *aft. del.* 'But this a mean appeal.' |

55.14   This] *alt. fr.* 'These'

55.21   Bunge . . . read] ('B' *of* 'Bunge' *ov.* 'Lel'); *added w. finer pen*

55.22   vs] *bef. del.* 'clear as bell and'

55.22   ¹as] *ov. doubtful* 'or'

55.28   If] *aft. del.* 'No da' |

55.28   ideal] *aft. del.* 'turbid,'

5. LECTURES ON ABNORMAL PSYCHOLOGY 1895, 1896 #4404, #4405, #4403, #4402

Various manuscripts are associated with James's lectures on Abnormal Psychology. The first, #4404, holds notes for a Lecture on Degeneration, written on rectos only of laid paper watermarked L. L. Brown, measuring 10⅞ x 8½″. The six leaves are foliated 4–9, centered, the last a part-page, the final item written later in a lighter ink.

Manuscript #4405 continues the inscription with six leaves of the same paper foliated 16 20–24, fol. 16 headed 'Genius & Insanity', underlined. The writing is in ink with ink and pencil revisions; at 58.3–5 James drew a pencil line against 'Myers . . . genius.' and wrote 'omit' in the margin.

Manuscript #4403 consists of twelve leaves of wove paper, measuring 10 x 8″, watermarked Invincible Linen Bond. The leaves are foliated in ink in the upper right corner 20–28; fols. 29–31 are numbered in pencil, also in the upper right corner. Pencil inscription begins on the lower two-thirds of fol. 28 ('Give Gurney's Expts.' 62.33, originally written before 'Dessoir's case.' at 62.29) and continues through fol. 29 ('Mediumships.' 63.1). Although fols. 30–31 are written in ink (63.2–23), the foliation remains in pencil. All the leaves have a roman 'II' written in the upper left corner, this changing to pencil also on fol. 29.

Manuscript #4402 is written in ink on seventy-three leaves of white wove paper, the first twenty-six leaves measuring 10 x 8″, the remaining leaves measuring 10½ x 8⅛″, the paper watermarked MERCHANTS PURE BOND. Found with the manuscript is a fragment of a torn manila envelope, stamped in the upper right corner 'William James, | 95 Irving St., | Cambridge, Mass.' To the right of the name James wrote in ink 'Property of' and centered on the envelope he wrote 'Lowell lectures on psycho-pathology'. Also included with this manuscript is a single leaf containing ink notes in James's hand: 'Mosso Kreislauf etc, p. 94+ | Schrader found that his brainless pigeons slept at night. | Heerwagen in Phil. Stud. V, 301 | Dreams, F. P. Cobbe D. in M. p. 335 (1872) | Heerwagen in Wundt vol. 5'.

The first leaf (unnumbered) is headed 'Lowell Lectures', underlined, and then beneath a section number 'I' James wrote 'Dreams—Hypnotism', double underlined. The leaves are foliated upper center, and versos are ordinarily blank. Folio [1] ('Unwholesome . . . gives' 63.29–35) is written on the back of a deleted leaf numbered 5 containing an early version of the first notes on fol. 5 ('*in gear* . . . VIII. 31.' 64.20–31) and is thus identified as a revision. Similarly, fol. 2 is a revision written on the back of a leaf numbered 4 over 3 and providing an early version of fol. 4 ('3 types . . . ideas' 64.11–20). Folio 7 ('Hypnotic . . . awake.' 64.41–65.7) is numbered 7 over 6 and is written on the back of a false start numbered 4 which continues the deleted text at the foot of fol. 3 (see Alterations entry 64.10). Folio 8 is numbered after a deleted 8 over a 7 (65.8–18), but fols. 9–11 have not been altered (although on fol. 10 the 10 is written to the left of a deleted start of a number or letter). Folio 12 (67.9–17) is numbered to the right of deleted 10, and its first three lines, which seem to have continued present fol. 10 text, are deleted. It would seem that this fol. 12 was written on a discarded early 10 but James, unusually, did not turn it over when he came to 12 but instead wrote below its deleted first three lines. A slip is pasted on fol. 14 verso (see footnote 5). Folio 24 (70.26–33) is numbered 24 over 23, and fol. 25 ('This . . . dwelt' 70.34–71.4) over 24. This fol. 25 is written on the back of an undeleted false start numbered 23 for the first four lines of present fol. 24 (over 23). Folio 26 ('on to . . . right' 71.4–13), its numbering unaltered, used the back of a leaf numbered 25 over 24 which contains the first few words of a trial for the first line of present fol. 25 over 24. Folio 35 is a revised part-page, repeating text that was first written in the margins of fol. 36 and then deleted. It begins with the syllables '*antes*' (73.17) completing the 'summis desider' (in roman) that had been inserted at the foot of fol. 34. After 'Antediluvian ['A' *ov.* 'a'] etc.' (73.24), James started a new line 'Ghast' but deleted it before finishing the word since 'Ghastly' was already on fol. 36 below the deleted text now found on fol. 35. This fol. 36 is numbered in the upper right corner, the original centered 4 having been deleted. The 9 of fol. 39 (74.12–23) is written over a 6, and the number 40 of the next leaf (74.24–31) comes at the right of a deleted 7. Folios 43–45 ('In the eyes . . . delusion,' 75.18–76.11) are altered from 42, 43, and 44 respectively. Disruption is clearly evident when fol. 47 is found to consist of no more than three lines ('mind, . . . hope.' 76.21–22), and fol. 48, written to the right of a deleted false start for a number, the 8 over a five, begins with six lines of deleted text that has no counterpart elsewhere in the lecture. Again, it would seem that James wrote fol. 48 ('I have . . . of' 76.23–27) using the recto of a discarded leaf instead of turning it over and using the back. Thus fol. 48 need not and probably does not represent revised text. Folio 49 ('intolerance . . . world' 76.27–34) begins with ink text through 'hands.' (76.30), but pencil text, probably added later, makes up the rest of the page. Folio 52 (77.19–32) was written on the back of a few words under the foliation 52 and so was immediately turned over and used.

Folios 57–59 (78.30–79.21) were renumbered from 17–19 and fols. 60–61 (79.22–80.25) were numbered above deleted 58 and 59 respectively. Folios 69–71 ('The . . . life?' 82.20–83.10) were renumbered from 66–68. Folio 72 is altered from 67 ('that . . . with that' 83.10–16), and the single line on the final leaf is foliated 73 altered from 72.

The two sections of text, fols. 39 and 40 originally numbered 6 and 7, and also fols. 57–59 originally numbered 17–19 indicate that an earlier document for these lectures existed from which James in the revision was able to abstract five pages.

Found with the notes for these lectures are two typescripts, signed in ink 'Alice Vanderbilt Morris.', the leaves of wove paper, measuring 10 x 8″, watermarked Chinese Linen. The typing is not James's, but the leaves are foliated in ink by him: the first leaf, headed 'Skating.', is numbered 'p. 9^a' on the recto and 'p. 9^b' on the verso; the second, headed 'Singing.', is numbered 'p. 9^c' on the recto, the verso blank. It is probable that these typescripts were intended for insertion after fol. 9, which contains the reference to 'Mrs. Morris's cases' (65.25). Since fol. 9 continues in mid-sentence to fol. 10, the typescripts have been transcribed in footnote 2.

Reports of the lectures appeared in several newspapers, and these are reprinted in Appendix III.

Emendations

☞ 59.2 (confession)] (~$_\wedge$ (*similar* 73.37,39;77.26,40)	72.27 Verzegnis] Verzegniss
60.11 *a priori*] *a* | priori	73.17 *summis desiderantes*] summis desider-|*antes*
60.13–14 anaesthesias] anaesthesas	73.21 inquisitors] inquisitor's
61.5 green] red	74.24 $_\wedge$he] "~
62.1 governs] govern	75.10 persons] persons'
62.9 instances] instance	75.29 doctors] doctor's
66.4 Tissié$_\wedge$] ~)	76.12 agents] agent's
67.4 throws] throw	76.26 imaginary] imagnary
67.5;79.5 anaesthesias,] ~$_\wedge$	76.34 world.] ~$_\wedge$
67.11 Sovereign] Soereign	76.38 seem] seems
68.19 inflammation,] ~$_\wedge$	77.9 $_\wedge$Two] (~
69.15 *Something*] *Somethings*	78.37 madman.""] ~."$_\wedge$
69.36 m."] ~.$_\wedge$	79.8 utopists,] ~$_\wedge$

79.21   Lombroso] Lombros
80.29   irritability] irritibility
80.39   ∧neuropathic] (∼

81.4   the] the of
82.12   Everywhere] Everwhere

Alterations in the Manuscripts

55.34   when unnerved] *penc. added; period not moved fr. aft.* 'people' *in error*
56.2   We ... delusion.] *added to the right of del.* 'Anxiety—relief. | Obsessive idea'
56.5   In] *aft. del.* 'Action gives relief. | In [*illeg.*] case idea returns. | Attempts to exorcise it of all sorts.' |
56.8   Folie] *aft. del.* 'Grubel Qu'
56.11   photographs] *added*
56.12   *Arithmomania*] *aft. del.* 'Legrand du Saulle's case of pretty women.' |
56.12   *Normal germ,*] *penc. underl.; period alt. to comma*
56.12   Candlesticks] *penc. added*
56.13–14   Counts ... stones] *added*
56.15   orange] *aft. del.* 'Apple—'
56.16   fig] *aft. del.* 'Pear—'
56.17   lemon] *aft. del.* 'Quince—'
56.20   Dressing] *aft. del.* 'Acts'
56.21   *Here ... germ.*] *penc. underl.; aft. del.* 'Case, Am. J., I.240'
56.24–25   Harm ... system] *added*
56.31   Different] *ov.* 'New'
56.33   We] *aft. del.* 'Wh'
56.40   germ] *bef. del.* 'in all'
57.1   but] *aft. del.* 'by'
57.5   musician] *penc. ab. del.* 'actor'
57.10   anti- ... impulses.] *intrl.*
57.11   always] *ab. del.* 'often'
57.11   Cunning.] *ab. del.* 'Pomeroy.'
57.14   obsession] *aft. del.* 'impulse &'
57.19–20   Superior ... genius.] *penc. added*
57.21   These] *aft. del.* 'The peculiarity is a divided' |
57.25   They] *aft. del.* ' 'Déséquilibrés.' Horses & driver.' |
57.30   The] *aft.* 'All people who *feel* challenged—transition to *genius*' | *added in lighter ink, then penc. del.*
57.30   strong] *bef. del.* 'as to coerce attention.'
57.31   such] *bef. del.* 'dissociation'

57.33   When bad enough] *ab. del.* 'In the extremes'
57.36   In some cases] *ab. del.* 'To some extent'
58.3   Myers] *aft. penc. del.* 'Recap. Showed existence of sublim. C.' |
58.5   another] *ab. del.* 'a'
58.5   genius.] *period added bef. del.* 'somewhat akin.'
58.8   Not] *aft. del.* 'Contrast with | *Now we see the **tendency [2'e' *ov.* 'a'] of our realistic and scientific view of human nature. Not only blots on sun, but sun itself a blot. [*written around del.* 'Formerly there could be no']' |
58.8   only] *bef. del.* 'Not'
58.9   jealousy] *aft. del.* 'van'
58.14   rules.] *bef. del.* 'AB [*space; beg. of letter*]'
58.15   count ... count.] *insrtd.*
58.17   to] *bef. del.* 'estimate psychopaths to population | p' |
58.20   sedentary ... men] *penc. added*
58.23   Let] *aft. del.* '[Nisbet's diseases?] *Nisbet's diseases—mortality p. 315 [*penc. del.*]' |
58.25   does s'thing] *intrl.*
58.26   psych] *intrl.*
58.27   No] 'N' *ov.* 'C'; *aft. del.* 'Paganini—Newton; Rousseau—Bonaparte; *Saint-Paul [*ab. del.* 'Gen. Booth']—Jay Gould.' |
58.27   Paderewski] *penc. ab. del.* 'Paganini'
58.27   Shelley] *aft. del.* 'Sarah Bernhardt and Sai'
58.28   Washington ... Platt.] ('St' *aft. del.* 'Thos. C. Platt'); *penc. ab. del.* 'St Paul'
58.37   Men ... men] *penc. added*
59.1   Goethe] *final 's' del.*
59.3   De ... Sand] *intrl.*
59.4   If] *aft. penc. del.* 'Kipling Ste-

venson | *Compare [*ov.* 'It does']
freedom of artist with constraint of
scientist or statesman in execution |
*Not even or [*ink del.*]' |

59.10 Moltke] *penc. ab. del.* 'Washington'

59.16 not] 't' *penc. added*

59.16 Englishman] *penc. added*

59.17 *Liability*] *ov.* 'That'

59.20 Howard] *ab. del.* 'F. Willard'

59.20 F. Willard] *insrtd.*

59.27 ideas] *intrl.*

59.30 Washington] *ov.* 'Mol'

59.35 Poe] *aft. del.* 'or'

59.36 Gladstone . . . Longfellow]
insrtd. for del. 'Gladstone ['G' *ov.*
'D'], Napoleon'

59.40 — — —it] *aft. penc. del.*
'Nordau's book'

60.3 Venn's . . . 5] *penc. added*

60.5 Nordau . . . profi] *penc. added*

60.8 proportionate] *aft. del.* 'varying'

60.9 a] *alt. fr.* 'an'

60.9 strong degree] *ab. del.* 'abundant
way'

60.11 in] *aft. del.* 'to a degree'; *bef.
del.* 'pe'

60.12 many] *intrl.*

60.12 cases of] *ab. del.* 'class'

60.13 of] *bef. del.* 'anaesthesas'

60.14 may] 'a' *intrl.*

60.17 began to be] *ab. del.* 'was fully'

60.17 up,] *period alt. to comma bef.
del.* 'The patient in fact feels and
sees'

60.19 an] *aft. del.* 'and'

60.20 about] *aft. del.* 'ag'

60.22 relations] *ab. del.* 'respects'

60.24 and malingerers.] *added aft. del.
period*

60.25 left] *ab. del.* 'right'

60.26 supposed to be] *intrl.*

60.26 Lying] *intrl. bef.* 'W' *not reduced
in error*

60.26,27 he] *alt. fr.* 'she'

60.27 pinch] *bef. del.* 'and "no" when
the pinch is unfelt'

60.28 power] *aft. del.* 'state of things'

60.29 yes] *insrtd. for del.* 'no,'

60.31 says] *bef. del.* 'no. How could he
say no unless he felt the'

60.32 reply] *bef. del.* '['to' *del.*] thus
aptly to the touch.'

60.33 who] *aft. del.* 'with'

60.33 closed] *aft. del.* 'open'

60.36 patient] *ab. del.* 'two eyes'

60.37 which] *bef. del.* 'one eye is red
the other green'

60.37 right] *ab. del.* 'left'

60.37 , being] *comma added;* 'being'
ab. del. 'is'

60.37 stops all] *aft. del.* 'and'; *bef. del.*
'green'

60.37 coming . . . green] *ab. del.* 'whilst
it lets rays pass from red'

61.1 objects,] *comma alt. fr. period*

61.1 making . . . it] *ab. del.* 'The right
glass ['co' *del.*] on the contrary is
green and makes red objects invisible.'

61.2 patient,] *comma added bef. del.*
'a card'

61.3 red] *alt. fr.* 'read'

61.4 cannot] *bef. del.* 'see'

61.7 optically] *intrl.*

61.7 be] *ab. del.* 'were'

61.9 contrivances originally] *ab. del.*
'devices' *ab. del.* 'inventions'

61.11 hysterics] *final* 's' *added*

61.12 as] *bef. del.* 'an'

61.12 impostors] *final* 's' *added*

61.12 certain] *aft. del.* 'hypnotic'

61.12 analogous] *ab. del.* 'hypnotic'

61.13 in . . . has] *ab. del.* 'has enabled
us'

61.13 revealed] *aft. del.* 'by'; 'ed' *ov.
hyphen bef.* | 'ing' *undel. in error*

61.14 to . . . sympathetically.] *tr. by
guideline fr. aft. del.* 'has enabled us'

61.15 subject₍ₐ₎] *comma del.*

61.15 may] *ab. del.* 'can'

61.17 they] *alt. fr.* 'these'

61.17 to him] *intrl.*

61.18 sheet of] *intrl.*

61.18 1only] *intrl.*

61.20 sentence,] *bef. del.* 'a p'

61.21 object] *aft. del.* 'thing' *ab. del.*
'person'

61.21 words.] *ab. del.* 'voice.'

61.22 many] *aft. del.* 'that'

61.23 things,] *intrl.*

61.23 being] *aft. del.* 'objects, [*intrl.*]
voices, etc,'

61.24 object] *aft. del.* 'proper'

61.24 identical] *insrtd.*

61.24–25 whose presence] *ab. del.* 'which'

61.25 be] *bef. del.* 'blind, or deaf or otherwise'

61.27 rest.] *bef. del.* 'Or if the *operator [*undel. ab. del.* 'person' *aft. del.* 'operator to whos'] to whose voice he has been made deaf says to him "you can hear me now," he forthwith hears perfectly well.'

61.28 Dʳ] *aft. del.* 'Mr.'

61.29 subject] *bef. del.* '*whom he [*undel. in error*] ordered to be deaf no'

61.32 forthwith . . . subject.] ('forthwith' *added;* 'subject.' *bef. del.* 'forthwith.'); *ab. del.* 'immediately proceeded to do so,'

61.32–33 She had doubtless] ('had' *aft. del.* 'doubtless'); *ab. del.* 'showing that she had on all probably been'

61.33 heard] 'd' *ov.* 'ing'

61.33 with her ears] *insrtd.*

61.33–34 entered . . . with] *ab. del.* 'made no impression on'

61.34 thoughts] *ab. del.* 'ideas'

61.36 real] *intrl.*

61.37 insensibility produced] *ab. del.* 'blindness or deafness,'

61.38 a . . . is] *ab. del.* 'something'

61.39 complex,] *comma alt. fr. period*

61.39 something like an] *ab. del.* 'An'

61.39 shutting out] *insrtd. for del.* 'exclusion' *ab. del.* 'cutting out'

62.1 counts as] *ab. del.* 'governs'

††62.1 govern] *intrl.*

62.3 one] *aft. del.* 'on the margin of one's consciousness'

62.3 remains] *bef. del.* 'aware.'

62.5 even] *ab. del.* 'is whether'

62.5 cases] *aft. del.* 'sample' *ab. del.* 'hypnotic and hysteric'

62.5 is . . . idea] *ab. del.* 'the [*undel. in error*] sha s'

62.7 altogether] *bef. del.* 'for the most part'

62.7 coexistent] *bef. del.* 'field of con bit'

62.12 its] *bef. del.* 'chara'

62.13 fields‸] *comma del.; aft. del.* 'dissociated and dissevered'

62.13 genuinely . . . yet] *intrl.*

62.13–14 outside . . . functionally.] *insrtd. for del.* 'dissociated with one another.'

62.20 In] *aft. del.* 'Per'

62.21 an] *ab. del.* 'and'

62.21 induced sleep,] *ab. del.* 'trance-state'

62.22 designated] *aft. del.* 'determ'

62.22 be] *bef. del.* 'obeyed, although'

62.23 even] *intrl.*

62.24 will] *bef. del.* 'hold no re'

62.26 appointed] *intrl.*

62.27 a designated] *ab. del.* 'an appointed'

62.27 days] *aft. del.* 'hours'

62.29–63.1 Dessoir's . . . Mediumships.] *penc. added*

62.32–33 Give . . . 282+] *tr. by guide-line fr. bef.* 'Dessoir's'; 'Give' *and* 'G' *of* 'Gurney's' *traced ov. in ink*

62.37 Binets] *aft. del.* 'Mrs. Sh'

62.38 birth] *aft. del.* 'her'

62.38 of] *ov.* 'etc.'

62.38 Adrienne] *added*

62.39 Hysteric] *aft. del.* 'Automatisms, Mrs. Shaler. | Janet's subject with apron | Automatic writing | Gift of tongues.'

63.3 The] *aft. del.* 'Such oddi'

63.7 bring] *aft. del.* 'pro'

63.8 ¹ordinary] *ab. del.* 'routine'

63.8 medical] *bef. del.* ', or to the routine p'

63.8–9 or . . . has] *intrl.*

63.9 its] *aft. del.* 'with'; *bef. del.* 'routine'

63.9 routine] *aft. del.* 'its'; *bef. del.* 'medical'

63.10 appliances‸] *semicolon del.*

63.10 the . . . has] *ab. del.* 'or ['th' *del.*] to the ordinary psychological mind with'

63.13 it is] *intrl.*

63.13 humoring] *aft. del.* 'humb'

63.15 orderly] *bef. del.* '['smooth-shaven and eminently respectable p' *del.*] and conventionally tame'

63.17 as . . . were] *ab. del.* 'as if it were'

63.17 among the] *ab. del.* 'an'

63.21   the] *intrl.*

63.35   Melancholy] *aft.* 'life [*undel. in error*]' *ab. del.* 'Into a healthy'

63.35   gives truer values] *insrtd.*

63.36   must] *intrl.*

63.36   have] *alt. fr.* 'has'

63.36   some] *intrl.*

64.2   for] *aft. del.* 'but'

64.10   "House on fire."] *insrtd. for del.* ' "House ['H' *ov.* 'C'] on fire." | 3 cases. | In dreams. ideas appear detached: My dream of Seth ['see back of 2' *del.*] | Field narrowed—vividness | 2 conditions. 1) narrowness, 2) vivid-[*fol.* 7ᵛ, *orig. fol.* 4]ness of field. | Hard to understand, but electric wire and gas jet metaphors.'

64.12   detached] *aft. del.* 'don't come'

65.5   Main] *aft. del.* 'What makes a subject is this dissociability. | Ideas that remain have the vividness.'

65.7   awake.] *bef. del.* 'Peggy on bicycle.'

65.8   is] *ab. del.* 'are'

65.9   Hammond's . . . table.] *insrtd. for del.* 'Subject on chair.'

65.24   d.] 'd' *ov.* 'e'; *aft. del.* 'd. In both, memory s'ts gone.' |

65.25   Mrs. Morris's cases] *insrtd. for del.* 'f [*ov.* 'd']. Posthypnotic suggestions as in the hysteric dreams.'

66.3   Bernheim] *intrl.*

66.12   Proved] *insrtd. bef.* 'Not' *not reduced in error*

66.14   Line] *aft. del.* 'Prism doubles' |

66.14   2not] *intrl.*

66.16   subject] *ab. del.* 'girl'

66.16   he] *alt. fr.* 'she'

67.4   suggestion] *final* 's' *del.*

67.9   Gurney's experiments:] *bel. del.* 'Two parts of mind not on speaking terms. | *System* ['abolished' *del.*] thrown out of gear. Head story. | 2) *Post hypnotic suggestion.* They fall again — —'

67.16   talking] *aft. del.* 'or'

67.18   Same] *aft. del.* 'Two simultaneous conscious systems.' |

67.18   (to sleep)] *intrl.*

67.23   think.] *bef. del.* 'Barkworth, Dessoir.'

67.25   automatism in Bark] *aft. del.* 'in Bark-' |

67.25   adding . . . or] *ab. del.* '&'

67.26   alternation in] ('in' *insrtd.*); *tr. by guideline fr. aft.* 'Possible'

67.31   Andrew . . . case] *insrtd.*

67.32   us] *ov.* 'in'

67.34   Glines case] *intrl.*

68.4   immediate] *aft. del.* 'tri'

68.11   Nichols] 's' *ov.* 'as'

68.12   Lately] *aft. del.* 'Myers'

68.17   Pains] *aft. del.* 'Ana ['a' *ov.* 'e']'

68.18–19   Loss . . . vomiting.] *intrl.*

68.19   mimicries] *aft. del.* '['Mimicri' *del.*] Vomitings, loss of voice,'

68.26   Among] *aft. del.* 'Among them'

68.26   wh.] *ab. del.* 'of'

68.26   has seen,] *intrl.*

68.29   Charcot's] 's' *ov. semicolon*

68.29   school] *insrtd. bef. del.* 'Janet; Breuer; Freud; | The nature of this disease best seen'

68.31   genuine] 'g' *ov.* 'r'

69.6   1a] *aft. del.* 'an'; *opp. this line in the left mrgn. is insrtd. but then del.* '*elective* blindness | The Mouse; match'

69.6   black] *aft. del.* 'p'

69.8–10   Elective . . . Match!] *insrtd. for del.* 'suggested here from within. The mind is split into two parts. Pt agrees not to see anything with left eye *alone*, etc | This condition ['is obvious' *del.*] is ['realized' *del.*] obvious in a number of curious observations | Touch anaesthetic hand several times'

69.11   Self] *ov.* 'Auto'

69.13   hypnotic] 'hy' *ov.* 'ca'

69.15–17   That . . . well.] *insrtd.*

69.18   Alterations . . . 190] *insrtd.*

69.19   Binet's] 'B' *ov.* 'J'

69.23   field.] *bef. del.* 'Bin'

69.24   Adamson] *ab. del.* 'Car' *ab. del.* 'Big-elow'

69.27   Janet] *final* 's' *del.*

69.29   Question] 'Q' *ov.* 'q'

69.32   becomes] *ab. del.* 'sinks'

70.1   Cause . . . awake] *insrtd.*

70.6   New . . . delusions] *insrtd. for del.* 'Of course these are'

70.8 that] *aft. del.* 'of'

70.9 ordinary] *aft. del.* 'orgin'

70.13 certain] 'c' *ov.* 'h'

70.13 by] 'b' *ov.* 'w'

70.13–14 whether . . . Janet . .] *intrl.*

70.21 Tissié's case.] *insrtd. bef. del.* ' "f'

70.21 O] *ov.* 'C'

70.24 Norristown] 'N' *ov.* 'M'

70.26 Mason . . . Boy.] *insrtd.*

70.29 Janet's] 'Jan' *ov.* 'Bin'

70.29 theory] 'y' *ov.* 'ies'; *aft. del.* 'vs. [undel. in error] Myers' '

70.30 589] '8' *ov.* '7'

70.31 Mediumship.] *bel. del.* 'Here we are at a great bifurcation of our interpretations. If we take one path . . . if the other we lead to psychical research. I said I would not enter there. Myers's theory' |

70.37 we say] 'we' *ov.* 'the'; 's' *ov.* 'u'

70.39 formula] *ab. del.* 'explanation'

71.4 relation] *final* 's' *del.*

71.9 admit] *bef. del.* 'anything new'

71.9 even] *aft. del.* 'if'

71.12 Of] *ab. del.* 'Both'

71.12 one] *intrl.*

71.12 pursues] *final* 's' *added*

71.12 tribe] *ab. del.* 'cave'

71.14 formula] *aft. del.* 'spl'

71.15 for] *bef. del.* 'most of'

71.15–17 Hypnotism . . . phrase] *ab. del.* 'Janet's phrase'

71.19 Whether] *ov.* 'That'; *intrl. bef.* 'Supernormal' *not reduced in error*

71.20–21 is . . . that] *ab. del.* 'I am convinced. For them to occur,'

71.22 more] *ab. del.* 'a'

71.23 or tho't transference] *intrl.*

71.25 if] *aft. del.* 'be'

71.25 yield] *aft. del.* 'be'

71.25 their] *ov.* 'an'

71.27 real] *intrl.*

71.27 Thus] *bef. del.* 'the truth'

71.29 theories,] *bef. del.* 'are real'

71.39 Insane . . . Cadwell] *penc. intrl.*

72.2 History . . . . -possession.] *tr. by penc. guideline fr. aft.* 'altered personality.' |

72.5 the belief] *aft. del.* 'this doctrine'

72.5–6 Xian belief] *penc. insrtd.*

72.8 Egypt Africa,] *insrtd.*

72.8 Polynesia] 'P' *ov. start of poss.* 'D'

72.9 disorders] *alt. fr.* 'diseases'

72.14 4th type mediumship] *penc. insrtd.*

72.17 Supernormal] *aft. del.* 'Amnesia.'

72.19 Ontaké] *penc. insrtd.*

72.19 153] *penc. ab. del.* '134 177'

72.19–20 Nevius . . . Foxes!] *insrtd.*

72.21 Capt.] 'C' *ov.* 'd'

72.23–24 One . . . country.] *tr. by guideline fr. aft.* 'p. 23.' |

72.24 Globus. Hysteria.] *insrtd.*

72.25 69] *penc. insrtd.*

72.29–30 Michael . . . Bavaria] *insrtd. in ruled frame; poss. intended to foll. the brace ab.*

72.31 suggestive disease.] *insrtd.*

72.33 cracked] 'ed' *ov.* 's in'; *bef. del.* 'the'

72.36 Witchcraft] 'W' *ov.* 'A'

73.4 1475] *bel. del. doubtful* '1487'

73.10 Arts] *ab. del.* 'Architecture &'

73.11 Bacon] *aft. del.* 'Kepler'

73.13 Evil] *aft. del.* 'Apply to our time. Don't judge an age by the evil it contains . . . or by any one of its features.' |

73.20 canon-] *intrl.*

73.24 Babylonian] 'B' *ov.* 'b'

73.24 Antediluvian] 'A' *ov.* 'a'

73.24 etc.] *bef. del.* 'Ghast'

73.25 Ghastly] *aft. del.* '*Dominican inquisitors worked up the whole business—no witch burned except in name of pope—though protestants must not throw stones—Scotland. [insrtd. in left mrgn.; position indicated by guideline] *Malleus 1487 confirmed by successive popes as autho[penc. insrtd.]rized canon-law manual. *Regret! [penc. del.] | *Quote Snell. Drips with blood [penc. insrtd.] Antediluvian monster—cuneiform inscription' |

73.27 timorousness] *aft. del.* 'and'

73.29 raised] *ab. del.* '['often thinking that' del.] heated'

73.30 battle] *aft. del.* 'batl ['l' ov. 't']'

73.31 feeling—] *bef. del.* 'Quote Snell.'

73.32   W] *ov.* 'w'

73.33   their . . . proofs] *intrl.*

74.11   themselves &] *intrl.*

74.19   Crimen exceptum] *insrtd.*

74.20   May . . . suspicion] *intrl.*

74.21–22   ; No . . . etc.] ('v' *of* 'wives' *ov.* 'f'); *insrtd.*

74.23   extorted.] *bef. del.* | 'Torture "continued"—not "repeated"' '

74.27   (Diabolically malicious!)] *aft. del.* 'Ordeals by fire & water, *not much used [*penc. insrtd.*]'; *ab. del.* | 'Many of the *signs [*ab. del.* 'things'] ascribed to devil we now understand ['as hysteric symptoms' *del.*] | Hysteria. Anaesthesia particularly.'

74.28   Accused] *insrtd.*

74.29   fasting] *intrl.*

74.30   confession] *bef. del.* 'S'

74.31   Torture] 'To' *ov.* 'Co'

74.36   Baissac 592] *intrl.*

74.37   1692:] *intrl.*

75.6   Weier's &] *intrl.*

75.6   aconite, belladonna] *intrl.*

75.8   Stramonium] *aft. del.* 'Me'

75.12   Remember] *aft. del.* 'Medical marks of witch disease.' |

75.15   halls. . . . "pinched"] *insrtd.*

75.17   have] *bef. del.* 'delusion'

75.19   fraud] *aft. del.* 'humbug.'

75.22–23   "Carried . . . acting."] *insrtd. in right mrgn.*

75.26   where the] *ab. del.* 'from the'

75.28   prefacing] *aft. del.* 'and'

75.31   doctors] *apostrophe bef.* 's' *del.*

76.2   (Tituba)] *penc. insrtd.*

76.6   beyond] *aft. del.* 'unquesti'

76.6   accounts] 'acc' *ov.* 'was'

76.6   for] *insrtd.*

76.7   Philip von Schönborn.] *insrtd.*

76.11   by . . . made] *penc. ab. penc. del.* '& leading to the *acts [*ab. del.* 'horrors'] which we have seen through medical & *theological [*intrl. bef. del.* 'religio' *ab. del.* 'priestly'] delusions in which whole populations sh⟨are⟩d. It is all'

76.12   friars] *aft. del.* 'dominic'

76.12   & other judges] *intrl.*

76.14   story] *aft. del. illeg.*

76.15   To . . . power] *ab. del.* 'Detestation'

76.17   & Man] *intrl.*

76.21–22   evil and dread] *ab. del.* 'fear'

76.22   rather] *aft. del.* 'tha'

76.23   I have] *bel. del.* 'was [*ab. del.* 'has been'] a dropping fire, and even in the XIX Century Soldan reports a large number of case of witch slaying in all parts of Europe. ['in' *del.*] At S. Jacopo in Mexico 5 witches were burnt together *in [*intrl.*] 1877 by legal process. This very year in Ireland' |

76.27   but] *insrtd.*

76.27   devil] *final* 's' *del.*

76.27   of] *bef. del.* 'ignorance, [*illeg. del.*] intoler⟨ance⟩'

76.29   legitimate] *intrl.*

76.29–30   authority] *aft. del.* 'power into'

76.30–34   Strange . . . world] *penc. added*

76.38   makes] *bef. del.* 'them loom'

76.38   deep.] *bef. del.* 'and squee'

77.4   Human] *aft. del.* 'Guiteau's trial bro't in "crank."' ' |

77.4   these] *alt. fr.* 'this'

77.5   Screw . . . temperament] *intrl.*

77.14   fear . . . fainting] *intrl.*

77.24   Recherche] *aft. del.* 'Munsterberg's case.' |

77.32   scientific] *aft. del.* 'theory'

77.35   Exorcism] *aft. del.* 'Pretty'

77.36   Van] *aft. del.* 'Impulses.'

77.38   Münsterberg's] *aft. del.* 'Money spending.' |

78.10–11   Anti Viv. Moreau.] *penc. added*

78.12   Love] *aft. del.* ' "Antivivisectionist-mania."' ' |

78.20   Frances Willard.] *penc. insrtd. for ink del.* 'Bryan'

78.21–23   Lecture . . . kinds!] *tr. by guideline fr. bef.* | 'Love.' [78.12]

78.28   p. 57] *penc. insrtd.*

78.30   Lélut,] *aft. del.* 'Not only blots on sun, but sun a blot! | I will briefly mention and exemplify' |

78.31   Lélut] *aft. del.* 'Nisbet 1891'

78.31   halluciné] 'é' *ov.* 'a'

78.33   and] *aft. del.* 'to'

78.35   purely] *aft. del.* 'purlely'

††78.37 madman."] *bef. del.* | 'All because he stood once motionless for many hours in the cold, and spoke of having a guiding demon. Even if *by [*intrl.*] this demon were really meant hallucinations of hearing, we know now that ['about' *del.*] one in 8 or 10 of the population has had such an experience at least once, and that for insanity we must resort to ['oth' *del.*] other tests than these.'

79.1 by] *penc. intrl. ab. two dashes undel. in error; bef. penc. del.* 'Pascal a real psychopath.'

79.1 who] *penc. intrl.*

79.2–4 Madness . . . *conveniunt.*] *insrtd.*

79.4 tree:] *bef. del.* 'Insanity proper; various paralyses, spasmodic and neuralgic affections; psychopathy; and genius'

79.7 excentrics] *init.* 'e' *ov.* 's'

79.10 squarely] *aft. del.* 'fairly'

79.10 Explain] *penc. intrl.*

79.11 g.] *ov.* 'N.'

79.11 variety).] *bef. penc. del.* 'Nisbet (1891). Read p XV *without exception unsound. [*insrtd.*] | Nordau *hysteria [*enclosing parens del.*]—invasion.'

79.17 many] *aft. del.* 'much'

79.21 first.] *bef. ink and penc. del.* | 'Begin with p. 6 — — — | Entartung u. Genie—begin with 1st Chap. Replies ['t' *del.*] obj. p. 15. Dante & Michelangelo. | Exhaustion theory, ['57.' *del.*] 63 *PORTRAITS [*penc. insrtd.*] | Nisbet's mortality theory, 315 | Stimson's enumeration.'

79.24 Leanness] *aft. penc. del.* 'Pallor' |

80.18 Drunkenness] *aft. del.* 'Alcoholism'

80.37 book.] *aft. del.* 'list'

81.3 said] 'a' *ov.* 'et'

81.5 By] *bef. del.* 'fel ['e' *doubtful*]'

81.7 To] *aft. del.* 'Let us examine significance ourselves.' |

81.7 nothing] *bef. del.* 'proved' *ab. del.* 'no essential connection'

81.8 Sunday] *aft. del.* 'Tues'

81.10 No] *aft. del.* 'Simple enumeration. | It leaves the negative instances out.' |

81.11 alone] *intrl.*

81.15 Negative] *aft. del.* 'So genius *is* not a morbid state. | How account for its frequency?' |

81.17 Take] 'Ta' *ov.* 'Wh'

81.17 Longf.] *intrl.*

81.20 look] *aft. del.* 'we must'

81.21 homogeneous] 'homo' *ab. del.* 'hetero ['o' *undel. in error*]'

81.23 person's] 'p' *ov.* 'n'

81.26 Rockefeller . . . Twain &] *penc. intrl. bef.* '&' *in error*

81.26 Washington] *ab. del.* 'St Paul'

81.27 Rudyard] *aft. del.* 'Thos. C. Platt.' |

81.27 St Paul] *tr. by guideline fr. bef.* '& [*not tr. in error*] ['Thos. C. Platt.' *del.*]'

81.29 *intellect.*] *bef. del.* 'First'

81.36 Feeling] *aft. del.* 'Dogged or' |

82.1 This] *aft. del.* 'This being the case, with' |

82.1 case,] *bef. del.* 'where is'

82.2 Those] *aft. del.* 'We all know mediocre intellects who impress their time: In public affairs, notorious. Bismark. Cleveland.' |

82.2 ambition] 'a' *ov. doubtful* 'an'

82.5 We] *bef. del.* 'all'

82.9 Most] 'M' *ov.* 'B'

82.14 (Myself . . . -books)] *insrtd.*

82.20 neurosis] *aft. del.* 'insane'

82.24–32 Let . . . health.] *drawn lines frame this text*

82.25 taken . . . tamer.] *ab. del.* 'reduced things flatter.'

82.28 Double] *aft. del.* 'Demon ['em' *ov. illeg.*] possession . . . . hysteria' |

82.33 Affair . . . leg"] *insrtd.*

82.36 Jury of] *penc. insrtd.*

82.37 The] *aft. del.* 'Welcome . . . if useful.' |

82.38 S̄.] *aft. del.* 'Biceps'

83.7 geniuses . . . peculiarities] *ab. del.* 'things'

83.9–10 about the] *aft. del.* 'to make.'; *bef. del.* 'truth of'

83.12 fear] 'fea' *ov.* 'vio'

83.16 you] *aft. del.* 'they may leave you *in more of that sort of an [*ab. del.* 'in that'] attitude than'

Deleted and Undeleted Versos (#4402)

[*del. fol.* 1ᵛ: *orig. fol.* 5, *corresponding to text* 64.20–24] 'in gear with each other. "Integrated." | The abstract law is that each idea by itself tends to be believed & acted out | But in normal life we have no single ideas | Field—focus—margin. | Margin controls focus.'

[*del. fol.* 2ᵛ: *orig. fol.* 4(*ov.* 3), *corresponding to text* 64.11–20] '*1) level-headed | 2) rattled [*braced to right*] waking. | 3) asleep | In dreams, ideas are detached from the *usual consorts [*intrl.*] | Mine of Seth. | ['Fundamental' *del.*] | 2 conditions *1) **negative ['nega' *ov.* 'posi']—narrowness | 2) positive—vividness [*braced to left and right*] of field. | These 2 conditions found in many *of the [*intrl.*] disorders | So get an emphatic idea of the fundamental psychological point. | The sound mind a system, of ideas'

[*undel. fol.* 25ᵛ: *orig. fol.* 23, *corresponding to text* 70.26–30] 'Mollie Fancher | Felida & Madame B.—no need of Europe. | Birth of "Adrienne" Rev. Phil. XXII, 589 | Janet's view vs. Myers's.'

[*undel. fol.* 26ᵛ: *orig. fol.* 25(*ov.* 4), *corresponding to text* 70.34] 'To these cases Janet's conception fits'

[*del. fol.* 52ᵛ: *orig. fol.* 52, *corresponding to text* 77.19] '['Psychopa' *del.*] These are for our por'

6. SUMMER SCHOOL OF THEOLOGY LECTURES ON "INTELLECT AND FEELING IN RELIGION" 1902 #4479, #4513

These lectures are contained in #4479, which includes the original manila envelope container, on which James wrote 'Theological School lectures' and, later, added in pencil (probably in 1906) 'Trash | never to be printed'. The original manuscript is written on the rectos of a cheap buff wove unwatermarked paper 10¾ x 8¼", foliated in the upper right corner, with some interspersed leaves from another version written on a fine white laid paper, unwatermarked, and some insertions on a white wove paper watermarked Agawam Bond. Interspersed here and there throughout the sequence are foliated leaves written in pencil on a lightweight wove paper watermarked L. L. Brown Co. These appear to be attempts to alter some of the text when the lectures were redelivered in the summer of 1906. On occasion, to admit these leaves, portions of the buff-paper leaves were deleted in pencil. The added L. L. Brown leaves do not always fit into the text and appear to be memoranda notes from which James could talk, merging their content with the original as he spoke. The manuscript consists of 53 leaves; as presently constituted there are 21 leaves in the 1906 form with the abstracted 1902 leaves making up the remaining 32. However, since this later form does not always offer coherent connected discourse, the present text rearranges the manuscript to reproduce the 1902 version, including all pencil-deleted matter. The 1906 leaves are transcribed separately as Appendix IV, with notation of their place in the 1902 text and with an alterations list recording the 1906 pencil alterations made in the 1902 ink text.

The original buff fol. 1 (83.21–31) was removed for 1906 and replaced by an unnumbered leaf on L. L. Brown paper, in pencil, headed '*Devotion*', written on the back of a reversed unnumbered false start. The manuscript continues with the original buff text on fol. 2, but some disruption begins at the foot of fol. 3 where a passage after 'the whole matter.' (84.29) beginning '*Reactions on my book*' has been deleted in ink. The deleted text originally continued on fol. 4 with 'and if the world' (85.11), but the excised matter was replaced with a leaf foliated 3½ (84.30–85.4), which at the foot ('Reactions . . . *won't*' 85.5–6) began a new version of the passage deleted at the foot of fol. 3. These two lines (here transcribed) are separated from the preceding text by a pencil line and are deleted in pencil by five vertical lines, alterations made by James when he rearranged the material in 1906. This material at the foot of fol. 3½ was continued for six lines on a leaf foliated 4, which then ran into the text of original 4 'and if the world . . .' which was then renumbered 4½. But this fol. 4 proved to be a false start and was discarded, its verso used to replace it with a new fol. 4 part-page ('train . . . faculties.' 85.6–10), ending with notes to save James from writing out the passage once again. As a result, earlier renumbered 4½ starts in mid-sentence, disconnected from the notes on the revised fol. 4. At the foot of 4½ the beginning of a sentence (here transcribed) ('Even . . . who are' 85.22–24) was deleted in pencil and a pencil 'Omit' added in the margin in order to introduce 1906 L. L. Brown leaves foliated 5 and 5½ which replaced original buff fols. 5 and 5½ ('non-religious . . . possible.]' 85.24–86.2), fol. 5½ ('"religion." . . . possible.]' 85.34–86.2) being added as a revision of the deleted first two lines of fol. 6 ('If . . . immanent' 86.3–15).

The next 1906 alteration starts with a pencil sentence added at the foot of fol. 7 ('perfection . . . him.' 86.15–28), followed by 8–10 on the L. L. Brown paper, the last being a part-page. Folio 8 is written on the back of a reversed unnumbered pencil trial, deleted by two vertical lines, that was revised to begin added fol. 5. These three leaves took the place in 1906 of a 1902 sequence beginning with buff fol. 8 ('I call these . . .' 86.29) and ending with buff fol. 23 ('. . . they are *too individual*.' 93.23), altered from 22½. Within this series fol. 9½ ('world . . . altogether.' 87.19–36) links with fol. 9 ('inroads . . . against the natural' 87.5–19). Since fol. 10½ (88.14–22) is a part-page, it seems evident that revision and expansion have taken place between 9½ and 10½. Folio 10 (87.37–88.13) is written on the back of a reversed three-word false start numbered 10 in the upper right corner. Folio 10½ is written on the back of a reversed unnumbered page containing a false start for the first three lines (88.14–16) on present 10½.

Folios 14–17 ('questions concerning . . . the whole divine.' 89.22–90.17) introduce leaves of a white laid unwatermarked paper 9 x 6¾", their left margins cut to fit. These leaves are foliated in the right upper corner, 50–53, deleted, and evidently were cut out from the notebook (#4513) that holds several numbered pages in the same manner. On fol. 14 the upper quarter of the text is deleted in ink. A notation 'Continued from p. 30 of yellow sheets', set off by lines above and below, is also deleted in ink (as is the first line of the following text). The 'p. 30' referred to by James is not the present buff fol. 30, however, as the text ending buff fol. 30 does not link with the text on this fol. 14. The final leaf of this white paper ending 'the whole divine.' (90.17) has been cut off about a quarter of the way from the foot as a means of removing original text.

With fol. 18 ('Natural Supernaturalism . . .' 90.18) the buff paper returns, continuing on fol. 19, which is written on the back of a reversed numbered trial (deleted) for the start of fol. 18. Folio 19 (90.37–91.7) ends with four lines of undeleted text ('I wish . . . that God' 92.18–20) that link in mid-sentence with lines deleted at the head of fol. 20 ('is one element . . . against me.' 92.20–22), but restored in the present edition. Between buff fol. 19 and buff fol. 20 come four leaves of white wove paper 11 x 8¼″ watermarked Agawam Bond. The first three leaves are numbered, centered, 19a, 19b, and 19c, but the fourth is unnumbered. The first three pages are largely quotations (91.8–92.6) but the fourth (92.7–17) consists of notes for continuing the lecture. On fol. 19a and continuing at the head of 19b part of a quotation ('The reconciliation . . . knowledge." ' 91.16–27) has been deleted by a vertical ink stroke but is reprinted here within the text on the assumption that James removed it to shorten the series of quotations for public delivery. Correspondingly, the ink deleted continuation of fol. 20 from the last words on fol. 19, which were not deleted, raises a question of James's intentions for delivery, even though the odds favor the guess that the start of the paragraph on fol. 19 was not deleted in error. The completion of the paragraph on fol. 20 originally differed: fol. 20 is written on the back of a false start for the leaf.

Buff leaf 23 (93.20–23) is a part-page, originally numbered 22½, that leads into 24, originally numbered 23. Starting with fol. 24 ('Too . . . home to' 93.24–38) James in 1906 added in pencil, top centered, a different series of numbering, beginning with 11. Folios 25–26 ('*him*, . . . tradition.' 93.38–94.27) are normal buff leaves dual numbered 25–26 in ink and 12–13 in pencil. Folio 26 is written on the back of a false start for its first words.

Folio 27 (94.28–95.6) was not included in the 1906 series; hence fol. 28 (95.7–20) follows with centered 14 after the 13 of fol. 26. The lower half of this fol. 28 (95.12–20) is set off with a pencil line drawn across the page and deleted with a single vertical line. Thereafter the 1906 series concluded with L. L. Brown paper, written in pencil, and numbered in the upper center 15–16 16½ 17. The original 1902 continuation of fol. 28 consists of numbered folios 29–33 plus an unnumbered part-page at the end. Folio 29 starts at 95.21 with 'Nevertheless investigation,'. Folio 31 is written on the back of a reversed unnumbered deleted false start for the leaf. With fol. 32 (96.34–97.6) we come to the last of the inscription on buff paper, fol. 33 and the final unnumbered leaf being written on the white Agawam Bond paper earlier used for the insertion of leaves starting with 19a. James's brackets are found at 94.37–95.4 '[Genius . . . loathsome.]'.

[Appendix: Notes on Religion]

The bound notebook #4513 holds among various other items fragmentary notes on religion. These cannot be associated with the Theology School lectures but presumably are part of the background for them and perhaps for *The Varieties of Religious Experience*. The notebook has numerous missing leaves, attested by their stubs; some leaves have had sections cut out, and others conceal the text by blank paper pasted over the inscription. The notebook was written on the rectos, but when James came to the end he turned the book around and wrote toward the front on the versos. Various sections have been deleted in ink or pencil, as well as pasted over. Some fragments written just before and after the notebook was turned are foliated in the upper right corner. Remarks headed '*Ecclesiasticism*' on a leaf foliated 12 are continued on numbered fols. 13 and 14 ('you that the two . . . prim temper.' 97.30–98.5), this subject ending above a quotation from Sainte-Beuve, which is deleted by a single vertical line but is transcribed here (98.6–8). Deleted text follows the quotation.

The subject of religion is missing until we reach fols. 19–20, a discussion of reasonable versus passionate religion (98.9–24), again apparently ending a section. Next preserved are fols. 26–27 containing a discussion on the religion of the 'well-mixed' man (98.26–99.6), which ends in mid-sentence. This discussion begins on fol. 26 beneath a short line that separates it from the line above (98.25) that ended a section, now lost. We catch a glimpse of another subject on the verso of a slip headed '*Critical points.*' and beginning an anecdote about Ostwald. The verso of this slip was pasted over with a blank, but removal of this blank shows a fragment of text numbered 29 beginning with a deletion and itself deleted by the beginning of a vertical line (99.7–9). The next preserved text comes on fols. numbered 35–37 with a discussion on Consecration (99.10–32), which ends with 'this world's values.' followed by the deleted start (here transcribed) of another paragraph (99.30–32). The text on fol. 37 has been cut off below the fourth line of this deletion. Beneath paste-overs are found fragments of text on versos numbered 45 (99.33–37) and 48 (100.1–4). The last numbered page preserved is 57 (100.5–18).

Emendations

83.29	temperamental] temperamtal	95.28	Myers's] Myer's
85.2	gives] give	95.31	Xian"] ~∧
87.37	anthropologists] anthopolists	95.31	Granger]] ~)
90.9	characterizes] chacterizes	96.3	phenomena,] ~∧
91.20	conflict∧] ~.	97.13	these] there
92.5	*religion.*"] ~·∧	98.10	emphasis] imphasis
93.28	joins] join	98.27	infinite,] ~∧
93.29	"reasonable,"] "~∧"	100.7	possibility] possibly
94.10	religion,] ~∧		

Alterations in the Manuscripts

83.23 needed,] *alt. fr.* 'need,'
83.27 First] 'F' *ov.* 'f'; *aft. del.* 'The'
83.27 of term &] (*comma aft.* 'term' *del.*); *ab. del.* '&'
83.27–28 , which] *comma and* 'w' *ov. three ellipsis dots; bef. del.* 'term'
84.1 nothing if not] *intrl.*
84.2 Others,] 's,' *added*
84.2 *private*] *ab. del.* 'personal'
84.4 *morality*] *aft. del.* 'and'
84.5 *Pessimists*] *final* 's' *ov.* 'ic'; *bef. del.* '—twice born'
84.6 in] *intrl.*
84.6 a] *intrl.*
84.9 *lives*] *aft. del.* 'cons'
84.10 beliefs] *aft. del.* 'religious'
84.17 enthusiastic] *ab. del.* 'zealous'
84.17 the] *final* 'ir' *del.*
84.19 formalist] 'ist' *added*
84.19 &] *intrl.*
84.21 On] *ov.* 'To'
84.22 spiritual] *intrl.*

84.29 matter.] *bef. del.* '*Reactions on my book.* *dislike of saintly char [intrl.]* [¶] It is of no use to try to conciliate these subjective antipathies. They are fundamental. They depend on radical divergencies of human character, on different needs and faculties in individuals,'
84.35 *onesided*] *intrl.*
84.36 of] *ov.* 'to'
85.11 individualities of] *intrl.*
85.12 character] *final* 's' *del.*
85.12 surely] *aft. del.* 'to'
85.13 what] *ab. del.* 'a religion to'
85.14 suits] *final* 's' *added*
85.14 his] 's' *ov.* 'm'
85.14 own] *insrtd.*
85.17 oneself] *alt. fr.* 'onesself'
85.20 objectively] *ab. del.* 'in religion'
85.20 that] *bef. del.* 'there are'
85.24 has ... do] *ab. del.* 'does not coincide'

85.27 another] 'an' *insrtd. aft. del.*
    'the'
85.28 because of] *ab. del.* 'by'
85.29 in him] *insrtd.*
85.29 human . . . some] *intrl.*
85.29 kind] 'k' *ov.* 'c'
85.29 mental] *intrl.*
85.30 may be] *ab. del.* 'are'
85.31 We] *ab. del.* 'Mankind'; *aft. del.*
    '[¶] We must not use the word
    "religious" merely eulogistically.'
85.31 need] *final* 's' *del.*
85.31 types∧] *comma del.; aft. del.* 'its'
85.31 the] *intrl.*
85.31 revelations.] 's' *and period
    added; bef. del.* '['which is the fruit'
    del.]* of all *human [ab. del.* 'its']
    experience. We must neither narrow
    the significance of such a wide word
    as ['a' *ov.* 'i'] religion'
86.3 If] *aft. del.* '"religion." We
    must [ab. del. 'need'] not use it
    merely *eulogistically.* Terrible to use
    words so . . .'
86.6 faculties] 'ies' *ov.* 'y'
86.6 would then] *ab. del.* 'may well'
86.7 perfect] *aft. del.* 'wisdom.'
86.9 interests,] *comma ov. period bef.*
    'It' *not reduced in error*
86.10 breadth] *aft. del.* 'ideal of'
86.12 called] 'ed' *added*
86.14 wise man like] *intrl.*
86.18 latter] *intrl.*
86.19 be] *aft. del.* 'pay with'
86.23 Wesley] *added*
86.24 take] *aft. del.* 'decide for'
86.25 even] *intrl.*
86.26 In] *aft. del.* 'The individual'
86.27 gravitate] *aft. del.* 'gratif'
86.30 are] *ab. del.* 'deal'
86.34 real] *intrl.*
86.36 They must] *insrtd. for del.*
    'They ar'
86.36 men's] *ab. del.* 'the'
86.36 ways] 's' *added*
87.1 one of them] *intrl.*
87.3 dumbly or explicitly] *intrl. w.
    caret orig. placed aft.* 'been' *but
    then orig. caret del.*
87.3 been] *bef. del.* 'in'
87.3 centre] *ab. del.* 'foreground'

87.6 philosophizing.] *period ab. del.
    comma*
87.6 It] *ab. del.* 'which'
87.6 an issue] *intrl.*
87.6 settled.] *ab. del.* 'solved, and
    which, [comma undel. in error]'
87.6 think∧] *comma del.*
87.7 it] *intrl.*
87.8 it] *poss. added*
87.9 other.] *bef. del.* 'It'
87.11 Contradictories] 'ories' *aft. del.*
    'ions'
87.16 bluntly & grossly] *intrl.*
87.17 it] *aft. del.* 'blunt'
87.18 set] 's' *ov.* 'g'
87.23 sympathetic magic.] *intrl.*
87.37 many] *ab. del.* 'the'
87.38 obscene] *alt. fr.* 'obscence'
88.5 on] *aft. del.* 'of'
88.20 to] *intrl.*
88.21 abandoning] *aft. del.* 'waiving'
88.27 Nature] 'e' *ov.* 'al'
88.31 religious] *aft. del.* 'reg'
88.33 reactions.] *bef. del.* 'Ethni'
88.34 Ethnic] *ov. illeg.; bef. del.* 'to'
89.1 deemed] *intrl.*
89.2 (absoluteness)] *parens and* 'ness'
    added
89.10 very] *intrl.*
89.11 have] *aft. del.* 'ha'
89.12 why] *aft. del.* 'it u'
89.14 Transcendentalism] 'T' *ov.* 't';
    aft. del. 'In'
89.16 Truth] *aft. del.* '[¶] The total is
    divine anyhow'
89.18 So,] *comma added; bef. del.*
    'we are'
89.21 seems] *aft. del.* 'is this'
89.22 questions] *aft. del.* 'religion is
    accustomed to, is thus in principle
    not at all at variance with our
    spontaneous tendencies as *active
    [ab. del.* '['mor' *del.*] practical and
    moral'] agents. *[line]* Continued
    from p. 30 of yellow sheets *[line]*
    seems *[ab. del.* 'is'] this general
    ['alist' *del.*] total insight *to the
    transcendentalist *[intrl.]* that *for
    him *[intrl.]* all'
89.23 dwindle] *bef. del. intrl. illeg.*
89.23 insignificance] 'ce' *ov.* 't'

89.25–26 supposable or proposable]
each 'able' *ab. undel.* 'ed'

89.26 is] *ab. del.* 'becomes'

89.27 chokes] *bef. del.* 'and coughs'

89.29 stones] *aft. del.* 'stones towards'

89.29 of Spirit] *ab. del. intrl.* 'to
Heaven'; *caret aft.* 'stones' *formed fr.
comma and comma aft.* 'Spirit' *om.
in error*

89.30 "Miracles,"] 'M' *ov.* 'm'; 'a'
intrl.; aft. del. 'When he hears the
old fashioned pietist talk of'

89.33 wholly] *intrl.*

89.33 matter] *ab. del.* 'flesh'

89.34–35 antitheses] *aft. del.* 'co'

89.36–37 without cavil] *intrl.*

89.37 ²of] *aft. del.* 'by'; *bef. del.* 'the'

89.38–39 a cerebral . . . without a]
ab. del. ', to accept without'

89.39 to] *intrl.*

89.40 system.] *period aft. del. comma
bef. del.* 'for'

89.40 He] *ov.* 'he'

90.1 total,] *comma ov. period bef. del.*
'The old fashioned'

90.2 tendency] *aft. del.* 'old fas'

90.2 religious thought] *ab. del.*
'theology'

90.3 spiritual] *ab. del.* 'divine'

90.4 material] *bef. del.* ', or'

90.5 diabolical] *aft. del.* 'ant'

90.6 *Divine*] 'D' *ov.* 'd'

90.8 This] *alt. fr.* 'These'; *bef. del.*
'two'

90.10–11 to . . . supernaturalism]
ab. del. 'monistic'

90.12 with] *aft. del.* 'which'

90.13 joining] *aft. del.* 'and'

90.14 oracles and] *intrl.*

90.16 Either nowhere or] *intrl. bef.*
'Here' *not reduced in error*

90.17 ²this] *ab. del.* 'my'

90.20 Universal] *final* 'ism' *del.*

90.22 circuits] *init.* 'c' *ov.* 's'

90.25 &] *intrl.*

90.29 All . . . faith.] *insrtd.*

90.36 is it] *intrl.*

90.36 ¹as . . . goes] *intrl.*

90.37 new views make] *ab. del.* 'a'

90.40 Question] *intrl.*

91.1 individual] *aft. del.* 'fact'

91.5 Is] *intrl.*

91.5 the] 't' *ov.* 'T'

91.5 one] *intrl.*

91.8 pretension] *orig.* 'prentesion', *then*
'n' *bef.* 's' *intrl. but* 'n' *bef.* 't'
undel. in error

91.18 training the] ('training' *aft. del.*
'getting'); *ab. del.* 'raising the'

91.18 mind] *ab. del.* 'consciousness'

91.18 those] *alt. fr.* 'the'

91.19 different orders of] *intrl.*

91.19 reality] 'y' *ov.* 'ies'

91.19 natural] *aft. del.* 'relig'

91.21 belong] *ab. del.* 'refer'

91.21 "We] 'W' *ov.* 'w'; *aft. del.*
' "[undel. in error] As men'

91.22 that] *bef. del.* | 'that'

91.22 events enjoy,] *ab. del.* 'existence
gives'

91.24 they] 'y' *added; bef. del.* 'events'

91.24–25 on . . . gain] *ab. del.* 'of
them is found'

91.25 scientific] *ab. del.* 'theoretic'

91.25–26 and . . . becomes] *ab. del.*
'and in it, ['thus' *del.*] is founded
['the' *del.*]'

91.26 independent] 't' *ov.* 'ce'; *bef. del.*
'of religion'

91.26 particular] *intrl.*

91.27 the . . . as a] ('es' *of* 'rages' *ov.*
'ing'); *intrl.*

91.27 ground] *final* 's' *del.*

91.29 organisms] *aft. del.* 'animal'

91.29 God] 'G' *ov.* 'g'

91.30 unapproachable] *ab. del.* '['un'
del.] intangible height'

91.30 down] *ab. del.* 'and'

91.31 degrades] *ab. del.* 'lowers'

91.31 being] *ab. del.* 'a part'

91.33 . . . .] *intrl.*

91.33 what] *aft. del.* 'how'

91.35 actual] *intrl.*

91.38 adding] *ab. del.* 'construction'

91.39 existence.] *period ov. comma*

91.39 . . . . .] *insrtd.*

91.39 But] 'B' *ov.* 'b'

91.40 so much] ('so' *aft. del.* 'so')·
intrl.

91.40 existence] 'ence' *ov.* 'ing'

91.40 simply] *aft. del.* 'as'

92.4 material] *ab. del.* 'fact'

92.12   rule . . . facts . . .] *insrtd. for del.* 'say particular facts irrelevant. | Spontaneous thought'

92.15   are] *aft. del.* 'do'

92.21   be left] *intrl.*

92.23   One] 'O' *ov.* 'o'

92.24   This] *aft. del.* 'Miracle'

92.26   Genuine . . . repulsive.] *intrl.*

92.30   Great] *aft. del.* 'Some of *you* ashamed to look at me! | So, to gain even a hearing, I must make a preliminary distinction.'

93.2   No] *final* 't' *del.*

93.2   *principle!*] *bef. del.* | 'Only question of *fact!*'

93.4   simply.] *bef. del.* | 'Transcendentalism submits to science in denying fact. (M___g)'

93.8   What] *aft. del.* ' "If facts be there, Science of religions ought to acknowledge." ' |

93.10   mystical] *aft. del.* 'regenerative changes,'

93.17   *level*] *aft. del.* 'lve'

93.18   Science] *aft. del.* 'Significant primarily for life | Even for subject, doctrine secondary. [Leuba]' |

93.20   hysterics] *bef. del.* | '[Munsterberg]'

93.21   universally.] *bef. del.* | 'But Science only a *method*—any facts may be studied scientifically.'

93.22   is] *aft. del.* 'ob'

93.33   escape] *ab. del.* 'exceed'

93.33   general] *aft. del.* 'form'

93.36   Individuality] 'I' *ov.* 'i'; *aft. del.* 'The'

93.40   the] *ov.* 'all'

94.3   Procrustes'] 'P' *ov.* 'p'

94.11   intellectualized] 'ized' *insrtd. bel. del. insrtd. colon*

94.11   classifications . . . by] *ab. del.* 'ways of judging re['c' *del.*]actions of'

94.13   only] *aft. del.* 'abs'

94.15–16   abstract] *intrl.*

94.17   which] *bef. del.* 'meets it.'

94.19   realities] *aft. del.* 'not'

94.21   Whose . . . philosophizing] *insrtd. ab. line drawn across the page*

94.30   religious] *ab. del.* 'those'

94.31   ourselves] *aft. del.* 'others.'

94.36   We . . . elsewhere—] *insrtd. bel. line drawn across the page*

95.3   lovers are] *intrl.*

95.9   that] *bef. del. intrl.* 'positively'

95.20   fence.] *bef. del.* | 'It temperamentally loathes psychical researcher, even as Saint is loathed by strong men.'

95.21   continue] *final* 's' *del.*

95.26   Myers's] *bef. del.* 'book—his'

95.27   Dissolutive] *ov.* 'If [*illeg.*]'

95.36   bearings] *ab. del.* 'importance'

95.36   all.] *bef. del.* | 'In the first place it gi'

96.16   Science . . . method] *intrl.*

96.17   "rot."] *period ov. comma bef. del.* 'as by ' "*Scientist [alt. fr.* 'Science."].'

96.18   "scientists."] *ov.* 'him.'

96.21   Still] 'S' *ov.* 'O' *ov.* 'T'

96.39   difference] *aft. del.* 'g'

97.4   God] *aft. del.* 'Read'

97.15   ¹to] *aft. del.* 'to as[*start of letter*]'

97.17   Universe] *final* 's' *del.*

97.23   science] *aft. del.* 'natural'

97.24   stand] *aft. del.* 'also'

97.24–25   specially loving] *intrl. aft. del.* 'friendly' *ab. del.* 'positive'

97.25–26   or . . . clergymen] *intrl.*

97.27   to an imagination] *ab. del.* 'if'

97.28   yield] *ab. del.* 'afford *any real [intrl.]'*

97.28–29   sustenance.] *period added bef. del.* '['to the' *del.*] ['They require different facultie' *del.*] With'

97.29   be] *aft. del.* 'f'

97.30   are] *bef. del.* 'two'

97.30   and] *ab. del.* 'which'

97.34   importance] *ab. del.* 'meaning'

98.1   a] *ab. del.* 'any'

98.1–2   pride . . . laymen,] ('pride' *ab. del.* 'delight'; 'more' *intrl.*; 'clergymen,' *bef. del.* 'even though deacons'); *insrtd. for del.* 'complacency at ['being immediately' *del.*] having closer relations with the clergy than with the laity, or at taking particular pride in ['be' *del.*] the distinction'

98.3   phraseology] *aft. del.* 'fr'

98.3   intonation,] *comma insrtd.*
98.3   or] *intrl. ab. del. period*
98.3–4   a sweet . . . bishops.] *period added; tr. by guideline fr. aft.* 'find' [98.2]
98.9   former] *aft. del.* 'latter'
98.10   uses] *aft. del.* 'simply' *ov. illeg.*
98.11   its] *aft. del.* 'this'
98.14   own] *intrl.*
98.19   In] *aft. del.* 'The'
98.23   to] *intrl.*
98.27   and . . . infinite] *intrl.*
98.29   like.] *period aft. del. comma*
98.29   him] *intrl.*
98.35   ways that] *intrl.*
98.36   inconvenient.] *aft. del.* 'highly'; *period added bef. del.* 'sense.'
99.1   centre] 'c' *ov.* 'm'
99.1   emphasis] *aft. del.* 'g'
99.7   Against] *aft. del.* 'despise them, and holds to its own norms and averages, adequately accounted for by general formulas.'
99.11   active] *aft. del.* 'any' *ab. del.* 'all'
99.11–12 überhaupt.] *ab. del. period*
99.12   is] *ab. del.* 'should'
99.12   species] *aft. del.* 'so'
99.13   distinct] *aft. del.* 'wi'

99.13   specific] 'fic' *ab. del.* 'al'
99.13   willing] *aft. del.* 'wil' |
99.17   powers,] *bef. del.* 'from'
99.17–18 our . . . whom] *tr. by guideline fr.* 'with whom our relations'
99.18   ²the] *intrl.*
99.19   assert that] *ab. del.* 'tend to place'
99.19   the] *final* 'y' *del.*
99.20   and even] *ab. del.* '['in a s' *del.*] if not'
99.20   lies] *insrtd.*
99.21   while] *ab. del.* 'would'
99.23   or] *insrtd. aft. del.* 'made'
99.25   an] *final* 'd' *del.*
99.27   finite,] *bef. del.* 'but not a destroyer or [start of letter]'
99.28   Religion] 'R' *ov.* 'r'; *final* 's' *del.; aft. del.* 'The'
99.28   has] 's' *ov.* 've'
99.31   habit] *ab. del.* 'tendency'
100.1   in . . . places] *intrl.*
100.1   vinegar] *bef. del.* 'of a pickle'
100.1   bitter] *bef. del.* 'in a cocktail'
100.2   characteristic] *intrl.*
100.10 tradition.] *period added bef. del.* 'of'
100.13 experimental] *ab. del.* 'natural'

Deleted and Undeleted Versos

[*del. fol.* 4ᵛ: *orig. fol.* 4; *orig. continuation of fol.* 3½, *corresponds to text* 85.6–10] 'train with that band, that gang. | Useless to try to conciliate these subjective antipathies. They are fundamental. They depend on radical divergencies of character, on different needs and faculties in ['d' *del.*] individuals,'

[*del. fol.* 10ᵛ: *orig. fol.* 10; *false start for present fol.* 10] 'But simultaneously religion'

[*del. fol.* 10½ᵛ: *false start for present fol.* 10½, *corresponds to text* 88.14–16] 'Christian controversy has of course been largely over matters of fact. | Facts revealed by Bible, within the church | Facts about Bible's origin.'

[*del. fol.* 19ᵛ: *orig. fol.* 18; *trial for fol.* 18, *corresponds to text* 90.18–24] 'Universalistic *or natural [intrl.] supernaturalism *thus [intrl.] makes piecemeal or particular supernaturalism unnecessary. | It ['is a' *del.*] short-circuits the problem of whether the world is divine. | ['It thus' *del.*] Rescues religion compro*m[intrl.]ised by scientific naturalism. | It is clean, intellectual, abstract. | It gratifies a certain subjective temperament.'

[*undel. fol.* 20ᵛ: *orig. continuation of fol.* 19, *corresponds to text* 92.20–21] 'may be not the whole of things but a part of things, ['may not be closed' *smudged out*]' [*undel. fol.* 26ᵛ: *orig. continuation of fol.* 25, *corresponds to text* 94.11–12] 'reactions of his fellows,'

[*undel. fol.* 31ᵛ: *orig. continuation of fol.* 30, *corresponds to text* 96.15–16] 'to *study facts* without destroying function. | Medical materialism does so off hand, altho' sense physiology does n't displace sense knowledge.'

7. DRAFTS AND NOTES FOR ADDRESSES TO GRADUATE CLUBS
    1902–1906   #4523, #4524

A draft (#4523) is written in black ink on the rectos of nineteen leaves of un-watermarked wove paper measuring 10½ x 8¼″, foliated, centered, 1–4 4½ 5–12 12½ 13–17. In this sequence fol. 4½ ('All . . . history, the' 102.25–28) replaces deleted matter at the start of fol. 5. Its paper is slightly heavier. Folio 8 ('follow . . . haunts her.' 103.35–104.8) is written on the back of an unnumbered and undeleted line and a half that originally continued text at the foot of fol. 5 that is now deleted (see Alterations entry 103.7). Folio 9 contains a pencil vertical line through the text 'The . . . sod.' (104.13–18). Folio 10 is numbered to the right of what appears to be a deleted 9. Although there is a considerable deletion at the foot of fol. 8, this fol. 10 (if it had been 9) does not link either with the undeleted or the deleted text, and hence it would seem that the leaf ('than those . . . disturbance.' 104.24–37) was misnumbered inadvertently and not as the result of preceding textual disturbance. This folio also contains a pencil oblique line through the text 'The . . . sophist,' (104.26–28). Folio 12 is a part-page ('a harder . . . intellectual' 105.12–18), added as a revision of deleted text at the top of present fol. 12½ ('onlooker . . . ²must' 105.18–29), which had been the original fol. 12. The 6 of fol. 16 is written over an illegible figure that could be 5. Again, inadvertency seems to be the cause of the alteration, for fol. 16 ('setting . . . men must' 106.30–107.6) links without evidence of revision.

A piece of a manila envelope is preserved with this manuscript which reads 'Possible Assembly address—. | Graduate Club address | (possibly ['re' *del.*] work up for Commencement)'.

What appear to be notes (possibly for speaking) and drafts are preserved in #4524 written on different papers. The manuscript starts with two leaves, each a half of a torn-apart unwatermarked wove sheet measuring 11 x 8½″. These are paged 1–4 and written on rectos and versos (107.11–108.20). This is followed by a single sheet of wove L. L. Brown G paper, measuring 10½ x 8″, written on recto and verso (108.21–109.24). Next come two folds (4 leaves) of L. L. Brown wove paper. The first leaf is written on recto and verso, the second on recto only (109.25–110.30). The third is inscribed on the recto and halfway down the verso (110.31–111.10), but the fourth leaf contains only one line 'expectation—failure [*period del.*; *vert. stroke*] serves individual [*vert. stroke*]' written vertically on the verso, the recto blank.

Another section begins, written on different papers and containing a mixture of discourse with topic memoranda for speaking. The first three leaves (unnumbered) are of an unwatermarked wove paper from a notebook, measuring 10½ x 8¼″, written on the recto of the first leaf, the recto and verso of the second leaf, and the recto of the third leaf (111.11–112.24). Next come 4 quired leaves from a ruled notebook, measuring 8¼ x 6¾″, unnumbered, written on the rectos except for a footnote written on the verso of the second leaf. The first leaf starts in mid-sentence 'fortunate enough' (112.25) written above the deleted continuation (see Alterations entry 112.25) of a deleted folio (see Alterations entry 114.3); the fourth leaf ends with 'a Cromwell, a Gari-' (113.20). The text continues ('baldi or . . .' 113.20) on two detached leaves of the same notebook paper, this section ending in mid-sentence with 'See the' (113.30), obviously with succeeding leaf or leaves missing. The final sequence consists of three leaves, measuring 8¼ x 7", irregularly torn from two ruled notebooks (the first leaf with wider spaces between the rules). The leaves, written on rectos and versos except for the last verso which is blank, are numbered 1–4, but the numbering skips the deleted verso of the first leaf (transcribed in the Alterations entry 114.3). These notes run from 113.31 to 114.32.

Emendations

101.7   expire.] ∼∧
103.37   unhesitating] unhestitating
105.21   also∧] ∼.
105.30   country] coutry

106.13   strikes] strike
106.29   ¹and] *om.*
108.2   disappointed] dissappointed
111.3   prophets] prohphets

Alterations in the Manuscripts

100.26   culture &] *intrl.*
100.27   500] *ab. del.* '1000 of'
100.29   wonderful] *ab. del.* 'so'
100.30   the] *aft. del.* 'an'
100.31   had] 'd' *ov.* 's'
100.31   that] *aft. del.* 'a t'
101.1   a] *bef. del.* 'p'
101.4–5   As . . . lecture.] *intrl.*
101.9   thing] *intrl.*
101.9   natural] *bef. del.* 'thing'
101.10   be] *bef. del.* 'the upshot of his experience of the worth of the profession.' *bef. del.* 'his practical'
101.16   ¹education∧] *comma del.*
101.18   three] *alt. fr.* 'the'
101.18   schools &] *intrl.*
101.18   popular] *aft. del.* 'edu'
101.19   pet] *aft. del.* 'darling'
101.19   panacea] *ab. del.* 'measure'
101.20   The] *aft. del.* 'Ed'
101.20   have] *aft. del.* 'were to be'; *bef. del.* 'always'
101.20–21   always . . . ¹to] *ab. del.* 'been [*undel. in error*] ['considered [*ab. del.* 'relied on'] ['to' *del.*] as our best' *del.*] relied on'
101.21   moral] *aft. del.* 'national'; *bef. del.* 'lief'
101.22   what is right,] *ab. del.* 'the better course,'
101.22   them] *bef. del.* 'reason straightly,'
101.22   and] *intrl.*

101.23   discontent] *ab. del. insrtd.* 'unhappiness'
101.23   of which evils] ('of' *aft. undel.* 'for'; *bef. del.* 'these evils'); *ab. del.* 'of which'
101.24   natural source.] *ab. del.* 'chief promoter.'
101.25   defects] *ab. del.* 'evils'
101.25   an] *ab. del.* 'the'
101.26   charged] *ab. del.* 'said'
101.32   popular instruction] *ab. del.* 'book learning'
101.33   our] *bef. del.* 'midst, that a survey'
101.34   of] *bef. del.* 'the facts is calculated to p'
101.35   moralizing] 'izing' *added*
101.36   but] *aft. del.* '(though negro-*hunting [*ab. del.* 'burning'] ['has' *del.*] as a great popular sport seems to have *revived) [*paren ov. comma*]'
101.38   find] *bef. del.* 'co' *ab. del.* 'univers'
101.39   both] *intrl.*
101.40   the] *intrl.*
102.3   either] *aft. del.* 'however'
102.4   that] *bef. del.* 'it [*undel. in error*] is a neccessar'
102.5   The] 'T' *ov.* 't'; *aft. del.* 'The editorial page of'
102.6   truth] *bef. del.* ', ha'
102.10   almost] *intrl.*
102.10   old] *bef. del. intrl.* 'shameless'

102.11 bravoes & panders] *intrl.*

102.11 whom] *ab. del.* 'of the'

102.11 supported to do] *ab. del.* 'who did'

102.11–12 & criminal] *intrl.*

102.12 work.] *bef. del.* 'for pay. They even glory in their shame'

102.12 glory] *aft. del.* 'do the'

102.13 For] 'F' *ov.* 'f'

102.13–14 Reason] 'R' *ov.* 'r'

102.14 invent] *ab. del.* 'find'

102.14 reasons] *aft. del. intrl.* 'good-sounding'

102.17 set forth] *intrl.*

102.18 instincts] *aft. del.* '['passion' *del.*] man's'

102.18 fixed] *ov.* 'set.'

102.19 father] *final* 's' *del.*

102.22 Look . . . war.] *intrl.*

102.22 has] *bef. del.* 'made me'

102.23–24 in . . . right.] *ab. del.* 'as our own Philippine way. In my eyes it has seemed war of conquest in the Philippines.'

102.25 an . . . enterprise.] *ab. del.* '['and' *del.*] an almost insane ['abandonment of *our*' *del.*] *a most blundering [*insrtd. bel.*] repudiation of our national Soul.'

102.28 spontaneous] *aft. del.* '*I can see in it only an almost insane [*ab. del.* 'a blundering'] adventure [*insrtd.*]. To crush out *the beginnings of a [*ab. del.* 'another'] national soul, to nip in the bud [*intrl.*] one of the most interesting experiments in the world's history, ['the promising beginning of a yellow' *del.*] the leading spirits of *an ['n' *added*] asiatic [*ab. del.* 'yellow'] race, to organize itself spontaneously, as Japan had already done, *according to [*ab. del.* 'on lines of'] western ideals'

102.28 effort] *ab. del.* 'attempt'

102.29 after] *ab. del.* 'on'

102.29 ideals.] *period alt. fr. comma bef. del. intrl.* '&'

102.29 We . . . doing] *ab. del.* 'to do'

102.29 all] *insrtd. for del.* 'no ['inher' *del. when* 'h' *crossed in error*] inherit'

102.30 no] *final* 't' *del.; bef. del.* 'fatal'

102.30 imperial] *intrl.*

102.31 England] *aft. del.* 'England'

102.32 doing] 'ing' *added; aft. del.* 'to'; *bef. del.* 'this by'

102.32–33 making . . . friends,] ('making ['ing' *added*]' *aft. del.* 'and' *ab. del.* 'to'; 'implacably' *intrl.*; 'already' *ab. del.* 'once'; 'beloved' *intrl.*); *tr. by guideline fr. aft.* 'revolution.' [102.35]

102.33 and] *bef. del.* 'lose'

102.34 spitting upon] (*aft. del.* 'in doing it to'; 'ting' *added*); *intrl.*

102.34 taking on] ('ing' *added*); *intrl.*

102.35 to execrate] *ab. del.* 'to boast *of [*undel. in error*]'

102.35 since . . . revolution.] ('own' *intrl.; period alt. fr. comma*); *ab. del.* 'in the bargain,'

102.35 All] 'A' *ov.* 'a'

102.36 makes] *ov.* 'seems'

102.36 it seem] *insrtd.*

102.36 as I said,] *intrl.*

102.36 insane] *bef. del.* 'piece of'

102.37 friends] *aft. del.* 'men'; *bef. del.* 'br'

102.37 own] *intrl.*

102.37 educated] *ab. del.* 'brought *up [*undel. in error*]'

102.37 in] *insrtd.*

102.37 liberalism] 'ism' *ov.* 's'

102.37–38 philanthropism] 'm' *ab. del.* 'ts'

102.38 abolitionism] 'ism' *ab. del.* 'ists'

102.38–103.1 men . . . it,] ('ex' *of* 'expected' *ov.* 'in'); *intrl.*

103.2 dictated by unmistakeable] *ab. del.* 'in accordance with unambiguous'

103.2–3 will . . . in] *ab. del.* 'return'

103.3 an . . . youth] ('youth' *aft. del.* 'birth'); *ab. del.* 'a second *youth [*ab. del.* 'birth']'

103.5 ¹as . . . right] *intrl.*

103.5 in] *bef. del.* 'an ['a' *ov.* 's'; 'n' *added*]'

103.5 issues] *final* 's' *added; ab. del.* 'matter'

103.5 simple] *aft. del.* 'big and'

103.5 these] *alt. fr.* 'this'

103.7 passion?] *bef. del.* '[*on fol.* 5]
*Passion for old american sentiment
on the one hand, for power & pride
& enlargement on the other? [*intrl.*]
And if so, *need* a nation full of PhD's
be anything more than a more
rottenly sophistical nation? Nobody
can live till 60 and not [*undel. fol.*
8ᵛ] have some of his youthful faiths
disappointed. It must be confessed'

103.7 in . . . is] ('the philippine' *ab.
del.* 'our own'); *ab. del.* 'is'

103.8 new responsibility] *ab. del.*
'pride'

103.9 certainly] *intrl.*

103.10 are] *bef. del.* 'more learned in
histor'

103.10 Harvard] *intrl.*

103.10 I] *aft. del.* 'I might myself be a
PhD. But'

103.10 a PhD, tho'] *ab. del.* 'one, but'

103.11 a] *ab. del.* 'all the'

103.12 and] *ab. del.* 'about the right.
Need it be anything but a more'

103.12–13 sophisticated] 'ted' *ov.* 'l';
bef. del. 'nation?' *bef. del.* 'crowd of
men.'

103.14 faiths] *aft. del.* 'ideal'

103.15–16 Yet . . . are] ('Yet,' *added*;
'Although' *not reduced in error*); *ab.
del.* 'Pessimism as to the moral value
of intellectual culture is ['a' *del.*]'

103.16 to . . . widely,] *ab. del.* 'it must
be confessed to be *such [*ab. del.*
'a rather'] widespread kind of
*pessimism, [*comma ov. period*]'

103.16 &] *intrl. bef.* 'Some' *not reduced
in error*

103.17 are] *ab. del.* 'have'

103.17 touched] *aft. del.* 'been'

103.17 their] *ab. del.* 'its'

103.17 wing,] *comma ov. period bef.
del.* 'And yet'

103.17–18 myself still] *intrl.*

103.18 give . . . them.] *ab. del.* 'abandon
*ourselves ['ves' *ov.* 'f'] to it.'

103.19 indeed] *aft. del.* 'we cannot'

103.19–20 we . . . in.] *insrtd. for del.*
'*give way [*ab. del.* 'commit ourselves'] to.'

103.20 But] *aft. del.* 'But in spite of
sober restriction I still think that'

103.20 when] *bef. del.* 'its'

103.20 the intellect's] *ab. del.* 'its'

103.22 Ph.D's . . . our] *insrtd. bel.*
'candidates' *del. in error*

103.24 customs,] *intrl.*

103.25 moral,] *comma added bef. del.*
'habits, its customs ob'

103.25 and these are] *ab. del.* 'its'

103.25 not . . . as] *intrl.*

103.26 blindly.] *period aft. del. comma*

103.26 They] *alt. fr.* 'these'; *aft. del.*
'and'

103.26 ²at] *ov.* 'in'

103.26 home] *final* 's' *del.*

103.27 clubs . . . at] *intrl.*

103.28 on] *aft. del.* 'and'

103.29 admires,] *ab. del.* 'trusts,'

103.29 calls &] *intrl.*

103.30 leaders,] *bef. del.* 'the kind of
action it will tolerate, and the kind
it will stop business for and take up
arms against,'

103.30–31 public] *intrl.*

103.31 it will] *ab. del.* 'it will tolerate
and wink at, these are the things
which make the health of nations,
and'

103.32 license] *ab. del.* 'action'

103.34 national] *ab. del.* 'public'

103.34 crazes] *aft. del.* 'hysteria'

103.34 can . . . it] *ab. del.* 'it [*undel.
in error*] is liable to'

103.35 that . . . it,] *bel. del.* 'it is not
liable to,'

103.36–37 because . . . and] ('its' *bef.
del.* 'impulses'); *ab. del.* 'and ['its'
del.] the *& [*insrtd. and undel. in
error*]'

103.38 such] *insrtd. bef. del.* 'and
criticize ['; an' *del.*] the'

103.38 one] *aft. del.* 'them'

103.39 ²is] *ov.* 'a'

104.1–2 , ²and . . . on,] *intrl.*

104.2 force] *aft. del.* 'function'

104.5 after] *intrl.*

104.5–6 too . . . upon] *ab.* 'on' *undel.
in error*

104.6 bird] *aft. del.* 'bird abandons her
young, but'

104.8 her.] *bef. del.* 'A small force *like this [*intrl.*]* if constant, will accumulate effects. Much greater forces if wayward, will *alternately undo [*ab. del.* 'neutralize'] each other. When a popular craze is going, it *may [*intrl.*]* sweep['s' *del.*] even ['the' *del.*] PhD's before it. Their critical poise *may [*ov.* 'is'] be [*insrtd.*]* lost for the moment. *When [*ov.* 'A'] one's personal *or corporate [*ab. del.* 'interests and'] passions are engaged on *the [*alt. fr.* 'one'] side *of some selfish interest [*intrl.*]* one's intellect plays readily the sophist.'

104.10 ¶ It] *orig. run on; line to indicate indention insrtd.*

104.13 intellect's] *intrl.*

104.14 sober.] *period alt. fr. comma*

104.14 But] 'B' *ov.* 'b'

104.15 evil] *aft. del.* 'mis'

104.15 its] *aft. del.* 'and the appeal is'

104.15 later] *intrl.*

104.16 unjustly] 'un' *added*

104.16 comes as a derisive] ('a' *bef. del. illeg.*); *ab. del.* 'is but a poor'

104.17 Dreyfuss] *aft. del.* 'Of what'

104.17 Filipino] *alt. fr.* 'Philippine'

104.17 patriots] *aft. del.* '*homes lie now [*ab. del.* 'Islands are dep'] desolated.'

104.18 under the sod.] *ab. del.* 'decimated.'

104.19 We . . . a] *ab. del.* 'As a present'

104.19 present] *intrl.*

104.20 present] *ab. del.* 'opposite'

104.20 of . . . sort ['are' *del.*]] *intrl.*

104.20 are] *aft. del.* ', [*undel. in error*] not intellectual judgments,'

104.21 we] *intrl.*

104.21 trust to.] *ab. del.* 'be relied on.'

104.21 all present] *ab. del.* 'the greater'

104.21 passions_∧] *comma del.*

104.22 revulsions,] *comma ov. period*

104.22 while Cortical] *ab. del.* 'Intellectual'

104.22 judgment,] *comma added*

104.22–23 on . . . hand,] *intrl.*

104.23 function.] *period added*

104.23 Now] *ab. del.* 'on the contrary [*comma del.*] and'

104.23 if] *bef. del.* 'co'

104.25 but] *intrl.*

104.25 one] *ab. del.* 'each'

104.26 another] 'an' *added*

104.27 our] *ab. del.* 'the'

104.27 interest] *ab. del.* 'or corporate p'

104.28 our] *ab. del.* 'ones'

104.28–29 for us,] *intrl.*

104.29 bird,] *comma ov. period*

104.29 and] *ab. del.* 'And'

104.29 face] *ab. del.* 'feel'

104.31 even] *ab. del.* 'then'

104.33 are] *bef. del.* 'usually'

104.33 often] *intrl.*

104.33 unwilling] *insrtd.*

104.35 most of] *ab. del.* 'all'

104.35 institutions] *aft. del.* 'orderly'

104.37 delaying] *aft. del.* 'evening out' *ab. del.* 'levelling down and ['making modi' *del.*] minimizing the disturbances which would ['be' *del.*] get by'

104.37 disturbance.] *bef. del.* | 'If this be so, the'

104.38 then,] *ab. del.* 'that'

104.38 mission] *ab. del.* 'function'

104.38 ²the] *ov.* 'an'

104.38 society_∧] *comma del.*

104.39 to] *ab. del.* 'that of'

104.39 find] *final* 'ing' *del.*

104.39 invent] *final* 'ing' *del.*; *bef. del.* 'argumen'

104.39 for] *bef. del.* 'the'

104.39 demands] *ab. del.* 'needs'

104.40 small, but incessant] *intrl.*

105.1 because . . . forgets] *intrl.*

105.1–2 of . . . and] *ab. del.* 'and puts thin'

105.2 proper] *intrl.*

105.2 scale] *aft. del.* 'relative'

105.4 motive] *ab. del.* 'one'

105.4 and neutral] *ab. del.* 'unsympathetic'

105.4 attitude] *aft. del.* 'wears' *ab. del.* 'and and superior'

105.4–5 sometimes ['it' *del.*] . . . it] *ab. del.* 'is, it'

105.5–6 a . . . generally] *intrl.*

105.6 critic] *ab. del.* 'man,'

105.7 of] *intrl.*

105.7 partisan] *ab. del.* 'bystander'

105.8 have] *aft. del.* 'be'

105.8 of] *bef. del.* '['re' *del.*] moral reptile'

105.8 bore and] *intrl.*

105.9 Those] *aft. del.* '['He' *del.*] The'; *line to indicate indention insrtd.*

105.9 history] 'i' *ov.* 'y'

105.9 abolitionists,] *aft. del.* '['abolitio' *del.*] earliest'; *bef. del.* 'th'

105.10 were] *aft. del.* 'wh'

105.10 called‸] *comma del.*

105.11 etc.,] *intrl.*

105.12 corporeal] *ab. del.* 'physical'

105.12 Living . . . indeed] ('Living' *insrtd. bef.* 'Mugwumps [*not reduced in error*]' *insrtd. bef. del.* 'They'); *insrtd. bel. del.* '['Yet, if you wish to inherit' *del.*] It *is* a much'

105.13 members] *aft. del.* 'do the'

105.14 first] *aft. del.* 'honored'

105.18 intellectual] *ab. del.* 'man'

105.18 onlooker] *aft. del.* 'harder *row to hoe [*ab. del.* 'places ['s' *added*] to fill'] in society than do the members of *any of [*intrl.*] the regular ['partisan' *del.*] organizations. ['Oscar Wilde' *del.*] Often [*intrl.*] their ['t' *ov.* 'T'] only [*intrl.*] audience is posterity, ['and' *del.*] their names *are honored [*ab. del.* 'flourish'] only when the *breath is out of [*ab. del.* 'worms feast on'] their bodies, *and like the holders of insurance policies they must die to win. [*intrl.*] Oscar Wilde, *once, [*intrl.*] extolling the intellectual'

105.18 said] *aft. del.* 'once'

105.19 The] 'T' *ov.* 't'; *aft. del.* 'But'

105.20 of . . . always] *ab. del.* 'not only'

105.20 write] *final* 's' *del.*

105.20–21 sometimes] *intrl.*

105.21 even . . . it] *ab. del.* 'very'

105.21 slowly.] *period added bef. del.* '*it is true yet [*ab. del.* 'but'] very surely.'

105.22 truth] *intrl. bef. del.* 'right' *ab. del.* 'truth'

105.22 small] *ab. del.* 'modest'

105.22 his] *alt. fr.* 'he'

105.22 strength] *intrl.*

105.23 at the moment,] *ab. del.* 'at his own moment,'

105.23 for] *ab. del.* 'and'

105.23 ['though' *del.*] insensible] *ab. del.* 'endless'

105.25 are] *bef. del.* 'then'

105.27 then] *intrl.*

105.28 possibly] *insrtd.*

105.28 somewhat] *aft. del.* 'a'

105.28 places] 's' *added*

105.28 this] *alt. fr.* 'the'

105.29 stand . . . of] *ab. del.* 'even out the scales of truth by not following'

105.29 even] *intrl.*

105.30 time, and country,] *ab. del.* 'century'

105.32 names] *ab. del.* 'is,'

105.32 ¹as] 's' *added*

105.32–33 fine . . . any ['to a' *del.*]] *ab. del.* '['patent of nobility' *del.*] ['noble title and a noble band to rally to' *del.*] noble society to ['as any' *del.*]'

105.33 be] *alt. fr.* 'become'

105.34 truth] *aft. del.* 'reason to w'

105.35 an American] *ab. del.* 'a man'

105.37 the sake of] *intrl.*

105.38 envious] *intrl.*

105.38 at] *aft. del.* 'and *growling [*ab. del.* 'yelping'] which in every co'

105.39–40 unless . . . intellectuals] ('unless' *aft. del.* 'unless it be the'); *intrl.*

105.40 see] *final* 's' *del.*

105.40 all] *intrl.*

105.40 proportions?] *qst. mk. added bef. del.* 'save these intellectuals? Every'

106.1 day‸] *comma del.*

106.2 weak] *ab. del.* 'slight'

106.2 to be] *intrl.*

106.4 is] *intrl. bef. del.* 'looks' *ab. del.* 'was'

106.5 transient] *intrl.*

106.6 turns away from] *ab. del.* 'is [*undel. in error*] opposed in ways ['opposed to' *del.*]'

106.6 some of] *intrl.*

106.6 ideals] *ab. del.* 'notions'

106.7 us] *intrl.*

106.7 never] *aft. del.* 'do not'

106.8 imitated] *aft. del.* 'ca'

106.10 appear isolated.] *ab. del.* 'be alone.'

106.10 idol] *aft. del.* 'ideal'

106.12 and] *aft. del.* 'and as the test of every good is the willingness of men to pay for it, it has come about that the only proof that'

106.12 always] *ab. del.* 'th'

106.14 as big] *intrl.*

106.14 may indeed] *ab. del.* 'can'

106.15 when . . . it,] *intrl.*

106.16 in] *ov.* 'a'

106.16–17 contemptuous] *intrl.*

106.17 street,] *insrtd. for del.* 'time,'

106.17 ⋏not] *db. qt. del.*

106.18 tide] *aft. del.* 'pre'

106.21 with] *bef. del.* 'goods,'

106.21 bric a brac] *ab. del.* 'burdens'

106.21 responsibilities,] *bef. del.* 'all undertaken to be like'

106.22 a] *intrl.*

106.22 like] *ab. del.* 'like'

106.23 correct . . . eyes,] *intrl.*

106.23 mean,] *intrl.*

106.25 created.] *ab. del.* 'ever born.'

106.26–27 If . . . happier;] *insrtd. for del. intrl.* '& happier'

106.28 the idol . . . tribe,] *intrl.*

106.28–29 both accomplices] *intrl.*

106.29 blindly⋏] *comma del.; aft. del.* 'obeyed'

106.29 the] *aft. del.* 'the herd' *ab. del.* '['the' *del.*] instead of setting an ['an' *del.*]'

106.29 herd] *bef. del.* 'instead of'

106.29–30 ²and . . . ¹of] *insrtd.*

106.31 Ruskin] 'R' *ov.* 'r'

106.34 only] *aft. del.* ', that'

106.34 lights] 'l' *ov.* 'r'

106.37 smeared all over] *ab. del.* 'in the midst of precept'

106.39 ripe] *ab. del.* 'sure'

107.2 intellectual] *bef. del.* 'f'

107.4 now] *intrl.*

107.4 without] *alt. fr.* 'with out'

107.6 must] *bef. del.* 'go in for smaller *worldly [intrl.] successes, of the mast and'

107.9 vitality.] *bef. del.* | 'One more word, since I am giving advice. Don't you, as intellectual men and women, care too much for academic distinctions. I hear Radcliffe in agony . . . ['They produce along with' *del.*] Stimulus to learning, but incidental

evils. Years wasted. failure. psychopaths. Inoculation of all america with mandarin ideas. Bad as Germany or Britain. | ['The university st' *del.*] ['The man's the man for a th' *del.*] Instructorships. | Every one who refuses to take it, every college who refuses to demand it, deserves well of our country. | Contemptible to go round asking ['for' *del.*] to be stamped. *A [*ov.* 'T'] man's a man for a' that.'

107.21 Recently] 'R' *ov.* 'r'

107.25 Corporation] 'C' *ov.* 'S'

107.30 for] *bef. del.* 'instincts'

107.30 ends] 'e' *ov.* 'd'

107.30 . . .] *intrl.*

108.3 expect] *aft. del.* '['ha' *del.*] am'

108.3 but] *aft. del.* 'I se'

108.20 blow] *aft. del.* 'co'

109.8–9 normal . . . values] *intrl. to right of these two lines is del.* '"liberal"'

109.11 bore] *bef. del.* | '[*short rule*] les intellectuels. | posterity! [*short rule*]'

109.17 Liberal] *aft. del.* 'Be judges *Know ['K' *ov.* 'D'] difference. | Discern gold from brass. | ['Women' *del.*] | ['Prophets' *del.*] Point out true prophets. Support the⟨m⟩. | Carry to extreme, you have' |

109.35 blindly.] *bef. del.* rule and 'Customs change'

110.14 condemnation] *aft. del.* 'Constant force'; *bef. del.* | 'quiet'

110.19 justice.] *bef. del.* 'So many inte | hot—cold. mugwump'

110.35 anchor.] *bef. del.* 'Yet critical intellect does work'

111.1 B] *intrl.*

111.2 Kipling.] *insrtd.*

111.10 order.] *on the verso of this folded sheet is written vert.* 'expectation—failure [*period del.*] [*vert. stroke*] serves individual [*vert. stroke*]'

111.11 Brooks] 'B' *ov.* 'C'

111.14 The] *aft. del.* 'Sin'

111.17 about your profession.] *intrl.*

111.18 the] *bef. del.* 'extr'

111.18 One] *aft. del.* '['The go-betweens . . . .' *del.*] Commerce the go between but we also on a higher'

111.20   where.] *bef. del.* 'I find this institution individualistic.'

111.22   This] *aft. del.* 'Prem'

111.23   in] *bef. del.* 'such'

111.23   encouraged.] *bef. del. intrl.* 'Contrast with teacher-class'

111.29   not art as such] *intrl.*

111.31   To] *intrl. bef.* 'Imitate' *not reduced in error*

111.35   our] *bef. del.* 'profession.'

112.6   Academic] *aft. del.* 'Lotze' |

112.10   Claimed] 'C' *ov.* 'A'

112.15   We] *aft. del.* 'Small systems'

112.18   worthwhile.] *bef. del.* | 'Compare British. | Big systems always unjust'

112.19   I . . . etc] *insrtd.*

112.23   small] *alt. fr.* 'samall'

112.25   fortunate . . . their] *ab. del.* 'endowed with the power of making their'

112.25   These] *bef. del.* 'contagious'

112.28   Butler] *intrl.*

112.28   Bryan.] *intrl.*

112.28   stand] *ab. del.* 'stood'

112.28   are] *ab. del.* 'were'

112.29   make] *alt. fr.* 'made'

112.30   great] *intrl.*

112.30–31   a . . . . It] ('temporarily' *intrl.*); *ab. del.* 'it'

112.32   with] *del.* 'me' *in left mrgn.*

112.35   crowd.] *ab. del.* 'party.'

112.35   The] *aft. del.* 'These'

112.35   who,] *comma added bef. del.* 'can effectively'

112.35   appealing] 'ing' *added*

112.35   can] *aft. del.* 'is a great man'

112.36   certainly] *intrl.*

112.36   for that occasion.] *ab. del.* 'in his way.'

112.37   are] *bef. del.* 'always two'

112.37   in] *bef. del.* 'the'

112.38   nation:] *bef. del.* 'the party of instinct and the party of reason.'

112.39   fun, excitement, ['& violence &' *del.*]] *ab. del.* 'brute force and'

113.1   reason,] *bef. del.* '['tolerance' *del.*] order,'

113.1   order . . . by] *insrtd. for del.* '['gradual growth,' *del.*] compromise, ['gra-' | *del.*] gra[*insrtd.*]dual'

113.1   2and] *bef. del.* 'toleration. One favors'

113.2   force] *ab. del.* 'violence'

113.4   nor] *ab. del.* 'and you'

113.4   can] *alt. fr.* 'can't'

113.4   2you] *insrtd.*

113.5   tendencies_∧] *comma del.*

113.5   wholesale,] *intrl.*

113.5   play] *final* 'ed' *del.; aft. del.* 'have'

113.5   a] *ab. del.* 'an essential'

113.6   that is indispensable.] *ab. del. period*

113.6   now it is] *ab. del.* 'wildness'

113.7   from] *ab. del.* 'for'

113.7   reign . . . jingo,] *insrtd. for del.* 'jingo party,' *ab. del.* 'good of one time,'

113.7   now] *intrl.*

113.8   from] *insrtd.*

113.8   ['that' *del.*] the . . . moderation,] (*comma ov. period*); *insrtd. for del.* 'the other' *ab. del.* 'for that of another.'

113.8–9   and . . . direction.] ('oscillating [*alt. fr.* 'oscillation']' *aft. del.* 'alternate' *and bef. del.* 'alternat'); *written on facing verso, position in text indicated by asterisks*

113.10   in any country] *intrl.*

113.11–12   when . . . and] ('as' *aft. del.* 'and'); *insrtd. for del.* 'and between them'

113.13   millstone] *bef. del.* 'unless it gets a magnetic leader.'

113.13   it] *aft. del.* 'they'

113.13   has] *alt. fr.* 'have'

113.13   no] *ab. del.* 'a'

113.14   they] *aft. del.* 'it is without one.'

113.15   speed &] *intrl.*

113.15   Over . . . again] *ab. del.* 'Sometimes'

113.15   generations get into] *aft. del.* 'things [*undel. in error*] *get to [*ab. del.* 'are at']'

113.16   in the dam] *intrl.*

113.17   A] *ov.* 'a'; *intrl. aft. del.* 'Where' *ab. del.* '['But' *del.*] A'

113.17   makes] 's' *added; aft. del.* 'will'; *bef. del.* 'a whole where'

113.18   where] *ab. del.* 'where'

113.18   a] *ab. del.* 'a mass with a vastly'

113.19 But] *intrl. bef.* 'Occasionally'
not reduced in error

113.19–20 with . . . bullet] ('vis' *aft. del.*
'rifle'); *ab. del.* 'rises ['who' *del.*]
with the rifle-bullet speed but with
liberal aims and *ambitions [*ab. del.*
'purposes']'

113.20 may] *ab. del.* 'is apt to'

113.21 Bismarck,] *comma ov. period
bef. del.* 'In any case, happy is the
country ['of whose liberal whist' *del.*]
whose liberals can use'

113.21 like] *bef. del.* 'the two'

113.22 that . . . to] *insrtd. for del.*
'that ['can ['be' *del.*] use such m'
del.] is [*insrtd.*] ['wise en' *del.*]
"educated" enough to'

113.22 men] *bef. del.* 'without being
victimized by'

113.23 to] *insrtd.*

113.23 country] *intrl.*

113.24 educated] *final* 'ed' *ov.* 'ion'; *aft.
del.* 'national'

113.24 But] *aft. del.* 'The endemic
disease of public opinion is liability
to infection by ['false heroes' *del.*]
cheap heroes and false leaders. ['Who'
del.] Every generation forgets his'

113.25 Heaven] 'H' *ov.* 'I'

113.26 assemblages . . . politics] *ab.
del.* 'political organisms'

113.28 Great . . . crises] *aft. del.* 'Along
the whole'; *bef. del.* 'are ['always led
up to by long growth towards them.'
del.] ['How' *del.*] ['Which of us can

enumerate all the steps that to day'
del.] *led up to [*insrtd. for del.*
'determined'] by a long chain of
causes that have made the tone of
the country.'

113.28 us] *insrtd. for del.* 'the country'

113.29 we . . . or] *ab. del.* 'are [*insrtd.
for del.* 'shall be'] met'

113.30 unsuccessfully] 'un' *added*

114.3 community.] *bef. del.* | 'That is
the training school of character. | The
tone of every nation results from a
long historic sequence of causes. | It
is taught far, *far*, less in schools and
colleges *than ['n' *ov.* 't'] at home
and in the streets. It defines itself by,
etc. [*space*] | It is of this general tone
that I want to say a few words. It is
here that education means the ability
to know a good man when you see
him. It *can [*ab. del.* 'should'] *mean
nothing [*intrl.*] else! For how are
these tones ['grad' *del.*] historically
built up? By nothing but the *setting
of fashions and patterns* by individuals'

114.4 crises.] *bef. del.* | 'France—
Germany— [*vert. stroke*] Russia—
Japan'

114.8 Habits,] *insrtd. bef.* 'Catchwords'
not reduced in error

114.9 abuses,] *insrtd.*

114.13 reflection.] *bef. del.* | 'spirit—
tameness'

II. Courses

8. FRAGMENTS OF EARLY COURSES 1875–1885 #4415, #4393

The first part of #4415 consists of eight leaves in folds or separately torn from
a sheet of laid unwatermarked paper 12½ x 8¾", the leaves written on rectos
and versos. The (a) section on Reasoning (117.3–119.10) takes up three leaves,
a fold and a single leaf. The (b) section consists of two folds, or four leaves,
of the same paper plus a single leaf. The text of the first two pages ('Find . . .

everywhere' 119.12–35) is written on the rectos of the first fold and is continued written vertically on the respective versos ('2) or to . . . biscuit etc' 119.35–120.27), and continued further on the recto of the first leaf of the second fold ('we shall . . . however.' 120.27–121.2). The text then goes to the recto of the second leaf in the fold ('A similar . . . concluded that' 121.3–19), continues on the verso of the first leaf ('this concrete . . . knowledge' 121.19–31) and concludes on the verso of the second ('goes . . . goes.' 121.31–32). On this verso, turned, at its original top, is written a note in pencil, 'Describe elephants fore-limb. ['Who' *del*.]'. The separate leaf (c), headed 'Syllogism', underlined, is written vertically on the recto, the verso blank, of a single leaf of a torn-apart sheet.

The next item (122.25–123.19) is a sheet of laid unwatermarked paper 10 x 7¾" dittographed from typed capitals, corrected and revised in black ink, with a few words underlined in red crayon for emphasis. The heading used here is written on the verso in black ink, the sheet turned lengthwise as if the heading were to be the recto of the first leaf of a fold. The typing ends with 'ESSENCE THAN M.' (123.11) at the foot of the recto, the text then being continued written vertically in the left margin in black ink ('But . . . judgment.' 123.11–14). The final paragraph is written in the same ink on the left side of the turned verso as if it would have been the verso of the second leaf of a fold.

Section (d) (123.21–28) is written in black ink on the recto of a single leaf (verso blank) torn in half from what would have been a full sheet 12½ x 8¾" of light-blue laid paper unwatermarked.

This assemblage of notes is completed with #4393 headed 'Aesthetics.', starting with the same unwatermarked light-blue laid paper 12½ x 8¾" as the last leaf in section (d) above, arranged in folds and single leaves written in pencil and in black ink. The first part ('Aesthetics . . . experience.' 123.29–125.10) consists of a fold and two single leaves. The text of the first single leaf (124.30–40), headed 'Aesthetics.', underlined, in the upper right corner, is written in pencil on recto and verso. The text of the second leaf (125.1–10), again headed 'Aesthetics.', underlined, in the upper right corner, is written in pencil on the recto only. The second part (125.11–126.8) has a title page on which is written 'Aesthetics', underlined, and the ink text, on rectos only (with the title repeated on the first recto), is on a laid white unwatermarked paper, in a fold of two leaves and a single leaf, written in ink on recto and verso, made from sheets measuring 12½ x 8¾". 'Authoritativeness . . . &c.' (125.33–35) is inscribed in Alice's hand. A single leaf of white wove paper, watermarked LINEN LEDGER, written on recto and verso and numbered 77 on the verso, is of a much later date and is not included in the present edition.

Emendations

117.27 "Rubbish."] "~·ᴀ
119.15 -evaporation)] -~ᴀ

120.19 , grease,] ᴀ~ᴀ
123.34 nonsensical,] ~ᴀ

Alterations in the Manuscripts

[*begin* MS]
117.6 sensation] *final* 's' *del.*
117.7 concept or] *intrl.*
117.12 reasoning.] *bef. del.* 'Transformation of'

117.12 In . . . study] *insrtd. for del.*
  ' "Notice." Inner field of view & point of sight.'
117.22 -existence] *ab. del.* 'sence'
117.24 matrix] *ab. del.* 'notice'

117.26 "Foreign stuff"] *intrl.*
117.27 "Experiment failed."] *intrl.*
117.27 vs] *intrl.*
117.29 in florence.] *intrl.*
118.1 in] *aft. del.* 'by di'
118.8 in] *aft. del.* 'in'
118.34 Reasoning] 'R' *ov.* 'r'
118.35 given] *bef. del.* 'connex'
118.35 connexion] *bef. del.* '—theoretic R'
119.1 word,] *comma tr. by guideline fr. aft.* 'we'
119.5 With] 'W' *ov.* 'In'
119.15 solution‸] *closing paren del.*
119.22 principle. It] *period added;* 'It'.*ab. del.* 'which'
119.30 coupling] *bef. del.* 'w'
120.5 either one] *ab. del.* 'each'
120.5 may] *bef. del.* 'on occasion'
120.9 marks] *aft. del.* 'spots;'
120.10 indelible ink] *ab. del.* 'a photographers hands'
120.10 In] *aft. del.* 'In each of the'
120.11 that . . . say] *intrl.*
120.12 rejection] *aft. del.* 'need of some remedy or the'; *bef. del.* 'by a purchaser, say,'
120.13 article.] *bef. del.* 'But as regards'
120.13 all] *alt. fr.* 'also'; *bef. del.* 'th'
120.14 cases] *intrl.; caret aft. comma in error*
120.19 grease] *intrl.*
120.23 this] *alt. fr.* 'these'
120.23 jar be] *ab. del.* 'sweetmeats are'
120.27 ¹be] 'b' *ov.* 'w'
120.31 though] *final* 't' *del.*
120.32 tasting] *bef. del.* 'food"'
120.34 its] *alt. fr.* 'is'
120.35 latter] *aft. del.* 'raison'
120.39 mould] *bef. del.* 'from [*undel. in error*] sealing'
121.1 Retention] *aft. del.* 'Prevention of dr'
121.4 spoils] *ab. del.* 'destroys'
121.6 syrup] *aft. del.* 'wine, or'
121.11 argentic] 'a' *ov.* 'n'
121.13 any] *insrtd. for del.* 'the'
121.16 thought] 'ou' *ov.* 'at'
121.17 insensibility] *ab. del.* 'sleep'
121.27 terms] *ab. del.* 'consequents'

121.31 they] 'ey' *ov.* 'at'; *bef. del.* 'cannot'
122.19 Mill's] *intrl.*
122.20 to] *intrl.*
[*end MS; begin TMs*]
122.28 is] *intrl.*
122.34 as] *bef. del.* 'individuals, but as'
122.35–37 (that . . . name,)] *parens added*
122.35 "all things"] 's' *added; db. qts. added*
122.36,38 M,] *intrl.*
123.2 M.] *intrl.*
123.2 premiss] *ab. del.* 'term'
123.5 M,] *comma added*
123.6 the] *ab. del.* 'Rome'
123.7 them] *ab. del.* 'A, B, & C, & *S [*undel. in error*]'
[*end TMs; begin MS*]
123.19 there] 're' *ov.* 'se'
123.22,23 nervous] *ab. del.* 'physical'
123.23–24 1 . . . 2 . . . 3 . . . 4] *each intrl.*
123.23 outward] *intrl.*
123.24 ¹its] *insrtd. bef.* '3' *in error*
123.24 nervous] *aft. del.* 'phy'
123.25 Each] 'E' *ov.* 'C'
123.25 & 4] *intrl. bef.* 'covers' *not alt. in error*
123.26 intensities] 'ies' *ov.* 'y'
123.30–124.6 Influence . . . body.] *penc.*
123.32 has] *ov.* 'as'
123.32 matters,] *bef. del.* 'according to one school'
123.34 nonsensical] 'no' *ov. poss.* 'cu'
124.3 Pleasure] 'P' *ov.* 'O'; *aft. del.* 'Habit' |
124.7 habit] *aft. del.* 'repetition'
124.7 aesthetic] *aft. del.* 'effect'
124.9 uneasiness] *aft. del.* 'distress,'
124.14 strong] *intrl.*
124.16 positively] *intrl.*
124.21 The] *aft. del.* 'Hunger, w'
124.21 warmth] *aft. del.* 'clot[*start of* 'h']'
124.22 air] *aft. del.* 'bre'
124.22 organized] *aft. del.* 'cre'
124.24–25 a particular] *intrl.*
124.28 bladder] *aft. del. poss.* 'various'
124.28 rises] *aft. del.* 'is'
124.30–125.10 The question . . . experience.] *penc.*

124.31 powers] *ab. del.* 'denominations'	125.12 nerve] *aft. del.* 'a'
124.32 on] *ov.* 'of'	125.14 they] *alt. fr.* 'their'
124.32 plane] *ab. del.* 'denomination'	125.28–29 veils & smothers] ('ve' *ov.*
124.35 and] *aft. del.* '&c &c'	'ma'); *tr. fr.* 'smothers & veils'
125.9 formal] *insrtd.*	125.36–37 Ennui ... change—] *penc.*
125.10 experience.] *bef. del.* | 'The	126.4 an] *aft. del.* 'one'
question whether'	[*end* MS]

9. NOTES FOR NATURAL HISTORY 2: PHYSIOLOGICAL PSYCHOLOGY 1876–1877 #4490

Two sheets of white laid unwatermarked paper 12½ x 8¾″, made into two folds of two leaves, plus a single sheet of the same paper, cut in half, measuring 6¼ x 8¾″ constitute #4490. The text is written on rectos and versos (except for the single sheet whose verso is blank) in black ink. The pages are unnumbered but the recto of the first leaf of the second fold is numbered 2. James's brackets are found at 129.6–16 '[Substantialists . . . say]'.

Emendations

126.27 sensation] sensa- |	128.19 farther] father
127.37 Nor] No	

Alterations in the Manuscript

126.12 This] 'T' *ov.* 't'; *aft. del.* 'In'	128.22 in all cases] *intrl.*
126.19 truth] *aft. del.* 'th'	128.24 ¹as] *intrl.*
126.21 explains] *bef. del.* ', [*undel. in error*] or assigns'	128.27 precipitated out] *intrl.*
	128.28 sensation] *bef. del.* ', either'
126.26 at] 't' *ov.* 'n'	128.29 reduce] *final* 's' *del.*
126.27 the] *intrl.*	128.29 &] *ov.* 'or'
126.27 possess. For] *period ov. comma;* 'For' *ab. del.* 'as'	128.30–31 (and ... truth.)] *parens added*
126.28 is] *aft. del.* 'show'	128.30 counted] *intrl.*
127.5 in] *aft. del.* 'whilst'	128.31 facts &] *insrtd.*
127.10 succession,] *comma added bef. del.* 'of'	128.32 is] *ab. partially del. comma*
	128.33 2&] *intrl.*
127.17 flickering] 'f' *ov.* 'n'	128.37 ignores] *aft. del.* 'wholly'
127.20 namely] *bef. del.* 'constancy'	128.38 relates] *aft. del.* 'the phenom-
127.26 ²the] 't' *ov.* 'e'	enal facts about our actual'
127.35 our] *aft. del.* 'of'	129.1 prevents] *ab. del.* 'deprives'
127.38 do] *final* 'es' *del.*	129.2 from] *aft. del.* 'of the chara'
127.39 make] *final* 's' *del.*	129.6 things?] *bef. del.* 'Scrutiny re-
128.1 is given to] *ab. del.* 'lies with'	duces them to groups of'
128.2 lie] *final* 's' *del.*	129.11 know] *aft. del.* 'truly'
128.7 Such] *aft. del.* 'Helmholtz's discoveries have'	129.11 like] *aft. del.* 'known'
	129.17 ¹its] *bef. del.* 'outward'
128.8 that] *bef. del.* 'we overlo'	129.20 had] *aft. del.* 'was related'
128.13 are,] *comma added*	129.23 analysis] ²'a' *ov.* 'y'
128.14 reveal] *final* 'ed' *del.*	129.24 particular] *intrl.*

10. Notes for Philosophy 4: Psychology 1878–1879 #4494, #4493, #4491

Manuscript #4494 is written on sheets of laid unwatermarked paper 12½ x 8¾″ in folds of two leaves, inscribed rectos and versos. The first fold (129.28–130.34), written in black ink is headed '*Spencer's Psych. [*underl.*] i. 146'. The second fold continues, headed '*Spencer's Psych. p. 158', followed by a short rule, and concludes with a third fold headed 'Spencer's ['Sp' *ov.* 'Co'] Psych p. 158. (2)' (130.35–133.7), its last verso blank. The next part (133.8–135.12) is written in blue-black ink on a single leaf and then a fold of the same paper, paged top center 1–6. The last part of the final sentence is written vertically in the left margin of the last page to squeeze in the text on the verso of the fold's second leaf. #4494 concludes with a single leaf of the same paper. The text begins on the verso (as the leaf is now positioned) ('Picture . . . genesis of' 135.13–26), the number 11 (or possibly 1 L) centered, written in light ink. The text continues with one line on the recto ('C. . . . 560' 135.26–27). Below this line of text James drew a line across the page in black ink and wrote 'To sum . . . ideal.' (135.28–38) in the same black ink.

Almost all of #4493 is in Alice's hand. James wrote the heading 'Spencer's "Law of Intelligence" ', followed by a short rule, on the first recto and on its verso, numbered 1, began the text (136.2–7). Alice took over on the next recto, paged 2 (136.8), and continued to the end with some additions and revisions in James's hand. Starting with p. 3 James himself numbered the pages of Alice's text, omitting 4–5, up to 9. After p. 9 two leaves are inserted paged 9a–d (138.3–37). Pagination resumes with 10 and continues to the recto p. 14. On the lower half of p. 13, below a line drawn across the page, 'C . . . *regulates.*' (139.28–39) is in James's hand. Pages 15–19 are unnumbered. On the recto of the final leaf James wrote the last line in pencil (141.3). The verso (141.4–18) is in Alice's hand.

Manuscript #4491 contains two sets of quired folds of laid unwatermarked paper 8¾ x 6¼″, written on rectos and versos. On the recto of the outermost page Alice wrote the title, 'Spencer's Chapter on the Assumptions of Metaphysicians.', and on the verso James wrote an introductory statement (141.20–33), probably after the text, in Alice's hand, had been completed as evidenced by the last six words written vertically in the right margin. The second leaf of the fold is blank, recto and verso, and serves as the back cover. The text begins on the recto of the next leaf and is numbered roman I (centered) by Alice who numbered every other leaf (I–IV). Starting with the fourth page someone, perhaps James (?), inserted D in the upper right or left corner of each page, except for the tenth and the last. The text of the manuscript ends with four lines ('sense . . . sensations.' 145.40–146.2) on the last verso, a part-page. Below a white space James added 146.3–5.

Emendations

130.1   judgment] judment
130.35   Fragments] Fragment's
133.1   considered] considerered
133.3   pleasurable] pleasureable
133.36   revelation,"] ~.∧
[*begin* Alice James *hand*]
136.25   as] a

138.38   Monthly] Monthy
[*end* Alice James *hand*]
141.21   chapters] chapter's
141.22   times] & times
[*begin* Alice James *hand*]
144.20   procedure] proceedure
[*end* Alice James *hand*]

Psychology

Alterations in the Manuscripts

129.30 of] *aft. del.* 'of'
130.1 their] *ab. del.* 'such a'
130.1 implies] *bef. del.* 'the no'
130.1–2,4 that they have] *intrl.*
130.3 is] *alt. fr.* 'it'
130.4 or more *real*] *intrl.*
130.7 them] *bef. del.* 'thus'
130.14 unifier] *bef. del.* 'of'
130.16 from] *intrl.*
130.20 *such,*] *bef. del.* 'as'
130.22 but] *ov.* '&'
130.22 particular] *intrl.*
130.23 on] *alt. fr.* 'in'
130.23 a] *ab. del.* 'the'
130.26 there] *alt. fr.* 'this'
130.27 Then] *ab. del.* 'For'
130.28 or . . . act] *intrl.*
130.29 must] *aft. del.* 'must) [paren undel. in error]'
130.30 argument] *intrl.*
130.31 If] *insrtd. bef.* 'on ['o' *ov.* 'O']'
130.33 it] *final* 'self' *del.*
130.36 the] *ov.* 'con'
130.36–37 consciousness] *bef. del.* 'of nerve'
131.1 psychic] *aft. del.* '['the' *del.*] the tremors'
131.4 or nervous system] *intrl.*
131.5 The] *aft. del.* 'What the brain's movements are conscious of is, whatever it may be, not themselves.'
131.9 intelligence] *alt. fr.* 'intelligent'
131.14 The] *final* 'y' *del.*
131.16 as] *intrl.*
131.17 as . . . &c] *intrl.*
131.19 to] *ov.* 'be'
131.20 i.e] *aft. del.* 'It'
131.20 anteriority] 'an' *ab. del.* 'pos'
131.21 anteriority] 'an' *ov.* 'pos'
131.21–22 supporting] *bef. del.* 'to one to that w'
131.22 first] *aft. del.* 'tho't'
131.28 with] *bef. del.* 'or revel'
131.29 representation] *aft. del.* 'brain'
131.31 there] *alt. fr.* 'their'
131.34 cologne] *aft. del.* 'putrid flesh is not'
131.37 existing] *aft. del.* 'that'
132.7 changes] *ov.* 'nerv'
132.9 pleasure] *aft. del.* 'feeling'

132.9 also] *aft. del.* 'should'
132.15 an] *ab. del.* 'our'
132.15 judgment] *final* 's' *del.*
132.18 judgment] *aft. del.* 'the'
132.20 some] *insrtd. for del.* 'much greater'
132.20 propriety.] *period added*
132.20 Not so] *ab. del.* 'than'
132.20 pure] 'p' *ov.* 's'
132.21 cognitions,] *comma ov. period bef. del.* 'may claim to replace the *outward events [ab. del.* 'matter'] consciously cognized.' *bef.* 'For' *not reduced in error*
132.21 that] *alt. fr.* 'they'
132.21 logical] *intrl.*
132.22 latter.] *ab. del.* 'former.'
132.25 conclusion] *aft. del.* 'given'
132.29 by] *intrl.*
132.30 conscious] *intrl.*
132.32 uses] *bef. del.* '(as morality to social approbation)'
132.37 Pleasure] *bef. del.* 'itself'
133.1 by it, a world] *ab. del.* 'a life'
133.1 still] *intrl.*
133.13 cognizing just] *intrl.*
133.13 these] 'se' *added*
133.20 Existence] *ov.* 'The'
133.22 *et seq. similar* R] *db. underl.*
133.22 sensibiles] *ab. del.* 'intelligibiles'
133.25 of] *intrl.*
133.27 2I] *aft. del.* 'But'
133.29 truth] *alt. fr.* 'true'
133.30 at least] *intrl.*
133.30–31 *existence* in] *intrl.*
133.37 Real] *aft. del.* 'truth'
133.37 simply] *intrl.*
133.38 true] *intrl.*
133.38 &] *ab. del.* 'but no'
134.4 psychogenetic] *alt. fr.* 'psychogenesis.'
[*begin Alice James hand*]
134.15 an] 'n' *added*
134.15 inseparable] *intrl.; orig. intrl. bef.* 'aspects'
134.15 Phenomenon] 'P' *ov.* 'p'
[*end Alice James hand*]
134.16 some] *aft. del.* 'all o'
134.26 "outer] *aft. del.* 'physical'

134.30 subjective Idealism] *ab. del.*
'Hegelism'

134.37 & coequals] *intrl.*

134.40 also?] *intrl.*

135.1 this] *aft. del.* 'then'

135.9 for] *ov.* 'by'

135.10–12 The . . . scale.] ('sticking'
aft. del. 'adding [*doubtful*] the');
insrtd.

135.21–23 Note . . . else.] *insrtd.*

135.30 real] *aft. del.* 'really'

135.34 those] *ab. del.* 'such'

135.34 aggregations] 's' *ov.* 'as'

135.36 aggregate] *aft. del.* 'to'

135.37 habits & actions] *ab. del.*
'individual actions'

136.4 Empirical] *bef. del.* 'f'

136.5 *thinker*] 'inker' *ov.* 'ough'

[*begin* Alice James *hand*]

136.18 shape taken by] *ab. del.* 'way
in which' (AJ)

136.25 facts] *aft. del.* 'natural' (AJ)

136.30 if] *aft. del.* 'to' (AJ)

136.39–137.2 Heredity . . . variation]
brace del.

137.10 Operative] *insrtd. bef.* 'factors
['f' *ov.* 'F']'

137.10–11 —acorn . . . pot.] (*dash ov.
period*); *added*

137.12–13 variations.] *bef. del.* 'E' (AJ)

137.19 in] *bef. del.* 'that' (AJ)

137.25 relations] *aft. del.* 'nature' (AJ)

137.27 ⱯXdoes] *db. qt. del.*

137.31 *itself.*] *period added bef. del.*
'indepen. | Read Wallace'

138.3 When I say that] *ab. del.* 'In
discussing'

138.11 is] *aft. del.* 'has' (AJ)

138.14 habitual expectation] 'ual'
added; 'expectation' *intrl. for del.
intrl.* 'association'

138.18 it] *aft. del.* 'I object' (AJ)

138.29 blanket] *aft. del.* 'metaphor'
(AJ)

138.30 or experience] *ab. del.* 'up over
our' (AJ)

138.33 to the sensible] *ab. del.* 'and'
(AJ)

138.35 mental] *aft. del.* 'oth' (AJ)

140.6 "Ces . . . herbivores.] ('ces naifs'
intrl.); *intrl.*

140.11–12 (Contem. . . . –9)] *added*

140.22 removing] 'r' *ov.* 'R' (AJ)

140.23 Scientific] 'S' *ov.* 'I' (AJ)

141.3 Many . . . corresponding.]
penc. added

141.8 Social] *aft. del.* 'Envir't preserves
or destroys' |

[*end* Alice James *hand*]

141.26 take] 't' *ov.* 'a'

141.29 *Subject*] 'S' *ov.* 's'

141.32 direct] 'd' *ov.* 'p'

141.33 perception . . . field.] *added in
left mrgn.*

[*begin* Alice James *hand*]

142.7 qualities] *bef. del.* 'Bu' (AJ)

142.16 "The] *db. qt. added;* 'T' *ov.* 't'
(AJ)

142.19 dawn of consciousness] *ab. del.*
'feeling'

142.23 one] *aft. del.* 'true attribu' (AJ)

142.27 in] 'n' *ov.* 's'; *bef. del.* 'that in
which' (AJ)

142.29–30 unknowable] 'able' *ov.* 'n'
(AJ)

142.30 in] *bef. del.* 'in' (AJ)

143.3 suddenly] *aft. del.* 'it'; *bef. del.*
'dawns' (AJ)

143.12 affirms] *ab. del.* 'holds' (AJ)

143.16 ²to] *bef. del.* 'the' (AJ)

143.18 were] *bef. del.* 'not' (AJ)

143.18 first] *bef. del.* 'th' (AJ)

143.23 puffs] 'p' *ov.* 'h' (AJ)

143.23 air] *bef. del.* 'in a' (AJ)

143.24 ¹of] *bef. del.* 'electrical ['al' *ov.*
'ity'] irritation of the ear and' (AJ)

143.25 until] *ab. del.* 'and' (AJ)

143.28 and] *bef. del.* 'the ap' (AJ)

143.34 belief] *ab. del.* 'idea'

143.37 of] *ov.* 'by' (AJ)

144.6 experience] *intrl.*

144.7 ¹the] *insrtd.*

144.7 one] *ov.* 'an'

144.7 immediately] 'ly' *added*

144.7 in hand] *ab. del.* 'experience'

144.8 ['and' *del.*] definitive, and
conceived] *intrl.*

144.9 primitive] *bef. del.* 'and'

144.9 & perceived] *insrtd.*

144.9–10 former] *insrtd. by* WJ *aft.
del.* 'conceived' *ab. del.* 'new-born
one' (AJ)

144.10 latter] *ab. del.* 'perceived one'

144.10 its] *ab. del.* 'an'

144.11–14 The . . . form.] ('that' aft. del. 'of'); insrtd.

144.16 rightly] bef. del. 'when'

144.22 of] insrtd. (AJ)

144.23 original] bef. del. 'egg from which you have st' (AJ)

144.23 not in] ab. del. 'which you have' (AJ)

144.23 making] 'king' ov. 'de' (AJ)

144.23 it] insrtd. for del. 'to' (AJ)

144.24 has] 's' ov. 'd' (AJ)

144.24 just] intrl. (AJ)

144.26 and] ov. 'but' (AJ)

144.26 we] ab. del. 'it is'

144.26 can never] intrl.

144.26 know] alt. fr. 'unknowable'

144.26 it] intrl.

144.30 rudimentary] 'rudi' ab. del. 'ele'

144.37 range] alt. fr. 'arrange'

144.39–145.4 One . . . O.] added

145.5 if] intrl.

145.5 or] ab. del. 'are'

145.6 when true] intrl. (AJ)

145.7 impressions,] comma added bef. del. 'when true'

145.7–8 than these impressions] intrl.

145.10 instances?] bef. del. 'It is that the perception cannot possibly be interpreted as a particular disguised case of the conception. We cannot believe that Venus is there on the Sun's face and yet invisible; nor can we believe that the solid in one scale which counterpoises the 2 grain'

145.13 what] aft. del. 'reali' (AJ)

145.16 this] alt. fr. 'the' (AJ)

145.27 The] aft. del. 'There is' (AJ)

145.35–36 But . . . following] added in space aft. 'overthrow' [145.34] for del. 'Thus there we have the' and joined by guideline to 'general' (AJ)

145.37 as] bef. del. 'experi' (AJ)

145.39 it,] bef. del. 'and where' (AJ)

[end Alice James hand]

11. Notes for Philosophy 3: The Philosophy of Evolution
1879–1885 #4487, #4489, #4488, #4484, #4492, #4486

These notes are contained in six manuscript files on an assortment of paper. The first, #4487, starts with a fold enclosing three separate leaves, all of wove paper watermarked Merchants Pure Bond, each leaf measuring, irregularly, 8 x 5". The fold is written on rectos and versos but the separate leaves (146.26–147.9) on rectos only. These single leaves are noted by Perry as found in James's copy of Spencer's *First Principles*. This part is unnumbered save for a centered 2 heading the second of the inserted leaves. The third of these leaves is a part-page, as is the verso of the second leaf of the fold (147.18–19). Next comes a single leaf, written on the recto and verso, of wove paper, measuring 8 x 5", watermarked Parchment Vellum (147.20–29), followed by a fold of wove unwatermarked paper 7¼ x 4¼", its second recto a part-page and its verso blank (147.30–148.23). Again Perry notes that this was found in James's copy of *First Principles*.

Further notes come on a fold of laid unwatermarked paper 8¾ x 6¼" followed by a single leaf, paged 1–6 (148.24–150.12). The upper half of the recto of the fold's second leaf (p. 3) has been pasted over by a blank, this text comprising 149.23–25, with three lines of circled text below it that is printed in the Alterations. The lower half of this page consists of 149.26–30, ending with 'Read!'. On the evidence of offset, the blank was attached after final part-page 6 ('it is . . . experience.' 150.10–12) had been newly written and the single leaf mistakenly placed inside the fold. The manuscript concludes with a fold (the second leaf badly torn in the right margin) of thin laid unwatermarked paper 8¼ x 4½" (150.13–151.7), the verso of its second leaf blank, the recto holding only four notes. The ink is blue-gray. Laid in the fold is a torn fragment 4½ x 3¼", irregular, written in black ink and deleted by vertical and cross strokes, verso blank; the inscription does not appear to be in James's hand.

Manuscript #4489 consists of five folds (ten leaves) of laid unwatermarked paper 8¾ x 6¼", the folds repeating the title and roman-numbered I–V. In this sequence IV is written after deleted III and V is altered from IV. It is likely that III has been made from a II. Apparently there is no significance in this corrected numbering, for the recto of the third fold follows in mid-sentence the verso of the second fold (153.11–12) with 'Force) | we ought'. James wrote the text from the first leaf, ending on the verso of the third fold with 'special conditions,' which Alice then continued with 'and says that' (154.13) on the recto of the fourth fold's first page, below James's heading 'Persistence of Force *IV [aft. del. 'III']'. Alice concluded on the recto of the first leaf of the fifth fold with 'nature allows' (155.10) and James completed the manuscript, writing to the end of the recto ('is conceivable' 155.11) and continuing on the verso, a part-page ('and is constantly . . . effort.' 155.11–15). The recto and verso of the second leaf of this last fold are blank.

The notes continue with #4488 starting on a single leaf of the same laid paper, unnumbered, written on recto and verso, headed 'Rythm of Motion.' Next comes a fold, similarly headed, containing the text for 156.2–157.2. The manuscript ends with a fold of wove paper, the leaves measuring 8 x 5", the text (157.4–158.7) headed 'The Direction of Motion.' At the upper right above this title James wrote in pencil, 'Ch IX'.

A fold of the same laid paper as before, written recto and verso, returns in #4484 (158.9–159.8) headed 'Concluding lecture on Spencer'. To the right, under the title, James added 'Trash!'.

The same laid paper continues in #4492, a series of folds interspersed with single leaves that seem to be additions. The numbering is irregular: the first leaf of each fold is numbered, a half-circle around the number, the other pages of the fold and the separate leaves usually silently paged, but occasionally numbered. The first fold, written on rectos and versos, is numbered 1 on the first page, but 2–4 are unnumbered. On the first page James squeezed-in in a smaller hand above the heading 'Spencer's First Principles' the names 'Guthrie, Bowne, Chauncey Wright, Martineau'. The first leaf of the second fold is numbered 5 and begins Chapter III at 160.31. Above its heading James pencilled a C. Laid in the fold between the first and second leaves is a separate leaf of the same paper in Alice's hand (except for the last line), her only appearance in this manuscript. The leaf is headed 6a, its verso blank. This text (printed here as 174.26–32) interrupts continuous text between the verso of the first leaf of the fold and the recto of the second ('Cannot be infinite, | but why not finite?' 161.16). On the verso of the second leaf James began Chapter IV, the IV written over III. The next leaf is separate, now printed as 175.1–25 and manifestly out of place although its recto is numbered 7 and its verso 8, both centered. This is followed by a fold, its first leaf (162.4–17) numbered 9 in the usual position of the right-hand corner and headed 'Ch. *IV [ov. 'III'] (cont'd)'. Chapter V heads its verso, continued (and concluded) on the fold's second leaf's verso with the notes James placed at the end of the lectures (163.12–17). The lower half of the page contains the brief passage headed 'Criticism' (163.18–28). The next fold is headed 'Spencer's 1st Princ.', a heading used for the first leaf of subsequent folds. It is numbered 13 in the upper right corner, which would have been its pagination if the preceding fold had been paged after its first leaf numbered 9. That it follows regularly is indicated by its original top item numbered 2, continuing the 1 at the foot of the preceding fold's verso, as well as by James inserting in pencil above this number 2 item the notation '1 Self existent', which repeats the heading for the item at the foot of the preceding verso (163.27). The text continues on this fold, ending on its second verso with deleted 'Dog in laboratory.' above a white space and below 164.36. Above this deleted line James wrote, with a finer pen, '(Skip to p. 18)'. The recto of the next fold is headed 17, centered, and beneath this the heading 'Spencer's 1st Principles' is deleted in blue crayon. The text of this recto is deleted by a cross stroke in ink, this deletion carrying over to the upper half of the verso (the deletion printed here as 165.1–22). On the recto, under the deleted heading and just above the start of the text, James wrote '(*Omit this in order*)'. The verso of this first leaf is numbered 18, the numbering being added later as shown by its offset on the second leaf recto, no offset being present for the deleting diagonal stroke of the upper half. Below the deletion the text begins with 'No doubt' (165.23) and continues on the recto of the second leaf of the fold. But six lines above the foot, starting with 'But we have seen' (166.6) and continuing with the end of the sentence beginning 'Some time back' on the verso, including a series of notes through 166.23, James again deleted the text with a diagonal stroke. The recto of the next fold begins 'Dog in Laboratory.' (166.24) repeating the deleted same line at the foot of the verso of the fold numbered 13 (163.29–164.36). The heading is the usual one and in the upper right corner the number 21 is written before a deleted 7, the 21 continuing the practice of numbering the first page in a fold. Squeezed in at the very foot of the page is 'End of mystery no 1.'

Starting on the verso of this first leaf James numbered the pages 22–24 in small figures at the upper right, p. 24 ending the fold's verso with only three lines of text (167.29–30), which may be an afterthought added on a blank verso since the text of p. 23 ends at 167.28 with an inch and a quarter of white space. The recto of the next fold begins Part II, Chapter I (167.31) below the usual heading, numbered 25 with the usual half-circle that James used for the first page of a fold, the numbering continuing with 26–27 on its verso and the second leaf recto of the fold. The text for a single leaf numbered 28–29 (168.35–169.23) continues the upper half of p. 27 (168.27–33) with the heading 'Spencer on the Data of Philosophy'. This single leaf is keyed in toward the foot of p. 27 by James's notation, circled, 'pp. 28. *& 29 [*intrl.*] on separate sheet'. This leaves the last two lines of text below the note (169.24–25) intended to follow 169.23 ending p. 29. Since the verso of p. 27 is then paged 30 it follows p. 29 regularly with the start of Chapter III. The next fold begins Chapter IV (below the usual heading), numbered 31. The other leaves of the fold are unnumbered, the verso of the first leaf headed 'Chap. V.', the second leaf recto 'Chap. VI', and its verso, a part-page (171.3–6), 'Chap. VII.' To this verso is hinged a leaf of thin laid paper $7\frac{1}{2}$ x $4\frac{1}{2}''$, written on recto and verso, headed 'Comment on Chap. VIII' (171.7–33).

A single leaf of the usual laid paper has the regular heading and the numbering 35 (171.34–172.17), a pencil note 'Leuba VII, 309' to the left of the heading. The lower half of its verso, ending in mid-sentence, is deleted. This is succeeded by a fold written on the recto of the first leaf only, numbered 37, the other three leaves blank. The next fold, with 'Chapter X' below the usual heading, is numbered 41 (172.32–173.25) and ends partway down on the recto of the second leaf, its verso blank. The final fold beginning Chapter XI is numbered 44, altered from 35. The second leaf recto begins Chapter XIII. **The** final notation halfway down on the second verso (174.23–25) is a later addition written with a finer pen.

The last manuscript placed in this section of notes is #4486, written on unwatermarked laid paper 8⅞ x 6¼″, starting with a single leaf and followed by a fold, the whole paged 1–6. The recto of the first leaf of the fold above 'an intrinsic worth, an ideal' (176.14) is headed 'Ethics 7'. The text runs along in mid-sentence but only after the deletion before 'an intrinsic' of 'an in', written over the start of what appears to be 'Not'.

James's brackets are found at 154.8–9 '[Mass . . . right.]', 167.29 '[Infinity' (opening bracket only), and 172.7 '[This' (opening bracket only).

Emendations

147.28   Pleiades] Pleides
148.6   achieve] acheive
148.21   who] we
☞148.29   relations)] ~∧ (*similar* 162.24;163.7;167.14;168.5;170.7,11,22, 23,24;172.26)
149.12   ceases] cease
149.16   it] in
150.10   it is] it is | it is
150.24   Lucretius,] ~∧
150.32   Lamarck] Lamark
150.37   Niebuhr] Niehbuhr
151.5   Brit.] Britt.
152.2   Karma] Kharma
152.21   *phenomenon*] *pheno-*|menon
152.26   arises] arise
153.9   we] *om.*
154.9   right.] ~∧
[*begin* Alice James *hand*]
155.1   karma] kharma
[*end* Alice James *hand*]
☞155.23   hand]] ~∧ (*similar* 155.30;

161.14,17;162.11;163.11;168.8;169.32; 173.31,39;174.19)
156.21   produce] produces
156.37   republics.] ~∧
157.13   with] with | with
158.18   this.] ~∧
158.33   vicious.] ~∧
160.4   ∧ṡ] (~
160.32   nor] no
161.13   neccessitating] neccessiting
161.39   important] importance
162.8   arguments] argumenents
162.20   phenomenal] phomemal
164.18   *sich.*] ~∧
166.19   Wordsworth's] Wordswoth's
168.15   (No] [~
169.1   seek] & seek
170.26   Bowne] Bown
171.32   symmetry] symetry
171.36   corollaries] corrollaries
173.3–4   be symbolically] by symbollically

Alterations in the Manuscripts

146.19   Not] *aft. del.* 'Not'
146.25   problem.] *bef. del.* | 'A sovereign purpose is only an hypothesis. | Absolute world soul'
146.28   By] *insrtd. bef.* 'What' *not reduced in error*
146.28   reasons] *aft. del.* 'arguments'
147.7   Sincerely] *aft. del.* 'Make any criticism you like of ['the' *del.*] Spencer's'
147.10   "Evolution"] *aft. del.* 'vs. republic of ends' |
147.10   an] *intrl.*

147.29   Orion] 'O' *ov.* 'o'
148.20   against] *insrtd.*
148.20   a] *aft. del.* 'and'
148.22   will] *bef. del.* 'op'
148.25   is] *bef. del.* 'monist'
148.30   validity] *bef. del.* 'denied to'
148.32   that] *bef. del.* 'our'
148.32   processes] *final* 'es' *added*
148.35–36   They . . . utilitarianism] *insrtd.*
148.36   Status] 'St' *ov.* 'Da'
149.7   Huxley's formulas.] *insrtd.*
149.8   for] *bef. del.* 'action'

149.10–12 We . . . etc] *tr. by guideline
fr. facing page; period aft.* 'etc' *om.
in error*

149.24 Great] *aft. del.* 'A *lack* in us.'

149.29 real.] *bef. del.* 'Back of Weld
bricks ['cor' *del.*] numbered.'

149.29–30 Coerciveness–Read!] *tr. by
guideline fr. aft.* 'transparency).'
[149.31]

149.32 This . . . actual.] *insrtd. for del.*
'What is this? merely the continuity
of a system? or a noumenal world?'

149.40 appearing] *bef. del.* 'I'

150.1 a] *alt. fr.* 'an'

150.8 perceive.] *bef. del.* 'Objectivity,
good, and pleasure thus are seen to
have a common root.'

150.24 Lucretius] *intrl.*

150.25 Platonic] 'Pla' *ov.* 'Ari'

150.29 Leibnitz] *insrtd.*

151.9 1I] *ov.* 'you'

151.11 itself] *intrl.*

151.14;152.15 Natura] 2'a' *ov.* 'e'

151.19 reason] *final* 's' *del.*

151.25 with,] *bef. del.* 'though he'

151.31–32 Say . . . inertia.] *insrtd.*

151.33 not] *ab. del.* 'have'

151.33 have] 'ha' *ov.* 'no'

152.2 Aesthetic] 'Ae' *ov.* 'Ee'

152.14 4] *ov.* '3'

152.26 disappears] *alt. fr.* 'dissapears'

152.32 sleep] 'sl' *ov.* 'it'

152.36 $] *intrl.*

152.37 to] *bef. del.* 'do what Spencer
does, call all these phenomena
manifestations of'

153.1 all] *aft. del.* 'each'

153.3 Masses] *aft. del.* 'Re'

153.3 Force] 'F' *ov.* 'f'

153.4 this] *bef. del.* 'p'

153.8 Were . . . find] *ab. del.* 'This
seems to presuppose'

153.9 have] *aft. del.* 'whe h'

153.10 Where] *aft. del.* 'Where the
cause is one'

153.12 ought] *bef. del.* 'to'

153.13 should] 's' *ov.* 'c'

153.13 At] *bef. del.* 'Or when mo'

153.14 motion] *bef. del.* 'is ex'

153.16 twice] 't' *ov.* '2'

153.17 lengthen] *final* 'd' *del.*

153.18 1] *aft. del.* '1 ft a'

153.20 with] *bef. del.* 'velocity of'

153.28 of] *bef. del.* 'motion'

153.29 1of] *bef. del.* 'which correspond'

153.30 different] *intrl.*

153.37 amounts] 'a' *ov.* 'm'

153.39 discriminating] *bef. del.* 'in a'

153.40 of] *bef. del.* 'ways in which
['motions and masses moving' *del.*]
moti'

153.40 and] *aft. del.* 'ang'

154.3 one] *aft. del.* 'one'

154.6 each of] *intrl.*

154.8 which] *bef. del.* 'it'

154.9 he] *aft. del.* 'is'

[*begin* Alice James *hand*]

154.14 sum] *aft. del.* 'mathe-' (AJ)

154.17 move] *bef. del.* 'onl' (AJ)

154.20–21 If . . . true.] *insrtd.*

154.23 Read.] *bef. del.* 'Observe' (AJ)

154.25 make] *bef. del.* 'theoreti' *ab.
del.* 'the practical reasons, so as to go
ahead with our understand' (AJ)

154.28 Identical] *aft. del.* 'Spencer's
inconsis' | (AJ)

154.35 Ask] *alt. fr.* 'Assume' (AJ)

154.35 now,] *intrl.* (AJ)

154.35 whether] *ov.* 'now' (AJ)

154.35 Uniformity] 'U' *ov.* 'u' (AJ)

154.35 follows] 'f' *ov.* 'F' (AJ)

154.35 either] *aft. del. intrl. start of* 'n'

[*end* Alice James *hand*]

155.13 combinations] 'c' *ov.* 'n'

155.14 world] *bef. del.* 'in'

155.20 body's] *alt. fr.* 'bodies'

155.21 the case will be] ('the ['t' *ov.*
'T']' *ov.* 'a'); *tr. fr.* 'will be the case'
aft. del. 'it' *ab. del.* 'there'

155.21 one] *intrl.*

155.22 rythm] *underl. del.*

155.24–26 send . . . be] *insrtd. for del.*
'reverse [*undel. in error*] the *motion)
[paren ov. period]' bef.* 'One' *not
reduced in error*

155.26 cycle] *bel. del.* 'beat'

155.26 of rythm] *underl. del.*

155.28 3] *insrtd. for del.* '3 [*ov.* '2'] If A
meanwhile has stopped acting this
will be all.'

155.28 and] *aft. del.* 'then'

155.28 then] *insrtd.*

155.31 1sometimes] *aft. del.* 'are'

155.31 stop acting] *ab. del.* 'finite'

155.31 go on,] *(comma ov. period)*; *ab. del.* 'permanent.'; *bef.* 'So' *not reduced in error*

155.32 may be] *ab. del.* 'are'

155.32 Class] 'C' *ov.* 'c'; *aft. del.* 'Those ['o' *ov.* 'e'] *of the [*intrl. and undel. in error*] 3rd'

155.32 3 is very] *ab. del.* 'are'

155.33 fact] *aft. del.* '['fact' *del.*] prevalence of continuously acting forces'

155.33 that] *bef. del.* 'media repulsive'

155.33 matter] *ab. del.* 'bodies'

155.33 exerts] 's' *added*; *bef. del.* 'are always acting ['and' *del.*] on everything ['that' *del.*] making everything move which comes into'

155.34 but] *ab. del.* 'acting and'

155.34 reversing all motions] ('and' *undel. in error bef.* 'reversing'); *ab. del.* '*first [*undel. in error*] stopping [*ab. del.* 'overcoming [*ab. del.* 'driving back']'] all bodies which ['move' *del.*] begin to move'

155.35 that begins] *intrl.*

156.4 In case] *aft. del.* 'In case of perfectly elastic bodies, ['m' *del.*] rythm whenever one ['p' *del.*] meets another. In case of inelastic bodies, no ry' |

156.11–12 constant.] *bef. del. intrl.* 'or self reproducing'; *period part of intrl. but left undel.*

156.13 reversed] *aft. del.* 'ry'

156.20 The] *aft. del.* '*One tribe [*ab. del.* 'The animals'] exhausts [*final* 's' *added*] itself [*ab. del.* 'themselves'] in destroying ['the' *del.*] ['each' *del.*] another ['an' *added*], the other reproduces itself and'

156.21–22 the constant . . . makes] *intrl.*

156.23 have time to] *intrl.*

156.23 high] *aft. del.* 'demand pr'

156.23 supply] *aft. del.* 'dema'

156.24–25 constant . . . ¹the] *intrl.*

156.25 rot] *final* 's' *del.*

156.25 till] *aft. del.* 'th'

156.27 regenerate] *aft. del.* 'reproduce'

156.32 describes] *aft. del.* 'takes'

156.32 the] *ov.* 'an'

156.36 predict] *aft. del.* 'tell'

156.36 may] *ab. del.* 'will'

157.4 account] *aft. del.* 'law'

157.6 the] *poss. alt. fr.* 'this'

157.6 next] *intrl.*

157.8 in] *ab. del.* 'on'

157.8 future] *ab. del.* 'whole'

157.9 overcome] *ab. del.* 'confront'

157.9 present] *intrl.*

157.10 facts] *aft. del.* 'resistances'

157.13 social] *intrl.*

157.13 present . . . resistances] *ab. del.* 'actually easiest paths,'

157.14 "social] *intrl.*

157.14–15 actual mechanical] *ab. del.* 'outer'

157.17 gaining] *intrl.*

157.18 notoriously] *intrl.*

157.18 attack a] *ab. del.* 'confront'

157.19 ²a] *ab. del. intrl.* 'a'

157.19–20 movement] *final* 's' *added aft. del. final* 's' *and then that* 's' *del.*

157.20 follows . . . ²the] *ab. del.* 'obey['s' *del.*] idea['s' *del.*] of greatest'

157.20 but] *aft. del.* 'or of least resistance, th'

157.20 it] *aft. del.* 'they obey'

157.21 idea] *bef. del.* 'to follow;' *ab. del.* 'or least resisting idea'

157.22 the most] *intrl.*

157.22 And] *insrtd. bef.* 'Since' *not reduced in error*

157.24 a] *intrl.*

157.24 movement] *final* 's' *del.*

157.24 is always] *ab. del.* 'are'

157.25 path] *final* 's' *del.*

157.26 attached] *bef. del. intrl.* 'to *that ['at' *ov. poss.* 'em'] path'

157.26 greatest] 'est' *added*

157.26 and] *aft. del.* 'and'

157.26 social] *ab. del.* 'social'

157.27 take] *ab. del.* 'in'

157.27 where] *ab. del.* 'of the greatest ['re' *del.*] outer'

157.27 resistances] *final* 's' *added*

157.27 empirical] *ab. del.* 'the'

157.28 the brain] ('brain' *bef. del.* 'paths'); *ab. del.* 'the easiest'

157.28 are the easiest,] *ab. del.* 'are' *tr. fr. bef. to aft.* 'followed'

157.28 none.] *period added bef. del.* 'of an empirical kind.'

157.29 can] *intrl.*

157.31 is . . . leads] ('leads' *bef. del.* 'him'); *ab. del.* 'is vain, leading him'

157.31 the] *alt. fr.* 'this'

157.32 confusions of] 'ions of' *ab. del.* 'ing between inner and outer, future and present, near and remote, ideal and mechanical, which characterizes'

157.32–34 are . . . openness] *ab. del.* 'are treated *mechanically [intrl.]* as [*undel. in error*] checking [*aft. del.* 'turning' *ab. del.* 'turning aside'] present movements, ['remote' *del.*] [*del.* 'openness of ['remote' *del.*] paths in *one [*ab. del.* 'other'] country ['y' *ov.* 'ies'] *as producing [*ab. del.* 'determining'] movement over ['closed' *del.*] obstructed paths in another, figure *mechanically [intrl.]* as present mechanical checks,'] ['remote' *del.*] the *case [*ab. del.* 'openness']'

157.34 one] *ab. del.* 'remote'

157.34 country] 'y' *ov.* 'ies'

157.34 is made to] *ab. del.* 'acts to'

157.34 determine] *final 's' del.*

157.34 over] *aft. del.* 'of'

157.35 closed] *ab. del. doubtful* '['close' *del.*] hard'

157.35 ¹in . . . as] ('in which' *intrl.*); *ab. del.* 'here,'

157.35–36 figure as] *ab. del.* 'appear['s' *del.*] as a'

157.37 pushed . . . but] *ab. del.* 'moved'

157.37–158.2 in . . . results.] ('clearly abstracted or' *intrl.*); *ab. del.* 'instead of *only [intrl.]* moving *the [intrl.]* brain molecules by which the outer things are discharged,'

158.2 policy] *intrl.*

158.3 in . . . page] *intrl.*

158.5 could] *alt. fr.* 'can'

158.17 mediation] *bef. del.* 'on this point his system is worthless. Read passages fm. his chloroform article. Mind Oct. 1878. There remain other modes. | G'al estimate. Learning? No desultory interests. | Read Phenomenalism 1, 2,'

158.20 Chloroform . . . 1878] *added*

158.21 what] *start of final letter del.*

158.25 expression] *intrl.*

158.31 So . . . reduces] *added bef. del.* | 'A phil. of ultimate kinds can accept the facts and by the notion of ultimate law not swamp them. | No philos. a substitute for the fullness of living.'

159.17 & . . . science?] *insrtd.*

160.2 (31)] '3' *ov. poss.* '2'

160.5 ditto] 'd' *ov. qst. mk.*

160.23 Grote's . . . XXIV] *insrtd.*

160.26 Wundt] *written ov. line intended to stand for* 'Renouvier'

160.31 [1. no attributes]] *insrtd.*

160.32 2] *insrtd.*

160.35 results] 'res' *ov. poss.* 'con'

160.36 terminable] *alt. fr.* 'terminate'

161.26 Problem] 'P' *ov.* 'C'

161.26 Chaps] *intrl.*

161.28 Jas. . . . XXI.] *added*

161.29 IV] *ov.* 'III'

161.32 a] *intrl.*

161.32 [yes . . . genus.]] (*opening bkt. ov. closing bkt.*); *added*

161.35 76–] '7' *ov. closing bkt.*

162.5 thinking] *alt. fr.* 'thing'

162.6 What] *aft. del.* 'Give Sp's arg<u>ts</u> for existence of Absolute?' |

162.13 the] *intrl.*

162.19–20 One . . . . But] *insrtd.*

162.21 (not . . . tho't)] ('we' *ov. illeg.*); *intrl.*

162.22 impute this] *alt. fr.* 'impugn ones'

162.23 our] *added*

162.23 as] *aft. del.* 'or not?'

162.23 cf. . . . bottom] *insrtd.*

162.27 108] *added*

162.28 Suppose] *aft. del.* 'What is the religious character' |

162.31 assertion?] *qst. mk. ov. colon*

162.31 Force] 'F' *ov.* 'f'

163.8 p. 111] *intrl.*

163.11 S] *ov.* 's'

163.16–17 esp. . . . Theism"] *added*

163.29 Self existent] *penc. added*

163.33 48,–58.] *intrl.*

163.33 the] *ov.* 'a'

163.36 infinite] 'fini' *ov.* 'com'

163.36 existence of the] *insrtd.*

163.36 proves] 'pr' *ov.* 'sa'

163.37 Absolute] 'A' *ov.* 'a'

164.5   7. *Bare*] *aft. del.* '['7. Most abstract element of our thing—' *del.*] 7 Bare Abstract Being, (residuary 91) bare existence [*opening paren del.*] indefinite (88) Something 95, objective reality' |

164.5   an] 'n' *added*

164.5   indefinite] *ov.* 'residu'

164.6   residuary] *aft. del.* ' "something" (95) general existence (95) objective reality (93)'

164.6   objective] *aft. del.* 'unformed & unlimited (94)'

164.7   unlimited] 'un' *intrl.*

164.10   So] *aft. del.* 'It is the mere'

164.13   of presence.] *ab. period undel. in error*

164.14   S'ts . . . 169] *insrtd. aft. del.* '8. Power, Substance. 98–99. Analogy of Soul.'

164.16   Unknowable] 'U' *ov.* 'u'

164.18   Ding *an sich*] *intrl.*

164.18   irrelative] 'ir' *added*

164.20   its] *intrl.*

164.22–23   Why . . . relation?] *insrtd.*

164.25–26   "Natur . . . Schale."] *insrtd.*

164.27   Its] *aft. del.* 'Spencer's Real motive: To make his system of phenomenalism absolute, & forestall criticism. *All ['A' *ov.* 'I'] I don't know is unknowable.'

164.35   plenty—3] *ab. del.* 'that of Truth yet to be known. That of Being as given. That of completed Infinite.'

164.36   known.] *on line bel.* WJ's *note* '(Skip to p. 18)' *is del.* 'Dog in laboratory.'

165.1   he] *aft. del.* 'he'

165.3   being] *aft. del.* 'to'

165.5   2nd)] *paren ov. period*

165.13   are] 're' *insrtd.*

165.16   believing] *aft. del.* 'belief'

165.20   selves] *alt. fr.* 'self'

165.25   he] *ov. illeg.*

165.29   takes] *aft. del.* 'does not'

165.30   of] *aft. del.* 'of confirmation'

165.32   Those] 'T' *ov.* 't'; *aft. del.* '['E *del.*] I think *exe [intrl.]*'

165.33   Hamilton & Mansel] *intrl.*

166.7   their] *aft. del.* 'givenness.'

166.25   Not] 'N' *ov.* 'I'

166.26   Read . . . 1884] *insrtd.*

166.30   Spencer] *apostrophe undel. in error when final 's' del.*

166.35   Read] *aft. del.* 'Read Jackman's Answer.'

166.36   in] *aft. del.* 'against'

167.1   (No. 2)] *intrl.*

167.3   ¹mystery] *aft. del.* 'the'

167.6   defines] *aft. del.* 'says'

167.11   *shall*] *ov.* 'will'

167.15–16   Perhaps . . . it.] *insrtd.*

167.20   an] *final 'd' del.*

167.23   past] *intrl.*

167.23   &c] *intrl.*

168.1   way] *aft. del.* 'ex'

168.9   (Objective] *paren ov. bkt.*

168.11   154] *intrl.*

168.13   156] *intrl.*

168.14   p] *ov. closing paren*

168.15   One] 'O' *ov.* 'o'

168.22   Each] *aft. del.* '4'; *w. guideline indicating 'Each' should foll.* 'series'

168.23   4] *ov.* '5'

168.25   5] *ov.* '6'

168.26   faint.] *bef. del.* | '6 [*ov.* '7'] Faint have traceable antecedents'

169.5   differing] *ab. del.* 'a'

169.5   realities] 'ies' *ov.* 'y'

169.7–8   Called . . . Powers"] *penc. added*

169.18   out] *ov.* 'of'

169.24   Part] 'P' *ov.* 'II'

169.28   159)] *paren ov. period*

170.2   remarks] *intrl.*

170.8   be indestructible?] *ab. del.* 'persist?'

170.10   whose] *ov.* 'having'

170.12–14   Recommend . . . Mechanics.] *added*

170.20   183] *insrtd.*

170.26   Controversy] *aft. del.* 'L'

171.12   motion] *bef. del.* ': [*undel. in error*] 192 *note [intrl.]* & d'

171.18   What] *ov.* 'In'

171.24   no] *intrl.*

171.27   etc.] *insrtd.*

172.17   effect.] *bef. del.* | 'These require not only *enough* force to unlock them, but the *right kind.* ['A f' *del.*] A very small force measured by impact *of the right kind [intrl.]* may unlock *more [ov. 'a'] ['vast discharge' *del.*] than a very large one of the wrong kind. | In such cases, ['we can only intelligibly talk of motion resulting in the line of least resistance, after we have defined where the existence is.' *del.*] there are two resistances—the internal and external. The larger external resistance may be vanquished, if only ['the' *del.*] overcome by a discharge whose'

172.23 Egypt] 'E' *ov.* 'e'

172.35 thrown] *intrl.*

173.2 map] *ab. del.* 'call'

173.2 as a line] *ab. del.* 'in one direction by a line, change in the other by another line, then we can diagrammatically represent the process of change by a passage from'

173.10 one] *intrl.*

173.12 Usually] *aft. del.* 'Wh [*beginning a new line*]'

173.16 Emerson's] 'E' *ov.* 'e'

173.16–17 5 . . . 3's] *penc. added*

173.19 Sexes at birth.] *insrtd.*

173.21 nothing] *penc. ab. del.* 'notion'

173.23 force] *aft. del.* 'outside'

173.31 p. 270] *intrl.*

173.37 279] *ov. closing bkt.*

174.1 both] *intrl.*

174.1 &] *insrtd. for comma undel. in error*

174.9 which] 'w' *ov. qst. mk.*

174.10 Evolution] 'E' *ov.* 'e'

174.15 Shaking] 'k' *ov.* 'd'

174.19 show] *bef. del.* 'eva'

174.20 chemical] *ab. del.* 'nitrogen'

174.23–25 What . . . 280] *added w. finer pen*

175.2 unclamp] *ab. del.* 'knock out'

175.2 ensue] *bef. del.* 'therefore'

175.11 Spencer] *final* ' 's' *erased*

175.11 wd] 'd' *ov.* 'h'

175.12 Single] 'S' *ov.* 'C'

175.23 starting] *aft. del.* 'telling'

175.30 parties.] *period added bef. del.* 'as see'

176.5 ¹is] *ab. del.* 'if'

176.7 but] *aft. del.* 'by'

176.8 that] *ov. poss.* 'as'

176.9 nothing] *red crayon underl. of* 'thing' *del. in ink*

176.12 But] *alt. fr.* 'Bot[*start of* 'h']'

176.14 ¹an] *aft. del.* 'an [*ov. poss.* 'Noeti']'

176.28,32 Ideal] 'I' *ov.* 'i'

177.1 an] *final* 'd' *del.*

177.7 Pessimism] *aft. del.* 'Waitz The more the' |

177.8 thorough] *aft. del.* 'would'

177.12 being] *aft. del.* 'etc.'; *bef. del.* 'So conclude'

---

12. Notes for Philosophy 5: Psychology 1880–1881 #4416

Manuscript #4416 consists of a single fold of unwatermarked laid paper, the unnumbered leaves measuring 8⅞ x 6¼", the first leaf headed 'Sentimentality', with a rule below. Alice wrote on the recto and verso of the first leaf and continued halfway down the recto of the second, at which point (178.10) James finished the page. The fourth page is blank.

Emendations

178.1 Kingsley,] ~∧

178.12 Emotion."] ~∧"

Alterations in the Manuscript

[*begin* Alice James *hand*]

177.23 will.] *bef. del.* 'One' (AJ)

177.30 perfect] *bef. del.* 'bl' (AJ)

177.31 manifestations,] *comma ov. period bef. del.* 'a' *ov.* 'A' (AJ)

178.2 see] *aft. del.* 'reali' (AJ)

178.7 landing.] *bef. del.* 'A' (AJ)

178.8 so] *ab. del.* 'now' (AJ)

[*end* Alice James *hand*]

178.12 Emotion] 'E' *ov.* 'e'

13. Notes for Philosophy 4: Contemporary Philosophy
1881–1882 #4441

Headed 'Mill on Induction', underlined, manuscript #4441 consists of four folds of unwatermarked laid paper, the leaves measuring 8½ x 6″. The first leaf of each fold has a similar heading and is numbered respectively 1, 2, III, and IV. Alice wrote the first fold of two leaves, rectos and versos, and the recto of the first leaf of the second. She continued halfway down the verso of this leaf, at which point (179.34) James took over and continued to the end. Starting with the fourth fold (181.31) James wrote on the rectos only, the versos remaining blank.

Emendations

[*begin* Alice James *hand*]
179.15   methods"] ~ₐ
[*end* Alice James *hand*]
180.8   "subsumption."] "~.ₐ

181.2   -undulation)] -~ₐ
181.21   410)] ~ₐ
181.32   privative] privitive

Alterations in the Manuscript

[*begin* Alice James *hand*]
179.10–11   Definite . . . heart.] *insrtd.*
179.18   Each] *ov.* 'The'
179.18   "law"] *final* 's' *del.*
179.18   is] *ab. del.* 'are'
179.20   Nature's] ' 's' *added*
179.20   couplings] *intrl.*
179.31   laws.] *bef. del.* 'He says we can make a weak induction strong by deducing it from a stronger.'
179.32   what] *aft. del.* 'how to find' (AJ)
[*end* Alice James *hand*]
179.35   kindₐ] *comma del.*

179.36–37   The . . . is.] *insrtd.*
180.1   Supposing] *aft. del.* 'Let us examine it.' |
180.7   x,] *intrl.*
180.15   Sun] 'S' *ov.* 's'
180.29   becomes] *bef. del.* 'true of'
181.7   that] *bef. del.* 'being'
181.9   the] *ov.* 'a'
181.10   direct] *intrl.*
181.12   b] *final* 'e' *del.*
181.20   1880] *insrtd.*
181.20–21   Bowen's Logic 410] *insrtd.*
181.27   141)] *bef. del.* | 'Taine's Positio'
181.32   motions] *intrl.*

14. Notes for Philosophy 4: Ethics—Recent English Contributions
to Theistic Ethics 1888–1889 #4427

Most of the notes in #4427 come in nine leaves, unnumbered, of a ruled exercise book from A. A. Waterman & Co., Boston, the verso of the ninth leaf blank, as are the remaining leaves in the book. On the first page James wrote the heading 'Resumé of my lectures in Ethics | 1888–9', followed by a short rule. In the panel on the front cover he wrote 'Ethics Course | 1888–1889'. In the same folder is added a leaf of L. L. Brown laid paper, written on recto and verso, paged 3–4 at upper right. The text of this inserted leaf constitutes 185.21–186.4.

Emendations

183.29   returning] return|ning

184.17   both] bothe

Alterations in the Manuscript

182.8   Preface] *ab. del.* '*1*'
182.9   Martineau's] *aft. del.* 'I began by noting the narrowness of'
182.9   is narrow] *ab. del. period*
182.11   we must] *aft. del.* 'it must'; *bef. intrl.* 'also'
182.11   objective] *ab. del.* 'canon of'
182.12   consequences] *bef. del.* 'also,'
182.12   rightness] *aft. del.* 'or [*del. in error*] goodness of'
182.13   best] *insrtd. for del.* 'only'
182.13   action] *bef. del.* 'that is of supreme worth'
182.13–14   do . . . knowledge.] ('do the best' *ab. del.* 'be as good as'; 'know.' *period insrtd. bef. del.* 'how.'; 'imperfect the' *ab. del.* 'erroneous one's'; 'knowledge.' *period insrtd. bef. del.* 'may be.'); *ab. del.* '*act for the best. The good will is the highest subjective good, is what makes a man meritorious. *Conscientiousness, [insrtd. for del.* 'Reverence,']'
182.14   The] 'T' *ov.* 't'
182.15   best,] *ab. del.* '['good which binds us,' *del.*] In pain'
182.15   ascertained] *ab. del.* 'sought'
182.18   ethical] *alt. fr.* 'ethicall'
182.19   merely "what] *insrtd. for del.* '"what'
182.19   are] *aft. del. doubtful* 'also'
182.20   1)] *aft. del.* '2)'; *bef. del.* '['What is the method of proof that a thing is good. Either it is immediately admitted' *del.*] Goods are either'
182.23   as . . . premise] *intrl.*
182.24   every] *aft. del.* 'as its major knowing'; *bef. del.* 'chain of'
182.26   2)] *bel. del. false start for fol.* [1] '1) [¶] I began by showing the method of reasoning in Ethics. There must be at least one ethical proposition (Balfour), one which asserts an ideal, and which is *admitted as [*intrl.*] ultimate, either absolutely, or for the time being (in the sense that *neither [*ab. del.* 'both'] disputant['s' *del.*] denies [*ab. del.* 'admit'] it.'
182.27   question is] *ab. del.* 'led us to a long'

182.27   psychological.] *period added bef. del.* 'discussion.'
182.29   The] *aft. del.* 'Bodily ['pains [*ov.* 'is'] are ['goo' *del.*] b' *del.*] pleasures are good & pains bad.'
182.29   or] *ab. del.* 'and'
182.30   From . . . between] ('between' *bef. smudged out* 'our'); *ab. del.* 'Out of the ins'
182.31   the . . . life] *intrl.*
182.32   social & physical.] *intrl. ab. comma ov. period*
183.1   either] *intrl.*
183.2   esteemed] *aft. del.* 'go'
183.3   Analogy] 'A' *ov.* 'a'; *aft. del.* 'All'
183.3   the] *insrtd. aft. del.* '['our primitive' *del.*] the instincts'
183.5–6   arising . . . variation"] *ab. del.* '*incidentally* to these. ['or by "spontaneous vari' *del. intrl.*] Many ['of them arising in the brain' *del.*] originally modelled'
183.6   minds] 's' *added aft. del.* 'a'
183.6   contain] *final* 's' *del.*
183.7   preferences] *aft. del.* 'moral preferences'
183.7   2by] *intrl.*
183.7   direct] *insrtd.*
183.8   prefe-|]] *aft. del.* 'moral'; *bef. del.* | 'rences [*del. in error*] ['of an indigenous sort' *del.*] of a spontaneously *arising [*insrtd.*] sort'
183.8   as] *ab. del.* 'moral preferences strictly so called, for'
183.9   etc.] *period aft. comma ov. period bef. del. intrl.* 'i.e moral or conscientious preferences strictly so-called.'
183.12   utter] *aft. del.* 'say'
183.13   absolutely best is] *intrl.*
183.13   approves] *bef. del.* 'is absolutely best'
183.14   like] *bef. del. intrl.* 'alt'
183.15   itself] *intrl.*
183.16   which] *bef. del.* 'which'
183.17   that] *ab. del.* 'which'
183.19   is . . . so.] ('seems' *ab. del.* 'does'); 'is' *added on line bef. del.* 'must be *absolutely [*intrl.*] good.'; 'better . . . so.' *intrl. bef. del.* 'The

preferences of the moral faculty *are stamped with [*ab. del.* 'bring'] the *feeling of obligation.*'

183.19 The] *aft. del.* '5)'; *bef. del.* 'usual'

183.20 school thereupon] *ab. del.* 'ethics therefore'

183.20 our] *insrtd.*

183.20 ethical] *alt. fr.* 'ethics'

183.20 system] *intrl.*

183.21 Things] *aft. del.* 'All *obligatory things [*insrtd. for del.* 'duties'] are *moral [*intrl.*] goods; conscience informs us ['what' *del.*] immediately which things *are* *obligatory, either absolutely or relatively, [*ab. del.* 'duties'] so a list of moral goods *is easily [*ab. del.* 'can be'] drawn up. Martineau makes this scheme more flexible by saying that conscience merely.'

183.21 are] *ab. del.* 'seem'

183.22 the sense . . . inexplicably.] ('sense' *insrtd. for del.* 'feeling'; 'attached ['d' *ov.* 's']' *aft. del.* 'is one of those inexplicable feelings'); *ab. del.* 'our [*insrtd.*] conscience *makes [*ab. del.* 'informs'] us immediately *feel [*ab. del.* 'of'] that.'

183.23 Our estimate] *ab. del.* 'The value'

183.23 the] *intrl.*

183.23 systems must thus] *ab. del.* 'thus ['amount' *del.*] hinges on ['the' *del.*] our'

183.25 this ['latter' *del.*] feeling] *ab. del.* 'it'

183.25 psychologically.] *bef. del.* 'How do *purely [*intrl.*] impulsive* tendencies or preferences become *imperative?* In one sense whatever we *do* is imperative, whether good or bad. Of course this is not the sense meant. In another sense, bad things *may be [*ab. del.* 'are'] as imperative as good: they *may worry [*ab. del.* 'haunt'] us and ['worry us until' *del.*] give us no peace so long as they are undone. This is not the sense either. The imperatives which are *obligations* return to plague us afterwards if

we don't do them; so may sensual opportunities lost'

183.25 notions of] *intrl. aft. del.* 'obligations imperative['s' *del.*] acts a'

183.27 together,] *comma ov. period bef. del.* 'In one sense whatever we *do* must have been imperative, but that is not the sense'

183.27 seem] *ab. del.* 'be'

183.27 to] *ab. del.* 'in'

183.28 so] *aft. del.* 'at all'

183.28 will] *intrl.*

183.29 or] *aft. del.* 'or'

183.29 if] *aft. del.* 'till'; *bef. del.* 'left *not [*ab. del.* 'un'] done'

183.30 serve] *aft. del.* 'will'

183.30 differentiate] *bef. del.* '['a [*doubtful ab. del.* 'the'] *morally* from the' *del.*] simply psychological['ly' *del.*] imperative ['action' *del.*] from'

183.30–31 impulses] *insrtd. for del.* 'acts'

183.31 *any*] *aft. del.* 'all'

183.31 imperative] *bef. del.* 'psychologically'

183.31 ways.] *bef. del.* '['Usually' *del.*] The ['T' *ov.* 't'] sense of obligation *usually [*intrl.*] means ['usually' *del.*] something ominous to our ego, from omission of the act. But the same ominousness ['belongs to ['aesthetic and othe' *del.*] many' *del.*] seems to reinforce certain immoral impulses connected with pride a [*illeg.*]. Bain *& [*ov.* 'et'] Co say obligation is sense of *responsibility.* True; but to whom; to your club? to *the laws of [*intrl.*] your country? to your better self? *or [*intrl.*] your God? Martineau himself admits that the "total wisdom" of an act (i.e. its definitive value) *is a [*ab. del.* 'is'] compound['ed' *del.*] of its *inner worth [*ab. del.* 'intrinsic feeling of *obligation [*ab. del.* 'rightness']'] with its utility, so that more utility *with [*ab. del.* '&'] less *inner urgency [*ab. del.* 'rightness'] might be best.*— It follows that [*insrtd. for del.* '[¶] I conclude that'] the feeling of obligation *if used alone, [*ab. del.* 'fluctuates too much to'] is too indefinite *a thing [*ab. del.* 'a thing to ['serve as' *del.*] use alone to'] to found a system of ethics *upon. [*ab. del.* 'on.'] It is fallible ['and like' *del.*] and wavering [*comma del.*] like other feelings, and its *dicta* must be *questioned & [*insrtd.*] discussed like theirs.'

183.32 sorts] *ab. del.* 'sources'

183.32 of] *bef. del. intrl.* 'the sense of'

183.32 1) . . . 2) . . . 1)] *each insrtd.*

183.33 dignity] *ab. del.* 'worth'

183.33 act] *bef. del.* 'in [*undel. in error*] | the way of nobility, dignity'

183.33–34 Our . . . urgency.] *del. but then underdotted for retention w. circled* 'stet' *in mrgn.*

183.36 (*twice*) dignity] *ab. del.* 'inner worth'

183.37 We] *ab. del.* 'And we may have to pock'

183.38 Our] 'O' *ov.* 'o'; *aft. del.* '2) [*insrtd.*] Responsibility to others has an urgency *sui generis.* But'

183.38 also may] *insrtd. for del.* 'often'

183.38 among themselves.] *intrl. ab. comma insrtd. for del. period*

183.39 taken alone] ('taken' *aft. del.* 'when'); *intrl.*

183.39–40 wavering and fallible] *ab. del.* 'indefinite'

183.40 definitive] *intrl.*

184.1 compared] *aft. del.* 'judged'

184.2 does] 'es' *added*

184.2 one] *ab. del.* 'it' *ab. del.* 'we'

184.2 by] *ab. del.* 'to' *ab. del.* 'by'

184.2 seeking] 'ing' *ab. del.* 'ing'

184.3 that] *bef. del.* 'one [*ab. del.* 'we'] demands [*ab. del.* 'demands [*ab. del.* 'postulates ['s' *added*]'] real goods as so'] some sort of ['uni' *del.*] order and reality in the kingdom of goods, that one comes to know of two seeming goods in conflict, ['which with real good' *del.*] an outer warrant *that [*intrl.*] for his ethical judgments ['which' *del.*] shall *be [*ab. del.* 'make them'] objectively true; and that'

184.3 true] *ab. del.* 'real'

184.4 and . . . true.] *intrl. ab. comma ov. period*

184.5 Now] *insrtd. aft. del.* 'The

condition whereby anything is good is that some one'; *bef.* 'Nothing' *not reduced in error*

184.5 at all] *intrl.*

184.5 by] *ab. del.* ', except *for*'

184.6 so.] *period ov. comma bef. del.* 'for me namely. But if I am to be *right* in my feeling, ['some' *del.*] I must not make it, but *find* it already made good. The quest of the real objective good supposed that some-one has been before the querist, and made good what the querist must discover.'

184.7 Good] *final* 's' *del.*

184.7 & bad] *intrl.*

184.7 can] *intrl.*

184.7 even] *intrl.*

184.8 judgments.] *bef. del.* 'Chaotic goods can exist where there are many such minds, independent of each other. *An ['n' *added*] orderly [*intrl.*] system of goods can only exist where *there ['re' *added*] *is some [*ab. del.* 'minds agree in some'] principle['s' *del.*] of unity *among the minds [*intrl.*]. The ['min' *del.*] simplest possible system is where two minds principle of unity would be the recognition of *one [*ab. del.* 'some'] of the minds as *authority ['y' *ov.* 'ies'] by the others. When I *demand ['de' *ov.* 'as'] that my own ethical judgments shall be *true* what I really postulate is a previous mind *to [*intrl.*] whose *ethical [*intrl.*] judgment it is my duty to conform *mine [*ov.* 'to.'].'

184.8 These] *alt. fr.* 'They'

184.8–9 judgments themselves] *intrl.*

184.9 or false,] *ab. del.* 'good and *true* bad'

184.11 that] *bef. del.* 'I ['recognize' *del.*] already recognize th'

184.12 are already] *ab. del.* 'to be'

184.12 a] *aft. del.* 'an'

184.14 is] *aft. del.* 'at least'

184.15 systematic] 'atic' *added*

184.15 But] *aft. del.* 'Without authority there is no unity or system. ['With willing' *del.*] But what does authority consti'

184.16 but] *bef. del.* 'willingness on one part or the other, the willingness to *be* it, the willingness to *be subject to it. [*ab. del.* 'have it.'] With both together the system ['h' *del.*] is harmonious.'

184.17 Where] *aft. del.* 'It is like love'

184.17 coexist] 'co' *intrl.*

184.18 imperfect.] *bef. del.* '[¶] Authority is thus a creation of the will, like love.'

184.19 refused] *alt. fr.* 'false'

184.20 submission] *init.* 's' *ov.* 'a'; *aft. del.* 'appeal to'

184.21 both] *insrtd. for del.* 'all'

184.21 acknowledge.] *bef. del.* 'A harmonious moral system must'

184.22 character of the] *intrl.*

184.23 relations] *bef. del.* 'of evils'

184.23 persons.] *bef. del.* 'Abolish persons, and what remains of the world is non-moral.'

184.23 These] 'se' *added; bef. del.* 'moral'

184.23 are] *aft. del.* '['pa' *del.*] between the'

184.24 wills] *aft. del.* 'persons' '

184.24 either] *intrl.*

184.24 the['se' *del.*] wills] *bef. del.* 'and their relations cease to be moral; abolish the persons'

184.25 in the universe] *intrl.*

184.26 system] *aft. del.* 'good or is a quest for that'

184.27–28 In . . . ¹we] *orig.* 'Subjectively the only good is the good will, or the will to acknowledge the objective Best, so that (as far as our theoretic life goes) we are already in possession of this good, *subjectively and [*intrl.*] we have already'; *then text was del. except for* 'subjectively' *alt. to* 'subjective' *and* 'In a' *and* 'sense [2's' *intrl.*] we' *added*

184.28 enter] *final* 'ed' *del.*

184.28 the moment] *aft. del.* '['by beco' *del.*] the act of'

184.29 serious] *intrl.*

184.29 We] *insrtd. bef. del.* 'Ethical skepticism *wont [*insrtd. for del.* 'will not']'

184.29 assumption] *bef. del.* 'which ethical faith makes,'

184.30 with] *ov.* 'we'

184.30 an . . . seek;] *ab. del.* 'make the assumption;'

184.31 we] *intrl.*

184.32 (what] *paren insrtd. aft. del.* 'of'

184.32 goods] 's' *added; aft. del.* 'the'

184.32 for that authority?)] 'for that authority?' *ab. del.* 'things?'; *paren orig. insrtd. aft. now del.* 'things?'

184.32 untouched.] *added aft. del.* 'still for our hands.'

184.33 Prima . . . form] *ab. del.* 'As goods present themselves they seem'

184.33–34 Must . . . unified?] *ab. del.* 'We *wish [*ab. del.* 'seek'] to make a system of them.'

184.34 were] *ab. del.* 'be'

184.34 any] *insrtd.*

184.34 quality] *ab. del.* 'genus'

184.36 principle.] *bef. del.* 'But examination proves goods to be of many heterogeneous kinds.'

184.36 proposed] *intrl.*

184.39 enjoyment is a] *ab. del.* 'it is'

184.39 perfection,] *comma insrtd. bef. del.* 'to enjoy,'

185.2 other.] *bef. del.* '[¶] 10) *A priori* they are indeterminate. *What* perfection? *whose* and *what* pleasure. All the actual *concrete [*init.* 'c' *ov.* 'd'] difficulties of ethical decision come from answering these questions. If we say the best pleasure the best perfection, we but fall back on the postulate we start with "there is a best," but know not which? [¶] 11) The only way out which I see is by Royce's "moral insight." '

185.4 treat] *aft. del.* 'th'

185.4 as] *bef. del.* 'an'

185.4 irreducibly] 'y' *ov.* 'e'

185.4 plural] *final* 'ity' *del.*

185.5 practically] *intrl.*

185.5 by] *bef. del.* 'any'

185.6 rules.] 's' *ov. period and period added bef. del.* '['Whose' *del.*] The difficulty of the moral life consists ['all' *del.*] wholly in the fact that goods are rival competitors for realization'

185.6 should be] *ab. del.* 'were'
185.9 sacrifice] *aft. del.* 'keep'
185.9 The] 'e' *ov.* 'is'
185.10 is . . . ¹and] *intrl.*
185.10–11 pleasures . . . perfections]
   each final 's' *poss. added*
185.11 have] *aft. del.* 'are'
185.12 shall] *aft. del.* 'The difficulty is
   the *good excluded.*'
185.17 That] 'at' *ov.* 'e'; *aft. del.* 'Act
   for the *best whole,* measured by every
   possible standard.'
185.17 is] *bef. del.* 'fo'
185.18 *whole,*] *comma ov. period*
185.18 the] 't' *ov.* 'T'

185.18 ²which] *aft. del.* 'in'
185.19 prevails] 's' *added; aft. del.*
   'the goods which'; *bef. del.* '['carry the
   most of' *del.*] preserve the most of
   what their vanquished rivals wished'
185.19 in] *intrl.*
185.19 which] *bef. del.* 'least completely annuls'
185.25 *fact*] *bef. del.* 'can prove or
   disprove that a thing is good, except'
185.25 prove] *bef. del.* 'its'
185.28 XIXth . . . 1880.] *insrtd. for del.*
   'Contemp. R.'; *bef. del.* 'The ultimate
   question'

15. NOTES FOR PHILOSOPHY 1: GENERAL INTRODUCTION TO
   PHILOSOPHY 1890–1891 #4455a

James's notes are contained in two ruled exercise books from A. A. Waterman
& Co., Boston. In the panel on the front cover of the first, James wrote 'Phil 1 |
1890–1' and numbered it 1. On the panel of the second notebook he wrote
'Phil I.' and numbered it 2. On the cover of the second book James wrote the
name 'F. W. Nichols' in pencil and on the inside back cover he wrote in pencil
the names 'Miss Hillard. | Mrs. Lord. | 8 Mᵗ Vernon St'. The first book is written
in ink up to the verso of the seventh leaf which starts 'Read more contents'
(191.33) in pencil and continues in pencil to the end of the book on 8 verso
(192.29). The passage 189.15–34 has been marked with diagonal lines through
the text. The second book is written throughout in ink, the text starting with
192.30 and ending on the verso of the seventh leaf. The eighth and last leaf has
been torn off irregularly in the upper third and is blank.

Emendations

186.29–30 undiscovered,] ~ₐ
187.9 Dialogs] Diaglogs
187.29 Cause,] ~ₐ |
188.27 ₐtalking] "~
188.28 Theaetetus] Thaeatetus
189.33 ₐSocrates] (~
190.33 Arcesilaus] Arcelisalaus
190.33 (Alexandria)] (~ₐ
191.28 Peirce] Pierce

192.36 "thing"] "~ₐ
193.1 Microcosmus] Microsmus
193.1 578)] ~ₐ
194.1 "What] ₐ~
194.21 Geulincx] Geulinx
194.25 Gita] Ghita
195.24 Mainz] Maunz
196.1 monadology] modadology

Alterations in the Manuscript

186.15–17 ontological . . . (2] *tr. by
   guideline fr. aft.* 'general.' | [186.12]
186.18 Absolute] 'A' *ov.* 'a'
186.27 talk!] *bef. del.* | '120 men would
   carry tradition to *black ['b' *ov.*
   'M'] unknown!'

186.28 Go back] *added in mrgn.*
186.28 years] *bef. del.* '–6 men!'
186.29 just] *aft. del.* 'C'
186.29 laws] *aft. del.* 'weight of
   atmosphere ignored,'
187.3 5] *ov.* '6'

187.5   Huxley] *insrtd. for del.* 'Darwin'
187.6–11   Kepler . . . 1687] *tr. by guideline fr. bef.* 'Go' [186.28]
187.8   Harvey 1628] *intrl.*
187.18–19   Atomism . . . determinism] *tr. by guideline fr. aft.* 'left—' [187.22]; *orig. tr. to aft.* '1890' [187.20]
187.27   criticizes] *bef. del.* 'Ph'
187.32   Kant] *aft. del.* 'Cousin's 4 kinds of Philosophy: | Sensualism, Idealism, Skepticism, Mysticism | Eclecticism' |
188.1   way] *aft. del.* 'phil'
188.10   Heracleitus] *underl. del.*
188.18   *Empedocles . . .* Evolutionism] *intrl.*
188.32   character] *aft. del.* 'martyrdom'
188.32   I] *aft. del.* 'II'
188.35   No writings] *aft. del.* 'No writing'
188.38   Aristippus b 435] *tr. by guideline fr. aft.* 'Xenophon' [188.36]
188.39   Morning!] *intrl.*
188.39–40   Journeys . . . Ægina] *insrtd.*
189.9–11   The . . . Sophists.] *tr. by guideline fr. bef.* 'All' [189.1]
189.9   logical] *intrl.*
189.10   teleology,] *bef. del.* 'ontology'
190.9   Nature] *aft. del.* 'Nature no'
190.28   322] *bef. del.* | '*Zeno 350–258 | Epicurus 341 270 [braced] | Both aim at *practice* | Stoicism a religion. | Cicero Lucretius Seneca Epictetus. | Philo BC–AD | Plotinus, Porphyry 3rd century A.D.'
190.29   322] 2'2' *ov.* '8'
190.33   1] *bef. del.* 'Œnisidemus'
190.35   life.] *bef. del.* 'Good is th'
190.37   Stoicism] 'm' *ov.* '2)'
190.39   Physics] *bef. del.* 'Virtue for its own sake.'
191.4   82] *intrl.*
191.12   Philo] *aft. del.* 'Augustine 354–430' |
191.12   BC] 'B' *ov.* 'A'
191.26   becomes] *aft. del.* 'ba'
[*begin penc.*]
191.35   Substance . . . them.] *ab. del.* 'Matter & form—substantial vs. accidental form.'
192.2   Not] *ov.* 'If'

192.2   *separable*] *bef. del.* '?—then'
192.10   Composite system.] *aft. del.* 'No materialism except | Atomism dead!'; *bef. del.* | 'Look back'
192.20   One] 'O' *ov.* 'o'
192.21   stands] *ab. del.* 'belongs'
192.21   what] *aft. del.* 'to determine the'
192.22   of truth] *tr. by guideline fr. aft.* 'ground'
192.22   or] *intrl.*
192.22   concrete] *intrl.*
192.23   explained] *intrl.*
192.25   face] *aft. del.* 'go back for the deepest reality to the'
192.27   abstract] *bef. del.* 'and general aspect'
192.29   from] *bef. del.* 'f'
[*end penc.*]
192.32   in . . . element] *tr. by guideline fr. aft. del.* 'than' [*see entry for* 192.33]
192.32   than] *intrl.*
192.33   thing.] *period added bef. del.* 'than'
192.36   ¹each] *aft. del.* 'qualities'
192.36   ²each] *ab. del.* 'the'
192.36   unfolds a great] *ab. del.* 'in a meeting place of'
193.4   Thing =] *added in mrgn.*
193.4   properties] *aft. del.* 'and'
193.5   Water] 'W' *ov.* 'w'
193.9   (p] *paren ov. start of* 'p'
193.11   Montaigne] *aft. del.* 'Renaissance' |
193.12   1543] *added in mrgn.*
193.12   de Revol.] *intrl.*
193.33   refraction] 'ra' *ov.* 'le'
194.7   Spinoza Leibnitz] *added*
194.8   Materialism] 'M' *ov.* 'C'
194.26   Spinoza] *aft. del.* 'Goethe' |
194.27   Walt] *aft. del.* 'Two attributes'
194.32   physicist] *bef. del.* | 'Deus quatenus'
194.34   p. 104] *added in mrgn.*
194.34   108] *intrl.*
194.36   Space] *aft. del.* 'No final cause' |
195.5   humility] *intrl.*
195.10   God's] 'G' *ov.* 'D'
195.22   ²at] *aft. del.* 'Studies law—'
195.22–23   Cartesian] 'C' *ov.* 'G'

195.27   London.] *insrtd.*
196.3   279] '2' *ov.* '3'
196.3   31] *bef. del.* | 'His'
196.5   live atoms] *intrl.*
196.5   indestructible] *insrtd.*
196.8   2) . . . life] ('2' *ov.* '7'); *tr. by*
   guideline fr. aft. 'Optimism' | [196.14]
196.9   3] *ov.* '2'
196.10   4] *ov.* '3'
196.11   5] *ov.* '4'
196.12   6) Evolution] *intrl.*
196.13   7] *ov.* '5'
196.14   8] *ov.* '6'
196.15   One] *aft. del.* 'Harder to give
   inner spirit | Read pp. 14–16 Nx Es.' |
196.17   Things] 'Th' *ov.* 'se'
196.17   changes,—] *intrl.*
196.21   But] 'B' *ov.* 'W'
196.21   primal] *intrl.*
196.23   simple homogeneous] *insrtd.*
   and circled
196.27   Contrapuntal] *insrtd.*

196.27   Read . . . 15] *tr. by guideline fr.*
   aft. 'change?' [196.25]
196.31   L.] *aft. del.* 'Idealism comes in' |
196.36   Substances] 'S' *ov.* 'M'
196.39   Make] 'M' *ov.* 'S'
197.2   Greek] *aft. del.* 'MB' |
197.12   Masham] 'M' *ov.* 'm'
197.15   Reasonableness] 'R' *ov.* 'C'
197.21   Read] *bef. del.* 'pp v, vi'
197.25   nominal] *ab. del.* 'real'
197.26   328] *intrl.*
197.27   in] *bef. del.* 'sub'
197.28   Progress] *aft. del.* 'His idea of
   eternal truth. | Irony of fate. Locke
   used as dogmatic text-book. Read
   pp. v, vi' |
197.29   1753] '3' *ov.* '2'
198.2   When] *aft. del.* 'or ob'
198.6   like . . . sk.] *ab. del.* 'like an
   antique skeptic—easy-going—'
198.8   Cause] *aft. del.* 'Belief—Ego'

16. Notes for Philosophy 10: Descartes, Spinoza,
   and Leibnitz 1890–1891 #4425

These notes (#4425) are contained in a ruled exercise book from A. A. Waterman & Co., Boston. In a panel on the front cover James wrote in pencil 'Des-
cartes *etc. [added] | Leibnitz Pluralism'. The writing is in pencil, except for
patches of ink, through the verso of the fifth leaf. On the recto of the sixth leaf
James began a listing, written vertically on the page (202.5–18), which he continued, also vertically, on one side of a loose leaf torn from the book (202.19–33),
this listing concluded, written horizontally, on the part-page verso of the sixth
leaf (202.34–204.2). On the other side of the loose leaf (199.24–200.6), James
started his notes on Descartes' chronology, which he completed on the recto
of the seventh notebook leaf (200.7–14). This Descartes material is printed out
of its notebook order on the evidence that after finishing the Leibnitz chronology in pencil starting on the recto of the third notebook leaf with 200.15,
James wrote in the upper right corner in ink: 'Descartes + 1650 | Spinoza
*1677 ['6' *ov.* '8'] | Locke 1704 | Newton 1717 | Leibnitz 1716' suggesting that
the Descartes matter was intended to precede the Leibnitz. On the verso of the
seventh leaf James made vertically a number of notations reproduced on
p. 203. He left a number of blank pages and turned the book end for end
and started to write forward starting with what would be the verso of the
eleventh leaf but the recto of the first leaf to be written from the end of the
book (204.3), finishing the inscription with the line and a half 'But . . . rational.'
(205.30). The recto of the twelfth leaf is blank, but on its verso James wrote in
ink 'A. I. Street | 12 Shepard St. | Dᵣ Hausknecht | 112 Boylston St.' James's
bracket is found at 199.16 '[No' (opening bracket only).

Textual Apparatus

Emendations

199.5   likes.] ~∧
200.29   1666] 1866
200.31   Rosicrucian] Roscicrucian
201.1–2   peaceable] peacable
201.32   indifference] indifferenc

202.34   Pomponatius] Pomponatious
204.22   actualized.] ~∧ |
204.23   –302.] –~∧ |
205.4   thoroughgoing,] ~. |
205.17   similarly] simarly

Alterations in the Manuscript

198.14   Bouillier . . . Rosmini] *penc. added*
198.15–16   , Renouvier . . . forms.] *penc. added bef. del. penc.* 'M'
[*begin penc.*]
198.27   founded] *ab. del.* 'pub.'
198.28   law of] *intrl.*
199.5   Cf. . . . 221] *insrtd.*
199.5   His] *intrl.*
199.8   either] *intrl.*
199.9   185] *insrtd.*
199.9   VI, VII] *intrl.*
199.10   p. 43 . . . 280] *insrtd.*
199.12   All] *ov.* 'Those'
199.14   288] *intrl.*
199.15   of] *ov.* 'in'
199.15   clear] *final* 'ly' *del.*
199.17   if . . . universe] *intrl.*
199.22   discussing] *aft. del.* 'the'
[*end penc.*]
199.25   1596] '9' *ov.* 'o'
199.27   no books] *intrl.*
199.28   etc.] *bef. del.* 'no books'
[*begin penc.*]
200.27   15 years old] *ink added*
200.30   Declines . . . Spinoza] *intrl.*
200.33   1667] '6' *ov.* '8'
200.36   more] *intrl.*
201.7   1676] '6' *ov.* '8'
201.11   knew] *ov. illeg.*
201.12   in] *ov.* 'at'
201.15   Guelph] *final* ' 's' *del.*
201.20   In . . . 90—] *intrl.*
201.22   1714] *aft. del.* '16'
201.32   accused . . . indifference.] *intrl.*
201.33   L's] *ov.* 'his'
201.34   Protestantism.] *bef. del.* |
'Akadem'
202.2   & Dresden] *added*
[*end penc.*]

202.14   Suarez] *alt. fr.* 'Suarz'
202.17   Montaigne's . . . 1580] *insrtd. aft. del.* 'Vanini's execution 1616 | Bacon's Novum organum 1620' |
202.18   Bruno burnt 1600] *aft. del.* 'O'; *bef. del.* | 'Vanini burnt 1618'
202.22   Shakespeare 1623] *insrtd.*
202.24   Descartes] *aft. del.* 'Shakes'
202.24   1637] '3' *ov.* '4'
202.31   Newtons . . . 1687] *insrtd. aft. del.* 'Leibnitz Theodicy 1716' |
202.32   1689] '9' *ov.* '8'
202.35   b.] *intrl.*
202.36   Picus] *added*
204.7   pity] 'p' *ov.* 'b'
204.8   the latter's] *ab. del.* 'its'
204.15   Spinoza's] *aft. del.* 'Spinoza's finale ↗ | Leibnitz ↘ | The voice of the silence' |
204.26   one] *aft. del.* 'i[illeg.]'
204.28   The] *ov.* 'Na'
204.34   unity?] *bef. del.* 'These ['kinds' *del.*] analogies—*1) [*intrl.*] space *2) [*ov. dash*] Thought'
205.1   of] *bef. del.* '['tho't' *del.*] thou'
205.4   3] *bef. del.* '& 4'
205.4   is] *ab. del.* 'are'
205.4   finite.] *period added bef. del.* 'parts of the object.'
205.5   No] *aft. del.* '4)'
205.9   being] *bef. del.* 'a'
205.13   conception] *aft. del. illeg.*
205.14   if] 'f' *ov.* 't'; *aft. del.* 'be'
205.14   finite] *bef. del.* 'or infinite'
205.17   T'] *aft. del.* 'the'; *bef. del.* 'know'
205.21   keep] *aft. del.* 'hold to'
205.28   easily] 'ily' *ov.* 'y'

608

17. Notes for Philosophy 20a: Psychological Seminary
1891–1892   #4392

The notes (#4392) are written in an exercise book of blue-ruled laid paper, measuring 8¼ x 6¾″, watermarked Pure Linen, the design of a cross between the two words. The notebook is from A. A. Waterman & Co., Boston, and in the blank panel on the front cover James wrote 'Aesthetics' in ink. To the right of the panel he sketched in pencil the outlines of two faces, and on the outside back cover he drew, again in pencil, what appears to be the back of a watch case. The leaves in the notebook are unnumbered; the writing on rectos and versos is in a mixture of ink and pencil, the ink predominating. Folio 1 recto contains only three lines of ink text (206.4–5), but its verso and 2 recto contain a number of pencil notations (206.6–15), those on the second leaf written vertically. Independent inscriptions in pencil and ink are found on fols. 2 verso through 4 recto ('*Essential* . . . unpleasantness' 206.16–207.25). The one reference on the verso of fol. 4 ('see . . . etc' 207.25–26) is in pencil as is the text on fol. 5, recto and verso (207.27–208.3). Folios 6–7 are blank, as is 8 recto, but the verso contains five lines of pencil text (208.4–6). Ink inscription begins again on fol. 9 (208.7–16) and continues through fol. 12 verso, a part-page ('with . . . way.' 209.36–39), although some pencil text (208.27–28 and 208.31–32) is found on fol. 10 recto (208.26–34). Folio 13 has an ink notation at its head (210.1), the lower half of the page having been irregularly torn off; its verso is blank. Folio 14 recto is blank, but pencil inscription fills the verso (210.2–17). The book ends with ink inscription on 15 recto (but with three pencil references) and verso, and 16 recto and verso, a part-page.

Emendations

206.28   Volkmann] Volkman
207.29   explained] explaned
208.6   Lehmann] Lehman
208.15   pain.)] ∼.ʌ

211.12   Levesque] Leveresque
211.15   –422)] –∼ʌ
211.21   Zurʌ] ∼.

Alterations in the Manuscript

206.6–15   *Major . . . scale*] *penc.*
206.6   big . . . top] *insrtd. at top of page aft. del.* '6 [*ov.* '5'; *poss. intended as a page no.*] S | 5 4'
206.9   mi⁴] *bef. del.* | 'or [*undel. in error*] ut⁴ mi⁴ sol⁴'
206.25–28   flickering . . . 306)] *penc.*
206.26   is] *ov.* 'are'; *aft. del.* '& hope'
207.1   or . . . activity] *insrtd.*
207.3–4   bad . . . vain] *penc.*
207.8   deferred] *aft. del.* 'deffer'
207.9   Insight . . . grounds] *penc.*
207.12   Pleasures] *bef. del.* | 'Blun'
207.13–16   The . . . intoxⁿ] *penc.*
207.17   pain] *bef. del.* 'or a'
207.19   *a triumph of*] *intrl.*

207.21–208.6   Food . . . tears.] *penc.*
207.35   47] '7' *ov.* '9'
208.2   is] *ov. poss.* 'are'; *aft. erased intrl.* '&'; *bef. erased intrl.* '[*illeg.*]a'
208.9   departs] *aft. del.* 'goes'
208.18   our] *ov.* 'us'
208.27–28   11 . . . (Sheffield)] *penc.*
208.31–32   13 . . . stimuli] *penc.*
208.32   weak,] *intrl.*
208.35   alternative] *aft. del.* 'great'
208.35   Dr] 'D' *ov.* 'M'
208.37   takes] *ab. del.* 'states'
209.6   seems] *aft. del.* 'is str'
209.8   that] *intrl.*
209.11   copious] *aft. del.* 'baffled expectatio'

209.11   stimulation] *bef. del.* 'the pains of craving and the pleasures of release.' *written vert. in left mrgn. and insrtd. aft.* 'stimulation' *w. guideline*

209.12   immediately] *aft. del.* 'in' *and poss. start of* 'p'

209.14   2a] *intrl. in error aft.* 'very'

209.16   bad] *aft. del.* '[*illeg. del.*] l'

209.18   1into] *intrl.*

209.18,19   nn.] *intrl.*

209.18   2into] *intrl.*

209.21   "disagreeables" and] *intrl.*

209.22   very] *ab. del.* 'more'

209.24   begun] *aft. del.* 'of'

209.27   pleasure] *ab. del.* 'nn'

209.31   bodily] *aft. del.* 'pain'

209.31   Not] *intrl. bef.* '*That*' *not reduced in error*

209.31-32   but . . . is] *ab. del.* 'is not'

209.32   form] *bef. del.* ', but only'

209.35   that] *bef. del.* 'from all the'

209.36   which] *bef. del.* ', [*undel. in error*] as Milton says'

210.2-17   The . . . McLeod] *penc.*

210.5   Spencer] *bef. del.* '— [*undel. in error*] Allen'

210.21   97] '7' *ov.* '5'

210.23   XIII] *ab. del.* 'XX'

210.26   Jas. . . . Psychology] *penc.*

210.28-29   Mosso . . . XXX.] *penc.*

210.29   XXX] *init.* 'X' *ov.* '3'

210.30   –210] *intrl.*

210.38   Essays] *intrl.*

211.8   355–60] *added*

211.9-10   vol . . . –207] *penc.*

211.14   E.] *intrl.*

211.16   pp. 129, 342] (2'p' *ov. period*); *intrl.*

211.16   p. 308] *intrl.*

211.16   III] *bef. del.* ', 308,'

211.22   to] *ab. del. vert. stroke*

211.23   386] *ab. del. poss.* '366'

211.26   Mill] *final* ' 's' *del.*

211.27   (The feelings)] *insrtd.*

211.28   Physiol.] *aft. del.* 'Phy'

211.29   System] *aft. del.* 'S [*ov.* 'P'] of'

211.30   T.] *aft. del.* 'F'

211.30   [Fortnightly] *bkt. ov. paren;* 'F' *ov.* 's'

211.30   Jan.] *intrl.*

211.30   1889] '9' *ov.* '8'; *bef. del.* '(?)'

18. Notes for Philosophy 20b: Psychological Seminary—The Feelings 1895–1896 #4504

Manuscript #4504 starts in a marbled hard-cover notebook from J. L. Fairbanks & Co., Boston. This notebook is the first of three in a series containing notes for various seminaries. (The second and third are transcribed as No. 20 and No. 25 in the present edition.) The text is written on rectos and versos in a mixture of pencil and ink on wove ruled paper, measuring 9¾ x 7½". The notebook was reversed and the text written from the back forward. The panel on the front cover is inscribed by James, 'Seminary of | 1895–6 | Book I.'; in the space between '1895–6' and 'Book I.' he wrote in pencil, probably at a later time, 'The Feelings', followed by a short rule. On the inside of this cover is pasted-in an envelope inscribed by James in pencil, 'Notes on Feeling | continued from page 31 | of this note book'. This is a reference to the loose leaves starting with p. 32 that continue the notebook and are contained in the envelope. All of the leaves are numbered in pencil, indicating that James added the numbers after he had assembled the text.

James wrote 212.3–15 on the verso of the first leaf (after 2 stubs) of the reversed notebook; the recto is blank but on what is now the foot (but was then the head) of the page there is a paste-over concealing nine deleted lines of text written at some earlier time before the notebook was reversed: 'Lehman: Hauptgezetze | Calls distinctness yet inseparableness of cognitive and | feeling elements the Kantian theory (15). Defends | this agst various attempts to prove two distinct | processes, as 1) ['the' *del.*] by the facts of retardation 2) | by

Schiff's sections of cord. [pain not pure when passed? | Columns cut, 47]; 3) Secondary sensation, | Not pure pain; 4) Külke's statement that our nicer | organs have feeling but no sensation'. A change of subject is begun on the second leaf recto, which is paged 1. Thereafter James foliated the leaves, but numbered them as if they were pages, the versos unnumbered: that is, the recto of the second leaf is 3, the recto of the third leaf is 5, and so on. At the foot of page 27 is an undeleted reference, 'Indiff. point. | Ziegler, 80 Lehman 182+', written before the notebook was reversed on what was then the head of the page and separated from the last line of the text, 'The *value* of the whole *attempt [ab. del. 'thing']* would' (225.33), by an ink line drawn across the page. Page [28] at the foot contains a paste-over that conceals several lines of deleted text again written at some earlier time before the notebook was reversed: 'Function. | Utility. Origin and evolution. | Cognitive function. | Question of primacy. Schop. II. 224 | Minot says (3rd Ed. 488) no ground to suppose | Feeling attached to one sensation rather than another | before ['general' *del.*] the *self* arose.' In the margin James had written '*paste*' and drawn directional lines to indicate the text that he wanted concealed. The text above the paste-over written after the notebook was reversed is continuous with the text at the head of p. 29 ('as immediate, | seems to be' 226.10). Page [30] (leaf 16ᵛ) has been glued over with a blank piece of paper, perhaps obliterating discarded or unpertinent notes. The text at the foot of p. 29, although continuous in sense with p. 31, shows some signs of disruption. The last words on p. 29 'divisions of its content' (226.27) end with a period; then after the glued-over p. [30], p. 31 begins with deleted 'but' followed by 'and the NS.' This p. 31 is the recto of the last preserved leaf in the notebook, its verso being glued-over with a blank and the leaf followed by 25 stubs of abstracted leaves.

A series of loose sheets written in pencil continues the text. At the foot of p. 31 after 'continuous at another?]' (227.10) James had written within brackets, 'see the loose sheets'. The first of the eleven sheets is headed in the pencil of the text, 'Continuation of blank-book on the Feelings, *p. 31*, beginning at back.' In the upper left corner James added later in ink, 'Book I. | "loose sheets" '. The text begins without paragraphing with 'The ejective data' (227.10). The paper of the sheets is thin wove, measuring 10¼ x 7", watermarked Merchant's Pure Bond in hollow letters. The sheets are written on the rectos only, foliated 32–42 in the upper right corners. Folio 33, starting 'between any "field" ' (227.21–22) after a deletion, is written on the reversed back of a deleted three-line trial also foliated 33. On the verso of fol. 35 and facing item 2 heading fol. 36 (228.13) James wrote in ink the reference transcribed in footnote 19 in the present edition. The text headed 'Lecture.' (229.19) heads fol. 40 and ends on the part-page 42. On the verso of this last leaf in the lower half, James wrote at some time in what is now brown ink, 'Chemicals that you can't make "pure" | Rau: Empfindung und Denken. | Râu'.

James's brackets are found at 221.8–13 '[These . . . respectively*].', 222.35–37 '[Of . . . described]', 223.5–6 '[Singer's . . . here.]', 223.11 '[Resemblance' (opening bracket only), 224.34 '[On' (opening bracket only), 225.33–36 '[The . . . world.]', and 227.7–10 '[Is . . . another?]'.

Emendations

213.16	phenomenon] phenomenen	215.17	mental.] ~ₐ
214.15	present.] ~ₐ	215.21	doesn't] doen't
214.32	foundation] fundation	215.25	reality).] ~)ₐ

216.22   me."] ~·ᴧ
216.35   2owns] own
217.9   transcendental] tran-|cendental
220.18   lose] lost
221.21   that] that | that
221.35   *We] ᴧ~
222.6   together.]ᴧ] ~.].
222.31   corrected.] ~ᴧ
222.37   described.] ~ᴧ

224.3   moment"] ~ᴧ
226.32   is.] ~ᴧ
227.13   g.)] ~·ᴧ
227.15   each)] ~ᴧ
227.20   tho'ts] thot's
228.28   known.'] ~·ᴧ
228.29   "respects"] "~'
229.18   (See] ᴧ~

Alterations in the Manuscript

212.3   it] *bef. del.* 'pleasant'
212.4   The] *aft. del.* 'The nature of the experience seems a rational ground'
212.4   logic] *aft. del.* 'f'
212.5   seems . . . be] *ab. del.* 'is'
212.6   he] *init.* 't' *del.; bef. del.* 'man'
212.6   would] *aft. del.* 'the'
212.6   deemed a rational] *aft. del.* 'a sufficient'
212.6   ground] *bef. del. intrl.* 'by others'
212.7   others] *ab. del.* 'the man'
212.8   what] *aft. del.* 'the'
212.9   objects] *aft. del.* 'experience'
212.10   what] *intrl.*
212.10   2feels] *intrl.*
212.10   be] *ab. del.* 'feel'
212.11   By] 'B' *ov.* 'A'
212.11   is] *ab. del.* 'has'
212.11–12 enabled] *aft. del.* 'the power'
212.14–15 why . . . man] ('why' *alt. fr.* 'what'); *intrl. for del.* 'by what *machin [del.* 'pow' *ab. del.* 'ery' *of* 'machinery'] the *fact comes about that the man [*undel. in error when* 'why . . . man' *intrl.*] ['has a' *del.*] has a feelin'
212.15   of essence] *ab. del.* 'about logical *ground* by'
212.18   Ego] *aft. del.* 'Self'
212.21   will] *bef. del.* 'elem'
212.24   is] *intrl.*
212.25–26 The . . . consciousness] *penc. added*
212.32   30,+ 37+] *penc. added*
213.3–6 Fouillée's . . . Meinong] *penc. except* 'Baldwin' *which is in ink*
213.4   Reid] 'i' *ov.* 'e'
213.8   Thinker?] *bef. del.* 'Subconsciousness & synthesis'

213.13   stuff] *bef. del.* 'or *Monistic ['M' *ov.* 'm'; 'n' *intrl.*] ego.'
213.14   Monistic] *aft. del.* 'Free will.'
213.16–18 All . . . content.] *penc.*
213.20   taking] *aft. del.* 'the'
213.23–214.7 First . . . this?] *penc.*
213.23   2the . . . experience] *ink added*
213.27   2in] 'n' *ov.* 's'
213.27–28 but . . . whatness.] *ab. comma ov. period*
213.28   conceived] *intrl.*
213.31   datum] *ab. del.* 'subjectivity'
213.31   subjectively] *intrl.*
213.31   as] 's' *ov.* 't'
213.32   but] *aft. del.* 'by'
214.11   It] *aft. del.* 'We'
214.13   he] *intrl.*
214.13   have] *intrl.*
214.13   been] 'en' *added*
214.21   immediately given] *intrl.*
214.28–29 By . . . datum] *intrl.; period om. in error*
215.3   "thises"] 'es' *ov. comma*
215.3   or whatnesses] *intrl.*
215.4   system] *init.* 's' *ov.* 'a'
215.7   involve] *final* 's' *del.*
215.7   2as] *ov.* 'in'
215.9   datum] *aft. del.* '['thing' *del.*] content as th'
215.10   unity] *aft. del.* 'y'
215.10   —That] *aft. del.* 'F'
215.15   one] *intrl.*
215.16   none of] *bel. del.* 'not'
215.20   Movement] *aft. del.* 'Repr'
215.24–27 A . . . come.] *penc.*
215.31   52] *aft. del.* '133'
215.33   Harder] *aft. del.* 'The datum, experience, phenomenon, content.'
215.35   in] *aft. del.* 'im'

216.1 Datum's] *aft. del.* 'da'
216.4–5 C. . . . states.] *penc.*
216.10 old] *intrl.*
216.12 every] *aft. del.* 'the d'
216.13 things] *aft. del.* 'the th'
216.14–15 the same] *intrl.*
216.15 as such] *intrl.*
216.16 mes] 's' *added*
216.16 fall] *final* 's' *del.; aft. del.* 'makes'
216.19 past and remote] *ab. del.* 'other'
216.20 past] *aft. del.* 'oth'
216.25 is] *intrl.*
216.25 given] *aft. del.* 'appears'
216.26 it] *aft. del.* 'the'
216.28 being] *final* 's' *del.*
216.30 are] *aft. del.* 'don't'
216.30–31 , but each other's.] *penc. comma ov. ink period; penc. added*
217.1–11 Things . . . present.] *penc.*
217.1 experiences] *bef. del.* 'of | Some of the things perceived'
217.13 an] *final illeg. del.*
217.15 entirety)] *paren ov. comma bef. del.* 'so to speak,'
217.15 so to speak] *ab. del.* 'wh'
217.16 associates] *aft. del.* 'inner'
217.18 when] *aft. del.* 'are'
217.26 Lasswitz . . . 1896] *penc. added*
217.28 *Stein*] *brace and* 'Stein' *penc. added*
217.35 Piat] *aft. del.* 'Maher'
217.35 *Spindler*] *penc. intrl.*
217.35 Knauer] *bef. penc. del. penc. added* '*Cushman*'
217.36 Nature] *bef. penc. del. penc. added* '*Stein*'
217.37 *Rice*] *penc. added*
217.38 l'Erreur.] *bef. penc. del. penc. added* '*Dearborn*'
218.1 Inquiry] *bef. penc. del. penc. added* '*Thorndike.*'
218.2 XXVI] *bef. penc. del. penc. intrl.* '*Hashell*'
218.4 *Huntington*] *penc. added*
218.6 *Thorndike.*] *penc. added*
218.7 *Holt.*] *penc. added*
218.9 *Solomons*] *penc. added*
218.10 *Cabell*] *penc. added aft. ink del. penc.* 'Rickaby'
[*begin penc.*]

218.21 Dozen] *aft. del.* ' "Mankind," '
219.13 neighbors] *aft. del.* 'contigua in the'
219.20 over] *aft. del.* 'of'
219.21 as] 'a' *ov.* 's'
219.29 there] *aft. del.* '(which'
219.29 seen] *aft. comma ov. period and del.* 'As they a'
219.30 will] *ab. del.* 'is'
219.31 appear] *aft. del.* 'be'
219.32 the] *ov. poss.* 'an'
219.33 all] *added*
219.33 this] *bef. del.* 'al'
220.2 expressed] *aft. del.* 'explained so'
220.4 increasing] *aft. del.* 'altering. The subjective part thereof shrinking con'
220.6 in] *bef. del.* 'concentrically'
220.6 2matter] *aft. del.* 'marginal'
220.10 represents] *bef. del.* 'this'
220.25–26 Imagined] *bef. del.* 'water wil'
221.2 absent] *aft. del.* 'utterly unimportant'
221.4 adjectives] *ab. del.* 'properties'
221.5 To] *aft. del.* 'A property is some'
221.6–7 limitations] *aft. del.* 'peculi'
221.8 1laws] *bef. del.* 'are all laws'
221.9 whereas] *intrl.*
221.10 subjective] *ab. del.* 'ideal'
221.10 attributes] 's' *added; aft. del.* 'an'
221.10 obey] *final* 's' *del.; ab. del.* 'has'
221.11 can't] *ov.* 'don't'
221.12 them] *ab. del.* 'those attributes'
221.17 parts] *aft. del.* 'separate ['and' *del.]*'
221.19 consisting] *aft. del.* 'consitin'
221.21–22 , analogously,] *insrtd. for del.* 'in the same way,'
221.22 abolish] *aft. del.* 'make no differ'
221.23 no] *ov.* 'it'
221.26 Each] *aft. del.* 'So'
221.30 whole] *intrl.*
221.30 mental] *aft. del.* 'the'
221.32 either the] *insrtd. for del.* 'the['re' *del.]*'
221.33 1changes,] *aft. del.* 'either'; *bef. del.* 'al'

221.35–38   We . . . –51.] *fn. written*
vert. in mrgn.

221.38   II, 548–51.] *ink alt. fr.* 'III, 549'

222.11   Substantive] *aft. del.* 'Subst'

222.12   a] *ov.* 'an'

222.12   yet] *intrl.*

222.12   other] *intrl.*

222.13   evasively] *aft. del.* 'el'

222.14–21   "Our . . . 196.] *ink*

222.16   area] *aft. del.* 'fog'

222.25   in] *ov.* 'it'

222.26   is] *ov.* 'w'

222.28   changed] *ab. del.* 'new'

223.2   Continuity] 'C' *ov.* 'T'

223.10   was] *aft. del.* 'we'

223.12   total] *intrl.*

223.12   of the field] ('o' *of* 'of' *ov.*
period); *insrtd.*

223.14   notion] *ab. del.* 'conception'

223.14   an inner] *insrtd. for del.* 'a'

223.20   to] *insrtd.*

223.23   every] *aft. del.* 'everyt'

223.27   &] *intrl.*

223.27   no)] *paren ov. period*

223.33   When] *intrl. bef.* 'Once' *not*
reduced in error

223.34   quite] *bef. del.* 'immaterial'

223.36   an] *aft. del.* 'a notion'

224.2   and] *intrl.*

224.2   actually] 'ac' *ov.* 'so' | *and bef.*
del. 'far as'

224.4   there is *something*] *intrl. ab.*
comma ov. period and period not
added to 'something' *in error*

224.10   whenever] *aft. del. comma and*
'that'

224.29   never are] *ab. del.* 'are not'

224.29   terms] *aft. del.* 'except'

224.30   But] *insrtd. bef.* 'Sameness' *not*
reduced in error

224.34   pluralistic] *intrl.*

224.35   Same] 'S' *ov.* 's'

225.2   Object] 'O' *ov.* 'o'

225.2   Object] 'O' *ov.* 'o'

225.3   Object] 'O' *ov.* 'o'; *bef. del.* 'is
*now [*insrtd. for del.* 'that object
plus'] the margin, i.e.'

225.10   stand] *aft. del.* 'serve'

225.13   not] *aft. del.* 'that'

225.17   growth or] *insrtd.*

225.19   2datum] 'd' *ov.* 'n'

225.22   meant] *aft. del.* 'that the other

part'; *bef. del.* '(even though not
completely given)'

225.23   only . . . neither] *ab. del.* 'either,
or both'

225.23   may] *bef. del.* 'not'

225.25   itself] *intrl. aft. del. intrl.* 'also'

225.30   proleptically] *intrl.*

225.33   attempt] *ab. del.* 'thing'

225.34   already] *insrtd.*

225.35   pretended] *intrl.*

225.36   in] *aft. del.* 'it'; *bef. del.* 'the'

225.36   its] *ov.* 'a'

226.2   is] 's' *ov.* 't'

226.4   "fact,"] *comma ov. period bef.*
del. 'The machinery'

226.5   in] *ab. del.* 'does n't'

226.5   implying] 'ing' *added*

226.5–6   an entire] *intrl.*

226.9   one] 'o' *ov.* 'd'

226.11   as] *aft. del.* 'it is'

226.15   many] *intrl.*

226.16   my] *aft. del.* 'data'

226.16   datum] 'um' *ov.* 'a'

226.18   *postulates*] *bef. del.* 'in that'

226.21   not] *bef. del.* 'a'

226.21   grenzbegriffe] *final* 'e' *added*

226.26   Cf.] *ov.* 'Vide'

226.27   outer] *intrl.*

226.27   and] *aft. del.* 'but'; *period foll.*
'content' | *undel. in error*

226.28   which] *aft. del.* 'comes'

226.28   one of the] *ab. del.* 'an'

226.28   realities] 'ies' *ov.* 'y'

226.28   believed] *alt. fr.* 'belief'

226.29   even] *ab. del.* 'also'

226.32   worlds] *bef. del.* '['begin' *del.*]
together'

226.32   I.e.] *bef. del.* 'from the point of
view of thatness'

226.34   datum] *bef. del.* 'to be'

226.35   1be] *bef. del.* 'at'

226.35   peculiar] *intrl.*

226.36   whose] *alt. fr.* 'which'; *bef. del.*
'is not'

227.4   do] *ab. del.* 'are'

227.5   But first] *intrl. bef.* 'In' *not*
reduced in error

227.13   field] *aft. del.* 'world'

227.13   also] *intrl.*

227.13   that] *bef. del.* 'their ['ir' *ov.* 'y']
['postulate' *del.*] identical content
resemb'

614

227.16 My] *aft. del.* 'I sa'
227.17 of thought,] *ab. del. comma*
227.19 (*twice*) your] *final* 's' *del.*
227.19 thoughts] *intrl.*
227.20 N.S.] *intrl.*
227.20 my] *alt. fr.* 'mine'
227.20 tho'ts] *intrl.*
227.21 between] *aft. del.* 'between [*undel. in error*] my tho'ts obtains just as much'
227.23 together] *aft. del.* 'con-comitantly.'
227.24 between the] *ab. del.* 'of'
227.24 of] *insrtd. for del.* 'between'
227.25 field] *aft. del.* 'same NS'
227.26 ¹of] *ab. del.* 'between'
227.26 to] *ab. del.* 'and'
227.27 when] *alt. fr.* 'which'; *aft. del.* 'in'
227.29 also] *insrtd.*
227.30 Immediate.] 'I' *ov.* 'i'; *period insrtd. bef. del.* 'field.'
227.31 differ?] *qst. mk. ov. comma*
227.36 both] *aft. del.* 'are'
227.36 ¹the] *ov.* 'sy'
227.37 And] *ab. del.* 'But'
227.37 not] *intrl.*
227.37 more] *bef. del.* 'than that'
227.37–228.1 than physical] *insrtd.*
228.1 ²physical] *aft. del.* 'more not yet given in the physical is tho't of as an extension'
228.1–2 completely] *aft. del.* 'from'
228.4 the physical system] *ab. del.* 'it'
228.6 describe] *aft. del.* 'express the fa'
228.8 categories] 'ies' *ov.* 'y'
228.9 other:—] *colon insrtd.; dash ov. period*

228.9 ¹sameness] *bef. del.* 'in ['objects' *del.*] things, and so'
228.10 fulfilment of] *insrtd. for del.* 'but no stuff that isn't in and of some field. *Why* *and by what "forces" [*intrl.*] they develope is another matter. | 2) Eventual relations among'
228.11 content,] *bef. del.* '['etc.' *del.*] cognitive'
228.11 another,] *bef. del.* 'etc.'
228.13 postulated] 'ed' *ov.* 'ion'
228.13 whose whatness] *blue penc. ab. del.* 'that'
228.13 some] *ab. del.* 'the'
228.17 &] *intrl.*
228.21 Transcendental] *final* 'ism' *del.*
228.27 or . . . fields,] ('S' *ov.* 's' in 'Same'); *intrl. w. caret ov. comma*
228.28 & known.] ('known.' *bef. erased word*); *insrtd. aft. erased period*
228.28 contents] *aft. del.* 'changing'
228.28 continuing] 'ing' *ov.* 'ous'
228.29 into] *ab. del.* 'with'
228.30 stable] *intrl.*
228.30 changing] *aft. del.* 'tho'ts'
228.31 substituting] *ab. del.* 'points of'
228.34 at any rate] *intrl.*
228.35 some] *intrl.*
228.37 memory] *aft. del.* 'etc point'
228.38 content] *bef. del.* 'actually'
229.1 given] 'g' *ov.* 'd'
229.4 &] *intrl.*
229.6 terms] *bef. erased word*
229.15 How] 'H' *ov.* 'W'
229.18 p] *aft. del.* 'last'
229.32 object] *aft. del.* 'more'
229.32 eject] *aft. del.* 'more'
229.37 mysterious] *aft. del.* 'continuo'

Deleted and Undeleted Versos

[*del. fol.* 33ᵛ: *orig. fol.* 33; *orig. continuation of fol.* 32, *corresponding to text* 227.21–22] '['the' *del.*] my own ['NS. [*ab. undel.* 'field'] and my' *del.*] tho'ts qua what (i.e. as my own NS. and any tho't of mine which it may condition'

[*undel. fol.* 42ᵛ, *written in brown ink on lower half*] 'Chemicals that you can't make "pure" | Rau: Empfindung und Denken. | Râu'

19. Notes on Stout's *Analytic Psychology* for Psychology Course 1896–1898 #4407

Manuscript #4407 consists of a series of ruled wove leaves, unwatermarked, made into a notebook by folding and quiring. The folded leaves measure 8¼ x

6¾″. The leaves are unnumbered and are inscribed in pencil on recto and verso through the second line on fol. 6 recto, ending 'The elements are habits' (233.7–8). Thereafter James shifts to ink up to the conclusion of part-page fol. 7 recto, ending 'to the old one.' (233.31). On the verso of this final leaf James added 233.32–34 in pencil, as well as the profile of a man's face and a decorative circle.

Emendations

230.18   267,] ~–
231.2   terms.''] ~.ᴀ
231.10   do] to

232.11   (But] ᴀ~
232.27   *Intussusception*] Intusception

Alterations in the Manuscript

[*begin penc.*]
230.10   247, 55] *insrtd.*
230.20   II. . . . 591] *insrtd.*
230.26   Ward] 'W' *ov.* 'S'
230.28   265] *ov.* 'Dis'
230.29   Compare] 'Com' *ov.* 'Say'
231.4   non-rational] *final* 'n' *of* 'non' *ov.* 't'; *bef. del.* 'trains'
231.7   an infinite] *alt. fr.* 'a finite'
231.19   its] *ov.* 'a'
231.21   suggested] *bef. del.* 'by'
231.23   Inchoate] *aft. del.* 'Deceptive: [*colon undel. in error*]'
231.25   function] *aft. del.* 'content'
231.27–29 Drunkenness . . . mind.] *circled and poss. added later*
231.29   *some*] *ov.* 'one'
231.32   hitherto] *aft. del.* 'th'
232.5–12 The . . . phrasemongers)] *circled*
232.8   single behavior] *ab. del.* 'sort of act'
232.13   time] *intrl.*
232.16   expressions] *ab. del.* 'results'
232.19   subjective,] *comma ov. period bef. del.* 'They ar'
232.19   in] *ab. del.* 'of'
232.20   Things,] *bef. del.* 'genera, cau'
232.24   with] *aft. del.* 'wh'

232.24   ¹the] *final* 'ir' *del.*
232.25   hate] 'te' *ov.* 'd'
232.25–26 (except . . . action)] *opening paren ov. comma; closing paren ov. vert. line ov. comma*
232.26   we] *intrl.*
232.30   lived] *aft. del.* 'living'
232.30   matter,] *comma ov. period*
232.30   a continuous broth] *added*
232.32   obeyed] *aft. del.* 'to'
232.33   abstracted] *aft. del.* 'recognized *& [undel. in error]'
233.1   from] *aft. del.* 'in what does it consist?'
233.2   See . . . reasoning.] *insrtd.*
233.4   ᴀconcrete] *db. qt. del.*
[*end penc.*]
233.10   There] *aft. del.* 'In the mental world there is always a residuum of'
233.11   configuration] *aft. del.* 'form of'
233.12   really] *aft. del.* 'new'
233.13   (Wundts . . . synthesis)] *intrl.*
233.13   mere] *aft. del.* 'element'
233.14   one] *aft. del.* 'a force'
233.16   For] *bef. penc. del.* 'in'
233.18   and] *bef. del.* 'far'
233.20–21 action] *aft. del.* 'reaction'
233.21   choice] *aft. del.* 'there is'

20. Notes for Philosophy 20b: Psychological Seminary—The Philosophical Problems of Psychology   1897–1898
#4505, #4506

This marbled hard-cover notebook (#4505) from J. L. Fairbanks is the second in a series of three containing notes for various seminaries. (The first notebook is transcribed as No. 18 in the present edition.) The notebook is reversed, the text written from the back forward in a mixture of ink and pencil. On what is now the front cover (but was originally the back) James has inscribed on the pasted-on panel: 'Book II | [short rule] | The Self.—Pure | Experience, etc. | 1897–8'.

The numbering of the thirteen leaves comprising this notebook presents something of a mystery. James uncharacteristically seems to have numbered the pages before he began writing. The numbers were then altered at two different times. James originally numbered the rectos only, silently numbering the versos, so that the rectos of the thirteen leaves are numbered 1–25, in the order 1 3 5 etc. At some point for reasons that remain obscure, this sequence was altered to take into account the numbering of the first five versos, so that the altered sequence is as follows: leaf 1 recto is numbered 1, leaf 1 verso is numbered 3, 2 recto is numbered 2 over 3, 2 verso is numbered 5, 3 recto is numbered 4 over 5, 3 verso is numbered 7, 4 recto is numbered 6 over 7, 4 verso is numbered 9, 5 recto is numbered 8 over 9, 5 verso is numbered 11. With the sixth leaf this sequence of numbering stops on the versos but continues on the rectos, so that the thirteenth leaf is numbered 18 after deleted 25. James started the notebook writing on the rectos only, but with the tenth leaf, numbered 15 over 19 on the recto ('The brain . . . in their' 237.37–238.10), he continued the inscription on its verso, numbered $15\frac{1}{2}$. He then continued on recto and verso, numbering the verso of the eleventh leaf $16\frac{1}{2}$ and the verso of the twelfth leaf $17\frac{1}{2}$. The verso of the thirteenth leaf had been numbered 26 (following the original 25 of its recto) at some earlier time. James deleted the 26 and after it wrote '19 to 26' while at the foot of the verso ('. . . we may' 241.23), he wrote '[Go back to page 27, on the reverse side of page 1]'. The text continues with the verso of the first leaf, numbered 27 after deleted 3. The following versos are numbered 28 (after deleted 5), 29 (over original 7), 30 (over original 9), and 31 (over original 11). He continued writing on the versos numbering them 32–35. Since these last four versos (through the ninth leaf) had originally been silently numbered, the numbering is new.

The case of these renumberings is not clarified by James's direction at the foot of leaf nine verso (paged 35): '[For continuation of this, see Book III, p. 18'. This 'Book III' is in a notebook (#4506) sold by Charles W. Sever, University Bookstore, Cambridge. On the original label James had written in ink 'Pleasure & Pain'. James reversed the notebook and on the pasted-on panel on what is now the front cover he wrote: 'Book III | Seminary of 1897–8'. Below a short rule he wrote, 'Theoretic Psychology | [short rule] | Seminary of 1903–4', the title of a later seminary. Inside the cover is inscribed 'William James | 95 Irving S^t | Cambridge | [rule]' in James's hand. Preceding the first leaf are eight stubs. On the sixth stub written vertically is '*You think you are moving, whereas it is the other *R.R. [*intrl.*] train that is moving.—You'.

The first leaf, numbered 18, was obviously inscribed after the completion of p. 35 of the preceding notebook since its text (which begins in mid-sentence of a deletion that began on p. 35) carries on the syntax and thought of p. 35 ('continuity in the ['noetic' *del.*] ['series is interest in the "topic" to which the terminus belongs, in the wider' *del.*] total series' 245.24). Moreover, the first line was inscribed lower than normal on the page following the heading 'The "pure experience" hypothesis | Continuation of Book II, p. 35 | [short rule]'. Why James numbered this first page as 18 is something of a mystery. It seems likely that he originally intended to write in this notebook as he had started with #4505, that is, on rectos only but silently paging the blank versos. For instance, the verso of the first leaf is blank and the recto of the second leaf is numbered 20, but starting with the verso of this second leaf James wrote in order on both rectos and versos and paged accordingly. One may guess, but it is only a guess, that he was still thinking in terms of modified foliation, and p. 35 would have been followed by 36, which would have been fol. 18. The pagination after 20 is regular except that 30 and 36 are not numbered. However, in error the verso of the thirteenth leaf is paged 42, the same as its recto. The recto of the next leaf is unnumbered, but its verso is paged 44, thus continuing the error with subsequent pages. The number for p. 51 was added ahead of the deletion of a 57 on the recto of the eighteenth leaf, and its verso is correctly 52. Whether this odd numeration 57 has anything to do with the conclusion on this p. 51 of the 1897–1898 seminary halfway down the page and the start, with heading, on the same page of the seminary of 1903–1904, transcribed here as No. 25, is obscure.

James's brackets are found at: 241.22–35 '[This . . . terminates.]', 242.19–22 '[Avenarius's . . . hypothesis.]', 243.38–40 '[Yet . . . that]', 244.5 '[The' (opening bracket only), 247.30–35 '[But . . . eye.]', 249.12–13 '[Does . . . relations?]', 249.17–18 '[I . . . being.]', 253.36–40 '[The . . . "experiences."]' (closing bracket deleted), 254.21–28 '[For . . . All.]', 256.38–257.36 '[The . . . whatever.]', 258.13–16 '[The . . . it.]'.

Emendations

235.11	the] the the	246.30	field)] ~ₐ
237.31	series"] ~ₐ	246.36	"double-] ₐ~-
238.6	2)] ~ₐ	247.20	creation] creatin
239.15	2*of*] *om.*	248.5	thought-] -~
240.18	*comparison.*] ~ₐ	248.18	"activity"] "~ₐ
240.35	are] are are	248.36	exists] exists | exists
241.10	desirability] desireability	253.23	ₐas] (as
241.35	3,)] ~,ₐ	255.30	search] seach
244.1	the] The	256.3	bewusstheit] bewussheit
245.3	Hodgson's] Hogdson's	258.30	P.ₐ] ~."
245.4	taken] take	258.33	explained.] ~ₐ
246.29	34)] ~ₐ		

Alterations in the Manuscripts

234.9   a)] *intrl.*
234.9   knowing] *aft. del.* 'knowledge'
234.9   b)] *intrl.*
234.10 c)] *intrl.*
234.12 division] *aft. del.* 'dif'
234.16 Suppose] 'S' *ov.* 's'; *aft. del.* 'If you'
234.21 Space . . . as] *insrtd. for del.* 'Mind'
234.23 action-] *aft. del.* 'point on which action takes place'
234.25 with] *ab. del.* 'to'
234.25 be] *aft. del.* 'correspond. Can'

234.26 obvious] *aft. del.* 'necces'
234.29 practically] *ab. del.* 'conc'
235.1   a] *aft. del.* 'at'
235.5   So] *bef. del.* 'the brain's own'
235.7   content] *aft. del.* 'mind's'
235.9   Where] *aft. del.* 'The self'
235.11 systematized] *ab. del.* 'ordered and graded'
235.12 a . . . feeling] *ab. del.* 'the self'
235.12 and] *bef. del.* 'which in fact seems to have no other content than ['the' *del.*] the feeling of the body for the kernel of its content.'

235.17   as a] *ab. del.* 'on the'
235.22   a] *aft. del.* 'dominate'
235.23   being] *bef. del.* 'C at'
235.25   keeps] *ov.* 'is'
235.26   masses] *aft. del.* 'amo'
235.27   positionally] *aft. del.* 'from the point of view'
235.27   as] *intrl.*
235.31   objects] *aft. del.* 'enti'
236.3   Activity] *bef. del.* 'in' *and start of* 'p'
236.6   chief] *bef. del.* 'immedi'
236.8   has] *bef. del.* 'its cause in con'
[*begin penc.*]
236.11   As . . . ¹in] ('incentives' *ink ab. del.* 'entering'); *ab. del.* 'In'
236.11   appear_∧] *comma del.*
236.13   such] *ab. del.* 'future' *bef. del.* 'is'
236.13   acts] *alt. fr.* 'active'
236.21   in . . . future] *ab. del.* 'therein'
236.22   also] *intrl.*
236.28   representation] 'ta' *intrl.*
236.30   fall] *aft. del.* 'stand or'
236.30   out] *ab. del.* 'now'
236.31   ¹of] *bef. del.* 'the'
236.39   field] *bef. del.* 'what'
237.1   were] *bef. del.* 'and inspissated'
237.2   in] *bef. del.* 'the [*'tendency' del.*] [*illeg. del.*] determination of one'
237.8   each] *bef. del.* 'mome'
237.9   process] *aft. del.* 'selection'
237.9–10   possible] *intrl.*
237.10   become] 'come' *ab. del.* 'real.'
237.16   issue.] *period added bef. del.* 'of the'
237.20   teleology] *aft. del.* 'effe'
237.22   short] *bef. del.* 'the monis'
237.23   PHENOMENISTIC] *ab. del.* 'MONISTIC'
237.28   & sensations] *ab. del.* 'of the body'
237.28   memories,] *bef. del.* 'feelings'
237.28   ideals_∧] *paren del.*
237.29   Physical] *aft. del.* '"Things"'
237.29   ditto.] *bef. del.* 'The "things," quâ actual, are percepts. ['When they are called termini' *del.*] It is as concepts that they are *Termini.* | Where does the *brain* come in on this [*illeg.*]? | ['The physical things' *del.*] ['Says' *del.*] The field'

237.32   transitive] *aft. del.* 'The positions of equilibrium ['are' *del.*] are substa'
237.35   The] *aft. del.* 'But'
237.37   called] *aft. del.* 'representative'
237.37   termini.] *bef. del.* 'From'
237.37   The] *aft. del.* 'The brain and its activities hardly ever appear perceptually, usually only as concepts. Concepts nowadays of something physically causative of ['phenom' *del.*] experience continua.'
237.39   as] *intrl.*
[*end penc.*]
238.4   self with] *ab. del.* 'field of'
238.4   fields] *alt. fr.* 'feelings'
238.7   to 1)] *intrl.*
238.10   abstract] *ab. del.* 'conceived'
238.12   no other] *ab. del.* 'the same'
238.17   the field] *ab. del.* 'it'
238.17   many] *bef. del.* 'termini, actual'
238.18   Prospectively] 'spective' *ov.* 'leptical'
238.20   objects known] *ab. del.* 'termini'
238.20   large] *aft. del.* 'the'
238.25   system] *ab. del.* 'world'
238.34   segregation] *aft. del. intrl.* 'su'
238.37   ends] *bef. del.* 'with "ideas" reporting'
238.38   to] *bef. del.* '"selves"'
239.2   however] *bef. del.* 'the original ['what' *del.*] immediate what or'
239.6   melting] *bef. del.* 'fringing margins'
239.8   earlier] *ab. del.* 'other'
239.10   and] *bef. del.* 'the'
239.11   fields] *bef. del.* 'report'
239.13–16   nothing . . . itself] *underl. added;* 'a definite' *not underl. in error*
239.15   certain . . . sorts] *intrl.*
239.19   the] *bef. del.* 'scr'
239.19–20   between] *aft. del.* 'of'; *bef. del.* 'phenom'
239.23   them] *intrl.*
239.29   terminate] *bef. del.* 'in'
239.30   relation] *ab. del.* 'logical connexion'
240.1   S] *ov.* 'A'
240.2   long] *aft. del.* 'large'
240.3   final] *ov.* 'ne'
240.4   M_∧] *comma del.*
240.5   ¹or] *bef. del.* 'ascribed to a'

240.7 classificatory] *aft. del.* 'logical'
240.9 fields.] *period alt. fr. comma bef.*
del. 'which'
240.9 These] *insrtd.*
240.9 in turn] *intrl.*
240.10 may] *bef. del.* 'also'
240.10 even as] *ab. del.* 'like'
240.10–11 has so figured.] *intrl.*
240.11 various original] *intrl.*
240.12 "logical"] *intrl.*
240.13 parts of] *intrl.*
240.13 diverse] *final* 's' *del.*
240.15 1)] *intrl.*
240.15 classificatory] *intrl.*
240.17 abstract] *intrl.*
240.17 or] *aft. del.* 'that may'
240.17 types] 't' *ov.* 'n'
240.17 appear] *final* 'ed' *del.; aft. del.*
'have'
240.19 system] *ab. del.* 'field'
240.19 ideal] *intrl.*
240.19 aesthetically] *alt. fr.* 'ethically'
240.20 those] *aft. del.* 'ide'
240.25 great] *aft. del.* 'verifi'
240.27 or] *bef. del.* 'lo'
240.28 psychologic] *intrl.*
240.30 more] *ab. del.* 'only'
240.30 streams] *bef. del.* 'or of such
union of them'
240.31 think] 'k' *ov.* 'g'
240.31 the] *bef. del.* 'termini'
240.32 it contains] *intrl.*
240.32–33 those . . . quality] ('those'
insrtd. for del. 'the immed'; 'quality'
orig. bef. del. 'that figure a sys-' |);
tr. by guideline fr. aft. 'contains'
240.35 that] *aft. del.* 'that'
240.36 given] *bef. del.* 'in system'
240.40–241.4 3 . . . respectively.]
insrtd. vert. in mrgn.
241.1 4] *bef. del.* 'f'
241.2 epistemological] *ab. del.* 'noetic'
241.3 exhibit] *aft. del.* 'show'
241.3 these] *alt. fr.* 'this'
241.6 that] *bef. del.* 'it'
241.9 system] *bef. del.* 'one'
241.10 2] *ov.* 'tw'
241.11 with] *aft. del.* 'as having a
permanent existence in space,'
241.11 measureable] 'ur' *ov. poss.* 'ea'
241.12 in] *aft. del.* 'and power of
movement in'

241.14 in their] *aft. del.* 'either'; *bef.*
del. 'sensational'
241.14 as] *aft. del.* 'or'
241.15 epistemologic] *ab. del.* 'noe-|*tic
[*undel. in error*]'
241.20 (where] *paren ov. comma*
241.20 or] *ab. del.* 'and'
241.21 make] *aft. del.* 'are'
241.21 &] *intrl.*
241.22 conation.] *period ov. comma*
bef. del. 'or'
241.25 be] *bef. del.* 'fe'
241.26 speak] *aft. del.* 'conceive fictit'
241.27 objects] *aft. del.* 'fictitious'
241.28 to] *aft. del.* 'outside'
241.30 and] *bef. del.* 'trans-s'
241.31 &] *intrl.*
241.33 of] *bef. del.* 'a ['sp' *del.*]
psychologic field'
241.35 a] *intrl.*
241.36–37 content] *ab. del.* 'object'
241.40 in] *bef. del.* 'the pl'
242.2 happens] *bef. del.* 'there'
242.4 "change of base"] ('change of'
intrl.; 'base' *alt. fr.* 'metabases'); *tr. by*
guideline fr. aft. '-experience' [242.5]
242.19 Avenarius's] *alt. fr.*
'Avenarious's'
242.19 being] 'ing' *added ov.* 'a'; *aft.*
del. 'seeming to'
242.19 a] *insrtd.*
242.20 absolute] *ab. del.* 'mere'
242.21 of] *bef. del.* 'pure materialism'
242.21 2system] *aft. del.* 'system.]'
242.23 on] *bef. del.* 'the'
242.24 first] *aft. del.* '—first'
242.26 a] *intrl.*
242.27 parts] *bef. del.* 'of other fields
which brains'
242.28 these] *alt. fr.* 'they'
242.28 latter] *intrl.*
242.33 such] *intrl.*
242.34 system] *final* 's' *del.*
242.39 as] *underl. del.*
243.2 (the . . . individual)] *intrl.*
243.4 that] *ab. del.* 'a'
243.4 2of] *bef. del.* 'that'
243.4 same] *intrl.*
243.6 3's,] *apostrophe ab. del. hyphen;*
bef. del. 'the parallelists say it does
not whilst'
243.19 each system 2] *ab. del.* 'two'

243.19 forms] 's' *ab. del.* 's'
243.19 severally] *intrl.*
243.20 be] *bef. del.* 'f'
243.21 simultaneously] *intrl.*
243.22 3] *ov.* '4'
243.22 same] 's' *ov.* 't'
243.23 3] *aft. del.* '4,'
243.28 ¹series˄] *comma del.*
243.28 representively] 'tive' *ov.* 'tati'
243.29 can figure] *ab. del.* 'as'
243.30 then] *ab. del.* 'in system 3'
243.31 the same] *intrl.*
243.31 system] *bef. del.* 'th'
243.31 only] *aft. del.* 'conceptually only'
243.35 different] 't' *ov.* 'ce'
243.39 a] *aft. del.* 'the whole'
244.3 originals] *bef. del.* 'belong'
244.7 its] *aft. del.* 'the'
244.7 third,] 'ird' *ov.* 'e'; *comma added bef. del.* 'disconti'
244.7 the] *intrl.*
244.13 By] *alt. fr.* 'But'
244.14 movement] *ab. del.* 'progress'
244.17 end with] *ab. del.* 'give'
244.18 worth] *bef. del.* ', or'
244.21 Should] *ab. del.* 'Does'
244.25 or] *aft. del.* 'from it'
244.25 gradual] *final* 'ly' *del.*
244.26 sort] *aft. del.* 'system'
244.26 4] *aft. del.* 'fou'
244.26 the relation] *ab. del.* 'that'
244.27 with] *aft. del.* 'betwee'
244.28 fact] *final* 's' *del.*
244.30 ultimate] *aft. del.* 'irre'
244.35–36 only . . . may] *ab. del.* 'or'
244.36 think˄] *comma del.*
244.37 seeing˄] *comma del.*
245.2 1)] *ab. del.* 'a sensation continuum'
245.3 2)] *intrl.*
245.4 his] *alt. fr.* 'this'
245.5 all] *aft. del.* 'all'
245.5 his] *ov.* 'the'
245.5 and] *aft. del.* 'about'
245.11 but] *bef. del.* 'continuous'
245.12 The] *aft. del.* 'But this leaves us in'
245.14 state] *bef. del.* 'without pas'
245.15 thither] *ov.* 'there'
245.18 may] *bef. del.* 'be'

245.19 or] *aft. del.* 'alone being the path'
245.21 previous . . . terminus,] *tr. by guideline fr. aft.* 'steps' [245.20]
245.22 within] 'in' *added*
245.23 experience] *final* 'e' *ov.* 'ed'
245.24 the] *bef. del.* 'noetic'
245.24 total series] *aft. del.* 'series is interest in the "topic" to which the terminus belongs, in the wider'; *bef. del.* 'it'
245.28 (Bk . . . 17½)] *insrtd.*
245.30 which] *aft. del.* 'of'
245.32 an] 'n' *added*
245.32 individual] *intrl.*
245.33 relation] *aft. del.* 'the'
245.34 actual] *intrl.*
245.34–35 which permits] *ab. del.* 'of'
245.35 to] *added*
245.35 fall] *final* 'ing' *del.*
245.36 objective condition] *ab. del.* '*possibility* of such falling'
245.36 be] *added aft. del.* 'follow'
245.36 fact] *aft. del.* 'logical'
245.36 that] *ab. del.* 'if'
245.37 are] *ab. del.* 'being fou'
245.39 *occurrence*] 'o' *ov.* 'r'
245.39 objects] *bef. del.* 'interrelated'
245.40 *specific*] *ab. del.* 'determinate'
246.2 recurrence] *alt. fr.* 'reccurrence'
246.4 such a] *ab. del.* 'the'
246.4 whether] *alt. fr.* 'where'
246.8 ²field] *bef. del.* 'with such or'
246.11 But] *bef. del.* 'so far,'
246.19 which] *aft. del.* 'wil'
246.24 field] *ab. del.* 'thing'
246.24 itself;] *semicolon ov. period bef. del.* 'The words'
246.24 any] *aft. del.* 'me'
246.27 object] *bef. del.* 'quâ terminus, and'
246.31 moving] *intrl.*
246.31 itself] *aft. del.* 'both'
246.32 remote] *intrl.*
246.33 Are] *aft. del.* 'Is the'
246.34 *seen*] *ab. del.* '*felt*'
246.35 *felt*] *ab. del.* '*seen*'
246.36 Taine] *bef. del.* 'identity theory'
246.37 we] *bef. del.* 'fall back on the distinction'
246.37 in] *underl. del.*
247.1 ¹cause˄] *qst. mk. del.*

247.6   entitatively] *intrl.*
247.8   entitatively] *aft. del.* 'the brain'
247.8   But] *intrl.*
247.8   if] 'i' *ov.* 'I'
247.9   in] *aft. del.* 'ho'
247.12   of] *aft. del.* 'whi'; *bef. del.* 'thing'
247.12   from] *ab. del.* 'and'
247.13   dualistic] *aft. del.* 'co'
247.16–17   concrete] *aft. del.* 'real'
247.20   nerve] *aft. del.* 'etc,'
247.21   latter] *intrl.*
247.25   each,] *bef. del.* 'cannot figure there in the same'
247.26   at] 't' *ov.* 'n'
247.27   such] *ab. del.* 'so'
247.27   that] *bef. del.* 'you'
247.27   up] *ab. del.* 'along'
247.30   on] *ov.* 'in'
247.30   plane] *alt. fr.* 'place'
247.32   stimuli] *aft. del.* 'etc'
247.33   physical] *intrl.*
247.34   as floating] *intrl.*
247.34–35   space between] *ab. del.* 'plane in front of'
247.36   Friday] *ab. del. insrtd.* 'Saturday'
247.36   15th] *aft. del.* '*16th* ['*16*' *ov. poss.* '*24*']'
248.1   not] *aft. del.* 'the'
248.1   contrast] *bel. del.* 'distinction'
248.1   I] *bef. del.* 'I'
248.1   between] *alt. fr.* 'been'
248.2   ¹brain] *ab. del.* 'entitative or'
248.7   of] *intrl.*
248.13   just] 'j' *ov.* 's'
248.21   activity] *intrl.*
248.25   which are] *intrl.*
248.27   a] *ab. del.* 'our'
248.28   ¹the] *ov.* 'an'
248.29   leading] *aft. del.* 'opening'
248.29   backward] *tr. by guideline fr. aft.* 'retrospectively'
248.31   which] *aft. del.* 'of'
248.33   conceptual] *aft. del.* ' "fields" '
248.34   puzzle] *bef. del.* 'or problem'
248.35   partly] *intrl.*
249.1   in] *ov.* 'to'
249.2   *e.g.*] *intrl.*
249.8   up on] *insrtd.*
249.8   too] *aft. del.* '& two;'
249.10   *former*] *aft. del.* 'ph'

249.16   (sensations] *paren ov. qst. mk.*
249.19   both] *ab. del.* 'by'
249.19   kinaesthetic,] *aft. del.* 'a certain number of'; *bef. del.* 'and a'
249.20   optical] *aft. del.* 'an'
††249.20   content,] *comma not alt. to period in error bef. del.* 'and'
249.26   developes] *aft. del.* 'def'
249.28   immediately] *aft. del.* 'originally and'
249.30   world] *aft. del.* 'field'
249.33   optical] *aft. del.* 'subject's'
249.37   The] *aft. del.* 'Suppose I see what comes of considering'
250.6   Tufts] *aft. del.* 'Truth'
250.10   *later*] *aft. del.* 'values'
250.12   thus] *bef. del.* '['has a' *del.*] retains'
250.17   dualistic] *aft. del.* 'w'
250.21   sensation] 'sen' *ov.* 'per'
250.22   over] *aft. del.* 'of'
250.26   fields] *ab. del.* 'things'
250.27   states";] *init.* 's' *ov. closing db. qt.; intrl.*
250.28   substantive] *final* 's' *del.*
250.28   states] *init.* 's' *ov. closing db. qt.; intrl.; closing db. qt. om. in error*
250.30–31   questions] *final* 's' *added*
250.31   are] *ab. del.* 'is'
250.35   under] *aft. del.* 'what the'
250.36   "minds"] *aft. del.* ' "egoes" are'
251.7   (loose] *paren poss. added*
251.7   pp. 32ff.)] *poss. added*
251.13   hereafter] *intrl.*
251.21   etc.)] *paren ov. comma*
251.21   experiencedₐ] *paren del.*
251.22   reply that] *ab. del.* '['do' *del.*] suppose'
251.23   do] *intrl.*
251.23   exist] *final* 'ing' *del.*
251.25   panpsychistic] *alt. fr.* 'panpsychism'
251.31   he] *aft. del.* 'the'
251.38   focal] *intrl.*
251.38   first] *ab. del.* 'already'
252.1   relation] *bef. del.* '['of one p' *del.*] the fo'
252.1   more and the that] *ab. del.* '['focus and' *del.*] margin & the focus'
252.2   whole] *intrl.*
252.5   immediate] *intrl.*
252.8   dualists] *aft. del.* 'trans'

252.13 truth] *ab. del.* 'it'

252.13 interpreted] 'ed' *added but* 'be' *not added in error aft. del.* '['give a' *del.*] seems to verif'; *bef. del.* 'truth'

252.18 merely] 'ly' *added*

252.18–19 another] *aft. del.* 'the' *and start of letter*

252.19 *that*] *ab. del.* 'the fact of'

252.19 between] *bef. del.* ' "truth" and "verification" which'

252.23 actually] 'c' *insrtd.; bef. del.* 'ready *a [*intrl.*]'

252.23–24 already] *intrl.*

252.24 Absolute] 'A' *ov.* 'a'

252.24 as] *bef. del.* 'a means of'

252.30 should] 'sh' *ov.* 'w'

252.34 gets] *aft. del.* 'is'

252.37 the] *ab. del.* ' "my" '

252.39 goes] *ab. del.* 'stops'

253.16 of] *intrl.*

253.17 sensible experience] 'ible' *ab. del.* 'ation'; 'experience' *intrl.*

253.18 sensible] *aft. del.* 'perceptual'

253.19 painted] *aft. del.* 'back'

253.21 Moreover] *bef. del.* 'in immediate memory'

253.28 dualism] *aft. del.* 'realism'

253.29 2the] *ov.* 'an'; *aft. del.* 'as'

253.33 as] *bef. del.* 'an['o' *del.*]'

253.34 deliverances] *bef. del.* 'to'

253.40 "experiences."ₐ] *bkt. del.*

254.3 "subjective"] *final* 'ly' *del.; db. qts. added*

254.3 "content."] *ab. del.* 'apprehended.'

254.10 ascribes] 'es' *ab. del.* 'ing'

254.11 thus] *intrl.*

254.13 as] *ab. del.* 'of'

254.16 apparent] 'arent' *ab. del.* 'earance'

254.16 vs.] *ab. del.* 'and'

254.16 is] *ab. del.* 'are'

254.22 common] *ab. del.* 'contermi'

254.28 All] 'A' *ov.* 'a'

254.31 contexts:] *colon ov. comma*

254.31 (inner)] *aft. del.* 'flux'

254.32 1as] *aft.* 'as' *intrl. and undel. in error*

254.32 the (outer)] *ab. del.* 'a'

254.37 is] *bef. del.* 'sensation.'

255.1 Monday] 'M' *ov. poss.* 'Th'

255.2 homogeneous] *alt. fr.* 'homog-| geneous'

255.19 presently] *ab. del.* 'soon'

255.19 and *b*] *intrl.*

255.19 are] *ov.* 'is'

255.19 vivid,] *bef. del.* 'to thog'

255.21 "there] *aft. del.* 'vividly always except'

255.22 as a] *poss. ov.* 'is in'

255.26 as on p. 41.] *intrl.*

255.28 the] *intrl.*

255.29 other] *ov. illeg.*

255.32 some] *ov. poss.* 'is'

255.33 a] *aft. del.* 'the'

255.33 time] *bef. del.* '-tag "always'

255.34 mental] 'm' *ov.* 'a'

255.35 so called] *ab. del.* 'taken'

255.35 dualistic] *alt. fr.* 'dualism.'

255.37 epistemology] *init.* 'e' *ov.* 's'

255.38 facts] *intrl.*

256.3 impersonal] *aft. del.* 'bess'

256.5 matter] *aft. del.* ' "experience" '

256.5 all] *ov.* 'is'

256.6 "for."] *aft. del.* 'there'

256.7 fact] *aft. del.* 'know'; *bef. del.* 'that some things knowl'

256.12 my] *aft. del.* 'the c'

256.12 That] *aft. del.* 'In that field ['I discern' *del.*] ['objects' *del.*] "physical things'

256.12 3of] *intrl.*

256.13 of] *aft. del.* 'of a personal self and'

256.14 margin] *final* 'al' *del.*

256.15 "other"] *ab. del.* 'more'

256.16 what I call] *intrl.*

256.17 selves] *aft. del.* 'self'

256.21 that] *bef. del.* 'a'

256.23 is] *ab. del.* '['certain' *del.*] being'

256.24 is] *ab. del.* ', the beyond, is'

256.26 began] *aft. del.* 'ended'

256.27 Absolute] 'A' *ov.* 'a'

256.30 *sames,*] *intrl.*

256.31 transcendent] *final* 'al' *del.*

256.32 *They*] *ov.* 'It'

256.32 BECOME] *final* 's' *del.*

256.33 *the field*] *intrl.*

256.33 *fields*ₐ] *comma del.*

256.34 the parts of] *intrl.*

256.35 succession & feeling] *intrl.*

256.39 the earlier] *ab. del.* 'each'

256.40 as if] *ab. del.* 'that'

257.1 might] *intrl.*
257.1 lodge] *final 'd' del.*
257.1 The] 'T' *ov.* 't'; *aft. del.* 'In'; *bef. del.* 'mo'
257.1 more,] *comma added*
257.1 we say,] *intrl.*
257.4 cut] *insrtd. for del.* 'line on the "more" '
257.4 ¹the] *ab. del.* 'any'
257.4 event] *aft. del.* 'flow'
257.5 from . . . view,] *(comma ov. period); tr. by guideline fr. aft.* 'field. *[period ov. comma]*' [257.7]
257.5–6 content] *insrtd.*
257.6 belongs] *aft. del.* 'blo'
257.7 These] *aft. del.* 'If the'
257.8 *being] aft. del.* 'entitative *[intrl.]* content in common, *[*'entitatively' *del.]*'
257.10 entitatively, or] *intrl.*
257.10–11 "intentionally" or] *intrl. orig. w. caret aft.* 'and' *but then that caret del. and new guideline placed bef.* 'and'
257.11 in . . . field.] *(*'other' *ab. del.* 'following'; *period ov. comma); tr. by guideline fr. bef.* 'as a knowledge'
257.12 bridged] *bef. del.* 'when we say the margins "overlap," '
257.13 whichever] *aft. del.* 'whether it'
257.14 state] *aft. del.* 'parts'; *bef. del.* 'resides'
257.17 bit of] *intrl.*
257.18 take] *aft. del.* '[*'bring them' del.]* place them'
257.20 as] *intrl.*
257.23–24 appears.] *period ov. comma*
257.24 And] 'A' *ov.* 'a'
257.26 experience] *final 's' del.*
257.26 changes] 's' *added*
257.31 thereby] *aft. del.* 'there-'
257.37 *that & thus] ab. del.* 'that' *and caret for intrl.*
258.1 all] *aft. del.* 'thos'
258.2 experiences] *aft. del.* 'objects'
258.2 by] *intrl.*
258.3 first] *aft. del.* 'doubl'
258.5 "then,"] *comma ov. period bef. del.* 'But when you think it'
258.6 of] *intrl.*
258.8 ¹the] *ab. del.* 'your'

258.8 you then had] *intrl.*
258.8 "the] *db. qt. added*
258.8 ᴧpresent."] *db. qt. del.; period added bef. del.* 'then,'
258.8 When,] 'W' *ov.* 'w'; *comma added*
258.9 however,] *intrl.*
258.9 along] *aft. del.* 'with'
258.9 *thats] aft. del.* 'things'
258.10 *real] aft. del.* 'the'
258.10 both] *ab. del.* 'then'
258.11 ¹a] *intrl.*
258.11 bit] *ab. del.* 'part'
258.11 the] *bef.* 'the *[repeated in error ab. del.* 'time']'
258.12 was] *aft. del.* 'takes place.'
258.15 ²to] *added*
258.16 incoherent] *aft. del.* 'discre'
258.19 objects] *bef. del.* 'that'
258.19 qualities] *intrl. aft. del.* 'adjectives' *ab. del.* 'attributes'
258.21 As] *aft. del.* 'In the latter case'
258.23 possesses] *insrtd. for del.* 'owns' *ab. del.* 'wears'
258.26 dynamically] *aft. del.* 'can'
258.27 towards] *ab. del.* 'with'
258.34 identical] *aft. del.* 'either'; *bef. del.* 'f'
258.35 else] *aft. del. poss.* 'as'
258.35 ²the] *intrl.*
258.37 supersedes] *aft. del.* 'replaces'
258.38 only] *intrl.*
258.38 substitute] *bef. del.* 'only'
259.1 bit of experience] *ab. del.* 'state'
259.5 querying] 'q' *ov.* 's'
259.6 In] *aft. del.* 'So far as'
259.6 relation] *aft. del.* 'noetic'
259.11 could] 'c' *ab. del.* 'w'
259.14 common to] *ab. del.* 'continuous with'
259.14 these points] *intrl.*
259.14 form] *aft. del.* 'lie'
259.15 is] *bef. del.* 'functional'
259.15 identical] *aft. del.* 'function'
259.21 is] *aft. del.* 'can'
259.21 the centre] *ab. del.* 'part'
259.22 on] *aft. del.* 'bol'
259.22 anatomy] *aft. del.* 'its'
259.23 summarily] *aft. del.* 'I'
259.26 side] *aft. del.* 'sig'

21. NOTES ON "CONCLUSIONS OF LOTZE COURSE" 1897–1898 #4549

The notes in #4549 are written in ink on folds made from sheets of a wove paper watermarked Old Berkshire Mills 1897, each leaf of the fold measuring 8 x 5″. The inscription, on rectos and versos, starts in mid-sentence on p. 11 and proceeds in order to p. 21, which has been altered from 20. This is the recto of the first leaf of a fold, and its verso is unnumbered, as is the recto of the second leaf. But this second leaf's verso is correctly numbered 24, followed by 25 on the recto of the next leaf whose verso is unnumbered as is the recto of the second leaf, the verso numbered 28. The first leaf recto of the next fold is 29. Its verso and the next recto are unnumbered, but the verso of the second leaf is numbered 32. The next fold is numbered 33–36. The rest of the manuscript is missing. In the folder with the manuscript is a piece cut off from a manila envelope that would originally have held the notes, on which James had inscribed, 'Unity [*underl.*] | Conclusions of Lotze Course etc.'

Emendations

261.22   "noetic] ∧~

262.35   simultaneous] simutaneous

263.5   things] thngs

264.2   Rev,)] ~, [*space*]

Alterations in the Manuscript

260.3   logically] *bef. del.* 'involve'

260.4   and . . . greatest,] *intrl.*

260.9   kinds of] *intrl.*

260.9   thing] *final* 's' *del.*

260.11   , or . . . differences] *insrtd.*

260.13   meant] *bef. del.* 'is either'

260.13   be] *aft. del.* 'permit'

260.17   other] *aft. del.* 'an'

260.21   kinds] *aft. del.* 'u'

260.21   are realized] *intrl.*

260.22   certain] 'c' *ov.* 'p'; *aft. del.*
'things are realized, in'

260.28   connexions.] *bef. del.* '[¶]
Generic unity seems in the case of
living beings to involve unity of
origin as a matter of fact *([*paren ov.
semicolon*] al-'

260.29   connexion] *ab. del.* 'unity'

260.31   generic] *ov.* 'dynamic'

260.31   where] *ab. del.* 'in [*intrl.*] e.g.,'

260.32   where] *ab. del.* 'that'

260.32   kind] 'k' *ov.* 'c'

260.34   connexions] *alt. fr.* 'connections'

260.34   (telegraphic] *paren ov. comma
bef. del.* 'though'

260.35   or] *aft. del.* 'and'

261.1   without] 'out' *added*

261.2   love] *aft. del.* 'love—in general

the more general without the more special. Many human interactions require noetic connexion between the human and the other term. [Conventional human connexions, *as [*intrl.*] wife-husband, etc. of course *involve [*ab. del.* 'require'] other material connexions between the things *concerned. [*ab. del.* 'involved.']]'

261.4   involve] *aft. del.* 'inf'

261.7   One] *ov.* 'The'; *bef. del.* 'n oli'

261.7   connexion] *aft. del.* 'does not seem n'

261.8   known] *aft. del.* 'conn'

261.10   seem] *ab. del.* 'are dee'

261.10   more] *aft. del.* 'shallower levels of connexion. The deeper'

261.12   ¹do] *aft. del.* 'are'

261.15   ways,] *comma ov. period*

261.15   some in one] *ab. del.* 'Any one way'

261.21   principle] *final* 's' *del.*

261.22   barely] *ab. del.* 'colle'

261.22   collective] 've' *ov.* 'on'

261.23   logical] *ab. del.* '['organ' del.] rational'

261.25   the] *ov.* 'we'; *bef. del.* 'should'

261.27 be] *intrl.*
261.28 attained;] *semicolon ov. period*
  bef. del. 'There'
261.28 though] 't' *ov.* 'T'
261.28 this] *bef. del.* 'at present'
261.31 that] *bef. del.* 'ever'
261.31 would] 'w' *ov.* 'c'
261.34 absolute] *ab. del.* 'organic'
261.37 that] 'at' *ov.* 'ose'
261.38 Royce] *aft. del.* 'Lotze and';
  bef. del. '['&' del.] [¶] 1. Commensurability. [¶] 2. Int. Lotze: [¶] 1
  *Intera ['I' *ov.* 'T']'
261.40 1. The . . . maintains] *insrtd.*
  ab. del. 'or *a [*intrl.*] universe which
  is a complete unity. Either no connexion, or the most absolute possible
  [¶] *Noetic* connexion deserves special
  attention. Monism argues'
261.40 if] *intrl.*
261.40 is] *aft. del.* 'can be no'; *bef. del.*
  'any'
262.1 between] *aft. del.* 'any'
262.1 also a wider] *ab. del.* 'an
  absolute'
262.4–5 Partial . . . elsewhere.] *intrl.*
262.7 knowers and known,] *intrl.*
262.8 an] *insrtd.*
262.9 form.] *ab. del.* 'argument.'
262.16 them] *aft. del.* 'outer'
262.17 from] 'f' *ov.* 'b'
262.18 from a] *intrl.*
262.22 Another] 'An' *ov.* 'Ca'
262.24 merely] *aft. del.* 'whether'
262.24 if] *ab. del.* 'that'
262.26 ₐmysteriously] *db. qt. del.*
262.26 object—] *dash ov. period*
262.28 imply] *intrl.*
262.29 connection] *bef. del.* 'between
  its objects.'
262.30 1the] *ov.* 'we'
262.31 ever shall] *intrl.*
262.31 know] *final* 's' *del.*; *bef. del.* 'of'
262.31 all] *intrl.*
262.33 of] *bef. del.* 'other'

262.36 if] *ab. del.* 'to make sure'
263.6 mutually] *aft. del.* 'of the same k'
263.7 logic] *aft. del.* 'principl'
263.7 an] 'n' *added*
263.8 efficient] *intrl.*
††263.9 comgeneric] 'g' *ov.* 'm'; 'com'
  not alt. to 'con' *in error*
263.11 fact] *bef. del.* ', assume'
263.13 1as] *ov.* 'or'
263.13 -Being] 'B' *ov.* 'be'
263.20 facts,] 's,' *ov. comma*
263.21 that] *ab. del.* 'it'
263.24 differences] 'diffe' *ov.* 'princ'
263.26 those] 'ose' *ov.* 'e'
263.32 1God] 'G' *ov.* 'g'
264.2 say['s' *del.*] the monists,] *intrl.*
264.4 still] *intrl.*
264.5–6 mutually] *intrl.*
264.7 to] *ov.* 'as'
264.12 on] *insrtd.*
264.13 abstract] *aft. del.* 'out of'
264.16 odd] *bef. del.* 'that there'
264.17 chance] *aft. del.* 'of [*del. in
  error*] alte'
264.18 something] 'some' *ab. del.* 'any'
264.22 typeₐ] *comma del.*; *aft. del.*
  'familiar'
264.22 connexion] *aft. del.* 'that'
264.23 us] *aft. del.* 'and'
264.25 its] *intrl.*
264.27 incredible] 'credible' *ab. del.*
  'conceivable'
264.27 said] *aft. del.* 'the'
264.30 is assumed] 'is' *ab. del.* '['must'
  del.] is'; 'assumed' *tr. by guideline
  fr. aft.* 'purposes'
264.35 just] 'j' *ov.* 'n'
264.39 needs] *ov.* 'is'
265.3 admitted] 'tt' *ov.* 'dd'
265.4 even,] *ab. del.* 'inwardly absurd,'
265.7 both] *aft. del.* 'Possibly'
265.8 not . . . but] *intrl.*
265.10 would] *intrl.*
265.10 answer] *final* 's' *del.*

22. NOTES FOR PHILOSOPHY 9: METAPHYSICS—THE FUNDAMENTAL PROBLEMS OF THEORETICAL PHILOSOPHY 1898–1899 #4507

These notes, in #4507, are written in ink on the unnumbered rectos and versos of a blue-paper covered exercise book from Amee Brothers, Cambridge, ruled wove paper measuring 8½ x 7″. In a panel on the cover James wrote 'Philosophy

9 | 1898–9 | (Concluding Lectures)'. In 1898 the 9 is written over what appears to be an 8. The inscription ends on the recto of the fifth leaf, its verso blank, followed by ten blank leaves. James's brackets are found at 265.15–17 '[But . . . picked]' and 266.24–25 '[Yet . . . acts.]'.

Emendations

265.17	picked.] ~∧		266.15	synchronous] synchonous
265.18	system.] ~∧		266.31	(pentadactyles.)∧] (~.).
266.5	(b).] (~)∧			

Alterations in the Manuscript

265.17–18 Bradley . . . system] *insrtd.*
265.20 to] *bef. del.* 'demand Unity. Discuss it.'
265.25 inward] *aft. del.* 'of inw'
265.30 But] *bef. del.* 'both the creator and the One Being, even if you take it psychically, have their ['cons' *del.*] inner constitution.' *bef.* 'It' *not reduced in error*
266.1 It] *aft. del.* 'Because as such they are separate in that mind as well as if they were outside of *it. [period ov. comma bef. del.* 'and'] All ['A' *ov.* 'a'] that the invocation of the mind ['does is to say that' *del.*] amounts to is that'

266.1 saying] *bef. del.* 'that'
266.3 run] *aft. del.* 'are'
266.9 singly] *ab. del.* 'in succession'
266.9 grew] 'g' *ov.* 'd'
266.9 &] *ab. del.* 'but'
266.13 fitness] *aft. del.* 'desire,'
266.13 sympathy] *aft. del.* 'etc.'
266.13 variations] *bef. del.* 'w'
266.19–20 understanding] *aft. del.* 'ex'
266.24 several] *ab. del.* 'single'
266.27 about] *aft. del.* 'in this being'
266.34 nor] *ab. del.* 'neither'
267.9 Whitman] *aft. del.* 'Trevor'
267.10 Trevor] 'T' *ov.* 'B'
267.20 2Time] *aft. del.* 'the'
267.21 are] *ov.* 'is'

23. SYLLABUS OF PHILOSOPHY 3: THE PHILOSOPHY OF NATURE
1902–1903   #4468, #4522, #4510

James's Syllabus of Philosophy 3, so headed, was printed on four leaves, paged [1] 2–7 [8], the last verso blank. Three copies are preserved in the Houghton Library. The first, #4468, has James's own ink annotation ' "Philosophy of Nature" 1st ½ year.' At the foot of p. 7 he wrote 'Jan. *20 ['20' *ov.* '18'] 1903'. On p. 5 at 271.6 he corrected in ink 'with the one, or in the many' to 'in the one, or with the many'. Folder #4522 holds two copies. The first is complete and without annotation. The second is missing pp. 3–4 ('II. Monistic . . . stable chance' 269.16–270.35). On p. 7 at 273.1 of this second copy James deleted in ink the misprint of a comma after 'between'. The missing leaf was abstracted for use, hinged to fol. 83 verso of #4510, No. 24 in the present edition. Obvious typographical errors have been corrected silently.

24. NOTES FOR PHILOSOPHY 20c: METAPHYSICAL SEMINARY—A
PLURALISTIC DESCRIPTION OF THE WORLD   1903–1904   #4510

These extensive notes and outlines (#4510) are contained in a marbled-board bound notebook of unlined blue paper 9¼ x 7½" sold by Partridge and Cooper, Chancery Lane, London. On a panel pasted on the front cover James wrote in ink 'Metaphysics—1903–4', and on the inner front cover 'Return this book to Prof. W. James | 95 Irving Street | Cambridge'. Directly below this he inscribed in pencil, 'Fröhlich extension of time'. Then after a white space, in ink, ' "Change"—How do such abstract | ideas lose all their *properties* yet retain their *meaning*, if they mean | their properties.'

The first notebook leaf is preceded by two leaves of white wove unwatermarked paper 8½ x 6½", ruled, taped in after the front cover, written on recto and verso in ink (273.8–274.18). The notebook proper begins on its first leaf recto with 'Hegelian whirlpool dialectic.' (274.19) in pencil, the text continuing on the verso. The text proceeds in pencil on rectos, with blank versos except for a reference note in ink on 4^v (fn. 5), through the recto of the fifth leaf. The first leaf is unnumbered, but thereafter the leaves are foliated 2, 3, 4, etc. Before fol. 5 (276.1–7), a leaf has been torn out, leaving a stub with some remains of ink inscription on its verso. On fol. 5^v ('What is matter?' 276.8) James started to write in ink on rectos and versos. After fol. 6 James pasted in at the top a fold of white wove unwatermarked paper, the unfolded sheet measuring 11 x 8½". This text, for which see fn. 8, ends on the second recto partway down, the verso blank, followed by a slip with pencil formulas in reversed position: 'S $= \frac{gt^2}{2}$ | gs (work) $= \frac{v^2}{2}$.'.

Folio 7 is a notebook leaf, recto and verso in ink (277.12–278.4), followed by an inserted sheet of white laid paper, unwatermarked, the sheet measuring 12 x 8½", folded to make two leaves. The text of the inserted leaves does not follow fol. 7^v in order. Folio 7^v ends with 278.4, and is continued on fol. 8 (278.5–12). But this text then skips from fol. 8 recto to the recto of the first leaf of the inserted fold and continues about two-thirds down that page to 278.19, at which point James inserts an item number 4a, with the circled note 'See end', referring to the text for 4a added at the foot of the verso of the second leaf (278.20–30), the latter part squeezed in by writing vertically in the right margin. The text continues on the first recto with item no. 5 (the 5 over a 4) at 278.31 and concludes at 279.11 with a short horizontal stroke separating it from the added item 4a. Folio 8^v continues the verso of the second leaf of the inserted fold with 279.12–18. Initially at the foot of the page James drew a horizontal line and beneath it wrote a series of five references in ink (adding two in pencil), but a pencil line moves these references from the foot of 8^v to (seemingly) follow 279.19, although in fact the proper place for them is very likely where placed in the present text, at 279.23–28.

Starting with fol. 9, headed by 279.19, the foliation changes from ink to pencil although much of the text inscription remains in ink. Blank versos also begin with 9^v although occasionally they are used for additional notes or references, these listed in footnotes in this edition, except that 287.10–15 on the verso of fol. 29 has been made a part of the text owing to a horizontal line after 287.9 that seems intended to mark its insertion. On the blank verso of fol. 36 James pasted a page of text (290.7–19), paged 37 over some illegible number. This addition caused him to foliate original 37 (290.20–32) as 37½. The verso of this leaf 37½ is paged 37° but contains notes to himself, not reproduced here in the text but instead in footnote 27.

Folios 38–40 are inscribed fully on their versos (footnotes 29–31), the text of footnote 30 on 39^v being paged 39½. Starting with fol. 40 ('A & B . . .' 292.6) the foliation reverts to ink, but almost immediately, with fol. 43 (293.26) changes back to pencil. Folio 47 (295.33–296.11) is numbered regularly as 47 but the text continues on its unnumbered verso (296.12–26). The next folio is also numbered 47 (ink numbered), which is a leaf written on recto and verso (296.27–297.10) of the same blue notebook paper that has been inserted by hinging in the inner margin. Actually the three lines of continuous text on the verso (297.9–10) at the head are followed by a memorandum (footnote 39). This fol. 47, which is numbered 'II' at its head, originally followed a verso numbered 46 that is found in #4429 (No. 49, "Hegelism," in *Manuscript Essays and Notes*, WORKS). The notebook from which these leaves were torn has not been identified. Folio 49ᵛ (298.2–18) follows the text of fol. 49 recto and continues on fol. 50. With fol. 53 (299.21) ink numbers start again. Folio 58 text covers 301.26–302.7 ('From . . . pluralism'). The top five lines on fol. 59 ('as of . . . admit it.' 302.7–11) follow regularly the text on fol. 58. But then on the verso (also numbered 58) of fol. 58 James continues the text to end it about halfway down the page with 302.12–18. Below, separated by a horizontal line, James wrote a passage beginning ' "Tychism" ' which is continued at the foot of fol. 59 below a horizontal line setting off a nine-line passage deleted by cross strokes. In turn, the foot of fol. 59 is concluded by two lines at the top of fol. 60, set off again by a horizontal line. This passage (302.19–32), transcribed here, has been marked through with a single vertical ink stroke on the three pages.

The unmarked text resumes on fol. 60 below the horizontal line (303.1). The text at the foot of fol. 61 is continued in mid-sentence on the next leaf, which is unnumbered ('such a relation | between two things' 303.25). On this leaf below 304.2 James left a white space. The context suggests that the text on the verso of fol. 61, numbered 61½ (304.3–25) belongs at this point, above the first line below the white space beginning ' "Tychism." ' (304.26). The unnumbered leaf after fol. 61 is followed without a break in the text by fol. 65, skipping 63–64 in error. Folio 65 is succeeded by silently numbered fol. [66] and then by 67. The text of fol. 68 (306.11–17) follows on that of fol. 67, but on the blank verso of fol. 67 James pasted a leaf of white paper on which he had inscribed 306.18–25 ('In . . . be their') to replace a massive deletion in the lower half of fol. 68 after 306.17. The text of this paste-on on the verso of fol. 67 is continued on another white-paper paste-on (' "Anerkennung" . . . knows.' 306.26–307.3) on the blank verso of fol. 68, followed by yet another paste-on (unnumbered) on the next recto that deletes the original text beneath the paste-on: 'continuity with other things, when it occurred would be a privileged case. Things would condition one another's possibility in the direction desired.' The paste-on is below the first six words on the original recto ('Since . . . it' 307.4), which lead into the text on the paste-on ('could . . . consci-' 307.4–18). At the foot of this recto paste-on the last two words ('Also consci-' 307.17–18) have been deleted and the continuation taking up all of the recto of the next (unnumbered) leaf has been marked by a single vertical ink stroke, transcribed here as 307.18–31 ('ousness in the sense . . . . Spencer.'). Written vertically in the left margin is 307.32–36. The opposite verso continues the text ('Peirce . . . beings' 307.37–308.13) which is then followed in mid-sentence by the recto of a leaf foliated 71 ('thus . . . associate' 308.13–309.7), succeeded by an unnumbered leaf silently foliated [72], and then by fol. 73. The lower half of 73 ('Two futures . . . the fact.' 309.33–310.7) is marked through by a single vertical ink stroke, and 310.7–12 ('When . . . being.') is written vertically in the left margin.

The text then continues on the verso of fol. [72]. Originally this verso had been blank, but then, about a quarter of the way down, James wrote in pencil, 'All pre-astronomic time for physics & chemistry to have consolidated'. However, when he wanted to extend the text from fol. 73 he drew a horizontal line under this pencil note and wrote-in 310.13–35, the latter part of this addition ('The whole . . . relations' 310.34–35) squeezed in vertically in the left margin. Only then did he continue the added material by writing 310.36–311.3 vertically in the space at the head above the horizontal line but carefully avoiding the pencil note. Folio 74 starts with 311.4 and continues to 311.14, at which point James drew a horizontal line and on fol. 73ᵛ continued the text with 311.15–32. Only then did he resume on fol. 74 with 311.33 below the line. This order is demonstrated by the last few words of the text on fol. 73ᵛ ('tion . . . demand.' 311.31–32) being written in the left bottom line of fol. 74 and brought over by a guideline, the inscription on fol. 74 of 311.36–37 ('In . . . suppose') at the foot by necessity avoiding it and written to the right of the spill-over from fol. 73ᵛ. In fact, the text beginning with the heading 'Question of Infinite' (with a line beneath) was written still later, for 'If we suppose' is interrupted by an inserted leaf torn from the same notebook which on its recto contains 312.25–313.3. The verso of this leaf was originally numbered 75 and is chiefly occupied by fourteen lines which have been deleted (see Alterations entry 311.39–40). Above this deletion the text continues from 'In . . . suppose' at the foot of fol. 74 with 311.37–40 ('the change . . . merely.'), the latter part ('¹Not . . . merely.') much squeezed in. James then reverted to fol. 74ᵛ and wrote 312.1–21 ('Infinitely . . . Tortoise.'). Later, on the bottom line after a space he added 'Principe du nom', which was completed by 'bre' inserted with a guideline on the verso of the inserted leaf below the deletion before the continued text ('Best . . . finite.' 312.21–24). It seems clear from the deletion on the present verso of the inserted leaf, which continues the Achilles and Tortoise notation at the foot of fol. 74ᵛ (and by its numbering as 75) that the inserted verso was originally the recto. Thus its present recto ('Fullerton . . . Phil. I, 29' 312.25–313.3) is transcribed as following 312.24 at the foot of its verso. This text for 312.25–313.3 on the added leaf is written with a different pen and a blacker ink than the rest and is thus a later addition.

Next comes a second inserted leaf of the same notebook paper, foliated 75 and containing 313.4–19, the last sentence ('Taken . . . philosophy.') squeezed in vertically in the left margin. Its verso (313.20–314.7) is headed 'Infinite, continued'. After 313.24 appears a short horizontal line in the left margin, and when James continued with 'The Russell-Cantor' he wrote in a smaller hand, and with a narrower left margin, the hand decreasing in size as he neared the foot, in order to work in all of the text.

The section ' "Free-Will" ' (with a line beneath) (314.8) marks the return to the regular bound notebook leaves and James's normal hand. Once again he wrote on the rectos only, leaving the versos blank or reserved for notes and memoranda. His system of numbering changes, however, and from this point to the end he numbers the versos silently: thus fol. 75 is followed by 77. On the verso of fol. 81 (p. [82]) there is pasted the recto of a leaf of white wove unwatermarked paper 9 x 5¾″ abstracted from some other work, since it is numbered 4 but followed by deleted added 5–6. At its foot James added '(over'. The continued text on the verso is numbered 5–6 (see fn. 67). On the verso of fol. 83 (p. [84]) James pasted pp. 3–4 of his printed syllabus for Philosophy 3 (see No. 23), a fact that explains the missing leaf in the second copy in folder #4522. The lower part of this hinged printed leaf obscures five handwritten lines (see fn. 68). Starting with fol. 89 (316.22) the numbering is in pencil instead of ink. With fol. 89ᵛ (p. [90]) the inscription is continuous on rectos and versos. This p. [90] is headed 'Last lecture' (with a line beneath) (317.1) and it and the succeeding text on pp. 91–93 are marked by a single vertical ink stroke through the text (317.2–318.18). Unmarked text begins again on the verso of fol. 93, that is, p. [94], and continues to the end at 319.19, an unnumbered recto (verso blank) that should have been p. 97.

James's brackets are found at 298.22 '[If' and 304.23 '[If' (opening brackets only).

Emendations

275.16　therefore] therfore
281.3　Maxwell] Maxwill
281.25　Conserved] Consered
282.27　413+)] ~+∧
284.13　Acquaintance] Aquaintance
☞288.27　world.] ~∧ (*similar* 290.18 (*first*);293.30;294.19;295.29;296.9; 310.35)
290.14　"between"] "~∧
293.9　monism."] ~·∧
294.17　² „] *om.*

295.5　required] require
299.26　classification,] ~∧
299.32　single] singly
301.6　some way] some-|way
302.18　aboriginal] aborinal
302.32　etc.)] ~·∧
305.22　appellatives] appelatives
310.38　contend] content
311.39　∧finite] "~
312.40　*The] ∧~
315.6　"comes."] "~·∧

Alterations in the Manuscript

273.9　monism.] *bef. del.* | '1. "Problem of evil" '
273.16　If] *aft. del.* '3.'
273.21–22　"Central . . . agitation."] *insrtd.*
273.23　Contrast] *aft. del.* 'Possibly too s' |
273.23　between] *bef. del.* 'reg'
273.24　Pluralism] 'Pl' *ov. ditto marks and* 'm'
274.12　12] '2' *ov.* '4'
274.16　Our] *bef. del.* 'the' [*begin penc.*]
274.19　dialectic] *bef. del.* | 'Idealism | Conceptual short hand'
274.22　Monism] *bef. del.* 'Royce'
274.25　Determinism] 'D' *ov.* 'Fr'
274.28　Pragmatism] *bef. del.* | ' "Ac'
274.35　adjacency] *insrtd.*
275.1　Being . . . Renouvier.] *ink*
275.6　this] *alt. fr.* 'the'
275.6　rather] *init.* 'r' *ov. illeg.*
275.11　Idealism] *bef. del.* | '(Idealism does n't settle religious question. [*closing paren del.*] Leave this open. | Royce's arguments.).'
275.14　outcome] *ab. del.* 'quality'
275.17,30　interests] *ab. del.* 'operations'

275.20–23　Statistics . . . light] ('Statistics . . . forces.' *in ink*); *insrtd. for del.* 'Explanations. | 1) Theistic. | 2) Selective short hand. (Ward, Pearson)'
275.35　Possibility.] *insrtd.*
276.2　υλη, υποκείμενον,] *intrl.*
276.3　T. . . . 189] *orig. bef.* | '(Confusion until Descartes betw. material & spiritual substance. Descartes made it sharp.)' *and then tr. by guideline to foll.* '(Confusion . . . sharp.)' *which was then del.*
276.3　School] *bef. del.* 'II' [*end penc.*]
276.12　In] *aft. del.* 'Reals'
276.14　1)] *penc.*
276.18　slumbered] *intrl.*
276.26　2)] *penc.*
276.26　33 . . . –9] *penc.*
276.27　–74] *penc.; bef. del.* | 'Get realistic point of view: *Object* remains. The first misapprehension: *head; "there"?* Absolute experience: Emerson's here or nowhere | Howison. | Edwards. | Divine visual Language | My Harvard Square experience.'

276.28–29   The . . . truth.] *insrtd.*
276.30–32   Don't . . . percept.] *vert. insrtd.*
276.30   means:] *ab. del.* 'says'
276.30   by] *aft. del.* 'that'
276.32   than] 'n' *ov.* 't'
277.3   idealism] *aft. del.* 'view'
277.4   (plural)] *penc. intrl.*
277.6   3)] *penc.*
277.6   argument] *aft. del.* 'step'
277.8   "infinite."] *bef. del.* | '"Unconditioned." *Totality of conditions must be given.*'
277.14   Composition?] *bef. penc.* 'req' *unrelated to text and undel. in error*
277.21   K's] *intrl.*
277.25   D.a.S.] *bef. del.* | 'General rationality of all things. | We don't follow them now. | *Monistic* idealism. Phil. of Absolute. | Rationalism! Ascend to Universal. Compare with empiricism, as grounded in sensations.'
277.26   reality.] *bef. del.* | 'Contrast of phenomenal and real'
277.27   (sing)] *intrl.*
278.1   Dialectic method] *intrl.*
278.3   Ego] 'E' *ov.* 'e'
278.4   Absolute.] *bef. del.* | 'Compare ['C' *ov.* 'E'] with empiricism.'
278.4   To . . . think.] *insrtd.*
278.5   Question] *aft. del.* 'Strong practical contrast! | Lower vs. higher. | "Materialism"—explain by lower. | Within Idealism there may be a materialistic wing.' |
278.15   facts] *ab. del.* 'objects'
278.17   facts] *insrtd. for del.* 'objects' *bel. del.* 'thoughts' *ab. del.* 'Minds'
278.18   thinker] 'inker' *ov.* 'ought'; *ab. del.* 'mind'
278.20   4a] *insrtd.*
278.20–30   not . . . so.] *orig. aft.* 'world.' [279.11] *but marked for tr. by* '(See end)' *aft. insrtd.* '4a'
278.20   not because] *aft. del.* '4a [undel. in error]* Mental facts are the only existences we can know'; *bef. del.* 'our knowing faculties would'
278.21   existences] *aft. del.* 'facts that exist'
278.22   Physical] 'P' *ov.* 'O'
278.23   S.] *aft. del.* 'S — I'
278.23   Object] *bef del.* | 'S with seconda'
278.26–30   I . . . so.] ('the matter' *aft. del.* 'our'); *insrtd. vert. in right mrgn.*
278.31   5] *ov.* '4'
278.31   exists . . . it.] *orig. del. and* 'his knowledge does not constitute, *but ['b' *ov.* 'f'] finds' *written ab.; then* 'his . . . finds' *del. and orig. text underdotted for retention and* '(stet)' *in mrgn.*
278.32   The] *ab. del.* 'Each has *thus [intrl.] a'
278.32   of . . . veracious.] *insrtd. for del.* 'of veraciously objective or cognitive *form. [undel. in error]*'
278.33   object] *ab. del.* 'fact' *ab. del.* 'object'
278.33   existing in] *insrtd. for del.* 'in'
278.35   object] *ab. penc. del.* 'fact' *aft. del.* 'object'
278.35   to . . . known] *intrl. w. penc. guideline*
278.35   conceived as] *ab. del.* 'transformed into'
278.37   theism] *alt. fr.* 'theistically'; *aft. del.* 'This is'
278.37   conceives it thus] *ab. del.* 'does this' *ab. del.* 'done'
278.37   saying] *ab. del.* 'believing'
278.37   *God means*] *intrl. aft. del.* '*God means that [alt. fr.* 'it is God's meaning that' *alt. fr.* 'it is the intention of God that']' *aft. del.* 'that the phenomenon'
278.37   think] *ab. del.* 'have the tho't of'
278.38   In knowing] *intrl. aft. del.* 'In thinking' *aft. del.* 'I think' *ab. del.* 'The *truth is that [aft. del.* 'object thus is']'
278.38   means] *alt. fr.* 'meaning'; *aft. del.* 'is ['thinking ['for my sake.' *del.*] I think truth. | 10.' *del.*]'
278.39   know] *ab. del.* 'think'
278.40   physical] *aft. del. intrl.* 'form of the'; *bef. del.* 'form.'
278.40   appearance.] *ab. del.* 'of the phenomenon.'
279.1   physical] *aft. del.* '*in se* of the'

279.1 fact] *aft. del. false start* '7 Suppose a number of these thinkers each
*cognitive ['tive' *ab. del.* 'zant'] of
the *others; [*semicolon alt. fr. period
bef. del.* 'All must think'] they must
have almost identical thoughts.'

279.6 of it] *insrtd.*

279.7 purposes . . . them] *intrl.*

279.7 same] *intrl.*

279.8 full] *intrl.*

279.10 thinker] *intrl.*

279.10 error] *aft. del.* 'truth will be
incomplete.'

279.24 Jas. Ward] *penc.*

279.28 Bergson] *penc.*

280.1 Ego] 'E' *ov.* 'e'

280.5 consciousnesses] *final* 'es' *added*

280.7 either] *aft. del.* 'any'

280.9 come] *final* 's' *del.*

280.27 light] *bef. del.* | 'Curves of coor'

280.31 Pearson] *aft. del.* 'Bos'

280.32 198] *bef. del.* | 'Ward | Ostwald
(why hypotheses false, 212)'

280.33 Triumph] 'Tri' *added in left
mrgn. when orig.* 'Tri' *del. aft. del.*
'Schiller'

280.37 (Boscovich)] *intrl.*

281.1 either] 'ei' *ov.* 'as'

281.9 try!] *bef. del.* 'Ostwald's
Energetik. (Cf. p. 212) | This leads
to a sceptical interpretation | Science
merely aesthetic. Le Roy | But what
on this view is Nature *objectively*? |
Wilbois vol IX, p. 636 | Schiller 59 |
Ostwald on hypotheses'

282.11 C.] *ov.* 'ct'

282.12 Const] 'C' *ov.* 'c'

282.14 "pure experience"] *intrl.*

282.20 formulas] *bef. del.* | 'But why so
hard to find?'

282.29 directly.ₐ] *db. qt. del.*

282.33 Nevertheless] *aft. del.* 'Suppo'

282.37 Pearson's: p. 100–104] *tr. by
guideline fr. line ab.* 'Ward's'

283.5 idealism] *aft. del.* 'view.'

283.11 Here] 'H' *ov.* 'R'

283.12 Our] *aft. del.* 'The'

283.25 remedy.] *bef. del.* 'he possesses
remedy as a term of comparison.'

283.26 world] *bef. del.* 'leaves no'

283.27–28 At . . . 2he] *insrtd. for del.*
'*Bare* versus *grounded* possibility |

The later involves phenomenal
sequence.'

283.29 For] *bef. del.* 'excluded'

284.8 Absolute] 'A' *ov.* 'a'

284.14–15 develope] *aft. del.* 'lead'

284.16 3] *ov.* '2'

284.17 truthsₐ] *comma partially erased*

284.22 Feeling] *final* 's' *del.*

285.6 that] *bef. del.* 'objects of know-'

285.9 possible] *intrl.*

285.10 our] *intrl.*

285.10 *perceive*] *intrl.*

285.12 General] *aft. del.* 'Give me
writte'

285.13 backing] 'b' *ov.* 'p'

285.18–23 The . . . check] *tr. by
guideline fr. bef.* 'Each'

††286.2–4 3) We . . . objects?] *tr. by
guideline fr. aft.* '2) "Possible" . . .
*possible?' and numbers not alt. in
error*

286.2 yet] *bef. del.* 'they'

286.3 one another] *intrl. bef. del.*
'other' *alt. fr.* 'the'

286.4 or the] *intrl.*

286.7 diverse] *aft. del.* 'different'

286.7 relationₐ] *qst. mk. del.*

286.11 how] *aft. del.* 'the'

286.25 conceptual] *init.* 'c' *ov.* 'p'

286.26 know] *ab. del.* 'have'

286.31 outer . . . with] *intrl.*

286.31 (Give] *aft. del.* 'My'

286.33 you] 'y' *ov.* 'I'

286.33 my] *ab. del.* 'your'

286.34 your] *ab. del.* 'my'

286.34 my] *aft. del.* 'If not my body?'

287.1 denial] *aft. del.* 'con'

287.2 My] *ov.* 'Your'

287.4 my] *aft. del.* 'the'

287.8 is] *ov.* 'be'

287.12 logical] *bef. del.* 'one'

287.13 described] *ab. del.* 'affirmed'

287.14 bringing] 'ing' *insrtd. bef. del.*
'about what is des-'

287.19 though] *bef. del.* | 'Dualism
supposes many inner worlds each
*"representing" the same [*ab. del.*
' "knowing" one'] outer world, the
latter not direct matter of experi-
ence. | *Minds* we will admit to be
ejective to one another—postpone
that question!'

287.20 Now] *aft. del.* 'My argument yesterday assumed that' |

287.22 lamp.] *bef. del.* | 'You infer my mind, why? Because it ['it' *del.*] seems to animate *that* body which is your object.'

287.23 , so] *comma alt. fr. period bef. intrl.* 'so' *bef.* 'You' *not reduced in error*

288.1 But . . . so] *insrtd. bef.* 'My' *not reduced in error*

288.1 taken] *aft. del.* 'thus'

288.1 as] *bef. del.* 'term'

288.3 ¹that] *ab. del.* 'your'

288.3 of yours] *intrl.*

288.3 all.] *bef. del.* | 'But that object *my body [intrl.] connects with the lamp, and thus with all other objects. If the bodies—'

288.4 object,] *bef. del.* 'are connected in the same experience, and since that experience is homogeneous with the lamp and other experiences, *the [alt. fr. 'they'] *minds both [ab. del. 'both'] terminate in a common world. Such in brief was the argument.'

288.4 (one] *paren ov. comma*

288.5 in] *bef. del.* 'the same exper'

288.15 our] *bef. del.* 'two'

288.18 me] *intrl.*

288.18 *my* lamp] ('*my*' *ab. del.* 'the'); *ab. del.* 'my body'

288.18 and] *bef. del.* 'I let you touch it'

288.19 perceive as] *ab. del.* 'call'

288.20 exist] *aft. del.* 'be mine'

288.22 2] *intrl.*

289.1 also] *intrl.*

289.7 Leibnitz] *aft. del.* 'Apply pragmatism:'

289.15 of] *ab. del.* 'allows for'

289.21 need] *ab. del.* 'may'

289.25 that] *bef. del.* 'External relations imply internal relations.'

289.30 about] *ab. del.* 'for'

290.13 several things,] *ab. del.* 'beings'

290.14 whatever] *aft. del.* 'between'

290.18 its] *bef. del.* 'parts'

290.19 some] *aft. del.* 'them.'

290.19 statements] *bef. del.* 'from P'

290.20 contrast] *ab. del.* 'position'

290.20 opposite] *aft. del.* 'sheet 16' *aft. del.* 'p'

290.25 ¹B] *ov.* 'be'

290.26 ground] *ab. del.* 'reason'

290.27 name] *ab. del.* 'identity'

290.30 not . . . facto] *intrl.*

291.7 they] *aft. four ellipsis dots del.*

291.7 somehow] *intrl.*

291.7 real,] *comma ov. period bef. del.* '. . . in such a way that *from ['fr' ov. 'to'] A to B'

291.9 from A or B] *intrl.*

291.18 separate] *aft. del.* 'same subject'

291.18 synthetic] *intrl.*

291.21 your] 'r' *added bef. del.* 'are to'

292.1 if] *bef. del.* 'they'

292.5 ¹B] *ov.* 'be'

292.7–8 falsifies] *alt. fr.* 'false' *aft. del.* 'is'

292.10 as] 'a' *ov.* 'n'

292.15 ever] *intrl.*

292.15 become] *ab. del.* 'be'

292.17 things] 's' *added*

292.21 pre-exists∧] *comma del.; aft. del.* 'exists'

292.21 and determines] *intrl.*

292.23 never] 'n' *ov.* 'c'

293.4 known] *aft. del.* 'pe'

293.5 however] *intrl. bef. del. intrl.* 'however'

293.5 But this] 'But' *intrl.;* 't' *of* 'this' *ov.* 'T'

293.5 as] *aft. del.* 'as fact, however'

293.8 the] *bef. del.* 'fe'

293.9 Pluralism] *aft. del.* 'Plur'

293.18 seems] *ab. del.* 'is'

293.20 know] *aft. del.* 'say'

293.20 how . . . out] *ab. del.* '['what' *del.*] whether it will happen or not'

293.22 the] *bef. del.* ' "po'

294.4,5 more] *intrl.*

294.18 In] *aft. del.* 'In some'

294.18 the nature of] *intrl.*

294.18 either] *ov.* 'one'; *ab. del.* 'the'; 's' *of* 'terms' *undel. in error*

294.22 on] *ab. del.* 'outside *of [undel. in error]'

294.29 Case:] *colon added bef. del.* 'of'

294.29 alongside of/] *intrl.*

295.3 Does] 'D' *ov.* 'I'

295.6 if there?] *intrl.*

295.6 ²n't] *intrl.*

295.7   intimacy of] *ab. del.* 'sense and transparency *of [*undel. in error*]*'

295.9   space] *aft. del.* 'objects got made, or'

295.11   but] *bef. del.* 'once being there'

295.11   their] 'ir' *added*

295.11   relation] *bef. del.* 'of them'

295.11   or is known-as] *intrl.*

295.13–17   If . . . facts.] *insrtd. vert. in left mrgn.*

295.14   if] *aft. del.* 'with'

295.17   ¹facts] *bef. del.* 'are the'

295.17   are] *ab. del.* 'were'

295.19   type] *ab. del.* 'order'

295.22   a] *ab. del.* '['th' *del.*] two'

295.22   thing] *final 's' del.*

295.23   logically] *intrl.*

295.25   quality] *aft. del.* 'determinate'

295.26   quality,] *comma alt. fr. semicolon bef. del.* 'already;'

295.27   ¹resemblance] *aft. del.* 'quality'

295.28   one] *ab. del.* 'the'

295.28–29   the other] ('other' *alt. fr.* 'either'); *ab. del.* 'both'; *bef. del.* 'qualities' *unalt. to* 'quality' *in error*

295.29   in . . . may] *intrl.*

295.29   just] *bef. del.* 'as they were.'

295.30   an] *intrl.*

295.30   relation] *intrl.*

295.31   on] *bef. del.* 'an exter-'

295.33   ¹the] *intrl.*

296.1   ground.] *period insrtd. bef. del. comma*

296.1   So . . . anything] *ab. del.* 'it is transparent; nothing'

296.1   being] *ab. del.* 'is'

296.1   required] *bef. del.* '*to make [*undel. in error*] it intelle' ab. del.* 'than the sight of the two things, the relation['s' *del.*] then instantly appears, it is only a name for the ['double' *del.*] fact that ['the two things' *del.*] no difference appears.'

296.2   absence] *ab. del.* 'failure'

296.3   difference,] *comma added bef. del.* 'to appear,'

296.4   It . . . difference.] *insrtd. for del.* | 'It thus remains a secondary phenomenon, ['additional ['to the ab' *del.*] and' *del.*] extraneous logically to the ['being' *del.*] nature of each particular thing,' *bef. del.* | 'It is

*logically [*intrl.*] grounded in *the [*intrl.*] nature *of any particular thing, the [*intrl.*] nature is not grounded in it. It is a ['relation' *del.*] possible'

296.5   grounded] 'ed' *ov.* 'in'

296.5   each] *ab. del.* 'a'

296.6   are] *bef. del.* 'only'

296.10   cut] *intrl.*

296.11   "manifolding" . . . etc.]] *added w. bkt. extended fm. orig. bkt. aft. first* 'etc.'

296.16   (p.] *paren ov. colon*

296.22   whole] *ab. del.* 'possibi'

296.22   complex] 'co' *ov. poss.* 'he'

296.25   then] *intrl.*

296.27   42] *intrl.*

297.4   Loyalty] *ab. del.* 'Pragmatism'

297.4–5   is . . . ¹is] *ab. del.* 'is'

297.5   ²is] *ab. del.* 'or'

297.8   words.] *bef. del.* | '3. Hegel & double negation: State the principle'

297.12   nature] *bef. del.* 'in no way de'

297.12   the] *intrl.*

297.13   figure as] *ab. del.* 'become'

297.13   term.] *bef. del.* | 'Case *3 [*ab. del.* '4' *ov. illeg.*] Partnership, marriage etc. Here every one admits that the being of the terms is one order of fact, *& [*intrl.*] that [*alt. fr.* 'the'] the [*intrl.*] relation depends for its existence on a fact of another order, *into [*intrl.*] which the terms may or *may not [*intrl.*] enter, ['after th' *del.*] ['when' *del.*] after they independently exist. *Such [*ov.* 'The'] 'entrance' is grounded on moral and physical conditions which may practically be called "changes" in the *beings' [*ab. del.* 'parties'] lives, [*comma ov. period*] ['The [*alt. fr.* 'They'] terms [*intrl.*] must already exist ['with' *del.*] ['out of the' *del.*] independently for the' *del.*] changes which thus appear to be ['among the' *del.*] as much among the ['terms' *del.*] beings' adventitious possibilities as space relations and resemblances are.'

297.14   how] *aft. del.* 'wh'

297.14   they] *ab. del.* 'it'

297.15   they are] *ov.* 'it is'

297.15 2they] *ab. del.* 'it'

297.15 have] *insrtd. for del.* 'does'

297.15 occurred]] 'ed' *added to* 'occur' *and* 'r' *not doubled in error; bef. del.* [*del.* 'It is known as ['the [*ab. del.* 'a'] growing differ' *del.*] a ['continued' *del.*] continuity of an experience through successive instincts, with'] It is experienced as ['continuity' *del.*] a blending of continuity and alteration—i.e., a succession in time of new ['pa' *del.*] elements, without a total disappearance of old ones.'

298.2 tho't of as] *ab. del.* 'a' *and start of letter*

298.3 even now] *intrl.*

298.6 possibles] *alt. fr.* 'possibiles'

298.8 1is] *bef. del. intrl.* 'either: 1)'

298.8 you] *ab. del.* 'an idea'

298.8 frame['d;—' *del.*]] *aft. del.* 'be'

298.8 an idea] *ab. del.* 'or 2'

298.9 neither] 'n' *intrl.; bef. del.* 'not'

298.9 nor] 'n' *intrl.*

298.14 By] *ov.* 'The'

298.14 the] *ov.* 'po'

298.14 grounded] *intrl.*

298.15 of these] *intrl.*

298.20 antecedent₍∧₎] *comma del.*

298.29 things] 'th' *ov.* 'so'

298.29 viz] *intrl.*

298.31 completed] 'co' *ov.* 'in'

299.1–2 or many] *intrl.*

299.2–3 non-contact, . . . outness] *intrl.*

299.3 "One."] *bef. del.* | 'It is a question not of logic, but of real process. | The many must not be separate enough to frustrate the amount of interaction observed, and the *One ['O' *ov.* 'o'] must [*ab. del.* 'should'] be connected enough to [*illeg. del.*] permit it, but no more.'

299.11 the denial of] *ab. del.* 'a false consequence of'

299.12 Many] 'M' *ov.* 'm'

299.13 interact] *aft. del.* 'have'

299.20 Affinity] *bef. del.* | 'But if beyond the fact of likeness between things we demand a principle, we should equally ask for one to account for unlikeness. | In point of fact we have both on an enormous scale, and after the monist has said "Unity" in the abstract, he has to allow us to interpret the unity concretely for him. It must be ['the' *del.*] a kind of union that is compatible with whatever multiplicity we actually find. Till that is done, it is *Machtspruch* merely, from which no practical deductions can be made.'

299.23 2. noetic . . . (Kant.)] ('2' *ov.* '3'); *tr. by guideline fr. aft.* '3 [*ov.* '2']. Likeness, and difference. [' "Law." classification' *del. added*]'

299.33 inter-] *intrl.*

300.1–2 6, . . . own hypo] *insrtd. fr. facing page w. arrow guideline for del.* 'My'

300.2 is] *insrtd. bef. del.* 'that although these latter for' *ab. del.* 'says to *6 [*ov.* 's']

300.4 that] *aft. del.* 'To 7.'

300.5 that] *aft. del.* 'To 8.'

300.6 Make] *written ov.* 'Make' *in a larger hand in order to indicate beginning of a new line*

300.21 I] *intrl.*

300.21 438–] *intrl.*

300.21 441] '1' *ov.* 'o'

300.28 ever] *insrtd. w. guideline*

300.30 (Maxwell)] *aft. del.* 'but'

300.31 made] *aft. del.* ' "for" '

300.34 can] *final* 't' *del.*

301.1 2whole] *aft. del.* 'first in order of existence is the'

301.2 comes] 'c' *ov. period*

301.4 1)] *intrl.*

301.13 Production] *ov.* 'The'

301.15 Absolute] 'A' *ov.* 'a'

301.17 Source] *aft. del.* 'origin'

301.17 whole.] *bef. del.* | 'The question is, is what we find *in*compatible with many sources?'

301.18 wd. be] *ab. del.* 'is, [*comma poss. erased*]'

301.23 ever] *intrl.*

301.28 Even] *aft. del.* 'Hegel. Oken'

301.28 the] *intrl.*

301.28 which] *aft. del.* 'non'

301.28 has] *ov.* 'is'

301.28 a] *intrl.*

302.1 facts] 's' *added*

302.5 and] 'an' *ov.* 'sa'

302.8 time—] *dash ov. period*

302.9   phenomenal] *alt. fr.* 'phenomal'
302.10   piecemeal coming] *ab. del.*
   'such'
302.10   must,] *ab. del.* 'can'
302.11   it.] *bef. del.* | 'Suppose, then,
   there were piecemeal coming, could
   n't things come so as to have relations
   with what they found pre existing? |
   Can't they, e.g. *resemble* them? | Take
   bare chance coming.? | Surely they
   may resemble. If not, why not? | If
   you need to postulate a higher principle of resemblance, why not also
   one of non-resemblance.'
302.13   been] *insrtd. for del.* 'got'
302.16   or . . . shapes] *intrl.*
302.20   that] *init.* 't' *ov.* 'c'
302.21   deduce] *aft. del.* 'neccessarily'
302.22   obtains] *aft. del.* 'obj'
302.32   can.]] *bef.* | 'Chan' *undel. in*
   error
303.6   union] *aft. del.* 'connection'
303.6   positive] *intrl.*
303.7   keeps] *bef. del.* 'them'
303.15   there] 're' *ov.* 'y'
303.15   a] *intrl.*
303.15   addition] *final* 's' *del.*
303.16   there] *aft. del.* 'in the'
303.18   is,] *comma ov. period*
303.18–19   even . . . is.] *added aft. del.*
   'Free will,' *beginning new line*
303.22   things] *bef. del.* ', arising'
303.23   In . . . be] *ab. del.* 'Turn to the
   concrete, with is'
303.25   Define chance.] *aft. del.*
   ' "Tychism." '; *bef. del.* 'Go back to
   page 58'
303.35   a] *ov.* 'an'
303.37   should] *ab. del.* 'do'
304.4   may] *bef. del.* 'nevertheless'
304.8   idea] *ab. del.* 'thing'
304.9   merely] *intrl.*
304.9   *possible*] *bef. del.* '*merely*'
304.14   latter] *intrl.*
304.14   single] *intrl.*
304.17   together.] *intrl. ab. caret ov.*
   period
304.21   My] *ov.* 'The'
304.22   effective] *intrl.*
304.22   regularities] *aft. del.* 'products,
   which may be'
304.22   because] *insrtd. aft. del.* 'and'

304.29   survival] *bef. del.* 'and'
304.30   among] *aft. del.* 'one of'
305.3   lead] *ab. del.* 'make'
305.3   to] *aft. del.* 'averse to supposing
   that'
305.6   variations] *aft. del.* 'an observed'
305.10   second.] *bef. del.* '*It would
   take [undel. in error]* 250 years to
   distinguish these vibrations if we
   could 500 a second.'
305.12   61½] *aft. del.* '62. ['6' *ov.* '5']'
305.13   In] 'I' *ov.* 'O'
305.26   admit₍ₐ₎] *comma del.*
305.27   variation₍ₐ₎] *comma del.*
305.30   experiences] 's' *ov.* 'd'; *aft. del.*
   'phenomena that we'
305.31–32   of conservation] *intrl.; orig.*
   caret bef. 'energy' *in error*
306.6   Many] 'M' *ov.* 'm'; *aft. del.* 'The'
306.6   things] *intrl.*
306.10   and interactions.] *added aft.*
   'interrelations. [*period undel. in*
   error]' |
306.17   *prevent?*] *bef. del.* | 'Is gre-
   gariousness, associability not only a
   condition of *there ['t' *ov.* 'w'] being
   universe *überhaupt* but of preservation of *the ['t' *ov.* 's'] several
   members. Is each helped ['to remain
   by' *del.*] not only to remain in that
   universe, but to remain in existence,
   by its fellow serving as its cue? | One
   does n't see it, *in abstracto* | But if
   one specify, one can find a case in
   which the elements would be
   "helped." | They must have the wish
   to *perseverare in* ['esr' *del.*] *esse*, and
   to rejoice in *increase*. | If these
   affections were among the chance
   variations,'
306.18   existence] *ab. del.* 'presence
   ['ce' *ov.* 't']'
306.20   They] *aft. del.* 'Such'
306.21   and emotional] *intrl.*
306.23   comes] *aft. del.* 'beco'
306.24   one] *aft. del.* 'to ea'
306.24   ¹to] *intrl.*
306.32   aggregate."] *bef. del.* | '*Nextness*
   would however be realized;—and
   how about overlapping or sharing
   the boundary? Refer to Peirce Monist
   II, 554, & to Clifford on Boundaries.'

306.33 such] *intrl.*

306.35 is] *insrtd. for del.* 'does n't enable them'

307.1–3 This . . . knows.] *insrtd.*

307.5 one] *ab. del.* 'Absolute'

307.6 many,] *ab. del.* 'universe,'

307.7 lie] *ab. del.* 'be'

307.8 could] 'c' *ov.* 'w'; *bef. del.* '['itself' *del.*] be an instance of the principle itself'

307.8 only] *intrl.*

307.9 possibility] *ab. del.* 'principle'

307.13 gregariousness] *aft. del.* 'habit forming,'

307.14 creation] 'cre' *ab. del.* 'form'

307.20 this latter] *ab. del.* 'it'

307.22–23 boundaries.] *bef. del.* 'It means memory—this is useful, and *positive [intrl.] variations of it would tend to accumulate.'

307.30 this] *bef. del.* 'th'

307.32–36 I . . . preserved.] ('ing' *added to* 'be' *aft. del.* 'to'; 'habit taking second' *intrl.*); *insrtd. vert. in left mrgn.*

307.37 Peirce . . . 531] *circled*

307.38 as gregariousness] *ab. del.* 'in proportion to'

307.40–308.1 "interact" by] *intrl.; caret bef.* 'things' *in error*

308.1 "integrating"] 'ing' *ov.* 'e'

308.1 2by] *insrtd.*

308.1 keeping] 'ing' *added; bef. del.* 'asunder.'

308.1 other] *intrl.*

308.7 memory & expectation,] *intrl.*

308.12 either] *intrl.*

308.15 come] *aft. del.* 'arise'

308.18–19 be admitted to] *intrl.*

309.1 only] *bef. del.* 'in th'

309.4 In our] *ab. del.* 'The'

309.6 inner] *aft. del.* 'conscio'

309.23 properly] 'ly' *added*

309.23 so-called] *intrl.*

309.24 a] *ab. del.* 'the'

309.27 small] *final illeg. letter del.*

309.27 in] *ab. del.* 'when'

309.28 when] *ov.* 'is'

309.33 alike] *intrl.*

310.7 means] *bef. del.* 'only'

310.7 fact.] *bef. del.* 'Individuality— *plurality ['p' ov. 'P'].'

310.7–12 When . . . being.] ('the ['e' *ov.* 'at']' *intrl.*; 'of *that* consequent' *intrl.*); *insrtd. vert. in left mrgn.*

310.14 one] *intrl.*

310.17 an] *intrl.*

310.17 ideal] *final* 's' *del.*

310.17 seems] *final* 's' *added*

310.17 a] *intrl.*

310.17 ground] *final* 's' *del.*

310.28 "laws"] 's' *added*

310.28 demand] *final* 's' *del.*

310.28 concrete] *intrl.*

310.29 abstract] *intrl.*

310.29 "ideas" etc,] *intrl.*

310.30 *What*] 'Wh' *ov.* 'The'

310.31 ever] *intrl.*

310.34–35 The . . . relations] (*final* 's' *of* 'conception' *del.*); *insrtd. vert. in left mrgn.*

311.16 *Anarchy*] '*A*' *ov.* '*a*'

311.17 means] *aft. del.* 'all'

311.23 or] *aft. del.* 'etc.'

311.31–32 In . . . demand.] *insrtd.*

311.33 Infinite] 'I' *poss. ov.* 'i'

311.37 change_∧] *comma del.*

311.38–40 Not . . . merely.] *insrtd. bef. del.* | 'Achilles & the Tortoise. | Generalizing this, we get Kants antinomies: 1) Extent & duration 2) Composition (Unconditioned) 3) Causation [4. Necessary being too obscure.] | Give K's solution by transcendental Idealism. | Renouvier's principe du nombre. | *Cauchy: Suppose an infinite-th number X. We can square or double & get new series of X terms. But by hypothesis X contains all. So first series is both equal & double to itself which is absurd. Ergo no X exists. Dedekind makes of this a definition. [*set off by lines*]'

312.11 formation.] *period added aft. del. comma*

312.18 series,] *comma ov. period bef. insrtd.* 'Is [*not reduced in error*] . . . infinite.' *bef. del.* | 'Principe du nombre.'

312.20 Can] *final* 'n' *del.*

312.21   Principe du no⟨m⟩bre] *added*
312.27   say] *final* 's' *del.*
312.27   expression] *ab. del.* 'word'
312.27   "never~] *db. qt. del.*
312.27–28 can overtake"] *penc. intrl.*
312.28   The words] *ab. del.* 'Zeno'
312.28   suggest['s' *del.*]] *ab. del.* 'says'
312.29   they] *intrl. for del.* 'it' *ab. del.* 'he'
312.29   mean['s' *del.*]] *ab. del.* 'ought to say'
312.30   and] *ab. del.* 'but'
312.31   difficulty in] *ab. del. illeg.*
312.33   distance] *aft. del.* '['dist' *del.*] traverse'
312.37   bounds] *aft. del.* 'a'
312.40   The . . . number] *insrtd. vert. in left mrgn.*
313.2   Essai . . . ff,] *intrl. w. caret ov. comma*
313.4   must.] *bef. del.* 'Every real must be finite in composition.'
313.8   form:] *bef. del.* '*Achilles*'
313.10   antinomies.] *bef. del.* 'Achilles. | Part time antinomy:'
313.13   question] *aft. del.* 'matter'
313.14   antinomies] *bef. del.* | '(Can't get from logic answers to fact. Ontologic *argt [*insrtd.*].) Idealistic hypothesis on all accounts satisfactory. | Nevertheless'
313.18–19 Taken . . . philosophy.] *insrtd. vert. w. arrow guideline in left mrgn.*
313.22   intuition] *bef. del.* 'of each'
313.33   ²classes] *aft. del.* 'real'
313.34   adding] *alt. fr. poss.* 'additing'
314.4   of number] *intrl.*
314.4   and] *aft. del.* 'is'
314.5   contradict] *aft. del.* 'do not apply imm'
314.16   that] 2't' *ov.* 'n'
314.22   1.] *aft. del.* '1. Nothing uniform can be found, outside' |
314.27   the] 'e' *ov.* 'is'
314.31   applicable.] *bef. del.* 'Graft'
314.38   only one future] *tr. by guideline fr.* 'future only one'
315.2   no] *final* 't' *del.*
315.4   What] *aft. del.* 'Retrospectively, the graft grows' |

315.19   ~involved."] *db. qt. del.*
315.21   constant.] *bef. del.* | 'Molecular naturalism takes this view. | But what then are the concrete experiences?'
315.22   *Teleology.*] '*T*' *ov.* '*t*'; *bef. del.* | 'Older teleology assumed'
316.1   to . . . out.] ('to' *ov. period*); *insrtd.*
316.3   1)] *intrl.*
316.18   in] *intrl.*
316.22   reason] *final* 'e' *del.*
316.22   suppose] *final* 'd' *del.*
316.23   neccessarily] *alt. fr. poss.* 'neccessary'
316.32   in] *bef. del. poss.* '&'
317.6   grounded] *intrl.*
317.7   g–d] *intrl.*
317.10   &] *aft. del.* 'ide'
317.11   Tychism] *aft. del.* 'Chance phil'
317.19   a] *ab. del.* 'the ['existent' *del.*]'
317.19   Divine~] '*D*' *ov.* '*d*'; *comma del.*
317.25   they] *ab. del.* '['they giv' *del.*] their non-re la'
317.25   and] *aft. del.* 'th'
317.28   From] *ov.* 'For'
317.28   ¹the] *ov.* 'in'
317.29   viz.~] *comma del.*
317.30   suo] 'o' *ab. del.* 'um'
317.30   perseverare] *final* 'e' *ov.* 'i'
317.30   is] *aft. del.* 'belong'
317.31   described] *ab. del.* 'expressed'
317.32   an] 'n' *added; bef. del.* 'full e'
317.33   *Anerkennung*] '*A*' *ov.* '*a*'
317.34   get] *aft. del.* 'must'
317.35   its] 'ts' *ov.* 'n'
317.36   say] *bef. del.* 'with'
317.38   experience] *aft. del.* 'the'
318.3   a] *intrl.*
318.5   be] *aft. del.* 'by'
318.7   for] *aft. del.* 'can'
318.9   by] *aft. del.* 'th'
318.14   seems] *bef. del.* 'to'
318.20   experienced] *aft. del.* 'facts,'
318.33   eventual] *init.* 'e' *ov.* 'd'
318.35   accidents.] *bef. del.* 'Perfectio'
319.3   *possibility*] *bef. penc. del.* | 'Depends on extension of consciousness—especially in upward direction. | My own reasons. Mysticism. | Our

moral consciousness is once for all
gregarious. Kingdom of Man | Our
ideals are *imposed*. We must be
loyal. | But this involves *requital.*'
319.5   actual,] *comma ov. period*

319.5–6   ³of . . . present.] *added aft.*
    del. 'If ideals' |
319.7   If] *bef. del. poss.* 'I___d'
319.11   be] *ov.* 'is'
319.13   Something] *aft. del.* 'Somethin' |

25. NOTES FOR PHILOSOPHY 20C: METAPHYSICAL SEMINARY 1903–1904   #4506

The notes for Philosophy 20c are contained in the notebook that completed the notes for the 1897–1898 Seminary (No. 20), which is identified on the panel pasted to the front cover and followed by 'Theoretic Psychology | Seminary of 1903–4'. The text, headed 'Seminary of 1903–4 | [short rule] | Cognition [*db. underl.*] etc', begins half way down on the eighteenth leaf of this notebook, directly beneath the conclusion of the 1897–1898 Seminary notes, on p. 51 (the 51 written-in for deleted 57) and is written on rectos and versos, paged 52–78 (but with four pages unnumbered), ending on the recto of the thirty-second leaf. The upper part of p. [53], including the numbering, has been deleted by a blank paste-over on which James wrote three lines of text ('another . . . else.]' 320.1–3), the continuation of an addition ('[One . . . "know" ' 319.30–320.1) on p. 52. These three lines are above the start of a new paragraph (320.15) on p. [53]. The transition, then, from the text ending 320.14 and that on 320.15 is not the original. Page [57] is unnumbered (' "Experiences," . . . content' 322.3–18) and its unnumbered verso is blank except for a four-line inscription at the foot that is a note and not part of the continuous text that on p. 59 ('as to eliminate . . .' 322.18–19) follows that at the foot of p. [57]. It will be observed that this otherwise blank page is silently numbered. For the text of the note, see footnote 3.

The unnumbered p. [57] starts a change in inscription in which James wrote only on the rectos, leaving the versos blank but silently paged. Thus the twenty-second leaf is paged 59 on its recto, its blank verso is silently numbered, and the recto of the twenty-third leaf is 61, and so on to p. 67 on the recto of the twenty-sixth leaf, which ends with a few inches of white space after 324.24. The next recto is numbered 68 (in error omitting the silent paging of the preceding verso) and this error is continued through the final leaf paged 78, p. [76] being unnumbered. In the upper left corner of p. 78, James wrote 'Truth' and drew a half circle around the word to set it apart from the first line of text.

James's brackets are found at 320.30–31 '[In . . . position.]' and 325.2–6 '[If . . . world.]'.

Emendations

320.36   (See] [~
320.36   G] C
321.12   ) .])∧
321.25   "adjectives."] "~,"

323.36   "systematic"] "~'
324.6   heterogenous] hetergenous
324.35–36   observer's] observers's

Alterations in the Manuscript

319.25   or] *bef. del.* 'whether'
319.27   represented,] *comma added bef. del. qst. mk.*

319.27   latter] *aft. del.* 'former term'
319.28   former,] *comma added aft. del. qst. mk.*

319.30–320.3 [One . . . else.]] *insrtd.*
320.5 assumes] *aft. del.* 'does n't'
320.7 quasi-] *aft. del.* 'unveriable'
320.9 Ego] 'E' *ov.* 'e'
320.10 the synthetic] *aft. del.* 'sy'
320.11 smallest parts] *ab. del.*
  'elements'
320.20 in so far] *intrl.*
320.20 should] 'sh' *ov.* 'w'; *aft. del.*
  'one'
320.21 we] *intrl.*
321.1 realized] *aft. del.* 'empirically'
321.1 two] *aft. del.* 'the ob'
321.3 singular] *bef. del.* 'Er'
321.4 I] *ov.* 'me'
321.5 just] *intrl.*
321.16 had] *aft. del.* 'ob'
321.16 definable] *aft. del.* 'deter'
321.27 here] *aft. del.* 'her'
322.7 simple] *intrl.*
322.8 then] *insrtd.*
322.8 one] *ab. del.* 'they'
322.8 there] *ab. del.* 'that'
322.8 an] *insrtd. for del.* 'the'
322.9 it.] *ab. del.* 'them.'
322.9 ¹it] *aft. del.* 'them.'
322.12 *reported*] 'ed' *ov.* 's'
322.13 now] *intrl.*
322.13 makes] *bef. del.* 'it'
322.14 a] *ab. del.* 'to'
322.14 perception] *alt. fr.* 'perceive'
322.14 of] *intrl.*
322.16 dead] *ab. del.* 'pure'
322.20 that] *aft. del.* 'thing'
322.21 *outcome*] *aft. del.* 'facts &'
322.26 are,] *ab. del.* 'start'
322.26 experience—] *dash ov. period*
322.28 that] *ab. del.* 'which'
322.28 better] *aft. del.* 'best'
322.33 content] *aft. del.* 'remains ar'
322.34 fact] *aft. del.* 'accidental fact'
323.2 *philosophy.*] *ab. del.* 'ism.'
323.10 more] *intrl.*
323.14 and share it] *intrl.*
323.23 his] *alt. fr.* 'he'; *bef. del.* 'says'
323.24 is] *aft. del.* '['den' *del.*] contra'
323.28 Truth] *aft. del.* 'throu'
323.32 *serial*] *intrl.*
323.35 is the] *intrl.*
323.36 carries] *aft. del.* 'conveys.'
324.3 There] *alt. fr.* 'They'

324.3 in] *intrl.*
324.5 series] *aft. del.* 'stat'
324.22 object] *aft. del.* 'the'
324.28 or] *aft. del.* 'of'
324.29 an external] *ab. del.* 'their
  knower or'
324.31 thus] *intrl.*
324.35 They] 'Th' *ov.* 'I[*poss. start
  of* 't']'
324.37 offered itself] *ab. del.* 'found
  to enter'
325.2 two] *aft. del.* 'the'
325.4 might] *intrl.*
325.4 perceive] *final* 'd' *del.*
325.5 observer] *aft. del.* 'obje'
325.6 continuous] *aft. del.* 'unite'
325.8 form] *aft. del.* 'be'
325.12 his] *aft. del.* 'the'
325.12 the] *aft. del.* 'experienced,'
325.12 one] *aft. del.* 'an'
325.12 It] *aft. del.* 'It would'
325.15 both] *intrl.*
325.18 contiguity] *aft. del.* 'pragmatic'
325.21 interpolation] *aft. del.* 'se'
325.23 and] *ab. del.* 'only'
325.27 towards a] *ab. del.* '&'
325.32 has] *aft. del.* 'is'
325.35 I] *insrtd. for del.* 'I [*ab. del.*
  'I'] work with'
325.35 constantly_∧] *comma del.*
325.35 feel] *final* 'ing' *del.*
325.35 namely that] *intrl.*
326.2 taste] *aft. del.* 'bad'
326.7 on] *ab. del.* 'a'
326.7 terms] *aft. del.* 'temper'
326.8 ¹the] *aft. del.* 'the abso'
326.10 in others] *intrl.*
326.12 ¹with] *aft. del.* 'of'
326.16 muddle] *aft. del.* 'stru'
326.19 to me,] *intrl.*
326.21 honour] *ab. del.* 'favor'
326.23 authorities] 'ies' *ov.* 'y'
326.24 & suppressions] *ab. del.* 'into'
326.25 -glory] *ab. del.* 'honour'
326.26 exist] *ab. del.* 'be there'
326.30 no] *ab. del.* 'a'
326.32 making] *aft. del.* 'keeping
  professorships going, and'
326.35 revelation] *aft. del.* 'expression.'
327.1 fr] *final* 'om' *del.*

26. Notes for Philosophy 9: Metaphysics 1904–1905 #4511

James wrote these notes in #4511, a hardbound notebook, blue marbled boards, of ruled white laid paper 9 x 7″. The notebook is reversed, the text written from the back forwards. The inscription in ink is chiefly on the rectos, the versos being reserved for occasional reference notes and memoranda and occasionally for continued text. The leaves are unnumbered. On the cover James wrote on a paste-on panel, 'Philosophy 9 | 1904–5 | [short rule] | William James | 95 Irving Street | Cambridge'. On the recto of the first leaf (the lower third of which is irregularly torn off), are four signatures and addresses: 'W. J. Mc-Cormick Jr Berkeley | R N Thompson 53 Dunster St | C. S Berry 13 Howland St. | J. R. White 378 Harvard St.' The text begins on the recto of the second leaf, headed 'Oct *6th. ['6' *ov.* '4'] 1904', a rule below; a note on the verso of the first leaf is transcribed in footnote 1. On leaf 4 (328.5–18), including the memoranda on the facing verso page (see fn. 4), James drew a single vertical ink stroke through the text, which is transcribed in the present edition.

The text of 329.14–23 was written on the lower half of the verso of leaf 6. A guideline from 329.13 on the recto indicates that this reference '(Read II, 12–16)' was intended to head the verso addition. The note at 330.20 is a later addition in pencil, as is 332.34–35 on leaf 16. Continuous text after leaf 15 recto is inscribed on 15 verso (332.16–31), which gives evidence that it was written before leaf 16 recto (332.32–35). The text then follows in order on 16 verso to 17 recto and 17 verso, ending with an incomplete sentence (334.3) and then a short horizontal line to the left below, indicating the end of a section. Starting with 334.4, leaf 18, James briefly resumed inscription on rectos only. Leaf 21 recto starting in mid-sentence with 'tute that has to be' (334.33) follows the text on leaf 20 recto, but then is continued on the verso of leaf 20, the facing page, with 335.8, which then carries on on 21 verso, and so recto and verso up to the recto of leaf 25 ('you offer me . . . adventitious.' 337.26–38), which resumes the recto-only inscription with occasional memoranda on versos. For some reason, probably as a later self-contained addition, James wrote on the whole of leaf 27 verso (338.22–29). The text of 345.22–27 is written on the verso of leaf 50, its position in the text indicated by a guideline on 51 recto. A guideline with an arrow at the foot of 53 recto indicates the position of a note found at the foot of leaf 52 verso (346.18). The recto of leaf 55 holds only the two lines of items 11 and 12 (346.31–32), but 55 verso is fully inscribed, the lower half (346.38–347.5) in smaller writing to crowd-in the text. The recto of the final leaf (347.6–10) is a half page, ending with a diagram. The verso of this leaf is the recto of the last page of the 1905–1906 notes (No. 27 in the present edition).

Emendations

327.15	change,] ~‿ₐ	337.10	"But] ₐ~
330.24	(multiverse)] (~‿ₐ	337.28	element."] ~·ₐ
331.4	"additives" "subtractives"]	338.12	fact,] ~. |
	ₐ~""~‿ₐ	338.27	you."] ~·ₐ
332.3	Describe] Decribe	339.35	302.)] ~·ₐ
332.8	footprint)] ~‿ₐ	342.23	*b*)] ~,
334.33	superseded.] ~‿ₐ	342.28	s'thing] s'ting
335.9	-as-] -~‿ₐ |	346.12	mysticism] mysticicism
337.4	(568)] ₐ~)	346.39	what] was

Alterations in the Manuscript

327.5   6th.] '6' *ov.* '4'
327.6   Ordinarily] 'ily' *ov.* 'y'
327.9   life] *intrl. ab. added s*emicolon;
  comma aft. 'life' *undel. in error*
327.13 find . . . world.] *intrl. ab.
  comma ov. period*
327.15 change] *intrl.*
327.21 basis] *insrtd.*
328.6,7 Change! | Being] *tr. by guide-
  line fr. left mrgn.*
328.8–9 definition!] *added*
328.24 etc] *added*
328.25 Empiricism] 'E' *ov.* 'D'
328.26 Rationalism] *aft. del.* 'Idealism'
328.31 problems] *bef. del.* | '(Teich-
  muller)'
329.1   Interpret] *aft. del.* 'I take pure
  "experience" | Conjunctive rela-
  tions . . | Give essence of this.' |
329.14–23 Growth . . . Panpsychism.]
  tr. by guideline fr. facing page
329.28 any] *intrl.*
329.28 datum] 'um' *ov.* 'a'
329.33 imperceptible] *insrtd.*
329.34 Organic] 'O' *ov.* 'G'
330.3   word.] *bef. del.* | 'Method'
330.4   Substance.] *intrl. bef. del. intrl.*
  'Self.'
330.6   Baldwin] *added*
330.7   connotations] *aft. del.* 'seems
  dualistic.'
330.9   concrete] *final* 'ness' *del.*
330.12 Ego] 'E' *ov.* 'e'
330.20 Noetic . . . about.] *penc.*
330.23 connexions] *bef. del.* | 'Deeper
  & shallower levels | Shallower involve
  deeper'
331.7   Generic] *aft. del.* 'Mechanical.'
331.9   mechanical] *bef. del.* 'Doesn't
  mo'
331.16 You] *aft. del.* '['You' *del.*]
  Incompletely reciprocal' |
331.18 *conceivable.*] *period added bef.
  del.* 'as'
331.29 It . . . but] *added*
331.36 Green etc.] *added*
331.39 25] '5' *ov.* '3'
332.1   Chaos] *penc.*
332.2   If . . . they] *ov. penc.* 'Consciousness'

332.7   Dreams] *aft. del.* 'Dyak's head.' |
332.14 reporting,] *comma ov. period*
332.14 awareness.] *added*
332.21 Admit] *aft. del.* 'What'
332.22–24 It . . . tendency.] *added*
332.26 E.g. . . . '04] *added*
332.29–31 Because . . . object.] *added*
332.34–35 We . . . cars.] *penc.*
333.7   naively] *aft. del.* 'has'
333.15 particle] 'cle' *aft. del.* 'cular'
333.18 Solipsism] *insrtd.*
333.22 interactions] *aft. del.* 'their'
333.34 *distinguons*] *aft. del.* 'disgi'
334.1   if] *bef. del.* 'we'
334.10 sense] *bef. del.* 'philosophy'
334.12 knowing] *ab. del.* 'having'
334.15 as] *aft. del.* 'w'
334.20 by] *aft. del.* 'but'
334.21 immediately] *aft. del.* 'really
  know'
333.22 actual] *intrl.*
334.24 experienced] *aft. del.* 'con'
335.5   ,, Unity of Things] *poss. added*
335.9   that] *bef. del.* 'the'
335.10,31 -C] 'C' *ov.* 's.'
335.11 its] *ab. del.* 'the'
335.11 what] *aft. del.* 'not'
335.12 mean, not] *ab. del.* 'are, but'
335.12 *are*] *insrtd. for del.* 'mean'
335.12 the real] *ab. del.* 'in'
335.13 experience.] *final* 's' *del.; period
  added bef. del.* 'which, as *they [ab.
  del.* 'it'] comes, contain a conjunctive
  transition.'
335.13 given;] *semicolon added bef.
  del.* '*& given [intrl.] as the same
  which is known (say) by A & knows
  C [ov. 'B'], or is above A & ['bl' *del.*]
  below *C [ov.* 'B'] etc. Its self sameness in the two relations is an original
  constituent of the experience'
335.14 its] *insrtd. for del.* 'the'
335.14 (*first two*) to] *intrl.*
335.15 latter] *insrtd. for del.* 'two
  latter'
335.16 No] *aft. del.* 'It is as ['one' *del.*]
  ['as the' *del.*] self same B ['to which'
  del.] that it thus functions conjunctively ['If you break it into two' *del.*]
  This [*alt. fr.* 'These'] is no warrant

643

in the immediate experience for breaking it'

335.17 one] *ab. del.* 'each'

335.17 C] *ov.* 'B'

335.18 B] *ov.* 'C'

335.18 experienced] *aft. del.* 'given as without'

335.19 a] *ab. del.* 'the'

335.19 mediates] *insrtd. for del.* 'functions *as a [intrl.]'

335.20 conjunctively] 'ly' *aft. del.* 'ly'; *bef. del.* 'intermediary' *ab. del.* 'towards'

335.20 between] *intrl.*

335.20 C.] *period added bef. del.* 'to which it is adventitiously related.'

335.21 being] *ab. del.* 'is'

335.22 from A to C] *intrl.*

335.22 point of] *intrl.*

335.23 or discontinuity] ('continuity' *ab. del.* 'integration'); *aft. del.* 'or separation about it.'

335.23 logical] *aft. del.* 'distinction of the'

335.25–26 by ... is] ('reflective' *aft. del.* 'some'); *ab. del.* 'it to be illusory, by substituting'

335.26 some deeper and] *ab. del.* 'a more real'

335.28 effect,] *comma added bef. del.* 'are either verbal or logical.'

335.30 integral] *intrl.*

335.30 "B] *aft. del.* 'A re'

335.30 A] *ov.* 'a'

335.31 is] *bef. del.* 'integrally'

335.31 But] *aft. del.* 'Each phrase ['one of' *del.*] denotes B in one of its two contexts. Each is a separate mental ['act of distinction;' *del.*] product'

335.32 we ... this] *ab. del.* '['this' *del.*] secondary wh'

335.33 successive] *intrl.*

335.33 phrases,] *bef. del.* 'has to use 2 Bs,'

335.33 phenomenon itself] *ab. del.* 'original experience'

335.34 been] *aft. del.* '['had one B' *del.*] ['run through one B,' *del.*] had one B'

335.34 distinguish] 'guish' *aft. del.* 'ctio'

335.35 Every] *aft. del.* 'If every'

335.37 The] *aft. del.* 'The mind using the words sees what they mean & restores the continuity of experience. Humes dictum, that'

335.37 B ... A] *ov.* 'A ... B'

335.38 fixes &] *intrl.*

335.39 them] *insrtd. for del.* 'it'

336.2 distinct] *aft. del.* 'its'

336.2 2in] *aft. del.* 'it'

336.6 test] *ab. del.* 'definition'

336.6 inability to show] *ab. del.* 'absence of'

336.9 differ] *ab. del.* 'are | *different [undel. in error]'

336.9 part] *bef. del.* ', which the'

336.12 relations ... linked] *intrl.*

336.13 118] *intrl.*

336.19 which] *bef. del.* 'ac'

336.21 appearance] *aft. del.* 'appeer'

336.26 Obviously] *aft. del.* 'Bradley begins by denying that pure experience gives conjunction.'

336.26 conjunctions] *aft. del.* 'g'

336.27 passing] *bef. del.* 'into memory leaves the sense'

336.31 experience] *bef. del.* '['contains objects' *del.*] ['objects ear' *del.*] gives space continuity. The ['ob' *del.*] central object is below the top one & above the bottom one.'

336.32 conjoined] 'c' *ov.* 'is'; *aft. del.* 'there'

336.32 placed,] *comma added bef. del.* 'in'

336.35 His] *ov.* 'Its'

336.37 ᴧBut] *db. qt. del.; aft. del.* 'But'

337.3 [in] *bkt. ov. paren*

337.14 as] *intrl.*

337.19 the] *ab. del.* 'a'

337.20 also] *aft. del.* 'by'

337.26 beside] *aft. del.* 'you'

337.33 p 86–91] *penc.*

337.35 Revert] *aft. del.* 'Leave Bradley! article!' |

338.8 & ... table] *intrl.*

338.11 ground] *aft. del.* 'previo'

338.20 intelligibility &] *intrl.*

338.22 Miss] *aft.* 'No ['N' *ov.* 'O'; *poss. false start for* 'Nov']' | *undel. in error*

338.27 "affirm] *intrl.*

338.31 idealistic] *aft. del.* 'arg'

339.6   A . . . Absolute.] *added*
339.21   negations] *aft. del.* 'dangerous'
339.34   Its] *aft. del.* '[we must take it radically as an instantaneity!] | 1. Its superfoetations—negativities, errors etc. | 2. Block universe' |
340.2   3] *aft. del.* '2 Lion's den character.' |
340.2–3   Abs. . . . ideas] *insrtd.*
340.4   4] *ov.* '3'
340.12   Raindrops etc] *insrtd.*
340.19   thing] *aft. del.* 'new'
340.23   the question is] *intrl.*
340.33   Other] *aft. del.* 'In the' |
341.4   two] *aft. del.* 'that'
341.6   occur] *aft. del.* 'ac'
341.8   *Ultimate*] *aft. del.* 'Having occu' |
341.14   no] *final* 'thing' *del.*
341.23   Conservation] *aft. del.* '"Summer"—"winter"' |
341.25   This table] *insrtd.*
341.34   1st] *aft. del.* 'U.S. Post Office.' |
342.7   Reality] 'R' *ov.* 'I'
342.8   Real] *aft. del.* 'Individualism.' |
342.22   Huxley] 'ey' *ov.* 'y'
342.30   kinetoscope] *bef. del.* | 'Continuous by interpolation, mixture, partial alteration partial identity.'
342.36   Zeno] *final* 's' *del.*
343.2   when] *bef. del.* 'it is habitual?'
343.14   Logic] 'L' *ov.* '§'
343.20   looking forward] *intrl.*
344.3   procession] *aft. del.* 'identity.'
344.7   variation] *aft. del.* 'f'
344.8   full] *bef. del.* 'meaning of the wor'
344.14   Either] *bef. del.* 'panpsychism or *a [*ov. start of* 'p'] purely devitalized s'
344.15   either] *init.* 'e' *ov.* 'a'

344.19   Healthy] *aft. del.* 'Suppose now | Strong's diagram: | [*diagram*] | Postpone Strong etc. | Assume panspsychism.' |
344.25   *conterminous*] *bef. del.* 'the reasons is dynamism'
344.29   How] *aft. del.* 'We have to interpolate | They may be *contiguous* at last | They *may* be *confluent*, like ['my ha' *del.*] sight & touch in "my hand." | (This would be *noetic* confluence) | Meanwhile chain of activities supposed. | [*diagram*]'
344.32   Idea] *final* 'I' *del.*
344.33   Percepts] *aft. del.* 'Ideas give rise'
345.7   instant] *intrl.*
345.12   Our] *ov. illeg.*
345.22–27   On . . . penetrate.] *tr. by guideline fr. facing page*
345.23   think] *ab. del.* 'say'
345.23   cortex] *aft. del.* 'brain.'
345.24   B.] *aft. del.* 'Stro'
345.26   But] *aft. del.* 'Tele'
345.28   brain . . . *action*] *insrtd.*
346.3   synthesis] *bef. del.* | 'Psych. Rev. Vol 2.'
346.5   2.] *bef. del.* | 'My [*undel. ab. del.* 'My'] ['bo' *del.*] | Varieties | Leuba | My reply | Wider world | Synthesis vs analysis'
346.7   private . . . done] *added*
346.16   an] *intrl.*
346.18   If . . . 74] *tr. by guideline fr. facing page*
346.23   3] *aft. del.* '3. Theory of Knowledge.'
346.25   Realistic] *ab. del.* 'no tr'
347.1   1of] *intrl.*
347.5   is] *aft. del.* 'has'
347.6   e.g] *intrl.*

27. Notes for Philosophy 9: Metaphysics 1905–1906 #4511, #4458

The notes (#4511) for the 1905–1906 course are found in the same hardbound notebook as those for the 1904–1905 (No. 26 in the present edition). On the inner cover is the label of Partridge and Cooper, Chancery Lane, London, above which James inscribed, 'Return this book, if found, to' and then inserted his name and Irving Street address by rubber stamp. The text is inscribed in the normal way from the front of the notebook to the back, but the first thirteen leaves plus two tipped-in leaves contain a class list and two examinations (reproduced on pp. 348, 350, and 352) as well as a number of notes that pertain to the 1904–1905 class. Why these leaves preface the 1905–1906 material is not to be ascertained, but there are notes within these pages that James probably intended for use in both courses. The arrangement of the material as found in #4511 has been preserved in the present edition.

On the recto of the first leaf a strange hand has written at upper left, 'Arthur Stanley Beale, | 6 Thayer Hall, | Cambridge.' To the right of this James wrote 'No philosophy | Told him I might let him in later'. A horizontal line then divides the page and beneath it James wrote the following series of notes: 'J. Petzoldt | ..*Einführung ['E' *ov.* 'e'] in d. Philosophie *der reinen Erfuhrung:" [*added in blue ink*] | Froeltsch Sunday | J. S. Moore, 74 Buckingham St | Abraham Baldwin, 26 Woodland Park | Chicago | J. L. French, 140 Boylston St'. On the verso of this first leaf appears the printed 1904–1905 class list mentioned above. James's notes start on the recto of the second leaf with 347.13 and continue on the rectos, each item widely spaced, except for an interpolation on the verso of the seventh leaf at 349.30–36. On the verso of leaf 12 James pasted a printed hour examination for November 1, 1904, and below it wrote 351.1–5. Then come two leaves tipped-in of light-blue laid unwatermarked paper, ruled, with a vertical marginal rule, on the recto, verso and next recto of which James inscribed 351.6–27. His notes begin again on leaf 13 (351.28–352.2), but on the verso of this leaf James pasted the printed midyear examination at the head of which he wrote '1904 ['4' *ov.* '3']–5 [*ov.* '4']'.

Leaf 14 recto contains a list of topics that could pertain to either the 1904–1905 or the 1905–1906 course, but leaf 14 verso and both sides of leaf 15 are occupied by a list of the theses that James's students in the 1905–1906 class were writing. In the upper right corner of leaf 15 recto James wrote, circled, 'Phil 9 | 1905–6' and beneath it, pasted on the page, is the calling card of one of his students (fn. 2). On the verso of leaf 15 James had pasted-on the printed class list for his 1905–1906 course (p. 354). The notes for the year start formally on the sixteenth leaf headed 'Sept 30. 1905', above a rule, and proceed mostly on the rectos, with the versos reserved for memoranda but occasionally inscribed with continuous text. The numbering is on the rectos only, but with the versos silently paged. Occasionally James made a slip in the numbering and then corrected himself as on p. 9 where the nine is written over an eight and p. 21 where the one is over a zero. Text for the seminar, not merely a memorandum, comes on the verso of leaf 21 (356.21–31), which would be p. [12]. After leaf 23, paged 15, a leaf has been torn out so that the inscription skips from p. 15 at 357.23 to 357.24 heading p. 19, the text of p. [17] now lost. Leaf 21 is correctly numbered, although, as mentioned above, the 21 is altered from the error 20. After leaf 25 (p. 21), with a one-line note on its verso, five of the original leaves have been cut out, representing pp. 23–31. Page [33] is preserved only with its upper third cut away, including the numbering, the text then beginning with 358.9. On the verso, below the cut-out, are two lines of notes, and the text continues on p. 35, the recto of the twenty-seventh preserved leaf with 'that or words' (358.18). Below 358.27 James drew a horizontal line and started circled 'Oct 14.' to the left below, but the lower third of the page is blank and 'Oct. 14' (358.28) with its text heads the recto of leaf 28, wrongly numbered with repeated 35, an error that is continued. Page 45, the recto of leaf 33 ('His reply . . . sense's notion' 360.19–361.1) is correctly numbered 45 over original error 44.

The recto inscription is interrupted by a verso addition (362.9–11), including a diagram, about halfway down the page, intended (although no guideline is present) presumably to follow 362.8 about two-thirds down on the facing recto of leaf 38 (p. 55) which then continues with 362.12. On the verso of leaf 37, in a larger hand, James wrote beneath 362.9–11 a note in the lower right corner (fn. 20). This note is written in pencil around a pencil-deleted false start 'Concate' that James had written in ink at an earlier time.

After leaf 38 five leaves have been cut out, some remnants of handwriting showing in the margin. When the text resumes on the preserved thirty-ninth leaf, headed 'Nov 5', circled, (362.16), the leaves are unnumbered for the rest of the notebook. The recto-only inscription, with blank or annotated versos, continues from the thirty-ninth leaf through leaf 43 ('s̄. love . . . Classic 363.31–364.7) and then to the recto of leaf 44 (364.8–13), ending with five deleted lines. The text of 44 recto is then continued on the facing page, 43 verso (364.14–22), which seems to be intended as a unit and probable addition, with the handwriting decreasing in size as the foot of the page approaches. Written vertically in the left margin of this page is a memorandum reproduced as footnote 24. The text of 43 verso continues on 45 recto (364.23–28) and then switches to the facing page, 44 verso (364.29–365.5). In turn this text is continued on the upper half (365.6–11) of 45 verso, the final clause 'and the privation . . . thought.' (365.10–11) written vertically in the left margin. Below this text, a horizontal rule separates three lines (fn. 28) that comment on the text on 46 recto (365.22–24), their position indicated by a guideline arrow. Below these three lines are five lines (365.17–19) positioned by a guideline to follow 365.16 in the text on 46 recto. Leaf 46 recto is continued on 46 verso (365.27–366.2) after a white space, with 365.33–366.2 written later in a different ink vertically in the left margin.

Leaf 47 recto (366.3–12) then begins once more the inscription on rectos only, with occasional notes on versos. After leaf 52 (367.19–28) twelve leaves have been cut out of the notebook. Two fragments of text written vertically in the margin can be observed on the stubs. On the verso of the fourth stub appears 'Possibility swings between 2 extremes, no', and on the recto of the tenth stub, 'Average human longevity'. After the stubs the fifty-third preserved leaf holds the text for 367.29–368.8, which ends with three deleted lines. The next, or fifty-fourth leaf, has its upper half irregularly cut off but the uncut margin shows that at least some of the text had been deleted. What appears to be a later added footnote asterisk indicator for ' "Design." ' (368.16) refers to text written without asterisk reference at the foot of the facing page, leaf 53 verso (368.29–33). Above this footnote, horizontal lines set off what appears to be a memorandum possibly written at the same time (fn. 35). Recto inscription continues. On leaf 57 recto the text for 369.20–23 is an afterthought, brought over from the facing verso by an arrow guideline. In the last leaves of the notebook James began writing on verso as well as recto. Leaf 59 recto (370.13–370.24) is continued on 59 verso, then 60 recto, and 60 verso. The text ends on 61 recto. On the verso of this page is the reversed recto of the last page of the notes for the 1904–1905 course (No. 26 in the present edition).

James's brackets are found at 358.21–26 '[Explain . . . pictures]', 362.17–18 '[It . . . change]', and 364.17–18 '[If . . . alone.]'.

Four leaves of laid note paper 8⅝ x 6½", unwatermarked, are present in a manila envelope on the cover of which James had written 'Possibility', underlined (#4458). The leaves (372.16–374.18) are written on rectos and versos in black ink. Prefixing these leaves is the upper half of a typescript on laid paper with a partial watermark THE BOS. This unidentified typed piece (not transcribed here) is numbered 16 and begins, 'Here is a passage which I have always loved of Emerson's', ending in mid-sentence.

James's brackets are found at 373.18–19 '[Meanwhile . . . p. 42]'.

Emendations

351.18   exist,"] ~,∧
351.25   account] acount
353.28   Mill)] ~∧
354.25   Gundersen] Gunderson
355.13   (Wolff.)] (~.∧
355.27   "Knowledge] ∧~
355.37   ∧Philosophers] "~
356.11   ∧How] "~
357.34   intellect.)] ~.∧
361.11;362.6   Heymans] Heymanns
363.13   backward."] ~.∧

365.3   esse] essi
365.3   cogitari] cogiti
367.10   intellectually)] ~,
368.13   "ontological"] "~∧
368.29   *Any] ∧~
370.6   "Souls"] "~'
371.21   des∧] ~.
371.21   Daseins] Dasein's
371.24   comparison.] ~,
373.19   42)] ~∧

Alterations in the Manuscripts

347.13–14   Dewey's . . . Price] *penc.*
347.20   Scot] 'S' *ov.* 's'
349.3   *Dorrance*] 'Darrance [*in error for* 'Dorrance']' *ab. del.* 'Foerster'
349.3–5   Fraser's . . . Huxley] ('Fraser's *aft. del.* 'Berkeley'); *added*
349.8–9   Foerster . . . books] *added aft. del.* 'Toll?' *ab. del.* 'Dorrance' *ab. del.* 'Dorrance:'
349.27   Necessity] *aft. del.* 'Epistemology'
349.32   either] *aft. del.* 'th'
349.34   progress.] *ab. del.* 'approach.'
350.9   *Byard*] *alt. fr.* 'Bayard'
350.23   Tait] *aft. del.* 'Mayer *Brain Physiology: My Principles. [insrtd.]'
351.6   term.] *bef. del.* 'Of what'
351.7   "knowing"] *bef. del.* 'help to'
351.10   structure.] *bef. del.* | 'Question of Being'
351.12   Build up] *ab. del.* 'Expound' *ab. del.* 'Defend a'
351.12   theory of the] *intrl.*
351.12   making] *aft. del.* 'by'
351.14   &] *intrl.*
351.14   these] 'se' *added*
351.15   Compare . . . irrationalities.] ('Compare' *ab. del.* 'Mention'); *tr. by guideline fr. bef.* 'How' [351.11]

351.17   be] *aft. del.* 'stan'
351.17   anything] 'any' *ab. del.* 'some'
351.19   'ideas.'] *period aft. del.* comma *and bef. del.* qst. mk.
351.20   properties?] *bef. del.* | 'Think of some examples'
351.21–22   any . . . you] *ab. del.* '['some of the places of its' *del.*] ['use in the course.' *del.*] where it was useful in the course'
351.23   "Radical] *aft. del.* 'Why was'
351.26   Can] *ab. del.* 'are'
351.36   Genesis] *aft. del.* 'Theory of knowledge.' |
351.37   Natl. Realism] *added*
353.17   D. Arnold] *ab. del.* 'Churchill'
353.19   Emerson] *penc.*
353.21   Sc) R. W. Pumpelly] *ab. del.* 'Elder'
353.25   J. . . . A] *penc.*
354.6   Kallen] 'Kallin [*in error for* 'Kallen'] *ab. del.* 'White'
354.8–9   Spencer's & Fiske's religion] ''s' *added to each name*; 'religion' *insrtd.*
354.11   Spencers Sociology] *penc.*
354.13   Brundage] 'a' *ab. del.* 'id'
354.17   Ogawa] 'w' *ov.* 'm'
354.18–19   & Santayana] *ab. del.* period

354.24 —Santayana's book] *added on facing page aft. del.* 'D Leavens'

354.25 D] *aft. del.* 'D Freeman'

354.25–26 Evolution & Immortality] ('& Immortality' *on facing page*); *penc.*

355.21 principles] | 'ciples' *aft. del.* | 'cip [*written flush left instead of indented for run-over*]'

355.29 Ward . . . 1890] ('8' *ov.* '9'); *added*

355.32 motto.] *bef. del.* | 'Real objection: unlike both scienc | Student last year. | Tendency of rationalists. | Closed systems. | Empiricism and Sci'

356.9 5th] '5' *ov.* '7'

356.12 higher or lower?] *insrtd.*

356.18 Mind] 'Mi' *ov.* 'Ho'

356.29 1I] *ov.* 'we'

356.29 What . . . hope?] *added*

356.31 do?] *bef. del.* | 'Answers so wide & abstract as to be full of ambiguity & misunderstanding'

356.33 opinion.] *bef. del.* | 'A priori? experience?'

356.35 One] *aft. del.* 'Antitheses:' |

356.35 continuity vs. discontinuity] *intrl.*

357.5 Renouvier's] *ov. start of* 'R'

357.6 facts] *intrl.*

357.6 ideas] *bef. del.* '(facts'

357.9 liberty] *bef.* 'happiness duty' *tr. by guideline to aft.* 'faith' *but then del.*

357.18 Terms] 'T' *ov.* 'D'

357.22 Substance] *bef. del.* | 'Jas. Mill on'

357.26 word] *bef. del.* 'Pragm̄'

357.28 Wider] *aft. del.* 'W[*start of* 'h']'

358.2 Roughly] 'R' *ov.* 'I'

358.8 1] *ov.* '3'

358.17 glass] *aft. del.* 'mosaic'

358.24 (Pearson)] *poss. added*

358.27 Empiricism uses "collection."] *bel. this line* WJ *drew a line across the page and bel. the line wrote and circled* 'Oct 14.'*, but then repeated* 'Oct. 14' *at top of foll. page without del. orig.* 'Oct 14.'

359.10 dont read it] *insrtd.*

359.17 17] '7' *ov.* '6'

359.23 act] *aft. del.* 'action'

359.29 19] '9' *ov.* '8'

360.10 would] *aft. del.* 'do we'

360.13 extrapolate] 'extra' *ov.* 'inter'

360.15 the] *intrl.*

360.15 termini.] *bef. del.* | 'But criticism of the senses reduces them to a *provisional ['on' *intrl.*] halting place.'

360.17 knowledge] 'kn' *ov.* 'Co'

360.20 pluralistic] *insrtd. w. guideline showing position*

360.27 act] *bef. del.* 'on it [*period del.*] or for it or'

361.2 Common] 'C' *ov.* 'h'

361.12 Conceptual] 'Con' *ov.* 'per'

361.13 original] *aft. del.* 'percepts'

361.13 things] *aft. del.* 'the real'

361.13 in themselves,] *intrl.*

361.15 But] *aft. del.* 'All the whole'

361.33 percept] *aft. del.* '['percep' *del.*] sense'

362.3 centre] *bef. del.* 'of action'

362.11 psychic] 'ps' *ov. poss.* 'ner'

362.24 way?] *bef. del.* | 'Take purpose, dramatic unity etc. | Lotze, Royce abandon it in detail. | Individualistic method the only possible one. | Paulsen p. 158.'

363.7 their unity] *ab. del.* 'it'

363.10 from] *aft. del.* 'Read Lotze'

363.12 205–] '5' *ov.* '6'; *aft. del. intrl.* '172'

363.15 I] *bef. del. illeg.*

363.15 such passages as] *penc. insrtd. bef. penc. del. ink intrl.* '421'

363.15 440–] 'o' *aft. del.* '1'

363.19 667] *bef. del.* | 'Royce. C of G. 292–4, 312–4 | Mill on number of elements'

363.22 not.] *bef. del.* | 'Knowableness together'

363.26 telegrafic] *aft. del.* 'Some conne'

363.31 knowledge] *aft. del.* 'ether'

363.31 copper] *ab. del.* 'water'

364.1 ⌃Shallower] *paren del.*

364.5 Network!] *poss. added*

364.6 not a dogma] ('a' *ab. del.* 'for'); *added*

364.8 Classic] *aft. del.* 'Hypothesis of absolute unity' |

364.8 our] *aft. del.* 'our exact'

364.11   vs.] *aft. del.* 'Absolute unity as sum of all partial ones.'

364.13   Criticize it.] *aft. del.* 'Objections to it.'; *bef. del.* | '1. Does ['de' *del.*] it demand through-and-through type? | It thinks things *as [*intrl.*] on time. | Need *their ['ir' *ov.* 'y'] age be identical?'; *in the left mrgn. bef.* '1.' WJ *insrtd.* 'barrenness ['b' *ov.* 'P'] lion's den,'

364.20   previous] *aft. del.* 'separ'

364.23   1] *penc. insrtd. for penc. and ink del.* '2'; *aft. ink del.* 'Compatible therefore with concatenated Universe & *empirical [*intrl.*] novelty. | Royce on free-will | Read C. of G. 292–4, 312–4' |

364.24   in] *aft. del.* 'of'

364.29   by] *aft. del.* 'on the'

364.29   think] *intrl.*

364.30   (A . . . etc)] ('b' *alt. fr.* 'be'); *intrl.*

364.31   simply] *intrl.*

364.32   the fact] *aft. del.* 'a n'

365.6   both] *aft. del.* 'a be an'

365.7   Its] *aft. del.* 'We have no other way of being than as *It ['I' *ov.* 'i'] thinks us. *B [*ov.* 'T' *and poss. start of* 'h']'

365.8   than its way] *intrl.*

365.9   our] *intrl.*

365.10–11   and . . . thought.] *insrtd. vert. in mrgn.*

365.17–19   Metaphysical . . . first.] ('A' *ov.* 'a' *in* 'Absolute'); *tr. by guideline fr. facing page*

365.24   freedom] *bef. del.* | 'of infinit'

365.32   they] 'y' *ov.* 'm'

365.32   2It] 'I' *ov.* 'i'

365.33–366.2   We . . . difference.] ('He' *ov.* 'W'); *insrtd. vert. in mrgn.*

366.4   Read blank book] *intrl.*

366.5   443–] '3' *ov.* '4'

366.20   excludes] 'exc' *ov.* 'sol'

366.23   What] 'W' *ov.* 'w'

366.34   Monists] 'M' *ov.* 'm'

367.1   1. . . . information.] ('1' *ov.* '2'; 'information' *aft. del.* 'completeness of'); *tr. by guideline fr. aft.* '2 [*ov.* '1'] . . . facts.'

367.6   one] *ov.* 'a'

367.10   intellectually] *aft. del.* 'f'

367.15   help] *aft. del.* 'ad'

367.17   work] *ab. del.* 'take it up'

367.28   Chance] 'C' *ov.* 'c'

368.1   to] *aft. del.* 'So far I have been atheistic.'

368.8   results.] *bef. del.* | 'Naturalism allows no mind above the human. | Yet there *may* be such. Their invisibility is no *disproof ['dis' *intrl.*]. Dogs.'

368.21   feeling] *ab. del.* 'belief'

368.21   friendly] *ab. del.* 'congenial'

368.25   example.] *bef. del.* ' "Slum" '

368.26   political] 'pol' *ov.* 'soc'

369.5–6   Ab- . . . congenial.] *tr. by guideline fr. aft.* 'Dogs.' [369.10]

369.19   Fechner's] 'F' *ov. illeg.*

369.20–23   All . . . God.] *tr. by guideline fr. facing page*

369.26   "say,"] *aft. del.* 'final'

369.28   guise.] *bef. del.* | 'In any case private experiences are the fully concrete ones. *All* life is more than the merely *intellectual* life. | Pure naturalism & objectivism an abstraction.'

369.30   Fechnerian] *bef. del.* '*, or [*undel. in error*] Roycian'

370.2   e.g.] *ov.* 'i.e.'

370.3–4   at . . . known] *added*

370.6   3 . . . experience.] *insrtd.*

370.9   "Monument] *aft. del.* 'Egoti'

370.10   Personal] *aft. del.* 'Private'

370.11   Whole] 'W' *ov.* 'In'

370.18   Royce] *bef. del.* 'and Bradley'

370.19   Bradley] 'B' *ov.* 'R'

370.28   in] *aft. del.* 'when'

370.29   does] *ov.* 'is'

370.29   copy] *ab. del.* ' "true" '

370.30   Is it true?] *insrtd. for del.* 'Does it copy.'

371.1   of relations.] *intrl. bef.* 'unlikeness' *l.c. in error*

371.4   works?] *bef. del.* | 'Two alleged objections: 1.'

371.6   have] *aft. del.* 'Discuss this latter proposition.' |

371.9   Are] *ov.* 'Has'

371.9   no] *aft. del.* 'it'

371.9   for it?] *intrl.*

371.10   have] *ab. del.* 'is'

371.10 accept] *aft. del.* 'a'
371.10 it] *bef. del.* ', nothing to do with its de jure'
371.17 Believe] 'B' *ov.* 'W'
371.23–24 ¹of . . . comparison] *intrl. ab. comma ov. period*
371.25 stay] *bef. del.* 'we must'
372.2 tent-] 'ten' *ov.* 'cos'
372.4 involved.] 'volved.' *intrl.*
372.7 immediate] *aft. del.* 'th'
372.8 One] *aft. del.* 'Subordinate'
372.9 useful] *aft. del.* 'rela'
372.11 am] 'm' *ov. illeg.*
372.11 you] *ab. del.* 'I'
372.14 or known] *intrl.*
372.16 from] *bef. del.* 'any'
372.16 one] *intrl.*
372.17 extant] *intrl.*
372.24 *Possibility*] *ink and penc. underl.*
372.24 *may*] *aft. del.* 'either'; *bef. del.* 'be'
372.25 &] *ov.* 'or'

372.26 twilight] *intrl.*
372.31 makes] 'm' *ov.* 'is'
372.31 existence] *aft. del.* 'actual'
372.32 make] *final* 's' *del.*
373.1 thing] *final* 's' *del.*
373.8 recovery] *aft. del.* 'cure of'
373.12 impossibility] *aft. del.* 'real'
373.12 necessity] *ab. del.* 'possibility'
373.12 conditions,] *bef. del.* | 'From condition to condition, world *changes*'
373.19 name] *aft. del.* 'finite'
373.22 *Change*] 'C' *ov.* 'c'
373.26 Alternatives:] *bef. del.* | 'Discontinuous: Kinetoscope,'
374.5 chance] *aft. del.* 'the'
374.9 fit] *insrtd. for del.* 'fulfill purposes belonging to'
374.11 debtor.] *bef. del.* 'R.Js hat & Foss'
374.13 for] *bef. del.* 'everything, ['in' *del.*] in i'

28. Lectures at Stanford 1906 #4516

James's essay on "Faith" comes toward the end of a full notebook (#4516) after an extended series of notes for his course in Philosophy 1a at Stanford University in 1906, not transcribed in this edition because of the considerable duplication with similar notes for his courses at Harvard. The notebook is from Partridge and Cooper, Chancery Lane, London, ruled white wove paper 9 x 7″, in boards. The essay itself takes up the rectos of three leaves.

The "Lecture to Miss Martin's Class" comes on the verso of the fourteenth leaf after the conclusion of "Faith," the intervening pages occupied by discussions for Philosophy 1a and a brief discourse of "Religion." In all the lecture occupies four pages of rectos and versos. The footnote is an afterthought, written vertically in the left margin of the first page.

Emendation

376.37 to] *om.*

Alterations in the Manuscript

374.21 fit] *aft. del.* 'may be,'
375.1 order in wh.] *ab. del.* 'way'
375.6 faculty] 'y' *ov.* 'ies'
375.7 indeed] *intrl.*
375.9 put] *ab. del.* 'made'
375.11 This] 'is' *ov.* 'e'

375.12 truths] *aft. del.* 'th'
375.15 meaning] 'ing' *added*
375.18 as to] *insrtd. for del.* 'between'
375.19 or] *ab. del.* 'and'
375.19 more] *aft. del.* 'phr'
375.20 one] 'o' *ov.* 'w'

375.32   man.*] *asterisk added*
375.33   live] *aft. del.* 'life'
375.34–36   *But . . . specific?]
('Evolutionists' *ab. del.* 'Geologists');
added vert. in left mrgn.
376.8   states.] *bef. del.* | 'Intoxicants—
normal consciousness only one case.'
376.13   case.] *bef. del.* | 'Conventional
people vs. Mind-curists. Little finger. |

Some *can't* pray; *can't* feel a God. |
Yet here a germ! amen!'
376.14–15   Partition moveable] *insrtd.*
376.25   Evangelical] 'E' *ov.* 'c'
376.30   this‸] *semicolon partially del.*
376.31   then] *intrl.*
376.32   resources] *aft. del.* 'new'
376.36   our] *aft. del.* 'the'

29. Talk with Cohen about Kant   1906   #4516

In #4516 after the "Lecture to Miss Martin's Class" (in No. 28), comes a scored-through "Talk to Psychology-Club at Harvard, May 18 '06," six pages of notes ending in a blank verso, printed as Appendix I in *Essays in Religion and Morality*, Works. The notebook ends with "Talk with Cohen" on the rectos of four leaves, with two blanks following.

No emendations

Alterations in the Manuscript

377.5   residual] 'l' *ov.* 'm'   377.28   principles] *aft. del.* 'content'

30. Syllabus in Philosophy D: General Problems of Philosophy   1906–1907   #4466, #4467, #4522, HUC 8906.370.56

James had two different printed syllabuses for Philosophy D: the first (without a designation) was used for the course which he gave at Stanford University in the spring of 1906; the second, somewhat revised and expanded, and in a different typesetting, was used for Philosophy D at Harvard in the following autumn of 1906. Each was printed on rectos only. The pagination 1–45 can be established only from the beginning and end of the Harvard printing. In James's own collection only two examples are preserved. In #4466 are found pp. 1–14 and 40–45 of the Harvard Philosophy D printing. This folder holds, also, two extra copies each of pp. 11–14. In folder #4467 one finds pp. 1–35 of the complete Stanford syllabus. In the Philosophy D folder p. 43 ends five lines short of the foot. On this page James wrote in pencil at the head 'only these two copies of this', and at the foot, in the white space, 'end of syllabus'. However, p. 44 begins a section entitled 'Materialism Again.', which concludes partway down the page on the final p. 45. James's statement that he has in 'these' the only two copies of 'this' coincides with the leaves in the two folders, but between the two one should notice that leaves 36–39 of the complete syllabus are missing in both folders. On the other hand, a scrapbook #4522, among a collection of examination papers and other such academic miscellanea, contains pp. 1–14 and 32–45 in the Harvard printing (thus filling in the missing pp. 36–39), and prefaces Harvard p. 32 by the four Stanford pages 28–31. Finally, in the Harvard Archives under HUC 8906.370.56: Morison, S. E.—Notes in Philosophy D, 1906–07, are preserved pp. 4–14 of the Harvard syllabus, pp. 14–21 and 24–30 of the Stanford syllabus, and finally pp. 32–45 of Harvard.

In summary, the situation is this. We have preserved pp. 1–14 and 32–45 of the Harvard syllabus and pp. 1–35 of Stanford's. The two overlap for pp. 1–14 and 32–35. In the Stanford syllabus p. 13 ends with the same text as Harvard p. 14 (394.3). The text of Stanford p. 14 ('Parallelists . . . exist-' 394.4–395.10), therefore, seems to continue the text of Harvard p. 14 without interruption and so begins the section of text in which the Stanford syllabus is uniquely preserved. The copy-text in this edition, therefore, is the revised Harvard syllabus for Philosophy D pp. 1–14, 32–45 made up from #4466 and #4522, confirmed by Archives HUC 8906.370.56, containing 378.9–394.3 and 414.29–428.28 in the present edition. The intervening text (394.4–414.28) is reprinted from the Stanford syllabus pp. 14–31 in #4467. Where the two texts parallel each other in pp. 1–14 and 32–35 the Historical Collation records their differences.

James annotated various pages in both the Stanford and the Harvard syllabuses. Some of these constitute revisions of the text and are therefore adopted as emendations of the printed copy-text whether made in the Stanford or the Harvard leaves. The more frequent annotations are memoranda on which James would have based his enlarged exposition in class of the syllabus. These are transcribed in Appendix V. The scrapbook leaves #4522 are unannotated. James annotated the Stanford leaves chiefly in ink but with some notes in lead pencil and once in blue pencil. These are present on pp. 4–10 (including the blank 8 verso), leaves also present and in part annotated in the Harvard series. In red-brown pencil a vertical line for emphasis is drawn at the left against the top lines on p. 16 (396.18–26) in the unique Stanford leaves and similar lines in ink at the right on pp. 20 (401.14–29) and 21 (402.30–403.3). A reference to Paulsen also appears to the left on p. 21. Pages 22–26 are not annotated. On p. 27 the printed text ends halfway down the page and in the white space below the last printed line James wrote a comment. On p. 30 he added a section heading, on p. 34 a note, and on the final p. 35 a revision of the text.

The annotations in the Harvard leaves in #4466 are in ink, mainly, but various in lead pencil. Two notes are in a red-brown pencil, which is used also to underline words in the text and in the ink annotations and to draw a guideline. James marked corrections, revisions, and notes on pp. 1–7 and 9–14. No markings are present in pp. 40–45 except for the note about the number of copies and the end of the syllabus on p. 43 remarked above. Since pp. 32–39 are known only from the scrapbook and the Harvard Archives leaves, both unannotated by James, any annotations he may have made in leaves not now present in #4466 are lost. The Archives copy belonged to Samuel Eliot Morison, a student of James, and contains his annotations, not reproduced in this edition.

James paid particular attention to the syllabus between pages 10 and 14. Page 10 (388.22–389.23) is heavily annotated, and between 10 and 11 is inserted a piece of exercise-book ruled paper 5¼ x 6¾", cut off from a larger leaf as indicated by the feet of some letters in the upper margin above the first line of text. The recto of this piece is written on the lines of the ruled paper, but its verso has been turned sideways and the writing is vertical to the rules (Appendix V, entry 389.23). The annotations on p. 10 are in ink, except for one note and some underlining in the red-brown pencil, and pretty well fill the margins, chiefly with memoranda notes but with four textual revisions.

Three copies of leaves 11–14 are present in #4466. The identification and the inferential order is, of course, arbitrary although some suggestive evidence is present. What may be identified as p. 11a (389.24–390.28) is heavily anno-

tated with memoranda in lead pencil and ink so that the margins are full.
Page 11b has extensive notes in ink in the lower half of the right margin and
the foot, filling these margins but leaving the upper part of the page unmarked.
Page 11c has only one marginal remark, in pencil. Page 12a ('*Read* . . . that'
390.30–391.33) has three major sections of ink notation in the left margin but
plenty of white space. Pages 12b and 12c are unannotated. Page 13a ('pop . . .
also?' 391.33–392.37) has three brief notes in ink, one note underlined in a
red-brown pencil as are some words in the other two notes as well as a line of
printed text. Pages 13b and 13c are unmarked. The margins of p. 14a (392.38–
394.3) are almost completely filled with annotation, all in ink except for one
note in red-brown pencil and a few underlinings. Page 14b has a single ink
revision (Emendation entry 394.2), and 14c is unmarked.

Given the heavy annotation of p. 11a (following heavy marking-up of p. 10),
it may seem that when James wanted to add to his notes on p. 11 he inserted
an extra page, 11b. These extra pages need not have been inscribed simultaneously, for the single note on p. 11c, for instance, could have been accommodated on 11b. The extra pages of 12b–c and 13b–c were not required,
nor was the 14c leaf (nor perhaps the 14b leaf although the extra annotation
on 14b might not have been accommodated on 14a). It is probable that James
abstracted the three leaves from two extra copies of the syllabus in anticipation
of heavy annotation, which was only partly fulfilled. The annotation of the
Stanford leaves is more laconic, and some, at least, is in a smaller hand and
differently placed. It is a reasonable conjecture that the Stanford annotation
was made for the purpose of the California class and has no relation to the
markings of the Harvard leaves. That the two sets were at one time assembled
may be suggested by the presence of the rare red-brown pencil markings on
pp. 10, 13, and 14 of the Harvard leaves and the same red-brown pencil used
for a vertical emphasis line against the text of 396.18–26 of Stanford p. 16.
However, in the uniquely preserved Stanford leaves for pp. 14–31, in addition
to the vertical line on p. 16, there is only a short reference note in ink on p. 21
(Appendix V, entry 402.20–23), a comment at the foot of p. 27 (Appendix V,
entry 410.7), and an added section title on p. 30 (413.3). Where for pp. 32–35
the two syllabuses overlap, Stanford has a note at the head of p. 34 (Appendix
V, entry 417.11–12), and a textual revision on p. 35 (Emendation entries 418.25)
which has not been made in the printed Harvard leaf in the Archives or the
scrapbook. Since p. 35 is one of the pages missing from James's own set of the
Harvard syllabus, we cannot tell whether he had made this change in his own
copy. The odds are: probably not, the more especially since the Harvard leaves
for pp. 40–45 in James's possession have no teaching notes. Indeed, it is of
interest that annotation of the Stanford leaves, never very heavy for teaching
purposes, trails off after the early pages, and is sparse indeed even when, as
conjectured below, James would need to have used these leaves from Stanford
p. 14 through p. 31 in his Harvard seminar. The total evidence suggests that
he lost interest and trusted to extemporary comments not triggered by written
notes. That he did expatiate in class on the syllabus, as would have been required, is indicated by the Morison notes attached to these pages in the
Archives copy.

The above represents the ascertainable facts from the preserved physical evidence. Conjecture alone can attack the interesting problem of the uneven
preservation of the leaves of the Harvard syllabus. One may start by suggesting
that since the Stanford spring semester was shorter than the Harvard autumn

semester, which ran over into 1907 after starting in September of 1906, the thirty-five pages of the Stanford syllabus are almost certainly complete, the extra ten pages of the Harvard syllabus extending to p. 45, plus the new p. 14, being accounted for by this disparity in the number of classes. That the Harvard syllabus was set from a marked-up copy of the Stanford, plus additional material as in the two different p. 14 texts, and the extension of the syllabus beyond p. 35, is evident from the general page for page format.

The odd fact must now be faced that no complete copy of the Harvard syllabus has been preserved. In #4466, James's working copy, only the first fourteen and the last six Harvard leaves are preserved, showing a gap and missing Harvard leaves for pp. 32–39 (as shown by their presence in #4522 and in the Archives copy). It is significant that James's scrapbook copy and the Archives copy are identical in pp. 4–14, 28–30, and 32–45. This suggests the hypothesis that James had a number of sets of his Stanford syllabus left over and therefore that he ordered only pp. 1–14 and 32–45 to be set to provide complete syllabuses for his Harvard seminar of 1906–1907. Why his own working copy (when combined with Stanford #4467) of this syllabus is incomplete is not to be ascertained. James's note in pencil at the head of p. 3 in #4466, 'Complete save for pp 18–24', corresponds to no known facts.

Emendations

The copy-text is SPD, *Syllabus in Philosophy D* (bMS Am 1092.9 [4466, 4522]), for 378.9–394.3 and 414.29–428.28 and SP, *Syllabus in Philosophy* (bMS Am 1092.9 [4467]), for 394.4–414.28. The sigil WJ followed by the appropriate symbol (as WJ/SPD and WJ/SP) indicates James's autograph revisions. All WJ annotations are in ink unless otherwise noted. Emendations marked as H (Harvard) are editorial and are not drawn from any authoritative document. Obvious typographical errors in SPD and SP have been corrected silently. The headnote to the Textual Apparatus may be consulted for general conventions of notation.

379.9   else to] WJ/SPD (*penc.*); else. To SPD
379.24   closed] SP,WJ/SPD; close SPD
379.33   Leibnitz] WJ/SPD; Leivnitz SPD
381.6   do] SP,WJ/SPD; know SPD
381.8   things.] H; things. | II. META-PHYSICS, THE STUDY OF SUCH QUESTIONS, CANNOT BE EVADED SP; things. | III. THE STUDY OF SUCH QUESTIONS CANNOT BE EVADED. SPD
381.28   course] SP;WJ/SPD (*penc.*); case SPD
382.25–26   necessary &] WJ/SPD; *om.* SP,SPD
383.6   2₁] SP,WJ/SPD; *om.* SPD
383.36   389] WJ/SP (*penc.*); 398 SP,SPD
385.9   conceptually] WJ/SPD; conceptionally SPD
385.15   This . . . proves] WJ/SP; These abstractions prove SP,SPD
385.15–16   abstract concepts] WJ/SP; them SP,SPD
385.16   deaf] H; dead SP,SPD
385.17   characters of the] WJ/SP; *om.* SP,SPD
385.34–35   A . . . instrument.] WJ/SPD; *om.* SP,SPD
386.22   occasions] WJ/SPD; occasion SPD
387.1   the . . . abstraction] WJ/SP; *all rom.* SP,SPD
387.33   essential] WJ/SPD; *rom.* SP,SPD
387.37   it is] SP; is it SPD
387.39   essence] WJ/SPD; *rom.* SP,SPD

389.6 things] WJ/SPD (*ink but w. red-brown penc. underl.*); facts SP; *om.* SPD

389.8 unless] WJ/SPD; unless there be SP,SPD

389.9 happen to exist] WJ/SPD; *om.* SP,SPD

389.10 they do] WJ/SPD; these are SPD

393.3 notion] SP; motion SPD

394.2 and . . . Paulsen] WJ/SPD; *om.* SP,SPD

395.31 140] H; [*space*] SP

413.3 *Melioristic Pluralism*] WJ/SP (MELIORISTIC PLURALISM); *om.* SP

418.25 not] WJ/SP; *om.* SP,SPD

418.25 won't] WJ/SP; will SP,SPD

420.13 344] H; 341 SPD

Historical Collation

The copy-text is *Syllabus in Philosophy D* (bMS Am 1092.9 [4466, 4522]), with reference to *Syllabus in Philosophy* (bMS Am 1092.9 [4467]). This list comprises the substantive variant readings that differ from the edited text where the two texts parallel each other (378.9–394.3 and 414.29–419.23). The reading to the left of the bracket is that of the present edition; the rejected variant in *Syllabus in Philosophy* is to the right of the bracket. The noting of variant readings is complete for the substantives; accidental variants may be recorded when they bear upon the substantive variant being shown. Variants are not repeated in the Historical Collation when the copy-text has been emended since the details may be found in the list of Emendations.

378.14–16 In . . . 'sciences.'] *om.*

378.30–31 'animistic' . . . the] *om.*

378.32 Fable] Fancy

379.5 aspects] relations

379.9–10 to . . . spiritual] *om.*

379.11–12 marvelously successful] *om.*

379.13 treatment.] treatment. In our own day we have seen general biology and psychology drop off from the parent trunk of philosophy, and grow into independent 'sciences.'

379.18 subjective] subjectivistic

379.21 , appeals . . . *priori*] *om.*

379.22 concrete] *om.*

379.30–31 , and . . . abstractions] *om.*

379.33–34 [Leibnitz . . . quoted.]] *om.*

380.4 worthy] ideal

380.7 II. . . . *Metaphysics*] *om.*

381.23 or] or made

381.33–34 (Examples: . . . SCHOPENHAUER.)] *om.*

381.37 facts.'] facts.' [¶] Examples of *a*: Older Greeks, ARISTOTLE, SCHOLASTICS, DESCARTES, SPINOSA, LEIBNITZ, KANT, HEGEL, SCHOPENHAUER, SPENCER.

382.1 (Examples] Of *b*

382.4 constructions.] constructions. Universally admired for the lofty and

inspiring character of their work.

382.5 More objective] Less subjective

382.10 of . . . inquiry] *om.*

382.16 just that] that one

382.29 of] *om.*

382.29–30 , and . . . definition] *om.*

383.5–7 Compare . . . –152.] *om.*

383.24–25 the . . . proximate] that

383.28 the *call* . . . ones] *call*

383.33 *V. The Problem*] SECOND PROBLEM: that

384.1 an . . . thing,] what is

384.12–13 being, . . . thought).] being). [The 'tree of Porphyry' in logic.]

384.16–18 A . . . concepts.] *om.*

384.19 *or sensible*] *om.*

384.21 experiencing] perceiving

384.23 always] *om.*

384.24 thing or] *om.*

384.24 every] or

384.26 may be] is

384.27 it is] *om.*

384.33 will] *om.*

384.33 character,] *om.*

385.18–19 for our partiality] *om.*

385.22 singleness,] *om.*

385.23 each concept] concepts

385.26 individual] single

385.32 they say,] *om.*

386.6   blind and] *om.*
386.20–22   particular .... What]
   content. Yet what
386.32   individual ... situation]
   experienced singular
386.33   situation] singular
386.38   , which ... facts,] *om.*
387.27   of ... world] *om.*
387.27   dogmatically] *om.*
387.34   and ... fact,] *om.*
387.38   the more] *om.*
387.38   Either ... little.] *om.*
388.2   This] His
388.3–4   The ... instructive.] *om.*
388.8   a] *om.*
389.2   apply] affirm of Nature
389.3   to ... realities] *om.*
389.9   own] *om.*
389.10   whether ... not] that
389.16–17   in its passage] *om.*
389.24   *Important Points in*] *om.*
389.32   and ... explain] explains
389.33   Being] essence
389.34–35   relating ... are] *om.*
389.35–36   the explanation] its
   explanations
390.20   109–113] 200
390.28   Journal] California University
   Chronicle, Sept. 1896, and Journal
390.28   677ff.] —.
390.30   –78] –86
390.33   in ... experience] *om.*
390.33–34   our ... minds] mind
390.34   our minds] mind
391.4–5   when ... fulfilled] *om.*
391.9   *correlated* with] an *effect* or
   product of
391.10   property] aspect
391.11   , he says] *om.*
391.20   , engendered ... ²them] *om.*

391.22   , P. says,] *om.*
391.35   such] the
391.39–392.1   cerebral cortex] *om.*
392.4–5   continuous] *om.*
392.6   well] then
392.7   111] 106–111
392.8   likely] *om.*
392.24   *action*] *motion*
392.33   all] *om.*
393.2   —it ... feeling] *om.*
393.5   by denying] in the sense
393.6   by seeing] in the sense
393.7   physical] mental
393.7   things] some things
393.7   external] accidental
415.11–24   Such ... live.] *om.*
415.25–26   ¹our ... believe,'] will
415.29   pluralistic] moral or personal
415.30–31   and ... concerned] of all
   concerned, theoretical as well as
   practical
415.35   really] truly
416.4   may] must
416.7   *How ... Probabilities*]
   FAITH—*Continued.*
417.9   Boston] San Francisco
417.10   the bridge] San Mateo
417.27   very serious business] business
   full of seriousness
417.30–31   To ... prevail.] *om.*
417.35   *The ... Universe*] *om.*
418.22   either] *om.*
418.24,26   or] *om.*
418.31   spells] means
419.18   may] may be trusted to
419.19   then] *om.*
419.20   ²the] *om.*
419.20   could] can
419.22–23   (Compare ... IV.)] *om.*

31. REPORT OF A DISCUSSION IN PHILOSOPHY 20e: SEMINARY IN
     THE THEORY OF KNOWLEDGE 1908 #4461

Folder #4461 contains twelve leaves of wove white paper 10½ x 8″, water-marked Merchants Bond. The ribbon-copy text is typed in single space with a white space between each item. The Report was prepared either by Ralph Barton Perry or at Perry's initiative. Ink markings which correct typographical errors and insert square brackets appear to be Perry's. A few ink revisions also appear to have been made by Perry and these have not been accepted in the present edition. Some few markings for emphasis in pencil may have been made by James.

Word-Division

The following is a list of compound words divided at the ends of lines in the manuscripts, which could be read either as one word or as a hyphenated compound. In a sense, then, the hyphenation or the non-hyphenation of possible compounds in the present list is in the nature of editorial emendation.

29.34	supernumerary	241.30	transsubjectively
72.32	supernormal	242.31	psycho-physical
86.8	one-sided	271.34;391.28	self-sufficing
86.22	workshop	277.17	extra-mental
99.1	supernaturalism	286.23	onrushing
103.29	catchwords	299.3	non-intercourse
140.14	wood-pile	310.32	non-deducibility
144.23	psychoplasm	315.40	Gun-powder
144.28;298.9	self-contradictory	319.17	everlasting
155.6	non-phenomenal	323.17	non-contradictory
180.4	non-rational	323.29	non-pragmatic
214.8	presupposes	412.14	common-sense
221.2	non-essential		

The following is a list of words divided at the ends of lines in the present edition but which represent authentic hyphenated compounds as found within the lines of the manuscripts. Except for this list, all other hyphenations at the ends of lines in the present edition are the modern printer's and are not hyphenated forms in the manuscripts.

22.11	philo-|progenitiveness	242.37	experience-|stuff
29.12	gaming-|table	246.28	*hand-*|illustrations
36.25	piano-|playing	247.7	thought-|*of*
39.9	after-|images	249.20	subject-|worlds
62.12	poly-|psychism	249.21	object-|world
85.27	non-|religious	252.15	Over-|Soul
87.37	demon-|worship	254.19	sense-|philosophy
126.21	non-|mathematical	257.12	self-|transcendency
144.7	new-|born	260.8	known-|as
157.24	*brain-*|*molecules*	270.12	Block-|universe
187.37	non-|philosophical	285.32	experience-|continuum
235.22	pre-|supposition	292.36	dollar-|given-
236.4	brain-|activities	293.29	self-|contradictory
242.16	pure-|experience	296.30	trump-|card

297.16	not-|existing
304.12	chance-|encounter
304.32	chance-|universe
307.35	Non-|interfering
315.38	log-|jam
318.13	Habit-|taking
321.1	object-|field
321.18	-con-|tinuity
321.29	quasi-|spontaneous
326.34	self-|revelation
351.9	world-|structure
380.5	co-|ordinated
386.38	fountain-|head

387.36	Mind-|produced-
397.19	free-|will
405.4	all-|inclusive
409.15	through-|and-
409.29	space-|relations
411.10	all-|knowing
417.21	hell-|fire
420.31	soul-|substance
423.21	brain-|excitements
425.10	pre-|existing
429.17	self-|sufficing
439.24	logically-|deductive

The following are actual or possible hyphenated compounds broken at the ends of lines in both the manuscripts and the present edition.

231.7 forward-|reference (*i.e.,* forward-reference)

246.4 time-|continuity (*i.e.,* time-continuity

326.21 -philosophy-|shop (*i.e.,* -philosophy-shop)

415.29 good-|will (*i.e.,* good-will)

Index

This index is a name and subject index for the text of *Manuscript Lectures* and Appendixes I–V. It is an index of names only for the "Notes" and "A Note on the Editorial Method."

Names of persons and institutions and titles of books are indexed. However, such items are not indexed if no information about them is provided—if they are only part of the identification of a discussed item or are merely used to indicate its location. Most of the time this excludes names of editors, translators, and titles of reference books consulted in connection with the present volume. James's class notes contain several biographical summaries of the philosophers whose works he was teaching, and in these summaries numerous persons and places are mentioned. Such items are not indexed. Except for articles by James himself, titles of articles in periodicals are not indexed. The Introduction to the present volume is not indexed.

Abbot, Francis Ellingwood, 534
Abelard, 191
Abercrombie, John, 35, 454
Absolute: and knowledge, 162, 252, 261–262, 298; and practicalism, 259; and interaction, 264; and explanation, 267; and Kant, 278; and perfection, 283; and infinity, 313–314; and ignorance, 339; and unity, 359, 408, 409; and negations, 364–365; and explanation, 365; and optimism, 366; and religion, 367; and possibility, 373; criticism of, 410–412
Absolutism, 290, 293
Abstractions, 384–385
Academy of Sciences, 198
Accommodation, 208
Achilles, 312
Acquaintance, 284
Action: and history, 105; and ideas, 157–158; worth of, 182; and novelty, 233; and brain, 234–235; and probabilities, 416–417
Activity: and habits, 39; and knowledge, 148; and language, 232; and direction,

236; and pure experience, 248, 318; analysis of, 325; paradigm, 344
Actuality, 311
Adamson (unidentified person), 69, 466
Adaptation, 136–137
Adler, Felix, 111, 480
Adrienne (mental patient), 62, 70, 463
Aesthetics: and philosophy, 25; and selection, 27; and pleasure, 123–126, 132–133, 206–211
Aeterni Patris, 191, 491
Affectibility, 307
Africa, 72
Agassiz, Louis, 531, 532
Agents, 36
Agnosticism, 126
Agnostics, 134
Agrippa von Nettesheim, Henricus Cornelius, 202, 204, 493
Albee, Helen Rickey, 67, 465
Albert (mental patient), 66, 464
Albigenses, 73
Alcohol: effects of, 43–46, 48–51, 52–55, 513, 514–515; and fashion, 46–48
Alexander, 189, 305

Alexandria, 190
Alice in Wonderland, 430
Alkoholfrage, Die (G. von Bunge), 457
Allen, Charles Grant Blairfindie: on
  consciousness, 28; and pleasure, 133;
  and great men, 138–139, 141; notes
  on, 454, 497; mentioned, 210, 211, 483
Altérations de la personnalité, Les
  (A. Binet), 69, 466
Alternative, The (E. Clay), 218n, 500
Americans, 106
American Society for Psychical
  Research, 469
American Society for the Prevention of
  Cruelty to Animals, 461
Ami Fritz, L' (Erckmann and Chatrian),
  54, 64, 464
*Analysis of the Phenomena of the
  Human Mind* (James Mill), 501
Analytic Psychology (G. F. Stout), 230–
  233, 501
Anarchism, 76
Anarchy, 311, 326
Anaxagoras, 188
Anaximander, 150, 188
Anaximenes, 188
Anesthesia: and alcohol, 50, 54; and
  hysteria, 60–62, 68–69; and multiple
  personality, 66–67
Angell, James Rowland, 210, 495
Anselm, Saint, 191, 347, 382
Anstie, Francis Edmund, 48, 456
Anthropology, 87
Antinomies, 313
Antisthenes, 188
Aphasia, 23, 41, 42, 231
Appearance, 144, 145, 254
Appearance and Reality (F. H. Bradley),
  217, 290, 291, 292, 293n, 294, 336, 337,
  338n, 499, 504
Apperception, 127, 231, 232
Approach to Philosophy, The (R. B.
  Perry), 368n, 511
Apriorists, 15–16
Arcesilaus, 190
Archibald, Warren Seymour, 354
"Are We Automata?" (W. James), 454,
  481
Aristippus, 188
Aristotle: and wonder, 166; his thought,
  189–190, 328; on matter, 276; and
  continuity, 324; on causes, 343; and
  possibility, 373, 374; and knowledge,
  386; and common sense, 389; and
  form, 400; mentioned, 140, 188, 191,
  347, 348, 349, 358n, 378, 381, 491,
  530, 532

Aristotle (G. Grote), 368n, 511
Arnold, D. (unidentified person), 353
Arnold, Harold Greene, 354
Arnold, Matthew, 46, 84, 456, 477
Arrian, 191, 491
Ashburner (unidentified person), 376
Assimilation, 117–118
Association, 117, 118, 230–233, 307
Associationism, 33–34
Assyriology, 150
Astronomia Nova (J. Kepler), 187, 193,
  202
Atherton, Henry Francis, 348, 353, 354
Attention: and vision, 6–7; and discrim-
  ination, 13; and sensation, 14–15;
  and interest, 117; and character,
  148; Stout on, 230
Attraction, 307
Attributes, 258
Augustine, Saint, 191, 347, 348
Authority, 184
Automatic or Spirit Writing (S. A. F.
  Underwood), 466
Automatism, 67–68
Automatisme psychologique, L'
  (P. Janet), 462, 467, 468
Avenarius, Richard: and pure experi-
  ence, 223, 225, 226, 242, 246n, 250n,
  253, 321; notes on, 498, 501; men-
  tioned, 213, 218
Azam, Eugène, 468

B., Madame. *See* Léonie
Bacon, Francis: note on, 491; mentioned,
  73, 141, 187, 193, 198, 202, 492
Bacon, Roger, 202
Bagehot, Walter, 140, 484
Bailey, Samuel, 15, 450
Bain, Alexander: on space, 15; on
  genius, 59; and external world, 169;
  and emotion, 178; and induction, 181;
  on feelings, 210; notes on, 462, 488,
  489, 490, 495; mentioned, 118, 164,
  218
Bainism, 230
Baissac, Jules, 74, 75, 472, 473
Bakewell, Charles Montague, 210, 495
Baldwin, James Mark: notes on, 498,
  500; mentioned, 213, 217, 315, 330
Baltimore, 447, 448, 449, 451, 452
Barkworth, Thomas, 67, 465
Barnett, Miss (unidentified person), 436
Bataille, Doctor. *See* Jogand-Pagès,
  Gabriel Antoine
Baumann, Julius, 212, 498
Baumgarten, Alexander Gottlieb, 355,
  509

Beard, George Miller, 64, 464
Beethoven, Ludwig van, 59, 152
Being, 382–383
Belief, 162, 413–416, 433
Bellanger, A., 532
Beneke, Friedrich Eduard, 211, 496
Benfey, Theodor, 150, 485
Berenson, Bernhard, 48, 53, 456
Berger, Jean, 72, 75, 471
Bergh, Henry, 57, 78, 461
Bergmann, Julius, 218, 500
Bergson, Henri: and brain, 234, 345; and time, 305; on memory, 318; notes on, 501, 505, 506, 507; mentioned, 279, 309n, 310, 313, 353
Berkeley, George: his thought, 197–198; and God, 249; and idealism, 268, 422, 423; and pragmatism, 275, 357; on space, 277; and science, 280; and laws, 282; and representationism, 284; and general ideas, 287; and economy, 289; and phenomenalism, 359, 362; and knowledge, 360; and nominalism, 385, 386; note on, 492; mentioned, 276, 328, 330, 348, 349, 355, 382
Berkeleyism, 321
Berlin, 47, 52, 514
Bernays, Albert James, 456
Bernhardt, Sarah, 58, 81, 461
Bernheim, Hippolyte: and hypnotism, 61; and suggestion, 66, 69; notes on, 462, 464; mentioned, 62, 67
Berry, Charles Scott, 353, 354
Bewusstsein, Das (J. Bergmann), 218
Bhagavad-Gita, 194, 267
Bible, the, 88, 191, 202
Binet, Alfred, 62, 69, 462, 466
Binz, Karl, 48, 456
Biology, 136–137, 141
Birks, Thomas Rawson, 170, 488
Bismarck, Otto von, 113, 140, 518
Blagden, Arthur Campbell, 348
Blaine, James Gillespie, 112, 480
Blavatsky, Elena Petrovna, 494
Blindness, mental, 40, 69
Block universe, 270, 293, 340, 341
Blood, Benjamin Paul, 267, 365n, 497, 502, 510
Bloomfield, Leonard, 353, 354
Bode, Boyd Henry, 361n
Body, 32
Boehme, Jacob, 204
Boer War, 102, 479
Boguet, Henri, 72, 470
Booth, William, 59, 78, 462
Bopp, Franz, 150, 485
Boredom, 125

Boscovich, Roger Joseph, 161, 280, 486
Bossuet, Jacques Bénigne, 201, 493
Bouillier, Francisque Cyrille, 198, 210, 211, 492–493
Boulanger, Georges Ernest Jean Marie, 112, 114, 480
Boundaries, 306
Bourne, Ansel, 70, 468
Bourne, Henry Richard Fox, 197, 492
Bowen, Francis, 181, 343, 490, 508
Bowne, Borden Parker: and God, 265, 266, 280; notes on, 488, 498, 502; mentioned, 170, 212, 342, 349, 353
Boyle, Robert, 197
Bradley, Francis Herbert: on pleasure, 210; and knowing, 285n; and relations, 286, 290, 291, 292, 294n, 334, 336–337, 338, 370; and monism, 293n, 406; and activity, 318; and intellectualism, 413; notes on, 495, 499, 504; mentioned, 217, 265, 266, 275, 348, 530
Brain: recent studies, 17, 31–32; and choice, 19; and memory, 20–21; and localization, 22–23; and mind, 23–29, 345; described, 32–33; and size, 35; functions, 35–36, 395; and experience, 37; and memory, 38–43; and degeneration, 77; and consciousness, 131–132; paths, 157; and association, 231; and action, 234–235; and time, 236; and the idealistic paradox, 246–247; and perception, 423
"Brain and the Mind, The" (W. James), 451–452
"Brain and the Senses, The" (W. James), 447–449
Breed, Frederick Stephen, 348
Brémaud, Paul, 460
Brentano, Franz, 212, 497
Breuer, Josef, 69, 70, 467, 468
Bridgman, Laura Dewey, 128, 482
Broca, Pierre Paul, 41–42, 454
Brochard, Victor Charles Louis, 217, 500
Brooklyn, 458
Brooklyn Eagle, 516
Brooklyn Institute of Arts and Sciences, 458–459, 516, 517
Brooklyn Museum Archives, 458
Brown, John, 59, 78, 82, 462
Browning, Robert, 81, 475
Brown-Séquard, Charles Édouard, 22, 453
Bruce, Edward Estabrook, 353, 354
Brundage, D. Earl, 354, 374n
Bruno, Giordano, 193, 202
Brunton, Thomas Lauder, 46, 456

"Brute and Human Intellect" (W. James), 118, 481

Bryan, William Jennings, 111, 112, 480

Bryant, William Cullen, 80, 475

Bryce, James, 110, 480

Büchner, Ludwig, 532

Bucke, Richard Maurice, 267, 376, 502

Buckle, Henry Thomas, 138, 483

Bulwer-Lytton, Edward George Earle Lytton, 80, 475

Bunge, Gustav von, 51n, 52, 55, 457

Burckhardt, Gottlieb, 208, 495

Burke, Edmund, 113, 481

Burnet, Arthur Russell, 348

Burns, Robert, 80, 475

Burroughs, John, 110, 480

Butler, Benjamin Franklin, 112, 480

Byard, Lee Brooks, 348, 350

Byron, Lord (George Gordon), 518

Cabanis, Pierre John Georges, 532

Cabell, Sears Wilson, 218, 222

Cabot, Richard Clarke, 323n, 507

Cadwell, J. W., 70, 71, 468, 469

Caesar, Julius, 191, 347, 395, 433

Caird, Edward, 198, 405, 410, 493

Caird, Edward or John, 283, 331

Caird, John, 161, 405, 410, 487

Caldwell, Morley Albert, 353, 354

Caldwell, Robert Charles, 72, 470

Caldwell (unidentified person), 442

California, 460, 479

Calkins, Mary Whiton, 219n, 500

Calmeil, Louis Florentin, 75, 473

Cambridge, Mass., 31, 458, 476

Campanella, Tommaso, 202, 494

Cantor, Georg, 312, 313, 506

Cape Cod, 72, 471

Carlyle, Thomas: and sentimentality, 178; notes on, 477, 488; mentioned, 90, 166, 369

Carneades, 190

Carnot, Nicolas Léonard Sadi, 281, 282, 504

Carpenter, Edward, 106, 109, 110, 345, 480, 509

Carpenter, William Benjamin, 19, 37, 453

Carthage, 172

Castillo (unidentified person), 49

Cate, Sheridan Read, 353, 354

Categories, 255

Catholicism, 73

Cattell, James McKeen, 458

Cauchy, Augustin Louis, 313, 506

Causality: physical, 5, 227; psycho-physical, 242; theories, 343–344; Hume's view, 389

Cause, 247

Cautio Criminalis (F. von Spee), 76, 473

Certainty, 5

Cesca, Giovanni, 206, 494

Chance: and unity, 182; and tychism, 271; meaning of, 302, 303, 341; and order, 304–305; and variation, 309; and external relations, 310; and direction, 317, 318; and empiricism, 367; and novelty, 374

Change, 342, 373, 411

Character, 85, 86, 148, 514

Charcot, Jean Martin, 68, 466

Charron, Pierre, 204, 494

Chasm, epistemological, 251–252, 257, 359

Chatrian, Louis Gratien Charles Alexandre, 464

Chesterton, Gilbert Keith, 111, 479, 480

Chiap, Giuseppe, 72, 470

Chicago, 54, 113, 366

Child, Francis J., 449

China, 72, 150

Chladni, Ernst Florens Friedrich, 26, 454

Choice, 19, 309–310, 397

Christianity, 72, 90, 150

Cicero, 150, 191

Cid, Le (Corneille), 198

Clairvoyance, 71

Classes, 311

Classification, 123

Clay, Edmund R., 218n, 500

Clemens, Samuel, 81

Clements, Edgar Thomas, 348, 350

Clifford, William Kingdon: on consciousness, 24, 28, 29; and ejects, 223; and double-aspect, 246; and mind-stuff, 404; and intellectualism, 413, 414; note on, 454; mentioned, 308, 350, 487, 533, 534

Cobb (unidentified person), 354

Cobden, Richard, 140, 484

Cochran (unidentified person), 56, 77, 460

Cognition, 71, 83

Cogswell, Walter Cleveland, 353, 354

Cohen, Morris Raphael: and transcendence, 332; and Kant, 377–378; note on, 508, 512; mentioned, 347, 348, 349

Colbert, Jean Baptiste, 198

Coleman, Albert John, 348

Coleman, Norman Frank, 353, 354

Coleridge, Samuel Taylor, 59, 80, 462, 475

Commentary on Kant's Critick of the Pure Reason, A (K. Fischer), 299n, 505

Common sense: and philosophy, 159; and data, 225; and knowledge, 229; and phenomenalism, 249–250; and pure experience, 287, 290; and activity, 325; categories of, 334; on perception, 360

Composition, 221–222

Comte, Auguste, 170, 186, 488, 491

Conception: and perception, 117–119, 143, 250, 253, 259, 386–387; and experience, 145

Conception of God, The (J. Royce), 283n, 300, 365, 504

Concepts: and life, 89; and objectivity, 213; and percepts, 239n, 360, 383–385, 530; and systems, 246

Concepts and Theories of Modern Physics, The (J. B. Stallo), 161, 486

Concepts de cause, Les (A. Bellanger), 532

Conceptualism, 385

Congress of Arts and Sciences, 507

Conscience, 104

Consciousness: and evolution, 4; and composition, 4–5, 221–222; and nervous system, 16; efficacy of, 24–29, 395; and habits, 39; unity of, 70, 218–219; and brain, 131–132; and knowledge, 142–143, 223; elements of, 144–145; and data, 170, 214–215; and self, 212; and solipsism, 224; and body, 234–235; and activity, 236; and phenomenalism, 237–238; and insufficiency, 238; and synthesis, 307; and coherence, 308; span, 309; extension, 318; James's view, 320–321; superhuman, 369; and automatism, 391; and matter, 392; and monism, 411; subliminal, 516; limits, 521

Conservation of Energy, The (B. Stewart), 170, 488

Consistency, 124–125, 435, 436–437

Constans, Augustin, 72, 470, 471

Conterminousness, 252–253

Contiguity, 218, 325

Continua, 243

Continuity: and discontinuity, 223; and monism, 224; and ejects, 226, 227; of fields, 239; and pure experience, 244; and interest, 245; and unity, 308–309, 320, 324–325

Contradictions, 87

Contrast, 208

Cope, Jackson I., 448

Copernicus, Nicolaus, 72, 186, 187, 193, 202

Copying, 370

Corin (literary character), 186

Corinthians (book of the Bible), 68n

Corneille, 493

Cornelius, Hans, 213, 217, 280, 498, 499

Corsica, 140, 141

Cosmos, 398–399

Coulomb, Charles Augustin de, 281, 504

Cournot, Antoine Augustin, 303, 505

Cours de philosophie positive (A. Comte), 170, 488

Cousin, Victor, 187, 198, 491

Couturat, Louis, 312, 506

Cowles, Edward, 56, 77, 460

Creation, 160

Crime, 101–102

Critique of Pure Reason (I. Kant), 277, 285, 489, 491

Cromwell, Oliver, 113

Crookes, William, 305n, 506

Crothers, Thomas Davison, 64, 464

Cuba, 262

Cudworth, Ralph, 385, 512

Culture and Anarchy (M. Arnold), 477

Culturgeschichte in ihrer natürlichen Entwicklung (F. A. H. von Hellwald), 489

Customs, 103, 109–110

Cuvier, Georges, 35, 385, 454

Cyples (unidentified person), 218n

Dailey, Abram Hoagland, 468

Dalton, John, 187, 491

Dante Alighieri, 80, 191, 202, 475, 517, 518

Danville, Gaston, 57, 78, 461

Darlington, Lionel Chester, 265, 502

Darwin, Charles: and survival, 26, 27; on instincts, 29; on conscience, 104; and evolution, 136, 137, 138, 139, 140, 141; note on, 484; mentioned, 80, 108, 109, 110, 117, 150, 151, 300n, 326, 475

Darwinism, 30, 374

Data, 215, 322

Data of Ethics, The (H. Spencer), 175–176, 484, 489

Datum: subject and object in, 216, 217, 219–220, 225; and nervous system, 226–227; and tychism, 270

Davidson, Thomas, 350, 509

Davidson (unidentified person), 348

Davis, Miss (unidentified person), 441–442

Dean, Sidney, 68, 466

Debs, Eugene Victor, 111, 480
Decision, 237
Dedekind, Richard, 313, 506
Deduction, 179–182
De Finibus (Cicero), 191
Degeneration, 55–57, 76–78, 79–80, 517–519, 524
Degeneration (M. Nordau), 475
De Incertitudine Scientiarum (Agrippa von Nettesheim), 202
De l'alcool (J. Jaillet), 455
De la recherche de la vérité (Malebranche), 202
De la suggestion (H. Bernheim), 66, 464
De la suggestion (J. Liégeois), 465
Delbœuf, Joseph Remi Léopold: and suggestion, 65; on desire, 207; notes on, 464, 489; mentioned, 171, 314n, 507
De l'erreur (V. C. Brochard), 217, 500
Deliberation, 20
De l'intelligence (H. Taine), 178, 490
Delusion of Spiritualism, The (J. W. Cadwell), 468
Democracy, 272, 311
Democritus, 188, 276, 328n, 532
Demon Possession (J. L. Nevius), 72, 469–470
Demons, 72
Depew, Chauncey Mitchell, 114, 481
Depth, 11
De Rerum Natura (Telesio), 202
De Revolutionibus (Copernicus), 193, 202
Descartes, René: and certainty, 5; his thought, 193–194, 198–200; and substance, 276; on God, 382; and innate ideas, 388; note on, 491; mentioned, 73, 167, 186, 187, 195, 202, 319, 350, 378, 379, 381, 492, 531
Descartes and His School (K. Fischer), 198–199, 493
Descent of Man, The (C. Darwin), 104
Descourtis, Gabriel, 57, 460
Description, 254
De Sensu Rerum et Magia (T. Campanella), 202, 494
Dessoir, Max, 62, 67, 463, 534, 535
Determinism, 140, 154, 310
Deuteronomy (book of the Bible), 507, 512
Dewey, John: and substitution, 320; on truth, 323; his ethics, 347; note on, 507; mentioned, 325, 353
Diable au XIXe-siècle, Le (Doctor Bataille), 72, 470–471

Dialogue on the Two Chief Systems of the World (Galileo), 187, 193, 202
Dialogues of Plato, The, 188–189, 491
Dickens, Charles, 58
Dickinson, Goldsworthy Lowes, 297n, 419, 512
Dictionary of Philosophy and Psychology, 297, 327, 342, 355, 505
Diderot, Denis, 150, 484
"Dilemma of Determinism, The" (W. James), 304n
Dionysius, 188
Discontinuity, 223, 244
Discours de la méthode (Descartes), 193, 198, 202
Discours exécrable des sorciers (H. Boguet), 470
Discrimination, 13, 118
Discussions on Philosophy and Literature (W. Hamilton), 159, 218, 486
Disputationes Metaphysicae (F. Suarez), 202
Disraeli, Benjamin, 113, 140, 481
Dissociation, 66, 118
Distance, 7, 10
Divine Comedy, The (Dante), 202, 475, 518
Dix, Dorothea Lynde, 78, 474
Dominicans, 73
Donders, Franciscus Cornelis, 8, 10, 450
Doppel-Ich, Das (M. Dessoir), 463
Dorrance, Samuel Martin, 348, 349
Dove, Heinrich Wilhelm, 8, 10, 11, 450
Dreams, 63–64, 65, 519
Dreyfus, Alfred: James's view, 479; mentioned, 102, 104, 105, 107, 108, 109, 114
Drunkenness, 49
Dualism: and religion, 87–88, 90; and God, 92; and psychology, 235; assumptions of, 238; and radical empiricism, 247–248; and duality, 253; and epistemology, 255–256; and experience, 256
Du Bois Reymond, Emil, 390, 512
Du démon de Socrate (L. F. Lélut), 78, 474
Dueberg, Helmuth Frederick Christian, 353
Du fractionnement des opérations cérébrales (G. Descourtis), 57, 460
Dühring, Eugen Karl, 198, 493
Dumont, Léon, 207, 210, 211, 494
Duns Scotus, John, 191, 192, 347
Du rôle de l'alcool (Lallemand, Perrin, Duroy), 457

Duroy, J.-L.-P., 48, 456
Duty, 76
Dwight, Sereno Edwards, 503
Dyak's head, 332, 333, 352
Dynamic Sociology (L. F. Ward), 489

Earle, Pinkston, 70
Ecclesiasticism, 97–98
Economy, 279
Edinburgh Review, 43, 46
Education: moral, 37; value of, 101–103, 107–114; and passion, 105–106; and success, 107
Edwards, Jonathan, 276, 277
Edwards (unidentified person), 348
"Effects of Alcohol, The" (W. James), 514
Ego, 212, 214, 228, 229, 320
Egypt, 72, 172
Einführung in die Metaphysik auf Grundlage der Erfahrung (G. Heymans), 395, 512
Einleitung in die Psychologie (P. Natorp), 212, 215, 320, 498
Ejects, 223, 224, 225, 226, 227, 251, 306
Eleatics, 192
Elementary Exposition of the Doctrine of Energy, An (D. D. Heath), 170, 488
Elements of Metaphysics (A. E. Taylor), 337, 338, 341n, 343, 356n, 508
Eliot, Charles William: on education, 101, 107, 108; and James, 447, 448; note on, 479; mentioned, 111
Eliot, George, 80, 475, 500
Emerson, Louville Eugene, 348
Emerson, Ralph Waldo: and the oversoul, 369; note on, 511; mentioned, 58n, 81, 90, 106, 109, 110, 164, 173, 191, 277, 353, 361n, 364n, 475, 477, 487, 518
Emotion, 124
Emotions and the Will, The (A. Bain), 169, 178, 218, 488, 490
Empedocles, 188
Empirical Logic (J. Venn), 343
Empiricism: and space, 15–16; British, 127; and Spencer, 136; on knowing, 257; and tychism, 272; and method, 301, 340; radical, 330, 331; and morality, 367; and rationalism, 381–382; and fact, 383; Paulsen's, 388–389; and pluralism, 403, 404
Energy, conservation of, 154, 155, 268, 305
England, 47, 52
Énigmes de l'univers, Les (E. Haeckel), 533

Enquiry Concerning Human Understanding, An (D. Hume), 334, 492, 531
Entartung (M. Nordau), 475
Entartung und Genie (C. Lombroso), 80, 475
Entretiens sur la métaphysique (Malebranche), 206, 494
Environment, 138
Epictetus, 191, 491
Epicureanism, 190, 191
Epicurus, 190
Epidemia di istero-demonopathie in Verzegnis, L' (F. Franzolini), 470
Epiphenomenalism, 393, 396, 397, 427
Epistemology, 227, 255–256
Erckmann, Émile, 464
Erigena, John Scotus, 191, 347
Error, 333–334
Esquisse d'une classification systématique des doctrines philosophiques (C. Renouvier), 313, 506
Essai sur les données immédiates de la conscience (H. Bergson), 310, 313, 506
Essai sur l'évolution psychologique du jugement (T. Ruyssen), 505
Essay Concerning Human Understanding, An (J. Locke), 197, 202, 276, 378, 492
Essay on the Foundations of Our Knowledge, An (A. A. Cournot), 505
Essays (R. W. Emerson), 511
Essays (M. de Montaigne), 202
Essays, Comments, and Reviews (W. James), 452, 454, 455, 456, 457, 461, 462, 465, 467, 468, 469, 470, 475, 476, 480, 481, 482, 483, 484, 485, 487, 497, 498, 509
Essays in Philosophy (W. James), 482, 483, 487, 488, 502, 504, 505, 507, 509, 510, 532, 533
Essays in Psychical Research (W. James), 461, 462, 463, 465, 466, 469, 471, 472, 478
Essays in Psychology (W. James), 449, 450, 454, 455, 462, 466, 467, 468, 481, 482, 500
Essays in Radical Empiricism (W. James), 498, 506, 507
Essays in Religion and Morality (W. James), 477, 487, 532
Essays, Philosophical and Theological (J. Martineau), 161, 163, 486
Essays: Scientific, Political, and Speculative (H. Spencer), 161, 487
Essays: Speculative and Suggestive (J. A. Symonds), 211, 497

Essay towards a New Theory of Vision, An (G. Berkeley), 197

État mental des hystériques (P. Janet), 467

Ethics: and selection, 27; and evolution, 158; and survival, 175–177; and goodness, 182; and utility, 183; and obligation, 183–184

Ethics (Spinoza), 202, 382, 388, 492

Europe, 72, 117

Evans, Glendower, 529, 531

Eve, Anna, 74, 472

Evellin, François Jean Marie Auguste, 312, 313, 506

Evidence, 414

Evil, 204, 272, 411

Evolution: and mind, 4; law, 135; factors, 136–137; social, 138–141; and purpose, 147, 315–316; and ideals, 148–149; meaning of, 158; and organisms, 174; and ethics, 175–177; and chance, 304; and habit, 307; and wills, 318; and empiricism, 367; and epiphenomenalism, 396

Evolutionism, 133–135, 316, 358

Examination of Sir William Hamilton's Philosophy, An (J. S. Mill), 159, 160, 211, 486

Exner, Sigmund, 4, 45, 449

Experience: religious, 93; and truth, 96; primitive, 142; and conception, 145; and purpose, 146; neutral, 215, 216; described, 228, 256; and knowledge, 238; and points of view, 244; and duality, 253, 254; and categories, 255; and objects, 257–258; and reality, 277; moment of, 308, 311, 315; and ideals, 317–318; and rationality, 327; defined, 331; and reflection, 334; and language, 335; religious, 368–369; and novelty, 383; and monism, 411

Experience, pure: described, 213, 237–238; problems solved by, 242; and continua, 243; and systems, 244; and activity, 248; and solipsism, 251–252; and description, 254, 287; and epistemology, 256; and common sense, 268; and idealism, 282; and transcendency, 284n; and nextness, 285–286; and common objects, 287–289; and infinity, 311; and uniformity, 314–315; and activity, 318; and knowledge, 319–320; and philosophy, 320–321; and dualism, 322; and neutrality, 329, 330; and conjunctions, 336; and pluralism, 362

Explanation, 42, 119, 143, 161, 164–165

Exposition de la doctrine de l'église catholique (J. B. Bossuet), 201, 493

Fact and Fable in Psychology (J. Jastrow), 378, 478

Facts, 88, 166–167, 390, 532

Facts and Comments (H. Spencer), 479

Faith, 374–375, 404, 413–415, 419, 426

Faith-ladder, 415

Fanaticism, 76

Fancher, Mollie, 70

Faraday, Michael, 306, 506

Fatalism, 148, 411

Faust (J. W. von Goethe), 488, 510

Fechner, Gustav Theodor: and double-aspect, 246; and world soul, 309, 393; and panpsychism, 345; notes on, 482, 505; mentioned, 123, 210, 301n, 369, 534

Feelings, 5, 93, 126, 215

Félida X (mental patient), 70, 468

Ferrier, David: and localization, 21, 22, 40, 41, 42; note on, 453

Ferrier, James Frederick: notes on, 487, 498; mentioned, 161, 162, 165, 213

Fichte, Immanuel Hermann, 211, 497

Fichte, Johann Gottlieb, 277, 354

Fields: mental, 64, 65; and datum, 220n; and composition, 221, 222; and knowledge, 223; and solipsism, 224; and ejects, 225; and continuity, 228, 239; completeness of, 230; and insufficiency, 238, 250; described, 256

First Principles (H. Spencer), 158, 159–164, 168–174, 484, 485, 491

First Principles of Moral Science (T. R. Birks), 488

Fischer, Kuno, 196, 198, 299n, 492, 493

Fisher, Galen Merriam, 348

Fisk, James, Jr., 35

Fiske, John: his learning, 158; notes on, 485, 487; mentioned, 151, 163, 186, 354

Flechsig, Paul Emil, 34, 454

Flint, Austin, 17, 452

Flourens, Jean Pierre Marie, 21, 40, 453

Flournoy, Théodore, 95, 478, 501

Focus, 64

Foerster, Robert Franz, 348, 349

Folie du doute, La (H. Legrand du Saulle), 460

Fonsegrive, George, 217, 500

Foods (E. Smith), 455

Force, 151–154, 161, 170, 172

Foster, Michael, 71, 469

Fouillée, Alfred, 213, 498

Foundation of Death, The (A. C. J. Gustafson), 46, 455

Fragments of Science for Unscientific People (J. Tyndall), 130, 453
Fragments of the Work of Heraclitus of Ephesus on Nature, 491
France, 524–525
Franco-Prussian War, 114, 140
Frantz, Orville Gish, 295n, 338
Franzolini, Fernando, 470
Fraser, Alexander Campbell, 349, 491, 503
Frazer, James George, 96, 379, 478, 512
Freedom: and intelligence, 36; and mind, 136; and tychism, 272, 372; and monism, 273, 411; and pragmatism, 289; and habit, 310; and novelty, 314, 412; value of, 342; and world's outcome, 397; and possibility, 424–427
Freeman, Lemuel Elmer McMillan, 354
Freer, Ada Goodrich, 62, 67, 463
French Academy, 198
Freud, Sigmund, 69, 70, 467, 468
Froude, James Anthony, 178, 490
Fugues, 70, 522, 533
Fullerton, George Stuart: notes on, 486, 503, 506, 510; mentioned, 160, 274n, 312, 313, 314, 356n, 531
"Function of Cognition, The" (W. James), 504

Galileo Galilei, 73, 187, 193, 202, 281, 282
Garfield, James, 474
Garibaldi, Giuseppe, 82, 113, 476
Gassendi, Pierre, 194, 202, 493
Gefühlsleben, Das (J. W. Nahlowsky), 210, 495
General Metaphysics (J. Rickaby), 276, 343, 503
Genie und Entartung (W. Hirsch), 82, 476
Genius: described, 27; and insanity, 58–60, 78–83; and progress, 83; and value, 94; and degeneration, 517–519, 524
Geoffroy Saint-Hilaire, Étienne, 150, 484
George III, 59, 462
Georgette (mental patient), 56
Gerlach, Joseph von, 17, 33, 35, 452
Germany: and alcohol, 47, 48, 52, 54, 514; education in, 111, 112; study of vision in, 127; ethics in, 176; and intellectualism, 413
Geschichte der Hexenprozesse (W. G. Soldan), 74, 75, 472
Geschichte der neueren Philosophie (K. Fischer), 200–202, 492, 493
Geulincx, Arnold, 194, 276n, 503, 531

Gib. (mental patient), 70, 467
Gilman, Daniel Coit, 447–448, 451
Gladstone, William Ewart, 59, 82, 462
Gleam, The (H. R. Albee), 465
Gleanings from a Literary Life (F. Bowen), 343, 508
Glines (unidentified person), 67
Gluziński, C. Anton, 49, 457
Gnosticism, 186
God: and religion, 88; and dualism, 92; pragmatic view, 97, 263; and the past, 167; James's view, 266; and evolution, 368; and pluralism, 369; and the ontological argument, 382; meaning of, 387–388; and the teleological argument, 400; and faith, 404
Goethe, Johann Wolfgang von: quoted, 47, 52, 167; notes on, 456, 488; mentioned, 59, 81, 82, 86, 194, 510, 518
Golden Bough, The (J. G. Frazer), 379, 512
Goldsmith, Oliver, 102, 107, 108, 109, 479
Goltz, Friedrich Leopold, 21, 23, 41, 453
Goodness, 175–176, 182–185, 372
Gould, Jay, 58, 81, 461
Graduate Club, 111
Graefe, Alfred Karl, 7, 10, 450
Graft-theory, 310–311
Grammar of Science, The (K. Pearson), 282, 502
Grands jours de la sorcellerie, Les (J. Baissac), 74, 75, 472
Granger, Frank Stephen, 95, 478
Gray, Thomas, 340, 348
Great Britain, 102, 140, 514
Great men, 138–141
"Great Men and Their Environment" (W. James), 304n, 483
Greece, 72, 150, 167, 378
Green, Thomas Hill: on sensation, 226; on ego, 331; and monism, 410; notes on, 482, 501, 509; mentioned, 128, 213, 218, 349
Greene, John Arthur, 348
Grimm, Jakob Ludwig Karl, 150, 484
Grote, George, 160, 368n, 486, 511
Grundlinien einer Theorie des Bewusstseines (J. Bergmann), 500
Grundriss der Erkenntnistheorie und Logik (W. Schuppe), 499
Grundtatsachen des Seelenlebens (T. Lipps), 210, 496
Grundzüge der Naturphilosophie (H. Lotze), 205, 494
Grundzüge der physiologischen Psychologie (W. Wundt), 481

Grundzüge der Psychologie (H. Münsterberg), 92, 477, 507
Guiteau, Charles, 77, 474
Gulick, Addison, 348
Gundersen, Alfred Ludvig Georg, 354
Gurney, Edmund: and hypnotism, 62; and suggestion, 67; and multiple personality, 520; notes on, 463, 465; mentioned, 210, 495
Gustafsen, Axel Carl Johann, 46, 455
Guthrie, Malcolm, 161, 164, 487

Habit: utility of, 18–19; and instinct, 29, 140; and intelligence, 36–37; and nerve tissue, 38–39; and drinking, 46–48, 51; and national life, 103; and pleasure, 123–124, 125; and apperception, 231; and association, 233; and order, 307; and freedom, 310; and fashion, 514
Hackett, Lewis Wendell, 348
Haeckel, Ernst Heinrich, 151, 533, 534
Hague Tribunal, 104, 109
Hale, Robert Lee, 353, 354
Hale, Swinburne, 348
Hall, Granville Stanley, 346, 451, 509
Hallucinations, 61, 66
Hamilton, William: Spencer on, 158; and absolute, 162; his mysticism, 165; note on, 486; mentioned, 159, 210, 211, 213, 218, 382
Hamlet (W. Shakespeare), 135
Hammond, William Alexander: and alcohol, 43, 45, 49, 53; note on, 455; mentioned, 65
Handbuch der physiologischen Optik (H. Helmholtz), 128, 482
Harper, Thomas Morton, 276, 503
Harris, William Torrey, 355, 510
Harvard Divinity School, 476, 477, 478, 526
Harvard Graduate Club, 478–479
Harvard Library, 496
Harvard Total Abstinence League, 46, 48, 52, 455, 456, 513, 514
Harvard University, 103, 112, 147, 447, 448, 457, 478–479, 507
Harvey, William, 187, 491
Hatch, Roscoe Conkling, 353, 354
Healing, 71
Health, 82–83
Healthy-mindedness, 83
Hearing, 4
Heath, Douglas Denon, 170, 488
Heathcote, George Milton, 348
Hebraism, 84, 85
Hebrews, 150

Hegel, Georg Wilhelm Friedrich: and dialectic, 274, 432; and things in themselves, 277; and transcendentalism, 280; and being, 301, 330, 382; and the Absolute, 334; and negation, 340; and monism, 405, 406; and intellectualism, 413; and pragmatism, 433; mentioned, 128, 173, 186, 219n, 311, 381
Hegelianism, 87
Heim, Karl, 377n, 512
Helen of Troy, 305, 314n, 507
Hellenism, 84
Hellwald, Friedrich Anton Heller von, 176, 489
Helmholtz, Hermann Ludwig Ferdinand von: on sensation, 4, 6, 12, 15; on space, 7, 8–9; and perception, 128; and postulates, 151; and conservation, 154; notes on, 449, 482, 485, 500; mentioned, 59, 171, 193, 220n, 450, 499
Helmont, Jean Baptiste van, 204, 494
Hemispheres, cerebral, 19–21, 25–26, 35–36, 38–43
Henle, Jakob, 17, 35, 453
Heracleitus, 188, 190
Herbart, Johann Friedrich, 207, 210, 495
Heretics (G. K. Chesterton), 479, 480
Hering, Ewald, 15, 450
Hero-worship, 311
Herrick, Clarence Luther, 210, 496
Herschel, John Frederick William, 534
Hertz, Heinrich Rudolf, 306, 434, 436, 506
Herz (unidentified person), 72, 75, 471
Hexenprozesse und Geistesstörung (O. Snell), 471, 473
Heymans, Gerardus: and phenomenalism, 362; and panpsychism, 395, 396, 428; notes on, 510, 512; mentioned, 353, 361, 534
"Hidden Self, The" (W. James), 466, 467
Hindoos, 150
Hirsch, William, 82, 476
Histoire de la philosophie cartésienne (F. C. Bouillier), 493
Historical Account of the Belief in Witchcraft in Scotland, A (C. K. Sharpe), 471
History, 105, 267
History of Materialism, The (F. A. Lange), 394
History of Philosophy, A (W. Windelband), 508
Hitzig, Eduard, 21, 40, 453
Hobbes, Thomas, 193, 199, 276, 493, 503
Hobhouse, Leonard Trelawney, 343, 508

Hodder, Alfred, 210, 290n, 495, 504
Hodgson, Richard, 71, 95, 469
Hodgson, Shadworth Hollway: and
  perception, 245; and experience, 286;
  notes on, 487, 498, 504; mentioned,
  163, 164, 213, 214n, 218, 499
Hoernlé, R. F. Alfred, 371, 511
Höffding, Harald: and feelings, 210; on
  knowledge, 274; his lecture, 330n; on
  irrationality, 351; and monism, 367n;
  and religion, 369; notes on, 495, 508,
  509, 511; mentioned, 211, 231, 371,
  503
Holmes, Oliver Wendell (senior), 44, 58,
  59, 81, 455, 475
Holt, Edwin Bissell: and pragmatism,
  429–431, 434–436; note on, 499;
  mentioned, 217, 218, 436, 512
Holt (unidentified person), 173
Homer, 519
Homme de génie, L' (C. Lombroso), 78,
  79, 474, 475
Homme et l'intelligence, L' (C. Richet),
  210, 496
Hooper, William Everett, 348
Horace, 191
Horwicz, Adolf, 210, 211, 495, 497
Houghton Library: James Collection in,
  447; mentioned, 451, 459, 463, 467,
  469, 470, 471, 472, 474, 475, 476,
  486, 502
Howard, John, 59, 462
Howe, Samuel Gridley, 128, 482
Howison, George Holmes, 277, 347, 356,
  503
Hudson, Thomson Jay, 65, 464
Humanism, 357, 371
Humanism: Philosophical Essays
  (F. C. S. Schiller), 357, 510
Humanities, 111
Human Nature (T. Hobbes), 276, 503
*Human Personality and Its Survival of
  Bodily Death* (F. W. H. Myers), 95,
  461
Human Submission (M. I. Swift), 356,
  510
Hume, David: and skepticism, 198; his
  triumph, 265; and relations, 334; and
  causality, 343, 389; and pragmatism,
  357; and connection, 405; notes on,
  492; mentioned, 167, 274n, 349, 353,
  382, 503, 531, 532
Hume (T. H. Huxley), 492
Huntington, Edward Vermilye: and
  pragmatism, 438–440, 442; notes on,
  500, 509; mentioned, 218, 344n, 434,
  512

Hutcheon, Robert James, 354
Huxley, Thomas Henry: on conscious-
  ness, 23, 24, 28, 29; notes on, 453, 492;
  mentioned, 30, 123, 149, 187, 198,
  342, 349, 350, 482, 533, 544
Hyde, Mr. (literary character), 525
Hypnotism: and suggestion, 61, 62, 65,
  67; history of, 64–65; and memory,
  66; and anesthesia, 69; and sleep, 71,
  82, 524; and multiple personality,
  516–517, 520, 521–522; and dreams,
  519
Hypnotism (A. Moll), 464
Hypnotisme, suggestion, psychothérapie
  (H. Bernheim), 462
Hypotheses, 141
Hyslop, James Hervey, 95, 478
Hysteria: and anesthesia, 60–62; and
  sleep, 64; and multiple personality,
  68–70, 522–523; and fixed ideas, 71;
  and hypnotism, 82; described, 520–
  521; and therapy, 524–525

Ibsen, Henrik, 81, 475
Iceland, 140
Idea, fixed, 71
Idealism: subjective, 134; and perception, 141; and religion, 149; and
  Spencer, 169; and materialism, 187–
  188, 422; medieval, 192; modern, 196;
  Berkeleyan, 197; paradox, 246–247;
  absolute, 254; and ideality, 268; and
  pluralism, 269–270; and realism, 275;
  and matter, 276; kinds, 279–280; and
  coherence, 308; and antinomies, 313;
  and unity, 339; Paulsen's, 393, 420–
  421; absolute, 410–412; and objec-
  tivity, 422–423; and realism, 423–424;
  thinness of, 436; and truth, 443
Idealists, logical, 128
Ideals: and matter, 26; and religion, 99;
  and evolution, 148–149; and choice,
  310; objectified, 317; and materialism,
  394
Ideas, 33–34, 157–158, 238
Identity, 120
Ignorance, 339, 364
Images, double, 7, 8, 9, 10–12, 14
Imagination, 220
Imitation, 94
*Immanuel Kant's Critique of Pure
  Reason*, 485
Immediacy, 238, 245
Imperatives, 183, 185–186
Imperialism, 102
Impossibility, 373
India, 72, 470

670

Individualism, 99, 311
Induction, 178–182
Inference, 122–123
Infini et quantité (F. J. M. Evellin), 312, 506
Infinity: and causality, 160; and process, 167; and wholeness, 218; meaning of, 272–273; Kant on, 277; kinds, 311–313; and the absolute, 313–314; and regress, 424
Inhibition, 59
Innocent VIII, 73, 471
Inquiry into the Human Mind on the Principles of Common Sense, An (T. Reid), 500
Inquisition, 73, 76
Insanity, 57, 58–60, 77, 78–83
Insanity of Genius, The (J. F. Nisbet), 80, 475
Insight, moral, 185
Instincts, 19, 29, 140
Institutes of Metaphysic (J. F. Ferrier), 161, 162, 487
Intellect: and insanity, 57; and order, 63; and feeling, 93; and passion, 103–106, 107–109; and attention, 117
"Intellect and Feeling in Religion" (W. James), 476
Intellectualism: and space, 15–16; and religion, 92; on faith, 374–375; and concepts, 386; and faith, 413–415, 419
Intelligence, 19, 36, 43–44, 50, 54
Intelligibility, 151–152, 154
Interaction, 265–266, 270–271, 298–299, 306, 394–395
Interactionism, 396, 428
Interest, 26, 234, 245
Interpretations of Poetry and Religion (G. Santayana), 477
Introduction to Philosophy (G. S. Fullerton), 531
Introduction to Philosophy (F. Paulsen), 300, 356n, 363, 378, 383–396, 399–406, 412, 419–421, 423, 505, 512, 533, 535
Introduction to Psychological Theory (B. P. Bowne), 212, 498
Introduction to Systematic Philosophy, An (W. T. Marvin), 289n, 356n, 504
Introduction to the History of Religion, An (F. B. Jevons), 379, 512
Introduction to the Philosophy of Religion, An (J. Caird), 487
Introduction to the Science of Religion (F. M. Müller), 511
Introspection, 3, 17–18, 31, 33–34
Isabella (mental patient), 69, 467

Is Life Worth Living? (W. H. Mallock), 177, 390, 489
Italy, 73

Jackman, Wilbur Samuel, 166, 487
Jackson, John Hughlings, 23, 43, 453, 454
Jack the Ripper, 57
Jäger, H., 211, 497
Jaillet, Jules, 44, 455
James, Alice Gibbens (wife), 51n, 174n, 449, 452, 484, 537, 539
James, Henry (brother), 458
James, Margaret Mary (daughter), 65, 464
James Collection, 447, 449, 481
Janet, Paul, 354, 509
Janet, Pierre: and suggestion, 62, 67; and hysteria, 64, 68, 69, 70; and multiple personality, 71, 251, 517; notes on, 462, 463, 467, 468; mentioned, 95, 346, 466, 469
Japan, 114, 470
Jastrow, Joseph, 95, 378, 478, 534
Jefferies, Richard, 376, 511
Jefferson, Joseph, 454
Jeffries, Benjamin Joy, 7, 10, 450
Jekyll, Dr. (literary character), 525
Jenckes, Edward Nathaniel, 353, 354
Jerome, William Travers, 111, 480
Jevons, Frank Byron, 379, 512
Jevons, William Stanley, 141, 349, 484
Joachim, Harold Henry, 296, 505
Job (biblical figure), 147
Jogand-Pagès, Gabriel Antoine, 470–471
Johns Hopkins University, 447–449, 451, 452
Johnson, Samuel, 198, 492, 519
Johnson, W. E., 210, 495
Jordan, David Starr, 479
Jowett, Benjamin, 188
Judaism, 191
Judgment, 117, 123, 390
Junius, John, 74, 472
Justine (mental patient), 69, 467

Kaan, Hanns, 56, 460
Kallen, Horace Meyer, 354
Kant, Immanuel: on space, 15; Spencer on, 158; his forms, 160; and noumena, 164; and philosophy, 167, 356, 381; and ethics, 175; and imperatives, 183, 185; and reason, 187; and the *that*, 254; and idealism, 268; and infinity, 272, 277, 313; and Absolute, 278, 334; and science, 279, 280; and knowing, 285; on the permanent,

297n; and unity, 299; and possibility, 314; and categories, 325; on the ego, 330; and causality, 343; Cohen on, 377; and antinomies, 382, 423–424; and monism, 408, 410; note on, 512; mentioned, 9, 63, 77, 150, 159, 177, 204, 213, 348, 349, 350, 355, 364n, 383, 410, 489, 491, 531

Kantians, 134, 217

Kantism, 357

Karma, 152

Kepler, Johannes, 73, 179, 187, 193, 202

Kettle (unidentified person), 67

Keyser, Cassius Jackson, 313, 506

Kierkegaard, Søren, 363, 510

Kingsley, Charles, 178, 489

Kipling, Rudyard, 81, 111, 476

Kleutgen, Joseph, 198, 493

Knapp, J. H., 348

Knauer, Vincenz, 217, 500

Knower, 130

Knowing, 361

"Knowing of Things Together, The" (W. James), 504

Knowing-together, 229

Knowledge: and sensation, 5–7, 126–129, 144, 169, 245; reasoned, 118; and relativity, 129–130; of external objects, 133–135; and consciousness, 142–143; revisions in, 143–144; and activity, 148; Spencer on, 158; expansion of, 165–166; and common objects, 217, 269, 288–289; and fields, 223; described, 228–229, 256; and systems, 238, 240–241; and phenomenalism, 239, 250, 359; and Absolute, 252, 298; empiricism on, 257; and substitution, 258–259; practicalism on, 262; problem of, 283–285; objects of, 285; and pure experience, 319–320; and pragmatism, 332; and practice, 360; and universals, 386

Knowledge-about, 284

Knox, Howard Vincenté, 358n, 510

Körperliche Gefühl, Das (E. Kröner), 495

Krafft-Ebing, Richard von, 64, 463

Kraft und Stoff (L. Büchner), 532

Kramer, Henry, 471

Krieger (unidentified person), 69, 466

Kritik der reinen Erfahrung (R. Avenarius), 498, 501

Kröner, Eugen, 209, 211, 495, 497

Külpe, Oswald, 211, 497

Kwo, case of, 72, 470

L., J., 213

Laas, Ernst, 218n, 500

Lallemand, Ludger, 43, 48, 456

Lamarck, Jean Baptiste Pierre Antoine de Monet de, 150

Lambe, Roland, 353, 354

Landmann, Samson, 67, 465

Lang, Andrew, 67, 465

Lange, Carl Georg, 220, 500

Lange, Friedrich Albert, 198, 394, 493

Language, 85–86, 232, 335

Lao-tse, 348

Laplace, Pierre Simon, marquis de, 150

Lasswitz, Kurd: quoted, 91; notes on, 477, 486, 499; mentioned, 160, 167, 217

Lathrop, John Howland, 348

Lavoisier, Antoine Laurent, 170

Law of Psychic Phenomena, The (T. J. Hudson), 464

Laws, 92, 268, 279, 280–282

Leaders, 112–113

Leading, 320, 361

Leavens, Robert French, 354

Le Baron, Albert. *See* Waters, Henry Guy

LeBon, Gustave, 339n, 508

Lebon (unidentified person), 34

Lecky, William Edward Hartpole, 75, 472

Leçons de philosophie (E. Rabier), 211, 496

Leçons sur les maladies du système nerveux (F. Raymond), 468

Lectures and Essays (W. K. Clifford), 454, 534

Lectures on Diseases of the Nervous System (S. W. Mitchell), 470

Lectures on Metaphysics and Logic (W. Hamilton), 159, 211, 218, 486

Lectures on Some Recent Advances in Physical Science (P. G. Tait), 170, 488

Legrand du Saulle, Henri, 56, 460

Lehmann, Alfred Georg Ludwig, 208, 495

Lehrbuch der allgemeinen Psychologie (J. Rehmke), 212, 215, 498

Lehrbuch der Philosophie (A. Stöckl), 343, 355, 509

Lehrbuch der Psychologie (F. E. Beneke), 211, 496

Lehrbuch der Psychologie (W. F. Volkmann), 206, 211, 494

Lehrbuch der Psychologie (T. Waitz), 211, 497

Lehre von den Tonempfindungen, Die (H. Helmholtz), 499

Leibniz, Gottfried Wilhelm von: his
thought, 195–196, 200–202; and
reality, 204, 205; and harmony, 265,
289; and evil, 273; and Newton, 281;
and creation, 301; Lotze on, 346,
365n; and optimism, 356, 379; and
phenomenalism, 362; on possibility,
373; notes on, 492, 493; mentioned,
59, 150, 167, 186, 194, 198, 202, 276n,
381, 494, 510, 530
Leib und Seele (H. Ulrici), 211, 496
Leland, Charles Godfrey, 51, 55, 457
Lélut, Louis François, 78, 79n, 474, 517
Leo XIII, 191, 491
Léonie (mental patient), 70, 468
Le Roy, Édouard, 279, 280n, 282, 503,
504
Letter on Toleration (J. Locke), 197
Letters of William James, The, 479,
498, 501, 503, 508
Leuba, James Henry, 171n, 346, 376,
489, 509
Leucippos, 188
Levesque de Pouilly, Louis Jean, 211,
496
Leviathan (T. Hobbes), 193
Lewes, George Henry: on consciousness,
24; on truth, 119; notes on, 453, 508;
mentioned, 18, 146, 161, 343, 481
Lewis, Clarence Irving, 348
Liberalism, 90, 101, 113
Liebreich, Matthias Eugéne Oscar, 121,
481
Liégeois, Jules, 67, 465
Life, 83, 89, 334, 359
Life of John Locke, The (R. F. Bourne),
492
Life of President Edwards, The (S. E.
Dwight), 276, 503
Life of Reason, The (G. Santayana),
359, 368, 509, 530
Limits of Religious Thought, The
(H. L. Mansel), 159, 486
Lindley, Ernest Hiram, 348
Lipps, Theodor, 210, 211, 496, 497
Lipsius, Justus, 202, 494
Lisbon, 301
Literature and Dogma (M. Arnold), 456
Littré, Émile, 186, 491
Localization, 21, 22–23, 33, 42
Locke, John: his thought, 196–197; and
mechanism, 276; and representation-
ism, 284; and pragmatism, 357; and
empiricism, 388–389; note on, 492;
mentioned, 167, 198, 200n, 202, 326,
349, 378, 382

Logic, 123
Logic (A. Bain), 181, 490
Logic (C. Sigwart), 343, 508
Logik (C. Sigwart), 179, 490
Lombroso, Cesare: on genius, 58, 78,
79–80, 81, 517–518; notes on, 461,
474, 475; mentioned, 63
Longet, François Achille, 208, 495
Longfellow, Henry Wadsworth, 58n,
59, 81, 461, 475, 518
Lord, Robert Howard, 348
Lotze, Rudolph Hermann: on space, 15;
and induction, 178; his aim, 192;
and monism, 205, 261, 264, 265, 266,
271, 275, 286, 289n, 290, 297, 300, 335,
337, 351, 352, 358, 405; and evil, 273;
and interaction, 289, 292, 298, 299;
on Leibniz, 346, 365n; notes on, 490,
494, 496; mentioned, 111, 112, 187,
194, 196, 210, 211, 213, 231, 259, 278,
279, 301n, 354, 363, 371, 490, 492, 502
Lovejoy, Arthur Oncken, 365, 366n, 510
Lowell, Augustus, 451–452, 459
Lowell, James Russell, 58n, 81, 449,
461, 475
Lowell, Percival, 72, 469, 532
Lowell Institute: James's lectures at,
449, 451–452, 454, 459–460; mentioned,
20, 21, 31, 39, 41, 63, 480, 516, 519,
520, 521, 522, 523, 524
Lubbock, John, 151, 485
Lucie (mental patient), 62, 67, 69, 463
Lucretius, 150, 191, 284, 393
Lucy (mental patient), 70, 468
Luke (book of the Bible), 477
Luther, Martin, 86, 140, 192, 376, 395
Lutoslawski, Wincenty: James's letter
to, 476–477; notes on, 502, 505, 509;
mentioned, 266, 298n, 354
Luys, Jules, 17, 33, 35, 131–132, 452
Lyceum, 189
Lyell, Charles, 140, 329, 484, 508

McCleod, Keith, 348
McCormick, Washington Jay, 354
McLeod (unidentified person), 210
McTaggart, John McTaggart Ellis, 330,
508
Mach, Ernst: and laws, 280, 421; and
intellectualism, 413; and phenomenal-
ism, 421; note on, 501; mentioned,
170, 198, 227n, 279, 349, 488
Madagascar, 152
Madura, 72, 470
Maeterlinck, Maurice, 92n, 477
Magic, 87

Magnan, Valentin, 56, 77, 460
Mahaffy, John Pentland, 198, 299n, 493, 505
Maher, Michael, 211, 284, 348, 496
Maillat, Louyse, 470
Maine de Biran, François Pierre, 213, 498
Malebranche, Nicolas de, 194, 202, 206, 276n, 494
Malleus Maleficarum (Sprenger and Kramer), 73, 74, 75, 471, 472, 473
Mallock, William Hurrell, 177, 390, 489
Man, 83, 113
Manhood, 47
Manias, 56–57, 59
Mansel, Henry Longueville, 159, 161, 162, 165, 486
Man's Place in the Cosmos (A. Seth Pringle-Pattison), 290n, 504
Mantegazza, Paolo, 207, 210, 495
Manual of Practical Hygiene, A (E. A. Parkes), 46, 455, 457
Manuscript Essays and Notes (W. James), 478, 481, 482, 484, 485, 504
"Many and the One, The" (W. James), 478
Marcelle (mental patient), 69, 467
Marcus Aurelius, 191, 354
Margin, 64
Marie (mental patient), 62, 69, 467
Marion, Henri, 462
Marion (unidentified person), 59
Mariotte, Edme, 171, 489
Marryat, Frederick, 47, 456
Marshall, Henry Rutgers: on pleasure, 207, 208, 210; notes on, 494, 508; mentioned, 339n
Martin, Henry Newell, 49, 53, 457
Martin, Lillien Jane, 375, 511
Martineau, James: his ethics, 182, 183; notes on, 481, 486, 490; mentioned, 118, 161, 163, 349
Marvin, Walter T., 289n, 356n, 504
Mason, Rufus Osgood, 70, 468
Massachusetts Medical Society, 463
Materialism: and mind, 23; and science, 29, 30–31; and evolution, 148; and purpose, 158; and idealism, 187–188; and ideality, 283; and spiritualism, 387–388; Paulsen on, 389–393; and minds, 393–396; and freedom, 397; kinds, 427; Paulsen's, 428
Matière et mémoire (H. Bergson), 305, 505
Matter: and ideals, 26; conservation of, 170; discussions of, 275–276; and

ideality, 283; and consciousness, 392; pragmatic view, 398; idealism on, 422
Matter and Motion (J. C. Maxwell), 170, 488
Maudsley, Henry: and explanation, 23; and introspection, 34; on conduct, 125; and knowledge, 131–132; note on, 453; mentioned, 454, 458
Maury, Louis Ferdinand Alfred, 65, 464
Maxwell, James Clerk: and unity, 340; note on, 504; mentioned, 170, 281, 299, 300, 306, 488
Mayer, Leo, 348
Meaning of Truth, The (W. James), 502, 504, 510
Mechanik, Die (E. Mach), 170, 488
Medicinische Psychologie (H. Lotze), 211, 496
Méditations métaphysiques, Les (R. Descartes), 199, 200, 202, 382, 493
Mediumship: and multiple personality, 63, 70, 71; and possession, 72, 82, 523; and mental continuity, 251
Mehrheit geistiger Persönlichkeiten, Die (S. Landmann), 465
Meinong, Alexius, 213, 217, 223, 498, 499
Mejer, Ludwig Christian, 75, 473
Meliorism, 412–413, 417–419
Memorial Hall, 332
Memory, 20–21, 38–43, 66
Menschliche Denken, Das (W. Schuppe), 499
Menschliche Weltbegriff, Der (R. Avenarius), 498
Mental and Moral Science (A. Bain), 489, 490
Merriman, Daniel, 46, 456
Merrington, Ernest Northcroft, 348
Mersenne, Marin, 199
Mesmer, Friedrich Anton, 521
Metaphysica (A. G. Baumgarten), 509
Metaphysic of Experience, The (S. Hodgson), 286, 504
Metaphysics: described, 186, 327, 355–357; and consciousness, 318; James's, 329–330; problems of, 380–381; and being, 382–383; and universals, 383–385; and abstraction, 387–388; and probabilities, 417
Metaphysics (Aristotle), 276
Metaphysics (B. P. Bowne), 212, 498
Metaphysics (H. Lotze), 213, 289n, 299
Metaphysics of the School, The (T. M. Harper), 276, 503
Metaphysik (H. Lotze), 178, 490
Method, 140, 141, 179

Methodism, 96, 97
Methods of Ethics, The (H. Sidgwick), 489
Meynert, Theodor: on brain, 17, 32, 33; notes on, 452, 496; mentioned, 35, 209, 210
Michelangelo, 80, 517
Michelet, Jules, 75, 76, 473, 525
Microcosmus (H. Lotze), 193, 211, 213, 231, 289n, 290, 300, 301, 363, 492, 501, 502
Milhaud, Gaston Samuel, 304n, 505
Mill, James: and nominalism, 385; notes on, 482, 501; mentioned, 127, 213, 382
Mill, James or John Stuart, 314, 353, 354
Mill, John Stuart: on space, 15; and juxtaposition, 119; and syllogisms, 122; and great men, 140; and external world, 169; and induction, 178–181; and mental chemistry, 231; on substance, 357; and phenomenalism, 362, 421, 424; on laws, 363n; James's courses on, 490; notes on, 486, 501; mentioned, 159, 160, 163, 164, 197, 210, 211, 343, 348, 349, 382, 481, 530
Miller, Dickinson Sergeant: and knowledge, 284; and will to believe, 375; as student, 494; notes on, 499, 511; mentioned, 207, 210, 217, 359n, 361n
Miller-Bode Notebooks (W. James), 479
Mind: atomistic view, 4–5; and nervous system, 5, 21–22; and reduction, 9; and sensation, 12; and brain, 17, 23–29, 345; materialists on, 23, 393–396; study of, 30–32, 63; signs of, 36; and sensation, 39–40; and degeneration, 55–57; focus and margin in, 64; and hysteria, 68; unity, 70; and therapy, 75; diseases, 77; health, 82–83; spontaneity, 136–137; evolution, 138; and selection, 148; and extensivity, 216; and composition, 221–222, 258; and continuity, 226, 227; and ejectivity, 251; and common objects, 269, 287–289; and repetition of states, 310; and philosophy, 392; and choice, 397; pragmatic view, 398; and body, 428; types, 521; Paulsen on, 533
Mind, 501
Mind cure, 106
Mind-stuff, 4–5
Miner, Charles Everett, 348
Miracles, 89, 92, 93, 389, 532

Mitchell, Silas Weir, 72, 470, 523, 525
Mitchell (unidentified person), 353
Modern Physical Fatalism (T. R. Birks), 488
Modoc Indians, 176
Mohammed, 140
Moll, Albert, 67, 464
Mollie Fancher (A. H. Dailey), 468
Moltke, Helmuth von, 59, 462, 518
Monadology (Leibniz), 196, 202
Monasmith, Harold Benjamin, 348
Monck, William Henry Stanley, 159, 486
Monism: and religion, 87; and evolution, 148, 158; and rationality, 182; Lotze's, 192; and continuity, 224; and fields, 228; and phenomenalism, 249; and unity, 260, 289; and knowledge, 261–262; and commensurability, 262–263; and interaction, 264–265, 265–266, 271, 298–299; arguments for, 269–270; criticism of, 273, 293–297; and possibility, 297–298; and explanation, 299–300, 301, 302; and unity of origin, 300–302; and relations, 335–337; and pluralism, 338–339; and activity, 344; and mysticism, 346; abstractness of, 388; and panpsychism, 403; and pluralism, 404–405; and pragmatism, 406–410; absolute, 410–412; and freedom, 424–427
Montague, William Pepperell, 366n, 510
Montaigne, Michel de, 72n, 193, 202, 204
Mont Pelée, 402
Montpellier, University of, 75, 473
Moore, George Edward, 320, 505, 507
Morality: and habits, 37; and religion, 84, 273; and education, 101–103; and pleasure, 124–125; and unity, 148; and perfection, 149; and conflicting goods, 184–185; and pluralism, 311; and empiricism, 367
Moreau, Jacques Joseph, 78, 79, 474, 475
Morel, Bénédict Auguste, 77, 474
Morris, Alice Vanderbilt, 65n–66n, 464
Morris, William, 81, 475
Morzine, 72, 470, 471
Moseley, Henry Nottidge, 71, 469
Mossner, Ernest Campbell, 492
Mosso, Angelo, 210, 496
Motion: and space, 4; conservation of, 152–154; rhythm of, 155–157, 172–173, 175; and ideas, 157–158
Motley, John Lathrop, 298n, 505
Movement, 248

Mozart, Wolfgang Amadeus, 59
Mugwumps, 105
Muir, Matthew Moncrief Pattison, 484
Müller, Friedrich Max, 159, 375, 511
Müller, Johannes, 15, 450
Munk, Hermann, 21, 22, 40, 453
Münsterberg, Hugo: on consciousness, 234; and pure experience, 320, 321; James's view, 325–326; notes on, 461, 477, 498, 499, 507; quoted, 91–92; mentioned, 57, 77, 95, 212, 213, 215, 317, 476, 511
Musgrove, William James, 353, 354, 433–434, 512
Musset, Alfred de, 59, 461
Myers, Frederic William Henry: on genius, 58; and subliminal self, 67, 95, 100, 376; and multiple personality, 70, 520, 525; and psychical research, 71; and telepathy, 309; notes on, 461, 465, 469; mentioned, 478
Mystery, 164–165
Mysticism, 94, 165–166, 204, 267, 346
Myths, 88, 89

Nahlowsky, Joseph Wilhelm, 210, 495
Napoleon Bonaparte, 58, 59, 81, 113, 156, 518
Nations, 103, 112–113
Natorp, Paul, 212, 215, 320, 321, 498
Natural History 2, 482, 483
Naturalism, 87–88, 98–99, 370
Naturalism and Agnosticism (J. Ward), 280, 282, 353, 502
Nature: and the supernatural, 87–88; and reason, 151, 268, 275, 280; uniformity of, 154–155, 178–179, 265, 305; and artificiality, 326
Nature, 170
Nature of Truth, The (H. H. Joachim), 296, 505
Necessity, 119, 304, 372–373
Negations, 364–365
Nelson, Horatio, 47, 514
Nervous system: and consciousness, 16, 25–29; functions of, 18–19, 35–36; and mind, 21–22; and habit, 29; described, 32–33; and experience, 37; and thought, 226
Neurasthenia, 51, 55–56
Neurasthenische Angstaffect, Der (H. Kaan), 460
Nevius, John Livingston, 72, 469–470
Newbold, William Romaine, 68, 70, 466
New England, 471
Newman, John Henry, 214n, 499
Newport, R. I., 451

Newspapers, 102, 107
Newton, Isaac: and Leibniz, 281; mentioned, 64, 187, 197, 200n, 201, 202, 220, 279, 435, 463
New York Neurological Society, 457, 469
Nextness, 285–286, 308, 324
Nichols, Herbert: and automatism, 68, 70; and pleasure, 208, 209, 210; notes on, 466, 495
Niebuhr, Barthold Georg, 150, 485
Nihilism, 129
Nisbet, John Ferguson, 80, 81, 475
Nominalism, 192, 385
Nordau, Max Simon: on genius, 81, 517–518; notes on, 462, 475; mentioned, 60, 82
"Notes on Automatic Writing" (W. James), 465, 466
Noumenon, 164
Nouveaux essais sur l'entendement humain (Leibniz), 196, 492
Novelty: and reasoning, 141–142; and action, 233; and tychism, 271, 372; and pluralism, 311; and freedom, 314, 412, 424–427; and chance, 341, 374; and experience, 383; and monism, 411–412
Novum Organum (F. Bacon), 187, 193, 202, 491
Novum Organum Renovatum (W. Whewell), 181, 490
Number, 313–314

O., Miss (mental patient), 70, 468
Obermann (É. P. de Sénancour), 376, 511
Objectivity, 213
Objects: and subjects, 214, 220; unity of, 215; and thoughts, 257–258; common, 269, 287–288, 361; types, 422–423
Obligation, 183–184, 185
Occult Japan (P. Lowell), 72, 469
Œuvres de Malebranche, 494
Œuvres de Spinoza, 492
Œuvres philosophiques de Leibniz, 492
Ogawa, Chuzo, 354
Oken, Lorenz, 301, 383, 505, 512
Oliver, James Edward, 228n, 501
Omniscience, 364
On Intelligence (H. Taine), 483
On Mr. Spencer's Formula of Evolution (M. Guthrie), 161, 164, 487
On Sameness and Identity (G. S. Fullerton), 503
Ontaké, Mount, 72, 469
"On the Function of Cognition" (W. James), 502

On the Sensations of Tone (H. Helm-
 holtz), 449
On the Soul (Aristotle), 276
Optimism, 84, 89–90, 356, 366, 412
Opus Majus (R. Bacon), 202
Order, 309, 341
O'Reilly, William Francis, 354
*Origin and Growth of Plato's Logic,
 The* (W. Lutoslawski), 509
Origin of Species, The (C. Darwin), 140,
 484
Ostwald, Wilhelm: on hypothesis, 281,
 282; notes on, 503, 504; mentioned,
 279, 330
Outlines of Cosmic Philosophy (J.
 Fiske), 163, 487
Outlines of Metaphysic (H. Lotze), 187,
 289n, 490
Outlines of Psychology (H. Höffding),
 210, 211, 495
Over-belief, 99
Oversoul, 252

P. (mental patient), 70
P____ll (mental patient), 67
Packer Collegiate Institute, 458
Paderewski, Ignace Jan, 58, 461, 518
Padua, University of, 480
Paganini, Nicolo, 81, 476
Paganism, 376
Paget, James, 456
Pain, 206–211, 212
Palgrave, Francis Turner, 211, 497
Palmer, George Herbert, 437, 490
Panpsychism: and experience, 146;
 described, 198, 395–396; theses, 278–
 279; and opacity, 308; and freedom,
 397; kinds, 403, 404; and epiphenom-
 enalism, 427
Parallelism, 242–243, 393–394, 396, 427
Parties, political, 112–113
Parts, 358
Pascal, Blaise, 504
Passion, 103–106, 107–109, 113
Pasteur, Louis, 119, 481
Pathology of Mind, The (H. Maudsley),
 458
Patrick, George Thomas White, 188, 491
Patrizi, Francesco, 202, 493
Paul, Saint, 58, 63, 68, 81
Paulhan, Frédéric, 163, 487
Paulsen, Friedrich: and panpsychism,
 266, 399–400, 427, 428; and monadism,
 278; and pluralism, 300; and world
 soul, 309; and science, 344; and em-
 piricism, 388–389; and materialism,
 389–396; and theology, 400–404; and

monism, 404–406, 412; and intellectualism, 413; on nature, 415; and
 skepticism, 420; and idealism, 420–
 421, 423; notes on, 488, 505; mentioned, 167, 198, 353, 356n, 363, 378,
 383, 512, 531, 533, 535
Pearson, Karl: and order, 268; on laws,
 279, 280; and intellectualism, 413;
 note on, 502; mentioned, 282, 349, 358
Peirce, Benjamin, 531, 532
Peirce, Charles Sanders: and idealism,
 128; his criterion, 150; on mental
 states, 217; and order, 268; and evolution, 275; and laws, 303n; and
 tychism, 304, 341; and habit, 307; and
 boundaries, 308; and chance, 358;
 notes on, 482, 491, 499, 500, 505;
 mentioned, 191, 484
Perception: and sensation, 9–10; of
 depth, 11; and selection, 27; and
 conception, 117–119, 143, 250, 253,
 259, 386–387; direct, 141; authority of,
 145; Stout on, 230; possible, 285;
 and practice, 346
Percepts, 239n, 360, 361, 383–385, 530
Perfection, 89, 149, 184–185, 283
Perrin, Maurice Constantin, 48, 456
Perry, Everett Robbins, 353, 354
Perry, Ralph Barton: on Royce, 366n;
 and James's library, 447; notes on,
 509, 510, 511, 512; mentioned, 350n,
 368n, 482, 492, 493, 537. *See also
 Thought and Character of William
 James, The*
Personal Idealism (H. Sturt), 280n, 283,
 357n, 503
Personalism, 272, 311
Personality, 235
Personality, multiple: and degeneration,
 57; and hysteria, 62, 68–70, 522–523;
 and suggestion, 66–67; theories, 70–71,
 525; types, 71–72; and religion, 95;
 and continuity, 251; and suffusion,
 309; James on, 516–517; and hypnotism, 520, 521–522
Perspective, 11
Pessimism, 84, 177, 412
Peterson, Henry, 353, 354
Phenomena, 134, 148, 149, 162, 322
Phenomenalism: and duality, 213;
 described, 237–238; and knowledge,
 239; and solipsism, 249; and common
 sense, 249–250; types, 358; and
 knowledge, 359; and Berkeley, 422
Philip II, 59, 462
Philippines, 96, 102, 103, 104, 107, 108,
 109

Index

Phillips Brooks House, 111, 479

Philo, 191

Philosophiae Naturalis Principia Mathematica (I. Newton), 187

"Philosophical Conceptions and Practical Results" (W. James), 97, 398, 478

Philosophical Discussions (C. Wright), 163, 170, 487, 488

Philosophie als Denken der Welt (R. Avenarius), 498

Philosophie als Orientierung über die Welt (J. Baumann), 212, 498

Philosophy: and physiology, 3, 31; motives of, 25; and science, 30, 378–380; and religion, 84; and generality, 93; and mysticism, 94; and doctrinairism, 96; British, 126–127; and mind, 136; definition, 146; task of, 148; postulates, 149; factors, 159; assumptions, 168; Spencer's, 173; and ultimate kinds, 174; described, 186, 187, 267; Greek, 188–191; medieval, 191–192; modern, 193–198, 202–204; Descartes', 198–200; Leibniz's, 200–202; as absolute system, 240–241; professional, 326; and life, 334, 359; and systems, 355; problems, 356, 380–381; types, 358; and mental types, 381–382; and intellectualism, 415; and pragmatism, 438; divisions, 530

Philosophy 1, 490

Philosophy 1a, 511

Philosophy 3, 146–147, 484, 502

Philosophy 4, 482, 483

Philosophy 5, 489

Philosophy 9, 346, 350, 351, 352, 502, 507

Philosophy 15, 458

Philosophy 20a, 494

Philosophy 20b, 457, 458

Philosophy 20c, 507

Philosophy 20e, 512

Philosophy D, 512, 529

Philosophy of Reflection, The (S. Hodgson), 163, 487

Philosophy of Theism, The (B. P. Bowne), 280, 502

Phobias, 55–56

Phrenology, 22, 42

Physics, 126

Physiological Æsthetics (G. Allen), 211, 483

"Physiological Effects of Alcohol, The" (W. James), 513

Physiologie de la douleur (P. Mantegazza), 207, 210, 495

Physiologische Diagnostik der Nervenkrankheiten, Die (G. Burckhardt), 495

Physiology: and psychology, 3, 17–18, 22, 30–32, 33–34, 41; and sensation, 6; and mind, 9

"Physiology and Hygiene" (W. James), 455

Piat, Clodius, 217, 500

Pico della Mirandola, Giovanni, 202, 493

Pierce, Arthur Henry, 67, 465

Piper, Leonora Evelina, 262, 502

Planchettes, 67

Plato: his genius, 188; Aristotle, 189; and ideas, 240, 388; and relations, 292; on knowledge, 328; and concepts, 385; and intellectualism, 386; and hallucinations, 517; mentioned, 347, 348, 349, 354, 531

Plato (G. Grote), 160, 486

Platonism, 150

Platt, Thomas Collier, 58, 461, 518

Pleasure: and utility, 28, 132–133; and habit, 123–124, 125; moral, 124–125; and goodness, 184–185; and aesthetics, 206–211

Pliny the Younger, 191

Plotinus, 191, 267, 347, 407

Pluralism: Leibniz's, 204, 205; and unity, 224–225; and points of view, 229; and interaction, 265–266; and idealism, 269–270; and tychism, 272; James's, 274–275; and pragmatism, 296; and monism, 300, 338–339, 404–405; and chance, 303; and affecting, 307; and anarchy, 311; described, 345; and pure experience, 362; and God, 369; and change, 373; and abstractness, 388; and panpsychism, 403; and religion, 412; and meliorism, 412–413, 417–419; and freedom, 424–427

"Pluralistic Mystic, A" (W. James), 502

Pluralistic Universe, A (W. James), 506

Poe, Edgar Allan, 59, 462

Poincaré, Henri, 280, 503

Point of view, 228, 244

Pole, Captain, 72, 470

Politics, 76

Polynesia, 72

Polytheism, 87

Pomponazzi, Pietro, 202, 493

Pope (unidentified person), 436–438

Popular Lectures on Scientific Subjects (H. Helmholtz), 220n, 500

Popular Science Monthly, 16, 30, 31, 452

Index

Porphyry, 191

Positivism, 186

Possession, 72, 82, 523

Possibility: and infinity, 167; and absolutism, 293; described, 297–298, 301, 372–373; bare, 303; and necessity, 304; grounded, 416; and freedom, 424–427

Post-Kantians, 164

Postulates, 149, 151–152, 154

Power of Sound, The (E. Gurney), 495

Practicalism, 259–260, 262

Pragmatic method, 398

"Pragmatic Method, The" (W. James), 390

Pragmatism: and meaning, 97, 370, 398; and monism, 263, 406–410; on time, 267; and relations, 269; on infinity, 272–273; on common objects, 288–289; and pluralism, 296; and pure experience, 319–320; and skepticism, 322–324; and tastes, 325–326; and knowledge, 332; on sameness, 336; and transcendence, 349; Papini on, 357; and unity, 364, 366; and Protagoreanism, 377; and the cosmological problem, 403; as method, 429; and satisfaction, 430–431, 441–442; and ultimate truth, 432–434; and consistency, 435, 436–437; and philosophy, 438; and deduction, 439–440

Pragmatism (W. James), 478, 503, 505, 510, 529, 531, 532

Prat, Louis, 529

Pre-Raphaelites, 81

Preyer, Wilhelm Thierry, 309, 506

Price, Junius Lucien, 354

Prichard, James Cowles, 57, 461

Primitive Culture (E. B. Tylor), 378–379, 512

Prince, Morton, 62, 67, 95, 463

Principes de la philosophie, Les (R. Descartes), 187, 200, 202, 491

Principes de philosophie positive (A. Comte), 186, 491

Principles of Biology, The (H. Spencer), 137, 162, 483, 487

Principles of Empirical or Inductive Logic, The (J. Venn), 508

Principles of Psychology, The (W. James): and habits, 230; and automatism, 237; and mind, 384; and consciousness, 395; mentioned, 279, 449, 450, 452, 453, 454, 460, 462, 463, 464, 466, 467, 468, 469, 482, 486, 495, 498, 499, 500, 501, 503, 509, 512, 534

Principles of Psychology, The (H. Spencer), 129n, 130n, 132n, 135, 136, 137, 140, 158, 162, 169, 211, 482, 483, 484, 485

Principles of Science, The (W. S. Jevons), 484

Probabilities, 416–417

Problems of Life and Mind (G. H. Lewes), 146, 161, 343, 481, 508

Problems of Philosophy, The (H. Höffding), 509, 511

Proclus, 191

Professors, 100–101, 111

Progress, 150, 367, 378, 379

Prolegomena to Ethics (T. H. Green), 349, 509

Protagoras, 276, 377, 382, 388

Protestantism, 73

Psychiatrie (T. Meynert), 210, 496

Psychical research, 63

Psychologie (I. H. Fichte), 211, 497

Psychologie de l'amour, La (G. Danville), 461

Psychologie der Veränderungsauffassung (W. Stern), 362, 510

Psychologie morbide, La (J. J. Moreau), 78, 79, 474

Psychologie physiologique, La (G. Sergi), 211, 496

Psychologie vom empirischen Standpunkte (F. Brentano), 212, 497

Psychologische Analysen (A. Horwicz), 211, 497

Psychologismus oder Antipsychologismus? (K. Heim), 377n, 512

Psychology: and physiology, 3, 17–18, 22, 30–32, 33–34, 41; condition of, 5; and sensation, 12; and association, 33; and explanation, 42; abnormal, 63, 64, 71; and hysteria, 68; and psychical research, 71; and logic, 123; physiological, 124; and free will, 136; and environment, 137; and dualism, 235; and philosophy, 378; and mind, 521

Psychology (M. Maher), 496

Pumpelly, Raphael Welles, 353, 354

Purkinje, Johannes Evangelista, 15, 450

Purpose: and explanation, 119, 301; and experience, 146; and evolution, 147, 315–316; and materialism, 158; and habit, 230; and mechanism, 401; and point of view, 402

Pyle, Charles Bertram, 354

Pyrrho, 190

Pythagoras, 188

Quetelet, Lambert Adolphe Jacques, 305, 506

R., Mrs., 463
Rabier, Élie, 211, 496
Radcliffe College, 458, 502
Radcliffe Graduate Club, 479
Rankin, Henry William, 469, 476
Rationalism: and philosophy, 187; and empiricism, 381–382; limits of, 383; and monism, 403, 404, 412
Rationality, 18–19, 24, 36, 123–124, 182
Raymond, Fulgence, 70, 468
Reaction time, 117
Read, Louis H., 70
Realism, 142, 275, 423–424
Reality: spheres, 92; and generality, 99; external, 127, 134; and appearance, 144, 254; criteria, 149; and relations, 164–165; mystery of, 166–167; Spencer's, 169; and perception, 219; and law, 220; pragmatism on, 429, 430
Reason, 94, 98–99, 187, 268, 280
Reasoning: and selection, 27; described, 118–119; examples, 120–121; and syllogisms, 122–123; and novelty, 141–142; and reality, 143
"Recent Researches into Exceptional Mental Phenomena" (W. James), 458, 516
"Recent Researches into Exceptional Mental States" (W. James), 459–460, 519, 520, 521, 522, 523, 524
Recherches sur les centres nerveux (V. Magnan), 56, 77, 460
Reed, Charles Clarence, 347, 348
Reed, Warren Whittemore, 353, 354
Reflection, 334
Reflex action, 24
Regulus, Marcus Atilius, 172, 489
Rehmke, Johannes, 212, 214, 215, 498
Reich, Emil, 530
Reid, Thomas, 213, 218, 233, 353, 500
Relation sur une épidémie d'hystéro-démonopathie en 1861 (A. Constans), 470
Relations: and knowledge, 164–165; and data, 223; adventitious, 269; external, 272, 290, 337–338; Bradley's, 291–292; and monism, 293–296, 335–337; and experience, 334, 377
Relativity, 129–130
Relaxation, 106
Religion: types, 83–85; and tolerance, 85; and wisdom, 86; and science, 86, 91–92; and the supernormal, 87–88; and values, 88; and knowledge, 89;

and liberalism, 90; and experience, 93, 96; and mysticism, 94; and the subliminal, 95; and ecclesiasticism, 97–98; reasonable, 98–99; task of, 148; and perfection, 149; meaning of, 177; and morality, 273; motives of, 318; and Absolute, 367; described, 368–369; and private life, 370; psychology, 375–376; and pluralism, 412–413; and intellectualism, 414–415; and probabilities, 417; and personality, 526–527
Religion: A Criticism and a Forecast (G. L. Dickinson), 419, 512
Religious Aspect of Philosophy, The (J. Royce), 283n, 337, 366, 490, 504
"Religious Philosophy and Individualism" (W. James), 477, 526
Reni, Guido, 80, 475
Renouvier, Charles: and evolutionism, 133–134, 135; and *principe du nombre*, 272, 312; on reality, 275; his categories, 357; notes on, 483, 486, 506; mentioned, 160, 164, 198, 313, 503, 529
Repetition, 310
Representation, 236
Resemblance, 227, 294–296
Restitution, 23
Rêves, Les (P. A. Tissié), 464
Reynolds, Mary, 70, 468, 522, 523, 525
Reynolds, Osborne, 305, 505
Ribet, Jérôme, 267, 502
Ribot, Théodule, 505
Rice (unidentified person), 217, 225n
Richardson, Benjamin Ward, 49, 457
Richelieu, Armand Jean du Plessis, duc de, 198
Richet, Charles Robert, 210, 496
Rickaby, John, 276, 343, 503
Rickert, Heinrich, 217, 500
Ridge, John James, 46, 455
Rieger, Conrad, 466
Riehl, Alois, 279, 343, 503
Rip van Winkle (literary character), 19, 37, 454
Roberts (unidentified person), 210
Robespierre, Maximilien Marie Isidore, 76
Robin, Charles Philippe, 18, 32, 35, 39, 453
Robins, Sidney Swaim, 348
Robinson (unidentified person), 348
Rockefeller, John Davison, 81, 476
Roff, Mary, 469
Rogers, William Barton, 7, 10, 450
Rollande (unidentified person), 72, 471
Romanes, George John, 4, 167, 449

Index

Rome, 72, 140, 150

Roosevelt, Theodore, 111, 480

Rosmini-Serbati, Antonio, 198, 493

Rousseau, Jean Jacques, 150, 177

Royce, Josiah: and moral insight, 185;
and unity, 205; and continuity, 224,
226; and monism, 261, 262, 264, 266,
269, 338, 339, 405, 406, 408, 410;
and time-span, 271, 309; and knowledge, 274; and perfection, 283; and
Absolute, 284, 298, 365, 366; and
relations, 286, 290n, 291n; and
realism, 288n, 292, 335, 337; and
pluralism, 293, 296; and error, 297,
333, 334; and infinity, 313; and
pragmatism, 322, 323, 433, 443; and
causality, 343; on negation, 364; on
identity, 370; and intellectualism,
413; notes on, 490, 503, 504; mentioned, 213, 218, 300, 308n, 315, 328n,
342, 345, 352, 501, 506, 507, 508, 511

Ruloff, Edward Howard, 35, 454

Ruskin, John, 81, 106, 178, 475

Russell, Bertrand, 313, 332, 506, 508

Russia, 114

Ruyssen, Théodore, 505

Sacerdotalism, 84

Sainte-Beuve, Charles Augustin, 98, 478

Salem, Mass., 74, 75, 473

Salem Witchcraft (C. W. Upham), 473

Salvation Army, 462

Sameness, 229, 255, 336

Sämmtliche Werke (I. Kant), 512

Samoa, 72

Sanchez, Francisco, 204, 494

Sand, George, 59, 81, 461

Sanskrit, 150

Santayana, George: on Schiller, 322;
notes on, 477, 509; quoted, 91;
mentioned, 210, 219n, 354, 359, 368,
490, 500, 530, 533

Sardinia, 140

Sartor Resartus (T. Carlyle), 166, 369,
477, 488

Satan, 73

Satisfaction, 371, 430–431, 437, 439–440

Savage, Theodore Fiske, 353, 354

Schelling, Friedrich Wilhelm Joseph
von, 280

Schiller, Ferdinand Canning Scott: and
monism, 264; on truth, 322, 323, 433;
and humanism, 357; on Royce, 366n;
notes on, 502, 503, 510, 511; mentioned, 280n, 283, 289n, 298n

Schiller, Johann Christoph Friedrich
von, 59

Schlesinger, Armin Ardery, 348

Schliemann, William Emil, 210, 495

Schmidt, Henry D., 17, 33, 452

Scholasticism: and religion, 89; vice of,
96; vulgar, 169; development, 191;
and common sense, 389; and form,
400; mentioned, 150, 186

Schönborn, Johann Philip von, 76, 474

Schopenhauer, Arthur: and ethics, 175;
and philosophy, 186; on metaphysics,
329, 382; and optimism, 379; note
on, 491; mentioned, 211, 314, 353,
381, 534, 535

Schulinus, Hugo, 48, 53, 457

Schuppe, Ernst Julius Wilhelm, 214,
215, 499

Science: and verification, 4; standards
of, 29–30; and mind, 30–31; and
mental types, 63; and data, 71; and
religion, 86, 91–92, 93; and the supernatural, 87; and the subliminal, 95;
as method, 96; and ecclesiasticism,
97–98; and vagueness, 138; limits of,
166; and philosophy, 168, 378–380;
history of, 186–187, 202–203; and
things, 254; laws in, 271, 280–282; and
truth, 279; and statistics, 305; and
metaphysics, 327; and systems, 355;
logic of, 436

Science and Culture (T. H. Huxley),
533, 534

Scotland, 73, 471

Scott, Frederick J. Down, 477

Scott, Walter, 81, 475

Sears, Miss (unidentified person), 293,
338

Seipt, Howard Anders, 353, 354

Selection: and sensation, 4, 27; and consciousness, 26–28; natural, 136–137;
and mind, 148; and will, 237; and
systems, 245

Selections from Berkeley, 276, 503

Self: meanings, 212; as knower, 213, 214,
241; and time, 234; and pure
experience, 320

Semicircular canals, 5

Sénancour, Étienne Pivert de, 511

Seneca, 150, 191

Sensation: and selection, 4, 27; and
knowledge, 5–7, 126–129, 144, 169,
245; as sign, 8; and perception, 9–10,
253; and mind, 12; and intensity,
12–13; and extension, 13; and attention, 14–15; elementary, 39–40;
interpretation of, 141; as fact, 226;
role of, 254; and conjunction, 336

Sensationalism, 15–16

Sentimentality, 177–178
"Sentiment of Rationality, The" (W.
  James), 167, 181, 382, 388, 417, 488, 532
Sergi, Giuseppe, 211, 496
Seth Pringle-Pattison, Andrew, 218,
  290n, 355, 500, 504
Seth (unidentified person), 64
Sextus Empiricus, 190, 388
Sexuality, 56, 124
Shaftesbury, Anthony Ashley Cooper,
  first Earl of, 197
Shakespeare, William, 26, 73, 202, 302,
  485, 518
Shaler, Mrs. (unidentified person), 67
Sharpe, Charles Kirkpatrick, 471
Shaw, George Bernard, 114, 481
Sheffer, Henry Maurice, 438, 512
Sheffield, Joseph Buckingham, 208, 210
Shelley, Percy Bysshe, 58, 59, 81, 461, 518
Shocks, 69
Shurtleff, Harold Robert, 354
Sicily, 188
Sidgwick, Henry: and psychical re-
  search, 71; and ethics, 176, 185; notes
  on, 469, 489, 490; mentioned, 349
Sigwart, Christoph, 179, 279, 343, 490,
  508
Similarity, 218
Singer, Edgar Arthur, 213, 218, 223,
  224, 498
Sir William Hamilton (W. H. S. Monck),
  159, 486
Skepticism: and sensation, 12; value of,
  76; and relativity, 129; ethical, 184;
  history, 190; and pluralism, 311; and
  pragmatism, 322–324; James on,
  419–420
Skrupskelis, Ignas K., 529, 537
Sleep, 63–64, 65, 82
Smith, Arthur George, 348, 349
Smith, Edward, 46, 455
Snell, Otto, 73, 75, 471, 473
Society, 101–103
Society for Psychical Research, 63, 465,
  469
Socrates: and insanity, 78, 517; his
  philosophy, 188–189; mentioned, 190,
  382
Soldan, Wilhelm Gottlieb, 74, 472
Solipsism: and consciousness, 224; static,
  225; and phenomenalism, 249; and
  pure experience, 251–252; and
  pragmatism, 333; and idealism, 424
Solomons, Leon M., 218, 305n, 341n,
  500, 506
Some Problems of Philosophy (W.

James), 490, 491, 492, 503, 504, 505,
  506, 507, 509, 511, 512, 531
Somerset, Isabella Caroline, 57, 78, 461,
  524
Sommeil et les rêves, Le (F. H. A.
  Maury), 464
Sophists, 189, 388
Sorcière, La (J. Michelet), 473
Sorel, Georges, 210, 496
Soul, 212
Soul of a Christian, The (F. S. Granger),
  95, 478
Space, 4, 8–9, 160
Space, perception of, 11, 13–14, 15–16
Spalding, Douglas Alexander, 19, 37,
  453, 454, 534
Spamer, Karl, 125, 482
Spanish Gypsy, The (G. Eliot), 222, 500
"Spatial Quale, The" (W. James), 449,
  450
Spee, Friedrich von, 76, 473
Speech, 41
Spencer, Herbert: on mind, 4, 7; and
  skepticism, 12; on space, 15; and
  explanation, 23; and usefulness, 28;
  on education, 101; and knowledge,
  126–129, 130–131, 158; on pleasure,
  132; on reality, 134; his influence,
  135; and law of intelligence, 136–137,
  141; and great men, 138–139, 140;
  on reasoning, 141–142, 144; and
  perception, 145; examination questions, 146–147; and ideals, 148; and
  his age, 150; criticism of, 151, 153, 154,
  155, 156, 164–167, 174–175; and social
  movements, 157; his *First Principles*,
  159–164, 168–174; his *Data of Ethics*,
  175–176; and equilibrium, 177; and
  agnosticism, 186; and unity, 309; on
  religion, 375; on philosophy, 380;
  and metaphysics, 381; and mind-stuff,
  404; notes on, 450, 479, 482, 483, 484,
  485, 487, 489; mentioned, 108, 117,
  192, 198, 210, 211, 213, 218, 307, 329,
  347, 354, 382, 449, 451, 452, 488, 534
Spinal cord, 32–33
Spindler, Frank Nicholas, 217, 500
Spinola, Cristobal Rojas de, 201, 493
Spinoza, Baruch: and God, 192, 382;
  his thought, 194–195; and mysticism,
  204; and rationalism, 388; and
  parallelism, 393; and monism, 412;
  note on, 492; mentioned, 51, 52, 53,
  147, 198, 200, 201, 202, 306, 341, 350,
  381, 531
Spirits, 71

Spiritualism, 387–388
Sprenger, James, 73, 471
Springfield Republican, 102n, 480
Spurzheim, Johann Kaspar, 35, 454
Stallo, John Bernard, 161, 279, 486
Stanford University, 374, 479, 511, 512
Stanley, Hiram Miner, 210, 495, 496
Starbuck, Edwin Diller, 346, 509
Statistics, 305, 309, 416
Stein, Gertrude, 217, 499
Stephen, James Fitzjames, 177, 489
Stephen, Leslie, 93, 100, 477
Stern, William, 362n, 510
Stevens, Lewis T., 457
Stevenson, Robert Louis, 311, 506
Stewart, Balfour, 170, 488
Stimulation, 125–126
Stöckl, Albert, 198, 343, 355, 493, 509
Stoicism, 190
Stout, George Frederick: his psychology, 230–233; on relations, 336; notes on, 501, 508; mentioned, 234
Stowe, Ancel Roy Monroe, 348
Stream of consciousness, 214, 219, 240
Strong, Charles Augustus: on brain, 345; and thing in itself, 361; and phenomenalism, 362; and panpsychism, 395, 428; notes on, 499, 512; mentioned, 213, 348, 350, 353, 534
Strother, Shelby French, 354
Studien über Hysterie (Breuer and Freud), 467, 468
Studies in Logical Theory (J. Dewey), 507
Studies in Theism (B. P. Bowne), 170, 488
Study of Religion, A (J. Martineau), 490
Stumpf, Carl: on space, 15; notes on, 450, 499; mentioned, 213, 217
Sturt, Henry, 357n, 510
Suarez, Francisco, 202, 493
Subject, 214, 220
Substance, 130, 147–148
Substantialism, 129
Substitution, 258–259
Success, 106–107
Suffusion, 308
Suggestibility, 65
Suggestion: and hypnotism, 61, 62, 65, 67, 519, 521; and multiple personality, 66–67; and mysticism, 94; and therapy, 524–525
Suicide, 57
Sully, James, 210, 495

Summa Theologica (Thomas Aquinas), 87, 202
Summation of stimuli, 5
Summis desiderantes affectibus, 73, 471
Sunshine in Thought (C. G. Leland), 51, 457
Supernatural, 87–88, 136
Supernaturalism, 90, 98–99, 99–100
Surrey, Frank Miller, 348
Survival, 26–27, 175–177
Swain, Prescott Leggett, 348
Swift, Jonathan, 80, 475
Swift, Morrison Isaac, 356, 379, 510
Switzerland, 471
Syllogism, 122–123
Symonds, John Addington, 211, 497
Synechism, 331, 347
Syntagma Philosophiae Epicuri (P. Gassendi), 202, 493
System der Philosophie (W. Wundt), 315n, 316, 507
System of Logic, A (J. S. Mill), 179–181, 490
System of Metaphysics, A (G. S. Fullerton), 356n, 510
System of Psychology, A (D. G. Thompson), 211, 495
Systems: criterion, 150; knowledge of, 238, 240–241; and continua, 243; and pure experience, 244; and selection, 245; and fields, 246; partial, 363

Tagesansicht gegenüber der Nachtansicht, Die (G. T. Fechner), 301n, 505
Taine, Hippolyte Adolphe: on mind, 4, 7; and synthesis, 119; on history, 138; and induction, 178, 181; and double-aspect, 246; and mind-stuff, 404; notes on, 481, 490; mentioned, 449, 450, 483
Tait, Peter Guthrie, 170, 488
Tait, William Dunlop, 350, 354
Talks to Teachers (W. James), 463, 474, 480, 489
Tarde, Jean Gabriel, 111, 112, 350, 480
Taylor, Alfred Edward: and monism, 344; and truth, 351, 371; and intellectualism, 413; notes on, 508, 511; mentioned, 334, 337, 338, 341n, 343, 353, 356n
Taylor, Eugene, 460, 463, 468
"Teaching Philosophy in Our Colleges" (W. James), 482
Teichmüller, Gustav, 327, 507
Telepathy, 71, 309, 345, 360

Telesio, Bernardino, 202, 493
Temperance, 51, 55
Tempest, The (W. Shakespeare), 485
Templars, 73
Ten Lectures on Alcohol (B. W. Richardson), 457
Termination, 236, 239, 259
Text-Book of Pharmacology, A (T. L. Brunson), 46, 456
Thackeray, William Makepeace, 58, 461
Thales, 188, 378
Theaetetus (Plato), 188
Theism, 398–400
Théodicée (Leibniz), 196, 202, 204, 494, 510
Theology, 30, 96, 527
Théorie scientifique de la sensibilité (L. Dumont), 494
Theory, 346, 532
Theory of Agreeable Sensations, The (L. J. Lévesque de Pouilly), 211, 496
Therapy, 75
Things, 5–7, 254, 258
Thinker, 213, 214
Thomas Aquinas, Saint: on God, 382, 387; mentioned, 191, 192, 202, 347, 349, 378
Thomas (unidentified student), 210, 431–433
Thompson, Daniel Greenleaf, 210, 211, 495
Thompson, Richard Henry, 354
Thomson, Joseph John, 276n, 305, 503, 505
Thoreau, Henry David, 109, 110
Thorndike, Edward Lee, 218, 219n, 500
Thought, 67, 226
Thought and Character of William James, The (R. B. Perry), 448, 456, 460, 476, 497, 507, 537
Thucydides, 114
Tilley (unidentified person), 348, 349
Timaeus (Plato), 189
Time, 160, 234, 267
Time and Space (S. Hodgson), 213, 498
Time-span, 271, 309
Tissié, Philippe Auguste, 65, 66, 70, 464, 523
Tituba, 76, 473
Tolerance, 85, 96, 311
Toll, Charles Hansen, 348
Tolstoi, Lev Nikolayevich, 81, 106, 109, 111, 475
Tonpsychologie (C. Stumpf), 499
Touch, 4, 8
Touchstone (literary character), 186

Tractatus Theologico-Politicus (Spinoza), 202
Traité de logique générale (C. Renouvier), 160, 486
Traité des dégénérescences (B. A. Morel), 474
Trance State of Inebriety, The (T. D. Crothers), 464
Transcendence, 332, 349
Transcendentalism, 89–90
Treatise Concerning the Principles of Human Knowledge, A (G. Berkeley), 197
Treatise of Human Nature, A (D. Hume), 198, 492
Treatise on Insanity, A (J. C. Prichard), 461
Treatise on Logic, A (F. Bowen), 181, 490
Trevor, John, 267, 502
Trotter (unidentified person), 514
Truth: and morbidity, 83; and value, 89; and character, 94; and experience, 96; and necessity, 119, 170; and convergence, 128; and explanation, 143; and totality, 146; and system, 149–150; and panpsychism, 198; as destiny, 278; and science, 279; and absolutism, 290; and skepticism, 322–324; and taste, 325–326; and error, 333–334; and timelessness, 346–347; and humanism, 371; and goodness, 372; as ideal goal, 432; and belief, 433; and disagreement, 434; and consistency, 435; ultimate, 436, 437; and satisfaction, 441–442
Tufts, James Hayden, 250, 501
Tuke, Daniel Hack, 353, 509
Tupper, George William, 353n, 354
Turley, Louis Alvin, 354
Turner (unidentified person), 292n
Twardowski, Kazimierz, 217, 499
Tychism: and spontaneity, 270; reasons for, 271–272; and origin, 302; and Peirce, 304, 341; and uniformity, 306; and direction, 317, 318; and novelty, 372
Tylor, Edward Burnett, 151, 378, 485, 512
Tyndall, John: and brain, 23; and materialism, 390; note on, 453; mentioned, 123, 130, 482, 533
Type-phenomenon, 358
Types of Ethical Theory (J. Martineau), 490

Index

Überwindung des wissenschaftlichen Materialismus (W. Ostwald), 282, 504

Ulrici, Hermann, 211, 496

Unconscious, 4, 67

Underwood, Sara A. Francis, 68, 70, 466, 468

Uniformity, 154–155, 178–179, 314–315

United States, 51, 52, 102, 106–107, 178–179, 513

Unity: as postulate, 149; meanings of, 204–205; and similarity, 218; and pluralism, 224–225; kinds of, 260–261, 331, 339, 363–364, 406–409; extent of, 264–265; grades, 268; and tychism, 272; and pure experience, 288–289; and monism, 289; and explanation, 301, 302; and chance, 303; and variation, 307; and continuity, 308–309, 320, 324–325; static, 311; of origin, 340; pragmatic view, 366

Universals, 383–385

Universe: unity of, 92; and individuality, 111; explanations of, 166–167; and conclusion, 267; and boundaries, 306; and coherence, 308; and stability, 309

Unknowable, 163–165, 169

Upham, Charles Wentworth, 75, 473

Uphues, Goswin K., 217, 499

Utilitarianism, 191

Utility, 183

Vaihinger, Hans, 163, 487

Vail, Albert Ross, 348

Value, 88, 89, 390

Van Eeden, Frederik Willem, 56, 77, 460

Vanini, Lucilio, 193, 202, 492

Variation: and evolution, 136–137; and social development, 138, 139, 141; and ethics, 183; and unity, 307; and chance, 309

Varieties of Religious Experience, The (W. James), 83, 376, 477, 478, 480, 502, 509

Vaughan, Diana, 471

Vedantism, 407

Vel. (mental patient), 70, 467

Venice, 125

Venn, John, 60, 178, 343, 462, 508

Vennum, Lurancy, 70, 468, 469

Venus, 145

Verification, 251–252

Versuch den Begriff der negativen Grössen (I. Kant), 512

Verzegnis, 72

Vesalius, Andreas, 73, 471

Vie des abeilles, La (M. Maeterlinck), 477

Vierordt, Karl von, 4, 219n, 449

Virchow, Rudolph, 210

Vision: and touch, 5; and attention, 6–7; and distance, 7, 10; and double images, 7–8, 10–12; and thought, 9–11

Vivekananda, Swami, 267, 502

"Vocation of a Scholar, The" (W. James), 479

Voice of the Silence, The (E. P. Blavatsky), 494

Volition, 236–237, 394–395

Volk, Douglas, 111, 480

Volkmann, Wilhelm Fridolin, Ritter von Volkmar, 206, 210, 211, 494

Voltaire, François Marie Arouet de, 150, 187, 340

Wagner, Richard, 81, 475

Waitz, Theodor, 211, 497

Waldenses, 73

Wallace, Alfred Russel, 137, 141, 483

Walsh, W. (unidentified person), 284n

War, 104

Ward, James: on force, 280; on nature, 282; on philosophy, 378; notes on, 491, 496, 501, 502; mentioned, 187, 210, 230n, 231, 279, 353, 355, 510

Ward, Lester Frank: notes on, 485, 486, 489; mentioned, 151, 160, 167, 173

Warren, Joseph Weatherhead, 49n, 457

Washburn, Claude Carlos, 348

Washington, Booker Taliaferro, 111, 480

Washington, George, 58, 59, 81

Waters, Henry Guy, 68, 466

Watts, Rowland Howard, 348

Wauchope, William Crawford, 354

Waugh, Karl Tinsley, 348

Weber, Ernst Heinrich, 123, 482

Webster, Daniel, 35, 454

Wellington, Arthur Wellesley, first Duke of, 47, 514

Welt als Wille und Vorstellung, Die (A. Schopenhauer), 186, 211, 491, 496

Wemding, Bavaria, 72, 471

Wesley, John, 86, 198, 477, 492

Wheeler (unidentified person), 354

Whewell, William, 181, 198, 490

Whitby, Charles Joseph, 274, 503

Whitman, Walt, 194, 267, 407

Whittier, John Greenleaf, 81, 476

Wholes, 358

Why the Mind Has a Body (C. A. Strong), 348, 395, 512
Widener Library, 447, 460, 462, 466, 471, 473, 474, 486, 487, 495, 496
Wier, Johann, 75, 473
Wilbois, Joseph, 283, 504
Wilde, Oscar, 105, 109, 480
Wiley, Fred Talmadge, 354
Will, 136, 184, 310, 318
Willard, Frances Elizabeth Caroline, 59, 78, 462, 524
William I, 140
William James on Exceptional Mental States (E. Taylor), 460, 463, 468
William of Occam, 191, 192, 347
Will to believe, 415
"Will to Believe, The" (W. James), 338, 417
Will to Believe, The (W. James), 382 388, 474, 484, 490, 505, 508, 511, 512, 532
Windelband, Wilhelm, 198, 328n, 493, 508
Wirklichkeiten (K. Lasswitz), 91, 477
Wisdom, 86, 527
Witchcraft: history, 72–73; works, 73–74; cases, 74–75; theories, 75; James's view, 76, 525; explanations, 82
Wolff, Christian, 355, 509
Wolfman, Nathan, 354
Wollowicz, Cyprian, 455
Wordsworth, William, 166, 194, 487, 503
Work, 50, 54

Working, 371
Works of Epictetus, The, 191, 491
Works of George Berkeley, The, 491
World and the Individual, The (J. Royce), 283, 290n, 291, 292, 293, 297, 309, 339, 503, 504, 506, 508
World as Will and Idea, The (A. Schopenhauer), 382
World soul, 309
Wright, Chauncey: and rationality, 125; notes on, 482, 487; mentioned, 163, 170, 484, 488
Wundt, Wilhelm: on space, 7, 8–9, 15; his law, 10, 11; on sensation, 12; and suggestion, 64; and perception, 117; and Horwicz, 210; and psychic synthesis, 233; and novelty, 315n, 316; notes on, 464, 481, 486, 497, 507; mentioned, 123, 160, 167, 211, 450, 495
Wyckoff, A. E., 458

X, Miss. *See* Freer, Ada Goodrich
Xenophanes, 188
Xenophon, 188

Zeno of Citium, 190
Zeno of Elea, 161, 188, 272, 312, 342, 486
Zilk, Michael, 72, 471
Zola, Émile, 81, 475
Zulu tribe, 176
Zur Lehre vom Inhalt und Gegenstand der Vorstellungen (K. Twardowski), 499